UNIVERSITY CASEBOOK SERIES®

MATERIALS FOR A BASIC COURSE IN

CIVIL PROCEDURE

CONCISE THIRTEENTH EDITION

RICHARD H. FIELD

Late Story Professor of Law Emeritus, Harvard University

BENJAMIN KAPLAN

Late Royall Professor of Law Emeritus, Harvard University, and
Associate Justice, Supreme Judicial Court of Massachusetts

KEVIN M. CLERMONT

Ziff Professor of Law, Cornell University

FOUNDATION
PRESS

University Casebook Series is a trademark registered in the U.S. Patent and Trademark Office.

© 2011 By THOMSON REUTERS/FOUNDATION PRESS
© 2014, 2017 LEG, Inc. d/b/a West Academic
© 2020 LEG, Inc. d/b/a West Academic
    444 Cedar Street, Suite 700
    St. Paul, MN 55101
    1-877-888-1330

Printed in the United States of America

ISBN: 978-1-68467-021-5

PREFACE

This Thirteenth Edition represents another updating and a thorough rewriting. Nevertheless, the revision also reflects a basic satisfaction with the objectives, with the methods, and generally with the depth and range of coverage that have characterized this casebook since its beginnings. Therefore, I appropriately begin with the words that Professors Field and Kaplan used to describe their trailblazing First Edition:

"Traditional courses in Civil Procedure suffered from being too much concerned with detail and too diffuse. These defects were perhaps due to an overscrupulous regard for the obligations which Procedure was thought to owe to other courses in the curriculum; in all events Procedure often seemed to underplay the fact that it had distinctive missions of its own. And in straining either for omnibus coverage or for the satisfactions that came from historical exposition, the traditional courses dwelt too long on the common law and older code systems and gave less than adequate attention to current practice.

"We have sought to avoid these errors even if we have succeeded only in committing others. A basic course should, we think, lay stress on the fundamental and recurrent problems of litigative procedure as against particular procedural devices. To be sure, the course should insist on the mastery of specifics, but the larger picture should be kept in view. As a second objective, not antithetical but rather intrinsic to the first, the course should give a rounded understanding of a single, modern system of procedure. The choice naturally falls on the Federal system. The common law and older codes may come in by way of comparison and as a reading of the minutes of yesterday's meeting, but the Federal Rules should be a principal theme.

"The belief that the course should deal in a large way with the litigative process has impelled us at various points to deal explicitly with the general attitudes that underlie and characterize current procedural modes. . . .

"On the side of method, we set much store by the pedagogical device which will be found early in this book in Part One, Topic B, entitled 'Phases of a Lawsuit.' Here we have about 150 pages of text interspersed with cases, statutes and questions, describing and analyzing the conduct of litigation in the Federal courts from the institution of suit through appeal. We have sought here to convey bedrock information and to locate and expose significant questions which provide the basis for much of the rest of the book. This initial survey makes considerable demands on students but it seems to us to have the virtues of giving them a sense of procedure as a whole, of raising at the threshold and keeping steadily before them the fundamental and recurrent problems of adjudication, and of enabling them to proceed thereafter on a more profound level than they might otherwise attain. Perhaps we should add that after this survey we have felt less than the usual scruples of conscience about making some omissions later in the course as pressure of time has compelled it.

. . . .

"Teachers of Procedure have differed widely about the route to be travelled, but they have not differed much about the ultimate goal. They have sought in their separate ways to turn out lawyers who will not approach a practice question as just an exercise in using the index to the practice act or the rule book, but who will go about the job with a lively awareness of the importance of farsighted procedural strategy, a sense of the total procedural resources of the law, and a feeling of personal responsibility for the fair and efficient running of procedural machinery. We have hoped in this book to help students toward the vital skills and attitudes."

Those words still stand as a statement of our views on what a Civil Procedure course should try to do. Also, we continue to rely on the concentric series of three surveys of the whole in Topics A, B, and C of Part 1. These give the student a solid grounding in the subject and thereby free the teacher to pick and choose among the theoretical and practical problem areas explored in the subsequent Parts of the current edition.

As many teachers today have witnessed the contraction of civil procedure courses into as few as three semester-hours, perhaps all in the first semester of law school—a contraction imposed just when the subject has dramatically expanded and diversified—they have come to realize that conciseness in teaching materials is no longer merely a virtue but is now an essential. The technique of an initial but substantial survey seems more and more appropriate for, and indeed uniquely suited to, the modern compact course.

Overall Aim. Teachers of civil procedure have widely shared goals, in addition to the practical ones mentioned by Field and Kaplan. First, we want students to perceive the essence and ultimately the thematic coherence of the adversary system prevailing in U.S. courts. The survey is the tool here. Second, we want to convey an understanding of the constitutional and legal structure in which those courts operate. Selecting certain major problems for in-depth study can facilitate this goal. Third, we believe that the whole course serves another purpose, namely, to develop a sense of the importance of any given procedural system in constructing the surrounding body of substantive law. Indeed, all U.S. civil procedure professors recognize that no one can begin to understand any legal system without a careful dissection of its procedural component.

The materials' arrangement allows accomplishing these goals effectively. By utilizing the survey the teacher can fulfill the responsibility of getting across the essential information, while reserving enough time to do the more significant and palatable. However, the structure of the casebook is not a straitjacket. Some teachers, for example, might prefer to begin with the jurisdictional materials.

Pedagogic Theory. The suggestion of flexibility in pursuing the overall aim does not mean that the book arrives with no thought behind the order of materials. Nor does the emphasis on brevity imply that the resort to a survey method is a simple-minded concession to the press of time. A pedagogic theory definitely lies behind the book.

Teaching basic civil procedure has its problems. The first one the teacher meets is getting into a subject so marked by *interdependencies of parts.* To understand anything the student must understand everything. Where to approach a truly seamless web constitutes a tricky problem indeed.

This casebook's solution is not to find a seam, but to present the whole. Part 1 of the casebook in fact provides a series of three concentric overviews of increasing breadth and depth. Each is small enough in scope for the students to absorb when they reach it, but each stretches their minds sufficiently to prepare them for the greater effort of assimilating the succeeding materials. Topic A examines a single case, providing the students enough introductory information to understand that case adequately and to create a context for the more detailed study to come. Topic B presents the step-by-step survey of a procedural system, giving the students sufficient detail to develop a working knowledge of federal procedure but not so much detail as to obscure for all time the big picture. Topic C unveils that big picture, looking broadly at a system of justice and thus rounding out the students' introduction to procedure.

The step-by-step survey of the entire subject in Part 1 is more than an introduction, though. It suffices to give the students a complete and solid grounding in civil procedure. Between the opening case of Sibbach v. Wilson & Co. in Topic A and the closing overview in Topic C based on the Lassiter case, there is a tight comprehensive treatment of modern civil procedure, 200+ pages comprising cases and commentaries and text and questions that progress from pretrial to settlement to trial to judgment to appeal to jurisdiction to complex litigation. In many civil procedure casebooks, a desire to expose the students to, say, discovery entails covering (or hopping through) more than a hundred pages and expending several weeks of precious class hours. And comprehensibly piecing a number of such hasty forays together into a compact course appears to expect too much. In our casebook, brief yet thorough coverage can be effected through its efficient and systematic step-by-step survey.

This scheme allows the student to build up to a solid grasp of procedure as a whole, with a minimum of real confusion. With the foundation laid by the survey and with relative freedom from concerns about coverage, the teacher can turn to the theoretical, doctrinal, and practical problem areas addressed in depth in the rest of the casebook, to the extent that time permits. The student is ready for the challenges of in-depth study of some of the fundamental problems of procedure: those relating to federalism, jurisdiction, res judicata, or whatever, the study of which will in turn illuminate the opening coverage. Along the way through Part 1, the student has also picked up the necessary bedrock information concerning the mechanics of procedure. This permits the teacher freely to pick and choose among the theoretical and practical problems addressed in the subsequent Parts of the casebook, selecting materials or supplementing them to suit particular tastes and needs and to fit a course of any length. Ideally, then, the compactness of Part 1 enhances the student's basic comprehension, while its comprehensiveness frees the teacher of worries about coverage.

Thus, the casebook's approach is to present the subject of civil procedure to the students in a series of waves, each successive one of greater sophistication. This allows the students to understand far more broadly and to probe far more deeply than an approach that seemingly goes neatly from area to area in covering the law of civil procedure without any doubling back. Moreover, the casebook's approach is much more effective at addressing another major problem in teaching basic civil procedure: the *latency of values* that marks the subject. Only after some time and considerable effort can the students perceive and weigh the fundamental values at play in any area of procedure. It would be a shame to complete the study of a particular area before the students were prepared to begin that study.

Stories' Methodology. One seemingly odd decision made in seeking conciseness was to include five (heavily re-edited) stories from the acclaimed Civil Procedure Stories (2d ed. 2008). The story of Hickman or the story of Hansberry can work wonders in quickly conveying a sense of a whole field such as pretrial discovery or class actions. At the same time, pausing for a while on one case can do a lot to counter the modern teaching tendency to rush through cases in order to lecture on the rule of the case. Today's teacher faces lots of temptations to go in that direction, in the pursuit of speedy coverage of the vast and rich subject and in the pursuit of delivery of knowledge rather than creation of understanding. The story method is an antidote. Studying a selected few cases with special care, criticism, and activism best allows the student to create that understanding.

Other benefits flow from the stories' eschewing the acontextual presentation of a case. A thorough treatment of the facts and proceedings shows the law in action, along with its various actors (and especially lawyers) likewise in action; it helps students to understand the legal process, as to both dispute-processing and lawmaking; it instructs on what the law values, and what the law does not value; and, at the same time, it humanizes the law, showing the roles people play in creating law and the effects law has on people's lives. Putting the case into its socio-economic-political context can illuminate the reasons for a judicial decision and its truer meaning, while simultaneously attuning the students to the importance of viewing the law from the perspectives of many different academic disciplines. All these benefits are not a bad payoff for a method that incidentally makes the course more interesting and even more fun for teacher and students.

In sum, including these stories in the Unabridged Edition seems a no-brainer. But inclusion of a few stories fits with even the Concise Edition's mission of delivering a compact book for short courses without substantial pedagogic sacrifices, and might even lead to a better course.

Current Revision. Each succeeding edition has altered the emphases and refined the techniques, of course. In recent editions, for example, we have further attempted to foster diverse teaching by facilitating digression during the survey at one or more points to the more advanced subsequent materials. Moreover, we rely ever more on excerpted commentary to convey a sense of the intellectual richness of Procedure.

The law persists in its refusal to stand still, fortunately. So the contents of this latest edition—as opposed to its structure—are again newfashioned. We undertook this unavoidable part of the rewriting task with a renewed determination to integrate rather than append new developments. Our regard for earlier editions of this casebook has not constrained alterations in coverage to those forced upon us by legislators, rulemakers, and courts. Thus, we have tried to keep the focus moving to the significant new ideas in the field. The result of this enrichment of subject is a very slightly longer casebook. Nevertheless, this increase in length should not diminish the casebook's teachability—thanks to its structure, which permits the instructor to convey an effective compendium and then to select among problem areas according to tastes and needs.

In summary, the Thirteenth Edition represents growth along lines consistent with the First Edition's conception of stressing the current and pursuing Procedure's own distinctive and evolving missions. Yet concerned with methodology, we pruned and trained that growth within the casebook's proven structure. Also wary of letting the new growth obscure the basics, we did not forget the abiding importance of typical litigation in American courts today as a locus of lawmaking and value-articulation as well as of dispute resolution, nor did we abolish among Procedure's missions its supporting role in the law-school curriculum as a source of illumination.

Some Miscellanea. We strive to reproduce the original materials as accurately as possible. Thus, what may appear to be a typographic error is more likely a faithful reproduction of an official court document.

"It's downright embarrassing. Thirty years on the bench and just today I find out judgment is spelled without an 'E'."

We continue our practice of using the original numbers for footnotes by judges in judicial opinions and by authors in quoted materials, when we retain such footnotes; we omit other such footnotes without any statement to that effect. Editors' footnotes are lettered rather than numbered.

In some of the cases the editors' bracketed statement of the facts includes information culled from the record. We specifically comment on any such supplementation in our version of the case only when the original omission of information by the opinion-writer could conceivably have had some significance.

We do not advise the student to turn regularly to treatises or law review articles in preparing for class discussion, but we do note their availability for research and other special purposes. In our text we make frequent reference to the two major multivolume works—Federal Practice and Procedure by Professors Charles Alan Wright and Arthur R. Miller and others, and James Wm. Moore's Federal Practice—which we simply cite respectively as Wright & Miller and as Moore. We also often cite Charles Alan Wright & Mary Kay Kane, Law of Federal Courts (8th ed. 2017), a single-volume hornbook on the jurisdiction and practice of the federal courts, and Geoffrey C. Hazard, Jr., John Leubsdorf &

Debra Lyn Bassett, Civil Procedure (6th ed. 2011), a single volume dealing with procedure more generally. We cite other treatises and law review articles on a highly selective basis, usually when we think they are especially useful adjuncts to our cases and text.

For the final note, I should explain why I use "we" in writing this preface to mean the three of us even though Professor Field died in 1978 and the late Justice Kaplan's absorption in judging precluded active participation after the Second Edition in 1968. My reason lies in their original conception and their powers to convey it, which give me the sensation of a continuing collaboration that prevails over the bounds of time.

K.M.C.

January 2020

FEDERAL RULES BOOKLET

The Federal Rules of Civil Procedure (together with the Advisory Committee's notes on the major amendments), many of the Federal Rules of Appellate Procedure, selected provisions of the Constitution of the United States and title 28 of the United States Code and other procedural statutes, and the Federal Rules of Evidence are integral to this book. They are printed in a separate booklet by Foundation Press.

ACKNOWLEDGMENTS

We gratefully acknowledge the permission extended by the following publishers and authors to reprint excerpts from the works indicated: American Bar Association Journal: Joint Conference on Professional Responsibility, Report, 44 A.B.A.J. 1159 (1958) ("Reprinted with permission from American Bar Association Journal"), and ABA Comm. on Prof'l Ethics & Grievances, Formal Op. 280, 35 A.B.A.J. 876 (1949); Foundation Press, Inc.: L. Fuller, The Problems of Jurisprudence (1949), and J. Maguire, Evidence: Common Sense and Common Law (1947); American Bar Association Reports: Pound, The Causes of Popular Dissatisfaction with the Administration of Justice, 29 A.B.A.Rep. 395 (1906); Princeton University Press: J. Frank, Courts on Trial (1949) ("Reprinted by permission of Princeton University Press"); West Publishing Co.: Schaefer, Is the Adversary System Working in Optimal Fashion?, 70 F.R.D. 159 (1976), Clark, Simplified Pleading, 2 F.R.D. 456 (1943), B. Shipman, Handbook of Common-Law Pleading (3d ed. 1923), and P. Carrington, D. Meador & M. Rosenberg, Justice on Appeal (1976); Notre Dame Lawyer: Barrett, The Adversary System and the Ethics of Advocacy, 37 Notre Dame Law. 479 (1962) ("Reprinted with permission. © by the Notre Dame Lawyer, University of Notre Dame.") (We bear responsibility for any errors which have occurred in reprinting or editing.); American Law Institute: Morgan, Foreword to Model Code of Evidence (1942) ("Copyright 1942 by The American Law Institute. Reprinted with the permission of The American Law Institute."), Restatement of Judgments (Am. Law Inst. 1942), Restatement (Second) of Conflict of Laws (1971) (revised 1988) ("Copyright 1971 by The American Law Institute. Reprinted with the permission of The American Law Institute."), and Restatement (Second) of Judgments (1982) ("Copyright 1982 by The American Law Institute. Reprinted with the permission of The American Law Institute."); Stanford Law Review: Curtis, The Ethics of Advocacy, 4 Stan.L.Rev. 3 (1951) ("Copyright 1951 by the Board of Trustees of the Leland Stanford Junior University"), and Scott, Two Models of the Civil Process, 27 Stan.L.Rev. 937 (1975) ("Copyright 1975 by the Board of Trustees of the Leland Stanford Junior University"); New York University School of Law: Simpson, "The Problem of Trial," in David Dudley Field Centenary Essays 141 (A. Reppy ed., 1949); Yale Law Journal: Smith, Components of Proof in Legal Proceedings, 51 Yale L.J. 537 (1942) ("Reprinted by permission of The Yale Law Journal Company and Fred B. Rothman & Company from The Yale Law Journal, Vol. 51, pp. 537, 575"), and Crick, The Final Judgment as a Basis for Appeal, 41 Yale L.J. 539 (1932); Harcourt, Brace & Co.: G. Joughin & E. Morgan, The Legacy of Sacco and Vanzetti (1948); Abram Chayes: The Role of the Judge in Public Law Litigation, 89 Harv.L.Rev. 1281 (1976); Columbia University Press: N.Y. Cty. Lawyers' Ass'n Comm. on Prof'l Ethics, Op. 309 (1933); Marvin E. Frankel: The Search for Truth: An Umpireal View, 123 U.Pa.L.Rev. 1031 (1975); Buffalo Law Review:

Kaplan, Civil Procedure—Reflections on the Comparison of Systems, 9 Buff.L.Rev. 409 (1960); Cambridge University Press: F. Maitland, The Forms of Action at Common Law (1936), F. Maitland, The Constitutional History of England (1908), and F. Maitland, Equity (1909); Harvard Law Review Association: Morgan, Some Observations Concerning Presumptions, 44 Harv.L.Rev. 906 (1931), Morgan, Instructing the Jury upon Presumptions and Burden of Proof, 47 Harv.L.Rev. 59 (1933), Henderson, The Background of the Seventh Amendment, 80 Harv.L.Rev. 289 (1966), and Note, Appealability in the Federal Courts, 75 Harv.L.Rev. 351 (1961); Stevens & Sons, Ltd.: C. Fifoot, History and Sources of the Common Law (1949); Columbia Law Review: Adams, The Origin of English Equity, 16 Colum.L.Rev. 87 (1916); Methuen & Co., Ltd.: W. Holdsworth, A History of English Law (7th ed. 1956); University of Michigan Law School: Z. Chafee, Some Problems of Equity (1950); Little, Brown and Company: Bowen, "Progress in the Administration of Justice During the Victorian Period," in 1 Select Essays in Anglo-American Legal History 516 (1907), G. Hazard, J. Leubsdorf & D. Bassett, Civil Procedure (6th ed. 2011), F. James, G. Hazard & J. Leubsdorf, Civil Procedure (5th ed. 2001), F. James & G. Hazard, Civil Procedure (3d ed. 1985), and F. James, Civil Procedure (1965); Macmillan Co.: The Diary of George Templeton Strong (A. Nevins & M. Thomas eds., 1952); Georgia Law Review: Wright, Procedural Reform: Its Limitations and Its Future, 1 Ga.L.Rev. 563 (1967); Minnesota Law Review: Wolfram, The Constitutional History of the Seventh Amendment, 57 Minn.L.Rev. 639 (1973); and Michigan Law Review: Reed, Compulsory Joinder of Parties in Civil Actions (pt. 1), 55 Mich.L.Rev. 327 (1957).

Also: Greenwood Press, Inc.: Golding, "On the Adversary System and Justice," in Philosophical Law 98 (R. Bronaugh ed., 1978); West Publishing Co.: Sander, Varieties of Dispute Processing, 70 F.R.D. 111 (1976), and Current Developments in Judicial Administration: Papers Presented at the Plenary Session of the American Association of Law Schools, December, 1977, 80 F.R.D. 147 (1979); Buffalo Law Review: Landsman, The Decline of the Adversary System: How the Rhetoric of Swift and Certain Justice Has Affected Adjudication in American Courts, 29 Buff.L.Rev. 487 (1980); National Clearinghouse for Legal Services, Inc.: Singer, Nonjudicial Dispute Resolution Mechanisms: The Effects on Justice for the Poor, 13 Clearinghouse Rev. 569 (1979); American Judicature Society: Luskin, Building a Theory of Case Processing Time, 62 Judicature 115 (1978); Joseph W. Bartlett: The Law Business: A Tired Monopoly (1982); American Bar Foundation Research Journal: Brazil, Improving Judicial Controls over the Pretrial Development of Civil Actions: Model Rules for Case Management and Sanctions, 1981 Am.B.Found.Res.J. 873; Harvard Law Review Association: Resnik, Managerial Judges, 96 Harv.L.Rev. 374 (1982) ("Copyright © 1982 by the Harvard Law Review Association."), Chayes, The Supreme Court, 1981 Term—Foreword: Public Law Litigation and the Burger Court, 96 Harv.L.Rev. 4 (1982) ("Copyright © 1982 by the Harvard Law Review

Association."), and Miller, Of Frankenstein Monsters and Shining Knights: Myth, Reality, and the "Class Action Problem," 92 Harv.L.Rev. 664 (1979) ("Copyright © 1979 by the Harvard Law Review Association."); American Bar Association: Ebersole, "Discovery and Pretrial Procedures," in The Improvement of the Administration of Justice 137 (F. Klein ed., 6th ed. 1981); Michigan Law Review: Note, A Probabilistic Analysis of the Doctrine of Mutuality of Collateral Estoppel, 76 Mich.L.Rev. 612 (1978); Frank M. Coffin: The Frontier of Remedies: A Call for Exploration, 67 Calif.L.Rev. 983 (1979); Stanford Law Review: Rhode, Class Conflicts in Class Actions, 34 Stan.L.Rev. 1183 (1982) ("Copyright 1982 by the Board of Trustees of the Leland Stanford Junior University"); Harvard Civil Rights-Civil Liberties Law Review: Jones, Litigation Without Representation: The Need for Intervention to Affirm Affirmative Action, 14 Harv.C.R.-C.L.L.Rev. 31 (1979); and U.C. Davis Law Review: Friedenthal, Increased Participation by Non-Parties: The Need for Limitations and Conditions, 13 U.C.Davis L.Rev. 259 (1980).

More recently: American Bar Association: Model Rules of Professional Conduct (1983) ("Excerpted from the Model Rules of Professional Conduct, copyright by the American Bar Association. All rights reserved. Reprinted with permission."); Minnesota Law Review: Shapiro, Some Problems of Discovery in an Adversary System, 63 Minn.L.Rev. 1055 (1979); Academic Press: Hans & Vidmar, "Jury Selection," in The Psychology of the Courtroom 39 (N. Kerr & R. Bray eds., 1982); Van Nostrand Reinhold: M. Saks & R. Hastie, Social Psychology in Court (1978); Journal of Legal Education: Spiegelman, Integrating Doctrine, Theory and Practice in the Law School Curriculum: The Logic of Jake's Ladder in the Context of Amy's Web, 38 J.Legal Educ. 243 (1988); Texas Law Review: Abel, Why Does the ABA Promulgate Ethical Rules?, 59 Tex.L.Rev. 639 (1981) ("Published originally in 59 Texas Law Review 639–88 (1981). Copyright © 1981 by the Texas Law Review. Reprinted by permission."); University of Florida Law Review: Sander, Alternative Methods of Dispute Resolution: An Overview, 37 U.Fla.L.Rev. 1 (1985); Little, Brown and Company: S. Goldberg, F. Sander & N. Rogers, Dispute Resolution (2d ed. 1992); National Clearinghouse for Legal Services, Inc.: Simon, Legal Informality and Redistributive Politics, 19 Clearinghouse Rev. 384 (1985); Wisconsin Law Review: Bush, Dispute Resolution Alternatives and the Goals of Civil Justice: Jurisdictional Principles for Process Choice, 1984 Wis.L.Rev. 893; Stephen N. Subrin: How Equity Conquered Common Law: The Federal Rules of Civil Procedure in Historical Perspective, 135 U.Pa.L.Rev. 909 (1987); Columbia Law Review: Marcus, The Revival of Fact Pleading Under the Federal Rules of Civil Procedure, 86 Colum.L.Rev. 433 (1986) ("Copyright © 1986 by the Directors of the Columbia Law Review Association, Inc. All Rights Reserved. This article originally appeared at 86 Colum.L.Rev. 433 (1986). Reprinted by permission."); UCLA Law Review: Menkel-Meadow, For and Against Settlement: Uses and Abuses of the Mandatory Settlement Conference,

33 UCLA L.Rev. 485 (1985); Jeffrey W. Stempel: A Distorted Mirror: The Supreme Court's Shimmering View of Summary Judgment, Directed Verdict, and the Adjudication Process, 49 Ohio St.L.J. 95 (1988); The Michie Company: J. Frederick, The Psychology of the American Jury (1987); Kentucky Law Journal: Stephens, Controlling the Civil Jury: Towards a Functional Model of Justification, 76 Ky.L.J. 81 (1988); Plenum Publishing Corp.: V. Hans & N. Vidmar, Judging the Jury (1986); Cornell Law Review: Idleman, The Emergence of Jurisdictional Resequencing in the Federal Courts, 87 Cornell L.Rev. 1 (2001); North Carolina Law Review: Tobias, Rule 19 and the Public Rights Exception to Party Joinder, 65 N.C.L.Rev. 745 (1987) ("Reprinted with permission from 65 N.C.L.Rev. 745 (1987). Copyright © 1987 by the North Carolina Law Review Association."); American Law Institute: Complex Litigation (1994) ("Copyright 1994 by The American Law Institute. Reprinted with the permission of The American Law Institute."); Roger H. Trangsrud: Joinder Alternatives in Mass Tort Litigation, 70 Cornell L.Rev. 779 (1985); Indiana Law Journal: Rosenberg, Class Actions for Mass Torts: Doing Individual Justice by Collective Means, 62 Ind.L.J. 561 (1987); and South Carolina Law Review: Carrington, The Function of the Civil Appeal: A Late-Century View, 38 S.C.L.Rev. 411 (1987).

SUMMARY OF CONTENTS

PART 1. A FIRST VIEW OF THE SUBJECT

PART 2. GOVERNING LAW

PART 3. AUTHORITY TO ADJUDICATE

PART 4. FORMER ADJUDICATION

TABLE OF CONTENTS

PART 2. GOVERNING LAW

PART 3. AUTHORITY TO ADJUDICATE

PART 4. FORMER ADJUDICATION

TABLE OF CASES

The principal cases are in bold type.

TABLE OF STATUTES

TABLE OF RULES

MATERIALS FOR A BASIC COURSE IN

CIVIL PROCEDURE

CONCISE THIRTEENTH EDITION

PART 1

A FIRST VIEW OF THE SUBJECT

TOPIC A

OPENING STATEMENTS

This course treats "Civil Procedure." For the purpose of putting general boundaries to the course, what meanings do we ascribe to these words? We shall not attempt here to define them in any formal way, but shall rather begin at this point to convey a sense of the meanings we attach to them.

Nature of civil controversies.—The word "civil" appears in the present context in contradistinction to "criminal." The typical criminal case is one that the government initiates for the purpose of securing obedience to its laws by the punishment, correction, or incapacitation of a lawbreaker. In a civil case, ordinarily the government is not seeking a sanction against a lawbreaker, nor is it even a party in the proceedings. The typical civil case is one initiated and maintained by a person who seeks redress for some wrong alleged to have been committed against him by another. The redress he seeks is commonly, although by no means always, the payment of money to him by the wrongdoer.[a]

Wrongs can arise when people interact. In their interactions, people living together in organized society are bound by rules governing their day-to-day conduct, imposed in one way or another by the government. These are rules of substance, or of substantive law. A rule of substantive law may be embodied in a legislative enactment—an act of Congress, an act of a state legislature, or a municipal ordinance. Often it finds its source instead in the "common law," the decisions and opinions of the courts.[b] Whatever the source of a rule of substantive law, one may cast it in the form of a proposition such as the following:

If B knowingly strikes A, and . . . , then, unless A consented, or . . . , A is entitled to a judgment of a court that he recover money damages from B.

---

[a] What cases suggest themselves where the payment of money would not be a satisfactory form of redress? What other forms of redress might be appropriate? After considering these questions, see infra p. 230.

[*Note:* Editor's footnotes throughout this casebook are lettered. Footnotes by the court in judicial opinions and by authors in quoted materials, when retained, will bear the numbers of the originals; we shall omit the other footnotes without any statement to that effect.]

[b] "With the common law, unlike the [European] civil law and its Roman law precursor, the formulation of general principles has not preceded decision. In its origin it is the law of the practitioner rather than the philosopher. Decision has drawn its inspiration and its strength from the very facts which frame the issues for decision. Once made, the decision controls the future judgments of courts in like or analogous cases. General rules, underlying principles, and finally legal doctrine, have successively emerged only as the precedents, accumulated through the centuries, have been seen to follow a pattern, characteristically not without distortion and occasional broken threads, and seldom conforming consistently to principle." Harlan F. Stone, The Common Law in the United States, 50 Harv.L.Rev. 4, 6 (1936).

This particular proposition refers to an event that the law calls a battery. Rules of this sort state the rights and duties among people and suggest the circumstances in which a person may seek redress against another.

The government establishes and maintains a system of courts to which a person may resort, if the person chooses to do so, to obtain such redress. Predominantly, then, the task of courts in civil cases is to decide specific cases brought before them by people who cannot or will not follow the usual course of settling their disagreements by themselves. True, in deciding a case a court will apply or generate general rules that guide other people later involved in similar disagreements. Much of the law student's work entails the appraisal and use of past decisions, and judicial opinions explaining these decisions, as precedents to aid in predicting how courts would likely decide future cases. These decisions and opinions are tools of the lawyer's trade. They help him or her, as adviser, to resolve the client's difficulties short of litigation and, as advocate, to further the client's cause if litigation comes. This constant resort to precedents tends, however, to becloud the proposition that a traditional purpose of a typical lawsuit is to decide a very real dispute between flesh-and-blood people and, where possible, to resolve it once and for all.[c] What, then, is the nature of these disputes with which the courts have to deal in civil cases?

In many cases that come to the courts there is dispute over what the rule of substantive law is. Legislation may be of doubtful meaning, or precedents may not speak with a clear voice. New sets of circumstances arise to pose problems for which neither existing legislation nor the precedents afford a ready answer. A court must nevertheless decide the case before it and will do so with a view to existing rules of substantive law and upon some consideration of historical continuity, of institutional competence, of prevailing morals, of policy goals, and of other factors.

In other cases the substantive law will be pretty clear, and the contest will be over what happened. The parties may agree that the pertinent rule of substantive law is the one given schematically above, but they may differ as to whether *B* struck *A,* whether she did so knowingly, or whether *A* consented.

In still other cases there will be a contest both as to what occurred and as to what the applicable rule is. In lawyers' language, such a dispute presents both questions of fact ("What happened?") and questions of law ("What is the substantive rule?").

A first word of warning is in order here. Although we have spoken of the "typical civil case," the student should not let this focus create blinders. Of late, interest in several quarters has shifted toward complex

---

[c]   There are elaborate rules designed to prevent the relitigation of disputes once adjudged by a court. Reference to these rules, which cluster under the banner of "res judicata," recurs throughout this book. We treat them in detail in Part 4.

litigation, exemplified prototypically by desegregation cases and characterized by vastly intensified public concern and participation. Concomitantly, interest has also shifted toward alternatives to litigation, whereby almost all grievances conclude short of judicial adjudication. In some significant senses, so-called public law litigation and alternative dispute resolution both are more important than the typical civil case. Accordingly, this book will eventually turn to those matters, and the student should meanwhile bear them in mind. Nevertheless, we begin our study with so-called ordinary litigation, partly because it has abiding importance, and partly because one must begin somewhere, but mainly because we view this as the pedagogically sound place to begin.

Nature of procedural rules.—In statutes enacted by the legislature, in sets of general rules promulgated by the courts, and in specific judicial rulings having the force of precedent, the government prescribes the procedures by which persons may bring disputes before its courts, by which they must unfold and conduct those disputes once in the courts, and by which they can enforce the resulting decisions of the courts. The scope of procedural provisions may be roughly gauged by examining the table of contents of the "Federal Rules of Civil Procedure." This course deals with all such procedures, which you may consider as the mechanics of litigation.

Rules of procedure, in this broad sense, provide among other things the means of laying bare what the contest is about. The court, in theory at least, knows nothing of the state of affairs between the contestants until one of them formally presents a claim to it. The rules of procedure regulate how he must do this, and also how his adversary must present the adverse side of the matter, so that the court can judge between them and grant or refuse redress. One aim of the rules is to disclose the real dispute in a minimum of time and with least expense, and thus to avoid the vexatious and wasteful business of dealing with questions on which the parties are actually not in disagreement. Another aim is to confine the parties to presenting only materials relevant to the real dispute and helpful in its resolution. Yet another is to give neither side an undeserved forensic advantage in persuading the court.

Litigation could perhaps proceed without general procedures established in advance. The parties or the court could conceivably determine as an original matter, case by case, the procedures that they consider appropriate to the particular dispute to be resolved. In out-of-court arbitration, procedures are in fact frequently improvised for the particular case. But this has not been the mode of our courts' litigation. The conduct of litigation follows existing rules of more or less general application.

Nevertheless, there remains room within the rules for a certain amount of individualized treatment of cases, and room also for discretion, experimentation, and invention as well as for argument. Perhaps procedural rules ought to be so definite and clear-cut as always to furnish a sure guide for the behavior of the parties and the courts. Whether or not this would be the ideal situation, one can say at the outset that it has not been attained, and one may doubt whether it ever could be attained.

Moreover, the rules are subject to change, have changed from time to time, and will undergo change in the future. Some of the rules look principally to preserving a settled order of proceeding. The system could radically alter them without important consequence. In respect to other rules, there are powerful reasons of policy why they should be as they are, or should not be as they are. The competing considerations in such areas of procedure will absorb much of our attention in this course.

So, it is mainly by this apparatus of malleable and changeable procedural rules, and their application by parties and courts, that society seeks to ensure that litigation will be accurately resolved in a fair and orderly way and as expeditiously and economically as may be practicable. It is this apparatus that we shall study.

We must nevertheless approach the study of procedure with full awareness that we shall be bedeviled by many of the same doubts and difficulties about what the rule is, or ought to be, that characterize the study of substantive law. Therefore, although the rules of procedure aim to isolate and sharpen the issues in controversy and thus to simplify the dispute, the uncertainties in the procedural law may serve to inject a further disputatious ingredient into a lawsuit. Procedural problems are more obtrusive in our law than a beginner is likely to suppose, and perhaps more obtrusive than they ought to be.[d]

The substance/procedure distinction.—It may already be apparent that there will be difficulties in assigning particular rules to the category of substance or the category of procedure. These difficulties will sometimes defy the most careful and circumspect attempts to delineate the categories. For example, take a "statute of limitations" laying it down that a plaintiff must commence an action for battery within two years after the event. One might say that this is a rule of substance, for it expresses a firm condition on the plaintiff's right to recover. Yet, another might say that this is a rule of procedure, for it regulates a step in a lawsuit, the first step, the time within which the plaintiff must sue. We shall see many instances, and many more poignant instances, where classification will be difficult.

---

[d]   Compare the following statement: "It is characteristic of the prevailing rationalistic systems of legal philosophy that they minimize the importance of procedure by calling it adjective law, etc. But the tendency of all modern scientific and philosophic thought is to weaken the distinction between substance and attribute . . . and to emphasize the importance of method, process, or procedure." Morris R. Cohen, "The Process of Judicial Legislation," in Law and the Social Order 112, 128 (1933). Or, "The history of American freedom is, in no small measure, the history of procedure." Malinski v. New York, 324 U.S. 401, 414, 65 S.Ct. 781, 787 (1945) (Frankfurter, J., concurring). Or, "Procedure is the bone structure of a democratic society . . . ." Abe Fortas, Concerning Dissent and Civil Disobedience 104 (1968). Or, "I'll let you write the substance . . . and you let me write the procedure, and I'll screw you every time." Regulatory Reform Act: Hearings on H.R. 2327 Before the Subcomm. on Admin. Law and Gov'tal Relations of the House Comm. on the Judiciary, 98th Cong. 312 (1983) (statement of Rep. John Dingell).

But why should we be concerned with mere classification? Certainly difficulties of classification are of small consequence if the aim is the lowly one of assigning subject matter to courses in a law school, so that if we conceive the statute of limitations to be a rule of procedure, its study would fall within Civil Procedure, but if conceived to be a rule of substance, it would be dealt with elsewhere. We shall be casual about course boundaries; if a problem arises in the heartland of Civil Procedure and takes us beyond that field, we shall follow it; and we shall often trespass on other courses without even that excuse. It is, indeed, one of our main tasks to observe how a legal problem may cut across many conventional departments of the law, and extend beyond the law.

There is, however, another and graver matter. It happens that legislatures and courts constantly use such titles as "civil procedure" or "civil practice," and they also constantly use the words "procedure" and "substance" and cognate words. Moreover, they attach serious consequences to these labels. Thus, the matter of classification may become important.

Our first case, Sibbach v. Wilson & Co., raises a question of the meaning of "practice and procedure" and "substantive rights" as those words appear in the very Act of Congress that originally empowered the Supreme Court of the United States to promulgate the Federal Rules of Civil Procedure.

———

Sibbach v. Wilson & Co.

Supreme Court of the United States, 1941.
312 U.S. 1, 61 S.Ct. 422.

Certiorari to the Circuit Court of Appeals for the Seventh Circuit.

■ MR. JUSTICE ROBERTS delivered the opinion of the Court.

This case calls for decision as to the validity of Rules 35 and 37 of the Rules of Civil Procedure for District Courts of the United States.

In an action brought by the petitioner[e] in the District Court for Northern Illinois to recover damages for bodily injuries, inflicted in Indiana, respondent answered denying the allegations of the complaint, and moved for an order requiring the petitioner to submit to a physical examination by one or more physicians appointed by the court to determine the nature and extent of her injuries. The court ordered that the petitioner submit to such an examination by a physician so appointed.

---

[e] The petitioner is the party who seeks review in the Supreme Court by writ of certiorari; the respondent is her adversary. The name of the petitioner appears first in the caption of the case in the Supreme Court. In this case the petitioner and the respondent happened to be the plaintiff and the defendant, respectively.

Compliance having been refused, the respondent obtained an order to show cause why the petitioner should not be punished for contempt. In response the petitioner challenged the authority of the court to order her to submit to the examination, asserting that the order was void. It appeared that the courts of Indiana, the state where the cause of action arose, hold such an order proper [citing Indiana precedents], whereas the courts of Illinois, the state in which the trial court sat, hold that such an order cannot be made [citing Illinois precedents]. Neither state has any statute governing the matter.

The court adjudged the petitioner guilty of contempt, and directed that she be committed until she should obey the order for examination or otherwise should be legally discharged from custody. The petitioner appealed.

The Circuit Court of Appeals decided that Rule 35, which authorizes an order for a physical examination in such a case, is valid, and affirmed the judgment. The writ of certiorari was granted because of the importance of the question involved.

The Rules of Civil Procedure were promulgated under the authority of the Act of June 19, 1934, which is:

"Be it enacted [Sec. 1.] That the Supreme Court of the United States shall have the power to prescribe, by general rules, for the district courts of the United States and for the courts of the District of Columbia, the forms of process, writs, pleadings, and motions, and the practice and procedure in civil actions at law. Said rules shall neither abridge, enlarge, nor modify the substantive rights of any litigant. They shall take effect six months after their promulgation, and thereafter all laws in conflict therewith shall be of no further force or effect.

"Sec. 2. The court may at any time unite the general rules prescribed by it for cases in equity with those in actions at law so as to secure one form of civil action and procedure for both: *Provided, however,* That in such union of rules the right of trial by jury as at common law and declared by the seventh amendment to the Constitution shall be preserved to the parties inviolate. Such united rules shall not take effect until they shall have been reported to Congress by the Attorney General at the beginning of a regular session thereof and until after the close of such session."[f]

---

[f]   The Rules Enabling Act of 1934 has since undergone amendment and now primarily appears as § 2072 of title 28 of the United States Code, which is cited as 28 U.S.C. § 2072.

Title 28 contains most of the statutes dealing with procedure in the courts of the United States, as distinguished from the courts of the states. It was revised and recodified in 1948.

The Rules booklet that accompanies this casebook sets out portions of title 28, along with selected provisions of the Constitution of the United States.

[The Supreme Court here quoted the relevant portions of Rules 35 and 37.ᵍ]

The contention of the petitioner, in final analysis, is that Rules 35 and 37 are not within the mandate of Congress to this court. This is the limit of permissible debate, since argument touching the broader questions of Congressional power and of the obligation of federal courts to apply the substantive law of a state is foreclosed.

Congress has undoubted power to regulate the practice and procedure of federal courts [citing Wayman v. Southard, 23 U.S. (10 Wheat.) 1, 21 (1825), among other cases,] and may exercise that power by delegating to this or other federal courts authority to make rules not inconsistent with the statutes or constitution of the United States; but it has never essayed to declare the substantive state law, or to abolish or nullify a right recognized by the substantive law of the state where the cause of action arose, save where a right or duty is imposed in a field committed to Congress by the Constitution. On the contrary it has enacted that the state law shall be the rule of decision in the federal courts.[8]

Hence we conclude that the Act of June 19, 1934, was purposely restricted in its operation to matters of pleading and court practice and procedure. Its two provisos or caveats emphasize this restriction. The first is that the court shall not "abridge, enlarge, nor modify substantive rights," in the guise of regulating procedure. The second is that if the rules are to prescribe a single form of action for cases at law and suits in equity, the constitutional right to jury trial inherent in the former must be preserved. There are other limitations upon the authority to prescribe rules which might have been, but were not mentioned in the Act; for instance, the inability of a court, by rule, to extend or restrict the jurisdiction conferred by a statute.

Whatever may be said as to the effect of the Conformity Actʰ while it remained in force, the rules, if they are within the authority granted by Congress, repeal that statute, and the District Court was not bound

---

ᵍ   Both of these Rules underwent heavy amendment in 1970. Rule 37(b)(2)(iv), which is now Rule 37(b)(2)(A)(vii), formerly read: "In lieu of any of the foregoing orders or in addition thereto, an order directing the arrest of any party or agent of a party for disobeying any of such orders except an order to submit to a physical or mental examination." None of the other changes bears on the Sibbach problem.

The original and amended texts of Rule 37 appear in the Rules booklet. See the section of the Rules booklet containing the amendments and the Advisory Committee's notes thereon.

⁸   [In a footnote here the Court cited the Rules of Decision Act of 1789, now embodied in 28 U.S.C. § 1652. We consider this important statute more extensively in connection with Erie Railroad Co. v. Tompkins in Part 2.]

ʰ   The Conformity Act of 1872, old 28 U.S.C. § 724, provided: "*Conformity to practice in State courts.* The practice, pleadings, and forms and modes of proceedings in civil causes, other than equity and admiralty causes, in the district courts, shall conform, as near as may be, to the practice, pleadings, and forms and modes of proceedings existing at the time in like causes in the courts of record of the State within which such district courts are held, any rule of court to the contrary notwithstanding."

to follow the Illinois practice respecting an order for physical examination. On the other hand if the right to be exempt from such an order is one of substantive law, the Rules of Decision Act required the District Court, though sitting in Illinois, to apply the law of Indiana, the state where the cause of action arose, and to order the examination. To avoid this dilemma[i] the petitioner admits, and, we think, correctly, that Rules 35 and 37 are rules of procedure. She insists, nevertheless, that by the prohibition against abridging substantive rights, Congress has banned the rules here challenged. In order to reach this result she translates "substantive" into "important" or "substantial" rights. And she urges that if a rule affects such a right, albeit the rule is one of procedure merely, its prescription is not within the statutory grant of power embodied in the Act of June 19, 1934. She contends that our decisions and recognized principles require us so to hold.

[After discussing a number of prior decisions relied on by the petitioner, the Court continued:]

We are thrown back, then, to the arguments drawn from the language of the Act of June 19, 1934. Is the phrase "substantive rights" confined to rights conferred by law to be protected and enforced in accordance with the adjective law of judicial procedure? It certainly embraces such rights. One of them is the right not to be injured in one's person by another's negligence, to redress infraction of which the present action was brought. The petitioner says the phrase connotes more; that by its use Congress intended that in regulating procedure this court should not deal with important and substantial rights theretofore recognized. Recognized where and by whom? The state courts are divided as to the power in the absence of statute to order a physical examination. In a number such an order is authorized by statute or rule. The rules in question accord with the procedure now in force in Canada and England.

The asserted right, moreover, is no more important than many others enjoyed by litigants in District Courts sitting in the several states, before the Federal Rules of Civil Procedure altered and abolished old rights or privileges and created new ones in connection with the conduct of litigation. The suggestion that the rule offends the important right to freedom from invasion of the person ignores the fact that, as we hold, no invasion of freedom from personal restraint attaches to refusal so to comply with its provisions. If we were to adopt the suggested criterion of the importance of the alleged right we should invite endless litigation and confusion worse confounded. The test must be whether a rule really regulates procedure,—the judicial process for enforcing rights and duties recognized by substantive law and for justly administering remedy and redress for disregard or infraction of them. That the rules in question are such is admitted.

---

[i]   Assume for the present that the petitioner's dilemma was as stated by the Court. Later cases will shed a different light upon the problem.

Finally, it is urged that Rules 35 and 37 work a major change of policy and that this was not intended by Congress. Apart from the fact already stated, that the policy of the states in this respect has not been uniform, it is to be noted that the authorization of a comprehensive system of court rules was a departure in policy, and that the new policy envisaged in the enabling act of 1934 was that the whole field of court procedure be regulated in the interest of speedy, fair and exact determination of the truth. The challenged rules comport with this policy. Moreover, in accordance with the Act, the rules were submitted to the Congress so that that body might examine them and veto their going into effect if contrary to the policy of the legislature.

The value of the reservation of the power to examine proposed rules, laws and regulations before they become effective is well understood by Congress. It is frequently, as here, employed to make sure that the action under the delegation squares with the Congressional purpose. Evidently the Congress felt the rule was within the ambit of the statute as no effort was made to eliminate it from the proposed body of rules, although this specific rule was attacked and defended before the committees of the two Houses.[18] . . . We conclude that the rules under attack are within the authority granted.

The District Court treated the refusal to comply with its order as a contempt and committed the petitioner therefor. Neither in the Circuit Court of Appeals nor here was this action assigned as error. We think, however, that in the light of the provisions of Rule 37 it was plain error of such a fundamental nature that we should notice it. Section (b)(2)(iv) of Rule 37 exempts from punishment as for contempt the refusal to obey an order that a party submit to a physical or mental examination. The District Court was in error in going counter to this express exemption. The remedies available under the rule in such a case are those enumerated in [today's (b)(2)(A)(i)–(vi)]. For this error we reverse the judgment and remand the cause to the District Court for further proceedings in conformity to this opinion.

Reversed.

■ [JUSTICE FRANKFURTER, in an opinion concurred in by Justices Black, Douglas, and Murphy, took issue with the reasoning of Justice Roberts, who had been joined by Chief Justice Hughes and Justices McReynolds, Stone, and Reed.]

. . . .

Speaking with diffidence in support of a view which has not commended itself to the Court, it does not seem to me that the answer to our question is to be found by an analytic determination whether the

---

[18]   Hearings before the Committee on the Judiciary, House of Representatives, 75th Cong., 3rd Sess., pp. 117, 141; Hearings before a Subcommittee of the Committee on the Judiciary, U.S. Senate, 75th Cong., 3rd Sess., pp. 36, 37, 39, 51. [A few witnesses in the hearings briefly testified that Rule 35 was substantive and otherwise troublesome, thus aggravating concerns among some senators at least.—Ed.]

power of examination here claimed is a matter of procedure or a matter of substance, even assuming that the two are mutually exclusive categories with easily ascertainable contents. The problem seems to me to be controlled by the policy underlying the [traditional immunity from physical examination]. To be sure, the immunity ... has no constitutional sanction. It is amenable to statutory change. But the "inviolability of a person" was deemed to have such historic roots in Anglo-American law that it was not to be curtailed "unless by clear and unquestionable authority of law" [quoting Union Pac. Ry. Co. v. Botsford, 141 U.S. 250, 251–52, 11 S.Ct. 1000, 1001 (1891)]. . . .

So far as national law is concerned, a drastic change in public policy in a matter deeply touching the sensibilities of people or even their prejudices as to privacy, ought not to be inferred from a general authorization to formulate rules for the more uniform and effective dispatch of business on the civil side of the federal courts. I deem a requirement as to the invasion of the person to stand on a very different footing from questions pertaining to the discovery of documents, pre-trial procedure and other devices for the expeditious, economic and fair conduct of litigation. That disobedience of an order under Rule 35 cannot be visited with punishment as for contempt does not mitigate its intrusion into an historic immunity of the privacy of the person. Of course the Rule is compulsive in that the doors of the federal courts otherwise open may be shut to litigants who do not submit to such a physical examination.

In this view little significance attaches to the fact that the Rules, in accordance with the statute, remained on the table of two Houses of Congress without evoking any objection to Rule 35 and thereby automatically came into force. Plainly the Rules are not acts of Congress and can not be treated as such. Having due regard to the mechanics of legislation and the practical conditions surrounding the business of Congress when the Rules were submitted, to draw any inference of tacit approval from non-action by Congress is to appeal to unreality. And so I conclude that to make the drastic change that Rule 35 sought to introduce would require explicit legislation.

   . . . .

———

In reading any case in this course, the student should seek to visualize the successive steps taken by the parties and the courts. Topic B of this Part, "Phases of a Lawsuit," should facilitate understanding of the scenario. Briefing of the cases will aid in this process of visualization and comprehension, as the following sample brief and accompanying notes and questions illustrate.

———

Sample Brief

Facts: Mrs. Sibbach claimed to have received bodily injuries in Indiana, presumably caused by an employee of Wilson & Co.

Notes and Questions

(1) In this part of your brief you should state who the parties are and what happened to them before reaching the courthouse. Limit yourself to the legally relevant facts. For example, Hertha J. Sibbach's case actually arose from a serious automobile accident occurring on September 3, 1937, on a country highway near Gary, Indiana, and involving the truck of Wilson & Co., a giant Chicago-based meatpacker. These facts are not relevant to the issue and so should be omitted from your brief, just as they were omitted from the Supreme Court opinion itself. Sometimes, however, judicial opinions will include a great many irrelevant facts, and you must sift through them for the essence. Moreover, write the "Facts" (and the other entries) in your own words. Nothing is gained by transcribing the opinion.

In briefing a case, you should follow a logical and set format. As to choice of format, many possibilities are defensible. We choose to begin with the out-of-court facts in the interest of chronology and as an indication of their enormous importance in shaping decision. However, we do not here record the fruits of some abstract historical inquiry. Instead, we record the facts as they are accepted by the court for the purpose of decision. These emerge from the procedural maneuvers in the case, and the condition of the facts depends on the procedural posture of the case at the time of decision. For example, in Sibbach the facts rest upon the plaintiff's allegations, because the issues arose at the case's beginnings. Given this legalistic meaning of facts, your job of fixing the facts will prove difficult, meaning that you cannot write this first part of your brief until you have thought about the rest of your brief. This warning reflects the view that competent briefing serves as a record of thorough reading and study, as well as a stimulus to further reading and study.

Prior Proceedings: Plaintiff Sibbach (*P*) sued the corporate

(2) This portion of your brief should be detailed, covering everything that happens from crossing the threshold of the trial court to the moment as of which the opinion before you speaks. This is especially important for this

Sample Brief

defendant (*D*) in the United States District Court for the Northern District of Illinois, alleging negligence and seeking money damages.

Notes and Questions

course because detailed briefing here can be very helpful in mastering procedure and also because the issues presented by a procedure case always arise here. Yet even in your other courses, you should give attention to this aspect of the brief, because it is often impossible to know precisely what or why a court is deciding without knowing the procedural background of the case. To put it better: "Now a case never reaches a court of review until it has first been through a tribunal of trial—else there would be nothing to review. But the cases, so-called, in your case-books are almost exclusively chosen from courts of review. To understand them, therefore, you must get at least some quick picture of what has gone on before they got there." Karl N. Llewellyn, The Bramble Bush 20 (7th printing 1981).

(3) There is a considerable amount of learning between the lines of the sample brief's first short entry concerning "Prior Proceedings." We shall attempt to sketch it out, previewing material you will soon study and also using some information concerning the case that appears in the court record but does not appear in the opinion itself.

First, Sibbach's suit was one of the sort that can be brought in either state or federal court. An essential concept here is that federal courts, unlike many state courts, are courts of limited jurisdiction. This means that federal courts normally have the power to hear only those kinds of cases that are within the constitutional grant of federal judicial power (see Article III, Section 2 of the Constitution) and that are also within some congressional enactment entrusting jurisdiction to the federal courts. There are three classes of these statutes that embrace the largest numbers of federal lawsuits. The first class comprises "federal question" cases—actions arising under the Constitution, laws, or treaties of the United States. There is a statute conferring jurisdiction over such cases in general terms. See 28 U.S.C. § 1331. But a good many statutes specify details on jurisdiction over specific kinds of such cases. See, e.g., 28 U.S.C. §§ 1337(a), 1338(a). The

Sample Brief

Notes and Questions

second class comprises "diversity" cases—actions where there is diversity of citizenship between the parties, of which the most important category is actions between citizens of different states. See 28 U.S.C. §§ 1332(a), 1335. A statutory requirement that the matter in controversy exceed, or sometimes merely equal, some sum of money, in order that the case be cognizable in a federal district court, applies to a very few actions in the first class and to all actions in the second class. The third class comprises cases to which the United States itself is a party. See §§ 1345, 1346. To come back to the present case, Sibbach based her suit in federal district court on 28 U.S.C. § 1332(a). She could do this because there was diversity of citizenship (*P* was a citizen of Illinois; *D* was a Delaware corporation, making it a citizen of that state for diversity purposes) and her claimed damages exceeded the jurisdictional amount (she claimed $10,000 in damages, but at the time of suit the jurisdictional amount was $3000—Congress raised the jurisdictional amount under the relevant statute from $500 to $2000 in 1887, to $3000 in 1911, to $10,000 in 1958, to $50,000 in 1988, and to $75,000 in 1996).

Second, Sibbach sued in a United States District Court. The ninety-one United States District Courts are the trial courts of the federal system. A district is coterminous with a state or constitutes part of a state; thus, there is a United States District Court for the District of Delaware, and United States District Courts for the Southern, Central, and Northern Districts of Illinois. See 28 U.S.C. § 133.[j] On the next higher

---

[j]   However, the District of Hawaii includes certain Pacific islands not part of that state, and the District of Wyoming includes those portions of Yellowstone National Park situated in Montana and Idaho.

    The District of Columbia is a judicial district, and the District Court for the District of Columbia is a United States District Court. (Prior to 1970, it had a combined federal and local jurisdiction. It now exercises only federal jurisdiction like the other United States District Courts; Congress has vested local jurisdiction in local courts.)

    The Commonwealth of Puerto Rico is also one of the ninety-one judicial districts, and the District Court for the District of Puerto Rico is a United States District Court (exercising federal jurisdiction).

    Additionally, the Federal Rules are applicable by statute to the three so-called territorial district courts of the Virgin Islands, Guam, and the Northern Mariana Islands (exercising both federal and at least some local jurisdiction).

Sample Brief

Notes and Questions

level of the federal court system, twelve United States Courts of Appeals (formerly called Circuit Courts of Appeals) each cover a circuit comprising a number of districts. See 28 U.S.C. § 41.[k] The primary function of the courts of appeals is to hear appeals from decisions of the district courts in their respective circuits. At the summit of this pyramid of courts is the Supreme Court of the United States.

Third, she sued in the Northern District of Illinois, where she lived and where the defendant did much business. She had had a choice on the place of federal suit. Under the choice-of-forum law then in effect, she could have sued there, or in the District of Delaware where the defendant was incorporated, or in the Northern District of Indiana where the accident had taken place.

Fourth, when we say that she "sued," we mean that she made her grievance and request for redress known to the court by a complaint filed with the court in November 1937. See Rules 3, 10(a) and (b), 8(a), and 11(a). Following these Rules would yield a result looking much like former Federal Form 11 (which is in the Appendix of Forms after the Federal Rules in the Rules booklet). In fact, Sibbach's complaint was a bit unnecessarily flamboyant, as compared to that form. Her complaint alleged in part: "As a direct and proximate result of said acts of negligence of the defendant, the plaintiff Hertha J. Sibbach was greatly cut, wounded, lacerated, and contused in and about the head, body, arms, and legs, and divers bones in plaintiff's body were broken and fractured, and plaintiff became and was and has so remained from thence hitherto sick, sore, lame, diseased, and disordered, and has suffered great pain; all of which injuries are permanent and lasting."

---

[k]   However, the United States Court of Appeals for the District of Columbia Circuit covers only a single district.

Additionally, there is a thirteenth court of appeals—the United States Court of Appeals for the Federal Circuit—which hears appeals from a number of specialized tribunals and also hears appeals from all of the nation's ninety-four district courts in cases involving certain special areas such as patents or certain claims against the United States. See 28 U.S.C. § 1295.

Geographical Boundaries of
United States Courts of Appeals and United States District Courts

LEGEND
— Circuit Boundaries
— State Boundaries
···· District Boundaries

Sample Brief	Notes and Questions

Fifth, it is not enough to file the complaint: the defendant must be notified. This is done by serving the complaint, and a summons issued by the clerk of the court, in conformance with Rule 4. See Form 3.

D answered by denial.

(4) Again, a lot is buried here. Various responses are available to a defendant served with process. In this case, *D* filed an answer containing a denial of the allegations in the complaint. See Rule 8(b). Its answer looked much like the first part of Form 30, with a suitable caption and signature.

D moved for an order requiring *P* to submit to a Rule 35 physical exam, and the court granted that motion.

(5) D proceeded here by motion, as the express terms of Rule 35(a)(2)(A) require. What is a motion? See Rule 7(b); Form 40.

(6) An order is simply a command of the court. It may be oral or written; it may be rather formal or may be simply the words "so ordered" written at the foot of the motion; it may be accompanied by an opinion explaining the court's reasoning or, as in this case, it may not be. Selected district court opinions are printed in reporters, usually either in Federal Supplement or in Federal Rules Decisions. Many others now appear in online services.

P refused to comply, so *D* obtained an order to show cause, which required *P* to prove why the court should not hold her in contempt under Rule 37.

(7) An order to show cause serves the same purpose as a motion, but the court handles it more expeditiously. It is actually an order of the court, usually drafted by the attorney for one side and submitted to the court for signature, directing the other side to appear as specified and present to the court such reasons as it has to offer that some consequence (in this case, a finding of contempt) should not ensue. The court usually grants an order to show cause only on a showing of urgency or of special need (as here, where *D* was seeking to force compliance with a court order, for which *D* had already once gone through the slower motion procedure).

(8) Contempt is a disregard or disobedience of public authority, such as a court order. There are two types of contempt proceedings, criminal and civil. The difference, it should be noted, is not necessarily in the nature of the

Sample Brief   **Notes and Questions**

contemptuous act but in the proceedings consequent thereto—the same contemptuous act might give rise to either or both types of proceedings. For the time being, distinguish the two as follows. Criminal contempt proceedings serve the interests of society by punishing and deterring deliberate disrespect of public authority; accordingly, the procedure is relatively protective of the defendant's rights, but an unconditional fine or prison term is the form of sanction. Civil contempt proceedings more directly help the party who would benefit from the contemnor's obedience; accordingly, the form of sanction either is a compensatory payment to such party or is a conditional fine or imprisonment that need not be paid or further suffered by the contemnor if he obeys (thus the maxim that these contemnors "carry the keys of their prison in their own pockets"). In short, the design of criminal contempt proceedings is to punish and deter, and that of civil contempt proceedings is to compensate or compel.

In response to the order to show cause, *P* argued that the court had no authority to order a physical exam. The court rejected *P*'s argument, found her in contempt, and ordered her imprisoned until she submitted to a physical exam.

(9) Was this a civil or a criminal contempt sanction?

P appealed to the United States Court of Appeals for the Seventh Circuit.

(10) In the federal system, the first level of appeal is a matter of right, not judicial discretion. Sibbach had the right, at some time, to appeal to the appropriate court of appeals.

As to the timing of appeal, a party can normally take one appeal at the conclusion of the case. See 28 U.S.C. § 1291. Here, however, *P* took an interlocutory appeal before the case proceeded. Possibly she was not then entitled to

Sample Brief	Notes and Questions

appeal, but the question was not raised by the parties or the courts.

There are provisions for staying a lower court's order pending appeal. So chances are that Sibbach never saw the inside of "the common jail of Cook County," to which the court had ordered her committed.

The Seventh Circuit affirmed.

(11) The courts of appeals normally act by written decision and opinion, and many of these are printed. They appear in Federal Reporter. In this case, the affirmance appears in volume 108 of Federal Reporter, Second Series, at page 415. The Seventh Circuit handed down the affirmance on December 13, 1939. The citation is therefore 108 F.2d 415 (7th Cir.1939).

P petitioned the Supreme Court of the United States for a writ of certiorari, and the Court granted the writ because her case involved an unsettled, important question of federal law.

(12) There are a couple of routes from a court of appeals to the Supreme Court. See 28 U.S.C. § 1254.

The most common route is by writ of certiorari. Review thereby is not of right, but is discretionary. The party seeking review must petition the Supreme Court for the writ, and hence that party is called the petitioner. The Supreme Court decides whether to review the case pursuant to United States Supreme Court Rule 10, which provides in part: "A petition for a writ of certiorari will be granted only for compelling reasons. The following, although neither controlling nor fully measuring the Court's discretion, indicate the character of the reasons the Court considers: . . . a United States court of appeals has entered a decision in conflict with the decision of another United States court of appeals on the same important matter; . . . a United States court of appeals has decided an important question of federal law that has not been, but should be, settled by this Court, or has decided an important federal question in a way that conflicts with relevant decisions of this Court."

Sibbach told the Supreme Court in her petition that her case presented this question: "Does Rule 35 of the Federal Rules of Civil Procedure abridge or modify the substantive

Sample Brief   **Notes and Questions**

rights of the petitioner contrary to the provisions of the Rules Enabling Act?" You should ask yourself why the Supreme Court bothered to hear this case. What sense does it make to have the Supreme Court review the validity of rules it itself promulgated? Assuming that the Supreme Court would not have promulgated rules it thought invalid, how could this case present "an important question of federal law that has not been, but should be, settled by" the Supreme Court?

At any rate, on April 8, 1940, the Court did grant the writ and thereby agree to review the case. Actions by the Supreme Court are reported officially in United States Reports. The grant of the petition for a writ of certiorari in this case appears in volume 309 of United States Reports, at page 650. It also appears in volume 60 of the parallel, unofficial Supreme Court Reporter, at page 809. The citation is therefore 309 U.S. 650 (1940) or, more expansively, 309 U.S. 650, 60 S.Ct. 809 (1940).

Statutes and Rules Involved: Rules Enabling Act; Rules 35 and 37.

(13) This entry in your brief serves only as a handy reference, so at a glance you can later recall what the case was about. But we shall take this opportunity to give you some historical background on the statute and Rules here involved. For greater detail, reference should be made to Charles Alan Wright & Mary Kay Kane, Law of Federal Courts §§ 61–63 (8th ed. 2017).

(14) To understand the Rules Enabling Act, one must go back to the Process Act of 1789. This Act, and the subsequent Process Acts, required the procedural practices in the newly created federal courts to conform in each and every state to the practices "as are now used or allowed in the supreme courts of the same." Conformity to state procedure flowed, in contemporary phraseology, from a fear of an "injurious clashing" with the procedure of the states. What the statutes called for, however, was a *static* conformity; a federal court in, say, 1850 had to apply the state procedure of 1789. Moreover, the early statutes did not cover the problem of new states; federal courts in the new states were at

Sample Brief   **Notes and Questions**

first free to apply any procedure they wished; later statutes forced the procedure of federal courts in those states to conform to the state procedure of 1828, 1842, or the date of admission, the choice among these base dates depending on when the state in question had been admitted. The situation was even more complicated than this description suggests, because there were exceptions, and exceptions to exceptions. However, the basic idea here is that of static conformity, meaning that the federal courts had to ignore recent developments and reforms in state procedure and instead follow an outmoded and abandoned version of the state procedure.

Congress reworked all this by the Conformity Act of 1872, which instituted *dynamic* conformity. From then on, in theory, the same procedure prevailed in state and federal court, and the practitioner could switch courts without relearning procedure. The first question one might ask is why it took Congress almost a century to make this obvious change. One reason was that it was not until the mid-nineteenth century that state reform started snowballing by adoption of "codes" of procedure, leaving the procedure applied in federal courts far behind. Another reason might have been that Congress feared that such a change constituted an unconstitutional delegation of federal rulemaking power to the states, as the Supreme Court itself had suggested in Wayman v. Southard, 23 U.S. (10 Wheat.) 1 (1825); after the change in 1872 the issue of constitutionality never came up for decision in this procedural context, although the Court upheld dynamic conformity to state law in a different context in United States v. Sharpnack, 355 U.S. 286, 78 S.Ct. 291 (1958). The second question one might ask is whether dynamic conformity worked. The answer would be that the simplicity of theory was never realized in practice. Instead, the Conformity Act became riddled with exceptions, both judge-made and statutory (note the phrasing "conform, as near as may be" in the

Sample Brief   **Notes and Questions**

Conformity Act itself, quoted in footnote h to the Sibbach case). Federal courts in the course of a litigation consequently used some state procedure and some home-brewed procedure to create a rampantly confusing federal practice: "To the average lawyer it is Sanskrit; to the experienced federal practitioner it is monopoly; to the author of text books on federal practice it is a golden harvest." Report of the Committee on Uniform Judicial Procedure, 46 A.B.A.Rep. 461, 466 (1921).

It is against this backdrop that one can best view the Rules Enabling Act of 1934. This Act again seems the obvious answer, but it actually represented reformist agitation by the bar and bench dating back to the previous century. Finally, in 1934, reform secured the support of the national administration, and quickly Congress enacted the Rules Enabling Act. See generally Stephen B. Burbank, The Rules Enabling Act of 1934, 130 U.Pa.L.Rev. 1015 (1982).

Even after that statute passed, it took the Supreme Court a year to act on it; but when the Court eventually did act, it acted in grand style, appointing a highly distinguished Advisory Committee to assist in drafting the rules. The Advisory Committee prepared three drafts for debate and discussion in the legal community. The first draft was circulated in May 1936. The third draft was submitted in November 1937 to the Supreme Court, which promulgated it with minor changes the following month. Congress having taken no action, the Federal Rules of Civil Procedure became effective on September 16, 1938. (For the curious: although as we have seen the Sibbach complaint was filed in 1937 before the Rules were promulgated, the defendant's motion for a physical exam was filed on May 6, 1939, and was thus subject to the new Rules; cf. current Rule 86(a)(2).) Thus ended the long reign of the Conformity Act, which was apparently superseded in toto by the new Rules and which was in any case formally repealed by Congress in 1948.

Sample Brief   **Notes and Questions**

The success of the Federal Rules has been, in Professor Wright's words, "quite phenomenal," creating "a uniform procedure that is flexible, simple, clear, and efficient" and that has had a tremendous impact on the development of procedure in other jurisdictions. A less restrained commentator wrote that the Rules were "one of the greatest contributions to the free and unhampered administration of law and justice ever struck off by any group of men since the dawn of civilized law." B.H. Carey, In Favor of Uniformity, 3 F.R.D. 507, 507 (1944).

Of course the Rules have not proved perfect or timeless, and so they have undergone a continuing review. The old Advisory Committee was discharged in 1956; and in 1958 the Judicial Conference of the United States, a body of federal judges headed by the Chief Justice that has long been charged with improving the administration of federal courts, took over the advisory function with respect to the Supreme Court's rulemaking power. See 28 U.S.C. § 331. There were important amendments to the Rules in 1948, 1961, 1963, 1966, 1970, 1980, 1983, 1985, 1991, 1993, 2000, 2003, 2006, 2009, 2010, and 2015. Additionally, in 2007 the rulemakers "restyled" the Rules by rewriting every single one to make it clearer and simpler, but supposedly without alteration to its meaning, and in the process redesignated some of the Rules' lettered or numbered subdivisions.

More change surely lies in the future, and you should not infer that this change will be merely in the nature of further refinement. Indeed, citing increasing dissatisfaction, some commentators have been predicting the imminent end of the Federal Rules' era itself. One of their major arguments is that the Federal Rules' preference for transsubstantive rules, or very general rules that apply to all sorts of cases, has worn out, and the time has come for returning explicitly to specialized rules tailored to particular subsets of cases.

This background allows you to focus in on the Rules involved in Sibbach. Rules 35 and 37

Sample Brief   **Notes and Questions**

are part of the so-called discovery Rules, which run from Rule 26 to Rule 37. The rulemakers heavily redid the discovery Rules in 1970.

(15) This brings us to an important point. When reading an older case, it is important to know how any rule or statute in question read at the time of decision; you have to know this in order to know what the court is referring to and often what it is deciding. For example, the Sibbach Court refers to Rule 37(b)(2)(iv). Today there is no such numbered Rule. You will find the old version of the Rule in the Rules booklet.

(16) There is also the converse problem. An old case might quote an obsolete version of a statute or rule. You should look up the current version, and ask yourself how and why it has changed. For example, the Sibbach Court quotes the Rules Enabling Act. This is now 28 U.S.C. §§ 2072–2074. Comparison shows that Congress has changed the original statute in several important ways.

First, there is now a reference in § 2072 to the courts of appeals. This extension of the Supreme Court's rulemaking power under § 2072 came in 1966, and the eventual result thereof was the Federal Rules of Appellate Procedure (portions of which appear in the Rules booklet). Prior to the adoption of those Appellate Rules in 1968, each court of appeals had a fairly wide power to make rules for its own proceedings. (To complete the procedural rulemaking picture, note that under 28 U.S.C. § 2071(a) the Supreme Court can make its own rules for its own business; recall S.Ct. Rule 10 above. Note further that all federal courts have the power under §§ 2071 and 2077 to promulgate interstitial rules for themselves; see Rule 83 and App. Rule 47.)

Second, there is no longer a reference in § 2072 to the courts of the District of Columbia. Although the Federal Rules apply to the District Court for the District of Columbia because it is a United States District Court, the Supreme Court never used the statutory authorization to make

Sample Brief   **Notes and Questions**

rules for the *local* courts of the District of Columbia. Today Congress handles directly the matter of rules for the District of Columbia's local courts.

Third, current § 2072 omits the term "at law." This omission is profoundly significant, but to understand it you must appreciate the important distinction between law and equity, two historically distinct systems of courts, of remedies, and of procedures. Again for purposes of introduction, and at the price of oversimplification, law courts in old England typically gave relief only in the form of money damages. Old England's equity courts, on the other hand, typically gave relief only in the form of an order commanding the defendant to do or not to do something, such as to convey land he had promised to sell ("specific performance") or to remove a dam he had wrongfully constructed ("injunction"). The procedures of the two court systems were very different, but one of the more salient differences was that law courts offered trial by jury while equity courts did not.

The equity system was transported to the infant United States. In the federal system, parties instituted and litigated equity and law cases separately in different divisions, or sides, of the lower federal courts, although the same judges sat on both sides. The history of federal procedure on the equity side was quite distinct from that of the procedure used on the law side. (The history imparted under (14) above concerned actions at law, not suits in equity.) Congress never required federal equity procedure to conform to state equity procedure, largely because some of the newly independent states had not developed formally any such procedure. Instead, Congress instructed the federal courts to follow generally the procedure of English equity, but gave rulemaking power to the Supreme Court. The Court did not exercise that power until 1822, but thereafter it promulgated successive sets of equity rules for use in the federal courts. The last set of these was the modernizing Equity Rules of 1912,

Sample Brief   **Notes and Questions**

which served as one of the models for the Federal Rules of Civil Procedure.

As we have already noted, throughout this long period the Supreme Court, while making rules in equity, was doing nothing with respect to rulemaking for the separate realm of actions at law. The Rules Enabling Act was the legislative response. Section 1 thereof authorized the Supreme Court to do for law as it had been doing for equity all along, and section 2 permitted the Supreme Court to unite the two procedures. The Supreme Court did exercise its section 2 powers right away, so that the new Federal Rules united equity and law, this being the greatest single achievement of the Rules. See Rules 1 and 2. In summary, it is by reason of this union that § 2072 can now omit "at law."

A related change in § 2072 is the omission of old section 2. Congress could omit this from the current statute because the union of equity and law under the Rules had been achieved. Yet with regard to other matters—especially the extent of the right to trial by jury in civil actions—the equity/law distinction remains very important.

Fourth, § 2072 now refers broadly to "cases" rather than to "civil actions." This change encapsulates the long-term trend toward a broader scope of the Rules Enabling Act.

The Federal Rules of Civil Procedure themselves have broadened to cover "admiralty and maritime" cases. Again, this broadening is significant, but complex in meaning. A leading text in this area explains that "the terms 'admiralty' and 'maritime law' are virtually synonymous in this country today, though the first derives from the connection of our modern law with the system administered in a single English court, while the second makes a wider and more descriptive reference." Grant Gilmore & Charles L. Black, The Law of Admiralty 1 (2d ed. 1975). We essay only the oversimplified statement that admiralty and maritime cases comprehend torts occurring upon, or contracts having to do with commerce or navigation upon,

Sample Brief   **Notes and Questions**

the high seas or the navigable waters of the United States. The history of federal procedure in this realm is analogous to that in equity. Congress never required conformity to state practice. Instead, federal courts followed English admiralty practice, with rulemaking power having been given to the Supreme Court. The Court exercised this power by promulgating successive sets of admiralty rules, starting in 1844. Finally, in 1966, the Court brought admiralty and maritime cases within the coverage of the Federal Rules of Civil Procedure, with certain minor special treatment. See Rule 9(h) and the Supplemental Rules (which appear after the Appendix of Forms in the Rules booklet).

This extension of the Federal Rules of Civil Procedure leads to the question of what cases are not covered by those Rules. Most importantly, criminal cases are not so covered. These cases were handled in the federal courts by uncodified procedure until 1946, and since then by the Federal Rules of Criminal Procedure. Several other special kinds of proceedings are not covered by the Federal Rules of Civil Procedure. See Rule 81(a).

Fifth, the Rules Enabling Act has undergone changes with respect to the process for composing the rules, § 2073, and the mechanism by which promulgated rules take effect, § 2074. Under § 2073, the Judicial Conference—directed to carry on a continuous study of the rules of practice prescribed by the Court for the inferior federal courts and to make recommendations to the Court—works through a standing committee, appointed by the Chief Justice, and advisory committees, also appointed by the Chief Justice, which report to the standing committee. There are now five advisory committees respectively for Civil, Criminal, Evidence, Bankruptcy, and Appellate Rules, each assisted by a reporter who is usually a law professor. The advisory committees draft new or amended rules with explanatory notes, circulate them under the aegis of the standing committee

Sample Brief	**Notes and Questions**

to the bench and bar and public for comment, rework the rules in the light of the comments, and transmit them to the standing committee. The standing committee in turn makes recommendations to the Judicial Conference, which finally advises the Court. At this point the specific procedure of the Rules Enabling Act, in § 2074, takes over with respect to submission of the rules to Congress.

Issues:

(17) In this part of the brief you should list the precise questions the court is to decide. Often the issues are far from obvious, and so this entry in the brief requires digging and careful analysis on your part.

1. Are Rules 35 and 37 valid, insofar as being within the congressional delegation to the Supreme Court expressed in the Rules Enabling Act?

An unavoidable difficulty lies in stating an issue neither too broadly nor too narrowly. There is no foolproof approach or unarguable resolution. You must tie your statement of the issue to the facts of the case, but you must also suggest any resultant rule of law that will be applicable to future cases. Try to state that legal point narrowly enough to exclude future cases not covered by the ruling but broadly enough to include all those cases within it. Obviously, room for argument exists about the scope of precedent, and arguing about that is one thing lawyers do. So, your statement of the issue can represent only your best judgment on a difficult matter. At any rate, by the time you complete studying the Sibbach case, you might be able to come up with a formulation of the first issue better than this sample brief's entry.

2. If so, was the contempt sanction imposed by the district court proper under Rule 37? (N.B.: This second issue was raised by the Supreme Court, not by *P*.)

(18) In appellate cases, the issues normally center on those lower-court actions that the appealing party designates as improper in his papers on appeal, i.e., the points assigned as error. It is generally for the aggrieved parties, through their lawyers, to specify those lower-court actions with which they are dissatisfied, and so to shape the issues for resolution by the appellate court. The appellate court generally does not "notice" other errors on its own, leaving ours a party-propelled adversary system.

Sample Brief   **Notes and Questions**

What are the reasons behind this policy that allows the parties to select the issues? If such a policy is generally a good one, why did the Supreme Court by noticing the error here reach out to decide this second issue? That is, why did the Supreme Court consider the propriety of the contempt finding and the commitment order if, as the Supreme Court noted, "[n]either in the Circuit Court of Appeals nor here was this action assigned as error" by Sibbach? What special circumstances were present to prompt the Court to decide the issue? Incidentally, the Supreme Court's attention was first drawn to this second issue by William D. Mitchell, who was Chairman of the Advisory Committee that had drafted the Federal Rules and who filed a brief as amicus curiae in this case when it reached the Supreme Court.

Decisions:

1. Yes (5–4).

2. No.

(19) Here you should give the decision on each one of the above-listed issues. Incidentally, were they decisions on issues of fact, substantive law, or procedural law?

(20) Note that the first decision was five to four, with Justice Frankfurter writing for the minority. So this was a very close vote in a very important case, one that was to determine the vitality of the new Federal Rules. However, no one dissented on the second issue.

Judgment reversed and case remanded to the district court, because the district court had imposed an improper sanction on *P*.

(21) Also indicate the court's disposition of the case. (This case soon disappeared on remand, after the Supreme Court's action on January 13, 1941. The district court vacated its contempt order on April 9, 1941. The next day, that court dismissed the action, "this cause having been settled.")

Reasons: As to the Court's first decision, Justice Roberts uses deductive reasoning to come to the conclusion

(22) In this part of your brief you should state the gist of the court's reasoning, probably even more briefly than we have. Needless to say, sometimes a great deal of work is necessary in order to perceive the court's reasoning, especially if the opinion is expressed in the form of free association. After all, Justice Owen

Sample Brief

that Rules 35 and 37 are valid. The major premise of his syllogism is that all rules that deal with procedure are valid, because Congress in the Rules Enabling Act delegated to the Supreme Court the power to make rules throughout the whole realm of procedure; thus, the Court reads narrowly the Act's limitation on the Court's power, reading the reference to "substantive rights" to mean only substantive law, i.e., things other than procedure. His minor premise is that Rules 35 and 37 deal with procedure. So, because all procedural rules are valid, and because Rules 35 and 37 are procedural, the conclusion is that Rules 35 and 37 are valid. Q.E.D.

Derivation of Roberts' major premise

Notes and Questions

Roberts himself seemed unable to state his own reasoning simply (but note how Justice Felix Frankfurter immediately grasped, and attacked, Roberts' major premise). When you are processing the court's reasoning, another difficult and important task is separating, as well as possible, statements of law directly involved in and necessary to the decision ("holdings") from asides unnecessary to the decision ("dicta").

Why have we not included in the sample brief Roberts' observations on the importance of the particular right here involved?

Of course, this sample brief is not intended to be definitive. The entry here represents only one way of distilling and analyzing the supposed holdings. Do you see another way?

Sometimes, in uncovering the issues and the court's essential reasoning, it is helpful to reconstruct what the parties were arguing. What precisely was Mrs. Sibbach's dilemma, as stated by the Court? What did she argue in order to refute that dilemma? What did the defendant argue in response?

(23) Under Roberts' reading of the Rules Enabling Act, exactly what does the Act's limitation on the Court's power, located in the

Sample Brief

essentially entails divining congressional will. Roberts offers three arguments in support of his reading of the Rules Enabling Act. First, in demarking the Supreme Court's authority Congress must have meant to draw the line between substantive law and procedure, because any other division would "invite endless litigation and confusion worse confounded." Second, Congress intended that a comprehensive system of court rules be adopted, and therefore envisaged that "the whole field of court procedure be regulated." Third, the Federal Rules as promulgated by the Court did in fact cover the whole field of procedure, and Congress took no action to "veto their going into effect."

Notes and Questions

second sentence of section 1, add to the meaning of the Act? What of the canon of statutory construction that "every word and clause must be given effect"? Karl N. Llewellyn, Remarks on the Theory of Appellate Decision and the Rules or Canons About How Statutes Are to Be Construed, 3 Vand.L.Rev. 395, 404 (1950); see Jonathan R. Macey & Geoffrey P. Miller, The Canons of Statutory Construction and Judicial Preferences, 45 Vand.L.Rev. 647 (1992).

Does the Act's proviso regarding the jury right cut against Roberts' reading, in that Congress was thereby specifically telling the Court not to affect an important procedural right? But would that proviso be necessary if the Act's second sentence of section 1 had already instructed the Court not to affect important rights?

Sample Brief

The primary support for Roberts' minor premise is that Sibbach conceded that Rules 35 and 37 are procedural. Other support comes from Roberts' definitions of procedure ("the judicial process for enforcing rights and duties recognized by substantive law and for justly administering remedy and redress for disregard or infraction of them") and substantive law ("rights conferred by law to be protected and enforced in accordance with the adjective law of judicial procedure").

As to the Court's second decision, Roberts holds the sanction improper as being simply contrary to the express provisions of the former version of Rule 37(b)(2).

Separate Opinions: Justice

Notes and Questions

(24) Do you find Roberts' definitions useful or satisfying?

(25) Is it really so clear under old Rule 37(b)(2)(iv) that the sanction imposed was improper? What is the definition of "arrest" in your legal dictionary? Assuming contempt and commitment were not permissible, what kind of order might the district court have properly made in this case?

(26) Here you should sketch out in briefest form the reasoning of the minority. You might

Sample Brief

Frankfurter likewise argues deductively. His major premise is that all rules affecting (very) important rights are invalid, because in his view Congress in the Rules Enabling Act did not intend to empower the Supreme Court to make rules in derogation of important rights. His minor premise is that Rule 35 affects an important right, the inviolability of person. Because all rules affecting important rights are invalid, and because Rule 35 affects an important right, Rule 35 is invalid.

Remarks:

Notes and Questions

omit supporting arguments. But think about those arguments. How did Frankfurter support his major premise? his minor premise? Do you agree? Do you see that Frankfurter may possibly have been right as to his minor premise, but that the correctness of his minor premise is rendered irrelevant if Roberts' major premise is accepted? Do you also see that Frankfurter's major premise may very well have been closer to specific congressional intent, but that Roberts' major premise may have been superior from a policy viewpoint? Should such policy notions play a role in a court's decision?

(27) Here you should jot down your comments on and criticisms of the case. You might make a preliminary attempt before class, but you should certainly supplement this during and after class. There should be special emphasis on the significance of the decision and the validity of the reasoning. For example, what is the significance of Sibbach v. Wilson & Co.? Surely it represents more than a mere "Rule 35 case."

What kind of job do you think Justice Roberts did? It may seem a bit premature in your career to judge Justices. But they are only human, and some more than others. As one

Sample Brief

Notes and Questions

scholar said of Roberts, "There was an almost terpsichorean quality about this benign, conscientious jurist who established a record of inconsistency probably difficult to equal in his voting on the bench." Henry J. Abraham, Justices, Presidents, and Senators 152 (1999).

What kind of job did Sibbach's lawyer do? Why did he not assign as error the improper sanction? Why, in the first place, did he not sue in Illinois state court, instead of federal court, and thus avoid the whole problem of a physical exam? Possible explanations include mistake, or perhaps this was a test case. Do you see any more subtle explanations?

Does it affect your theorizing to know that, prior to Rule 35, the federal courts had shown hostility to the idea of physical examinations? See, e.g., Union Pac. Ry. Co. v. Botsford, 141 U.S. 250, 11 S.Ct. 1000 (1891). That case was one for negligence, brought by Clara Botsford against a railroad. She complained of head injuries, caused when an upper berth in a sleeping car fell and hit her in the head. Although there were only head injuries, and although the defendant proposed that the physical examination "should be made in manner not to expose the person of the plaintiff in any indelicate manner," the Court denied the defendant's request for a physical examination, observing: "The inviolability of the person is as much invaded by a compulsory stripping and exposure as by a blow. To compel any one, and especially a woman, to lay bare the body, or to submit it to the touch of a stranger, without lawful authority, is an indignity, an assault and a trespass; and no order or process, commanding such an exposure or submission, was ever known to the common law in the administration of justice between individuals, except in a very small number of cases, based upon special reasons, and upon ancient practice, coming down from ruder ages, now mostly obsolete in England, and never, so far as we are aware, introduced into this country." Botsford ended up with $10,000 for her troubles.

Sample Brief   Notes and Questions

Times do change. All the states now provide for physical and mental examinations, with Mississippi in 2003 being the final state to fall into line. Does this trend represent progress? Is Rule 35 a good rule? What makes for a "good" procedure? Why are we raising such basic questions only at the end of this treatment of Sibbach v. Wilson & Co., almost as an afterthought?

————

We shall have many more occasions to observe how legislatures and courts go about this business of classification with which the Sibbach case was concerned—and to observe whether a rule is uniformly assigned to the same category, such as substance or procedure, or whether it may be assigned to one category when the classification's aims and consequences are such-and-such and to another category when they are thus-and-so.

On attitudes toward the subject and the course.—We shall confine our consideration mainly to procedure in civil cases *in courts*. Such an initial focus on courts is not nonsensical. One reason is that early mastery of the official procedural system helps in comprehending the cases read in other law courses. The primary reason, however, is that litigation in court remains so extremely important to society and to citizens. The courts act, when other mechanisms default to them, as the last-line enforcer of law and resolver of disputes. Litigation not only produces singular decisions that restructure society but also serves as a major vehicle for lawmaking in our government and for articulation of societal values. Meanwhile, the courts' adjudications enunciate the law that sets the standards under which potential litigants resolve their disputes alternatively, "bargaining in the shadow of the law" by nonlitigation processes to reach outcomes that generally conform to the law and thereby further the law's purposes.

Nevertheless, we should observe at the outset that there is in fact a great volume of controversies adjudicated outside the courts. The modes of operation of tribunals like workers' compensation boards, the National Labor Relations Board, and the Federal Communications Commission, to name but a few of them, will be beyond our scope, except that we shall note some interrelations between courts and administrative agencies. Nor shall we do more than touch upon adjudicative procedures within corporations, labor unions, clubs, associations, or churches—or do much more than describe procedures for arbitration, mediation, and other alternative dispute-resolution mechanisms.

This notice of exclusion leads to another caveat. The stress laid on court procedure in the first year of law school sometimes leads to an unhappy insularity or provincialism among some students. They get the notion that the general style of procedure used in the courts is the only really viable one for the resolution of controversies and that other styles, being different and being studied later, are necessarily inferior. But students should suspend judgment on this matter until they have examined the other procedures. They may find that procedure relates to setting, structure, and purpose. Although it is likely that certain fundamentals must be observed in handling any civil controversy if the handling is to be accurate and fair and efficient, it is also likely that various rules of procedure appropriate to the regular grist of court business would be quite unsuitable for resolving a controversy over collective bargaining before the NLRB or a question of licensing before the FCC. It may even be that the courts have something to learn in the way of procedural finesse from administrative agencies and other bodies that deal with civil controversies.

Another common superstition is that the particular rules making up the court procedure of one's own time and place are the only rules that would really work in courts. A possible corrective for this kind of intransigence lies in the realization that court procedures have undergone drastic changes in this country without cataclysm. Another lies in realizing that today significant differences exist among federal and various states' procedures; moreover, foreign countries have procedures very different from our own, and many of them appear to work fairly well. A proposal for change certainly deserves consideration on the merits without any arbitrary assumption that sudden doom will attend change. It is, indeed, part of the purpose of this course to evolve meritorious proposals for change, some of which we shall suggest by means that include looking at other times and places.

By the way, we have been talking of "court procedure." Do not let this mode of expression seduce you into error. One kind of error is to think of "court" entirely in the abstract as the equivalent of a disembodied law and to assume that steps of "procedure" somehow are taken without any human actors at all. A more common kind of error is to think that it is the court (in the sense of the judge, or perhaps some parajudge or clerk) that alone initiates the procedural steps. The fact is that under the current system, as under the traditional Anglo-American scheme, it is typically the contending parties through their lawyers who take most of the initiative in the court process.

The judge's role is predominantly that of deciding the issues put before the judge by the lawyers in their procedural thrusts and parries. All this has lent to the entire court process an air of battle or strife in which the lawyers play the part of combatant champions and the judge (and jury) the part of passive umpire. However, modern complex lawsuits, often of considerable social significance, and other modern developments seem destined to demand increased judicial initiative and control. The extent to which the judge currently plays a more active role varies from jurisdiction to jurisdiction and from judge to judge and especially from case to case. We shall consider what the judicial role ought to be.

Just as it is true that court procedure is not self-propelled but is for the most part propelled on the initiative of the lawyers, so it is true that the lawyers may exercise this initiative in a variety of ways. The lawyer at various stages of a lawsuit may have a choice whether to make one or another move. Now we must add the notable fact that success or failure in the lawsuit may well turn on the wisdom, ingenuity, and skill with which the lawyer makes those moves. Although it is indeed the object of rules of procedure to facilitate the just resolution of controversies, there is no avoiding the fact that good claims are sometimes lost, and bad claims sometimes won, because of the quality of counsel's use of procedural rules—and it is implausible that any now foreseeable improvement in the rules themselves could altogether eliminate these miscarriages. It is part of the task of a course in procedure to give you training in the strategy and tactics of controversy so that missteps by you will not contribute to such miscarriages. Another part of the task is to impress upon you that, with the lawyer's freedom of motion, comes a personal responsibility for the fair and efficient running of the procedural machinery. It will help if you constantly ask this question as you read the following materials, just as we asked about Sibbach's attorney: why did the lawyer make this particular move rather than another that was open to him or her?

TOPIC B

PHASES OF A LAWSUIT

Our purpose in this Topic is to describe the major phases in the conduct of a lawsuit. Procedure too often appears to the student as a maze of unrelated rules to be painfully mastered. We hope in the sketch that follows to give a sense of the subject as a whole and to point out some fundamental problems. In taking a look at the entire organism before examining the separate parts, we have not allowed to deter us the knowledge that later amplification will throw additional light on many of the matters here discussed.

Focus on procedure in the United States District Courts.— Our sketch focuses on the current procedures in civil actions in the United States District Courts. The Federal Rules of Civil Procedure regulate these procedures to a large extent. See Rules 1 and 81.

Our reasons for selecting these procedures as the basis not only for the sketch but for much of the course will appear more plainly as the course develops. Some of them may, however, be worth noting here. (1) Focusing on a single procedural system most efficiently presents the essential. (2) Spotlighting a complete system enables the student to reach those problems of theory and practice that require consideration of one system in its entirety. (3) The Federal Rules are a concise corpus, from the study of which the student can grasp rather quickly how a going system of procedure functions in a general way. (4) The federal system is generally considered to be a fairly successful, but by no means perfect, representative of modern procedure. (5) Although the federal procedural system created by the Rules differs in various respects from the systems of procedure prevailing in other times and places, which of course differ among themselves, it provides a model by reference to which the student can later study and evaluate those systems.[a] (6) A majority of the state systems are now based in substantial part on the Federal Rules, and still others adopt particular features of the Rules.[b] (7) Although litigants

---

[a]   We shall not often interrupt the sketch by contrasting the terminology and provisions of the Federal Rules with those of predecessor procedure. Of course, some provisions of the Federal Rules will become more meaningful when considered in the light of what they superseded, so we shall later treat some of the predecessors.

[b]   Nor shall we often interrupt this presentation by contrasting the terminology and provisions of the Federal Rules with those of the state systems of procedure. However, it would be useful for the student to examine the procedural statutes and rules of his or her home state, or the state where he or she expects to practice, to see the extent to which they are comparable to the Federal Rules. There is no state that remains wholly unaffected by the federal reform, but some populous states remain importantly distinctive. See John B. Oakley & Arthur F. Coon, The Federal Rules in State Courts: A Survey of State Court Systems of Civil Procedure, 61 Wash.L.Rev. 1367 (1986); John B. Oakley, A Fresh Look at the Federal Rules in State Courts, 3 Nev.L.J. 354 (2003). But perhaps the trend favoring the federal model is on the verge of reversing. See Stephen N. Subrin & Thomas O. Main, Braking the Rules: Why State Courts Should Not Replicate Amendments to the Federal Rules of Civil Procedure, 67 Case W.Res.L.Rev. 501 (2016).

commence vastly more civil cases in state courts than in federal courts, the United States District Courts are important courts that handle a large volume of cases, many of which are of major significance.

Selection of a proper forum.—The first step in instituting a lawsuit is to select a proper court to hear the case. Each state has its own set of courts exerting the judicial power of the state, and there is an overlay of United States courts exerting the judicial power of the nation. Sometimes there is only one proper court for a particular controversy, but often two or more are available. Then a choice must be made, and that initially is the plaintiff's. However, situations exist where a suit properly lodged by the plaintiff in one court can be moved to a different one by the defendant at her option or with the court's permission.

We shall not now undertake the survey of the judicial systems of the states and the United States that would be necessary in order to determine which court or courts may properly be selected to hear a given case. (We instead defer such a survey to Sections 6 and 7 of this Topic.) Rather we shall assume during the following discussion, except when we specially raise the question, that a plaintiff has properly instituted a case in a United States District Court—that the case is of a type that such a court has the authority to adjudicate, and that the particular district court has authority over the particular case through the proper filing of a complaint with it (see Rule 3) and the proper service upon the defendant (see Rule 4).

———

SECTION 1.   PRETRIAL

(a) STATING THE CLAIM[c]

[Rules 8(a), (c), (d), and (e), 9(b), 11; Form 11]

So, according to Rule 3, the plaintiff has commenced an action by filing a complaint with the court. What is a complaint, how is it written, and what are its purposes?

---

[c]   Immediately under this and later captions we shall give references to the most important of the relevant Federal Rules and forms. Students should read each of these Rules and forms with particular care. Other Rule and form references in text and questions are less important, but still students should examine those Rules and forms.

Note that the rulemakers abandoned the official forms in 2015, because their usefulness in practice did not justify their upkeep. The Advisory Committee explained:

Rule 84 was adopted when the Civil Rules were established in 1938 "to indicate, subject to the provisions of these rules, the simplicity and brevity of statement which the rules contemplate." The purpose of providing illustrations for the rules, although useful when the rules were adopted, has been fulfilled. Accordingly, recognizing that there are many alternative sources for forms, including the website of the Administrative Office of the United States Courts, the websites of many district courts, and local law libraries that contain many commercially published forms, Rule 84 and the Appendix of Forms are no longer necessary and have been abrogated. The abrogation of Rule 84 does not alter existing pleading standards or otherwise change the requirements of Civil Rule 8.

Rule 8(a) indicates that a complaint shall contain "a short and plain statement of the claim showing that the pleader is entitled to relief" (as well as a statement of the grounds for the court's jurisdiction, and a demand for the relief sought). Here, then, is the first step in laying bare what the dispute is about. By his complaint the plaintiff is to inform his adversary and the court of the basis of his contention that he can invoke the court's aid in redressing a grievance.

Rule 8(a) by itself, however, does not go far in describing what the form of the complaint should be or just what the complaint should set forth. Other Rules are helpful on these matters. But perhaps the way to begin is to look at Forms 10 to 21, inclusive, which are illustrations of proper complaints in various kinds of lawsuits.

Who has the burden of allegation?—Surely the plaintiff need assert only relevant matters, but by reference to what is the plaintiff to determine relevancy? Doubtless the rule of substantive law that the plaintiff seeks to invoke establishes the contours of relevancy. Reconsider the rule shown schematically in the earlier example of battery:

If *B* knowingly strikes *A,* and . . . , then, unless *A* consented, or . . . , *A* is entitled to a judgment . . . .

Now examine with special care Form 11, a "Complaint for Negligence." You will observe that the plaintiff has there given a somewhat particularized statement within the compass of a rule of substantive law regarding liability for negligence. The complaint does not explicitly state the applicable substantive rule, but it implicitly invokes it.

Question: (1) Can you phrase schematically the rule of substantive law that the plaintiff is probably seeking to invoke in the forms' Complaint for Negligence?

After putting into words the rule of law that the Form 11 plaintiff is probably seeking to invoke, you will notice that he appears to have limited himself in the complaint to a somewhat particularized statement of the "if" part of the rule; he has not concerned himself with negating the "unless" part. To put the matter more concretely, plaintiff may also have been negligent at the time, which would normally bar his recovery at least in part; yet plaintiff does not in his complaint assert that he was himself free of negligence or, equivalently, that he was exercising due care. It thus appears that a plaintiff need not allege in his complaint all the conditions of the defendant's liability. He may confine himself to the "ifs" and omit any reference to the "unlesses."

Unfortunately, the "if, unless" form of statement is not the only meaningful one that someone could employ. Someone could state a substantive rule—the conditions under which a court will grant a

---

We nevertheless continue to cite those forms because they remain useful as illustrations for pedagogic purposes.

remedy—altogether in "if" fashion, without any "unless" clauses, simply by altering the form of the statement thus:

If B knowingly strikes A, and if A has not consented, and . . . ,
then A is entitled to a judgment . . . .

So why do we use the "if, unless" form? Because it is a convenient way to make the point that indeed the law divides the burden of allegation between the parties. The plaintiff must assert the matters in the "if" clauses, and the defendant must assert such of the matters in the "unless" clauses as she proposes to raise. As we shall see later, an omitted matter that the plaintiff need not assert and that the defendant chooses not to assert is ordinarily not in issue in the case.

But then which matters belong on the "if" side and which on the "unless"? The law's placing of the dividing line, and the corresponding assignment of the respective burdens of allegation to the parties, does not follow from an exercise of pure logic.[d] Reconsider the Complaint for Negligence. The law might well require the plaintiff to assert that he was using due care for his own safety when the defendant drove a motor vehicle against him. Indeed, as we shall see, in some state judicial systems the law did cast the burden on the plaintiff to assert his due care rather than on the defendant to assert the contrary.

Question: (2) What are the considerations that ought to govern the allocation between the parties of the burdens of allegation?

The Federal Rules provide a guide, although not a complete one, to the way in which the law actually allocates these burdens in the United States District Courts. Rule 8(c), entitled "Affirmative Defenses," is a catalogue of certain matters that the defendant must assert in her answer, if she wishes to put them in issue, and that the plaintiff need not assert in the complaint. Note that "contributory negligence" of the plaintiff is such an affirmative defense. Beyond Rule 8(c), statutes and precedents and form books and websites provide further guidance to the pleader.

All this gives at least an idea of what elements the parties respectively must plead. Generally, a pleader is well advised to avoid saying much more than the minimum required. We shall see later that any excess will risk causing problems—such as putting into issue matters that otherwise would not be in the case or boxing the pleader in—even though the Federal Rules try to mitigate most of such risks.

How particularized must allegations be?—We have said that the plaintiff's statement of claim appears to be a somewhat particularized rendering of the "if" part of a rule of law. This leaves at large, however, the question of the degree to which the plaintiff must

---

[d]   For the logical involvements of the scheme here presented, see H.L.A. Hart, "The Ascription of Responsibilities and Rights," in Essays on Logic and Language 145 (Antony Flew ed., 1951). But see H.L.A. Hart, Punishment and Responsibility, at v & n.1 (1968). See generally Richard A. Epstein, Pleadings and Presumptions, 40 U.Chi.L.Rev. 556 (1973).

carry particularization. Within the contours of relevancy, how much detail is necessary?

This is the big problem. There is no easy or simple answer, but the Rules and forms throw some light upon it. The statement of the claim is, according to Rule 8(a), to be "short" as well as "plain." And Rule 8 goes on, in its subdivisions applicable to all pleadings, to prescribe, for example, that each allegation of a pleading shall be "simple, concise, and direct."

Question: (3) Does a negligence plaintiff really need to plead the amount of his medical expenses, as Form 11 does?

Rule 9, "Pleading Special Matters," gives a number of further directions. Consider Rule 9(b). On the one hand, it tells us that in all allegations of fraud or mistake, the pleader must state "with particularity" the circumstances constituting fraud or mistake. On the other hand, it says that the pleader may allege generally malice, intent, knowledge, and other conditions of mind.

Question: (4) What is the reason for the distinction that Rule 9(b) draws? Is it not becoming plain that to answer such a question you must first decide what the system intends to accomplish by the pleadings? For example, would it not be desirable to know whether the pleadings will serve any purpose later during the course of trial?

If you were now asked to draft a complaint in a battery case, would these Rules and illustrative forms provide enough light to go by? Your client has given you, probably very volubly, a detailed account of what happened. It is your task to cull from this account a properly particularized statement of claim invoking the pertinent rule of substantive law. Should you state in your complaint when and where the attack took place? how your client happened to be there at the time? who witnessed the incident? what were the dimensions of the stick with which the defendant beat your client? the nature and extent of your client's injuries? the conversation between the parties before the attack? what the police officer who arrived on the scene said and did? Let us see what the courts have told us, after first reviewing how one lawyer read the Rules and illustrative forms.

————

Plaintiff's Amended Statement of Claim
Filed Nov. 17, 1938, amending complaint of Sept. 13, 1938.

Martin Sierocinski, also known as Martin Selensky, the plaintiff above named, brings this action in trespass against E.I. DuPont DeNemours & Company upon a cause of action whereof the following is a statement:

1. The plaintiff is a resident of the City and County of Philadelphia.

2. The defendant, E.I. DuPont DeNemours & Company, is and was at the time of the occurrences hereinafter described, a corporation duly organized and existing under the laws of the State of Delaware, and duly authorized to transact business in the Commonwealth of Pennsylvania, in accordance with the Business Corporation Law, having its registered office at 3500 Gray's Ferry Road, Philadelphia.

3. The defendant is engaged in the business of manufacturing and distributing, and does manufacture and distribute, inter alia, blasting caps for use by the public.

4. On or about September 24, 1936, and for a long period of time prior thereto, the plaintiff was an employee of Ehret Magnesia Manufacturing Company, which has and had its principal place of business located in the vicinity of Valley Forge, Pa.

5. The plaintiff, in the course of his duties as servant, agent or employee of the said Ehret Magnesia Manufacturing Company, was charged with the responsibility and duty of handling, preparing and exploding the explosives used by the said Ehret Magnesia Manufacturing Company in certain of its quarrying operations, and had occupied this position and performed these duties for a long period of time prior to September 24, 1936, as well as on said date.

6. The Ehret Magnesia Manufacturing Company furnished to the plaintiff dynamite caps manufactured by the defendant, which dynamite caps were in the same condition as they were when distributed by the said defendant.

7. On or about September 24, 1936, the plaintiff was engaged in crimping a dynamite cap, manufactured and distributed by the defendant, when it prematurely exploded causing the injuries hereinafter set forth.

8. In the crimping of the said dynamite cap, the plaintiff acted in the usual and customary manner, the process being a necessary one in the using of the said dynamite cap for the purpose for which it was manufactured and distributed, and such action on his part having been anticipated by defendant.

9. The aforementioned premature explosion, and the injuries resulting therefrom, were caused solely by the carelessness and negligence of the defendant, in:

    (a) manufacturing a dynamite cap in such a fashion that it was unable to withstand the crimping which defendant knew it would be subjected to,

    (b) distributing a dynamite cap which was so constructed that it was unable to withstand the crimping which defendant knew it would be subjected to,

    (c) distributing a dynamite cap which was so constructed that it would explode, upon being crimped, without warning or in any fashion indicating that the said dynamite cap would explode upon being crimped,

(d) distributing a dynamite cap which it knew would be crimped when the said dynamite cap would explode upon said crimping, and such fact was known or should have been known to defendant.

10. By reason of the said premature explosion of the said dynamite cap, manufactured and distributed by the defendant, the plaintiff did suffer the following injuries: Loss of great toe of left foot; loss of sight of both eyes; lacerations of the legs, arms, shoulders, thighs, face and neck; gravel and grit were driven into various and sundry portions of his body, including his face, legs, arms, shoulders, thighs, trunk and torso; a severe shock to his nerves and nervous system; and various and sundry other injuries of a serious and permanent nature.

11. As the result of the aforesaid occurrence, the plaintiff has undergone and will undergo great pain and suffering. He was confined to his bed for a long period of time and will be blind for the rest of his life. He has required and will require medical attention and treatment, thereby incurring great expenses. He has been deprived of his sole means of livelihood, and he is otherwise greatly injured and damaged.

Wherefore, the plaintiff claims to recover from the defendant the sum of Two Hundred Thousand Dollars ($200,000) as damages for the aforesaid injuries caused directly by the negligence of the defendant as aforesaid.

(S) RAYMOND A. WHITE, JR.,
ATTORNEY FOR PLAINTIFF.

Sierocinski v. E.I. Du Pont De Nemours & Co.
United States Circuit Court of Appeals, Third Circuit, 1939.
103 F.2d 843.

■ Before MARIS, BIDDLE, and BUFFINGTON, CIRCUIT JUDGES.

■ BIDDLE, CIRCUIT JUDGE. The plaintiff's "statement of claim" (complaint), amended under an order of court [25 F.Supp. 706 (E.D.Pa. Nov. 10, 1938) (Kalodner, J.)] granting defendant's motion for a more definite statement under Rule 12(e), Rules of Civil Procedure for District Courts . . . , alleged that he was injured by the premature explosion of a dynamite cap. Specifically the plaintiff claimed as negligent acts the manufacturing and distributing of the cap "in such a fashion that it was unable to withstand the crimping which defendant knew it would be subjected to"; and distributing a cap so constructed that it would explode upon being crimped, without warning, the defendant knowing it would be crimped. Judge Kalodner granted the defendant's motion to strike this amended statement, as failing to set forth any specific act of negligence, and dismissed the action. [His unpublished opinion explained: "The allegations as amended in Paragraph 9 . . . are not sufficiently specific and do not afford the Defendant opportunity to know what issue or issues it might have to meet upon trial in regard to negligence. In brief, the amended statement of claim still fails to set forth any specific act of negligence. The allegations consist of conclusions and not facts."] From his order the plaintiff appealed to this court.

The plaintiff, as alleged, was injured while "crimping" a dynamite cap manufactured by the defendant and supplied to him by his employer. "Crimping" is a necessary and anticipated process in using the cap.

Appellee, admitting that a manufacturer is liable for injuries to a person from the use of a defectively manufactured article, argues that it is not put on notice by the complaint as to whether it must meet a claim of warranty, of misrepresentation, of the use of improper ingredients, or of faulty inspection.

But there is a specific averment of negligent manufacture and distribution of the cap in such a fashion as to make it explode when crimped. A plaintiff need not plead evidence. He "sets forth a claim for relief" when he makes "a short and plain statement of the claim showing that the pleader is entitled to relief (Rule 8(a)(2))." The same rule [Rule 8(d)(1)] requires that "each averment of a pleading shall be simple, concise, and direct. No technical forms of pleading or motions are required"; and [(e)] "all pleadings shall be so construed as to do substantial justice". Form [11] in the Appendix of Forms attached to the Rules, "intended to indicate . . . the simplicity and brevity of statement which the rules contemplate [Rule 84]",[e] contains this concise allegation of negligence: "defendant negligently drove a motor vehicle against plaintiff who was then crossing said highway". If defendant needs further information to prepare its defense, it can obtain it by interrogatories (Rule 33).

The judgment is reversed, and the cause remanded for further proceedings.

––––––––

Question: (5) How convincing are Judge Biddle's arguments drawn from (a) the valid proposition that the plaintiff need not plead evidence, (b) the style of Form 11, and (c) the fact that the defendant might resort to Rule 33?

---

e   The omission in the quotation of Rule 84 was by Judge Biddle. Note that, at the date of this decision, Rule 84 read: "The forms contained in the Appendix of Forms are intended to indicate, subject to the provisions of these rules, the simplicity and brevity of statement which the rules contemplate." It was not until 1948 that Rule 84 came to declare the forms "are sufficient under the rules and are intended to indicate the simplicity and brevity of statement which the rules contemplate."

Upon remand, the Sierocinski case went to trial before a new judge and a jury. The jury brought in a verdict for the plaintiff. Denying the defendant's motions for a directed verdict and for judgment notwithstanding the verdict, the judge entered judgment for the plaintiff. From this judgment, the defendant took an appeal to the circuit court of appeals. The appellate court reversed the judgment, 118 F.2d 531 (3d Cir.1941) (Jones, J., joined by Maris & Clark, JJ.), on the ground that the judge should have taken the case away from the jury. The appellate court said: "No proof, . . . either direct or circumstantial, was adduced to support a finding of any of the specific acts of negligence alleged." The appellate court also rejected the plaintiff's attempt on appeal to switch to a contractual theory of breach of warranty.

Questions: (6) Does this subsequent history demonstrate that the decision on the first appeal was wrong?

(7) After decision on the second appeal, should it be open to the plaintiff to commence a new action, basing his claim on a legal theory not exploited before, for example, on a theory of breach of warranty?

————

CONLEY v. GIBSON, 355 U.S. 41, 78 S.Ct. 99 (1957). African American members of the Brotherhood of Railway and Steamship Clerks brought suit under the Railway Labor Act to compel the union to represent them in collective bargaining without discrimination because of race. There were in the complaint allegations that the union had not done so, mainly concerning its passivity after the employer, the Texas & New Orleans Railroad, replaced 45 plaintiff-jobholders with white hires. On motion to dismiss, defendants' principal contention was that the National Railroad Adjustment Board had exclusive jurisdiction of the dispute, but defendants also moved to dismiss on the ground that the complaint was defective for failure to state a claim upon which relief could be granted.

Ultimately the Supreme Court upheld the jurisdiction of the district court. See Emily Sherwin, "The Story of Conley: Precedent by Accident," in Civil Procedure Stories 295 (Kevin M. Clermont ed., 2d ed. 2008). On the pleading point, Justice Black for the Court made two significant pronouncements, albeit without a lot of thought.

First, before addressing the factual detail required, the Court addressed the test of legal sufficiency. It looked to see if any legal claim existed that would be consistent with the words of the complaint. The Court said the complaint must conceivably encompass a legal claim, without including extra allegations that would establish a defense to the claim and hence defeat the complaint.

Second, after the Court held that the plaintiffs passed the legal test, it disposed of any contention that dismissal was proper for the complaint's failure to set forth enough specific facts to support the general allegations of discrimination. The Court said: "The decisive answer to this is that the Federal Rules of Civil Procedure do not require a claimant to set out in detail the facts upon which he bases his claim. To the contrary, all the Rules require is 'a short and plain statement of the claim' that will give the defendant fair notice of what the plaintiff's claim is and the grounds upon which it rests. The illustrative forms appended to the Rules plainly demonstrate this. Such simplified 'notice pleading' is made possible by the liberal opportunity for discovery and the other pretrial procedures established by the Rules to disclose more precisely the basis of both claim and defense and to define more narrowly the disputed facts and issues. Following the simple guide of Rule 8([e]) that 'all pleadings shall be so construed as to do substantial justice,' we have no doubt that [the] complaint adequately set forth a claim and gave the [defendants] fair notice of its basis. The Federal Rules reject the approach that pleading is a game of skill in which one misstep by counsel may be decisive to the outcome and accept the principle that the purpose of pleading is to facilitate a proper decision on the merits."

———

BELL ATLANTIC CORP. v. TWOMBLY, 550 U.S. 544, 127 S.Ct. 1955 (2007). Telephone and internet subscribers brought a class action against the telecommunications giants, claiming an illegal conspiracy in restraint of trade. Under antitrust law, however, parallel and even consciously identical conduct unfavorable to competition is not illegal if it comprises only independent acts by competitors without any agreement. The complaint alleged parallel conduct in great detail, explaining how each company sought to inhibit upstarts in its own region and refrained from entering the other major companies' regions. The complaint also alleged an agreement in conclusory terms upon information and belief, because the plaintiffs had no proof yet in hand.

The obvious concern in this big complex case was with opening the door to the plaintiffs' expensive discovery. So, the Court upheld dismissal on a pre-answer motion for failure to state a claim upon which relief could be granted, holding that the complaint failed to show an agreement to be plausible. According to the Court, the defendants' behavior was what each company would naturally have done in pursuit of its own interests. The plaintiffs needed to give factual detail to make their complaint plausible, yet they "mentioned no specific time, place, or person involved in the alleged conspiracies." Dismissal followed for these plaintiffs who "have not nudged their claims across the line from conceivable to plausible."

In so ruling, the Court added a plausibility test for claimants to pass at the pleading stage. This move represented the Court's first unmistakable step backward from the modern conception of so-called notice pleading blessed in Conley. The Court did not step in the direction of reverting to a requirement of heightened detail in factual allegations, but instead it instituted a judicial inquiry into the pleading's convincingness. Such an innovation—testing factual strength at the pleading stage—would prove momentous *if* it were not limited to antitrust cases. Justice Souter for the Court explained the new test, and did so in generally applicable wording:

"This case presents the antecedent question of what a plaintiff must plead in order to state a claim under § 1 of the Sherman Act. Federal Rule of Civil Procedure 8(a)(2) requires only 'a short and plain statement of the claim showing that the pleader is entitled to relief,' in order to 'give the defendant fair notice of what the . . . claim is and the grounds upon which it rests,' Conley v. Gibson, 355 U.S. 41, 47, 78 S.Ct. 99 (1957). While a complaint attacked by a Rule 12(b)(6) motion to dismiss does not need detailed factual allegations, [citations omitted], a plaintiff's obligation to provide the 'grounds' of his 'entitle[ment] to relief' requires more than labels and conclusions, and a formulaic recitation of the elements of a cause of action will not do, see Papasan v. Allain, 478 U.S. 265, 286, 106 S.Ct. 2932 (1986) (on a motion to dismiss, courts 'are not bound to accept as true a legal conclusion couched as a factual allegation'). Factual allegations must be enough to raise a right to relief above the speculative level . . . .

"In applying these general standards to a § 1 claim, we hold that stating such a claim requires a complaint with enough factual matter (taken as true) to suggest that an agreement was made. Asking for plausible grounds to infer an agreement does not impose a probability requirement at the pleading stage; it simply calls for enough fact to raise a reasonable expectation that discovery will reveal evidence of illegal agreement. . . . It makes sense to say, therefore, that an allegation of parallel conduct and a bare assertion of conspiracy will not suffice. Without more, parallel conduct does not suggest conspiracy, and a conclusory allegation of agreement at some unidentified point does not supply facts adequate to show illegality. Hence, when allegations of parallel conduct are set out in order to make a § 1 claim, they must be placed in a context that raises a suggestion of a preceding agreement, not merely parallel conduct that could just as well be independent action.

"The need at the pleading stage for allegations plausibly suggesting (not merely consistent with) agreement reflects the threshold requirement of Rule 8(a)(2) that the 'plain statement' possess enough heft to 'sho[w] that the pleader is entitled to relief.' A statement of parallel conduct, even conduct consciously undertaken, needs some setting suggesting the agreement necessary to make out a § 1 claim; without that further circumstance pointing toward a meeting of the minds, an account of a defendant's commercial efforts stays in neutral territory. An allegation of parallel conduct is thus much like a naked assertion of conspiracy in a § 1 complaint: it gets the complaint close to stating a claim, but without some further factual enhancement it stops short of the line between possibility and plausibility of 'entitle[ment] to relief.' [Citation omitted.]

Thus, in this case the Court did not credit as true the conclusory allegation of agreement. It had to accept as true the allegations of parallel conduct, but it could still treat them as an inadequate "showing" of entitlement to relief because they did not make plausible the existence of an agreement.

Justice Stevens, joined in relevant part by Justice Ginsburg, dissented. He saw the decision as a "dramatic departure from settled procedural law," and an unjustified one because it should have come if at all by amendment of the Federal Rules or by statute. He lamented that by imposing a plausibility test on pleadings, "the Court succumbs to the temptation that previous Courts have steadfastly resisted. . . . Here, the failure the majority identifies is not a failure of notice—which 'notice pleading' rightly condemns—but rather a failure to satisfy the Court that the agreement alleged might plausibly have occurred. That being a question not of *notice* but of *proof*," courts will now have "to engage in armchair economics at the pleading stage" in order to ascertain somehow whether the complaint's pleaded facts adequately show liability.

Justice Stevens noted the inconsistency of the majority's holding with the simple reference to "negligently" in Form 11. "Whether the Court's actions will benefit only defendants in antitrust treble-damages cases, or whether its test for the sufficiency of a complaint will inure to the benefit of all civil defendants, is a question that the future will answer." The answer came in the next case, two years later.

———

ASHCROFT v. IQBAL, 556 U.S. 662, 129 S.Ct. 1937 (2009). Here the civil rights plaintiff, a Pakistani Muslim arrested post-9/11 in the United States, sued high federal officials upon allegations of harsh conditions of confinement on account of his race, religion, or national origin. After interlocutory appeal, the Court overturned the lower courts' approval of the complaint, while ruling that Twombly applied to all federal complaints.

The Court did not credit conclusory allegations of the cause of action's elements, such as that the top-level defendants knowingly condoned a discriminatory policy. The Court then said the remaining allegations did not suffice to make plausible that Attorney General John Ashcroft and FBI Director Robert Mueller subjected the plaintiff to harsh confinement *because of* his race, religion, or national origin. The issue was whether the content of the nonconclusory factual allegations "allows the court to draw the reasonable inference that the defendant is liable for the misconduct alleged."

"Two working principles underlie our decision in Twombly. First, the tenet that a court must accept as true all of the allegations contained in a complaint is inapplicable to legal conclusions. Threadbare recitals of the elements of a cause of action, supported by mere conclusory statements, do not suffice. Id., at 555, 127 S.Ct. 1955 (Although for the purposes of a motion to dismiss we must take all of the factual allegations in the complaint as true, we 'are not bound to accept as true a legal conclusion couched as a factual allegation' (internal quotation marks omitted)). Rule 8 marks a notable and generous departure from the hyper-technical, code-pleading regime of a prior era, but it does not unlock the doors of discovery for a plaintiff armed with nothing more than conclusions. Second, only a complaint that states a plausible claim for relief survives a motion to dismiss. Id., at 556, 127 S.Ct. 1955. Determining whether a complaint states a plausible claim for relief will, as the [Iqbal] Court of Appeals observed, be a context-specific task that requires the reviewing court to draw on its judicial experience and common sense. 490 F.3d, at 157–158. But where the well-pleaded facts do not permit the court to infer more than the mere possibility of misconduct, the complaint has alleged—but it has not 'show[n]'—'that the pleader is entitled to relief.' Fed.Rule Civ.Proc. 8(a)(2).

"In keeping with these principles a court considering a motion to dismiss can choose to begin by identifying pleadings that, because they are no more than conclusions, are not entitled to the assumption of truth. While legal conclusions can provide the framework of a complaint, they must be supported by factual allegations. When there are well-pleaded factual allegations, a court should assume their veracity and then determine whether they plausibly give rise to an entitlement to relief."

Now Justice Souter was in dissent, joined by Justices Stevens, Ginsburg, and Breyer. He agreed that nonconclusory allegations are to be taken as true, unless they "are sufficiently fantastic to defy reality as we know it: claims about little green men, or the plaintiff's recent trip to Pluto, or experiences in time travel"; yet he disagreed with the majority's classifying the key allegations here as conclusory.

In a separate dissent, Justice Breyer would have also relied on the lower court's using case-management tools to structure minimally intrusive discovery in anticipation of a summary judgment motion (a pretrial device invoked—often after pleadings, motions to dismiss, and discovery—to test whether the available evidence was sufficient to generate a genuine dispute of fact requiring trial); but the majority expressly rejected such a route in lieu of dismissal.

———

Thus, the Twombly-Iqbal Court was adding a requirement, only for claimants, above and beyond their having to give notice. The Court just unearthed, in Rule 8(a)(2)'s required "showing," a requirement that at the pleading stage the plaintiff must establish by nonconclusory allegations the complaint's plausibility. Although much puzzlement persists, nonconclusory-and-plausible pleading apparently works this way now:

First, upon a challenge to the complaint's *legal sufficiency*, the judge should proceed in the traditional way by asking whether any legal claim exists that would be consistent with the words of the complaint—that is, the complaint must encompass a legal claim without including factual allegations that would defeat it. Henceforth, however, the plaintiff must do more to identify the complaint's legal theories as a practical matter, because the plaintiff must be specific enough for the judge to weigh the complaint's factual sufficiency under the next test.

Second, to satisfy the test for *factual sufficiency*, the plaintiff must plead facts and perhaps some evidence. The plaintiff should give a particularized mention of the factual circumstances of each element of the claim. The degree of particularization should be sufficient to make liability reasonably possible, with the judge testing that plausibility not of each fact but only of the moving defendant's ultimate liability on the claim. The judge performs the decisional task (1) by ignoring, except for contextual purposes, any conclusory allegation, such as a bald assertion that an element exists; and (2) if any inference is necessary after accepting as true the nonconclusory and nonfrivolous allegations, by weighing the plausibility of ultimate liability in light of his or her judicial experience and common sense as applied in the case's context. This new approach will most seriously impact the potential plaintiff who needs discovery to learn the required factual particulars—although uncovering the empirical impact has proved elusive so far. See David Freeman Engstrom, The Twiqbal Puzzle and Empirical Study of Civil Procedure, 65 Stan.L.Rev. 1203 (2013).

———

Questions: (8) In first embracing notice pleading and then inventing nonconclusory-and-plausible pleading fifty years later, the Court was interpreting the same Rule 8(a). Should the Court's activism in interpreting a Federal Rule substantially differ from its role in interpreting a statute like the Rules Enabling Act? See Catherine T. Struve, The Paradox of Delegation: Interpreting the Federal Rules of Civil Procedure, 150 U.Pa.L.Rev. 1099 (2002) (arguing in the negative).

(9) Could Mr. Conley pass the Twombly-Iqbal test? Could Mr. Sierocinski?

———

Menard v. CSX Transportation, Inc.

United States Court of Appeals, First Circuit, 2012.
698 F.3d 40.

■ Before LYNCH, CHIEF JUDGE, BOUDIN and THOMPSON, CIRCUIT JUDGES.

■ BOUDIN, CIRCUIT JUDGE. Mark Menard and Carol Menard appeal from a district court order dismissing their complaint for failure to state a claim and denying their motion to amend the complaint. Mark Menard, whom we refer to as "Menard," was permanently injured while crossing through a railroad freight yard; the district court ruled that his complaint against CSX Transportation, Inc. ("CSX") failed to assert sufficient facts to overcome his status as a "trespasser" and thereby state a claim under Massachusetts law.

. . . .

In July 2008 Menard lived in West Springfield, Massachusetts, near a rail freight yard owned and operated by CSX, and he regularly walked across the rail yard on his way to and from his home, as did others who lived in the area. This included, as it turned out, crossing active railroad tracks. Heading home on July 30, 2008, Menard entered the rail yard; he says that at least three CSX employees saw him enter, he made eye contact with some and none told him to leave. Menard says that signs did not clearly warn him of the dangers of entering the yard but does not deny knowing that it was railroad property used to switch and store trains.

Once inside the rail yard, Menard saw several trains on different tracks, including one train on the track nearest to him that was moving very slowly under the control of an engineer and the guidance of a conductor on the ground. Menard made eye contact with both. Neither warned him to leave although the conductor waved his right arm, apparently to indicate that Menard should move in one direction. Menard continued to walk across the rail yard until, at some point, his right foot was pinned as an activated rail switch moved a segment of track.

With his foot crushed and in great pain, Menard freed himself and staggered about 30 feet, where he was struck by an oncoming train. Grabbing the train to prevent being dragged under it, he nevertheless ultimately fell under the train and his left leg was severed, his left arm was badly damaged in the encounter and his right foot was later amputated. . . .

. . . .

Thereafter, the district court ruled that Menard was indisputably a trespasser in the rail yard so that the only duty that CSX owed to Menard under Massachusetts law was a duty to refrain from willful, wanton or reckless conduct—with one qualification, namely, that state law imposes a duty of reasonable care on the property owner where a trespasser is in a position of "peril" inside the property and his presence is known to the owner. *Menard v. CSX Transp., Inc.*, 840 F.Supp.2d 421, 424 (D.Mass.2012).

Given this legal framework, the district court held that the ... complaint failed to state a claim and ... did not allege that any employee knew that Menard was in the vicinity of the switch or otherwise in a position of peril; and, even if a CSX employee did see Menard staggering across the rail yard after he freed himself from the switched rails, Menard alleged no facts to suggest that any reasonable steps were available to CSX to protect Menard from being struck or falling under the train. *Id.* at 424–28.

On Menard's appeal, this court reviews the dismissal de novo . . . .

. . . .

In any event, if Menard is deemed a trespasser, the duty owed to him—unless and until a specific peril threatened him and this became known to CSX—was only to avoid willful, wanton or reckless conduct. Whatever the risk in crossing a railroad yard, the dangers of injury in this case were apparently not so severe as to prevent regular crossings of the yard by Menard and others like him. Absent aggravating circumstances, the case law in Massachusetts makes clear that an adult who chooses without permission to trespass upon railroad tracks is not entitled to recover.

Neither in the district court nor on appeal does Menard ever directly dispute that he was a trespasser or argue that he was there by permission or as a licensee. . . .

. . . .

. . . In substance, Menard says that . . . "[u]pon information and belief, employees and/or agents of CSX knew that Mr. Menard had been injured by the rail switch and had sufficient time to take action to prevent further injury to him."

The quoted statement clearly aims to invoke the exception to the trespasser rule for those perceived to be in peril, [citation omitted], but nothing in the complaint provides any facts to support the general statement either that Menard was seen by CSX workers after he was hit or, if seen, could have been rescued by reasonable care. Menard says the allegation is made on "information and belief"; but if he had any facts to support this assertion, they should have been set forth. "Information and belief" does not mean pure speculation.

As the district judge observed, [the complaint does not] "allege that Mr. Menard saw any employees in the vicinity of the railroad switch when he was injured, that he called to anyone for help, or that any specific person saw Mr. Menard's peril." *Menard*, 840 F.Supp.2d at 428. Nor [does it] "even allege how much time passed between Mr. Menard's first and second injuries," let alone identify even briefly what could have been done by CSX workers in the interval. *Id.*

. . . .

. . . Here, one might not expect precise recollection from a man badly injured by a switched track and shortly thereafter hit and dragged under the train. By contrast, CSX likely made its own investigation which, if not privileged, could easily reveal just what its employees saw between the switch accident and the denouement.

Where modest discovery may provide the missing link, the district court has discretion to allow limited discovery and, if justified, a final amendment of the complaint. . . . If tempered by sound discretion, Twombly and Iqbal may produce the best that can be expected in human affairs which is a sensible compromise between competing legitimate interests.

In the end, the response to Twombly and Iqbal is still a work in progress; and we think that a limited remand is appropriate to allow Menard to explain to the district judge what basis he has to believe that narrow discovery is warranted as to the brief interval between the switch incident and Menard's fall under the wheels of the train. If anything beyond speculation supports Menard's "information and belief" allegation, that too can be disclosed. After that, the matter is confided to the discretion of the district judge.

The judgment is vacated and the matter remanded for further proceedings consistent with this decision. If Menard on remand offers no solid basis for the remaining peril-and-negligence allegation and limited discovery is not shown to be promising, the judgment should be reinstated. Each side shall bear its own costs on this appeal.

[On remand, discovery subject to some limits ensued. The district judge denied the defendant's motions for summary judgment. At trial, the jury found for the defendant.]

———

Statement of claim in the alternative.—Rule 8(d)(2) says that a party may set out two or more statements of a claim or defense "alternatively" (either-or) or "hypothetically" (if-then), whether in a single account or in separate ones. As applied to the complaint, the main function of this provision is to assist a plaintiff who is genuinely uncertain about the facts that he will be able to prove or the substantive law that will apply. The Rule permits that plaintiff to take advantage of whatever pleaded version of the claim he may eventually establish to the satisfaction of the adjudicator.

It may seem obvious to you that statements of claim in the alternative should be permissible, but it is worth pointing out that the Rule represents a departure from the practice permitted at common law. Does this not tell us more about the purposes of federal pleading?

Definition of "claim."—Throughout Rule 8, the word "claim" appears. This word is analogous to the phrase "cause of action" as it appears in cases and various state codes of procedure, but one should not assume that "claim" and "cause of action" necessarily mean the same thing. Nor should one assume that either "claim" or "cause of action" necessarily means the same thing whenever and wherever it is used, irrespective of context.

In all events, what does "claim" mean as it appears in Rule 8's provision for alternative statements of claim? We can say at least that the drafters of the Rule thought that a plaintiff may in some cases state a *single claim* in different ways. Yet how far can the statements vary before they produce not alternative statements of a single claim, but a set of *multiple claims*?

Consider here that the differing statements may all invoke the same rule of substantive law, or they may each allege a violation of a distinct legal right and thereby invoke a distinct rule of substantive law (say, negligence and warranty). Does this have a bearing on whether the statements are alternative statements of one claim or constitute a number of distinct claims? Shall we say narrowly that the "legal theory," or the substantive right, is the measure of what is a claim?

Consider further that a single, straightforward statement of an episode may implicitly invoke a number of rules of substantive law, each casting liability on the defendant. Thus, if *B* sells to *A* a device negligently constructed, and by reason of the defect it injures *A* in the course of operation, *B* may be liable by reference to a rule of tort law (negligence) or by reference to a rule of contract law (warranty). When *A* sets forth a recounting of the accident in her complaint, is she alleging one claim or two? Shall we say broadly that the "transaction or occurrence," or the natural grouping or congeries of events, is the measure of what is a claim?

The importance of this question—what is the distinction between alternative statements of a single claim, on the one hand, and multiple claims, on the other hand—may be minimal in the present context, because Rule 18(a) complements Rule 8(d)(2) by permitting the plaintiff to join in the complaint, either as independent or as alternative claims, as many claims as he has against the defendant. Nevertheless, we put the question here to call attention to a problem that later appears in various guises in other contexts and can sometimes be highly significant: what is the meaning of "claim"? of "cause of action"?

Consistency and truth in pleading.—Rule 8(d)(3) goes on to provide that a party may state as many separate claims or defenses as the party has against the opponent, "regardless of consistency."

Nevertheless, all statements in pleadings are subject to the obligations of Rule 11. Note thereunder that the pleader ordinarily need not verify or swear to the pleading, but presenting a pleading constitutes a certification that there is good ground to support it and that it is not interposed for improper purpose. The Rule sets forth sanctions for violations of its obligations.

Questions: (10) What obligation does Rule 11 impose on an attorney to investigate, before signing the complaint, the motivation and the legal and factual bases for the client's claim? See the section of the Rules booklet containing the 1983 and 1993 amendments to Rule 11 and the Advisory Committee's notes thereon.

(11) Considering the state of knowledge, information, and belief of Mr. Sierocinski's lawyer as to the cause of the accident, did he violate his duty under original Rule 11 when he signed the amended complaint in that action? Would Mr. White's signature have violated current Rule 11?

————

MURPHY v. CUOMO, 913 F.Supp. 671 (N.D.N.Y.1996). Murphy brought suit in February 1994 against a variety of defendants for injuries arising from an incident in which a New York State Police officer had sprayed Murphy with a pepper spray called CAP-STUN. The police argued that during post-arrest processing, while Murphy was intoxicated and belligerent, he had lunged at one of the officers and so prompted the spraying.

Murphy named as one of the defendants Zarc International, the manufacturer of CAP-STUN. Murphy alleged in detail that Zarc had conspired with the police to spray innocent people for testing the spray and then to forward the results to Zarc. Murphy further alleged that he had been one of those innocent people and that the incident had violated his federal statutory and constitutional rights. He sought $20 million in compensatory and punitive damages.

With the trial date fast approaching, Zarc moved for summary judgment under Rule 56 and sought sanctions pursuant to Rule 11. In granting the defendant's motion for summary judgment, the court determined that the "plaintiff has offered absolutely no evidence that Zarc conspired with the New York State Police to conduct an illegal experiment whereby officers would subject innocent and unwitting citizens to CAP-STUN in order to study the spray's effects. . . .

"The Pilot Study undertaken by the State Police appears to have been properly intended 'to evaluate the use of chemical agents [that] could be used as a non-lethal, alternative weapon to the issue side arm and the baton,' (Def.'s Mem.Supp.Summ.J. at 11), and plaintiff has presented no evidence to the contrary. In other words, the Court has no reason to believe that the Pilot Study was intended to test the effects of CAP-STUN on innocents, rather than to test whether CAP-STUN met the State Police's needs in situations where the use of some force was justified. Moreover, even if the State Police were involved in some kind of diabolical experiment, no evidence has been put forth that defendant Zarc had anything at all to do with the experiment, or with the officer's decision to use CAP-STUN on plaintiff as opposed to someone else.

"As late as his deposition in August, 1995, when discovery was supposed to be complete, plaintiff was unable to clarify the basis for his claim of conspiracy:

Q. Do you have any information that Zarc did anything other than provide the product Cap-Stun to the New York State police department?

A. I personally don't have any knowledge of that.

Q. Do you know of anyone who does have any knowledge of that?

A. No.

Q. Do you plan on calling any witnesses at the trial of this action to testify that Zarc did anything other than provide the New York State police with Cap-Stun?

A. We may.

Q. Who would that be?

A. I'm not sure right now.

. . . Now that discovery is complete and plaintiff has another opportunity to proffer evidence of an illegal plan to test CAP-STUN on innocent citizens, he does not fare much better. Plaintiff argues in his opposition memorandum that '[i]t is undisputed that Zarc provided the [pepper spray] for the State Police test.' (Pl.'s Mem.Opp.Summ.J. at 6.) Furthermore, '[t]o the extent that Zarc knowingly provided the State Police with training in the application of Cap-Stun . . . it helped to create the experimental protocol.' (Id.) Lastly, Zarc 'was informed of the results of the pilot study . . . and uses the results . . . as part of its advertising.' (Id. at 11.)

"The Court simply believes that, based on plaintiff's evidence, no reasonable jury could find that defendant Zarc was significantly involved in the Pilot Study. Nor could a reasonable jury find that the Pilot Study was intended to do anything but evaluate a chemical agent that could be used by police as a non-lethal, alternative weapon when the use of some force was justified."

Because no reasonable jury could find for the plaintiff, the court granted summary judgment for Zarc. It then moved on to Zarc's separate motion for sanctions.

"The objective of Rule 11 is to deter dilatory and abusive tactics in litigation, and to streamline the litigation process by lessening frivolous claims or defenses. . . . Imposition of Rule 11 sanctions does not require a finding of bad faith. Rather, '[t]he test as to whether an attorney made a reasonable inquiry prior to signing a pleading is an objective standard of reasonableness under the circumstances at the time the attorney acted.' EEOC v. Tandem Computers, Inc., 158 F.R.D. 224, 227 (D.Mass.1994).

"Rule 11 requires attorneys to take responsibility for the claims they present by requiring them to make a reasonable inquiry to assure that the claims represented by them are well-grounded in both law and fact. Id. At its simplest, Rule 11 'continues to require litigants to "stop-and-think" before initially making legal or factual contentions.' Fed.R.Civ.P. 11, Advisory Committee Notes (1993 Amendment). However, under the 1993 revisions to the rule the imposition of sanctions is always discretionary with the Court rather than mandatory. See Fed.R.Civ.P. 11(c); Knipe v. Skinner, 19 F.3d 72, 78 (2d Cir.1994). As a procedural matter, Rule 11 forbids the imposition of sanctions unless the challenged pleading has not been withdrawn or corrected within 21 days of service of the motion for sanctions. . . .

"The Court realizes that Rule 11 sanctions must be imposed with caution, so as not to chill the prosecution of meritorious claims. Knipe, 19 F.3d at 78; MacDraw, Inc. v. CIT Group Equip. Fin., Inc., 73 F.3d 1253, 1258–59 (2d Cir.1996). Furthermore, a district court must 'articulate with specificity the sanctionable conduct and the reasons supporting the sanctions.' MacDraw, 73 F.3d at 1258–59.

"[First, in applying these generalities the court concluded that plaintiff's counsel, Robert Ballan, had failed to make a reasonable inquiry into the legal viability of one of his claims against Zarc based on a federal drug statute, a statute that creates no private right of action—as would have been shown by] a mere cursory review of the applicable caselaw . . . . Defendant's counsel seems to have notified plaintiff's counsel of this reality on numerous occasions, but with no effect.

"Second, in regard to plaintiff's claims against defendant Zarc for other violations of his statutory and constitutional rights, plaintiff's counsel knew at the time he signed the Complaint that plaintiff had no basis in fact for his allegations. Another perusal of plaintiff's deposition, taken 20 months after plaintiff's counsel signed a document in which he seeks $20 million, makes this fact abundantly clear . . . . Thus even 20 months after the Complaint was signed, neither plaintiff nor his counsel knew if any facts existed that would support the serious allegations they had made in the Complaint.

"It is true that the law does not require a plaintiff to be able to prove his case prior to discovery. However, . . . a complaint must always be based 'on more than pure speculation and fantasy.' In re Keegan Management Co., 154 F.R.D. 237, 241 (N.D.Cal.1994). [After discovery, this] plaintiff's complaint is *still* based on mere speculation and fantasy. In sum, federal courts 'cannot tolerate complaints grounded solely on metaphysical inferences nor those filed without an informed basis for the allegations.' Id. at 242. Plaintiff and his counsel have taken a colorable claim of excessive force against certain police officers and turned it into a conspiratorial burlesque. Monetary sanctions against plaintiff's counsel are warranted under Rule 11.

"The only question that remains is the amount of sanctions the Court should assess. Monetary sanctions must be reasonable as well as consistent with the purpose of Rule 11—to deter baseless filings and dilatory or abusive pretrial tactics. Cooter & Gell v. Hartmarx Corp., 496 U.S. 384, 393, 110 S.Ct. 2447, 2454 (1990). In determining the amount, the district court must strike a balance that furthers the purpose of the rule without chilling meritorious litigation. See id. To this end, a court may consider not only the conduct itself, but also the offending party's ability to pay. The Court will reserve on this issue pending its receipt of submissions from the parties concerning a proper amount that is consistent with the objectives of Rule 11, the egregiousness of Mr. Ballan's conduct, and the burden this suit has imposed on defendant Zarc."

By about a year later, the court had imposed $4451.49 in sanctions against Ballan and also dismissed Murphy's entire case.

———

Questions: (12) Rule 11 prescribes a different type of cure for the problem of a plaintiff's getting a foot in the federal courthouse door too easily. It requires knowing more, rather than pleading more. In place from 1938 and later tightened, it now seems a necessary requirement—if only to avoid a plaintiff's circumvention of Twombly-Iqbal by pleading factual details without any basis. Would you expect Rule 11 to be effective in regulating behavior? What are the drawbacks of Rule 11?

(13) Rule 11 will have a differentially heavier impact on certain categories of cases, like civil rights. Does Rule 11 thereby affect substantive rights in violation of the Rules Enabling Act? Does Rule 8(a)(2), as interpreted by Twombly-Iqbal (or by Conley)?

(b) INTERPOSING DEFENSES AND OBJECTIONS

[Rules 7(b), 8(b), 12; Forms 30, 40]

A defendant who has been served with a summons and complaint pursuant to Rule 4 must make known her defenses—the grounds upon which she resists the relief demanded against her in the complaint—and must do so within certain time limits.[f] So also she has opportunity to object to the complaint for vices such as undue vagueness.

Questions: (14) Suppose the defendant does nothing during the prescribed time period. What should the plaintiff do to take advantage of the default? See Rule 55(a) and (b).

(15) What steps may the defendant take to cure such a default? See Rule 55(c). What sort of showing should she have to make? Compare Tesillo v. Emergency Physician Assocs., 230 F.R.D. 287 (W.D.N.Y.2005) (granting motion to set aside default, where defendant "forgot" to answer but plaintiff

---

[f]   Ordinarily the time limit is twenty-one days after service of the summons and complaint. See Rules 12(a)(1) and 6(a). May the parties stipulate, i.e., agree, to enlarge this time? See Rule 6(b).

suffered no prejudice and defendant had a meritorious defense), with In re Hein, 341 B.R. 903, 905 (Bankr.N.D.Ind.2006) ("Stupidity—acting without sufficient forethought—is a legitimate basis for imposing sanctions upon an attorney. . . . An empty head but a pure heart is no defense.").

Types of defenses and objections.—Let us consider the kinds of defenses and objections that may be available to a defendant. Imagine that the defendant faces the complaint of a single plaintiff attempting to state a single claim.

1. In the first place, there may be reasons why the court should not proceed with the case that have no bearing on the intrinsic merits of the plaintiff's claim. The defendant may wish to contend that the case is of a type the plaintiff cannot maintain in any federal district court (see Rule 12(b)(1)), that the particular district court selected by the plaintiff as the place of trial—the venue—is wrong (see Rule 12(b)(3)), or that there is another party who ought to be joined before the action goes forward (see Rule 12(b)(7)). We shall consider later the possible bases for such defenses (as well as for the defenses referred to in Rule 12(b)(2), (4), and (5), which involve failure to get the defendant properly before the court).

2. The defendant may take the position that, assuming for the sake of argument the truth of the basic allegations in the complaint, they do not invoke any rule of substantive law that casts liability on the defendant. For example, plaintiff alleges merely that defendant gave him a dirty look, or plaintiff follows Form 11 but omits any charge of negligence. Here, in the language of the common-law pleader, is ground for "demurrer" or, in the words of Rule 12(b)(6), a defense of "failure to state a claim upon which relief can be granted." It is plainly desirable that there should be some procedural device for exposing the futility of the plaintiff's claim without further inquiry as to whether his allegations are true.

3. Assuming for the sake of argument that the plaintiff's statement of claim does allege all the "if" clauses in a rule of substantive law casting liability on the defendant, the defendant may wish to challenge the truth of one or more of the allegations by "denying" it. See Rule 8(b) regarding defense by way of denial.

4. A further possibility is that, assuming without granting that all of the plaintiff's basic allegations are true and do invoke a rule of substantive law casting liability on the defendant, there are additional matters that will "avoid" that liability. In other words, the defendant may wish to activate one or more of the "unless" clauses in the relevant rule of law, such as the plaintiff's contributory negligence, the running of the period of limitations before the commencement of suit, or some other affirmative defense listed in the nonexhaustive Rule 8(c).

5. A complaint may be so vague or ambiguous that the defendant cannot reasonably prepare a responsive pleading. In that case it is open to the defendant to object and require the plaintiff to give "a more definite

statement." See Rule 12(e) and the Sierocinski case. Or the complaint may be objectionable because it contains "redundant, immaterial, impertinent, or scandalous matter" that causes prejudice to the defendant. In that case Rule 12(f) permits the defendant to have the court strike that matter out.

Question: (16) Is there any other position that a defendant might conceivably want to take?

The defendant may wish to take two or more of the positions outlined above. For example, suppose the plaintiff claims damages for mental anguish suffered by him because of the defendant's negligence. The defendant's counsel knows that according to the law of some states there exists a right of action for mental anguish inflicted in the alleged circumstances; that other states recognize no such right; and that the courts of the state in which the event occurred have not yet spoken on the question. Further, her investigation of the facts indicates considerable likelihood that the plaintiff cannot prove negligence. Further still, she wishes to challenge the venue, and also to argue that the plaintiff was contributorily negligent. In what manner should she present these defenses to the court? That is, should the defendant's counsel set up multiple defenses successively or simultaneously—and, indeed, may she set up all these defenses or do the Rules limit her to some lesser number?

Manner of presenting defenses and objections.—The pattern starts with Rule 12(b). It is, incidentally, very much at odds with the practice at common law.

1.   It is clear from Rule 12(b) that the defendant may raise all defenses to a claim in the answer.

Form 30 is an example of an answer. There the answer denies certain allegations of the complaint, and it also raises the defenses that the complaint fails to state a claim and that the plaintiff has failed to join a required party. Its fourth defense asserts additional matter, namely, the affirmative defense that the applicable period of limitations had expired. Note that defenses are to be stated "in short and plain terms," the aim being to give notice. Rule 8(b)(1)(A).

Defendant serves the answer by delivering or transmitting a copy to plaintiff's attorney. Within a reasonable time after service on plaintiff's attorney, defendant must file the answer in court, along with a certificate of service. See Rules 5 and 6(d). A similar pattern of service and filing normally applies to other papers subsequent to the complaint.

2.   Rule 12(b) states that the defendant can instead choose to assert any of seven enumerated defenses by motion, before answer.[g] Most of

---

[g]   See Rule 12(a)(4), which prescribes when to serve the answer if the defendant makes such a motion and the court denies it. Why does it make this extension?

these seven go to matters not affecting the merits of the claim, the obvious exception being Rule 12(b)(6)'s defense of failure to state a claim.

"Motion" receives no formal definition in the Rules, but Rule 7(b)(1) suggests that it is a request for a court order. (What order does the defendant seek when presenting each of the seven enumerated defenses by motion?) Unless made during a hearing or a trial, which is not the present circumstance, a motion must be in writing, must state with particularity its grounds, and must set forth the relief sought. Read Form 40, which is a form of motion, and then match the defenses presented there with the terms of Rule 12(b).

When a moving party wishes to bring up matters of fact in support of his motion, he may do so by affidavits. The opposing party then has an opportunity to serve and file counteraffidavits. The court may either decide the motion upon the affidavits or proceed to take oral testimony. See Rules 6(c) and 43(c). On disputes over the relevant law, the lawyers will usually support their respective positions by filing memoranda of law, and the court will sometimes entertain oral argument. Sometimes the movant instead just piles facts and law into a much lengthier motion. See David F. Herr, Roger S. Haydock & Jeffrey W. Stempel, Motion Practice (7th ed. 2016).

Rule 12(i) provides with respect to the seven enumerated defenses that, whether raised in an answer or by a motion, the court will hear and determine them before trial on application by any party, unless the court orders a deferral until trial. Why does the Rule pick these enumerated defenses for preliminary hearing? Consider with respect to each of the enumerated defenses whether it is likely to involve only a question of law resolvable on memoranda and arguments of counsel, or whether it is likely to involve disputed issues of fact. Is the circumstance that a defense will involve only a question of law a sufficient reason for seeking to dispose of it at an early stage before trial? No. Therefore, consider with respect to each of the enumerated defenses whether it is likely to spell the end of the lawsuit.

3.   We can deal summarily with the objections under Rule 12(e) and (f) for vagueness or redundancy or the like. These objections are not frequent, and they should rarely succeed. In the nature of things, the defendant makes them by motion before answer.

Consolidation and waiver of defenses and objections.—We shall now mention some consequences that attach to the defendant's actions and failures to act at the answer-or-move stage.

———

1.   Consider the seven defenses listed in Rule 12(b). The effects of Rule 12(g) and (h) are as follows:

First. If the defendant makes a pre-answer motion based on any of the seven defenses but omits another of those defenses then available to her, she may not make a further pre-answer motion based on the defense omitted. In other words, Rule 12(g) contemplates that the defendant will consolidate these defenses in her initial motion if she chooses to make a motion.

Example: Defendant moves before answer on the ground of improper venue. The court denies the motion. She may not move again before answer to assert the defense of failure to state a claim (assuming that this defense was available to her when she first moved).

There is one exception to the consolidation requirement: the defendant may raise the defense of lack of subject-matter jurisdiction (Rule 12(b)(1)) by a second motion—indeed, Rule 12(h)(3) implies that anyone may suggest this defense at any time in any manner and that the court ought to raise it even if the defendant does not.

Second. By contrast, if the available defense omitted from the pre-answer motion was lack of jurisdiction over the person, improper venue, insufficiency of process, or insufficiency of service of process (Rule 12(b)(2)–(5)), not only is the defense disallowed as the subject of a second pre-answer motion, but also it is waived, i.e., lost altogether. See Rule 12(h)(1)(A).

Example: Defendant moves before answer on the ground of failure to state a claim. Motion denied. Defendant loses any defense of improper venue (assuming that this defense was available to her when she moved).

If the defendant makes no pre-answer motion, defenses under Rule 12(b)(2)–(5) are nevertheless waived if the defendant does not include them in the answer or in an amendment thereof permitted to be made under Rule 15(a)(1) "as a matter of course," i.e., without applying to the court for permission. See Rule 12(h)(1)(B).

Example: Defendant makes no motion; she answers without making any reference to venue; and the time expires to amend the answer without the court's permission. The defense of improper venue is no longer open to the defendant.

Third. Notwithstanding any omission otherwise to assert the defenses of failure to state a claim upon which relief can be granted and of failure to join a party under Rule 19 (Rule 12(b)(6) and (7)), they are preserved and may be included in the answer or made the subject of a post-answer motion for judgment on the pleadings under Rule 12(c) or presented at trial. See Rule 12(h)(2).

Questions: (17) What does "available" mean as used in Rule 12(g)(2)?

(18) Why are the defenses enumerated in Rule 12(b)(2)–(5) disfavored in this way? Why are those in Rule 12(b)(6) and (7) preserved? Why is the Rule 12(b)(1) defense treated with unique solicitude?

————

2.   The proper way for the defendant to raise other defenses is by answer. So, suppose the defendant serves and files an answer. The effects of the Rules are as follows:

First. To the extent that the answer, after any amendment "of course" under Rule 15(a)(1), fails to deny allegations of the complaint, those allegations stand admitted for purposes of the litigation. This follows from Rule 8(b)(6), which states that allegations in a pleading to which a responsive pleading is required are admitted if the responsive pleading does not deny them.[h]

Second. Any affirmative defenses omitted from the answer, after any amendment "of course," are presumptively lost. This waiver is not explicit in the Rules, but follows from the pattern of the Rules, including Rules 8(c) and 12(b).

Third. Those two effects were overstatements, however. Amendments of the answer, if allowed to the defendant by leave of court under Rule 15(a)(2), may alleviate the described waivers as to denials and affirmative defenses. But this somewhat uncertain step will entail, like any extra step, extra expense in attorney's fees.

Example: *A* for consideration releases his claim against *B,* thus giving *B* a perfect defense to *A*'s suit. *A* can nevertheless proceed with his action, and possibly get judgment, if *B* fails to present this defense in her answer or by an amendment.

Questions: (19) Can Rule 15(a) on amendments, either as a matter of course or by leave of court, furnish any escape from the other waivers, for example, a waiver under Rule 12(h)(1)(A)?

(20) Take the case of alleged mental anguish set out above in this subsection and, on behalf of the defendant, describe the manner and sequence in which you might present your defenses. Mention any strategic or tactical considerations that would affect your choices.

———

3.   The defendant should raise objections under Rule 12(e) and (f), dealing with vagueness or redundancy or the like, in the initial pre-answer motion. The defendant may not interpose an objection under Rule 12(e) if she has omitted it from such motion (see Rule 12(g)) or if she has answered (see Rule 12(e)). The same is true of a Rule 12(f) objection to redundancy or the like, although the Rule allows the court to act on its own initiative and so gives the court discretion to entertain a later request to strike.

Questions: (21) Assume that on Day 1, a Wednesday, a summons and complaint are served; on Day 15 defendant serves a 12(f) motion to strike scandalous matter from the complaint; and on Day 42 defendant receives notice that the court granted the 12(f) motion and thereby struck the

---

[h]   There is one exception: allegations as to the amount of damages, although not denied in the answer, are not taken as admitted. Why this exception?

scandalous passage. Assume further that defendant was a private party and that the manner of all service was ordinary in-hand service within the state. How much time does defendant have to serve an answer?

(22) Assume that on Day 0, the first Monday in October, a summons and complaint are served; on Day 15 defendant serves a 12(e) motion for a more definite statement; on Day 43 the court grants the 12(e) motion; on Day 56 plaintiff serves the more definite statement as an amended complaint, revealing for the first time possible grounds for a 12(b)(6) motion; on Day 60 defendant serves a 12(b)(6) motion; and on Day 74 defendant receives notice that the court denied the 12(b)(6) motion. Assume further that defendant was a private party and that the manner of all service was ordinary in-hand service within the state. How much time does defendant have to serve an answer?

————

When learning the mechanics of the Rules, you should give thought to the policies behind them. A general policy underlying many of the Rules is the facilitation of deciding cases on their merits, rather than on procedural points. Another is the elimination of traps for the unwary or, often equivalently, the protection of clients from the effects of their lawyers' mistakes. Yet Rule 12 bristles with notions of waiver. What countervailing policies account for this?

————

Coleman v. Frierson

United States District Court, Northern District of Illinois, 1985.
607 F.Supp. 1566, aff'd sub nom. Coleman v. Smith, 814 F.2d 1142 (7th Cir.1987).

■ SHADUR, DISTRICT JUDGE.

[In late 1982 Samuel Coleman sued the Village of Robbins, its mayor, and its police chief under 42 U.S.C. § 1983, a very important civil rights statute that appears in the Rules booklet. Coleman alleged, among much else, that he had been a special investigator for that suburb of Chicago, authorized to investigate police corruption; that his investigation had led to the mayor's office; and that then Coleman had been summarily fired as part of a cover-up. He sought two million dollars in damages for lost wages and for injuries that allegedly included mental, emotional, and ultimately physical harm resulting from the defendants' so depriving him of property or liberty without due process of law in violation of the Fourteenth Amendment.

[The defendants' answer denied many allegations. However, the defendants were willfully delinquent during the discovery phase, and eventually the judge imposed a sanction of default as to liability.

[A jury then tried the issue of damages, giving the plaintiff a verdict for more than a half million dollars in compensatory and punitive damages. The judge entered judgment on the verdict. The defendants promptly made several motions to set aside the judgment.

[One of these motions] asserts three grounds:

1.   Coleman's claims are barred by res judicata principles because they could have been raised in the context of his lawsuit against Robbins for unpaid wages, filed in the Circuit Court of Cook County in March 1980. There, claiming to have served as Special Investigator for a period of 107 weeks at a salary of $225 per week, Coleman sought a judgment of $24,000. That action was terminated January 29, 1982 when the parties filed a stipulation to dismiss the cause with prejudice.

2.   Coleman's factual allegations in the Complaint, deemed admitted as a consequence of the default judgment, are insufficient to state a claim upon which relief can be granted.

3.   Coleman had no property or liberty interest in his employment . . . . Robbins was therefore not required to afford him a pre-termination hearing. Under prevailing law, his due process rights were adequately guarded by the availability of an adequate state remedy.

But the short answer is that this Court need not consider the merits of those contentions at this late stage of the litigation, though different reasons for that answer attach to the differing attacks.

Defendants' first argument is an affirmative defense to liability, essentially asserting defendants (though otherwise liable) are not subject to suit because of facts outside the Complaint. Ordinarily such a defense must be pleaded in a defendant's answer to the complaint. At the least it must be raised by motion [to amend] at trial. See 5 Wright & Miller § 1277, at 328–29, 332; id. at § 1278. In any event such a defense may not be raised for the first time after judgment has been entered and the record in the case established. See Johnson v. Rogers, 621 F.2d 300, 305 (8th Cir.1980) (defense of res judicata may not be raised for the first time in a motion for judgment n.o.v.). Clearly the strong policy in favor of certain and final judgments on the merits compels such a rule.

Defendants' second argument is of the variety normally and properly raised in a Rule 12(b)(6) motion. In that regard Judge Weinfeld said . . . in Snead v. Department of Social Services of the City of New York, 409 F.Supp. 995, 1000 (S.D.N.Y.1975) (emphasis in original):

If, as stated in Bell v. Hood, [327 U.S. 678, 682, 66 S.Ct. 773, 776 (1946),] "the failure to state a proper cause of action calls for a judgment on the merits," then a litigant should not be permitted to raise such a failure after a determination on the merits. This view finds support in Rule 12(h)(2) of the Federal Rules of Civil Procedure, which provides that "[a] defense of failure to state a claim upon which relief can be granted . . . may be made in any pleading . . . or by motion for judgment on the pleadings, or at trial on the merits." The clear thrust of the Rule is that a failure to state a claim may be raised at any time *before* a disposition on the merits but not *after*. Any other construction would not only add to intolerable delay, but create uncertainty as to the validity of a final judgment on the merits.

See also 5 Wright & Miller § 1392, at 861–62 (1969 & Supp.1984).

Defendants' third argument is not technically an affirmative defense (for it challenges one of the elements of Coleman's cause of action, rather than acknowledging the validity of the claim as pleaded by plaintiff but urging its defeat because of other factors; see Rule 8(c)), nor is it strictly speaking a Rule 12(b)(6) contention (for it asserts facts outside the Complaint itself . . .). But the same reasoning applies. See Breuer Electric Manufacturing Co. v. Toronado Systems of America, Inc., 687 F.2d 182, 186 (7th Cir.1982). Once the record in the case has been made at or before the trial on the merits, every principle of orderly jurisprudence forbids an assault on the judgment for reasons dehors the record—unless of course any of the bases for post-judgment attack under Rule 60(b) applies. Defendants do not even hint at a right to relief under that Rule, so far as the three grounds discussed in this section are concerned.

In both legal and practical contemplation a default judgment is the equivalent of a trial on the merits. That makes all the foregoing reasoning fully applicable here. Between the time Coleman filed the Complaint and the time the default . . . was entered nearly a year and a half elapsed, affording defendants ample time to have raised the arguments they only now put forward. If defendants could not with reasonable diligence have discovered the factual predicate for those arguments, the principles embodied in Rule 60(b) might perhaps compel a different analysis. But in‛ the absence of such a showing—and defendants have made none—the default . . . as to liability must be seen as the analogue of a judgment on the merits. Its entry foreclosed arguments challenging the sufficiency of Coleman's claim for relief. Any other result would effectively allow defendants the opportunity now to press arguments they wholly neglected to advance, for no excusable reason, when they should have. Doing justice between litigants, after all, hinges as much on respect for the procedural rules governing the progress of the lawsuit as on affording parties liberal scope in making their arguments on the merits.

[The other sections of the opinion, denying the defendants' other motions, are omitted.]

———

SUA SPONTE POWERS

An odd aspect of upholding waiver of a Rule 12(b)(6) defense is that the outcome could be that the court might decide the case on the basis of nonexistent law. At common law such a defense was largely unwaivable. Although today it is waivable, the judge retains the power to raise the Rule 12(b)(6) defense sua sponte when the public interest strongly calls for doing so, which it might because this defense raises an issue of law rather than fact and usually raises a matter of substance rather than procedure.

The more generally stated problem is when may a trial judge raise an issue that the parties cannot or will not raise, either by virtue of forfeiture or waiver or by virtue of consent or stipulation. The answer is not often. Consistent with the background norm of party-propelled adversary presentation, the parties can shape the litigation, either inadvertently or intentionally, and could even customize their litigation by creating their own procedure. The trial judge should not intercede unless interests beyond the parties' are at stake.

If such externalities are in play, the judge has the residual power to raise the issue, but will discretionarily exercise that power only when various factors counsel doing so. Those factors primarily include the public's, the court system's, and any third parties' interests and only secondarily include such matters as the parties' behavior and their strictly private interests. Sometimes the factors could be so strong that failure to raise the issue would be an abuse of discretion. And sometimes the positive law expressly regulates the judge's particular sua sponte powers. An incisive example would be Rule 12(h)(3), which provides against party waiver and imposes a duty on the judge to act sua sponte.

––––––––

Question: (23) There is in the folklore of the common law the famous Case of the Kettle. The plaintiff claimed damages for a kettle that assertedly the defendant had borrowed and had allowed to become cracked while in his possession. The defendant is reputed to have pleaded (a) that he did not borrow the kettle, (b) that it was never cracked, and (c) that it was cracked when he borrowed it. See Andy Wible, "Kettle Logic," in Bad Arguments 174 (2018) (claiming this pleading to be a logical fallacy). Would this pleading be permissible today under the Federal Rules?

––––––––

ABA, Model Rules of Professional Conduct
(2008).

Preamble: A Lawyer's Responsibilities

A lawyer, as a member of the legal profession, is a representative of clients, an officer of the legal system and a public citizen having special responsibility for the quality of justice.

As a representative of clients, a lawyer performs various functions. As advisor, a lawyer provides a client with an informed understanding of the client's legal rights and obligations and explains their practical implications. As advocate, a lawyer zealously asserts the client's position under the rules of the adversary system. As negotiator, a lawyer seeks a result advantageous to the client but consistent with requirements of honest dealing with others. . . .

. . . .

A lawyer's responsibilities as a representative of clients, an officer of the legal system and a public citizen are usually harmonious. Thus, when an opposing party is well represented, a lawyer can be a zealous advocate on behalf of a client and at the same time assume that justice is being done. . . .

In the nature of law practice, however, conflicting responsibilities are encountered. Virtually all difficult ethical problems arise from conflict between a lawyer's responsibilities to clients, to the legal system and to the lawyer's own interest in remaining an ethical person while earning a satisfactory living. The Rules of Professional Conduct often prescribe terms for resolving such conflicts. Within the framework of these Rules, however, many difficult issues of professional discretion can arise. Such issues must be resolved through the exercise of sensitive professional and moral judgment guided by the basic principles underlying the Rules. These principles include the lawyer's obligation zealously to protect and pursue a client's legitimate interests, within the bounds of the law, while maintaining a professional, courteous and civil attitude toward all persons involved in the legal system.

. . . .

Scope

The Rules of Professional Conduct are rules of reason. They should be interpreted with reference to the purposes of legal representation and of the law itself. Some of the Rules are imperatives, cast in the terms "shall" or "shall not." These define proper conduct for purposes of professional discipline. Others, generally cast in the term "may," are permissive and define areas under the Rules in which the lawyer has discretion to exercise professional judgment. No disciplinary action should be taken when the lawyer chooses not to act or acts within the bounds of such discretion. Other Rules define the nature of relationships between the lawyer and others. The Rules are thus partly obligatory and disciplinary and partly constitutive and descriptive in that they define a lawyer's professional role. Many of the Comments use the term "should." Comments do not add obligations to the Rules but provide guidance for practicing in compliance with the Rules.

. . . .

RULE 3.1   Meritorious Claims and Contentions

A lawyer shall not bring or defend a proceeding, or assert or controvert an issue therein, unless there is a basis in law and fact for doing so that is not frivolous, which includes a good faith

argument for an extension, modification or reversal of existing law. A lawyer for the defendant in a criminal proceeding, or the respondent in a proceeding that could result in incarceration, may nevertheless so defend the proceeding as to require that every element of the case be established.

COMMENT:

[1] The advocate has a duty to use legal procedure for the fullest benefit of the client's cause, but also a duty not to abuse legal procedure. The law, both procedural and substantive, establishes the limits within which an advocate may proceed. However, the law is not always clear and never is static. Accordingly, in determining the proper scope of advocacy, account must be taken of the law's ambiguities and potential for change.

[2] The filing of an action or defense or similar action taken for a client is not frivolous merely because the facts have not first been fully substantiated or because the lawyer expects to develop vital evidence only by discovery. What is required of lawyers, however, is that they inform themselves about the facts of their clients' cases and the applicable law and determine that they can make good faith arguments in support of their clients' positions. Such action is not frivolous even though the lawyer believes that the client's position ultimately will not prevail. The action is frivolous, however, if the lawyer is unable either to make a good faith argument on the merits of the action taken or to support the action taken by a good faith argument for an extension, modification or reversal of existing law.

. . . .

RULE 3.2   Expediting Litigation

A lawyer shall make reasonable efforts to expedite litigation consistent with the interests of the client.

COMMENT:

[1] Dilatory practices bring the administration of justice into disrepute. Although there will be occasions when a lawyer may properly seek a postponement for personal reasons, it is not proper for a lawyer to routinely fail to expedite litigation solely for the convenience of the advocates. Nor will a failure to expedite be reasonable if done for the purpose of frustrating an opposing party's attempt to obtain rightful redress or repose. It is not a justification that similar conduct is often tolerated by the bench and bar. The question is whether a competent lawyer acting in good faith would regard the course of action as having some substantial purpose other than delay. Realizing financial or other benefit from otherwise improper delay in litigation is not a legitimate interest of the client.

(c) Replying to Defenses

[Rule 7(a)]

If the defendant's answer includes only denials, there is no occasion for a response by the plaintiff, because the matters in dispute appear on the face of the complaint and the answer.

Suppose, however, that the answer sets up an affirmative defense. May the plaintiff respond to it? Must he respond to it or have it taken as admitted? Rule 7(a)(7)—differing sharply from the practice at common law and under many state codes of procedure—not only declines to require the plaintiff to plead in response, but does not permit him to do so unless the court orders a reply. The court ordinarily will not order a reply unless it is the defendant who moves for such an order, and there are relatively few cases in which it will order a reply even on the defendant's motion.

Questions: (24) What is the purpose of the general prohibition on replies to defenses?

(25) In what circumstances should the court order a reply?

Rule 8(b)(6) is the necessary complement of Rule 7(a)(7). Its second sentence provides that allegations in a pleading to which no responsive pleading is required will be considered *denied* or *avoided*.

If, then, plaintiff makes allegations 1, 2, 3, and 4, and defendant in her answer denies 1 and asserts 5, 6, and 7 by way of affirmative defense, and there is no order by the court that plaintiff reply, what are the matters in dispute?

Allegation 1 is in dispute because the plaintiff asserts the affirmative and the defendant the negative of it. But allegations 2, 3, and 4 stand admitted under the first sentence of Rule 8(b)(6).

Allegations 5, 6, and 7 are in dispute by reason of the second sentence of Rule 8(b)(6). Defendant asserts the affirmative on these allegations. The pleadings do not disclose plaintiff's position with respect to them. At the trial, or otherwise, he may (a) assert the negative (denial), (b) assert that, granting for the sake of argument the truth of the allegations, there are further matters that vitiate their effect (avoidance), or (c) take both such positions. For instance, if defendant alleges the affirmative defense that plaintiff for consideration released his claim against defendant, plaintiff without filing a reply is free at trial to deny that he received consideration for the release, or he can assert that defendant procured the release by fraud, or both.

Furthermore, by a motion to strike under Rule 12(f), the plaintiff may raise the point that a defense in an answer is "insufficient"—a point that Rule 12(h)(2) preserves through the stage of trial. This is the plaintiff's analogue of a defendant's Rule 12(b)(6) motion addressed to the complaint.

Finally, under Rule 12(f), the plaintiff may move to strike matter from an answer as being redundant or the like, much as a defendant can object to a complaint.

(d) INTERPOSING COUNTERCLAIMS

[Rule 13]

Defendant, whether or not she asserts defenses or objections to plaintiff's statement of claim, may desire to assert one or more claims against plaintiff. Must she resort to a separate action against plaintiff, or may (or must) she assert such claims as "counterclaims" in her answer to plaintiff's complaint?

You may first wonder whether we are repeating ourselves. Did we not consider counterclaims already in our discussion of contributory negligence? In a word, no. That discussion involved an affirmative defense, not a counterclaim. Imagine that A sues B for negligence, based on a two-car accident. B can (1) deny B's negligence and (2) affirmatively defend by alleging that A's contributory negligence helped to cause the accident. Her aim in pleading the second defense, as well as the first defense, is to defeat A's suit that seeks damages for A's injuries. Yet in that accident, B might have suffered injuries too. B might then want to counterclaim by alleging that A's negligence caused the injurious accident. Her aim in counterclaiming would be to recover damages for B's injuries, which are of course a thing different from A's injuries. Although beginning students always confuse affirmative defenses and counterclaims, the two are not at all the same. Here, the same acts characterizable as A's lack of due care constitute both contributory negligence and also negligence, but the former is an affirmative defense to A's claim for A's injuries and the completely distinguishable latter can generate B's counterclaim seeking compensation for B's damages caused by A's negligence.

Rule 13 deals with this new question of counterclaims. Rule 13(a) covers "compulsory counterclaims" and Rule 13(b) "permissive counterclaims." It is important to examine the differences between the two.

Compulsory counterclaims.—Now imagine instead that A sues B for slander. B wishes to contend (1) that she has a good defense to A's claim, because she did not use the slanderous words alleged, and (2) that A struck her at the time and place of the alleged slander, so that she has a claim against A for battery. The events involved in these two claims for slander and battery are closely interwoven. If it were necessary for B to bring a separate action, the same witnesses might well have to be brought to court again, and much of the same testimony would have to be repeated. There is a generally recognized wisdom in permitting enlargement of plaintiff's action to encompass defendant's claim when the latter arose out of the same "transaction or occurrence" that is the subject matter of plaintiff's claim. The Federal Rules, however, go further, making enlargement in those circumstances compulsory and not merely permissive. Note that the plaintiff can thus choose the forum for the defendant's claim, a choice that can constitute a significant advantage.

The language of Rule 13(a) is mandatory, so that the defendant must state the counterclaim. Of course, this does not mean that the defendant is jailed or fined for failing to assert a compulsory counterclaim. It does suggest that if she fails to assert the claim in her answer or an amendment to her answer, she is thereafter precluded from asserting it against the plaintiff in an independent action. This preclusion involves an application of the principle of finality in litigation. If a person who has failed to assert a compulsory counterclaim later sues on that claim, the opponent can then plead res judicata or the like as a defense.

Question: (26) *E* sues *F,* who moves under Rule 12(b)(6) for failure to state a claim upon which relief can be granted. The court grants the motion and dismisses the case, *F* never having filed an answer. There is no appeal. Then *F* sues *E* on a claim arising out of the same transaction or occurrence as *E*'s earlier attempted claim. *E* defends solely on the ground that *F*'s claim is precluded by *F*'s failure to interpose it as a counterclaim in the first action. What judgment? Does the word "pleading" as used in the first sentence of Rule 13(a) include a motion? Consider Rule 7. See Lawhorn v. Atl. Ref. Co., 299 F.2d 353 (5th Cir.1962) (judgment for *F*). (Always herein, when a cited case or other authority seems to provide the law's answer, you should think further to construct reasons for that outcome and to question its soundness.)

Permissive counterclaims.—*A* and *B* have a troubled relationship. Suppose now that when *A* sues *B* for breach of a contract, *B* has a claim against *A* for another battery arising out of a transaction or occurrence wholly unrelated to the subject matter of *A*'s contract claim. Rule 13(b) permits but does not compel *B* to assert such an unrelated claim by way of counterclaim in her answer in *A*'s action. If *B* chooses not to assert the counterclaim, she is free to bring an independent action for this battery.

We should mention here that, in furtherance of convenience or to avoid prejudice, the court may order a separate trial of any claim, counterclaim, or issue in an action. See Rule 42(b). There will naturally be more frequent occasion to apply Rule 42(b) to permissive than to compulsory counterclaims.

Furthermore, Rule 42(a) allows the court to combine separate actions pending before it if they involve a common question of law or fact. Thus, the two parts of Rule 42 provide the court with a means to take into account the peculiarities of particular cases, by appropriately peeling off compulsory counterclaims or piling on separate claims, without having to twist Rule 13's dividing line for compulsoriness completely out of shape.

Definition of "transaction or occurrence."—Having been warned that words like "procedure" and "claim" are legal chameleons that may change their meaning as the context changes, you may wonder whether the key phrase of Rule 13(a) and (b), "transaction or occurrence," has proven to be a chameleon.

There are relatively few cases in which a party has invoked Rule 13(a) in an attempt to bar a later suit, and hence there is a dearth of judicial decisions defining "transaction or occurrence" for purposes of Rule 13 in those circumstances.

Question: (27) What probably accounts for the dearth of case law on this point?

A minority of states make no provision for a compulsory counterclaim. Indeed, a code of procedure might permit the defendant to interpose only certain kinds of counterclaims. In such a code, the definition of permitted kinds of counterclaims is commonly this: "a cause of action arising out of the contract or transaction set forth in the complaint as the foundation of the plaintiff's claim, or connected with the subject of the action." This code language has generated case law defining "transaction."

Question: (28) Consider whether the defendant may interpose her counterclaim in the following cases under that state code language. Then consider whether the counterclaim would be compulsory under Federal Rule 13(a).

(a) Lyric Piano Co. v. Purvis, 194 Ky. 826, 241 S.W. 69 (1922): *P* sues *D* for the balance due on an installment contract for the sale of a piano. *D* seeks to counterclaim for a battery by *P*'s representative while engaged in collecting the sum due.

(b) Mulcahy v. Duggan, 67 Mont. 9, 214 P. 1106 (1923): *P* sues *D* for a battery occurring on May 17. *D* seeks to counterclaim for a libel published by *P* about *D* on May 8, with *D* alleging that the subsequent altercation was the result of the publication of the libel.

Obviously, the question posed by the state code is different from the question of compulsoriness under Rule 13, and so the definitions given in answer do differ. But the meaning of "transaction or occurrence," even only for the purposes of a particular Rule such as Rule 13, does in fact vary with the type of circumstances of the case and the consequent effects on the parties and the public. As Justice Oliver Wendell Holmes, Jr., put it in Towne v. Eisner, 245 U.S. 418, 425, 38 S.Ct. 158, 159 (1918): "A word is not a crystal, transparent and unchanged, it is the skin of a living thought and may vary greatly in color and content according to the circumstances and the time in which it is used."

Thus, you will certainly find it wise, in seeking the meaning of a phrase in a certain type of circumstances under a particular Rule, to bear steadily in mind what the purposes of the Rule may be in that context. For an example in regard to counterclaims, expand your focus to the statute of limitations. Although the limitation period's application to counterclaims is a complicated subject, one popular approach allows assertion of a counterclaim on which the statute of limitations expired between the filing of the complaint and the filing of the counterclaim *provided that* the counterclaim arises out of the same transaction or occurrence as the main claim. (That approach may seem to address a bizarrely rare scenario, but some plaintiffs have an inclination to wait until the last moment to file.)

Question: (29) Now imagine the facts of the Mulcahy case arising recently in Montana, which adopted a replica of Federal Rule 13 in 1962. Would the court, facing a slightly late counterclaim and applying that popular approach, uphold or reject a statute of limitations attack by the plaintiff on the counterclaim?

———

Williams v. Robinson

United States District Court, District of Columbia, 1940.
1 F.R.D. 211.

■ LETTS, JUSTICE.

By way of background it may be stated that the following matters transpired in sequence as related; the defendant's wife filed a suit for maintenance; the defendant filed his answer with a cross-complaint[i] seeking an absolute divorce upon the ground of adultery, [joining in accordance with the old practice] this plaintiff as co-respondent; in his answer to such cross-complaint this plaintiff contented himself with denying the acts of adultery with which he was charged; such maintenance cause is identified as Civil Action No. 5224, and is pending in this court.

Plaintiff brings this suit entitling his complaint as one for libel and slander. He alleges that he was libeled and slandered by the matters set up by the defendant in the cross-complaint wherein the defendant falsely and maliciously charged that this plaintiff had been guilty of adultery with the defendant's wife.

The defendant has filed no answer but moves to dismiss the complaint upon the ground that plaintiff has failed to assert his claim, if any he has, in his answer to the cross-complaint in the maintenance suit. Defendant invokes Rule 13(a) of the Federal Rules of Civil Procedure . . . and insists that plaintiff was obliged thereunder to then assert the claim which he now brings as an independent action. It is the defendant's position that since plaintiff failed so to do by way of counterclaim he is now precluded from asserting it here.

---

[i]   In the terminology of the Federal Rules, this cross-complaint would properly be called a counterclaim. Note, incidentally, Rule 13(h).

Rule 13(a) relates to compulsory counterclaims and clearly required this plaintiff in the maintenance suit to state as a counterclaim any claim which at the time of filing his answer in the maintenance case he had against this defendant if such claim arose out of the transaction or occurrence that was the subject matter of the defendant's cross-complaint in the maintenance suit.

But one question arises for consideration: was the slander and libel of which plaintiff complains part and parcel of the transaction or occurrence that was the subject matter of the defendant's cross-complaint in the maintenance suit? The question may be otherwise stated; the defendant in his cross-complaint charged this plaintiff with specific acts of adultery; these charges were in response to the wife's complaint for maintenance; can it be said that the acts of adultery alleged and relied upon by defendant and his subsequent accusations respecting such adultery may be grouped together as one and the same transaction or the same occurrence within the meaning of the rule?

The word "transaction" has abundant use in many statutes as; requiring or permitting joinder of causes of action growing out of the same transaction; making it necessary or optional for a defendant to plead as a counterclaim a cause of action arising out of the transaction which is the subject matter of the plaintiff's suit; relating to the admissibility of evidence pertaining to personal transactions with persons since deceased; statutes of limitation and many others which the courts have had occasion to construe. As a result of judicial determination the word "transaction" as so used has acquired a well defined meaning which, if applied to Rule 13(a), will give to it the intended sense and meaning.

The decided cases indicate that the word "transaction" denotes something done; a completed action; an affair as a whole; in Craft Refrigerating Mach. Co. v. Quinnipiac Brewing Co., 63 Conn. 551, 29 A. 76, 25 L.R.A. 856, the word "transaction" is defined to mean something which has been acted out to the end. In Cheatham v. Bobbitt, 118 N.C. 343, 24 S.E. 13, it is said the word "transaction" as found in the North Carolina Code in reference to the joinder of actions is used in the sense of the conduct of finishing up an affair, which constitutes as a whole the subject of an action. A right of action for slander and one for false imprisonment of plaintiff at the time the words were uttered cannot be united in one action, under the New York Code of Civil Procedure, as being causes arising out of the same transaction; DeWolfe v. Abraham, 151 N.Y. 186, 45 N.E. 455 [(1896)].

The use of the word "occurrence" in the rule in connection with the word "transaction" can serve no other purpose than to make clear the meaning of the word "transaction". An "occurrence" is defined to be a happening; an incident; or event. The word "transaction" is somewhat broader in its scope than the word "occurrence". The word "transaction" commonly indicates an act of transacting or conducting business but in the rule under consideration it is not restricted to such sense. It is broad enough to include an occurrence. It seems apt to say that the words "transaction" and "occurrence" as used in Rule 13(a) include the facts and circumstances out of which a cause of action may arise; Scarborough v. Smith, 18 Kan. 399. The words "transaction" and "occurrence" probably mean, whatever may be done by one person which affects another's rights and out of which a cause of action may arise. Whether the subject matter of opposing claims is the same requires an examination into the basic facts underlying each of them. A familiar test may be applied by inquiring whether the same evidence will support or refute the opposing claims.

It is clear that the use of the defamatory language of which plaintiff complains constituted no portion of the facts or circumstances alleged and relied on by this defendant in his cross-complaint filed in his wife's maintenance suit. There is no common point between the causes of action. The rule is in accordance with modern trend and the general prevailing policy to have the whole subject matter of any controversy settled in one action. It does not apply to causes growing out of separate transactions.

To sustain defendant's motion to dismiss would be in effect to require plaintiff to admit that there was a transaction or occurrence within the meaning of the rule, and as alleged by defendant in his cross-complaint in the maintenance suit. He makes no such admission but specifically denies the acts of adultery with which he is charged.

It follows that defendant's motion to dismiss the complaint must be overruled.

————

Questions: (30) Some have suggested that the test of compulsoriness should be whether there is a "logical relationship" between claim and counterclaim. What do you think of this possible criterion?

(31) Is there an undesirable inconsistency between Rule 18(a), which states that a plaintiff *may* join his claims, and Rule 13(a), which states that a defendant *must* assert her claims arising from the same transaction or occurrence as the plaintiff's claim?

Response to counterclaim.—A counterclaim, whether compulsory or permissive, is treated very much like a complaint for pleading purposes, with the counterclaiming defendant assuming to that extent the role of a plaintiff, and the original plaintiff the role of a defendant. See Rules 7(a) and 12(a). Note that the plaintiff must file an answer (formerly called a reply) to the counterclaim in much the same way as a defendant must answer a complaint. And, reading the remainder of Rule 12, you will see that the plaintiff may make motions in respect to the counterclaim in much the same way that a defendant may move against a complaint.

Questions: (32) What would be the consequence if the plaintiff failed to answer or to move with respect to the counterclaim? See Rule 55.

(33) *P* sues *D* on a contract. *D* sets up in her answer a counterclaim on an unrelated contract. *P* answers, denying that he committed any breach of the second contract. The court eventually gives judgment on the merits of the action, including the counterclaim. Thereafter *P* sues *D* for a breach of the second contract occurring before he interposed his answer to *D*'s counterclaim in the first suit. *D* sets up a defense based upon *P*'s failure to counterclaim in the first suit. Is *P*'s second suit precluded? See Wright & Miller § 1188. Why were we careful to say that the breach of the second contract occurred before the interposition of *P*'s answer?

Recovery on claim and counterclaim.—In an action that involves a counterclaim, the plaintiff may prevail on his claim and the defendant on the counterclaim. If the defendant's recovery is for a smaller sum than the plaintiff's, the result is a judgment in favor of the plaintiff for the difference, unless some special statute or contract provides against offset. Likewise, if the defendant's recovery is for a larger amount than the plaintiff's, there will be an affirmative judgment in favor of the defendant for the difference. See Rule 13(c). An affirmative judgment for the defendant will also follow where the plaintiff fails on his claim and the defendant succeeds on the counterclaim.

(e) AMENDING THE PLEADINGS

[Rule 15]

Rule 15 reflects the idea that a party ought not to be irretrievably bound to stand by his first formulation of a pleading of either claim or defense—that the contours of the controversy should not become frozen beyond change too soon. A party may commit an innocent mistake in framing his pleading; or a need for altering it in the light of his opponent's subsequent pleading may appear; or the investigation of the facts, carried on privately or by means of the discovery methods soon to be described, may show that the matters in dispute are not as the party first supposed. A party who finds himself in such a situation will naturally want to amend his pleading.

The question of the degree of freedom of amendment that the system should permit turns on the answer to the general question already posed: what are the purposes of the pleading process? In this light consider why Rule 15 attaches importance to the stage of the lawsuit at which the party seeks to amend.

Amendments before trial.—Rule 15(a)(1) permits a party to amend his pleading once as a matter of course during a certain limited time. The length of this period of grace turns on whether his pleading requires a responsive pleading.

Afterwards, unless the party obtains his opponent's written consent, the allowance of an amendment rests in the discretion of the court. Rule 15(a)(2) says that the trial-court judge "should freely give leave when justice so requires." Courts have interpreted this to mean that the judge should balance the equities, although it is up to the opponent (O) of the amendment's movant (M) to convince the judge to disallow the amendment. Because the equities involve a set of offsetting factors that fall on either side of the balance, the amendment's opponent must show:

$$(M's \text{ fault} - \text{prejudice to } M) > (O's \text{ fault} - \text{prejudice to } O + \text{net public interest}),$$

where M's fault comes from any delay in moving to amend; the prejudice to M means detriment to a full presentation of the merits that would be unavoidably caused by denying the amendment; O's fault comes from any inducing of the delay; and the prejudice to O means the disadvantage to reliance interests attributable to the delay that would be unavoidably caused by allowing the amendment. Then the court must throw onto the scales of the balance the considerations of public interest, which usually favor amendment.

Question: (34) Under that approach, should a court generally be more ready to allow amendment of an answer than of a complaint?

The party seeks leave to amend by a motion made in accordance with Rule 7(b). The party should present the proposed amendment with the motion. As a general rule the court on such a motion will not pass on the sufficiency of the proposed amended pleading under the pleading Rules, and clearly the granting of the motion is not an adjudication on this point. If, however, it is obvious that the proposed amended pleading is insufficient, the court is likely in the exercise of its discretion to disallow the amendment.

Question: (35) Are there still other factors that should influence the court in granting or refusing amendment?

An amended pleading supersedes the original pleading, which drops out of the case. Note the time that Rule 15(a)(3) gives the opposing party to respond to an amended pleading.

[handwritten margin note: within time remaining to respond to original pleading or w/in 14 days of service of amended pleading, whichever is later]

Beeck v. Aquaslide 'N' Dive Corp.

United States Court of Appeals, Eighth Circuit, 1977.
562 F.2d 537.

■ Before BRIGHT and HENLEY, CIRCUIT JUDGES, and BENSON, DISTRICT JUDGE.*

■ BENSON, DISTRICT JUDGE.

This case is an appeal from the trial court's exercise of discretion on procedural matters in a diversity personal injury action.

Jerry A. Beeck was severely injured . . . while using a water slide. He and his wife, Judy A. Beeck, sued Aquaslide 'N' Dive Corporation

---

*   The Honorable Paul Benson, Chief Judge, United States District Court for the District of North Dakota, sitting by designation.

(Aquaslide), a Texas corporation, alleging it manufactured the slide involved in the accident, and sought to recover substantial damages on theories of negligence, strict liability and breach of implied warranty.

Aquaslide initially admitted manufacture of the slide, but later moved to amend its answer to deny manufacture; the motion was resisted. The district court granted leave to amend. On motion of the defendant [under Federal Rule 42(b)], a separate trial was held on the issue of "whether the defendant designed, manufactured or sold the slide in question." This motion was also resisted by the plaintiffs. The issue was tried to a jury, which returned a verdict for the defendant, after which the trial court entered summary judgment of dismissal of the case. Plaintiffs took this appeal. . . .

A brief review of the facts found by the trial court in its order granting leave to amend, and which do not appear to have been in dispute, is essential to a full understanding of appellants' claims.

In 1971 Kimberly Village Home Association of Davenport, Iowa, ordered an Aquaslide product from one George Boldt, who was a local distributor handling defendant's products. The order was forwarded by Boldt to Sentry Pool and Chemical Supply Co. in Rock Island, Illinois, and Sentry forwarded the order to Purity Swimming Pool Supply in Hammond, Indiana. A slide was delivered from a Purity warehouse to Kimberly Village, and was installed by Kimberly employees. On July 15, 1972, Jerry A. Beeck was injured while using the slide at a social gathering sponsored at Kimberly Village by his employer, Harker Wholesale Meats, Inc. Soon after the accident investigations were undertaken by representatives of the separate insurers of Harker and Kimberly Village. On October 31, 1972, Aquaslide first learned of the accident through a letter sent by a representative of Kimberly's insurer to Aquaslide, advising that "one of your Queen Model #Q-3D slides" was involved in the accident. Aquaslide forwarded this notification to its insurer. Aquaslide's insurance adjuster made an on-site investigation of the slide in May, 1973, and also interviewed persons connected with the ordering and assembly of the slide. An inter-office letter dated September 23, 1973, indicates that Aquaslide's insurer was of the opinion the "Aquaslide in question was definitely manufactured by our insured." The complaint was filed [in the Southern District of Iowa on] October 15, 1973. Investigators for three different insurance companies, representing Harker, Kimberly and the defendant, had concluded that the slide had been manufactured by Aquaslide, and the defendant, with no information to the contrary, answered the complaint on December 12, 1973, and admitted that it "designed, manufactured, assembled and sold" the slide in question.

The statute of limitations on plaintiff's personal injury claim expired on July 15, 1974. About six and one-half months later Carl Meyer, president and owner of Aquaslide, visited the site of the accident prior to the taking of his deposition by the plaintiff.[5] From his on-site inspection of the slide, he determined it was not a product of the defendant [but instead a counterfeit slide]. Thereafter, [on February 26, 1975,] Aquaslide moved the court for leave to amend its answer to deny manufacture of the slide.

. . . .

It is evident from the order of the district court that in the exercise of its discretion in ruling on defendant's motion for leave to amend, it searched the record for evidence of bad faith, prejudice and undue delay which might be sufficient to overbalance the mandate of Rule 15(a) . . . that leave to amend should be "freely given." Plaintiffs had not at any time conceded that the slide in question had not been manufactured by the defendant, and at the time the motion for leave to amend was at issue, the court had to decide whether the defendant should be permitted to litigate a material factual issue on its merits.

In inquiring into the issue of bad faith, the court noted the fact that the defendant, in initially concluding that it had manufactured the slide, relied upon the conclusions of three different insurance companies, each of which had conducted an investigation into the circumstances surrounding the accident. This reliance upon investigations of three insurance companies, and the fact that "no contention has been made by anyone that the defendant influenced this possibly erroneous conclusion," persuaded the court that "defendant has not acted in such bad faith as to be precluded from contesting the issue of manufacture at trial." The court further found "[t]o the extent that 'blame' is to be spread regarding the original identification, the record indicates that it should be shared equally."

In considering the issue of prejudice that might result to the plaintiffs from the granting of the motion for leave to amend, the trial court held that the facts presented to it did not support plaintiffs' assertion that, because of the running of the two year Iowa statute of limitations on personal injury claims, the allowance of the amendment would sound the "death knell" of the litigation. In order to accept plaintiffs' argument, the court would have had to assume that the defendant would prevail at trial on the factual issue of manufacture of the slide, and further that plaintiffs would be foreclosed, should the amendment be allowed, from proceeding against other parties if they were unsuccessful in pressing their claim against Aquaslide. On the state of the record before it, the trial court was unwilling to make such assumptions, and concluded "[u]nder these circumstances, the Court deems that the possible prejudice to the plaintiffs is an insufficient basis on which to deny the proposed amendment." The court reasoned that the amendment would merely allow the defendant to contest a disputed

---

[5]   Plaintiffs apparently requested Meyer to inspect the slide prior to the taking of his deposition to determine whether it was defectively installed or assembled.

factual issue at trial, and further that it would be prejudicial to the defendant to deny the amendment.

The court also held that defendant and its insurance carrier, in investigating the circumstances surrounding the accident, had not been so lacking in diligence as to dictate a denial of the right to litigate the factual issue of manufacture of the slide.

On this record we hold that the trial court did not abuse its discretion in allowing the defendant to amend its answer.[j]

. . . .

The judgment of the district court is affirmed.

———

Amendments during or after trial.—Rule 15(b) shows that a motion to amend made during the course of the trial is not necessarily too late, and indeed that there are circumstances in which a party may seek and a court may allow an amendment even after the conclusion of trial and the entry of judgment.

Question: (36) Why would a party ever seek amendment of the pleadings after judgment, and why would a court ever allow it?

Rule 15(b) handles two late situations. Rule 15(b)(1) makes provision for allowing amendment in this situation: where a party seeks to amend after the opposing side has successfully objected to trial evidence as going beyond the pleadings. Rule 15(b)(2) provides for treating the pleadings as amended in this situation: where the opposing side, having failed to object fully to trial evidence unambiguously going beyond the pleadings, thereby consented to the trial of those new issues.

Questions: (37) How does an objecting party show, under Rule 15(b)(1), that she will suffer adequate "prejudice" by the admission of evidence not within the issues made by the pleadings? How does the rule of decision here compare with the rule applicable under Rule 15(a)(2)?

(38) What is a "continuance," referred to in Rule 15(b)(1)? Is this device feasible in jury trials?   ⌐ postponement or adjournment

Relation back of amendments.—What is the purpose of Rule 15(c)?

———

[j]   The reference here is to a deferential standard of review called abuse of discretion. For a decision that depends on the presence of the judge upon the trial-court scene to get a feel for the case, an appellate court will not overturn the decision unless clearly convinced there was error. This contrasts with the de novo standard of review for a decision on pure law, where the appellate court will substitute its view whenever it thinks the decision was wrong.

Blair v. Durham

United States Circuit Court of Appeals, Sixth Circuit, 1943.
134 F.2d 729.

■ Before HICKS, SIMONS, and HAMILTON, CIRCUIT JUDGES.

■ HAMILTON, CIRCUIT JUDGE. Appellant, Algernon Blair,[k] doing business as the Algernon Blair Construction Company, was general contractor for the repair of and improvements on, the United States Post Office, Customs House and United States Court Building in the city of Nashville, Tennessee, and appellant, C.W. Roberts, was the Superintendent and Manager for his co-appellant. The work was being done while the building was occupied and in use by officers and employees of the United States.

On or about August 17, 1938, appellee, Nelle B. Durham, a stenographic clerk in the Social Security Division in the office of the Collector of Internal Revenue, while at work in one of the rooms where the rebuilding under appellant's contract was going on, was struck in the head and injured by a heavy piece of timber falling from a scaffold.

Appellee originally filed this action [in the Middle District of Tennessee] on January 14, 1939, and alleged in her complaint that "by reason of the negligence and carelessness of defendants, their agents and servants in handling certain heavy timbers on and about the scaffolding that was erected in the office in which the plaintiff was working, a large and heavy piece of board approximately 2 x 4 inches in width and thickness and about 3 feet long was permitted to fall from said scaffolding, which was about 10 feet above the floor, and onto plaintiff's head with great force and violence injuring her."

Issue was joined on this complaint and the cause came on for trial before a jury. In the course of the trial on August 15, 1940, appellee with the consent of the court filed an amended complaint alleging the same facts with the following revision: "The defendants had erected said scaffolding and provided it for the use of persons engaged in the installation of air-conditioning equipment in said building and said scaffold was erected in such a manner that it did not protect persons, including the plaintiff, who were required to work thereunder, but was erected in such a manner that the defendants might have reasonably anticipated that heavy objects would be likely to fall therefrom."

---

[k]   Blair was a defendant.

In the district court, the caption of the case is, of course, in the form of Plaintiff v. Defendant; if there are several parties on either side, only the first is named in citing the case. Cf. Rule 10(a). In the courts of appeals, it was long the usual practice to reformulate the caption as Appellant v. Appellee; but since 1968, when the Federal Rules of Appellate Procedure were adopted, the title given to the action in the district court is retained on appeal. See App. Rule 12(a). In the Supreme Court, the practice is still to caption the case thus: party who seeks review versus adverse party.

So in this case from a court of appeals in 1943, because defendants were appealing plaintiff's victory in the district court, the caption of the case is Appellant (i.e., defendant) v. Appellee (i.e., plaintiff).

At the time the amendment was filed, the empanelling of the jury was set aside and the cause continued. Thereupon appellants moved to dismiss the amended complaint on the ground it stated a new cause of action and was barred by the Tennessee Statute of Limitations of one year. (Code of Tennessee, Sec. 8595.) Said motion was overruled by the court.

On retrial, the jury returned a verdict on behalf of plaintiff for $6,500. Appellants assign the following points:

1. Appellee's amended complaint was barred by the one-year statutory period of limitation.

[Two other assignments of error are omitted.]

Rule 15(a) of the Rules of Civil Procedure . . . provides that a party may amend his pleadings by leave of court, which leave shall be freely given when justice so requires at any time during the proceedings, and subsection (c) of the rule provides that whenever the amended pleading arose out of the conduct, transaction or occurrence set forth or attempted to be set forth in the original pleadings, the amendment relates back to the date of the original pleading. The issue here as to whether the statute of limitations was tolled by the original complaint depends upon whether the amendment stated a new cause of action.

A cause of action is the unlawful violation of a right or failure to discharge a duty which the facts show. The variety of facts alleged does not establish more than one cause of action so long as their result, whether they be considered severally or in combination, is the violation of but one right by a single legal wrong. A multiplicity of grounds of negligence alleged as causing the same injury does not result in pyramiding as many causes of action as separate allegations of actual negligence.

An amendment does not set up a new cause of action so long as the cause of action alleged grows out of the same transaction and is basically the same or is identical in the essential elements upon which the right to sue is based and upon which defendant's duty to perform is alleged to have arisen. As long as a plaintiff adheres to a legal duty breached or an injury originally declared on, an alteration of the modes in which defendant has breached the legal duty or caused the injury is not an introduction of a new cause of action. The true test is whether the proposed amendment is a different matter or the same matter more fully or differently laid.

A comparison between the appellee's original complaint and the amendment leaves no room for doubt that in both she relies on the same unlawful violation of a duty which appellants owed her at the place and in the position where she worked.

The original complaint which alleged that appellee's injuries were due to the negligence of appellant's employees in the use of the scaffold states no different cause of action as respects limitation than the amended complaint which stated that her injuries were due to the negligent manner in which the scaffold was constructed, because the two acts alleged were but different invasions of appellee's primary right and different breaches of the same duty. There was but one injury and it is immaterial whether it resulted from the negligence of the users of the scaffold or from its construction, since in either case it was a violation of the same obligation. [Citations omitted.]

[The remainder of the opinion, dealing with the other assignments of error, is omitted. However, in the course of its discussion the court did mention this: the evidence at trial had shown that at the time of the accident, the scaffold was being used not by Blair's employees but solely by employees of a subcontractor.]

. . . Judgment affirmed.

———

Questions: (39) How could the plaintiff have pleaded originally to avoid all this trouble?

(40) It does not appear that the defendants objected to the making of the amendment itself. Why did they not do so?

(41) Some state codes prohibit amendments that would have the effect of changing or substantially changing the "cause of action" or "defense." Do you find a comparable limitation in Rule 15? So, do you agree with the court's statement in Blair v. Durham that "[t]he issue here . . . depends upon whether the amendment stated a new cause of action"?

"Cause of action" and "claim."—Of "cause of action" the Supreme Court has said: "One of the most theory-ridden of legal concepts is a 'cause of action.' This Court has recognized its 'shifting meanings' and the danger of determining rights based upon definitions of 'a cause of action' unrelated to the function which the concept serves in a particular situation." United States v. Dickinson, 331 U.S. 745, 748, 67 S.Ct. 1382, 1385 (1947) (quoting United States v. Memphis Cotton Oil Co., 288 U.S. 62, 67, 53 S.Ct. 278, 280 (1933)). The Federal Rules avoid use of "cause of action," but do use the word "claim" in a good number of places. We shall have to observe how far the avoidance of the former phrase actually obviates the difficulties to which the Court referred.

Definition of "conduct, transaction, or occurrence."—Federal courts today read the transactional test of Rule 15(c)(1)(B) in light of its putting-on-notice function and therefore usually read the test loosely to require for relation back no more than "a common core of operative facts." Wright & Miller § 1497, at 97. For example, a mere switch in a complaint's legal theory from negligence to warranty will relate back. Hood v. P. Ballantine & Sons, 38 F.R.D. 502 (S.D.N.Y.1965). So also, there should be relation back for an amendment adding a count of false imprisonment to a complaint alleging battery in the very same incident.

Questions: (42) An associate professor brings a federal civil rights action against her college and its president based on the failure to renew her contract of employment. Much later, her amended complaint also alleges defamation by the college's president near the time of and in connection with her termination. Does the defamation count relate back? See Pendrell v. Chatham College, 386 F.Supp. 341 (W.D.Pa.1974) (Teitelbaum, J., holding no and saying, "A more reasonable interpretation of F.R.Civ.P. 15(c) does not permit lawyers to endlessly answer the question: How many causes of action can you find in this fact situation? much as they might have done years earlier in law school examinations.").

(43) Do you see any disadvantages in the prevailing functional reading of certain malleable terms in the Federal Rules?

A recent case suggests that Rule 15(c)(1)(B) will not reach what is factually the same conduct, transaction, or occurrence if the original complaint failed to give fair notice of the amended claim. Glover v. FDIC, 698 F.3d 139 (3d Cir.2012). The plaintiff sued lawyers, claiming violations of the Fair Debt Collection Practices Act in the defendants' trying to foreclose on the plaintiff's mortgage. She then amended the complaint after the statute of limitations had run. The original complaint had recounted the whole episode but stressed a debt-collection phone call and the filing for foreclosure, while the amended complaint stressed failure to withdraw the filing after the plaintiff had reached a loan modification with the bank and thus stressed a continuing representation that the plaintiff was in arrears. The court ruled that the factual overlap did not suffice for relation back, because the original complaint had not made clear "the factual predicate and legal theory of the amended claim."

(f) DISCLOSURE AND DISCOVERY

[Rules 26, 30–37]

General purposes.—The pleadings, as well as the motions attacking the pleadings, serve among other things to acquaint the parties with the character and scope of the controversy. But the pleadings contain limited detail on facts or contentions (for example, Form 11 does no more than identify the accident and charge the defendant with negligence: the plaintiff does not describe the accident with precision, nor does the plaintiff state in what way the defendant was negligent). Moreover, even when the pleadings do go into detail, they do not often disclose the witnesses, documents, or other evidence by which the parties propose to make their proof.

If, apart from the pleadings, the parties knew all about the relevant facts and contentions and how the proof would be made by both sides at the trial, the pretrial exchange of information might stop with the pleadings. But this is rarely the situation in practice. The parties are often quite in the dark about the facts and about each other's positions and sources of proof. Indeed, they may not know precisely what detailed positions they themselves will ultimately take or how they will prove their own claims or defenses.

Private investigation is possible for those with means. But no one is bound to talk or display papers to an investigator, and an adverse party or a person friendly to an adverse party is unlikely to cooperate voluntarily.

When the time for trial comes, a party may compel by subpoena any local person, including an adverse party, to attend court and testify; and the person may also be commanded by subpoena duces tecum to bring with him and produce designated documents and the like. See Rule 45 (setting geographical limits). Knowledge acquired through such trial testimony or evidence, however, may well not come in time for effective use. It may, for instance, point to a new line of inquiry, revealed too late to undertake. Moreover, in the event of unexpected and unfavorable testimony, the surprised party may suffer seriously from lack of opportunity for further investigation to rebut it. And counsel's decision whether to call a given witness may quite properly turn on advance knowledge of what the witness will say—the practical hazard in calling a witness whose testimony may boomerang is obvious.

The Federal Rules on "disclosures and discovery" add another machinery, much of which is a striking departure from tradition, for sifting of facts and exploration of positions and evidence before trial. As a result of disclosures and by the use of the discovery devices, a party may learn facts or sources of proof not hitherto known to him that will aid him in establishing his own contentions, or he may obtain leads that will help him to search out and uncover such facts or sources of proof for himself. He may also uncover to a considerable extent what his adversary will seek to prove in support of a claim or defense and how his adversary expects to prove it. He may simply discover what a particular witness will say in court. Or, by the skillful use of the discovery devices he may eliminate from the trial issues on which there is no real dispute.

A major motive behind these Rules is to prevent the trial from being a drama of surprises with the happy ending for the side with the more extensive facilities for private investigation or the more agile court performer. Accordingly, the disclosure and discovery provisions not only shape the preparation for trial but also profoundly affect the strategy and tactics of the trial itself.

The disclosure and discovery provisions affect other aspects of procedure as well. For example, as the Sierocinski case suggested, the availability of discovery devices might influence decision on how much detail the pleadings must supply. Indeed, as Twombly-Iqbal suggested, the whole problem of pleading under the Federal Rules is bound up with the discovery provisions and ultimately cannot be fruitfully considered apart from them. All this implies that another major motive behind the disclosure and discovery Rules is to facilitate the efficient presentation and resolution of controversies.

General provisions governing disclosure (Rule 26(a), (f), and (g)).—In 1993, amid much controversy, the rulemakers introduced a new phase of procedure called disclosure. Elaborating on the pleaded facts, parties now must disclose certain core information, without awaiting a discovery request.

Disclosure aims at achieving some savings in time and expense, and also at moderating litigants' adversary behavior in the pretrial process. At least intuitively, this innovation makes some sense. Opponents find the core information useful in virtually all cases. Almost all the information would be discoverable anyway. Disclosure essentially makes the obvious discovery automatic, so that parties just hand over the information without awaiting a request.

According to Federal Rule 26(a), there are three distinct types of disclosure. However, the judge by order, or the parties by stipulation, may alter these disclosure obligations.

1. Rule 26(a)(1) requires disclosure, at the outset, of routine evidentiary and insurance matters, except in certain special categories of cases. These initial disclosures comprise (i) witnesses likely to have discoverable information that the disclosing party may use to support its claims or defenses, unless solely for impeachment, (ii) documents, electronically stored information, and tangible things that the disclosing party has in its possession, custody, or control and may use to support its claims or defenses, unless solely for impeachment, (iii) computation of claimed damages, and (iv) insurance agreements that might cover part or all of an eventual judgment.

2. Rule 26(a)(2) requires a party to disclose, at a specified time, information regarding any expert whom it may call at trial. Most of these experts must also deliver a detailed report, which must include all opinions the witness will express and the underlying reasons, as well as details about qualifications, compensation, and previous experience as a witness.

3. Rule 26(a)(3) requires disclosure, shortly before trial, of trial witness lists and the like regarding nonimpeachment evidence. In particular, the party must disclose trial exhibits, which allows airing evidentiary disputes in advance of trial.

Disclosure under the Federal Rules is meant to proceed in an atmosphere of cooperation. Still, there are rules. First, all disclosures are to be in writing, signed, and served. See Rule 26(a)(4). Second, an attorney, or if there is no attorney then the party, must sign each disclosure under (a)(1) or (a)(3); the signature is a certification, to the best of the signer's knowledge, information, and belief formed after reasonable inquiry, that the disclosure is complete and correct as of the time it is made; the court must punish violations. See Rule 26(g), which imposes this certification requirement, analogous to the provision for pleadings and motions in Rule 11, for each *discovery* request or response also. Third, the disclosing party must promptly file pretrial disclosures under (a)(3) with the court. See Rule 5(d), which provides that the other disclosures, like most *discovery* items too, must not be filed until used in the proceeding.

An increasingly key feature of the disclosure and *discovery* schemes lies in Rule 26(f): very early on, the attorneys and unrepresented parties normally must confer to consider the case and the disclosures, as well as attempt in good faith to develop a proposed discovery plan and promptly submit a written report to the court along the lines of Form 52. Under Rule 26(d), discovery normally cannot proceed until this conference takes place. Under Rule 26(a)(1)(C), initial disclosures are normally due within fourteen days after the conference.

General provisions governing discovery (Rule 26(b), (c), and (d)).—Disclosure conveys only basic or core information about the case. A great deal more information is discoverable through the various discovery devices introduced in 1938.

What may a discovering party inquire into? The scope of discovery is wide. Fundamental is Rule 26(b)(1). As a general proposition,[1] the party may obtain discovery regarding any *nonprivileged*[m] matter that is *relevant* to the claim or defense of any party and that is *proportional* to the needs of the case in the sense of its benefit exceeding its expensiveness.

Relevance embraces, among much else, the existence and location of documents or other things and the identity and whereabouts of persons having knowledge of any discoverable matter. Relevant information need not be evidence admissible at trial. Thus, in an action based on alleged negligence of the defendant in maintaining a skylight through which the plaintiff fell, the plaintiff can discover from the defendant what repairs it made to the skylight following the accident. See Caulk v. Baltimore & Ohio R.R., 306 F.Supp. 1171 (D.Md.1969). This is true even though evidence law makes evidence of such subsequent remedial measures inadmissible at trial, in order not to discourage persons from making repairs. See Federal Rule of Evidence 407, which is in the Rules booklet.

Question: (44) In an action for alleged violation of the federal antitrust laws, plaintiff during discovery refuses to answer (a) questions concerning the circumstances surrounding the bringing of the suit, including possibly unethical financial arrangements between plaintiff and his counsel for bearing the costs of this litigation, and (b) questions concerning plaintiff's net worth, including his ability to satisfy a judgment for costs if defendant were to prevail in the action. Defendant moves to compel answers. What

---

[1]   The introductory clause of Rule 26(b) provides a significant exception for contrary orders of the court. See, e.g., Rule 26(c) (protective orders).

[m]   The reference is to such limitations as the attorney-client privilege. We shall soon consider the law of privileges, infra p. 208, as part of a general treatment of the admissibility of evidence in connection with study of the trial.

should be the decision? See Bogosian v. Gulf Oil Corp., 337 F.Supp. 1228 (E.D.Pa.1971) (discovery disallowed); Moore § 26.45[1].

Rule 26 follows these general formulae with specific provisions not only authorizing case-by-case judicial supervision of duplicative discovery (see Rule 26(b)(2)), but also limiting the discovery of so-called work product (see Rule 26(b)(3) on discovery of the critically useful materials prepared by or for a party or his representative in anticipation of litigation or for trial) and the discovery of expert information (see Rule 26(b)(4) on discovery regarding these players who have become so important in modern litigation) in ways that we save for later study.

Question: (45) What if the defendants in a suit for sexual harassment during state-police training sought discovery of the plaintiffs' sexual history? their sexual behavior during the training period? See Mitchell v. Hutchings, 116 F.R.D. 481 (D.Utah 1987) (allowing discovery, but only for contemporaneous work-environment behavior); Herchenroeder v. Johns Hopkins Univ. Applied Physics Lab., 171 F.R.D. 179 (D.Md.1997) (further subjecting such discovery to a confidentiality order). Do such judicially imposed restrictions on discovery rest on privilege, irrelevance, disproportionality, or something else? Where do the current Federal Rules authorize such restrictions? What if the plaintiffs seek to discover the *defendants'* sexual history or behavior?

Theory expects discovery to work almost wholly by action of the parties without intervention by the court. Physical or mental examination under Rule 35, already considered in Sibbach v. Wilson & Co., is the only discovery device that the discovering party must initiate by motion addressed to the court. The five other devices—depositions by oral examination, depositions by written questions, interrogatories to parties, production of documents and things, and requests for admission—generally start and move along by party initiative alone. A party makes application to the court only in special situations or when something goes awry, as when a request for discovery is resisted or a misuse of discovery is threatened.

Question: (46) Why should a request for a physical or mental examination require an order made only on motion for good cause?

Incidentally, the six devices may proceed in any sequence according to Rule 26(d), unless a party gets the court to order otherwise or unless the parties agree otherwise. In practice, much of discovery proceeds in accordance with negotiated agreement between the parties, as Rule 29 recognizes. A litigator should beware of pursuing a defiant or aggressive tactic without contacting the other counsel informally. And the litigator should certainly hesitate before involving the court.

Depositions by oral examination (Rule 30).—This method of discovery comprises oral examination of anyone, party or nonparty, thought to have information within the scope of discovery as set out in Rule 26. In considering this surprisingly awesome power bestowed on parties, it may be well to begin by asking why a party might want to take a deposition. Here are some possible reasons, which in a sense particularize the purposes of discovery discussed above:

1.   The discovering party may know or suspect that some person has information that would aid him in his own investigation and preparation for trial. For example, under Rule 26(b)(1) he can force the person deposed to reveal the names and addresses of other witnesses to the events in suit.

2.   He may be left genuinely in the dark by his adversary's pleadings and disclosures, and so may want to take the adversary's deposition to uncover the nature of the claim or defense that he must prepare to meet in settlement negotiations or at trial.

3.   He may have a witness with whose story he is fully familiar, so there is no occasion to "discover" it. But the witness may be old and likely to die before trial, or she may be young and about to join the armed forces, or she simply may live far from the place of trial, or there may be some other danger that she will be unavailable to testify at trial. A deposition serves to record testimony and, as we shall see, may be used at trial upon a proper showing that the witness is unavailable.

4.   He may know the story some other witness will tell well enough for purposes of his own preparation. But he nevertheless may want a deposition to pin the witness down by sworn testimony in advance of trial. If, as sometimes happens, the witness tells a different story at trial, he may use the deposition to discredit the witness.

5.   He may hope that he can by a deposition expose a fatal weakness in his adversary's claim or defense, and thus be able to avoid a trial altogether by a motion for summary judgment.

To follow the main features of the oral-deposition process, read these provisions in order: Rules 30(a) and (b); 45(a), (b), (c), and (g); 28(a); and 30(c), (e), and (f).

In the usual case, leave of court is not necessary to initiate the deposition procedure.[n] The discovering party gives reasonable notice in writing to the other parties to the action, specifying the time and place of the deposition and naming the person to be examined ("deponent"). On the one hand, service of a subpoena upon a nonparty deponent officially summons her to appear at the deposition. Under Rule 45(a)(1), a subpoena duces tecum may command the nonparty deponent to bring with her and produce documents and other things. On the other hand, if the deponent is a party, a subpoena is not necessary, because the notice of examination itself suffices as a command. Under Rule 30(b)(2), a request under Rule 34 to produce documents and other things at the taking of the deposition may accompany the notice to the party deponent.

---

[n]   Reread Rule 30(a)(2), describing the situations in which leave of court is necessary, and consider why. Cf. Rule 27 (discovery to perpetuate testimony, before an action's commencement or after judgment pending appeal).

Question: (47) With regard to the place specified by the discovering party for taking the deposition, what is the effect of the geographical limits set by Rule 45(c)(1)?

The actual taking of the deposition resembles the taking of testimony at a trial.° The deponent is sworn, interrogated by counsel for the discovering party, cross-examined by counsel for the other party or parties, and so on, the questions and answers being taken down stenographically or otherwise recorded.

There is, however, no judge present as at a trial. The person presiding at the deposition does not have judicial powers. This difference becomes important upon an objection to a question. At a trial, the judge would rule on the objection and the witness would answer or not, depending on the ruling. At the deposition, no one is on hand to make the ruling. How, then, is the objection disposed of?

Consider the possible reasons for objection: (1) A question put at deposition may be within the scope of discovery described in Rule 26, but would be objectionable at trial under the rules of evidence. (2) A question may be objectionable as not falling within the scope of discovery (in such case, it would in all likelihood also be objectionable at the trial proper).

In situation (1)—where the examining party puts a question at deposition that is within the scope of discovery—the Rules contemplate that the deponent will answer the question and that the objection will simply be recorded. See Rule 30(c)(2). Then, if the deposition is offered in evidence at trial, the objection will in effect be renewed and the trial judge will pass on it as if the deponent were testifying orally. (In fact, when a deposition is offered at trial, a party may ordinarily object under the rules of evidence to deposition questions even without an objection during the deposition. However, if the ground for objection is one that might have been obviated if presented at the taking of the deposition, the party cannot raise the objection for the first time at trial. It would be patently unfair to exclude deposition testimony at trial if the examining party, upon alert, could have remedied the error during the deposition. For example, a leading question on direct examination is objectionable in form, but a rephrasing of the question provides a ready corrective; yet the error would be fatal if the opponent could object for the first time at trial and if the deponent was then unavailable to answer the rephrased question. See Rule 32(b) and (d)(3)(A) and (B). But see Rule 26(a)(3)(B). Other problems are more difficult. Suppose at deposition a party asks a doctor a question calling for an expert opinion on a medical question, and at trial the opponent objects on the ground that her expert qualifications were not sufficiently shown: is the objection untimely because the ground for it was obviable? Uncertainty in the few precedents in this area often leads lawyers either to attempt to protect themselves by excessive

---

° But see again Rule 30(b)(4), which permits a stipulation or order that a deposition be taken by telephone or by other remote electronic means.

objections at the deposition or to stipulate at the time of the deposition that all objections except as to form may be first made at the trial.)

Even in situation (2)—where the examining party puts a question at deposition that is not within the scope of discovery—the deponent and the other parties may be willing to have it answered, and excluded at trial, as long as merely answering it would not prove damaging or offensive. But suppose the question is thought to enter the field of privilege. Here there may be strong reason to decline to give an answer unless the court actually orders one, for the answer may be harmful in itself, and ruling the question improper at the subsequent trial would not cure that harm. The system indulges such reasons by allowing refusal to answer.

In summary, the deponent should answer, under any appropriate objection, all questions, except for particular questions thought to fall outside the scope of discovery and to call for an answer that would infringe on privilege in a damaging or offensive fashion.

If the examining party is unhappy regarding a deponent who chooses to refuse to answer or who has accepted advice by an opposing party not to answer, the examining party can complete or adjourn the deposition and then seek an enforceable court order to answer. See Rule 37(a). Note that the examining party may request payment of expenses for proceedings occasioned by unreasonable failure to answer a proper discovery question, and the deponent or opposing party may make a corresponding request in case of unreasonable insistence on an answer to an improper discovery question. The court may oblige counsel advising unreasonable action to pay these expenses personally.

———

UMPHRES v. SHELL OIL CO., 15 Fed.R.Serv.2d (Callaghan) 1116 (S.D.Tex.1971). This case involved a Rule 37(a) motion to compel the plaintiff, who was formerly a Shell retailer in the Houston area, to answer certain questions asked of him during the taking of his oral deposition by the defendant.

"Apparently, defendant commenced plaintiff's deposition as scheduled, on August 30, 1971. As pointed out by the defendant in its memorandum in support of its motion to compel answers, counsel for the defendant commenced interrogating the plaintiff with regard to an alleged conspiracy [with other oil companies to fix prices around Houston in violation of the antitrust laws] pleaded by him. Plaintiff's counsel advised his client not to answer any questions about conspiracy, to which the attorney for the defendant observed, in effect, that conspiracy is a question of fact and the proper subject for interrogation, and the defendant should be entitled 'to inquire of him what he thinks the conspiracy was.' Plaintiff's counsel, Mr. Conde Anderson, replied, 'Well, you know full well, Mr. Kingdon, that I prepared the complaint and that Mr. Umphres didn't. And I attempted to prepare it, keeping in mind what

I understood the law to be, and I don't think this is a proper line of inquiry and I'm going to instruct him not to answer.'

"Mr. Kingdon then continued with his next question, being, 'Mr. Umphres, do you have any information regarding the allegation in the complaint that Shell exercised control of numerous retail dealers with whom it contracted in areas elsewhere in the state of Texas other than Harris County, Texas, and in many other states, do you have any information to support that claim that there was a conspiracy in areas other than Harris County, Texas?' The plaintiff did not answer this question under instructions from his counsel.

"The court is of the opinion that the oral interrogatory may very well ask for plaintiff's conclusion as to the legal meaning of conspiracy, and, if so, since plaintiff is not an experienced man in the field and the subject matter which is involved in such question, he should not be required to answer the question as asked. However, it seems to the court that defendant is certainly entitled to interrogate plaintiff about the facts upon which the claim of conspiracy was based. But, up to now, defendant's counsel has not asked Mr. Anderson for the details upon which he relied to plead conspiracy.

"This court considers any motion relating to discovery to be premature until the party making such request has first explored all reasonable avenues of agreement as to discovery problems by conference with counsel for the other side. Therefore, counsel for the plaintiff and counsel for the defendant are here directed to sit down, face to face, and in good faith discuss the question of conspiracy as alleged by the plaintiff, and the attorney for the plaintiff is to detail for the benefit of the defendant those facts which he took into account in making his allegations of conspiracy. Upon the furnishing of such factual information to the defendant, then the deposition of plaintiff should resume and the defendant's counsel is at liberty to interrogate the plaintiff with regard to the particular facts which his counsel has divulged, or which may be developed during the interrogation."

Note that the court ordered such a conference long before the rulemakers imposed duties to confer under Rules 26(f) and 37(a) in 1993. Note further that at trial the plaintiff eventually lost by directed verdict because of lack of evidence, a result affirmed at 512 F.2d 420 (5th Cir.), cert. denied, 423 U.S. 929, 96 S.Ct. 278 (1975).

———

BRANDENBERG v. EL AL ISRAEL AIRLINES, 79 F.R.D. 543 (S.D.N.Y.1978). Plaintiff sued two airlines for $900,000, alleging negligent and reckless treatment that had caused physical stress and mental injuries. Mrs. Brandenberg's position was "that in view of her age and physical condition (she suffered from diabetes), the airlines were obligated to treat her with particular care, and that they failed in that obligation, on the contrary, 'abandoning' her in times of need."

Defendants deposed the 72-year-old plaintiff. Counsel for British Airways questioned her concerning the events of its leg of the flight that had carried her abroad to visit her daughter. "It is fair to say that the plaintiff . . . had some difficulty in remembering the sequence of events." The court further noted: "It is also fair to say that, having studied her account of the events involving British Airways, the precise complaint or complaints which the plaintiff makes concerning her treatment at the hands of that defendant are not clear." Contrariwise, her criticism of the other airline had been "entirely clear."

"In these circumstances, counsel for British Airways posed, or attempted to pose, the following questions to plaintiff at the end of the deposition:

'Q. Do you know of any factual basis to support the allegations in your complaints against British—'

'Q. Do you know of anything that British Airways did that was not proper treatment of you at Heathrow Airport in March of 1976?'

'Q. Mrs. Brandenberg, can you tell me in your own words what the basis of your claim against British Airways—'

'Q. Do you know of anything that British Airways did to you that was not in accordance with the way you thought you should be treated by them?'

'Q. What facts do you contend show that British Airways did not properly treat you?'

"On direction of her attorney, the plaintiff declined to answer any of these questions. British Airways now moves for an order under Rule 37(a) compelling answers. Plaintiff resists on the ground that the questions call for legal conclusions of a lay witness."

The court concluded that such contentions were discoverable: "British Airways is understandably left in the dark, on the present deposition record, as to the factual basis perceived by plaintiff for the charge of negligence against it. British Airways is entitled to inquire on that score, and plaintiff is directed to respond to such questions, at a continuation of her deposition at a place and time to be mutually agreed or, failing such agreement, as directed by the Court."

The Rules give a party (or the deponent) certain opportunities to take the initiative against the examining party, halt the examination, and obtain a court order to terminate or limit the deposition if it is going too far afield or becoming abusive or to furnish other kinds of protection. See Rule 30(d)(3); also consider Rule 26(c), which in certain circumstances allows seeking court protection against the deposition before its stated starting time. Again, the court may order an offending person to pay expenses.

Moreover, recall that Rule 26(b)(2)(C) encourages district courts on their own to curb discovery overuse. Thus, the court can limit disproportionate discovery.

After examination of the deponent and upon prior request, the deponent has a chance to review the transcript or recording, and then append any changes with the deponent's reasons. Finally, the person who presided at the deposition certifies and delivers the transcript or recording to the deposing attorney.

Depositions by written questions (Rule 31).—The typical notice to take a deposition by oral examination does not specify the particular matters to be inquired into, but rather might at most refer generally to some matters involved in the action. The notice for taking a deposition by written questions, however, comes with the questions to be put to the deponent, who may be a nonparty or party and who is summoned to appear in the same way as for a Rule 30 deposition. Within 14 days after being served with the Rule 31 notice and questions, any party may serve questions for cross-examination, and then questions for redirect and recross may follow. The deposing party delivers all questions to the person designated to preside at the deposition. He swears the deponent, and he reads the questions one by one, with the deponent responding orally. As for an oral deposition, the testimony is recorded, reviewed, certified, and delivered.

Again consult Rule 37(a) to see when and how an examining party may secure an order directing a deponent to answer a written question, and see Rule 26(c) as to when and how a party or deponent may secure a protective order in respect to a deposition by written questions.

Questions: (48) Why is there no equivalent in Rule 31 of Rule 30(d)(3)'s motion to terminate or limit?

(49) Is it proper for counsel, who has received the Rule 31 questions from her opponent in advance, to rehearse her client or a friendly nonparty deponent by reading the questions to him? Compare Moore § 31.02, with Wright & Miller § 2133.

Rule 31 depositions by written questions are typically much cheaper than Rule 30 depositions by oral examination. The saving under Rule 31 arises from the fact that counsel can with reasonable safety absent themselves from the examination. Yet depositions by written questions are rare. One reason is that counsel labor under the handicap of having to frame questions without knowing what answers the deponent will have given to the previous questions. Hence they must frame questions on predictions or on alternative assumptions about the content of the prior answers. This procedure is uncertain and cumbersome. And if the deponent is unfriendly to the examining side, it may be harder to pin him down by written questions than by oral examination.

Question: (50) What may a party do in an effort to save the expense of attending another party's oral deposition of, say, a nonparty deponent of

who is other?
What if deponent
refuses?

peripheral importance who lives far away? See Rule 30(c)(3). What difficulties can you foresee?

Interrogatories to parties (Rule 33).—This method of discovery is relatively simple and inexpensive. The discovering party can serve a limited number of written questions, each of which is called an interrogatory and is similar to a written question in a Rule 31 deposition, upon any other party to the action. The served document would consist of the usual caption and signature components bracketing a set of straightforward questions, which would look much like the interrogatories quoted in the upcoming O'Brien case.

The responding party and his lawyer, on their own, sit down to prepare responses. They have to answer each interrogatory separately and fully in writing under oath—unless they object to the particular interrogatory, in which event they have to state the reasons for objection with specificity. Answers are signed by the party making them, but objections are signed by the attorney.

Questions: (51) Give some typical reasons why the attorney might fairly object to an interrogatory.

file motion
to compel

(52) What may an interrogating party do to compel an answer when she considers an objection insufficient? when she considers an answer, unaccompanied by an objection, insufficient?

(53) May a responding party seek any protection against the interrogatories otherwise than by written objections in lieu of answers?

(54) So the general provisions governing discovery extend to interrogatories much as they do to depositions, but not completely. For example, a responding party may not serve cross-interrogatories, i.e., interrogatories directed to himself. But a party who is being deposed by oral examination may have his own counsel cross-examine him or may initiate a deposition by oral examination in which he himself is the deponent. Similarly, a party who is being deposed by written questions may direct cross-questions to himself or may depose himself by written questions. What explains this divergence between interrogatories (which may not be self-directed) and deposition questions (which may be)? What useful purpose might be served by self-directed deposition questions?

Under Rule 33(d), instead of actually answering interrogatories involving business records, the responding party sometimes may invite the interrogating party to inspect the records from which answers can be derived. The very extensive 1970 discovery amendments added this subdivision. See the Advisory Committee's notes thereon in the Rules booklet.

———

O'Brien v. International Brotherhood
of Electrical Workers

United States District Court, Northern District of Georgia, 1977.
443 F.Supp. 1182.

■ EDENFIELD, DISTRICT JUDGE.

This action was brought pursuant to the Labor Management Reporting and Disclosure Act, 29 U.S.C. §§ 401, et seq., against a local union and its parent international union. . . .

Plaintiff was charged by a fellow union member with violating certain sections of the IBEW constitution when he distributed certain information which was allegedly detrimental to the union. Local 613's executive board heard the charges on January 27, 1976 and found plaintiff guilty, fining him $2,725.00 and temporarily suspending him from local union activities. The decision of Local 613 was rescinded when it was discovered that defendant IBEW, not Local 613, had jurisdiction over the charges pursuant to the IBEW constitution. On March 15, 1976 plaintiff was notified of a new hearing to be held before the International Executive Council of IBEW on May 6, 1976. At this hearing, plaintiff was found guilty and fined $100. Thereafter, plaintiff filed this action [for damages].

Plaintiff has alleged that the charges, trials and disciplinary measures violated plaintiff's rights of free speech and assembly as guaranteed by the LMRDA in 29 U.S.C. § 411(a)(2).*. . .

[The court first disposed of a number of other motions.]

Lastly, the court must concern itself with plaintiff's motion to compel answers to interrogatories from Local 613. Plaintiff's interrogatories, filed May 18, 1977, seek to have defendants explain why they found plaintiff guilty of the union charges. Local 613 has registered a general objection to plaintiff's interrogatories which may be readily disposed of. Local 613 claims that since its decision to fine and suspend [plaintiff] was rescinded, its reasons for trying plaintiff and finding him guilty are now irrelevant. However, plaintiff is charging that both defendants in their respective actions taken against plaintiff violated plaintiff's free speech rights under the LMRDA. Plaintiff seeks, among other relief, the

---

*   Section 411(a)(2) of Title 29, U.S.C., provides:

"Every member of any labor organization shall have the right to meet and assemble freely with other members; and to express any views, arguments, or opinions; and to express at meetings of the labor organization his views, upon candidates in an election of the labor organization or upon any business properly before the meeting, subject to the organization's established and reasonable rules pertaining to the conduct of meetings: *Provided,* That nothing herein shall be construed to impair the right of a labor organization to adopt and enforce reasonable rules as to the responsibility of every member toward the organization as an institution and to his refraining from conduct that would interfere with its performance of its legal or contractual obligations." [Footnote by court.—Ed.]

expenses incurred in defending and appealing Local 613's decision. While the decision may have been rescinded, the expenses were not.

A second objection listed by Local 613 is that plaintiff has not sought to compel discovery as against IBEW. While that is a matter for plaintiff to decide, it must be noted that plaintiff cannot expect the local union to answer interrogatories that are within the distinct knowledge of the international union, specifically interrogatories numbered 1(c) and (d), 2(2), and 5.

Interrogatory numbers 1(a) and (b) ask for the specific statements allegedly made by plaintiff for which he was tried. The court sees no reason why defendant should not be required to set out these statements, despite the fact that plaintiff might be able to cull this information from the hearing transcript. The same may be said with respect to interrogatory number 2, wherein plaintiff asks that defendant Local 613 state which provisions of the IBEW constitution were violated by which statements.

Interrogatory number 3 seeks an explanation as to why these statements violated these constitutional provisions. While defendant Local 613 argues that this question seeks a legal theory which is not discoverable, when the constitutional provisions presumably involved are examined, the interrogatory appears to be one that Local 613 should answer. All but one of the provisions proscribe false statements. Plaintiff is entitled to know the facts which render his utterances untrue. One constitutional provision deals with conduct which causes dissension and dissatisfaction among union members. Plaintiff is entitled to know the facts which, in Local 613's view, constituted dissension caused by plaintiff's statements.

Interrogatory number 4 provides as follows:

> In respect to each act and/or utterance listed in response to Interrogatory 1. above, explain the manner in which each said act and/or utterance (a) violated plaintiff's responsibility toward Local 613, IBEW and IBEW as institutions, and (b) interfered with Local 613, IBEW's, and IBEW's performance of their respective legal or contractual obligations. (If any of said acts/utterances violated neither standard, please indicate which did not.)

Clearly this question seeks to discover defendant's legal theory based on the facts elicited from the other interrogatories. Interrogatory number 4 is based on the exceptions in the free speech section of the LMRDA [the court here quoted again the proviso of 29 U.S.C. § 411(a)(2)]. Anticipating that defendant will rely on this language as a defense to this action, plaintiff asks defendant to explain its application to the communications made by the plaintiff.

Rule 33 . . . makes clear that such discovery is in fact permissible [the court here quoted what is now Rule 33(a)(2) treating opinion and contention interrogatories]. This rule cuts against many older cases which imposed a strict rule against opinions, contentions and conclusions. The Advisory Committee Note only excludes those interrogatories which "extend to issues of 'pure law,' i.e., legal issues unrelated to the facts of the case." Note to 1970 Amendment of Rule 33 . . . , 48 F.R.D. 485, 524 (1970), see Wright & Miller, Federal Practice and Procedure, § 2167 at 513. Interrogatory number 4 seeks an application of law to the central facts of the case, and accordingly is permissible under Rule 33 . . . . Since the discovery period is nearly complete, there is no danger of tying defendant to a legal theory before he has had an opportunity to fully explore the case, see Wright & Miller, supra, at 514.

Interrogatory number 6 reads as follows:

> In respect to each and every constitutional provision listed in response to Interrogatory 2., state and explain the reasons why each provision is *not* deprived of force and effect by operation of 29 U.S.C. § 411(b)[p] in respect to plaintiff and the acts and utterances listed in response to Interrogatory 1.

In contrast to the interrogatory previously discussed, this question seeks pure legal conclusions which are related not to the facts, but to the law of the case. While the line demarcating permissible discovery under Rule 33 . . . may be obscure, the court concludes that this interrogatory exceeds the bounds of permissible discovery under the rule.

For these reasons, plaintiff's motion to compel discovery is DENIED as to interrogatories numbered 1(c) and (d), 2(2), 5 and 6, but is GRANTED as to the balance of the interrogatories in dispute. The court further concludes that each party should bear the cost incurred in bringing and opposing these discovery motions.

. . . .

Questions: (55) In the Sierocinski case, would it be proper under present Rule 33(a)(2) for the defendant to put to the plaintiff the interrogatory: "What specific acts or omissions by the defendant do you contend constituted negligence?" How about the interrogatory: "Do you intend to rely on the doctrine of res ipsa loquitur?" How about: "What do you contend are the contours of the doctrine of res ipsa loquitur in this state?"

(56) If Mr. Sierocinski were to answer any such interrogatory, how binding on him should his answer be?

(57) Would it be proper for the defendant instead to put those same questions when deposing Mr. Sierocinski? when deposing Mr. White, the plaintiff's lawyer?

---

p   That statute provides: "(b) Any provision of the constitution and bylaws of any labor organization which is inconsistent with the provisions of [29 U.S.C. § 411(a)] shall be of no force or effect."

A most significant point is that interrogatories, unlike depositions, cannot be used to question nonparties. But both devices serve to question parties.

So, what is the difference between depositions by written questions, when addressed to parties, and interrogatories to parties? In the former case, the party as deponent is at least formally on his own when he testifies and gives answers to the written questions read out to him. In the latter case, the party answering can and commonly does sit down with his attorney, examine the questions at leisure, and make use of his attorney's advice in framing the answers. Despite the often studied and artful answers consequently returned to Rule 33 interrogatories, this discovery method is a good and relatively cheap means of obtaining evidence or leads to evidence, or of obliging one's adversary to specify positions on the issues arising in the case. Indeed, interrogatories are so much cheaper than a written deposition that one would employ the latter only when interrogatories just cannot do the job, as when the desired respondent is a nonparty (and there is insufficient need for the very expensive effectiveness of an oral deposition).

The expenses incurred in discovery can sometimes be enormous. Normally, they fall ultimately on the party who initially incurred them; for example, the discovering party pays the small cost of preparing interrogatories, and the responding party pays the potentially huge cost of answering them. However, the court may eventually award certain, relatively insignificant discovery expenses as costs to the party who prevails in the lawsuit, as we shall see. More importantly, as we have suggested, the Rules have ample provisions for shifting reasonable discovery expenses (including attorney's fees) as a condition of approving discovery; for ordering parties, deponents, or counsel to reimburse anyone's reasonable expenses incurred in successfully invoking the court's assistance in a discovery dispute or resisting such an attempt; and for requiring reimbursement of reasonable expenses as a discovery sanction.

––––––––

Martin H. Redish, Pleading, Discovery, and the Federal Rules: Exploring the Foundations of Modern Procedure

64 Fla.L.Rev. 845, 877–79 (2012).

It should be clear that ... the costs of discovery are properly attributable, in the first instance, to the requesting party. By imposing the costs of discovery on the responding party, then, our system effectively requires the responding party to provide a subsidy to the requesting party. To be sure, assuming no constitutional problems, the system may choose to order such a subsidy. But because those who created the system implicitly—and inaccurately—assumed that the cost of discovery was properly seen as a cost to be borne by the responding party, our system provides for a hidden subsidy, one recognized by no one. At the very least, democracy demands that the decisions of those who make fundamental choices of social policy make clear what those choices actually are, so a transparent debate of whether it is fair to impose such a subsidy may finally take place. This has never been done in the case of discovery costs.

Wholly apart from this complete lack of transparency, the implicit assumption that the costs of discovery are to be attributed to the responding party makes little sense, from any theoretical or practical perspective, particularly when coupled with the broad scope of discovery in the age of informational technology. In addition to its moral and legal bases, attribution of the costs of discovery to the discovering party, rather than the responding party, is likely to have significant instrumental benefits because it would cure a fundamental economic pathology plaguing the discovery process: the externality inherent in the choice to invoke discovery. Simply put, under the prevailing practice the cost-benefit decision of whether or not to invoke the discovery process is made by a party who risks incurring no cost, only benefit, even though it is quite conceivable that the choice will impose a significant cost on others. This lack of economic disincentive underscores what may be a far greater harm to the system than intentionally abusive discovery: "excessive" discovery. This concept includes discovery that, while not consciously interposed for purposes of delay or harassment, nevertheless gives rise to costs greater than its benefits in finding truth.... [T]he value of finding truth cannot be considered in a vacuum, wholly divorced from the costs to which the effort gives rise.... Yet when the responding party, rather than the requesting party, bears the costs of this process, the requesting party has absolutely no economic disincentive not to make the request, regardless of its costs. Indeed, given that it is the requesting party's opponent who will bear that cost, one might even perversely suggest that the higher the cost, the greater the incentive to invoke the discovery process.

This focus on the subtle but important differences between "abusive" and "excessive" discovery underscores the manner in which a reversal in the ex ante presumption of discovery cost attribution can function in a symbiotic manner with [other] methods of discovery control. While those more judicially-driven practices are more likely to punish or deter abusive discovery, it is the self-executing shift in discovery cost allocation that is far more likely to deter the practice of excessive discovery.

The key social problem to which imposition of discovery costs on the requesting party might give rise derives from its inherently regressive nature: the poor will be more immediately and seriously impacted by such costs than will the rich. To be sure, this is also true of all litigation costs, though this fact has never prompted a shift all of the poor's litigation costs to the wealthier party. Moreover, particularly in the case of complex class action lawsuits, the real party in interest will not be the individual plaintiff but rather the plaintiff's attorneys, for whom the funding of such suits is simply a cost of doing business. In these cases, it would be wrong to see this alteration in discovery cost allocation as an inherently regressive practice. In any event, if there are particular substantive rights which the governmental body decides require procedural subsidization, that body may say so at the time it creates those rights. Therefore even if one were to find the regressive impact of this reversal in cost allocation to be a matter of concern, a wholesale rejection of the cost allocation model would not be justified.

Even if society were to decide to subsidize a poorer litigant's discovery in particular suits, it hardly makes sense to impose that cost on his opponent, rather than on society as a whole. . . .

A conceivable objection to the reversal of the current cost allocation model might be that such a practice would simply shift the externality, for under the new model the responding party will have no incentive to keep costs down. But it is the discovering party who sets the contours of the response by the scope of its inquiries or production requests. In an important sense, then, the outer limits of the costs that the responding party will incur are set out by the requesting party. In any event, there always exists the possibility of judicial intervention to determine that the submitted costs are excessive. While one might respond that such intervention would significantly increase the systemic burdens of the discovery process, it is highly unlikely that judicial intervention would be required in many instances. If the responding party knows that any excessive costs it incurs may well not be reimbursed, it is unlikely to risk incurring them in the first place.

———

But does the argument in the preceding paragraph address the risk that potential defendants might store their electronic records in an inexpensive way that happens to make retrieval costly, thus making discovery more expensive to plaintiffs? Does the author's argument more generally ignore the fact that unequal costs for discovery will skew results away from accurate resolution? See Robert D. Cooter & Daniel L. Rubinfeld, An Economic Model of Legal Discovery, 23 J.Legal Stud. 435, 456 (1994) ("A discovery rule of 'each pays his own costs' encourages discovery abuse by the plaintiff. Alternatively, a rule that shifts all discovery costs . . . will impose much larger costs on the plaintiff than the defendant. Consequently, the rational settlement will be less than the expected judgment, thus favoring the defendant. So the simple rules ('each bears his own costs' or 'all cost shifted') result in discovery abuse or inaccuracy."); Benjamin Spencer, Rationalizing Cost Allocation in Civil Discovery, 34 Rev.Litig. 769 (2015) (plotting a *via media*).

Requests for admission (Rule 36).—A party may serve upon any other party a written request to admit the truth of matters separately set forth in the request or to admit the genuineness of described documents. See Form 51. Observe what action or inaction by the requested party may result in an admission, what the requesting party may do about inadequate answers or improper objections, and what the effect of an admission is.

Question: (58) Prior to 1970, a party could seek Rule 36 admissions only as to genuineness of described documents and as to matters of "fact." Compare present Rule 36(a)(1)(A), and see Booth Oil Site Admin. Group v. Safety-Kleen Corp., 194 F.R.D. 76 (W.D.N.Y.2000) ("where the question of the meaning of the document is at issue in the case, a request directed to another party seeking an admission or denial of a document's meaning or intent . . . is authorized by Rule 36"). Was the earlier version preferable?

A denial defeats the attempt to obtain an admission. But consider the sanctions contained in Rule 37(c)(2), which aim to discourage capricious denials.

Questions: (59) What is the meaning of "fails to admit" and "proves" in Rule 37(c)(2)? What, in your opinion, is the practical likelihood of securing a Rule 37(c)(2) order?

(60) How do Rule 36 requests for admission differ from Rule 33 interrogatories, and wherein do the functions of these devices differ?

Production of documents and things (Rule 34).—Witnesses, including parties, may be compelled to produce documents and other things during trial, but this may be too late for effective use. Rule 34(a)(1) enables a party to anticipate trial and compel any other party to produce any designated documents, electronically stored information, or tangible things within his possession, custody, or control, so that the discovering party may inspect, copy, test, or sample them. (Also, Rule 34(a)(2) provides for securing entry on any other party's land or property for the purposes of inspection, measuring, or the like.) All this must of course be within the scope of Rule 26.

In modern litigation, this discovery device receives heavy use, and ever more so with the advent of e-discovery. The Rule 34 process begins by service of a request in writing. See Form 50. The requested party serves a written response either acquiescing in the request or objecting with specific reasons. The discovering party has a remedy under Rule 37(a) for an insufficient response.

Questions: (61) Rule 34(a)(1)(A) refers to "designated documents." What should a party do if she does not know enough to identify the documents she wants?

(62) A party can address requests under Rule 34 only to other parties. Suppose a document or thing is under the control of a nonparty. How can the party compel its production? See Rule 34(c).

Material may be protected from discovery (and from use at trial) by an evidentiary privilege such as attorney-client privilege. It may also be protected by the work-product protection recognized in Rule 26(b)(3). Both types of protection can be waived through the disclosure of protected information, although the standards for finding such a waiver differ as between the two protections. See, e.g., United States v. MIT, 129 F.3d 681 (1st Cir.1997). Concerns about waiver lead litigants to engage in meticulous (and, thus, sometimes very costly) review prior to producing documents to an adversary. Congress in 2008 enacted Federal Rule of Evidence 502, which addresses some, but not all, questions of waiver and which may help to reduce the costs of document review.

Physical and mental examinations (Rule 35).—Physical or mental condition is frequently in question in lawsuits, and almost invariably in actions for personal injuries. In a personal-injury case, the defendant will generally want his physician to conduct an examination of the plaintiff. Otherwise he will be at a disadvantage in meeting an exaggerated or fraudulent claim by the plaintiff, or in evaluating a valid claim for purposes of settlement.

The plaintiff will often agree to examination by the defendant's physician because she also has interest in settlement. Moreover, she is aware that the trier might draw unfavorable inferences from revelation at trial that she has refused an examination. But when for any reason a person declines to allow an examination, Rule 35 is useful.

Question: (63) The Rule reaches only a party (or a person in the custody or under the legal control of a party). How, then, does a litigant prepare on the condition of a nonparty, e.g., the eyesight of a witness to the accident in suit?

The discovering party initiates the Rule 35 procedure by a motion. The physical or mental condition must be "in controversy" in the action, and the movant must show "good cause." In the Schlagenhauf case below, the Supreme Court said this about these requirements of "in controversy" and "good cause": "They are not met by mere conclusory allegations of the pleadings—nor by mere relevance to the case—but require an affirmative showing by the movant that each condition as to which the examination is sought is really and genuinely in controversy and that good cause exists for ordering each particular examination. Obviously, what may be good cause for one type of examination may not be so for another. The ability of the movant to obtain the desired information by other means is also relevant. Rule 35, therefore, requires discriminating application by the trial judge . . . ."

Question: (64) The Court further noted: "Of course, there are situations where the pleadings alone are sufficient to meet these requirements. A plaintiff in a negligence action who asserts mental or physical injury, cf. Sibbach v. Wilson & Co., supra, places that mental or physical injury clearly in controversy and provides the defendant with good cause for an examination to determine the existence and extent of such asserted injury."

In what circumstances would it be necessary in a personal-injury case to establish "in controversy" and "good cause" otherwise than by the pleadings?

———

SCHLAGENHAUF v. HOLDER, 379 U.S. 104, 85 S.Ct. 234 (1964). In a diversity action involving a collision between a bus and the rear of a tractor-trailer, the plaintiff bus passengers named as defendants the bus owner, bus driver, tractor owner, tractor driver, and trailer owner. Bus owner crossclaimed against tractor owner, tractor driver, and trailer owner for damage to the bus, alleging that the tractor-trailer was driven at a dangerously low speed; alleging that it had not remained in lane; and alleging that it was not equipped with proper rear lights. Tractor owner and driver, answering the crossclaim, denied their own negligence; alleged contributory negligence on the part of the bus driver, one Schlagenhauf; and further alleged that Schlagenhauf was "not mentally or physically capable" of driving a bus at the time of the accident.

Tractor owner, tractor driver, and trailer owner together moved for an order directing Schlagenhauf to submit to mental and physical examinations by one specialist each in the fields of internal medicine, ophthalmology, neurology, and psychiatry. They accompanied the motion with an affidavit of counsel stating that Schlagenhauf admitted on deposition that he had seen the red lights of the trailer 10 to 15 seconds prior to the collision and yet had driven on without change of speed or course; stating that the only eyewitness testified that he also had been approaching the trailer from the rear and had seen the lights from three-quarters to one-half mile away; and stating that Schlagenhauf also admitted in his deposition that he had been involved in a prior rear-end collision of a similar type.

While the motion was pending, trailer owner answered the crossclaim and included a counterclaim against bus owner and Schlagenhauf for damage to the trailer caused by his negligence when both knew he had defective vision.

The district court granted the requested examinations, and the court of appeals refused to vacate this order upon a petition for mandamus.[q] The denial of mandamus reached the Supreme Court upon its granting Schlagenhauf's petition for certiorari.

After considering the threshold problem whether mandamus was a proper avenue for review and deciding that it was, the Supreme Court dealt with Schlagenhauf's contentions that application of Rule 35 to defendants was a violation of the Rules Enabling Act and an unconstitutional invasion of privacy. (Although no federal court had previously applied Rule 35 to a defendant, how could Schlagenhauf argue that these issues remained open after Sibbach v. Wilson & Co.?) The

---

[q]   Petitioning for the extraordinary remedy of mandamus sometimes functions as a kind of irregular means of securing interlocutory review of district-court action by the court of appeals. See 28 U.S.C. § 1651 (authorization); App. Rule 21 (procedure).

Court also considered Schlagenhauf's contentions that he was not an opposing party vis-à-vis the discovering parties, that his physical and mental condition was not "in controversy," and that the movants had not shown "good cause."

How should the Court decide the case?

————

Question: (65) Justice Douglas dissented, with the thought that the Court should refer the problem to the Civil Rules Advisory Committee so that, if the Rule were to be apply to defendants, the rulemakers might make the standards and conditions discriminating and precise. He referred to the need to safeguard "against the awful risks of blackmail." What do you think he meant by "blackmail"? What standards and conditions would you prescribe to safeguard against those "risks"?

The party against whom an order is made has the right upon request to receive from the discovering party a detailed written report of the examination made under Rule 35(a) and also like reports of earlier examinations of the same condition to which the latter may have access.

Questions: (66) If a discovering party delivers these reports, to what does he become entitled? See Rule 35(b)(3) and (4).

(67) Should an examined party hold the right to have her attorney present during the physical or mental examination? See Brandenberg v. El Al Israel Airlines, 79 F.R.D. 543 (S.D.N.Y.1978) (no, with respect to a court-ordered psychiatric examination of Mrs. Brandenberg).

Sanctions for failure to make disclosures or to cooperate in discovery (Rule 37).—We have referred at a number of points to a party's motion under Rule 37(a) for a directive order, that is, an order compelling disclosure or discovery. Note the court to which the party addresses such a motion; the use of the motion to enforce various duties under Rules 26(a), 30, 31, 33, and 34; and the possibilities of securing reimbursement of expenses incurred in making or opposing the motion. Although it may be open to another party or a deponent to seek a protective order under Rule 26(c) in anticipation of an application for a directive order, this is an optional route and is not a condition of that person's resisting and avoiding a directive order.

In general, when the party encounters recalcitrance, he must assume the burden: first, of conferring with the recalcitrant person; second, in case of nonagreement, of going to court to get a directive order; and, third, in case of continued recalcitrance, of going to court to obtain a sanction. Rule 37(b) states the sanctions for refusals to obey such directive orders.

Some qualifications to this general scheme are needed, however. As to disclosure, a less elaborate procedure must additionally be available to allow disclosure to work. So, Rule 37(c)(1) provides that a party who without substantial justification fails to make a mandatory disclosure, unless such failure was harmless, is subject to appropriate sanctions, which will usually prohibit use of the undisclosed evidence. Now, as to discovery:

First, Rule 37(d) provides that in certain cases of gross failure of a party to comply with the process for giving discovery, the discovering party need not apply for a directive order but instead may move for a sanction forthwith; and the party from whom discovery is sought cannot excuse his failure on the ground that the discovery sought was objectionable unless he had made a motion for a protective order. The gross failures referred to are failure to appear to be deposed and refusal to serve any answers or objections to interrogatories or to serve a written response to a request for inspection. Consider also the contempt sanction that Rule 45(g) provides against nonparties.

Second, because Rule 35 requires a preliminary court order, Rule 37(a) and (d) has no application. The discovering party may proceed immediately to seek sanctions for disobedience under Rule 37(b), as in the Sibbach case.

Third, as already mentioned, orders and sanctions for failure to make discovery under Rule 36 receive special treatment in Rules 36(a) and 37(c)(2).

Supplementing disclosures and discovery responses (Rule 26(e)).—If a party's disclosures or discovery responses that were actually or presumably complete and correct when given come to appear incomplete or incorrect by reason of later events or newly acquired knowledge, they may seriously mislead other parties who rely upon them. But a full obligation to supplement would be extremely onerous because it would force the disclosing or responding party's lawyer to keep checking for new bits of information and matching them against the prior documents.

Rule 26(e) now deals with the problem, in a way designed to limit the burden on the disclosing or responding party and at the same time to protect the other parties. It provides that the party has a duty to supplement disclosures under Rule 26(a) and responses under Rules 33, 34, and 36 if the party learns that they are in some material respect incomplete or incorrect, unless the other parties are aware of the additional information.

Questions: (68) Apart from any provision by Rule, is an attorney ethically justified in standing silently by and letting answers that the attorney knows are no longer true mislead an opponent? Cf. N.Y. Cty. Lawyers' Ass'n Comm. on Prof'l Ethics, Op. 309 (1933), which suggests that, although the attorney has an ethical duty of truthfulness, there is no general duty of candor.

(69) What might a federal trial judge appropriately do if a party calls at trial a witness whose identity the party had not revealed despite a Rule 26(e)(1) duty to do so? See Rule 37(c)(1).

(70) Suppose you are counsel in a personal-injury case in which, during the disclosure and discovery phases, you have fully complied with a duty to identify all known witnesses with knowledge of the facts in litigation. When the trial is nearly over, a witness previously unknown to you appears and tells you that she read of the case in the newspaper and that she was an eyewitness to the accident. Her story is favorable to your client's case. What should you do? Suppose instead her story is very unfavorable to your client's case. What, if anything, should you do?

David L. Shapiro, Some Problems of Discovery in an Adversary System

63 Minn.L.Rev. 1055, 1055–58, 1073–75, 1090 (1979).

[I]n a recent article, Professor [later Magistrate Judge] Brazil has argued that the present adversary character of civil discovery systematically encourages obstruction of the goals of discovery and that substantial changes in the pretrial environment must be made if those goals are to be achieved.[3] He would "curtail substantially" the role of the adversary system at the pretrial stage, preserving it in its present form primarily for the "dialectical evaluation of the relevant evidence" at the trial itself.

He may be right. Surely, there is considerable tension between the apparent duty of the lawyer, in response to discovery requests, to reveal information, opinion, and even belief, and the duty and desire of that same lawyer to represent his client zealously and effectively. Perhaps such tension may be found in every corner of litigation, both civil and criminal. But it may well be more acute in the civil arena, where the client is not entitled to stand mute in the dock, and especially in the realm of discovery, where the lawyer may be asked to act as investigator, counselor, advocate, witness, and officer of the court all at the same time.

. . . .

But a drastic change in the nature of litigation of the sort suggested by Professor Brazil would be hard to legislate and even harder to implement. Is it possible, then, that at least some of the difficulty may be due not to the inevitability of conflict between the goals of discovery and the nature of the adversary system, but rather to a gap between the theory and practice of discovery? Is it also possible that the present rules . . . do not speak to practitioners and judges with a sufficiently clear

---

[3]   Brazil, The Adversary Character of Civil Discovery: A Critique and Proposals for Change, 31 Vand.L.Rev. 1295 (1978). . . . The core of his proposed changes includes shifting the lawyer's obligation before trial away from the client's interest and "toward the court"; imposing a duty on counsel to investigate thoroughly the factual background of disputes; imposing a "duty" on counsel and client to disclose "voluntarily" all relevant information and evidence (how can there be a duty to volunteer?); narrowing the scope of the attorney-client privilege and the work product doctrine; expanding the role of the court in supervising discovery; and requiring "judicial review of, or participation in, all settlements that exceed a specified dollar amount." Id. at 1349.

voice? If so, there may be hope for reducing the conflict without so thorough an overhaul of the system itself.

[Professor Shapiro surveyed litigators with a questionnaire that included the following hypothetical case:]

1.   You represent *A,* executor of *B,* in a Superior Court action for negligence arising out of an automobile accident at a highway intersection in the state. The intersection contained a stop sign at all access roads. *B* died in the accident and *C,* a passenger in the car *B* was driving, stated to you in an interview that *B* did not come to a full stop before entering the intersection. *C* too has since died, from causes unrelated to the accident, and none of the other witnesses you have spoken to claims to have seen *B* enter the intersection. You have no reason to doubt the correctness of *C's* statement. *D,* the defendant in the action, has alleged contributory negligence as a defense and has submitted the following interrogatory to *A* under Rule 33 of the state rules of civil procedure:

"Did *B* come to a full stop before entering the intersection where the accident in suit occurred?"

What should be the response to this interrogatory?

[Eighty to ninety percent of the respondents said that they would have their client in effect refuse to answer such an interrogatory, most by saying something like: "I do not know." Is such a response proper?]

I think not. In the first place, there is substantial authority for the view that if the party interrogated does not know the answer to a question, he must specify in some detail the effort he has made to find out.[67] Such detail in this case should probably include a reference to *C's* [inadmissible hearsay] statement and its contents, though it might also add that *C* is dead and that other witnesses interviewed were unable to corroborate or refute that statement.

Moreover, failure to disclose information relevant to the question is, in my view, a failure to answer the question. Every interrogatory of this type—which asks directly about the fact and not for information relating to the fact—is in substance a two-part question: (1) what information do you have that relates to this fact? and (2) what is your evaluation of that information? Assuming that the discoveree is unable or for some proper reason unwilling to answer the second part of the question with a clear statement, that should not shield him from answering the first. The purpose of an interrogatory is not simply to determine a party's position with respect to a fact, or to extract an admission, but to get information. Nor should the discoveror be required to break the question down into its components to get that information. The failure to break down into

---

[67]   See, e.g., Miller v. Doctor's Gen. Hosp., 76 F.R.D. 136, 140 (W.D.Okla.1977); Cohn v. Dart Industries, Inc., 21 Fed.R.Serv.2d 792, 793 (D.Mass.1976); Breeland v. Bethlehem Steel Co., 179 F.Supp. 464, 467 (S.D.N.Y.1959); 4A Moore's Federal Practice ¶ 33.26, at 33–140 (2d ed. 1979).

components an interrogatory seeking disclosure of the existence of a fact may result in the discoveror receiving an answer to only the second implicit part when the discoveree is willing to swear to an unqualified "yes" or "no." I do not think it should have this result, however, if the answer falls short of an unqualified response.

The matter was well put in Riley v. United Air Lines, Inc.,[68] where the plaintiff served interrogatories asking the defendant to state in detail how the accident in suit occurred. In holding insufficient the defendant's response that it had "no knowledge sufficient to answer the said interrogatories because all the crew members died in the accident," the court said:

> It is apparent from the opposing affidavit that the defendant has already obtained certain information from third persons relating to some of the interrogatories .... In this situation, defendant should furnish whatever information it now has, regardless of when or from whom it acquired it. ...
>
> Defendant may state in its answers what the source of the information is, if it so desires, [but when] the information has been obtained by persons under defendant's control solely from [questions they have addressed to] third persons, defendant is not required to admit its accuracy. If no one under defendant's control now has any information from any source as to a particular interrogatory, defendant may so state under oath, and such a statement shall be a sufficient answer.

While the suggestion in Riley that the discoveree has no duty to investigate is contrary to my own view as well as to respectable authority,[70] the Riley court's statement of the obligation to disclose information a party does have, regardless of its reliability or credibility, seems eminently sound. The fact that so many respondents to question 1 took a different and less forthcoming approach can perhaps be explained by the failure of rule 33 to make this obligation sufficiently clear. It may also, as Professor Brazil might argue, be attributable to the bias against disclosure inherent in the adversary system. But before that conclusion is reached and its implications explored, the less drastic remedy of writing a clarifying amendment to rule 33 should be considered.

. . . .

One would be hard pressed to deny the tension between the tenets of the adversary system and the goals of pretrial discovery. Certainly it is difficult to square some expansive theories of discovery expressed or implicit in the rules and supported by commentators with the protective attitudes of litigating lawyers.

---

[68]   32 F.R.D. 230 (S.D.N.Y.1962). See, e.g., Coyne v. Monongahela Connecting R.R., 24 F.R.D. 357, 359 (W.D.Pa.1959); Stom v. Pennsylvania R.R., 15 F.R.D. 284, 285 (E.D.Pa.1953).

[70]   See note 67 supra and accompanying text.

But tension is not always evil. A system of adjudication single-mindedly dedicated to total pretrial disclosure, or to maximum pretrial secrecy, might be found more wanting than the present uneasy compromise. If things are now more confused than they need to be, it is possible that some clarifying changes in the rules—here in the direction of disclosure and there in the direction of protecting the lawyer in his function as advocate—may improve matters and render unnecessary more drastic remedies.

————

Question: (71) In the Sierocinski case, would it be improper under the present Rule 11(b) for the plaintiff's lawyer to continue to pursue the case if discovery revealed to him that there had been no good ground to support the complaint?

Using disclosures and discovery products in court proceedings (Rule 32).—The mere presence of, say, a deposition in an attorney's files or even in the court's files does not mean that the court will consider it in deciding the action. Usually the court will ignore a deposition unless a party elects to offer it in evidence. Indeed, the use by the court of a deposition that a party has not introduced into evidence is often improper and may amount to reversible error.

Rule 32 deals with the use by parties of depositions. The big barrier to introducing a deposition at a hearing or trial is the hearsay rule, which as we shall soon see is a rule of evidence that renders most out-of-court statements inadmissible and thus would tend to exclude all depositions. So Rule 32(a) lists a series of circumstances—such as some situations when the deponent is presently unavailable to testify—in which the hearsay rule should not apply to exclude a deposition simply because it embodies out-of-court statements. In those circumstances, a party may use a deposition so far as admissible under the rules of evidence applied as though the deponent were then present and testifying.

Questions: (72) Rule 32(a)(4)(E) overrides the hearsay rule if the court finds "exceptional circumstances," but in making its finding the court is to give due regard to the importance of presenting witnesses' testimony orally in open court. See also Rule 43(a). Why the preference for live testimony? See John Leubsdorf, Presuppositions of Evidence Law, 91 Iowa L.Rev. 1209, 1234–44 (2006).

(73) What explains the special treatment in Rule 32(a)(3) of the deposition of a party-opponent?

Rule 32 regulates the use in court proceedings only of depositions, and it exists mainly to facilitate admission of these rather formal records of testimony. What about the use in court proceedings of disclosures and the products of other discovery methods—answers to interrogatories, documents, etc.? In general, it is correct to say simply that a party may use these items so far as admissible under all the usual rules of evidence. See, e.g., Rule 33(c). Thus, the plaintiff in the Freed case below could introduce at trial the defendant's answer to an interrogatory under the rule that relevant out-of-court statements by the party-opponent are admissible in evidence, as we shall soon explain.

———

Freed v. Erie Lackawanna Railway Co.

United States Court of Appeals, Sixth Circuit, 1971.
445 F.2d 619, cert. denied, 404 U.S. 1017, 92 S.Ct. 678 (1972).

■ Before PECK, BROOKS and KENT, CIRCUIT JUDGES.

■ BROOKS, CIRCUIT JUDGE. Plaintiff-appellant, Floyd W. Freed, III, brought this action under the Federal Employers' Liability Act against defendant-appellee, Erie Lackawanna Railway Company, for personal injuries sustained when he was struck by a train. This appeal follows a jury verdict for the defendant [in 1969].

At the time plaintiff was injured, he was the head brakeman on a freight train running from Cleveland to Youngstown, Ohio. The accident occurred in the North Randall switching area where there were numerous sets of tracks and switching operations were frequent. The plaintiff and the fireman, a fellow crewman, had just dropped off their train and had started walking down a right-of-way adjacent to a side track on their way to lunch when plaintiff was struck by a caboose, which was the lead car of a switching train that was slowly backing in performance of its switching assignment. Seconds before getting in the path of the train, plaintiff's attention was diverted when the fireman turned and called to the engineer of the freight train to throw him his cigarettes which he had forgotten and left in the cab of the locomotive.

The principal issue raised by plaintiff on appeal is whether an answer made by the defendant to an interrogatory is binding on it although contradicted by other evidence adduced by the defendant. In response to one of plaintiff's interrogatories, defendant stated that the location of the switch train at the time of the accident was not within the yard limits. A train that is not within yard limits was subject to road rule Number 103 which requires cars being pushed by engines in an area outside the yard limits to have a lookout posted on the lead car. There was no such lookout on the car of the switch train that injured the plaintiff. At trial the defendant produced testimony that the switch train was actually operating within the yard limits and, therefore, no lookout on the lead car was required, thus contradicting the answer given in the interrogatory as to the location of the train at the time of the accident.

While the jury was deliberating, the jury foreman submitted a question to the court asking if the switch train was within the yard limits at the time of the accident. The court declined to answer the question on the grounds that it involved a question of fact which it was the duty of the jury to resolve. Plaintiff argues that the answer to the interrogatory, when introduced in evidence, was ... binding on the defendant, and therefore the court should have answered the jury's question in accordance with the answer given in the interrogatory. ... As stated in Victory Carriers, Inc. v. Stockton Stevedoring Company, [388 F.2d 955 (9th Cir.1968)]:

> "An answer to an interrogatory is comparable to answers, which may be mistaken, given in deposition testimony or during the course of the trial itself. Answers to interrogatories must often be supplied before investigation is completed and can rest only upon knowledge which is available at the time. When there is conflict between answers supplied in response to interrogatories and answers obtained through other questioning, either in deposition or trial, the finder of fact must weigh all of the answers and resolve the conflict."

The court properly declined to answer the question dealing with the location of the switch train at the time of the accident.

. . . .

Affirmed.

■ [The concurring opinion of JUDGE PECK is omitted.]

———

Questions: (74) Would the result in the Freed case have been different under Rule 26(e)(1), which was added in 1970 and amended in 1993? Assume that the defendant had discovered the error and chose not to supplement, but then at trial tried to contradict its discovery response.

(75) Would the decision in the Freed case have been different if the plaintiff had utilized Rule 36 rather than Rule 33? Assume that the defendant had admitted the point, and then at trial tried to contradict it.

General problems.—Gradually the bar came generally to accept discovery on the broad scale envisaged by the Federal Rules, but not universally and not without some lingering doubts and second thoughts. Thus, some critics of discovery have suggested that compliant or unscrupulous witnesses, having gone through the informing experience of testifying on deposition, or having learned about the results of other discovery, can contrive to manipulate their stories to meet all exigencies when they finally testify at trial. Some view "surprise" at trial—at least up to a point—as a promoter of truth rather than the opposite.

Apart from that dispute over the value of discovery, there is the trumpeted risk of discovery overuse and the even greater problem in practice of improper resistance to discovery. Thus, for example, all would agree that if carried on without decent restraint, discovery could give wealthy litigants excellent opportunities to browbeat their weaker adversaries. Lawyers can make discovery very expensive, or embarrassing. And, of course, the oppressive sword of discovery cuts both ways. Plaintiffs may use nuisance suits to extort unjust settlements from wealthy litigants, who realize it is sometimes cheaper to buy off opponents than to defend. Empirical surveys have tended to indicate that discovery has generally kept within reasonable bounds of expense. See Daniel Klerman, The Economics of Civil Procedure, 11 Ann.Rev.L. & Soc.Sci. 353, 361–67 (2015). The typical case sees little discovery. But the possibility that a party will attempt through discovery to price a lawsuit out of the market for his adversary—and might succeed despite the protections offered by such provisions as Rule 26(c)—must be real in more than a few cases.

Added to these truth and fairness costs are simple laments over the time and expense consumed even by proper discovery, especially in those occasional cases where that consumption mounts to almost unimaginable heights. Ultimately, one could argue, albeit without real empirical support, that together all these different kinds of costs outweigh any benefits of discovery. At the least, one could argue convincingly that the system must make an effort to lower those costs.

During the 1970s these complaints about the burdens of discovery grew more intense. Various proposals to limit and control discovery circulated. In response, the Supreme Court in 1980 and 1983 adopted a series of amendments to the discovery Rules, changes that were relatively modest but may have succeeded in changing emphasis and the resultant atmosphere. See the section of the Rules booklet containing those amendments and the Advisory Committee's notes thereon. Innovations such as Rule 26(b)(2)(C) should to some degree facilitate a more active but selective case-by-case supervision of discovery by the court. The motivating ideas behind that Rule were that such supervision, despite its obvious and serious shortcomings, is the most effective of feasible remedies for discovery abuse and that explicit amendments to the Rules were necessary to overcome longstanding judicial reluctance to use existing powers of control.

In 1993, the Supreme Court made more significant Rule amendments, the most dramatic of which was the addition of the disclosure requirements in Rule 26(a). Because the notion of lessening the burdens of discovery by overlaying a whole new system of mandatory disclosure is, at least on first impression, bizarre, the result was torrid controversy.

Question: (76) In dissenting from the promulgation of the disclosure Rules, Justice Scalia's big argument was the increase in direct costs that would accompany this new system of disclosure. See Order of April 22, 1993, 507 U.S. 1089, 1099. Moreover, the reform would impose these costs even in the majority of cases where there was currently no discovery or at least no real dispute over discovery, and also in the many cases where disclosure already occurred on a voluntary basis between cooperative lawyers. Meanwhile, the costs of the discovery system itself would largely persist. How could the rulemakers have responded to this argument? See the 1993 Advisory Committee's note on Rule 26(a) in the Rules booklet.

Unsurprisingly, the controversy surrounding the disclosure and discovery provisions did not end with the 1993 changes. A new round of amendments became effective in 2000, making several changes aimed at achieving cost reduction: the rulemakers sharply reduced the scope of initial disclosures in recognition of that provision's ineffectiveness, so that the disclosing party now has to initially disclose only *favorable* witnesses, documents, and things; the usual scope of discovery, which had reached information relevant to the subject matter, now reached information relevant to claims and defenses only; and a presumptive one-day limit came to apply to depositions. In 2006, the rulemakers moved to control the fire ignited by the astounding upswing in e-discovery. In 2015, the rulemakers acted again to tighten discovery slightly. See the section of the Rules booklet containing those amendments and the Advisory Committee's notes thereon. One must still wonder whether this tinkering with the Rules will have the desired effects.

In addition, a basic controversy remains that is as old as the Federal Rules themselves: whether downplayed pleading with the consequently broad scope of discovery is the best allocation of issue-narrowing and fact-alleging functions, or whether the barriers at the pleading stage should be higher even than those Twombly-Iqbal erected. One academic has pointed out that, "[w]hether we like it or not, whether we admit it or not, the harsher reality is that procedural rules allocate power and advantage. . . . It is no secret that the anti-discovery pressure has come from defendants, especially defendants in product liability, securities, and antitrust cases." Elizabeth G. Thornburg, Giving the "Haves" a Little More: Considering the 1998 Discovery Proposals, 52 SMU L.Rev. 229, 230, 243 (1999). Can the rulemakers allocate functions between the pleading stage and the discovery stage in a value-neutral way? Indeed, should they?

———

Richard L. Marcus, "The Story of Hickman: Preserving Adversarial Incentives While Embracing Broad Discovery"

Civil Procedure Stories 323 (Kevin M. Clermont ed., 2d ed. 2008), with case documents at http://civprostories.law.cornell.edu.

"The federal rules of civil procedure pertaining to discovery admittedly were written with a view toward eliminating the adversary system." So pronounced a brief in the classic case of Hickman v. Taylor.[2] Was this really true?

Embracing broad discovery was a big step, no doubt. Discovery has become central to the American system of litigation . . . . The American system relies on suits brought by private lawyers using broad discovery

———

[2]   329 U.S. 495 (1947).

as a crucial element of our governance . . . . Widespread reliance on private attorneys to enforce public law was largely a product of the mid-twentieth century. Broad discovery came into being at roughly the same time, as a result of the adoption of the Federal Rules of Civil Procedure in 1938.

. . . But were the Rules, with both their implicit emphasis on private law enforcement and their institution of a discovery scheme, designed to end the adversary system? On the one hand, a change as earthshaking as the Rules might have worked to displace the adversary system, even though it had been around for centuries. On the other hand, private law enforcement relies on adversariness. . . .

Private law enforcement depends also on broad discovery. . . . It thus would be odd if discovery were intended to eliminate the adversary system wholesale, along with its litigant (often lawyer) initiative. Yet, discovery might be employed by the other side to capture the fruits of preparation, thereby eroding the very incentive on which the structure relies. As we shall see, there is an inevitable tension between broad discovery and adversarial prerogatives.

The extent to which the adversary system had been supplanted by full discovery became in fact a major controversy soon after the adoption of the Federal Rules. Hickman served as the central response, stating the enduring importance of maintaining adversarial incentives despite also recognizing a general commitment to broad discovery.

The precise question in Hickman was whether the rulemakers' invention of broad discovery should be taken to erode adversarial incentives to the extent of permitting one side to capture the other side's trial preparation, thereby blunting an important incentive for full trial preparation. The case was thus the story of both rulemaking and adversarial litigation incentives. Although its holding was largely superseded by Rule amendments in 1970 (and although since the 1970s, concern about adversarial excesses in civil litigation has prompted rulemakers and judges to intrude into areas protected by Hickman, while controversy has shifted to claims that discovery imposes excessive burdens), the case remains a defining feature of our overall adversary system.

Social and Legal Background

Adversary System. The emergence of the Anglo-American adversary system has been a gradual process of evolution from a nonrational trial method a millennium ago to reliance on competing in-court presentations of evidence. Other modern systems do not rely so heavily on the parties and their lawyers to prepare and present the evidentiary material on which the decision should be based, which has led some Americans to argue for shifting that responsibility to judges.

Excessive adversarialism has been a target of reform efforts in America since the beginning of the twentieth century. In 1906, Dean

Roscoe Pound gave a speech to the American Bar Association that sounded many themes pursued in ensuing procedural reform. One of his main themes was to denounce "our American exaggerations of the common law contentious procedure":

> The sporting theory of justice . . . is so rooted in the profession in America that most of us take it for a fundamental legal tenet. But it is probably only a survival of the days when a lawsuit was a fight between two clans in which change of venue had been taken to the forum. So far from being a fundamental fact of jurisprudence, it is peculiar to Anglo-American law; and it has been strongly curbed in modern English practice. With us, it is not merely in full acceptance, it has been developed and its collateral possibilities have been cultivated to the furthest extent. . . . The idea that procedure must of necessity be wholly contentious disfigures our judicial administration at every point. It leads the most conscientious judge to feel that he is merely to decide the contest, as counsel present it, according to the rules of the game, not to search independently for truth and justice. It leads counsel to forget that they are officers of the court and to deal with the rules of law and procedure exactly as the professional football coach with the rules of the sport.[13]

Discovery Before the Rules. The common-law system did not offer significant discovery opportunities. Instead, it relied on self-interested investigation by the parties to produce evidence for the trial.

Equity, lacking the jury trial, did not rely on evidence produced in court, and thus something like discovery developed in equity as a method for providing the chancellor with written information upon which to decide the case. On occasion, a party with a case before the law courts could file an ancillary bill for discovery in the equity courts, and judicially aided fact-gathering for litigation at law gradually began to take shape. . . .

In the United States, discovery slowly expanded. By the nineteenth century, discovery opportunities were considerably more significant than they had been in the old days. There were states with broader discovery provisions than those available in the federal courts. American discovery was already distinctive and unwelcome in the rest of the world. . . .

Still, until 1938 there was little opportunity to obtain the sort of thing that came to be critical in Hickman—material that the other side would use to support its own case. Discovery was nothing like what we know today.

Rulemaking Causes a Revolution. . . .

Then, Pound's clarion call for reform stimulated efforts that led eventually to the adoption of the Rules Enabling Act of 1934, which in

---

[13]   Roscoe Pound, The Causes of Popular Dissatisfaction with the Administration of Justice, 29 A.B.A.Rep. 395, 404–05 (1906).

turn became the vehicle for finally curtailing the gamesmanship that had typified American litigation. . . . Pleading reform was not, however, the biggest change wrought by the new Rules. That honor belonged to the discovery Rules.

. . . .

Resulting Controversy and Rulemakers' Reactions. . . .

There was [a great], and almost immediate, reaction to the breadth of the new discovery Rules. As the Third Circuit wrote in its decision in Hickman v. Taylor: "Some, but not an overwhelming preponderance, of the judges have difficulty in believing that the Rules Committee really meant what it said." Most significantly, courts sometimes held that discovery was allowed only as to things that would themselves be admissible, thereby excluding hearsay evidence from discovery. They also construed the scope of discovery to be narrower for interrogatories. . . .

Perhaps the lower courts could have sorted out these differences with time, but the rulemakers set to work on many of these questions four years after the new Rules went into effect. Along with amendments that would clarify a number of topics (but not the standard for pleading the claim), they set out to make clear that they had indeed meant what they had said about discovery. Most importantly, Rule 26(b) was to be amended by adding a sentence to specify that inadmissible materials such as hearsay were discoverable . . . . On that point, the Advisory Committee's Note in 1946 rebuked the courts that had "erroneously limited discovery on the basis of admissibility." Similarly, the scope of discovery by interrogatories was to be explicitly made as broad as that allowed for depositions under Rule 26(b). Despite questioning by some courts, the Advisory Committee declared in its Note that there "is no reason why interrogatories should be more limited than depositions" and that under "present Rule 33 some courts have unnecessarily restricted the breadth of inquiry on various grounds." Overall, then, the discovery proposals pervasively weighed in on the side of courts that had taken a broader, more flexible view of the new discovery procedures.

It is hardly surprising that the Hickman problem—discoverability of material that the other side would use to support its own case—emerged soon after the new Rules were in place, for they directed that discovery could be had of "any matter, not privileged, which is relevant to the subject matter involved in the pending action." Because a lawyer's investigation for trial would normally be relevant . . . , it would seem to be subject to discovery unless it were privileged. But allowing discovery of the lawyer's activities would be anathema to the core values of the adversary system. Eventually, there was much conflicting authority, as set forth at great length in the Advisory Committee's Note to its proposed amendment to the pertinent Rule in 1946.

On this particular topic, however, the Advisory Committee itself seemed of two minds about whether to take the broadest view of its new discovery procedures. Initially, in its first preliminary draft of proposed amendments in 1944, the Advisory Committee proposed to deal with the problem by putting the burden on the adverse party resisting discovery to seek a protective order providing "that designated restrictions be imposed upon inquiry into papers and documents prepared or obtained by the adverse party in the preparation of the case for trial." Consistently with the overall tenor of the first draft of these proposed amendments to favor broadening discovery, the Advisory Committee's Note confirmed that the new provision "does not suggest, as some courts have done, that such an inquiry may not be made." A year later, in its second draft of proposed amendments, the Committee stuck with the protective order approach. This time the Note expanded on the disagreement among courts and noted that some had held such materials entirely beyond discovery. Although making it clear that a court had authority to limit access to litigation-preparation materials, the Note emphasized that "such files and their contents are not absolutely privileged."

A year after that, and evidently without any public comment, the Committee did an about-face in its final report to the Supreme Court on the proposed amendments. Rather than impose on the responding party the obligation to move for a protective order, the first draft of these proposed amendment put litigation-preparation materials beyond the grasp of the discovering side unless it made a showing justifying discovery:

> The court shall not order the production or inspection of any writing obtained or prepared by the adverse party, his attorney, surety, indemnitor, or agent in anticipation of litigation or in preparation for trial unless satisfied that denial of production or inspection will unfairly prejudice the party seeking the production or inspection in preparing his claim or defense or will cause him undue hardship or injustice. The court shall not order the production or inspection of any part of the writing that reflects an attorney's mental impressions, conclusions, opinions, or legal theories, or, except as provided in Rule 35, the conclusions of an expert.

In its Note, the Committee acknowledged that the Supreme Court had granted certiorari in Hickman v. Taylor. The scene was thus set for the Court to deal with the question, either by rulemaking or by decision of the case.

Factual Background

As the Supreme Court was to observe, Hickman v. Taylor resulted from an accident that was "unusual in nature, the cause of it still being unknown." Because that uncertainty explains the plaintiff's desire to obtain all possible information about the accident, it is worthwhile to detail the surrounding events, as presented at the time of the Court's decision.

In 1939, Norman Hickman began working as a deckhand on tugs operated by the Taylor & Anderson Towing and Lighterage Co. (Taylor & Anderson), which was a partnership of John M. Taylor and George H. Anderson. Taylor & Anderson operated seven tugs, being one of the larger tug operations in Philadelphia. The unmarried Hickman lived with his parents (his father worked for Taylor & Anderson as a watchman). While working, however, he slept on the tug.

On Saturday, February 6, 1943, Hickman was working on the 115-ton tug J.M. Taylor when it was directed to proceed (along with another Taylor & Anderson tug called Philadelphia) to Pier 12 in Philadelphia for towing a sunken car float of the Baltimore & Ohio Railroad (B & O) across the Delaware River to Camden, New Jersey. A car float is a barge-like vessel designed to transport railroad cars; this one was 220 feet long and 34 feet wide, with a total weight of 500 to 600 tons. When the two tugs arrived at Pier 12, the car float was largely submerged, although the shore-end of the car float was above the surface.

According to Taylor & Anderson, a B & O representative told the tug crew that the car float would rise to the surface when freed from the mud at the pier. A diver attached two towing hawsers to the river-end of the car float. The Philadelphia attached the two hawsers to its stern, and the J.M. Taylor attached a line from its stern to the bow of the Philadelphia. The two tugs then began to tow the car float, but instead of rising to the surface, it sank entirely. The tugs kept going. As the tugs approached the eastern side of the shipping channel, about 1,000 feet from the Camden shore, the car float hung up on an obstruction on the bottom, and one of the towing hawsers parted.

The J.M. Taylor then returned to Pier 12, while the Philadelphia remained with the car float, secured by the remaining hawser. When the J.M. Taylor was at Pier 12, there was telephone contact with George H. Anderson, and it was concluded that the J.M. Taylor should relieve the Philadelphia and stand by the sunken car float to display danger signals for passing navigation. The J.M. Taylor took up this position between 6:00 and 7:00 p.m. It was cold, and there were cakes of ice floating in the river, which was about 43 feet deep at the point where the car float was stuck. The J.M. Taylor kept a full head of steam throughout the operation. Hickman had watch from 6:00 p.m. until midnight, and was to begin his next watch at 6:00 a.m. He would ordinarily have been awakened for breakfast at 5:30 a.m.

At about 6:00 a.m., in the words of the Philadelphia Inquirer, the car float "shot to the surface" and "ripped into the port side of the tug, and the craft capsized." One of the surviving crew members, who was asleep at the time, reported being awakened by the sensation of being thrown— "everything seemed topsy-turvy." He fought his way up the companionway against "a flood of water" and turned to assist another crew member out of the hold, after which the other crew member was quickly washed overboard. The tug sank so rapidly that there was never an order to abandon the vessel. In the words of the Evening Bulletin, this was an "unusual accident, first of its kind in the memory of river men."

Three of the survivors managed to cling to the tug's hatch, and were rescued by a police launch. One of them reported that "we were nearly frozen." The fourth survivor had clung to a ladder as he was swept downstream by "a strong running tide." When a harbor patrol boat found him, he was too weak to grasp the life ring thrown to him, and the boat had to be maneuvered alongside him to rescue him. The other five crew members, including the captain, perished. Hickman's body was found on the floor of the forward cabin when the tug was raised several days after the accident.

Given the unusual nature of the accident, it must have been apparent that there could be accusations about the hazards of towing a sunken car float and of leaving a tug tied to it overnight. Three days after the sinking of the tug, Taylor & Anderson retained attorney Samuel B. Fortenbaugh, Jr., to represent them in connection with possible claims. About three weeks after the sinking, a public hearing was held before the United States Steamboat Inspectors. The four surviving crew members testified at the hearing. Fortenbaugh did not attend the hearing, but someone from his office was there. The testimony was recorded, and a transcript made available. Shortly after the hearing, Fortenbaugh interviewed the four survivors about the sinking and obtained signed statements from them about the event. In addition, he interviewed others he thought had information about the sinking, and sometimes made memoranda for his files about those interviews.

Claims were presented on behalf of four of the five crew members who died in the sinking.[42] All the claims but Hickman's were settled [without litigation].

Prior Proceedings

The District Court. About nine months after the accident, Hickman's father, as the administrator of his estate, filed suit against Taylor & Anderson and B & O, alleging that Hickman's death was due to defendants' negligence. He alleged that the car float had surfaced several times before capsizing the tug. A month later Taylor & Anderson, represented by Fortenbaugh, filed an answer denying negligence in connection with the sinking of the tug, and denying that the car float had surfaced other times before causing the accident. [B & O answered too.]

Nearly a year later, plaintiff served a set of interrogatories on Taylor & Anderson and also served a set of interrogatories on B & O. These interrogatories sought many details about the sinking, as well as the towing of the car float that preceded it. Eventually, the defendants

---

[42] As Fortenbaugh reported in his deposition, there was no contact from the heirs of deckhand Ole Knudsen. . . .

provided answers with considerable information, as well as some finger-pointing between them about who was responsible for the decisions to tow the sunken car float and to have the J.M. Taylor stand by it overnight in mid-river.

The initial package to Taylor & Anderson contained Interrogatory 38, which the Supreme Court addressed in its decision.[43] Responding to the interrogatories, Fortenbaugh objected that this question sought privileged matter.[44] Plaintiff also served supplemental interrogatories seeking more detailed information about any statements. It was apparent from the detail of the questions that plaintiff's lawyers had mastered the use of the new discovery tools. Ten days after the supplemental interrogatories were served, Fortenbaugh answered some of them and objected that the "answering of the very minute and detailed [other questions] would involve practically turning over not only the complete files, but also the telephone records and, almost, the thoughts of counsel." Plaintiff moved to compel discovery from Taylor & Anderson.

From this point forward, what appeared to be an ordinary case took on extraordinary aspects, probably due to the widespread interest in the issue presented by the discovery dispute. In order to explore that issue, Fortenbaugh submitted to what was called a deposition. This event more closely resembled what is ordinarily called an evidentiary hearing, as it occurred in the courthouse and the questions were asked by the assigned judge. The question whether Fortenbaugh's objection to the interrogatories should be sustained was then ripe for decision, but the extraordinary progress of the case continued. Rather than decide the question himself, the assigned judge convened an en banc session of all the judges of the district, and the eventual decision was by all of them.

The district court ordered Taylor & Anderson to answer the interrogatories. It started by emphasizing the broad grant of discovery of all nonprivileged, relevant material: "The guiding principle is the broad conception of the Rules that discovery of all matters relevant to a suit should be allowed to the fullest extent consistent with the orderly and efficient functioning of the judicial process." It rejected the idea that statements taken from witnesses would be covered by the attorney-client privilege, saying that "the mere fact that statements of third parties have been taken by an attorney does not itself give rise to the privilege. In such case the lawyer is merely the medium through which his client becomes apprised of facts and his intention to transmit them to his client does not

---

[43]   Interrogatory 38 was as follows, Transcript of Record at 17a:

(38) State whether any statements of the members of the crews of the Tugs "J.M. Taylor" and "Philadelphia" or of any other vessel were taken in connection with the towing of the car float and the sinking of the Tug "John M. Taylor." Attach hereto exact copies of all such statements if in writing, and if oral, set forth in detail the exact provisions of any such oral statements or reports.

[44]   The response was as follows, id. at 28a:

38. Respondents except to this interrogatory as calling for privileged matter obtained in preparation for litigation. Statements were taken.

make the facts privileged from disclosure in answer to interrogatories." Counsel's activities were entitled to no protection because "Mr. Fortenbaugh was acting primarily as an investigator. The liberal scope of discovery under the Rules displaces any concept of proprietary or quasi-proprietary interest which, under the prior practice, a party to a suit may have claimed to the fruits of his investigation." But the court did recognize that protection should be accorded to Fortenbaugh's theories of the case:

> Discovery should not be abused to become an instrument for obtaining knowledge of the opponent's theories of the case or the opinions, impressions or the record of mental operations of his attorney. . . . If Mr. Fortenbaugh's record of the oral statements made to him by witnesses also contain notations of mental impressions, opinions, legal theories or other collateral matter these memoranda should be submitted by him to the Court. The Court will then direct disclosure to the opposite party of those portions of the memoranda containing statements of facts obtained from witnesses which it considers to be within the proper scope of discovery.

When the district court's order was not obeyed, the assigned judge held Taylor, Anderson, and nonparty Fortenbaugh in contempt and ordered that they be confined in the Philadelphia County Prison until they complied. Nobody was actually imprisoned as a result. Instead, the contempt citation provided an [arguably] appealable order permitting immediate appellate review. The notice of appeal was filed on the same day the contempt order was entered. . . .

The Court of Appeals. Like the district court, the court of appeals heard the case en banc with all judges sitting. The case had attracted enough attention that two amicus curiae briefs were filed.

The appellate court began by noting that the discovery "Rules probably go further than any State practice," and agreed with the district court that there is no proprietary right in information obtained in preparation for trial: "We have no desire to restrict the operation of the rules on discovery by the application of any notion of semi-property right in information one secures to use in a pending lawsuit against another. Nor do we balk at the notion that the hare may by discovery avail himself of the diligence of the tortoise." . . . It disavowed putting the lawyer's files entirely beyond the reach of discovery: "A piece of a machine which has hurt someone, a document needed to show a fact, many things required in a lawsuit find their way from client's hands to lawyer's file and are not to be concealed until the day of trial for that reason."

Nonetheless, the court reversed, concluding that "there is more in the exception of 'privilege' than has been so far developed," so that the information involved could be protected from discovery even though not covered by the attorney-client privilege. In the case before it, there was a basis for extending the new privilege to the newly minted concept of "work product of the lawyer." It explained that this extension should be adopted for purposes of public policy, in order to aid parties involved in litigation in obtaining "whole-souled efforts" from their lawyers.

In closing, the court acknowledged that its protection of lawyers could be contested: "The soundness of this policy is not capable of laboratory demonstration. Enunciated and applied as it necessarily is by members of the guild which derives incidental benefit from its application, it is open to the gibes of the cynical."

The Supreme Court. Thus was the scene set for the Supreme Court to reconcile the demands of the adversary system with broad discovery. . . . Yet the Court did not immediately seize the opportunity to put the matter to rest. It first denied certiorari, and took the case only after Hickman's lawyer filed a petition for rehearing. In its eventual opinion, the Court explained that it granted certiorari due to the "importance of the problem, which has engendered a great divergence of views among district courts," citing the Advisory Committee's Note accompanying the proposed amendment.

But the Court had an alternative way of dealing with the general question, that is, adoption of the Rule amendment proposed by the Advisory Committee to handle the problem. Even though it had granted certiorari, the Court could have proceeded by amendment. On the one hand, as the Court noted, the "problem thus far transcends the situation confronting this petitioner." In an amicus curiae brief in Hickman, the American Bar Association opposed general resolution of the question via a decision but also urged that more discussion should occur before an amendment. On the other hand, the Advisory Committee's about-face regarding this particular amendment might have counseled in favor of a Supreme Court decision. The plaintiff's lawyer in Hickman left no doubt about his views, saying in his brief that the proposed amendment was even worse than the Third Circuit's decision. One can certainly debate whether procedural developments are best accomplished by rulemaking amendment or by judicial decision. In any event, the Court chose the decisional route. Some have suggested that it withheld the proposed amendment from the package of amendments that it did approve because there was insufficient time to decide the case and still meet the deadline for submitting the other Rule amendments.

The Supreme Court Decision

There was another easy way to dispose of this particular case. But like the lower courts, the Supreme Court did not hesitate over the technical problem presented by the fact that plaintiff's discovery seemed to be trying to use interrogatories in order to obtain production of documents. The Court addressed the problem of determining whether plaintiff was principally relying on Rule 33 (interrogatories) or Rule 34 (document production, which [at that time] required a court order [based on "good cause"]), but concluded that this difference did not matter and that "the basic question at stake is whether any of those devices may be used to inquire into materials collected by an adverse party's counsel in the course of preparation for possible litigation. The fact that the petitioner may have used the wrong method does not destroy the main thrust of his attempt. Nor does it relieve us of the responsibility of dealing with the problem raised by that attempt."

Then the Court, in its opinion by Justice Murphy, endorsed the regime of broad discovery introduced in 1938, recognizing and embracing the breadth of the discovery revolution wrought by the adoption of the Federal Rules:

> We agree, of course, that the deposition-discovery rules are to be accorded a broad and liberal treatment. No longer can the time-honored cry of "fishing expedition" serve to preclude a party from inquiring into the facts underlying his opponent's case. Mutual knowledge of all the relevant facts gathered by both parties is essential to proper litigation.

The rulemakers' discovery revolution had clearly carried the day at the highest level of the American court system.

. . . The Court insisted that the materials in question fell outside the realm of privilege, but it proceeded to hold that the material was not discoverable without a showing of need or necessity. At heart, it determined that the policies underlying the adversary system would be compromised were discovery routinely available:

> [I]t is essential that a lawyer work with a certain degree of privacy, free from unnecessary intrusion by opposing parties and their counsel. . . . That is the historical and the necessary way in which lawyers act within the framework of our system of jurisprudence to promote justice and to protect their clients' interests.

In his concurring opinion, Justice Jackson was more emphatic in a famous passage: "But a common law trial is and always should be an adversary proceeding. Discovery was hardly intended to enable a learned profession to perform its functions either without wits or on wits borrowed from the adversary." This adversary orientation was "necessarily implicit in the rules as now constituted" and "so well recognized and so essential to an orderly working of our system of legal procedure that a burden rests on the one who would invade that privacy."
. . .

At least from an academic perspective, there certainly were grounds to question the Court's rationale in affirming. Both the majority opinion and the concurrence appeared intent on protecting the profession against something that would be "demoralizing." Given the public uneasiness that immunity for lawyers would likely engender, as had been noted by the Third Circuit, this seemed an odd justification. Discovery was not restricted in order to spare the sensibilities of any other profession.[71] And the Court was seemingly willing to countenance some consequences that would be demoralizing for attorneys, because it unequivocally called for discovery without any special showing of pertinent information counsel learn through assiduous preparation.[72] The lawyer also had to confront the risk that the protection Hickman granted would be overcome by a showing of need.

It is not clear what harmful consequences would come from allowing discovery without an extra showing, except for being demoralizing. The Court's suggestion that "much of what is now put down in writing would remain unwritten" seems relatively mild. Altogether, then, one might be tempted to view Hickman in rough political terms "as the compromise most likely to achieve final, general acceptance of the still new discovery machinery."[74] Today one might go further to agree with those academics who now argue that there should be no protection of work product at all, by privilege or otherwise.

But it is difficult to blink the fact that Hickman was a unanimous decision, with a concurrence that was, if anything, more emphatic about the need for this insulation of the lawyer's work. The Third Circuit, sitting en banc, had been similarly unanimous about the need for a new form of protection against discovery. . . . Indeed, it may be that this attitude transcends the dynamics of litigation and reflects an important feature of American political arrangements. This country's conduct of its affairs is singularly reliant on an adversarial method that depends on self-interested citizens acting through lawyers. Although one element of this mode of political organization is broad discovery, another is to protect the incentives for this adversarial activity against governmentally authorized intrusion. This respect for lawyers' latitude is consistent with another distinctive feature of American lawyering— reduced insistence that lawyers forgo one-sided adversarialism and instead pursue society-wide objectives. Putting all these strands together

---

[71]   In 1984, the Court was presented with a request to recognize similar protection for the work product of outside auditors, and it rejected the auditors' attempt to rely by analogy on Hickman because independent auditors perform a different role from lawyers' and have a public responsibility that transcends any duty owed to the client. United States v. Arthur Young & Co., 465 U.S. 805, 817 (1984).

[72]   See 329 U.S. at 504 ("A party clearly cannot refuse to answer interrogatories on the ground that the information sought is solely within the knowledge of his attorney."), 508–09 ("Full and honest answers to such broad inquiries [as plaintiff's interrogatories] would necessarily have included all pertinent information gleaned by Fortenbaugh through his interviews with the witnesses."). So the lawyer who investigates vigorously must bear the risk that unpalatable evidence will be unearthed in the process. To get this information, of course, the other side must ask a question about the subject to which the information relates. A question like "Describe all facts counsel has encountered in her preparation for trial" would not do. But a question like "Identify all witnesses to the accident" would cover the identity of a witness whom counsel had identified only through remarkable initiative. (Moreover, at least since the 1983 amendment to Rule 11, the lawyer has a duty to investigate that is a product of professional obligation, and not solely a matter of fealty to the client under the dynamics of the adversary system.)

[74]   Edward H. Cooper, Work Product of the Rulemakers, 53 Minn.L.Rev. 1269, 1273 (1969).

involves speculation beyond the scope of conventional caselaw analysis or a functional analysis of legal rules of litigation, but it also suggests deep reasons for Hickman's basic orientation.

Moreover, even for the skeptical, there remains a core of good sense in Hickman's insistence that lawyers enjoy some privacy in preparing their cases . . . . Proof of Hickman's good sense comes from a situation that was undoubtedly rare or unknown in 1947 but has since become more commonplace. Although Fortenbaugh submitted to a "deposition" before the court in connection with his discovery dispute, lawyers and judges of the mid-twentieth century did not expect litigants to depose opposing counsel. Yet by the end of the century, that was a growing phenomenon [limited by courts to special circumstances]. So at some point, Hickman's protection is central to adversary litigation: if all one had to do to prepare for trial were to take opposing counsel's deposition, there would be little incentive to prepare vigorously in any other way.

The Immediate Impact of Hickman

Subsequent Proceedings. After remand from the Supreme Court, the case was tried to the court, and the judge entered judgment against Taylor & Anderson and in favor of B & O.[80] The judge found that Taylor & Anderson was negligent in two ways. First, it was negligent in allowing the tug to be moored overnight to the car float. In the judge's view, the natural buoyancy of the car float made it likely that it would rise to the surface. Indeed, the extraordinary feature of its behavior was that it "sank a half dozen times in spite of having enough buoyancy to rise." A better alternative would have been to improvise a buoy and have the tug stand by nearby, out of danger from the car float. Second, the failure to sound a general alarm on the morning of the sinking was also negligent. The judge concluded that the car float had actually risen more than once shortly before the occasion on which it caused the tug to capsize, and that these events sufficed to call for a warning. On this score, the judge noted that Hickman's body was clothed only in his underwear, indicating that he was asleep in his bunk when the tug went down. The district judge determined that the pecuniary loss suffered by Hickman's parents due to the death was $4,000, and that $1,000 was appropriate compensation for Hickman's pain and suffering.

. . . .

Impact on the Rules. In a real sense, the problem presented by Hickman was the product of rulemaking, namely, the rulemakers'

---

[80] Hickman v. Taylor, 75 F.Supp. 528 (E.D.Pa.1947), aff'd, 170 F.2d 327 (3d Cir.1948), cert. denied, 336 U.S. 906, reh'g denied, 336 U.S. 921 (1949). During the trial, Fortenbaugh evidently tried to offer in evidence the witness statements he had withheld as work product, and plaintiff successfully objected. In 1977, the Harvard Law Record ran a story on the case. Paul Coady, Dredging the Depths of Hickman v. Taylor, Harv.L.Rec., May 6, 1977, at 2, 7. It reported that Fortenbaugh had offered the statements in evidence to dispel any suspicions that might have arisen about his earlier resistance to producing them. Plaintiff's counsel explained that he had opposed their admission because "the statements must have been all favorable to Fortenbaugh's client, or else he would not have taken them."

revolutionary adoption of broad discovery. Hickman addressed the question that had been addressed by the most recent Rule amendment proposals—whether there should be routine discovery of materials that lawyers developed in anticipation of litigation, as opposed to facts they unearthed. But the Court's answer lacked clarity. There were many important details still to be worked out. . . .

. . . The scope of the basic protection was not clear. For example, did the protection apply only to the lawyers' personal work (as in Hickman) or also to the work of others under the lawyers' direction? And what was to be done about experts hired by the lawyers to assist in preparation of the case? Hickman certainly said nothing about that.

Moreover, the showing needed to obtain production of materials that were protected as work product remained uncertain after Hickman. In that case, the plaintiff had not attempted to make any such showing, standing instead on the Rules as sufficient to guarantee access. With regard to the witness statements of the survivors, at least, it might well have been possible to make a showing. Although at first blush the availability of the transcript of the hearing before the Steamboat Inspectors might seem sufficient, it also appears that Fortenbaugh had not thought so, as he took the statements in question after that hearing occurred. So, what was to be the standard? . . .

One obvious reaction would be to accomplish the needed clarification by rulemaking. . . . Perhaps the Hickman Court was suggesting that a Federal Rule should be developed when it said that "until some rule . . . definitely prescribes otherwise, we are not justified in permitting discovery in a situation of this nature as a matter of unqualified right." But the topic had already proved very controversial and divisive. The Advisory Committee had done a flip-flop on how to approach the problem between 1945 and 1946. Perhaps it was not surprising, then, that it did not embark immediately on another attempt, despite the multitude of open questions. Yet a number of states reacted to Hickman by adopting statutory or rule provisions to address work-product issues.

. . . .

[Finally, the Advisory] Committee turned to discovery and commenced a comprehensive review of the discovery Rules. This multi-year effort produced the 1970 amendments to the Rules, which rearranged a number of discovery provisions and modified several.

One significant change was to remove the requirement of a motion and order based on good cause for document production. But certainly the most significant Rule changes had to do with work product and related concerns. The Committee explained its adoption of Rule 26(b)(3): "In deciding the Hickman case, the Supreme Court appears to have expressed a preference for an approach to the problem of trial preparation materials by judicial decision rather than by rule. Sufficient experience has accumulated, however, with lower court applications of the Hickman decision to warrant a reappraisal."

The new Rule 26(b)(3), then, was intended largely to supplant the caselaw, including Hickman itself. . . . [I]t remains important to appreciate the differences between Hickman and the Rule and to perceive the continued role of the Hickman holding in constituting today's Rule-based law:

Documents and Tangible Things. Rule 26(b)(3) is, in effect, a limitation on discovery of otherwise discoverable materials, but it limits discovery of only that which is a document or tangible thing. That would cover Mr. Fortenbaugh's witness statements and memoranda to his file, but not his recollections. For the latter, Hickman continues to provide protection.

Litigation Preparation by Nonlawyers. The Hickman case seemed to deal only with the work of lawyers, and perhaps those working under their direction, such as private investigators and paralegals. Rule 26(b)(3), on the other hand, provides protection for the work not only of lawyers, but also of a party's consultant, surety, indemnitor, insurer, or agent. Of course, there is no protection under the Rule for intangible information possessed by these people, but as to many of them there will probably be no recollections needing protection.

. . . .

Anticipation of Litigation. When protection applied only to the work of lawyers, the problem whether given materials were created in anticipation of litigation rarely presented difficulties. But with the introduction in Rule 26(b)(3) of protection for the work of nonlawyers, the number of occasions when it could be argued that materials were created in the party's normal business multiplied. So the subject has grown in importance.

Showing Necessary to Obtain Protected Materials. After Hickman, courts had used the malleable "good cause" phrase to describe the standard for production of protected materials. Rule 26(b)(3) substituted a much more focused inquiry: "a showing that the party seeking discovery has a substantial need of the materials in the preparation of the party's case and that the party is unable without undue hardship to obtain the substantial equivalent of the materials by other means." . . .

Opinion Work Product. Rule 26(b)(3) also made explicit something implicit in Hickman—that "mental impressions, conclusions, opinions, or legal theories" should receive special protection.

Witness Statements. Rule 26(b)(3) significantly changed the treatment of these items, which were, of course, the main focus in Hickman. It provides that a party may obtain its own statement without the showing usually required, and that a nonparty may similarly do so without making a showing. Had this been the rule when Hickman was filed, it is likely that Norman Hickman's father could have persuaded the survivors to request copies of their statements and thus side-stepped the entire problem that made the Supreme Court's decision necessary.

Experts. Since Hickman was decided, the importance of experts to litigation has mushroomed, but Hickman said nothing explicitly about them. The 1970 amendments directly addressed the question by adding a new Rule 26(b)(4), which regulated discovery regarding experts who will testify at trial and which forbade discovery in almost all circumstances regarding the work of expert consultants who will not testify at trial. . . .

In sum, the work-product problem could be seen ultimately as a success story for rulemaking. At first, there was division over what rule should be adopted, and the controversy surrounding the topic impeded solution by rule. Hickman resolved the biggest issue, and caselaw provided the experience to inform rulemaking more than two decades later. For most purposes the Rules now provide the starting point. But this is not to say that the Rules have answered all questions. . . .

The Continuing Importance of Hickman Today

As we have seen, except for cases involving intangible work product, Hickman has largely been superseded by the 1970 amendments to the Rules. So today the case might be seen as largely a relic. To the contrary, it still stands as a signpost representing the American commitment to preserving adversarial incentives, one that is relevant not only within but also outside the civil litigation arena. Thus, in 1975 the Supreme Court recognized that the work-product doctrine applies in criminal cases because "we have placed our confidence in the adversary system," and Hickman's protection for trial preparation is "grounded in the realities of litigation in our adversary system."[103] . . .

Getting back to ordinary civil litigation, the enduring importance of the principles of Hickman was evidenced in the intense controversy about initial disclosure [under Rule 26(a) in the 1990s]. . . .

. . . .

Judicial Management and Protection of Litigation Strategy. If the initial-disclosure furor showed the enduring strength of the central principles of Hickman, the emerging importance of judicial management of litigation shows the limits of those principles. This new movement thus illustrates again the eternal tension concerning the amount of latitude the litigator should have in our adversary system.

Judicial management began as an innovation in the 1970s in a number of metropolitan district courts, prompted by judges concerned that unrestrained adversarialism of lawyers caused undue delay and cost in litigation. The judges' method of taking control of litigation usually

---

[103]   United States v. Nobles, 422 U.S. 225, 230, 238 (1975). The Court went on to hold that, in the case before it, the defendant had waived work-product protection by using a private investigator's work product as evidence at the trial.

consisted of conferences in which they would ask the lawyers about their plans for the case. . . . Not surprisingly, then, there has been vigorous criticism of this managerial activity on the ground that it frees judges from traditional tethers and it risks undermining their impartiality. . . .

Such judicial views have struck a responsive chord. . . . For our purposes, the important thing to appreciate is that the Rules are now full of directives that intrude into the lawyer's control of case preparation. . . .

All of these requirements call for the lawyer to reveal the sorts of things that the work-product principle seemed designed to insulate. Within the Rules, therefore, the judicial management movement may be said to have eroded the protections Hickman tried to provide. Is there any limit on the power of the activist judge to pierce the sanctity of the lawyer's work-product protections? That is not a question often addressed, but when it is raised the answer given is that the work-product doctrine places far fewer limits on the judge's inquiries or requirements than on those of the opponent.

. . . .

Enduring Controversy over Discovery. Hickman addressed the most controversial dispute that had erupted from the introduction of broad discovery under the Federal Rules. . . . But that controversy has since subsided.

Perhaps the work-product controversy subsided because of the adoption in 1970 of Rule 26(b)(3) and (b)(4). In any event, it is certain that controversy about discovery since 1970 has focused elsewhere. And there has been plenty of such controversy about discovery. Beginning in the 1970s, discovery indeed became the most controversial topic of all under the Federal Rules. It was on the Advisory Committee's agenda relatively continuously for the remainder of the century.

One could say that this new controversy was an attempt at counterrevolution, an effort to undo the transformation of discovery worked by the original Federal Rules. Hickman's dictum embraced wide-open discovery, but since its time voices have been heard sounding a very different note. . . .

. . . .

Conclusion

If nothing else, Hickman v. Taylor shows that the discovery Rules were not intended to eliminate the adversary system, even though they very substantially transformed the role of the advocate. . . .

The Hickman story involved intertwined tales of rulemaking and the adversary system. Rulemaking effected a sea change in American litigation by dramatically expanding discovery, a point the Supreme Court recognized in its decision. But the Court's decision, rather than rulemaking, preserved the adversary system against the possible erosion of adversary incentives to prepare fully using the new tools and traditional techniques of investigation. More than twenty years after the Court's decision, rulemaking articulated that case's principles more fully—based in large measure on the intervening caselaw—and the courts have since then shouldered the task of implementing both Hickman and Rule 26(b)(3) and (b)(4).

. . . .

In the end, we see that both the discovery saga and the adversary system tale are likely to endure and evolve for decades to come. Despite repeated invitations to do so, we have not jettisoned broad discovery. And despite broad discovery, and despite developments like managerial judging, this country is not abandoning its adversary traditions. So this seems to be a story that, in some ways, will never end.

———

(g) PRETRIAL CONFERENCES

[Rule 16]

Playing in with pleadings and with disclosure and discovery—serving some of the same functions and also having the distinct missions of *propelling* and *focusing* the case—are the pretrial conferences under Rule 16. Note the objectives and range of this procedure as given in Rule 16(a) and (c).

The original Rule 16 was a brief and relatively simple Rule. Practice thereunder, although highly variable in response to obvious tensions of policy, was generally rather *informal, uncomplicated, noncoercive, and nonbinding*. See McCargo v. Hedrick, 545 F.2d 393 (4th Cir.1976). The court could call the attorneys for a talk and typically would do so once late in the litigation to consider with them what the points in controversy were and how together they might facilitate the trial of the action.

In 1983, however, the rulemakers rewrote Rule 16 in expansive form, certainly changing the tone thereof if not the practice thereunder. Judicial case management from the institution of suit was the new emphasis, motivated by the "widespread feeling" that modern litigation demanded a move in that direction. See the lengthy 1983 Advisory Committee's note on the amended Rule in the Rules booklet. The empirical and theoretical bases for this change were, respectively, scanty and disputed. Moreover, it was not clear that such detailed rulemaking, rather than some form of more tentative and flexible experimentation, was the most desirable route to reform. Yet in 1993, the rulemakers chose to make Rule 16 even more detailed.

The initial step in the current procedure is the scheduling order of Rule 16(b). In most cases, within about three months of commencement, the court *must* after consultation fix time limits for settling pleadings, filing motions, and completing discovery. In actuality, however, the court often finds a way not to do so.

Then there *may* be one or more pretrial conferences. (Indeed, a scheduling conference may have preceded the scheduling order under Rule 16(b).) The use of pretrial conferences is optional with the court. The court may hold one or more pretrial conferences relatively early in the litigation to address some of the pretrial concerns listed in Rule 16(c). A final pretrial conference, which can be especially useful when the parties have obtained substantial discovery, may occur shortly before trial to formulate a plan for trial, as prescribed in Rule 16(e).

The actual practice varies from district to district. In some districts the judges hold a conference in each case, in other districts they confine conferences to selected cases, and in still others they resort to Rule 16 perfunctorily if at all.

The degree to which particular judges actively employ the pretrial conference also varies considerably. It depends not only upon the temperaments of the judges but also upon their views of what their role is or should be in the litigation process.

The use of the pretrial conference likewise varies from case to case. A small, simple case may not warrant the expense and effort entailed in a conference. In an average case there might be a single, "final" pretrial conference. And in large or complex litigation, such as antitrust cases and class actions, all judges find extensive use of conferences nearly indispensable. (The Manual for Complex Litigation gives elaborate advice about how to employ multiple conferences at intervals to elucidate the issues, organize and control discovery, and otherwise prepare the "big case" for trial. More generally, that semi-official Manual, which is the product of the drafting and revising efforts of a committee of judges over the last few decades, serves as a tracking mechanism by suggesting specialized guidelines for handling complex actions.)

If held, a pretrial conference culminates in an order that, according to Rule 16(d) and (e), controls the subsequent course of the action unless modified. The order may articulate in a convenient and helpful way the remaining controverted issues. Even though the order does not in terms amend the pleadings (as it may do), in practice the order has the effect of superseding the pleadings. And because the order is binding on the parties, they need not offer evidence at the trial to prove a proposition established in the order, nor will the court admit contrary evidence.

Question: (77) Should the court permit a party to offer evidence on a proposition established in her favor in the pretrial order? Why might she want to do so?

Finally, Rule 16(f) expressly provides for sanctions that the court might impose for certain violations of the Rule.

In summary, the changes from the original to the current Rule 16 are massive, but still the practice remains variegated. To the extent any generalizations are meaningful, what can we say about how *informal, uncomplicated, noncoercive, and nonbinding* today's pretrial conferences remain? Not too much.

First, as a marker of informality, consider whether courts should hold pretrial conferences in chambers or in open court, and off the record or on a record taken down by some means. The fact is that there is still no consensus on such practices. But another fact is that a greater need for formality now exists, given current Rule 16's increased judicial activity.

Second, although Rule 16 does not in terms provide for it, most courts now require the attorneys for both sides to meet prior to a pretrial conference and to agree if possible upon a joint pretrial statement, or to file separate pretrial statements indicating their respective positions. (By virtue of Rule 83, many districts have complicated local rules on this subject, some of which at least literally require fairly extensive and detailed preparation by counsel. Also, many individual district judges issue standing orders that operate in the judge's own courtroom. More generally, throughout the phases of a lawsuit, counsel must keep a sharp eye on local rules and standing orders, which are often surprisingly and unfortunately voluminous, restrictive, and demanding.)

Third, Rule 16 does not well specify the appropriate coerciveness of a pretrial conference, and so the result is considerable disagreement. For example, judges differ in their views about the propriety and wisdom of introducing the subject of settlement or urging it on the parties. Perhaps settlement talk should arise, if at all, only as a natural by-product of a businesslike pretrial conference aimed at shaping the litigation. Or perhaps judges should take an active role in pushing for settlement. There has long been a wide range of judicial practice regarding settlement, but in recent decades there has been a noticeable shift toward activism. Since 1983, Rule 16(a)(5) and (c)(2)(I) expressly mentions settlement and the Advisory Committee's note thereon even suggests the possibility of a settlement conference. This emphasis has accelerated that shift toward activism. The Identiseal case below explores the appropriate limits on activism.

Fourth, as to bindingness, there is the usual tension between freezing things and allowing amendments. The following Shuber case considers whether to modify what was the final pretrial order.

————

Identiseal Corp. v. Positive Identification Systems, Inc.

United States Court of Appeals, Seventh Circuit, 1977.
560 F.2d 298.

■ Before SWYGERT and BAUER, CIRCUIT JUDGES, and JAMESON, SENIOR DISTRICT JUDGE.[1]

■ SWYGERT, CIRCUIT JUDGE. The outcome of this appeal turns on whether the district court, in presiding over the pretrial phase of the case, had the power to compel plaintiff to conduct discovery instead of permitting it to litigate the entire suit at trial. We conclude that the district court lacked the authority to compel involuntary discovery and we reverse the court's order dismissing the complaint.

. . . .

On April 26, 1973, plaintiff Identiseal Corporation of Wisconsin filed a complaint against defendant Positive Identification Systems, Inc. in the district court for the Eastern District of Wisconsin. The complaint charged that defendant induced plaintiff to enter into a franchising agreement for the sale of a product known as "Identiseal"; that defendant represented to plaintiff that defendant was successful in the promotion of its products, causing plaintiff to invest $15,000 in defendant's products; and that in fact defendant was not successful in the promotion of its products. Plaintiff sought relief under a common law theory of misrepresentation and under Wisconsin statutes relating to franchising. Jurisdiction was based on diversity of citizenship.

After a delay caused by the death of plaintiff's attorney, the litigation proceeded and a final pretrial conference was held on February 26, 1976. On March 8, 1976, the district court issued an order in which it concluded "that the pretrial work necessary to efficiently try this action had not been done." It ordered that the action be dismissed for want of prosecution, but stayed the order until June 4, 1976 and stated that the order would be vacated if plaintiff's counsel had conducted specified discovery . . . by that date.[2]

---

[1]   The Honorable William J. Jameson, Senior District Judge for the District of Montana, is sitting by designation.

[2]   The court held that its order of dismissal would be vacated if plaintiff's counsel satisfied the following conditions:

     1. Counsel shall, by means of discovery such as written interrogatories, requests for production of documents, or requests for admissions, ascertain the identity of those persons who have knowledge of the facts relevant or material to the issues of this action and those documents containing information relevant or material to the issues of this action.

     2. Counsel shall then, by means of further discovery such as oral depositions or deposition on written questions, determine the actual knowledge of such persons disclosed as having knowledge of the facts. Counsel shall also, by means of requests for production of documents or requests for admissions, obtain copies of relevant documents not already within their possession.

. . . .

. . . Plaintiff's counsel [subsequently argued to no avail] that he had "made a considered judgment that discovery would in no way be beneficial to the plaintiff's interest and would at most be of some significant support or assistance to the defendant." He also asserted that the court had exceeded its authority under the Federal Rules of Civil Procedure in ordering plaintiff to conduct discovery or suffer dismissal of the complaint.

[Pursuant to the March 8 order the district court ultimately dismissed the action without prejudice, and the plaintiff appealed. The defendant had not moved for the March 8 order, but was willing to ride that order to judgment rather than pursue its own discovery.]

Discovery in lawsuits in the federal courts is governed by Rules 26 to 37 of the Federal Rules of Civil Procedure. Although these rules provide for judicial intervention to settle disputes about the scope of discovery and to enforce a legitimate request by one party for information or documents from the other party, they do not give district judges the authority to compel a litigant to engage in discovery in the first place.

Therefore, the district court's March 8 order can only be upheld if the court had the power, under its general authority over the pretrial phase of a lawsuit, to compel plaintiff to conduct discovery. Pretrial procedure in the district courts is governed by Fed.R.Civ.P. 16, which states in relevant part that "the court may in its discretion direct the attorneys for the parties to appear before it for a conference to consider . . . [t]he possibility of obtaining admissions of fact and of documents which will avoid unnecessary proof." Under the rule, "the court has wide discretion and power to advance the cause and simplify the procedure before the cause is presented to the jury." O'Malley v. Chrysler Corp., 160 F.2d 35, 36 (7th Cir.1947).

This discretion, however, is not unlimited. The language of the rule does not, by its terms, confer upon the court the power to *compel* the litigants to obtain admissions of fact and of documents even if it is clear that such admissions would simplify the trial of the case. Instead, the rule requires the parties to appear and *consider the possibility* of admissions which would lessen their task at trial.

We have recently decided a case in which we made clear that there are limitations on the district court's power at the pretrial conference. In J.F. Edwards Construction Co. v. Anderson Safeway Guard Rail Corp., 542 F.2d 1318 (7th Cir.1976) (per curiam), we held that a district court lacks the authority under Rule 16 to dismiss an action because one of the parties would not agree to a stipulation of facts. We noted that Rule 16 was noncoercive in nature, and we concluded that a dismissal based on a party's refusal to follow the trial judge's wishes expressed at the pretrial conference could only be upheld if that refusal could be characterized as a "failure to prosecute." Because the party that would not agree to the stipulation of facts was clearly not attempting to avoid trial, the district court's order could not stand.

In our judgment this appeal is controlled by J.F. Edwards. Like the appellant in J.F. Edwards, plaintiff in the case at bar did not engage in conduct that could be characterized as a failure to prosecute. Plaintiff was ready to go to trial, and simply disagreed with the district court about the desirability of eliminating the need to develop all of the facts at trial. Although we recognize that its order was based on a commendable desire to simplify the lawsuit, the court had no more authority under Rule 16 to command discovery than the district court in J.F. Edwards had to require a stipulation of facts. The limit of the court's power was to compel plaintiff to consider the possibility of conducting discovery,[7] and there is no evidence in the record that plaintiff's attorney rejected the district court's preferred method of litigating the action without giving it serious consideration.

Our decision is predicated on more than the absence of express authority in Rule 16 authorizing compulsory discovery. It is also based on the traditional principle that the parties, rather than the court, should determine litigation strategy. See Chayes, The Role of the Judge in Public Law Litigation, 89 Harv.L.Rev. 1281, 1283 (1976); Developments in the Law—Class Actions, 89 Harv.L.Rev. 1318, 1414 (1976). It was the judgment of plaintiff's attorney that his client's chances of prevailing would be maximized if he did not conduct discovery but instead developed his entire case at trial. We cannot say whether this decision was correct. We can say, however, that the decision was for plaintiff's attorney, and not the district court, to make.

The judgment of the district court is reversed and the cause is remanded for further proceedings consistent with this opinion.

––––––

Question: (78) Is Identiseal still good law under amended Rule 16? Is J.F. Edwards? Compare Strandell v. Jackson Cty., 838 F.2d 884 (7th Cir.1987) (in holding that Rule 16 does not permit district judge to compel a nonbinding summary jury trial as a pretrial device for encouraging settlement, the Seventh Circuit relied on Identiseal and J.F. Edwards), with G. Heileman Brewing Co. v. Joseph Oat Corp., 871 F.2d 648 (7th Cir.1989) (6–5 en banc decision) (while acknowledging Identiseal and J.F. Edwards, the Seventh Circuit held that district court has inherent power to order a represented party to attend a settlement conference in person, a power since recognized by amendment to Rule 16(c)(1)). Are Identiseal and J.F. Edwards still good law despite other Rule amendments, such as the continuing obligation under amended Rule 11 to make reasonable inquiry into the facts?

––––––

SHUBER v. S.S. KRESGE CO., 458 F.2d 1058 (3d Cir.1972), aff'g 55 F.R.D. 52 (W.D.Pa.1970). Wife-plaintiff brought a diversity action against Kresge in federal court for personal injuries, in which her

––––––––––––––––––––––

[7]   We note that our resolution of this issue is in conflict with the Third Circuit's decision in Buffington v. Wood, 351 F.2d 292 (3d Cir.1965). . . .

husband joined with a claim for her medical expenses and the loss of her services. The theory of recovery was that defendant had been negligent in installing or having installed a light fixture that fell upon wife-plaintiff while she was working for an independent concessionaire in defendant's store in 1965. As required by the local rule for pretrial procedure, plaintiffs set forth this theory in a narrative pretrial statement and also listed therein "plaintiff" (not "plaintiffs") as a witness on the issue of liability. There was no indication that husband-plaintiff, an electrician by trade, was to testify concerning the fixture.

At trial around the beginning of 1970, plaintiffs' evidence, including wife-plaintiff's testimony, pointed to the contention that the fixture had been negligently installed by an electrical subcontractor to the construction company employed by Kresge's landlord. But the evidence failed to connect Kresge with the negligence. Kresge moved for judgment as a matter of law at the close of plaintiffs' case. After argument on the motion, plaintiffs moved for leave to reopen to call a witness not listed in the pretrial statement. Their counsel announced that he intended to call husband-plaintiff to testify that Kresge itself installed the ceiling tiles and, in doing so, disconnected the light fixtures and reinstalled them negligently. Defendant objected to the complete change of the theory of liability. Wife-plaintiff had testified on deposition that her husband had no knowledge of the facts of the accident, and he had been present throughout the trial without any suggestion that he had such evidence to offer.

The trial judge referred to the statement in Washington Hospital Center v. Cheeks, 394 F.2d 964, 965 (D.C.Cir.1968) (Burger, J., who became U.S. Chief Justice in 1969), that liberal modification of pretrial orders encourages careless preparation but that an unbending attitude may work grave injustice. In that case, a medical malpractice action against a hospital, the testimony as to causation on defendant's cross-examination of plaintiff's attending physician genuinely surprised plaintiff's counsel, who sought leave the next day to offer an expert medical witness not on the pretrial list. The district court modified the final pretrial order and let the expert testify the following day, first giving defendant a chance to depose him. Defendant did not request a longer continuance or mistrial, but took the deposition and sought only to exclude the new testimony. The expert's testimony supported plaintiff's claim, and verdict and judgment were for plaintiff. The Court of Appeals for the District of Columbia Circuit held that there had been no abuse of discretion by the district judge, who was in a superior position to evaluate the situation.

Nevertheless, the trial judge here refused to allow the Shubers to reopen their case and granted defendant's motion for judgment, saying that the "Court has an interest to support the integrity of its pretrial procedures. The Pretrial Order in the case binds and limits the parties to what they have presented and revealed in their Pretrial Narratives and at the Pretrial Conference. Neither at the Pretrial Conference, nor in the trial was this new line of evidence suggested. We must either require adherence to our Pretrial Rules or abandon them utterly in this case. We think that the interests of the efficient administration of justice require their enforcement."

The Court of Appeals for the Third Circuit affirmed, expressing itself as thoroughly in accord with the trial judge's quoted statement. The court of appeals commented that counsel's inadequate prosecution of his plaintiff-clients' cause "would appear to be in violation of the Code of Professional Responsibility of the American Bar Association requiring a lawyer to represent his client competently and zealously within the bounds of the law."

———

Question: (79) A complaint alleged that *P* and *D* had entered into an oral partnership to sell certain oil-well drilling equipment on commission, that they were to divide equally any commission, and that *D* had received a commission of over $39,000 but had paid *P* only $3000. The answer denied any partnership, and stated that *P* had demanded a portion of the commission for services performed in the sale and that *D* had paid *P* $3000 in full settlement of *P*'s claim. The final pretrial order included agreement as to the amount of the commission and the amount paid to *P,* and it recited that the only matter of controversy for determination by the jury was whether a partnership existed. At trial the judge charged the jury on the question of partnership without any objection, but at the end of the charge the judge refused a request to instruct on the issue of compromise settlement on the ground that it was not within the pretrial order. Should the appellate court sustain *D*'s appeal from this refusal? See Case v. Abrams, 352 F.2d 193 (10th Cir.1965) (no). Should it matter that *D*'s proof in support of the compromise settlement had been admitted without objection? Of what relevance is Rule 15(b)(2)? See Monod v. Futura, Inc., 415 F.2d 1170 (10th Cir.1969) (suggesting that Rule 15(b)(2) applies to Rule 16(e) by analogy, if amender makes adequate showing of issue's trial by consent).

———

MAGISTRATE JUDGES AND MASTERS

Rule 16(c) mentions two principal kinds of parajudges in the federal system.

Congress created the corps of magistrates in 1968 and has since expanded their jurisdiction several times. See 28 U.S.C. § 636 and Rules 72 and 73. Magistrate judges are salaried judicial officers appointed for an eight-year term, a number being appointed for each district by the district judges of that district. They number more than 500 nationwide. In addition to a good deal of criminal work, magistrate judges exercise the following civil jurisdiction:

1.   a district judge may designate a magistrate judge to hear and determine any so-called nondispositive pretrial matter, examples being discovery disputes and pretrial conferences; the district judge will consider any party's objections to the magistrate judge's determination, setting aside any portion shown to be clearly erroneous or to be contrary to law;

2.   a district judge may designate a magistrate judge to conduct hearings, make proposed findings of fact when appropriate, and recommend disposition with respect to a so-called dispositive pretrial matter, an example being a motion for summary judgment; the district judge must make a de novo determination (upon the record or after additional evidence) on those portions of the magistrate judge's findings and recommendation that any party objects to;

3.   a district judge may designate a magistrate judge to serve as a special master, a role explained below;

4.   upon consent of all the parties, the court clerk may refer to a specially designated magistrate judge all proceedings in any case, including trial of a jury or nonjury case and entry of judgment; appeal from the magistrate judge's judgment goes to the appropriate court of appeals; and

5.   district judges may assign to a magistrate judge "such additional duties as are not inconsistent with the Constitution and laws of the United States."

Although this procedural innovation has enjoyed heavy use in many districts and with many district judges, and proved generally successful, the broad extent of the magistrate judges' jurisdiction raises some unsettled constitutional questions of due process and separation of powers. See generally Tim A. Baker, The Expanding Role of Magistrate Judges in the Federal Courts, 39 Val.U.L.Rev. 661 (2005).

The use of masters has ancient roots, and Rule 53 continues to authorize that use while limiting and regulating it. Today the only kind of master is what was formerly called a special master, i.e., someone specially appointed by the district judge to help handle a particular action. The judge supposedly can appoint a master only upon the parties' consent or in complicated cases where there is exceptional need, and the master must assist rather than displace the judge. The judge gives the master specific assignments, traditionally most often involving ascertainment of facts in nonjury cases but today also involving an impressive range of pretrial and posttrial tasks. Ultimately, the master files a report with the judge, and the master's factual findings as well as his legal conclusions are normally subject to de novo review by the judge. The master's compensation, fixed by the judge, falls on the parties upon terms directed by the judge. See generally David R. Cohen, The Judge, the Special Master, and You, Litigation, Summer 2014, at 32.

Question: (80) Can a question of propriety ever arise as to whether the pretrial judge should preside at the trial? For context, you should be aware that the now commonly prevailing "individual assignment system" randomly assigns a case to a federal judge for all purposes; thus as a usual matter under the typical local scheme, the same judge will sit in pretrial and at trial, unless that judge decides that it would be proper to delegate a pretrial task to a parajudge or, eventually, to shift the case itself to another judge.

———

(h) DEVICES FOR TERMINATING LITIGATION WITHOUT TRIAL

[Rules 12(c) and (f), 56]

We have already seen a number of ways in which a case may terminate short of trial. For example, if defendant presents by motion under Rule 12(b)(6) the defense that the complaint fails to state a claim, and the court grants the motion, and plaintiff does not thereafter manage to amend the complaint, then the case is ripe for a judgment for defendant.

Question: (81) In what other ways may a case terminate short of trial? See Rules 41 and 55.

Motion for judgment on the pleadings.—We call attention now to another device that may conclude the case without trial. Rule 12(c) provides for a motion for judgment on the pleadings. A party can make this motion after the pleadings are closed, and it asserts that upon the pleadings the moving party is entitled to judgment in his favor. In deciding it, the court can resolve only questions of law, not contests as to facts.

For purposes of the Rule 12(c) motion, the moving party admits his adversary's allegations, but his own allegations stand as true only if his adversary's pleading has admitted them. A motion for judgment on the pleadings by defendant rather than by plaintiff ordinarily challenges the sufficiency of the complaint only, just as does a motion under Rule 12(b)(6). It invokes Twombly-Iqbal. But it takes on no added strength by reason of one or more affirmative defenses in the answer. For, as we have seen, the allegations of such defenses are taken as denied or avoided under Rule 8(b)(6).

Question: (82) P files a complaint attempting to allege defamation. D answers, admitting P's factual allegations and attempting to assert the defense of immunity by an allegation that the statement in question was pertinently uttered in the course of judicial proceedings. D moves for judgment on the pleadings. What are the facts for purposes of the motion? What legal issues does the motion raise? P also moves for judgment on the

P's factual allegation was admitted by D)

pleadings at the same point. What are the facts for purposes of this motion? What legal issues does this motion raise?

Suppose the complaint adequately alleges a claim, and the answer admits the allegations of the complaint but sets up two purported affirmative defenses with new allegations of facts. If one but not both of the defenses is insufficient as a matter of law, a timely motion by plaintiff lies under Rule 12(f) to strike that defense; the court's grant of that motion will eliminate the insufficient defense, but the case will then stand for trial on the other defense. If both defenses are insufficient as matters of law, plaintiff may move for judgment on the pleadings. However, if defendant, besides setting up the two insufficient defenses, had denied in her answer material allegations of the complaint, the court would have to deny plaintiff's motion for judgment on the pleadings, although it might grant a motion under Rule 12(f) to strike the affirmative defenses.

Question: (83) Suppose in the preceding question's defamation case that, instead of admitting *P*'s factual allegations, *D* denies them and also attempts to assert the defense of immunity. *D*'s motion is unaffected. But what relief can *P* get if the immunity defense is insufficient as a matter of law? In what manner may *P* pursue that relief? Does it matter how much time has elapsed since service of *D*'s answer?

Thus, the plaintiff can use the Rule 12(f) motion to strike an insufficient defense to challenge the legal sufficiency of a defense. Such a motion to strike, if granted, will dispose of a question of law in advance of trial and may significantly simplify the trial. But courts show reluctance to strike a defense as insufficient. If the defense presents a question of law that the court can better determine in the context of facts proved at trial, the court plainly should not strike it. Yet there are many cases involving a purely legal question where the court strangely says that its function on a motion to strike is not to determine disputed questions of law.

Motion for summary judgment.—The motion for judgment on the pleadings is available where a pleading is legally insufficient. But must there necessarily be a trial whenever the pleadings show a disputed issue of fact, either by an actual denial of an adversary's allegation or through the operation of Rule 8(b)(6)?

If so, the system could not deliver "the just, speedy, and inexpensive determination of every action" set forth as the ideal in Rule 1. In certain district courts, the trial list for civil cases is in such a congested condition that the median lapse of time between the filing of an answer and a trial on the merits is over two years. A defendant against whom the plaintiff has asserted a just claim is likely to want to put off the day of reckoning as long as possible: there is thus a temptation, despite Rule 11, to file an answer with denials or affirmative defenses for purposes of delay, even though the defendant knows that certain defeat awaits at trial. Similarly, a plaintiff may assert a baseless claim in vain hope or in order to extort.

To prevent such behavior, Rule 56 on "summary judgment" provides a means of going behind the pleadings to see whether there really is a genuine dispute as to any material fact. If there is not, there is no occasion for a trial, and so the case is ripe for a successful motion for summary judgment. Such a motion may be filed by either a plaintiff or a defendant in any type of case. The motion may be made even before the pleadings are closed, but ordinarily only until thirty days after the close of all discovery.

The court may grant a summary judgment on the entire case or on only a part of it. For example, the court may grant summary judgment on the issue of liability alone, although a genuine dispute on the amount of damages remains. Furthermore, upon motion for summary judgment the court may specify that certain facts are not genuinely in dispute, thus narrowing the issues for trial in a way somewhat similar to the pretrial procedure under Rule 16.

On a summary judgment motion, the movant maintains that there is no genuine dispute of material fact and that, upon resolution of any disputed questions of law, he is entitled to judgment. The movant must show the absence of factual dispute by citing specifically to the record for support of the movant's view of the facts. See Rule 56(c)(1). Ordinarily the movant will accompany the motion with affidavits (of the movant or of others) in support of the contention that there is no genuine dispute over fact. The affidavits may incorporate exhibits; the affidavits must be on the personal knowledge of the affiants; and the contents of the affidavits must be such as would be admissible in evidence. The opposing party may file like counter-affidavits. On the motion the court will also consider the pleadings—and normally will consider depositions, answers to interrogatories, documents, admissions, and similar material on file, to the extent they represent admissible evidence.

Question: (84) Recall that Rule 32(a)(1) speaks of the use of a deposition not only at trial, but also upon the hearing of a motion. Can the court apply Rule 32 according to its terms when it uses depositions upon a motion for summary judgment under Rule 56(c)? (You should renew this question after reading the next case.)

If the movant's affidavits convincingly maintain that there is no genuine factual dispute but the opponent then contests that point by counter-affidavits, the judge faces a subtlety. This subtlety has generated the following standard of decision: the judge can agree with the movant that no genuine dispute exists as to a particular factual matter only if a reasonable trier of fact could not find for the opponent on that matter.

Under this standard of decision, in a medical malpractice case where the plaintiff is contending that under the law the claim accrued on the date of discovery of the harm and the defendant is contending that it accrued on the date of the surgery, a defendant could obtain summary judgment on a statute-of-limitations defense if the judge decides that legally the time of accrual is the date of the surgery and if, given the detailed affidavits for the defendant and given the plaintiff's lack of any statement as to the date of surgery, a trier could not reasonably find that the operation took place within the three-year statutory limitations period preceding the action's commencement.

Bear in mind, however, that a motion for summary judgment is not a means of trying questions of fact upon conflicting affidavits. The function of the court on this motion is to determine whether there is a genuine factual dispute, not to resolve a genuine factual dispute found to exist. Hence, if on the motion the judge encounters a genuine factual dispute, he must deny the motion even though he has strong ground for the belief that one set of affidavits is true and the other false.

Thus, the defendant in the medical malpractice case could not obtain summary judgment on a statute-of-limitations defense if under the law the time of accrual is the date of the discovery of the harm and if, given conflicting affidavits, a trier deciding within the outer bounds of reason could go either way on whether that discovery date came within the three-year statutory limitations period preceding the action's commencement. Likewise, the plaintiff could not obtain summary judgment.

Question: (85) May a judge ever grant summary judgment when the case is of a type in which trial by jury is constitutionally guaranteed and proper demand for a jury has been made?

American Airlines v. Ulen

United States Court of Appeals, District of Columbia Circuit, 1949.
186 F.2d 529.

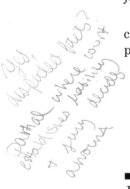

■ Before [Bennett] Clark, Wilbur K. Miller, and Prettyman, Judges.

■ Clark, Judge. Appellant, American Airlines, Inc., a certified carrier engaged in the business of transporting passengers for hire, separately appeals from two final judgments of the District Court. The appeal in No. 9921 attacks the judgment based upon a jury verdict for $25,000 in favor of appellee, Violet Ulen, for personal injuries and property damage. The appeal in No. 9922 was taken from a judgment based on a jury verdict for $2,500 in favor of appellee, Francis Graeme Ulen, husband of Violet Ulen, for medical and other expenses resulting from his wife's injuries and for loss of her services. These two appeals were consolidated for the purpose of filing briefs and for hearing and decision by order of this court dated July 24, 1948. Accordingly, this opinion shall dispose of both appeals.

At about midnight on February 22–23, 1945, Violet Ulen boarded appellant's plane at Washington National Airport with a ticket entitling her to transportation to Mexico City, Mexico. The plane took off from

Washington at 12:15 A.M. on February 23, 1945. At approximately 2:25 A.M. that morning, appellant's plane, with Violet Ulen aboard, crashed close to the summit of Glade Mountain near the town of Rural Retreat in Southwest Virginia. The crash, in which both the pilot and the co-pilot of the plane lost their lives, resulted, admittedly, in very serious and aggravated injury to Violet Ulen and in her permanent partial disability.

On January 11, 1946, the Ulens both filed complaints in the District Court alleging that their injuries and losses directly resulted from the negligence of agents of the appellant in carelessly planning and approving the flight and in unskillfully operating the plane. The complaint filed by Violet Ulen sought recovery in the amount of $257,500. Mr. Ulen's complaint asked for $50,000 in damages. Appellant carrier answered both complaints by admitting the facts alleged but denying that the injuries were caused by its negligence and disclaiming any knowledge of the extent of Violet Ulen's injuries. Thereupon the Ulens served a set of 55 interrogatories on appellant and these were answered in detail by appellant. The Ulens then filed motions for summary judgment in their favor and to impanel a jury for the purpose of determining damages. As grounds for these motions the Ulens asserted that the pleadings together with the carrier's answers to the interrogatories demonstrated that there was no genuine issue as to any material fact except as to damages. After these motions for summary judgment came on for oral argument in the court below, appellant carrier filed a motion for leave to amend its answers to the complaints by including additional defenses. At the same time appellant filed its opposition to the motions for summary judgment. On July 14, 1947, Judge Morris entered a memorandum opinion in which he indicated his intention of granting the motions for summary judgment in favor of the Ulens, but in which he also indicated that decision on the motions would be continued in order to allow the filing by the carrier of an amended answer. A court order to that effect was entered below and appellant filed its amended answer which added the additional [affirmative] defense that Violet Ulen was a passenger in international transportation within the purview of the Warsaw Convention,[1] and hence that total recovery, if any, is limited thereby to the sum of $8,291.87.[2]

On November 12, 1947, the motions for summary judgment were granted and the cases were assigned for inquisition by a jury as to the amount of damages. The court expressly reserved the defense based upon the Warsaw Convention for disposition . . . at the time of such inquisition. In April, 1948, the two cases were tried together before a jury. Defendant-appellant moved for directed verdicts both at the close of plaintiffs' case and at the close of all the evidence, but said motions were overruled. The

---

[1]   49 Stat. (Part 2) 3000 (1929).

[2]   Under Article 22 of the Warsaw Convention the liability of the carrier for each passenger was limited to the sum of 125,000 francs. It is agreed by the parties to this appeal that the figure above is the equivalent, in United States currency, of $8,291.87.

jury then returned verdicts for Violet Ulen in the amount of $25,000 and for her husband in the amount of $2,500 and judgments thereon were entered. Following the denial of various other motions of the carrier, separate appeals were taken from those judgments.

Appellant raises two major issues on these appeals which shall be dealt with separately herein. First, appellant asserts that plaintiff-appellees were not entitled to summary judgment. Second, it is vigorously urged that, if there is any liability at all, it is definitely limited in amount by the applicable provisions of the Warsaw Convention.

Appellant's first point is that summary judgment was erroneously granted and to its great prejudice, because the *pleadings* (that is, the complaint alleging negligence and the answer as amended denying any negligence) raised genuine issues as to material facts which could only have been properly determined by a trial on the merits. Thus far, we have no difficulty in agreeing with appellant and, in fact, appellees concede that this contention, so far as it goes, is correct. However, it is vitally significant that *before* summary judgment was granted the trial judge had before him not only the complaint and the answer as amended but also the 55 interrogatories of plaintiffs and all of defendant's detailed, sworn answers thereto as well as a lengthy "Defendant's Brief in Opposition to Motion for Summary Judgment." . . .

The answers to the interrogatories which Judge Morris had before him in this case show undeniably that appellant was negligent. The answers show that appellant's authorized and experienced agents planned, agreed upon, and were in the process of executing, a flight plan which called for the plane to fly at an altitude of 4000 feet on the leg of the flight on which the accident occurred (Pulaski to Tri-City). From the flight log kept by the pilot during this particular flight it is clear that he was following this flight plan up to the time of his last entry. The last radio contact with the plane while in flight was received at 2:05 A.M. (about 20 minutes before the crash) when the pilot reported his altitude as 4000 feet. At the time this flight was planned and flown there was in effect a Civil Air Regulation [No. 61.7401] promulgated by the Civil Aeronautics Board which read as follows:

"No scheduled air carrier aircraft shall be flown at an altitude of less than 1000 feet above the highest obstacle located within a horizontal distance of 5 miles from the center of the course intended to be flown . . . ."

The answers to the interrogatories show further that appellant's plane crashed at an elevation of 3910 feet near the summit of Glade Mountain which was located near the center of Green Airway No. 5, a strip ten miles wide over which the plane was scheduled to, and did, fly. The answers admit that a certain chart apparently in appellant's possession indicates that "the terrain [Glade Mountain] is more than 3500 ft. high but less than 4000 ft. above sea level."

We have no difficulty in finding, as did the lower court, that negligence and proximate cause were sufficiently established so as to justify entry of summary judgment in favor of appellees subject only to a determination of the amount of damages and the applicability of the Warsaw Convention.

Appellant's second major contention is that, because of the applicability of the Warsaw Convention, appellant's liability is limited to the sum of $8,291.87. This Convention, to which the United States was not a signatory but to which, pursuant to Presidential Proclamation, this country adheres, applies to "all international transportation of persons, baggage, or goods performed by aircraft for hire." In the view which we take of this case it is unnecessary for this court to decide whether or not the Convention applies since the result would be the same either way. Assuming, without deciding, that the Convention does apply here, we are of the opinion that one of the Articles of the Convention itself precludes appellant's claim of limited liability in this case. Article 25(1) of the Convention as it appears in the official translation from the original French reads as follows:

"The carrier shall not be entitled to avail himself of the provisions of this convention which exclude or limit his liability, *if the damage is caused by his wilful misconduct or by such default on his part as, in accordance with the law of the court to which the case is submitted, is considered to be equivalent to wilful misconduct.*" (Emphasis supplied.)

The words "wilful misconduct" as they twice appear in the language quoted above were represented in the original French of the Convention by the word "dol." Appellant vigorously urges that the word "dol" was improperly translated and that properly translated it means "fraud" or "deceit." As we understand appellant's argument, the carrier must be guilty of well-nigh criminal intent before Article 25(1) has application. Stated somewhat differently, it is appellant's claim that its liability, if any, is limited unless it can be successfully shown that the pilot, or other agents of appellant, with malicious or felonious intent, planned to fly the plane into the mountain to the injury of its passengers. We cannot agree that the language of Article 25 quoted above goes, or was intended to go, this far.

Appellant has gone to the trouble of having translated (by a translator of its own selection) a portion of the official minutes of the Conference which later formulated the Convention. We see nothing in these minutes which would justify a holding that the official translation of "dol" into "wilful misconduct" is incorrect. Those minutes show little more than that the delegates were at the time in disagreement as to what terms would express their intent when translated into various languages. In fact, one statement by an English delegate to the Conference lends force to appellees' claim that the term is properly translated. That delegate said: "We have in English the expression 'wilful misconduct'. I think that it covers all that you want to say; it covers not only the acts accomplished deliberately, but also of insouciance, without concern for the consequences."

We, therefore, see no basis for questioning the correctness of the official translation as quoted above. The problem thus becomes one of deciding whether the trial judge properly applied the "law of the court to which the case is submitted" when, in his charge to the jury he said as follows:

"Now, wilful misconduct is not, as I have said, merely misconduct, but wilful misconduct. So if the carrier, or its employees or agents, wilfully performed any act with the knowledge that the performance of that act was likely to result in injury to a passenger, or performed that act with reckless and wanton disregard of its probable consequences, then that would constitute wilful misconduct; and if the result of that wilful misconduct was injury to Mrs. Ulen, then her recovery would not be limited by this sum of some eight thousand dollars.

. . . .

"Now, the mere violation of those [safety rules and regulations], . . . even if intentional, would not necessarily constitute wilful misconduct, but if the violation was intentional with knowledge that the violation was likely to cause injury to a passenger, then that would be wilful misconduct, and likewise, if it was done with a wanton and reckless disregard of the consequences."

We are of the opinion that this charge to the jury was substantially correct and that there was ample evidence upon which the jury could base its verdict, finding appellant guilty of wilful misconduct. One recent federal court decision defines the term as follows: " 'Wilful misconduct' means a deliberate purpose not to discharge some duty necessary to safety."[15] This definition squarely fits the facts in the instant case. The obvious and sole purpose of Civil Air Regulation 61.7401, supra, is safety. It imposed a duty upon all scheduled carriers which appellant deliberately, knowingly and intentionally violated. Appellant attempts to excuse itself by stating that the "center of the course intended to be flown" is not the same as the center of the airway and by arguing that it was possible for the airplane, by zigzagging first to the right of the airlane and then to the left, to fly at 4000 feet and still more than five miles distant from and 1000 feet above the highest obstacle and thereby comply, appellant says, with Regulation 61.7401. We need not pass upon the technical distinction between "center of the course" and "center of the airway," because, even adopting appellant's theory, the evidence clearly establishes a deliberate violation of the safety regulation.

---

[15] Circuit Judge Minton in Rowe v. Gatke Corporation, 7 Cir., 1942, 126 F.2d 61, 66. [A later and more complete definition of wilful misconduct's dual requirements in the Warsaw Convention context comes from Bayer Corp. v. British Airways, LLC, 210 F.3d 236, 238 (4th Cir.2000): "Negligence will not suffice, nor even recklessness judged objectively. Rather, a plaintiff must show that a defendant either intended to cause the damage or acted recklessly with *subjective* knowledge that the damage would probably result."—Ed.]

The flight plan, drawn up, approved, and partially executed by appellant's admittedly experienced and otherwise qualified personnel, indicates that the "course intended to be flown" by this plane from Pulaski to Tri-City (the leg of the flight on which the accident occurred) was 246 degrees magnetic. The aeronautical chart introduced in evidence at the trial shows Glade Mountain to be 4080 feet in elevation and lying very close to the center of the *airway* over which this plane was to fly. That chart also shows clearly that a plane proceeding at an altitude of 4000 feet from Pulaski toward Tri-City on a magnetic bearing of 246 degrees—*the course intended to be flown*—would pass *within 1½ miles, or at most 2 miles, from Glade Mountain, a mountain 4080 feet high!* Under these circumstances, it requires no stretch of the imagination whatever to visualize what *could* happen and what *did* happen in this case. Appellant's case is only weakened by its proof that the same pilot had flown this same route in the same manner several times before. This is only evidence of deliberateness and full knowledge which renders appellant's actions the more reprehensible. One further fact of record cannot escape note. In appellant's answers to the interrogatories it made the astonishing admission that "we do not know the official elevation of Glade Mountain." From the foregoing it is evident that wilful misconduct in planning and executing this flight has been completely and conclusively shown in this case. Finally, there is nothing in either the flight plan or the flight log of this plane to show that the zigzag course, which appellant now argues would safely carry the plane through the mountains in compliance with Regulation 61.7401, was ever contemplated or attempted in the case of this flight. The fact that there might have been a safe way to fly this flight over this route cannot help this appellant where all the evidence of record shows indisputably that an obviously unsafe method was employed and planned.

It follows that the Warsaw Convention, by its own terms, is inapplicable and does not operate to limit appellant's liability in these cases.[r] Both judgments appealed from in these cases must be, and are hereby

---

[r]   On or after September 28, 1955, a good number of countries including the United States signed the Hague Protocol. This was a new treaty incorporating important amendments to the Warsaw Convention. The Protocol doubled the Convention's limitation on liability for personal injury or death to passengers. However, the Protocol eliminated the Convention's reference to "dol" or "wilful misconduct," and instead provided that the limitation on liability was not to apply "if it is proved that the damage resulted from an act or omission of the carrier, his servants or agents, done with intent to cause damage or recklessly and with knowledge that damage would probably result." Although in force elsewhere, the Protocol was not ratified by the United States.

On November 15, 1965, the United States gave notice of "denunciation" of the Warsaw Convention (meaning withdrawal in accordance with the terms of the Convention), emphasizing that such action was solely because of the Convention's low limitation on liability. The notice was to become effective six months later. Within that period, the International Air Transport Association made efforts to effect an arrangement among domestic and foreign air carriers that would raise the limitation and provide a basis upon which the United States could rescind its notice of denunciation. The result was the so-called Montreal Agreement among numerous

Affirmed.

────────

One could disagree with the appellate court's view of the record. American Airlines had a decent argument, although its counsel failed to express it very clearly even on appeal. The argument ran that the evidence showed the pilot was probably flying not on instruments but by Contact Flight Rules, whereby the pilot would maneuver the plane by simple adjustments of direction to maintain the appropriate five-mile distance from terrestrial obstacles as the pilot flew visually from flight beacon to flight beacon; that the bearing given in the flight plan, which contemplated a CFR flight, properly was only an indication of the general direction of the flight, and therefore the center of the airway was not "the course intended to be flown"; that it was for the pilot in flight to decide whether circumstances warranted sticking with CFR, which was a routine and acceptable practice and, under certain higher-altitude weather conditions, would be the most prudent course for this particular flight; and that the crash could have resulted from a nonnegligent cause such as the unexpected squall that blew through the area that night at the right time and in the right direction and could have pushed the airplane miles off course. Actually, the airline's interrogatory answers implied this argument and its witnesses so testified explicitly at trial, and the plaintiffs offered no evidence to refute this theory of how *the appellant had not violated the Civil Air Regulation.* If the appellate court had so understood the appellant's argument, would its decision have changed on either of the two issues before it?

──────────────────────────

carriers by which they bound themselves to include in their tariffs a special contract providing for liability regardless of fault up to $75,000 per passenger. There was no change in the wilful misconduct exception to limited liability. This contract was to be applicable to international transportation that included a place in the United States as a point of origin, point of destination, or agreed stopping place. Thereupon, the United States officially rescinded its notice of denunciation of the Convention.

Since then, on March 8, 1971, in Guatemala City and on September 25, 1975, in Montreal, the United States and other countries signed controversial new treaties in an attempt to amend further the Warsaw Convention. These treaties provided for no-fault liability of the airline up to approximately $100,000 per passenger, with the possibility of a country's imposing supplemental mandatory insurance coverage. However, there was to be no exception, on wilful misconduct or other grounds, to this limited liability. Of these treaties, the United States ratified only Montreal Protocol No. 4, by which, as of March 4, 1999, the United States finally adhered to the old Hague Protocol and its defined exception to limited liability.

Meanwhile, the IATA was taking steps to get the airlines unilaterally to eliminate the cap on liability. It adopted the Intercarrier Agreement on Passenger Liability on October 31, 1995, in Malaysia, by which the airlines would "take action to waive the limitation on liability." By subsequent IATA agreements, effective January 1, 1997, there was strict liability of the airline up to about $140,000 per passenger and, further, there was full compensation unless the airline could prove the absence of fault on its part.

Finally, activity shifted back to the treaty front, culminating in the Montreal Convention of May 28, 1999. It replaces the Warsaw Convention and adopts the above-stated terms of the IATA Intercarrier Agreements. After the United States ratified it, it went into force on November 4, 2003. The limit on strict liability was adjusted for inflation in 2009 to about $170,000.

In any event, Mrs. Ulen died in 1979. Her obituary in the Washington Post, Sept. 24, 1979, at C4, recounted the crash:

"Mrs. Ulen later recalled for reporters that it was snowing, and she did not move for some time because when she first tried to move she had disturbed a badly injured Marine Corps colonel. 'He begged me to shoot him,' Mrs. Ulen said. 'The colonel died about daybreak,' she went on, 'then I dug myself out of the wreckage.'

"After trying to find her shoes, she gave up, and began a barefoot seven-hour trek over mountainous terrain in an effort to find aid for the other survivors. She was discovered by a farmer who helped her to a phone to call for help.

"According to newspaper accounts at the time, Mrs. Ulen accomplished this even though she herself was suffering from a fractured collar bone, broken ribs, and assorted cuts as a result of the crash.

"Her search for help resulted in additional injuries, including frostbitten hands and feet, and torn ankle ligaments. During the three months she spent in the hospital, it also was discovered that she had a brain concussion, according to later newspaper stories.

"Mrs. Ulen was awarded a bronze medal by the Carnegie Hero Fund Commission of Pittsburgh and honored by the Commission for 'risking her life to save others.' She was one of five persons to survive the crash."

Questions: (86) How did the plaintiffs in the American Airlines case go about proving to the jury the defendant's "wilful misconduct"? Could they have relied simply on the answers to interrogatories? *through interrogatories*

(87) Would you expect courts often to grant summary judgment in favor of plaintiffs in actions based on charges of negligence?

(88) What did the district court in the American Airlines case accomplish by granting summary judgment as to liability?

In your mind, try to pin down the standard of decision applicable upon a motion for summary judgment. The motion can be granted only if the judge believes that a reasonable factfinder could not find for the opponent. When determining whether there is a reasonable dispute in this sense, the court construes all factual matters in the light reasonably most favorable to the party opposing the motion and then asks whether reasonable minds could differ as to the fact's existence. Overwhelming evidence could remove all reasonable doubt from disputes existing on the face of the pleadings, but it is said that summary judgment cannot reach disputes that turn on credibility.

As a practical matter, it is easiest to rely on lack of proof and so obtain summary judgment against the party who will have to prove some key fact at trial. The burden of proof at trial often falls on the plaintiff, so think of a summary judgment motion by the typical defendant. The moving defendant might preliminarily show, by citing specifically to the record, that the plaintiff will be unable to produce admissible evidence to support the fact. Then, the plaintiff cannot rely on her pleading allegations, but must respond with sufficient support of the fact, see Rule 56(e), or a justification for postponement, see Rule 56(d), to avoid summary judgment.

The Supreme Court elaborated this shifting of burdens with regard to summary judgment in Celotex Corp. v. Catrett, 477 U.S. 317, 106 S.Ct. 2548 (1986), one of the most cited cases of all time and one described in David L. Shapiro, "The Story of Celotex: The Role of Summary Judgment in the Administration of Civil Justice," in Civil Procedure Stories 359 (Kevin M. Clermont ed., 2d ed. 2008). The Court confirmed that the movant ultimately has the burden of persuasion that summary judgment should be granted to him, by showing that no genuine issue exists and the substantive law favors him. However, if the movant supports his motion sufficiently to make a prima facie showing that summary judgment should be granted on the basis of what is then before the court, the opponent normally cannot rest upon her pleading but instead must produce a real response or suffer summary judgment. So, if a defendant moves by specifically describing the basis of the motion and demonstrating the absence of evidence in the record on an element of the plaintiff's claim, the plaintiff cannot hold back her evidence but instead must respond to the motion by showing that there will be enough evidence on the element at trial to allow a reasonable factfinder to decide for the plaintiff.

In your opinion, has the Rule, so interpreted, struck the right balance between providing open access and ending hopeless cases?

———

SCOTT v. HARRIS, 550 U.S. 372, 127 S.Ct. 1769 (2007). Just three weeks before Bell Atlantic Corp. v. Twombly, the Supreme Court stepped in to encourage use of summary judgment as another way for judges to short-circuit litigation, with the Court taking a very activist role in drawing inferences from the record in order to reverse a denial of summary judgment.

The case was a civil rights action complaining of the conduct of a police officer in pursuing an automobile, which he had clocked at 73 mph in a 55-mph zone. The officer ultimately bumped the car, causing it to crash and thereby grievously injuring the plaintiff driver. The plaintiff invoked the Fourth Amendment as requiring the police behavior to be objectively reasonable, and so the defendant's summary judgment motion boiled down to whether as a matter of law the defendant could defeat a finding of violation of the Fourth Amendment. The Supreme Court, after viewing a videotape of the chase (available at http://www.youtube.com/watch?v=qrVKSgRZ2GY), held on the key factual issue that the plaintiff's conduct posed a risk of imminent harm to others. That is, the plaintiff's "version of events is so utterly discredited by the record that no reasonable jury could have believed him."

Justice Stevens, the sole dissenter, objected to "this unprecedented departure from our well-settled standard." He contended that the videotape "surely does not provide a principled basis for depriving [Harris] of his right to" trial. Indeed, he found the video ambiguous. "In my judgment, jurors in Georgia should be allowed to evaluate the reasonableness of the decision to ram respondent's speeding vehicle in a manner that created an obvious risk of death and has in fact made him a quadriplegic at the age of 19."

———

The Scott Court seemed to rely on logic and anecdote when reining in the perceived excesses of today's litigation, rather than on an accurate sense of how often parties were making and winning summary judgment motions. By contrast, the Federal Judicial Center has released the premier published study of summary judgment. Joe S. Cecil, Rebecca N. Eyre, Dean Miletich & David Rindskopf, A Quarter-Century of Summary Judgment Practice in Six Federal District Courts, 4 J.Empirical Legal Stud. 861 (2007). That study looked at a sample of federal civil cases (excluding prisoner, Social Security, and benefit repayment cases) in six districts from 1975 to 2000. While emphasizing that summary judgment practice varies considerably with locale and case type, it found overall that the percentage of cases involving one or more summary judgment motions increased from 12% in fiscal year 1975 to 20% in calendar year 2000; the court granted such a motion in full or in part in 6% and 12%, in those respective years, of all cases in the sample; and grant of summary judgment resulted in termination of 3.7% and 7.8%, respectively, of all cases in the sample. It suggested that the modern ascendancy of summary judgment dates from the upswing in the late 1970s of judicial case management and its emphasis on motion practice. Incidentally, among all the summary judgment motions over the whole time period studied, viewed on a motion level rather than a case level, 72% were motions by defendants (with about half granted in full or in part), while 28% were plaintiffs' motions (with an analogous success rate of about a third).

Thus, summary judgment is an important procedural device on the modern scene, especially for defendants. Yet it is doubtful that the peculiar Scott case will have a general impact in further raising the rate of granting these motions. See Tolan v. Cotton, 572 U.S. 650, 134 S.Ct. 1861 (2014) (per curiam) (reverting to the traditional standard that a judge on summary judgment is not to weigh the evidence but merely to determine whether there is a genuine dispute for trial).

Interchangeability of motion for summary judgment and motion for judgment on the pleadings.—It is clear under Rule 56 that if the moving party is legally entitled to judgment solely based on the pleadings, unassisted by affidavits or other factual materials, the court should give summary judgment in his favor. Correspondingly, Rule 12(d) states that if on a motion for judgment on the pleadings the court chooses to receive factual materials outside the pleadings, the court must treat the motion as one for summary judgment, which would include giving the parties an opportunity to present any further material they may have pertinent to a summary judgment motion. There is no point in insistence on mere form—here the names of the motions.

Questions: (89) Why, then, would a party ever use Rule 12(c) in preference to Rule 56?

(90) What can be said of the interchangeability of a motion for summary judgment and a motion under Rule 12(b)(6) for failure to state a claim upon which relief can be granted or a motion under Rule 12(f) to strike an insufficient defense?

(i) PROVISIONAL REMEDIES

[Rules 64, 65]

It is worth pausing to make the point that although we are canvassing the "phases of a lawsuit"—a phrase that might suggest a set order of proceedings—modern lawsuits do not exhibit an invariant pattern. They are fluid affairs. It is true that under the Rules certain moves necessarily precede other moves, and in this sense any lawsuit has a certain sequential order. The complaint precedes the answer, and a motion for a more definite statement necessarily follows the pleading that it addresses, and so on. But a lawsuit is not a cotillion in which the litigants take the same steps according to a definite routine. In a particular litigation, the litigants will make only some of the large variety of moves that are theoretically available under the Rules; they will not make those moves in an absolutely fixed order; they may carry out a number of moves more or less simultaneously; and they may respond to a given move in one or more of a variety of ways.

It is the mark of the first-class litigating lawyer to be able to hold the entire litigation in view while considering particular steps. One of the things he or she must bear in mind is that the adversary will sometimes not remain in a condition of repose while the lawsuit is taking its course.

Provisional remedies from common law.—Suppose plaintiff begins an action for a money judgment. If he wins, he can then take steps to have defendant's property in the court's jurisdiction seized and sold to satisfy the judgment. But what is to prevent defendant from concealing her property or removing it from the jurisdiction so that plaintiff cannot reach it? Or, for that matter, what is to prevent her from dissipating her property? In either case, plaintiff's victory might be a hollow one, leaving him with an uncollectible judgment.

The common law and now state legislatures have provided various devices designed to secure a plaintiff against these hazards, and Federal Rule 64 makes available in the district court whatever remedies of this sort are available under the law of the state in which the district court sits. There are considerable differences in the remedies available to plaintiff from state to state, in the circumstances where plaintiff can use them, and in the types of property that plaintiff can reach thereby. Because the district courts follow the local state practice, the result is a divergence in practice among the district courts. Note, however, that Rule 64's adoption of state law by reference is subject to the qualification that any statute of the United States governs in federal court as far as applicable.

Speaking generally, the most important of the state remedies are attachment and garnishment. Attachment is the seizure of defendant's property in advance of judgment, commonly at a very early stage in the proceedings, to give security to plaintiff that the judgment he hopes to obtain will be collectible. Garnishment is a process that makes a debt owed by a third person to defendant, or more generally property in the hands of a third person but belonging to defendant, similarly subject to plaintiff's claim. A typical example of a garnishable debt is defendant's bank deposit: the service of proper process upon the bank warns it not to pay defendant the amount deposited and garnished, but to hold that amount for application to plaintiff's judgment if he gets one; the garnishment excuses the bank from paying defendant in the meantime; indeed, if the bank nevertheless does pay defendant, the successful plaintiff can make it pay again.[s]

These remedies are drastic ones, particularly if the seizure takes effect upon plaintiff's say-so, thus depriving defendant of control of property before there has been any sort of impartial adjudication that plaintiff's claim is sound or even prima facie sound. Accordingly, in recent times lawsuits have repeatedly challenged, and often with success, the fundamental fairness of these remedies and therefore their constitutional validity. Of course, much turns on the details of the attachment or garnishment procedure provided by the particular state, the kinds of claims and the classes of creditors and debtors covered by the procedure, the type of property involved, and the like. We shall examine this question later, in Topic B of Part 3. In any event, we can summarize here that the district courts follow the local statutes unless those statutes are determined to be unconstitutional.

Provisional remedies from equity.—Attachment and garnishment are possible provisional remedies when plaintiff is seeking a money judgment. But the ultimate relief sought may be a judgment

---

[s]   Similarly, state statutes have long provided for garnishment of wages by service of proper process upon the employer. However, over the years, varying but increasing statutory restrictions have come to regulate this power to garnish wages.

Most significantly, in 1970 by Title III of the Consumer Credit Protection Act, Congress greatly restricted this device not only in the federal courts but in the state courts as well. Title III overrode state law except to the extent that state law imposes more stringent restrictions on wage garnishment. Title III generally provides that the maximum amount subject to wage garnishment is the lesser of (1) 25% of the defendant's weekly disposable earnings or (2) the amount by which those earnings exceed 30 times the federal minimum hourly wage. Title III also makes it a criminal offense to discharge an employee because of a single garnishment of the employee's wages. See 15 U.S.C. §§ 1671–1677.

directing defendant to do or to refrain from doing particular acts. In appropriate circumstances, the court will issue such ultimate relief, denominated a final injunction, after a decision for plaintiff on the merits of the dispute. Defendant's disobedience of such an order will result in severe action by the court. Yet here again intervening events may frustrate the effectiveness of this final relief. Suppose defendant is about to conduct blasting operations in dangerous proximity to plaintiff's property, and plaintiff seeks an injunction directing defendant to desist. Defendant may inflict the harm feared by plaintiff before the court can hear and decide the case.

Rule 65 draws on the traditions of equity to provide that plaintiff is not helpless in this situation. On a sufficient showing of urgency and irreparable harm, the court may issue a "temporary restraining order" without a hearing and, in particularly exigent cases, even without notice to the adverse party. But plaintiff should promptly follow up such an order with an application for a "preliminary injunction," which requires notice and hearing under Rule 65(a)(1).

It is hard at this point of your study to appreciate just how much is at stake here. Perhaps the best we can do for you is to allude to the dark history of federal labor injunctions, wherein broad temporary injunctions against strikes proved so effective at busting unions that in 1932 Congress had to step in to impose procedural and substantive limits on the federal-court injunctive power in labor disputes. More broadly, we can merely pronounce that temporary injunctive relief is a breathtakingly effective remedy, enforceable as it is by the unignorable power of contempt. Furthermore, in practical terms, the grant or refusal of this provisional remedy often spells the outcome of the dispute, as many parties cannot persevere until trial.

Accordingly, the law must concern itself with when and how a judge is to decide on this remedy, knowing that the judge must decide without all the procedural safeguards of a trial. Note the strict limitations imposed by Rule 65. In what manner do the Rule's various limitations channel the judge?

The working of the security requirement, for example, is a bit tricky. The court must require security, which comes usually in the form of a bond. However, the court can discretionarily fix the amount at a nominal level for a poor but deserving plaintiff. The defendant who ultimately prevails on the propriety of the provisional injunctive relief, by any means from a full-blown trial down to a voluntary dismissal without her consent, can recover her actual economic losses resulting from obeying the wrongfully imposed injunction. She can ordinarily recover these losses up to the amount of the bond, but not beyond. This cap follows from the proposition that a plaintiff is ordinarily not liable for the harm that a defendant suffers from litigation.

Question: (91) Most importantly, what should be the standard for granting a preliminary injunction? Begin by considering the standard stated in Sonesta International Hotels Corp. v. Wellington Associates, 483 F.2d 247, 250 (2d Cir.1973): "The settled rule is that a preliminary injunction should issue only upon a clear showing of either (1) probable success on the merits *and* [likely] irreparable injury, *or* (2) sufficiently serious questions going to the merits to make them a fair ground for litigation *and* a balance of hardships tipping decidedly toward the party requesting the preliminary relief." But the standard for granting a preliminary injunction is worth worrying about some more.

American Hospital Supply Corp. v. Hospital Products Ltd.

United States Court of Appeals, Seventh Circuit, 1986.
780 F.2d 589.

■ Before POSNER, CIRCUIT JUDGE, and SWYGERT and PELL, SENIOR CIRCUIT JUDGES.

■ POSNER, CIRCUIT JUDGE.

A supplier terminated a distributor, who sued for breach of contract and got a preliminary injunction. The supplier has appealed under 28 U.S.C. § 1292(a)(1). The appeal raises issues of procedure and contract law.

The supplier, Hospital Products (as we shall call the affiliated corporations that are the defendants), a small firm now undergoing reorganization in bankruptcy, is one of the world's two principal manufacturers of "reusable surgical stapling systems for internal surgical procedures" ("surgical stapling systems," for short). The terminated distributor, American Hospital Supply Corporation, the world's largest distributor of medical and surgical supplies, in 1982 became the exclusive distributor in the United States of Hospital Products' surgical stapling systems. The contract of distribution was for three years initially, but provided that it would be renewed automatically for successive one-year periods (to a limit of ten years) unless American Hospital Supply notified Hospital Products at least 90 days before the three years were up [on September 1, 1985] (or any successive one-year period for which the contract had been renewed) that it wanted to terminate the contract; and this meant, by June 3, 1985.

On that day Hospital Products hand-delivered a letter to American Hospital Supply demanding to know whether it intended to renew the contract and reminding it that if it failed to respond by the end of the day this would mean that the contract had been renewed. American Hospital Supply responded the same day in a letter which pointed out that since it wasn't terminating, the contract was, indeed, renewed. But on the next day Hospital Products announced that it was going to treat the contract as having been terminated, and on June 7 it sent a telegram to American Hospital Supply's dealers informing them that effective June 3 American

Hospital Supply was "no longer the authorized distributor of [Hospital Products'] stapling products."

American Hospital Supply forthwith brought this diversity breach of contract suit against Hospital Products and moved for a preliminary injunction, which was granted on July 8 after an evidentiary hearing. The injunction forbids Hospital Products to take any action in derogation of American Hospital Supply's contract rights so long as the injunction is in force (i.e., pending the outcome of the trial). It also requires Hospital Products to notify American Hospital Supply's dealers that American Hospital Supply is still Hospital Products' authorized distributor, and this has been done. Hospital Products counterclaimed, alleging breach of contract, fraud, and unfair competition.

Two months after the entry of the injunction, Hospital Products, which had been in parlous financial state even before this litigation began, filed a petition for bankruptcy under Chapter 11 of the Bankruptcy Act (reorganization). . . .

A district judge asked to decide whether to grant or deny a preliminary injunction must choose the course of action that will minimize the costs of being mistaken. Because he is forced to act on an incomplete record, the danger of a mistake is substantial. And a mistake can be costly. If the judge grants the preliminary injunction to a plaintiff who it later turns out is not entitled to any judicial relief—whose legal rights have not been violated—the judge commits a mistake whose gravity is measured by the irreparable harm, if any, that the injunction causes to the defendant while it is in effect. If the judge denies the preliminary injunction to a plaintiff who it later turns out is entitled to judicial relief, the judge commits a mistake whose gravity is measured by the irreparable harm, if any, that the denial of the preliminary injunction does to the plaintiff.

These mistakes can be compared, and the one likely to be less costly can be selected, with the help of a simple formula: grant the preliminary injunction if but only if $P \times H_p > (1 - P) \times H_d$, or, in words, only if the harm to the plaintiff if the injunction is denied, multiplied by the probability that the denial would be an error (that the plaintiff, in other words, will win at trial), exceeds the harm to the defendant if the injunction is granted, multiplied by the probability that granting the injunction would be an error. That probability is simply one minus the probability that the plaintiff will win at trial; for if the plaintiff has, say, a 40 percent chance of winning, the defendant must have a 60 percent chance of winning ($1.00 - .40 = .60$). The left-hand side of the formula is simply the probability of an erroneous denial weighted by the cost of denial to the plaintiff, and the right-hand side simply the probability of an erroneous grant weighted by the cost of grant to the defendant.

This formula, a procedural counterpart to Judge Learned Hand's famous negligence formula, see United States v. Carroll Towing Co., 159 F.2d 169, 173 (2d Cir.1947); [other citation omitted], is not offered as a new legal standard; it is intended not to force analysis into a quantitative straitjacket but to assist analysis by presenting succinctly the factors that the court must consider in making its decision and by articulating the relationship among the factors. It is actually just a distillation of the familiar four (sometimes five) factor test that courts use in deciding whether to grant a preliminary injunction. The court asks whether the plaintiff will be irreparably harmed if the preliminary injunction is denied (sometimes also whether the plaintiff has an adequate remedy at law), whether the harm to the plaintiff if the preliminary injunction is denied will exceed the harm to the defendant if it is granted, whether the plaintiff is reasonably likely to prevail at trial, and whether the public interest will be affected by granting or denying the injunction (i.e., whether third parties will be harmed—and these harms can then be added to H_p or H_d as the case may be). See, e.g., Palmer v. City of Chicago, 755 F.2d 560, 576 (7th Cir.1985). The court undertakes these inquiries to help it figure out whether granting the injunction would be the error-minimizing course of action, which depends on the probability that the plaintiff is in the right and on the costs to the plaintiff, the defendant, or others of granting or denying the injunction. All this is explained at length in Roland Machinery Co. v. Dresser Industries, Inc., 749 F.2d 380, 382–88 (7th Cir.1984) [(Posner, J.)], where a panel of this court applied the verbal counterpart to our algebraic formula, as did a different panel in Maxim's Ltd. v. Badonsky, 772 F.2d 388, 391 (7th Cir.1985). See also Leubsdorf, The Standard for Preliminary Injunctions, 91 Harv.L.Rev. 525 (1978). The formula is new; the analysis it capsulizes is standard.

The formula does not depend on the legal basis of the plaintiff's claim, whether it is antitrust law (Roland) or trademark law (Badonsky) or, as here, the common law of contract, although the nature of the right asserted by the plaintiff may affect the weighting of the harms, see, e.g., Shondel v. McDermott, 775 F.2d 859, 866–67 (7th Cir.1985). So may the nature of the permanent remedy to which the plaintiff would be entitled if he prevailed at trial. For example, prevailing parties in breach of contract cases normally are not awarded specific performance, that is, a mandatory injunction to perform. Since many breaches of contract are involuntary, implying that performance would be very costly, routinely ordering specific performance would create situations where the defendant was forced to bargain desperately to buy his way out of the injunction. The high bargaining costs that would result are a dead-weight cost of equitable relief. To the extent that those costs attend a preliminary injunction, they are of course relevant to the decision whether to issue such an injunction. But the formula takes account of this; the case we have described would be one where the harm to the defendant from granting the injunction would be very great. Thus the fact that a plaintiff might have no hope of getting specific performance ordered at the conclusion of the trial need not prevent him from obtaining a preliminary injunction. Cf. Roland v. Dresser Industries, Inc., supra, 749 F.2d at 386. The premise of the preliminary injunction is that the remedy available at the end of trial will not make the plaintiff whole; and, in a sense, the more limited that remedy, the stronger the argument for a preliminary injunction—provided that the remedy is not limited for reasons that would make a preliminary injunction equally inappropriate.

As explained in Roland, the scope of judicial review of a district judge's decision to grant or deny a preliminary injunction is limited. See 749 F.2d at 384–85, 388–91. The usual formulation is that the decision will be reversed only if it is found to be an "abuse of discretion." Unfortunately this phrase covers a family of review standards rather than a single standard, and a family whose members differ greatly in the actual stringency of review. See, e.g., id. at 388–91; Metlyn Realty Corp. v. Esmark, Inc., 763 F.2d 826, 831–32 (7th Cir.1985); Friendly, Indiscretion About Discretion, 31 Emory L.J. 747 (1982). For example, when we review an order granting or denying a preliminary injunction, we do not do so with as much deference (virtually complete deference) as when reviewing a criminal sentence that is within legal limits but is challenged as too harsh; we do "not simply engage in a perfunctory rubber-stamping of the district court's decision." Olin Water Services v. Midland Research Laboratories, Inc., 774 F.2d 303, 307 n. 7 (8th Cir.1985). But we do give that decision substantial deference, bearing in mind that the district judge had . . . to balance factors which, though they can be related in a neat formula, usually cannot be quantified, and that in dealing with the parties and their witnesses and counsel in the hectic atmosphere of a preliminary-injunction proceeding the judge may have developed a feel for the facts and the equities that remote appellate judges cannot obtain from a transcript. To reverse an order granting or denying a preliminary injunction, therefore, it is not enough that we think we would have acted differently in the district judge's shoes; we must have a strong conviction that he exceeded the permissible bounds of judgment. And although recognizing that the order granting such an injunction must set forth the judge's reasons, see Fed.R.Civ.P. 65(d), we also recognize that the haste with which the judge must act precludes as full a statement of reasons as could reasonably be demanded of a final decision.

We have now to apply these precepts, and we begin with the balance of harms. . . .

[The appellate court saw a threat of substantial irreparable harm to the plaintiff, in its being stuck with excess inventory upon the loss of distributorship status and likely being unable eventually to recover damages from the insolvent defendant for breach of contract. The court saw harm to the defendant from the preliminary injunction in the increased risk of bankruptcy, but this harm was offset at least in part by the $5 million bond that the plaintiff posted under Rule 65(c). The court remained unpersuaded "that the district judge erred in concluding that the balance of harms inclined in favor of granting the preliminary injunction."]

. . . Even if there were no clear basis for differentiating between the irreparable harms to American Hospital Supply from denying and to Hospital Products from granting a preliminary injunction, in which event those harms would have to be treated as equal, Hospital Products' appeal would fail. If the harms to the plaintiff and the defendant of denying and granting the injunction, respectively, are equal, the injunction must be granted if the plaintiff has a better than 50 percent chance of winning the case, for then P in our preliminary-injunction formula must exceed 1 − P, and therefore $P \times H_p$ must exceed $(1 - P) \times H_d$ from the assumption that $H_p = H_d$.

The district judge was persuaded that Hospital Products, not American Hospital Supply, had broken the contract, implying a very high P. He undoubtedly was correct if the contract was renewed on June 3 and in force the next day when Hospital Products announced that the contract was terminated. But we must consider as did he whether American Hospital Supply repudiated the contract before this announcement. That would make this a case of anticipatory breach of contract . . . .

[The appellate court, by lengthy discussion, concluded that "as nearly as we can determine, the able and experienced district judge who resolved the uncertainty in American Hospital Supply's favor was on solid ground in doing so." The appellate court indicated that findings of fact were subject to a clearly erroneous standard of review, while conclusions of law were subject to nondeferential review.]

. . . In thus commenting on the merits, however, as we must do to review the district court's action in granting the injunction, we do not mean to prejudge the outcome of the full trial, which may cast the facts in a different light from how they appeared in the preliminary injunction proceeding. This caveat applies to all the discussion of the merits of the case in this opinion.

. . . .

We comment briefly on the term of the preliminary injunction. Since federal litigation is sometimes protracted and since the contract entitles American Hospital Supply to renew the contract annually for six more years after this year, there is a theoretical possibility that the injunction will remain in effect for many years. Over such a period the balance of harms and impact on the public interest may of course change. We trust that the district judge will bear this in mind in considering any requests to modify the injunction.

. . . .

Affirmed.

■ SWYGERT, SENIOR CIRCUIT JUDGE, dissenting.

[Among other lines of attack, the dissenting judge argued that "the district court clearly erred in finding that the balance of harms weighed in AHS's favor" and argued that there was an insufficient showing of likelihood of success on the merits.]

I would have preferred to avoid commenting on the majority's attempt to reduce the well-developed and complex law of preliminary injunctions to a "simple" mathematical formula. But because of the potentially far-reaching and baneful consequences of today's decision, I must regretfully voice my concerns.

Henceforth, the district courts of this circuit should grant a preliminary injunction if, "but only if," $P \times H_p > (1 - P) \times H_d$ . . . .

The majority describes its formula as a procedural counterpart to Judge Hand's negligence formula first appearing in United States v. Carroll Towing, 159 F.2d 169, 173 (2d Cir.1947). Carroll Towing was an admiralty case in which a shipowner's duty to provide against injuries resulting from the breaking of a vessel's moorings was expressed in algebraic terms. In Hand's formula the liability of the shipowner depends on whether $B < PL$, where P is the probability that the ship will break away; where L is the gravity of the resulting injury if she does; and where B is the burden of adequate precautions. . . . My quarrel, however, is not with Carroll Towing but rather with the majority's attempt today to create its equitable analogue. A quantitative approach may be an appropriate and useful heuristic device in determining negligence in tort cases, but it has limited value in determining whether a preliminary injunction should issue. Proceedings in equity and cases sounding in tort demand entirely different responses of a district judge. The judgment of the district judge in a tort case must be definite; the judgment of the district judge in an injunction proceeding cannot, by its very nature, be as definite. The judgment of a district judge in an injunction proceeding must be flexible and discretionary—within the bounds of the now settled four-prong test.

I question the necessity and the wisdom of the court's adoption of a mathematical formula as the governing law of preliminary injunctions. The majority claims that its formula is merely a distillation of the traditional four-prong test. But if nothing is added to the substantive law, why bother? The standard four-prong test for determining whether a preliminary injunction should issue has survived for so many years because it has proven to be a workable summation of the myriad factors a district court must consider in deciding whether to grant an injunction. The test articulated in Technical Publishing v. Lebhar-Friedman, 729 F.2d 1136, 1138 (7th Cir.1984), and in countless other cases, may not exhibit the "precision" the majority seems to demand, but such "precision" is antithetical to the underlying principles of injunctive relief. Equity, as the majority concedes, involves the assessment of factors that cannot be quantified. A district court faced with the task of deciding whether to issue a preliminary injunction must to some extent, the majority concedes, rely on the "feel" of the case. See generally my discussion in Roland, 749 F.2d at 396 [(dissenting opinion)]. The majority's formula will not assist the district courts in their assessment of this aspect of the decision to grant a preliminary injunction. The traditional element of discretion residing in the decision of a trial court to grant a preliminary injunction has been all but eliminated by today's decision.

Ironically, the majority never attempts to assign a numerical value to the variables of its own formula. We are never told how to measure P or H_p or H_d. I believe, and the majority appears to concede, that a numerical value could never be assigned to these variables. Who can say, for instance, what *exactly* the probability is that the granting of the injunction was an error? How then will the majority's formula ease in a meaningful way the responsibilities of the district courts? Judges asked to issue a preliminary injunction must, in large part, rely on their own judgment, not on mathematical quanta.

We must, of course, be mindful not to vest too much imprecision in the preliminary injunction standard, for law implies a system of known and generally applicable rules. See Fiss & Rendleman, Injunctions 104 (2d ed. 1984). The existing four-prong test, however, represents the historical balance struck by the courts between the rigidity of law and the flexibility of equity.

The majority disavows any effort to force the district courts into a "quantitative straitjacket," but I suspect that today's decision may lead to just that. District judges operate under enormous pressure to be decisive and precise. Much rides on their smallest decisions. Like a Homeric Siren the majority's formula offers a seductive but deceptive security. Moreover, the majority's formula invites members of the Bar to dust off their calculators and dress their arguments in quantitative clothing. The resulting spectacle will perhaps be entertaining, but I do not envy the district courts of this circuit and I am not proud of the task we have given them.

I would reverse the district court's issuance of the preliminary injunction.

. . . .t

---

t   Compare Linz Audain, Of Posner, and Newton, and Twenty-First Century Law: An Economic and Statistical Analysis of the Posner Rule for Granting Preliminary Injunctions, 23 Loy.L.A.L.Rev. 1215 (1990), with Linda S. Mullenix, Burying (with Kindness) the Felicific Calculus of Civil Procedure, 40 Vand.L.Rev. 541 (1987). For a startlingly different economic approach, taking as its premise that the purpose of preliminary injunctions is mere efficiency rather than the minimization of the interim loss of legal rights, see Richard R.W. Brooks & Warren F. Schwartz, Legal Uncertainty, Economic Efficiency, and the Preliminary Injunction Doctrine, 58 Stan.L.Rev. 381 (2005). For a psychological approach to this sort of problem, see Hal R. Arkes & Victoria A. Shaffer, "Should We Use Decision Aids or Gut Feelings," in Heuristics and the Law 411 (G. Gigerenzer & C. Engel eds., 2006).

The American Hospital formula has enjoyed only a smattering of judicial support. For later treatment of the formula by other panels of the same court of appeals, see, e.g., Lawson Products, Inc. v. Avnet, Inc., 782 F.2d 1429 (7th Cir.1986) (Flaum, J.) (politely but explicitly

———

COUNTRY FLOORS, INC. v. A PARTNERSHIP COMPOSED OF CHARLEY GEPNER AND GARY FORD, 930 F.2d 1056 (3d Cir.1991). Country Floors, a manufacturer of upscale ceramic tiles, brought a suit for trademark infringement against a partnership selling tiles under the name Country Tiles. At the outset, the district court denied plaintiff's motion for a preliminary injunction, which plaintiff supported by its employees' testimony of customer confusion between the tile products, with the court ruling in part that plaintiff had not made a sufficient showing of a likelihood of confusion. Later, after complete discovery, the court granted defendant's motion for summary judgment, relying in part on credibility determinations that it had made in connection with the preliminary injunction motion.

The court of appeals reversed, on the ground that the court could not so use such determinations and that indeed a genuine dispute of fact existed as to the likelihood of confusion. It wrote:

"[C]redibility evaluations are inappropriate in deciding a motion for summary judgment. It is error to rely on the previous resolution of credibility issues in deciding a motion for summary judgment because such reliance cannot co-exist with the requirement of [the summary judgment Rule that no genuine disputes] of material fact remain outstanding.

. . . .

" . . . [O]n a motion for summary judgment the responsibility of the district court is to determine if there are triable issues, rather than to try those issues and make findings based on the affidavits and other materials accompanying the motion.

---

endorsing the circuit's traditional approach). But Abbott Laboratories v. Mead Johnson & Co., 971 F.2d 6, 11–12 (7th Cir.1992) (Flaum, J.) (some citations omitted), ruled:

"As a threshold matter, a party seeking a preliminary injunction must demonstrate (1) some likelihood of succeeding on the merits, and (2) that it has 'no adequate remedy at law' and will suffer 'irreparable harm' if preliminary relief is denied. If the moving party cannot establish either of these prerequisites, a court's inquiry is over and the injunction must be denied. If, however, the moving party clears both thresholds, the court must then consider: (3) the irreparable harm the non-moving party will suffer if preliminary relief is granted, balancing that harm against the irreparable harm to the moving party if relief is denied; and (4) the public interest, meaning the consequences of granting or denying the injunction to non-parties.

"The court, sitting as would a chancellor in equity, then 'weighs' all four factors in deciding whether to grant the injunction, seeking at all times to 'minimize the costs of being mistaken.' American Hosp. Supply, 780 F.2d at 593. We call this process the 'sliding scale' approach: the more likely it is the plaintiff will succeed on the merits, the less the balance of irreparable harms need weigh towards its side; the less likely it is the plaintiff will succeed, the more the balance need weigh towards its side. This weighing process, as noted, also takes into consideration the consequences to the public interest of granting or denying preliminary relief. While we have at times framed the sliding scale approach in mathematical terms, see American Hosp. Supply, 780 F.2d at 593–94, it is more properly characterized as subjective and intuitive, one which permits district courts to 'weigh the competing considerations and mold appropriate relief.' Lawson Prods., 782 F.2d at 1436."

"Accordingly, inferences concerning credibility that were previously made in ruling on the Corporation's motion for a preliminary injunction cannot determine the Partnership's Rule 56[(a)] motion and should not be used to support propositions that underpin the decision to grant the motion for summary judgment. . . .

. . . .

"Additionally, in the context of this case, we note that the considerations that determine a motion for a preliminary injunction are foreign to those that govern decision on a motion for summary judgment."

SECTION 2.   SETTLEMENT

(a) INCIDENCE

Most lawsuits do not make it all the way through the pretrial practice we have studied. Indeed, most disputes do not even become lawsuits. Aggrieved persons abandon or settle the overwhelming majority of grievances at some point along the line.

A useful image is the so-called grievance pyramid:

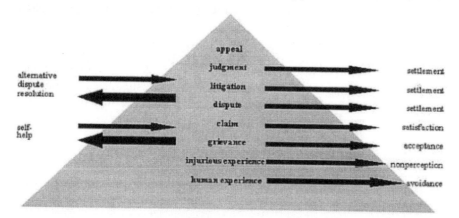

This image represents, as one progresses up the steps of the pyramid, how the whole realm of experiences narrows to disputes, a subset that produces in turn those selected cases we study in law school. Infinite experiences produce countless disputes, which yield few cases. For example, only a small percentage of grievances ripen into claims, by the aggrieved's voicing the grievance to the injurer; most aggrieved persons accept their injury as part of life or just figure that there is no remedy available; tellingly, the theorists in this subject sometimes refer to acceptance as "lumping it." Similarly, most disputants never make it to a lawyer, much less to a courthouse. So this image of a pyramid suggests another image: in this book we have thus far focused on the tiny tip of a huge iceberg.

The slope of the sides of the pyramid is quite gentle. That is, a huge percentage of situations leaves the pyramid at each step upward. A survey of more than five thousand households indicated that during the previous three years just over a third of them had perceived one or more grievances of certain litigable types; 71.8% of those grievances produced a claim informally; 62.6% of those claims met an initial rebuff to produce a dispute; and 11.2% of those disputes resulted in filing a lawsuit. See David M. Trubek, Austin Sarat, William L.F. Felstiner, Herbert M. Kritzer & Joel B. Grossman, The Costs of Ordinary Litigation, 31 UCLA L.Rev. 72, 86–87 (1983). Indeed, these percentages are exaggeratedly high, because the survey limited its inquiries to grievances involving $1000 or more. Even for such substantial grievances, litigation is by no means a knee-jerk or common reaction in the United States, because these numbers mean that overall only about 5% of those grievances ultimately resulted in a court filing.

In the world of litigation at the top of the pyramid, the slope remains gentle. Of the relatively few filed cases, only a small percentage make it through the procedural system to a contested judgment. We can look at all the 271,753 federal civil cases terminated during fiscal year 2005. Of these, at least 67.7% were settled in one way or another; approximately 20.7% were adjudicated at the pretrial stage, as by a motion under Rule 12 or 56; about 1.3% were adjudicated at the trial stage; and the other 10.3% of the cases fell into a welter of other disposition method codes, such as remand or transfer to another court, whereby most result in an eventual settlement rather than a final adjudication.

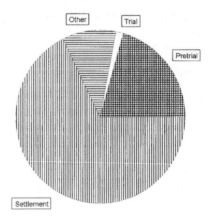

We can combine all these rough numbers with the visual presentation of the grievance pyramid. From the experiential infinitude, imagine that 1000 sizable grievances arise. This typical thousand will decrease to 718 claims, 449 disputes, 50 filed cases, 12 litigated judgments, and 1 decided appeal. Thus, we advisedly described the pyramid's sides by saying that their slope is gentle.

Merely stating such numbers, as rough as they are, constitutes a major step forward for students as well as for proceduralists. A new wave of empirical research is giving a fresh sense of reality to the field of procedure. Moreover, there is a growing need for such study, because in recent years anecdotal evidence has created a frenzy about the current state of litigation and led to a host of ill-conceived reform efforts. Before undertaking reform, one should know whether and to what extent there really is a problem.

Although these new empirical studies are a step in the right direction, their reader of course needs to be careful. Interpreting them can be difficult, risky, and subjective. Looking at actual court statistics is far from a controlled experiment, which means that it is hard to compare court outputs (say, jury verdicts and bench trial judgments) when the streams of cases under comparison vary. This so-called selection effect has a major impact. Indeed, interpretation ends up being almost as much art as science. See generally Kevin M. Clermont & Theodore Eisenberg, Litigation Realities, 88 Cornell L.Rev. 119 (2002) (also explaining how to gain access to raw court data on the internet); Kevin M. Clermont, Litigation Realities Redux, 84 Notre Dame L.Rev. 1919 (2009).

(b) IMPORTANCE

From the viewpoint of the civil justice system, settlement is a critical need. Ours is a slow and expensive procedure. The system simply would not be able to adjudicate all cases currently filed. We depend on the parties' using alternatives to adjudication. Accordingly, reformers are constantly seeking ways to increase the settlement rate (which is a loose term that measures the percentage of cases leaving the sides of the grievance pyramid, whether by abandonment, concession, or privately negotiated settlement or by more formal alternative dispute resolution such as arbitration, mediation, and conciliation).

Nevertheless, the system must adjudicate some cases in order to pronounce the law. These cases set the standards under which the parties negotiate settlement of their disputes. The parties "bargain in the shadow of the law" to reach outcomes that generally conform to the law and thereby further the law's purposes. Thus, the settlement rate could conceivably become too high. If parties settled all cases, there would be big gaps in the law that is supposed to be setting the standards for settlement. If courts adjudicated some cases, but still too few, the gaps might be smaller but the law would remain not only inefficiently fuzzy but also insufficiently conformed to social purposes. At some lower settlement rate, the law would be optimally set so that further adjudication would be wasteful.

Reformers might nonetheless contend that the settlement rate in America today lies below that optimum and therefore push to increase the settlement rate. In reality, however, they would not find it easy to raise, or for that matter lower, the rate. Almost all reform attempts to enhance settlement will be largely offset by consequential increases in the amount of litigation. See George L. Priest, Private Litigants and the Court Congestion Problem, 69 B.U.L.Rev. 527 (1989).

Shifting from the viewpoint of the system to that of the disputants, settlement is also of critical importance. For them in the usual course, settlement *is* our system of justice. For their "trial" lawyers, negotiating settlements—and pursuing other alternatives to adjudication—is what their profession primarily comprises. All those alternatives usually offer procedural and substantive advantages to the disputants. Again, however, some optimal settlement rate exists, above which increases in external pressure to settle would impose undesirable costs on party autonomy. See Stephen McG. Bundy, The Policy in Favor of Settlement in an Adversary System, 44 Hastings L.J. 1 (1992).

So why are we postponing focused study of all these important alternative dispute-resolution mechanisms? We have already explained that early mastery of the official procedural system helps in comprehending the cases read in other law courses. More importantly, litigation remains extremely important to society and to citizens. By it, courts act as the default enforcer of law and resolver of disputes. Litigation not only produces singular decisions that restructure society but also serves as a major vehicle for lawmaking in our government and for articulation of societal values. And the legal system's adjudication enunciates the law, in the shadow of which the grievance pyramid lies and the potential litigants operate those nonadjudicative processes.

However, negotiating settlements, which constitutes the preeminent alternative dispute-resolution process, is too essential an appendage of the litigation process to ignore even temporarily. Indeed, some theorists propose renaming litigation as "litigotiation." Accordingly, we find it necessary to pause here and consider settlement itself in some detail.

———

MARC GALANTER, THE EMERGENCE OF THE JUDGE AS A MEDIATOR IN CIVIL CASES, 69 Judicature 257, 257 (1986). "Typically, settlement negotiations involve only counsel for the respective parties. But in many instances the negotiations are encouraged, brokered, or actively mediated by the judge. Most American judges participate to some extent in the settlement of some of the cases before them. Indeed, this has become a respectable, even esteemed, feature of judicial work.

"There have always been a lot of settlements in American civil courts. It remains unclear whether the percentage of cases terminated by settlement has increased in recent years. And, if there has been an increase, it is unclear whether it is caused by the increased intervention of judges. There has been a sea change, however, in the way judges talk about settlement and think about their roles as judges."

There are "two recurrent themes that impel and justify judicial involvement in the settlement process. We might call these the 'warm' theme and the 'cool' theme. The 'warm' theme refers to the impulse to replace adversary conflict by [for example] a process of conciliation to bring the parties into a mutual accord that expresses and produces community among them. The 'cool' theme emphasizes not a more admirable process but efficient institutional management: clearing dockets, reducing delay, eliminating expense, unburdening the courts."

––––––––

Question: (1) With our focus now squarely on settlement, consider again how actively should the judge push for it. What would be the effect of activism on the direct costs of operating the legal system, taking into account the time and expense of public judges and officers as well as private lawyers and parties, and subtracting litigation savings but only to the extent that settlement would not have occurred anyway? What would be the other costs, taking into account the negative impact on a range of values regarding fair process and accurate outcome, some of which are not obvious as the next excerpt will illustrate, but all of which offset the gains in the "warm" values served? Bear in mind that the costs vary with different kinds of settlement techniques, different kinds of cases, and different courts and judges.

––––––––

OWEN M. FISS, AGAINST SETTLEMENT, 93 Yale L.J. 1073, 1075, 1085 (1984). "I do not believe that settlement as a generic practice is preferable to judgment or should be institutionalized on a wholesale and indiscriminate basis. It should be treated instead as a highly problematic technique for streamlining dockets. Settlement is for me the civil analogue of plea bargaining: Consent is often coerced; the bargain may be struck by someone without authority; the absence of a trial and judgment renders subsequent judicial involvement troublesome; and although dockets are trimmed, justice may not be done. Like plea bargaining, settlement is a capitulation to the conditions of mass society and should be neither encouraged nor praised."

Adjudication employs *public* officials, whose "job is not to maximize the ends of private parties, nor simply to secure the peace, but to explicate and give force to the values embodied in authoritative texts such as the Constitution and statutes: to interpret those values and to bring reality into accord with them. This duty is not discharged when the parties settle."

––––––––

CARRIE   MENKEL-MEADOW,   FOR   AND   AGAINST SETTLEMENT: USES AND ABUSES OF THE MANDATORY SETTLEMENT CONFERENCE, 33 UCLA L.Rev. 485, 504–05, 507–11, 513–14 (1985). "I will not repeat the often stated assertion that settlement is a 'docket-clearing' device. We have examined the efficiency argument and found it wanting. What settlement offers is a substantive justice that may be more responsive to the parties' needs than adjudication. Settlement can be particularized to the needs of the parties, it can avoid win/lose, binary results, provide richer remedies than the commodification or monetarization of all claims, and achieve legitimacy through consent. In addition, settlement offers a different substantive process by allowing participation by the parties as well as the lawyers. Settlement fosters a communication process that can be more direct and less stylized than litigation, and affords greater flexibility of procedure and remedy.

. . . .

"For those who seek to use the settlement conference as a docket-clearing device, the conference becomes most problematic in terms of the substantive and process values (i.e., *quality* of solution) previously discussed. . . .

"A much touted settlement technique is the use of the 'Lloyds of London' formula: The settlement judge asks the parties to assess the probabilities of liability and damages and, if the figures are within reasonable range, to split the difference. The difficulty with such settlement techniques is that they tend to monetarize and compromise all the issues in the case. Although some cases are reducible to monetary issues, an approach to case evaluation on purely monetary grounds may decrease the likelihood of settlement by making fewer issues available for trade-offs. Furthermore, a wider definition of options may make compromise unnecessary. As the recent outpouring of popular and scholarly literature on negotiation illustrates, the greater the number of issues in controversy between the parties, the greater the likelihood of achieving a variety of solutions. Parties may place complementary values on different items. The irony is that settlement managers, who think they are making settlement easier by reducing the issues, may in fact be increasing the likelihood of deadlock by reducing the issues to one. Furthermore, [their approach] may thwart the possibilities for . . . mutual gain.

"In addition to foreclosing a number of possible settlements, the efficiency-minded settlement officer seems prone to use coercive techniques such as suggesting a particular result, making threats about taking the case off the docket, directing meetings with clients or parties. Lawyers find these techniques problematic. Thus, the quest for efficiency may in fact be counterproductive.

"Some recent data seem to indicate that greater satisfaction can be achieved with a different settlement management role—the facilitator of good settlements. [Examples included] judges who analyzed the particular facts of the case (as opposed to those who used formulas like 'Lloyds of London'), offered explicit suggestions and assessments of the parties' positions, occasionally spoke directly to recalcitrant clients, and expressed views about the unfairness of particular results. . . .

. . . .

"Judges who perform these functions are not necessarily mediators, though they are frequently called that by themselves and others. Strictly speaking, a mediator facilitates communication between the parties and helps them to reach their own solution. As a mediator becomes more directly involved in suggesting the substantive solution, his or her role can change and he or she can become an arbitrator or adjudicator. It appears that the role judges and magistrates assume in many settlement conferences is this hybrid form of med-arb. Med-arb uses all the techniques associated with mediation and arbitration—caucusing (meeting with the parties separately), making suggestions to the parties, allowing closed or best-offer bidding, and meeting with principals (clients) who have authority to settle or to reconsider and reconceive the problem. As the med-arb process moves toward arbitration, 'settlements' may closely resemble adjudication with rationalized, normative, or law-based solutions.

. . . .

"We might ask the procedural question: Who should bear the burden of proof on success? Critics like Fiss . . . assume that adjudication is the preferred process and challenge the 'settlors' to prove up their claims. Judges and judicial administrators argue vehemently that settlement devices speed cases along and provide better settlements, and assert that adjudication be used only when a strong need for it can be shown. My own view is that settlement is now the norm. The pertinent question is how can it be used most effectively (for the parties and for other users of the system) when traditional adjudicators are brought into the process. . . . Thus, on balance I support the movements toward mandatory settlement conferences, as long as they are 'properly' conducted by settlement officers sensitive to the efficiency-quality problem."

———

Kothe v. Smith

United States Court of Appeals, Second Circuit, 1985.
771 F.2d 667.

■ Before LUMBARD, VAN GRAAFEILAND and PIERCE, CIRCUIT JUDGES.

■ VAN GRAAFEILAND, CIRCUIT JUDGE:

Dr. James Smith appeals from a judgment of the United States District Court for the Southern District of New York (Sweet, J.), which directed him to pay $1,000 to plaintiff-appellee's attorney, $1,000 to plaintiff-appellee's medical witness, and $480 to the Clerk of the Court. For the reasons hereinafter discussed, we direct that the judgment be vacated.

Patricia Kothe brought this suit for medical malpractice against . . . Dr. Smith . . . , seeking $2 million in damages. . . .

Three weeks prior [to trial], Judge Sweet held a pretrial conference, during which he directed counsel for the parties to conduct settlement negotiations. Although it is not clear from the record, it appears that Judge Sweet recommended that the case be settled for between $20,000 and $30,000. He also warned the parties that, if they settled for a comparable figure after trial had begun, he would impose sanctions against the dilatory party. Smith, whose defense has been conducted throughout this litigation by his malpractice insurer, offered $5,000 on the day before trial, but it was rejected.

Although Kothe's attorney had indicated to Judge Sweet that his client would settle for $20,000, he had requested that the figure not be disclosed to Smith. Kothe's counsel conceded at oral argument that the lowest pretrial settlement demand communicated to Smith was $50,000. Nevertheless, when the case was settled for $20,000 after one day of trial, the district court proceeded to penalize Smith alone. In imposing the penalty, the court stated that it was "determined to get the attention of the [insurer]" and that "the [insurers] are going to have to wake up when a judge tells them that they want [sic] to settle a case and they don't want to settle it." Under the circumstances of this case, we believe that the district court's imposition of a penalty against Smith was an abuse of the sanction power given it by Fed.R.Civ.P. 16(f).

Although the law favors the voluntary settlement of civil suits, ABKCO Music, Inc. v. Harrisongs Music, Ltd., 722 F.2d 988, 997 (2d Cir.1983), it does not sanction efforts by trial judges to effect settlements through coercion. Del Rio v. Northern Blower Co., 574 F.2d 23, 26 (1st Cir.1978) (citing Wolff v. Laverne, Inc., 17 A.D.2d 213, 233 N.Y.S.2d 555 (1962)); [other citations omitted]. In the Wolff case, cited with approval in Del Rio, supra, the Court said:

> We view with disfavor all pressure tactics whether directly or obliquely, to coerce settlement by litigants and their counsel. Failure to concur in what the Justice presiding may consider an adequate settlement should not result in an imposition upon a litigant or his counsel, who reject it, of any retributive sanctions not specifically authorized by law.

17 A.D.2d at 215, 233 N.Y.S.2d 555. In short, pressure tactics to coerce settlement simply are not permissible. [Citations omitted.] "The judge must not compel agreement by arbitrary use of his power and the attorney must not meekly submit to a judge's suggestion, though it be strongly urged." Brooks v. Great Atlantic & Pacific Tea Co., 92 F.2d 794, 796 (9th Cir.1937).

Rule 16 of the Fed.R.Civ.P. was not designed as a means for clubbing the parties—or one of them—into an involuntary compromise. [Citations omitted.] Although subsection [(c)(2)(I)] of Rule 16, added in the 1983 amendments of the Rule, was designed to encourage pretrial settlement discussions, it was not its purpose to "impose settlement negotiations on unwilling litigants." See Advisory Committee Note, 1983, 97 F.R.D. 205, 210.

We find the coercion in the instant case especially troublesome because the district court imposed sanctions on Smith alone. Offers to settle a claim are not made in a vacuum. They are part of a more complex process which includes "conferences, informal discussions, offers, counterdemands, more discussions, more haggling, and finally, in the great majority of cases, a compromise." J. & D. Sindell, Let's Talk Settlement 300 (1963). In other words, the process of settlement is a two-way street, and a defendant should not be expected to bid against himself. In the instant case, Smith never received a demand of less than $50,000. Having received no indication from Kothe that an offer somewhere in the vicinity of $20,000 would at least be given careful consideration, Smith should not have been required to make an offer in this amount simply because the court wanted him to.

Smith's attorney should not be condemned for changing his evaluation of the case after listening to Kothe's testimony during the first day of trial. As every experienced trial lawyer knows, the personalities of the parties and their witnesses play an important role in litigation. It is one thing to have a valid claim; it is quite another to convince a jury of this fact. It is not at all unusual, therefore, for a defendant to change his perception of a case based on the plaintiff's performance on the witness stand. We see nothing about that occurrence in the instant case that warranted the imposition of sanctions against the defendant alone.

Although we commend Judge Sweet for his efforts to encourage settlement negotiations, his excessive zeal leaves us no recourse but to remand the matter with instructions to vacate the judgment.[a]

————

JEFFREY A. PARNESS, IMPROVING JUDICIAL SETTLEMENT CONFERENCES, 39 U.C.Davis L.Rev. 1891, 1908 (2006). Professor Fiss, among others, has "expressed concerns about the unbounded, unchecked, unbridled, and virtually unfettered judicial discretion of trial judges who preside over civil case settlement conferences. I, too, am concerned. But the best response is not to abolish or severely restrict judicial settlement conferences. Rather, it is to add more formality and more written guidelines. . . . These guidelines should involve . . . both more adversary

---

[a]   In a later case Judge Sweet imposed a $1000 fine on defendant for criminal contempt of a pretrial conference order to submit a "bonafide" settlement offer. In an opinion by Judge Van Graafeiland, another panel of the Second Circuit reversed, finding the order too vague and imprecise. Hess v. N.J. Transit Rail Operations, 846 F.2d 114, 104 A.L.R.Fed. 455 (2d Cir.1988). Other courts have held as a matter of law that a party's failure to talk settlement, by refusing to make or accept an offer of settlement, is not sanctionable by itself. E.g., Old Reliable Wholesale, Inc. v. Cornell Corp., 635 F.3d 539, 549–50 (Fed.Cir.2011). But cf., e.g., White v. Raymark Indus., Inc., 783 F.2d 1175 (4th Cir.1986) (upholding assessment of juror costs on defendant, upon notice and hearing and pursuant to local rule, for delaying settlement until morning of trial); Andrew J. Wistrich & Jeffrey J. Rachlinski, How Lawyers' Intuitions Prolong Litigation, 86 S.Cal.L.Rev. 571 (2013).

control and more detailed and written criteria. In addition, new guidelines should expressly recognize that the claims and interests that might be discussed at judicial settlement conferences are far more expansive than the justiciable claims that might be discussed at trial preparation conferences. Thus, civil case settlements . . . can involve many more claims, interests, and people than would have been involved in any adversarial proceedings in the same case."

———

J. MARIA GLOVER, THE FEDERAL RULES OF CIVIL SETTLEMENT, 87 N.Y.U.L.Rev. 1713, 1715–18, 1778 (2012). "The Federal Rules of Civil Procedure . . . were designed to achieve a fundamental goal: to facilitate the resolution of cases on their merits. To accomplish that goal, the reformers behind the Federal Rules eschewed technical formalities in favor of a streamlined procedural system, one for which plenary truth-seeking followed by trial was the 'gold standard.' However, federal civil cases today are virtually never resolved through trial. Rather, settlement has emerged as the dominant endgame." Today, "there is reason to worry that case outcomes—now the product of settlements—correspond to the legal merits of a given dispute in only the coarsest of ways. . . . [T]he 'shadow of the law' cast upon settlement outcomes is growing faint." The author calls for redesign of the current procedural rules into a "system designed for a world of settlement—in particular, one that would convert what is now a largely detached relationship between pretrial procedure and the substantive merits of a given case into one . . . that expressly integrates pretrial procedure with meaningful merits-based determinations."

———

WAYNE D. BRAZIL, EFFECTIVE LAWYERING IN JUDICIALLY HOSTED SETTLEMENT CONFERENCES, 1988 J.Disp.Resol. 1, 54. "Lawyers who are good settlement negotiators understand clearly that the hat they wear during negotiations is very different from the hat they might wear at an adversarial hearing or during a trial. They know that effectiveness in the settlement dynamic requires careful preparation (by them and of their clients), tight reasoning, unusual levels of candor about strengths and weaknesses, calm and open-minded exchanges of views, a quiet, understated confidence, flexibility, and the capacity to make controlled concessions. Good settlement lawyers pay attention to the needs (economic and psychological) of others and know that they have an advantage if, by the reasonableness and professionalism of their presentations, they can convert the settlement judge to an advocate of a solution that they can recommend to their client."

———

(c) MODEL

The "law and economics" movement has enjoyed great success as an analytic aid since its birth around 1960, and it promises to continue to do so. See generally Richard A. Posner, Economic Analysis of Law (9th ed. 2014). We have already seen an example in the American Hospital Supply case, and we can further demonstrate its usefulness by constructing a simple explanatory model of the disputants' settlement decision.

The aim is to construct the condition for litigation under a number of simplifying assumptions, including known recovery, equal costs, risk neutrality, rational decisionmaking by lawyers acting in their clients' best interests, and absence of impediments to bargaining. In that situation, settlement negotiations will collapse and litigation will proceed only if the minimum amount that the potential plaintiff will accept in settlement exceeds the maximum amount that the potential defendant will pay. The plaintiff's minimum is the eventually recoverable judgment (J) discounted by his estimated probability of winning (P_p), minus his future cost of litigating (L) that he would save by settling, plus his transaction cost of settling (S) that he would incur in arranging a settlement. The defendant will pay up to the eventual judgment times her estimate of the probability of the plaintiff's winning (P_d), plus litigation cost, minus settlement cost. That is to say, the necessary condition for litigation is

$$P_p J - L + S > P_d J + L - S.$$

The lessons become clearer upon rewriting the inequality as

$$(P_p - P_d) J > 2 (L - S).$$

If the two disputants agree on the probability of the outcome, and given that litigation is normally more expensive than settlement, then the left side of the second inequality is zero and the right side is positive, so that the condition for litigation will never be met—in other words, a settlement range running from the plaintiff's minimum demand up to the defendant's maximum offer will always exist, and the parties will negotiate a settlement amount that divides the range between themselves somehow. Thus, litigation should ensue only when each disputant persists in viewing his or her chance more favorably than the opponent does. That represents a significant insight.

Questions: (2) Create a numerical example in which the condition for litigation is met. Now, what changes to J, L, and S will produce a settlement range?

(3) If a critical condition for litigation is that each side be relatively optimistic about its chances, what effect would you expect a robust discovery scheme to have on the settlement rate? But what if psychologists are correct in teaching that humans tend to assimilate information in a self-serving way,

so that each side interprets new information in a way that is relatively favorable to its position? See Samuel Issacharoff, The Content of Our Casebooks: Why Do Cases Get Litigated?, 29 Fla.St.U.L.Rev. 1265, 1284–86 (2002) (discussing self-serving assessments of fairness in pretrial bargaining).

To proceed much further in analysis with assurance, one would obviously have to relax the simplifying assumptions, such as damages known by both sides to be a certain amount. Also, one would have to supplement this economic technique with other methods, such as game theory or behavioral decision theory. See Robert G. Bone, Civil Procedure: The Economics of Civil Procedure (2003). Nevertheless, simple modeling, even if based on somewhat unrealistic assumptions, can prove quite helpful to the student.

Consider, for example, the problem of frivolous litigation. The right side of the first of the two inequalities suggests why a defendant facing expensive litigation might be willing to make an offer, even if P_d is near zero. The right side will still be positive. So, the defendant can save most of her cost of litigating by settling.

But if the legal system could shift the defendant's cost of litigating to the frivolous plaintiff, which is an indemnification that Rule 11 permits, then the plaintiff's cost of litigating goes to $2L$ and the defendant's cost of litigating falls to zero. In this way, making frivolous litigation costless for the defendant would theoretically be a way for the system to remove the frivolous plaintiff's ability to threaten litigation in order to extort a nuisance settlement from the defendant.

Nonetheless, a glance at the left side of the first inequality suggests that the real world of frivolous litigation is a complex one. The left side should be negative, in that a straightforwardly frivolous suit has a negative expected value for the plaintiff, rendering mysterious why a rational plaintiff would file suit, and why a rational defendant would offer to settle. As a matter of strategy, the defendant, especially if concerned about her reputation for fighting frivolous lawsuits, would be tempted to call the plaintiff's bluff. The plaintiff, facing an out-of-pocket loss, would then cave. For frivolous litigation to be frequent enough to constitute a social problem, which it seems to be, it therefore must often involve some other factor. It could be asymmetric information, such that either the plaintiff or the defendant wrongly thinks that the plaintiff has a decent chance of winning. Then the plaintiff would be willing to file a suit, and the defendant would be willing to offer a settlement. Such situations of asymmetric information therefore call for regulation that goes beyond cost-shifting—perhaps regulation both to require prefiling investigation, as Rule 11 does, and to provide for early judicial screening, as Rule 56 does to some extent. See Robert G. Bone, Modeling Frivolous Suits, 145 U.Pa.L.Rev. 519 (1997). But cf. Chris Guthrie, Framing Frivolous Litigation: A Psychological Theory, 67 U.Chi.L.Rev. 163 (2000) (supplementing rational-actor model with law-and-psychology's framing theory, which predicts litigants' overvaluing of low-probability litigation).

———

SECTION 3.   TRIAL

If the case has survived the pretrial maneuvers and has not been settled by the parties or otherwise accelerated to termination, a trial is in order. Bear in mind that fewer and fewer trials take place each year. Nevertheless, the vanishing civil trial retains importance because it is the last-line resolver of factual disputes. Any settlement of the case will proceed in the shadow of trial's potential outcome.

Rule 40 directs each district court to provide by local rule for the placing of cases upon the calendar for trial. These local rules vary. In some districts, one of the parties must take the initiative in order to secure a trial; in others, the court exclusively handles the matter. One way or another, the case is set for trial, with or without a jury. About two-thirds of federal civil trials are jury trials.

(a) JURY

[Rules 38, 39, 47, 48]

Jury right.—Our legal system can be fairly clearly traced back to roots in the English system of a millennium ago. Over the ensuing centuries, England's system fundamentally divided into common law and equity, which as already explained were two distinct sets of courts, procedure, remedies, and substantive law. The system of common law was the older of the two. Its eventual marker was that its courts offered trial by jury, but gave relief only in the form of money damages or recovery of possession pursuant to a rigid regime of substantive law. The system of equity arose to overcome the growing inadequacies of the common law. Equity's eventual marker was that its courts did not conduct jury trials, but did give relief in the form of ordering the defendant to do or not to do something pursuant to a relatively dynamic substantive law.

Today, will the trial be to a judge alone or to a jury (under the supervision of a judge)? For the answer, begin by reading the Seventh Amendment to the Constitution of the United States.

Until relatively recently, we could have said with a fair amount of accuracy that the measure of the jury right preserved by the Constitution was whether the case was of a type that was triable by jury in a superior court of common law in England, rather than triable to a chancellor in equity, when the United States adopted the Seventh Amendment in

1791.[a] The constitutional test for the jury right thus turned on a historical dividing line.

Although that historical test is still of central importance, it no longer tells the whole story. Complications arise primarily from the fact that under the Federal Rules the federal courts hear cases in a procedural context unknown to the English courts, with the Rules' merger of law and equity being particularly significant here because it allows legal and equitable claims to be brought together. The resulting question is a difficult one. The Supreme Court has generally resolved the procedural complications in a way that preserves the jury right for both parties on any common-law cause of action appearing in a modern federal lawsuit. Likewise, the Court has simplified the application of the historical dividing line with respect to newly created causes of action by looking primarily at the form of relief, so that any action for damages will usually fall into the category of common law and thus afford a jury right.

The fact that a case falls into a category making it triable by jury as a matter of right does not necessarily mean that a jury will ultimately render a verdict upon it. The parties waive the jury right unless a party makes timely demand for it in accordance with Rule 38(b) and (c). At any rate, even if a jury is impanelled, it may never be given anything to decide, for the jury's sole function is to pass upon genuine disputes of material fact. If, for instance, the judge has reserved until trial the question whether the plaintiff has stated a claim upon which relief can be granted, the judge's determination of this question of law adversely to the plaintiff may dispose of the case without the intervention of the jury. Similarly, a ruling of law that the proof is insufficient to warrant a reasonable jury in finding that a claim or defense has been established may result in withdrawal of the case from the jury.

Jury characteristics.—A common-law jury numbered twelve, and its verdict had to be unanimous. It was long accepted without question that the jury right preserved by the Seventh Amendment entitled a party in a federal civil case to a unanimous verdict of twelve jurors. See Maxwell v. Dow, 176 U.S. 581, 586, 20 S.Ct. 448, 450 (1900). But does the Seventh Amendment actually preserve these incidents of a civil jury trial?

Consider first the *number* of jurors. Even assuming that the Seventh Amendment entitled a party in federal court to a twelve-person jury, the Seventh Amendment itself does not restrict the states. Some states had thus provided in certain civil cases for juries of fewer than twelve persons. A few states had gone further, prescribing juries of fewer than

---

[a]   The superior courts of common law were the Court of Common Pleas, the Court of King's Bench, and the Court of Exchequer. The Court of Chancery, which had jurisdiction of suits in equity, did not use the jury method of trial, except that the chancellor sometimes referred a case to a jury for advisory purposes. See generally John Baker, An Introduction to English Legal History (5th ed. 2019).

twelve in certain criminal cases, despite the fact that the criminal jury right of the Sixth Amendment does restrict the states.[b]

Yet, in Williams v. Florida, 399 U.S. 78, 90 S.Ct. 1893 (1970), the Supreme Court rejected precedent to hold that a six-person jury, acting unanimously, in a state criminal trial does not constitute a violation of the Federal Constitution. Encouraged by these developments on the criminal side, most federal district courts came to provide by local rule for six-person civil juries.[c]

Colgrove v. Battin

Supreme Court of the United States, 1973.
413 U.S. 149, 93 S.Ct. 2448.

■ MR. JUSTICE BRENNAN delivered the opinion of the Court.

Local Rule 13(d)(1) of the Revised Rules of Procedure of the United States District Court for the District of Montana provides that a jury for the trial of civil cases shall consist of six persons. When respondent District Court Judge set this diversity case for trial before a jury of six in compliance with the Rule, petitioner sought mandamus from the Court of Appeals for the Ninth Circuit to direct respondent to impanel a 12-member jury. Petitioner contended that the local Rule (1) violated the Seventh Amendment; (2) violated the statutory provision, 28 U.S.C. § 2072, [which until 1988 provided] that rules "shall preserve the right of trial by jury as at common law and as declared by the Seventh Amendment . . ."; and (3) was rendered invalid by Fed.Rule Civ.Proc. 83 because "inconsistent with" Fed.Rule Civ.Proc. 48 [which until 1991 provided in its entirety: "The parties may stipulate that the jury shall consist of any number less than twelve or that a verdict or a finding of a stated majority of the jurors shall be taken as the verdict or finding of the jury."]. The Court of Appeals found no merit in these contentions, sustained the validity of local Rule 13(d)(1), and denied the writ, 456 F.2d 1379 (1972). We granted certiorari, 409 U.S. 841, 93 S.Ct. 44 (1972). We affirm.

---

[b]   By interpretation of the Fourteenth Amendment, the Supreme Court has held most of the rights in the Bill of Rights to be fundamental enough to be guaranteed against invasion by the states, but the Seventh Amendment right to a civil jury has not been one of those. See, e.g., Walker v. Sauvinet, 92 U.S. 90 (1876); Gonzalez-Oyarzun v. Caribbean City Builders, Inc., 798 F.3d 26 (1st Cir.2015). That is to say, the Seventh Amendment applies to actions in the federal courts, but not to state-court actions. State constitutions, however, most often contain provisions similar to the Seventh Amendment.

In contrast, the Sixth Amendment right to a criminal jury does apply to the states through the Fourteenth Amendment. Why this distinction?

[c]   Federal district courts could not experiment with their criminal juries, because the Federal Rules of Criminal Procedure, independently of the Constitution, did and still do require normally in federal criminal cases a twelve-person jury that acts unanimously.

I

In Williams v. Florida, 399 U.S. 78, 90 S.Ct. 1893 (1970), the Court sustained the constitutionality of a Florida statute providing for six-member juries in certain criminal cases. The constitutional challenge rejected in that case relied on the guarantees of jury trial secured the accused by Art. III, § 2, cl. 3, of the Constitution and by the Sixth Amendment. We expressly reserved, however, the question whether "additional references to the 'common law' that occur in the Seventh Amendment might support a different interpretation" with respect to jury trial in civil cases. Id., at 92 n. 30, 90 S.Ct., at 1901 n. 30. We conclude that they do not.

The pertinent words of the Seventh Amendment are: "In Suits at common law . . . the right of trial by jury shall be preserved . . . ." On its face, this language is not directed to jury characteristics, such as size, but rather defines the kind of cases for which jury trial is preserved, namely, "suits at common law." And while it is true that "[w]e have almost no direct evidence concerning the intention of the framers of the seventh amendment itself,"[7] the historical setting in which the Seventh Amendment was adopted highlighted a controversy that was generated, not by concern for preservation of jury characteristics at common law, but by fear that the civil jury itself would be abolished unless protected in express words. Almost a century and a half ago, this Court recognized that "[o]ne of the strongest objections originally taken against the constitution of the United States, was the want of an express provision securing the right of trial by jury in civil cases." Parsons v. Bedford, 3 Pet. 433, 445 (1830). But the omission of a protective clause from the Constitution was not because an effort was not made to include one. On the contrary, a proposal was made to include a provision in the Constitution to guarantee the right of trial by jury in civil cases but the proposal failed because the States varied widely as to the cases in which civil jury trial was provided, and the proponents of a civil jury guarantee found too difficult the task of fashioning words appropriate to cover the different state practices. The strong pressures for a civil jury provision in the Bill of Rights encountered the same difficulty. Thus, it was agreed that, with no federal practice to draw on and since state practices varied so widely, any compromising language would necessarily have to be general. As a result, although the Seventh Amendment achieved the primary goal of jury trial adherents to incorporate an explicit constitutional protection of the right of trial by jury in civil cases, the right was limited in general words to "suits at common law." We can only conclude, therefore, that by referring to the "common law," the Framers of the Seventh Amendment were concerned with preserving the *right* of trial by jury in civil cases where it existed at common law, rather than the various incidents of trial by jury. In short, what was said in Williams

---

[7]   Henderson, The Background of the Seventh Amendment, 80 Harv.L.Rev. 289, 291 (1966).

with respect to the criminal jury is equally applicable here: constitutional history reveals no intention on the part of the Framers "to equate the constitutional and common-law characteristics of the jury." 399 U.S., at 99, 90 S.Ct., at 1905.

Consistently with the historical objective of the Seventh Amendment, our decisions have defined the jury right preserved in cases covered by the Amendment, as "the substance of the common-law right of trial by jury, as distinguished from mere matters of form or procedure . . . ." Baltimore & Carolina Line, Inc. v. Redman, 295 U.S. 654, 657, 55 S.Ct. 890, 891 (1935). The Amendment, therefore, does not "bind the federal courts to the exact procedural incidents or details of jury trial according to the common law in 1791," Galloway v. United States, 319 U.S. 372, 390, 63 S.Ct. 1077, 1087 (1943); see also Ex parte Peterson, 253 U.S. 300, 309, 40 S.Ct. 543, 546 (1920); Walker v. New Mexico & S.P.R. Co., 165 U.S. 593, 596, 17 S.Ct. 421, 422 (1897), and "[n]ew devices may be used to adapt the ancient institution to present needs and to make of it an efficient instrument in the administration of justice. . . ." Ex parte Peterson, supra, 253 U.S., at 309–310, 40 S.Ct., at 546; Funk v. United States, 290 U.S. 371, 382, 54 S.Ct. 212, 215 (1933).

Our inquiry turns, then, to whether a jury of 12 is of the substance of the common-law right of trial by jury. Keeping in mind the purpose of the jury trial in criminal cases to prevent government oppression, Williams, 399 U.S., at 100, 90 S.Ct., at 1905, and, in criminal and civil cases, to assure a fair and equitable resolution of factual issues, Gasoline Products Co. v. Champlin Refining Co., 283 U.S. 494, 498, 51 S.Ct. 513, 514 (1931), the question comes down to whether jury performance is a function of jury size. In Williams, we rejected the notion that "the reliability of the jury as a factfinder . . . [is] a function of its size," 399 U.S., at 100–101, 90 S.Ct., at 1906, and nothing has been suggested to lead us to alter that conclusion. Accordingly, we think it cannot be said that 12 members is a substantive aspect of the right of trial by jury.

It is true, of course, that several earlier decisions of this Court have made the statement that "trial by jury" means "a trial by a jury of 12 . . . ." Capital Traction Co. v. Hof, 174 U.S. 1, 13, 19 S.Ct. 580, 585 (1899); see also American Publishing Co. v. Fisher, 166 U.S. 464, 17 S.Ct. 618 (1897); Maxwell v. Dow, 176 U.S. 581, 586, 20 S.Ct. 448, 450 (1900). But in each case, the reference to "a jury of twelve" was clearly dictum and not a decision upon a question presented or litigated. . . . Insofar as the Hof statement implied that the Seventh Amendment required a jury of 12, it was at best an assumption. And even if that assumption had support in common-law doctrine, our canvass of the relevant constitutional history, like the history canvassed in Williams concerning the criminal jury, "casts considerable doubt on the easy assumption in our past decisions that if a given feature existed in a jury at common law . . . then it was necessarily preserved in the Constitution." 399 U.S., at

92–93, 90 S.Ct., at 1902. We cannot, therefore, accord the unsupported dicta of these earlier decisions the authority of decided precedents.

There remains, however, the question whether a jury of six satisfies the Seventh Amendment guarantee of "trial by jury." We had no difficulty reaching the conclusion in Williams that a jury of six would guarantee an accused the trial by jury secured by Art. III and the Sixth Amendment. Significantly, our determination that there was "no discernible difference between the results reached by the two different-sized juries," 399 U.S., at 101, 90 S.Ct., at 1906, drew largely upon the results of studies of the operations of juries of six in civil cases. Since then, much has been written about the six-member jury, but nothing that persuades us to depart from the conclusion reached in Williams.[15] Thus, while we express no view as to whether any number less than six would suffice,[16] we conclude that a jury of six satisfies the Seventh Amendment's guarantee of trial by jury in civil cases.

[Parts II and III of the Court's opinion rebuffed the petitioner's arguments based on § 2072 and on Rules 48 and 83. They are omitted.]

Affirmed.

. . . .

■ Mr. Justice Marshall, with whom Mr. Justice Stewart joins, dissenting.

Some 30 years ago, Mr. Justice Black warned his Brethren against the "gradual process of judicial erosion which . . . has slowly worn away a major portion of the essential guarantee of the Seventh Amendment." Galloway v. United States, 319 U.S. 372, 397, 63 S.Ct. 1077, 1090 (1943) (dissenting opinion). Today, the erosion process reaches bedrock. . . .

. . . No one need be fooled by reference to the six-man trier of fact utilized in the District Court for the District of Montana as a "jury." . . . We deal here not with some minor tinkering with the role of the civil jury, but with its wholesale abolition and replacement with a different institution which functions differently, produces different results, and was wholly unknown to the Framers of the Seventh Amendment.

. . . .

---

[15] Arguments, pro and con, on the effectiveness of a jury of six compared to a jury of 12 will be found in Devitt, [The Six Man Jury in the Federal Court, 53 F.R.D. 273 (1971)]; . . . Zeisel, . . . And Then There Were None: The Diminution of the Federal Jury, 38 U.Chi.L.Rev. 710 (1971) . . . . [On the dangers of the use by courts of social science research, see Jeffrey J. Rachlinski, "The Story of Colgrove: Social Science on Trial," in Civil Procedure Stories 389 (Kevin M. Clermont ed., 2d ed. 2008).—Ed.]

[16] What is required for a "jury" is a number large enough to facilitate group deliberation combined with a likelihood of obtaining a representative cross section of the community. Williams v. Florida, 399 U.S., at 100, 90 S.Ct., at 1905. It is undoubtedly true that at some point the number becomes too small to accomplish these goals, but, on the basis of presently available data, that cannot be concluded as to the number six. [Citations omitted.]

When a historical approach is applied to the issue at hand, it cannot be doubted that the Framers envisioned a jury of 12 when they referred to trial by jury. . . .

. . . .

The Court today elects to abandon the certainty of this historical test, as well as the many cases which support it, in favor of a vaguely defined functional analysis which asks not what the Framers meant by "trial by jury" but rather whether some substitute for the common-law jury performs the same functions as a jury and serves as an adequate substitute for one. . . .

. . . But the composition of the jury itself is a matter of arbitrary, a priori definition. As Mr. Justice Harlan argued "[t]he right to a trial by jury . . . has no enduring meaning apart from historical form." Williams v. Florida, 399 U.S., at 125, 90 S.Ct., at 1919 (separate opinion).

It is senseless, then, to say that a panel of six constitutes a "jury" without first defining what one means by a jury, and that initial definition must, in the nature of things, be arbitrary. . . . There is no way by reference to abstract principle or "function" that one can determine that six is "enough," five is "too small," and 30 "too large."[8] These evaluations can only be made by reference to a hypothetical ideal jury of some arbitrarily chosen size. All one can say is that a jury of six functions less like a jury of 12 than would a jury of, say eight, but more like a jury of 12 than would a jury of three.[9] Although I think it clear that my Brethren would reject, for example, a jury of one, the Court does not begin to tell us how it would go about drawing a line in a nonarbitrary fashion, and it is obvious that in matters of degree of this kind, nonarbitrary line drawing is a logical impossibility.

Of course, there is nothing intrinsically wrong with drawing arbitrary lines and, indeed, . . . in order to resolve certain problems they are essential. Thus, this Court has not hesitated in the past to rely on arbitrary demarcations in cases where constitutional rights depend on matters of degree. See, e.g., Burns v. Fortson, 410 U.S. 686, 93 S.Ct. 1209 (1973) [(upholding fifty-day pre-election cutoff on voter registration, while saying this approaches constitutional limit)]. But in cases where

---

[8]   The Court asserts that "[w]hat is required for a 'jury' is a number large enough to facilitate group deliberation combined with a likelihood of obtaining a representative cross section of the community." See ante, at . . . n. 16. We can bypass for the moment the intriguing question of where the majority finds this requirement in the words of the Seventh Amendment. For our purposes, it is sufficient to note that, upon examination, this "test" turns out to be no test at all. It may be that the ideal jury would provide "enough" group deliberation and community representation. But the question in this case is how much is "enough." Obviously, the larger the jury the more group representation it will provide. . . . Merely observing that a certain level of group representation is constitutionally required fails to tell us what that level is. And, more significantly, it fails to tell us how to go about deciding what that level is.

[9]   It thus will not do to argue, as has my Brother White, that one "can get off the 'slippery slope' before he reaches the bottom. . . ." Williams v. Florida, 399 U.S. 78, 91 n. 28, 90 S.Ct. 1893, 1901 n. 28 (1970). This begs the question how one knows at what point to get off—a question for which the Court apparently has no answer.

arbitrary lines are necessary, I would have thought it more consonant with our limited role in a constitutional democracy to draw them with reference to the fixed bounds of the Constitution rather than on a wholly ad hoc basis.

I think history will bear out the proposition that when constitutional rights are grounded in nothing more solid than the intuitive, unexplained sense of five Justices that a certain line is "right" or "just," those rights are certain to erode and, eventually, disappear altogether. Today, a majority of this Court may find six-man juries to represent a proper balance between competing demands of expedition and group representation. But as dockets become more crowded and pressures on jury trials grow, who is to say that some future Court will not find three, or two, or one a number large enough to satisfy its unexplicated sense of justice? It should be clear that constitutional rights which are so vulnerable to pressures of the moment are not really protected by the Constitution at all. . . .

. . . It may well be that the number 12 is no more than a "historical accident" and is "wholly without significance 'except to mystics.'" Williams v. Florida, supra, 399 U.S., at 102, 90 S.Ct., at 1907. But surely there is nothing more significant about the number six, or three, or one. The line must be drawn somewhere, and the difference between drawing it in the light of history and drawing it on an ad hoc basis is, ultimately, the difference between interpreting a constitution and making it up as one goes along.

. . . .

■ [JUSTICES DOUGLAS and POWELL dissented on other grounds, allowing them to avoid reaching the constitutional issue. Their opinions are omitted.]

———

A strong majority of states have since moved to juries smaller than twelve. However, in Ballew v. Georgia, 435 U.S. 223, 98 S.Ct. 1029 (1978), the Supreme Court held that in a state criminal trial a five-person jury, even though acting unanimously, constitutes a violation of the Federal Constitution. All the Justices supported this holding, although the case produced five opinions. Justice Blackmun, through a lengthy review of the numerous post-Williams empirical studies on the jury, explained that reducing the jury below six members would adversely affect group deliberation and cross-sectional representation. Among other points, he observed that the smaller the jury, the less likely is the group to remember accurately, to overcome the biases of its members, and to exhibit self-criticism; also, "the data now raise doubts about the accuracy of the results achieved by smaller and smaller panels," as well as about the consistency thereof. Furthermore, reducing jury size erects barriers to "the representation of minority groups in the community." Meanwhile, he argued, reducing the jury below six members would offer only minimal savings in court time and financial costs. Accordingly, the Court drew the line.

In the meantime, a roughly similar scenario is working itself out on the *unanimity* front. It has long been the general assumption that the Seventh Amendment entitles a party in federal court to a unanimous verdict. Indeed, here it is more than assumption, the Supreme Court having in fact so held in Springville v. Thomas, 166 U.S. 707, 17 S.Ct. 717 (1897), and apparently also in American Publishing Co. v. Fisher, 166 U.S. 464, 17 S.Ct. 618 (1897). Some states, on the other hand, abolished the unanimity requirement for certain civil and criminal cases. When the issue finally arose, in Apodaca v. Oregon, 406 U.S. 404, 92 S.Ct. 1628 (1972), and Johnson v. Louisiana, 406 U.S. 356, 92 S.Ct. 1620 (1972), a sharply divided Supreme Court held that a nonunanimous verdict, by a twelve-person jury, in a state criminal trial passes federal constitutional muster. There was some indication by the Court, however, that a "substantial majority of the jury" is necessary and that a 9–3 verdict is at or very near the constitutional floor for twelve-person state criminal juries.

Questions: (1) The winds of change are obviously buffeting Springville and American Publishing. Do you see any way that their constitutional requirement of unanimity for federal civil juries could survive the trend of the modern cases, if somehow a challenge were to arise? Is there an argument in the fact that the Court here faces actual holdings directly in point, unlike the situation confronting the Court in Colgrove? If not, is there an argument you can build on the fact (a) that Apodaca and Johnson are criminal cases, as contrasted to civil cases governed by the Seventh Amendment, or (b) that Apodaca and Johnson are state cases, thus leaving open the question whether unanimity is still a requirement for federal juries? Or is there an argument tied to the questionable belief that unanimity is a more important concern than is the number of jurors, thus allowing Colgrove to be distinguished? Note that the Supreme Court has granted certiorari, after a 10–2 verdict in a state criminal trial, on "whether the Fourteenth Amendment fully incorporates the [supposed] Sixth Amendment guarantee of a unanimous verdict." Ramos v. Louisiana, 139 S.Ct. 1318 (2019).

(2) Assuming nonunanimous verdicts by federal civil juries are authorized, what combinations of reduced numbers of jurors and majority verdicts would you deem constitutionally permissible? Eight-out-of-nine?

In Burch v. Louisiana, 441 U.S. 130, 99 S.Ct. 1623 (1979), the Court held that in a state criminal trial a nonunanimous verdict, by a six-person jury, violates the Federal Constitution. All the Justices were in agreement that a 5–1 verdict is invalid. Writing for the Court, Justice Rehnquist addressed this " 'close' " question "at the intersection of our decisions concerning jury size and unanimity" by first noting that "having already departed from the strictly historical requirements of jury trial, it is inevitable that lines must be drawn somewhere if the substance of the jury trial right is to be preserved." He then quickly concluded that "much the same reasons that led us in Ballew to decide that use of a five-member jury threatened the fairness of the proceeding and the proper role of the jury, lead us to conclude now that conviction for a nonpetty offense by only five members of a six-person jury presents a similar threat to preservation of the substance of the jury trial guarantee and justifies our requiring verdicts rendered by six-person juries to be unanimous."

Given all this, where do we stand on unanimity for civil juries? Well more than half of the states permit a less than unanimous verdict in a civil case, with three-quarters or even two-thirds of the jurors being sufficient for a verdict. In New York, under NY CPLR § 4113, a verdict may be rendered by five-sixths of the six jurors. See generally Hans Zeisel, The Verdict of Five out of Six Civil Jurors: Constitutional Problems, 1982 Am.B.Found.Res.J. 141, 155.

On December 1, 1991, Rule 48 took on essentially its present form, expressly specifying the key characteristics of the federal civil jury and thus restricting further experimentation by any federal district court's local rule. The new Rule 48 invoked the Colgrove holding to provide for juries of at least six persons, who act unanimously, unless the parties otherwise stipulate.

Interestingly, the rulemakers worked this reform soon after the American Bar Association, upon a weighing of the evidence and values, had called for returning to a federal civil jury of twelve but allowing 10–2 verdicts. 58 U.S.L.W. 2474, 2478 (Feb. 20, 1990). More recently, the ABA, in its Principles for Juries & Jury Trials princs. 3–4 (2005), threw its support to twelve-person juries acting unanimously.

Still more interestingly, after the 1991 amendment of Rule 48, the civil rulemaking committees proposed amending it to require the seating of twelve-person juries that act unanimously. The Advisory Committee's note had explained its proposal's purpose:

"Rule 48 [would be] amended to restore the core of the twelve-member body that has constituted the definition of a civil jury for centuries. Local rules setting smaller jury sizes [would be] invalid because inconsistent with Rule 48.

"The rulings that the Seventh Amendment permits six-member juries, and that former Rule 48 permitted local rules establishing six-member juries, do not speak to the question whether six-member juries are desirable. Much has been learned since 1973 about the advantages of twelve-member juries. Twelve-member juries substantially increase the representative quality of most juries, greatly improving the probability that most juries will include members of minority groups. The sociological and psychological dynamics of jury deliberation also are strongly influenced by jury size. Members of a twelve-person jury are less easily dominated by an aggressive juror, better able to recall the evidence, more likely to rise above the biases and prejudices of individual members, and enriched by a broader base of community experience. The wisdom enshrined in the twelve-member tradition is increasingly demonstrated by contemporary social science."

But when this proposal reached the Judicial Conference in 1996, it rejected the proposal as inefficient. So, read Rule 48 as it exists today. The drafters envisaged as the normal course the seating of juries somewhat larger than six members, but not more than twelve, to insure against attrition during the trial. If the judge excused one or more jurors pursuant to Rule 47(c), as for illness, there should then still be at least six persons to render verdict. So today, eight-person federal civil juries are most commonly impanelled.

Jury selection.—The Jury Selection and Service Act of 1968, 28 U.S.C. §§ 1861–1869, aims at ensuring selection of federal jurors at random from a fair cross section of the community without discrimination on account of race, color, religion, sex, national origin, or economic status. Each district court must adopt a selection plan, normally tied to voter lists.

The Act otherwise leaves the selection of the actual jury largely to local rule and practice. Still, some general description is possible. From the list of available citizens, the statutory officials summon to the courtroom a panel of jurors. From that panel, they draw by lot the tentative jurors for the particular trial. These jurors then undergo the questioning process referred to in Rule 47(a), which is called the voir dire examination and which in federal court is usually conducted by the judge. Its purpose is to determine whether good reason exists why any of them should not serve in the case.

If, for example, a juror is related to a party, or if she has a financial interest in the outcome of the case, or if she is prejudiced against a party, she may be challenged "for cause." The court will exclude the juror if it finds that the cause exists. In addition, at some point in the process, each side can exercise a limited number of "peremptory challenges" (28 U.S.C. § 1870 provides each party in a civil case with three peremptory challenges, but when there are multiple plaintiffs or defendants, the court in its discretion may treat each side as a single party or may allow additional peremptory challenges). A party may exercise peremptory challenges at the party's mainly uncontrolled pleasure.

Jurors who have been excluded by either type of challenge are replaced by other persons similarly drawn by lot from the panel and similarly subjected to questioning and challenge. When the process of selection is completed, the jury is sworn. The trial proceeds.

———

VALERIE P. HANS & NEIL VIDMAR, "JURY SELECTION," in The Psychology of the Courtroom 39, 63–64, 68 (Norbert L. Kerr & Robert M. Bray eds., 1982). "Trial tactics handbooks used in the training of lawyers provide us with some indirect evidence about the theories of 'good' jurors and 'bad' jurors that guide selection practices. The handbooks . . . consist of a mixture of legal lore, streamlined social science findings, and common sense. Some of the advice extended to lawyers betrays an obvious trafficking in stereotypes. A case in point is provided by Bailey and Rothblatt[, Successful Techniques for Criminal Trials] (1971), who suggest that defense lawyers choose women for the jury if the principal witness against the defendant is female, since women are 'somewhat distrustful' of other women; they also caution that the occupation of a prospective woman juror's husband is of importance, since generally a woman 'will feel and think in the same manner as her husband [p. 105].' Given that the information about jurors is often minimal, the trial tactics manuals do display a remarkable ingenuity in developing generalizations about those characteristics typically available to lawyers, such as occupation. For example, Bailey and Rothblatt maintain that salesmen, actors, artists, and writers are highly desirable as defense jurors, reasoning that because their occupations have exposed them to varied aspects of life, these individuals are not so easily shocked by crime as are people in less adventuresome occupations. [Another manual] warns defense lawyers to beware of individuals who are employees of large bureaucratic organizations, since these persons are less inclined to sympathize with the nonconforming behavior of the defendant. Also of note in the trial tactics manuals is an emphasis on fitting juror characteristics to the details of the specific case (e.g., women jurors for an attractive male defendant but male jurors when the offense is rape).

"In addition to providing a wealth of information about demographic predictors of the sympathetic juror (information that is of dubious value), trial manuals also suggest strategies for the conduct of the voir dire. Lawyers are advised [for example] to use the voir dire not only to ferret out those who are unfavorable to their case but also to ingratiate themselves with the jury. . . .

. . . .

"There is, therefore, scanty concrete information about the effectiveness of lawyers' selection techniques although what we do know indicates that generally selection strategies may be only minimally effective. From a psychological perspective, it seems unlikely that future studies of lawyer effectiveness would substantially alter the current conclusion that attorney strategies have minimal impact on the jury's verdict. . . . In real jury trials, the voir dire may be effective in eliminating openly prejudiced persons, but we cannot expect too much more.

"On the other hand, the most useful function of the voir dire may be its ability to indoctrinate and sensitize jurors about the need to set aside prejudices and participate in the trial with an impartial mind. This function of the voir dire . . . awaits systematic empirical examination.

. . . .

"In the late 1960s and early 1970s, social scientists became directly involved in jury selection in a series of political trials evolving out of racial protests and the Vietnam War. Variously labeled 'scientific' or 'systematic' jury selection, the techniques provide the defense with an alternative to traditional jury selection [and include community opinion surveys, investigation of jury panel members, and courtroom observation of prospective jurors]."

————

MICHAEL J. SAKS & REID HASTIE, SOCIAL PSYCHOLOGY IN COURT 49, 66–71 (1978). "The theory underlying the core hypothesis, that the characteristics of jurors affect the decision they reach, can be stated fairly simply. A person's demographic background (socioeconomic class, race, religion, sex, age, education, and so forth) denotes a particular kind of socializing history for that person. If you are poor, young, black, and female, you will have been conditioned to view the world differently, to react to it differently, and to hold different attitudes compared with a person who is wealthy, old, white, and male. These perceptions, attitudes, and values, in turn, help determine the decision you make as a juror. In addition to demographic characteristics, personality type (whether personality arises through genetics, psychodynamic development, or conditioning history) is thought to predispose a juror to a particular decision. If you are highly dependent on order, for example, you might be conviction-prone. It is unclear whether the theory holds that personality type determines the substantive preference one has (e.g., always wanting to be punitive) or whether it influences the way one processes the evidence (giving more weight to the government's evidence than to the defense's). Thus, juror demographic characteristics, personality, and attitudes are thought to have substantial impact on their decisions.

. . . .

"Despite a good deal of excitement about scientific jury selection . . . , and despite the apparently widely held assumption that the kind of person making a decision affects the decision made, the evidence consistently indicates that a jury's composition is a relatively minor determinant of the verdict. In the face of such enthusiastic countervailing belief, this conclusion may seem surprising. However, it should not. Small-group researchers have long recognized that individual difference variables account for little of the variation in group performance . . . . Juries are merely a special case of small-group decision making and are not exempt from the principles that apply to small groups generally. Nor should small-group researchers be surprised by the lack of impact of personality and attitude variables. The relative unimportance of personality . . . and attitudes . . . as determinants of behavior has become increasingly evident in the study of human behavior generally. What, then, does determine the verdict a jury will render if it is not the characteristics of the group members? . . .

. . . .

"In another study [Michael J. Saks, Carol M. Werner & Thomas M. Ostrom, The Presumption of Innocence and the American Juror, 2 J.Contemp.L. 46 (1975)], a sample of former jurors from Columbus, Ohio, were asked to indicate their certainty of a defendant's guilt or innocence in a series of brief hypothetical cases, each consisting of a set of evidentiary statements. They were given cases in which the crime alleged differed, where the amount of evidence against the defendant differed, and in which the strength of the evidence varied; it was either moderately (prescaled to reflect a .44 probability of guilt) or highly (.77) incriminating. Jurors were also tested with a scale of defendant-related attitudes in order to classify them as favorable or unfavorable to the defense. The attitude scale did predict how the jurors would respond. Jurors designated 'antidefendant' gave an average rating of guilt of 58 while 'prodefendant' jurors gave ratings that averaged −20. (A score of zero would indicate a juror thought it was equally likely that the defendant was guilty as not guilty; positive scores are in the guilty direction; negative scores in the not guilty direction.) That is a spread of 78 points. But the point spread between average certainty of guilt in response to one item of evidence compared to six items of evidence was 143 points. And presenting moderately incriminating evidence compared to highly incriminating evidence produced a spread of 172 points. In terms of the proportion of variance accounted for by each of the independent variables, the amount of evidence was more than three times as powerful, and the strength of evidence was more than seven times as powerful as attitudes were in determining the jurors' verdicts. Juror characteristics made a difference, but not nearly so much of a difference as characteristics of the trial evidence.

. . . .

"The studies are unanimous in showing that evidence is a substantially more potent determinant of jurors' verdicts than the individual characteristics of jurors. Indeed, the power of evidence is so well recognized by jury researchers that when studying processes other than evidence, they must calibrate the evidence to be moderate so that it leaves some variance to be influenced by the variables under study. Manipulating the evidence powerfully influences the verdict the group renders. This finding also is consistent with findings from elsewhere in psychological research. However important personality and attitudes may be in determining overt behavior, they generally are not as important as stimulus features of the situation . . . . What this implies about human behavior, on juries or off, is that while we are unique individuals, our differences are vastly overshadowed by our similarities. Moreover, the range of situations we are likely to encounter is far more varied than the range of human beings who will encounter them.

. . . .

"From the viewpoint of the jury system, [all the research] findings mean that jurors [especially] are much more responsive to the evidence placed before them than to their own personalities and attitudes. Our educated speculation is that this may well be due to the special social situation created by the court. Through learning outside of court and by the court's atmosphere, the judge's charges, and the rules of the game, jurors adopt a role of 'fairness' and 'objectivity' which may be as extreme as they ever have had or will have in their lives. That jurors are selected who do not have ongoing relationships with the parties or interests at stake in the case further enhances the success of the 'objective factfinders' role. Common-sense assumptions that the personal politics and prejudice which characterize much of human life invade the jury box ignore the special situational characteristics of the court and the human relationships constructed there.

. . . .

"From the viewpoint of attorneys and social scientists, working to serve a particular side of a particular case, these findings mean that while jury selection will have some impact on the outcome of the case, it is not as effective as directing their efforts at building and structuring the evidence to be presented to the jury."

————

KEVIN M. CLERMONT & THEODORE EISENBERG, TRIAL BY JURY OR JUDGE: TRANSCENDING EMPIRICISM, 77 Cornell L.Rev. 1124, 1151–55 (1992) (footnotes omitted). "Indeed, one of the more remarkable lessons that empirical study has to offer the law is that virtually no evidence exists to support the prevailing ingrained intuitions about juries [as biased and incompetent, relative to judges]. In fact, existing evidence is to the contrary.

"Admittedly, not much effective empirical work exists on the quality of the jury's performance, and there is even less on juries' performance as compared to that of judges. Studies on broad questions regarding the jury are difficult to do, and correspondingly shaky to interpret. But the evidence, such as it is, consistently supports a view of the jury as generally unbiased and competent, or at least so compared to a judge. The fact that jury and judge show a high degree of agreement is better supported.

"Research, for example, indicates that the strength of the trial evidence is the most important determinant of the verdict. Evaluated over the run of cases, juries are good factfinders. More specifically, research does not support a view of the jury as overly generous on awards, frequently ignoring the law, or institutionally unable to handle complex cases. Related research indeed suggests that a jury could even outperform a judge, because the judge is also human and groups typically outperform individuals by virtue of superiority in such tasks as recall of facts and correction of errors.

"The classic work in this area by Kalven and Zeisel[, The American Jury 63–64 (2d ed. 1971),] addressed reliability (the ability to treat like cases alike) rather than the validity or correctness of jury decisionmaking. Their questionnaires to presiding judges in some 4000 actual civil jury trials in the 1950's yielded data showing a 78% agreement between judge and jury on liability. When judge and jury disagreed, they exhibited no distinct pattern other than the juries' very small tendency to favor plaintiffs relative to judges.

"When compared to other human decisionmakers, the rate of agreement is more impressive than it first appears. This 78% agreement rate is better than the rate of agreement [on dichotomous decisions] between scientists doing peer review, employment interviewers ranking applicants, and psychiatrists and physicians diagnosing patients, and almost as good as the 79% or 80% rate of agreement between judges making sentencing decisions [of custody or no custody] in an experimental setting. So although theory plausibly suggests some judge/jury differences—such as that juries, because of a need for compromise to produce a unanimous verdict, would tend to give plaintiffs more wins but less money—the significance of any such differences seems to fade in actuality. Apparently, judge trial and jury trial combine to operate a decisionmaking system that is, at least in one sense, highly reliable.

"Much of the recent research has focused on jury verdicts, revealing trends such as the average award markedly increasing in recent years. Even if accurate, these observations do not bear on the issue of jury performance versus judge performance. Judges, who go wholly unobserved in this research, might be responding similarly to similar forces. For a specific example, [the following graph] presents from our data, in millions of 1989 dollars, the mean recovery in judge and jury trials of successful product liability cases over the calendar years covered by this study. The similarity of the recovery trends suggests that the explanation for trends in awards lies somewhere other than in peculiarities of the jury system."

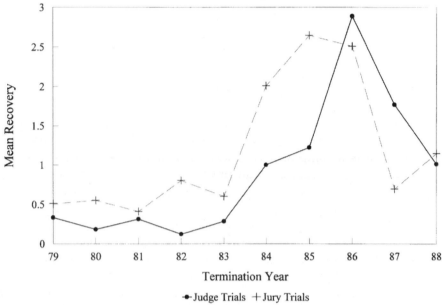

Mean Recovery vs. Termination Year:
Product Liability Cases

-•-Judge Trials +Jury Trials

Source: Administrative Office Data, 1979-1989

PEREMPTORY CHALLENGES

Amidst this swirl of deleterious, negligible, and beneficial effects, one might presume that the permissibility of peremptory challenges has little net effect on outcome. Then why should the law permit this questionable type of challenge, which comes into play only when the court does not find cause to excuse? What are the benefits and costs of peremptory challenges?

Could one defend permitting these challenges on the ground that, all else being equal, we have a better process, as a process, when people have a say in selecting their own adjudicator? At least, one could pragmatically argue that the availability of these challenges helps to ensure sound operation of challenges for cause, in that peremptories enable the litigator to question aggressively in pursuit of an exclusion for cause, without too much concern that an especially alienated juror will remain on the jury if the challenge for cause fails.

But even if those assertions were true, counter-values would seem also to be at stake. Most obviously, parties can surely misuse peremptory challenges of jurors. Although recent cases prohibit their use on invidious bases such as race, that imperfect regulation obviously increases the costs of administration. See Minetos v. CUNY, 925 F.Supp. 177, 183 (S.D.N.Y.1996) (dictum) ("All peremptory challenges should now be banned as an unnecessary waste of time and an obvious corruption of the judicial process.").

Perhaps those counter-values explain why no equivalent of the peremptory challenge exists under 28 U.S.C. §§ 144 and 455, which provide the standards for disqualification of federal district judges.

———

KEVIN M. CLERMONT, ROBERT A. HILLMAN, SHERI LYNN JOHNSON & ROBERT S. SUMMERS, LAW FOR SOCIETY: NATURE, FUNCTIONS, AND LIMITS 101 (2010). "[Process-oriented] law, if well designed, will reflect a variety of important values. These values generate standards or criteria for judging the goodness or badness of processes such as adjudication, legislation, and administration. The important point here is that one has not exhaustively accounted for the total significance of such values merely by stressing their relationship to quality of outcome. Some processes have significance quite apart from their impact on outcome, and some indeed lead to a negative impact on outcome. This point is overlooked by some contemporary reformers who have their tunnel vision focused on result and result alone.

"There is independent worth, for example, in having processes in which those most vitally affected can be meaningfully heard and in having processes free of the taint of undue influence. The kinds of values reflected thereby, in contrast to *outcome values,* we shall call *process values.* To speak somewhat more carefully, then, we shall use the phrase 'process values' to refer to values by which we can judge a legal process to be good as a process, apart from any good outcome it may yield in the case at hand. We might use the phrase 'outcome-value efficacy' to refer to the tendency of a legal process to favor the desired winner.

"We do not mean to suggest that process values are beyond argument. Indeed, the word 'value' suggests just the opposite. They are latent and subtle. Moreover, much room remains for debate as to what they mean precisely (think particularly of equality) and how much weight they deserve relatively (think generally of process versus outcome values) and also as to whose values they are and how they come into play. Nevertheless, process values do seem to exist, independent of outcome values. One proof of the independent importance of process values is that we all know from experience that we would condemn public processes that did not reflect such values even if the processes' decisional output were invariably good. That is, for reasons independent of outcome, we want processes in which affected parties are heard and in which decision makers are free of undue influence. All that ends well is not well after all."

———

Question: (3) What would be an example of a rule that serves process values without serving, or while even undercutting, outcome values?

(b) ORDER AND METHOD OF PROOF

[Rules 50(a), 52(c)]

The law largely confides the conduct of a trial to the trial judge's discretion, rather than governing it by specific Rules. Therefore we resort in much of the following description to an account of the traditional course of a usual trial. For the purpose of this account, we assume that the judge-run trial includes a jury. But the main elements of that traditional course are much the same whether the trial is by jury and judge or by the judge alone.

Burden of proof.—Who must prove what? What happens if the burdened party does not present enough evidence to persuade the jury?[d]

Speaking broadly, the law allots between the parties the burden of persuasion on particular disputed issues in the same way that the rules of pleading assign the burden of allegation.[e] Thus, plaintiff will lose if the jury is not persuaded of the truth of the allegations of the complaint that defendant has denied in the answer. So also, defendant's affirmative defenses will fail if the jury is not persuaded of their truth.

What happens if no evidence is presented on a disputed issue? Ordinarily, plaintiff has the initial burden of production, obliged to bring forward evidence in support of the disputed issues in his claim or suffer defeat.

Question: (4) Why is this ordinarily so? Suggest cases where it is not so.

Opening statements.—Before calling his witnesses, plaintiff's attorney customarily makes an opening statement in which he tells the jury what the issues in the action are and what he proposes to prove. The purpose of the opening is to explain the case in such a way that the jury will be better able to follow the testimony. Commonly, defendant's attorney follows immediately with a comparable opening statement, although defendant's attorney sometimes can choose to postpone this until the beginning of defendant's case.

Plaintiff's case.—Plaintiff's first witness is called to the stand, sworn to tell the truth, and questioned first by plaintiff's attorney (direct examination) and next by defendant's attorney (cross-examination), following which there may be redirect examination, recross-examination, and so on. Other witnesses for plaintiff are called and subjected to the same process of examination until plaintiff's attorney is satisfied that he

---

[d]   We pass over at this point the question of the degree of persuasion to which the evidence must bring the minds of the jurors before they can properly accept a proposition as established. Suffice it now to say that in a civil case the required degree of persuasion, or standard of proof, is normally "preponderance of the evidence," which is said to require a showing of more-likely-than-not.

[e]   This is not invariably so. For example, the defendant is to plead contributory negligence as an affirmative defense under Rule 8(c)(1), but we shall see that the substantive law has sometimes cast upon the plaintiff the burden of proving the absence of contributory negligence.

has done all that he feasibly can to establish the elements of the claim. In theory he is not supposed at this stage of the case to anticipate defenses and rebut them; but matters of claim and defense are frequently so interwoven that it is not practicable to try to separate them, and so the trial judge usually allows considerable leeway. Upon the completion of the testimony in support of his "case in chief," plaintiff's attorney announces that he rests his case.

Motion at the close of plaintiff's case.—When plaintiff rests, he may have failed to present any evidence on an issue upon which he has the burden of production, or his evidence on it may be so insufficient that it could not persuade any reasonable trier of fact. In such a situation, defendant may move for judgment as a matter of law pursuant to Rule 50(a), a motion formerly called a motion for a directed verdict. If the judge grants such a motion, the judge will withdraw the case from the jury. Judgment will be entered for defendant.

Question: (5) The corresponding motion by the defendant where the action is being tried without a jury is a motion for a judgment on partial findings under Rule 52(c). However, here the standard that the defendant must meet is the much less stringent one that "the court finds against" the plaintiff on a dispositive issue. Do you see why such very different standards should prevail under Rules 50(a) and 52(c)?

Defendant does not risk all by making a motion at the close of plaintiff's case. If the judge does not grant the motion, defendant may proceed with her case just as if she had not made the motion.

Defendant's case.—If plaintiff has presented evidence sufficient to permit a reasonable trier to find in plaintiff's favor, defendant's motion would be futile because the judge will not withdraw such a case from the jury. Yet defendant may still cut short the scenario—by resting without offering proof.

Why would defendant rest right away? After plaintiff rests, the condition of the evidence may be such that reasonable triers could differ. For example, the situation may be that plaintiff has sustained the burden of production only if the jury believes a given piece of evidence, and a reasonable jury might either believe or disbelieve it. By resting, defendant stakes her chances upon argument to the jury that they should not accept plaintiff's story as true. Defendant would do so where she has little evidence to offer or a lot of confidence, or perhaps where defendant's only evidence would entail great expense or would risk backfiring.

Ordinarily, however, defendant will proceed to offer her own evidence. Defendant may design this evidence to disprove one or more of the disputed issues on which plaintiff has the burden of proof. Or defendant's evidence may break new ground, being designed to prove matters of affirmative defense upon which defendant has the burden of proof. The process of direct examination by defendant's attorney and cross-examination by plaintiff's attorney is the same as that already described. Upon completion of her presentation of evidence, defendant's attorney rests.

Motion at the close of defendant's case.—When defendant rests, plaintiff may move for judgment as a matter of law pursuant to Rule 50(a), without waiving his right to put in rebuttal evidence if the judge does not grant his motion.

Questions: (6) May plaintiff make a corresponding motion at this point if the case is being tried without a jury? See Rule 52(c).

(7) May defendant, at this point, make a motion for judgment as a matter of law or a motion for a judgment on partial findings? See Rules 50(a) and 52(c).

Rebuttal and rejoinder.—Assuming that plaintiff has not moved for judgment as a matter of law, or that the judge has not granted his motion, he now has the chance to offer rebuttal evidence. Properly speaking, plaintiff should limit rebuttal to evidence that meets new facts put in evidence by defendant.

On the one hand, rebuttal can nevertheless go beyond evidence designed to meet an affirmative defense. For instance, defendant may have presented a supposed eyewitness to an automobile accident whose testimony contradicted that of plaintiff's witnesses. It would be proper rebuttal on the part of plaintiff to put on a witness to testify that defendant's witness was elsewhere at the time of the accident.

On the other hand, mere reiteration of plaintiff's own evidence for the purpose of giving it added emphasis so as to overcome the effect of contradictory testimony is improper rebuttal. It is also improper to reserve for rebuttal material that was properly a part of the case in chief, as defendant may have supposed that the case in chief was the entire case to meet. However, the trial judge has a wide discretion in these matters. The judge is likely, for example, to permit testimony in rebuttal that plaintiff inadvertently omitted earlier. Indeed, even after both parties have rested at the end of all the evidence, the court has some discretion in the interests of justice to permit the introduction of evidence to repair the damage of an inadvertent omission in a party's proof.

Again, examination of rebuttal witnesses is the same as that already described. After presenting all his evidence in rebuttal, plaintiff rests. And again, defendant may move for judgment as a matter of law.

After the rebuttal, the defendant may present evidence in rejoinder, as to which rebuttal's general principles apply. And there may be still further stages until finally both parties rest.

In Subsection (d) we shall pick up with the motions that are available at the stage when both parties have rested. But first we should digress to consider what all this evidence coming to the trier of fact comprises.

(c) RULES OF EVIDENCE

The process of proof that we have just described in general terms is subject throughout to the rules of evidence. These rules originated in the decisions of common-law judges and changed over the years by the traditional common-law method of case-by-case adjudication. Progress was inevitably sporadic, uncertain, and unsystematic, with the result that accidents of history hampered the administration of justice.

The rules of evidence developed differently from jurisdiction to jurisdiction, just as did the rules of substantive law. The original Federal Rules of Civil Procedure contained only minimal provisions about evidence, not a detailed set of evidence rules for actions in federal courts. Rule 43(a) provided for admissibility of evidence if it fell in any one of three categories: (1) evidence admissible under federal statutes, of which there were few; (2) evidence admissible under the rules "heretofore" applied in federal courts in suits in equity; or (3) evidence admissible under the law applied in the courts of the state in which the federal court sat. This was a rule of admissibility, not a rule of exclusion, so that any of those provisions favoring reception of the evidence governed.

As the culmination of years of study by an advisory committee, publication of two drafts, revision in light of comments from bench and bar, and approval by the standing committee and the Judicial Conference of the United States, the Supreme Court prescribed Federal Rules of Evidence on November 20, 1972, to be effective on July 1, 1973, that would govern civil and criminal cases in federal courts. However, taking into account serious objections that had arisen concerning some of those rules, Congress enacted a statute, signed by the President on March 30, 1973, as Pub.L. No. 93–12, 87 Stat. 9, that provided those rules should have no force or effect without express congressional approval. A two-year redrafting project produced a substantially revised and less revolutionary House bill (see H.R.Rep. No. 93–650), Senate amendments that moved back toward the Court-proposed rules (see S.Rep. No. 93–1277), and a compromise conference bill (see H.R.Conf.Rep. No. 93–1597), which was finally passed and signed into law on January 2, 1975, as Pub.L. No. 93–595, 88 Stat. 1926. That law (1) adopted the redrafted rules of evidence, *as a statute*, (2) amended the Rules Enabling Act specifically to treat rules of evidence in the future, and (3) made minor conforming changes to the Federal Rules of Civil Procedure and the Federal Rules of Criminal Procedure. The effective date for the new Federal Rules of Evidence[f] and the conforming changes was July 1, 1975.

The following pages constitute a brief survey of the law of evidence.[g] Focus will center on the Evidence Rules, not only because they are

---

[f]   Hereinafter cited as Evidence Rules. This set of provisions is in the Rules booklet.

[g]   Certainly, the brevity will raise some questions without answering them. Answers are often readily available, however. Many are available by reading the Evidence Rules themselves; where the text or footnotes refer to particular Evidence Rules, it is meant that you should read

controlling in the federal courts but also because to an extent they reflect current thinking as to what modern rules of evidence should be—they have already spurred most states to adopt similar rules, and other states are likely to follow, just as was the case with the Federal Rules of Civil Procedure. Nevertheless, for the purpose of contrast, we shall make frequent reference to the practice at common law and to the practices prevailing in the several states.

Kinds of evidence.—Testimony does not always consist of the simple narration by a witness of what he observed. Sometimes a witness may give *opinion evidence*.

When the evaluation of evidence calls for specialized knowledge not possessed by the ordinary juror, a qualified expert may testify to assist the jury. On a given point, the needed expert may be a doctor, a chemist, a fingerprint specialist, a musician, a carpenter, or anyone with a specialty. The expert may express reliable opinions in his field of expertness. See Evidence Rules 702, 703, and 705. Determination of an expert's qualifications is in the first instance for the judge. See Evidence Rule 104(a) and (c). Counsel examine and cross-examine experts much as they examine and cross-examine lay witnesses. The testimony of experts is of course often in sharp conflict. The credibility of experts and the weight to be given their testimony are for the jury. See Evidence Rule 104(e).

How about opinion evidence from a lay witness? Clearly he cannot give an opinion upon a matter as to which he is not qualified, but there are many matters upon which an ordinary adult is capable of giving a valid opinion. Indeed, it is perhaps already obvious that what we above called "the simple narration by a witness of what he observed" necessarily embodies a certain quantum of inference and hence in a sense is opinion evidence. "I saw *B*" is a product of inference and hence an opinion. "*B* was drunk" is more obviously a matter of opinion, and a useful one. Nevertheless, the jury is presumably equally capable of forming its own opinion if it has before it the data on which the witness bases his opinion. Is not the forming of such opinions precisely what the jury's job is? If the witness is allowed to express his opinion, is he not usurping the jury's function? Shall we then confine the non-expert witness to matters of "fact"? See Evidence Rules 701, 704(a), and 602.

Question: (8) Consider the admissibility under the Evidence Rules of the following statements by an ordinary witness, who was a bystander to the automobile accident at issue in a personal-injury suit: (a) "The road was very slippery." (b) "The defendant's automobile was going very fast" (or "too fast").

---

them. In further study of a particular Evidence Rule, the original Advisory Committee's notes, together with the above-cited legislative reports, are often invaluable; a multivolume work, keyed to the Evidence Rules and including the notes and the legislative history, is Weinstein's Federal Evidence (Mark S. Brodin ed., 2d ed. 2012). See also Daniel J. Capra, Case Law Divergence from the Federal Rules of Evidence (2000). If you desire further information of a more general nature, an excellent compact treatise is McCormick on Evidence (Kenneth S. Broun gen. ed., 7th ed. 2013).

(c) "The defendant's automobile was going 30 miles per hour" (or "about 30 miles per hour"). (d) "The defendant was driving the automobile in a very negligent manner."

We have so far spoken of testimony given in court by witnesses. There is also, as it is sometimes rather uninformatively called, *real evidence*: a person or thing shown to the jury for use of the jurors' own powers of direct observation. A jury might be shown a scarred face, a bloodstained garment, a sample of seized narcotics, or a document. If an object cannot be produced in court, the jury may at the court's discretion be taken elsewhere to view it. For example, the jury might be taken to the scene of an automobile accident to observe how the roads intersect. Before the jury views real evidence, the introducing party must authenticate that evidence. See Evidence Rule 901(a). Authentication in the first instance is a question for the judge, not the jury. However, the jury again has the ultimate say, because it has the option of giving no weight to the evidence offered.

A word on the best-evidence rule should suffice to drive home the point that the parties' choice of the kind of evidence is not entirely free. Suppose a defendant wishes to prove payment by means of proving the content of a written receipt given by the plaintiff. The defendant can prove payment otherwise than through the receipt, even if the plaintiff in fact gave a receipt. But suppose that the defendant intends to rely on showing the content of the receipt. The "best evidence" of the content consists of the original paper, which the judge will admit upon sufficient authentication. May the defendant prove the content not by means of the original paper but by means of a copy of the paper, or by means of oral testimony regarding the content by a witness who read it? Evidence Rules 1001 and 1002 tell us that the defendant usually may not do this. But exceptions exist, as explained in Evidence Rules 1003, 1004, and 1007.

Experiments performed in the presence of the jury fall into the same general category as real evidence. So do charts, models, and diagrams. These items, which have not played a part in the events in suit but which are offered to illustrate or explain testimony, are sometimes called *demonstrative evidence*.

Finally, *judicial notice* may appear to be another medium of presenting evidence at a trial, but it is actually a means of dispensing with proof. When the judge can safely assume that a matter to be proved is indisputably true as a matter of public knowledge (not his own private knowledge), he may "notice" it, that is, instruct the jury that it is true. The judge may have to inform himself of the fact before "noticing" it. For example, he may consult a calendar to ascertain that August 25, 2020, fell on a Tuesday, or an almanac to ascertain that the sun set at 4:43 p.m. on December 31, 1977. The object of judicial notice is to save the time and expense of proving matters not subject to reasonable dispute. See Evidence Rule 201.

With the new ease of research on the internet, some judges have slipped into the questionable practice of investigating their cases' facts. They supposedly limit their own research to background context, without touching contested facts. This practice could still represent a radical expansion of judicial notice. In Rowe v. Gibson, 798 F.3d 622 (7th Cir.2015) (researching a medical condition), Judge Posner oddly defended his practice. He argued that we should not "make a fetish of adversary procedure." Thus, judges should not "confine their role to choosing between the evidentiary presentations of the opposing parties, much like referees of athletic events. . . . There is a high standard for taking judicial notice of a fact, and a low standard for allowing evidence to be presented in the conventional way, by testimony subject to cross-examination, but is there no room for anything in between?" But cf. ABA Comm. on Ethics & Prof'l Responsibility, Formal Op. 478 (2017) (condemning judicial research into adjudicative facts).

Relevance.—With regard to admissibility of evidence, regardless of kind, we take it as our starting point that the judge will allow evidence only if it is relevant, that is, only if it has some rational tendency to make more or less probable any proposition of fact that is of consequence to the action. See Evidence Rules 401 and 402.

First, to determine what propositions are of consequence, or material, we look to the issues shown by the pleadings as narrowed and clarified by the pretrial techniques already considered. When proof of a proposition of fact could have no proper effect on the outcome of the case, either because the parties have not chosen to put it in issue or because as a matter of substantive law it makes no difference whether it is true or false, evidence bearing only on that proposition is inadmissible.

Accordingly, what is in appearance a ruling on evidence is often actually a ruling on substantive law. Sherrod v. Berry, 856 F.2d 802 (7th Cir.1988) (en banc), provides an example. A police officer stopped a robbery suspect and then fatally shot him when, according to the officer's testimony, the suspect made a quick hand movement into his coat as if going for a weapon. The resultant civil rights action turned on the objective reasonableness of using deadly force under the circumstances then known by the policeman. The divided appellate court overturned a $1.6 million award because of error in admitting irrelevant evidence, namely, the later discovery that the suspect had been unarmed. Not wanting to second-guess the police, it said, "Knowledge of facts and circumstances gained after the fact (that the suspect was unarmed) has no place in the trial court's or jury's proper post-hoc analysis of the reasonableness of the actor's judgment." The dissents argued that the absence of a weapon was relevant to evaluating the totality of the circumstances and also the credibility of the officer's testimony.

Second, relevant evidence may be probative of propositions of consequence with varying degrees of directness and persuasiveness. For illustration, imagine that A sues B on a promissory note and that the genuineness of *B*'s signature on the note is in dispute. On the one hand, *W-1*'s testimony for *A*, "I saw *B* sign the note," bears directly on the disputed issue, and if the jury believes *W-1*'s testimony the jury may so determine. On the other hand, *W-2*'s testimony for *B*, "I saw *B* in bed in a Boston hospital on the morning of July 1, 2020" (the day the note was allegedly signed in Los Angeles), bears more remotely on the disputed issue. In each case the witness is testifying to what she observed, but in the latter case what she observed is significant only if the jury takes account of certain general propositions and infers that *B* did not sign the note in Los Angeles. The general propositions are that a flight to Los Angeles takes a certain number of hours, that a man in a hospital bed is probably sick and unable or unwilling to fly, and so on. In order to introduce evidence thus inferentially connected—lawyers often term such evidence "circumstantial"—the inference need not be a necessary one. *W-2*'s testimony is admissible although *B* has not excluded the possibility that he left his hospital bed and went by plane to Los Angeles in time to sign the note. It is open to *A* to attempt to overcome *W-2*'s testimony by proving these facts.

Question: (9) There may of course be several links in the chain of inference between the evidence and the proposition to be proved. Suppose the proposition for the plaintiff to prove is that *Y* killed *X*, and the plaintiff offers in evidence a love letter from *Y* to *X*'s wife.[h] Spell out the series of inferences that the plaintiff is asking the jury to make.

Thus, not all relevant evidence deserves the same amount of weight. The weight of a piece of evidence depends upon the number of successive inferences necessary to connect it with the proposition to be proved and upon the probability of each inference. Sometimes a single piece of evidence will be enough to induce the jury to infer the proposition. Often the party must present many pieces of evidence before their cumulative effect is such as to induce the jury so to conclude. (And remember, of course, that the testimony may be subject to an initial discount if there is a question whether the witness correctly and truthfully reported her observation. The man in the hospital bed may not have been *B*, but *Z*. The witness may be mistaken or lying.)

Third, here is a procedural note on relevance. Often a party offers a piece of evidence that will become relevant only after or in connection with other evidence not yet presented. Practical necessities prevent excluding it. A party must start somewhere, and the connecting evidence would very likely be subject to the same infirmity if presented first. The judge resolves the dilemma by admitting the piece of evidence conditionally on the assurance of counsel that it will be "connected up" later. If it turns out not to be, the judge will strike it on motion and instruct the jury to disregard it. See Evidence Rule 104(b).

---

[h]   The illustration comes from Edmund M. Morgan, "Introduction to Evidence," in Austin W. Scott & Sidney P. Simpson, Cases and Other Materials on Civil Procedure 941, 943 (1950).

Is it realistic to assume that the jurors can or will eliminate from their minds evidence that they have heard or seen, merely because the judge instructs them to do so? "Indeed, instructions to disregard seemingly important, damaging evidence may be like telling someone to ignore the elephant that is in the room with them." Paul F. Rothstein, Myrna S. Raeder & David Crump, Evidence in a Nutshell 14–15 (6th ed. 2012); see J. Alexander Tanford, The Law and Psychology of Jury Instructions, 69 Neb.L.Rev. 71 (1990).

Rules excluding relevant evidence.—So, to be admissible, evidence must be relevant. It is not true, however, that all relevant evidence is admissible. The rules of evidence sometimes have the effect of excluding relevant evidence. Some persons who could give relevant testimony cannot testify at all; some witnesses cannot give certain kinds of testimony although relevant; and some kinds of relevant evidence are inadmissible no matter who the witness is. To return to the case of the promissory note, testimony tending to show that *B* signed the note is relevant. Yet the judge may not permit an insane person, prepared to swear that she saw *B* sign, to testify (a question of *incompetency*). Nor can *B*'s attorney testify that *B* told her the signature was genuine (a question of *privilege*). Nor can any witness testify that *X* told him or her that he, *X*, saw *B* sign (a question of *hearsay*).

As we examine these three major rules that prevent relevant evidence from being presented to the jury, you should ask yourself whether the claimed justification for each is valid.

Incompetency.—We have said that some persons cannot testify at all. For example, some states have the rule that a particular person may be so lacking in mental capacity that he is unfit to be a witness. The judge would therefore not allow a two-year-old child or a wildly insane person to testify. But how about a four-year-old, six-year-old, or eight-year-old child? How about a patient in a mental hospital who although "of unsound mind" has sufficient mental capacity to observe an event, remember it, and narrate what he saw?

Question: (10) Of what effect is lack of understanding of the nature and meaning of an oath? What about an atheist who says that the oath means nothing to him? See Evidence Rule 603; Federal Rule 43(b); 28 U.S.C. § 1746; cf. Evidence Rule 610.

How does the judge go about determining whether a person is incompetent to be a witness? In some instances, such as extreme infancy or insanity, mere observation may be enough. In others, preliminary questioning of the prospective witness may satisfy the judge. But it may become necessary to supplement these methods by calling witnesses to testify about the mental capacity of the witness in question. Suppose instead that the incapacity appears for the first time in the course of the direct examination or cross-examination of the witness: the judge may then strike out the testimony already given and tell the jury to disregard it.

It is well to remember that although the judge has the first word as to the competency of a witness, the jury will have the last as to his worth if the judge allows him to testify. The judge may decide that a six-year-old child has sufficient mental capacity to testify, but the jury may give no weight or credence to what he says. Does this suggest that in a doubtful case the judge should allow the testimony to come in and leave it to the jury to appraise it? The modern approach is to exclude testimony only from witnesses so lacking in mental capacity that no reasonable jury could believe them.

Some other competency rules persist in the several states. For one example, a very few states still hold to an old common-law rule rendering a person incompetent as a witness if he has been convicted of a serious crime.

Questions: (11) What justification could exist for this rule? Is the rule a sound one?

(12) Assuming that a state has no such rule rendering incompetent a person convicted of a crime, to what extent if any should it be permissible to inform the jury of the witness's conviction? Cf. Evidence Rule 609.

Another type of incompetency demands a word. Until the middle of the nineteenth century the common-law courts took the cynical view that a party's interest in the outcome of the litigation rendered him so unreliable that he should not testify at all. This rule frequently produced the bizarre result of silencing those who knew most about the controversy. Nowadays the states have entirely abolished this disqualification in its broad form. Instead, the judge warns the jurors to take into account the interest of the party when they come to appraise the credibility of his testimony.

A vestige of party incompetency remains, however, in the many states that have a so-called Dead Man's Act. The various states' statutes vary widely in scope, and their interpretation has given rise to much litigation. But generally, in suits prosecuted or defended by an executor or administrator on behalf of the decedent, these statutes render the surviving opponent-party incompetent as a witness against the estate concerning some or all matters in issue. Note that this incompetency question arises only with respect to a survivor testifying against an executor or administrator. Thus, there is no general rule silencing a party where the only person who could have contradicted him has died before trial.

Question: (13) Do these Dead Man's Acts reflect merely the same purpose as the old disqualification of parties for interest? Do you think the statutes are wise?

Enough examples of state law: how do the rules of incompetency work in federal court? Against the patchwork background of the states' incompetency rules, Evidence Rule 601 as originally proposed by the Supreme Court represented a major advance. It simply provided that "[e]very person is competent to be a witness except as otherwise provided in these rules," thus virtually abolishing the concept of incompetency in federal court because the Evidence Rules "otherwise provided" in only the very special circumstances of Evidence Rules 605 and 606. Included among the grounds of incompetency to be abolished were mental incapacity, conviction of crime, and party status; also, state Dead Man's Acts would become ineffective in federal court. The common law's total exclusion of testimony from a doubtful witness, the reformers thought, was a rather inept and primitive manner of handling the problem. Instead, the reformers said, the judge should let in the testimony of almost all witnesses, and the jury could appraise its weight and credibility. Their rationale was that it is generally better to let a witness testify and then—in order to counter the effects of mental incapacity, moral turpitude, and interest—to rely on cross-examination, extrinsic evidence, and warnings by the judge to the jury. Judges, however, could still exclude testimony from witnesses so mentally deficient that no reasonable jury could believe them, using Evidence Rule 403 to invoke the requirement of personal knowledge and capacity for truthfulness embodied in Evidence Rules 602 and 603.

The congressional redrafting of Evidence Rule 601 cut back the extent of this proposed advance. The redraft added a second sentence providing that in civil cases "with respect to an element of a claim or defense as to which State law supplies the rule of decision, the competency of a witness shall be determined in accordance with State law." You will not fully understand this change until you have studied Part 2 of this book. However, in very gross terms, we can describe the new sentence, its significance, and its rationale respectively as follows.

As you have already seen in several cases, federal courts sometimes apply state substantive law; that is to say, state law sometimes supplies the rule of decision. For example, if a New Jersey driver runs down a New Yorker in Manhattan and if the New Yorker sues in the United States District Court for the Southern District of New York, that court will apply New York State's negligence law, not some uniform federal law of negligence. Evidence Rule 601 now says that as to testimony tending to support or defeat a finding of negligence in such a suit, New York State's law as to competency will control. The federal court will apply not only state substantive law, but also state evidence law dealing with competence.

What this signifies in practical terms is that the Evidence Rules do not provide for uniform practice in federal district courts on the subject of competency. The federal court will treat the competency of some witnesses under the uniform federal rule embodied in the first sentence of Evidence Rule 601, while the judge will determine the competency of others under diverse state rules incorporated by the second sentence thereof. So, in the area of testimonial competency, the federal practitioner must be the master of both federal and state evidence law.

The legislators' rationale for introducing this note of confusion into the Evidence Rules was, in part, that the federal interest in a uniform law of evidence for federal courts is not strong enough to override the state policies embodied in the states' competency rules. The states had no strong policies wrapped up in rules of, say, judicial notice, but Congress thought that competency rules such as the Dead Man's Acts might involve more important state policies.

Privilege.—There are various rules protecting certain persons from disclosure of particular matters. To take a familiar example: if a party calls *L*, a lawyer, as a witness and asks about what *B*, her client, confidentially told her in the course of seeking legal advice, *B* may prevent *L* from responding. Assuming, as we shall see may be the case, that if *B* told the same things to a layperson, the layperson could testify to what *B* said, why does the law deal differently with statements to a lawyer? The law also commonly privileges confidential communications between husband and wife, patient and physician, and penitent and clergyman. What are the reasons for and against each of these privileges?

What would you say about confidential communications to an accountant by her client? How about confidential communications between parent and child? How about a communication made to any person on a pledge of secrecy? The communications just listed are commonly not privileged. Should they be?

Would you compel a newspaper reporter to disclose the source of information given to her in confidence? See the absorbing case of Branzburg v. Hayes, 408 U.S. 665, 92 S.Ct. 2646 (1972) (regarding newspaper reporters' obligation to testify before grand juries), which held that the First Amendment does not give rise to a general journalists' privilege but which left plenty of room for distinguishing the holding. And, of course, the absence of a privilege of constitutional origin does not preclude a judge-made or statutory privilege. Thus, most of the federal circuits have molded some degree of qualified privilege for journalists, and more than half the states have enacted shield legislation that accords reporters some form of privilege as to their confidential sources. See generally Wright & Miller § 5426.

In addition to privileged communications and sources, there are topics privileged from disclosure. For example, the public interest may require that state secrets be privileged. Within limits, trade secrets important to the existence of a particular business may be privileged too. Here also falls the familiar privilege against self-incrimination. A witness can claim this constitutional privilege in all kinds of proceedings: criminal and civil actions, administrative hearings, and legislative investigations. Although a witness in a civil action is thereby privileged not to reveal facts appreciably tending to subject himself to criminal liability, he has no such privilege as to facts incriminating someone else.

We might mention here as well the restrictions on use in criminal cases of confessions and evidence illegally obtained. Under "privilege," broadly defined, we would also class the question of whether the President, a state governor, or a foreign ambassador can claim immunity from compulsory process to testify as a witness.

However, we do not here attempt to draw a logically satisfying distinction between incompetency and privilege. We shall just observe that the key to it would lie in the differing purposes of the two doctrines. Incompetency rules centrally concern the reliability of evidence, whereas privilege rules foster social policies extrinsic to the courtroom. That is, privilege does not aim at the ascertainment of truth, but rather at some other goal often pursued at the price of shutting out the truth.

A telling contrast lies in the common-law rule that husband and wife were incompetent to testify either for or against each other in any case, civil or criminal. Today in the states this rule has largely disappeared, first eroding and transmuting into a privilege in criminal cases whereby the accused may elect to keep his or her spouse off the stand (except when the charge is the commission of a crime against the spouse) and whereby the accused's spouse may refuse to testify adversely, but most often eroding still further to some narrower version of this privilege that is even more readily distinguishable from the old rule of incompetency. Note that both the dying rule of spousal incompetency and the eroding criminal privilege to avoid adverse spousal testimony are distinguishable from the above-mentioned privilege against disclosure of confidential communications between husband and wife.

Questions: (14) If a judge erroneously upholds a witness's privilege and excludes testimony, should the party damaged by the ruling be able to attack it on appeal?

(15) What if the judge erroneously denies the privilege and admits the testimony? See McCormick on Evidence § 73.1 (Kenneth S. Broun gen. ed., 7th ed. 2013).

Each particular privilege, being tied to a certain extrinsic social policy, requires individual consideration as to how broad it is in scope, as to who may claim it, and as to how it may be waived. It is worth thinking about the answer the law should give to these three questions for each of the privileges mentioned above.

As to privilege in general, we again need to consider separately the situation in federal court. Against the background of the states' accepted rules regarding privilege, the Evidence Rules as originally proposed by the Supreme Court represented another major change. Thirteen proposed Evidence Rules codified the rules of privilege for federal courts in accordance with modern thinking on the subject. Thus, their effect was, in general, to restrict the realm of privilege, eliminating some common-law privileges and modifying others. However, these privilege provisions generated more controversy in Congress than did any other aspect of the Evidence Rules, and the result was both the enactment of a redrafted version of Evidence Rule 501 in lieu of the codification and also the passage of 28 U.S.C. § 2074(b).

Evidence Rule 501, as enacted, is similar in effect to Evidence Rule 601. It provides for the application of federal privilege rules in certain circumstances and state privilege rules in others. Thus, just as for competence, the federal practitioner must be the master of both federal and state privilege law. But there is an important difference between Evidence Rules 501 and 601. The first sentence of Evidence Rule 601 represents a codification of federal competence law. In contrast, the first sentence of Evidence Rule 501, along with the congressional deletion of the codification attempted by the rulemakers in their proposed Evidence Rules, leaves federal privilege rules to a continuing case-by-case development. This change was a reflection of the furor that the proposed privilege provisions generated in Congress.

Section 2074(b) was a further reflection of that controversy. This statutory provision specifically restricted the Supreme Court's rulemaking power in the area of privilege. The congressional concern expressed here was more with separation of powers than with federalism.

Question: (16) Would the codification of privilege rules as proposed by the Supreme Court have been within the terms of 28 U.S.C. § 2072?

Hearsay.—We have already given one example of hearsay: in the suit on the promissory note, W testifies that X told her that X saw B sign the note. This testimony is objectionable as hearsay. See Evidence Rule 802. Why is it objectionable? Because W may be mistaken in her memory as to what X said? Suppose then that W produces in court a written statement that X prepared. The testimony is still objectionable. Is this because X was not under oath? Suppose then that W is a notary public and has taken X's oath that the statement is true. Even this does not cure the hearsay difficulty. Why all this squeamishness about hearsay? Responsible persons daily make important decisions in their own lives in reliance upon patent hearsay—indeed, normal life could hardly go on if this were not so. Why should courts reject a type of evidence so commonly relied upon outside the courtroom?

The heart of the objection to hearsay is the absence of an opportunity for cross-examination of the declarant (the person who made the out-of-court statement offered in evidence by the testimony of another). Cross-examination may lay falsehood bare; it may expose errors in observation, memory, or narration; it may bring out important matters omitted from the original statement; or it may at least raise doubts as to the credence and weight the jury should give to the testimony. Often, of course, cross-examination fails of its reliability purposes and, particularly if it is unskillful, may serve only to reinforce the original story. But cross-examination also serves parties' dignity interests in facing in court the witnesses against them. The law regards the chance for cross-examination as such an essential check that where cross-examination is not possible the testimony is ordinarily not admissible. For example, if a witness dies immediately after direct examination, thus defeating the opportunity for cross-examination, the judge may strike the testimony already given under oath in open court.

The concerns generated by lack of an opportunity for cross-examination largely explain the hearsay rule, but not entirely. The rule will apply even when the declarant is sitting in court, readily available for cross-examination. Indeed, testimony in a previous trial or hearing where the declarant was in fact subject to cross-examination will in certain circumstances run afoul of the hearsay rule. In such situations the hearsay rule applies simply because calling the declarant to the stand to testify as to what he has to say is usually superior, as a method of proof, to letting some witness testify as to what the declarant previously said. If a party calls the declarant, the factfinder can consider his demeanor on the stand along with his in-court statements.

How sound is the hearsay rule? Granting that there is a value to cross-examination and demeanor, does this value so overcome the probative value of the testimony that the factfinder should not get the chance to hear and appraise it, while making what the factfinder thinks is due allowance for its infirmity? Basic to the rule excluding hearsay and to some other exclusionary rules is a distrust of the capacity of the jury to appraise the evidence properly. You will find that such rules frequently do not apply when the trier of fact is an expert administrative tribunal, even though this contrary practice equally rests on untested empirical assumptions.

Question: (17) Should the hearsay rule apply when the trier of fact is a judge sitting in a nonjury case? See McCormick on Evidence § 60 (Kenneth S. Broun gen. ed., 7th ed. 2013).

Do not fall into the fallacy of assuming that repetition in court of an out-of-court statement of another person invariably raises a hearsay problem. Assume that *A* is suing *B* for slander, alleging that *B* called her a thief, and *B* by answer has denied that he made such a statement. *W* testifies that at the time and place in question he heard *B* say that *A* was a thief. In this case, although *W* is testifying to what he heard *B* say, *W*'s testimony is admissible. No question of hearsay is involved. What is the difference between this case and the one where *W* testified as to what *X* had said about seeing *B* sign the note? There the purpose of the testimony was to prove that *B* had signed the note, and the credibility and weight of *X*'s out-of-court statement were therefore important. In the present case, the purpose of offering *W*'s testimony is simply to prove that *B* made the slanderous statement that *W* says he made, and for that purpose the credibility and weight of *B*'s statement are unimportant. The credibility and weight of *W*'s testimony are important, but *W* is on the stand and subject to cross-examination. We can generalize and say that it is only when the statement of the declarant is offered to prove the truth of the statement—when, in effect, testimony by the declarant is being offered through the mouth of another—that a question of hearsay arises. See Evidence Rule 801(c).

Question: (18) *P* sued Dr. *D* for negligence in leaving a sponge in the incision after an operation on *P*'s spine. Several doctors had operated on *P*'s spine at various times prior to the discovery of the sponge. To establish liability it was necessary to prove (a) that a sponge was left in the incision by Dr. *D* and (b) that, if he left it there, it was left as the result of Dr. *D*'s failure to exercise proper skill and care. Among other evidence, *P* offered testimony by an assisting physician, *W*, that in the operating room an unidentified nurse had told Dr. *D* that "the sponge count did not come out right." The judge excluded this testimony on the ground that it was hearsay. There was a verdict and a judgment for Dr. *D*, and *P* appealed. The question on appeal was the propriety of excluding the proffered testimony. What argument would you make for *P*, and what do you think the decision should be? See Smedra v. Stanek, 187 F.2d 892 (10th Cir.1951) (reversal).

Exceptions to the hearsay rule.—The rule excluding hearsay is riddled with exceptions. We shall not catalogue them all or probe the refinements of any of them. Were we to do so, you would quickly see that the pattern is haphazard rather than logical. Not only does the law differ greatly from state to state, but the law of any one state is likely to be shifting, uncertain, and abounding in inconsistencies; on the federal level, the thirty exceptions listed in Evidence Rules 803, 804, and 807 suggest a similar complexity. Rather we shall consider in a general way why the rejection of hearsay has not been complete and what conditions must exist before making an exception to the rule.

In the first place, it is apparent that not all forms of hearsay are inherently unreliable, and a rational system would attempt to segregate and admit hearsay evidence that falls high on the reliability scale. In the second place, although an out-of-court utterance might be a less desirable method of proof than in-court testimony, it is further apparent that a rigorous exclusion of all hearsay, or of all but the most reliable hearsay, would sometimes block effective proof of an essential issue. Because of these two considerations, courts have always admitted some types of hearsay.

Exceptions to the hearsay rule have accordingly arisen where there is something about the out-of-court utterance that justifies trusting that evidence even in the absence of accompanying demeanor evidence and cross-examination. Thus, these exceptions demand that the circumstances in which the declarant made the statement must be such as to make it seem reliable. See Evidence Rule 803. Absolute trustworthiness is not, of course, the test—even the testimony of a witness on the stand and subjected to cross-examination does not approach that ideal.

When the circumstances surrounding the declarant's statement suggest some lesser degree of reliability, they do not constitute a sufficient condition for admission, and so the law imposes the additional requirement that the declarant be unavailable to testify (for example, because she is dead or absent from the jurisdiction). Thus, these hearsay exceptions impose an explicit requirement of need. See Evidence Rule 804. However, careful examination of most hearsay exceptions, including those that apply whether or not the declarant is unavailable, will reveal implicit notions of need or at least of practicality.

With these generalities in mind, consider the following examples of major exceptions to the hearsay rule.

1.   Our first illustration comes originally from the criminal law. *A* is charged with the murder of *B*. Testimony of *W* is offered to the effect that *B*, knowing that death was imminent, said, "*A* shot me," or, for that matter, "*C* shot me." *W*'s testimony is clearly hearsay, but the likelihood that *B* told the truth under the circumstances set forth is supposedly strong enough to justify admitting *W*'s account. Of course, *B* may have been mistaken or may have lied to get revenge upon *A* or *C*, to protect someone, or for some other reason; but these considerations will go only to the credence to be given to the evidence.

You may well ask how much scientific support there is for the supposition upon which this "dying declaration" exception rests.[i] Indeed, distrust of its scientific support perhaps explains the fact that the common law and many states have construed this exception narrowly. Traditionally, for it to apply, (a) the case has to be a criminal prosecution for homicide, (b) the declarant has to have died, a victim of that homicide, (c) the declarant had to make the utterance while believing that the declarant's own death was imminent, and (d) the utterance had to concern the circumstances of that impending death. In many states, then, *W*'s testimony of *B*'s dying declaration, admissible in a murder trial, is oddly not admissible in a civil action for *B*'s wrongful death.

Evidence Rule 804(b)(2) significantly expands the exception by modifying requirements (a) and (b), although the drafters based that expansion not on a belief in the reliability of dying declarations, but rather on a feeling that the traditional requirements were illogical and arbitrary. You should specially note that the dying declaration exception to the hearsay rule is now available in civil cases in federal court.

2.   *A*, injured by a hit-and-run driver, civilly sues *B* as the alleged driver. The identity of the driver remains in dispute. *B* offers the testimony of *W* that *C*, now dead, said to *W*, "I ran over *A* and was lucky enough to get away." Should the court admit it? How is the requirement

---

[i]   "The existing rule, with its strict limitations, has been introduced into India where it appears to have worked badly, according to Mr. Justice Stephen, who says: 'I have heard that in the Punjab the effect of it is that a person mortally wounded frequently makes a statement bringing all his hereditary enemies on to the scene at the time of his receiving his wound, thus using his last opportunity to do them an injury. A remark made on the policy of the rule by a native of Madras shows how differently such matters are viewed in different parts of the world. "Such evidence," he said, "ought never to be admitted in any case. What motive for telling the truth can any man possibly have when he is at the point of death." ' (1 Stephen's Hist. Crim. Law of England, 448, 449.)" People v. Becker, 215 N.Y. 126, 147, 109 N.E. 127, 133 (1915).

of reliability satisfied? The theory is that a person is unlikely to make a statement against the person's own interest unless it is true.

This "declaration against interest" exception to the hearsay rule is well recognized. It is, however, narrowly limited. Traditionally, (a) the declarant had to be unavailable and (b) the statement had to have been against a *proprietary* or a *pecuniary* interest. Some state courts still say that a statement that would inferentially subject the declarant to tort liability is not sufficiently against pecuniary interest to be admissible, and such courts would therefore exclude the statement of the hit-and-run driver given above. Is there any rational basis for this limitation?

Evidence Rule 804(b)(3)(A) extends the exception to cover a statement of a declarant unavailable as a witness that "a reasonable person in the declarant's position would have made only if the person believed it to be true because, when made, it was so contrary to the declarant's proprietary or pecuniary interest or had so great a tendency to invalidate the declarant's claim against someone else or to expose the declarant to civil or criminal liability."

3. "Admissions" form another traditional exception, and an extremely important one. These are out-of-court statements by a party or the party's representative offered by an opponent as evidence of their content.[j] If *A* is suing *B* for negligently inflicted injuries, *A* can introduce testimony of *W* that *B* said, "It was all my fault," or, "I had only one drink before the accident, but I didn't see *A* until after I hit her."

Admissions and declarations against interest are frequently confused. But note: (a) admissions are utterances attributable to parties, while a declaration against interest can be uttered by anyone; (b) for admissions availability of the declarant is immaterial, while for a declaration against interest the declarant must be unavailable; and (c) admissions need not be against interest when made, while a declaration against interest obviously must be. Usually admissions were against interest when made, but they need not have been so. Dean McCormick cited this example: if someone has stated that a note is a forgery, but then buys the note and sues on it, the statement can come in against him as an admission. McCormick on Evidence § 254 (Kenneth S. Broun gen. ed., 7th ed. 2013).

Question: (19) What is the justification for the exception regarding admissions?

Admissions receive the traditional treatment under the Evidence Rules, in that they are still admissible. However, the analytic approach differs. As just explained, courts have traditionally treated admissions as an exception to the hearsay rule, but the Evidence Rules treat admissions as simply not hearsay in the first place. See Evidence Rule 801(d)(2). The Advisory Committee's note thereto says: "Admissions by a party-

---

[j]   Contrast these "evidential" admissions with binding "judicial" admissions such as those made under Federal Rule 36. See Freed v. Erie Lackawanna Ry. Co., supra p. 114.

opponent are excluded from the category of hearsay on the theory that their admissibility in evidence is the result of the adversary system rather than satisfaction of the conditions of the hearsay rule."

4. Courts have also created a hearsay exception for statements relating to a startling event made while the declarant was under the stress of excitement caused by the event. This is one of several hearsay exceptions often lumped together under the label "res gestae" without serious analysis.[k]

Questions: (20) What is the voucher of trustworthiness for this "excited utterance" exception?

(21) Should it make any difference whether the declarant is available?

———

Handel v. New York Rapid Transit Corp.

Supreme Court of New York, Appellate Division, Second Department, 1937.
252 App.Div. 142, 297 N.Y.S. 216, aff'd mem., 277 N.Y. 548, 13 N.E.2d 468 (1938).

■ TAYLOR, J. In an action to recover damages for the death of plaintiff-appellant's intestate alleged to have resulted from the negligence of the defendant-respondent, judgment dismissing the complaint, entered upon a nonsuit, affirmed, with costs. The plaintiff's proofs failed to establish, prima facie, a cause of action. The claimed declaration of the intestate after the happening of the accident, to wit, "Save me. Help me—why did that conductor close the door on me," was incompetent as evidence and properly excluded by the trial court. The declaration was not admissible as part of the res gestae. [Citations omitted.] It was narrative of a past event and within the hearsay rule.

■ DAVIS, ADEL and TAYLOR, JJ., concur; CLOSE, J., with whom HAGARTY, J., concurs, dissents and votes for reversal of the judgment and for a new trial, with opinion.

■ CLOSE, J. (dissenting). In my opinion the evidence, offered in behalf of the plaintiff, of a statement made by the decedent after the accident was admissible as a part of the res gestae, and the trial court erred in excluding it. A recital of the circumstances under which the statement was made will serve to define the point of law.

The decedent was a police officer attached to Precinct 60, located at West Eighth street, Brooklyn. At some time between three-forty and four o'clock in the morning of April 22, 1934, Timothy Downing, another policeman, saw him coming from a nearby lunch wagon. Handel was off

———

[k]   "The marvelous capacity of a Latin phrase to serve as a substitute for reasoning, and the confusion of thought inevitably accompanying the use of inaccurate terminology, are nowhere better illustrated than in the decisions dealing with the admissibility of evidence as 'res gestae.' It is probable that this troublesome expression owes its existence and persistence in our law of evidence to an inclination of judges and lawyers to avoid the toilsome exertion of exact analysis and precise thinking." Edmund M. Morgan, A Suggested Classification of Utterances Admissible as Res Gestae, 31 Yale L.J. 229, 229 (1922).

duty, having finished at midnight, and was not due back at the station house until the following afternoon. After a brief conversation, the two policemen crossed the street to the West Eighth Street station of the defendant's elevated railroad, located almost opposite the precinct station house. Handel passed through the door, and Downing last saw him as he was going up the stairs toward the elevated platform. As Downing walked back across the street he heard the rumble of an approaching train. It was then about four o'clock.

Mrs. Ida Pfeifer lived on the top floor of an apartment house on West Third street, with her bedroom window directly facing the elevated structure. She slept with the window open. She testified that at about four o'clock in the morning she was awakened by the sound of someone screaming. Looking out the window, she saw a train come to a stop and something that looked like "a big bundle" fall from the side door of the last car down to Park place. The screaming continued. Mrs. Pfeifer put on a bathrobe and slippers, ran down three flights of stairs to the front entrance of her house, and proceeded from there to Park place, a distance of about seventy feet. There she found the body of Handel. He was moaning, and made a statement to the witness which was excluded from evidence on the defendant's objection. The record shows that the witness would have testified, if permitted, that Handel said, "Save me. Help me— why did that conductor close the door on me."

John Leyton also lived in the vicinity of West Third street and Park place. A little before four o'clock in the morning he had taken his dog out for a walk. When he returned it was "Pretty near four o'clock." As he approached the house he heard the noise of an elevated train, and looking up he saw a train stop near West Third street. Leyton put the dog in the house and stepped out again. As he did so he heard someone moaning under the elevated structure. He estimated that it took him about half a minute to get to where Handel lay, and that about two and one-half minutes elapsed between the time when he heard the train and his arrival at the place where the deceased lay. Mrs. Pfeifer was already there. Leyton would also have testified to Handel's statement if permitted to do so. One of Handel's shoes was missing, and his pants were torn off from the hips down.

Officer Downing testified that he received word of the accident about three-quarters of an hour after he had left Handel at the station entrance. In company with a detective named Fitzsimmons, he went up to the station platform, walked to the end of the platform, and then proceeded along a "catwalk" beside the tracks. The "catwalk" ended about fifty feet from West Third street. The two men then walked on the ties between the rails to a point just over the curb of West Third street, about 1,000 feet distant from the station entrance. There they found a shoe, with the laces broken out of it, wedged between the rail and a wooden beam. The toe of the shoe pointed back toward West Eighth street.

Downing returned and examined the station platform. He found two dark marks running parallel with the edge of the platform for a distance of about 125 to 150 feet, increasing in width as they approached the end of the platform. The inference is that the marks were made by the rubber heels of Handel's shoes as he was dragged along by a moving train. Beyond the end of the platform no marks were visible.

When the decedent was examined by a doctor it was found that, in addition to numerous lacerations and contusions, he had suffered a concussion of the brain, a broken right hand, a fracture of the right femur, a broken pelvis, and a ruptured bladder. He was also in profound shock. Of course, this must have been his condition at the time when he made his statement to Mrs. Pfeifer and Leyton. Apparently, he died later in the day.

The foregoing is substantially all the evidence offered by the plaintiff. At the close of the plaintiff's case, the trial court dismissed the complaint. We are all agreed that the dismissal was proper if the declaration of the decedent was properly excluded; because without that declaration the record is wholly lacking in proof of negligence on the part of the defendant. From the drag marks on the platform, the broken shoe wedged between the rails, and the fact that the deceased was seen to fall from the car door at just about the point where the shoe was found, it might reasonably be inferred that the deceased had, in some manner, been caught in the door at the station platform; that he had been dragged along with his body hanging outside the train as far as West Third street; that his foot had then become caught between the ties or the rails; and that his shoe had been torn off and his body jerked from the train at the same time. But the circumstances throw no light on how the deceased came to be trapped in the door, and the proof is therefore insufficient to warrant an inference of negligence.

However, the declaration of the deceased, if admissible, would constitute some evidence of negligence. . . . The question to be determined is whether this evidence was competent as a part of the res gestae. The trial court concluded . . . that the evidence was not admissible under that exception to the hearsay rule. A majority of this court are of the same opinion. With that conclusion I disagree.

. . . .

. . . We must answer two questions: (1) Was the declaration "spontaneously expressive of the injured person's observation" of the occurrence? (2) Was the utterance made "within such limit of time as presumably to preclude fabrication?"

Handel's statement was of a spontaneous character. It was not made in response to any question . . . . The spontaneous nature of the utterance is shown by the words "Save me. Help me," which preceded the reference to the action of the conductor. . . . The statement about the conductor took the form of a question, "why did that conductor close the door on me," which in itself is an indication of spontaneity. A construction which holds this declaration merely a narrative of a past event ignores the language used and its plain implications.

The other element is that of time. We are asked to consider the fact that the deceased had traveled from West Eighth street to West Third street before he fell. I would disregard that entirely. On a journey so perilous, one has little leisure for plotting fiction. The only material period of time is that which elapsed after the deceased fell to the street. The best estimate of the interval is that given by the witness Leyton, who said that about two and one-half minutes elapsed between the time when he heard the train and his arrival at the place where Handel was found. . . . But it is not a question of precisely how many seconds or minutes elapsed. The question is whether "the utterance is made within such limit of time as presumably to preclude fabrication."

My conclusion is that Handel's utterance came within the confines of the rule. It seems to me incredible that a man so broken in body and so profoundly shocked in mind could have spent the slight interval before aid arrived in manufacturing a false explanation of the extremity in which he was found.

If there is a "spontaneous exclamation exception to the hearsay rule," here is a case for its application. In my opinion the evidence was wrongly excluded, and the error requires a reversal of the judgment and a new trial.

———

Questions: (22) Assuming that the Handel case arose today in federal court, would the evidence be admissible under Evidence Rule 803(2)? under Evidence Rule 803(1)? See Brunsting v. Lutsen Mountains Corp., 601 F.3d 813 (8th Cir.2010) (admitting statement under Evidence Rule 803(2) despite four or five minutes' lapse of time).

(23) Adopting the same assumption, would Handel's statement be admissible as a dying declaration under Evidence Rule 804(b)(2)? See Shepard v. United States, 290 U.S. 96, 100, 54 S.Ct. 22, 24 (1933) (Cardozo, J.) ("There must be a 'settled hopeless expectation' [citation omitted] that death is near at hand, and what is said must have been spoken in the hush of its impending presence.").

5.   Entries contemporaneously made in books and records in the ordinary course of business generally may come into evidence without producing the persons who actually made the entries. For the contours of the business records exception under federal law, see Evidence Rule 803(6), as well as the subsequent subdivisions of that Evidence Rule.

This "business records" exception serves to point up again the important fact that writings may present hearsay problems, e.g., where a party offers a document in evidence to prove the facts it relates. See Evidence Rule 801(a). In order to get such evidence in, the introducing party must authenticate the document, and also find an applicable hearsay exception (such as business records).

Incidentally, nonverbal conduct may similarly present hearsay problems, e.g., where a witness testifies that someone nodded his head to show assent. Was there a hearsay problem with Mrs. Pfeifer testifying that she had heard someone scream?

6.   We close with some brief observations on other illustrative exceptions to the hearsay rule. (a) *Testimony given at another hearing during the same or a different proceeding by a witness now unavailable.* This is an easy exception to justify when the parties to the former hearing were the same and the issues substantially identical. But suppose the testimony is now offered against a person not a party before. Should the opportunity for cross-examination by someone else with similar motive and interest suffice as a voucher of reliability? See Evidence Rule 804(b)(1)(B). Apparently, Federal Rule of Civil Procedure 32(a) provides alternative exceptions to the hearsay rule, so that a deposition satisfying an exception under either the Civil Rules or the Evidence Rules is admissible in a civil case. See Evidence Rule 802. (b) *Declarations concerning family history.* See Evidence Rule 804(b)(4); cf. Evidence Rule 803(13). If it were not for this exception, proof of matters of pedigree might be extremely difficult. But what is the basis for holding such declarations reliable? (c) *Other exceptions.* Consider the potential of Evidence Rule 807. Do you think that this residual exception portends the demise of the hearsay rule?

Multiple hearsay.—Finally, there is the problem of, as Evidence Rule 805 puts it, "hearsay within hearsay." The rule here is that when testimony includes multiple levels of hearsay, each level must come within a hearsay exception in order for the testimony to be admissible.

Question: (24) In a civil wrongful-death action brought in federal court by X's wife against K, plaintiff calls W to testify that W saw X and his wife walking together, that X fell, that W ran over, that X was then dead, and that W heard X's wife cry, "X just groaned that K wasn't joking in telling him that K had poisoned him." Can the quoted testimony come in, over objection?

Remote, confusing, and prejudicial evidence.—The fact that a piece of relevant evidence does not run afoul of any of the three foregoing exclusionary rules does not necessarily mean that the judge will admit it. The judge has discretion to exclude evidence of comparatively slight probative value when the judge believes that it is not nearly worth the time required to hear it. See Evidence Rule 403. Thus, to prevent the piling up of merely cumulative testimony, the judge has discretion to limit the number of witnesses on a particular issue, a discretion frequently exercised with respect to the number of expert witnesses and often specified in a pretrial order under Federal Rule 16.

A similar discretion exists when the confusion or the prejudice that the evidence would produce substantially outweighs its probative value.

For example, will the plaintiff suing for injuries from an allegedly defective condition on the defendant's premises be permitted to prove that other accidents occurred there, for the purpose of showing that the situation was dangerous? Generally yes. Will the defendant be allowed to show an absence of other accidents, as evidence of nonexistence of danger? Generally no. Why the distinction? Should this plaintiff be permitted to prove that liability insurance covers the defendant, as the basis for an inference that he had nothing to lose by his carelessness and hence was less likely to be careful? See Evidence Rule 411.

Still in that suit for injuries allegedly due to a defective condition on the defendant's premises, should the plaintiff's evidence that the defendant made repairs after the accident be admissible, as some proof of negligence? See Evidence Rule 407. Should the defendant's pretrial offer to make a compromise settlement be admissible, as evidence for the plaintiff? See Evidence Rule 408. Are your conclusions with respect to these last two questions tied exclusively to notions of remoteness, confusion, and prejudice?

Objecting to inadmissible evidence.—When a party offers evidence that the opponent believes to be inadmissible, the opponent should object specifically, with grounds. Examine Federal Rule 46, and you will find that a formal "exception" is not necessary after an adverse ruling. This is a reference to the old requirement of such ritualistic words as, "I except," or, "Please note my exception," in order for a party to have the right to appeal eventually. Although in some states the old ritual still prevails, in the federal courts it is now necessary only to state an objection.

The objection should come immediately, as soon as possible after the ground for objection appears. Indeed, pretrial disclosures under Federal Rule 26(a)(3)(A) should trigger the opponent's listing of objections under Rule 26(a)(3)(B) and, possibly, the court's advance evidential rulings. More generally, the opponent can make a motion to exclude evidence in advance of trial, which is called a motion in limine and which the court in its discretion may choose to decide immediately or to postpone until trial. Usually, however, the opponent has the option of waiting to object upon the evidence's offering at trial.

The objection has a two-fold purpose: (1) to keep the evidence out, or to have it stricken; and (2) to lay the foundation for a later appeal if the judge admits the evidence. The jury may give any evidence admitted without objection such weight and credence as the jury thinks it deserves, and usually the opponent has waived any error in its admission. See Evidence Rule 103(a)(1) and (e). For instance, the jury may properly base a finding upon hearsay testimony to which no objection was made. In any such case, of course, the jury may nevertheless discount or disregard the testimony because of the inherent weakness that gave rise to the exclusionary rule in question.

It will often happen that offered evidence is properly admissible for one purpose but inadmissible for another. The risk that the jury might improperly apply it to the inadmissible purpose does not ordinarily require its exclusion. But the opponent may acquire some protection by asking the judge to instruct the jury as to the limited purpose for which it is being admitted. See Evidence Rule 105. If the judge gives no such instruction, the jury may properly give the evidence its natural probative force for any purpose.

Question: (25) In the case in the earlier question involving the statement that the sponge count did not come out right, if the judge admitted the proffered testimony over objection, what should the objecting party then do?

If the judge erroneously admits proffered evidence over objection, the record is clear for purposes of appeal. If, however, the judge sustains the objection and excludes the evidence, the proffering party should make known to the judge by "offer of proof" the substance of the proffered evidence (for example, the answer the party expected from the witness), unless the substance is apparent from the context. If not, the party cannot predicate error on the exclusion, because the appellate court could not appraise the seriousness of the error. See Evidence Rule 103(a)(2). For obvious reasons the party should make the offer of proof out of the hearing of the jury. See Evidence Rule 103(d).

Question: (26) Suppose the opponent does not agree that the witness would answer the objectionable question as the proffering party expected. How can this difficulty be resolved?

Cross-examining witnesses.—A conventional method of cross-examination is to put "leading questions," that is, questions that suggest the desired answer. One such type is, "Isn't it a fact that . . . ?" Leading questions are usually improper on direct examination, although they generally pass without objection on routine matters of a preliminary nature, and also the judge may permit them in specified situations including interrogation of a hostile witness. See Evidence Rule 611(c); cf. Evidence Rule 611(a).

Question: (27) Why are leading questions ordinarily objectionable on direct but permissible on cross-examination?

How far does the scope of cross-examination extend? That is, how far may the cross-examining party go in seeking to support his own case out of the mouth of the witness? Not far, according to the rule in most states and in the federal courts. See Evidence Rule 611(b). Accordingly, the party may cross-examine the witness only as to facts and circumstances connected with the matters covered in direct examination, in addition to matters affecting credibility. Departures from this rule are, however, permissible in the discretion of the trial judge, but then direct examination's predisposition against leading questions will apply to the cross-examiner.

Given the restricted scope of cross-examination, a party who has cross-examined may find it necessary to recall the witness at a later stage of the trial to get additional testimony. In doing so the party is held to "make the witness his own," thus subjecting the questioning on recall to the rules governing direct rather than cross-examination.

By contrast, in some states the scope of proper cross-examination extends to all aspects of the case, so that the cross-examining party may interrogate as to matters on which he has the burden of proof and may even use leading questions thereon. Evidence Rule 611(b) as originally proposed by the Court adopted this minority "wide-open" position. However, in the final version of the Evidence Rules enacted as a statute, Congress had redrafted the Rule to return to the traditional "restrictive" practice.

Question: (28) What reasons can you advance for and against the majority rule of limiting the scope of cross-examination?

Impeaching and contradicting admissible evidence.—Let us assume that a party has called a witness whose direct testimony, if believed, will be damaging to the opponent. What may the opponent do to combat it?

The opponent may try in various ways to impeach (that is, discredit) the witness. See, e.g., Evidence Rules 608 and 609. His first chance is on cross-examination, when he may ask questions designed to bring out bias; prior inconsistent statements; weakness of observation, of memory, or of narration; bad character; or the like. The opponent has a second chance, in that he may wait until he puts on his own case, and then impeach the witness by the testimony of other witnesses or documentary evidence bringing out similar defects. However, to prevent unreasonable excursions, the rules limit such impeachment by extrinsic evidence to the more significant defects, and so on lesser matters the opponent must "take the witness's answer" on cross-examination. See, e.g., Evidence Rule 608(b). (The other side may attempt the counterstep of rehabilitating an impeached witness.)

In addition to impeaching the witness in these ways, the opponent may introduce other evidence to contradict (that is, disprove) the story of the witness. In line with the constant objective of keeping a trial within bounds, there are again limitations on the extent to which the judge will permit contradiction of "collateral" matters in a witness's testimony.

Now let us assume instead that a witness has unexpectedly given testimony damaging to the party who called her. The combination of Evidence Rules 607 and 801(d)(1)(A) turns out to be especially helpful in dealing with the turncoat witness, who changes her story and deprives the party calling her of essential testimony.

First, that party may of course contradict the witness through other evidence. However, the traditional rule has been that a party cannot "impeach his own witness," that is, discredit a witness he himself has called. This rule has long been subject to criticism. It was rejected in a few states, and inroads upon it by way of limitations and exceptions were made in others. Evidence Rule 607 abandons it entirely. The Advisory Committee's note thereto says that the traditional rule was "based on false premises. A party does not hold out his witnesses as worthy of belief, since he rarely has a free choice in selecting them."

Second, an especially effective form of impeachment is a prior statement inconsistent with the testimony of the witness on the stand. A prior inconsistent statement has traditionally been admissible for the purpose of discrediting court testimony, but normally not for the purpose of proving the truth of what the witness previously said. For the former purpose, it is not hearsay, because the point is just to show that the witness earlier uttered an inconsistent statement. For the latter purpose, the great majority of courts, including the Supreme Court of the United States, Bridges v. Wixon, 326 U.S. 135, 65 S.Ct. 1443 (1945), have considered it hearsay. However, Evidence Rule 801(d)(1)(A) alters the definition of hearsay somewhat so that when a declarant testifies and is subject to cross-examination concerning a prior inconsistent statement made under certain formal circumstances, that statement is not hearsay and can therefore be used for its truth in order to contradict. The argument for this Rule is that the trier of fact, being able to observe demeanor and consider the nature of the testimony, is in as good a position to determine the truth or falsity of such a prior statement as it is to determine the truth or falsity of the inconsistent testimony given in court.

(d) Motions at the Close of All the Evidence

We resume our consideration of the course of a jury trial. When all the evidence is in, either party may move for judgment as a matter of law. See Rule 50(a). Note that the motion must state specific grounds. The granting of this motion results in the withdrawal of the case from the jury. When may the judge take this drastic step without impinging upon the constitutional right to trial by jury? This brings us to examine in greater detail the difficult question of the standard for granting judgment as a matter of law.

Suppose that plaintiff has the burden of proof on propositions A, B, and C, all essential to his case, and defendant has the burden on defensive propositions D and E. When the evidence is closed, no evidence bearing on A has been offered by either party. The judge should grant defendant's motion for judgment as a matter of law. It is immaterial that there may be a conflict in the evidence as to B, C, D, and E, because the jury's resolution of these conflicts could make no difference in the result. There is no more infringement of the right to trial by jury here than there would be if plaintiff failed to allege A and the judge dismissed his complaint for failure to state a claim upon which relief could be granted.

Next let us assume that there is some evidence bearing on *A* but so little that the judge is satisfied that, looking only to the evidence favorable to the plaintiff, a reasonable jury would not be justified in finding *A*. Conceding that it is the function of the jury and not of the judge to resolve disputed issues of fact, is it not wholly proper to say that here there is no basis for a genuine dispute as to *A*? The almost universal answer to this question, and the answer given by the federal courts, is that judgment as a matter of law is proper in these circumstances.

Suppose, however, that there is testimony that, standing alone, would warrant a finding of *A*, but there is overwhelming testimonial evidence to the contrary. If the judge is satisfied that no jury reasonably considering the evidence could find *A*, must the judge nevertheless submit the case to the jury? This is a debated question. It is argued, on the one hand, that to grant judgment as a matter of law here would be an invasion of the jury's authority to determine the credibility of witnesses and, on the other hand, that the judge ought not to permit a jury to act unreasonably.

Now let us assume that the plaintiff has offered highly persuasive testimony as to *A, B,* and *C* and that the defendant has rested without impeaching the testimony and without putting in any evidence of her own.[1] We know that in a courtroom, as well as outside, people sometimes lie and honest people are sometimes mistaken. It could be argued, then, that the credibility of the testimony is necessarily at issue and, because credibility is a matter for the jury to decide, the defendant has the right to argue to the jury that it should disbelieve the plaintiff's witnesses. So, can the party with the burden of proof ever obtain judgment as a matter of law when highly persuasive testimony in support of all of his essential allegations is unimpeached and uncontradicted? The usual answer to this question, and the answer given by the federal courts, is that such a judgment is theoretically available in such circumstances.

Finally, suppose that the defendant has offered only some slight impeachment or contradiction of highly persuasive testimony tending to establish *A, B,* and *C* and that the testimony in support of the plaintiff's essential allegations is still overwhelming. If the judge is satisfied that no jury reasonably considering the evidence could find for defendant, must the judge nevertheless submit the case to the jury? This is a much debated question.

How can one generalize? There is some formula to be applied that is tied to a notion of whether reasonable minds could not differ. But this formula is applied only to a certain portion of the evidence, including all evidence that is favorable to the opponent of the motion and also apparently including unquestionable evidence (such as unimpeached and uncontradicted testimony from disinterested witnesses) that is favorable

---

[1]   The same problems are raised if the defendant offers highly persuasive evidence as to *D* or *E*, constituting a complete defense if believed, and the plaintiff offers nothing to counteract it.

to the movant. How does the standard for granting judgment as a matter of law compare with the standard for granting summary judgment? May judgment as a matter of law ever properly be granted when summary judgment for the same movant has properly been denied?

Question: (29) Is there, in an action tried without a jury, any motion analogous to a motion for judgment as a matter of law at the close of all the evidence? Is there a need for one?

(e) SUBMISSION TO JURY AND RETURN OF VERDICT

[Rules 49, 51, 52]

If a motion for judgment as a matter of law at the close of all the evidence is not made, or is made but not granted, the disputed issues of fact will be submitted to the jury for decision (at least in the first place). The jury will announce its decision in the form of a verdict.

Closing arguments and jury instructions.—Before the judge gives the case to the jury, however, counsel for the plaintiff and the defendant will make closing arguments to the jury that the proof is with their respective side. Normally, the party who could make the first opening statement can now make both initial and final closing argument.

Then, typically, the judge will instruct, or charge, the jury as to the law. This subject is treated in Rule 51, which leaves the timing to the judge's discretion.

Question: (30) In some states, instructions to the jury precede closing arguments. What are the advantages and disadvantages of the traditionally contrary federal practice?

The judge in his instructions to the jury will customarily state the issues that are in dispute and the contentions of the parties with respect to them; state who has the burden of persuasion on which issues, and what degree of persuasion the jury must reach before it decides that a party has successfully carried the burden; and analyze or at least summarize the evidence. A federal judge may also, if he chooses, express his views on the facts by "commenting on the evidence," provided he makes clear to the jury that matters of fact are for its determination and that his views are not binding.

Question: (31) Despite this acknowledged power to comment on the evidence, including the power to indicate who in their judgment should prevail on the facts, many federal judges refrain from expressing their views. In the majority of state courts, the judges do not have the power. What arguments can be made for and against the federal position of allowing comment?

What is the lawyers' role in connection with the judge's instructions? Rule 51(a) gives the parties the right to file written requests for specific instructions. But the lawyers have other opportunities to urge on the judge what the instructions should include.

Question: (32) *P* sues *D* for damage to *P*'s truck allegedly caused by *D*'s negligence. Because of industry-wide shortages *P* cannot obtain the requisite repair parts for some time, nor can *P* obtain a substitute truck. As a result, *P* loses the anticipated profit from a trucking contract. *P*'s attorney wants the jury to award as an element of damages the loss of this profit. Suppose: (a) *P*'s attorney requests an instruction that the jury may properly consider the loss of this profit as an element of damages, and the judge refuses so to instruct; (b) *P*'s attorney makes no such request, and the judge's charge expressly excludes from the jury's consideration every element of damages except the diminution in value of the truck caused by the accident; or (c) *P*'s attorney makes no such request, and the judge's charge makes no specific reference to the matter. In case (a), what must *P*'s attorney next do if she thinks the judge is in error on the law and if she wants to preserve the point for appeal? By not requesting an instruction, has she lost rights to assign error on appeal in case (b) or (c)?

Verdict.—Because the nature of the attorneys' arguments and of the judge's instructions is affected by the kind of verdict that the jury will be asked to return, it is appropriate concurrently to ponder the kinds of verdict authorized by the Rules. This subject is treated in Rule 49.

The verdict may be and most usually is a general one, for example, "The jury find for the plaintiff and assess damages in the sum of $_____," or, "The jury find for the defendant." Or the verdict may be a general one accompanied by written questions upon one or more issues of fact necessary to decision. Rule 49(b). Or the verdict may be special, in the form of a special written finding upon each issue of fact. Rule 49(a).

Questions: (33) Who determines which kind of verdict will be used, and when is the determination made?

(34) On what basis should the determination be made?

(35) How would the kind of verdict to be rendered affect the nature of the attorneys' arguments?

Whenever the jury has to return a general verdict, whether or not accompanied by written questions, the judge must determine and then instruct the jury on the rules of substantive law that govern the case. For the jurors cannot rationally find a verdict "for the plaintiff" or "for the defendant" without applying the rules of substantive law to the facts as they find them, and they do not and should not know these rules except as the judge states them. The rules of substantive law that the judge imparts to the jury may be rather vague or general, leaving a considerable range of judgment to the jury (instructions on the standard of due care in most negligence cases are perforce general), or they may be fairly specific. In all events, the judge's instructions on the law will usually be a good deal more particularized than the legal rubrics that the pleadings invoked or implied. For example, in an action for battery the defendant may have pleaded self-defense in a general way, but the judge may have to explain to the jury in detail the factors that should go into a determination of whether a defendant can justifiably strike a plaintiff in response to what appears to be a threatened attack.

If the jury is to return only a special verdict, the judge may reduce in scope his instructions on the applicable rules of substantive law, because the judge will himself apply those rules to the jury's special findings on the issues of fact.

Whatever the kind of verdict, the jury, after hearing arguments and receiving instructions, retires to deliberate in private. The jury is occasionally kept sequestered the entire time from when it retires until the judge finally discharges it. If the jurors are unable to reach a verdict, the judge will discharge the jury; and the case may have to be retried. If the jurors reach decision, the foreperson of the jury will appropriately complete and sign a given form of verdict; the verdict will be returned in open court with the jury present and will then be recorded; and the jury will be discharged.

Questions: (36) In an action tried without a jury, should the parties have a right to make closing argument to the judge?

(37) Our discussion of instructions and verdict is obviously inapplicable in an action tried without a jury. In a nonjury case, "the court must find the facts specially" and state separately its conclusions of law. Rule 52(a)(1); see Rule 52(c). Why should the judge be required to find the facts specially even though the jury is not required to do so (at least when it returns a general verdict)?

(f) MOTIONS AFTER VERDICT

[Rules 50, 59]

Suppose the jury has come in with a verdict for one of the parties. Will the result of the litigation in the district court necessarily conform to the verdict? No. Judgment is normally entered (at least in the first place) in accordance with the verdict. But even after that judgment has been entered, the party against whom the judgment went still has two motions available to him that may change the result.[m]

Renewed motion for judgment as a matter of law.—You will note that Rule 50(b) permits a party, whose motion for judgment as a matter of law under Rule 50(a) has been denied or not granted, to move to have the verdict and any judgment entered on the verdict set aside and to have judgment entered in his favor despite the adverse verdict. This later motion for judgment as a matter of law was formerly called a motion for judgment notwithstanding the verdict, a name often shortened to judgment n.o.v. from the Latin *non obstante veredicto*. The verdict-loser must file it not later than the twenty-eighth day after entry of judgment on the verdict.

---

[m]   Besides the renewed motion for judgment as a matter of law (Rule 50(b)) and the motion for a new trial (Rule 59(a)(1)) discussed in the text, see Rule 59(e) (motion to amend judgment) and Rule 60 (motion for relief from judgment).

Note carefully that it is a condition of a party's making an effective *renewed* motion for judgment as a matter of law under Rule 50(b) that he previously moved for judgment as a matter of law under Rule 50(a). The movant is thereby reasserting the same grounds. Indeed, as the text of Rule 50(b) suggests, the standard for granting a renewed motion for judgment as a matter of law is in theory the same as the standard for granting a motion for judgment as a matter of law, say, one made at the close of all the evidence. What hope is there, then, that the judge will grant a renewed motion for judgment as a matter of law when the judge has previously declined to grant the same party's motion for judgment as a matter of law at the close of all the evidence? Will not the jury's verdict against that party fortify the judge in the view supposedly expressed in ruling on the earlier motion?

In seeking an answer to these questions, consider a situation where defendant moves for judgment as a matter of law in his favor at the close of all the evidence, and the judge inclines to the belief that the motion is well-founded but she is not certain and wants time to reflect. Will she perhaps deny the motion, or refrain from granting it, and pass the case to the jury believing that the jury will probably find for defendant, thus rendering it unnecessary to deal further with the difficulty posed by the motion for judgment as a matter of law? And if the jury does find for defendant, has not the judge avoided the appearance of intruding into the sphere of the jury and obviated the appellate court's close scrutiny of judgment as a matter of law? But if the jury returns a verdict for plaintiff, may she not grant defendant's renewed motion for judgment as a matter of law in accordance with her original inclination? The value of this judicial approach will be more apparent if we anticipate the course of later proceedings on appeal.

Questions: (38) Suppose the judge grants defendant's motion for judgment as a matter of law at the close of all the evidence. The appellate court later decides that she was wrong and that the case should have gone to the jury. What happens after that? *retrial.*

(39) Suppose the judge instead denies defendant's motion, submits the case to the jury, and grants judgment as a matter of law on defendant's renewed motion after a verdict for plaintiff. The appellate court later finds her in error in granting that motion. What then happens?

(40) So there are excellent reasons for a judge to deny a motion for judgment as a matter of law even though the judge would feel bound to grant the same party's renewed motion, if necessary. Then why would judges ever grant judgment as a matter of law before a verdict, as they sometimes do?

Motion for a new trial.—A party dissatisfied with a verdict has yet another motion—the motion for a new trial under Rule 59(a)(1)—that the party may file not later than twenty-eight days after entry of judgment on the verdict. A new trial motion asks that the verdict and any judgment entered on the verdict be set aside and that the case be retried. The judge may grant such a motion on any of numerous grounds.

1.   One possible ground is that the verdict is, as is said, "against the weight of the evidence." The jury by its verdict will have decided one or more disputed factual issues. If the judge, looking at all the evidence including its credibility, is clearly convinced that the jury was wrong in deciding as it did—that is, if the judge is convinced that the jury grossly misjudged the credibility of the testimony or grossly misconceived where the weight of the evidence lay—the judge should order a new trial.

Here we touch upon a difficult problem. On the one hand, the judge should not order a new trial merely because the judge disagrees with the jury's resolution of the issues. On the other hand, there are cases where the verdict is so far against the general current of the evidence that to let it stand would be to countenance injustice. In the latter situation, the judge may properly set aside the verdict and order a new trial.

Questions: (41) What is the difference in practical result between (a) granting the defendant's renewed motion for judgment as a matter of law and (b) setting aside a verdict for the plaintiff and ordering a new trial?

(42) How does the standard for ordering a new trial on the ground that the verdict is against the weight of the evidence compare with the standard applied under Rule 50(a) and (b)? May a party's new trial motion on such ground ever properly be granted when the same party's motions for judgment as a matter of law have properly been denied?

(43) Suppose the jury returns a verdict, but the judge sets aside the verdict as against the weight of the evidence and orders a new trial. On the second trial before a new jury and possibly before a new judge, the same verdict is returned. May a new trial be ordered? Should there be a limit to the number of times a new trial may be ordered?

2.   Another possible ground for a new trial is some irregularity during the trial, such as misbehavior by a participant. Sometimes the judge will order a new trial because it is clear that the jury has failed to follow her instructions.

Question: (44) Can you imagine a situation where it would be manifest from a general verdict that such error has occurred?

A similar reason for granting a new trial is that the judge believes that she herself committed an error, for example, in instructing the jury or ruling on the admissibility of evidence. The motion for a new trial in a sense gives the judge a chance to reconsider her own actions; if she believes they need correction, she may order a new trial. Indeed, Rule 59(d) provides that within twenty-eight days "the court, on its own, may order a new trial for any reason that would justify granting one on a party's motion."

The list of such irregularities that might occur during the course of a trial, and on the basis of which the court could justifiably grant a new trial after verdict and judgment to prevent injustice, is a lengthy one. But see Rule 61.

3. The judge may also grant a new trial on the ground of newly discovered evidence.

Joinder of motions.—The verdict-loser may, and usually does, make a motion for a new trial together with any renewed motion for judgment as a matter of law. See Rule 50(b). If the judge denies both the renewed motion for judgment and the motion for a new trial, judgment on the verdict will stand. If the judge denies the renewed motion for judgment but grants the motion for a new trial, the judge will set aside the verdict and any judgment entered thereon, and the case will again stand for trial. If the judge grants the renewed motion for judgment, the judge will set aside the verdict and any judgment entered thereon, and the contrary judgment will be entered; in such case, the judge will also rule on the new trial motion, either *conditionally* granting or *conditionally* denying it pursuant to Rule 50(c)(1): if the judgment entered is reversed on appeal, there will be a new trial or not, ordinarily in accordance with the trial judge's decision on the new trial motion, which was *conditional* on such reversal.

Question: (45) Is there, in an action tried without a jury, any motion analogous to a renewed motion for judgment as a matter of law? Cf. Rule 52(b) (motion to amend findings). Is there any motion analogous to a motion for a new trial? Cf. Rule 59(a) (motion for a new trial, which in a nonjury case is usually only for taking additional testimony).

———

Section 4.   Judgment

(a) Entry of Judgment

[Rule 58]

The upshot of litigation in the district court is a judgment that sets out any relief the parties have won. This may come about short of, or after, completed trial.

Where the judgment is a simple one—a jury has returned a general verdict, or in a nonjury case the court has decided that a party shall recover a sum of money or has denied all relief—the clerk prepares, signs, and enters the judgment immediately. In more complicated cases, the court promptly approves the form of judgment and the clerk enters it. See Rule 58(b); Forms 70 and 71.

(b) Kinds of Relief Afforded by Judgment

[Rules 54; 57]

It is worth pausing on the kinds of relief that a judgment may afford. We should perhaps have dealt with this subject at the outset of our discussion of the phases of a lawsuit, because the questions, "What kinds of relief are available in this type of case?" and, "Which should I choose if

I have a choice?" are often of first importance to an intending plaintiff, and he will consider them before he frames his complaint. Observe, however, that under Rule 54(c), every final judgment should grant the relief to which the party is entitled, even if the party has not demanded such relief in the pleadings—except that a judgment by default must not be different in kind from or exceed in amount what the party requested in the demand for relief.

Question: (1) What are the reasons for these provisions of Rule 54(c)?

Coercive relief.—A common type of judgment for a successful plaintiff is one for money damages designed to compensate him for the defendant's wrong. Thus, an ordinary measure of damages for breach of contract is the difference between what the defendant promised and what the plaintiff got. In an action for personal injuries, the measure of damages is the sum that will supposedly restore the plaintiff as nearly as possible to the position he would have been in had the defendant not committed the tort, even though the difficulties in putting a dollar figure on such things as pain and suffering or facial disfigurement are obvious. In other kinds of cases the provision of nominal damages, which is a trifling sum given in recognition of the plaintiff's legal right, or a restitutionary measure of damages, which prevents the defendant's unjust enrichment, may be appropriate. In some kinds of cases the judgment may give the plaintiff punitive damages, designed to punish or make an example of the defendant. Additionally, the judgment may award interest, accruing after and in some kinds of cases before judgment.

Another type of judgment may allow a government official to restore property wrongfully withheld by the defendant from the plaintiff, as where the defendant has wrongfully appropriated the plaintiff's watch and retains it, or where the defendant has wrongfully entered upon the plaintiff's land and occupies it.

The foregoing types of judgment trace historically from the courts of common law. There is another type of judgment, historically associated only with the courts of equity, that orders the losing party to do or to refrain from doing some act. Orders in suits in equity were called decrees, while actions at law resulted in judgments. Note that Rule 54(a) now defines "judgment" as including a decree.

For an equitable example, in proper cases the judge may direct a party in default under a contract to carry out the contract according to its terms (specific performance). In some such situations the judgment will not go so far as to order the party to carry out her promise, but it will order her to refrain from acting inconsistently with her promise (injunction). So, if the defendant, a famous opera singer, has promised to sing exclusively for the plaintiff over a certain period of time and wrongfully refuses to perform, the judgment may order the defendant not to sing for the plaintiff's competitors during the time in question.

An equitable judgment may order the defendant to refrain from committing some other kind of wrong. If the defendant is wrongfully selling chewing gum packaged so as to imitate plaintiff Wrigley's, the judgment may order it to desist from this unfair competition. Or if the defendant has wrongfully constructed a dam that floods the plaintiff's land, the judge may enjoin her to tear it down.

A judgment may combine one kind of relief with another. Thus, a judgment for plaintiff ordering defendant to perform a promise may also award damages to plaintiff for past breaches by defendant.

————

RITTER v. RITTER, 381 Ill. 549, 46 N.E.2d 41 (1943). Joseph Ritter agreed with a relative, named Louis Ritter, that they would buy two pieces of real estate upon foreclosure sale, taking title in their names as joint tenants; and that if there was no redemption, Joseph would take the "Nixon property" and Louis the "brick building." After the purchase Joseph became critically ill; he asked Louis whether, in case of his death, his wife and daughter would have any trouble securing the Nixon property; and Louis assured him they would not. Nevertheless, after Joseph had died and the redemption period had passed, Louis procured a master's deed to both properties in his own name. Thus, Joseph's widow and daughter had to start a chancery suit against Louis in order to impose a constructive trust upon the Nixon property in their favor. They succeeded in the suit.

The widow and daughter then sued Louis to recover the expenses of the chancery suit that had not been assessed therein as costs. After trial without jury, judgment was entered in plaintiffs' favor for $2007, representing primarily counsel fees paid in prosecuting the prior suit. On appeal, the intermediate appellate court affirmed.

But the Supreme Court of Illinois reversed, holding that the subsequent action would not lie. Among the reasons given were the following: (1) Under Illinois law recovery of litigation expenses depends on statute, and here there is none in point. (2) As defendant had the "right" to resist plaintiffs' claim, on general principles he should not be liable for the consequences of his conduct in refusing to convey the property. (3) It is true that cases exist where A has been liable to B for wrongful conduct that involved B in litigation with a third party, and that the measure of damages there has included B's expenses of litigation with the third party, but those cases are not relevant to an attempt by successful litigants to recover their expenses against their immediate adversary. (4) The rule urged by plaintiffs would involve endless litigation, because if plaintiffs recover here, they could institute another action for expenses of the present action, and so on in an infinite series. (5) True, some jurisdictions consider litigation expenses in situations where they allow punitive damages, but that is different from recovery in a separate action. (6) Because Illinois has permitted an action for "malicious prosecution of a civil suit without probable cause" only if arrest, seizure of property, or other special injury accompanied the wrong (in refusing to extend this tort, this court has stressed the need to leave the courts "open to every citizen"), the converse must be true, namely, that a plaintiff cannot bring an action against a defendant who made a "groundless and causeless defense."

———

COSTS

"Costs" are normally awarded to the prevailing party, either plaintiff or defendant, as a part of any judgment. See 28 U.S.C. § 1920. After decision in the case, the clerk "taxes" these costs, subject to the judge's review and to the judge's possible refusal to award costs. See Rule 54(d)(1).

Taxable costs may include certain direct expenses incurred in conducting the litigation, such as fees of clerk and marshal, statutory fees and disbursements for witnesses, docket fees, some deposition expenses, and like items. Defining the bounds on such costs is a complicated and variable matter, but suffice it to say that such costs certainly do not reimburse total out-of-pocket expenditures. Of crucial importance is the precept that costs in American courts (other than in Alaska) ordinarily cannot include counsel fees, so that each party ordinarily pays his own lawyer. Thus, although sometimes rather significant in absolute terms, costs represent only a small percentage of the total expenses of litigation.

In most of the rest of the world, including England, the losing party also pays the attorney's fees of the prevailing party. Indeed, the so-called American rule against fee-shifting might be better termed the "American exception." But using comparative law to leap to conclusions of heresy must be resisted. It is true that the historical reasons for our early departure from the English rule are murky and largely obsolete. Nevertheless, the reasons behind the persistence of the difference in practice may well lie in profound societal differences, especially in differing views on the nature of law, the role of courts, and the desirability of litigation.

Here and today, the American rule appears firmly entrenched. See Alyeska Pipeline Serv. Co. v. Wilderness Soc'y, 421 U.S. 240, 95 S.Ct. 1612 (1975). Yet academic criticism of that rule remains high, and exceptions to it are slowly multiplying on both federal and state levels. Therefore, the complexities of adopting the English rule in America deserve consideration.

Considering the effects of a change to fee-shifting on the litigants' economic incentives, there has been little effective empirical work. There has been some theoretical work, but it is surprisingly inconclusive. For purposes of illustration, picture the Ritter plaintiffs' initial chancery suit under a regime that would require the loser to pay, in addition to his own counsel fees, the winning side's counsel fees as costs; so victory will be more complete, but the risk of loss is greater. First—on the decision to pursue the claim—probably the English rule relatively encourages small meritorious suits, while somewhat discouraging larger dubious suits and nuisance suits; however, risk aversion discourages the middle class from resorting to litigation under the English rule. Second—on the subsequent decision whether to settle—although the effects of implementing the English rule on the likelihood and timing of settlement are rather unclear, strong claims would tend to be settled for more and weak claims for less than under the American rule. Third—on the conduct of litigation—although the English rule might relatively encourage the litigants to escalate expenditures, its influence on the overall economic costs of the litigation system is unknown and arguably unknowable. Fourth—on the incentive to comply with substantive law—the comparison between English and American rules gets really complex, because the interaction or interplay of effects on all these various incentives can no longer be ignored. In any event, predicting the direction of an effect tells us nothing of the size of the effect or the importance of side effects. The lesson seems to be this: beware of simplistic analysis of the English-American dispute.

There are many considerations other than these economic concerns, of course. In a perspicacious article, Professor Rowe lists five other common rationales for fee-shifting: "The first is a sense of simple fairness: the idea that it is only just for the loser to have to pay, at least in considerable part, the winner's legal costs appears to be a major underpinning of the English indemnity rule. The second, the theme of making a litigant financially whole for a legal wrong suffered, is probably most familiar as the idea of compensation in the substantive law of remedies. A punitive emphasis on fee shifting to deter and punish misconduct, either in litigation or in the underlying transaction, is a third rationale. Fourth, the 'private attorney general' theory justifies a fee award on the basis of the public usefulness of advancing a particular type of claim. A fifth justification is a desire to affect the relative strengths of the parties, a theme that appears in discussion of schemes for fee shifting against government, particularly when the private party involved is an individual or a small concern." Thomas D. Rowe, Jr., The Legal Theory of Attorney Fee Shifting: A Critical Overview, 1982 Duke L.J. 651, 653. But as he goes on to demonstrate, the validity or at least the reach of each of these arguments is open to serious question or qualification. And counterarguments remain, including an effective claim that the weak rationales for the English rule fail generally to justify the undeniably substantial transaction costs of adopting and then operating a system of fee-shifting. Moreover, all these conflicting policies must be considered in a broader context, which would take into account at least the presence or absence of contingent fees, litigation funding, legal insurance, legal aid, small-claims courts, other alternative dispute-resolution mechanisms, class actions, and other representative litigation and also the effects of any security-for-costs or offer-of-judgment provisions. See, e.g., Rule 68. The lesson here seems to be this: beware of thinking too narrowly.

One should recognize that neither the English rule nor the American rule exists in pure form anywhere. There are exceptions on whether to shift fees and, given shifting, there are variations on how much of the fees should shift in the particular case. One should also recognize that the English and American rules do not exhaust the possible fee-shifting regimes. An obvious alternative is one-way fee-shifting, such as shifting only in favor of a prevailing plaintiff. Indeed, Professor Rowe apparently supported a one-way pro-prevailing-plaintiff scheme, although he would have allowed a shift in favor of any prevailing defendant who had faced a truly baseless action. Very importantly, because of the interplay of policies, the chosen rules for fee-shifting should probably differ according to the type or size of the case or the characteristics or behavior of the litigants. The lesson here seems to be this: beware of thinking too generally.

In summary, the English-American dispute raises very complex issues. In all likelihood, we shall retain the American rule; but the courts and especially the legislatures will continue to move cautiously by a sort of common-law incremental method away from that polar position, adopting numerous targeted exceptions such as the federal ones that currently allow discretionary shifting of reasonable fees, under the case law, when the opponent has litigated in bad faith; or, under 42 U.S.C. § 1988(b), when in a civil rights action a plaintiff has prevailed or a prevailing defendant has faced a truly baseless suit; or, under 28 U.S.C. § 2412, when certain private parties have prevailed against the federal government. Perhaps by now this approach does not appear as inappropriate as it might at first have seemed to you. See generally Avery Wiener Katz & Chris William Sanchirico, "Fee Shifting," in Procedural Law and Economics 271 (Chris William Sanchirico ed., 2d ed. 2012).

———

Declaratory relief.—The judgments so far considered are plainly coercive. The power of government is behind them, as we shall see shortly.

A judgment for the defendant is less plainly coercive, because the result of the litigation is a denial rather than a grant of the relief sought. The force of government may, however, secure the recovery of the costs awarded to the prevailing defendant, doing so by execution against the defeated plaintiff. More importantly, such a judgment for the defendant is a determination of rights and other legal relations, which the principle of res judicata may make conclusive.

Finally, Rule 57 speaks of declaratory judgments and refers to 28 U.S.C. § 2201. See also § 2202. The action for a declaratory judgment differs from the usual action in that the plaintiff instituting it need not seek the imposition of any sanction apart from a declaration of rights and other legal relations. He may, for example, seek a declaration as to whether a particular act that he proposes to commit will be tortious, by suing in a situation where the defendant, a person whom the act would affect, has asserted that she will so regard it.

Questions: (2) Rule 57 says that the "existence of another adequate remedy" does not prevent a judgment for declaratory relief in cases where it is otherwise appropriate. What does Rule 57 mean thereby? Why does Rule 57 so provide?

(3) What is the "further relief" that is mentioned in § 2201, and what is the "further relief" mentioned in § 2202? Why do these statutes so provide?

Section 2201(a) limits the remedy to "a case of actual controversy," much as Article III, Section 2 of the Constitution limits federal courts to cases or controversies. Courts have given the statute's limit of justiciability an operational definition in terms of balancing the benefits of immediate decision against its costs. The former factor comprises the need of the *plaintiff* for a declaration. The costs include the unfairness to the *defendant* of opening the courthouse doors. But the costs surely include much more in the way of the *system*'s interests. Restricting the federal courts to an actual controversy not only keeps them out of the states' domain and more significantly out of the other branches' business of prospective lawmaking, but also improves the judicial function itself. Courts as we know them will perform better if they decide based on focused facts presented by interested adversaries; moreover, entertaining only concrete disputes will keep many actions out of court, so allowing courts to handle their business more effectively.

————

American Machine & Metals, Inc. v. De Bothezat Impeller Co.

United States Circuit Court of Appeals, Second Circuit, 1948.
166 F.2d 535.

■ Before SWAN, CHASE and FRANK, CIRCUIT JUDGES.

■ SWAN, CIRCUIT JUDGE. This appeal presents a question under the Declaratory Judgment Act, 28 U.S.C.A. § 400,[a] which authorizes the courts of the United States "in cases of actual controversy" to declare "rights and other legal relations of any interested party petitioning for such declaration," without regard to whether further relief is or could be sought. . . . From the judgment of dismissal the plaintiff [American Machine] has appealed.

---

[a] With changes this section, originally enacted in 1934, now appears as 28 U.S.C. §§ 2201 and 2202.

In summary the allegations of the complaint are the following:

In 1934 the parties entered into a contract under which the defendant conveyed to the plaintiff certain patents and certain physical equipment for the making of fans and other products and the plaintiff agreed to pay the defendant license fees (not less than $5,000 annually) based on the "net sales" of its products. So long as the contract continued the fees were to be paid on "net sales" regardless of whether the plaintiff's products were covered by the patents or whether the patents had expired. The contract contained no expiration date but could be terminated at any time by the plaintiff on six months' notice. In the event of such termination the plaintiff was to transfer the patents back to the defendant and to cease using the name "De Bothezat," which it agreed to use in its literature and sales promotion while the contract continued. Since February 19, 1946, the plaintiff has neither manufactured nor sold any product for which possession of the patents is essential. The plaintiff "desires and intends" to exercise its right of termination under the contract and "desires and intends" to continue in the business of selling fans and ventilating equipment. The defendant at various times has made claims and assertions to the plaintiff and other persons to the effect that upon termination of the contract the plaintiff will no longer have the right to continue the manufacture of fans and ventilating equipment, and "has led plaintiff to believe" that upon termination of the contract defendant will sue plaintiff if it does not cease the manufacture and sale of fans and ventilating equipment. Said claims and assertions by defendant "are without basis and an actual controversy exists between the parties," and plaintiff seeks a declaration of the rights of the parties in order to avoid the possible accrual of avoidable damages. The prayer [in this diversity action] requests a declaration "particularly with respect to the proper interpretation and effect of the agreement" and that the court declare the right of plaintiff to continue to manufacture and sell fans and other noninfringing products after termination of the agreement and without the payment of further sums to defendant.

In concluding that no controversy exists the district judge noted that the plaintiff has not yet given notice of termination of the contract and may never do so; the opinion states [75 F.Supp. 421, 424]:

"In this case, if the court should decide that plaintiff might terminate and continue its manufacture and sale of products other than those covered by patents, plaintiff might and probably would terminate. If the court should decide otherwise, plaintiff would probably continue under the agreement until its termination and no controversy such as now claimed to exist might ever be present. In other words, plaintiff has not elected what it wishes to do and its action might and could render academic the very declaration which it seeks.

"The complaint is, therefore, dismissed because no justiciable controversy exists which would justify the maintenance of an action under the Declaratory Judgment Statute. The relief prayed for should not be granted at this time either as a matter of discretion or otherwise."

We think the judge construed the statute too narrowly. . . . After [giving notice of termination] it will be too late to avoid an action for damages if the plaintiff acts as he intends by continuing the business. The very purpose of the declaratory judgment procedure is to prevent the accrual of such avoidable damages. . . .

. . . .

Judgment reversed and cause remanded for trial on the merits.[b]

───────

PRASCO, LLC v. MEDICIS PHARMACEUTICAL CORP., 537 F.3d 1329 (Fed.Cir.2008). Prasco, the eventual plaintiff, marketed a generic benzoyl peroxide cleansing product called OSCION. Defendant Medicis made another such product called TRIAZ, which it marked as covered by four patents owned by the defendants. Prasco asked the defendants to agree not to sue for its selling OSCION, but the defendants declined.

Prasco then brought an action for a declaration that OSCION does not infringe those four patents. The U.S. District Court for the Southern District of Ohio dismissed for lack of jurisdiction because of the absence of an "actual controversy."

The court of appeals, on appeal under 28 U.S.C. § 1295(a)(1), began by explaining the context: "The Declaratory Judgment Act is not an independent basis for subject matter jurisdiction. Skelly Oil Co. v. Phillips Petroleum Co., 339 U.S. 667, 671–72, 70 S.Ct. 876 (1950). Rather, it provides a remedy available only if the court has jurisdiction from some other source. [Citation omitted.] Such jurisdiction is limited by Article III of the Constitution, which restricts federal judicial power to the adjudication of 'Cases' or 'Controversies.' [Citations omitted.] The Declaratory Judgment Act's requirement of 'a case of actual controversy' simply affirms this Constitutional requirement, having long been interpreted as referring to any case and controversy that is justiciable under Article III. . . .

"For there to be a case or controversy under Article III, the dispute must be 'definite and concrete, touching the legal relations of parties having adverse legal interests,' 'real and substantial,' and 'admi[t] of specific relief through a decree of a conclusive character, as distinguished from an opinion advising what the law would be upon a hypothetical state of facts.' MedImmune, [Inc. v. Genentech, Inc., 549 U.S. 118, 127, 127

───────

[b]   After the decision set out in the text, defendant again moved to dismiss the complaint and to obtain other relief, this time presenting affidavits to show that there was no controversy. The motion was denied, 8 F.R.D. 324 (S.D.N.Y.1948). Later reported steps in the case will be found at 8 F.R.D. 306; 8 F.R.D. 459; 82 F.Supp. 556; and 173 F.2d 890. Finally, plaintiff obtained a declaration that it could terminate the contract and continue to sell "any and all fans, ventilating equipment and other products, not infringing upon valid patents owned by defendant after such termination." This judgment was affirmed, 180 F.2d 342 (2d Cir.), cert. denied, 339 U.S. 979, 70 S.Ct. 1025 (1950).

S.Ct. 764, 771 (2007)] (quoting Aetna Life [Ins. Co. v. Haworth, 300 U.S. 227, 240–41, 57 S.Ct. 461, 464 (1937)]). As the Supreme Court has recently reiterated, however, there is no bright-line rule for determining whether an action satisfies the case or controversy requirement. Id. To the contrary, '[t]he difference between an abstract question and a "controversy" contemplated by the Declaratory Judgment Act is necessarily one of degree, and it would be difficult, if it would be possible, to fashion a precise test for determining in every case whether there is such a controversy.' Md. Cas. Co. v. Pac. Coal & Oil Co., 312 U.S. 270, 273, 61 S.Ct. 510 (1941). Instead of a bright-line rule, 'the analysis must be calibrated to the particular facts of each case,' Cat Tech LLC [v. TubeMaster, Inc., 528 F.3d 871, 879 (Fed.Cir.2008)], with the basic standard being whether 'the facts alleged, under all the circumstances, show that there is a substantial controversy, between parties having adverse legal interests, of sufficient immediacy and reality to warrant the issuance of a declaratory judgment,' MedImmune, 127 S.Ct. at 771 (quoting Md. Cas. Co., 312 U.S. at 273); see also Caraco Pharms. Labs. Ltd. v. Forest Labs., 527 F.3d 1278, 1290 (Fed.Cir.2008)."

The court of appeals then affirmed: "Considering the totality of the circumstances, Prasco has not alleged a controversy of sufficient 'immediacy and reality' to create a justiciable controversy. . . . Absent an injury-in-fact fairly traceable to the patentee, there can be no immediate and real controversy.

" . . . The mere existence of a potentially adverse patent does not cause an injury nor create an imminent risk of an injury; absent action by the patentee, 'a potential competitor . . . is legally free to market its product in the face of an adversely-held patent.' [Teva Pharms. USA, Inc. v. Novartis Pharms. Corp., 482 F.3d 1330, 1345 (Fed.Cir.2007).]

"Prasco argues that a case and controversy has nevertheless been created because Medicis has caused Prasco to suffer an actual harm— namely, 'paralyzing uncertainty' from fear that Medicis will bring an infringement suit against it. Appellant's Br. 23. As Prasco admitted at oral argument, however, any uncertainty has not been paralyzing. To the contrary, notwithstanding this lawsuit, Prasco has launched its OSCION product. . . . [T]he bedrock rule [remains] that a case or controversy must be based on a real and immediate injury or threat of future injury that is caused by the defendants—an objective standard that cannot be met by a purely subjective or speculative fear of future harm. . . .

"Rather than a purely subjective fear or the mere existence of a potentially adverse patent alone, the alleged injury at the root of most justiciable declaratory judgment controversies in the patent context is a 'restraint on the free exploitation of non-infringing goods,' or an imminent threat of such restraint. Caraco, 527 F.3d at 1291 (quoting Red Wing Shoe Co., Inc. v. Hockerson-Halberstadt, Inc., 148 F.3d 1355, 1360 (Fed.Cir.1998)).

"A patentee can cause such an injury in a variety of ways, for example, by creating a reasonable apprehension of an infringement suit, [citation omitted], demanding the right to royalty payments, [citation omitted], or creating a barrier to the regulatory approval of a product that is necessary for marketing, [citation omitted]." But here the court noted by contrast that "the defendants have not accused Prasco of infringement or asserted any rights to OSCION, nor have they taken any actions which imply such claims. Instead, all we have before us is Prasco's allegation that its product does not infringe the defendants' patents."

In sum, "where Prasco has suffered no actual present injury traceable to the defendants, and the defendants have not asserted any rights against Prasco related to the patents nor taken any affirmative actions concerning Prasco's current product, one prior suit [by Medicis against Prasco] concerning unrelated patents and products and the defendants' failure to sign a covenant not to sue are simply not sufficient to establish that Prasco is at risk of imminent harm from the defendants and that there is an actual controversy between the parties of sufficient immediacy and reality to warrant declaratory judgment jurisdiction. Although we understand Prasco's desire to have a definitive answer on whether its products infringe defendants' patents, were the district court to reach the merits of this case, it would merely be providing an advisory opinion. This is impermissible under Article III."

International Longshoremen's Local 37 v. Boyd

Supreme Court of the United States, 1954.
347 U.S. 222, 74 S.Ct. 447.

■ MR. JUSTICE FRANKFURTER delivered the opinion of the Court.

This is an action by Local 37 of the International Longshoremen's and Warehousemen's Union and several of its [permanent resident] alien members to enjoin the District Director of Immigration and Naturalization at Seattle from so construing § 212(d)(7) of the Immigration and Nationality Act of 1952* as to treat aliens domiciled in the continental United States returning from temporary work in Alaska as if they were aliens entering the United States for the first time. Declaratory relief to the same effect is also sought. Since petitioners asserted in the alternative that such a construction of the challenged statute would be unconstitutional, a three-judge district court was

---

*   This section states that the exclusionary provisions of § 212(a) shall, with exceptions not here relevant, "be applicable to any alien who shall leave Hawaii, Alaska, Guam, Puerto Rico, or the Virgin Islands of the United States, and who seeks to enter the continental United States . . . ." 8 U.S.C. § 1182(d)(7). [Footnote by Court. "Alien" is a perhaps unfortunate term that is used frequently in statutes and cases to refer to a person who is not a U.S. citizen.—Ed.]

convened.[c] The case came before it on stipulated facts and issues of law [by pretrial order], from which it appeared that the union has over three thousand members who work every summer in the herring and salmon canneries of Alaska, that some of these are aliens, and that if alien workers going to Alaska for the 1953 canning season were excluded on their return, their "contract and property rights [would] be jeopardized and forfeited." The District Court entertained the suit but dismissed it on the merits. 111 F.Supp. 802 [(W.D.Wash. Apr. 10, 1953)]. . . .

On this appeal,[d] appellee contends [inter alia] that the District Court should not have reached the statutory and constitutional questions—that it should have dismissed the suit for want of a "case or controversy" . . . .

Appellants in effect asked the District Court to rule that a statute the sanctions of which had not been set in motion against individuals on whose behalf relief was sought, because an occasion for doing so had not arisen, would not be applied to them if in the future such a contingency should arise. That is not a lawsuit to enforce a right; it is an endeavor to obtain a court's assurance that a statute does not govern hypothetical situations that may or may not make the challenged statute applicable. Determination of the scope and constitutionality of legislation in advance of its immediate adverse effect in the context of a concrete case involves too remote and abstract an inquiry for the proper exercise of the judicial function. United Public Workers v. Mitchell, 330 U.S. 75, 67 S.Ct. 556; see Muskrat v. United States, 219 U.S. 346, 31 S.Ct. 250, and Alabama State Federation of Labor v. McAdory, 325 U.S. 450, 65 S.Ct. 1384. Since we do not have on the record before us a controversy appropriate for adjudication, the judgment of the District Court must be vacated, with directions to dismiss the complaint.

It is so ordered.

■ MR. JUSTICE BLACK, with whom MR. JUSTICE DOUGLAS concurs, dissenting.

This looks to me like the very kind of "case or controversy" courts should decide. With the abstract principles of law relied on by the majority for dismissing the case, I am not in disagreement. Of course federal courts do not pass on the meaning or constitutionality of statutes

---

c   For the three-judge district court referred to, see 28 U.S.C. § 2284.

Prior to 1976, federal law required three-judge district courts not infrequently. Most importantly, a district court composed of three judges had to hear federal actions seeking injunctive relief against the enforcement of a federal or state statute on the ground that the statute in question was contrary to the Federal Constitution.

Now, the three-judge requirement is much more limited in scope, applying primarily to reapportionment suits and to certain cases under the 1964 Civil Rights and 1965 Voting Rights Acts. See generally Charles Alan Wright & Mary Kay Kane, Law of Federal Courts § 50 (8th ed. 2017).

d   There are special situations in which decisions of the district courts are subject to direct review by the Supreme Court. See Wright & Miller §§ 4039–4040 (citing and summarizing these few statutes). For example, 28 U.S.C. § 1253 gives any party a right of direct appeal from an order granting or denying an interlocutory or permanent injunction in an action required to be heard by a three-judge district court.

as they might be thought to govern mere "hypothetical situations . . . ." Nor should courts entertain such statutory challenges on behalf of persons upon whom adverse statutory effects are "too remote and abstract an inquiry for the proper exercise of the judicial function." But as I read the record it shows that judicial action is absolutely essential to save a large group of wage earners on whose behalf this action is brought from irreparable harm due to alleged lawless enforcement of a federal statute. My view makes it necessary for me to set out the facts with a little more detail than they appear in the Court's opinion.

Every summer members of the appellant union go from the west coast of continental United States to Alaska to work in salmon and herring canneries under collective-bargaining agreements. As the 1953 canning season approached the union and its members looked forward to this Alaska employment. A troublesome question arose, however, on account of the Immigration and Nationality Act of 1952, 66 Stat. 163. Section 212(d)(7) of this new Act has language that given one construction provides that all aliens seeking admission to continental United States from Alaska, even those previously accepted as permanent United States residents, shall be examined as if entering from a foreign country with a view to excluding them on any of the many grounds applicable to aliens generally. This new law created an acute problem for the union and its numerous members who were lawful alien residents, since aliens generally can be excluded from this country for many reasons which would not justify deporting aliens lawfully residing here. The union and its members insisted on another construction. They denied that Congress intended to require alien workers to forfeit their right to live in this country for no reason at all except that they went to Alaska, territory of the United States, to engage in lawful work under a lawfully authorized collective-bargaining contract. The defendant immigration officer announced that the union's interpretation was wrong and that workers going to Alaska would be subject to examination and exclusion. This is the controversy.

It was to test the right of the immigration officer to apply § 212(d)(7) to make these workers subject to exclusion that this suit was filed by the union and two of its officers on behalf of themselves and all union members who are aliens and permanent residents. True, the action was begun before the union members went to Alaska for the 1953 canning season. But it is not only admitted that the Immigration official intended to enforce § 212(d)(7) as the union and these workers feared. It is admitted here that he has since done precisely that. All 1953 alien cannery workers have actually been subjected to the wearisome routine of immigration procedure as though they had never lived here. And some of the union members are evidently about to be denied the right ever to return to their homes on grounds that could not have been legally applied to them had they stayed in California or Washington instead of going to Alaska to work for an important American industry.

Thus the threatened injury which the Court dismisses as "remote" and "hypothetical" has come about. For going to Alaska to engage in honest employment many of these workers may lose the home this country once afforded them. This is a strange penalty to put on productive work. Maybe this is what Congress meant by passing § 212(d)(7). And maybe in these times such a law would be held constitutional. But even so, can it be that a challenge to this law on behalf of those whom it hits the hardest is so frivolous that it should be dismissed for want of a controversy that courts should decide? Workers threatened with irreparable damages, like others, should have their cases tried.[e]

Question: (4) Four years after the International Longshoremen's case, an appeal came to the Supreme Court from dismissal of an action on the ground that there was no "actual controversy." The plaintiff's complaint sought a declaration that a Tennessee statute requiring segregated seating arrangements in transportation facilities on account of race was unconstitutional, and also sought an injunction against enforcement of this statute. The three-judge district court found that the plaintiff had boarded a bus in Memphis, Tennessee, and seated himself in the front; that the driver told him that he must move to the rear, the driver stating that the law required it because of his color; that the plaintiff refused; that two police officers shortly thereafter boarded the bus and ordered the plaintiff to go to the back of the bus or get off, or he would be arrested; and that thereupon the plaintiff left the bus. The record further showed that the defendants, who were officials and officers of the City of Memphis and of the company operating the bus, intended to enforce the Tennessee statute until final adjudication of unconstitutionality. The Supreme Court decided the appeal in a per curiam opinion without hearing argument. What would you expect the decision to be? Is the case distinguishable from the International Longshoremen's case? Should it matter that the plaintiff boarded the bus for the purpose of instituting this litigation? See Evers v. Dwyer, 358 U.S. 202, 79 S.Ct. 178 (1958).

(c) ENFORCEMENT OF JUDGMENT

[Rule 69]

Do not make the mistake of thinking that an unappealed judgment concludes the scenario. The maneuvering may have just begun. An unsatisfied judgment often does the victor little good, and the losing party is not always a good sport about compliance. In short, there are frequently extensive post-judgment proceedings.

---

[e]   Eventually, United States ex rel. Alcantra v. Boyd, 222 F.2d 445 (9th Cir.1955) (habeas corpus case by a person detained for deportation after the 1953 cannery season), held § 212(d)(7) inapplicable to any permanent resident alien who went from the continental United States to work temporarily in Alaska, and so who was not using the territories as stepping stones to "enter" the continental United States from a foreign land.

An equitable judgment is in the form and nature of a court order directed to the defendant. If she disobeys, the judge could imprison the defendant or increasingly fine her until she complies, and thus coerce her into compliance. This enforcement derives from the court's civil contempt powers. Criminal contempt is not, strictly speaking, a means of enforcement, but the possibility of criminal contempt incidentally benefits the plaintiff by encouraging compliance with the judgment.

A legal judgment, by contrast, typically does not express its relief as an order to the defendant to pay or to restore, but rather as a statement that the plaintiff shall recover a sum of money or certain property from the defendant. This signifies more than a matter of form or a historical oddity. A legal judgment is not an order directed to the defendant, and so it is up to the plaintiff to enforce the judgment.

Take as an example a judgment for money damages, and assume that the defendant does not voluntarily pay it. The initial step for the plaintiff is to identify and locate the defendant's assets. This sometimes requires investigation. The plaintiff can utilize the discovery devices of the Federal Rules for this purpose; state law may provide other means of discovery, which the plaintiff can use in connection with the enforcement of a federal judgment. See Rule 69(a)(2).

The plaintiff is then in a position to invoke the force of government in order to obtain the relief to which the court has found the plaintiff entitled. In federal court the procedure for this generally conforms to the local state law. The interplay of federal and state law here is similar to that prevailing under Rule 64 for provisional remedies. See Rule 69(a)(1).

Question: (5) What are the advantages and disadvantages of such incorporation of state procedure by the Rules?

Typically, the plaintiff will obtain from the federal court a writ of execution addressed to the district's federal marshal. Pursuant to this writ and with information from the plaintiff, the marshal (or deputy marshal) will levy on, or seize, so much of the defendant's nonexempt property within the state (state laws provide many and varied exemptions) as is necessary to pay the judgment. See Rule 4.1. If the defendant still does not pay, the marshal will sell that property, use the proceeds to cover the marshal's own fees and expenses and to satisfy the plaintiff's judgment, and then give any remainder to the defendant.

If execution is less than fully successful, there are other remedies available to the plaintiff by permission of the federal court, namely, state-law devices called supplementary proceedings. For example, state statutes commonly provide a means for compelling the judgment debtor to appear for sworn examination before the court as to her assets and her ability to pay the judgment; if the court finds that she has property not exempt from execution, the court may order her to turn over the property so that the marshal may take it on execution. For another example, under the law of some states, the court may order the debtor to make installment payments on the judgment debt, from time to time out of future income; the court will fix the payment schedule after taking into account the reasonable requirements of the debtor and her dependents. Now the defendant is the subject of a court order, and failure to obey an order of the court in supplementary proceedings is punishable as contempt.

As is the case with provisional remedies, some of the more pro-plaintiff enforcement mechanisms may be quite drastic in effect. Consequently, some have of late been attacked in lawsuits, and a few struck down, on the ground of fundamental unfairness. As a matter of constitutional law, then, the state legislatures must carefully draw their remedial procedure to accord with the dictates of procedural due process that we shall explore in Topic B of Part 3.

––––––––

GABOVITCH v. LUNDY, 584 F.2d 559 (1st Cir.1978). A federal-court judgment creditor of appellee Lundy obtained a writ of execution from the clerk for the District of Massachusetts. "The writ was returned on May 5, 1976, certifying a levy on appellee Taunton Co-Operative Bank in the amount of $3000, representing Lundy's deposits in the bank. The bank ignored appellant's numerous demands that it pay over the $3000. On February 24, 1978, appellant petitioned the district court" to enforce the writ. The district court denied relief, holding the writ ineffective because of the creditor's failure to comply with state procedure. The creditor appealed.

The court of appeals affirmed. The appellant had argued that Rule 69(a) makes state law applicable to procedures in aid of execution but not to the mere issuance of process. "Unfortunately for appellant, the legislative history and judicial application of Rule 69(a) make clear that the first sentence of the Rule expresses a limitation on the means of enforcement of money judgments and does not create a general power to issue writs of execution in disregard of the state law incorporated by the rest of the Rule."

Rule 69(a) was meant only (1) to adopt a prior practice of following state law on both the procedure for obtaining process and the effect of such writs and (2) to extend this practice to purely monetary equitable judgments.

"Finally, the courts have consistently read Rule 69(a) as limiting all federal process on money judgments to the type of process available under state law. This court held in First National Bank of Boston v. Antonio Santisteban & Co., Inc., 285 F.2d 855 (1st Cir.1961), that a federal writ of execution did not reach unearned wages of a Puerto Rican judgment debtor because Puerto Rican law gave no effect to such a writ. See Travelers Insurance Co. v. Lawrence, 509 F.2d 83, 86–88 (9th Cir.1974) (Rule 69 makes availability and effect of federal process subject to state law); United States ex rel. Marcus v. Lord Elec. Co., 43 F.Supp.

12 (W.D.Pa.1942) (bank deposits affected by writ of execution because state law so provides). Thus, we have no difficulty concluding that the writ of execution issued by the clerk had no effect. Under Massachusetts law, attachment of bank accounts takes place by trustee process. Mass.Gen.Laws Ann. ch. 246. Attachment on trustee process requires court approval. Mass.Rules Civ.Proc. 4.2(c). Because a writ issued solely on the authority of a court clerk has no effect on a bank account under Massachusetts law, it has no effect under Rule 69(a).[3]"

Question: (6) In a state where a plaintiff's lawyer can issue the documents for execution, as under NY CPLR § 5230(b), must the holder of a federal-court judgment go to the court clerk for a writ of execution?

SECTION 5.   APPEAL

(a) APPEAL TO THE COURT OF APPEALS

Appealability.—According to 28 U.S.C. § 1291, a party, claiming that a "final decision"[a] of a district court is erroneous, has a right to appeal to the appropriate circuit's United States Court of Appeals for correction of the error, that is, for reversal or modification of the decision. What a final decision is within the meaning of § 1291 may become a serious question, but the basic design is to accord an appeal of right when the court below has fully treated the case, save for award of costs and enforcement of judgment.

Question: (1) What are the arguments for and against generally limiting the right of appeal to final decisions?

When the Federal Rules came in to permit the inclusion in a single action of a number of claims to be litigated among a number of parties— a condition that could exist in the prior practice but was now to become more common—the rulemakers thought it desirable to permit a discretionary appeal from the disposition of a clearly divisible part of a complicated case. Under Rule 54(b), the district court must make an

---

[3]   Although the forms of the process would, of course, be federal, the essential elements of state procedure for obtaining the writ must be followed. Mass.Gen.Laws Ann. ch. 246 § 5 and Mass.Rules Civ.Proc. 4.2(a) provide for trustee process to attach the "credits" of a defendant. Receipt of a trustee summons notifies a bank of attachment of a depositor's credits. Mass.Gen.Laws Ann. ch. 246 § 20; Mass.Rules Civ.Proc. 4.2(b). But a trustee summons cannot issue without a prior court approval of the attachment. Mass.Rules Civ.Proc. 4.2(c). Under the same rule, the attachment usually will not be approved without a prior adversary hearing. Once the trustee process issues, the trustee must answer specifying the property subjected to the attachment. Mass.Gen.Laws Ann. ch. 246 § 10. If the court then adjudges the bank to be a trustee, it must pay over to the creditor or be subject to a trustee writ of execution. Mass.Gen.Laws Ann. ch. 246 § 45. Because appellant failed to obtain court approval of his process, it could not be effective to attach the property held by the bank.

[a]   We shift here from the word "judgment" because the appeals statutes usually do not use that term, which is more inclusive than final decision. Note again the wording of Rule 54(a).

express determination that "there is no just reason for delay" before it directs the entry of a final decision as to one or more of several claims or parties, which in effect releases a part of the case for appeal under § 1291.

There is also a right of appeal from certain "interlocutory decisions" of the district court, that is, nonfinal decisions. The most important class is described in 28 U.S.C. § 1292(a)(1) as interlocutory orders that grant, refuse, modify, or otherwise affect injunctions. By interpretation, preliminary injunctions are within § 1292(a)(1)—the statute allowed the appeal in the American Hospital case—but temporary restraining orders generally are not.

Question: (2) Why has Congress singled out these particular interlocutory orders for appeal of right?

Section 1292(b) permits appeal of an interlocutory order other than one covered by § 1292(a) when, first, the district judge states that it "involves a controlling question of law as to which there is substantial ground for difference of opinion" and that immediate appeal "may materially advance the ultimate termination of the litigation" and, second, the court of appeals in its discretion agrees to hear the appeal. Because of these multiple requirements, appeals under § 1292(b) are not at all common.

Dilly v. S.S. Kresge

United States Court of Appeals, Fourth Circuit, 1979.
606 F.2d 62.

■ Before RUSSELL and WIDENER, CIRCUIT JUDGES, and HOFFMAN, DISTRICT JUDGE.*

■ WIDENER, CIRCUIT JUDGE:

The plaintiffs, Bernard and Eleanor Dilly, brought this action against her employer, S.S. Kresge Co., for injuries she received during the course of employment. The uncontested facts are that an assistant manager of Kresge came to the soda fountain area of the store, where Eleanor Dilly worked, and ordered a cup of hot chocolate. After he was told that they had no hot chocolate, the assistant manager grabbed Mrs. Dilly, shook her and said "What the hell do you mean running out of hot chocolate?" Eleanor Dilly stated in her deposition that she thought the assistant manager was serious and angry. The assistant manager contends that he was joking. As a result of the assistant manager's action, Mrs. Dilly claims her neck was injured.

The parties filed cross-motions for summary judgment. The district court granted summary judgment for the plaintiffs on the issue of liability and set a hearing to ascertain the amount of damages, if any,

---

*   U.S. District Court for the Eastern District of Virginia, sitting by designation.

due the plaintiffs. Kresge filed a motion to set aside the district court's order pursuant to FRCP 59. This motion was denied. A notice of appeal was then filed and an appeal was taken to the order granting summary judgment in favor of the plaintiffs.

The defendant takes the position that the appeal from the grant of summary judgment for the plaintiffs and the denial of its Rule 59 motion is an appeal from a final order. We do not agree. The notice of appeal was filed and the appeal was taken prior to the ascertainment of damages; therefore, it was not a final order within the meaning of 28 U.S.C. § 1291. Neither has an interlocutory appeal been perfected as provided for in § 1292(b). Thus, we are without jurisdiction to hear this appeal. . . .

Accordingly, the appeal is dismissed.[1]

_____

Question: (3) Would the Dilly result on appealability change if the district court had entered judgment after granting summary judgment in favor of the defendant? What if there had been two defendants and if it had granted summary judgment in favor of one of the defendants?

Reviewability.—An appellant takes an appeal from and formally attacks the "final decision" or "interlocutory decision," but what the appellant really claims in many appeals is that some action of the district court taken prior to the entry of the final or interlocutory decision, appearing in the record and objected to at the time, was erroneous and that this error has infected the final or interlocutory decision with substantial error. The district court during the course of the litigation may have ruled on a variety of questions—motions attacking a pleading, objections to the admission and exclusion of evidence, motions for judgment as a matter of law, and so on. On appeal the losing party may be urging that one or more of these rulings were wrong and, hence, that

---

[1]   The question concerning the dismissal of the appeal and the jurisdiction of the court was initiated by the court at oral argument. The briefs did not address that subject. The subject briefed, however, and also argued was the question of whether or not summary judgment for the plaintiffs was appropriate.

While what follow are dicta, the case must be reconsidered by the district court, so what we say may not be too far a departure from appropriate judicial restraint. Perhaps another appeal on the same record can be avoided.

West Virginia law exempts employers, who pay into the workmen's compensation fund, from liability for injuries to employees which occur in the course of their employment unless the injury results "from the deliberate intention of [the] employer to produce such injury." West Virginia Code §§ 23–2–6, 23–4–2.

The West Virginia court recently held that these provisions meant that "an employer loses immunity from common law actions where such employer's conduct constitutes an intentional tort or willful, wanton, or reckless misconduct." Mandolidis v. Elkins Industries, Inc., 246 S.E.2d 907, 914 (W.Va.1978).

In view of the fact that the testimony of the assistant manager was that his touching of the plaintiff, Eleanor Dilly, was in a joking manner, and the testimony of her that his touching of her was not in a joking manner, rather serious or angry, we think the district court should carefully reconsider its grant of summary judgment. It recognized this very conflict in its opinion. The key and essential evidence in the case appears to be in direct conflict, and if that be true, as the record before us now indicates, the entry of summary judgment is open to serious question.

the final or interlocutory decision appealed from is wrong. For example, a losing plaintiff may be urging on appeal that the judgment for the defendant is wrong, and that the appellate court must reverse the judgment and order a new trial, because the district court erroneously excluded evidence offered by the plaintiff that, had it been received and considered, might have caused the jury to bring in a different verdict. It is of the utmost importance to our understanding of any case in an appellate court to single out the precise act or acts of the lower court that the appellant complains of as having been erroneous.

This is a convenient point to ask whether it makes sense to have any system of appeals and, if so, what limits should exist on appellate review. It would seem that there is no constitutional right to appeal, see Nat'l Union of Marine Cooks & Stewards v. Arnold, 348 U.S. 37, 43, 75 S.Ct. 92, 95 (1954) ("While a statutory review is important and must be exercised without discrimination, such a review is not a requirement of due process."), except perhaps in criminal cases where the defendant is sentenced to death, see Noel v. Norris, 322 F.3d 500, 503 (8th Cir.2003). In all events, why do we have the particular arrangements set out in the current statutes and doctrines with their emphasis on the distinction between final decisions and interlocutory decisions and their peculiar mix of appeals of right and discretionary appeals?

Appellate procedure.—The Federal Rules of Appellate Procedure outline the procedure for taking appeals. We do not recount this procedure here, but students should familiarize themselves with it in a general way, especially App. Rules 3 and 4 (appeal of right), 5 (appeal by permission), 7 (bond for costs), 10 and 11 (record on appeal), 12 (docketing appeal; required filings), 28 and 30–32 (briefs), 34 (oral argument), and 35 (possibility of en banc hearing). For detail, see Wright & Miller §§ 3945–3994.

In addition to the uniform provisions of the Federal Rules of Appellate Procedure, the courts of appeals may severally adopt their own rules of procedure not inconsistent with them. See 28 U.S.C. § 2071; App. Rule 47.

Despite local variations, the courts of appeals conduct their chief business in much the same way throughout the country, and it is largely the way traditional to our appellate courts. The appellate court hears the appeal on the record and on the briefs of counsel, and sometimes there is also oral argument. The appellate court applies to the alleged reviewable errors the appropriate standard of review, which might be a nondeferential redetermination by the appellate judges or might involve some or much deference to the trial judge's view. By majority vote of the usual three-judge panel, the appellate court affirms, reverses, or modifies the decision appealed from. If it follows from the view of the case adopted by the appellate court that further testimony should be taken, this will not be done by the appellate court, but rather by the lower court on remand. See 28 U.S.C. § 2106.

Stay of proceedings to enforce a judgment.—What happens to an appealable decision before the appellate court can dispose of any appeal? Does it remain effective or rest in abeyance until the court of appeals finishes? The arrangements are rather complex.

Where the judgment is an ordinary one, such as the usual one for money, there is an automatic stay of enforcement for thirty days after entry of judgment under Rule 62(a), unless the district court orders otherwise. The district court may further stay enforcement under Rule 62(b), as a matter of discretion and on appropriate conditions for the security of the adverse party. Normally such a bond is in an amount sufficient to cover the judgment, interest, damages for delay consequent to the stay, and costs on appeal.

Consider now an interlocutory or final judgment in an action for an injunction. There is no provision for an automatic stay. However, the district court in its discretion may order a stay (or modify, restore, or grant an injunction) in the period prior to appeal, see Rule 62(c), or after an appeal is taken, see Rule 62(d), always upon such terms as to bond or otherwise as it considers proper for the security of the adverse party's rights.

Matters regarding stays of enforcement are, in the first instance, within the purview of the district court. But if a party could not there obtain a stay, and if an appeal has been taken, the party can seek relief in the court of appeals. See Rule 62(g); App. Rule 8(a); 28 U.S.C. § 1651(a). In exceptional situations where a hearing by a panel of the court of appeals would be impracticable because of time, the party may apply for a stay to a single judge of that court. See App. Rule 8(a)(2)(D). Again, the appellate "court may condition relief on a party's filing a bond or other security in the district court." App. Rule 8(a)(2)(E).

————

LONG v. ROBINSON, 432 F.2d 977 (4th Cir.1970). In a class action a federal district court declared unconstitutional a Maryland statute and the corresponding local ordinance exempting Baltimore City from the uniform state definition of juvenile age as under 18 years and providing that a person in Baltimore City ceases to be a juvenile at the age of 16. (The age for determining who is a juvenile is important because the criminal justice system treats accused juveniles differently from accused adults.) The order required the authorities to turn over to the juvenile system as expeditiously as possible all persons 16 or 17 years of age currently in jail in Baltimore City awaiting trial. It was on August 6, 1970, that the district court entered this judgment, 316 F.Supp. 22 (D.Md.1970).

The district judge refused a stay. The defendants applied to a single judge of the court of appeals, Circuit Judge Winter, for a stay pending appeal. They asserted that the district judge's legal conclusions were incorrect and that the administrative and economic burdens in complying with the order would be very heavy. They estimated that the order would double the yearly caseload of juvenile cases in the city and would require expansion of detention facilities, training schools, courts and court personnel, social workers, and other personnel. They said that until these facilities and personnel became available, the treatment program for juveniles under 16 would suffer adverse effects. Finally, they argued that the unavailability of sufficient funds to meet the costs of the additional juvenile cases might necessitate a special session of the General Assembly of Maryland to make the needed appropriations.

Judge Winter stated the legal principles governing such an application: "a party seeking a stay must show (1) that he will likely prevail on the merits of the appeal, (2) that he will suffer irreparable injury if the stay is denied, (3) that other parties will not be substantially harmed by the stay, and (4) that the public interest will be served by granting the stay." He found: (1) that the defendants' probability of success on appeal was not substantial; (2) that the principal irreparable injury that the defendants claimed they would suffer was of their own making (the state legislature had abolished the lower age for juveniles in Baltimore City in 1966, to be effective in 1969, but nothing had been done to effectuate the change; the legislature had twice postponed the effective date for a year, but still no steps beyond some preliminary planning had been taken; and it "would seem elementary that a party may not claim equity in his own defaults"); (3) that a stay's deleterious consequences to the 16- and 17-year-old members of the plaintiff class by reason of their incarceration with older persons were clear; and (4) that the public interest lay in the immediate implementation of the order.

Judge Winter denied the stay on August 11, 1970, but ordered an expedited hearing of the appeal. The court of appeals heard argument on September 17, 1970. It affirmed the district court's decision on the merits on January 18, 1971, 436 F.2d 1116 (4th Cir.1971).

If the court of appeals denies a stay of enforcement of the district court's judgment, a party may seek immediate relief in the Supreme Court. See 28 U.S.C. § 1651(a). The party makes application to the single Justice assigned to oversee the particular circuit from which the case comes. If the Justice grants the stay, he or she may condition it upon the giving of adequate security. If the Justice denies the stay, the applicant may (with scant hope of success) renew the request to any other Justice, and so on. Any Justice may refer a request for a stay to the entire Court for action, which the Justice would tend to do in an important or difficult case.

If the party obtains a stay somewhere along this line, the adverse party may seek to modify or vacate the stay, on good grounds shown, by pursuing relief up the line in similar manner.

If no stay issues, the party who prevailed in the district court may proceed to enforce his money judgment or take the benefit of an injunction in his favor.

Question: (4) After an unstayed party enforces the judgment, what happens if the court of appeals ultimately reverses on the merits?

(b) REVIEW BY THE SUPREME COURT

After appeal, the litigant disappointed by an adverse decision of the court of appeals has still another chance. See 28 U.S.C. § 1254, which provides for review by the Supreme Court of cases in the courts of appeals by certiorari or by certified questions. Review via certification of questions by a court of appeals is extremely unusual, on the order of once per decade. The usual avenue to the Supreme Court is the petition for certiorari.

Review on certiorari is not a matter of right, but of discretion, and "will be granted only for compelling reasons." S.Ct. Rule 10, further quoted supra p. 20. A showing of a conflict in decisions of the courts of appeals on a point involved in the case is likely to weigh strongly with the Court as a factor favoring review, but the fact that it is strongly arguable that the decision below was wrong is not in itself a compelling reason for review. So a denial of certiorari, theoretically, says nothing as to the merits of the case.

Question: (5) Is certiorari available to review a decision of the court of appeals that is nonfinal? Is it actually necessary to await a decision by the court of appeals before applying for certiorari? At what point, precisely, can certiorari be sought, and by whom?

The Rules of the Supreme Court of the United States prescribe the procedure for review by the Court. Return your focus to certiorari. The petition for a writ of certiorari must contain the questions presented for review, a concise statement of the case, and an argument regarding the reasons for allowance of the writ. The Court denies or grants certiorari upon consideration of the petition and any brief in opposition and reply brief, there being no oral argument at this stage. If the Court grants the petition, a step that requires the vote of only four of the nine Justices, the Court has thereby agreed to consider the merits. The case is normally then briefed on the merits and heard on oral argument. Ultimately, the Supreme Court—by majority vote, with six Justices constituting a quorum—affirms, reverses, or modifies the decision being reviewed, possibly remanding to a court below for further proceedings.

A stay with respect to the adverse decision of the court of appeals is available from that court or a judge thereof, or from a Justice or the Supreme Court, under circumstances and in a manner analogous to the stay procedure described above for a district court's judgment.

Final decision in the Supreme Court brings the federal court case to the end of the line, and to the end of this survey of the conduct of a lawsuit. As Justice Jackson observed in Brown v. Allen, 344 U.S. 443, 540, 73 S.Ct. 397, 427 (1953) (concurring opinion), "We are not final because we are infallible, but we are infallible only because we are final."

SECTION 6.   SELECTION OF A PROPER FORUM: LIMITATIONS ON JURISDICTION OVER SUBJECT MATTER

Having described the conduct of lawsuits in the district courts and their review in the courts of appeals and the Supreme Court, we shall now return to a question put at the beginning of the survey: in which courts may the plaintiff institute a particular action? Our concern shifts first to jurisdiction, and to its component called more specifically jurisdiction over the subject matter. We start with a consideration of the division of business between the state court systems, on the one hand, and the federal court system, on the other hand. The grand themes of federalism and separation of powers reenter the stage.

(a) THE JUDICIAL POWER OF THE STATES

The Tenth Amendment to the Constitution of the United States, which is largely declaratory of the relationships created by the Constitution proper, declares: "The powers not delegated to the United States by the Constitution, nor prohibited by it to the States, are reserved to the States respectively, or to the people." The Constitution nowhere expressly denies any judicial power to the states.

First, as we shall see, Article III declares that the federal judicial power shall extend to various enumerated "cases" and "controversies," but these constitute only a small fraction of all disputes that require adjudication. The rest of those disputes constitutionally can proceed in the state courts exclusively.

Second, the states may handle even the Article III cases and controversies, except as Congress decides that the states shall not. In other words, although Article III gives a limited judicial power to the federal government, the Constitution does not provide that the states may not exercise that power also. The states are free to exercise it, unless Congress steps in and says no, and Congress seldom does so. Much of the jurisdiction of the federal courts is thus *concurrent* with that of the state courts. That is, a plaintiff instituting a particular action often has a choice between a federal court and a state court.

Third, there are indeed a few acts of Congress that declare the federal courts must exclusively handle certain classes of Article III cases and controversies. Examples of this *exclusive* federal jurisdiction are bankruptcy proceedings and actions under the federal antitrust laws.

The net result is that the states are free to handle a very large amount of business. A state may choose not to exert its full judicial power: subject to some vague but slight constitutional limitations not of immediate concern, a state may by provisions in its constitution or statutes restrict the kinds of disputes that its courts will handle. Nevertheless, state courts handle a very large percentage of this nation's judicial business, indeed well over 99% of civil cases in state and federal courts.

Of course, a state may set up a hierarchy of courts as it wishes and allocate business among its courts as it sees fit. There is no uniformity of pattern among the states in these respects.

(b) THE JUDICIAL POWER OF THE UNITED STATES

Article III of the Constitution fixes the outer bound on the judicial power of the United States. After reading the entire Article, consider Section 2, Paragraph 1;[a] Section 1, first sentence; and Section 2, Paragraph 2. Try to get a sense of what is meant by the statement that the federal courts are courts of *limited* jurisdiction, as opposed to *general* jurisdiction.

Questions: (1) Is it constitutionally required that federal courts have jurisdiction over all or any of the enumerated cases and controversies?

(2) Is it constitutionally required that there be a Supreme Court? that there be inferior federal courts such as the district courts and the courts of appeals?

The federal government may choose not to exert its full judicial power: again apart from other fairly slight but vague constitutional limitations not of immediate concern (although potentially of great political import), Congress appears to have a free hand in allocating to the inferior federal courts that it establishes,[b] and consequently in

---

[a]   You should read this provision in conjunction with the Eleventh Amendment. The Supreme Court in Chisholm v. Georgia, 2 U.S. (2 Dall.) 419 (1793), allowed an action in a federal court by a citizen of South Carolina against the State of Georgia. Dissatisfaction with that decision led to the adoption of the Eleventh Amendment, providing that the federal judicial power should not be construed to extend to any action brought against one of the states by citizens of another state or by citizens or subjects of any foreign state.

On the theory that the Amendment intended simply to overturn the Chisholm holding and return thereby to the original understanding of Article III, and that the original understanding was that no one other than a sister state or the United States could sue a nonconsenting state in federal court, the Supreme Court has far departed from the wording of the Amendment to shape a broad, but complicated and contested, principle of state sovereign immunity.

[b]   The most important "inferior Courts" established by Congress are the district courts and the courts of appeals. Congress has also established certain other Article III courts of specialized jurisdiction—currently including most significantly the United States Court of International Trade, which handles certain civil actions relating to import transactions. In fact, the United States has long shown a strong preference for Article III courts of nonspecialized and broad jurisdiction, with judges who necessarily have life tenure and salary protection and who tend to be diverse generalists and independent actors. An incidental benefit of thus putting most cases into one set of courts is the minimization of boundary problems regarding which courts hear which cases or parts of cases.

withholding from them, *original* jurisdiction over the enumerated cases and controversies within the federal judicial power. Thus, when the problem is whether such a federal court is authorized to hear a particular case or controversy, resort must be had (1) to federal statutes to determine whether Congress has allocated jurisdiction and (2) to Article III to determine whether it authorizes the particular statute bestowing jurisdiction.

Questions: (3) To what extent can you classify the cases and controversies enumerated in Article III, Section 2, Paragraph 1 as dependent on the nature of the claim asserted? as dependent on the types of parties involved?

(4) Examine, as examples of how Congress has vested original jurisdiction in the district courts, 28 U.S.C. §§ 1331 (federal question), 1332 (diversity of citizenship), 1337 (commerce), 1338 (patents and the like), and 1343 (civil rights) and 15 U.S.C. §§ 15(a) and 15a (antitrust). With respect to each of these statutory provisions: (a) Can you relate it to one of the classes of cases and controversies enumerated in Article III, Section 2, Paragraph 1? (b) Does it comprehend the entire class or only a portion of the class? (c) Is the jurisdiction conferred exclusive or concurrent? (d) Is the jurisdiction dependent upon the amount in controversy?

(5) What is the relation between § 1331 and § 1337? between § 1331 and § 1338? between § 1331 and § 1343?

Similarly, the Constitution appears to confide the *appellate* jurisdiction of the federal courts largely to congressional control. So, when considering an issue of federal jurisdiction, one should refer first to congressional enactment and then to Article III. Generally, for such jurisdiction to exist, the particular action must fall within the bounds of both.

(c) "FEDERAL QUESTION" PROVISION

Congress could constitutionally have given the district courts jurisdiction over all civil actions arising under the Constitution, laws, or treaties of the United States and made such jurisdiction exclusive. It has not done so. The basic federal question statute is 28 U.S.C. § 1331.

———

Distinguishably, Congress has established certain Article I bodies that are called legislative courts and are not part of the judicial branch itself—such as the United States Court of Federal Claims, the United States Tax Court, and each district's bankruptcy court.

Louisville & Nashville Railroad Co. v. Mottley

Supreme Court of the United States, 1908.
211 U.S. 149, 29 S.Ct. 42.

The appellees (husband and wife), being residents and citizens of Kentucky, brought this suit in equity in the Circuit Court of the United States for the Western District of Kentucky[c] against the appellant, a railroad company and a citizen of the same State. The object of the suit was to compel the specific performance of the following contract:

"Louisville, Ky., Oct. 2nd, 1871.

"The Louisville & Nashville Railroad Company in consideration that E.L. Mottley and wife, Annie E. Mottley, have this day released Company from all damages or claims for damages for injuries received by them on the 7th of September, 1871, in consequence of a collision of trains on the railroad of said Company at Randolph's Station, Jefferson County, Ky., hereby agrees to issue free passes on said Railroad and branches now existing or to exist, to said E.L. & Annie E. Mottley for the remainder of the present year, and thereafter, to renew said passes annually during the lives of said Mottley and wife or either of them."

The bill alleged that in September, 1871, plaintiffs, while passengers upon the defendant railroad, were injured by the defendant's negligence, and released their respective claims for damages in consideration of the agreement for transportation during their lives, expressed in the contract. It is alleged that the contract was performed by the defendant up to January 1, 1907, when the defendant declined to renew the passes. The bill then alleges that the refusal to comply with the contract was based solely upon that part of the act of Congress of June 29, 1906, 34 Stat. 584, which forbids the giving of free passes or free transportation.[d] The bill further alleges: First, that the act of Congress referred to does not prohibit the giving of passes under the circumstances of this case; and, second, that if the law is to be construed as prohibiting such passes, it is in conflict with the Fifth Amendment of the Constitution, because it deprives the plaintiffs of their property without due process of law. The defendant demurred to the bill. The judge of the Circuit Court overruled the demurrer, entered a decree [in 1907] for the relief prayed for, and the defendant appealed directly to this court.

■ MR. JUSTICE MOODY, after making the foregoing statement, delivered the opinion of the court.

---

[c]   Congress has since abolished these circuit courts, which exercised much original jurisdiction. Do not confuse them with the present United States Courts of Appeals, formerly called United States Circuit Courts of Appeals.

[d]   This Hepburn Act, very unpopular with the railroads, gave the Interstate Commerce Commission power to limit their rates. It also prohibited giving free passes and fare rebates, often used formerly to curry favor with politicians and journalists and to give an edge to favored shippers.

Two questions of law were raised by the demurrer to the bill, were brought here by appeal, and have been argued before us. They are, first, whether that part of the act of Congress . . . , which forbids the giving of free passes or the collection of any different compensation for transportation of passengers than that specified in the tariff filed, makes it unlawful to perform a contract for transportation of persons who, in good faith, before the passage of the act, had accepted such contract in satisfaction of a valid cause of action against the railroad; and, second, whether the statute, if it should be construed to render such a contract unlawful, is in violation of the Fifth Amendment of the Constitution of the United States. We do not deem it necessary, however, to consider either of these questions, because, in our opinion, the court below was without jurisdiction of the cause. Neither party has questioned that jurisdiction, but it is the duty of this court to see to it that the jurisdiction of the Circuit Court, which is defined and limited by statute, is not exceeded. This duty we have frequently performed of our own motion. [Citations omitted.]

There was no diversity of citizenship and it is not and cannot be suggested that there was any ground of jurisdiction, except that the case was a "suit . . . arising under the Constitution and laws of the United States." [Citation to predecessor of § 1331.] It is the settled interpretation of these words, as used in this statute, conferring jurisdiction, that a suit arises under the Constitution and laws of the United States only when the plaintiff's statement of his own cause of action shows that it is based upon those laws or that Constitution. It is not enough that the plaintiff alleges some anticipated defense to his cause of action and asserts that the defense is invalidated by some provision of the Constitution of the United States. Although such allegations show that very likely, in the course of the litigation, a question under the Constitution would arise, they do not show that the suit, that is, the plaintiff's original cause of action, arises under the Constitution. In Tennessee v. Union & Planters' Bank, 152 U.S. 454, 14 S.Ct. 654, the plaintiff, the State of Tennessee, brought suit in the Circuit Court of the United States to recover from the defendant certain taxes alleged to be due under the laws of the State. The plaintiff alleged that the defendant claimed an immunity from the taxation by virtue of its charter, and that therefore the tax was void, because in violation of the provision of the Constitution of the United States, which forbids any State from passing a law impairing the obligation of contracts. The cause was held to be beyond the jurisdiction of the Circuit Court, the court saying, by Mr. Justice Gray (p. 464), "a suggestion of one party, that the other will or may set up a claim under the Constitution or laws of the United States, does not make the suit one arising under that Constitution or those laws." Again, in Boston & Montana Consolidated Copper & Silver Mining Company v. Montana Ore Purchasing Company, 188 U.S. 632, 23 S.Ct. 434, the plaintiff brought suit in the Circuit Court of the United States for the conversion of copper ore and for an injunction against its continuance. The plaintiff then alleged, for the purpose of showing jurisdiction, in substance, that the defendant would set up in defense certain laws of the United States. The cause was held to be beyond the jurisdiction of the Circuit Court, the court saying, by Mr. Justice Peckham (pp. 638, 639):

"It would be wholly unnecessary and improper in order to prove complainant's cause of action to go into any matters of defence which the defendants might possibly set up and then attempt to reply to such defence, and thus, if possible, to show that a Federal question might or probably would arise in the course of the trial of the case. To allege such defence and then make an answer to it before the defendant has the opportunity to itself plead or prove its own defence is inconsistent with any known rule of pleading so far as we are aware, and is improper.

"The rule is a reasonable and just one that the complainant in the first instance shall be confined to a statement of its cause of action, leaving to the defendant to set up in his answer what his defence is and, if anything more than a denial of complainant's cause of action, imposing upon the defendant the burden of proving such defence.

"Conforming itself to that rule the complainant would not, in the assertion or proof of its cause of action, bring up a single Federal question. The presentation of its cause of action would not show that it was one arising under the Constitution or laws of the United States.

" . . . Under these circumstances the case is brought within the rule laid down in Tennessee v. Union & Planters' Bank, 152 U.S. 454, 14 S.Ct. 654. That case has been cited and approved many times since."

[The Court here cited sixteen more of its cases applying the rule.] The application of this rule to the case at bar is decisive against the jurisdiction of the Circuit Court.

It is ordered that the

Judgment be reversed and the case remitted to the Circuit Court with instructions to dismiss the suit for want of jurisdiction.

———

Question: (6) Suppose the action were instead one for a declaratory judgment under a statute analogous to present 28 U.S.C. § 2201, with the railroad as plaintiff seeking a declaration of its obligation in light of the statute prohibiting free passes and with the Mottleys threatening suit. Would federal question jurisdiction then exist?

(d) "DIVERSITY OF CITIZENSHIP" PROVISION

Congress could constitutionally have given the district courts jurisdiction over all civil actions comprehended in Article III's Diversity and Alienage Clauses. It has not done so. The basic diversity statute is 28 U.S.C. § 1332(a)–(c).

Question: (7) Does the required diversity under § 1332(a) exist in each of the following cases? Imagine each case is for an alleged vehicular tort occurring in Kansas City, Mo. The matter in controversy exceeds $75,000 in each case.

(a) *A*, a citizen of New York, sues *B*, a citizen of Missouri.

(b) *A*, a citizen of New York, sues *B*, a citizen and resident of England.

(c) *A*, a citizen and resident of Canada, sues *B*, a citizen and resident of England. See Hodgson v. Bowerbank, 9 U.S. (5 Cranch) 303 (1809) (Marshall, C.J.) (holding that a federal suit, brought under a statute that gave jurisdiction when "an alien is a party," fell outside Article III bound).

(d) *A*, a citizen of Canada and legal permanent resident of the United States domiciled in New York, sues *B*, a citizen and resident of England.

The general rule with respect to federal jurisdiction is to determine it as of the time it was invoked. Although jurisdiction can be saved by certain corrective steps (which comprise the party's amendment of defective jurisdictional allegations under 28 U.S.C. § 1653 or perhaps, in compelling circumstances, the court's dropping of jurisdiction-impeding parties under Federal Rule 21), jurisdiction is ordinarily not ousted by subsequent events. For a named party, it is normally citizenship at the time of the federal action's commencement that controls, and so any change thereafter is immaterial. So, suppose that *A*, a citizen of New York, sues *B*, a citizen of Missouri, in a United States District Court. While the suit is pending, *A* becomes a citizen of Missouri. That change does not destroy diversity.

In the ordinary case there is little difficulty in determining the citizenship of a litigant. At times, however, the parties seriously dispute the facts regarding citizenship, and the court must determine it.

———

Baker v. Keck

United States District Court, Eastern District of Illinois, 1936.
13 F.Supp. 486.

■ LINDLEY, DISTRICT JUDGE. Plaintiff has filed herein his suit against various individuals and the Progressive Miners of America charging a conspiracy, out of which grew certain events and in the course of which, it is averred, he was attacked by certain of the defendants and his arm shot off. This, it is said, resulted from a controversy between the United Mine Workers and the Progressive Miners of America.

Plaintiff avers that he is a citizen of the state of Oklahoma. Defendants filed a motion to dismiss, one ground of which is that plaintiff is not a citizen of the state of Oklahoma, but has a domicile in the state of Illinois, and that therefore there is no diversity of citizenship. To this motion plaintiff filed a response, with certain affidavits in support thereof.

Upon presentation of the motion, the court set the issue of fact arising upon the averments of the complaint, the motion to dismiss, and the response thereto for hearing. A jury was waived. Affidavits were received and parol evidence offered.

It appears that plaintiff formerly resided in Saline county, Ill., that he was not a member of United Mine Workers, but was in sympathy with their organization. The averment of the declaration is that he was attacked by members of, or sympathizers with, the Progressive [Miners of America, a union formed in 1932 as a rival to the UMW just for Illinois miners and today defunct]. He was a farmer, owning about 100 acres of land. After his injury, he removed to the state of Oklahoma, taking with him his family and all of his household goods, except two beds and some other small items. His household furniture was carried to Oklahoma by truck, and the truckman was paid $100 for transportation. Near Ulan, Okl., he rented 20 acres and a house for $150 per year, and began occupancy thereof October, 1934. He testified that he had arrangements with another party and his own son, living with him, to cultivate the ground, but that [the Dust Bowl] farming conditions were not satisfactory, and that it was impossible, therefore, to produce a crop in 1935. He produced potatoes, sweet corn, and other garden products used in the living of the family. He had no horses or other livestock in Oklahoma. He was unable to do any extensive work himself because of the loss of his arm. In the summer of 1935 he leased for the year 1936 the same 20 acres and an additional 20 acres at a rental of $150.

At the first opportunity to register as a qualified voter in Oklahoma after he went there, he complied with the statute in that respect and was duly registered. This was not until after he had been in the state for over a year, as, under the state statute [then in effect], a qualified voter must have resided within the state for twelve months prior to registration. He has not voted, but he testified that the only election at which he could have voted after he registered was on a day when he had to be in Illinois to give attention to his lawsuit. He has returned to Illinois for short visits three or four times.

He testified that he moved to Oklahoma for the purpose of residing there, with the intention of making it his home and that he still intends to reside there. He testified that the family started out to see if they could find a new location in 1934. Upon cross-examination it appeared that the funds for traveling and removal had been paid by the United Mine Workers or their representative; that he left his livestock on the Illinois farm, but no chickens; that he had about 60 chickens on his farm in Oklahoma; that, when he removed to Oklahoma, he rented his Illinois farm for a period of five years; that the tenant has recently defaulted upon the same.

In the affidavits it appears that plaintiff's house in Illinois was completely destroyed by fire shortly after he left. It was not insured and was a total loss. Witnesses for the defense testified that he had told them that he intended to move back to Illinois after he got his case settled; that he had told one witness in 1935 that he was going to Oklahoma but did not know for how long. Plaintiff denies that he told these witnesses that he expected to return to Illinois as soon as his litigation was completed.

I think it is a fair conclusion from all the evidence that at the time plaintiff removed to Oklahoma one of his motives was to create diversity of citizenship so that he might maintain a suit in the United States courts. But that conclusion is not of itself decisive of the question presented. There remains the further question of whether there was at the time this suit was begun an intention upon his part to become a citizen of Oklahoma. One may change his citizenship for the purpose of enabling himself to maintain a suit in the federal court, but the change must be an actual legal change made with the intention of bringing about actual citizenship in the state to which the removal is made.

Citizenship and domicile are substantially synonymous. Residency and inhabitance are too often confused with the terms and have not the same significance. Citizenship implies more than residence.[e] It carries with it the idea of identification with the state and a participation in its functions. As a citizen, one sustains social, political, and moral obligation to the state and possesses social and political rights under the Constitution and laws thereof. . . . Change of domicile arises when there is a change of abode with the absence of any present intention not to reside permanently or indefinitely in the new abode. This is the holding of the Supreme Court in Gilbert v. David, 235 U.S. 561, 35 S.Ct. 164, 167, 59 L.Ed. 360, where the court said: "As Judge Story puts it in his work on 'Conflict of Laws' (7th Ed.) § 46, page 41, 'If a person has actually removed to another place, with an intention of remaining there for an indefinite time, and as a place of fixed present domicil, it is to be deemed his place of domicil, notwithstanding he may entertain a floating intention to return at some future period.' 'The requisite animus is the present intention of permanent or indefinite residence in a given place or country, or, negatively expressed, the absence of any present intention of not residing there permanently or indefinitely.'"

It will be observed that, if there is an intention to remain, even though it be for an indefinite time, but still with the intention of making the location a place of present domicile, this latter intention will control, even though the person entertains a floating intention to return at some indefinite future period. In this respect the court in Gilbert v. David, supra, further said: "Plaintiff may have had, and probably did have, some floating intention of returning to Michigan after the determination of certain litigation. . . . But, as we have seen, a floating intention of that kind was not enough to prevent the new place, under the circumstances shown, from becoming his domicil. It was his place of abode, which he had no present intention of changing; that is the essence of domicil."

. . . .

---

[e]   The Fourteenth Amendment defines citizenship in terms of residence. However, that definition is not controlling for diversity-jurisdiction purposes.

The statement of the Restatement of the Law, Conflict of Laws, § 15, Domicil of Choice, is as follows:

"(1) A domicil of choice is a domicil acquired, through the exercise of his own will, by a person who is legally capable of changing his domicil.

"(2) To acquire a domicil of choice, a person must establish a dwelling-place with the intention of making it his home.

"(3) The fact of physical presence at a dwelling-place and the intention to make it a home must concur; if they do so, even for a moment, the change of domicil takes place."f

In Holt v. Hendee, 248 Ill. 288, 93 N.E. 749, 752, 21 Ann.Cas. 202, the court said: "The intention is not necessarily determined from the statements or declarations of the party but may be inferred from the surrounding circumstances, which may entirely disprove such statements or declarations. On the question of domicile less weight will be given to the party's declaration than to his acts."

Though it must be confessed that the question is far from free of doubt, I conclude that, under the facts as they appear in the record, despite the fact that one of the plaintiff's motives was the establishment of citizenship so as to create jurisdiction in the federal court, there was at the time of his removal a fixed intention to become a citizen of the state of Oklahoma. He testified that he worked on a community project in that state without compensation. It appears that he registered as a voter; he thus became a participant in the political activities of the state. Such action is inconsistent with any conclusion other than that of citizenship, and in view of his sworn testimony that it was his intention to reside in Oklahoma and to continue to do so, it follows that the elements constituting the status of citizenship existed.

True, there is some evidence that he had said he might return to Illinois as soon as his case was settled. The language of the cases above indicates that such a floating intention is insufficient to bar citizenship, where active participation in the obligations and enjoyment of the rights of citizenship exist.

Defendants contend that the fact that the costs of plaintiff's transportation and maintenance were paid by the United Mine Workers is of decisive weight upon this issue. I cannot agree. It seems to me immaterial what motives may have inspired the United Mine Workers to help him, and the court is not now concerned with their alleged charitable and philanthropic practices.

---

f   Among the changes in § 15 made by Restatement (Second) of Conflict of Laws § 15 (Am. Law Inst. 1971) is the omission of the phrase "through the exercise of his own will," this being omitted to avoid any implication that the significant intention is one to acquire a domicile rather than one to make a home. Section 16, "Requisite of Physical Presence," now provides: "To acquire a domicil of choice in a place, a person must be physically present there; but a home in a particular building is not necessary for the acquisition of a domicil." Section 18, "Requisite Intention," now provides: "To acquire a domicil of choice in a place, a person must intend to make that place his home for the time at least."

I conclude, therefore, that plaintiff was at the time of the commencement of the suit, and is now, a citizen of the state of Oklahoma. The findings herein embraced will be adopted as findings of fact of the court and entered as such. It is ordered that the motion to dismiss because of lack of diversity of citizenship be, and the same is hereby, denied. An exception is allowed to defendants.

. . . .

Question: (8) Does the required diversity under § 1332(a) exist in each of the following cases? The matter in controversy exceeds the jurisdictional amount in each case.

(a) The soprano Felice Lyne, born in Missouri, abandoned her home there and took up residence in London, England, declaring it to be her home and that it was her intention to remain there indefinitely. She has taken no steps toward naturalization in England. Oscar Hammerstein, a citizen of New York, sues her in a Missouri federal court while she is on a temporary visit to her former home in Missouri. In the course of reaching decision, the court finds that she is domiciled in England. See Hammerstein v. Lyne, 200 F. 165 (W.D.Mo.1912) (not within jurisdictional statute, although possibly within Article III bound).

(b) *A*, a citizen of New York, sues *B*, a Cuban refugee domiciled in Florida with the status of stateless and undocumented alien.

(c) *A*, a citizen of New York, sues *B*, a Cuban citizen domiciled in Florida with the status of undocumented alien.

Domicile of students.—An unemancipated minor normally has the same domicile as the parent on whom he or she is dependent, but the student who is emancipated or who is not a minor may acquire a domicile of choice. See ConnectU LLC v. Zuckerberg, 482 F.Supp.2d 3 (D.Mass.2007) (finding, on Zuckerberg's motion to dismiss the Winklevoss twins' suit, that the dropout, adult, California-based, multimillionaire founder of Facebook was still domiciled with his parents in New York in 2004, which would have destroyed diversity jurisdiction), rev'd on other grounds, 522 F.3d 82 (1st Cir.2008); Ceglia v. Zuckerberg, 772 F.Supp.2d 453 (W.D.N.Y.2011) (upholding removal jurisdiction based on diversity because by 2010 Zuckerberg had changed domicile from New York to California); cf. Restatement (Second) of Conflict of Laws § 22 (Am. Law Inst. 1971).

Question: (9) Should students be free to select either their parent's home or their college residence as their domicile? If not, what should be the standards for determining domicile? Should it matter whether a student lives in a dormitory or rented apartment or buys a house? whether the student returns to his or her parent's home during vacations? Should the student's present intention regarding post-educational residence matter: what if he or she intends to return to the parent's home, intends to remain in the college community, intends to move elsewhere, or does not know? Cf.

Restatement (Second) of Conflict of Laws § 18 cmt. f, illus. 13–14 (Am. Law Inst. 1971).

Although the issue of interest here is jurisdiction, the determination of a student's domicile may carry with it other consequences. For instance, domicile may affect voting rights, state income tax liability, and automobile registration and insurance premiums. For these different purposes, a student may have different domiciles under different definitions. Restatement (Second) of Conflict of Laws § 11(2) (Am. Law Inst. 1971) (amended 1988) recognized this possibility by providing: "Every person has a domicil at all times and, at least for the same purpose, no person has more than one domicil at a time." The conventional learning, reflected in Restatement of Conflict of Laws § 11 (Am. Law Inst. 1934), had been simply that every person has one and only one domicile at a time.

Domicile of wives.—At common law, a wife was not able to acquire a domicile of choice, but instead received the domicile of her husband by operation of law. This rule is close to expiration. Today a wife, particularly when she lives apart from her husband, may acquire a separate domicile of choice. Cf. Restatement (Second) of Conflict of Laws § 21 (Am. Law Inst. 1971) (amended 1988).

"Citizenship" of corporations.—What about diversity of citizenship with respect to corporations? The Constitution does not mention corporations, and for various constitutional purposes a corporation is not a citizen. For instance, a corporation cannot claim the benefits of Article IV, Section 2 of the Constitution, which provides: "The Citizens of each State shall be entitled to all Privileges and Immunities of Citizens in the several States." So, does this imply that corporations are excluded from diversity jurisdiction?

The Supreme Court of the United States avoided this result by deciding early that the citizenship of the stockholders effectively determined the citizenship of a corporation, and the Court later blandly laid down the conclusive presumption that for diversity purposes all the stockholders were citizens of the state of incorporation. See Marshall v. Balt. & Ohio R.R. Co., 57 U.S. (16 How.) 314 (1853). Thus courts would treat the General Motors Corporation as though it and all its stockholders were citizens of Delaware, the state of incorporation. Here is one of the many instances where the law achieved results thought desirable through the use of transparent fictions.

However, by statute enacted in 1958 and amended in 2011, a corporation for diversity purposes is now deemed a citizen of each and every American state and foreign country by which it has been incorporated (a corporation may be incorporated by more than one place), and also of any American state or foreign country in which it has its principal place of business (there can be only one). Given the intention of § 1332(c)(1), the more places of which a corporation is a citizen, the less likely diversity jurisdiction is to exist.

Hence, no diversity jurisdiction exists for a French corporation with its principal place of business in New York versus a New Yorker. This is citizen versus co-citizen. Also, there is no jurisdiction for a French corporation with its principal place of business in New York versus a German person, and there is no jurisdiction for a New York corporation with its principal place of business in Paris versus a German person. These are treated as alien versus alien.

What about jurisdiction for a New York corporation with its principal place of business in Paris versus a German corporation with its principal place of business in New Jersey? The multiple citizenships of the corporations mean that the court should look to either of the citizenships that defeats diversity jurisdiction. So this suit between foreign corporations fails. (The presence of American citizenships on both sides of this hypothetical is not sufficient to get within § 1332(a)(3)'s jurisdiction over actions between "citizens of different States and in which citizens or subjects of a foreign state are additional parties." Each side does not involve "additional parties" but rather a single entity with multiple citizenships. Whenever the jurisdictional law has bestowed extra citizenships in order to curtail diversity jurisdiction, the courts follow this approach of using any of the citizenships to create co-citizenship or to treat the suit as one between aliens.)

Next, the meaning of the statutory phrase "principal place of business" is obviously unclear. Should the principal place of business be where the company's headquarters are? Or should it be the place where the corporation's activities are heaviest? Or do we need a more complicated formula to account for the infinite variety of corporate structure and business—all in the attempt to attain the statute's primary purpose of attributing citizenship in the state where the corporation looks least like an outsider and so is least likely to suffer prejudice in the local courts against out-of-staters? Thus, statutory construction generated a longstanding and severe split among the circuits.

A unanimous Supreme Court settled the question in Hertz Corp. v. Friend, 559 U.S. 77, 130 S.Ct. 1181 (2010). "In doing so, we place primary weight upon the need for judicial administration of a jurisdictional statute to remain as simple as possible. And we conclude that the phrase 'principal place of business' refers to the place where the corporation's high level officers direct, control, and coordinate the corporation's activities. Lower federal courts have often metaphorically called that place the corporation's 'nerve center.' "

The Court provided a hypothetical: "For example, if the bulk of a company's business activities visible to the public take place in New Jersey, while its top officers direct those activities just across the river in New York, the 'principal place of business' is New York. One could argue that members of the public in New Jersey would be less likely to be prejudiced against the corporation than persons in New York—yet the corporation will still be" deemed a citizen of New York. "Accepting occasionally counterintuitive results is the price the legal system must pay to avoid overly complex jurisdictional administration while producing the benefits that accompany a more uniform legal system."

Anticipating occasional hard cases, the Court specified that the nerve center would be the actual center of overall direction, control, and coordination, not some formally declared headquarters where, say, only the board of directors meets. "Our approach provides a sensible test that is relatively easier to apply, not a test that will, in all instances, automatically generate a result."

Finally, the narrow direct-action exception at the end of § 1332(c)(1), added in 1964, aimed at preventing the exercise of diversity jurisdiction where it would exist only because under local law the injured plaintiff could sue the liability insurer directly without joining the insured.

"Citizenship" of unincorporated associations.— Unincorporated associations include partnerships, LLCs, fraternal benefit societies, trade associations, and labor unions. For the usual diversity purposes, neither the judicial fiction extended to corporations nor their legislative treatment covers unincorporated associations. Hence, courts treat an unincorporated association like a group of individuals, and so deem it a citizen of each and every state and country of which one of its members is actually a citizen. The Supreme Court reconsidered this rule in United Steelworkers v. R.H. Bouligny, Inc., 382 U.S. 145, 86 S.Ct. 272 (1965), but it there decided that change was a task for Congress and not for the courts. The rule remains the same today. See Americold Realty Trust v. Conagra Foods, Inc., 136 S.Ct. 1012 (2016) (extending its reach to real estate investment trusts).

Question: (10) Consider the case of a dual citizen, a man who is a citizen of both the United States and Ireland, and who is a party in a lawsuit against either a citizen of an American state or a citizen or subject of a foreign country. His treatment for diversity purposes is not clear. Unlike the preceding cases of multiple citizenship, here the law did not create the extra citizenship to curtail diversity jurisdiction, and so a different approach is arguable. The leading approach concludes that only any American state citizenship is attributed to him: thus, if domiciled in New York, he could bring a big case in federal court against a citizen of Ireland for an alleged vehicular tort occurring in Kansas City, Mo. Do you agree that this is the proper approach—even though it would defeat diversity jurisdiction if the dual citizen were domiciled in Ireland?

Desirability of diversity jurisdiction.—It is not too early to ask whether Congress has been wise in its allocation of diversity of citizenship cases to the federal courts. Compare § 1332(a) to 28 U.S.C. §§ 1332(d), 1335, and 1369, the latter being more recent utilizations of the Diversity Clause for special functions. In forming a judgment on this question you should consider the following: What were the possible purposes of the Founders in extending the federal judicial power to diversity cases? Have any changes come about since 1789 that have bearing on the general problem? What are the current costs and benefits of having federal courts entertain numerous state-law cases?

These questions were among the many considered by the American Law Institute before it proposed rather drastic restrictions on the scope of diversity jurisdiction. See Study of the Division of Jurisdiction Between State and Federal Courts 99–110 (Am. Law Inst. 1969) (recommending "that the right of a plaintiff to institute a diversity action in the federal court of his home state be abrogated"). More recently—and primarily in an effort to lessen congestion in federal court—numerous commentators, judges, legislators, and others have called for virtually complete abolition of federal jurisdiction based solely on diversity of citizenship. Congress has so far taken only the traditional step of raising the jurisdictional amount requirement of § 1332, increasing it in 1988 to $50,000 and in 1996 to $75,000.

This is not to say that diversity jurisdiction has no champions. See Adrienne J. Marsh, Diversity Jurisdiction: Scapegoat of Overcrowded Federal Courts, 48 Brook.L.Rev. 197 (1982); cf. Scott Dodson, Beyond Bias in Diversity Jurisdiction, 69 Duke L.J. 267 (2019) (shifting justification to facilitating multistate aggregation). Compare H.R. 3487, 115th Cong. (2017) (proposing massive expansion of diversity jurisdiction), with Diane P. Wood, The Changing Face of Diversity Jurisdiction, 82 Temp.L.Rev. 593 (2009) (defending the allocation of diversity jurisdiction for special functions).

As you read the next Subsection, ask yourself what difference there is between original and removal jurisdiction as to the parties' right of access to a federal court for a case involving diverse citizens. Is the difference a logical one?

(e) "REMOVAL" PROVISION

Suppose the plaintiff commences in a state court an action that he could instead have commenced in one of the federal district courts. Are there circumstances in which either party may remove the case from the state system into the federal system of courts? What reasons of policy suggest that such a course should at least in some situations be open? The basic removal statute is 28 U.S.C. § 1441.

Questions: (11) Can defendant properly remove in each of the following cases? Assume that the matter in controversy exceeds any jurisdictional amount and that service of process was made in the forum state.

(a) *A*, a citizen of New York, has a dispute with *B*, a citizen of Missouri. The only available basis of federal jurisdiction is diversity of citizenship. Although *A* could sue in a New York federal court, he chooses to sue in a New York state court.

(b) *A*, a citizen of New York, sues *B*, a citizen of Missouri, in a Missouri state court. The only available basis of federal jurisdiction is diversity of citizenship.

(c) A corporation incorporated in Delaware and having its principal place of business in New York commences a trademark action based on federal statute in a Massachusetts state court against a corporation incorporated in New York and having its principal place of business in Massachusetts.

(12) Suppose the Mottleys had instead brought the Louisville & Nashville Railroad Co. v. Mottley litigation originally in Kentucky state court. Could defendant railroad have properly removed the action to federal court under a statute analogous to present 28 U.S.C. § 1441? See Curran v. Price, 150 F.R.D. 85, 87 (D.Md.1993) (sanctioning under Rule 11 the defendant's attorney, who had removed on the basis of a federal defense, and ordering him "to copy out, legibly, in his own handwriting, and within 30 days of the date hereof, the text (i.e., without footnotes) of section 3722 in 14A C. Wright, A. Miller, and E. Cooper, Federal Practice and Procedure: Civil (1985), together with the text of that section's update").

On the one hand, there are exceptions to § 1441's general rule of removability, as is indeed suggested by the opening clause of the statute. For example, 28 U.S.C. § 1445(a) provides that a civil action arising under the Federal Employers' Liability Act (45 U.S.C. §§ 51–60) and commenced in a state court may not be removed to a federal district court. The FELA is a statute designed to make it easier for an injured railroad worker engaged in interstate commerce to recover damages from the employer. Substantively, it abrogates the common-law rule that prevented an employee from recovering from the employer for injuries sustained through the negligence of a fellow servant; and it provides that the plaintiff's contributory negligence is not a complete defense, but works only to reduce damages on a comparative-negligence basis. Procedurally, it gives the injured worker a choice between a state court and a federal district court that the defendant employer cannot frustrate by removal. (We note parenthetically that the Jones Act (46 U.S.C. § 30104) gives to seamen the same substantive benefits in actions against their employers for injuries suffered in the course of their employment that the FELA gives to railroad workers. It also gives seamen the same procedural benefits by allowing them the choice between state and federal court and forbidding removal by the employer. Indeed, the Jones Act incorporates by reference all laws of the United States regulating recovery in cases of personal injury or death to railway employees.)

On the other hand, there are a few special removal statutes that go beyond § 1441 in allowing removal. These statutes might allow removal of cases that are outside the district court's original jurisdiction, although within the bounds of Article III, such as those cases specified in 28 U.S.C. § 1442 (federal officers asserting a federal defense) and § 1443 (certain civil rights matters).

Finally, the mechanics of removal appear in 28 U.S.C. §§ 1446–1450. The defendant must seek removal promptly, normally within thirty days of receipt of the complaint. In the United States District Court sitting in the same locality as the state court, the defendant files a notice of removal, subject to Rule 11 and setting forth the grounds that justify removal. The defendant then gives the plaintiff and the state court notification of the filing. By this activity solely on the part of the defendant, removal is complete. The state court can proceed no further with the action unless and until the United States District Court remands it to the state court, as upon a finding that it was by law not removable. See also Federal Rule 81(c).

CHOICE OF FORUM

The existence of federal jurisdiction often gives a litigant's lawyer a choice between federal and state court. There are many considerations that might affect the choice, according to empirical studies of attorneys' preferences. See Kevin M. Clermont & Theodore Eisenberg, Do Case Outcomes Really Reveal Anything About the Legal System? Win Rates and Removal Jurisdiction, 83 Cornell L.Rev. 581, 599 (1998). Most of these considerations group under four general headings: expected bias against a litigant; logistical and practical concerns; perceived disparity in quality and other characteristics between federal and state judges and between federal and state juries; and the different procedures offered by one or the other court system.

First, the importance of these considerations can vary with the situation. An out-of-state defendant insurance company, for example, would expect more bias in an action brought by a resident individual plaintiff in state court than would an out-of-state individual defendant being sued by a resident insurance company in state court. A resident litigant from a city sued in a rural county court could conceivably expect as much bias as a litigant from another state. Whether or not all these kinds of prejudices still exist, many litigants think they do.

Second, logistical concerns include the parties' relative distances from the courthouse or the place where most of the legal action will take place. Sometimes a litigant's lawyer may choose a court far from the opponent's residence to increase leverage in settlement. Very importantly, a litigant's lawyer may be more familiar with the practices of a local state court, where also there may be less expense involved. Likely one's purposes would be served by a longer or shorter docket.

Third, federal judges often are seen as being of higher quality and greater independence than are state judges. Federal juries are drawn from a wider geographical area than are state juries.

Fourth, the different procedures offered by the court systems require a lawyer to consider many other variables when choosing a court. Many preferences regarding federal court turn on its pleading practices, discovery devices, pretrial conferences, summary judgment, and judicial activism in procedural matters. The state courts' trial rules of evidence might differ. The two systems' effectiveness of appellate review might affect choice. The transfer and joinder rules in federal court, which we shall next study, surely affect choice.

Whatever lawyers' reasons might be, and no matter how intangible those reasons might seem, the choice of forum apparently makes a significant difference. In recent years, the plaintiffs' win rate in nonprisoner federal question cases brought as original actions in federal court has been 52%; for such cases removed to federal court, the plaintiffs' win rate was only 25%. In diversity jurisdiction, the plaintiffs' win rate in original actions has been 71%; for removed cases, it was 34%. One must be wary in analyzing win rates because the groups of compared cases comprise different cases, which may differ in many respects. But here when the statistician controls for as many variables as possible, that robust result survives: removal seems seriously to affect case outcome. After all, that result accords with removal's purpose of protecting defendants.

For a consistent anecdote, consider Finding the Forum for a Victory, Nat'l L.J., Feb. 11, 1991, at S3:

"Choosing the right forum for a lawsuit can mean the difference between winning and losing.

"In his hate-crimes civil lawsuit against [pro se] white supremacist Tom Metzger, [plaintiffs'] attorney Morris Dees feels his selection of Oregon state court over federal court was critical.

" 'When we filed this lawsuit, we had a choice between state and federal court. We chose state court because Oregon discovery rules are quite different than the federal rules. You can do trial by ambush in Oregon. You have no interrogatories, no production of evidence; you don't have to give the names of witnesses or give the other side your documents.' As a result, Mr. Metzger had no idea how much evidence Mr. Dees had, and this ignorance would prove fatal."

(f) SUPPLEMENTAL JURISDICTION

Even at this early stage of your study, it is useful to acquire the idea of supplemental jurisdiction. The idea is that a federal court, if it has federal subject-matter jurisdiction over a claim, can hear at the same time certain other claims that would normally be within exclusive state jurisdiction. Think of two classic situations, which are often called respectively pendent jurisdiction and ancillary jurisdiction.

First, suppose a corporation brings a federal trademark action in federal court, but it also wants to assert a state claim against the defendant for unfair competition in the same transaction. The two claims may be joined in the federal complaint. The court has supplemental jurisdiction over the additional claim, which obviates a disincentive to accessing the federal system.

Second, parties other than the plaintiff might want to add additional, related state claims to a federal lawsuit. Imagine a diversity case in which the defendant wants to plead a compulsory counterclaim that fails to meet the jurisdictional amount. She may do so by supplemental jurisdiction. Given subject-matter jurisdiction over the main claim, and in order to protect the defendant from splitting up the claims, the federal court can hear the counterclaim that did not independently satisfy federal jurisdictional requirements.

The justification for supplemental jurisdiction is that the related federal and state claims form a single case in the constitutional sense, giving the federal court power. Then, in the exercise of discretion, the federal court can choose to entertain the claims together when considerations of fairness, convenience, efficiency, and comity so counsel.

Nonetheless, the doctrine poses an obvious threat to state sovereignty. Thus, supplemental jurisdiction is subject to limits, which are expressed by Congress's codification of the doctrine in 28 U.S.C. § 1367. But we leave the details to Topic C of Part 3.

(g) REVIEW OF STATE-COURT ACTIONS BY THE SUPREME COURT

If an action is properly commenced in or removed to a federal district court, it will normally remain in the federal court system to the end. There is no such thing as removal from a federal court to a state court.

But can an action that the plaintiff commenced in a state court appear in the federal court system at any later stage if it was not removable to a federal court, or if it was removable but was not in fact removed? Congress treated this matter in 28 U.S.C. § 1257, which you should read in contrast to 28 U.S.C. § 1254, discussed supra p. 252.

Questions: (13) What are the purposes, in a state/federal arrangement of courts, of § 1257?

(14) Why does § 1257 confine review by the U.S. Supreme Court of state-court decisions to "[f]inal judgments or decrees rendered by the *highest* court of a State in which a decision could be had" (emphasis added)?

Consider the subsequent history of Louisville & Nashville Railroad Co. v. Mottley, that 1908 decision you read. After the federal court dismissed their suit for want of jurisdiction, the Mottleys brought a new action in a state circuit court in Kentucky seeking the same relief. The railroad company again based its defense upon the federal statute prohibiting free passes. By its judgment granting the relief requested, the state circuit court required the railroad company to issue annual passes over its lines to the plaintiffs during their respective lives. On appeal, the Kentucky Court of Appeals, the highest court of the state, affirmed the judgment by construing the federal statute as nonretroactive and hence inapplicable. Then the railroad company put the case before the Supreme Court of the United States again, for determination of the same federal issue that the Mottleys had unsuccessfully relied upon to give the federal court original jurisdiction in the first suit. And the Supreme Court, viewing the federal statute as applicable and constitutional, now reversed on the ground that the railroad company had rightly refused further to comply with its agreement to issue passes to the plaintiffs and that judicially requiring performance of the agreement was erroneous. Louisville & Nashville R.R. Co. v. Mottley, 219 U.S. 467, 31 S.Ct. 265 (1911).

Question: (15) Was U.S. Supreme Court review in the second Mottley action statutorily and constitutionally within the Court's jurisdiction?

(h) TRIBAL COURTS

In setting up the distinction between state and federal courts, we did not mean to suggest that those two systems have a monopoly on civil controversies or even on civil court cases.

Native American tribes retain the typical attributes of governmental power except to the extent that those attributes have been removed by treaty, federal statute, or federal common law. A great many federally recognized Indian tribes have formal court systems. Much variation exists among their court structures, and in their governmental structures more generally. Perhaps the most prominent is the Navajo Nation's court system, which handles more than 50,000 cases each year in its trial courts and supreme court. Smaller tribal court systems might handle only a few hundred cases per year. Some tribes have a trial-level tribal court, with appeals taken to an inter-tribal appellate court such as the Southwest Intertribal Court of Appeals.

There is no mechanism for an appeal (on questions of federal law or otherwise) from a tribal court to a federal court. The federal district courts have jurisdiction to hear certain challenges to the subject-matter jurisdiction of a tribal court, but not to review the merits of a decision rendered by a tribal court that has jurisdiction (except upon habeas corpus brought by a person in tribal custody). During recent decades, the U.S. Supreme Court on review of the lower federal courts has significantly limited tribal-court jurisdiction with respect to nonmembers of the tribe, but Congress has altered a few of those limits. In any event, tribal courts continue to hear many cases, involving both members and nonmembers. See generally Matthew L.M. Fletcher, Federal Indian Law (2016).

SECTION 7.   SELECTION OF A PROPER FORUM: LIMITATIONS ON TERRITORIAL AUTHORITY TO ADJUDICATE

Suppose a person has a case that fits within Article III as well as within one of the sections of the United States Code vesting original jurisdiction in the United States District Courts, so that she may (if the jurisdiction is concurrent) or must (if it is exclusive) commence her action in one of those courts. Is she free to select any federal district court in any state? Manifestly she should not be altogether free to do so.

Question: (1) What are the factors that should enter rationally into a solution of the general problem here posed? (When you complete your study of this Section, try to make a tentative determination of how well the federal scheme takes these factors into account.)

For a court properly to undertake a civil adjudication, the law says that the court must have territorial authority to adjudicate. This requirement confines the place of litigation, by putting restrictions on the court's authority to entertain litigation with nonlocal elements. The scope of territorial authority to adjudicate is defined in terms of the geographic relationship among the forum, the parties, and the litigation.

In fact, territorial authority breaks down into two types of regulation that control the plaintiff's choice of a district court in which to commence the lawsuit. That is to say, territorial authority to adjudicate comprises both territorial jurisdiction and venue as requirements. The defendant, however, must raise any failure to satisfy these requirements.

Federal courts generally exercise territorial jurisdiction only where authorized by Congress or its rulemaker. Congress and the Supreme Court, the latter acting as Congress's rulemaker, have explicitly or implicitly authorized varying degrees of federal-court territorial jurisdiction in the confusing complex of statutes and Rules that treat service of process. So, we must give some initial attention to that topic.

(a) SERVICE OF PROCESS AS A REQUIREMENT

Service of process is the required means (1) of officially informing the defendant that an action has been brought against him and that he must defend himself or suffer the entry of judgment by default and (2) of formally subjecting the defendant to the adjudicatory authority of the sovereign. The first function of giving notice reflects an obvious fairness concern. The second function reflects the underlying requirement that the court have territorial jurisdiction. Service bridges the two functions. Fulfillment of the two functions is enforceable by, among other means, Rules 12(b)(5) and 12(b)(2), respectively.

You already know Rule 3 of the Federal Rules, which tells us that a plaintiff commences a civil action by filing a complaint with the court. Further now, Rule 4(b) says that, upon or after the filing of the complaint, the clerk must issue a summons, which is called process. Rule 4(a) states the formal requirements, and you should note how Form 3, the form of summons, carries out these requirements, which are enforceable by Rule 12(b)(4). Rule 4(c) provides that a copy of the summons must be served together with a copy of the complaint, and then it goes on to specify who can serve—ordinarily any nonparty at least eighteen years old. Incidentally, note that Rule 4(*l*) treats proof of service and that Rule 4(m) sets a time limit for service.

Question: (2) Consider the likely reaction of an inexperienced layperson when confronted with these formidable documents. Would it be desirable to couch the summons in simpler language? Or can something be said for the more formidable style? Why not require the use of both styles, as suggested by Oregon Rule of Civil Procedure 7C?

Manner of service.—Rule 4(e)–(j) describes the manner of service, i.e., the mechanics of delivering process to different kinds of defendants. The point here is *notice*. Take a typical lawsuit for a money recovery against an individual in the United States who is neither a minor nor an incompetent. Rule 4(e)(2) says that the service may be made by delivering a copy of the summons and of the complaint to the defendant personally, or by leaving these papers at his dwelling or usual place of abode with some person of suitable age and discretion residing there, or by delivering them to an agent authorized to receive them. According to Rule 4(e)(1), it is also sufficient if the papers are served in the manner prescribed by the law of the state in which the district court is held or in which service is made.

Question: (3) How is service to be made on a corporation? on an unincorporated association?

Rule 4(d) provides that a plaintiff suing an individual (who is neither a minor nor an incompetent), a corporation, or an unincorporated association can opt to mail or transmit to the defendant a notice requesting a waiver of service. If the defendant complies, the suit can proceed without need for the sometimes expensive formality of service. If the defendant fails to comply, the plaintiff needs to arrange for service of process, but the defendant normally will have to pay the expenses of that service. As the Advisory Committee explained: "The aims of the provision are to eliminate the costs of service of a summons on many parties and to foster cooperation among adversaries and counsel." In actuality, however, the waiver provision does not get heavy use. See David D. Siegel, The New (Dec. 1, 1993) Rule 4 of the Federal Rules of Civil Procedure: Changes in Summons Service and Personal Jurisdiction (pt. 1), 151 F.R.D. 441, 457 (1994) ("the waiver procedure may be seen as toothless by canny defendants," because costs are relatively small and because refusal to cooperate may produce timing advantages).

Circumstances of service.—Rule 4(k) and (n) regulates the circumstances of service, i.e., the "Territorial Limits of Effective Service." Its essential premise is that service will be effective only if *territorial* *jurisdiction* exists. It accordingly provides how far the federal court's territorial jurisdiction reaches for each of the six types of service listed therein. Its approach is ordinarily to adopt the local state's law (so that a federal court reaches only as far as a local state court could), but federal lawmakers have implicitly or explicitly extended the federal court's reach for certain special service types.

Rule 4 is somewhat intricate because, by the nature of its historical growth, it combines specific federal regulations with adopted features of state law. But the basic idea is that the federal authorities use it to specify the extent of the federal courts' territorial jurisdiction, either by adopting the necessarily restrictive state law or by imposing federal extensions.

(b) TERRITORIAL JURISDICTION AS A LIMITATION

The concept of territorial jurisdiction comprises the more important rules of territorial authority to adjudicate. Indeed, territorial jurisdiction rests heavily on the Due Process Clause of the Federal Constitution as its outer limit. That limit demands a connection or nexus between the sovereign's court and the target of the action that is adequately strong to justify imposing the judicial relief sought. Thus, in the typical case, adequate connections include the defendant's being served with process in the sovereign's territory, being domiciled there, consenting to suit there, or committing certain acts there such as a tort. These connections will fairly support "jurisdiction over the person" of the defendant. But this is huge subject, the bulk of which we put off until Topic A of Part 3.

Reach of territorial jurisdiction.—Within that outer constitutional limit, the service provisions in Rule 4(k) and (n) authorize territorial jurisdiction only in certain circumstances.

For a readily generalizable example, consider the familiar "nonresident motorist" statute as a state law that is applicable in federal court through Rule 4(k)(1)(A): where *A* suffers injuries on a State *X* highway through the alleged negligence of a nonresident motorist *B*, a State *X* statute says that *A* may start her action in State *X* and serve effective process upon *B* in his home state. So, a federal court in State *X* could reach B. But if State *X* had not chosen to stretch its territorial jurisdiction to get nonresident motorists, then the federal court in State *X* could not have reached *B*.

For a more specialized example, consider the federal "bulge" provision in Rule 4(k)(1)(B), which is very narrowly available but may be useful in a metropolitan area spanning more than one state: when a pending federal action is enlarged to bring in certain kinds of additional parties that we shall study in the next Section ("third-party defendants" under Rule 14 or "persons needed for just adjudication" under Rule 19), effective service upon those parties may be made at any place in the United States within the sweep of a radius of 100 miles from the courthouse. Here the federal lawmakers have promulgated an extension of the federal court's territorial jurisdiction, expressing that extension through the service provision of Rule 4(k).

Rule 4(n) supplements Rule 4(k). An example of a law within Rule 4(n)(2) is a State X statute permitting A, who claims as a creditor of a nonresident debtor B, to commence an action against B in State X by attaching property of B located in State X and providing some form of reasonable notice to B as prescribed in the statute. Such an attempt to base a suit on the attachment of property is called a nonpersonal action, which we shall study later.

Effect of requiring territorial jurisdiction.—To go back to the heading of this Subsection, it is clear that the place-restrictions of territorial jurisdiction impose limits on the plaintiff's choice of a district court in which to commence the action.

Thus, for simple illustration, in a diversity action for breach of contract, the territorial jurisdiction requirement might disable a plaintiff from suing in her home district court and oblige the plaintiff to sue in the district court at the defendant's home (or wherever else personal jurisdiction exists and venue is proper). We are not at the moment intimating any opinion that this result is bad or regrettable, although we shall have to come finally to the question whether the territorial limitations of Rule 4 do make sense. Here we are simply noting the fact that the result comes about through the current rules regarding effective service of process.

We should further note that those rules do not seem to follow from any constitutional requirement. One function of service of process, already explained, is to provide notice. Because the Due Process Clause requires adequate notification to the defendant for the exercise by any American court of the authority to adjudicate, the power to loosen the service of process is not unlimited. Nevertheless, this consideration of *adequate notice* creates no constitutional barrier to obliterating *territorial limitations* on service of process.

The other function of service of process is to subject the defendant to the adjudicatory authority of the sovereign. Because the Fifth Amendment's Due Process Clause requires an adequate connection between the federal sovereign and the defendant, it does result in some territorial limitations on the federal power to extend effective service of process on foreigners. By analogy, the Fourteenth Amendment's Due Process Clause requires an adequate connection between state and defendant for state-court actions, resulting in some territorial limitations on the state's power to extend effective service of process on out-of-staters. Again, there is no constitutional barrier to obliterating, for service of process in *federal actions*, the territorial limitations of Rule 4 adopted from state law and hence related to *state boundaries*. For example, the federal sovereign would have an adequate connection with a defendant domiciled in any American state, not just in the local state.

Federal courts thus could constitutionally reach much farther than state courts, even though the federal lawmakers by Rule 4(k)(1)(A) have chosen ordinarily to restrict the federal court's reach to the local state's reach.

All this goes to support the proposition that Congress has the power to provide for nationwide service of process issuing from federal courts, as indeed it has done in infrequent instances such as by the Federal Securities Exchange Act.

But all this is not to say that a federal court anywhere in the United States could conduct a particular federal action against a particular defendant consistently with the Fifth Amendment's Due Process Clause. Due process may prohibit the place of federal suit from being so arbitrarily distant as to be basically unfair for the defendant. This constitutional constraint would be not so much a restriction on territorial jurisdiction, however, as one on venue.

(c) VENUE AS A LIMITATION

Rules of venue specify where the sovereign will exercise its authority to adjudicate, i.e., in what place it will exercise its jurisdiction. The place-restrictions of venue pursue primarily the lower-level concerns of convenience and efficiency, and find expression mainly in statutes that do not employ the language of service of process.

General provision.—The general precepts regarding venue in the federal system appear in 28 U.S.C. § 1391. Under § 1391(b), venue lies in a district (1) where any defendant resides if all defendants reside in the same state or (2) where a substantial part of the events or omissions giving rise to the claim occurred or a substantial part of property that is the subject of the action is situated; however, (3) the statute effectively waives this venue requirement in the rare circumstance when it would block suit in every federal court, and it then requires satisfaction of only the requirement of personal jurisdiction.

Question: (4) In which United States District Courts would venue be proper in each of the following cases? Subject-matter jurisdiction exists and in-state service is possible in each case.

(a) *A*, a resident of the Southern District of New York, wishes to sue *B*, a resident of Vermont. The claim arose solely in Buffalo in the Western District of New York.

(b) Same as the preceding case, except that the claim arose solely in Quebec.

Note the use of the word "reside" in § 1391. Strangely, the case law had generally equated this term for individuals with "citizenship" as used in the diversity statute. Congress codified this approach in 2011 by § 1391(c)(1).

Question: (5) Is there any policy that should prevent a person from having more than one residence for venue purposes? (Note that Congress had mitigated the restrictive consequences of "residence" with respect to venue by the 1966 amendment that made the place where the claim arose a proper venue.)

Special provisions.—Read carefully § 1391(c)(2), which defines the residence of a defendant corporation or unincorporated association by tying it to the requirement of personal jurisdiction. Compare § 1391(c)(2) to 28 U.S.C. § 1332(c)(1). This means that as to such a defendant, the venue requirement does not place a substantial additional limitation on the plaintiff's choice of a district court. See also § 1391(d), which treats states with multiple districts and which should be read to mean that mere incorporation or license to do business in a state extends residence not to all of the state's districts, but only to a district containing the corporation's designated home office.

As for a defendant not "resident" in the United States according to these definitions, whether an individual or an entity, § 1391(c)(3) means that venue lies in any district. So, as to that defendant, the venue requirement places no limitation on the plaintiff's choice of a district court.

In particular, consider aliens who are natural persons. Their treatment is not expressed felicitously, but at least the intent is relatively clear in the 2011 legislative history. First, the history explains that all natural persons with a "lawful" domicile in the United States reside in the judicial district where domiciled. Subsection (c)(1) thus would include U.S. citizens domiciled here and also resident aliens with "green cards." Second, the history explains that all natural persons who are not lawfully domiciled in the United States are irrelevant for venue purposes. Subsection (c)(3) thus would include U.S. citizens domiciled abroad and also aliens present in the United States without a green card.

There are various statutes and a few judge-made doctrines that lay down special venue rules for particular classes of cases. Some of these turn on the plaintiff's residence. The courts have interpreted most of these special rules to supplement § 1391, thus broadening the choice of venue. E.g., 28 U.S.C. § 1401. But the courts have read some of these special rules to override § 1391, thus controlling venue for the particular class of cases. E.g., 28 U.S.C. § 1397.

One such exclusive provision is unique and deserves special mention: when a defendant removes a case from a state court to a federal district court, it passes "to the district court of the United States for the district and division embracing the place where such action is pending." 28 U.S.C. § 1441(a). Incidentally, Congress has subdivided many districts into divisions, but these divisions have significance only for local judicial administration.

Question: (6) Assume that the individual defendant properly removes a case from state court to the federal district court sitting in the same locality. Is that district court necessarily a court in which, under venue requirements for actions originally brought in the district courts, the plaintiff might initially have commenced the action?

Transfer of cases from one proper district court to another.— Operation of the ordinary rules will often result in a case being commenced in or removed to a federal district court that is constitutionally fair but nevertheless is not the most convenient for the conduct of the action. Congress has sought to meet this shortcoming principally by 28 U.S.C. § 1404(a).

Question: (7) What problems of interpretation are raised by the language of § 1404(a)?

(d) ADDENDUM ON ALLOCATION OF COURT BUSINESS AMONG THE STATES

A word is in order about the allocation of court business among the states. With fifty states, each having a court system, the country would seem to require some allocation among the states. The Constitution of the United States does the most to provide it, particularly through the Due Process Clause of the Fourteenth Amendment as interpreted. The constitutional control is largely negative: a defendant who has no adequate connection with a particular state is beyond that state's adjudicatory authority.

1. A highway accident occurs in Nebraska, both parties are domiciled there, the defendant has never gone outside the state and has no property outside the state, and all the witnesses reside in the state. It would seem that Nebraska is a proper state in which to conduct any resulting lawsuit. If Wyoming or some other state purports to handle the case at the plaintiff's request and to give judgment upon the defendant's default, its judgment should be open to attack or denied recognition.

2. But suppose the defendant wanders into Wyoming and is there handed summons and complaint in an action commenced in a Wyoming court based on the Nebraska accident. Does Wyoming now have constitutional authority to adjudicate? Yes.

The broad question later considered in detail is this: what must be the relation between a given state and the defendant, in light of the nature of the particular matter in dispute, so that the state will have the constitutional authority to render a judgment?

Again, we should note that a state may, by statute or otherwise, decline to exert its utmost constitutional powers of adjudication. For example, even though service of process on the defendant in the state would be sufficient, constitutionally, to support a valid default judgment, Wyoming law might say that there are reasons of fairness, convenience, and efficiency for declining to exercise territorial jurisdiction, and so its court would dismiss the action.

Each state naturally makes its own internal arrangements for allocating business among the various courts in its court system. For instance, in personal-injury cases between residents, a state may provide by its venue statute that the plaintiff must bring the action in the county of residence of the plaintiff or of the defendant.

Parenthetically, you should note that much of the law on territorial jurisdiction applicable to the state courts, but not state venue law, is relevant to the federal litigator. Remember that by Rule 4, the federal courts can reach only as far as the forum state court could, except when some specialized federal provision has extended their reach.

———

Section 8.   More Complex Litigation: Multiple Parties and Multiple Claims

Thus far we have spoken of lawsuits mostly in terms of two parties— one plaintiff and one defendant. Even within this two-party framework, litigation may become ramified by the assertion of a considerable number of claims. Rule 18 permits a plaintiff to join in a single proceeding as many claims as he may have against the defendant, however unrelated they may be. Similarly, the defendant may by counterclaim under Rule 13 expand the lawsuit so as to include whatever claims she may have against the plaintiff. And of course, in such multiclaim litigation, each claim may generate a number of defenses.

Further complication of a lawsuit may follow from the presence in it of more than two parties and also from the parties' assertion of various claims among themselves. The number of these multiparty actions in the courts has increased markedly in modern times. This is owing not only to the adoption of rules and statutes liberalizing the joinder of parties and claims, but also to the increased complexity of financial and other transactions in our society.

The subject of multiple parties and multiple claims is a large and difficult one, as even a casual reading of Rule 14 and Rules 19 through 24 (and a rereading of Rules 13 and 18) will indicate. We shall survey the field in a very general and necessarily superficial way. But first we must refer back to jurisdiction and venue.

There is a certain fitness in dealing with this subject of complex litigation after the Sections on subject-matter jurisdiction, territorial jurisdiction, and venue, for among the major difficulties is that of finding a proper court for the multiparty, multiclaim lawsuit. We shall illustrate this point by touching upon three problems of federal jurisdiction and venue in actions involving more than one plaintiff or defendant.

First, the diversity of citizenship required to satisfy 28 U.S.C. § 1332(a) is complete diversity (that is, no two opposing parties can be citizens of the same state). See Strawbridge v. Curtiss, 7 U.S. (3 Cranch)

267 (1806) (Marshall, C.J.). Here is an illustration: a plaintiff who is a citizen of New York cannot invoke § 1332(a) when joining as defendants a citizen of Missouri and another citizen of New York, because the presence of a New Yorker on each side of the controversy destroys the required diversity.

We are speaking here only about the general diversity statute. Courts have not so narrowly interpreted the Diversity and Alienage Clauses of Article III. Thus, Congress has considerable constitutional power to bestow jurisdiction based on minimal diversity (that is, any two opposing parties are of diverse citizenship). Indeed, Congress has sometimes done so, as for complex actions under 28 U.S.C. § 1369.

The alignment of the parties as plaintiffs and defendants in the pleadings is not conclusive in determining diversity jurisdiction. The court will realign the parties for such purpose according to their ultimate interests. For a frequently cited statement of the principles involved in determining ultimate interests, see Indianapolis v. Chase National Bank, 314 U.S. 63, 62 S.Ct. 15 (1941) (realignment to defeat jurisdiction in that case). Realignment may either defeat or create jurisdiction.

Question: (1) Does the required diversity under § 1332(a) exist in each of the following cases? The matter in controversy exceeds the jurisdictional amount in each case.

(a) *A*, a citizen of New York, and *B*, a citizen of Ohio, sue *C*, a citizen of Missouri.

(b) *A*, a citizen of New York, and *B*, a citizen of Ohio, sue *C*, a citizen and domiciliary of France.

(c) *A*, a citizen of New York, and *B*, a citizen and domiciliary of France, sue *C*, a citizen of Ohio.

(d) *A*, a citizen of New York, and *B*, a citizen and domiciliary of France, sue *C*, a citizen of Ohio, and *D,* a citizen and domiciliary of France.

(e) *A*, a citizen of New York, and *B*, a citizen and domiciliary of France, sue *C*, a citizen and domiciliary of France.

(f) A partnership of *A*, a citizen of New York, and *B*, a citizen and domiciliary of France, sues *C*, a citizen of Ohio, and *D*, a citizen and domiciliary of Germany.

Second, the basic removal statute, 28 U.S.C. § 1441, provides that "the defendant or the defendants" have the right, under the conditions there prescribed, to remove an action to the federal court. This means, by 28 U.S.C. § 1446(b)(2)(A), that all properly joined and served defendants must agree to removal.

Question: (2) In the following cases, assume that the matter in controversy exceeds any jurisdictional amount and that service of process was made in the forum state.

(a) *A*, a citizen of California, sues *B*, a citizen of Connecticut, and *C* Company, a Connecticut corporation with its principal place of business in

Connecticut, in a California state court, seeking joint relief. *B* is content with the state court. Can *C* Company alone properly remove the action to the local United States District Court?

(b) *A*, a citizen of California, sues *B*, a citizen of California, and *C* Company, a Connecticut corporation with its principal place of business in Connecticut, in a California state court, seeking joint relief. Can *B* and *C* Company together properly remove?

(c) *A*, a citizen of California, sues *B*, a citizen of California, in a California state court, seeking damages for personal injuries. *C* Ins. Co., *B*'s liability insurer, refuses to defend, contending that its policy does not cover the kind of accident in question. Thereupon *B* brings an action in the same state court for a declaratory judgment of coverage, naming as defendants *A* and *C* Ins. Co., a Connecticut corporation with its principal place of business in Connecticut. Can *C* Ins. Co. properly remove? See Bonell v. Gen. Accident Fire & Life Assur. Corp., 167 F.Supp. 384 (N.D.Cal.1958) (yes).

Third, multiparty actions also create problems with reference to venue. Note that the general venue statute, 28 U.S.C. § 1391(b)(1), refers to "all defendants."

Question: (3) In which United States District Courts would venue be proper in each of the following cases? Subject-matter jurisdiction exists in each case.

(a) *A*, a resident of Maine, wishes to sue *B*, a resident of Buffalo lying in the Western District of New York, and *C*, a resident of Manhattan in the Southern District of New York. The claim arose solely in Maine.

(b) *A*, a resident of Maine, wishes to sue *B*, a resident of Vermont, and *C*, a resident of New Hampshire. The claim arose solely in Maine.

(c) *A*, a resident of Buffalo, and *B*, a resident of Manhattan, wish to sue *C*, a resident of Vermont, and *D*, a resident of New Hampshire. The claim arose solely in Quebec. (Would it matter that *D* works in a factory in Vermont?)

We have couched the foregoing cases in terms of the plaintiff or plaintiffs "wishing" to sue. Insofar as the venue requirement—especially when taken together with the limitations on territorial jurisdiction—imposes obstacles to a *permissive* joinder of parties, the consequence is merely that the federal plaintiff must content himself with suing fewer defendants than he would like, or that several intending coplaintiffs will have to sue separately. But we shall see shortly that there is a graver problem. Sometimes party joinder is *required* (that is, the action cannot go forward in the absence of certain parties plaintiff or defendant). When this situation exists, the requirements of territorial authority to adjudicate may result in closing the doors of the federal courts to a meritorious claim cognizable there in point of subject-matter jurisdiction. Indeed, it may also turn out to be impossible to find a suitable state or foreign court for the action because no state or country is in a position to issue process that will be effective to bring in the defendants.

For the most part we shall postpone until Part 3 further study of the interplay between joinder rules and the law of subject-matter jurisdiction, territorial jurisdiction, and venue. As our mention of supplemental jurisdiction suggested, such problems rapidly become much thornier and require extensive treatment. So, with this introduction on jurisdiction and venue behind us, we turn to a consideration of the Federal Rules dealing with multiple parties and multiple claims. For the moment, your task is primarily to understand how the mechanics of these particular Rules work.

(a) PERMISSIVE JOINDER OF PROPER PARTIES

[Rules 17, 20]

There are numerous situations where a group of plaintiffs, each of whom would be free to sue separately as a litigant qualified under Rule 17, may consider it desirable to pool their resources and join in a single action. Rule 20(a)(1) permits them to do this, subject only to the requirements that their rights grow out of the same transaction, occurrence, or series of transactions or occurrences and that some question of law or fact common to all of them will arise in the action. Thus, for instance, ten passengers in a bus may join in suing the bus company for personal injuries sustained by them in a collision. On the one hand, such joinder may not only be advantageous to the parties, but also serve the public interest by preventing relitigation of the same facts in a succession of actions—and with a possibility of inconsistent results. On the other hand, if passengers in a series of bus accidents join in a single suit, they could be seeking an unfair advantage by suggesting gross wrongdoing by the defendant or by confusing the factfinder. Overall, the tests for permissive joinder receive flexible, but rather generous, interpretation.

Correspondingly liberal provisions allow a plaintiff (or several plaintiffs) to join a number of defendants in one action. Here are some examples of situations in which a plaintiff may join all persons claimed to be liable to him: plaintiff A suffers injuries in a collision of three cars owned and negligently driven by B, C, and D respectively; or plaintiff T suffers injuries through the negligence of employee S for which employer M is also responsible by the rule of respondeat superior. In situations of these concurrent-negligence and employee-employer types, the plaintiff may select his targets—he may sue all or any of those liable.

Questions: (4) A sues C and D for libel, alleging that C falsely wrote of her on May 1 that she was a thief and that D did the same on July 1. Is the joinder proper under Rule 20?

(5) A and B sue C and D for libel, alleging that C falsely wrote of A on May 1 that she was a thief and that D wrote the same of B on July 1. Is the joinder proper under Rule 20? See Wynn v. Nat'l Broad. Co., 234 F.Supp.2d 1067, 1078 (C.D.Cal.2002) (holding that Rule 20 generally does not allow

joinder of a plaintiff-versus-defendant claim with a different-plaintiff-versus-different-defendant claim).

(6) What is the Federal Rules' remedy for an attempted joinder that is improper under Rule 20?

Rule 20(a)(2)(A) expressly allows an action by a plaintiff who is in doubt as to which of two or more defendants is liable to him. Form 12 is illustrative of such a claim for relief against defendants "in the alternative."

The territorial limitations on effective service of process impose practical restrictions on joinder of defendants. Moreover, any joinder proper under Rule 20 may be prevented by requirements of subject-matter jurisdiction or venue, of course.

Suppose a defendant to an action wishes to assert a counterclaim that involves persons not already joined. Think of Mr. Robinson in Williams v. Robinson, and see again Rule 13(h).

(b) REQUIRED JOINDER OF PERSONS NEEDED FOR JUST ADJUDICATION

[Rule 19]

The party-structure of a lawsuit is in the first instance determined by the plaintiff (or plaintiffs) instituting the action. But he is not entirely free to do as he pleases. As we have just seen, there are outer limits on who *may* be joined as proper parties. And inner limits exist to tell the plaintiff who *must* be joined, limits enforceable by the defendant or the court: there are occasions when he must enlist other persons who should have joined him as plaintiffs, and there are also occasions when he must bring in certain additional persons to defend the lawsuit.

Rule 19(a)(1) declares that persons sustaining certain relationships to the action must be joined as parties if their *joinder is feasible*, that is, if effective service of process can reach them and if their joinder will not deprive the court of subject-matter jurisdiction. Ultimately, venue will also have to be satisfied unless the point is waived.

Rule 19(a)(1) expresses the relationships necessitating joinder in terms of, first, whether the court can give "complete relief" to those already parties if the particular person is not joined and remains outside the action and, second, whether the disposition of the action in the absence of the particular person either may as a practical matter impair the person's ability to protect a claimed interest relating to the subject of the action[a] or may leave those already parties exposed to a substantial

---

[a]   Ordinarily the judgment in an action between *A* and *B* cannot affect *C in a legal sense.* The law ordinarily dictates that no judgment can go against *C* or alter her legal position unless she has been summoned as a party and has had an opportunity to present her side of the case.

An action between *A* and *B* may, however, affect *C in a practical sense.* Here is a simple example: *B* is holding a certain amount of money for *A* and *C* in disputed shares, and *A* recovers

risk of incurring double liability as the result of a later suit by that person. These relationships, as described, are rather broadly inclusive. So, for example, if *P* sues *D* for specific performance on a contract, *P*'s joint obligee is a necessary party.

Rule 19(a)(1) is not so broad, however, as to take in the concurrent-negligence and employee-employer cases hypothesized above in connection with Rule 20(a)(2). Rule 19 does not require joinder of defendants in those cases, even if feasible. Joinder is entirely optional with the plaintiff, who can select targets under Rule 20. The explanation lies in the character of the substantive rights and duties of the persons involved. The traditional version of the substantive law here is often summed up as "joint-and-several" liability, but that term really represents the joinder conclusion that the plaintiff can sue the defendants together or separately. The better description of the substantive law is "entire" liability, meaning that *each* defendant is liable for *all* of the plaintiff's damages. The plaintiff who has sued and won against a number of defendants can recover the whole judgment from any judgment debtor, although the plaintiff of course cannot recover more than the amount of the judgment by going after other of the judgment debtors. The substantive policy is to make the plaintiff whole, and to leave the defendants to squabble among themselves about relative overpayment of their shares by invoking whatever law of contribution happens to exist. Because the absence or presence of other potential defendants has no legal effect on the joined defendants vis-à-vis the plaintiff, and because the substantive law intends the practical effect of disadvantaging defendants, Rule 19(a)(1) leaves it up to the plaintiff whom to sue. As usual, then, much is left to party autonomy.

Now suppose instead that some missing person is within the net of subdivision (a) of Rule 19 and thus termed "necessary," but *joinder is not feasible.* The court then faces the alternatives of dismissing the action or of continuing it without the full cast of characters that we would prefer to have as parties. Rule 19(b) sets out a series of factors to consider in deciding between these alternatives. Examine the statement of factors. Sometimes the case should continue: try to imagine situations in which the second and fourth factors would tend to the conclusion that the action should go forward notwithstanding the absence of a person embraced by the definition of subdivision (a). But sometimes the factors counsel dismissal: if upon consideration of the terms of subdivision (b) of Rule 19, the court finds that the person whose joinder is not feasible is so urgently needed for just adjudication that the court should dismiss the case, the person is labeled "indispensable."

---

the whole sum from *B* by an action in which *C* has not been joined; the judgment does not preclude *C* from suit—she is unaffected legally—but as a practical matter she may be left without an adequate remedy against either *B* or *A* once the money is spent.

Question: (7) Under the Federal Rules, how and when does the defendant raise the defense of a failure to join persons as required by Rule 19?

(c) INTERPLEADER

[Rule 22]

As stated above, Rule 20 makes provision for a plaintiff who is doubtful which of two or more defendants is liable to him. But what of the prospective defendant who is in doubt as to which of two or more claimants has the right to payment of a debt admittedly owed to one of them?

Assume, for example, that the *A* Life Insurance Co. insured *B*'s life. *B* has died, and *C* and *D* each claim to be the sole beneficiary under the terms of the policy. There is the uncomfortable possibility that *C* might sue *A* Co. and recover, and that *D* might thereafter sue *A* Co. and likewise recover. The imposition of such a double recovery is unjust to *A* Co., but it can easily happen if each claimant sues separately. The parties might present different evidence in the two cases, or different factfinders might take different views of substantially identical evidence. And *A* Co. cannot defend in *D*'s action by saying, "We do not have to pay you because we have already been held liable to *C* on this policy." (Why is this not a defense?)

Rule interpleader.—Rule 22(a) provides an escape from this quandary. *A* Co. may commence a suit against *C* and *D* and require them to make their respective claims in the same action, thus avoiding the hazard of double liability. Moreover, suppose *A* Co. contends that it is not liable to either *C* or *D* because *B* had procured the policy by false representations. The interpleader machinery is still available, because an admission of liability to one of the claimants is not a prerequisite to its use. See Form 20.

If one of the claimants sues *A* Co., it may still interplead. The Rule provides that a defendant in such a position may interplead the other claimant and say in effect to the two of them, "Fight it out and we'll pay the winner," or, "We'll pay the winner unless it is held that we don't have to pay either." See Form 31.

If jurisdiction for interpleader in federal court rests only on a federal question, the procedure of Rule 22(a) must be utilized, and the usual rules of subject-matter jurisdiction, venue, and service apply. Venue for such an interpleader action initiated by the stakeholder generally must satisfy 28 U.S.C. § 1391. And process runs within the usual territorial limits of Rule 4.

But most interpleader cases in federal court rest on diversity of citizenship. When the interpleader action rests on diversity jurisdiction and proceeds under Rule 22(a), the general diversity statute (28 U.S.C. § 1332(a)) is applicable, so that the stake must exceed $75,000 and the diversity of citizenship must be complete diversity between the stakeholder on the one side and the adverse claimants on the other.

Statutory interpleader.—When diverse citizenship exists, however, the stakeholder may have a choice between two devices: rule interpleader under Rule 22(a) or the statutory interpleader that is cross-referenced in Rule 22(b). The cross-reference is to the federal statute providing for interpleader (see 28 U.S.C. §§ 1335, 1397, 2361).

Here the jurisdictional amount is "$500 or more," and the required diversity has a special definition—the statute looks to diversity of citizenship among the claimants, and the Supreme Court has held that minimal as distinguished from complete diversity suffices. State Farm Fire & Cas. Co. v. Tashire, 386 U.S. 523, 87 S.Ct. 1199 (1967). Venue for such an interpleader action initiated by the stakeholder lies in any district in which any claimant resides. Also, process runs nationwide. In other words, Congress has appropriately invoked its broad constitutional authority to handle cases that are beyond the state courts' reach.

(d) THIRD-PARTY PRACTICE

[Rule 14]

A defendant may wish to extend the lawsuit in another way. He may want to reach a third person, not joined in the action, who he believes is or may contingently be liable to him for all or part of the claim that the plaintiff is making against him. In our economy and society, such a situation is common.

Assume, for example, that *A* sues *B*, a restaurant proprietor, claiming damage as a result of eating contaminated food. *B*'s contention is that if *A* can hold him liable, then the loss ought to fall on *C*, his supplier, who furnished the food. If *B* waits until *A* has recovered a judgment against him and he has paid it, and then brings a separate action against *C*, *B* may find himself in a position not dissimilar to that of the insurance company in the interpleader situation described above. *C* is not bound by what occurred in the *A* versus *B* litigation in her absence; and the two factfinders may arrive at inconsistent findings. Even if this inconsistency does not occur, there will remain the wasteful business of reworking the ground already covered in the first action.

Rule 14(a) permits such a defendant to bring the third person into the case as a party, if effective service of process can reach her. (Note when the Rule requires leave of court, and see Forms 4, 16, and 41.) This device, called impleader, is optional with the defendant, so that he is free to wait and bring a separate action if he chooses. For instance, the defendant may not wish yet to arouse the third person's hostility, and inspire possibly more adverse testimony, by suing her now.

If the defendant uses Rule 14(a), the result is a kind of lawsuit within a lawsuit. The defendant becomes a "third-party plaintiff" and the impleaded newcomer becomes a "third-party defendant" with respect to the claim between them. The premise of the claim between them is not that the third-party defendant might be liable to the original plaintiff, but rather that the third-party defendant should cover part or all of the third-party plaintiff's liability to the original plaintiff. The substantive theory of the claim might be indemnity, contribution, subrogation, or warranty. So the focus of this lawsuit within a lawsuit will be on whether, under the substantive law and the actual facts, such secondary liability exists.

What then is the strategic structure of the *A-B-C* litigation above sketched, after *B* has impleaded *C*? *A* wants to establish the primary case against *B*. *B* wants to defeat *A*'s claim against him, especially if he lacks confidence in his claim against *C* or in *C*'s ability to satisfy a judgment; *B* also wants to establish *C*'s liability to him if *A*'s claim succeeds. *C* wants to see *A*'s claim against *B* defeated; *C* also wants to prove that in no event does *B* have a right of reimbursement from her, *C*.

Question: (8) Referring to Rule 14(a)(2), how should *C* plead?

The original plaintiff may have a related claim of his own against the impleaded newcomer, but originally elected not to press it. Injection of the third-party defendant into the case cannot of itself force the plaintiff to sue an unwanted adversary. Nevertheless, a plaintiff who finds a potential adversary injected into the case may well change his mind. See Rule 14(a)(3). Likewise, the third-party defendant may wish to assert a related claim against the original plaintiff. See Rule 14(a)(2)(D). Once a two-party lawsuit has become a three-cornered affair through a Rule 14 impleader, the whole matter of claims and counterclaims among the parties requires careful examination. See generally Wright & Miller §§ 1455–1459.

Questions: (9) *S*, driving her employer *M*'s car on *M*'s business, collides with an automobile owned and operated by *T*. Both cars receive damage, and both *T* and *S* suffer injuries. It is a matter of doubt whether *T* or *S* or both were negligent. Under the applicable substantive law of contributory negligence: (a) *if S was negligent and T was not*, *T* can recover from *S* and can recover also from *M*, although *T* of course cannot actually collect from *M* and *S* more than the total amount of his damages; if *M* has to pay because of *S*'s negligence, *M* is entitled to repayment from *S*; *M* is also entitled to recover against *S* for the damage to *M*'s car; (b) *if S was not negligent and T was*, *S* can recover against *T* for *S*'s personal injuries, and *M* can recover against *T* for the damage to *M*'s car; and (c) *if both S and T were negligent*, *M* can recover against *S* for the damage to *M*'s car but cannot recover against *T* for that damage. Furthermore, under that traditional law, there is no doctrine of comparative negligence, no right to contribution among concurrent tortfeasors, and no workers' compensation law. Assume that *T*, who might sue *M* or *S* or both, elects to sue *M* only; and *M* brings in *S* as a third-party defendant. Further assume no problems of subject-matter jurisdiction, venue, or service exist. If the three parties wish to assert all the claims that they may assert under Rule 14, how should they plead? And how should they respond to the claims made against them? What claims will be foreclosed from presentation in a later lawsuit if they are not asserted here?

(10) Suppose M, more than fourteen days after serving its answer to T's complaint, had sought leave to implead S under Rule 14(a)(1); T had opposed the impleader on the ground that S is impecunious and without personal-liability insurance and would be unable to reimburse M to any substantial extent; and T had also argued that the jurors would likely render a smaller verdict if they knew that S is ultimately responsible for payment. What action should the court have taken on leave to implead? Would your answer be different if M had impleaded S at the time it served its answer and T had moved to strike the third-party claim under Rule 14(a)(4)?

Now suppose a plaintiff against whom a counterclaim has been asserted wishes to reach a third person who is or may be liable to him for the counterclaim. See Rule 14(b); cf. Rule 14(a)(5).

(e) INTERVENTION

[Rule 24]

Rule 19(a)(1)(B)(i) requires that persons claiming interests at risk in the subject of an action must be joined as parties, if feasible; and if joinder is not feasible, Rule 19(b) indeed puts the question whether the court should not dismiss the action. Rule 24(a) takes the plausible position that when such a person, instead of waiting to be forced into the action, applies to the court by timely motion to intervene, the court must allow him to do so—assuming that one of the parties does not adequately represent his interest already. This is "intervention of right."

There is also "permissive intervention," that is, intervention in the discretion of the court under the terms of Rule 24(b). This subdivision echoes Rule 20 in part.

Rule 24(c) prescribes the procedure for intervention. See also Form 42. Intervention normally means that the intervenor becomes a full party on the appropriate side of the action, but the court may impose some conditions or restrictions on an intervenor's participation.

(f) CROSSCLAIMS

[Rule 13(g)]

Once you recognize that there may be several plaintiffs, several defendants, and several third-party defendants in an action, the possibility of conflict among the coparties (meaning any parties who are not opposing parties) should become apparent. The effect of Rule 13(g) is to permit, but not to compel, coparties to assert against one another any claims that bear certain prescribed relations to the rest of the controversy—such claims are called crossclaims. This provision is but another reflection of the general aim of the Rules to allow the court to dispose of related quarrels under the umbrella of a single action.

To illustrate with a simple example, assume that *A* sues *B* and *C*. *B* has a claim against *C* arising out of the same transaction. *B* may proceed by crossclaim against *C*, or he may instead elect to bring a separate action against *C*.

Questions: (11) Why should a counterclaim arising out of the same transaction be compulsory while a crossclaim against a coparty is merely permissive?

(12) Why must a crossclaim bear a certain prescribed relation to the rest of the controversy while a counterclaim may be entirely unrelated?

Rule 13(g) specifies no time limit for asserting crossclaims, leaving it to judicial discretion.

Now suppose *A* and *B* sue *C* for breach of contract. *C* pleads a permissive counterclaim against *A* and *B* for negligence. According to the second sentence of Rule 13(g), *A* may plead a crossclaim against *B* to establish that *B* is liable over to *A* in respect to *C*'s counterclaim. If *A* pleads this crossclaim against *B* and if *B* has a claim against *A* arising out of the transaction or occurrence that is the subject matter of that crossclaim, *B* must assert his claim as a compulsory counterclaim under Rule 13(a), because *A* has become an opposing party within the Rule.

––––––––

HENZ v. SUPERIOR TRUCKING CO., 96 F.R.D. 219 (M.D.Pa.1982). Husband and wife sued for the wife's personal injuries. Defendant sought to implead the husband, who was allegedly at fault. But Rule 14(a)(1) was unavailable because the husband was not a "nonparty"; Rule 13(g) was unavailable because the husband was not the defendant's "coparty"; and Rule 13(a) and (b) was unavailable because the contribution or indemnity claim was not a mature claim.

"The parties have suggested alternative ways of proceeding. The actions of the plaintiffs might be severed under Rule 21 and then the defendant could join Mr. Henz as a third party defendant in the action by Mrs. Henz. At this point, the action of Mr. Henz against the defendants could be left for a separate trial or Mr. Henz might raise his claims for loss of association and medical expenses as counterclaims."

District Judge Rambo accepted the suggestion of severance, while observing that any separate actions might also be consolidated or joined for trial.

––––––––

(g) CLASS ACTIONS

[Rules 23, 23.1, 23.2]

We have thus far considered who may and who must be included in an action as parties plaintiff, parties defendant, and third-party defendants, and what claims may be tried out among the parties. Rule

23 opens up a different concept, the class action, by which persons may sue or defend not merely on their own behalf but also on behalf of others not before the court as parties.

The law knows a variety of people who as parties in litigation are "stand-ins" for, or represent, others not joined as parties, just as they may represent those others in ordinary transactions. Thus a trustee sues or defends on behalf of the beneficiaries in respect to the trust property; a guardian stands in for the ward; an executor represents the estate or those interested in it. And similarly an adjudication in an action by or against a person owning an interest in land may inure to the benefit of or limit the rights of successors to that interest in the land by purchase or devolution—the predecessor may be thought of as representing those who follow her in ownership.

Class actions also involve a version of representation, but of a somewhat different order. Suppose a large number of persons have similar claims (or similar liabilities) arising from the same matrix of facts. If each person had to commence his own individual action (or defend an action brought against him alone), we would have repetitious proceedings with a large expenditure of time, money, and effort; we would also run into the possible embarrassment of inconsistent results, and this would be especially painful where the party opposing numerous claimants would find himself unable or very hard put to carry out the conflicting commands comprised in the inconsistent judgments; furthermore, the inability to hear from all interested persons, or indeed the practical inability to maintain small individual actions, might have deleterious effects on the full realization of substantive policies.

The operation of Rules 19 and 20 might result in a joinder of the claimants (or defenders) in a single action, which would be helpful as far as it went. But joinder under either Rule encounters obstacles of subject-matter jurisdiction, venue, and service; as the group reaches a certain size, presence of all the members makes the action unmanageable; furthermore, Rule 19 is narrow in scope, and Rule 20 joinder depends heavily on cooperative action.

So, to meet the unmet problems, the class action envisaged by Rule 23, as reconceived in its 1966 amendment, invoked the justificatory principle of adequate representation: under stated conditions and subject to certain safeguards, one or a few members may sue (or defend) on behalf of the class. Plainly, the rulemakers had to delimit and control such a class device lest it run roughshod over the "represented" absentee members of the class or abuse the parties or overwhelm the court. Moreover, the rulemakers had to keep an eye on the inevitable substantive effects of enabling a lawsuit in situations where practicalities previously prohibited the lawsuit.

Subdivision (a) of Rule 23 sets out four prerequisites for maintaining any class action: the class must be so numerous as to make joinder of all members impracticable; there must be questions of law or fact common to the class; the claims or defenses of the representative parties must be typical of the class; and there must be assurance that the representatives will be vigorous and competent champions of the class objectives. These are necessary conditions for maintaining a class action, but they are not sufficient. The case must also satisfy the provisions of subdivision (b), in that it must fit into one of the three categories of that subdivision. Those categories require the absentees to be related to the representative party in a certain way, either that the absentees share common and thus aligned substantive interests with their representative or that the former somehow consented to representation by the latter. The aim of both (a) and (b) is to ensure that class treatment promises considerable benefits and acceptable costs.

Subdivision (b)(1) contemplates the evident inconveniences, absurdities, or unfairnesses involved in individual adjudications. Illustrative of (1)(A) is a taxpayers' suit against a municipality to declare a bond issue invalid, and (1)(B) would include an action involving numerous persons claiming against a fund insufficient to satisfy all the claims.

Subdivision (b)(2) takes in cases where a defendant has made the characteristics of the class a basis for his own conduct, and final class-wide injunctive or corresponding declaratory relief is thus appropriate. The prime example is a desegregation case.

Coming to subdivision (b)(3), we find situations that are not as readily amenable to class treatment as those in (b)(1) and (b)(2), but in which that procedure may yet have definite advantages. For example, hypothesize false statements in a stock prospectus: any element of reliance may vary among the purchasers making up the class, and the amount of damages certainly will vary; there may, in addition, be quite legitimate reasons why the individual defrauded purchasers would want to institute and control their own lawsuits. Note that (b)(3) permits a class action only upon findings, first, that the questions common to the class "predominate" over those affecting individual members and, second, that a class action is "superior" to other methods of handling the controversy. Examine the factors listed in (b)(3) as pertinent to these findings.

Even when the court is prepared to make the findings favorable to maintaining a (b)(3) class action, the individual member may "opt out" of the class by simply informing the court and then proceed on his own. Under subdivision (c)(2)(B), the court must give the best notice practicable to the members of a (b)(3) class of the right of any member to withdraw from the class.[b] If the member does not opt out, he remains tied into the class. He then has the option of entering an appearance in

---

[b]　The best notice practicable might consist of notice by mail to reasonably identifiable individuals together with notice addressed to the class as a whole and published in newspapers, trade magazines, or the like. The plaintiff must initially bear the cost of this notice.

the action through counsel, which would ensure his being kept currently informed about the case.

Question: (13) Why did the drafters of Rule 23 not prescribe this notice and opting-out procedure for (b)(1) and (b)(2) cases?

Soon after commencement of the proposed class action, the court must determine under subdivision (c)(1) the propriety of allowing maintenance as a class action. Under (c)(4), class treatment may be possible or advisable only as to certain issues in a case, while the other issues would receive individual treatment. Similarly, under (c)(5), the court may deem class treatment proper only for certain subclasses of a proposed class.

Apart from any (c)(2) notice, Rule 23 has ample provision for discretionary notices as part of the process of the court's running any class action. See the variety of "management" provisions in subdivision (d). You will notice that Rule 23(d)(1)(B)(iii) reminds the court that it may on occasion decide to give notice to class members of their opportunity to intervene. Intervention is common in class actions. The intervening class member is typically claiming that for one reason or another the representative parties do not adequately represent his particular interest.

A class action, when carried out to the end (you should note subdivision (e) on dismissal and settlement), results in a judgment extending by its terms to the class, but excluding in (b)(3) cases the opters-out. The judgment so extends whether it is favorable to the class or not. See subdivision (c)(3). The design is that the judgment will receive respect according to its terms as res judicata in subsequent litigation, but the system cannot assure that result until the subsequent litigation occurs and a plea of res judicata is made and decided. If, for instance, a (b)(3) plaintiff-class action is sloppily handled and no reasonable effort is made to notify class members, a member who got no notice of the class action may pursue his separate action and therein attack the prior class-action judgment that nominally included him.

The amount-in-controversy requirement of 28 U.S.C. § 1332(a) applies to the claim of each class member, albeit in a complicated way to be treated later. As to satisfying its diverse-citizenship requirement, however, the court considers only the citizenships of the named parties, not the citizenships of all the members of the class—if it instead were to consider the citizenships of the absentee members, the federal court would of course more often lack jurisdiction. Similarly, for purposes of venue and service, the court considers only the named parties.

Actions relating to unincorporated associations.—The preceding paragraph leads to a mention of Rule 23.2 governing actions involving unincorporated associations, such as labor unions. Instead of joining all the association's members, lawyers have used a class action naming a few members as representatives in order to satisfy any diversity requirement and to ease venue and service requirements. Because of the special reasons for utilizing the class device here, the rulemakers added the specifically tailored Rule 23.2 in 1966, with references where appropriate therein to Rule 23.

Derivative actions by shareholders.—A derivative action allows one or more persons to sue for the benefit of similarly situated persons on a claim that their common fiduciary refuses to assert. Imagine that a shareholder of a corporation (or a member of an unincorporated association), believing that the corporation should be asserting a right of action against another person (who may be a wrongdoing director or officer of the corporation), makes demand on the directors, and if necessary on the shareholders, to sue. The demand is refused. A right to sue upon the corporation's claim may then accrue to the shareholder. If she succeeds in the suit, the recovery goes into the treasury of the corporation to be shared, in a manner of speaking, by all the shareholders.

These derivative actions have their place even when there are few shareholders. When the number of shareholders is large, the derivative action has the character of a class action, with one or several shareholders suing on behalf of all. See Rule 23.1, also added in 1966 but having antecedents in the original Rule 23.

Only the corporation's claim need satisfy any jurisdictional amount requirement. Although the corporation must be joined as a defendant with the alleged wrongdoer, the court very occasionally realigns it with the plaintiff-shareholder for diversity of citizenship purposes. Note also the special supplementary provisions for venue and service in these actions: 28 U.S.C. §§ 1401 and 1695.

(h) GENERAL OBSERVATIONS

Even taking into account the practical restrictions imposed by territorial limitations on effective service, by the venue requirement, and by limits on the kinds of cases that the federal courts may entertain, it is clear that an action under the Federal Rules may abundantly proliferate.

The issues of fact and law may of course be highly complex even when the action involves few claims and few parties. An antitrust case by a single plaintiff against a single defendant, for instance, may produce issues of vast difficulty. But multiclaim actions sometimes pose peculiarly perplexing problems of both management for the court and planning for the parties. And multiparty actions raise even more intense problems of management and planning. How far, for a minor example, may a court justifiably limit examination and cross-examination of a particular witness by the several parties to a lawsuit, and may the court require that parties aligned in interest speak through one lawyer only? Often problems of this order are solved by informal arrangements. Multiparty actions may also aggravate the strategic problems of counsel.

The tactic of divide and conquer, for example, is not unknown in the courtroom: plaintiff may join two defendants for the very purpose of driving between them.

Criticism of the Rules has been made on this account: it is said that they allow litigation to get "too big" in terms of claims and parties. On the one hand, the Rules themselves recognize the dangers of delay, expense, confusion, and prejudice that spring from attempting to handle too many claims and parties as a bundle. Accordingly, the Rules give the court certain discretionary powers to reshape the litigation. That is, even for a case properly pleaded between the limits of required and permissive joinder, the court can reduce the bundle in the interests of fairness and efficiency. See Rules 42(b) (separate trials in general), 21 (severance in general), 13(i) (separate trials of counterclaims and crossclaims), 14(a) (discretion in allowing third-party claims; severance and separate trials of third-party claims), 20(b) (protective orders and separate trials in relation to permissive joinder of parties), 23(c) (effective discretion in allowing class actions), and 24(b) (discretion in allowing permissive intervention). On the other hand, the court also has discretion to make the bundle larger when this will avoid inconvenience or reduce costs. See Rule 42(a) (joint trials and consolidation).

———

Jay Tidmarsh, "The Story of Hansberry: The Rise of the Modern Class Action"

Civil Procedure Stories 233 (Kevin M. Clermont ed., 2d ed. 2008), with case documents at http://civprostories.law.cornell.edu.

October 25, 1940, was a cloudy day in Washington, D.C., and it had turned chilly by the time that Earl Dickerson finished his argument in Hansberry v. Lee.[1] Had Dickerson stopped for a moment on the top of the stairs leading from the Supreme Court to the street, he might have reflected on the remarkable journey that had taken him to this place. Some 850 miles distant, on his left and over the Statue of Freedom facing him from the top of the Capitol dome, lay Canton, Mississippi, where he had been born. Some 600 miles distant, on his right and beyond the Oval Office in which he would soon become an unwelcome visitor [as an activist member of the Federal Employment Practices Committee], lay Chicago, Illinois, where he had migrated as a penniless teenager.

Now almost fifty years old, Dickerson had risen to become the "dean of Chicago's black lawyers." He had spent a generation trying to build up African-American businesses and tear down racism in employment, education, and housing. Hansberry v. Lee had opened a new front in Dickerson's war: turning to the courts to seek relief against racist behavior. What Dickerson wanted the courts to do in *Hansberry* was to

---

[1]   311 U.S. 32 (1940).

declare all racially restrictive covenants—private agreements among landowners not to sell their homes to African-Americans—illegal as a matter of property law and unenforceable in court as a matter of constitutional law. What he got in *Hansberry* was something rather different: a procedural ruling that allowed him to try to invalidate one covenant in one small neighborhood on the South Side of Chicago. Dickerson won the case, thus garnering an exceedingly rare—and by far the most notable—victory in the years before the Supreme Court ultimately decided in 1948 that courts could not constitutionally enforce racially restrictive covenants.[3] But Dickerson had not won his years-long battle against restrictive covenants.

Although Dickerson himself had to settle for less than half a loaf, *Hansberry* is regarded today as one of the great cases in American law. On one level, *Hansberry* is a leading example of a more general strategic shift among civil rights lawyers during the late 1930s toward a litigation-based approach to civil rights—an approach that ultimately paved the way for Brown v. Board of Education a generation later. On a second level, the case is a wonderful study of the ethics of adversarial deception, for the Supreme Court based its ruling on a critical fact that was, as Dickerson well knew even as he drove it home in his briefs, demonstrably false. On a third level, the Court's holdings in *Hansberry* established the foundations for the modern doctrines of claim preclusion and class actions. As such, *Hansberry* provides a fascinating lens through which to view the interaction between substantive rights and procedural enforcement—and between the simple demands of human justice and the complex intricacies of law.

Social and Legal Background

Driven out by the South's repressive Jim Crowism and lured in by the North's promise of good industrial jobs, a million African-Americans flowed into northern cities during the first decades of the twentieth century. No city felt the effects of the migration more than Chicago. In 1900, Chicago had a small African-American population—around 30,000, or about 2% of its total population. No neighborhood was more than 70% black, and a significant number of African-Americans lived in predominantly white neighborhoods. Over the next twenty years, the African-American population in Chicago more than tripled, to 109,000; between 1920 and 1930, the population doubled again, to more than 233,000. Neighborhoods on the west and south sides of Chicago's Loop became predominantly black. As the migration continued, these neighborhoods could no longer hold the burgeoning African-American population. Overcrowding became endemic, and African-Americans began to spread southward and westward.

Along the path of this movement stood the Washington Park subdivision, a three-block-by-nine-block tract about six miles south of the

---

[3]   Shelley v. Kraemer, 334 U.S. 1 (1948). . . .

Loop and due west of the University of Chicago. Washington Park had once been the site of a race track, and was built up between 1908 and 1912 with multi-family homes and a few apartment buildings. Its residents were solidly middle-class. Four of five were born in the United States. Among the immigrants, the plurality were Irish, German, or Russian. The neighborhood was religiously diverse: a synagogue, a Catholic church, and several Protestants churches (at least one of which might have had ties to the Ku Klux Klan) served the neighborhood's residents. There was, however, no diversity in race. In 1920 the neighborhood, which had 8100 residents at its pre-1934 peak, was 99.76% white, 0.00% African-American, and 0.24% "other."

Many neighborhoods in Chicago, Washington Park included, wanted to stem the tide of black migration for what can today be described as stereotypically racist reasons: residents feared that black people trashed homes, drove down property values, and left neighborhoods blighted as they rolled on to consume the next neighborhood. Property owners decided to draw a line in the sand at Washington Park. The problem was how to do so. One obvious solution—legislative action—was forbidden, for the Supreme Court, in Buchanan v. Warley,[8] had recently invalidated racially restrictive zoning ordinances.

Washington Park's residents hit on another solution: a racially restrictive covenant. *Buchanan* had forbidden *governments* from creating racial living patterns. It did not—indeed, it could not—ban *private* discrimination. Hence they turned to the racially restrictive covenant, under which private landowners banded together and voluntarily agreed not to sell or lease their properties to African-Americans—"negroes" or "coloreds," as the covenants usually described them. The covenant "ran with the land," which meant that subsequent property owners were obliged to honor the covenant even though they had not themselves agreed to it.

. . . .

Factual Background

1.   The Washington Park Covenant. Residents of Washington Park and the adjacent Woodlawn neighborhood created the Woodlawn Property Owners' Association in 1926. Its primary function during the years of its existence was to prevent African-Americans from moving into the area. The Association, which received moral and, more significantly, financial support from the University of Chicago, organized the effort to put a racially restrictive covenant into place in the Washington Park subdivision. During the fall of 1927 and January 1928, a member of the Association, accompanied by one of two notaries public and sometimes by "Reverend Father Gilmartin, and the Jewish Rabbi," knocked on doors

---

8   245 U.S. 60 (1917).

throughout the neighborhood, asking that the property owners sign the covenant.[23]

The covenant was as straightforward as it is to modern eyes abhorrent. It provided that:

> 1. ... [N]o part of said premises shall in any manner be used or occupied directly or indirectly by any negro or negroes, provided that this restriction shall not prevent the occupation, during the period of their employment, of janitors' or chauffeurs' quarters in the basement or in a barn or garage in the rear, or of servants' quarters by negro janitors, chauffeurs, or house servants, respectively, actually employed as such for service in and about the premises by the rightful owner or occupant of said premises.

> 2. ... [N]o part of said premises shall be sold, given, conveyed or leased to any negro or negroes, and no permission or license to use or occupy any part thereof shall be given to any negro except house servants or janitors or chauffeurs employed thereon as aforesaid.

The covenant was not enforceable immediately. Instead, in the part of the covenant that became the focus of *Hansberry*, the agreement provided:

> This agreement and the restrictions herein contained shall be of no force or effect unless this agreement or a substantially similar agreement, shall be signed by the owners above enumerated of ninety-five per centum of the frontage [of the Washington Park subdivision], or their heirs or assigns, and recorded in the office of the Recorder of Deeds of Cook County, Illinois, on or before December 31, 1928.

Once effective, the agreement was to run at least until January 1, 1948, after which the owners of 75% of the frontage could abrogate the agreement.

Ultimately the Association collected signatures for 542 of the 560 parcels listed on the covenant. The signatories included not only the bulk of home owners but also a business, a hospital, a synagogue, and several Protestant churches. According to one affidavit, whose content must be taken with a grain of salt, the Association eventually experienced difficulty in signing up the few remaining home owners. The Association nonetheless filed the covenant with the recorder of deeds on February 1, 1928. From that day forward, the Association enforced the covenant against black migration into the neighborhood—although the degree of strictness and regularity of enforcement was the subject of considerable dispute at the *Hansberry* trial.

---

[23]   Testimony [in *Hansberry* trial].

In retrospect, the Association was destined to lose its battle. It was a simple matter of economic and social pressure. By the early 1930s the neighborhoods to the north, west, and south of Washington Park were solidly African-American. The City of Chicago had recently condemned almost a-mile-and-a-half-long tract of houses on the South Side to begin construction of housing projects; as a result, 1,400 buildings were demolished and 18,000 African-Americans landed on the street. An estimate in 1937 put at 50,000 the total number of African-Americans in Chicago looking for housing. Overcrowding was acute, and sale and rental prices for good-quality housing stock for African-Americans were rising. Meanwhile, as a result of "white flight," the desire for newer homes, and the Depression, few whites were interested in moving into Washington Park. Apartments were vacant. Houses sat unsold on the market. The inexorable law of supply and demand had already washed away restrictive covenants in other areas, and it seemed unlikely that the Association could keep its homeowners from eventually breaking rank.

Nonetheless, the Association tried. Its membership met monthly, and the main focus of the discussion was "to keep our property for our own race, and . . . how we could best do that." The most influential of the Association's leaders was a shadowy figure who lay at the heart of the *Hansberry* case: James Joseph Burke. We know little about Burke. His wife, Olive Ida Burke, owned a house in Washington Park. She bought the house from Hannah M. Studdert, who had signed the restrictive covenant and allegedly represented to the Burkes that the covenant was valid. James Joseph Burke became active in the Association. At various times he was either its president or its secretary. His principal source of income appears to have been his salary from the Association. He went door to door to collect dues; he set up block captains; he ran the monthly meetings. "He was interested in the restrictive agreement, and in keeping the subdivision white."

2. Enforcing the Covenant Prior to Lee v. Hansberry. One of the principal tools that the Association used to keep the neighborhood white was to file lawsuits against those that tried to breach the covenant. The Burkes were in the thick of the litigation.

a. Burke v. Kleiman as the Key Case. The first case to enforce the Washington Park covenant was filed by Olive Ida Burke against Isaac Kleiman, Sam Kleiman, Charles Sopkin, and James Hall on October 21, 1932, in Cook County Superior Court. Isaac Kleiman had purchased a three-story brick apartment building at 417–19 East 60th Street from Ben Piser, who had signed the restrictive covenant. His half-brother, Sam Kleiman, held a mortgage on the property, and appeared as well to be involved in rental decisions. Charles Sopkin, the Kleimans' attorney, was the trustee on the mortgage and held a contingent interest in the property. James Hall was a prominent African-American physician and community leader.

Because Burke v. Kleiman figures so centrally in the outcome of Hansberry v. Lee, it is necessary to spend some time describing it. The case commenced after the Kleimans rented an apartment to Dr. Hall. Olive Ida Burke sought an injunction to remove Hall and to prevent the remaining defendants from renting any other apartments to "any person or persons of the negro race." In the critical phrase in her bill of complaint, Olive Ida Burke stated that she was bringing the case:

> on behalf of herself and on behalf of all other property owners in the district covered and affected by the [covenant], and who are, or whose grantors, direct or otherwise, were parties to said [covenant], and whose property interest will be adversely and injuriously affected by the violation . . . of the covenants and terms of said agreement.

This phrase is code, well understood by lawyers then and now to mean that Olive Ida Burke was purporting to bring a class action. . . .

After receipt of the bill of complaint, Sopkin put in an appearance for himself and the other three defendants. He also filed answers, containing general denials, on behalf of all four. Sopkin's theory of the defense was that changes in the neighborhood made it inequitable to enforce the covenant. The argument was legally reasonable, and Sopkin had some factual evidence to back it up. Prior to the time that Hall moved in, three other properties on the edge of the restricted area already had African-American occupants—the South Way Hotel with 60 African-American occupants, an apartment building with 24 African-American tenants, and another apartment building with 12 African-American tenants.

Burke's lawyer and Sopkin entered into a stipulation of Agreed Facts, and further agreed that the trial court could decide the case on the basis of this stipulation, without the need for a trial. Included in the stipulation was the following critical "fact":

> That, on, to-wit: the 30th day of September, 1927, about five hundred or over white persons duly executed and entered into a Restrictive Agreement described in the Bill of Complaint herein, said white persons constituting and comprising more than 95% of then owners of said frontage described in said Agreement, . . . which Agreement with respect to recordation and execution thereof was fully completed within the time set forth, and was on February 1, 1928, recorded in the Recorder's Office of the Recorder of Deeds of Cook County, Illinois . . . .[41]

On October 2, 1933, Judge Robert E. Gentzel issued a decree in favor of Olive Ida Burke. Judge Gentzel first found that he had "jurisdiction of

---

[41]   . . . This stipulation actually agrees to an irrelevant fact. The Washington Park covenant required that the owners of 95% of the *frontage* in the subdivision agree to the restrictions before they came into force. Sopkin's stipulation, however, stated only that 95% of the *owners* of frontage (who might have owned less than 95% of the frontage) had signed the agreement. No one in Burke v. Kleiman noticed this glitch.

the subject matter of this cause and of the parties thereto." He then found that "the material allegations in said bill of complaint are true." Next, he accepted the Agreed Facts, finding that "the facts and each of them [in the stipulation] are true and constitute the evidence in this cause." On the basis of this "evidence," he then found:

> that said indenture agreement is and has been in full force and effect at all times since the first day of February, 1928, and that all terms of said indenture agreement are entirely valid and binding upon the defendants until January 1, 1948, and is binding upon the defendants and each of them and all persons claiming under any contract, agreement, assignment, lease, bill of sale, or other conveyance . . . .

Judge Gentzel made no specific mention of Sopkin's argument concerning the change in the neighborhood, but he seemed to have rejected this defense implicitly.

The defendants took a timely joint appeal. On November 27, 1934, the appellate court affirmed the judgment, holding that, in light of all the material circumstances, the change in three parcels subject to the agreement was not "such a change in the character of the neighborhood as to warrant a presumption of abandonment of the agreement." The appellate court also expressed sympathy with Olive Ida Burke's uncontested, and entirely beside-the-point, argument that the covenants were valid under state and federal law.

The absolutely essential aspect of *Burke* was Judge Gentzel's finding, premised on the Agreed Facts, that the Washington Park covenant was valid. As we shall see in detail shortly, in *Hansberry* white home owners again filed suit when African-Americans sought to move into the neighborhood. The *Hansberry* defendants wanted to prove that the covenant was invalid, both as a matter of law and on the particular facts of this covenant. Their principal theory for the covenant's *factual* invalidity was the Association's failure to obtain the signatures of the owners of the requisite amount of frontage. The plaintiffs' response in *Hansberry* was to argue that the defendants could not challenge Judge Gentzel's determination that the covenant was valid. The defendants responded by arguing that the determination did not bind them because, first, they were not parties to the Burke case and, second, *Burke* was a fraudulent lawsuit purposely rigged by the Association and Sopkin to obtain a judicial determination that an invalid covenant was valid.

Sopkin's behavior in *Burke*, which was crucial to this second response, is subject to different interpretations. One question involves figuring out whom exactly Sopkin was representing. Although Sopkin was certainly capable of representing himself, it is not clear that he had in fact the authority to represent the others. . . .

Even if he had the authority to represent the other defendants, Sopkin's half-hearted efforts on behalf of his clients raise lingering doubts about whom he was really working for. He made two critical strategic decisions—to enter into an arguably incorrect stipulation of Agreed Facts and to submit the case to the judge without presenting evidence—that turned out very badly. In concentrating on his "changed neighborhood" argument, Sopkin sacrificed valuable legal and factual ground. Legally, Sopkin failed to make any of the arguments urged with vigor in prior cases . . .—that restrictive covenants violated state public policy, state and U.S. constitutions, and federal statutes; he made only a tepid argument that restrictive covenants violated state freedom-of-alienation principles. Factually, Sopkin failed to contest one issue on which the *Hansberry* case would turn—that the restrictive covenant was unenforceable because it had never been signed by the owners of the requisite amount of frontage.

    b.   Other Cases to Enforce the Agreement. As black Chicagoans moved into properties along the perimeter of the Washington Park subdivision, members of the Association brought other cases to enforce the covenant. . . .

    . . . .

    [One such] case, Plath v. De Launty, led on its facts directly to *Hansberry*. *Plath* began as a foreclosure action against an apartment building on the outer perimeter of Washington Park. In September or October 1936, a woman named Ruth Hoffman showed up at the real estate office in charge of leasing apartments for the building's receiver. Hoffman stated that she was from "Philadelphia or Washington" and was moving to the area. She agreed to a lease until September 30, 1937, and paid rent for two months. In fact, Hoffman, who was white, subleased her apartment to her cousin, Carl Hansberry, who was a leading figure in Chicago's African-American community. After discovering that the Hansberrys had moved in, the receiver petitioned the court handling the foreclosure proceeding to disavow Hoffman's lease. Two grounds were given: that the receiver had no power to agree to a lease that continued beyond February 1937, and that the lease had been obtained by fraud. The fraud claim again hinged on the validity of the covenant, because if the covenant was invalid, it would not have been fraudulent for Hoffman to sublease to the Hansberrys. The circuit court ducked the validity issue, holding on November 10, 1936, that the receiver had no power to enter into a long-term lease. The appellate court affirmed on this ground.

    The *Hansberry* battle began on May 7, 1937, when the receiver obtained a writ of assistance to evict the Hansberrys. A sheriff's deputy told the Hansberrys to leave by May 18, but he did not evict them then because the receiver had not advanced the sheriff's costs for eviction. No matter. Unknown to the sheriff, the Hansberrys had agreed to buy a home in Washington Park, and they would move into it by May 27.

    3.   The Hansberrys Buy a Home. Until February 1937, no one doubted Burke's tenacity or devotion to the cause of the Woodlawn Property Owners' Association. From his service as secretary of the

Chicago chapter of the NAACP, Carl Hansberry knew Burke's name. Earl Dickerson, who had led the fight against Chicago's restrictive covenants for years, "had heard of him and cursed him out a few times." In February 1937, however, Burke abruptly resigned from the Association, declaring to several people in the neighborhood that "I will plant colored people in every block in this region to show the people what I can do" . . . .

We do not know the motivation behind Burke's abrupt change of heart. His language suggests that he underwent no conversion on the road to Damascus. A few facts are clear. One is that the University of Chicago, unhappy with the image created by its affiliation with the Association, decided to switch tactics away from covenant enforcement toward building up stable and desirable African-American neighborhoods that would tamp down the desire for middle-class black Chicagoans to move into white areas. By early 1937, the University had hired a person to implement the new plan. At about the same time, the Association underwent a name change, to the Woodlawn Property Owners' League. Consistent with these facts, Burke told some residents that he felt the Association had treated him unfairly, that he would not participate in the work of the Association if he had to work under other people, and that he would seek revenge on members of the Association. It also appears that the Association owed Burke a lot of salary—perhaps as much as eight hundred dollars at one point and at least several hundred dollars in early 1937. Perhaps Burke's change of heart was simple economic opportunism. In his answer [in *Hansberry*], Burke alleged that he had discovered a few months before March 1937 that the covenant had never been signed by the requisite 95% of the frontage and that the covenant was therefore invalid. In a chance meeting in early 1937, he told the plaintiffs' attorney in *Hansberry* that he had just obtained a real estate license. Burke was on the verge of losing his salary, his job, and his home. With the standard 5% commission and six hundred homes that African-Americans would snap up, Burke must have realized that his intimate familiarity with the subdivision could lead to a financial boon.

Whether it was anger, revenge, greed, or some combination of the three, Burke was instrumental in finding homes for two African-American families: the Paces and the Hansberrys.

a.   *Harry Herbert Pace and 413 East 60th Street.* On March 5, 1937, just after he quit the Association, James Joseph Burke showed up at Johnson Realty Company and told the broker that he had a buyer for 413 East 60th, a two-story house on the edge of the subdivision just a couple of doors down from the apartment that the Kleimans had rented to Dr. Hall. The building was owned by Walter and May Harrower, who had signed the restrictive covenant. The Harrowers no longer occupied the house, and it had been on the market for rent or sale for more than a year. Mr. Harrower had a longstanding offer from an African-American to buy the property at a very good price, but he refused to sell to anyone other than a white person. The broker told Burke that he "couldn't sell to colored," and Burke replied, "This is a white man that wants to buy it."

The buyer whom Burke was referring to was Henry Aloysius Lutz, a wholesale clothier who dabbled in real estate. Lutz was simply a middleman. Burke had come into Lutz's office with an attorney named Joseph Bibb. According to Lutz, Burke had some credentials showing that he was from Johnson Realty, and Bibb said that he had a relative from New York who wanted to buy the property from Lutz, if Lutz would buy the property from the Harrowers. Lutz was to be paid a 5% commission, and Bibb was to supply all the money for the purchase. Not one to turn down easy money, Lutz bought the property from the Harrowers on April 14, 1937. At virtually the same moment, Lutz turned around and resold the property to Edward and Aeolian Parrish, Bibb's New York relatives. The sale price was $3,000. To finance the purchase, the Parrishes took out a mortgage for $3,500 with Supreme Liberty Life Insurance Company. Within 12 days, Harry Herbert Pace, the president of Supreme Liberty, had leased and moved into the house. Three weeks later, on May 17, 1937, Pace bought the house from the Parrishes.

Pace needed no introduction to African-Americans in Chicago or elsewhere. Born in Covington, Georgia, in 1884, Pace graduated as valedictorian of Atlanta University. He was a student of W.E.B. DuBois, and briefly collaborated with him on a newspaper. He taught Latin and Greek for a time, and then worked in banks and life insurance companies in Atlanta and Memphis. While working in Memphis in 1912, he met W.C. Handy, the "father of the blues," and wrote the lyrics for some of Handy's early hits. The two formed the Pace and Handy Music Company, which Pace left in 1921 to start Pace Phonograph Company. Pace Phonograph became a trailblazer in the music industry. Before 1921, recording companies had used only white artists on their labels. Seeking to tap into the black music market, Pace Phonograph created Black Swan Records, the very first black-owned record label for which the recording artists and musicians were African-American. Although it was initially an enormous success, and had profound effects on the recording industry, Black Swan Records went into bankruptcy within a couple of years. Pace got back on his feet, and established Northeastern Life Insurance Company in Newark, which quickly became one of the largest African-American businesses in the North. In 1929 he moved to Chicago after Northeastern Life merged with two other African-American insurance companies to create Supreme Liberty. Pace became president of Supreme Liberty, which sold insurance and other financial services, including mortgages, to African-Americans. Studying nights and weekends, Pace graduated in 1933 from law school, finishing fourth in his class.

Pace was not simply an entrepreneur; he was also deeply interested in issues of race. He was one of the founders of the Atlanta chapter of the NAACP, served as the chapter's first president, and was active in the affairs of the national NAACP. He gave a young Walter White, who would go on to lead the NAACP for many years, his first job as secretary of the Atlanta chapter. He also tried to promote black entrepreneurship. In 1936, he paid college expenses and found a job for the promising John H. Johnson, and in 1942 gave Johnson space in the Supreme Liberty building to start his own company. Johnson went on to become one of America's great entrepreneurial successes, building a publishing empire that included Ebony and Jet magazines. In short, Pace was what was sometimes called a "race man": a person who believed in establishing African-American businesses to serve the needs of the African-American community.

The cloak-and-dagger transactions that put Pace into a home in Washington Park were almost certainly engineered as a way to test the covenant. Although Pace denied at the trial that he had any affiliation with it, a law firm in the Supreme Liberty building was called Bibb, Tyree & Pace. No one denied that the first-named partner in the firm was Joseph Bibb, the man who had shown up with Burke at Lutz's office. Pace's wife was named Ethlynde Bibb, and one of the directors of Pace Phonograph had been Viola Bibb. Pace admitted that he had known the Parrishes for a few years before he bought the property from them. The Parrishes took out their mortgage with Pace's company, which lent almost exclusively to African-Americans, with Pace himself voting to approve the loan. Although Pace steadfastly claimed at trial that he was rather disinterested in Supreme Liberty's decision to provide a mortgage to the Parrishes, had no intention of moving into the property until the mortgage had been given, and had no intention of buying the property until he had moved in, Pace also admitted that he had met James Joseph Burke at some point before he moved into his home. A strong inference exists that Pace knew what was happening all along.

   b. Carl and Nannie Hansberry and 6140 South Rhodes Avenue. The transactions that led to the Hansberrys' purchase had a striking similarity to the Pace transactions, albeit with one fewer middlemen. In 1919 Eva Somerman and her husband had purchased 6140 South Rhodes, a three-story red-brick building containing three flats and a basement apartment. The Somermans had signed the restrictive covenant in 1928. In 1933, the Somermans sold their home to Joseph Stoltz, who then immediately conveyed the property to the First National Bank of Englewood. The Somermans continued to live in the building as tenants, along with two other tenants.

   In April 1937, Burke called on Albert Olsen, a cashier at the First National Bank who had known Burke from his time with the Association, and asked if the bank had any available properties. Olsen said that the bank had one property it had been trying to sell, 6140 South Rhodes. Burke returned a week later and told Olsen that he had a buyer, the unfortunately named Jay B. Crook.

Crook, a white man, was in the coal and stoker business. Crook had known Burke for three or four years, and he had also had business dealings with Carl Hansberry for four or five years. Carl Hansberry had told Crook earlier in the spring of 1937 that his family was looking for a place to move. When Burke casually ran into Crook during the same period, Burke asked him whether he was interested in, or knew of anyone who was interested in, property in Washington Park. Crook thought of the Hansberrys.

Like Harry Pace, Carl Augustus Hansberry was a well-known figure in the Chicago African-American community. He had been born in Glaston, Mississippi, in 1895. After graduation from Alcorn College in 1913, he moved to Chicago, eventually setting up a bank and his own accounting practice. He became an accountant with Chicago's Board of Education, and was a U.S. Deputy Marshal between 1929 and 1931. At the same time, he began to buy or lease apartments and rooming houses on the South Side. His signature tactic was to lease an apartment building and then cut the building up into smaller "kitchenette" apartments that he subleased—taking his profit on the difference between the rent he paid and the rent sublessees paid him. He had a reputation—whether deserved or not—of being a slumlord; at a minimum, according to his youngest child, Lorraine, he "utterly subscribed" to "private enterprise."[83]

Like Pace, Carl Hansberry saw business success and racial advancement as two sides of the same coin. The brother of William Leo Hansberry, a professor at Howard University and a founder of the African-studies movement, Carl Hansberry was active in the Chicago chapter of the NAACP. In 1936 he established the Hansberry Foundation with an endowment of $10,000 and a mission of fighting racial discrimination in Chicago; in 1938, he sued a railroad over its practice of segregating African-American passengers in inferior cars. The Hansberry home was a center of African-American intellectual life; visitors included W.E.B. DuBois, Langston Hughes, Duke Ellington, Jesse Owens, and Paul Robeson.

Less is known about Carl's wife, Nannie. The daughter of a minister, she was born in Columbia, Tennessee, in 1897 or 1898. She graduated from Tennessee Agricultural and Industrial University, where she trained to be a teacher. On Lorraine's birth certificate, she listed her occupation as "ward committeeman"; she and Carl were active in Republican Party politics. Both parents had an intensity of purpose, a regal bearing, and a certain flamboyance. Lorraine wrote that her parents' attitude toward their four children was "utilitarian": they were well cared for, but there was little overt affection or love. The Hansberrys taught their children that they must never betray "the family and the race," and that they "were the products of the proudest and most

---

[83]   Lorraine Hansberry, To Be Young, Gifted and Black: Lorraine Hansberry in Her Own Words 7 (Robert Nemiroff adaptor, 1969).

mistreated of the races of man; that there was nothing enormously difficult about life; that one *succeeded* as a matter of course."

Before they moved into Washington Park, the Hansberrys lived about four blocks away. Carl Hansberry said that he moved his family into the Washington Park neighborhood because the public school in Washington Park was less crowded and had a full-day program for his children; schools in African-American neighborhoods were so crowded that the children attended for only half a day. Perhaps also feeding into the desire to move was an incident when Lorraine was five; her kindergarten classmates threw ink on a white fur coat she had received for Christmas.

Although Carl Hansberry had never met Burke, Burke lay behind the Hansberrys' move into the neighborhood. Crook and Burke agreed with Olsen on a price of $6,500, and then made a deal with the Hansberrys to sell the property to them for $7,000. Crook put none of his own money into the purchase. The Hansberrys supplied the escrow money, and most of the remainder came from a mortgage, again financed by Supreme Liberty, for which Crook had applied. Crook testified that he was aware of the covenant when he was arranging the sale, but that he had been led to believe that the covenant was not effective.

The bank sold the property to Crook and his wife on May 19, 1937— Lorraine Hansberry's seventh birthday. For his efforts, Burke received a 5% commission, presumably paid by the bank, of $325. Crook and his wife quitclaimed the property to the Hansberrys on May 27, 1937. When Olsen heard that the Hansberrys had moved into the Somermans' first floor and basement apartments, he desperately tried to hold up delivery of the deed to Crook. But it was too late.

A comparison of the Pace and Hansberrys deals points toward a common architect. Although Harry Pace had known Carl Hansberry for a couple of years before they both moved into the Washington Park neighborhood, Pace claimed at trial that he was unaware that the Hansberrys intended to move into the property on South Rhodes Avenue. Pace also testified that, when he voted to approve Crook's mortgage application, he never questioned why Crook was applying for a mortgage with Supreme Liberty. Crook's testimony that he had "a couple of colored loans" with Supreme Liberty lends some credence to Pace's claim. But the striking similarities in method, and the incredibility of Pace's claim that he knew nothing of the mortgage loan to the Parrishes, suggest that a larger plan was afoot to crack open the Washington Park covenant.

The neighborhood lashed back. During the few months that the Hansberrys lived in the house on South Rhodes Avenue, Lorraine Hansberry was "spat at, cursed and pummelled in the daily trek to and from school." Angry white mobs sometimes "howl[ed]" outside the house, and Nannie Hansberry patrolled the house at night with a "loaded German luger" whenever Carl was out for the evening. Lorraine was nearly killed once, when an object thrown through a window narrowly missed her.

The neighborhood also resorted to more traditionally legal means to enforce the covenant. One lawsuit went after Pace, Lutz, the Parrishes, and Supreme Liberty. Another lawsuit, Anderson v. Hansberry, sought damages from Hansberry, Pace, Burke, Crook, and Supreme Liberty. The third lawsuit, Lee v. Hansberry, sought an injunction that would not only dislodge the Hansberrys from the neighborhood, but also shut down the entire enterprise whose machinations seemed to lie behind the purchases by Pace and the Hansberrys. In filing Lee v. Hansberry, however, the neighborhood made its first critical mistake, for the scope and stakes of the lawsuit brought into the case Earl Burrus Dickerson and a cadre of talented civil rights lawyers that the Hansberrys alone could not have hoped to muster.

Prior Proceedings

1.   **The Litigants and Lawyers.** Lee v. Hansberry was filed on June 7, 1937, in Cook County Circuit Court. The plaintiffs were six residents of the neighborhood, including the neighbors on each side of the Hansberrys. All of the plaintiffs or their predecessors in interest had signed the restrictive covenant. The plaintiffs brought the case as a class action "on behalf of themselves and on behalf of other plaintiffs similarly situated."

There were nine defendants. Two of the defendants, W.T. Mooney and Elizabeth Cotzones, were the tenants of the second-floor and third-floor apartments of 6140 South Rhodes. They never hired lawyers or appeared in the case. They had no reason to, as the plaintiffs' theory was that they should not pay rent to the Hansberrys because the Hansberrys were illegal owners of the property. In a preliminary injunction of July 8, 1937, the trial court agreed, and ordered the tenants to pay their rent to the clerk of the court.

The other seven defendants were Carl and Nannie Hansberry, Harry Herbert Pace, Supreme Liberty, James Joseph Burke, Jay Crook, and Israel Katz. The inclusion of Katz showed the extent of the neighborhood's paranoia and willingness to intimidate waffling neighbors. Katz, who had signed the restrictive covenant, lived just down the street from the Burkes. Earlier in 1937, he had been subpoenaed by Harry Raymond, the attorney who had represented Olive Ida Burke in Burke v. Kleiman, in an administrative proceeding before the Department of Education and Registration. The proceeding concerned William Sexton, an African-American real estate broker. At the hearing Raymond asked Katz whether he would ever sell his property to an African-American. Katz reportedly answered: "Yes I would. I would sell it to anybody that I could get a buyer to purchase it. I would sell it now if I could." Even though Katz claimed—in testimony that the court said "wasn't very satisfactory and convincing"—that he had never talked with

Burke about selling his home, the neighborhood evidently feared that his property would be the next one to be sold in violation of the covenant.

Charles Churan, who lived in Washington Park, was the plaintiffs' lead counsel. Churan's theory of the case was that the seven defendants had engaged in a conspiracy, with Burke as the ringleader, to place African-Americans into Washington Park by means of dummy sales to middlemen. The lawsuit therefore sought a series of injunctions, including the removal of the Hansberrys; the sale of their home either back to Crook or to another white person; a prohibition against Burke from arranging sales that would lead to African-Americans living in the neighborhood; a prohibition against Pace and Supreme Liberty from making loans that would help African-Americans buy property in the subdivision; and an order barring Katz from selling his property to an African-American.

On the other side stood a group of talented lawyers that might be described as the "dream team" of Chicago's civil rights bar. . . .

. . . .

2. *Cook County Circuit Court.* The pleadings in Lee v. Hansberry make for good review of the rules for equity and code pleading. Suffice it to say that motions to dismiss, motions to strike, answers, objections to answers, motions to dissolve, rejoinders, objections to rejoinders, replies, demands for bills of particulars, and amendments flew back and forth for nine months. By the time of trial, the basic issues had been sketched out: The plaintiffs were claiming a conspiracy to violate the covenant. The defendants were contesting the validity of the covenant on both legal and factual grounds. In reply, the plaintiffs argued that racially restrictive covenants were legally and factually valid. As for the covenant's factual validity, the plaintiffs relied on the res judicata (or, in modern parlance, preclusive) effect of Burke v. Kleiman. In particular, they argued that the defendants or their predecessors in interest were parties to *Burke* and, under ordinary principles of res judicata, were therefore bound by the judgment in *Burke* and, in particular, by the finding that the covenant was effective. In rejoinder to the res judicata argument, the defendants claimed that *Burke* was a fraudulent and collusive suit not worthy of preclusive effect.

Prior to the trial, the most significant event was the July 8, 1937, decision of Judge Michael F. Feinberg to grant the plaintiffs' request for a preliminary injunction. Judge Feinberg ordered the Hansberrys out of their home within 90 days and forbade the other defendants from taking any action that might result in more African-Americans in Washington Park. Reportedly, Judge Feinberg ended his decision from the bench with the remark: "Negroes should not live where they are not wanted. I do not go where I am not wanted."

An appellate court affirmed the preliminary injunction on October 7, 1937. Shortly afterwards, the plaintiffs obtained a writ of assistance from the sheriff to evict the Hansberrys. The deputy sheriff went to the Hansberrys' home on October 22 and announced his business to a daughter, Mamie. He did not then dispossess them, because the plaintiffs had not advanced the funds for him to do so. The Hansberrys left of their own volition shortly afterwards, sometime in October 1937.

Trial commenced before Judge George W. Bristow on March 7, 1938. The trial was not scintillating. The thrust of the plaintiffs' case was to prove the chain of title to the Pace and Hansberrys properties, the convoluted artifices through which both properties came to be owned by African-Americans, and the deceitful involvement of Burke and Supreme Liberty in the artifices. The trial produced no smoking gun showing that a conspiracy existed, but a strong implication lingers from the testimony that Burke and Supreme Liberty, perhaps acting in parallel as much as in concert, were both playing a role in bringing African-Americans into the neighborhood.

The defendants' focus at trial was the invalidity of the covenant. Aside from their arguments that no restrictive covenant was legally enforceable, the defense offered numerous theories to prove that the Washington Park covenant in particular was invalid: that owners of less than 95% of the frontage had signed; that some owners signed without knowing the content of the covenant; that some of the signatures had not been notarized properly; that some of the signatures were not those of the true property owners; that Burke v. Kleiman was a fraud; that numerous blacks already lived in the subdivision (an argument that was relevant both to a changed-neighborhood argument and to a laches or negligence argument); that black Chicagoans needed more living space; and that black ownership resulted in higher rather than lower property values.

At trial the plaintiffs' only response to the argument of the covenant's factual invalidity was res judicata: that Burke v. Kleiman . . . had already determined the validity of the covenant; that the First National Bank of Englewood (the prior owner of the Hansberrys' property) was a member of the *Burke* class and was bound by the finding of validity; and that the Hansberrys, as successors to the property, were class members also bound by this judgment. As a result, the plaintiffs repeatedly objected to the admissibility of the defendants' evidence seeking to prove the covenant's invalidity. At no point did the plaintiffs produce evidence that the covenant was actually signed by the requisite 95% of the frontage—even though they had some evidence, of uncertain quality, by which they might have tried to make such a proof.

Judge Bristow made oral findings of fact on June 17, 1938, followed by a written decree and judgment on August 19, 1938. In his oral findings, he admitted that he thought the case was a hard one, and that he had not finally made up his mind about it until about twenty minutes before he got on the bench. His oral findings were a mixed bag, with something for each side. He ruled for the plaintiffs, finding a conspiracy among the various defendants—including, rather incredibly, Katz—to violate the restrictive covenant. On the covenant's validity, he found that *Burke* had been a class action, that the Hansberrys were in effect members of the class, that *Burke* had determined the question of the covenant's validity, that *Burke* also settled the question of the constitutionality of the covenant because the question could have been raised in *Burke*, and that *Burke* was therefore res judicata on the issue of the covenant's factual and legal validity. Judge Bristow had particularly harsh words for [James Joseph] Burke. He described Burke as a "villain" who turned on the Association that "he had lived off for years" and as the "principal force" in bringing the *Burke* "dummy proceeding," which "was all a fraud." Burke, the judge declared, "is just the same sort of wrongdoer and evil minded person when he threatened to and did carry out his threats that he was going to see that colored people were allowed to purchase in this area." But Judge Bristow's findings also gave the defendants some ammunition. He made clear that he thought that the covenant was not in fact valid, stating that "[t]he proof unquestionably shows that . . . the agreement was not signed by ninety-five per cent of the owners of the frontage in the restricted area." In a line of his opinion that became a central "fact" in the case as it proceeded through appeal, the judge stated, "I did not check up the exact figures, but counsel in their brief indicate that it was something like fifty-five per cent instead of ninety-five per cent."

Judge Bristow's written decree was far more tempered. (One reason, undoubtedly, is that the decree had been drafted by Churan.) To begin with, the decree never put an exact figure on the percentage of frontage that signed. Nor, for that matter, did it ever acknowledge that the covenant was factually invalid. It simply noted that the defendants had objected to introduction of evidence regarding the covenant until there was proof that the covenant had been signed by owners of the requisite frontage, and that the plaintiffs "offered no proof upon this subject." Accepting the res judicata argument, however, the court overruled the defendants' objection to introduction of the covenant. The written decision also contained three other significant dimensions. First, on the question of the class action, the court repeated its oral finding that Burke v. Kleiman was a class action; it also found that Lee v. Hansberry was a class action. Second, the court rejected the defendants' arguments that the covenant was unconstitutional, illegal as a restraint on trade or as against public policy, or otherwise violative of their civil rights under the Constitution. Third, because Burke was the "arch conspirator" who had "inaugurated" the entire "fraudulent scheme and conspiracy" of the defendants, the court found that "Burke and his associated conspirators come into this court with unclean hands and cannot by reason of their misconduct avail themselves of the argument that Burke v. Kleiman does not constitute res adjudicata." At no point on appeal did the plaintiffs rely on this third finding. This failure was another, and perhaps fatal, strategic mistake of Churan and the lawyers who represented the plaintiffs, for the finding of unclean hands might well have insulated the case from Supreme Court review [as an independent and adequate state ground].

In short, the trial's outcome hinged on certain factual determinations: whether *Burke* was in fact a class action; whether the covenant had been signed by owners of the requisite frontage; and whether *Burke* was a fraudulent, collusive suit. The trial court agreed with plaintiffs' position on the first question, with the defendants' position on the second, and with the defendants' position on the third. As I shall now explain, my reading of the records suggests that the court might have been mistaken about the second and third findings.

a.   *Was Burke v. Kleiman Even a Class Action?* . . .

With our modern understandings, *Burke* does not look like a class action. . . .

Nonetheless, it appears that *Burke* was in fact a class action. Illinois class-action decisions of the period required no further action beyond pleading a claim as a class action. . . .

b.   *Was the Covenant Effective?* . . . The U.S. Supreme Court would accept the defendants' version of the story—that owners of only "about 54%" of the frontage had signed the covenant, so that the covenant was never effective—and that finding would help to shape the Court's ultimate decision to reverse.

The truth, however, is less certain than this conventional answer. On at least one possible construction of the covenant, the requisite 95% had signed—or, put differently, the plaintiffs had a credible argument that the covenant was effective. The notion that only 54% of the frontage had signed—an important part of the *Hansberry* lore—is demonstrably false. . . .

. . . .

c.   *Was Burke v. Kleiman a Fraudulent, Collusive Suit?* Another "fact" that colored the Supreme Court's view of *Hansberry*, as well as our understanding of class actions ever since, was the fraudulent and collusive nature of *Burke*. Trying to vitiate its preclusive effect, the defendants vigorously insisted that *Burke* was a set-up from start to finish. In his oral findings, Judge Bristow agreed, calling the suit "all a fraud." But was it? From a distance of almost 75 years, the bona fide nature of *Burke* is the hardest question of all to answer. My own judgment is that *Burke* was not fraudulent or collusive—or at least that the *Hansberry* defendants never proved it to be so at trial.

. . . .

3.   Illinois Supreme Court. The defendants, minus Crook, appealed to the Illinois Supreme Court. The defendants' brief raised twelve arguments over 106 pages; the plaintiffs' brief raised fourteen arguments over 124 pages; and the defendants' reply brief urged thirteen arguments over 52 pages. All that needs to be said about the briefs on both sides is how poorly they anticipated the ultimate disposition of the case in the U.S. Supreme Court. The defendants' brief began with an attack on the factual validity of the covenant, and then moved through the legal arguments, under both state law and the U.S. Constitution, against racially restrictive covenants. It was not until the ninth argument, in the third subpart of the fifth part, that anything remotely resembling the Supreme Court's ultimate rationale appeared; a bit more emerged in the tenth argument. The defendants' case primarily concerned the factual and legal validity of the racially restrictive covenant, not class actions. Because the plaintiffs' brief led with the res judicata effect . . . , the defendants' reply brief finally moved their class-action argument into first position. But even here, their arguments were grounded in state law—that *Burke* . . . did not meet the class-action requirements under Illinois law, and that Illinois's principles of res judicata did not extend to issues that were not actually litigated. The argument that the *Burke* class action violated the Due Process Clause was never precisely presented.

Against that backdrop, the opinion of the Illinois Supreme Court makes sense. In a 5–2 decision entered on October 10, 1939, the court found that *Burke* was a class action, that the present defendants (as either class members in *Burke* or successors in interest to class members) were bound by that judgment, and that Illinois's res judicata principles bound the defendants to the finding that the covenant was effective. Responding to the argument that the covenant had never been effective, the court stated: "The principle of res judicata covers wrong as well as right decisions, for the fundamental reason that there must be an end to litigation." Responding to the argument that fraud and collusion in *Burke* undermined its res judicata effect, the court noted: "There is no evidence of fraud or collusion in that case. . . . [T]here is no showing of fraud or collusion in procuring that stipulation, or that there was not an actual controversy in the case. . . . As far as the record shows, if any fraud was committed, it was by Burke after he left the association."

Having thus dealt with the covenant's factual validity, the Illinois Supreme Court next rejected the argument that the covenant was legally invalid. It did so not on the merits, but again on res judicata grounds. Res judicata "extends not only to matters actually determined in the former suit, but also embraces all grounds of recovery and defense involved and which might have been raised." Because the constitutional and state-law policy arguments were available to the defendants in *Burke*, the court reasoned, the *Hansberry* defendants were unable to raise the question in their case.[131]

---

[131] You might have noticed that this logic holds no water. Under the court's reasoning, the persons bound by the judgment, and thus unable later to raise the constitutional and state-law defects with the covenant, were the defendants in *Burke*—the Kleimans, Sopkin, and Hall. But the *Hansberry* defendants, or their predecessors in interest, had been *plaintiffs*, not *defendants*, in *Burke*; they had no incentive to raise the legal invalidity of the covenant.

Significantly, the majority did not address the question of whether the class action in *Burke* denied the *Hansberry* defendants their due process right to be heard—in large measure because the defendants themselves did not well articulate such an argument. But the point did not escape Justice Elwyn R. Shaw, who filed a dissent. Taking as true Judge Bristow's oral finding that fraud lay at the heart of *Burke*, the dissent articulated the argument that *Burke* violated due process: "[E]ven the humblest of these five hundred [absentees in *Burke*] had a right to his day in court, to be made a party to the suit and to be given an opportunity to defend it." In a draft of his opinion, Justice Shaw had been more pointed, writing that if a person could be fraudulently bound to an agreement signed by a stranger, "it would be a good idea to repeal the 14th amendment because that is exactly what we are doing."

    4.   *United States Supreme Court.* After unsuccessfully seeking rehearing in the Illinois Supreme Court, the Hansberrys, Pace, Supreme Liberty, Burke, and Katz petitioned the U.S. Supreme Court for a writ of certiorari on March 11, 1940. The Supreme Court granted the writ on April 22, 1940.

    In their petition for a writ of certiorari and briefs, the petitioners argued that the Equal Protection and Due Process Clauses of the Fourteenth Amendment forbade the application of res judicata to the members of a class action who had received neither notice of the class action nor an opportunity to defend their own interests; that *Burke* was not a proper class action, given the individual and potentially conflicting interests of various property owners; and that racially restrictive covenants were unconstitutional under the Fourteenth Amendment. The respondents' brief countered by arguing that the petitioners' arguments regarding res judicata and class actions involved matters of Illinois law beyond the Supreme Court's power to review; that the petitioners' arguments lacked an evidentiary foundation because their evidence had been admitted subject to the plaintiffs' res judicata objection, which Judge Bristow ultimately sustained; and, unsurprisingly, that [past cases] had upheld the constitutionality of racially restrictive covenants. Although the petitioners' briefs got progressively better, they were never successful in shaping the due process argument into the form that the Supreme Court ultimately articulated.

    Argument was held on October 25, 1940. Dickerson argued for the petitioners. McKenzie Shannon, who had been brought into the case when it reached the Supreme Court, argued for the respondents; Churan, who had primarily handled the litigation for the plaintiffs until that point, did not even appear on the respondents' brief. . . .

The Supreme Court Decision

    The Supreme Court issued its opinion quickly, on November 12, 1940. Justice Stone's opinion was joined by five other justices. Justices McReynolds, Roberts, and Reed concurred in the result without opinion. There were no dissents. The opinion is not a model of clarity, which, in light of the opacity of the briefs and the novelty of the petitioners' argument, is not surprising. Two aspects of the opinion, however, stand out.

The first is the Court's holding—not new, perhaps, but stated with a power that has made it the standard citation on the point ever since—that:

> It is a principle of general application in Anglo-American jurisprudence that one is not bound by a judgment in personam in a litigation in which he is not designated as a party or to which he has not been made a party by service of process.

Thus, res judicata can later be asserted against only those who were parties to a case. That principle, on its own, did not resolve *Hansberry*, for the plaintiffs had argued from the beginning that the *Hansberry* defendants, as class members, were parties in *Burke*. Indeed, the Court itself said that a "recognized exception" to the "no joinder, no binding effect" principle—one that was "not precisely defined by judicial opinion"—was that a judgment in a class action "may bind members of a class action or those represented who were not made parties to it."

The Court's second central point was that a court could not, consistent with due process, bind the *Hansberry* defendants to the judgment in *Burke*. This holding was novel. For the first time, the Court recognized that the Due Process Clause in some fashion regulated or constrained state class actions. At one level, the Court's syllogism is clear enough. *Burke* failed to afford its class members constitutionally adequate process. Because the class action was inconsistent with the Constitution, the *Hansberry* defendants (or their predecessors in interest) were not proper members of the class. Because they were not proper members of the class, they were not proper parties. Because they were not proper parties, they were not bound by the judgment and findings in *Burke*. Because they were not bound, they were free to argue that the covenant was ineffective. The holding of the Illinois Supreme Court to the contrary was wrong, and the judgment in favor of the plaintiffs was reversed.

Today we accept every step of this logic—except for the first—as self-evidently correct. It is the first step that continues to create problems in understanding *Hansberry*. The problem is that the Court was never clear about exactly how *Burke* failed to afford its class members due process. The Court observed:

> It is familiar doctrine of the federal courts that members of a class not present as parties to the litigation may be bound by the judgment where they are in fact adequately represented by parties who are present, or where they actually participate in the conduct of the litigation in which members of the class are present as parties, or where the interest of the members of the class, some of whom are present as parties, is joint, or where for

any other reason the relationship between the parties present and those who are absent is such as legally to entitle the former to stand in judgment for the latter.

The Court went to some pains to acknowledge the force of the respondents' arguments that the scope of res judicata and the requirements for class actions are matters of state law. Granting "a proper regard for divergent local institutions and interests," however, the Due Process Clause came into play "in those cases where it cannot be said that the procedure adopted, fairly insures the protection of the interests of absent parties who are bound by it." Thus, a state class action passed muster "provided that the procedure were so devised and applied as to insure that those present are of the same class as those absent and that the litigation is so conducted as to insure the full and fair consideration of the common issue."

Applying these ideas to *Burke*, the Court stitched the *Hansberry* defendants' constitutional and state-law arguments into a holding that the *Burke* plaintiffs who sought to enforce the covenant "could not be said to be in the same class with or represent those whose interest was in resisting performance." *Burke* involved "dual and potentially conflicting interests" that made it "impossible to say . . . that any two of [the putative class members] are of the same class." The Court concluded:

> [A]ll those who are free alternatively either to assert rights or to challenge them [cannot be] deemed adequately to represent any others in the class in litigating their interests in either alternative. Such a selection of representatives for the purposes of litigation, whose substantial interests are not necessarily or even probably the same as those whom they are deemed to represent, does not afford that protection to absent parties which due process requires. . . . Apart from the opportunities it would afford for the fraudulent and collusive sacrifice of the rights of absent parties, we think that the representation in this case no more satisfies the requirements of due process than a trial by a judicial officer who . . . may have an interest in the outcome of the litigation in conflict with that of the litigants.

To ask class representatives in *Burke* to represent the interests of the *Hansberry* defendants was to ask them to shoulder "a responsibility which, in view of their dual interests it does not appear they could rightly discharge."

Hansberry, then, establishes the constitutional floor for all class actions, state or federal: class representatives must "adequately represent" absent class members. The facts and language of *Hansberry* link adequate representation with the avoidance of conflicts of interest within the class. That approach worked in *Hansberry*, because the interests were binary and mutually exclusive—either a property owner wanted the covenant enforced or it did not—and determining a conflict of interest in such a case is fairly simple. Looking beyond the facts of

Hansberry, the Court provided no guidance about how tightly aligned the class members' interests must be. Must all class members have *identical* interests in order for one class member to adequately represent another? The Court mentioned joint liability cases as an example of a situation in which all class members had undivided interests, but such cases are very rare in the law. In many large-scale disputes, interests are more varied and nuanced. One plaintiff, for instance, might prefer his case to be filed in one forum, while another might want her case filed in a second and a third plaintiff in a third. Or one plaintiff might be so angry with the defendant that she will not settle at any price, a second will settle only for a high price, and a third who dislikes controversy will settle for a low price. After *Hansberry*, can the first plaintiff adequately represent the latter two in either of these situations?

Indeed, the notions of adequate representation and conflict of interest prove elusive even on the seemingly egregious facts of *Hansberry*. At the time that *Burke* was filed, the Hansberrys' predecessors in interest, the Somermans, were as interested in enforcing the covenant as Olive Ida Burke; the First National Bank of Englewood, which bought the property while *Burke* was pending, was so interested in enforcing the covenant that it sought to revoke the deed after it found out about the Hansberrys' purchase in 1937. From all appearances, Olive Ida Burke shared these interests. The record contains no evidence that, *during* the time that *Burke* was being litigated, any member of the *Burke* class had a conflict of interest because they did not wish to enforce the covenant in the way that Olive Ida Burke did. Nor is there evidence that Olive Ida Burke failed to represent adequately the interests of those who wished the covenant enforced. If *Hansberry*'s point is that a class member's shift in interests, years after the class action is over, can undo a judgment decided when the member's interests were well represented, then few class judgments could ever bind class members.

It was too much to expect that *Hansberry* would articulate answers to these questions. The constitutional principle was new, and the petitioners' brief gave the Court little assistance in framing a precise rule. Moreover, the case seemed to involve egregious facts—a 54% signing rate and fraud in the prior class action—that did not require the Supreme Court to specify the decision's outer boundaries.

A fascinating question is whether the Supreme Court would have decided the case as it did if it had known the actual facts: that the covenant had been signed by far more than 54% of the neighborhood and even might have been effective, and that *Burke* was probably not a fraudulent or collusive action. Would the Court have then chosen to reach the constitutionality of the restrictive covenant, and would it have decided the issue in the same way that Shelley v. Kraemer did eight years later? Would it have granted certiorari at all if it had known that the facts were closer and murkier than the petitioners represented? On the one hand, nothing in the Court's opinion hinges on either the ineffectiveness of the covenant or the fraudulent, collusive nature of *Burke*. As long as the effectiveness of the covenant was debatable, which it certainly was, potential conflicts of interest existed concerning its enforceability. Moreover, as the Court noted, adequacy problems can exist even without fraud and collusion by the class representative. On the other hand, the Court recited the 54% figure in its description of the facts, and the apparent fraud and collusion in *Burke* twice in the opinion. These "facts" have always been the compelling and memorable part of the *Hansberry* story. I doubt that the Justices of the Supreme Court were immune to the power of these facts or to the injustice of which they spoke. It's just that the facts might not have been true.

The Immediate Impact of Hansberry

1.   Further Proceedings. The Supreme Court's decision did not end the *Hansberry* case, as the plaintiffs were quick to point out when the case was remanded. A live controversy still existed over the validity of the covenant. Nonetheless, the steam went out of the plaintiffs. Maybe they saw the handwriting on the wall, realizing the futility of stemming the African-American migration into the neighborhood. Maybe they knew they could not prove the effectiveness of the covenant. Maybe their funding dried up. Whatever the reason, the final document in the *Hansberry* file, signed by the lawyer who appeared after Churan withdrew, was an undated memorandum in support of a motion to retry the case. . . . And that's it. The defendants filed no response, and the case trailed into oblivion.

2.   Influences on the Neighborhood. The Washington Park neighborhood quickly switched from white to black occupancy, and has remained primarily an African-American neighborhood since that time. Today conditions in the neighborhood are changing. On the one hand, many buildings are boarded up, and empty lots bear the earmark of urban blight. Vacancy rates are high. On the other hand, the exteriors of most buildings are well-kept. There are some signs of revitalization, rehabilitation, and community involvement. The Hansberrys' home, 6140 South Rhodes Avenue, is still standing, huddled tightly in the middle of nearly identical three-story homes along the block. It shows signs of recent renovation. No plaque or marker informs the passer-by of the home's historical significance.

3.   Effects on the Litigants and Lawyers. Of Charles Churan and the plaintiffs who fought to keep their neighborhood segregated, I have discovered little. Churan's first appearance in a reported decision in Illinois was in 1903, so he was already nearing retirement age when he handled *Hansberry*. After *Hansberry*, he made appearances in only two more reported cases. In a 1941 case, a procedurally messy affair in which he represented a defendant class of Washington Park property owners, he was still arguing the preclusive effect of *Burke*. The Illinois appellate court had no choice but to follow *Hansberry*, which was barely two months old, and to reject his arguments. He also lost a 1943 case, which involved an unrelated probate matter, and then disappeared from the legal records.

George Bristow, the trial judge who sloppily constructed the "facts" on which the myth of *Hansberry* has been built, was appointed to an appellate judgeship in 1942. He served in that position until his election as a justice on the Illinois Supreme Court in 1951. He died on November 12, 1961.

On the defendants' side, it is fair to say that *Hansberry* treated the lawyers better than it treated the litigants. Seeking to ride on his notoriety from *Hansberry* all the way to the halls of Congress, Hansberry sought the Republican nomination for the House of Representatives in 1940. He lost in the primary. He eventually became disillusioned chasing the American dream in a racist society. In 1945, while living in a home within a stone's throw of Washington Park, he decided to emigrate to Mexico City, where he became "a permanently embittered exile." As he was preparing to move his family to join him there, he was stricken with an undetermined disease, and after languishing in a sanatorium for nine days, died on March 10, 1946, at the age of 50. He left his family an estate valued at more than $83,000—an amount equivalent to about $960,000 in current dollars. He never received any satisfaction from knowing that his name was attached to a famous Supreme Court decision, because, to his mind, the case had cost much and changed nothing.

Harry Pace, the combative, unsatisfactory witness whose company was the driving force behind *Hansberry*, died in 1943. In the last year of his life he moved to River Forest, a white suburb. Some black Chicagoans, including his young protégé John H. Johnson, claimed that Pace, who was very light-skinned, was trying to pass as white. In response to this criticism, he became more withdrawn and secretive.

. . . .

The Continuing Importance of Hansberry Today

Hansberry is one of the enduring cases in American civil procedure. It restated or established two principles of importance. The first is that generally a person must be joined as a party in a case for the person to be bound by its judgment. The other is that the Due Process Clause demands adequate representation for class members. Both principles continue to influence American law.

1. Party Joinder and Preclusion. The idea that every person is entitled to his or her day in court is deeply ingrained in American culture. Tied to individual liberty and the adversarial system, the "day in court" ideal long preceded *Hansberry*. But *Hansberry* stated the principle in clear language that suggested a constitutional linkage between party joinder and preclusion. Because the process of becoming a party is governed by procedural rules on joinder, this first *Hansberry* principle makes the scope of joinder rules a critical fulcrum in the American procedural system.

Our joinder rules are based on the expansive model of equity. They were promulgated at the federal level in 1938, just two years before *Hansberry*. The rules authorize joinder on a scale as large as the transaction or factual occurrences that form the basis of the dispute. In an important tip to individual liberty, however, the joinder rules do not generally require the joinder of all affected persons. Typically, the plaintiff can join other plaintiffs only with their consent. Together, these plaintiffs decide which defendants (out of the universe of possible defendants) to sue. Defendants have some opportunities to expand the plaintiffs' party structure, but it remains a defendant's choice whether to do so. For the most part, ours is a system of voluntary joinder, in which we give the parties the tools to effect broad joinder but do not require that they do so. Because of various strategic considerations, plaintiffs and defendants often decline to join all of the parties that might be joined in a case. As a result, the judgment in the case often does not bind all of the persons affected by a dispute.

For the most part, less-than-maximal joinder—and consequently, a judgment's less-than-maximal preclusive effect—creates no serious difficulties. In a small subset of cases, however, failing to extend preclusive effect to nonjoined parties is a problem. Factually related cases that repetitively litigate the same issues over and over strain a litigation system, especially when the individual cases are dispersed geographically and temporally. Think, for instance, of the thousands of asbestos cases that clog our courts; in case after case after case, courts are asked to decide the same questions of whether asbestos was dangerous, whether it could cause a particular type of injury, and so on. From a social viewpoint, it might be better if our system could decide these issues once, and then bind future litigants to this judgment. A number of commentators have urged this solution, and a few cases have utilized it, but most cases have rejected this approach.

The fundamental roadblock, of course, is the first principle stated in *Hansberry*—that only parties who are properly joined to a lawsuit can be bound by its outcome. The problem is well presented by Martin v. Wilks.[156] In 1974 African-American city workers sued Birmingham, Alabama, for racially discriminatory hiring and promotions practices. The parties ultimately settled, with Birmingham accepting a consent decree that provided for the hiring and promotion of African-American firefighters. A group of white firefighters tried to intervene as parties to this proceeding in order to argue that the racial preferences of the consent decree were themselves racially discriminatory and unlawful, but their request to intervene was denied.

A different group of white firefighters, including Robert Wilks, then brought suit against Birmingham. The court allowed a group of African-Americans, including John Martin, to intervene as parties in order to

---

[156]   490 U.S. 755 (1989).

protect the rights that they had obtained under the consent decree. Among the arguments of the *Martin* intervenors was the claim that the new lawsuit constituted an impermissible collateral attack on the consent decree. Effectively the intervenors were arguing that the judgment obtained in the prior case should preclude white firefighters who had not been joined as parties in that case.

Martin v. Wilks pitted two critical procedural policies against each other. On the one hand, to permit the white firefighters to undo the finality of a hard-fought remedy would make the rights of prior parties less secure, and might threaten the rights of many African-American or other civil rights litigants who had obtained relief through consent decrees or judgments. On the other hand, Martin v. Wilks is in many ways indistinguishable from Hansberry v. Lee, both saying that persons should be able to collaterally attack a judgment entered in a case to which they had not been joined as parties and in which they had no opportunity to participate.

In a 5–4 decision, the Court held that the consent decree did not bind Wilks. Chief Justice Rehnquist's decision led with *Hansberry*, noting: "All agree that '[i]t is a principle of general application in Anglo-American jurisprudence that one is not bound by a judgment in personam in a litigation in which he is not designated as a party . . . .'" The *Martin* intervenors had argued that, despite this rule, an obligation should have been imposed on Wilks, who knew of the original suit, to join the case; his failure to do so bound him to the consent decree. The Court rejected this approach, stating: "Joinder as a party, rather than knowledge of a lawsuit and an opportunity to intervene, is the method by which potential parties are subjected to the jurisdiction of the court and bound by a judgment or decree." In an ironic twist, the *Hansberry* principle, which the Court had developed to evade a racially restrictive covenant, was thus invoked to dismantle an affirmative action program.

Congress legislatively overturned Martin v. Wilks the following year, when it passed a statute providing that, in Title VII employment-discrimination claims, any person who had notice of a discrimination case and an opportunity to intervene, or whose interests were adequately represented by a party in the case, was bound by the outcome. But the statute applies only in the context of Title VII; beyond that, Martin v. Wilks remains good law. The statute has led to broader proposals, applicable to other types of repetitive litigation, that a person who has notice of and an opportunity to intervene in a case should be bound by its judgment, but so far courts and legislators have not adopted these proposals.

An obvious question about such proposals is their constitutionality. That question brings to light a curious feature of Hansberry v. Lee and Martin v. Wilks: although it is the clear implication of both decisions, neither case precisely held that the "no joinder, no binding effect" principle was of constitutional dimension. Any doubt on that score was removed in Richards v. Jefferson County, Alabama,[161] a case coincidentally arising in Birmingham. The county had passed a tax that some taxpayers felt was unconstitutional. In a lawsuit brought by a Birmingham city official and others, the tax was declared constitutional. In *Richards*, county taxpayers again challenged the tax. The Alabama Supreme Court held that the new challenge was precluded by the prior judgment. The U.S. Supreme Court unanimously reversed, holding that Alabama's preclusion of the second suit violated the Due Process Clause. The opening lines of Justice Stevens' opinion gave this construction of *Hansberry*: "In Hansberry v. Lee, we held that it would violate the Due Process Clause of the Fourteenth Amendment to bind litigants to a judgment rendered in an earlier litigation to which they were not parties and in which they were not adequately represented." Relying again on *Hansberry*'s language that " 'one is not bound by a judgment in personam in a litigation in which he is not designated as a party,' " and sprinkling the opinion liberally with other quotations from *Hansberry*, the Court finally rested the "no joinder, no binding effect" principle on a constitutional foundation.

At the same time, the *Richards* Court recognized exceptions to this principle. It mentioned, in particular, that class actions and special remedial schemes such as bankruptcy and probate were exceptions to *Hansberry*'s "no joinder, no binding effect" rule. Therefore, *Richards* should be read conservatively, so that party joinder as a condition of constitutionally appropriate preclusion is the default approach, not the necessary one. Another approach, such as adequate representation, could substitute for party joinder as the condition for preclusion. Nonetheless, until legislatures and courts devise and employ a constitutionally acceptable alternate approach, *Hansberry*'s default rule makes the once-and-for-all resolution of complex, repetitive litigation impossible.

Whether that result is right is a matter of debate; good arguments lie on both sides. In a big-picture sense, the issue boils down to how much you value each litigant's control over his or her day in court, in comparison to the court system's need for expeditious resolution of litigation. In thinking through the issue and evaluating approaches other than party joinder for achieving preclusion, a good gut check is to return to the facts of *Hansberry* and to ask how the alternative approaches might have affected the Hansberrys' ability to contest the covenant's validity.

2. Class Actions. As *Hansberry* and *Richards* state, the class action is an exception to the "no joinder, no binding effect" principle. Class members never consent to join the litigation, as ordinary plaintiffs do. Nor do class members enjoy the rights or shoulder the burdens of participation, as ordinary plaintiffs do. Although courts say that a class action "joins" the class members to the case, this joinder is purely a legal

---

[161]   517 U.S. 793 (1996).

fiction. What *Hansberry* did was to establish a constitutional quid pro quo: It swapped out party joinder for adequate representation, thus recognizing a "no adequate representation, no binding effect" alternative principle. In order for a class judgment to bind the class members, due process demands that those who have rights of participation and control (the class representatives) adequately represent those who do not (the class members).

The idea that class actions must ensure the adequate representation of class members' interests was hardly new when *Hansberry* was decided in 1940. For instance, as long as certain criteria were met, the 1938 Federal Rules of Civil Procedure permitted class actions to be brought by "such [class members], one or more, as will fairly insure the adequate representation of all." Illinois had no class-action rule as such; its class-action practice developed entirely out of case law. Although the cases did not usually recite adequacy of representation as an element of a class action, the notion was not foreign to Illinois courts. . . .

Hansberry's innovation in the law of class actions was to elevate adequacy of representation to a constitutional sine qua non for achieving binding effect on class members. In the years immediately following *Hansberry*, courts tended to read this constitutional requirement in light of the specific deficiencies of *Hansberry*: conflicts of interest within the class, especially those involving the potential for fraud or collusion. In 1966, Rule 23 underwent its first revamping since 1938. We can see the imprint of *Hansberry* all over the revised Rule 23, especially on Rule 23(a).

A principal function of Rule 23(a) is to give effect to *Hansberry*'s requirement of constitutionally adequate representation. Put differently, most of the conditions contained in Rule 23(a) aim to filter out class actions that would fail the *Hansberry* due process inquiry. Rule 23(a) contains four explicit and two implicit conditions that must be satisfied in order for a court to certify a class action. The implicit conditions are that a definable class must exist and that the class representative must be a member of the class. The explicit conditions are that class members must be so numerous that other joinder methods are impracticable (the "numerosity" inquiry of Rule 23(a)(1)), that a common question of law or fact must exist among all class members (the "commonality" inquiry of Rule 23(a)(2)), that the representative's claim must be typical of the claims of the class members (the "typicality" inquiry of Rule 23(a)(3)), and that the representative must adequately represent the class (the "adequacy" inquiry of Rule 23(a)(4)). An obvious connection between Rule 23 and *Hansberry* lies in the adequacy inquiry of Rule 23(a)(4). In fact, however, of the six conditions in Rule 23(a), all but the numerosity requirement help to work out the meaning of "adequate representation."[166]

Begin with the requirement that a definable class must exist. This requirement delineates who is and who is not in the class—an essential first step if we are to examine a class for possible internal conflicts and if we are to figure out who is bound by a judgment. Likewise, the reason that the class representative must be a member of the class is to ensure that the class representative has a stake in the case and is therefore more likely to adequately represent those with a comparable stake. With the commonality inquiry of Rule 23(a)(2), the rule takes the first rough pass at exploring the connection between the representative and the class; if the class representative and all class members share absolutely no common questions, the representative is unlikely to represent the class adequately. The typicality inquiry of Rule 23(a)(3) then takes a second, deeper cut at the adequacy question; in requiring a typical claim, the rule makes sure that the class representative argues the case in the way that most class members would wish it to be argued. Finally, the adequacy inquiry of Rule 23(a)(4) trims closest to the ground, exploring whether any individualized reasons or personal characteristics—such as physical or mental deficiencies; conflicts of interest; or evidence of fraud, collusion, or untrustworthiness in this or other matters—call into question the representative's vigor. Traditionally included within this (a)(4) inquiry, but now broken out separately in Rule 23(g), is the question of the adequacy of class counsel; the court must be satisfied that the attorney is competent, has no potential conflicts of interest, and is not engaging in fraud or collusion with the opponent.

More subtly, *Hansberry* influences portions of Rule 23(b). The biggest innovation in the 1966 amendments—the one that made Rule 23 the most controversial of all the Federal Rules of Civil Procedure and one of the most controversial rules in all of American law—was Rule 23(b)(3). It dramatically expanded the circumstances in which a class action was permissible, principally by making class actions available in cases seeking damages. The two criteria for class certification under Rule 23(b)(3) are that the common questions identified in Rule 23(a)(2) "predominate" over individual questions and that class treatment is "superior to other available methods for fairly and efficiently adjudicating the controversy." Although they also help to ensure that the class action is an economical approach to resolve the case, these criteria—especially predominance—further cement the cohesion between class representative and class members.

It is important not to press *Hansberry*'s influence on Rule 23 too far. *Hansberry* states a constitutional floor for all class actions, federal and state. Rule 23 cannot drop below that floor, but it can impose adequacy

---

[166]   The conditions are also doing other work at the same time. In particular, they are trying to ensure that the joint handling of related claims will achieve greater efficiencies than individual litigation would.

standards that are more stringent than due process requires. Thus, even though a case falls short of satisfying Rule 23(a), (b)(3), or (g), it would not necessarily fall short of satisfying due process; or just because a class action satisfies due process, it does not necessarily satisfy Rules 23(a), (b)(3), and (g). *Hansberry* adumbrated the adequacy issue, but Rule 23 has taken on a life of its own. Decision by decision, judicial interpretations of Rule 23 have built a complex coral reef of case law. Beneath that reef, acting as its foundation and giving it general shape, is *Hansberry*. But it is important to distinguish between that bedrock and the coral that overlays it.

Rule 23 has also had a fascinating reciprocal influence that continues to shape our understanding of *Hansberry*. As mentioned, the present Rule 23 is controversial largely because of Rule 23(b)(3). This new form of class action had no direct relationship to *Hansberry*, but it did increase significantly the circumstances in which class actions were permissible. In part because these cases often seek damages on behalf of large numbers of individuals, the stakes of class certification can be high. A person seeking to defeat a class certification motion can take two lines of attack: by arguing head-on that the standards of Rule 23(b) do not allow certification, or by arguing that the class representatives fail to meet one of the Rule 23(a) criteria designed to ensure adequate representation. Lawyers being practical people, they often take the second tack when it serves their interests. Thus, the expansion of class-action practice after 1966 has occasioned courts to look much harder at questions of adequate representation, and thus to return to *Hansberry* to seek guidance about how to handle class actions in factual and legal circumstances that were unimaginable in 1940. Each re-reading of *Hansberry* in light of modern circumstances yields new insights into and generates new uncertainties about the message that the case sends to us some 70 years later.

The Supreme Court's most recent examination of Rule 23(a) reflects this reality. In Amchem Products, Inc. v. Windsor,[170] the Court faced an asbestos class action that had settled the claims of thousands, and perhaps millions, of asbestos victims. Included in the class were both those who had present injuries and those who were presently healthy but whose injuries would manifest themselves in the years and decades to come. The settlement provided a schedule of compensation for injuries, but the schedule did not increase over time to account for inflation. Moreover, a limited number of plaintiffs were entitled to opt out of the compensation scheme and bring individual lawsuits, but that opt-out right was almost meaningless for victims whose injuries manifested themselves in later years. The Supreme Court invalidated the settlement on both (a)(4) and (b)(3) grounds. The (a)(4) holding trod familiar ground. As in *Hansberry*, the Court found conflicts of interest within the class— especially between those presently injured and those whose injuries lay

---

[170]   521 U.S. 591 (1997).

far in the future. Present victims wanted as much money as possible now, and for them the opt-out right had some value. Far-future victims had a primary interest "in ensuring an ample, inflation-protected fund for the future," and for them the opt-out right was nearly worthless. Lumping present and future victims into one class created "no assurance—either in the terms of the settlement or in the structure of the negotiations— that the [class representatives] operated under a proper understanding of their representational responsibilities." The conflicts in *Amchem* were certainly less acute than those in *Hansberry*, which had mainly a binary "yes" or "no" choice on the covenant's enforcement. But like the *Hansberry* opinion, *Amchem* thought of adequacy of representation in conflict-of-interest terms, and again found such conflicts to exist.

Hansberry also casts its shadow over one of the most significant issues in present class-action practice: whether a class member can collaterally attack a class-action judgment in a subsequent case by claiming that the representation in the class action was inadequate. If absent class members can engage in such collateral attacks, then they might avoid, as the *Hansberry* defendants avoided, the binding effect of the class action's unfavorable outcome. If they cannot, they must attack inadequacy within the confines of the original class action, and they will be bound by that action's unfavorable outcome if their attack fails or if they fail to mount an attack at all.

Although you might think that *Hansberry* answers the question in favor of collateral attack, the issue is not quite so simple. In *Hansberry*, the trial judge in *Burke* never certified the class. In most modern class actions, however, the trial judge does enter an order certifying the class. When a class member tries to collaterally attack the judgment in such a case, the class member must first show why he or she should not be bound by the finding of adequacy of representation. In other words, to avoid the claim-preclusive effect of the judgment, class members must first avoid the issue-preclusive effect of the finding that representation was adequate. That additional issue-preclusive step was not one that the *Hansberry* defendants had to deal with, and thus *Hansberry* provides no direct guidance about how to answer the question.

The stakes in this debate are high. Increasingly, defendants are taking advantage of class actions to settle all or most litigation concerning their alleged wrongdoing. A classwide settlement buys the defendant "global peace," to use the class-action vernacular. It also saves the court system from a great deal of repetitive and costly litigation. But there is a potential dark underbelly to this process. Sometimes a defendant shops a settlement among competing groups of plaintiffs' lawyers, pitting them against each other in their efforts to gain the attorney's fees that come with a successful settlement of a class action. This dynamic creates a risk of collusion between class counsel and the defendant, in which class counsel essentially sells the clients' claims down the river for pennies on the dollar. This sell-off might not become apparent until long after the class action is certified and concluded. Whether the benefits of global peace (hence no collateral attack) outweigh concerns for fair and noncollusive treatment of class members (hence collateral attack) is a matter presently dividing courts and commentators.

It has also divided the Supreme Court. In Dow Chemical Co. v. Stephenson,[173] the Court addressed the question in the context of the Agent Orange settlement. The Agent Orange settlement, which was achieved in 1984, provided no benefits for victims whose injuries first manifested themselves after the fund had been fully distributed in 1997. Two victims whose injuries manifested themselves after 1997 brought claims against the defendants. Just as Charles Churan had done in *Hansberry*, the defendants pointed to the prior class action, of which the plaintiffs were class members, and argued that they were bound by the terms of the settlement—even though the late onset of their injuries meant that they received nothing from it. The district court agreed, and dismissed their cases. The Second Circuit reversed, holding that a class member should be able to collaterally attack a class action in subsequent litigation upon a showing that the prior class representatives were inadequate. After granting certiorari to resolve a split among the circuit courts on the point, the Supreme Court split 4–4, with Justice Stevens not participating. Under the Court's rules, the Second Circuit's opinion was therefore affirmed, but the Court's affirmance has no precedential value.

As of this writing, the issue remains very much alive, with courts trending toward the view that class members cannot in most circumstances collaterally attack a finding that they were adequately represented in the first case. If the Supreme Court does not permit such collateral attacks, then class members will no longer be able to benefit from the *Hansberry* principle in the way that the *Hansberry* defendants did. *Hansberry*'s only influence will lie in how its holding shapes the judge's adequacy-of-representation determination in the original class action. But perhaps the *Hansberry* story can shed some light on this issue. If the judge in *Burke* had been asked to do so, he undoubtedly would have found that Olive Ida Burke was an adequate class representative; indeed, she certainly seemed to be. Would the Supreme Court have let such a finding bar the Hansberrys from challenging the covenant? It seems unlikely.

Conclusion

Carl and Nannie Hansberry's youngest child, Lorraine, grew up to become a world-renowned playwright. Her most famous work, A Raisin in the Sun, became required reading for a generation of American students struggling to understand racial identity and racism. First performed in 1959, the play tells the story of a poor African-American family living in a kitchenette apartment on Chicago's South Side, struggling with the decision whether to move into a white neighborhood

---

[173]   539 U.S. 111 (2003).

whose residents alternatively intimidate or bribe the family to remain in the ghetto. Widely misunderstood as a paean to integration, A Raisin in the Sun develops a complex portrait of African-American identity. Although it is impossible to know exactly how her family's move into Washington Park shaped her views, the racial reality of Hansberry v. Lee lies just beneath the surface of the play's aesthetic poignancy.

Yet Lorraine Hansberry had nothing but contempt for Hansberry v. Lee. She ridiculed the case as an example of "progress" that left "the Negroes of Chicago . . . as ghetto-locked as ever" despite the "sacrificial efforts" of her father and family. Viewed strictly from a lawyer's perspective, [she] judged too harshly and too soon. Too harshly, because some of the lawyers used *Hansberry* as a springboard to achieve great things, and because *Hansberry* itself was an early, tentative step on the path toward the litigation strategy that resulted in Brown v. Board of Education. Too soon, because her death in 1965 at the age of 35 prevented her from seeing the long shadow that *Hansberry* cast over the 1966 amendments that created the modern class-action rule.

Rule 23 has been an important instrument, achieving some notable successes, in the fight for racial justice in America. Perhaps Lorraine Hansberry, whose meteoric career has always put a human face on Hansberry v. Lee, would have taken satisfaction in knowing that her parents' lawsuit poured the foundation for one of the most powerful and controversial devices in American law. Or perhaps not. On November 16, 1940, the headline splayed across the top of the Chicago Defender, the most influential African-American weekly in the country, proclaimed in large block typeface "HANSBERRY DECISION OPENS 500 NEW HOMES TO RACE." For the litigants, the lawyers, and the African-Americans of Chicago, Hansberry v. Lee was never about class actions, adequacy of representation, or conflicts of interest. Those procedural principles can blind us to the true struggle in which the Hansberrys, Pace, and Dickerson were engaged.

Lorraine Hansberry
1930–1965

" . . . That fight also required that our family occupy the disputed property in a hellishly hostile 'white neighborhood' in which, literally, howling mobs surrounded our house. One of their missiles almost took the life of the then eight-year-old signer of this letter. . . ."

—Lorraine Hansberry, To Be Young, Gifted and Black 20–21 (Robert Nemiroff adapter, 1969)

(Photo: Courtesy Robert Nemiroff)

Closing Arguments

Elizabeth G. Thornburg, "The Story of Lassiter: The Importance of Counsel in an Adversary System"

Civil Procedure Stories 509 (Kevin M. Clermont ed., 2d ed. 2008), with case documents at http://civprostories.law.cornell.edu.

Abby Gail Lassiter first became a mother when she was fourteen years old. She was poor, black, single, and largely uneducated. Juvenile court records suggest that she was of low intelligence. Abby Gail continued to live with her mother, Lucille Lassiter, who helped her care for this child so that Abby Gail could go back to high school. Lucille also helped care for Abby Gail's four other children as they came along.[4] The fourth baby of the five, William (called Billy), was taken from the family when he was about eight months old by a social worker who claimed to be taking him to the doctor. Thus began state custody of Billy and the process that led to the termination of Abby Gail's parental rights. In neither the original hearing removing Billy from his home, nor in the hearing permanently severing the parent-child relationship, was Abby Gail represented by a lawyer.

Should an indigent parent have the right to appointed counsel before the state takes such drastic measures? That was the question before the Supreme Court in Lassiter v. Department of Social Services.[5] The answer to that question raises important issues about the role of counsel in our court system.

Litigation in the United States is organized around the adversary system. Technically, "adversary system" merely means that "neutral and passive factfinders . . . resolve lawsuits on the basis of evidence presented by contending litigants during formal adjudicatory proceedings."[6] Functionally, however, it means that the parties are responsible for investigating the relevant facts, preparing evidence for trial, presenting that evidence in the most persuasive way possible, and pointing out the weaknesses in the adversary's evidence. The judge (at least in theory) is a passive audience, making decisions based on the information put before

---

[4] The five children were Angelia, Candida, Felicia, William, and a baby boy [Bobby] born in the spring of 1976 after William was taken by the state. The other four children all remained with Lucille, their grandmother. The social worker Bonnie Cramer testified that Lucille did "a very fine job" caring for them. Transcript of the Evidence at August 31, 1978, Termination Hearing, reprinted in Reply to Respondent's Brief in Opposition app. IV, at 13 [hereinafter TR].

[5] 452 U.S. 18 (1981).

[6] Stephan Landsman, Readings on Adversarial Justice: The American Approach to Adjudication 1 (1988).

him or her by the litigants. This system is supposed to result in accurate and reliable outcomes, because these clashing presentations will allow the judge (or jury) to weigh the evidence and discern something close to the truth. Our faith in the adversary system rests on an assumption that the parties will be represented by equally prepared and equally competent advocates. When one party is represented by counsel and the other is not, will the system's ability to arrive at an acceptable result be compromised?

The court system also functions as a way to ritualize the resolution of disputes and to treat the participants with dignity. Researchers have determined that people care very much about how decisions are made, and not just about the outcomes reached. Participating in the trial of a legal dispute can provide the parties an opportunity to tell an important story in a culturally meaningful context demonstrating that society values them and takes their rights seriously. When people are represented by lawyers, is it more likely that the hearing will be conducted so that they will be treated with dignity and will feel that their voices have been heard? Indeed, will the community have more faith in the fairness of trials in which all parties have the ability to be taken seriously?

The Lassiter case gives us an opportunity to consider the difference a lawyer makes. The American Bar Association has said that "the integrity of the adjudicative process itself depends upon the participation of the advocate."[10] If this is correct, we must also ask whether there are some civil cases in which the government should be compelled to provide an indigent party with a lawyer, on the ground that not to do so would deprive the party of the constitutional right to due process of law.

Social and Legal Background

American policy regarding neglected or abused children has swung back and forth during the last several decades. Sometimes it emphasizes keeping children at home and rehabilitating families. At other times it leans toward removing children from suspect homes. The Lassiter case came during a period in which the dominant philosophy was the "rescue" of children who were seen to be at risk. In 1974 Congress passed the Child Abuse Prevention and Treatment Act, which required states to develop reporting systems for abuse and neglect. At the same time, there was a growing trend toward removing children from apparently unsafe environments. The result was a surge in the number of children taken from their families and placed in foster care.

Termination of parental rights is a comparatively recent development. It was not until the 1950s that states began enacting termination legislation. Until about 1980, termination was used mostly in cases in which parents voluntarily gave up their rights. The twin

---

[10]   Joint Conference on Professional Responsibility, Report, 44 A.B.A. J. 1159, 1160 (1958) (primarily written by Professor Lon L. Fuller).

trends toward putting children in foster care and toward wanting to free them to be adoptable, however, led to an increasing use of petitions by the state to terminate involuntarily the legal ties between parent and child. Because many of the parents involved were indigent, the states also had to decide whether to provide attorneys to represent the parents in those termination proceedings. By the time Abby Gail's case reached the Supreme Court, thirty-two states (plus the District of Columbia) provided a right to counsel by statute. In the remaining states, however, the legislature had not chosen to provide counsel. North Carolina was one of those states.

In states in which no statute provided for appointment of counsel, advocates for parents argued that the Constitution guaranteed counsel as part of the Due Process Clause of the Fourteenth Amendment. This contention relied on two lines of Supreme Court cases: (1) cases about right to counsel; and (2) cases about the more general requirements of procedural due process.

1. Counsel Right. The right to appointed counsel developed slowly, and it started in criminal cases. The Court derived this right from the Sixth and Fourteenth Amendments. The Sixth Amendment required appointed counsel in all federal criminal cases. Only gradually did the Supreme Court apply this requirement to the states through the Fourteenth Amendment. In Powell v. Alabama,[18] the state charged nine young black men with the rape of two white girls on a freight train. The trial judge purported to appoint "all members of the local bar" to defend them, but no one appeared at trial to do so. At the last minute, a local lawyer defended the men "with reluctance," and they were convicted and sentenced to death. The Supreme Court held that the failure to provide them with counsel to prepare their defense violated their due process rights. The Court did not, however, immediately extend this holding beyond cases in which the defendant was charged with a capital crime.

Instead, ten years later in Betts v. Brady,[19] the Court held that in non-capital cases due process required the state to provide a lawyer only if "a denial of fundamental fairness" would occur without one. The state court was to do a case-by-case analysis, requiring defendants to show "special circumstances" before they were entitled to state-provided counsel. This test proved unworkable, and became "a continuing source of controversy and litigation in both state and federal courts."[20]

---

[18]   287 U.S. 45 (1932). Powell is one of the notorious "Scottsboro Boys" cases. . . .

[19]   316 U.S. 455, 462 (1942) ("Asserted denial is to be tested by an appraisal of the totality of facts in a given case. That which may, in one setting, constitute a denial of fundamental fairness, shocking to the universal sense of justice, may, in other circumstances, and in light of other considerations, fall short of such denial."). The Court in Betts, like the Court in Powell, based its decision solely on the Due Process Clause of the Fourteenth Amendment, rather than on the Sixth Amendment. In Gideon, the Court would switch from the Due Process Clause to the Sixth Amendment as the ultimate source of the right to counsel in criminal cases.

[20]   Gideon v. Wainwright, 372 U.S. 335, 338 (1963) (habeas corpus case).

It was not until 1963 that the Supreme Court overruled Betts. Clarence Earl Gideon, a fifty-one-year-old white man, was charged by the state of Florida with the felony of breaking and entering. Unable to afford a lawyer, Gideon asked that one be appointed to represent him. The state refused, finding no special circumstances, and so he defended himself. He was convicted and sentenced to five years in state prison. The Supreme Court, which appointed an attorney to represent Gideon before it, held that "in our adversary system of criminal justice, any person haled into court, who is too poor to hire a lawyer, cannot be assured a fair trial unless counsel is provided for him." Thus, with Gideon v. Wainwright,[21] the requirement of appointed counsel under the Sixth Amendment extended to all felonies even in state court.

What about non-felonies? In Argersinger v. Hamlin,[22] the Court made clear that it was not the category of offense that determined whether the Sixth Amendment required appointment of counsel. Argersinger was convicted in a Florida court of carrying a concealed weapon, a crime punishable by imprisonment up to six months. The Court held that "absent a knowing and intelligent waiver, no person may be imprisoned for any offense, whether classified as petty, misdemeanor, or felony, unless he was represented by counsel at his trial." Seven years later the court qualified this holding a bit. Scott v. Illinois[23] restricted Argersinger to cases in which the defendant was actually imprisoned as a result of his conviction. Scott was convicted of shoplifting. Although he could have been sentenced to a year in jail, he received only a $50 fine. The Court held that he was therefore not entitled to appointed counsel.

In the meantime, the Court had also recognized a right to counsel in cases that were not strictly criminal, and in which the Due Process Clause thus operated unaided by the Sixth Amendment. For example, In re Gault[24] held that a child whose family could not afford counsel was entitled to appointed counsel in state delinquency proceedings that could result in the juvenile's confinement. The Court based its decision on the importance of counsel to a fair hearing. Because juvenile delinquency hearings are civil rather than criminal, Gault opened the door for the Court to expand the due process right to counsel in civil cases.

In some civil cases, however, the Betts case-by-case analysis still determined whether a right to counsel existed. In the context of parole

---

[21]   Id. at 344. The Court appointed Abe Fortas, then an attorney with the high-powered firm of Arnold, Fortas, and Porter, to represent Gideon. In 1965, President Johnson would appoint Fortas to serve as a Justice on the Supreme Court. For the story of Gideon and his case, see Anthony Lewis, Gideon's Trumpet (1989).

[22]   407 U.S. 25, 37 (1972).

[23]   440 U.S. 367 (1979). But cf. Alabama v. Shelton, 535 U.S. 654 (2002) (holding that actual confinement is not always required, so that a suspended jail term may not be imposed without assistance of counsel).

[24]   387 U.S. 1 (1967).

revocation, the Court in Morrissey v. Brewer[25] held that although revocation would result in a return to custody, the defendant was deprived only of "the conditional liberty properly dependent on observance of special parole restrictions" and rejected the claim of a per se right to counsel. Similarly, in the context of probation revocation, Gagnon v. Scarpelli[26] held that the possibility that the defendant would lose his physical liberty was not sufficient to require automatic appointment of counsel—in deciding that counsel was not required, the Court considered the state's interest in quick, simple procedures and the low risk of error; when the process involved is less formal and adversarial, a lay person was thought to be more able to represent himself without the aid of a lawyer. Both these parole and probation revocation cases allowed the authorities to engage in ad hoc, case-specific analysis to decide whether due process required an appointed attorney. In explaining the circumstances under which the indigent might be entitled to counsel, the Court noted in Gagnon v. Scarpelli:

> Presumptively, it may be said that counsel should be provided in cases where, after being informed of his right to request counsel, the probationer or parolee makes such a request, based on a timely and colorable claim (i) that he has not committed the alleged violation of the conditions upon which he is at liberty; or (ii) that, even if the violation is a matter of public record or is uncontested, there are substantial reasons which justified or mitigated the violation and make revocation inappropriate, and that the reasons are complex or otherwise difficult to develop or present. In passing on a request for the appointment of counsel, the responsible agency also should consider, especially in doubtful cases, whether the probationer appears to be capable of speaking effectively for himself.

In other civil circumstances, there might be a per se right to representation, even when the defendant's liberty had already been lost and no additional confinement would result. In Vitek v. Jones,[27] a prisoner was to be transferred from prison to a mental hospital. Four members of the Court found that the adverse change in the conditions of confinement and the stigma attached to being labeled mentally ill compelled the provision of counsel for any indigent prisoner facing a transfer hearing.[28]

All of these civil cases were decided in the fifteen years immediately preceding Lassiter. A number of them resulted in split opinions. The

---

[25]   408 U.S. 471, 480 (1972).

[26]   411 U.S. 778, 790–91 (1973).

[27]   445 U.S. 480 (1980).

[28]   Id. at 496–97 (plurality opinion of Justice White, joined by Justices Brennan, Marshall, and Stevens). Justice Powell agreed that an inmate facing involuntary transfer to a state mental hospital was entitled to representation, but left open the possibility that the representative did not need to be an attorney because the transfer hearing was informal and the central issue was a medical one. Id. at 498–500.

Court may have felt besieged with claims that due process required appointed counsel in various civil contexts. It had repeatedly been asked to expand the right, but it had failed to articulate any clear test explaining why due process did or did not require legal assistance. The Court was ripe for a "slippery slope" argument: recognize a due process right to counsel here and it will apply everywhere.

2. ***Due Process.*** A separate line of cases explored the right to procedural due process in the context of administrative hearings. Goldberg v. Kelly[29] found welfare recipients constitutionally entitled to trial-type hearings before the state could terminate their income maintenance payments under the Aid to Families with Dependent Children ("AFDC") program. The case was important because the Court expanded the scope of the rights protected by the Due Process Clause, extending the concept of due process to include a right to a pre-deprivation hearing.

It soon became clear, however, that the right to a hearing was not absolute. Critics of Goldberg expressed concern about the cost of procedural protections, arguing that the money spent on procedural measures administering benefits could be better spent on the benefits themselves. In Mathews v. Eldridge,[30] the Court tacitly accepted this critique. The plaintiff in that case was a recipient of Social Security benefits who suffered from back pain and chronic anxiety. The agency terminated his benefits without a hearing and he sued, claiming that the termination violated his due process rights. The Supreme Court disagreed, finding that he had no right to a pre-termination hearing. The Court adopted a utilitarian approach in which the costs of additional process are compared to its probable benefits, balancing three factors to decide what due process requires: (a) the private interests at stake (i.e., the nature and importance of the right being asserted by the nongovernmental litigant); (b) the government's interest (including the fiscal and administrative burdens that would result from additional procedural protections); and (c) the risk that the lesser procedures will lead to erroneous decisions and the probable value of additional procedural safeguards.

By 1978, the Court had issued nine opinions reducing the scope of due process protections required by the Constitution. One source of these limits was its restricted view of the "life, liberty, or property" protected by the Due Process Clause. The Court ruled that neither the Clause itself nor a person's expectation of a benefit creates a protected right—rather, before claiming a due process protection, the person must find the liberty or property interest elsewhere. Then, once such a right has been identified, the right is balanced against other factors under the Mathews test to see what due process requires.

---

[29]   397 U.S. 254 (1970). . . .

[30]   424 U.S. 319 (1976). . . .

Thus, the Court's championing of procedural due process, like its championing of the right to counsel, was fading during the 1970s. And along came Abby Gail Lassiter.

Factual Background

1. Neglect. William L. Lassiter was born on September 26, 1974, in Durham, North Carolina.[34] He was a small baby, and had some health problems from birth that required his mother to take him for repeated medical tests and checkups. In May of 1975, when Billy was eight months old, Duke Pediatrics became concerned because Billy had missed appointments and they were unable to contact his mother. The clinic asked the Department of Social Services ("Department") to try to find her. Social worker Sam Crawford went to Lucille's house. Abby Gail was not there, but Billy was there on his grandmother's lap. Crawford offered to take Billy to the hospital, and told Lucille that she should stay home and care for the other children. At Duke Pediatrics the doctors became more concerned, finding that Billy was having breathing difficulties, showed evidence of malnutrition, and had scars from an untreated infection. Crawford later informed Lucille that Billy would be kept at Duke for two weeks so that he could get medical care.

Shortly thereafter, the Department filed a petition alleging that Billy was neglected, seeking to remove him from his home. A hearing on this petition was first scheduled for May 19, 1975. Unfortunately, Abby Gail was in jail on that date, where she was being briefly held on a shoplifting charge.[35] The neglect hearing was rescheduled for June 16. Crawford called the Lassiter home that day, trying to secure Abby Gail's attendance at the hearing. The record conflicts about whom Crawford talked to and about whether the person refused to come or said that she had the other children and could not come. In any case, Abby Gail did not appear at this hearing, either personally or through counsel. The judge made findings of neglect and transferred custody to the Department on June 16, 1975. In December of 1975, Abby Gail visited with Billy at a meeting arranged by the Department. This was the only formal meeting reflected in the Department's records.

2. Murder. Soon Abby Gail's life went from bad to worse. Late on the evening of February 4, 1976, while Abby Gail was at Lucille's house, Lucille apparently had a dispute of some duration with a neighbor, one Linda Stanback. This dispute erupted into fatal violence. Both Lucille and Abby Gail were charged with the murder of Stanback. Both denied

---

[34]   William Boykin was identified as Billy's father. He was Abby Gail's boyfriend. It was alleged that Billy's AFDC checks were for a time mailed to Boykin's address, and he visited Billy in foster care in a visit set up by the Department. However, when the Department sought his consent to termination of parental rights, he denied being the father and did not contest the termination proceedings.

[35]   Lucille testified that the shoplifting charge was based on a mistake: "the man thought that she had picked up something but she didn't and they put her in jail but she had a lawyer and she came home." TR, supra note 4, at 45–46.

killing her. The murder trial took place in July of 1976 in Superior Court for Durham County.

A lawyer named Frank Bullock was appointed to represent Abby Gail, and another lawyer was appointed to represent Lucille. Bullock had attended law school at North Carolina Central University, graduated in 1973, and entered practice in 1974. He had handled ten to fifteen jury trials, mostly felonies, before representing Abby Gail. Her case was either his first or second homicide defense.

The actual trial transcript is no longer available, but the documents filed later as part of a collateral attack on the conviction reflect the trial testimony. Stanback and Lucille had had an argument, and Stanback left Lucille's house and sat outside on a wall. The Lassiters went out and talked to her, and Stanback came back in the house and talked some more. Then Stanback left and went back home. She was upset, angry, and crying. Stanback's autopsy revealed that she was 5′7″ tall, weighed 170 pounds, and had a 0.25 blood-alcohol level (more than twice the legal threshold of intoxication) at the time of her death. Although her cousin tried to stop her, Stanback ran back to the Lassiter house. During the ensuing scuffle, Lucille swung a broom at Stanback, Stanback grappled with and swung at Lucille, and the two of them tumbled into the Lassiter house, still fighting. Abby Gail ran into the house to defend her mother. Abby Gail must have been pregnant at the time, because in the spring of 1976 she gave birth to a baby boy, who would join his three older sisters in Lucille's household. Testimony diverged as to whether Abby Gail was seen to have actually struck Stanback. After the struggle, Stanback was found with seven stab wounds, one of which proved to be fatal.

On Bullock's advice, the defense called no witnesses, and neither Abby Gail nor Lucille testified to the events. This decision was based in part on Bullock's feeling that although Abby Gail had no prior criminal convictions, she did not communicate well and "she did not really explain herself. Now, I could understand her, but in looking at it from her sitting on the witness stand under cross examination it was just my opinion that she would not have made a good witness even though I felt she was telling the truth." Abby Gail and Lucille suggested to Bullock that Stanback had already been stabbed when she returned for the last time to the Lassiter home, but Bullock found no evidence to support this theory. Instead, Bullock's defense strategy, based on Abby Gail's and Lucille's denials, was to attack the credibility of the prosecution witnesses on cross-examination: (a) One witness did not see anyone stab Stanback. (b) Another witness testified that he could see the incident from across the street in the dark, but the layout of the house would have made it unlikely that he could see what he claimed to have seen. This witness was charged at the time with first-degree burglary and receiving stolen goods, and in return for his testimony the state promised to let him plead guilty to a lesser offense, to dismiss the serious charge, and to recommend probation. (c) His sister at first testified that the investigating detective had changed her statement and forged her signature. After a recess, she testified that the statement was correct. (d) Stanback's cousin testified that she saw Abby Gail stab Stanback three times, but she also testified that after seeing the stabbing she merely walked home and started talking with her mother. She gave no statement to the police concerning her knowledge of the incident until four months after it occurred.

During the trial, a surprising development revealed a different defense that would have been available to Abby Gail: Lucille and not Abby Gail stabbed Stanback. Lucille made a statement to that effect to a police officer, and the prosecution failed to reveal that statement during pretrial discovery. At the trial, a police officer attempted to testify that when he was called to the scene, Lucille stated that she had been the one who stabbed Stanback: "And I did it, I hope she dies."

Under North Carolina criminal procedure, the state was required before trial to turn over any oral statement allegedly made by a defendant, whether exculpatory, inculpatory, or neutral. The defense immediately objected that Lucille's statement had not been provided as required. After the trial judge announced his intention to grant Lucille a mistrial, the state withdrew its attempt to introduce the statement. At the end of the state's case, the judge granted Lucille's motion for dismissal of the charges against her.

The judge did not dismiss the charges against Abby Gail, and her defense rested without introducing any evidence. But with regard to Abby Gail, her mother's statement was exculpatory, and her lawyer should have been provided with it as a constitutional requirement. Nevertheless, Bullock failed either to raise this constitutional objection or to try to offer the statement in Abby Gail's defense. He stuck with his plan to argue for reasonable doubt based on the weakness of the evidence against her. The case against Abby Gail went to the jury, which found her guilty of second-degree murder. The judge sentenced her to a term of twenty-five to forty years in prison, and she was sent to the Raleigh Women's Prison on July 23, 1976.

Bullock failed to file any kind of motion for a new trial, even though Lucille repeated after the trial her statement that it had been she who had stabbed Stanback. He was appointed to handle Abby Gail's appeal, and he again failed to raise the issue of the unproduced statement. Her direct appeal was denied on June 1, 1977.

Bullock eventually felt so guilty about his failure to complain properly about the unproduced statement and to use it in Abby Gail's defense that he personally secured a lawyer to represent Abby Gail in her collateral attack on the conviction. In that attack, Abby Gail's new lawyer argued that the prosecution had violated Abby Gail's constitutional rights by failing to timely produce Lucille's statement. He also argued that Bullock had provided ineffective assistance of counsel by failing to use the statement in Abby Gail's defense. Since the double jeopardy clause would have prohibited retrying Lucille for the killing, Lucille could have safely testified in Abby Gail's defense that Lucille was the one who had stabbed Stanback. In the alternative, he argued that the police officer could have been called to testify to Lucille's statement and that it would have been admissible as an excited utterance, which is an exception to the hearsay rule. But the collateral attack failed, with the judge finding that Abby Gail's lawyer had waived the right to complain that the statement had not been produced before trial and that despite this waiver Bullock had not been constitutionally ineffective in representing her. The court believed that Abby Gail's failure to blame her mother was a matter of trial tactics, rather than a sign of ineffective assistance of counsel. So the conviction was upheld on March 20, 1979.

Bullock believed until the day he died that Abby Gail was not the person who had killed Stanback. At the hearing on the collateral attack, he testified that had he been informed of Lucille's statement before trial it would have changed his trial strategy:

> I am more than sure that it probably would have [had an effect on my trial strategy] . . . . [H]ad I had those statements earlier I am sure, as a matter of fact, I would probably have asked for a separate trial. I realize the strong feelings the mother has for the daughter and my client had for her mother, and I most certainly would have made a motion to sever the trials because I most certainly would have had to use that in defense of Miss Lassiter.

Prior Proceedings

1. State Trial Court. Meanwhile, the Department had decided that Abby Gail's parental relationship with Billy should be terminated. A new social worker, Bonnie Cramer, visited Abby Gail in prison in December of 1977 for the purpose of asking her to voluntarily relinquish her parental rights. Abby Gail strenuously objected, saying that she wanted Billy placed with her mother Lucille so that he could be raised by his grandmother with his brother and sisters. That plan was not acceptable to the Department, although the other four children remained with Lucille. On April 12, 1978, Abby Gail was served with formal notice of the Department's decision to seek termination. She asked a matron at the jail for help, but received none. Abby Gail corresponded with Thomas Loflin, the lawyer representing her in the collateral attack on her criminal conviction, but she did not discuss the parental rights matter with him; Loflin would not have been willing to handle the matter even if she had mentioned it, because his firm did criminal work and did not handle family law matters.

The case was originally set for hearing in June of 1978 in the District Court for Durham County; Lucille appeared at that time and stated Abby Gail's intention to contest termination; but the hearing was rescheduled because the judge was attending the state judicial conference. By this time Billy was almost four years old and had been in foster care for more than three years. The hearing on the Department's petition to terminate

Abby Gail's parental rights took place on August 31, 1978. Abby Gail had been brought from prison to attend the hearing, and Lucille was there as well. Abby Gail appeared at the hearing without any advance preparation and without a lawyer to represent her. The Department was represented by experienced counsel, Thomas Russell Odom, Assistant Durham County Attorney. Presiding was Judge Samuel F. Gantt, the same judge who presided over the 1975 hearing on Billy's neglect—he would rely on his earlier findings in this proceeding on Abby Gail's parental rights.

    a.   Opening. The hearing began with a colloquy between Judge Gantt and Odom concerning whether the hearing should be postponed to allow Abby Gail to retain an attorney. The very first exchange between Judge Gantt and Abby Gail went this way:

> THE COURT: And she has had over four months to speak to an attorney and has spoken to an attorney but has not consulted anyone with reference to this child. Isn't that true?
>
> MS. LASSITER: Say what now?

Although Odom told Judge Gantt, "if you want to give her a chance to talk with [Loflin] about this I don't object," Judge Gantt agreed with Odom's argument that if Abby Gail had really been concerned about her parental rights she would have discussed the problem with Loflin at their meeting the previous May. Judge Gantt stated that "she has had ample opportunity to seek counseling." He apparently did not consider her incarceration to be an adequate excuse not to have found a lawyer. The hearing therefore proceeded to the merits with Abby Gail attempting to represent herself. (Likewise, no attorney was appointed to represent Billy, because Abby Gail had not filed the written denial required to trigger the appointment of a guardian ad litem.[47])

    b.   Plaintiff's Case. Under North Carolina law, the Department had to show that Abby Gail had committed at least one of certain listed acts, and also that termination of her parental rights would be in Billy's best interests. The acts charged in her case were:

> (1) The parent has without cause failed to establish or maintain concern or responsibility as to the child's welfare; and
>
> (2) The parent has willfully left the child in foster care for more than two consecutive years without showing to the satisfaction of the court that substantial progress has been made within two years in correcting those conditions which led to the removal of the child for neglect, or without showing positive response within two years to the diligent efforts of a county department of social services . . . to encourage the parent to strengthen the

---

[47]   N.C.Gen.Stat. § 7A–289.29(b) ("If an answer denies any material allegation of the petition, the court shall appoint a licensed attorney as guardian ad litem for the child to represent the best interests of the child."). The child's own statutory right to representation therefore turns on his parent's awareness that a written answer should be filed.

parental relationship to the child or to make and follow through with constructive planning for the future of the child.

The Department thus had to demonstrate either that Abby Gail failed to take responsibility for Billy's welfare "without cause" or that she "willfully" left him in foster care for two years without taking appropriate corrective steps.

The Department called as its only witness Bonnie Cramer, the social worker assigned to Billy's case in August of 1977. She testified based on the contents of the Department's file, despite the fact that she had no personal knowledge of those earlier events. The file itself was not provided to Abby Gail, either before the hearing or at the hearing, nor was it introduced into evidence. The record does not make clear the extent of Abby Gail's reading skills. Had she had a lawyer, however, the lawyer could have obtained a copy of the file in advance of the hearing and been prepared to object to its use or to offer evidence contradicting its allegations where appropriate.

Cramer was allowed to testify in a conclusory manner about the circumstances that led to Duke Pediatrics' calling the Department and about the doctors' findings and reasons for keeping Billy. The record is therefore unclear as to whether the neglect that triggered Billy's involvement with the Department was a single missed appointment and its rescheduled date, was chronic failure to deal with serious health issues, or was something in-between. Similarly, Cramer was allowed to testify that the file showed only one contact between Abby Gail and Billy after he was taken from his home, and no requests from Abby Gail to see Billy even when she was out on bail. The file did not document any informal contacts between Abby Gail and Billy, or between Lucille and various social workers. Judge Gantt apparently inferred from the lack of recorded contacts that there were no other contacts.

Finally, even when the testimony turned to matters on which Cramer did have personal knowledge, her testimony consisted of an opinion that terminating Abby Gail's parental rights would be in Billy's best interest. At this point she presumably was testifying as an expert witness based on her training and experience as a social worker, because fact witnesses are generally not permitted to testify to such opinions. Her opinion was supported by generalized hearsay: "I don't feel that the home is conducive for William. I have checked with people in the community and from Mrs. [Lucille] Lassiter's church who also feel that this additional responsibility would be more than she can handle. Mrs. Lassiter herself has indicated that to me on a number of occasions." With no lawyer to test this testimony, the court got no further information on whom Cramer had talked to, what they actually told Cramer, or what basis they had for their opinions. Nor were these "people" present to be cross-examined. Nor were Cramer's own underlying assumptions or biases probed.

Judge Gantt then referred to his own findings from the 1975 neglect hearing: Lucille had complained to the Department on May 8, 1975, that Abby Gail often left the children with her for days without providing money or food and that Abby Gail's AFDC check did not come to Lucille's house. Neither Abby Gail nor Lucille was present at that hearing, and Lucille repeatedly denied having made the complaint. But Judge Gantt clearly regarded his prior findings as reliable and binding.

Judge Gantt offered Abby Gail the opportunity to cross-examine the social worker. The following excerpts give a partial picture of the futility of the exercise:

Q: The only thing I know is that when you say—

THE COURT: I don't want you to testify.

MS. LASSITER: Okay.

THE COURT: I want to know whether you want to cross-examine her or ask any questions.

MS. LASSITER: Yes, I want to. Well, you know, the only thing I know about is my part that I know about it. I know—

THE COURT: I am not talking about what you know. I want to know if you want to ask her any questions or not.

MS. LASSITER: About that?

. . .

THE COURT: Are there any questions you want to ask her about what she has testified to?

MS. LASSITER: Yes.

THE COURT: All right. Go ahead.

Q: I want to know why you think that you are going to turn my child over to a foster home? He knows my mother and he knows all of us. He knows her and he knows all of us.

THE COURT: Who is he?

MS. LASSITER: My son, William.

A: Ms. Lassiter, your son has been in foster care since May of 1975 and since that time—

Q: Yeah, yeah, and I didn't know anything about it either.

. . .

THE COURT: . . . All I want you to do is to ask her questions concerning your rights and your child.

Q: I think—Well, my rights, I think it's not right—

THE COURT: Don't tell us what you think. Ask her questions if you have any and if you don't, tell her to stand down.

MS. LASSITER: About my child?

THE COURT: Right.

Q: Well, what I want to ask about, what I want to know is why
you want to take the child and place it in adoption care?

This last question merely allowed the Cramer to repeat her original
testimony: Billy had been separated from the Lassiters since he was eight
months old, they had made no organized efforts to see him, and he
deserved a fresh start with an adoptive family.

   c.   *Defendant's Case.* Following this ineffective cross-examination,
it was time for Abby Gail's own case in defense. Because she had no
lawyer before the hearing, no one had prepared her by explaining the
requirements of a hearing, talked with her about what information would
be relevant, asked her to locate any documents or witnesses that might
support her story, or helped organize her testimony into a coherent
narrative.

   Because she had no lawyer at the hearing, there was no one to help
offer her testimony as direct evidence, in a supportive and
nonconfrontational way. Judge Gantt did try at first to elicit her
testimony in a way that might have worked with a witness who had been
prepared and who had good communication skills:

Q (by Judge Gantt): Tell us about your relationship with your
son, William L. Lassiter. I understand he was born September
26, 1974.

A (by Abby Gail Lassiter): Yes.

Q: Where was he born, Duke Hospital?

A: Yes.

Q: All right. Now tell us about your relationship with him and
his development and so forth from that time until you were
imprisoned.

A: When he was born, when I had him and everything?

Q: Yes, ma'am.

A: Okay. Well, he was born at Duke Hospital on September 26,
1974. . . . I brought him home, see, I was staying with my
mother. I brought him home and I carried—I'm going to tell you
what I did. I carried forth and back to the clinic for his checkups
and everything. And I took good care of him 'cause I've always
been a good mother. And I took care of them and everything and
did what a mother suppose to do for a child. And I love my child.
And took him back and forth to the clinic and I had
appointments and took him back and forth to Duke Hospital for
checkups and everything. So the doctors was in there, so I asked
him, the doctor was in there, I don't know, they didn't never say
what was wrong with him or nothing like that, you know. They
told me—I asked what was wrong with my child. I wanted to

know what was wrong with my child. They didn't tell me anything—nothing was wrong with him, they wouldn't tell me anything. They didn't tell me anything. And I wanted to know, you know, what was wrong with William. And I kept taking him and getting his checkup and everything. And I asked the lady, I said, what's wrong with William and they didn't never say anything, tell me anything, what was wrong with him or anything. And the day—

Rather than follow up on this information, Judge Gantt then skipped to trying to determine why Abby Gail had not attended the 1975 neglect hearing. He was apparently disturbed that Abby Gail's current testimony about her extensive efforts to get Billy medical care contradicted the findings that he had made at that hearing, although it was a hearing at which Abby Gail had not appeared. This exchange created mostly confusion. He turned instead to another finding from the 1975 hearing, this time questioning Abby Gail as a hostile witness:

Q: Your mother is Mrs. Lucille Lassiter, isn't she?

A: Yes, sir.

Q: Did you know that your mother filed a complaint on the 8th day of May, 1975, alleging that you had often left the children with her for days without providing money and food while you were gone?

A: No, 'cause she said she didn't file no complaint.

Q: That was some ghost who came up here and filed it I suppose.

Judge Gantt returned to questioning Abby Gail about the reasons she had not attended the 1975 hearing, and about other allegations apparently made at that hearing. When Abby Gail denied them, Judge Gantt's attempt at direct examination—Abby Gail's opportunity to tell her story—was over: "All right, Mr. Odom, see what you can do."

On cross-examination, Odom tried to pin down how many times Abby Gail had seen Billy between when he was taken away and her criminal trial. Everyone agreed that she had seen him once, in a visit arranged by the Department. Beyond that point, his effort was largely unsuccessful. She testified that she had seen him more than six times. She also tried to explain her failure to arrange more visits through the Department:

Q: But you haven't made any effort to really visit with him by calling the Department and setting it up, have you?

. . .

A: Yes, I have, yes, I have. Because she [Cramer] wasn't on the case working then, she wasn't on the case. It was another social worker on the case. She was saying the social worker was going to bring the child by the house and she was going to bring my baby home. She told me, she was a black lady, she said she was going to bring my baby home.

Odom also questioned Abby Gail about her plan for Billy's future, given the fact that Abby Gail was in prison and could not personally care for him until her release.[54] This is a question for which counsel would surely have prepared Abby Gail. Absent such preparation, she spoke her feelings:

Q: If you could decide right now what you plan to do with that child what would you plan to do for that child right now? What would you have happen to it?

A: If I do what now?

Q: What would you want to happen to your child if you could plan for him right now, what would happen to him? I mean, you can't take him over there and keep him with you.

A: Well, I'd be a mother for him like I always done, be a mother for him.

THE COURT: Just answer his question. He said what would you like to have done with your child since you can't take him with you?

Q: Do you want him to stay where he is?

A: No.

Q: You want him to go live with your mother?

A: Yes, I do. Because that's his family. She is his grandmother.

Q: And you think he knows her?

A: Yes, he does. He knows all of us, my children.

Q: How does he know you? How do you even know that he knows you if you haven't seen him in a year?

A: Well, he knows us.

Q: Just because you are his family?

A: He knows us. Children know they family. I don't care which way it is, children know they family. They know they people, they know they family and that child knows us anywhere. He got brothers and sisters. I got four more other children. Three girls and a boy and they know they little brother when they see him.

Q: He hasn't seen any of them in a couple of years.

A: Yes, he have, he have seen them since then.

Q: How do you know?

---

[54]   According to her counsel at the Supreme Court argument, Abby Gail was eligible for parole in 1982. In addition, at the time of the termination hearing, the collateral attack on Abby Gail's conviction was still pending.

A: Because I have been with them. They seen him because I had my children with me and when we meet and run into him and see him, they see him too. All of us be standing there. Because the last time when I ran into the store when that lady [Billy's foster mother] had him, that lady had him, she had him. And my other children were standing right there and she said there go our brother and that child got out of that cart, he didn't want to go with that lady. 'Cause she's not his mother, I'm his mother. I don't care which way it is, I'm his mother and that's his grandmother.

Q: And he has been in foster care for over three years of his four-year life, isn't that right? He was eight months old when he went into foster care, isn't that right?

A: Sir, how would you feel if somebody came and got your child and took it away like that?

Odom then turned to the judge and said that since Abby Gail's answers were "unresponsive," he had no further questions. He then made an argument to the court: "I know what she wants the child to feel and know, but I think it is unreasonable to suspect that he would know her after four years or even three." After another reference to the findings from the 1975 hearing, Abby Gail was told to step down.

Just as there was no lawyer to perform a supportive direct examination of Abby Gail, there was no lawyer to do that for Lucille. Judge Gantt once again attempted to perform this function. Lucille launched immediately into a narrative description of the facts she believed to be relevant:

She [Abby Gail] had been taking him, that child had been going to the hospital . . . . That youngun tended to her children, God knows that. She had been taking that child out to the hospital, back and forth. But it was something when the child was born, wasn't nothing wrong with the child but his 'pendix. . . . And he [Sam Crawford, the earlier social worker] sit there and talked to me for a while and I told him—he said where is Abby Gail. I said, I don't know. And I said—and he said—and I said—and I said that the baby was sick and he asked me how was the baby getting along and I said I don't know, she's taking him back and forth to the doctor, but I said it don't seem like the doctor is doing him any good. So he took the baby and looked at the baby and he said, well, do you want me to take this baby to the hospital today, this baby is ill, he said you said the doctor—I said well, she takes the baby to the doctor, because she have the papers—I have the papers there in my pocketbook now, where she'd taken that baby to the doctor. And her pocketbook hanging up in the closet, she took it and he said well—and I said, do you want me to go with you to the doctor and he said, no, you stay here with the rest of the children, he said, I'm going to the hospital. And so, when he went and he came back and he didn't come back that day and he come back he says your—he come back and he says the baby was sick and they said they were going to keep the baby for two weeks.

During further questioning by Judge Gantt, Lucille denied that she had filed a complaint about Abby Gail with the Department. Lucille confirmed Abby Gail's testimony that they had had difficulty learning which social worker was assigned to Billy's case. Lucille also denied that she had told Cramer that she could not care for Billy:

> She [Cramer] promised me faithfully—she said, now she was going to have me visit little Billy, that she was going to bring little Billy, William, to my house and play with the other little boy, you know, before she would bring him in to live with me because I definitely told her that I could take this child because I have four and I said now, the girl wants me to have the child and I would like for all of them to be together because she is—I got four children, she is the only one that have children and that's personally my family and it's all the family we have and I said I want all her children. And she said you're not—

At this point, when further testimony might have clarified the reason Cramer believed that Lucille could not handle another child, the judge interrupted her: "I tell you what, let's just stop all this. You [Odom] question her, please. Just answer his questions. We'll be here all day at this rate. I mean, we are just wasting time, we're skipping from one subject to another."

Odom's cross-examination of Lucille introduced an additional accusation, but indicated an awareness that Lucille had tried to arrange a visit with Billy. He asked: "Isn't it a fact, Mrs. Lassiter, that on the date that she said you could visit with the child you showed up and you had been drinking?" Lucille answered, "No. . . . Lord have mercy. I don't even drink. I'm a Christian. . . . Nor smoke either. My pastor—" Odom also tried to get Lucille to admit that she had called the Department in May of 1975 to complain about Abby Gail, and Lucille once again denied it.

After the close of Lucille's testimony, Judge Gantt asked Abby Gail whether she had any other witnesses. Given her limited understanding of the issues, and of the ways in which outside testimony might have bolstered her case, Abby Gail could think of no other witnesses: "Nobody else don't know nothing about this but me and momma."

   d.   Closing. Odom proceeded to make his closing argument, after which Judge Gantt asked Abby Gail if there was anything else she wanted to say. Her attempt at a response was met with argumentation:

MS. LASSITER: I don't think it's right.

THE COURT: Are you saying that you would rather let the child just float around?

MS. LASSITER: No, I want him to be with my mother.

THE COURT: Well, it has already been found as a fact in this matter [at the 1975 hearing] that she complained that you would leave the children for days without food or support of any kind.

MS. LASSITER: That's not true.

THE COURT: I have already found it as a fact at a hearing when you didn't show up and you were told to be here.

Finally, Judge Gantt informed Odom that he was ready to sign an order terminating Abby Gail's rights. He informed Abby Gail of her right to an appeal, suggesting that she go to North Central Legal Assistance Program to ask their advice. Finding that Abby Gail "wilfully failed to maintain concern or responsibility for the welfare" of her son, Judge Gantt entered his order terminating the parental relationship between Abby Gail and William Lassiter on September 8, 1978.

2.   State Appellate Courts. The North Carolina Court of Appeals affirmed the trial court's judgment on November 6, 1979. The court found that there was a "fundamental right to family integrity protected by the U.S. Constitution," but that there was no constitutional mandate to require the appointment of counsel for indigent parents. Rather, that decision was up to the legislature.

The North Carolina Supreme Court dismissed the further appeal and denied Abby Gail's petition for discretionary review on January 17, 1980.[65]

3.   The U.S. Supreme Court. The Court granted Abby Gail's petition for certiorari on October 6, 1980.

Abby Gail was represented at oral argument by Leowen Evans, her lawyer from the North Central Legal Assistance Program in Durham. He was quickly peppered with questions about the implications of establishing a right to counsel. When Evans argued that termination could be distinguished from the "vast majority" of civil cases based on the fundamental nature of parental rights, one Justice responded:

> I don't quite follow that. . . . There's certainly nothing in the explicit words of the Constitution that do protect that. But the words of the Constitution explicitly protect a person from being deprived of his property without due process of law. And that's what happens in the mine run of civil cases when the defendant loses. Why doesn't your argument apply in spades to every civil case?

---

[65]   In re William L. Lassiter, 262 S.E.2d 6 (N.C.1980). It was only at this point that the Department placed five-year-old Billy with a new set of foster parents who wanted to adopt him. Prior to that time, pre-adoptive placement was regarded as too risky, given the possibility of reversal of the termination order.

When Evans tried again to argue that the Court could distinguish termination cases based on the weight of the liberty interest involved, that Justice replied: "You think something this Court has dreamed up is more weighty than what's in the Constitution itself?" A number of hypotheticals followed: What about state condemnation actions? What if this case had been instituted by a foster parent rather than the state? What about an action to revoke a practitioner's license? Some Justices expressed concern that courts might also have to appoint counsel for the child, thus requiring the state to pay for two lawyers in every contested termination case.

Thomas Odom, the attorney who had tried the case below, argued for the Department. Odom first argued the merits: Abby Gail was a bad mother who did not take Billy to the doctor, did not bother coming to the initial hearing, only visited her child once after he was put in state care, and did not try to get a lawyer to represent her at the termination hearing. As to the impact a lawyer might have made at the termination hearing, he noted, "I'm not arguing that counsel wouldn't have been helpful—but the result [termination] was correct." Odom also pursued the slippery slope argument: "If this Court requires the appointment of counsel in a civil action, the Court will be hard pressed to limit it. The Court will have to decide which rights are fundamental enough to require it and which not."

Steven Shaber, arguing as amicus on behalf of the states of North Carolina, Delaware, Mississippi, Florida, Nevada, and Arkansas, also warned that indigent litigants would demand appointed counsel in all civil cases, that line-drawing among them would be difficult, and that the expense to the state in providing counsel would be much greater. The criminal/civil distinction, he argued, was much easier to administer. Shaber then raised the specter of another implementation problem: he asked the Court, if it were to rule for Abby Gail, to make the ruling explicitly prospective only; he warned that retroactive effect would risk upsetting numerous existing adoptions, if the termination orders that had preceded them were suddenly put in question.

The Supreme Court Decision

Lassiter sharply divided the Court, five to four. Justice Stewart wrote the opinion for the majority, joined by Chief Justice Burger and Justices White, Powell, and Rehnquist. Justice Blackmun dissented, joined by Justices Brennan and Marshall. Justice Stevens wrote a separate dissent.

1. Majority Opinion. Justice Stewart's opinion takes the trial court's findings at face value, despite the fact that some were made at a hearing at which Abby Gail was not even present, and the others at a hearing in which she was not represented by counsel. Thus the majority begins with the "bad mother" version of the story: Abby Gail failed to provide Billy with proper medical care, and he was found to be neglected. A year later, she was convicted of murder and sentenced to a long term of imprisonment. She was not married to Billy's father, and she was receiving AFDC payments. Abby Gail had not bothered trying to get a lawyer although she had ample opportunity to do so. Lucille was also a bad person, having committed murder despite the charges having been dropped against her.

Justice Stewart also gives a sanitized version of the termination hearing. He narrates the social worker's testimony. Of the disastrous attempt to cross-examine her, he merely notes, "Ms. Lassiter conducted a cross-examination of the social worker, who firmly reiterated her earlier testimony." Regarding Abby Gail's direct testimony, he quotes her for the only time in the opinion, choosing a particularly ungrammatical portion of her presentation. Regarding Lucille's testimony, he notes only her denial of the social worker's charges—not her positive testimony that Abby Gail was a good mother who took Billy to the doctor frequently and that Lucille wanted and was able to care for Billy.

Justice Stewart's take on the law melds the criminal right-to-counsel cases and the due process cases, and does so in a way that adds an enormous obstacle to obtaining appointed counsel in civil cases. His opinion begins by characterizing due process in general as extremely flexible. Looking then at the right-to-counsel cases, Stewart draws the conclusion that such a right exists "only where the litigant may lose his physical liberty if he loses the litigation." Surveying the cases, he notes that Gideon was sentenced to prison for five years, that Argersinger was also imprisoned if only briefly, that Gault was committed to an institution in which his freedom was curtailed, and that Scott had no right to counsel because he was not actually sentenced to confinement. Seen in this light, the cases before Lassiter recognized a right to counsel only when *physical* liberty, as opposed to some more intangible liberty interest, was involved. The Stewart opinion goes a step further by turning this into a presumption: "an indigent litigant has a right to appointed counsel only when, if he loses, he may be deprived of his physical liberty. It is against this presumption that all other elements in the due process decision must be measured."

Justice Stewart then switches to the procedural due process cases, applying the three Mathews v. Eldridge factors. These come out in Abby Gail's favor, even under the majority's view. First, although he avoids calling parental rights "fundamental," he notes that a parent's desire for and right to the "companionship, care, custody, and management of his or her children" is "important." A parent's interest in the accuracy and justice of the termination decision is therefore "a commanding one." Second, the state has two kinds of interests. It shares with the parent the interest in a correct outcome:

> If, as our adversary system presupposes, accurate and just results are most likely to be obtained through the equal contest of opposed interests, the State's interest in the child's welfare may perhaps best be served by a hearing in which both the

parent and the State acting for the child are represented by counsel, without whom the contest of interests may become unwholesomely unequal.

The state also has a conflicting interest in avoiding the expense of appointed counsel and the cost of lengthened proceedings that a lawyer's presence might cause. Justice Stewart's opinion does not give much weight to this financial interest:

> [T]hough the State's pecuniary interest is legitimate, it is hardly significant enough to overcome private interests as important as those here, particularly in light of the concession in the respondent's brief that "the potential costs of appointed counsel in termination proceedings . . . is [sic] admittedly de minimis compared to the costs in all criminal actions."

Third, the majority opinion considers the risk that a parent will be erroneously deprived of parental rights if not represented by counsel. This factor also seems to come out in favor of appointed counsel. Justice Stewart notes that the ultimate issues are not always simple, expert medical and psychiatric testimony may be involved, and the parents whose rights are at risk are "likely to be people with little education, who have had uncommon difficulty in dealing with life, and who are, at the hearing, thrust into a distressing and disorienting situation." He also recognizes that a majority of courts have held appointment of counsel to be required. The opinion cites a study of New York Family Court judges: more than six times as many judges agreed rather than disagreed that when a parent is unrepresented it becomes more difficult to conduct a fair hearing, and three times as many judges thought that it became difficult to develop the facts.

The Mathews balancing result, however, does not stand alone. It must overcome the presumption that there is no right to counsel in civil cases, and it is here that Abby Gail's argument seems to fail. The balancing favors her, but not by enough to overcome the presumption.

Moreover, the majority rejects any across-the-board right to counsel in parental termination cases. Instead, Justice Stewart's opinion recognizes only the ad hoc, case-by-case test it applies to Abby Gail. The strength or weakness of the Mathews balance will vary in other individual cases. "We . . . leave the decision whether due process calls for the appointment of counsel for indigent parents in termination proceedings to be answered in the first instance by the trial court, subject, of course, to appellate review." But the majority declines to formulate guidelines to help the lower courts in making their determination.

The one example we have of the standard in operation, then, is the majority's application of the new ad hoc test to Abby Gail's case. Justice Stewart points out that she faced no criminal charges. Since the nature of the right at stake otherwise does not change and the state interest is unlikely to change, from case to case, the variable that must make the difference is the probability that a lawyer could decrease the likelihood of error—greater legal or factual complexity would tip the balance toward requiring appointed counsel, while the existence of bad facts apparently would tip it toward requiring the accused parent to defend herself. Absolutely critical is Justice Stewart's view that in Billy's case the right result has prevailed (and perhaps that in general the right outcome matters more than the right process). He argues that no expert witnesses testified in this case, that it raised no difficult legal issues, and that the evidence against Abby Gail was so strong that presence of counsel could have made no difference. He reaches this conclusion despite explicitly conceding that:

- rampant hearsay evidence was admitted;

- Abby Gail "left incomplete" her defense that the Department had not adequately assisted her; and

- a lawyer might have done more with the argument that Billy should live with Lucille.

So, what can we learn from Lassiter about the application of the ad hoc test to future civil cases? The adversarial and formal nature of the termination proceeding is not enough to require appointment of counsel. Nor are the following flaws enough: the parent in fact did a wretched job of presenting her case; inadmissible evidence was introduced and relied on by the court; evidence in the parent's favor was not presented; and the decision was based on findings made in the parent's absence. Dictum in the opinion indicates that counsel might be required if the parent was also subject to criminal charges for child abuse or if the hearing would involve the testimony of expert witnesses other than the social workers.

Nevertheless, the majority opinion concludes by pointing out that states would be well advised to appoint counsel in termination cases:

> A wise public policy . . . may require that higher standards be adopted than those minimally tolerable under the Constitution. Informed opinion has clearly come to hold that an indigent parent is entitled to the assistance of appointed counsel not only in parental termination proceedings, but in dependency and neglect proceedings as well.

No Justice, then, questions whether counsel would make termination hearings fairer and more reliable. Their disagreement centers on whether appointed counsel is constitutionally required.[71]

2. Dissenting Opinions. Justice Blackmun's dissent largely agrees with the majority about the application of the Mathews balancing test, although he finds the result to be even more strongly in favor of the

---

[71]   Chief Justice Burger, concurring in the majority opinion, also writes separately to emphasize that cases terminating parental rights are not penal in nature, but instead aim to protect the child.

right to appointed counsel. The opinion characterizes "freedom of personal choice in matters of family life," including a parent's interest in retaining the custody and companionship of the child, as "fundamental" and entitled to great weight. It agrees with the majority that the state's interest in avoiding the cost and administrative inconvenience of providing counsel is insignificant. It finds the risk of error to be severe in all cases terminating the parental rights of an indigent parent without counsel: the proceeding is formal and adversarial, the state has great resources available, including experts and experienced counsel, the facts are complicated, and the legal issues are complex. But Justice Blackmun's opinion proceeds to disagree with the majority's legal analysis in important respects.

First, he rejects Justice Stewart's bright-line interpretation of the right-to-counsel cases as turning solely on the litigant's physical liberty. "Indeed, incarceration has been found to be neither a necessary nor a sufficient condition for requiring counsel on behalf of an indigent defendant." The dissent further rejects the slippery slope argument that the cost will grow as other civil cases are included in the ambit of required counsel, because "no difficult line-drawing problems would arise with respect to other types of civil proceedings."

Second, the dissent condemns the creation of a presumption against the right to counsel that must be overcome by the results of Mathews balancing. He contends that "the Court today grafts an unnecessary and burdensome new layer of analysis onto its traditional three-factor balancing test. Apart from improperly conflating two distinct lines of prior cases, . . . the Court's reliance on a 'rebuttable presumption' sets a dangerous precedent that may undermine objective judicial review regarding other procedural protections."

Third, he rejects the majority's case-by-case approach. He notes that this type of analysis creates insoluble practical problems. For appellate courts, review of the record of a hearing in which the party was unaided by counsel will not demonstrate what would have been possible had the party had an attorney. "Because a parent acting pro se is . . . likely to be unaware of controlling legal standards and practices, and unskilled in garnering relevant facts, it is difficult, if not impossible, to conclude that the typical case has been adequately presented." For trial courts, making case-by-case determinations will require advance analysis of the case, including the evidence that the state will offer, in order to reach an informed decision about counsel far enough in advance of a hearing for meaningful preparation.

Fourth, Justice Blackmun's dissent applies the due process test to Abby Gail's actual hearing in a way that differs dramatically from the majority's opinion. Rather than telling the bad mother story, the dissent notes that "the issue before the Court is not petitioner's character; it is whether she was given a meaningful opportunity to be heard when the State moved to terminate her parental rights." Justice Blackmun's view of the hearing includes a number of differences that counsel might have made. In addition to making proper objections to the Department's evidence, and to effectively cross-examining the social worker, the dissent lists areas in which evidence favorable to Abby Gail could have been (but was not) developed:

> A defense would have been that petitioner had arranged for the child to be cared for properly by his grandmother, and evidence might have been adduced to demonstrate the adequacy of the grandmother's care of the other children. . . . The Department's own "diligence" in promoting the family's integrity was never put in issue during the hearing, yet it is surely significant in light of [Abby Gail's] incarceration and lack of access to her child. . . . Finally, the asserted willfulness of [Abby Gail's] lack of concern could obviously have been attacked since she was physically unable to regain custody or perhaps even to receive meaningful visits during 21 of the 24 months preceding the action.

In light of these gaps, this dissent finds "virtually incredible the Court's conclusion today that her termination proceeding was fundamentally fair."

Justice Stevens' dissent goes even farther. While he agrees with the Blackmun dissent's analysis of the Mathews factors, he rejects a balancing approach. "The issue is one of fundamental fairness, not of weighing the pecuniary costs against the societal benefits." By analogy to the criminal cases, "even if the costs to the State were not relatively insignificant but rather were just as great as the costs of providing prosecutors, judges, and defense counsel to ensure the fairness of criminal proceedings, I would reach the same result in this category of cases. For the value of protecting our liberty from deprivation by the State without due process of law is priceless."

3.   Unwritten Opinions. *Lassiter* is also noteworthy for what it does not mention. Most obviously, race is completely swept under the rug. The Supreme Court's opinion never mentions the ethnicity of the participants, despite Abby Gail's having attacked in her brief the trial court's failure to consider placing Billy with his grandmother given the historical significance of the extended family within African-American culture. Further, an amicus brief argued that the discretionary nature of the termination decision, particularly when the indigent parent is unrepresented, allows decisions to be tainted by racial bias. The Court addressed neither argument.

The importance of poverty in the due process balance is also given little weight. Justice Stewart's opinion acknowledges that indigent parents in termination cases may lack coping skills, but the opinion does not appear to let that reality affect its assessment of Abby Gail's failure to attend her first hearing or her failure to retain an attorney. Nor do poverty and its consequences exert enough force in the Court's general

Mathews balance to tip the scale toward a right to counsel for all indigent parents.

Gender too plays a role in this case, but it is discussed nowhere. While fathers sometimes battle to keep their children, most of the cases like Abby Gail's will be about mothers . . . .

In many subtle ways, Abby Gail's gender in fact affected the Court's analysis. Her failure to take Billy to the doctor was not just a problem of balancing the needs of four children. It was a moral failure, a failure to be "worthy" of her child. The cult of motherhood can work to the advantage of women in some situations, but for one who has failed to live up to that ideal it is an uphill battle to regain her halo. No wonder Justice Stewart was unable to imagine a situation in which a lawyer would have made a difference in her case. In the majority's view Abby Gail was a woman of loose morals, a bad mother, a murderer—so a judge would inevitably choose to believe the Department's record despite any improved advocacy that a lawyer might have provided.

Without a lawyer, Abby Gail spoke in the language of feelings rather than linear logic. She talked about her love for her son and about the importance of family ties. Her appeal was an emotional one: "Sir, how would you feel if somebody came and got your child and took it away like that?" Her closing argument: "I don't think it's right." Abby Gail tended to use speech patterns that experts in linguistics associate with women and the powerless. These speech patterns include both content (concern for the everyday, the practical, and the interpersonal) and style (hesitant, qualified, question-posing). The tendency to speak in terms of relationships rather than rules means that these people do poorly in court . . . . Abby Gail's use of stereotypically female language cost her credibility both at trial and on appeal. The trial judge found her comments to be, on the whole, unbelievable or irrelevant. The Supreme Court majority doubted that a lawyer could have saved her case.

The decision about whether to terminate parental rights contains many elements of discretion. In the absence of a lawyer to help deflate unwarranted assumptions, and to translate the client's language into courtroom-speak, any biases that the judge might have may, despite his or her good faith, influence the outcome of the case. Should this possibility affect the Court's analysis of the right to counsel? Procedural rules are facially neutral, but to ignore the impact of gender and powerlessness on the "fundamental fairness" of the legal process ignores a factor that could have a very real effect on litigants and courts.

The Immediate Impact of Lassiter

Abby Gail failed in her effort to restore by appeal her lost parental rights, and so Billy did not grow up with his siblings and his grandmother. People believe that Abby Gail returned to the Durham area when she got out of prison, but there is currently no one by that name in the Durham phone book or elsewhere. Abby Gail, Billy, and Lucille quickly dropped off the pages of history.[a]

The immediate scholarly reaction to Lassiter was mixed, but mostly critical. The majority of commentators criticized the Court's creation of the presumption against right to counsel absent a deprivation of physical liberty and its adoption of the case-by-case approach. . . .

In its own context of termination proceedings, Lassiter failed to have much immediate impact on the law. Thirty-two states already provided a right to counsel for indigent parents. The case did not create a trend toward converting that absolute right to a conditional one. In those states that had denied a right to counsel in termination matters, the Lassiter approach actually increased the probability that an attorney would be appointed, as the trial court now had to consider whether the special circumstances of the case required a lawyer in order to ensure fundamental fairness. Indeed, from the viewpoint of trial judges, this permission to appoint counsel for the parent allowed them to make their own jobs easier and to eliminate a possible ground for appeal.

Today, every state provides at least a conditional right to appointed counsel, as they must under Lassiter. Indeed, mostly by statute (and occasionally by state constitutional law), all but seven states provide counsel as a matter of right in termination proceedings to indigent parents who request it. There is more. When the state intervenes in the family to protect children, termination proceedings are generally the end of a long series of formal and informal proceedings, generally beginning with an action to declare that the child has been subjected to abuse or neglect. Most states now provide indigent parents with counsel from the beginning of the process through the termination stage. Many also provide the right to counsel on appeal. Notice, though, that all these rights are primarily statutory. In this age of state budget crises, it is conceivable that a state might cut back to the constitutional minimum in order to save money, in which case the minimal protection provided by Lassiter and its progeny would assume greater importance.

Supreme Court cases since Lassiter have been more protective of parental rights. In Santosky v. Kramer,[83] Justice Blackmun wrote the majority opinion. The Court held that the Due Process Clause requires that the state prove its allegations supporting termination by at least clear and convincing evidence. Santosky also characterized the parents' interest in the care, custody, and management of their children as a "fundamental liberty interest." More recently, in M.L.B. v. S.L.J.,[84] the majority held that the state must provide a free transcript so that an indigent parent can appeal a termination decree. Relying more on equal protection, the Court commented that Lassiter and Santosky placed

---

[a]   Daughter Candida Lassiter, in Durham, now has a Facebook page featuring pictures of her mother, Abby Gail.

[83]   455 U.S. 745 (1982).

[84]   519 U.S. 102, 124, 127 (1996).

"decrees forever terminating parental rights in the category of cases in which the State may not 'bolt the door to equal justice.'" And the Court rejected the slippery slope argument it had found so convincing in Lassiter: "Respondents and the dissenters urge that we will open floodgates if we do not rigidly restrict [precedent] to cases typed 'criminal.' . . . But we have repeatedly noticed what sets parental status termination decrees apart from mine run civil actions, even from other domestic relations matters such as divorce, paternity, and child custody."

The Continuing Importance of Lassiter Today

Lassiter's most significant legacy is in the denial of appointed counsel in civil cases generally. Given the Court's presumption against a right to appointed counsel unless physical liberty is at risk, very few civil cases find a federal due process right to counsel. Lower courts have found no right to counsel in cases in which prisoners sue for damages or in pre-commitment psychiatric interviews, child custody proceedings, extradition cases, prison disciplinary hearings, or paternity cases. . . . The contingent fee system, pro bono volunteer lawyers, and legal aid are supposed to fill the gap.

From a theoretical standpoint, Lassiter is significant in its adoption of a balancing test to measure entitlement to appointed counsel in civil cases. The criminal right-to-counsel cases involve no such balancing. The Court no longer says "counsel makes a crucial difference in criminal defense, but that has to be balanced against the cost of providing counsel." Why was it not laughable, then, when the Department argued that requiring a lawyer for Abby Gail would require a lawyer "for any indigent faced with deprivation of a fundamental liberty interest"? Would that be a bad thing? In some areas, balancing is necessary or appropriate. But in other areas of basic rights, balancing itself has more costs than benefits. Justice Stevens made an argument like this, but his opinion garnered no additional votes.

In civil cases, balancing is now taken for granted. Yet a balancing methodology is problematic. It is largely free of objective criteria for valuing or comparing the interests at stake. In Lassiter, for example, one might be able to quantify the cost of providing lawyers in contested termination cases involving indigent parents. But what weight should be given Abby Gail's relationship with her child? And how do we measure the risk of error without counsel in termination cases, or the likelihood that a lawyer will make the result more reliable?

The problem is exacerbated when the result of the balancing must overcome a rebuttable presumption, such as the one added by Justice Stewart. First, the source and rationale of that presumption are unclear. The majority opinion makes a leap from surveying existing right-to-counsel cases, and deciding that imprisonment is the key, to creating a presumption against counsel. The incarceration requirement does not appear in the language of the Sixth Amendment, nor does the Fourteenth Amendment distinguish between physical liberty interests and other liberty interests, so the distinction cannot be explained as part of a literal reading of the Constitution. Perhaps it reflects an unspoken balancing test of its own: the seriousness of the deprivation of liberty is weighed against the cost of providing counsel. If that is the case, the Court is balancing both the rights and the costs twice, once in creating the presumption against counsel and again in the Mathews balance. Not only is this approach partially duplicative, but also it considers cost in a way that is inconsistent with the function of the cost element in the Mathews balance (which is more situation-specific) and with Lassiter's conclusion that the cost of counsel would be minimal in termination cases. Second, even if we accept the presumption as justified, the quantification of the balancing process is again a problem. When compared to the result of the Mathews balance, how much does the presumption weigh? How strongly would the Mathews balance have to come out in favor of a lawyer before it would tip the scale? Such indeterminacy allows the balancing court to reinforce the judge's own subconscious or conscious biases while appearing to apply a neutral test.

In addition, the Mathews factors omit relevant interests from the balance. Process has a value of its own, separate from its utilitarian function of leading the court to a more correct result. Where, for example, do a party's interests in dignity and a feeling of being taken seriously fit into the balance? Judging from the paper transcript, neither Abby Gail nor Lucille was treated with dignity. A lawyer might have made a difference, by improving their ability to present their case and by decreasing the judge's annoyance at them. But the Court generally has not included such dignitary interests in the due process balancing factors. Should it? Also, is there a separate interest in the community's believing that disputes are being resolved fairly? The community, especially those who are indigent, may lack confidence in the fairness of termination proceedings. Would providing a lawyer for the parent increase that level of confidence, and make people more likely to report suspected parental problems? These intangible factors do not "balance" well, but their exclusion slants the Mathews test toward less rather than more procedural protections.

Conclusion

Would a lawyer have prevented the termination of Abby Gail Lassiter's parental rights? Whatever their views about the requirements of due process, every Justice on the Supreme Court agreed that the presence of a lawyer would have resulted in a qualitatively different hearing. Every Justice agreed that providing a lawyer would be a wise policy. But because she did not get a lawyer, we shall never know what would have happened.

Lawyers perform a number of basic advocacy functions that clients cannot perform for themselves. Lawyers can delineate the issues, investigate and conduct discovery, present factual contentions in an orderly manner, cross-examine witnesses, make objections, and preserve a record for appeal. These capabilities go far beyond the setting of hearings to terminate parental rights. The "guiding hand" of the attorney is an important factor in every case. Yet parties to civil cases will not always have an attorney, and even when attorneys are present they will possess significantly different skills, experiences, and resources. Will this affect the outcome? Should the procedural rules recognize this potential imbalance and adjust for it in some way?

The adversary system generally, and the Federal Rules of Civil Procedure specifically, depends on competing litigants and their advocates to unearth the facts and explore the law, and then present the results to the court. You will soon be playing a role in this process as a participant. The process gives the attorney awesome power, as well as awesome responsibility. You may do pro bono work, representing clients who cannot afford to pay you. You may also be involved in creating or recommending changes in procedural systems as a committee member or as a judge. And you will surely have the opportunity, as an informed voter, to help make decisions about the level of support that the court system and the legal aid system will receive. Remember the story of Abby Gail Lassiter, and the difference a lawyer might make.

————

VALUES

The multiple and conflicting aims of our adversary system of justice, as well as their implementation, reflect underlying values. The ultimate values comprise both a complex variety of outcome values, because we care about the substantive resolution of disputes, and also a broad set of process values, because we care about how the system handles disputes and our care extends beyond the procedure's outcome-value efficacy. Your study of civil procedure should have already convinced you of the subtle latency of some of these values. Our current search for values should be convincing you of the contestable nature of all of these values— both as to what they mean precisely (think particularly of equality) and how much weight they deserve relatively (think generally of outcome and process values) and also as to whose values they are and how they come into play. Yet despite their latency and contestability, exploring and explicating values can be surprisingly practical, as for example when lawyers argue and judges decide a case such as Lassiter.

————

ECONOMIC ANALYSIS

To weigh the wisdom of procedural changes, an analytic framework is helpful. A framework that has come to enjoy wide acceptance is cost-minimization. Here is the description from a pioneering article by then Professor and now retired Judge Richard A. Posner, An Economic

Approach to Legal Procedure and Judicial Administration, 2 J.Legal Stud. 399, 400–02 (1973):

"An important purpose of substantive legal rules (such as the rules of tort and criminal law) is to increase economic efficiency [in the sense of maximizing economic value]. It follows . . . that mistaken imposition of legal liability, or mistaken failure to impose liability, will reduce efficiency. Judicial error is therefore a source of social costs and the reduction of error is a goal of the procedural system. . . .

"Even when the legal process works flawlessly, it involves costs—the time of lawyers, litigants, witnesses, jurors, judges, and other people, plus paper and ink, law office and court house maintenance, telephone service, etc. These costs are just as real as the costs resulting from error: in general we would not want to increase the direct costs of the legal process by one dollar in order to reduce error costs by 50 (or 99) cents. The economic goal is thus to minimize the sum of error and direct costs.

"Despite its generality, this formulation provides a useful framework in which to analyze the problems and objectives of legal procedure. It is usable even when the purpose of the substantive law is to transfer wealth or to bring about some other noneconomic goal, rather than to improve efficiency. All that is necessary is that it be possible, in principle, to place a price tag on the consequences of failing to apply the substantive law in all cases in which it was intended to apply, so that our two variables, error cost and direct cost, remain commensurable.

" . . . The cost inquiries required by the economic approach are not simple and will rarely yield better than crude approximations, but at the very least they serve to place questions of legal policy in a framework of rational inquiry."

This framework owes its success to its usefulness. To illustrate how well his approach worked, Posner considered the question whether to entitle the defendant to a trial-type hearing in an administrative action such as deportation or license revocation. He contrasted the traditional legal approach, which tended "to invoke either a purely visceral sense of fairness [Justice Stevens?] or a purely formal distinction between penal and nonpenal sanctions [Justice Stewart?]," with his economic approach: "We begin by asking, what is the cost of withholding a trial-type hearing in a particular type of case? This inquiry has two branches: first, how is the probability of an error likely to be affected by a trial-type hearing? If the legally dispositive issues are factual issues of the kind most reliably determined in trial-type hearings, the probability of error if such a hearing is denied may be high. Second, what is the cost of an error if one occurs? As a first approximation, if the stakes in the case are large, the cost of error in an individual case will be large, so if in addition the probability of error is high, total error costs will be very high. Having established the costs of error, we then inquire into the costs of measures—a trial-type hearing or whatever—that would reduce the error costs. If those direct costs are low . . . then adoption can be expected to reduce the sum of error and direct costs and thus increase efficiency.[2]"

For a further example of such a framework's usefulness, think still of the Lassiter case. Broadly conceived and properly utilized, economics insightfully suggests, first, that most process values played a negligibly small role in the prevailing formula and, second, that complex outcome values received a peculiarly fuzzy treatment in the clash of majority and dissent.

Lack of openness and rigor allowed Justices Stewart and Blackmun to state analyses that seemed essentially to differ only in conclusion. The two looked at the same three factors from Mathews v. Eldridge and gave them similar verbal weights: huge parental interest, key role for counsel, and small financial burden. As Justice Blackmun put it, "The Court's analysis is markedly similar to mine." How could the two come out differently? Something must have been going on behind the scenes.

It appears that Justice Stewart (and Chief Justice Burger's concurrence) stressed as the key outcome value the best result for little Billy, regardless of Abby Gail's legal rights: "the weight of the evidence that she had few sparks of [parental] interest was sufficiently great that the presence of counsel for Ms. Lassiter could not have made a determinative difference." Here the presence of counsel who would exclude all that hearsay evidence might even increase the odds of an incorrect refusal to terminate, a false negative in terms of the best real-world result for the child. The focus on the best outcome for the particular child necessitates a case-by-case approach.

By contrast, Justice Blackmun (and Justice Stevens's dissent) stressed as the key outcome value the system's respect for the parental legal rights: "the issue before the Court is not petitioner's character; it is whether she was given a meaningful opportunity to be heard." The routine presence of counsel would be hugely effective in reducing false positives, which would otherwise impede the correct legal result for the parent. The dissents also extended consideration beyond outcome values, giving heavy weight to process values. The focus on legal rights including process values suggests a categorical approach.

Thus, economic analysis reveals the real dispute between the Lassiter Justices. Indeed, a cost-minimization framework is useful enough to suggest consideration of its own costs. Among other drawbacks, it tends to distort analysis by ignoring or devaluing certain values, such as those hard to quantify, while injecting or exaggerating

---

[2]   [Although his 1973 article contained basically the same illustration, this last quotation comes from Richard A. Posner, Economic Analysis of Law 430 (2d ed. 1977), which here appended this footnote:] The Supreme Court has recently adopted essentially this approach as the standard guiding scrutiny of administrative hearing procedures for conformity with the requirements of due process. See Mathews v. Eldridge, 424 U.S. 319, 96 S.Ct. 893 (1976), and, for criticism of the Court's approach, Jerry L. Mashaw, The Supreme Court's Due Process Calculus for Administrative Adjudication in Mathews v. Eldridge: Three Factors in Search of a Theory of Value, 44 U.Chi.L.Rev. 28, 47–49 (1976).

others, such as efficiency. See Robert A. Baruch Bush, Dispute Resolution Alternatives and the Goals of Civil Justice: Jurisdictional Principles for Process Choice, 1984 Wis.L.Rev. 893, 929–32. Perhaps the Lassiter Court's very use of such a framework contributed to the opinions' inadequacies.

The best response to such a criticism is the simple but profound one that cost-minimization need not affect values. In a procedural system built on multiple and conflicting values, some analytic framework is necessary for weighing them against one another, and thus for evaluating procedural methods. Cost-minimization can play that role. It then is merely a tool for optimizing value, while the values can and should come from elsewhere. If used with careful thought about the inputted values, it does not have to denigrate or elevate any value. In other words, one can adopt a descriptive tool of economics without accepting any prescriptive baggage of economics.

———

T.S. Eliot, Little Gidding
14–15 (1942).

What we call the beginning is often the end
And to make an end is to make a beginning.

. . . .

We shall not cease from exploration
And the end of all our exploring
Will be to arrive where we started
And know the place for the first time.

PART 2

GOVERNING LAW

TOPIC A

FEDERAL COURTS

SECTION 1.   STATE LAW

We follow the preliminary overviews of litigation in the federal courts by now considering what law applies in particular federal actions. We know that the Federal Rules are the principal body of law governing matters of "practice and procedure" but that the Rules may not "abridge, enlarge or modify any substantive right." 28 U.S.C. § 2072. We have seen, too, that to draw the line between "procedure" and "substance," for this or any other purpose, is sometimes a difficult task. But assuming that we can classify a matter as one of substance, what then? Does federal or state substantive law apply in federal courts?

It comes as no surprise to the student by this time that not all courts arrive at the same answer to a given question of substantive law. The substantive law, both statutory and common, differs from state to state. But further: suppose that because diversity of citizenship exists and the jurisdictional amount is met, a plaintiff has a choice between bringing his action in the United States District Court for the Southern District of New York and instituting it in a state court of New York. Can he gain an advantage by examining the federal and state precedents and selecting the forum where the decisions on the relevant points of substantive law are more favorable to his case?

In the early years of our nation, the answer to this question was somewhat unclear. But for nearly a century after the unanimous decision in Swift v. Tyson, 41 U.S. (16 Pet.) 1 (1842) (Story, J.), the answer was clearly yes.

In the background of that classic case lay a land-fraud scheme in Maine, which had been perpetrated by two guys named Norton and Keith and which had unraveled as a consequence of the Panic of 1837. In the foreground was a bill of exchange or, in other words, a negotiable instrument by which one or more drawers (acting as a sort of check-writer) instruct a drawee (playing the role that a bank would play in the case of a check) to pay a certain sum to a payee or to the payee's designee by indorsement.

Here the shady Norton and Keith were drawers of the bill of exchange for $1540.30, the innocent Tyson was the drawee, and Norton the payee. Tyson accepted, or agreed to pay, the bill of exchange made out to Norton (or his indorsee) as part of the payment for land sold to Tyson by Norton and Keith.

Then Norton indorsed the bill to Swift in partial satisfaction of a prior, unrelated debt owing to Swift from Norton and Keith. Perhaps

Swift was in cahoots with them, as they inserted Swift as creditor in order to get money from Tyson, who was refusing to pay for the land.

Confusing? Maybe this will help. The bill in essence might have looked like the following. On this bill, Tyson later might have agreed to pay, by writing "Accepted at N.Y., N.Y." and signing his name. Still later, on the back of the bill, Norton might have indorsed it, by writing "Pay to the order of John Swift" and signing his name.

	Date: _____ May 1, 1836
To: George W. Tyson _____,	
Pay to the order of Nathaniel Norton _____	$ _____ 1540.30
Signed: _Nathaniel Norton_ & _Jairus S. Keith_ _____	

Now, however, Tyson refused to pay Swift, asserting that the original land sale had been induced by fraudulent representations on the part of the since bankrupt Norton and Keith. Consequently Swift, the indorsee from Maine, sued Tyson, the drawee-acceptor from New York, upon the bill of exchange in the federal court for the Southern District of New York. Jurisdiction rested on diversity of citizenship, with the claim exceeding the then jurisdictional amount of $500. Tyson's defense was that he had accepted the bill as the result of the drawers' fraud.

In certain circumstances—where the indorsee was a "bona fide holder without notice for valid consideration"—the indorsee would take a negotiable instrument free of most defenses otherwise available to the drawee-acceptor against the other original parties, such as the drawers' fraud. Swift, supposedly acting in good faith without notice of the alleged fraud, had taken the bill of exchange in satisfaction of a pre-existing debt. Did this make him a "bona fide holder without notice for valid consideration," so that Tyson's defense of fraud would be cut off as against him? Swift so contended, but Tyson countered that discharging a pre-existing debt was not a valid consideration under commercial law.

The issue thus narrowed to whether what Swift as indorsee had given in exchange for the indorsement was an invalid consideration in the eyes of the law. And the outcome turned on which sovereign's law should answer that purely legal issue.

It was assumed that under the common (that is, nonstatutory) law of New York (in this case, the place of acceptance of the bill), discharging a pre-existing debt would not serve as a valid consideration. The apparent purpose of this questionable New York law was to help prevent someone holding a note subject to defenses from signing the note over to someone in cahoots, who could then enforce it free from those defenses.

Nevertheless, Mr. Swift ultimately prevailed. The Supreme Court of the United States held that pre-existing debt would serve as a valid consideration under the true common law of commerce (a rule for negotiable instruments today adopted by U.C.C. § 3–303(a)(3)). In explaining its choice of law to govern the consideration issue, the Supreme Court said that the issue was one of general commercial law as to which the state-court decisions were not controlling. The Court conceded that if the New York rule had been laid down by state statute rather than developed through judicial decisions, or if the rule were a long-established local custom having the force of law, the Rules of Decision Act of 1789, now 28 U.S.C. § 1652, would have required the opposite result.

The essential holding of Swift, then, was that "upon its true intendment and construction" the phrase "laws of the several states" in § 1652 included, as being binding, only state statutes and local usages, not the state's general common law—and therefore, in this absence of a congressional directive, the federal courts had the power to come to an independent conclusion as to the "true" general common law. Justice Story elaborated: "In the ordinary use of language, it will hardly be contended, that the decisions of courts constitute laws. They are, at most, only evidence of what the laws are, and are not, of themselves, laws. They are often re-examined, reversed and qualified by the courts themselves, whenever they are found to be either defective, or ill-founded, or otherwise incorrect. The laws of a state are more usually understood to mean the rules and enactments promulgated by the legislative authority thereof, or long-established local customs having the force of laws." The true interpretation and effect of contracts and other commercial instruments lay "not in the decisions of the local tribunals, but in the general principles and doctrines of commercial jurisprudence."

What more detailed arguments could you marshal in favor of the Swift holding? What happened in the ensuing century to undercut those arguments? You can derive some answers to these two questions from a careful reading of the following case, which will allow you to flesh out Swift's above-sketched line of reasoning, its background jurisprudence regarding the nature of law and role of courts, and especially its motivating policies such as inducing legal uniformity, asserting federal authority, and ensuring a better commercial law. See also Richard H. Fallon, Jr., John F. Manning, Daniel J. Meltzer & David L. Shapiro, Hart and Wechsler's The Federal Courts and the Federal System 578–84 (7th ed. 2015).

———

Erie Railroad Co. v. Tompkins

Supreme Court of the United States, April 25, 1938.
304 U.S. 64, 58 S.Ct. 817.

■ Mr. Theodore Kiendl, with whom Messrs. William C. Cannon and Harold W. Bissell were on the brief, for petitioner.

. . . .

We do not question the finality of the holding of this Court in Swift v. Tyson . . . .

. . . .

The Pennsylvania decisions denying permissive rights on longitudinal pathways, as distinguished from crossings, declare a Pennsylvania rule sufficiently local in nature to be controlling . . . .

. . . .

■ MR. JUSTICE BRANDEIS delivered the opinion of the Court.

The question for decision is whether the oft-challenged doctrine of Swift v. Tyson shall now be disapproved.

Tompkins, a citizen of Pennsylvania, was injured on a dark night by a passing freight train of the Erie Railroad Company while walking along its right of way at Hughestown in that state. He claimed that the accident occurred through negligence in the operation, or maintenance, of the train; that he was rightfully on the premises as licensee because on a commonly used beaten footpath which ran for a short distance alongside the tracks; and that he was struck by something which looked like a door projecting from one of the moving cars. To enforce that claim he brought an action in the federal court for Southern New York, which had jurisdiction because the company is a corporation of that state. It denied liability; and the case was tried by a jury.

The Erie insisted that its duty to Tompkins was no greater than that owed to a trespasser. It contended, among other things, that its duty to Tompkins, and hence its liability, should be determined in accordance with the Pennsylvania law; that under the law of Pennsylvania, as declared by its highest court, persons who use pathways along the railroad right of way—that is, a longitudinal pathway as distinguished from a crossing—are to be deemed trespassers; and that the railroad is not liable for injuries to undiscovered trespassers resulting from its negligence, unless it be wanton or willful. Tompkins denied that any such rule had been established by the decisions of the Pennsylvania courts; and contended that, since there was no statute of the state on the subject, the railroad's duty and liability is to be determined in federal courts as a matter of general law.

Erie accident scene, in a trial exhibit—photographed from 150 feet southwest of the point of impact, which is marked with a small white x

The trial judge refused to rule that the applicable law precluded recovery. The jury brought in a verdict of $30,000; and the judgment entered thereon was affirmed by the Circuit Court of Appeals, which held (2 Cir., 90 F.2d 603, 604), that it was unnecessary to consider whether the law of Pennsylvania was as contended, because the question was one not of local, but of general, law, and that "upon questions of general law the federal courts are free, in absence of a local statute, to exercise their independent judgment as to what the law is; and it is well settled that the question of the responsibility of a railroad for injuries caused by its servants is one of general law. . . . Where the public has made open and notorious use of a railroad right of way for a long period of time and without objection, the company owes to persons on such permissive pathway a duty of care in the operation of its trains. . . . It is likewise generally recognized law that a jury may find that negligence exists toward a pedestrian using a permissive path on the railroad right of way if he is hit by some object projecting from the side of the train."

The Erie had contended that application of the Pennsylvania rule was required, among other things, by § 34 of the Federal Judiciary Act of September 24, 1789, c. 20, 28 U.S.C. § 725, which provides: "The laws of the several States, except where the Constitution, treaties, or statutes of the United States otherwise require or provide, shall be regarded as rules of decision in trials at common law, in the courts of the United States, in cases where they apply."[a]

Because of the importance of the question whether the federal court was free to disregard the alleged rule of the Pennsylvania common law, we granted certiorari. 302 U.S. 671, 58 S.Ct. 50.

First. Swift v. Tyson, 16 Pet. 1, 18, held that federal courts exercising jurisdiction on the ground of diversity of citizenship need not, in matters of general jurisprudence, apply the unwritten law of the state as declared by its highest court; that they are free to exercise an independent judgment as to what the common law of the state is—or should be; and that, as there stated by Mr. Justice Story, "the true interpretation of the 34th section limited its application to state laws strictly local, that is to say, to the positive statutes of the state, and the construction thereof adopted by the local tribunals, and to rights and titles to things having a permanent locality, such as the rights and titles to real estate, and other matters immovable and intraterritorial in their nature and character. It never has been supposed by us, that the section did apply, or was designed to apply, to questions of a more general nature, not at all dependent upon local statutes or local usages of a fixed and permanent operation, as, for example, to the construction of ordinary contracts or other written instruments, and especially to questions of general commercial law, where the state tribunals are called upon to perform the like functions as ourselves, that is, to ascertain, upon general reasoning and legal analogies, what is the true exposition of the contract or instrument, or what is the just rule furnished by the principles of commercial law to govern the case."

The Court in applying the rule of § 34 to equity cases, in Mason v. United States, 260 U.S. 545, 559, 43 S.Ct. 200, 204 [(1923)], said: "The statute, however, is merely declarative of the rule which would exist in the absence of the statute." The federal courts assumed, in the broad field of "general law," the power to declare rules of decision which Congress was confessedly without power to enact as statutes. Doubt was repeatedly expressed as to the correctness of the construction given § 34, and as to the soundness of the rule which it introduced. But it was the more recent research of a competent scholar, who examined the original document, which established that the construction given to it by the Court was erroneous; and that the purpose of the section was merely to make certain that, in all matters except those in which some federal law is controlling, the federal courts exercising jurisdiction in diversity of

---

[a]   With minor changes this section now appears as 28 U.S.C. § 1652. The words "in civil actions" were substituted for "in trials at common law" in the 1948 revision of title 28, but this change was intended only to conform the statute to the existing judicial interpretation.

citizenship cases would apply as their rules of decision the law of the state, unwritten as well as written.[5]

Criticism of the doctrine became widespread after the decision of Black & White Taxicab & Transfer Co. v. Brown & Yellow Taxicab & Transfer Co., 276 U.S. 518, 48 S.Ct. 404 [(1928)]. There, Brown & Yellow, a Kentucky corporation owned by Kentuckians, and the Louisville & Nashville Railroad, also a Kentucky corporation, wished that the former should have the exclusive privilege of soliciting passenger and baggage transportation at the Bowling Green, Ky., railroad station; and that the Black & White, a competing Kentucky corporation, should be prevented from interfering with that privilege. Knowing that such a contract would be void under the common law of Kentucky, it was arranged that the Brown & Yellow reincorporate under the law of Tennessee, and that the contract with the railroad should be executed there. The suit was then brought by the Tennessee corporation in the federal court for Western Kentucky to enjoin competition by the Black & White; an injunction issued by the District Court was sustained by the Court of Appeals; and this Court, citing many decisions in which the doctrine of Swift v. Tyson had been applied, affirmed the decree.

Second. Experience in applying the doctrine of Swift v. Tyson, had revealed its defects, political and social; and the benefits expected to flow from the rule did not accrue. Persistence of state courts in their own opinions on questions of common law prevented uniformity;[7] and the impossibility of discovering a satisfactory line of demarcation between the province of general law and that of local law developed a new well of uncertainties.

On the other hand, the mischievous results of the doctrine had become apparent. Diversity of citizenship jurisdiction was conferred in order to prevent apprehended discrimination in state courts against those not citizens of the state. Swift v. Tyson introduced grave discrimination by noncitizens against citizens. It made rights enjoyed under the unwritten "general law" vary according to whether enforcement was sought in the state or in the federal court; and the privilege of selecting the court in which the right should be determined was conferred upon the noncitizen. Thus, the doctrine rendered impossible equal protection of the law. In attempting to promote uniformity of law throughout the United States, the doctrine had prevented uniformity in the administration of the law of the state.

The discrimination resulting became in practice far-reaching. This resulted in part from the broad province accorded to the so-called

---

[5]   Charles Warren, New Light on the History of the Federal Judiciary Act of 1789 (1923) 37 Harv.L.Rev. 49, 51–52, 81–88, 108. [See Caleb Nelson, A Critical Guide to Erie Railroad Co. v. Tompkins, 54 Wm. & Mary L.Rev. 921, 951–56 (2013) (demonstrating the weakness of Warren's conclusion).—Ed.]

[7]   [The Court's footnote cited, among other writings, Felix Frankfurter, Distribution of Judicial Power Between United States and State Courts, 13 Cornell L.Q. 499, 524–30 (1928).]

"general law" as to which federal courts exercised an independent judgment. In addition to questions of purely commercial law, "general law" was held to include the obligations under contracts entered into and to be performed within the state, the extent to which a carrier operating within a state may stipulate for exemption from liability for his own negligence or that of his employee, the liability for torts committed within the state upon persons resident or property located there, even where the question of liability depended upon the scope of a property right conferred by the state, and the right to exemplary or punitive damages. Furthermore, state decisions construing local deeds, mineral conveyances, and even devises of real estate were disregarded.

In part the discrimination resulted from the wide range of persons held entitled to avail themselves of the federal rule by resort to the diversity of citizenship jurisdiction. Through this jurisdiction individual citizens willing to remove from their own state and become citizens of another might avail themselves of the federal rule. And, without even change of residence, a corporate citizen of the state could avail itself of the federal rule by reincorporating under the laws of another state, as was done in the Taxicab Case.

The injustice and confusion incident to the doctrine of Swift v. Tyson have been repeatedly urged as reasons for abolishing or limiting diversity of citizenship jurisdiction. Other legislative relief has been proposed. If only a question of statutory construction were involved, we should not be prepared to abandon a doctrine so widely applied throughout nearly a century. But the unconstitutionality of the course pursued has now been made clear, and compels us to do so.

Third. Except in matters governed by the Federal Constitution or by acts of Congress, the law to be applied in any case is the law of the state. And whether the law of the state shall be declared by its Legislature in a statute or by its highest court in a decision is not a matter of federal concern. There is no federal general common law. Congress has no power to declare substantive rules of common law applicable in a state whether they be local in their nature or "general," be they commercial law or a part of the law of torts. And no clause in the Constitution purports to confer such a power upon the federal courts. As stated by Mr. Justice Field when protesting in Baltimore & Ohio R. Co. v. Baugh, 149 U.S. 368, 401, 13 S.Ct. 914, 927 [(1893) (dissenting opinion)], against ignoring the Ohio common law of fellow-servant liability: "I am aware that what has been termed the general law of the country—which is often little less than what the judge advancing the doctrine thinks at the time should be the general law on a particular subject—has been often advanced in judicial opinions of this court to control a conflicting law of a state. I admit that learned judges have fallen into the habit of repeating this doctrine as a convenient mode of brushing aside the law of a state in conflict with their views. And I confess that, moved and governed by the authority of the great names of those judges, I have, myself, in many instances, unhesitatingly and confidently, but I think now erroneously, repeated the same doctrine. But, notwithstanding the frequency with which the doctrine has been reiterated, there stands, as a perpetual protest against its repetition, the constitution of the United States, which recognizes and preserves the autonomy and independence of the states— independence in their legislative and independence in their judicial departments. Supervision over either the legislative or the judicial action of the states is in no case permissible except as to matters by the constitution specifically authorized or delegated to the United States. Any interference with either, except as thus permitted, is an invasion of the authority of the state and, to that extent, a denial of its independence."

The fallacy underlying the rule declared in Swift v. Tyson is made clear by Mr. Justice Holmes [in his Black & White dissent]. The doctrine rests upon the assumption that there is "a transcendental body of law outside of any particular State but obligatory within it unless and until changed by statute," that federal courts have the power to use their judgment as to what the rules of common law are; and that in the federal courts "the parties are entitled to an independent judgment on matters of general law":

"But law in the sense in which courts speak of it today does not exist without some definite authority behind it. The common law so far as it is enforced in a State, whether called common law or not, is not the common law generally but the law of that State existing by the authority of that State without regard to what it may have been in England or anywhere else. . . .

"The authority and only authority is the State, and if that be so, the voice adopted by the State as its own [whether it be of its Legislature or of its Supreme Court] should utter the last word."

Thus the doctrine of Swift v. Tyson is, as Mr. Justice Holmes said, "an unconstitutional assumption of powers by the courts of the United States which no lapse of time or respectable array of opinion should make us hesitate to correct." In disapproving that doctrine we do not hold unconstitutional § 34 of the Federal Judiciary Act of 1789 or any other act of Congress. We merely declare that in applying the doctrine this Court and the lower courts have invaded rights which in our opinion are reserved by the Constitution to the several states.

Fourth. The defendant contended that by the common law of Pennsylvania as declared by its highest court in Falchetti v. Pennsylvania R. Co., 307 Pa. 203, 160 A. 859, the only duty owed to the plaintiff was to refrain from willful or wanton injury. The plaintiff denied that such is the Pennsylvania law. In support of their respective contentions the parties discussed and cited many decisions of the Supreme Court of the state. The Circuit Court of Appeals ruled that the question of liability is one of general law; and on that ground declined to decide the issue of state law. As we hold this was error, the judgment is reversed and the case remanded to it for further proceedings in conformity with our opinion.

Reversed.[b]

■ MR. JUSTICE CARDOZO took no part in the consideration or decision of this case.

■ [JUSTICE BUTLER filed a separate opinion concurred in by Justice McReynolds. In the course of arguing that Swift v. Tyson should not be overruled, Justice Butler gave attention to the Court's manner of proceeding:]

This Court has often emphasized its reluctance to consider constitutional questions and that legislation will not be held invalid as repugnant to the fundamental law if the case may be decided upon any other ground. In view of grave consequences liable to result from erroneous exertion of its power to set aside legislation, the Court should move cautiously, seek assistance of counsel, act only after ample deliberation, show that the question is before the Court, that its decision cannot be avoided by construction of the statute assailed or otherwise, indicate precisely the principle or provision of the Constitution held to have been transgressed, and fully disclose the reasons and authorities found to warrant the conclusion of invalidity. . . .

. . . Against the protest of those joining in this opinion, the Court declines to assign the case for reargument. It may not justly be assumed that the labor and argument of counsel for the parties would not disclose the right conclusion and aid the Court in the statement of reasons to support it. . . .

The course pursued by the Court in this case is repugnant to the Act of Congress of August 24, 1937, 50 Stat. 751.[c] . . .

. . . [N]ear the end of the last page the Court states that it does not hold § 34 unconstitutional, but merely that, in applying the doctrine of Swift v. Tyson construing it, this Court and the lower courts have invaded rights which are reserved by the Constitution to the several states. But, plainly through the form of words employed, the substance of the decision appears; it strikes down as unconstitutional § 34 as construed by our decisions; it divests the Congress of power to prescribe rules to be followed by federal courts when deciding questions of general law. In that broad field it compels this and the lower federal courts to follow decisions of the courts of a particular state.

---

b   On remand to the circuit court of appeals, the railroad's view prevailed regarding the content of Pennsylvania law, 98 F.2d 49 (2d Cir.), cert. denied, 305 U.S. 637, 59 S.Ct. 108 (1938). Thus Harry Tompkins, a young one-armed unemployed laborer and father, lost his sizable judgment.

c   This Act (with changes now 28 U.S.C. § 2403(a)) required, "whenever the constitutionality of any Act of Congress affecting the public interest is drawn in question in any court of the United States," that the court give notice to the Attorney General and allow intervention by the United States. This Act was not followed in this case, the majority apparently feeling that the Act did not apply. Why did it not apply?

I am of opinion that the constitutional validity of the rule need not be considered, because under the law, as found by the courts of Pennsylvania and generally throughout the country, it is plain that the evidence required a finding that plaintiff was guilty of negligence that contributed to cause his injuries and that the judgment below should be reversed upon that ground.

■ MR. JUSTICE REED. I concur in the conclusion reached in this case, in the disapproval of the doctrine of Swift v. Tyson, and in the reasoning of the majority opinion except in so far as it relies upon the unconstitutionality of the "course pursued" by the federal courts.

The "doctrine of Swift v. Tyson," as I understand it, is that the words "the laws," as used in § 34, line one, of the Federal Judiciary Act of September 24, 1789, did not include in their meaning "the decisions of the local tribunals." Mr. Justice Story, in deciding that point, said, 16 Pet. 1, 19: "Undoubtedly, the decisions of the local tribunals upon such subjects are entitled to, and will receive, the most deliberate attention and respect of this Court; but they cannot furnish positive rules, or conclusive authority, by which our judgments are to be bound up and governed."

To decide the case now before us and to "disapprove" the doctrine of Swift v. Tyson requires only that we say that the words "the laws" include in their meaning the decisions of the local tribunals. As the majority opinion shows, by its reference to Mr. Warren's researches and the first quotation from Mr. Justice Holmes, that this Court is now of the view that "laws" includes "decisions," it is unnecessary to go further and declare that the "course pursued" was "unconstitutional," instead of merely erroneous.

The "unconstitutional" course referred to in the majority opinion is apparently the ruling in Swift v. Tyson that the supposed omission of Congress to legislate as to the effect of decisions leaves federal courts free to interpret general law for themselves. I am not at all sure whether, in the absence of federal statutory direction, federal courts would be compelled to follow state decisions. There was sufficient doubt about the matter in 1789 to induce the first Congress to legislate. No former opinions of this Court have passed upon it. Mr. Justice Holmes evidently saw nothing "unconstitutional" which required the overruling of Swift v. Tyson, for he said in the very opinion quoted by the majority, "I should leave Swift v. Tyson undisturbed, . . . but I would not allow it to spread the assumed dominion into new fields." Black & White Taxicab & Transfer Co. v. Brown & Yellow Taxicab & Transfer Co., 276 U.S. 518, 535, 48 S.Ct. 404, 409. If the opinion commits this Court to the position that the Congress is without power to declare what rules of substantive law shall govern the federal courts, that conclusion also seems questionable. The line between procedural and substantive law is hazy but no one doubts federal power over procedure. Wayman v. Southard, 10 Wheat. 1. The Judiciary Article and the "necessary and proper" clause of Article One may fully authorize legislation, such as this section of the Judiciary Act.

In this Court, stare decisis, in statutory construction, is a useful rule, not an inexorable command. Burnet v. Coronado Oil & Gas Co., 285 U.S. 393, [406 n.1, 52 S.Ct. 443, 447 n.1 (1932) (Brandeis, J., dissenting). Other citations omitted.] It seems preferable to overturn an established construction of an act of Congress, rather than, in the circumstances of this case, to interpret the Constitution. [Citation omitted.]

There is no occasion to discuss further the range or soundness of these few phrases of the opinion. It is sufficient now to call attention to them and express my own non-acquiescence.

(refusing to ask state common law)

Questions: (1) What exactly did the Erie Court hold unconstitutional? Is that holding a restriction on the federal legislative power, or only on the federal judicial power?

(2) According to Justice Brandeis, why would a lower federal court sitting in New York apply the law of Pennsylvania?

(3) According to Justice Brandeis, how should the federal court determine what the law of Pennsylvania is? If the federal court were to resolve an unclear point of state law, what effect would the federal declaration of state law have in future state cases?

no fed. common law
(4) According to Justice Brandeis, in diversity and other cases, what matters will be decided under state law and what matters will be governed by federal law? Where would Justice Reed apparently draw that line?

BURDEN OF PROOF IN DIVERSITY ACTIONS

In Cities Service Oil Co. v. Dunlap, 308 U.S. 208, 60 S.Ct. 201 (1939), the plaintiff sued in diversity jurisdiction to remove a cloud on its title to certain Texas land that its deed covered. The defendants alleged in a counterclaim that the deed had included the land by mistake. The plaintiff replied that it had purchased the land in good faith, without notice of mistake, and for value. No evidence was offered by either side on the question raised by the plaintiff's reply. The district court and the circuit court of appeals found for the defendants by taking the view that the "burden of proving" bona fide purchase without notice for value was on the plaintiff, with the circuit court explaining that a federal court could ignore the recognized Texas rule to the contrary because the burden of production in a diversity case like this was "a matter of practice or procedure and not a matter of substantive law." The Supreme Court unanimously reversed, briefly explaining: "We cannot accept the view that the question presented was only one of practice in courts of equity. Rather we think it relates to a substantial right upon which the holder of recorded legal title to Texas land may confidently rely."

In Palmer v. Hoffman, 318 U.S. 109, 63 S.Ct. 477 (1943), the unanimous Court peremptorily disposed of the contention that an instruction to the jury, to the effect that the burden of persuasion as to contributory negligence in federal court is on the defendant, was proper because of Rule 8(c)(1). The Court said: "Rule 8(c) covers only the manner of pleading. The question of the burden of establishing contributory negligence is a question of local law which federal courts in diversity of citizenship cases . . . must apply." The Court cited Cities Service in support of this conclusion.

———

CHOICE OF LAW

Imagine a Pennsylvania railroad accident giving rise to a lawsuit in a New York *state* court. Which state's tort law should apply? What law governs burden of proof? As you undoubtedly perceive, a pervasive problem in litigation that involves nonlocal elements is choosing which sovereign's law to apply.

Generally, as between coequal sovereigns such as states (or countries), it is the forum court's task to choose the governing law under some technique for choice of law. The technique followed in any particular state's courts has typically evolved from (1) a traditional set of wooden and crude rules that pointed with relative certainty to the law of a particular place where some particular event occurred (e.g., the rule of lex loci delicti, or the law of the place of the wrong, controlled the choice for substantive issues in tort cases; but the lex fori, or the law of the forum, applied on all issues that the forum court characterized as procedural) to (2) a very flexible and sensitive but quite uncertain approach of comparing as to each issue the interests of the involved sovereigns in having their own law applied and then applying the law of the sovereign whose policies would be most impaired by nonapplication (so-called interest analysis). Nevertheless, this is a subject dominated today by competing subtheories that elaborate or alter interest analysis, and these subtheories conflict sharply at least on the verbal level. Many of these modern differences of opinion have arisen as theorists have worked to reinject some degree of practical certainty into the theoretical precision of interest analysis. For example, one might use interest analysis to create a new series of general rules to cover common situations. Such matters are the subject of study in the upperclass course of Conflict of Laws.

American states are under some constitutional restraint on their choice-of-law process. The Supreme Court has, however, interpreted the Federal Constitution in a way that gives state courts a very free hand in choosing the governing law and, in particular, in choosing to apply their own law. The Court summarized the constitutional restriction in Allstate Insurance Co. v. Hague, 449 U.S. 302, 308, 101 S.Ct. 633, 637–38 (1981) (plurality opinion): "In deciding constitutional choice-of-law questions, whether under the Due Process Clause or the Full Faith and Credit Clause, this Court has traditionally examined the contacts of the State, whose law was applied, with the parties and with the occurrence or transaction giving rise to the litigation. [Citation omitted.] In order to ensure that the choice of law is neither arbitrary nor fundamentally unfair, [citation omitted], the Court has invalidated the choice of law of a State which has had no significant contact or significant aggregation of contacts, creating state interests, with the parties and the occurrence or transaction."

Cases such as Erie, Cities Service, and Palmer treat a "vertical" choice of law that is similar to but distinguishable from this interstate and international, or "horizontal," choice of law. Those three cases concern a choice of law in the special sense that the federal authority is deciding whether federal law has been or should be generated to apply to a given issue, such as burden of proof, or whether state law should be left to govern.

Now return to a Pennsylvania railroad accident giving rise to a lawsuit in a New York *federal* court. Here the two types of choice of law intersect. There must be a vertical choice of law regarding the issue of horizontal choice of law. That is, does federal or state law decide which state's tort law to apply?

———

KLAXON CO. v. STENTOR ELECTRIC MANUFACTURING CO., 313 U.S. 487, 61 S.Ct. 1020 (1941). Plaintiff brought a diversity action for breach of contract in the United States District Court for the District of Delaware and obtained a verdict for $100,000. The court, applying the law of New York (the place of performance of the contract), added prejudgment interest to that sum. The Third Circuit affirmed this addition of interest, saying: (1) that the right to prejudgment interest is a matter of substance, not procedure, and so is governed by state law; (2) that such right "should be settled by reference to the law of the appropriate state according to the type of case being tried"; and (3) that in this contract case, under general principles of conflict-of-laws doctrine, the appropriate state is the place of performance.

On certiorari, the Supreme Court reversed. Passing over point (1), Justice Reed, for a unanimous Court, said:

"The principal question in this case is whether in diversity cases the federal courts must follow conflict of laws rules prevailing in the states in which they sit. We left this open in Ruhlin v. New York Life Insurance Company, 304 U.S. 202, 208, note 2, 58 S.Ct. 860, 862 n. 2. The frequent recurrence of the problem, as well as the conflict of approach to the problem between the Third Circuit's opinion here and that of the First Circuit in Sampson v. Channell, 110 F.2d 754, 759–762, led us to grant certiorari.

. . . .

"We are of opinion that the prohibition declared in Erie R. Co. v. Tompkins, 304 U.S. 64, 58 S.Ct. 817, against such independent determinations by the federal courts extends to the field of conflict of laws. The conflict of laws rules to be applied by the federal court in Delaware must conform to those prevailing in Delaware's state courts. Otherwise, the accident of diversity of citizenship would constantly disturb equal administration of justice in coordinate state and federal courts sitting side by side. See Erie R. Co. v. Tompkins, supra, 304 U.S. at 74–77, 58 S.Ct. at 820–822. Any other ruling would do violence to the principle of uniformity within a state upon which the Tompkins decision is based. Whatever lack of uniformity this may produce between federal courts in different states is attributable to our federal system, which leaves to a state, within the limits permitted by the Constitution, the right to pursue local policies diverging from those of its neighbors. It is not for the federal courts to thwart such local policies by enforcing an independent 'general law' of conflict of laws. Subject only to review by this Court on any federal question that may arise, Delaware is free to determine whether a given matter is to be governed by the law of the forum or some other law. Cf. Milwaukee County v. M.E. White Co., 296 U.S. 268, 272, 56 S.Ct. 229, 231. This Court's views are not the decisive factor in determining the applicable conflicts rule. Cf. Funkhouser v. J.B. Preston Co., 290 U.S. 163, 54 S.Ct. 134. And the proper function of the Delaware federal court is to ascertain what the state law is, not what it ought to be."

The Court remanded the case for determination of which state's law would be applied by Delaware state courts on the question of prejudgment interest. On remand, the circuit court of appeals found that Delaware would apply New York law, 125 F.2d 820 (3d Cir.), cert. denied, 316 U.S. 685, 62 S.Ct. 1284 (1942).

———

Question: (5) Reexamine Justice Roberts' statement of the plaintiff's dilemma in Sibbach v. Wilson & Co., supra p. 10. How did he handle the conflict-of-laws problem there? How is the plaintiff's supposed dilemma affected by the Court's later decision in Klaxon? (You should periodically renew this question—how to pose properly Sibbach's "dilemma" under prevailing doctrine—as you progress through this study of Erie's progeny.)

———

Edward A. Purcell, Jr., "The Story of Erie: How Litigants, Lawyers, Judges, Politics, and Social Change Reshape the Law"

Civil Procedure Stories 21 (Kevin M. Clermont ed., 2d ed. 2008), with case documents at http://civprostories.law.cornell.edu.

Erie Railroad Co. v. Tompkins is one of the most famous cases in American law, unusually important and also unusually puzzling. It is important because it implicated an extraordinary number of fundamental issues ranging from elevated questions of legal philosophy and constitutional structure to practical problems of judicial administration and manipulative litigation tactics. It is puzzling because the Court's opinion made a drastic change in the law on the basis of principles that were not fully specified and reasoning that was abbreviated and, in part, intentionally misleading.

Unfortunately for students of civil procedure, Erie's intrinsically puzzling qualities have been compounded by the extrinsic processes of historical change. When announced, Erie was a response to more than half a century of social and political conflict, and it represented the triumph of early twentieth-century progressive views on two major and sharply contested political issues: the proper institutional role of the federal courts and the relationship between those courts and the large national corporations that were coming to dominate the American economy. Rooted in that political and social context, Erie proved an awkward fit in the profoundly different world that began to coalesce almost immediately after its birth. . . .

. . . .

Social and Legal Background

"The question for decision," Erie tells us in its first sentence, "is whether the oft-challenged doctrine of Swift v. Tyson shall now be disapproved." From its very beginning, then, the opinion is puzzling, for the question before the Court was not the validity of Swift v. Tyson but only the scope of its doctrine. Neither party had questioned Swift or called for its overthrow. Indeed, both had explicitly relied on it, though construing it differently. Why, then, did the Court decide to alter the question it faced and disapprove the doctrine? To answer that query, as well as many others, we must begin where Erie did, with Swift v. Tyson.

. . . .

Although Swift enjoyed some success in achieving Story's goals, its practical significance changed after the Civil War. As the economy industrialized and American society grew more complex, the Court extended the idea of "general" law into common-law fields far removed from commercial law. Swift began to affect not just merchants but most Americans, and to affect them adversely. It was then that the Swift doctrine became "oft-challenged," and it was there that the road to Erie itself began.

. . . .

The resulting political battles gave Swift a new resonance. Increasingly, the federal courts were becoming identified with the new national economy and the protection of corporate rights, and their "general" law decisions spread from commercial issues into most common-law fields and seemed to grow ever more favorable to corporate interests. Further, for a variety of reasons, including the existence of the "general" common law, the federal courts were becoming increasingly burdensome and disadvantageous forums for individuals who were forced to litigate against large national corporations. On these two levels, then, the Swift doctrine came to symbolize the pro-corporate role of the federal courts and, consequently, to become part of the widening national political debate. Consequently, a succession of groups—populists, progressives, New Dealers, labor unions, plaintiffs' attorneys, and states' rights advocates—grew increasingly critical of the federal courts and the Swift doctrine, while a set of opposing groups—large-scale corporations, the elite corporate bar, and social and political conservatives—rallied vigorously to the defense of both.

. . . .

. . . The pattern was clear, widespread, and long established. Overwhelmingly, individual plaintiffs who sued national corporations brought their claims in their local state courts, and their corporate adversaries removed. . . .

. . . .

Factual Background

Lying in the heart of the old mining and industrial region of northeastern Pennsylvania, the small borough of Hughestown is situated roughly halfway between Scranton and Wilkes-Barre, almost a hundred miles north and slightly west of Philadelphia. In 1934 it was home to some 2,800 people, most of whom were experiencing first-hand the hardships of the Great Depression. Through the town ran a bare single-track rail line, a minor tributary to the main routes that shouldered the nation's heavy interstate traffic. Alongside the track a dirt footpath had been tramped into the ground by long decades of use.

William Colwell, who had labored in the local mines since he was a boy, lived in a house that bordered the track. Long before dawn on July 27, 1934, comfortably asleep in bed, he was suddenly roused by a loud banging on his front door. Two boys were outside, one running up and down the street and the other "hollering that there was a fellow run over." His wife warned him "that them fellows was crazy," but Colwell got up, stumbled downstairs, and peered out a side window. Next to the tracks he could make out what looked like a body. Hastily pulling on his pants, he rushed out. There on the footpath, sprawled next to the rails, he found the body and, between the rails, a severed arm. Then, he recognized the face. It was Harry Tompkins, his neighbor across the street. Colwell yelled at the two boys to run to a nearby house where there was a telephone and call an ambulance. He waited at the scene, a handful of neighbors straggling up through the darkness to join him. Finally, an ambulance arrived.

Harry James Tompkins was four days short of his twenty-seventh birthday at the time. Born and raised in Hughestown, he lived with his wife, Edith, and their three-year-old daughter, Naomi, in a small frame house that stood half a block from the spot where he lay that night. Like so many of his friends and neighbors, he knew the tracks well. Frequently he had walked beside them, and sometimes the trains they carried had awakened him in the middle of the night as they rumbled through town.

At fifteen, Tompkins had left school to get a job. Working first in a knitting mill and then a coal mine, he finally caught on at the nearby Pittston Stove Works where he became an iron molder, joined a labor union, and toiled for more than a decade. He and his co-workers, however, could not escape the depression. In early 1934 the stove works closed its doors. For the next two months Tompkins struggled to keep his family together, sometimes finding work repairing stoves or doing other pick-up jobs.

On the fateful night, he had been visiting his sick mother-in-law, who lived some five or six miles away. Shortly after midnight he left her house and walked several miles along the road until a car pulled over and a fellow iron molder from the foundry offered him a ride. Ferrying him the last mile or so to Hughestown, the co-worker dropped him off a couple of hundred feet from his house, at the familiar footpath along the tracks that would lead him homeward. As Tompkins headed down the path, he heard the whistle and saw the headlight of an oncoming train. "I kept right on walking," he recalled. "I had walked [along the path] plenty of times and I wasn't a bit afraid." The engine steamed by, and he glanced up at the rushing cars. Suddenly, "something came up in front of me, a black object that looked like a door." Tompkins tried to react. "I went to put my hands up and I guess before I got them up I was hit," he explained. "I didn't have a chance." Slammed in the head, he was knocked unconscious and hurled to the ground, his right arm flung under the passing cars. Hours later he awoke in a hospital.

Considering the nature of his injuries, his medical treatment went well. Doctors quickly sedated him and, after examination, amputated the remainder of his right arm, up to and including the socket. Although his injury would subsequently require further medical attention before it healed, the hospital released him after three weeks.

"Lefty" Tompkins, as he soon became known to his friends, was disabled and desperate, but he was not hesitant. He immediately looked for a lawyer, and friends quickly put him in contact with an attorney in New York City named Bernard G. Nemeroff. Only twenty-seven years old himself, Nemeroff had been scrambling to keep a law practice alive for five hard, depression-wracked years. He jumped at the opportunity to handle Tompkins' promising and potentially high-stakes claim. For litigation support he brought in his partner, who was another struggling young lawyer by the name of Bernard Kaufman, and retained a Columbia Law School student named Aaron L. Danzig to do legal research. The twenty-one-year-old Danzig soon developed a special affection for Tompkins. A victim of polio as a young boy, Danzig had also lost the use of one of his arms.

Prior Proceedings

1. The Art of Forum-Shopping. For what initially seemed like a routine personal injury suit, Danzig had to do a surprising amount of legal research. The nature of Tompkins' claim and the extent of his injuries were obvious, and there was no question that the train in question—the Ashley Special—belonged to the Erie Railroad Company. The matter of the controlling law, however, introduced some intricate doctrinal and tactical problems. Pennsylvania common law, Danzig discovered, would most likely deny Tompkins' claim. . . .

Fortunately for Tompkins, Danzig had been an enterprising lad in law school. When he took the course in Conflicts of Law, he prepared a detailed outline of the subject "and peddled it to my fellow students." Beyond the academic and financial rewards he reaped, Danzig gained something else. "I knew," he later recalled, "all about Swift v. Tyson." Assuring himself that its doctrine applied to torts and that most other courts rejected the Pennsylvania rule, Danzig informed Nemeroff that Tompkins could still prevail if his suit was filed in federal court. There, under Swift, the court could ignore Pennsylvania common law and apply the more generally accepted rule that railroads owed a duty of ordinary care to those using paths that paralleled their tracks.

. . . .

If the need to invoke Swift made a federal forum essential, Tompkins attorneys had a further question to answer. Should they choose a federal court in New York or Pennsylvania? They could get personal jurisdiction over the railroad in either state, and venue would be proper in both. Thus, more research was necessary, and it uncovered a sound reason to choose New York. The Third Circuit, which covered Pennsylvania, tended to encourage greater deference to the rulings of state courts, while the Second Circuit, which governed the New York federal courts, applied Swift more readily and broadly. Thus, a New York federal court would be more likely than a Pennsylvania federal court to ignore Pennsylvania "local" law and apply the Swift doctrine.

Accordingly, the attorneys chose to sue in the United States District Court for the Southern District of New York. There, on August 29, 1934, they filed Harry Tompkins' suit against the Erie Railroad. The complaint sought damages in the amount of $100,000.

2.   *The Adversaries.* Chartered in 1832, the Erie Railroad had a long and proud, if not always financially stable, history. . . .

If Tompkins and his attorneys—young, socially marginal, and legally inexperienced—seemed well-matched to each other, so did the Erie and its attorneys, the elite New York law firm of Davis, Polk, Wardwell, Gardiner & Reed. . . .

When Davis Polk received Tompkins' complaint, it assigned the Erie's defense to its chief trial lawyer, Theodore Kiendl. A forty-four-year-old graduate of Columbia Law School . . . , Kiendl had been a partner at the firm since 1923. Known for his exceptional thoroughness and ruthless cross-examinations, he specialized in defending the firm's corporate clients against negligence actions. In court, he was cool, analytical, and methodical, and his meticulous trial preparation included extensive and precisely drafted lists formulating every question that he planned to ask each witness he would examine. Indeed, Kiendl may have been a bit too cold and formal. He once introduced himself in court to a lawyer he thought was the opposing counsel only to learn that the person was one of his own firm's associates assigned to the case. To Danzig, the neophyte from New Jersey, Kiendl seemed the embodiment of the nation's social and economic elite. With "iron-gray hair" and a "striped iron-gray suit," he was "pure Westchester."

Kiendl positioned the railroad as best he could. His answer denied the critical allegations of the complaint and pleaded contributory negligence as an affirmative defense. The Erie was not liable because it had violated no duty of care owed to the plaintiff.

3.   *Trial and Appeal.* As trial approached, Nemeroff recognized that his inexperience could be costly, especially against an adversary like Kiendl. Accordingly, he brought in an experienced negligence lawyer, G. Everett "Stub" Hunt, to try Tompkins' case. Like Kiendl, Hunt was an astute and dangerous adversary. Unlike Kiendl, he was low-key, humorous, and immediately likeable. Fully at home before a jury, he was, "of course, a gifted actor." Although he knew Kiendl well and played bridge with him often, Hunt would give his friend no quarter in the courtroom.

The trial began on October 5, 1936. Hunt put Tompkins and five other witnesses on the stand, establishing the basic facts and deftly eliciting the jury's sympathy for his poor and injured client. The testimony stressed that the footpath had been long established and commonly used and that it was widely considered safe even when trains were passing. Kiendl cross-examined methodically, suggesting contradictions in the testimony of Tompkins and his witnesses and seeking to show that a reasonable person would have realized that the footpath was so narrow and close to the tracks that a passing train would obviously endanger anyone walking on it.

When Hunt rested, Kiendl moved to dismiss. He argued, first, that plaintiff had neither pleaded nor proved wanton negligence as required by Pennsylvania law and, second, that Tompkins had been guilty of contributory negligence as a matter of law. The court denied his motion.

Kiendl then proceeded with defendant's case. He called seventeen witnesses, seeking primarily to show that the railroad had repeatedly inspected the train in question and that all of the doors on its cars had been closed and securely fastened. On cross, Hunt chipped away at the railroad's witnesses, suggesting ways in which car doors could have jarred loose during operation and raising doubts about the thoroughness of the railroad's inspections and the accuracy of its supporting records.

After four days of testimony with a brief interruption, the trial ended on October 13. Rejecting Kiendl's request to charge on Pennsylvania law, the court instructed under the "general" law. The jury came back in ninety minutes, awarding Tompkins the munificent sum of $30,000, an amount equal to approximately forty-five times his annual salary.

Kiendl immediately appealed, raising several issues, including the argument that the court below had incorrectly ignored Pennsylvania law. Although his brief did not discuss Swift by name, it did argue that the "general" law should not apply on the facts of the case. A state's common law should control, Kiendl maintained, when its highest courts "have completely established a settled policy regarding local matters." In opposition, Nemeroff's brief stood squarely on the Swift doctrine and the applicable rule of "general" law. With barely a nod to Kiendl's argument about Pennsylvania law, the Second Circuit held that "general" law controlled, dismissed the railroad's other contentions, and unanimously affirmed the judgment below.

Kiendl's back was now to the wall.[62] His only remaining option was to file a petition for a writ of certiorari in the United States Supreme Court. Given the utterly routine nature of the suit and the fact that the Court granted only a small percentage of such petitions, it seemed highly unlikely that the railroad could gain another hearing, much less prevail ultimately on the merits. "There wasn't a chance in the world," Danzig believed.

Kiendl, however, persisted. Since the Second Circuit's affirmance ended the automatic stay of the judgment below, the Erie was faced with either paying Tompkins his $30,000 or securing a stay. Although the Court was in summer recess, Justice Benjamin N. Cardozo—who had

---

[62]   At some point after judgment the Erie offered to settle the case. Recollections recorded some thirty years after the fact, however, disagree about events in this informal part of the case. In 1978 Nemeroff recalled that the railroad contacted Tompkins after the original judgment was entered and offered him $7,500 to settle. In 1976 Danzig recalled an offer that came later, after the Second Circuit had affirmed the judgment, and that was for a much larger amount, $22,000. Both recollections agree that a settlement offer was made, that it came through one of Tompkins' acquaintances in Hughestown, that Tompkins' lawyers were confident of victory and dissuaded their client from accepting, and that for approximately two weeks his lawyers hid Tompkins away from the railroad at a location near Nemeroff's home on Long Island. . . .

succeeded Holmes after the latter's retirement in 1932—lived in a commuter town just north of New York City, and Kiendl hastily arranged for an appointment. On a warm July day, he met Nemeroff, Danzig, and one of Hunt's partners at the Justice's old Victorian house in Mamaroneck, New York. Greeting the lawyers in bedroom slippers and a black velvet jacket, Cardozo sat with a white handkerchief in his right hand, tamping his perspiration, while he listened to the lawyers argue. Faced with two unfavorable decisions below and an opposing brief that cited cases from 24 states rejecting the Pennsylvania rule, Kiendl decided to gamble. Knowing that Swift had many critics . . . , he rolled the dice. "Your Honor," he informed the judge, "I must be honest and say that if a stay is not granted, we will carry the case no further." At that, Cardozo paused and then turned reluctantly to Tompkins' attorneys. "[I]f I don't grant the stay it will end the case," he told them, "and I think the Court as a whole ought to have the opportunity to rule on the petition." Stay granted.

Three months later the other shoe fell. On October 11, 1937, to the surprise of everyone involved, the Court granted the railroad's petition for certiorari. After consecutive losses at trial and on appeal, Kiendl had now won his second consecutive victory. The fifth engagement would be decisive.

4. The Art of Appellate Lawyering. The Second Circuit's opinion had surely settled one matter. If Kiendl were to win the final battle, he had to develop some convincing theory that would enable him to avoid or defeat the Swift doctrine. After considerable thought and research, he settled on an approach that was both shrewd and nimble. He would stand squarely on the ninety-six-year-old precedent but reinterpret its doctrine to his advantage. "We do not," his brief announced emphatically, "question the finality of the holding of this Court in Swift v. Tyson." Embracing the doctrine firmly, he argued that it had a narrower scope than the court below had given it. Swift was good law, Kiendl insisted, but it called for the application of "general" law "only when the pertinent principle or rule of law has not been definitely settled, foreclosed or established" in an individual state. This Pennsylvania law had been clearly and authoritatively settled by the state's supreme court. Moreover, he argued that the Pennsylvania rule involved local policy regarding local rights of way, and so was "predominantly local in nature." Swift itself directed the federal courts to apply that "local" law.

Although Kiendl's argument adroitly transformed an obstacle into an ally, his brief raised an intriguing question. Why did he not also argue, in the alternative, that Swift should be overturned? . . .

. . . .

If Kiendl's instincts had, in fact, failed him, the oral argument before eight Justices on January 31, 1938, instantly sounded a clarion that he could not have missed.[72] He had hardly opened his mouth when Brandeis pounced. "Mr. Kiendl," the Justice asked bluntly, "do you think Swift v. Tyson was rightly decided?" Quickly the other Justices jumped in, and Kiendl was forced to spend most of his allotted time addressing the issue he had sought so assiduously to avoid, Swift's fundamental legitimacy. Despite Brandeis's direct invitation—and the promise of automatic victory if Swift were overturned—Kiendl still refused to criticize the case. Indeed, he actually argued that Swift was too well-established even to be questioned.

. . . .

Much more plausibly, Kiendl did not attack Swift for a simple but compelling reason: he did not want it overturned. He knew that his client would rather pay Harry Tompkins $30,000 than see the "general" law interred. Like other national corporations, the Erie Railroad put a high value on the Swift doctrine and wanted to preserve it at all costs. It was understandable, then, why Kiendl's brief not only failed to attack Swift but defended it explicitly. Attacks on the doctrine "have been largely misdirected," it argued, and the narrower interpretation he offered "furnishes the fundamental answer to the many criticisms of the doctrine of Swift v. Tyson."

Thus, Kiendl's strategy was even more clever and sophisticated than it initially appeared. His lawyering was brilliant not merely because he transformed a negative into a positive but because he did so while also shaping an argument that would protect his client's interests in both the short and the long term. His narrow interpretation would enable his client to triumph on narrow grounds in Tompkins' suit while safeguarding the Swift doctrine for its continued use in future disputes.[78] Had he prevailed, Kiendl would have saved the railroad the substantial sum of $30,000 while at the same time preserving the "general" law that served its interests in the great majority of cases. . . .

. . . .

The Supreme Court Decision

1.   The Justices Vote. It was no surprise that it was Brandeis who first challenged Kiendl at the oral argument. A dedicated progressive and a close friend and long-time admirer of Holmes, Brandeis was a resolute opponent of the "general" law. . . .

Brandeis had risen to national prominence at the turn of the century as a political activist and "people's lawyer" who warned repeatedly

---

[72]   Cardozo was absent, stricken with an illness that would take his life within months. . . .

[78]   Ordinarily, Kiendl's tactic would have succeeded. As a general matter, the Court refuses to address issues that have not been raised and briefed by the parties. Thus, Kiendl had strong grounds for thinking that his tactic would confine the Court to the question of Swift's applicability and prevent it from considering the question of its basic legitimacy.

against the dangers posed by the excessive and unchecked powers that national corporations wielded. . . .

Brandeis's progressive orientation led him to view the Swift doctrine as not only mistaken but also harmful. . . . He was determined to see it abolished [before his imminent retirement].

By the time of the oral argument in Erie, [the eighty-one-year-old] Brandeis sensed that at long last his opportunity was at hand. Only two members of the Taxicab majority, Pierce Butler and James C. McReynolds, remained on the bench. Stone, who had also joined Holmes's dissent, would surely favor overturning Swift, and all of the other four Justices sitting on the case seemed promising. Black and Reed were almost certain to agree with him, while either of the Court's two "swing" Justices, Hughes and Roberts, could provide the crucial fifth vote. Both had supported recent efforts to limit Swift, and both had joined the Court's "progressive wing"—Brandeis, Stone, and Cardozo—during the previous term to create the critical five-to-four majorities that had initiated the so-called New Deal constitutional revolution. Hughes, of course, was the key. If Brandeis could get him, the Chief Justice would most likely bring along Roberts, who frequently looked to Hughes for leadership.

When the eight Justices met in conference, the matter was quickly settled. Hughes himself opened the door. "If we wish to overrule Swift v. Tyson," he announced, "here is our opportunity." Scenting victory, Brandeis and Stone jumped to the attack. Butler and McReynolds objected fiercely, but the two old conservatives had no influence over their colleagues. In quick succession each of the three most junior Justices voted to overrule, creating a solid 6–2 majority to abolish the "general" common law. Acknowledging Brandeis's leadership on the issue, Hughes assigned him the task of writing the Court's opinion.

2. *Making Constitutional Law and Holding a Majority.* Although the conference vote had settled the basic issue, it had left an equally important matter unresolved. On what theory was Swift to be overruled? For his part, Brandeis had no doubt. The decision should turn on constitutional grounds. He wanted to repudiate Swift on the strongest possible basis and to bury its doctrine so decisively that it could never be revived. Accordingly, he drafted an opinion that referred to many practical criticisms of Swift but that rested on the Constitution.

In his earliest draft that reached the legal issue, dated March 7, Brandeis invoked Holmes's protest in the Taxicab case that Swift constituted "an unconstitutional assumption of powers by the courts of the United States." Further, he adumbrated the constitutional theory that would underlay his final opinion:

> Except where a rule of decision is one to be determined by the federal authority, the law to be applied is necessarily a state rule, whether it be enunciated by the legislature or by the courts

of the State. For there is no other authority. Congress has no power to declare the law general.

Brandeis, then, believed that Swift was unconstitutional because it allowed federal judicial lawmaking in areas that lay beyond the scope of "the federal authority." The scope of that authority was determined by the lawmaking powers the Constitution conferred on Congress and the federal government, and those powers did not include any power to make "general" law.

Unfortunately for Brandeis, the other Justices did not fully understand, or perhaps fully share, his theory. When he circulated a completed draft in late March, his majority immediately began to wobble. Stone questioned the statements about congressional power and asked Brandeis to "rephrase" his argument or "eliminate" some of his constitutional language. Reed likewise challenged the draft because, in his view, it suggested new substantive limits on the lawmaking powers of Congress. He proposed that the opinion avoid constitutional matters altogether and overrule Swift solely on statutory grounds by holding simply that the case misconstrued the word "laws" in the Rules of Decision Act.[87] To make matters worse for Brandeis, Hughes harbored similar reservations. The Chief Justice was uneasy about the constitutional language and preferred Reed's narrow statutory approach. Of the six Justices in the original majority, only Black expressed his unqualified acceptance of the draft.

Brandeis, however, was determined. He met with Stone on the afternoon of March 24, explained his theory in greater detail, and persuaded him to accept the constitutional language. Stone relented, in part, because Reed's proposal had reoriented his thinking. Stone was attracted to the simplicity of placing the decision on statutory grounds, but he was also troubled about the propriety of disturbing an issue of statutory construction that had been settled for almost a century. "In view of the long history of our support of Swift v. Tyson," he wrote to Brandeis the day after they had met, "I realize the force of the constitutional aspects of the case as an impelling reason for overruling Swift v. Tyson." Stone, in other words, had come to see Brandeis's constitutional argument as a necessary justification for the Court's decision to alter the construction of a statute that had been so long settled.[92] With Stone back on board, Brandeis turned to Hughes. He explained that Stone had agreed to accept his constitutional language and, indeed, that Stone now insisted that the decision had to turn on

---

[87]   ... Reed's suggestion that the case be resolved on statutory grounds highlighted the unshakeable nature of Brandeis's determination to dispatch Swift on constitutional grounds. The Court had often declared that it would not reach constitutional questions if it could decide cases on narrower grounds, and Brandeis had been one of the most forceful advocates of that practice. ... Brandeis, however, refused to accept Reed's suggestion. [Citation omitted.]

[92]   Accordingly, Stone asked Brandeis to alter the language in his draft to emphasize that it was precisely the command of the Constitution, not mere practical considerations of convenience, that required the Court to overrule Swift. ...

constitutional grounds. Sensitive to his responsibilities as Chief Justice and aware that a majority decision was essential in a case of such magnitude, Hughes reluctantly agreed to accept the draft's constitutional language. Likely influenced by the decision of Stone and especially Hughes to stay on board, Roberts also assented.

Reed held out. In spite of Brandeis's patient effort to explain his constitutional theory and assure him that it did not impose new limits on Congress, the Court's most junior Justice remained unpersuaded. Within days he circulated a draft concurrence that rested on statutory grounds. No one joined him.

Thus, Brandeis's constitutional language lost a vote but held a bare majority. Four other Justices accepted his opinion, while Reed concurred separately and Butler and McReynolds dissented. With a few relatively minor alterations—and with but a hair's breadth margin of victory— Brandeis's draft, with its original constitutional theory intact, became an opinion of the Court [on April 25, 1938].

   3. The Final Opinion. In shaping his opinion, Brandeis was animated by a variety of considerations. He had long been concerned with the proliferation of abusive procedural tactics and the social costs of forum-shopping, and overturning Swift would eliminate a doctrine that served as a major incentive for both. Similarly, overthrowing Swift appealed to his belief in the virtues of federalism. Making the decisions of state courts authoritative on common-law issues would limit federal power, enhance the authority of the states, and counter in some part the increasing centralization that the New Deal was bringing to American government. . . .

   . . . .

   The Social Issue: Progressive Reform and Judicial Art. In addressing the social issue, Brandeis confronted a delicate problem. Although he shared the progressive belief that Swift unfairly benefited large corporations and harmed individual litigants, he was wary of emphasizing that point lest his opinion seem partisan or "political." The time, after all, was early 1938, and the Court was in the middle of the New Deal constitutional revolution, apparently altering doctrine to accommodate the centralizing policies of the Roosevelt administration. Given the fact that he was overruling a ninety-six-year-old precedent that neither of the parties had challenged, and the further fact that the decision would surely provoke the wrath of political conservatives and the corporate bar, Brandeis thought it essential to avoid the slightest hint that progressive values had played any part in the result. Indeed, a distinctively progressive critique of the doctrine's social significance would endanger his shaky majority. Hughes and Roberts, after all, were moderate Republicans who might well bridle at such an approach, and even the more progressive Stone would consider it both unnecessary and unwise. . . . Finally, Brandeis's determination to rest his opinion on the Constitution sealed the matter. Repudiating Swift on constitutional grounds meant that there was simply no need to examine its social operations in any detail.

Thus, for overriding tactical reasons Brandeis decided to sterilize and depoliticize his opinion. Consequently, he obscured both the significance of the Swift doctrine in practice and the social consequences of its abolition. To that end, he structured an argument, condensed in barely four pages, that was both abstract and misleading.

. . . .

The analysis was spare and abstract, quite unlike the detailed and empirically based approach that Brandeis usually employed. . . .

. . . .

. . . Brandeis meticulously pruned his opinion of any . . . reference to either removal jurisdiction or its use by corporate defendants. . . .

. . . .

Thus, Erie's discussion of the Swift doctrine in practice was misleading by design. . . . To end the practical "injustice" that Swift caused while still preserving the image of strict judicial neutrality, he called on his ample legal skills to obscure and then repackage the social issue. His opinion altered the practical world of diversity litigation and deprived national corporations of one of their most cherished advantages, while ostensibly doing little more than eliminating an obviously indefensible "discrimination" that subjected innocent "citizens" to the abuses of scheming "non-citizens." Who could possibly object to that?

The Constitutional Issue: Separation of Powers and Legislative Primacy. Brandeis had, moreover, a larger and more fundamental goal in mind—restructuring the constitutional balance between Congress and the federal courts. If art allowed him to finesse the social issue, boldness almost cost him his majority on the constitutional question.

. . . .

Whatever its faults, however, Erie embodied a coherent and soundly based theory inspired by Brandeis's progressive faith in democratic government and legislative primacy, and one rooted in the Constitution's most fundamental structural principles. The first principle was that the Constitution made Congress the lawmaking branch of the national government and delegated to it the legislative powers of that government. Congress, therefore, was the federal government's paramount lawmaking authority. The second principle was that the Constitution made the federal judiciary the law-applying branch of that national government. Although exercising the nation's judicial power might allow the federal courts to engage in subsidiary and interstitial lawmaking on some occasions, their rulings could be authoritative only when they fell within those areas over which the Constitution gave Congress national legislative authority. The lawmaking powers of the federal judiciary, in other words, could be no broader than the lawmaking powers of Congress, and therefore Congress—the popularly elected and representative branch of government—would always be able to alter or negate any sub-constitutional rule that the federal courts adopted.

. . . .

If Brandeis was clear in his own mind about Erie's constitutional holding, however, his opinion failed to explain its underlying theory with sufficient clarity. Indeed, his laconic language raised two troubling and closely related questions.[118] One stemmed from that statement that Congress could not "declare substantive rules of common law." The other arose from the later statement that the Swift doctrine "invaded rights which in our opinion are reserved by the Constitution to the several States." Did the former mean that Erie's constitutional holding imposed substantive limits on the powers of Congress? Did the latter mean that Erie rested on the Tenth Amendment? . . .

As to the first question, Brandeis thought the Swift doctrine was unconstitutional because it allowed the federal courts to make law in areas where established law had held that Congress could not legislate. The doctrine, he pointed out explicitly, reached areas where "Congress was confessedly without power" to act.[123] Thus, Brandeis was not asserting any new restriction on the powers of Congress, nor was he arguing that Congress should be barred from legislating in any particular area. Erie held only that the federal courts were barred from making rules of law in an area *if* Congress was not authorized to make law in that same area. The Swift doctrine was unconstitutional because, under the law that stood in 1938, it allowed federal judicial lawmaking in areas that were, under the Court's prior decisions, beyond the scope of congressional power.

As to the second question, Brandeis not only refused to rely on the Tenth Amendment but sought, assiduously and quite obviously, to avoid it. First, had he intended to rely on the Amendment, he would surely have stated that fact, for citing it would have been the easiest and most unexceptionable action he could have taken. At no point, however, did he directly cite the Tenth Amendment, quote from it, or mention it by name. Second, only at the last minute and in response to Butler's dissent did he add the reference to reserved powers. He still refused, however, to refer

---

[118]   The opinion raised a third, though less substantial, constitutional question. On the ground that it used the phrase "equal protection," [304 U.S.] at 75, a few commentators have suggested that Erie might be based on the Equal Protection Clause. The suggestion seems implausible. First, the Equal Protection Clause does not apply to the federal government, and the Due Process Clause of the Fifth Amendment, which does so apply, was not held to have an "equal protection" component until 1954. Bolling v. Sharpe, 347 U.S. 497 (1954). Second, there is no indication in the opinion that the phrase "equal protection" was intended to refer to any specific constitutional clause. Third, Brandeis's overall analysis makes it relatively clear that he was using the phrase simply to dramatize the practical point that Swift created an unjust and unwarranted discrimination in the legal system.

[123]   . . . In his opinion Brandeis identified several areas (for example, torts committed within a state on residents or property there and contracts relating to real property located within a state) over which Congress did not legislate generally, and which were considered beyond its powers. . . .

to the Amendment or put the term "reserved" in quotation marks. Thus, even when directly challenged to identify some particular provision of the Constitution on which he based his opinion, Brandeis avoided any direct reference to the Tenth Amendment. Third, the successive drafts of his opinion demonstrate that he based his constitutional theory solely on the fact that the federal courts under Swift made laws that were beyond the delegated power of Congress. In those drafts he articulated the separation of powers holding that would appear in the final opinion, and he did so without any mention of reserved powers or the Tenth Amendment. Fourth, Brandeis had two compelling reasons for rejecting the Amendment as the basis of his opinion. One was that it had long been used by the Court's conservative majority to limit the powers of Congress and defeat progressive national legislation. The other was that the Court had previously used the Amendment as a basis for expanding the scope of the Swift doctrine and extending the power of the federal judiciary beyond the legislative authority of Congress. Relying on the Tenth Amendment, then, would have dragged a Trojan Horse within the gates of Erie's constitutional theory of legislative primacy.

Thus, the Tenth Amendment was relevant only as a corollary of Erie's constitutional holding. The Swift doctrine allowed federal judicial lawmaking in areas that lay beyond congressional power, and a fortiori it violated the Constitution's limits on the federal courts. As a corollary of that transgression, then, Swift also and automatically invaded the "reserved" powers of the states. Erie, in other words, did not imply that the Tenth Amendment created an independent and substantive limit on federal powers, but only that it stated the tautological principle that any powers not granted to the federal government remained with the states or the people. It was the nature and scope of those national powers, not the Tenth Amendment, that determined the limits of federal lawmaking authority.

The Immediate Impact of Erie

The Supreme Court's decision ordered Tompkins' suit remanded. Three months later the Second Circuit held that Pennsylvania law controlled, that the railroad owed him no general duty of care, and that he could not show wanton negligence. Unanimously, it directed judgment for the railroad. Tompkins' attorneys then filed their own petition for certiorari, but the Court denied it.

For Harry Tompkins and his attorneys, Erie was like the malicious wave of an evil wizard's wand. One flick and the $30,000 in their hands had vanished. They were, Danzig confessed, thrown into "desolation." Nemeroff heard the news from the Second Circuit while standing on the courthouse steps in what he had considered his "lucky blue suit." He raised his fist to the heavens and swore he would never again litigate a case. Harry Tompkins was crushed. Retreating to Hughestown and his family, he found himself unable to work and thrown onto welfare. Acute manpower shortages during World War II allowed "Lefty" Tompkins an opportunity once again to hold a job, but peace and the return of millions of two-armed veterans squeezed him out of the workforce and ended his chances for further employment. From then on, the family struggled to get by. From time to time Nemeroff sent him small amounts of money, but the attorney eventually lost track of his ex-client. Thirty years after the decision, no one involved in the case had any idea where Harry Tompkins was or what had happened to him. He had, in fact, lived on in Hughestown for more than two decades, noted for his love of music, singing, and fishing and for his skill in baiting a fishing line using his mouth and feet in place of his missing right arm. On August 27, 1961, he died quietly in a local hospital, leaving his wife, daughter, two sisters, and several nieces and nephews. He was fifty-four years old. The brief notice of his death that appeared in the local newspaper mentioned neither his chance encounter with the Erie Railroad that cost him so dearly nor his long journey to the United States Supreme Court that ultimately did the same.

For his adversaries, the case quickly faded. . . . Kiendl continued his distinguished legal career and four years later received a signal honor when he was elevated to the rank of name partner. . . . Davis, Polk, Wardwell, Sunderland & Kiendl. . . .

Although the public at large took no notice of such an arcane "procedural" decision [as Erie was], the legal profession reacted with shock and surprise. Given the mundane facts involved and the narrow focus of the briefs, no one had expected a decision of such reverberating import. Felix Frankfurter, then a professor at the Harvard Law School, was a specialist in federal jurisdiction who tracked the Court's business with a singular devotion, yet the decision stunned him. "Whhew!!! What will your Court do next?" he exclaimed to Stone two days after Erie was announced. "I haven't yet caught my breath over the Tompkins case." Stone understood the reaction. It was a "remarkable performance," the Justice replied. "I haven't gotten over my own surprise at it."

After shock came criticism and, from many, anger. A majority of legal writers—even some who shared Brandeis's progressive politics—criticized the Court for deciding an issue that had not been raised and for invoking the Constitution when, according to Reed at least, it was unnecessary to do so. Further, they criticized the decision for making a sweeping and radical change in the law. Indeed, Erie was bound to upset the profession, especially the elite bar. With a stroke it threw out a massive body of federal case law, overturned traditional legal assumptions and practices, subordinated the federal courts to state courts in common-law matters, and undermined the settled expectations of the corporate business community.

. . . .

Confusion quickly ensued, for Erie inevitably confronted the profession with a host of complex doctrinal questions that would take decades to resolve. How, for example, could one determine the common law of a state when the state's courts had not decided an issue, or when they had decided it unclearly or in conflicting ways? Additionally, which state's law should control in suits involving connections to different states (and why, in Erie itself, did Pennsylvania law apply when the case was heard in a federal court located in New York[145])? Most importantly, how were the federal courts to distinguish between the "substantive rules" of state law that the Court required them to follow and the state procedural rules that apparently lay beyond the mandate? How, indeed, did one reconcile Erie with the new Federal Rules of Civil Procedure that were about to establish nationally "uniform" procedural rules for the federal courts?

. . . .

The Continuing Importance of Erie Today

Over the decades since 1938, however, Erie's broad significance has changed substantially as American society, dominant litigation patterns, and the orientation of the federal courts themselves have evolved. The change was apparent, for example, in political terms. In the decades after Brown v. Board of Education the federal courts became identified with the values of post-New Deal "liberalism" and Warren Court "activism." In that context, Erie's theory of legislative primacy lost its progressive significance and more readily served conservative social and political ends. Then, in the last decades of the twentieth century, as the federal courts began to reflect the values of post-Reagan "conservatism" and Rehnquist Court "activism," Erie's significance was reversed. Restricting a conservative and pro-corporate judiciary, Erie once again served more progressive purposes.

. . . .

---

[145] In its final paragraph Erie remanded the case for decision under Pennsylvania law. Although the opinion made it clear that state law, not federal common law, should control, it merely assumed that the law of Pennsylvania was the properly controlling state law. Neither party had suggested that any other state's law should apply, and the standard choice-of-law rule held that the law of the place of injury should determine the substantive merits of a tort claim. Brandeis's opinion, however, failed to resolve or even note two related issues. First, it did not explain whether Pennsylvania law applied because (1) the choice-of-law issue was "procedural" and therefore controlled by a federal choice-of-law rule that called for the application of Pennsylvania law or (2) the choice-of-law issue was "substantive" and therefore controlled by some state law that called for the application of the law of the place of injury. Three years later, in Klaxon v. Stentor Electric Manufacturing Co., 313 U.S. 487 (1941), the Court adopted the second position, holding that under Erie a federal court was bound to follow the choice-of-law rules of the state within which it sat. Second, in the event that New York choice-of-law rules controlled and called, as they apparently did, for the application of Pennsylvania law, Brandeis's opinion did not consider what Pennsylvania law the New York courts would apply. New York was one of the states that recognized its own version of "general" law, and hence a New York court—looking to Pennsylvania law but finding no controlling statute—might have applied its own version of "general" law; that is, it might have ignored Falchetti and applied the more widely accepted rule that the railroad owed Tompkins the ordinary duty of care even though he was on a path that paralleled its tracks. See Alfred Hill, The Erie Doctrine and the Constitution, 53 Nw.U.L.Rev. 541, 598 (1958). Had the Court ordered reargument and considered the matter more fully, the latter issue might have surfaced, raising the possibility that Tompkins could win under New York "general" law or, at least, creating enough uncertainty in the minds of both parties to induce a settlement that would have given Tompkins something.

Yet in spite of such continuing and complex changes, Erie still stands at the beginning of the twenty-first century as a case of fundamental importance to the nation's legal system. The so-called doctrine that bears its name is only the most obvious reason for its exalted position.

. . . .

Guaranty Trust Co. v. York

Supreme Court of the United States, 1945.
326 U.S. 99, 65 S.Ct. 1464.

■ MR. JUSTICE FRANKFURTER delivered the opinion of the Court.

[In a class action brought in the United States District Court for the Southern District of New York on diversity-of-citizenship jurisdiction, noteholders of Van Sweringen Corporation sued Guaranty Trust Company, the noteholders' trustee, for its alleged breach of trust. The court granted the defendant's motion for summary judgment. The Second Circuit reversed (2–1), holding inter alia that the state statute of limitations did not apply in this federal-court case in the face of a federal tolling doctrine. On certiorari, the Supreme Court reversed the decision of the circuit court of appeals, saying: "Our only concern is with the holding that the federal courts in a suit like this are not bound by local law."]

Our starting point must be the policy of federal jurisdiction which Erie R. Co. v. Tompkins, 304 U.S. 64, 58 S.Ct. 817, embodies. In overruling Swift v. Tyson, 16 Pet. 1, Erie R. Co. v. Tompkins did not merely overrule a venerable case. It overruled a particular way of looking at law which dominated the judicial process long after its inadequacies had been laid bare. [Citations omitted.] Law was conceived as a "brooding omnipresence" of Reason, of which decisions were merely evidence and not themselves the controlling formulations. Accordingly, federal courts deemed themselves free to ascertain what Reason, and therefore Law, required wholly independent of authoritatively declared State Law, even in cases where a legal right as the basis for relief was created by State authority and could not be created by federal authority and the case got into a federal court merely because it was "between Citizens of different States" under Art. III, § 2 of the Constitution of the United States.

. . . .

In relation to the problem now here, the real significance of Swift v. Tyson lies in the fact that it did not enunciate novel doctrine. Nor was it restricted to its particular situation. It summed up prior attitudes and expressions in cases that had come before this Court and lower federal courts for at least thirty years, at law as well as in equity. The short of it is that the doctrine was congenial to the jurisprudential climate of the time. Once established, judicial momentum kept it going. Since it was conceived that there was "a transcendental body of law outside of any particular State but obligatory within it unless and until changed by statute," [Black & White Taxicab & Transfer Co. v. Brown & Yellow Taxicab & Transfer Co.,] 276 U.S. 518, 532, 533, 48 S.Ct. 404, 408, 409, State court decisions were not "the law" but merely someone's opinion— to be sure an opinion to be respected—concerning the content of this all-pervading law. Not unnaturally, the federal courts assumed power to find for themselves the content of such a body of law. The notion was stimulated by the attractive vision of a uniform body of federal law. . . .

. . . .

Matters of "substance" and matters of "procedure" are much talked about in the books as though they defined a great divide cutting across the whole domain of law. But, of course, "substance" and "procedure" are the same key-words to very different problems. Neither "substance" nor "procedure" represents the same invariants. Each implies different variables depending upon the particular problem for which it is used. See Home Ins. Co. v. Dick, 281 U.S. 397, 409, 50 S.Ct. 338, 341. And the different problems are only distantly related at best, for the terms are in common use in connection with situations turning on such different considerations as those that are relevant to questions pertaining to ex post facto legislation, the impairment of the obligations of contract, the enforcement of federal rights in the State courts and the multitudinous phases of the conflict of laws. [Citations omitted.]

Here we are dealing with a right to recover derived not from the United States but from one of the States. When, because the plaintiff happens to be a non-resident, such a right is enforceable in a federal as well as in a State court, the forms and mode of enforcing the right may at times, naturally enough, vary because the two judicial systems are not identic. But since a federal court adjudicating a State-created right solely because of the diversity of citizenship of the parties is for that purpose, in effect, only another court of the State, it cannot afford recovery if the right to recover is made unavailable by the State nor can it substantially affect the enforcement of the right as given by the State.

And so the question is not whether a statute of limitations is deemed a matter of "procedure" in some sense. The question is whether such a statute concerns merely the manner and the means by which a right to recover, as recognized by the State, is enforced, or whether such statutory limitation is a matter of substance in the aspect that alone is relevant to our problem, namely, does it significantly affect the result of a litigation for a federal court to disregard a law of a State that would be controlling in an action upon the same claim by the same parties in a State court?

It is therefore immaterial whether statutes of limitation are characterized either as "substantive" or "procedural" in State court opinions in any use of those terms unrelated to the specific issue before us. Erie R. Co. v. Tompkins was not an endeavor to formulate scientific legal terminology. It expressed a policy that touches vitally the proper distribution of judicial power between State and federal courts. In essence, the intent of that decision was to insure that, in all cases where a federal court is exercising jurisdiction solely because of the diversity of citizenship of the parties, the outcome of the litigation in the federal court should be substantially the same, so far as legal rules determine the outcome of a litigation, as it would be if tried in a State court. The nub of the policy that underlies Erie R. Co. v. Tompkins is that for the same transaction the accident of a suit by a non-resident litigant in a federal court instead of in a State court a block away should not lead to a substantially different result. And so, putting to one side abstractions regarding "substance" and "procedure," we have held that in diversity cases the federal courts must follow the law of the State as to burden of proof, Cities Service Oil Co. v. Dunlap, 308 U.S. 208, 60 S.Ct. 201, as to conflict of laws, Klaxon Co. v. Stentor Electric Mfg. Co., 313 U.S. 487, 61 S.Ct. 1020, as to contributory negligence, Palmer v. Hoffman, 318 U.S. 109, 117, 63 S.Ct. 477, 482. And see Sampson v. Channell, 110 F.2d 754. Erie R. Co. v. Tompkins has been applied with an eye alert to essentials in avoiding disregard of State law in diversity cases in the federal courts. A policy so important to our federalism must be kept free from entanglements with analytical or terminological niceties.

Plainly enough, a statute that would completely bar recovery in a suit if brought in a State court bears on a State-created right vitally and not merely formally or negligibly. As to consequences that so intimately affect recovery or non-recovery a federal court in a diversity case should follow State law. . . .

   . . . .

Diversity jurisdiction is founded on assurance to non-resident litigants of courts free from susceptibility to potential local bias. The Framers of the Constitution, according to Marshall, entertained "apprehensions" lest distant suitors be subjected to local bias in State courts, or, at least, viewed with "indulgence the possible fears and apprehensions" of such suitors. Bank of the United States v. Deveaux, 5 Cranch 61, 87. And so Congress afforded out-of-State litigants another tribunal, not another body of law. The operation of a double system of conflicting laws in the same State is plainly hostile to the reign of law. Certainly, the fortuitous circumstance of residence out of a State of one of the parties to a litigation ought not to give rise to a discrimination against others equally concerned but locally resident. The source of substantive rights enforced by a federal court under diversity jurisdiction, it cannot be said too often, is the law of the States. Whenever that law is authoritatively declared by a State, whether its voice be the legislature or its highest court, such law ought to govern in litigation founded on that law, whether the forum of application is a State or a federal court and whether the remedies be sought at law or may be had in equity.

■ [JUSTICES ROBERTS and DOUGLAS did not participate. JUSTICE RUTLEDGE, joined by Justice Murphy, dissented, and in passing observed:]

Applicable statutes of limitations in state tribunals are not always the ones which would apply if suit were instituted in the courts of the state which creates the substantive rights for which enforcement is sought. The state of the forum is free to apply its own period of limitations, regardless of whether the state originating the right has barred suit upon it. Whether or not *the action* will be held to be barred depends therefore not upon the law of the state which creates the substantive right, but upon the law of the state where suit may be brought.

————

Consider the following cases (all decided by the Supreme Court on the same day, June 20, 1949) in the light of the Erie Railroad Co. v. Tompkins doctrine as further spelled out in the Guaranty Trust case. The basis of jurisdiction in each case is diversity of citizenship.

RAGAN v. MERCHANTS TRANSFER & WAREHOUSE CO., 337 U.S. 530, 69 S.Ct. 1233 (1949). *P* sues *D* in the District Court for the District of Kansas for personal injuries arising out of a highway accident on October 1, 1943. The applicable state statute of limitations is two years. The complaint is filed with the court on September 4, 1945, and the summons and complaint are served on December 28, 1945. Rule 3 provides that a "civil action is commenced by filing a complaint with the court." A Kansas statute says that for statute-of-limitations purposes an action shall be deemed commenced on the date of the service of the summons. *D* pleads the statute of limitations and moves for summary judgment. Is the action barred? (8–1 decision.)

WOODS v. INTERSTATE REALTY CO., 337 U.S. 535, 69 S.Ct. 1235 (1949). *P*, a Tennessee corporation, sues *D*, a citizen of Mississippi, in the District Court for the Northern District of Mississippi for a broker's commission. A Mississippi statute requires a foreign corporation doing business in the state to file a written power of attorney designating an agent for service of process and provides that any foreign corporation not complying with this requirement "shall not be permitted to bring or maintain any action or suit in any of the courts of this state." The effect of the statute, as construed by the highest court of the state, is not to make the contracts of such a corporation void but only to make them unenforceable in the Mississippi state courts. Prior to the Erie case, in David Lupton's Sons v. Automobile Club of America, 225 U.S. 489, 32 S.Ct. 711 (1912), the Supreme Court had held that such a state statute was not a bar to a diversity suit by such a corporation, saying: "The State could not prescribe the qualifications of suitors in the courts of the United States, and could not deprive of their privileges those who were entitled under the Constitution and laws of the United States to resort to the

Federal courts for the enforcement of a valid contract." Note, although the Woods Court did not advert to it, Rule 17(b)(2). *P* has not complied with the state statute. *D* moves for summary judgment on that ground. Should the motion be granted? (6–3 decision.)

COHEN v. BENEFICIAL INDUSTRIAL LOAN CORP., 337 U.S. 541, 69 S.Ct. 1221 (1949). A small stockholder, *P*, brings a shareholders' derivative action in the District Court for the District of New Jersey, the defendants being the corporation and certain of its managers and directors who are alleged to have wasted or diverted corporate assets through mismanagement and fraud. A New Jersey statute provides that when stockholders whose holdings amount to less than 5% of the total stock outstanding and not more than $50,000 in market value bring an action of this type, the corporation can require the plaintiffs to give security for the reasonable expenses, including counsel fees, that it may incur in connection with the action, and against that security the corporation shall have recourse in such amount as the court may determine upon termination of the action. Compare Rule 23.1. The corporation moves to require *P* to give security as provided by the state statute, in the amount of $125,000. Is the statute applicable in the federal court? The Supreme Court divided on this question. One of the opinions said: "We see no reason why the policy stated in Guaranty Trust . . . should not apply." Another, which Justice Frankfurter joined, said: "The measure of the cause of action is the claim . . . against the alleged wrongdoers. This New Jersey statute does not add one iota to nor subtract one iota from that cause of action. . . . [It] regulates only the procedure for instituting a particular cause of action and hence need not be applied in this diversity suit in the federal court." Which do you think was the majority opinion and which a dissent? (6–3 decision.)

FEDERAL DETERMINATION OF STATE LAW

Questions as to scope of state-law applicability are not the only problem that Erie has intensified for the federal courts. What is to be done when a state's law clearly governs but the state has no clear law on the point in issue?

What if the only state-court decision is a very old one by the state's highest court but one that is wholly out of line with the modern trend of authority elsewhere? What if the highest court of the state has not passed upon the point but there is a decision of an intermediate state court of appeals? (The Supreme Court said in an early case that such a decision "is not to be disregarded by a federal court unless it is convinced by other persuasive data that the highest court of the state would decide otherwise," West v. AT&T, 311 U.S. 223, 237, 61 S.Ct. 179, 183 (1940), but where would a federal judge look for such "persuasive data"?) What if there is a recent decision of an intermediate state court that is inconsistent with an old decision of the state's highest court? What if, instead of any such decisions, there are only state-court dicta? What if there is no state law of any kind on the particular point in issue?

———

BERNHARDT v. POLYGRAPHIC CO. OF AMERICA, 350 U.S. 198, 76 S.Ct. 273 (1956). An employment contract made in New York between the plaintiff, an individual then residing in New York, and the defendant, a New York corporation, called in case of dispute for arbitration under the law of New York by the American Arbitration Association. The plaintiff subsequently moved to Vermont where he was to carry out the contract. In this action for wrongful discharge, removed on the basis of diversity of citizenship from the Vermont state court to the District Court for the District of Vermont, the defendant corporation applied for a stay pending resort to arbitration. The district court denied the application, on the ground that Vermont law controlled and provided for no stay, because agreements to arbitrate were not enforceable according to Mead v. Owen, 83 Vt. 132, 74 A. 1058 (1910). On appeal, the federal court of appeals reversed, holding that state law did not govern this matter, because it was not "substantive" in the Erie sense, and that federal law required a stay by the Federal Arbitration Act, 9 U.S.C. § 3, which the court construed to apply in any federal action with respect to any agreement to arbitrate.

On certiorari, the Supreme Court by Justice Douglas said that section 3 should be narrowly read and limited to arbitration agreements in maritime transactions or in interstate or foreign commerce transactions. Otherwise, "a constitutional question might be presented" in light of the Erie decision. (The student should attempt to formulate that question.)

With the Arbitration Act thus considered inapplicable to this particular contract, the Court next decided that state law applied to the issue of enforceability. "If the federal court allows arbitration where the state court would disallow it, the outcome of litigation might depend on the courthouse where suit is brought. For the remedy by arbitration, whatever its merits or shortcomings, substantially affects the cause of action created by the State. The nature of the tribunal where suits are tried is an important part of the parcel of rights behind a cause of action. The change from a court of law to an arbitration panel may make a radical difference in ultimate result."

As to what Vermont law was, Justice Douglas said: "That [Mead] case was decided in 1910. But it was agreed on oral argument that there is no later authority from the Vermont courts, that no fracture in the rules announced in those cases has appeared in subsequent rulings or dicta, and that no legislative movement is under way in Vermont to change the result of those cases. . . . Were the question in doubt or deserving further canvass, we would of course remand the case to the

Court of Appeals to pass on this question of Vermont law. But, as we have indicated, there appears to be no confusion in the Vermont decisions, no developing line of authorities that casts a shadow over the established ones, no dicta, doubts or ambiguities in the opinions of Vermont judges on the question, no legislative development that promises to undermine the judicial rule. We see no reason, therefore, to remand the case to the Court of Appeals to pass on this question of local law."

The Court, citing Klaxon, instead remanded the case to the district court with authority to consider whether, as a matter of conflict of laws, the Vermont Supreme Court would apply New York rather than Vermont law to the enforcement of this agreement to arbitrate. (It was not clear that the district court had considered that question in rendering its decision. On remand, the district court did decide to apply the Vermont law.)

Justices Frankfurter and Harlan, concurring separately, agreed that state law controlled, but they would have remanded to the court of appeals to consider whether the Vermont Supreme Court would not now change its attitude toward the enforcement of agreements to arbitrate. Justice Frankfurter said:

"As long as there is diversity jurisdiction, 'estimates' are necessarily often all that federal courts can make in ascertaining what the state court would rule to be its law. . . . The Supreme Court of Vermont last spoke on this matter in 1910. The doctrine that it referred to was not a peculiar indigenous Vermont rule. The attitude reflected by that decision nearly half a century ago was the current traditional judicial hostility against ousting courts, as the phrase ran, of their jurisdiction. . . . To be sure, a vigorous legislative movement got under way in the 1920's expressive of a broadened outlook of view on this subject. But courts do not always wait for legislation to find a judicial doctrine outmoded. . . .

"Surely in the light of all that has happened since 1910 in the general field of the law of arbitration, it is not for us to assume that the Court of Appeals, if it had that question for consideration, could not have found that the law of Vermont today does not require disregard of a provision of a contract made in New York, with a purposeful desire to have the law of New York govern, to accomplish a result that today may be deemed to be a general doctrine of the law. Of course, if the Court of Appeals, versed in the general jurisprudence of Vermont and having among its members a Vermont lawyer, should find that the Vermont court would, despite the New York incidents of the contract, apply Vermont law and that it is the habit of the Vermont court to adhere to its precedents and to leave changes to the legislature, it would not be for the federal court to gainsay that policy."

Justice Burton dissented, viewing arbitration as merely a "form of trial" as to which the federal courts were not bound to follow state law under Erie or Guaranty Trust.

These incidental problems of federal determination of state law persist to the present time. Consider this installment of the curious case of Factors Etc., Inc. v. Pro Arts, Inc., 701 F.2d 11 (2d Cir.1983), in which the majority opinion was as follows:

"On June 29, 1981, this panel of the Court, by a divided vote, issued an opinion reversing the District Court's grant of summary judgment in favor of the plaintiffs-appellees and the issuance of a permanent injunction barring the defendants-appellants from marketing a poster depicting Elvis Presley. Factors, Etc., Inc. v. Pro Arts, Inc., 652 F.2d 278 (2d Cir.1981). The basis for that ruling . . . was that in the absence of authoritative guidance from the courts of Tennessee, we would deem controlling in this diversity case the decision of the Sixth Circuit in Memphis Development Foundation v. Factors, Etc., Inc., 616 F.2d 956 (6th Cir.), cert. denied, 449 U.S. 953, 101 S.Ct. 358, 66 L.Ed.2d 217 (1980). Memphis Development, also a diversity case requiring application of Tennessee law, had held that Tennessee does not recognize a descendible right of publicity. Upon the return of the instant case to the District Court for the Southern District of New York, plaintiffs called to Judge Tenney's attention a decision of the Tennessee Chancery Court, issued October 2, 1981, which held that Tennessee law does recognize a descendible right of publicity. Commerce Union Bank v. Coors of the Cumberland, Inc., 7 Media L.Rptr. 2204 (Chan.Ct.Davidson Cty.Tenn.1981). That decision, not officially reported, was issued prior to the issuance of our mandate in the instant case.

"Judge Tenney thereupon stayed entry of judgment for the defendants pending an application by the plaintiffs to petition this Court to recall its mandate and consider an untimely petition for rehearing in light of the alleged intervening change in state law. [Citation omitted. (The mandate is the appellate court's clerical act that returns jurisdiction to the lower court. The appellate court retains a narrow power to recall its mandate, usually to correct what would otherwise be a miscarriage of justice in a still-pending case.)] Plaintiffs diligently sought such relief, and we granted leave to file their petition for rehearing to assess the significance of the Chancery Court's decision in Commerce Union Bank. Supplemental briefs have been received.

"Fortunately, a recent development in the Tennessee Chancery Court has made it unnecessary for us to determine whether Commerce Union Bank is of sufficient authoritativeness to warrant our disregard of the Sixth Circuit's decision in Memphis Development. On November 24, 1982, the Chancery Court, acting through a different judge from the one who rendered the decision in Commerce Union Bank, ruled that Tennessee does not recognize a descendible right of publicity. Lancaster v. Factors, Etc., Inc., [9 Media L.Rptr. 1109] (Chan.Ct.Shelby Cty.Tenn.1982). The Lancaster decision is surely entitled to no less weight than the decision in Commerce Union Bank and may even have a special pertinence since it involves a claim by the same parties who are plaintiffs in the instant litigation with respect to a descendible right of publicity concerning Elvis Presley. Whatever the weight to be given an unreported decision of the Tennessee Chancery Court by a diversity court at any stage of litigation, much less at the point where a mandate is sought to be recalled on the basis of an alleged intervening change of state law, we have no doubt that the appearance of two conflicting decisions of the Chancery Court on the precise point at issue affords us no basis for considering the law of Tennessee to have authoritatively been changed since our June 29, 1981, decision. The motion to recall the mandate and the petition for rehearing are denied."

Judge Mansfield dissented, saying that "the internal Tennessee state court conflict provides an additional reason for our following the usual practice, where we disagree with the reasoning of another circuit on an issue, of deciding a case according to what we believe to be the more rational basis."

Questions: (6) The general rule is that any federal court should use the latest available data in deciding what the state law is, to the extent that the forum state's supreme court would in the circumstances direct taking the recent data into account. Vandenbark v. Owens-Ill. Glass Co., 311 U.S. 538, 61 S.Ct. 347 (1941). Thus, a federal court of appeals should consider fresh state decisional law if the forum state would (this Elvis Presley case illustrates that even on a petition for rehearing, any federal cutoff for considering new state-law data has not yet kicked in). However, after the federal case finally ends, a federal cutoff has kicked in so that any change of state law, or discovered error in determining state law, is not by itself a ground for relief from judgment (this case's eventual victory for the defendants, 562 F.Supp. 304 (S.D.N.Y.1983), therefore survived the change several years later when Tennessee recognized a descendible right of publicity, Tenn. ex rel. Elvis Presley Int'l Mem'l Found. v. Crowell, 733 S.W.2d 89 (Tenn.Ct.App.1987)). But exactly when in-between should the cutoff occur?

(7) In a typical diversity case, assuming there are no last-minute revelations on state law, to what degree should a federal appellate court defer to the lower federal court's presumably more expert view on what the local state law is? See Salve Regina Coll. v. Russell, 499 U.S. 225, 111 S.Ct. 1217 (1991) (ordering nondeferential review by the courts of appeals, because such review "best serves the dual goals of doctrinal coherence and economy of judicial administration," even in the Erie setting), criticized in Jonathan Remy Nash, Resuscitating Deference to Lower Federal Court Judges' Interpretations of State Law, 77 S.Cal.L.Rev. 975 (2004) (arguing that courts of appeal do, and should, continue to afford some deference).

(8) The excerpted Elvis Presley case involves the oddity of the Second Circuit's bowing to a coordinate court (given that the Sixth Circuit covers Tennessee and so is the "home circuit"). Rather than doing so, should not the Second Circuit have been asking what consideration New York's highest

state court grants to a Sixth Circuit decision when determining and applying Tennessee law? See Wright & Miller § 4507, at 209.

————

STATE DETERMINATION OF STATE LAW

To sum up, Erie imposes on the federal courts the duty of, "in effect, sitting as a state court" when deciding certain issues of law. Comm'r v. Estate of Bosch, 387 U.S. 456, 465, 87 S.Ct. 1776, 1783 (1967). So, when facing unclear state law, the federal trial or appellate court should enunciate whatever state law governs as if it were then sitting as the forum state's highest court, taking into account all the latest precedent and other data that court would. The various burdens attendant upon such duty should now be obvious. Is there any way for the federal court to shift those burdens?

A possibility is abstention, a complex doctrine under which a federal court, in deference to a state's interests, declines to exercise the federal jurisdiction. There are a number of circumstances where a federal court might abstain. Along with a few other situations, the Supreme Court has indicated: "Abstention is also appropriate where there have been presented difficult questions of state law bearing on policy problems of substantial public import whose importance transcends the result in the case then at bar. Louisiana Power & Light Co. v. City of Thibodaux, 360 U.S. 25, 79 S.Ct. 1070 (1959), for example, involved such a question. In particular, the concern there was with the scope of the eminent domain power of municipalities under state law." Colo. River Water Conservation Dist. v. United States, 424 U.S. 800, 814, 96 S.Ct. 1236, 1244–45 (1976) (dictum). Accordingly, a district court faced under the Erie doctrine with an unsettled but publicly significant state-law issue might dismiss or stay the federal diversity case, leaving the parties to pursue a coercive or declaratory remedy in the state-court system.

There is a less drastic course that in this context is more broadly applicable, viz., a process of certification of the unsettled question of state law by the federal court directly to the highest court of the state, if the state is willing. By this device the federal court retains jurisdiction, eventually handling the case in accordance with the state court's answer. The first state provision for answering certified questions was a Florida statute, which had never been used until the Supreme Court gave its blessing to the procedure in Clay v. Sun Insurance Office Ltd., 363 U.S. 207, 80 S.Ct. 1222 (1960). Almost all states have since by statute or rule authorized their highest court to answer certified questions. The National Conference of Commissioners on Uniform State Laws in 1967 approved, and recommended for adoption by the states, a Uniform Certification of Questions of Law Act—and revised it in 1995. The Supreme Court emphatically restated its approval of certification in Lehman Brothers v. Schein, 416 U.S. 386, 94 S.Ct. 1741 (1974) (instructing the Second Circuit, in a diversity case, to reconsider the possibility of certifying a question of Florida law to the Florida Supreme Court).

Certification does offer a neat means of avoiding the anomaly of different answers to the same question of law from a state and a federal court. (Is this anomaly more of a reproach to the judicial process than the anomaly of different juries coming to opposite factual findings on the same evidence?) But this neat solution comes at a stiff price.

First, certification inevitably causes some delay and increased expense for the parties. At the least, this requires the federal court to balance the interests involved, taking into account the type of question and the circumstances of the particular case. Lehman Brothers v. Schein involved a question of corporate fiduciary obligation arising in a shareholders' derivative suit. By contrast, Clay v. Sun Insurance Office Ltd. involved an individual's suit against his insurance company seeking reimbursement for lost personal property, although other considerations pushed for certification of a statute-of-limitations point. But compare Thompson v. Johns-Manville Sales Corp., 714 F.2d 581 (5th Cir.1983) (2–1 decision) (holding in asbestosis action that state would not recognize market-share or enterprise liability, over colorful dissent urging certification), with Hatfield v. Bishop Clarkson Mem'l Hosp., 701 F.2d 1266 (8th Cir.1983) (4–3 en banc decision) (setting aside panel's decision in favor of plaintiff and certifying statute-of-limitations point in infant's medical-malpractice action, over dissent that includes a fable).

Second, certification imposes a burden on the state court. The unavoidably abstract nature of the question may make it difficult to answer. Indeed, a state certification provision may run aground if the state has a constitutional prohibition against giving advisory opinions. These problems are lessened by allowing certification, as Florida does, only from a federal appellate court, but most state provisions and the Uniform Act allow a federal district court to certify as well.

Third, certification poses a possible threat to the judicial function of the federal courts in diversity cases, diminishing their authority and their sense of responsibility. See generally Jonathan Remy Nash, The Uneasy Case for Transjurisdictional Adjudication, 94 Va.L.Rev. 1869 (2008).

Byrd v. Blue Ridge Rural Electric Cooperative

Supreme Court of the United States, 1958.
356 U.S. 525, 78 S.Ct. 893.

■ MR. JUSTICE BRENNAN delivered the opinion of the Court.

[This was a diversity action in a federal district court in South Carolina for injuries allegedly caused by the defendant's negligence. The plaintiff was employed as a lineman by a contractor, which held a construction contract with the defendant. The plaintiff had suffered injury while performing work under that contract.

[One of the defenses was that the South Carolina Workmen's Compensation Act imposed upon the plaintiff—because the work contracted to be done by his employer was allegedly work of the kind also done by the defendant's own construction and maintenance crews—the status of a "statutory employee" of the defendant. That classification would mean that the defendant was immune from an action at law, and the plaintiff had to accept workers' compensation benefits as his exclusive remedy.

[The Supreme Court on certiorari considered, among other things, whether the question raised by this defense—whether the work of the plaintiff's employer was work of the kind done by the defendant's crews—should be decided by the trial judge, as held in a South Carolina decision, Adams v. Davison-Paxon Co., 230 S.C. 532, 96 S.E.2d 566 (1957), or by a jury, in line with federal practice.]

First. It was decided in Erie R. Co. v. Tompkins that the federal courts in diversity cases must respect the definition of state-created rights and obligations by the state courts. We must, therefore, first examine the rule in Adams v. Davison-Paxon Co. to determine whether it is bound up with these rights and obligations in such a way that its application in the federal court is required. Cities Service Oil Co. v. Dunlap, 308 U.S. 208, 60 S.Ct. 201.

The Workmen's Compensation Act is administered in South Carolina by its Industrial Commission. The South Carolina courts hold that, on judicial review of actions of the Commission . . . , the question whether the claim of an injured workman is within the Commission's jurisdiction is a matter of law for decision by the court, which makes its own findings of fact relating to that jurisdiction. The South Carolina Supreme Court states no reasons in Adams v. Davison-Paxon Co. why [when such a question arises instead as a defense in an original court action], although the jury decides all other factual issues raised by the cause of action and defenses, the jury is displaced as to the factual issue raised by the affirmative defense . . . . The conclusion is inescapable that the Adams holding is grounded in the practical consideration that the question had theretofore come before the South Carolina courts from the Industrial Commission and the courts had become accustomed to deciding the factual issue of immunity without the aid of juries. We find nothing to suggest that this rule was announced as an integral part of the special relationship created by the statute. Thus the requirement appears to be merely a form and mode of enforcing the immunity, Guaranty Trust Co. v. York, 326 U.S. 99, 108, 65 S.Ct. 1464, 1469, and not a rule intended to be bound up with the definition of the rights and obligations of the parties. The situation is therefore not analogous to that in Dice v. Akron, C. & Y.R. Co., 342 U.S. 359, 72 S.Ct. 312 . . . .

Second. But cases following Erie have evinced a broader policy to the effect that the federal courts should conform as near as may be—in the absence of other considerations—to state rules even of form and mode where the state rules may bear substantially on the question whether the litigation would come out one way in the federal court and another way in the state court if the federal court failed to apply a particular local rule. E.g., Guaranty Trust Co. v. York, supra; Bernhardt v. Polygraphic Co., 350 U.S. 198, 76 S.Ct. 273. Concededly the nature of the tribunal which tries issues may be important in the enforcement of the parcel of rights making up a cause of action or defense, and bear significantly upon achievement of uniform enforcement of the right. It may well be that in the instant personal-injury case the outcome would be substantially affected by whether the issue of immunity is decided by a judge or a jury. Therefore, were "outcome" the only consideration, a strong case might appear for saying that the federal court should follow the state practice.

But there are affirmative countervailing considerations at work here. The federal system is an independent system for administering justice to litigants who properly invoke its jurisdiction. An essential characteristic of that system is the manner in which, in civil common-law actions, it distributes trial functions between judge and jury and, under the influence—if not the command[10]—of the Seventh Amendment, assigns the decisions of disputed questions of fact to the jury. Jacob v. City of New York, 315 U.S. 752, 62 S.Ct. 854.[11] The policy of uniform enforcement of state-created rights and obligations, see, e.g., Guaranty Trust Co. v. York, supra, cannot in every case exact compliance with a state rule[12]—not bound up with rights and obligations—which disrupts the federal system of allocating functions between judge and jury. Herron v. Southern Pacific Co., 283 U.S. 91, 51 S.Ct. 383 [(1931)]. Thus the inquiry here is whether the federal policy favoring jury decisions of disputed fact questions should yield to the state rule in the interest of furthering the objective that the litigation should not come out one way in the federal court and another way in the state court.

We think that in the circumstances of this case the federal court should not follow the state rule. It cannot be gainsaid that there is a strong federal policy against allowing state rules to disrupt the judge-jury relationship in the federal courts. In Herron v. Southern Pacific Co., supra, the trial judge in a personal-injury negligence action brought in the District Court for Arizona on diversity grounds directed a verdict for the defendant when it appeared as a matter of law that the plaintiff was

10   Our conclusion makes unnecessary the consideration of—and we intimate no view upon—the constitutional question whether the right of jury trial protected in federal courts by the Seventh Amendment embraces the factual issue of statutory immunity when asserted, as here, as an affirmative defense in a common-law negligence action.

11   The Courts of Appeals have expressed varying views about the effect of Erie R. Co. v. Tompkins on judge-jury problems in diversity cases. [Citations omitted.]

12   This Court held in Sibbach v. Wilson & Co., 312 U.S. 1, 61 S.Ct. 422, that Federal Rules of Civil Procedure 35 should prevail over a contrary state rule.

guilty of contributory negligence. The federal judge refused to be bound by a provision of the Arizona Constitution which made the jury the sole arbiter of the question of contributory negligence. This Court sustained the action of the trial judge, holding that "state laws cannot alter the essential character or function of a federal court" because that function "is not in any sense a local matter, and state statutes which would interfere with the appropriate performance of that function are not binding upon the federal court under either the Conformity Act or the 'Rules of Decision' Act." Id., 283 U.S. at page 94, 51 S.Ct. at page 384. Perhaps even more clearly in light of the influence of the Seventh Amendment, the function assigned to the jury "is an essential factor in the process for which the Federal Constitution provides." Id., 283 U.S. at page 95, 51 S.Ct. at page 384. Concededly the Herron case was decided before Erie R. Co. v. Tompkins, but even when Swift v. Tyson, 16 Pet. 1, was governing law and allowed federal courts sitting in diversity cases to disregard state decisional law, it was never thought that state statutes or constitutions were similarly to be disregarded. Green v. Neal's Lessee, 6 Pet. 291. Yet Herron held that state statutes and constitutional provisions could not disrupt or alter the essential character or function of a federal court.

Third. We have discussed the problem upon the assumption that the outcome of the litigation may be substantially affected by whether the issue of immunity is decided by a judge or a jury. But clearly there is not present here the certainty that a different result would follow, cf. Guaranty Trust Co. v. York, supra, or even the strong possibility that this would be the case, cf. Bernhardt v. Polygraphic Co., supra. There are factors present here which might reduce that possibility. The trial judge in the federal system has powers denied the judges of many States to comment on the weight of evidence and credibility of witnesses, and discretion to grant a new trial if the verdict appears to him to be against the weight of the evidence. We do not think the likelihood of a different result is so strong as to require the federal practice of jury determination of disputed factual issues to yield to the state rule in the interest of uniformity of outcome.

■ [JUSTICE WHITTAKER dissented from the ruling that the plaintiff was entitled to a jury determination of his status, arguing that Guaranty Trust required the application of state law. JUSTICES FRANKFURTER and HARLAN also dissented, but their opinions did not reach the jury-trial point.]

———

Question: (9) Reexamine Woods v. Interstate Realty Co. Do you think its decision to apply state law is still sound after Byrd?

———

Hanna v. Plumer

Supreme Court of the United States, 1965.
380 U.S. 460, 85 S.Ct. 1136.

■ MR. CHIEF JUSTICE WARREN delivered the opinion of the Court.

The question to be decided is whether, in a civil action where the jurisdiction of the United States district court is based upon diversity of citizenship between the parties, service of process shall be made in the manner prescribed by state law or that set forth in Rule 4(d)(1) of the Federal Rules of Civil Procedure [which is now Rule 4(e)(2)].

On February 6, 1963, petitioner, a citizen of Ohio, filed her complaint in the District Court for the District of Massachusetts, claiming damages in excess of [the then jurisdictional amount of] $10,000 for personal injuries resulting from an automobile accident in South Carolina, allegedly caused by the negligence of one Louise Plumer Osgood, a Massachusetts citizen deceased at the time of the filing of the complaint. Respondent, Mrs. Osgood's executor and also a Massachusetts citizen, was named as defendant. On February 8, service was made by leaving copies of the summons and the complaint with respondent's wife at his residence, concededly in compliance with Rule 4(d)(1) [the Court here quoted the Rule]. Respondent filed his answer on February 26, alleging, inter alia, that the action could not be maintained because it had been brought "contrary to and in violation of the provisions of Massachusetts General Laws (Ter.Ed.) Chapter 197, Section 9." That section provides:

> "Except as provided in this chapter, an executor or administrator shall not be held to answer to an action by a creditor of the deceased which is not commenced within one year from the time of his giving bond for the performance of his trust, or to such an action which is commenced within said year unless before the expiration thereof the writ in such action has been served by delivery in hand upon such executor or administrator or service thereof accepted by him or a notice stating the name of the estate, the name and address of the creditor, the amount of the claim and the court in which the action has been brought has been filed in the proper registry of probate...."
> Mass.Gen.Laws Ann., c. 197, § 9 (1958).

On October 17, 1963, the District Court granted respondent's motion for summary judgment, citing Ragan v. Merchants Transfer & Warehouse Co., 337 U.S. 530, 69 S.Ct. 1233, and Guaranty Trust Co. v. York, 326 U.S. 99, 65 S.Ct. 1464, in support of its conclusion that the adequacy of the service was to be measured by § 9, with which, the court held, petitioner had not complied. On appeal, petitioner admitted noncompliance with § 9, but argued that Rule 4(d)(1) defines the method by which service of process is to be effected in diversity actions. The Court of Appeals for the First Circuit, finding that "[r]elatively recent amendments [to § 9] evince a clear legislative purpose to require personal notification within the year,"[1] concluded that the conflict of state and federal rules was over "a substantive rather than a procedural matter," and unanimously affirmed. 331 F.2d 157. Because of the threat to the goal of uniformity of federal procedure posed by the decision below, we granted certiorari, 379 U.S. 813, 85 S.Ct. 52.

We conclude that the adoption of Rule 4(d)(1), designed to control service of process in diversity actions, neither exceeded the congressional mandate embodied in the Rules Enabling Act nor transgressed constitutional bounds, and that the Rule is therefore the standard against which the District Court should have measured the adequacy of the service. Accordingly, we reverse the decision of the Court of Appeals.

. . . Under the cases construing the scope of the Enabling Act, Rule 4(d)(1) clearly passes muster. Prescribing the manner in which a defendant is to be notified that a suit has been instituted against him, it relates to the "practice and procedure of the district courts." Cf. New York Life Insurance Co. v. Bangs, 103 U.S. 435, 439.

> "The test must be whether a rule really regulates procedure,— the judicial process for enforcing rights and duties recognized by substantive law and for justly administering remedy and redress for disregard or infraction of them." Sibbach v. Wilson & Co., 312 U.S. 1, 14, 61 S.Ct. 422, 426.[4]

In Mississippi Pub. Corp. v. Murphree, 326 U.S. 438, 66 S.Ct. 242, this Court upheld [former] Rule 4(f), which permits service of a summons anywhere within the State (and not merely the district) in which a district court sits:

> "We think that Rule 4(f) is in harmony with the Enabling Act . . . . Undoubtedly most alterations of the rules of practice and procedure may and often do affect the rights of litigants.

---

[1]   Section 9 is in part a statute of limitations, providing that an executor need not "answer to an action . . . which is not commenced within one year from the time of his giving bond . . . ." This part of the statute, the purpose of which is to speed the settlement of estates, Spaulding v. McConnell, 307 Mass. 144, 146, 29 N.E.2d 713, 715 (1940); Doyle v. Moylan, 141 F.Supp. 95 (D.C.Mass.1956), is not involved in this case, since the action clearly was timely commenced. (Respondent filed bond on March 1, 1962; the complaint was filed February 6, 1963; and the service—the propriety of which is in dispute—was made on February 8, 1963.) 331 F.2d, at 159. Cf. Guaranty Trust Co. v. York, supra; Ragan v. Merchants Transfer & Warehouse Co., supra.

Section 9 also provides for the manner of service. Generally, service of process must be made by "delivery in hand," although there are two alternatives: acceptance of service by the executor, or filing of a notice of claim, the components of which are set out in the statute, in the appropriate probate court. The purpose of this part of the statute, which *is* involved here, is, as the court below noted, to insure that executors will receive actual notice of claims. Parker v. Rich, 297 Mass. 111, 113–114, 8 N.E.2d 345, 347 (1937). Actual notice is of course also the goal of Rule 4(d)(1); however, the Federal Rule reflects a determination that this goal can be achieved by a method less cumbersome than that prescribed in § 9. In this case the goal seems to have been achieved; although the affidavit filed by respondent in the District Court asserts that he had not been served in hand nor had he accepted service, it does not allege lack of actual notice. [Incidentally, Massachusetts also had a general service provision similar to former Federal Rule 4(d)(1).—Ed.]

[4]   See also Schlagenhauf v. Holder, 379 U.S. 104, 112–114, 85 S.Ct. 234, 239–240.

Congress' prohibition of any alteration of substantive rights of litigants was obviously not addressed to such incidental effects as necessarily attend the adoption of the prescribed new rules of procedure upon the rights of litigants who, agreeably to rules of practice and procedure, have been brought before a court authorized to determine their rights. Sibbach v. Wilson & Co., 312 U.S. 1, 11–14, 61 S.Ct. 422, 425–427. The fact that the application of Rule 4(f) will operate to subject petitioner's rights to adjudication by the district court for northern Mississippi will undoubtedly affect those rights. But it does not operate to abridge, enlarge or modify the rules of decision by which that court will adjudicate its rights." Id., at 445–446, 66 S.Ct. at 246.

Thus were there no conflicting state procedure, Rule 4(d)(1) would clearly control. National Equipment Rental v. Szukhent, 375 U.S. 311, 316, 84 S.Ct. 411, 414. However, respondent, focusing on the contrary Massachusetts rule, calls to the Court's attention another line of cases, a line which—like the Federal Rules—had its birth in 1938. Erie R. Co. v. Tompkins, 304 U.S. 64, 58 S.Ct. 817, overruling Swift v. Tyson, 16 Pet. 1, held that federal courts sitting in diversity cases, when deciding questions of "substantive" law, are bound by state court decisions as well as state statutes. The broad command of Erie was therefore identical to that of the Enabling Act: federal courts are to apply state substantive law and federal procedural law. However, as subsequent cases sharpened the distinction between substance and procedure, the line of cases following Erie diverged markedly from the line construing the Enabling Act. Guaranty Trust Co. v. York, 326 U.S. 99, 65 S.Ct. 1464, made it clear that Erie-type problems were not to be solved by reference to any traditional or common-sense substance-procedure distinction:

> "And so the question is not whether a statute of limitations is deemed a matter of 'procedure' in some sense. The question is . . . does it significantly affect the result of a litigation for a federal court to disregard a law of a State that would be controlling in an action upon the same claim by the same parties in a State court?" 326 U.S. at 109, 65 S.Ct. at 1470.[5]

Respondent, by placing primary reliance on York and Ragan, suggests that the Erie doctrine acts as a check on the Federal Rules of Civil Procedure, that despite the clear command of Rule 4(d)(1), Erie and its progeny demand the application of the Massachusetts rule. Reduced to essentials, the argument is: (1) Erie, as defined in York, demands that federal courts apply state law whenever application of federal law in its stead will alter the outcome of the case. (2) In this case, a determination that the Massachusetts service requirements obtain will result in immediate victory for respondent. If, on the other hand, it should be held

---

5   See also Ragan v. Merchants Transfer Co., supra; Woods v. Interstate Realty Co., 337 U.S. 535, 69 S.Ct. 1235; Bernhardt v. Polygraphic Co., 350 U.S. 198, 203–204, 207–208, 76 S.Ct. 273, 276, 278–279; cf. Byrd v. Blue Ridge Rural Elec. Cooperative, 356 U.S. 525, 78 S.Ct. 893.

that Rule 4(d)(1) is applicable, the litigation will continue, with possible victory for petitioner. (3) Therefore, Erie demands application of the Massachusetts rule. The syllogism possesses an appealing simplicity, but is for several reasons invalid.

In the first place, it is doubtful that, even if there were no Federal Rule making it clear that in-hand service is not required in diversity actions, the Erie rule would have obligated the District Court to follow the Massachusetts procedure. "Outcome-determination" analysis was never intended to serve as a talisman. Byrd v. Blue Ridge Rural Elec. Cooperative, 356 U.S. 525, 537, 78 S.Ct. 893, 900. Indeed, the message of York itself is that choices between state and federal law are to be made not by application of any automatic, "litmus paper" criterion, but rather by reference to the policies underlying the Erie rule. Guaranty Trust Co. v. York, supra, 326 U.S. at 108–112, 65 S.Ct. at 1469–1471.

The Erie rule is rooted in part in a realization that it would be unfair for the character or result of a litigation materially to differ because the suit had been brought in a federal court.

> "Diversity of citizenship jurisdiction was conferred in order to prevent apprehended discrimination in state courts against those not citizens of the state. Swift v. Tyson introduced grave discrimination by noncitizens against citizens. It made rights enjoyed under the unwritten 'general law' vary according to whether enforcement was sought in the state or in the federal court; and the privilege of selecting the court in which the right should be determined was conferred upon the noncitizen. Thus, the doctrine rendered impossible equal protection of the law." Erie R. Co. v. Tompkins, supra, 304 U.S. at 74–75, 58 S.Ct. at 820–821.[7]

The decision was also in part a reaction to the practice of "forum-shopping" which had grown up in response to the rule of Swift v. Tyson. 304 U.S. at 73–74, 58 S.Ct. at 819–820.[8] That the York test was an attempt to effectuate these policies is demonstrated by the fact that the opinion framed the inquiry in terms of "substantial" variations between state and federal litigation. 326 U.S. at 109, 65 S.Ct. at 1469. Not only are nonsubstantial, or trivial, variations not likely to raise the sort of equal protection problems which troubled the Court in Erie; they are also unlikely to influence the choice of a forum. The "outcome-determination" test therefore cannot be read without reference to the twin aims of the

---

[7]   See also Klaxon Co. v. Stentor Electric Mfg. Co., 313 U.S. 487, 496, 61 S.Ct. 1020, 1021; Woods v. Interstate Realty Co., supra, note 5, 337 U.S. at 538, 69 S.Ct. at 1237.

[8]   Cf. Black & White Taxicab & Transfer Co. v. Brown & Yellow Taxicab & Transfer Co., 276 U.S. 518, 48 S.Ct. 404.

Erie rule: discouragement of forum-shopping and avoidance of inequitable administration of the laws.[9]

The difference between the conclusion that the Massachusetts rule is applicable, and the conclusion that it is not, is of course at this point "outcome-determinative" in the sense that if we hold the state rule to apply, respondent prevails, whereas if we hold that Rule 4(d)(1) governs, the litigation will continue. But in this sense *every* procedural variation is "outcome-determinative." For example, having brought suit in a federal court a plaintiff cannot then insist on the right to file subsequent pleadings in accord with the time limits applicable in the state courts, even though enforcement of the federal timetable will, if he continues to insist that he must meet only the state time limit, result in determination of the controversy against him. So it is here. Though choice of the federal or state rule will at this point have a marked effect upon the outcome of the litigation, the difference between the two rules would be of scant, if any, relevance to the choice of a forum. Petitioner, in choosing her forum, was not presented with a situation where application of the state rule would wholly bar recovery;[10] rather, adherence to the state rule would have resulted only in altering the way in which process was served.[11] Moreover, it is difficult to argue that permitting service of defendant's wife to take the place of in-hand service of defendant himself alters the mode of enforcement of state-created rights in a fashion sufficiently "substantial" to raise the sort of equal protection problems to which the Erie opinion alluded.

---

[9]   The Court of Appeals seemed to frame the inquiry in terms of how "important" § 9 is to the State. In support of its suggestion that § 9 serves some interest the State regards as vital to its citizens, the court noted that something like § 9 has been on the books in Massachusetts a long time, that § 9 has been amended a number of times, and that § 9 is designed to make sure that executors receive actual notice. See note 1, supra. The apparent lack of relation among these three observations is not surprising, because it is not clear to what sort of question the Court of Appeals was addressing itself. One cannot meaningfully ask how important something is without first asking "important for what purpose?" Erie and its progeny make clear that when a federal court sitting in a diversity case is faced with a question of whether or not to apply state law, the importance of a state rule is indeed relevant, but only in the context of asking whether application of the rule would make so important a difference to the character or result of the litigation that failure to enforce it would unfairly discriminate against citizens of the forum State, or whether application of the rule would have so important an effect upon the fortunes of one or both of the litigants that failure to enforce it would be likely to cause a plaintiff to choose the federal court.

[10]   See Guaranty Trust Co. v. York, supra, 326 U.S. at 108–109, 65 S.Ct. at 1469; Ragan v. Merchants Transfer Co., supra, 337 U.S. at 532, 69 S.Ct. at 1234; Woods v. Interstate Realty Co., supra, note 5, 337 U.S. at 538, 69 S.Ct. at 1237.

Similarly, a federal court's refusal to enforce the New Jersey rule involved in Cohen v. Beneficial Indus. Loan Corp., 337 U.S. 541, 69 S.Ct. 1221, requiring the posting of security by plaintiffs in stockholders' derivative actions, might well impel a stockholder to choose to bring suit in the federal, rather than the state, court.

[11]   Cf. Monarch Insurance Co. of Ohio v. Spach, 281 F.2d 401, 412 (C.A.5th Cir. 1960). We cannot seriously entertain the thought that one suing an estate would be led to choose the federal court because of a belief that adherence to Rule 4(d)(1) is less likely to give the executor actual notice than § 9, and therefore more likely to produce a default judgment. Rule 4(d)(1) is well designed to give actual notice, as it did in this case. See note 1, supra.

There is, however, a more fundamental flaw in respondent's syllogism: the incorrect assumption that the rule of Erie R. Co. v. Tompkins constitutes the appropriate test of the validity and therefore the applicability of a Federal Rule of Civil Procedure. The Erie rule has never been invoked to void a Federal Rule. It is true that there have been cases where this Court has held applicable a state rule in the face of an argument that the situation was governed by one of the Federal Rules. But the holding of each such case was not that Erie commanded displacement of a Federal Rule by an inconsistent state rule, but rather that the scope of the Federal Rule was not as broad as the losing party urged, and therefore, there being no Federal Rule which covered the point in dispute, Erie commanded the enforcement of state law.

> "Respondent contends, in the first place, that the charge was correct because of the fact that Rule 8(c) of the Rules of Civil Procedure makes contributory negligence an affirmative defense. We do not agree. Rule 8(c) covers only the manner of pleading. The question of the burden of establishing contributory negligence is a question of local law which federal courts in diversity of citizenship cases (Erie R. Co. v. Tompkins, 304 U.S. 64, 58 S.Ct. 817) must apply." Palmer v. Hoffman, 318 U.S. 109, 117, 63 S.Ct. 477, 482.[12]

(Here, of course, the clash is unavoidable; Rule 4(d)(1) says—implicitly, but with unmistakable clarity—that in-hand service is not required in federal courts.) At the same time, in cases adjudicating the validity of Federal Rules, we have not applied the York rule or other refinements of Erie, but have to this day continued to decide questions concerning the scope of the Enabling Act and the constitutionality of specific Federal Rules in light of the distinction set forth in Sibbach. E.g., Schlagenhauf v. Holder, 379 U.S. 104, 85 S.Ct. 234.

Nor has the development of two separate lines of cases been inadvertent. The line between "substance" and "procedure" shifts as the legal context changes. "Each implies different variables depending upon the particular problem for which it is used." Guaranty Trust Co. v. York, supra, 326 U.S. at 108, 65 S.Ct. at 1469; Cook, The Logical and Legal Bases of the Conflict of Laws, pp. 154–183 (1942). It is true that both the Enabling Act and the Erie rule say, roughly, that federal courts are to apply state "substantive" law and federal "procedural" law, but from that it need not follow that the tests are identical. For they were designed to control very different sorts of decisions. When a situation is covered by one of the Federal Rules, the question facing the court is a far cry from the typical, relatively unguided Erie choice: the court has been instructed to apply the Federal Rule, and can refuse to do so only if the Advisory

---

[12]   To the same effect, see Ragan v. Merchants Transfer Co., supra; Cohen v. Beneficial Indus. Loan Corp., supra, note 10, 337 U.S. at 556, 69 S.Ct. at 1230; id., at 557, 69 S.Ct. at 1230 (Douglas, J., dissenting); cf. Bernhardt v. Polygraphic Co., supra, note 5, 350 U.S. at 201–202, 76 S.Ct. at 275; see generally Iovino v. Waterson, [274 F.2d 41, 47–48 (2d Cir.1959)].

Committee, this Court, and Congress erred in their prima facie judgment that the Rule in question transgresses neither the terms of the Enabling Act nor constitutional restrictions.

We are reminded by the Erie opinion[14] that neither Congress nor the federal courts can, under the guise of formulating rules of decision for federal courts, fashion rules which are not supported by a grant of federal authority contained in Article I or some other section of the Constitution; in such areas state law must govern because there can be no other law. But the opinion in Erie, which involved no Federal Rule and dealt with a question which was "substantive" in every traditional sense (whether the railroad owed a duty of care to Tompkins as a trespasser or a licensee), surely neither said nor implied that measures like Rule 4(d)(1) are unconstitutional. For the constitutional provision for a federal court system (augmented by the Necessary and Proper Clause) carries with it congressional power to make rules governing the practice and pleading in those courts, which in turn includes a power to regulate matters which, though falling within the uncertain area between substance and procedure, are rationally capable of classification as either. Cf. M'Culloch v. Maryland, 4 Wheat. 316, 421. Neither York nor the cases following it ever suggested that the rule there laid down for coping with situations where no Federal Rule applies is coextensive with the limitation on Congress to which Erie had adverted. Although this Court has never before been confronted with a case where the applicable Federal Rule is in direct collision with the law of the relevant State,[15] courts of appeals faced with such clashes have rightly discerned the implications of our decisions.

> "One of the shaping purposes of the Federal Rules is to bring about uniformity in the federal courts by getting away from local rules. This is especially true of matters which relate to the administration of legal proceedings, an area in which federal courts have traditionally exerted strong inherent power, completely aside from the powers Congress expressly conferred in the Rules. The purpose of the Erie doctrine, even as extended in York and Ragan, was never to bottle up federal courts with 'outcome-determinative' and 'integral-relations' stoppers— when there are 'affirmative countervailing [federal] considerations' and when there is a Congressional mandate (the Rules) supported by constitutional authority." Lumbermen's

---

[14]   Erie R. Co. v. Tompkins, supra, 304 U.S. at 77–79, 58 S.Ct. at 822–823; cf. Bernhardt v. Polygraphic Co., supra, note 5, 350 U.S. at 202, 76 S.Ct. at 275; Sibbach v. Wilson & Co., supra, 312 U.S. at 10, 61 S.Ct. at 424; Guaranty Trust Co. v. York, supra, 326 U.S. at 105, 65 S.Ct. at 1467.

[15]   In Sibbach v. Wilson & Co., supra, the law of the forum State (Illinois) forbade the sort of order authorized by Rule 35. However, Sibbach was decided before Klaxon Co. v. Stentor Electric Mfg. Co., supra, note 7, and the Sibbach opinion makes clear that the Court was proceeding on the assumption that if the law of any State was relevant, it was the law of the State where the tort occurred (Indiana), which, like Rule 35, made provision for such orders. 312 U.S. at 6–7, 10–11, 61 S.Ct. at 423, 424–425.

Mutual Casualty Co. v. Wright, 322 F.2d 759, 764 (C.A.5th Cir.1963).

Erie and its offspring cast no doubt on the long-recognized power of Congress to prescribe housekeeping rules for federal courts even though some of those rules will inevitably differ from comparable state rules. Cf. Herron v. Southern Pacific Co., 283 U.S. 91, 51 S.Ct. 383. "When, because the plaintiff happens to be a non-resident, such a right is enforceable in a federal as well as in a State court, the forms and mode of enforcing the right may at times, naturally enough, vary because the two judicial systems are not identical." Guaranty Trust Co. v. York, supra, 326 U.S. at 108, 65 S.Ct. at 1469; Cohen v. Beneficial Indus. Loan Corp., 337 U.S. 541, 555, 69 S.Ct. 1221, 1229. Thus, though a court, in measuring a Federal Rule against the standards contained in the Enabling Act and the Constitution, need not wholly blind itself to the degree to which the Rule makes the character and result of the federal litigation stray from the course it would follow in state courts, Sibbach v. Wilson & Co., supra, 312 U.S. at 13–14, 61 S.Ct. at 426–427, it cannot be forgotten that the Erie rule, and the guidelines suggested in York, were created to serve another purpose altogether. To hold that a Federal Rule of Civil Procedure must cease to function whenever it alters the mode of enforcing state-created rights would be to disembowel either the Constitution's grant of power over federal procedure or Congress' attempt to exercise that power in the Enabling Act. Rule 4(d)(1) is valid and controls the instant case.

Reversed.

■ MR. JUSTICE BLACK concurs in the result.

■ MR. JUSTICE HARLAN, concurring.

It is unquestionably true that up to now Erie and the cases following it have not succeeded in articulating a workable doctrine governing choice of law in diversity actions. I respect the Court's effort to clarify the situation in today's opinion. However, in doing so I think it has misconceived the constitutional premises of Erie and has failed to deal adequately with those past decisions upon which the courts below relied.

Erie was something more than an opinion which worried about "forum-shopping and avoidance of inequitable administration of the laws," ante, . . . although to be sure these were important elements of the decision. I have always regarded that decision as one of the modern cornerstones of our federalism, expressing policies that profoundly touch the allocation of judicial power between the state and federal systems. . . .

    . . . .

. . . Whereas the unadulterated outcome and forum-shopping tests may err too far toward honoring state rules, I submit that the Court's [Federal Rules] test moves too fast and far in the other direction.

The courts below relied upon this Court's decisions in Ragan v. Merchants Transfer & Warehouse Co., 337 U.S. 530, 69 S.Ct. 1233, and Cohen v. Beneficial Indus. Loan Corp., 337 U.S. 541, 69 S.Ct. 1221. Those cases deserve more attention than this Court has given them, particularly Ragan which, if still good law, would in my opinion call for affirmance of the result reached by the Court of Appeals. Further, a discussion of these two cases will serve to illuminate the thesis I am advocating [whereby Justice Harlan would apply state law "if the choice of rule would substantially affect those primary decisions respecting human conduct which our constitutional system leaves to state regulation"].

In Ragan a Kansas statute of limitations provided that an action was deemed commenced when service was made on the defendant. Despite Federal Rule 3 which provides that an action commences with the filing of the complaint, the Court held that for purposes of the Kansas statute of limitations a diversity tort action commenced only when service was made upon the defendant. The effect of this holding was that although the plaintiff had filed his federal complaint within the state period of limitations, his action was barred because the federal marshal did not serve a summons on the defendant until after the limitations period had run. I think that the decision was wrong. At most, application of the Federal Rule would have meant that potential Kansas tort defendants would have to defer for a few days the satisfaction of knowing that they had not been sued within the limitations period. The choice of the Federal Rule would have had no effect on the primary stages of private activity from which torts arise, and only the most minimal effect on behavior following the commission of the tort. In such circumstances the interest of the federal system in proceeding under its own rules should have prevailed.

Cohen v. Beneficial Indus. Loan Corp. held that a federal diversity court must apply a state statute requiring a small stockholder in a stockholder derivative suit to post a bond securing payment of defense costs as a condition to prosecuting an action. Such a statute is not "outcome determinative"; the plaintiff can win with or without it. The Court now rationalizes the case on the ground that the statute might affect the plaintiff's choice of forum (ante . . . n. 10), but as has been pointed out, a simple forum-shopping test proves too much. The proper view of Cohen is, in my opinion, that the statute was meant to inhibit small stockholders from instituting "strike suits," and thus it was designed and could be expected to have a substantial impact on private primary activity. Anyone who was at the trial bar during the period when Cohen arose can appreciate the strong state policy reflected in the statute. I think it wholly legitimate to view Federal Rule [23.1] as not purporting to deal with the problem. But even had the Federal Rules purported to do so, and in so doing provided a substantially less effective deterrent to strike suits, I think the state rule should still have prevailed.

That is where I believe the Court's view differs from mine; for the Court attributes such overriding force to the Federal Rules that it is hard to think of a case where a conflicting state rule would be allowed to operate, even though the state rule reflected policy considerations which, under Erie, would lie within the realm of state legislative authority.

It remains to apply what has been said to the present case. The Massachusetts rule provides that an executor need not answer suits unless in-hand service was made upon him or notice of the action was filed in the proper registry of probate within one year of his giving bond. The evident intent of this statute is to permit an executor to distribute the estate which he is administering without fear that further liabilities may be outstanding for which he could be held personally liable. If the Federal District Court in Massachusetts applies Rule 4(d)(1) of the Federal Rules of Civil Procedure instead of the Massachusetts service rule, what effect would that have on the speed and assurance with which estates are distributed? As I see it, the effect would not be substantial. It would mean simply that an executor would have to check at his own house or the federal courthouse as well as the registry of probate before he could distribute the estate with impunity. As this does not seem enough to give rise to any real impingement on the vitality of the state policy which the Massachusetts rule is intended to serve, I concur in the judgment of the Court.

———

Questions: (10) Consider once again Woods v. Interstate Realty Co. Would you expect its result to be affected by Hanna v. Plumer (pronounced PLUM-er)? What of Rule 17(b)? See Wright & Miller § 1569. Assuming that Rule 17(b) does not extend to the situation in Woods (as the Supreme Court apparently assumed, knowingly or unknowingly, when it decided Woods itself, and also when it referred to Woods in Hanna), then reference must be made not to the portion of Hanna that deals with the applicability of the Federal Rules but rather to the discussion in Hanna of the more general Erie problem. So, under Hanna's refined outcome-determinative test, was Woods rightly decided?

(11) What exactly should be the meaning given "the twin aims of the Erie rule: discouragement of forum-shopping and avoidance of inequitable administration of the laws"? The former factor seems to focus on the systemic costs of the plaintiff or the defendant selecting federal or state court because of a difference in law. Under post-Hanna cases, the latter factor apparently refers to the unfairness of treating in a substantially different way any similarly situated individuals, given that certain classes of people have a choice of court systems. This latter factor, however, renders those forum-shopping concerns in large part redundant, and seemingly insignificant as to any remaining part. Should, then, the forum-shopping factor be seen instead to stand for the otherwise missing federalism factor expressed by Byrd or by Justice Harlan in Hanna, so recognizing that the "attempt to make the federal court function like the state court 'a block away' serves

federalism goals of allocating regulatory power [while it] deters shopping"? George D. Brown, The Ideologies of Forum Shopping—Why Doesn't a Conservative Court Protect Defendants?, 71 N.C.L.Rev. 649, 693 (1993).

———

SZANTAY v. BEECH AIRCRAFT CORP., 349 F.2d 60 (4th Cir.1965). Szantay bought a Beech aircraft in Nebraska and flew it to Florida and thence to South Carolina, where it was serviced by Dixie Aviation Co. during a brief stopover. Szantay and his passengers then left for Illinois, where they lived, but the plane crashed in Tennessee, killing all its occupants.

The Illinois personal representatives of the decedents each brought a diversity action in a federal district court in South Carolina against Beech and Dixie, alleging negligent design and manufacture on the part of Beech and negligent servicing by Dixie. The requirements for diversity jurisdiction were satisfied, as Beech was a Delaware corporation with its principal place of business in Kansas, Dixie was a South Carolina corporation doing business only in that state, and the amount in controversy exceeded the jurisdictional amount. By virtue of Beech's doing business in South Carolina, venue requirements were met and in-state service of process was properly effected under then-prevailing law.

Beech moved to dismiss the actions based on a South Carolina "door-closing" statute. It provided that a foreign corporation could be sued in a South Carolina court only by (1) any South Carolina resident for any cause of action or (2) a nonresident plaintiff when the cause of action arose in South Carolina. So, a South Carolina state court could not entertain a suit brought by a nonresident against a foreign corporation on a foreign cause of action. Beech maintained that this statute should likewise bar suit in the federal court. But the court denied the motion to dismiss.

On interlocutory appeal pursuant to 28 U.S.C. § 1292(b), the court of appeals, after discussing prior decisions that included the Erie, Guaranty Trust, Woods, Byrd, and Hanna cases, generalized: "If the state procedural provision is not intimately bound up with the right being enforced but its application would substantially affect the outcome of the litigation, the federal diversity court must still apply it unless there are affirmative countervailing federal considerations."

The appellate court proceeded by first considering the outcome-determinative factor. Rejection of the South Carolina statute in the federal court would have a forum-shopping effect. However, rejection of state law would not result in discrimination against South Carolina residents; indeed, such rejection would do no more than give to nonresidents what residents enjoyed anyway, viz., a South Carolina forum for a case such as this one.

The court next explored the state policies underlying the door-closing statute. Faced with a total absence of legislative history and prior judicial discussion, the court concluded that the state interests were uncertain and that the conceivable ones appeared weak. Among other possibilities, the statute could be viewed as a formulation of the doctrine of forum non conveniens or as a measure to relieve state docket congestion, but such interests would be irrelevant for Erie purposes "since federal cognizance of the case would in no way frustrate state policy."

The court then found the "countervailing federal considerations explicit, and they are numerous." The list included: (1) avoidance of discrimination against nonresidents, the very purpose of the Diversity Clause itself; (2) maximum enforcement in each state of the rights and duties created by sister states, the consideration underlying the Full Faith and Credit Clause; (3) the policy that a federal court sitting in diversity should hear and adjudicate the issues before it, citing Meredith v. Winter Haven, 320 U.S. 228, 64 S.Ct. 7 (1943); (4) encouragement of efficient joinder in multiparty actions, an interest otherwise threatened because at the time Dixie was subject to service only in South Carolina; and (5) the interest in providing a convenient forum for federal litigants, as expressed in provisions such as 28 U.S.C. § 1404(a).

After a final word distinguishing Woods, the court of appeals affirmed the decision below.

———

DAY & ZIMMERMANN, INC. v. CHALLONER, 423 U.S. 3, 96 S.Ct. 167 (1975). In May of 1970, in the midst of combat in Cambodia between American and North Vietnamese forces, a 105 mm. howitzer round prematurely exploded in a gun's barrel. The blast killed one of the gun's operators, a soldier named Daniel Nelms from Tennessee. It seriously wounded another soldier, Ken Challoner of Wisconsin. The round had been manufactured in Texas by Day & Zimmermann, a major military contractor incorporated in Maryland with its principal place of business in Pennsylvania.

Nelms's parents and Challoner brought a diversity action against the manufacturer in the United States District Court for the Eastern District of Texas. The district judge submitted the case to the jury under the strict liability principles of Texas law, as the plaintiffs had hoped it would. The jury returned sizable verdicts for the plaintiffs.

On appeal from judgment, the defendant contended that Klaxon compelled the district court to apply the Texas conflict-of-laws rule and that, because Texas then had a law-of-the-place-of-the-injury rule and because Cambodian law required proof of fault, the judgment based on a strict liability standard had to fall. The court of appeals nevertheless affirmed, 512 F.2d 77 (5th Cir.1975).

The court of appeals began by acknowledging that Klaxon "held, as a general rule," that the conflict-of-laws rules of the forum state apply in diversity cases. The court next conceded that a Texas state court would certainly look to Cambodian tort law in the wrongful-death action, and perhaps in the personal-injury action as well. Yet the Fifth Circuit went on to hold that a federal court in this situation could make an independent choice of law, thus permitting the district court here to look to the tort law of Texas rather than that of Cambodia.

The reasoning of the court of appeals in support of its assumed power to apply a federal conflict-of-laws rule was somewhat obscure. Yet its approach was unmistakably ad hoc, with the court weighing the federal interests at stake in this particular case against the forum state's interests in having its conflict-of-laws rule applied in this federal case. The federal interests predominated, and hence federal law applied.

In a per curiam opinion, the Supreme Court ruled curtly: "The Court of Appeals . . . supported its decision on the grounds that the rationale for applying the traditional conflicts rule applied by Texas 'is not operative under the present facts'; and that it was 'a Court of the United States, an instrumentality created to effectuate the laws and policies of the United States.'

"We believe that the Court of Appeals either misinterpreted our longstanding decision in Klaxon Co. v. Stentor Electric Mfg. Co., 313 U.S. 487, 61 S.Ct. 1020 (1941), or else determined for itself that it was no longer of controlling force in a case such as this. We are of the opinion that Klaxon is by its terms applicable here and should have been adhered to by the Court of Appeals. In Klaxon, supra, at 496, 61 S.Ct., at 1021, this Court said:

> 'The conflict of laws rules to be applied by the federal court in Delaware must conform to those prevailing in Delaware's state courts. Otherwise, the accident of diversity of citizenship would constantly disturb equal administration of justice in coordinate state and federal courts sitting side by side. See Erie R. Co. v. Tompkins . . . .'

"By parity of reasoning, the conflict-of-laws rules to be applied by a federal court in Texas must conform to those prevailing in the Texas state courts. A federal court in a diversity case is not free to engraft onto those state rules exceptions or modifications which may commend themselves to the federal court, but which have not commended themselves to the State in which the federal court sits. The Court of Appeals in this case should identify and follow the Texas conflicts rule. What substantive law will govern when Texas' rule is applied is a matter to be determined by the Court of Appeals.

"The petition for certiorari is granted, the judgment of the Court of Appeals is vacated, and the case is remanded for further proceedings in conformity with this opinion."

The court of appeals on remand ruled that Texas would apply Cambodian law, 546 F.2d 26 (5th Cir.1977) (per curiam). The plaintiffs lost for inability to show fault. Since that time, Texas has changed its conflicts approach, but too late for these plaintiffs.

WALKER v. ARMCO STEEL CORP., 446 U.S. 740, 100 S.Ct. 1978 (1980). This case from the United States District Court for the Western District of Oklahoma presented anew, on indistinguishably similar facts, the legal issue of Ragan v. Merchants Transfer & Warehouse Co. The district court and the Tenth Circuit barred suit by following Ragan, but the Supreme Court granted certiorari to resolve a conflict among the circuits. Justice Marshall, writing for a unanimous Supreme Court, affirmed on the basis of stare decisis. Ragan had survived Hanna.

First, the Hanna holding as to Sibbach did not apply. As recognized in Hanna's footnote 12, Rule 3 covers commencement for the internal purposes of case management, but not for stopping the statute of limitations.

Second, the Hanna dictum as to Erie called for state law to apply in Ragan and Walker. "It is sufficient to note that although in this case failure to apply the state service law might not create any problem of forum shopping, the result would be an 'inequitable administration' of the law." The explanation was that the "policies underlying diversity jurisdiction do not support such a distinction between state and federal plaintiffs."

Question: (12) In a prolonged diversity action, would the federal court apply a state statute that requires dismissal of actions not tried within five years of filing? See Olympic Sports Prods., Inc. v. Universal Athletic Sales Co., 760 F.2d 910 (9th Cir.1985) (2–1 decision) (no).

BURLINGTON NORTHERN RAILROAD CO. v. WOODS, 480 U.S. 1, 107 S.Ct. 967 (1987). After removal to the Northern District of Alabama on the basis of diversity jurisdiction, plaintiffs recovered $305,000 for personal injuries.

The defendant railroad obtained a stay pending appeal, but the Eleventh Circuit affirmed on the merits and then assessed a penalty against the railroad in accordance with an Alabama statute. This statute provided that upon any affirmance of a stayed money judgment, the appellate court must award a penalty equal to 10% of the judgment. Incidentally, Alabama also had a rule similar to Federal Rule of Appellate Procedure 38, a discretionary provision for frivolous appeals.

On certiorari, Justice Marshall, writing for a unanimous Supreme Court, concluded that the state statute did not apply in federal court. He explained that the Federal Rules of Appellate Procedure were within the Hanna holding on federal rulemaking. Then, quoting Walker, he decided that, "when fairly construed, the scope of Federal Rule 38 is 'sufficiently broad' to cause a 'direct collision' with the state law or, implicitly, to 'control the issue' before the court, thereby leaving no room for the operation of that law."

—————

Gasperini v. Center for Humanities, Inc.

Supreme Court of the United States, 1996.
518 U.S. 415, 116 S.Ct. 2211.

■ JUSTICE GINSBURG delivered the opinion of the Court.

Under the law of New York, appellate courts are empowered to review the size of jury verdicts and to order new trials when the jury's award "deviates materially from what would be reasonable compensation." N.Y.Civ.Prac.Law and Rules (CPLR) § 5501(c) (McKinney 1995). Under the Seventh Amendment, which governs proceedings in federal court, but not in state court, "the right of trial by jury shall be preserved, and no fact tried by a jury, shall be otherwise re-examined in any Court of the United States, than according to the rules of the common law." U.S.Const., Amdt. 7. The compatibility of these provisions, in an action based on New York law but tried in federal court by reason of the parties' diverse citizenship, is the issue we confront in this case. We hold that New York's law controlling compensation awards for excessiveness or inadequacy can be given effect, without detriment to the Seventh Amendment, if the review standard set out in CPLR § 5501(c) is applied by the federal trial court judge, with appellate control of the trial court's ruling limited to review for "abuse of discretion."

I

Petitioner William Gasperini, a journalist for CBS News and the Christian Science Monitor, began reporting on events in Central America in 1984. He earned his living primarily in radio and print media and only occasionally sold his photographic work. During the course of his seven-year stint in Central America, Gasperini took over 5,000 slide transparencies, depicting active war zones, political leaders, and scenes from daily life. In 1990, Gasperini agreed to supply his original color transparencies to The Center for Humanities, Inc. (Center) for use in an educational videotape, Conflict in Central America. Gasperini selected 300 of his slides for the Center; its videotape included 110 of them. The Center agreed to return the original transparencies, but upon the completion of the project, it could not find them.

Gasperini commenced suit in the United States District Court for the Southern District of New York, invoking the court's diversity jurisdiction pursuant to 28 U.S.C. § 1332. He alleged several state-law claims for relief, including breach of contract, conversion, and negligence. . . . The Center conceded liability for the lost transparencies and the issue of damages was tried before a jury.

At trial, Gasperini's expert witness testified that the "industry standard" within the photographic publishing community valued a lost transparency at $1,500. . . . This industry standard, the expert explained, represented the average license fee a commercial photograph could earn over the full course of the photographer's copyright, i.e., in Gasperini's case, his lifetime plus 50 years. . . . Gasperini estimated that his earnings from photography totaled just over $10,000 for the period from 1984 through 1993. He also testified that he intended to produce a book containing his best photographs from Central America. . . .

After a three-day trial, the jury awarded Gasperini $450,000 in compensatory damages. This sum, the jury foreperson announced, "is [$]1500 each, for 300 slides." . . . Moving for a new trial under Federal Rule of Civil Procedure 59, the Center attacked the verdict on various grounds, including excessiveness. Without comment, the District Court denied the motion. . . .

The Court of Appeals for the Second Circuit vacated the judgment entered on the jury's verdict. 66 F.3d 427 (1995). Mindful that New York law governed the controversy, the Court of Appeals endeavored to apply CPLR § 5501(c), which instructs that . . . the New York Appellate Division "shall determine that an award is excessive or inadequate if it deviates materially from what would be reasonable compensation." The Second Circuit's application of § 5501(c) as a check on the size of the jury's verdict followed Circuit precedent elaborated two weeks earlier in Consorti v. Armstrong World Industries, Inc., 64 F.3d 781, superseded [on other grounds], 72 F.3d 1003 (1995). Surveying Appellate Division decisions that reviewed damage awards for lost transparencies, the Second Circuit concluded that testimony on industry standard alone was insufficient to justify a verdict; prime among other factors warranting consideration were the uniqueness of the slides' subject matter and the photographer's earning level.

Guided by Appellate Division rulings, the Second Circuit held that the $450,000 verdict "materially deviates from what is reasonable compensation." 66 F.3d, at 431. Some of Gasperini's transparencies, the Second Circuit recognized, were unique, notably those capturing combat situations in which Gasperini was the only photographer present. Id., at 429. But others "depicted either generic scenes or events at which other professional photojournalists were present." Id., at 431. No more than 50 slides merited a $1,500 award, the court concluded, after "[g]iving Gasperini every benefit of the doubt." Ibid. Absent evidence showing significant earnings from photographic endeavors or concrete plans to publish a book, the court further determined, any damage award above $100 each for the remaining slides would be excessive. Remittiturs "presen[t] difficult problems for appellate courts," the Second Circuit acknowledged, for court of appeals judges review the evidence from "a cold paper record." Ibid. Nevertheless, the Second Circuit set aside the $450,000 verdict and ordered a new trial, unless Gasperini agreed to an award of $100,000 [as the maximum amount recoverable without being improperly excessive].

This case presents an important question regarding the standard a federal court uses to measure the alleged excessiveness of a jury's verdict in an action for damages based on state law. We therefore granted certiorari. 516 U.S. 1086, 116 S.Ct. 805 (1996).

II

Before 1986, state and federal courts in New York generally invoked the same judge-made formulation in responding to excessiveness attacks on jury verdicts: courts would not disturb an award unless the amount was so exorbitant that it "shocked the conscience of the court." See Consorti, 72 F.3d, at 1012–1013 (collecting cases). . . .

In both state and federal courts, trial judges made the excessiveness assessment in the first instance, and appellate judges ordinarily deferred to the trial court's judgment. [Citations omitted.]

In 1986, as part of a series of tort reform measures, New York codified a standard for judicial review of the size of jury awards. Placed in CPLR § 5501(c), the prescription reads:

> "In reviewing a money judgment . . . in which it is contended that the award is excessive or inadequate and that a new trial should have been granted unless a stipulation is entered to a different award, the appellate division shall determine that an award is excessive or inadequate if it deviates materially from what would be reasonable compensation."

As stated in Legislative Findings and Declarations accompanying New York's adoption of the "deviates materially" formulation, the lawmakers found the "shock the conscience" test an insufficient check on damage awards; the legislature therefore installed a standard "invit[ing] more careful appellate scrutiny." [Citation omitted.] At the same time, the legislature instructed the Appellate Division, in amended § 5522, to state the reasons for the court's rulings on the size of verdicts, and the factors the court considered in complying with § 5501(c). In his signing statement, then-Governor Mario Cuomo emphasized that the CPLR amendments were meant to rachet up the review standard: "This will assure greater scrutiny of the amount of verdicts and promote greater stability in the tort system and greater fairness for similarly situated defendants throughout the State." [Citation omitted.]

New York state-court opinions confirm that § 5501(c)'s "deviates materially" standard calls for closer surveillance than "shock the conscience" oversight. [Citations omitted.]

Although phrased as a direction to New York's intermediate appellate courts, § 5501(c)'s "deviates materially" standard, as construed by New York's courts, instructs state trial judges as well. [Citations omitted.] Application of § 5501(c) at the trial level is key to this case.

To determine whether an award "deviates materially from what would be reasonable compensation," New York state courts look to awards approved in similar cases. . . .

III

In cases like Gasperini's, in which New York law governs the claims for relief, does New York law also supply the test for federal court review of the size of the verdict? The Center answers yes. The "deviates materially" standard, it argues, is a substantive standard that must be applied by federal appellate courts in diversity cases. The Second Circuit agreed. See 66 F.3d, at 430; see also Consorti, 72 F.3d, at 1011 ("[CPLR § 5501(c)] is the substantive rule provided by New York law."). Gasperini, emphasizing that § 5501(c) trains on the New York Appellate Division, characterizes the provision as procedural, an allocation of decisionmaking authority regarding damages, not a hard cap on the amount recoverable. Correctly comprehended, Gasperini urges, § 5501(c)'s direction to the Appellate Division cannot be given effect by federal appellate courts without violating the Seventh Amendment's re-examination clause.

As the parties' arguments suggest, CPLR § 5501(c), appraised under Erie R. Co. v. Tompkins, 304 U.S. 64, 58 S.Ct. 817 (1938), and decisions in Erie's path, is both "substantive" and "procedural": "substantive" in that § 5501(c)'s "deviates materially" standard controls how much a plaintiff can be awarded; "procedural" in that § 5501(c) assigns decisionmaking authority to New York's Appellate Division. Parallel application of § 5501(c) at the federal appellate level would be out of sync with the federal system's division of trial and appellate court functions, an allocation weighted by the Seventh Amendment. The dispositive question, therefore, is whether federal courts can give effect to the substantive thrust of § 5501(c) without untoward alteration of the federal scheme for the trial and decision of civil cases.

A

Federal diversity jurisdiction provides an alternative forum for the adjudication of state-created rights, but it does not carry with it generation of rules of substantive law. As Erie read the Rules of Decision Act: "Except in matters governed by the Federal Constitution or by Acts of Congress, the law to be applied in any case is the law of the State." 304 U.S., at 78, 58 S.Ct., at 822. Under the Erie doctrine, federal courts sitting in diversity apply state substantive law and federal procedural law.

Classification of a law as "substantive" or "procedural" for Erie purposes is sometimes a challenging endeavor.[7] Guaranty Trust Co. v.

---

[7]   Concerning matters covered by the Federal Rules of Civil Procedure, the characterization question is usually unproblematic: It is settled that if the Rule in point is consonant with the Rules Enabling Act, 28 U.S.C. § 2072, and the Constitution, the Federal Rule applies regardless of contrary state law. See Hanna v. Plumer, 380 U.S. 460, 469–474, 85

York, 326 U.S. 99, 65 S.Ct. 1464 (1945), an early interpretation of Erie, propounded an "outcome-determination" test: "[D]oes it significantly affect the result of a litigation for a federal court to disregard a law of a State that would be controlling in an action upon the same claim by the same parties in a State court?" 326 U.S., at 109, 65 S.Ct., at 1470. Ordering application of a state statute of limitations to an equity proceeding in federal court, the Court said in Guaranty Trust: "[W]here a federal court is exercising jurisdiction solely because of the diversity of citizenship of the parties, the outcome of the litigation in the federal court should be substantially the same, so far as legal rules determine the outcome of a litigation, as it would be if tried in a State court." Ibid; see also Ragan v. Merchants Transfer & Warehouse Co., 337 U.S. 530, 533, 69 S.Ct. 1233, 1235 (1949) (when local law that creates the cause of action qualifies it, "federal court must follow suit," for "a different measure of the cause of action in one court than in the other [would transgress] the principle of Erie"). A later pathmarking case, qualifying Guaranty Trust, explained that the "outcome-determination" test must not be applied mechanically to sweep in all manner of variations; instead, its application must be guided by "the twin aims of the Erie rule: discouragement of forum-shopping and avoidance of inequitable administration of the laws." Hanna v. Plumer, 380 U.S. 460, 468, 85 S.Ct. 1136, 1142 (1965).

Informed by these decisions, we address the question whether New York's "deviates materially" standard, codified in CPLR § 5501(c), is outcome-affective in this sense: Would "application of the [standard] . . . have so important an effect upon the fortunes of one or both of the litigants that failure to [apply] it would [unfairly discriminate against citizens of the forum State, or] be likely to cause a plaintiff to choose the federal court"? Id., at 468, n. 9, 85 S.Ct., at 1142, n. 9.

We start from a point the parties do not debate. Gasperini acknowledges that a statutory cap on damages would supply substantive law for Erie purposes. See Reply Brief for Petitioner 2 ("[T]he state as a matter of its substantive law may, among other things, eliminate the availability of damages for a particular claim entirely, limit the factors a jury may consider in determining damages, or place an absolute cap on the amount of damages available, and such substantive law would be applicable in a federal court sitting in diversity."); see also Tr. of Oral

S.Ct. 1136, 1142–1145 (1965); Burlington Northern R. Co. v. Woods, 480 U.S. 1, 4–5, 107 S.Ct. 967, 969–970 (1987). Federal courts have interpreted the Federal Rules, however, with sensitivity to important state interests and regulatory policies. See, e.g., Walker v. Armco Steel Corp., 446 U.S. 740, 750–752, 100 S.Ct. 1978, 1985–1986 (1980) (reaffirming decision in Ragan v. Merchants Transfer & Warehouse Co., 337 U.S. 530, 69 S.Ct. 1233 (1949), that state law rather than Rule 3 determines when a diversity action commences for the purposes of tolling the state statute of limitations; Rule 3 makes no reference to the tolling of state limitations, the Court observed, and accordingly found no "direct conflict"); S.A. Healy Co. v. Milwaukee Metropolitan Sewerage Dist., 60 F.3d 305, 310–312 (C.A.7 1995) (state provision for offers of settlement by plaintiffs is compatible with Federal Rule 68, which is limited to offers by defendants).

Arg. 4–5, 25; Consorti, 72 F.3d, at 1011.[9] Although CPLR § 5501(c) is less readily classified, it was designed to provide an analogous control.

New York's Legislature codified in § 5501(c) a new standard, one that requires closer court review than the common law "shock the conscience" test.... More rigorous comparative evaluations attend application of § 5501(c)'s "deviates materially" standard.... To foster predictability, the legislature required the reviewing court, when overturning a verdict under § 5501(c), to state its reasons, including the factors it considered relevant. See CPLR § 5522(b).... We think it a fair conclusion that CPLR § 5501(c) differs from a statutory cap principally "in that the maximum amount recoverable is not set by statute, but rather is determined by case law." Brief for City of New York as Amicus Curiae 11. In sum, § 5501(c) contains a procedural instruction, ... but the State's objective is manifestly substantive. Cf. S.A. Healy Co. v. Milwaukee Metropolitan Sewerage Dist., 60 F.3d 305, 310 (C.A.7 1995).

It thus appears that if federal courts ignore the change in the New York standard and persist in applying the "shock the conscience" test to damage awards on claims governed by New York law, " 'substantial' variations between state and federal [money judgments]" may be expected. See Hanna, 380 U.S., at 467–468, 85 S.Ct., at 1142. We therefore agree with the Second Circuit that New York's check on excessive damages implicates what we have called Erie's "twin aims." ... Just as the Erie principle precludes a federal court from giving a state-created claim "longer life ... than [the claim] would have had in the state court," Ragan, 337 U.S., at 533–534, 69 S.Ct., at 1235, so Erie precludes a recovery in federal court significantly larger than the recovery that would have been tolerated in state court.

B

CPLR § 5501(c) ... is phrased as a direction to the New York Appellate Division. Acting essentially as a surrogate for a New York appellate forum, the Court of Appeals reviewed Gasperini's award to determine if it "deviate[d] materially" from damage awards the Appellate Division permitted in similar circumstances. The Court of Appeals performed this task without benefit of an opinion from the District Court, which had denied "without comment" the Center's Rule 59 motion. 66 F.3d, at 428. Concentrating on the authority § 5501(c) gives to the Appellate Division, Gasperini urges that the provision shifts fact-finding responsibility from the jury and the trial judge to the appellate court. Assigning such responsibility to an appellate court, he maintains, is incompatible with the Seventh Amendment's re-examination clause, and therefore, Gasperini concludes, § 5501(c) cannot be given effect in federal court. Brief for Petitioner 19–20. Although we reach a different conclusion than Gasperini, we agree that the Second Circuit did not

---

9   While we have not specifically addressed the issue, courts of appeals have held that district court application of state statutory caps in diversity cases, post verdict, does not violate the Seventh Amendment. [Citations omitted.]

attend to "[a]n essential characteristic of [the federal-court] system," Byrd v. Blue Ridge Rural Elec. Cooperative, Inc., 356 U.S. 525, 537, 78 S.Ct. 893, 901 (1958), when it used § 5501(c) as "the standard for [federal] appellate review," Consorti, 72 F.3d, at 1013; see also 66 F.3d, at 430.

That "essential characteristic" was described in Byrd, a diversity suit for negligence in which a pivotal issue of fact would have been tried by a judge were the case in state court. The Byrd Court held that, despite the state practice, the plaintiff was entitled to a jury trial in federal court. In so ruling, the Court said that the Guaranty Trust "outcome-determination" test was an insufficient guide in cases presenting countervailing federal interests. See Byrd, 356 U.S., at 537, 78 S.Ct., at 901. The Court described the countervailing federal interests present in Byrd this way:

> "The federal system is an independent system for administering justice to litigants who properly invoke its jurisdiction. An essential characteristic of that system is the manner in which, in civil common-law actions, it distributes trial functions between judge and jury and, under the influence—if not the command—of the Seventh Amendment, assigns the decisions of disputed questions of fact to the jury." Ibid. (footnote omitted).

The Seventh Amendment, which governs proceedings in federal court, but not in state court, bears not only on the allocation of trial functions between judge and jury, the issue in Byrd; it also controls the allocation of authority to review verdicts, the issue of concern here. . . .

Byrd involved the first clause of the Amendment, the "trial by jury" clause. This case involves the second, the "re-examination" clause. In keeping with the historic understanding, the re-examination clause does not inhibit the authority of trial judges to grant new trials "for any of the reasons for which new trials have heretofore been granted in actions at law in the courts of the United States." Fed.Rule Civ.Proc. 59(a). That authority is large. See 6A Moore's Federal Practice ¶ 59.05[2], pp. 59–44 to 59–46 (2d ed. 1996) ("The power of the English common law trial courts to grant a new trial for a variety of reasons with a view to the attainment of justice was well established prior to the establishment of our Government."); see also Aetna Casualty & Surety Co. v. Yeatts, 122 F.2d 350, 353 (C.A.4 1941) ("The exercise of [the trial court's power to set aside the jury's verdict and grant a new trial] is not in derogation of the right of trial by jury but is one of the historic safeguards of that right."); Blunt v. Little, 3 F.Cas. 760, 761–762 (Case No. 1,578) (C.C.Mass.1822) (Story, J.) ("[I]f it should clearly appear that the jury have committed a gross error, or have acted from improper motives, or have given damages excessive in relation to the person or the injury, it is as much the duty of the court to interfere, to prevent the wrong, as in any other case."). "The trial judge in the federal system," we have reaffirmed, "has . . . discretion to grant a new trial if the verdict appears to [the judge] to be against the weight of the evidence." Byrd, 356 U.S., at 540, 78 S.Ct., at 902. This discretion includes overturning verdicts for excessiveness and ordering a new trial without qualification, or conditioned on the verdict winner's refusal to agree to a reduction (remittitur). See Dimick v. Schiedt, 293 U.S. 474, 486–487, 55 S.Ct. 296, 301 (1935) (recognizing that remittitur withstands Seventh Amendment attack, but rejecting additur as unconstitutional).

In contrast, appellate review of a federal trial court's denial of a motion to set aside a jury's verdict as excessive is a relatively late, and less secure, development. Such review was once deemed inconsonant with the Seventh Amendment's re-examination clause. See, e.g., Lincoln v. Power, 151 U.S. 436, 437–438, 14 S.Ct. 387, 388 (1894); [other citations omitted]. We subsequently recognized that, even in cases in which the Erie doctrine was not in play—cases arising wholly under federal law—the question was not settled; we twice granted certiorari to decide the unsettled issue, but ultimately resolved the cases on other grounds. See Grunenthal v. Long Island R. Co., 393 U.S. 156, 158, 89 S.Ct. 331, 333 (1968); Neese v. Southern R. Co., 350 U.S. 77, 77, 76 S.Ct. 131, 131–132 (1955).

Before today, we have not "expressly [held] that the Seventh Amendment allows appellate review of a district court's denial of a motion to set aside an award as excessive." Browning-Ferris Industries of Vt., Inc. v. Kelco Disposal, Inc., 492 U.S. 257, 279, n. 25, 109 S.Ct. 2909, 2922, n. 25 (1989). But in successive reminders that the question was worthy of this Court's attention, we noted, without disapproval, that courts of appeals engage in review of district court excessiveness determinations, applying "abuse of discretion" as their standard. See Grunenthal, 393 U.S., at 159, 89 S.Ct., at 333. We noted the Circuit decisions in point, id., at 157, n. 3, 89 S.Ct., at 332, n. 3, and, in Browning-Ferris, we again referred to appellate court abuse-of-discretion review:

> "[T]he role of the district court is to determine whether the jury's verdict is within the confines set by state law, and to determine, by reference to federal standards developed under Rule 59, whether a new trial or remittitur should be ordered. The court of appeals should then review the district court's determination under an abuse-of-discretion standard." 492 U.S., at 279, 109 S.Ct., at 2922.

As the Second Circuit explained, appellate review for abuse of discretion is reconcilable with the Seventh Amendment as a control necessary and proper to the fair administration of justice: "We must give the benefit of every doubt to the judgment of the trial judge; but surely there must be an upper limit, and whether that has been surpassed is not a question of fact with respect to which reasonable men may differ, but a question of law." Dagnello v. Long Island R. Co., 289 F.2d 797, 806 (C.A.2 1961) (quoted in Grunenthal, 393 U.S., at 159, 89 S.Ct., at 333). All other Circuits agree. [Citations omitted]. We now approve this line of decisions, and thus make explicit what Justice Stewart thought implicit in our Grunenthal disposition: "[N]othing in the Seventh Amendment . . . precludes appellate review of the trial judge's denial of a motion to set aside [a jury verdict] as excessive." 393 U.S., at 164, 89 S.Ct., at 336 (Stewart, J., dissenting) (internal quotation marks and footnote omitted).

C

In Byrd, the Court faced a one-or-the-other choice: trial by judge as in state court, or trial by jury according to the federal practice.[21] In the case before us, a choice of that order is not required, for the principal state and federal interests can be accommodated. The Second Circuit correctly recognized that when New York substantive law governs a claim for relief, New York law and decisions guide the allowable damages. See 66 F.3d, at 430; see also Consorti, 72 F.3d, at 1011. But that court did not take into account the characteristic of the federal-court system that caused us to reaffirm: "The proper role of the trial and appellate courts in the federal system in reviewing the size of jury verdicts is . . . a matter of federal law." Donovan v. Penn Shipping Co., 429 U.S. 648, 649, 97 S.Ct. 835, 837 (1977) (per curiam); [other citation omitted].

New York's dominant interest can be respected, without disrupting the federal system, once it is recognized that the federal district court is capable of performing the checking function, i.e., that court can apply the State's "deviates materially" standard in line with New York case law evolving under CPLR § 5501(c).[22] We recall, in this regard, that the "deviates materially" standard serves as the guide to be applied in trial as well as appellate courts in New York. . . .

Within the federal system, practical reasons combine with Seventh Amendment constraints to lodge in the district court, not the court of appeals, primary responsibility for application of § 5501(c)'s "deviates materially" check. Trial judges have the "unique opportunity to consider the evidence in the living courtroom context," Taylor v. Washington Terminal Co., 409 F.2d 145, 148 (C.A.D.C.1969), while appellate judges see only the "cold paper record," 66 F.3d, at 431.

---

[21]   The two-trial rule posited by Justice Scalia . . . surely would be incompatible with the existence of "[t]he federal system [as] an independent system for administering justice," Byrd v. Blue Ridge Rural Elec. Cooperative, Inc., 356 U.S. 525, 537, 78 S.Ct. 893, 901 (1958). We discern no disagreement on such examples among the many federal judges who have considered this case.

[22]   Justice Scalia finds in Federal Rule of Civil Procedure 59 a "federal standard" for new trial motions in " 'direct collision' " with, and " 'leaving no room for the operation of,' " a state law like CPLR § 5501(c). . . . The relevant prescription, Rule 59(a), has remained unchanged since the adoption of the Federal Rules by this Court in 1937. 302 U.S. 783. Rule 59(a) is as encompassing as it is uncontroversial. It is indeed "Hornbook" law that a most usual ground for a Rule 59 motion is that "the damages are excessive." See C. Wright, Law of Federal Courts 676–677 (5th ed. 1994). Whether damages are excessive for the claim-in-suit must be governed by some law. And there is no candidate for that governance other than the law that gives rise to the claim for relief—here, the law of New York. See 28 U.S.C. § 2072(a) and (b) ("Supreme Court shall have the power to prescribe general rules of . . . procedure"; "[s]uch rules shall not abridge, enlarge or modify any substantive right"); [other citations omitted].

District court applications of the "deviates materially" standard would be subject to appellate review under the standard the Circuits now employ when inadequacy or excessiveness is asserted on appeal: abuse of discretion. [Citations omitted.] In light of Erie's doctrine, the federal appeals court must be guided by the damage-control standard state law supplies,[23] but as the Second Circuit itself has said: "If we reverse, it must be because of an abuse of discretion. . . . The very nature of the problem counsels restraint. . . . We must give the benefit of every doubt to the judgment of the trial judge." Dagnello, 289 F.2d, at 806.

IV

It does not appear that the District Court checked the jury's verdict against the relevant New York decisions demanding more than "industry standard" testimony to support an award of the size the jury returned in this case . . . . Accordingly, we vacate the judgment of the Court of Appeals and instruct that court to remand the case to the District Court so that the trial judge, revisiting his ruling on the new trial motion, may test the jury's verdict against CPLR § 5501(c)'s "deviates materially" standard.

It is so ordered.[d]

■ JUSTICE STEVENS, dissenting.

While I agree with most of the reasoning in the Court's opinion, I disagree with its disposition of the case. I would affirm the judgment of the Court of Appeals. I would also reject the suggestion that the Seventh Amendment limits the power of a federal appellate court sitting in diversity to decide whether a jury's award of damages exceeds a limit established by state law.

. . . .

■ JUSTICE SCALIA, with whom the CHIEF JUSTICE [REHNQUIST] and JUSTICE THOMAS join, dissenting.

. . . .

The Court's holding that federal courts of appeals may review district court denials of motions for new trials for error of fact is not the only novel [and, according to Justice Scalia, incorrect] aspect of today's decision. The Court also directs that the case be remanded to the District Court, so that it may "test the jury's verdict against CPLR § 5501(c)'s 'deviates materially' standard" . . . . This disposition contradicts the

---

[23]   If liability and damage-control rules are split apart here, as Justice Scalia says they must be to save the Seventh Amendment, then Gasperini's claim and others like it would be governed by a most curious "law." The sphinx-like, damage-determining law he would apply to this controversy has a state forepart, but a federal hindquarter. The beast may not be brutish, but there is little judgment in its creation.

[d]   On remand, the district court followed state law to order a new trial. Without explanation, it followed federal law, not state law, on the amount of remittitur to rule that Gasperini could avoid the new trial by agreeing to a reduction of the award to the maximum amount recoverable without being improperly excessive, which the court set at $375,000 and which he accepted. 972 F.Supp. 765 (S.D.N.Y.1997), modified, 149 F.3d 137 (2d Cir.1998).

principle that "[t]he proper role of the trial and appellate courts in the federal system in reviewing the size of jury verdicts is . . . a matter of federal law." Donovan v. Penn Shipping Co., 429 U.S. 648, 649, 97 S.Ct. 835, 837 (1977) (per curiam).

The Court acknowledges that state procedural rules cannot, as a general matter, be permitted to interfere with the allocation of functions in the federal court system . . . . Indeed, it is at least partly for this reason that the Court rejects direct application of § 5501(c) at the appellate level as inconsistent with an " 'essential characteristic' " of the federal court system—by which the Court presumably means abuse-of-discretion review of denials of motions for new trials . . . . But the scope of the Court's concern is oddly circumscribed. The "essential characteristic" of the federal jury, and, more specifically, the role of the federal trial court in reviewing jury judgments, apparently counts for little. The Court approves the "accommodat[ion]" achieved by having district courts review jury verdicts under the "deviates materially" standard, because it regards that as a means of giving effect to the State's purposes "without disrupting the federal system" . . . . But changing the standard by which trial judges review jury verdicts *does* disrupt the federal system, and is plainly inconsistent with "the strong federal policy against allowing state rules to disrupt the judge-jury relationship in federal court." Byrd v. Blue Ridge Rural Elec. Cooperative, Inc., 356 U.S. 525, 538, 78 S.Ct. 893, 901 (1958).[9] The Court's opinion does not even acknowledge, let alone address, this dislocation.

We discussed precisely the point at issue here in Browning-Ferris Industries of Vt., Inc. v. Kelco Disposal, Inc., 492 U.S. 257, 109 S.Ct. 2909 (1989), and gave an answer altogether contrary to the one provided today. Browning-Ferris rejected a request to fashion a federal common-law rule limiting the size of punitive-damages awards in federal courts, reaffirming the principle of Erie R. Co. v. Tompkins, 304 U.S. 64, 58 S.Ct. 817 (1938), that "[i]n a diversity action, or in any other lawsuit where state law provides the basis of decision, the propriety of an award of punitive damages . . . and the factors the jury may consider in determining their amount, are questions of state law." 492 U.S., at 278, 109 S.Ct., at 2921–2922. But the opinion expressly stated that "[f]ederal law . . . will control on those issues involving the proper review of the jury award by a federal district court and court of appeals." Id., at 278–279, 109 S.Ct., at 2922. "In reviewing an award of punitive damages," it said, "the role of the district court is to determine whether the jury's verdict is within the confines of state law, and to determine, by reference to federal standards developed under Rule 59, whether a new trial or remittitur should be ordered." Id., at 279, 109 S.Ct., at 2922. The same distinction necessarily applies where the judgment under review is for compensatory

---

[9]   Since I reject application of the New York standard on other grounds, I need not consider whether it constitutes "reexamination" of a jury's verdict in a manner "otherwise . . . than according to the rules of the common law."

damages: State substantive law controls what injuries are compensable and in what amount; but federal standards determine whether the award exceeds what is lawful to such degree that it may be set aside by order for new trial or remittitur.

The Court does not disavow those statements in Browning-Ferris (indeed, it does not even discuss them), but it presumably overrules them, at least where the state rule that governs "whether a new trial or remittitur should be ordered" is characterized as "substantive" in nature. That, at any rate, is the reason the Court asserts for giving § 5501(c) dispositive effect. The objective of that provision, the Court states, "is manifestly substantive," . . . since it operates to "contro[l] how much a plaintiff can be awarded" by "tightening the range of tolerable awards" . . . . Although "less readily classified" as substantive than "a statutory cap on damages," it nonetheless "was designed to provide an analogous control," . . . by making a new trial mandatory when the award "deviat[es] materially" from what is reasonable . . . .

I do not see how this can be so. It seems to me quite wrong to regard this provision as a "substantive" rule for Erie purposes. The "analog[y]" to "a statutory cap on damages" . . . fails utterly. There is an absolutely fundamental distinction between a *rule of law* such as that, which would ordinarily be imposed upon the jury in the trial court's instructions, and a *rule of review*, which simply determines how closely the jury verdict will be scrutinized for compliance with the instructions. A tighter standard for reviewing jury determinations can no more plausibly be called a "substantive" disposition than can a tighter appellate standard for reviewing trial-court determinations. The one, like the other, provides additional assurance *that the law has been complied with*; but the other, like the one, *leaves the law unchanged*.

The Court commits the classic Erie mistake of regarding whatever changes the outcome as substantive . . . . That is not the only factor to be considered. See Byrd, 356 U.S., at 537, 78 S.Ct., at 900 ("[W]ere 'outcome' the only consideration, a strong case might appear for saying that the federal court should follow the state practice. But there are affirmative countervailing considerations at work here"). Outcome-determination "was never intended to serve as a talisman," Hanna v. Plumer, 380 U.S. 460, 466–467, 85 S.Ct. 1136, 1141 (1965), and does not have the power to convert the most classic elements of the *process* of assuring that the law is observed into the substantive law itself. The right to have a jury make the findings of fact, for example, is generally thought to favor plaintiffs, and that advantage is often thought significant enough to be the basis for forum selection. But no one would argue that Erie confers a right to a jury in federal court wherever state courts would provide it; or that, were it not for the Seventh Amendment, Erie would require federal courts to dispense with the jury whenever state courts do so.

In any event, the Court exaggerates the difference that the state standard will make. . . . What seems to me far more likely to produce forum-shopping is the consistent difference between the state and federal *appellate* standards, which the Court leaves untouched. Under the Court's disposition, the Second Circuit reviews only for abuse of discretion, whereas New York's appellate courts engage in a de novo review for material deviation, giving the defendant a double shot at getting the damages award set aside. The only result that would produce the conformity the Court erroneously believes Erie requires is the one adopted by the Second Circuit and rejected by the Court: de novo federal appellate review under the § 5501(c) standard.

To say that application of § 5501(c) in place of the federal standard will not consistently produce disparate results is not to suggest that the decision the Court has made today is not a momentous one. The *principle* that the state standard governs is of great importance, since it bears the potential to destroy the uniformity of federal practice and the integrity of the federal court system. Under the Court's view, a state rule that directed courts "to determine that an award is excessive or inadequate if it deviates *in any degree* from *the proper measure of compensation*" would have to be applied in federal courts, effectively requiring federal judges to determine the amount of damages de novo, and effectively taking the matter away from the jury entirely. Cf. Byrd, 356 U.S., at 537–538, 78 S.Ct., at 901. Or consider a state rule that allowed the defendant a second trial on damages, with judgment ultimately in the amount of the lesser of two jury awards. [Citation omitted.] Under the reasoning of the Court's opinion, even such a rule as that would have to be applied in the federal courts.

The foregoing describes why I think the Court's Erie analysis is flawed. But in my view, one does not even reach the Erie question in this case. The standard to be applied by a district court in ruling on a motion for a new trial is set forth in Rule 59 of the Federal Rules of Civil Procedure, which provides that "[a] new trial may be granted . . . for any of the reasons for which new trials have heretofore been granted in actions at law *in the courts of the United States*" (emphasis added). That is undeniably a federal standard.[12] Federal district courts in the Second Circuit have interpreted that standard to permit the granting of new trials where " 'it is quite clear that the jury has reached a seriously erroneous result' " and letting the verdict stand would result in a " 'miscarriage of justice.' " Koerner v. Club Mediterranee, S.A., 833 F.Supp. 327 (S.D.N.Y.1993) (quoting Bevevino v. Saydjari, 574 F.2d 676, 684 (C.A.2 1978)). Assuming (as we have no reason to question) that this is a correct interpretation of what Rule 59 requires, it is undeniable that

---

[12]   I agree with the Court's entire progression of reasoning in its footnote 22, . . . leading to the conclusion that state law must determine "[w]hether damages are excessive." But the question of whether damages are excessive is quite separate from the question of when a jury award may be set aside for excessiveness. . . . It is the latter that is governed by Rule 59; as Browning-Ferris said, district courts are "to determine, by reference to *federal standards developed under Rule 59*, whether a new trial or remittitur should be ordered," 492 U.S., at 279, 109 S.Ct., at 2922 (emphasis added).

the federal rule is " 'sufficiently broad' to cause a 'direct collision' with the state law or, implicitly, to 'control the issue' before the court, thereby leaving no room for the operation of that law." Burlington Northern R. Co. v. Woods, 480 U.S. 1, 4–5, 107 S.Ct. 967, 969 (1987). It is simply not possible to give controlling effect both to the federal standard and the state standard in reviewing the jury's award. That being so, the court has no choice but to apply the Federal Rule, which is an exercise of what we have called Congress's "power to regulate matters which, though falling within the uncertain area between substance and procedure, are rationally capable of classification as either," Hanna, 380 U.S., at 472, 85 S.Ct., at 1144.

. . . .

Questions: (13) How does Justice Ginsburg meet Justice Scalia's point that statutory caps on damages are not analogous to standards for new trial, one being a rule of substantive law and the other a rule of review—his point being that the jury as the federal factfinder and law-applier must apply the New York tort damages law including any cap, but the trial judge as the federal reviewer should scrutinize the jury award for compliance in accordance with the federal standard for new trial? How does she meet his argument that strong federal interests are at stake in controlling the judge/jury relationship in the federal district courts—does she acknowledge those interests other than in footnote 21?

(14) Does the Court's decision to respect the federal interests in controlling the standard of appellate review in the federal courts of appeals prove that Byrd lives—that is, does the majority reach its trial/appeal holding by invoking Byrd's view that state interests can be outweighed by countervailing federal interests, such as those in not disrupting the federal courts' essentially characteristic allocation of trial and appellate functions? If so, did the majority perhaps reach its trial-level judge/jury holding by the same ad hoc balancing process, implicitly finding that the state interests in its own new trial standard outweigh the net of federal interests minus the Hanna-refined outcome-determinative effect—and thus, despite some loose language, the majority did not in fact resurrect the substance/procedure test or preserve a bare outcome-determinative test?

(15) Perhaps Gasperini throws some old answers back into doubt. What result in a converse-Byrd situation in a federal diversity case, where the state law would give a factual issue to the jury but the federal court would give it to the judge? Also, does federal or state law govern the directed-verdict standard in a federal diversity case?

SHADY GROVE ORTHOPEDIC ASSOCIATES, P.A. v. ALLSTATE INSURANCE CO., 559 U.S. 393, 130 S.Ct. 1431 (2010). The plaintiff sought to recover interest due by state statute for late payment of insurance benefits, doing so by means of a federal class action and thereby trying to join its individual claim for about $500 with many others' claims to create a single diversity action for more than $5 million under 28 U.S.C. § 1332(d)(2). New York law prohibits a class action to recover a "penalty" such as statutory interest, apparently for fear of annihilating the defendant. Accordingly, the lower federal courts applied the state prohibition to this case. But the Supreme Court narrowly reversed, through a fractured set of opinions. In the end, Federal Rule 23 applies to permit the class action.

The major doctrinal lesson to emerge was that the difference between Burlington Northern and Gasperini on how broadly or narrowly to read a Federal Rule potentially in conflict with state law—the question addressed in the last paragraph reprinted from the Gasperini dissents—remains a disputed question. In Shady Grove, five Justices, led by Justice Scalia against a dissent by Justice Ginsburg, read Rule 23 broadly enough to cover whether the suit "may be maintained" as a class action. It seems as if federal courts should construe a procedural Rule in a largely normal fashion but should, when alternative readings are defensible, read it to minimize its intrusion on substantive rights. That is, they should construe a Rule in a fashion that includes considering the impact on the generalized congressional and state interests in regulating substance, but they should not adopt a narrowed construction just to avoid conflict with the state's interests peculiarly in play in the particular situation presented by the case at bar.

Being so read to cover the point, and being a valid Rule under Sibbach because it was procedural, Rule 23 applies to displace any contrary state law, including the state prohibition invoked in this case. But that simple view of the case masks the fact that the five-Justice majority included Justice Stevens, who wrote separately to argue that under the Rules Enabling Act a Rule "cannot govern a particular case in which the rule would displace a state law that is procedural in the ordinary use of the term but is so intertwined with a state right or remedy that it functions to define the scope of the state-created right."

———

ROLE OF CONGRESS

Recall that in 1972 the Supreme Court, as article V of its proposed rules on evidence, sought to create uniform rules of privilege for the federal courts. Congress in 1975 provided instead for the application of state privilege rules in certain circumstances. It did so in Evidence Rule 501, a *statute* that receives insightful criticism from Earl C. Dudley, Jr., Federalism and Federal Rule of Evidence 501: Privilege and Vertical Choice of Law, 82 Geo.L.J. 1781 (1994). The House Committee on the Judiciary, in H.R.Rep. No. 93–650, explained Evidence Rule 501:

"The rationale underlying the proviso is that federal law should not supersede that of the States in substantive areas such as privilege absent a compelling reason. The Committee believes that in civil cases in the federal courts where an element of a claim or defense is not grounded upon a federal question, there is no federal interest strong enough to justify departure from State policy. In addition, the Committee considered that the Court's proposed Article V would have promoted forum shopping in some civil actions, depending upon differences in the privilege law applied as among the State and federal courts. The Committee's proviso, on the other hand, under which the federal courts are bound to apply the State's privilege law in actions founded upon a State-created right or defense, removes the incentive to 'shop'."

Question: (16) A diversity action is brought in a federal court in State *A*, based on an automobile accident in State *B*. During a doctor's deposition being taken in State *C* and bearing on the issue of negligence, the physician-patient privilege is asserted with respect to a consultation that took place in State *D*. A motion for an order compelling an answer is made in the federal court for State *C*. Which state's privilege law applies?

By way of contrast to Evidence Rule 501, Congress by Evidence Rule 407 apparently chose federal law to govern admissibility of subsequent remedial measures and then formulated an appropriate rule. So, in federal court, that rule should apply despite contrary state law. See Flaminio v. Honda Motor Co., 733 F.2d 463 (7th Cir.1984) (noting that the only limits on congressional choice of law are constitutional). But cf. 2 Christopher B. Mueller & Laird C. Kirkpatrick, Federal Evidence § 4:55 (4th ed. 2013).

In summary, if Congress chooses the applicable law, the only choice-of-law question remaining is whether that choice was constitutionally valid, because the Constitution imposes the only bounds on the congressional power. Within those constitutional limits Congress can expressly or impliedly make the choice between state and federal law, and its choice will bind the federal courts. So, Congress is the senior partner in the cooperative venture of drawing the appropriate line between state and federal law in federal court.

Ideally, when it legislates a choice between state and federal law, Congress would use a technique similar to the federal courts' Erie approach. However, Congress may properly opt for federal law more often than the federal courts would, because under our constitutional structure Congress should be the more active articulator of federal interests, while the courts should steer clear of blatantly formulating policies. And, of course, in practice Congress may be less systematic and rational than the courts.

Choosing the law and giving it content are two separate steps. If Congress chooses federal law, it can also generate the content of that federal law. Alternatively, it sometimes delegates to the federal courts the task of generating part or all of that federal law. It is important to keep clear the distinction between choosing the applicable law and specifying its content.

With this background, now reconsider each of the two sentences of Evidence Rule 501, and then contrast them with Evidence Rule 601.

_____

SECTION 2.   FEDERAL LAW

The Federal Constitution can dictate a choice in favor of federal law in federal courts, and of course this is binding. An example is the Seventh Amendment's guarantee of trial by jury. But most often, the Constitution does not so dictate, leaving the choice to other lawmakers.

In many of these circumstances, Congress can validly make a choice by statute in favor of federal law. That choice will bind the federal courts, as we have just seen in the discussion of the Evidence Rules.

What of federal common law? Justice Brandeis in Erie wrote: "There is no federal general common law." But have we not already seen post-Erie examples of federal common law being created and applied in federal courts?

_____

CLEARFIELD TRUST CO. v. UNITED STATES, 318 U.S. 363, 63 S.Ct. 573 (1943). Justice Douglas for a unanimous Court stated the facts as follows:

"On April 28, 1936, a check was drawn on the Treasurer of the United States through the Federal Reserve Bank of Philadelphia to the order of Clair A. Barner in the amount of $24.20. It was dated at Harrisburg, Pennsylvania and was drawn for services rendered by Barner to the Works Progress Administration. The check was placed in the mail addressed to Barner at his address in Mackeyville, Pa. Barner never received the check. Some unknown person obtained it in a mysterious manner and presented it to the J.C. Penney Co. store in Clearfield, Pa., representing that he was the payee and identifying himself to the satisfaction of the employees of J.C. Penney Co. He endorsed the check in the name of Barner and transferred it to J.C. Penney Co. in exchange for cash and merchandise. Barner never authorized the endorsement nor participated in the proceeds of the check. J.C. Penney Co. endorsed the check over to the Clearfield Trust Co. which accepted it as agent for the purpose of collection and endorsed it as follows: 'Pay to the order of Federal Reserve Bank of Philadelphia, Prior Endorsements Guaranteed.'[1] Clearfield Trust Co. collected the check from the United States through the Federal Reserve Bank of Philadelphia and paid the full amount thereof to J.C. Penney Co. Neither the Clearfield Trust Co. nor J.C. Penney Co. had any knowledge or suspicion of the forgery. Each acted in good faith. On or before May 10,

_____

[1]   Guarantee of all prior indorsements on presentment for payment of such a check to Federal Reserve banks or member bank depositories is required by Treasury Regulations. 31 Code of Federal Regulations § 202.32, § 202.33.

1936, Barner advised the timekeeper and the foreman of the W.P.A. project on which he was employed that he had not received the check in question. This information was duly communicated to other agents of the United States and on November 30, 1936, Barner executed an affidavit alleging that the endorsement of his name on the check was a forgery. No notice was given the Clearfield Trust Co. or J.C. Penney Co. of the forgery until January 12, 1937, at which time the Clearfield Trust Co. was notified. The first notice received by Clearfield Trust Co. that the United States was asking reimbursement was on August 31, 1937.

"This suit was instituted in 1939 by the United States against the Clearfield Trust Co., the jurisdiction of the federal District Court being invoked pursuant to the provisions of § 24(1) of the Judicial Code, 28 U.S.C. § 41(1).[e] The cause of action was based on the express guaranty of prior endorsements made by the Clearfield Trust Co. J.C. Penney Co. intervened as a defendant. The case was heard on complaint, answer and stipulation of facts. The District Court held that the rights of the parties were to be determined by the law of Pennsylvania and that since the United States unreasonably delayed in giving notice of the forgery to the Clearfield Trust Co., it was barred from recovery under the rule of Market St. Title & Trust Co. v. Chelten Tr. Co., 296 Pa. 230, 145 A. 848. It accordingly dismissed the complaint. On appeal the Circuit Court of Appeals reversed. 3 Cir., 130 F.2d 93."

Justice Douglas then said: "We agree with the Circuit Court of Appeals that the rule of Erie R. Co. v. Tompkins . . . does not apply to this action. The rights and duties of the United States on commercial paper which it issues are governed by federal rather than local law." Accordingly, the Court affirmed the application of old federal case law, under which mere delay in giving notice did not bar suit.

———

Questions: (17) Why did the Erie rule "not apply to this action"? Why did the Rules of Decision Act not require application of state law?

(18) Reconsider yet once again Woods v. Interstate Realty Co. Would that state door-closing statute apply in a federal question action asserting a patent claim? See Kinetic Concepts, Inc. v. Kinetic Concepts, Inc., 601 F.Supp. 496 (N.D.Ga.1985) (no). Would it apply in a diversity action to compel arbitration pursuant to the Federal Arbitration Act under a foreign-commerce contract? See Grand Bah. Petroleum Co. v. Asiatic Petroleum Corp., 550 F.2d 1320 (2d Cir.1977) (no).

(19) In a federal action under 28 U.S.C. § 1345 in the Western District of Texas, the United States sought to collect from Mrs. Yazell of Texas on a federal disaster loan. An issue arose as to the capacity of the defendant to bind herself personally by the loan contract. Under the peculiar Texas law of coverture that then existed, a wife could not so bind herself in the

---

e   Jurisdiction rested on that part of § 24(1) vesting original jurisdiction in the district courts over civil actions in which the United States is plaintiff, now 28 U.S.C. § 1345.

circumstances of this case. In the absence of a congressional directive, did that Texas law apply? See United States v. Yazell, 382 U.S. 341, 86 S.Ct. 500 (1966) (yes).

(20) In a diversity action, between two private parties and based on an alleged conversion of United States bonds, two issues arise: (a) who has the burden of proof on whether the defendant took the bonds in good faith; and (b) were the bonds, which had been called but were not yet mature, "overdue" at that time. Should these issues be governed by state law or federal common law? See Bank of Am. Nat'l Trust & Sav. Ass'n v. Parnell, 352 U.S. 29, 77 S.Ct. 119 (1956).

———

UNITED STATES v. KIMBELL FOODS, INC., 440 U.S. 715, 99 S.Ct. 1448 (1979). The two cases decided under this caption, both of which came from the Fifth Circuit, required a choice between federal and state law on "whether contractual liens arising from certain federal loan programs take precedence over private liens, in the absence of a federal statute setting priorities."

The first case, coming from Texas, involved a loan guaranteed by the Small Business Administration (SBA) and a debt to a private party, both obligations being secured by competing liens on the same collateral. The second case from a Georgia federal court arose in Georgia and involved loans from the Farmers Home Administration (FHA) to a farmer, secured in part by a lien on his tractor; when the farmer later brought the tractor to a private repairman but then could not pay for the repairs, the repairman retained the tractor and thus asserted a lien thereon; when still later the farmer defaulted on the federal loans, the United States sued the repairman to obtain the tractor, with jurisdiction invoked under 28 U.S.C. § 1345. State law concerning the relative priority of competing liens would have favored the private lienholders on the facts of these two cases, so the government argued for a more favorable federal common law.

On the vertical choice-of-law problem, Justice Marshall for a unanimous Supreme Court wrote:

"This Court has consistently held that federal law governs questions involving the rights of the United States arising under nationwide federal programs. As the Court explained in Clearfield Trust Co. v. United States, [318 U.S. 363, 366–67, 63 S.Ct. 573, 575 (1943)]:

'When the United States disburses its funds or pays its debts, it is exercising a constitutional function or power. . . . The authority [to do so] had its origin in the Constitution and the statutes of the United States and was in no way dependent on the laws [of any State]. The duties imposed upon the United States and the rights acquired by it . . . find their roots in the same federal sources. In absence of an applicable Act of Congress it is for the federal courts to fashion the governing rule of law according to their own standards.' (Citations and footnote omitted.)

"Guided by these principles, we think it clear that the priority of liens stemming from federal lending programs must be determined with reference to federal law. The SBA and FHA unquestionably perform federal functions within the meaning of Clearfield. Since the agencies derive their authority to effectuate loan transactions from specific acts of Congress passed in the exercise of a 'constitutional function or power,' Clearfield Trust Co. v. United States, supra, at 366, 63 S.Ct., at 575, their rights, as well, should derive from a federal source. When Government activities 'aris[e] from and bea[r] heavily upon a federal . . . program,' the Constitution and Acts of Congress ' "require" otherwise than that state law govern of its own force.' United States v. Little Lake Misere Land Co., 412 U.S. 580, 592, 593, 93 S.Ct. 2389, 2396, 2397 (1973) [(quoting the Rules of Decision Act's 'otherwise require or provide' language)]. In such contexts, federal interests are sufficiently implicated to warrant the protection of federal law.[19]

"That the statutes authorizing these federal lending programs do not specify the appropriate rule of decision in no way limits the reach of federal law. It is precisely when Congress has not spoken ' "in an area comprising issues substantially related to an established program of government operation," ' id., at 593, 93 S.Ct., at 2397, quoting Mishkin, supra, n. 19, at 800, that Clearfield directs federal courts to fill the interstices of federal legislation 'according to their own standards.' Clearfield Trust Co. v. United States, supra, at 367, 63 S.Ct., at 575.

"Federal law therefore controls the Government's priority rights. The more difficult task, to which we turn, is giving content to this federal rule.

. . . .

"Controversies directly affecting the operations of federal programs, although governed by federal law, do not inevitably require resort to uniform federal rules. See Clearfield Trust Co. v. United States, supra, at 367, 63 S.Ct., at 575; United States v. Little Lake Misere Land Co., supra, at 594–595, 93 S.Ct., at 2397–2398. Whether to adopt state law or to fashion a nationwide federal rule is a matter of judicial policy 'dependent upon a variety of considerations always relevant to the nature of the specific governmental interests and to the effects upon them of

---

[19]   See [citation omitted]; Mishkin, The Variousness of "Federal Law": Competence and Discretion in the Choice of National and State Rules for Decision, 105 U.Pa.L.Rev. 797, 800, and n. 15 (1957) (hereinafter Mishkin); Comment, Adopting State Law as the Federal Rule of Decision: A Proposed Test, 43 U.Chi.L.Rev. 823, 825 (1976); see also Bank of America National Trust & Savings Assn. v. Parnell, 352 U.S. 29, 33–34, 77 S.Ct. 119, 121–122 (1956); Miree v. DeKalb County, 433 U.S. 25, 29, 31–32, 97 S.Ct. 2490, 2493, 2494–2495 (1977).

applying state law.' United States v. Standard Oil Co., 332 U.S. 301, 310, 67 S.Ct. 1604, 1609 (1947).[21]

"Undoubtedly, federal programs that 'by their nature are and must be uniform in character throughout the Nation' necessitate formulation of controlling federal rules. United States v. Yazell, 382 U.S. 341, 354, 86 S.Ct. 500, 507 (1966); see Clearfield Trust Co. v. United States, supra, at 367, 63 S.Ct., at 575; United States v. Standard Oil Co., supra, at 311, 67 S.Ct., at 1609; Illinois v. City of Milwaukee, 406 U.S. 91, 105 n. 6, 92 S.Ct. 1385, 1393 n. 6 (1972). Conversely, when there is little need for a nationally uniform body of law, state law may be incorporated as the federal rule of decision. Apart from considerations of uniformity, we must also determine whether application of state law would frustrate specific objectives of the federal programs. If so, we must fashion special rules solicitous of those federal interests. Finally, our choice of law inquiry must consider the extent to which application of a federal rule would disrupt commercial relationships predicated on state law."

"[The Court decided 'to reject generalized pleas for uniformity as substitutes for concrete evidence.'] We are unpersuaded that in the circumstances presented here, nationwide standards favoring claims of the United States are necessary to ease program administration or to safeguard the federal treasury from defaulting debtors. Because the state commercial codes 'furnish convenient solutions in no way inconsistent with adequate protection of the federal interest[s],' United States v. Standard Oil Co., supra, at 309, 67 S.Ct., at 1609, we decline to override intricate state laws of general applicability on which private creditors base their daily commercial transactions.

. . . .

"Because the ultimate consequences of altering settled commercial practices are so difficult to foresee, we hesitate to create new uncertainties, in the absence of careful legislative deliberation. Of course, formulating special rules to govern the priority of the federal consensual liens in issue here would be justified if necessary to vindicate important national interests. But neither the Government nor the Court of Appeals advanced any concrete reasons for rejecting well-established commercial rules which have proven workable over time. Thus, the prudent course is to adopt the readymade body of state law as the federal rule of decision until Congress strikes a different accommodation.

. . . .

---

[21] As explained by one commentator:

"Whether state law is to be incorporated as a matter of federal common law . . . involves the . . . problem of the relationship of a particular issue to a going federal program. The question of judicial incorporation can only arise in an area which is sufficiently close to a national operation to establish competence in the federal courts to choose the governing law, and yet not so close as clearly to require the application of a single nationwide rule of substance." Mishkin, supra, n. 19, at 805.

"Accordingly, we hold that absent a congressional directive, the relative priority of private liens and consensual liens arising from these Government lending programs is to be determined under nondiscriminatory state laws. [The Court decided here to look at Texas and Georgia law, respectively, as being the appropriate states to provide the law.]"

The government had also argued that a federal rule was "needed to prevent States from 'undercutting' the agencies' liens by creating 'arbitrary' rules." The Court met this by noting: "Adopting state law as an appropriate federal rule does not preclude federal courts from excepting [particular] local laws that prejudice federal interests." The Court then cited again the Little Lake Misere Land Co. case, in which the Court had declined to borrow a recent Louisiana statute, which would have specially preserved private interests, when interpreting an earlier-consummated federal land contract.

Questions: (21) In 1990, when 28 U.S.C. § 1658 came into effect but only for future enactments, there were over two hundred federal statutes that had created causes of action but had failed to provide a limitations period. In such cases, federal courts ordinarily adopt the forum state's statute of limitations for the most closely analogous state cause of action. See, e.g., Owens v. Okure, 488 U.S. 235, 109 S.Ct. 573 (1989) (subjecting civil rights action to state's general personal-injury limitations period). How does this rule mesh with the Erie-Clearfield doctrine? When federal interests dictate, however, federal courts will instead choose to extend some analogous federal limitations provision to cover the federal cause of action. See, e.g., Agency Holding Corp. v. Malley-Duff & Assocs., 483 U.S. 143, 107 S.Ct. 2759 (1987) (subjecting civil RICO action to Clayton Act's four-year limitations period). How does this exception mesh with the Erie-Clearfield doctrine? Does not the key lie in the distinction between *applying* state law under Erie and merely *adopting* state law under Kimbell?

(22) Many other aspects of the statute of limitations for federal causes of action in federal court are governed by federal common law. See, e.g., West v. Conrail, 481 U.S. 35, 39, 107 S.Ct. 1538, 1541 (1987) (facing the limitations problem of Ragan and Walker, "we now hold that when the underlying cause of action is based on federal law ... the action is not barred if it has been 'commenced' in compliance with Rule 3 within the [limitations] period"). Where should the line lie between federally generated common law and adopted state law? See generally Mitchell A. Lowenthal, Brian E. Pastuszenski & Mark E. Greenwald, Special Project, Time Bars in Specialized Federal Common Law: Federal Rights of Action and State Statutes of Limitations, 65 Cornell L.Rev. 1011 (1980).

ILLINOIS v. CITY OF MILWAUKEE, 406 U.S. 91, 92 S.Ct. 1385 (1972). The State of Illinois brought a federal action against four cities and two local sewerage commissions in Wisconsin, seeking to abate the public nuisance allegedly caused by the defendants' pollution of the interstate waters of Lake Michigan. The Supreme Court held that here the federal court should, in the absence of applicable federal statutes, apply a uniform federal common law of nuisance (and further held that such an action founded on federal common law would arise under the "laws" of the United States within the meaning of 28 U.S.C. § 1331).[f]

After the lower courts gave injunctive relief under the federal common law, the parties once again came before the Supreme Court for review. City of Milwaukee v. Illinois, 451 U.S. 304, 101 S.Ct. 1784 (1981). In the meantime, however, Congress had enacted the Federal Water Pollution Control Act Amendments of 1972, "a comprehensive regulatory program supervised by an expert administrative agency." The Supreme Court concluded that here no remedy under the federal common law was still available, the statutory enactment having implicitly displaced the federal common law. The Court explained that "when Congress addresses a question previously governed by a decision rested on federal common law the need for such an unusual exercise of lawmaking by federal courts disappears."[g]

---

[f]   The Fourth Circuit refused to extend the reach of the federal common law to a suit by private citizens to enjoin intrastate stream pollution. Comm. for Jones Falls Sewage Sys. v. Train, 539 F.2d 1006 (4th Cir.1976) (in banc).

[g]   The Supreme Court later decided that the Act itself preserved some law of the pollution-source state even in the interstate setting. Int'l Paper Co. v. Ouellette, 479 U.S. 481, 107 S.Ct. 805 (1987).

STATE COURTS

HINDERLIDER v. LA PLATA RIVER & CHERRY CREEK DITCH CO., 304 U.S. 92, 58 S.Ct. 803 (1938). A Colorado corporation brought suit in a Colorado state court against the State Engineer of Colorado to enjoin him from depriving the plaintiff of the use of the water of the La Plata River, which runs from Colorado into New Mexico. An issue arose as to the relative rights of the two states to its water. On the very day that Erie was decided, a unanimous Court, again speaking through Justice Brandeis, held that "whether the water of an interstate stream must be apportioned between the two States is a question of 'federal common law' upon which neither the statutes nor the decisions of either State can be conclusive." This federal common law was applicable and binding in the state court, apparently by virtue of the Supremacy Clause of Article VI of the Constitution.

DICE v. AKRON, CANTON & YOUNGSTOWN RAILROAD CO., 342 U.S. 359, 72 S.Ct. 312 (1952). Plaintiff brought an FELA action in an Ohio state court. The railroad's defenses included a release of all claims signed by plaintiff. Plaintiff contended that the purported release was void because he had relied on the defendant's deliberately false statement that the document was merely a receipt for back wages. The Ohio Supreme Court, reversing the intermediate appellate court, sustained the trial court's entry of judgment for the defendant notwithstanding the verdict, holding that (1) Ohio, not federal, law governed the validity of the release; (2) under that Ohio law, the release bound plaintiff, a man of ordinary intelligence who could read, even though he had been induced to sign it by a deliberately false statement; and (3) under controlling Ohio law, all issues as to fraud in the execution of this release were properly decided by the judge rather than by the jury. Certiorari was granted.

The Supreme Court, in an opinion by Justice Black, held that federal common law controlled the validity of the release, that the correct federal rule was that a release of rights under the Act was void when induced by a deliberately false statement as to the contents of the release, and that the "factual" issues as to fraud had to be determined by the jury. On the last point, the Court said:

"*Third.* Ohio provides and has here accorded petitioner the usual jury trial of factual issues relating to negligence. But Ohio treats factual questions of fraudulent releases differently. It permits the judge trying a negligence case to resolve all factual questions of fraud [where the fraud is one of those kinds that constitute equitable defenses]. The factual issue of fraud is thus split into fragments, some to be determined by the judge, others by the jury.

"It is contended that since a state may consistently with the Federal Constitution provide for trial of cases under the Act by a nonunanimous verdict, Minneapolis & St. Louis R. Co. v. Bombolis, 241 U.S. 211, 36 S.Ct. 595,[a] Ohio may lawfully eliminate trial by jury as to one phase of fraud while allowing jury trial as to all other issues raised. The Bombolis case might be more in point had Ohio abolished trial by jury in all negligence cases including those arising under the federal Act. But Ohio has not done this. It has provided jury trials for cases arising under the federal Act but seeks to single out one phase of the question of fraudulent releases for determination by a judge rather than by a jury. Compare Testa v. Katt, 330 U.S. 386, 67 S.Ct. 810.

"We have previously held that 'The right to trial by jury is "a basic and fundamental feature of our system of federal jurisprudence"' and that it is 'part and parcel of the remedy afforded railroad workers under the Employers Liability Act.' Bailey v. Central Vermont R. Co., 319 U.S. 350, 354, 63 S.Ct. 1062, 1064. We also recognized in that case that to deprive railroad workers of the benefit of a jury trial where there is evidence to support negligence 'is to take away a goodly portion of the relief which Congress has afforded them.' It follows that the right to trial by jury is too substantial a part of the rights accorded by the Act to permit it to be classified as a mere 'local rule of procedure' for denial in the manner that Ohio has here used. Brown v. Western R. of Ala., 338 U.S. 294, 70 S.Ct. 105."

Justice Frankfurter, with whom Justices Reed, Jackson, and Burton joined, dissented from that portion of the opinion requiring a jury determination of those fraud issues. He said: "To require Ohio to try a particular issue before a different fact-finder in negligence actions brought under the Employers' Liability Act from the fact-finder on the identical issue in every other negligence case disregards the settled distribution of judicial power between Federal and State courts where Congress authorizes concurrent enforcement of federally-created rights.

. . . .

" . . . The fact that Congress authorized actions under the Federal Employers' Liability Act to be brought in State as well as in Federal courts seems a strange basis for the inference that Congress overrode State procedural arrangements controlling all other negligence suits in a State, by imposing upon State courts to which plaintiffs choose to go the rules prevailing in the Federal courts regarding juries. Such an inference is admissible, so it seems to me, only on the theory that Congress

---

a   This 1916 FELA case allowed the jury in state court, over the defendant's objection, to return a five-sixths verdict after at least twelve hours of deliberation, as permitted by the constitution and statutes of Minnesota. Although no one then questioned that the Seventh Amendment required a unanimous verdict in federal court, the Court did not view this requirement as controlling in a state-court action to enforce a right created by Congress.

included as part of the right created by the Employers' Liability Act an assumed likelihood that trying all issues to juries is more favorable to plaintiffs. At least, if a plaintiff's right to have all issues decided by a jury rather than the court is 'part and parcel of the remedy afforded railroad workers under the Employers Liability Act,' the Bombolis case should be overruled explicitly instead of left as a derelict bound to occasion collisions on the waters of the law. . . . It is one thing not to borrow trouble from the morrow. It is another thing to create trouble for the morrow."

————

BROWN v. WESTERN RAILWAY OF ALABAMA, 338 U.S. 294, 70 S.Ct. 105 (1949). Plaintiff brought an FELA action in a Georgia state court. He alleged that he had suffered injury while working when he stepped on a large clinker lying within the railroad yards, but did not allege the clinker's circumstances in a way to constitute negligence by the railroad and to exclude alternative causes. The railroad filed a general demurrer on the ground that the complaint failed to "set forth a cause of action and is otherwise insufficient in law." The trial court sustained the demurrer and dismissed the action, applying a Georgia rule to construe pleading allegations "most strongly against the pleader." The intermediate appellate court affirmed, and the Georgia Supreme Court denied review. Under Georgia law, this was a final adjudication barring recovery in any future state proceedings. Certiorari was granted.

The Supreme Court reversed in an opinion by Justice Black. He said:

"Strict local rules of pleading cannot be used to impose unnecessary burdens upon rights of recovery authorized by federal laws. 'Whatever springes the State may set for those who are endeavoring to assert rights that the State confers, the assertion of federal rights, when plainly and reasonably made, is not to be defeated under the name of local practice.' Davis v. Wechsler, 263 U.S. 22, 24, 44 S.Ct. 13, 14. Cf. Maty v. Grasselli Chemical Co., 303 U.S. 197, 58 S.Ct. 507. Should this Court fail to protect federally created rights from dismissal because of over-exacting local requirements for meticulous pleadings, desirable uniformity in adjudication of federally created rights could not be achieved. See Brady v. Southern R. Co., 320 U.S. 476, 479, 64 S.Ct. 232, 234.

"Upon trial of this case the evidence offered may or may not support inferences of negligence. We simply hold that under the facts alleged it was error to dismiss the complaint and that petitioner should be allowed to try his case."

Justice Frankfurter, with whom Justice Jackson joined, dissented. He said: "States have varying systems of pleading and practice. One State may cherish formalities more than another, one State may be more responsive than another to procedural reforms. If a litigant chooses to enforce a Federal right in a State court, he cannot be heard to object if he is treated exactly as are plaintiffs who press like claims arising under

State law with regard to the form in which the claim must be stated—the particularity, for instance, with which a cause of action must be described. . . .

. . . .

"The crucial question for this Court is whether the Georgia courts have merely enforced a local requirement of pleading, however finicky, applicable to all such litigation in Georgia without qualifying the basis of recovery under the Federal Employers' Liability Act or weighting the scales against the plaintiff. Compare Norfolk, Southern R. Co. v. Ferebee, 238 U.S. 269, 35 S.Ct. 781, with Central Vermont R. Co. v. White, 238 U.S. 507, 35 S.Ct. 865. Georgia may adhere to its requirements of pleading, but it may not put 'unreasonable obstacles in the way' of a plaintiff who seeks its courts to obtain what the Federal Act gives him. Davis v. Wechsler, 263 U.S. 22, 25, 44 S.Ct. 13, 14.

"These decisive differences are usually conveyed by the terms 'procedure' and 'substance.' The terms are not meaningless even though they do not have fixed undeviating meanings. They derive content from the functions they serve here in precisely the same way in which we have applied them in reverse situations—when confronted with the problem whether the Federal courts respected the substance of State-created rights, as required by the rule in Erie R. Co. v. Tompkins, 304 U.S. 64, 58 S.Ct. 817, or impaired them by professing merely to enforce them by the mode in which the Federal courts do business. Review on this aspect of State court judgments in Federal Employers' Liability cases presents essentially the same kind of problem as that with which this Court dealt in Guaranty Trust Co. v. York, 326 U.S. 99, 65 S.Ct. 1464, applied at the last Term in Ragan v. Merchants Transfer & Warehouse Co., 337 U.S. 530, 69 S.Ct. 1233, and Cohen v. Beneficial Industrial Loan Corp., 337 U.S. 541, 555, 69 S.Ct. 1221, 1229. Congress has authorized State courts to enforce Federal rights, and Federal courts State-created rights, but both may have their own requirements for stating claims (pleading) and conducting litigation (practice).

"In the light of these controlling considerations, I cannot find that the Court of Appeals of Georgia has either sought to evade the law of the United States or did so unwittingly."

———

Question: (1) In a reverse-Brown case brought in federal court, on a state-law claim where the state would employ notice pleading and the federal courts ordinarily follow Twombly-Iqbal, what is the appropriate pleading standard?

———

NORFOLK & WESTERN RAILWAY CO. v. LIEPELT, 444 U.S. 490, 100 S.Ct. 755 (1980). Plaintiff brought an FELA action in an Illinois state court for wrongful death. The trial court refused the defendant's request to instruct the jury that "your award will not be subject to any income taxes, and you should not consider such taxes in fixing the amount of your award." On appeal from verdict and judgment for plaintiff, the intermediate appellate court affirmed, and the Illinois Supreme Court denied review. Certiorari was granted.

The Supreme Court reversed in an opinion by Justice Stevens. He asserted, with no explanation, that this "is a matter governed by federal law." The result was a uniform federal common law that called for such an instruction. "It would not be prejudicial to either party, but would merely eliminate an area of doubt or speculation that might have an improper [inflating] impact on the computation of the amount of damages."

Justice Blackmun, with whom Justice Marshall joined, dissented. He said: "This Court, to be sure, has asserted federal control over a number of incidents of state trial practice that might appear to be procedural, and has done so out of concern, apparently, for protecting the rights of FELA plaintiffs. [Omitted citations include Dice and Brown.] I agree, of course, that state rules that interfere with federal policy are to be rejected, even if they might be characterized as 'procedural.' [Citations omitted.] I cannot conclude, however, that a purely cautionary instruction to the jury not to misbehave implicates any federal interest. This issue truly can be characterized as one of the 'ordinary incidents of state procedure,' Dickinson v. Stiles, 246 U.S. 631, 633, 38 S.Ct. 415, 416 (1918), which should be governed by state law.

"Since the law of Illinois, where this case arose, is that it is not error to refuse to instruct the jury as to the nontaxability of the award, . . . I would affirm the judgment of the Appellate Court of Illinois."

The dissent also argued that the required instruction was unnecessary and potentially misleading and that it opened the door to cautionary instructions on many other extraneous matters.

———

Felder v. Casey
Supreme Court of the United States, 1988.
487 U.S. 131, 108 S.Ct. 2302.

■ JUSTICE BRENNAN delivered the opinion of the Court.

[Alleging racially motivated police brutality, arrestee Bobby Felder brought a civil rights action under 42 U.S.C. § 1983 in a Wisconsin state court against Milwaukee and certain of its police officers. Although the plaintiff had satisfied Wisconsin's three-year statute of limitations for general personal-injury actions, the officers moved to dismiss for failure to comply with Wisconsin's notice-of-claim statute, which provides additionally that, before any suit may be brought in state court against a municipality or its officer, the plaintiff must give notice of the claim to

the defendant within 120 days of the injury; that the municipality then
has 120 days to act on the requested relief; and that the plaintiff must
bring the suit within six months after notice of the claim's disallowance.
The motion ultimately succeeded in state court. Certiorari was granted.]

No one disputes the general and unassailable proposition relied
upon by the Wisconsin Supreme Court below that States may establish
the rules of procedure governing litigation in their own courts. By the
same token, however, where state courts entertain a federally created
cause of action, the "federal right cannot be defeated by the forms of local
practice." Brown v. Western Railway of Alabama, 338 U.S. 294, 296, 70
S.Ct. 105, 106 (1949). . . . Because the notice-of-claim statute at issue
here conflicts both in its purpose and effects with the remedial objectives
of § 1983, and because its enforcement in such actions will frequently and
predictably produce different outcomes in § 1983 litigation based solely
on whether the claim is asserted in state or federal court, we conclude
that the state law is pre-empted when the § 1983 action is brought in a
state court.

[In the course of a long opinion, the Court noted that for suits under
§ 1983 the federal common law adopts the state's limitations period. The
Court further explained that both federal and state courts would apply
the same limitations period and, moreover, that in a § 1983 lawsuit a
federal court would not apply a state notice-of-claim statute. According
to the Court, most states have such statutes, which might encourage
prompt investigation of claims, but which benefit governmental
defendants as their primary purpose and thus discriminate against the
precise type of claim that Congress created.]

Respondents and their supporting amici urge that we approve the
application of the notice-of-claim statute to § 1983 actions brought in
state court as a matter of equitable federalism. They note that " '[t]he
general rule, bottomed deeply in belief in the importance of state control
of state judicial procedure, is that federal law takes the state courts as it
finds them.' " Brief for Amici Curiae 8 (quoting Hart, The Relations
Between State and Federal Law, 54 Colum.L.Rev. 489, 508 (1954)).
Litigants who choose to bring their civil rights actions in state courts
presumably do so in order to obtain the benefit of certain procedural
advantages in those courts, or to draw their juries from urban
populations. Having availed themselves of these benefits, civil rights
litigants must comply as well with those state rules they find less to their
liking.

However equitable this bitter-with-the-sweet argument may appear
in the abstract, it has no place under our Supremacy Clause analysis.
Federal law takes state courts as it finds them only insofar as those
courts employ rules that do not "impose unnecessary burdens upon rights
of recovery authorized by federal laws." Brown v. Western R. Co. of
Alabama, 338 U.S., at 298–299, 70 S.Ct., at 108; see also Monessen
Southwestern R. Co. v. Morgan, 486 U.S. 330, 336, 108 S.Ct. 1837, 1842–

1843 (1988) (state rule [against prejudgment interest] designed to encourage settlement cannot limit recovery in federally created action). States may make the litigation of federal rights as congenial as they see fit—not as a quid pro quo for compliance with other, incongenial rules, but because such congeniality does not stand as an obstacle to the accomplishment of Congress' goals. As we have seen, enforcement of the notice-of-claim statute in § 1983 actions brought in state court so interferes with and frustrates the substantive right Congress created that, under the Supremacy Clause, it must yield to the federal interest. This interference, however, is not the only consequence of the statute that renders its application in § 1983 cases invalid. In a State that demands compliance with such a statute before a § 1983 action may be brought or maintained in its courts, the outcome of federal civil rights litigation will frequently and predictably depend on whether it is brought in state or federal court. Thus, the very notions of federalism upon which respondents rely dictate that the State's outcome-determinative law must give way when a party asserts a federal right in state court.

Under Erie R. Co. v. Tompkins, 304 U.S. 64, 58 S.Ct. 817 (1938), when a federal court exercises diversity or pendent jurisdiction over state-law claims, "the outcome of the litigation in the federal court should be substantially the same, so far as legal rules determine the outcome of a litigation, as it would be if tried in a State court." Guaranty Trust Co. v. York, 326 U.S. 99, 109, 65 S.Ct. 1464, 1470 (1945). Accordingly, federal courts entertaining state-law claims against Wisconsin municipalities are obligated to apply the notice-of-claim provision. See Orthmann v. Apple River Campground, Inc., 757 F.2d 909, 911 (C.A.7 1985). Just as federal courts are constitutionally obligated to apply state law to state claims, see Erie, supra, 304 U.S., at 78–79, 58 S.Ct., at 822–823, so too the Supremacy Clause imposes on state courts a constitutional duty "to proceed in such manner that all the substantial rights of the parties under controlling federal law [are] protected." Garrett v. Moore-McCormack Co., 317 U.S. 239, 245, 63 S.Ct. 246, 251 (1942).

. . . Wisconsin . . . may not alter the outcome of federal claims it chooses to entertain in its courts by demanding compliance with outcome-determinative rules that are inapplicable when such claims are brought in federal court, for " '[w]hatever spring[s] [sic] the State may set for those who are endeavoring to assert rights that the State confers, the assertion of federal rights, when plainly and reasonably made, is not to be defeated under the name of local practice.' " Brown v. Western R. Co. of Alabama, 338 U.S., at 299, 70 S.Ct., at 108 (quoting Davis v. Wechsler, 263 U.S. 22, 24, 44 S.Ct. 13, 14 (1923)). . . . State courts simply are not free to vindicate the substantive interests underlying a state rule of decision at the expense of the federal right.

[Accordingly, the Supreme Court reversed and remanded.]

■ [JUSTICE WHITE concurred. JUSTICE O'CONNOR, with whom Chief Justice Rehnquist joined, dissented. Their opinions are omitted.]

PREEMPTION

Although the Felder Court expressed an overtly Erie-like analysis for judicial choice of law, it also threw into the mix the terminology of preemption. Analysts frequently so draw on the preemption doctrine, hoping to get more of a handle on judicial choice between federal and state law. They look to preemption because it is the most closely related doctrine in the task of determining the reach of federal law. It is in some senses a more important doctrine than judicial choice of law, with big consequences in both federal and state litigation as well as out in the real world.

Preemption, in brief, is an ill-bounded constitutional doctrine that invalidates state law if it interferes with federal law. See Erwin Chemerinsky, Constitutional Law: Principles and Policies § 5.2 (5th ed. 2015); Christopher R. Drahozal, The Supremacy Clause 89–125 (2004). Although preemption tends to focus on displacement of state substantive law by congressional statute, the judges and commentators recognize that it can occur by federal administrative act or even by the effect of federal common law, and that it can extend its effect to state procedural law. Preemption can be express or implied; and implied preemption can trump a state provision that conflicts by discrimination against or contradiction to federal law[b] or stands as an obstacle to federal law,[c] or can authorize federal law to occupy exclusively a whole field,[d] although of course all these categories are blurry.

Express preemption can follow from constitutional or congressional action. The Due Process Clause of the Fourteenth Amendment illustrates the former. For a congressional example, we can stick with the evidence area by referring to Evidence Rule 502(f), a statute enacted in 2008.

---

[b]   See Barnett Bank of Marion Cty. v. Nelson, 517 U.S. 25, 31, 116 S.Ct. 1103, 1108 (1996) (dictum) (saying that state law would be preempted if laws "impose directly conflicting duties on national banks—as they would, for example, if the federal law said, 'you must sell insurance,' while the state law said, 'you may not' "); Fla. Lime & Avocado Growers, Inc. v. Paul, 373 U.S. 132, 142–43, 83 S.Ct. 1210, 1217 (1963) (saying that state law would be preempted "where compliance with both federal and state regulations is a physical impossibility").

[c]   See Barnett Bank of Marion Cty. v. Nelson, 517 U.S. 25, 31, 116 S.Ct. 1103, 1108 (1996) (saying that state law would be preempted where "the Federal Statute authorizes national banks to engage in activities that the State Statute expressly forbids"); Hines v. Davidowitz, 312 U.S. 52, 67, 61 S.Ct. 399, 404 (1941) (saying that state law would be preempted where it "stands as an obstacle to the accomplishment and execution of the full purposes and objectives of Congress").

[d]   See Pac. Gas & Elec. Co. v. State Energy Res. Conservation & Dev. Comm'n, 461 U.S. 190, 212–13, 103 S.Ct. 1713, 1726–27 (1983) (saying that state law would be preempted when "the Federal Government completely occupies a given field or an identifiable portion of it"); Rice v. Santa Fe Elevator Corp., 331 U.S. 218, 230, 67 S.Ct. 1146, 1152 (1947) ("The scheme of federal regulation may be so pervasive as to make reasonable the inference that Congress left no room for the States to supplement it. . . . Or the Act of Congress may touch a field in which the federal interest is so dominant that the federal system will be assumed to preclude enforcement of state laws on the same subject.").

In further exploring preemption, when one gets into implied preemption by conflict and turns toward possible preemption of state procedural law otherwise applicable in state court, one encounters cases like Dice and Brown, which treatises often treat as sui generis under some heading like "State Court Procedures and Federal Law Claims" but which others see as ordinary preemption cases. When one pushes still further into judicial decisions like Norfolk where the courts on their own federalize some point of law for state courts, without any semblance of a search for actual congressional intent, one starts to see the wider relevance of preemption as it concerns the realms of federal and state law in state court. Then, if one perceives complementary methodologies at work in these two doctrines of implied preemption and judicial choice of law, one should begin sensing the significance of preemption.

In other words, implied preemption requires more attention at this stage of your study of vertical choice of law. Preemption obviously constitutes an important part of a broadly conceived "Erie doctrine" in federal court, calling for the application of much federal law without any resort to judicial balancing. Even more obviously, it is at work in state court too. Implied preemption works in favor of federal law by rejecting not only any state law that openly discriminates against or contradicts federal law but also any state law that otherwise imposes unnecessary burdens upon federal rights, as in Brown. It does so regardless of the outcome of any independent judicial choice-of-law balancing methodology. Valid federal law that directly collides with state law simply displaces that state law.

Preemption provides the explanation of why federal law spills down into state court more than state law applies in federal court, or why state courts must apply federal procedural law to federally created claims more extensively than federal courts must apply state procedural law to state-created claims. To explain that Brown example, the state's anti-plaintiff pleading rule fell because the Court saw it as directly colliding with the pro-plaintiff FELA. The result was preemption that rejected any state interests. In the reverse-Brown setting, when the question would be whether a state pro-plaintiff procedural law applies in a diversity case, the Erie balance manages to tilt in favor of federal pleading law. That is, federal procedural interests overcome the interests in favor of applying state law, even to the extent of establishing Hanna's blanket approach to the Federal Rules. In Brown the Supremacy Clause causes federal procedure to preempt state procedure, but in reverse-Brown the Supremacy Clause obviously plays no comparable role to cause the state sovereign's law to trump any conflicting rules of the home court.

————

JOHNSON v. FANKELL, 520 U.S. 911, 117 S.Ct. 1800 (1997). Kristine Fankell brought a federal civil rights action in an Idaho state court, alleging that she had been fired from her state-government job without due process. The defendant officials unsuccessfully moved for dismissal on the ground of qualified immunity for governmental officials, and then tried to appeal immediately. The state supreme court dismissed the appeal under its finality rule, even though federal law would have allowed an interlocutory appeal. Certiorari was granted.

The U.S. Supreme Court unanimously affirmed in an opinion by Justice Stevens. After noting "our normal presumption against pre-emption," it sequentially found (1) that the "dismissal of the appeal rested squarely on a neutral state rule regarding the administration of the state courts," (2) that the federal interests at stake lay in the procedural appealability doctrine rather than in the substantive qualified-immunity doctrine, and (3) that application of the state rule was not "outcome-determinative" in the Felder sense. It then balanced the state's "countervailing considerations" regarding "the operation of its courts" against the relatively weak federal interests, at least as the Court viewed them. Thus, the Court drew a limit on federal intrusion into state-court procedure.

———

Question: (2) In a converse-Brown case brought in state court on an FELA claim, where the state ordinarily employs notice pleading and the federal courts would follow Twombly-Iqbal, what is the appropriate pleading standard? Would your answer differ for a § 1983 case, which unlike an FELA case is removable.

———

REVERSE-ERIE

This, then, is the broadly conceived reverse-Erie doctrine: federal law—be it constitutional, statutory, or common law—will apply pursuant to the Supremacy Clause in state court, subject to the Constitution or Congress having already chosen the applicable law, whenever it preempts state law *or* whenever it prevails by an Erie-like judicial choice of law.

The reverse-Erie question is a relatively simple one if the Constitution or Congress actually chose to displace state law in state court. If the Constitution or Congress expressly or impliedly made federal law applicable in state court, that choice to preempt is binding on the state courts under the Supremacy Clause, provided that any such statutory choice was constitutionally valid. However, in the absence of such a constitutional or congressional directive, and in the absence of binding precedent, the state courts and ultimately the U.S. Supreme Court must decide whether the existing federal law applies in state court.

If the state and federal laws directly collide, then the state court must recognize that federal law preempts; if not, then the state court must perform the federally mandated accommodation of interests to choose the applicable law. This judicial choice-of-law methodology operates without the asymmetry of preemption, instead being the mirror image of the Erie balance. It complementarily smooths, while it explains, the outer reaches of preemption. On the one hand, in the setting that involves a matter more of inference by judge than of implication by statute, when state law would merely frustrate federal law, those Erie-like ideas provide refinement of how obstacle and field preemption should work: whenever federal interests outweigh state interests in an Erie sense, there should be preemption. On the other hand, as one gets into more independent judicial choice of law under reverse-Erie, the direct application of Erie-like ideas makes the precise location of the outer boundary of preemption unimportant, as that boundary becomes merely a transitional zone between implied preemption and judicial choice of law, somewhere in the middle of the broad subject of reverse-Erie.

The reverse-Erie doctrine, comprising preemption and judicial choice of law, tells the state court when to apply existing federal law to displace state law under the command of the Supremacy Clause. The state court may have to envisage an Erie analysis to determine the reach of federal law and its content in federal court. If the state court then determines that the federal law governs in state court, the state court must apply it.

Applying another sovereign's law is a task different from a court's deciding under its own sovereign's law. In the reverse-Erie setting, the state court is merely a law-applier and can never act as a creator of federal law. Although the state court is competent to decide questions of federal law, it must act as if it were a federal court and try to decide the federal questions in accordance with the U.S. Supreme Court's view of federal law. At the time of decision, the federal law might already be fully formulated or might still be simply incipient. Indeed, sometimes the state court has to be the very first to enunciate the federal law. It has this authority to enunciate federal law, as long as it decides in accordance with the federal law—by trying to discern what the Supreme Court would decide is the federal law, and not by undertaking to formulate federal law as an independent federal-law-creator acting in pursuit of the policies and principles that might guide it when serving as a state-law-creating court. That is, the state court should act in the same manner as federal courts do when applying state law under Erie. In both the reverse-Erie setting and the Erie setting, the court's job is to apply the other sovereign's "existing" law, not to "make" law for the other.

If the content of the governing federal law is really unclear, how should the state court determine that content? No undisputed answer exists to this pervasive and fundamental question, illustrating how unexplored all reverse-Erie matters remain. Specifically, the question of whether state courts are bound by lower federal courts on the federal law's content remains open. The better view—mainly trying to effectuate the constitutional status of state courts, while accepting some localized disuniformity in the short term—is that the state court should try to determine what the U.S. Supreme Court has ruled or would rule. On the one hand, the state court should not consider itself actually bound, rather than merely informed, by the local federal courts' rulings. On the other hand, the state court would naturally be bound under stare decisis by decisions within the state's hierarchy of courts as to the federal law's content. Note the profound implication of this view: it makes the state courts into judicial hierarchies that can independently enunciate federal law, parallel to the lower federal courts and subject only to rare U.S. Supreme Court review. See generally Donald H. Zeigler, Gazing into the Crystal Ball: Reflections on the Standards State Judges Should Use to Ascertain Federal Law, 40 Wm. & Mary L.Rev. 1143 (1999).

This all seems terribly complicated, in a way so typical of American law. But in fact there is nothing peculiarly American here. The complications come from federalism itself, which is a complex but common form of political organization. See Ronald L. Watts, Comparing Federal Systems 5 (3d ed. 2008) (40% of the world's population live under federalism, broadly defined but not classifying the European Union as federalism). Because federalism involves the people living under the authority of more than one sovereign, a problem of choosing between state and federal law is inevitably ubiquitous in any federal system. See Kevin M. Clermont, Book Review, 57 Am.J.Comp.L. 258 (2009).

PART 3

AUTHORITY TO ADJUDICATE

TOPIC A

TERRITORIAL AUTHORITY TO ADJUDICATE

SECTION 1.   THE FRAMEWORK

Pennoyer v. Neff

Supreme Court of the United States, 1878.
95 U.S. 714.

[Marcus Neff, an illiterate young settler, reached Oregon by wagon train in 1848. He homesteaded a 320-acre plot in what is now Portland. For some reason, perhaps in connection with perfecting his title to the land, he consulted a Portland attorney during 1862–1863. Neff moved on to California, and prosperity, sometime thereafter.

[That attorney was John H. Mitchell. Suffice it to say that this was a man of scandalous private life and questionable professional ethics. Neither trait impeded his election in 1872 to the United States Senate, where he was again serving at the time of his 1905 conviction for corruption. For intriguing detail on the dramatis personae, see Wendy C. Perdue, Sin, Scandal, and Substantive Due Process: Personal Jurisdiction and Pennoyer Reconsidered, 62 Wash.L.Rev. 479 (1987).

[At any rate, Mitchell sued Neff in Oregon state court, claiming $253.14 as allegedly unpaid fees for those legal services. He commenced suit by filing his complaint on November 3, 1865. He properly laid venue in the Circuit Court of the State of Oregon for the County of Multnomah.

[Service presented an obvious problem, as Neff was apparently an absent nonresident who would not be voluntarily appearing. Mitchell reasonably read Oregon's ambiguous statutory scheme as authorizing his action upon service by publication. So on November 13, 1865, Mitchell applied for an order of service by publication, with the required supporting affidavit stating in its entirety:

> I, J.H. Mitchell, plaintiff, being first duly sworn, say that the defendant, Marcus Neff, is a non-resident of this state; that he resides somewhere in the State of California, at what place affiant knows not, and he cannot be found in this state. That plaintiff has a just cause of action against defendant for a money demand on account. That this court has jurisdiction of such action. That the defendant has property in this county and state.

On that same date, the court ordered service of the summons by publication for six weeks successively in the Pacific Christian Advocate, a weekly newspaper published in Multnomah County with a denominational circulation inside Oregon and practically none outside Oregon. Mitchell complied, and he filed the required proof of service in the form of an affidavit by the paper's editor. No mention was made of specific property by Mitchell or the court. Yet Neff already had valid title to his Portland land, even though he had not yet received all the paperwork.

[Naturally enough, Neff defaulted. The result, without further evidence, was a judgment for Mitchell on February 19, 1866, in the amount of $294.98, which reflected the demand plus interest and costs. Mitchell now had a judgment, but no remedy as yet. So he went after Neff's Portland land by a writ of execution. At the resulting execution sale on August 7, 1866, Mitchell himself bought the land for $341.60.

[On August 10, 1866, Mitchell assigned his interest in the land to one Sylvester Pennoyer "for value received." Pennoyer, Harvard Law School '54, was another Portland resident. Incidentally, he went on in 1886 to become a populist Governor of Oregon, widely and somewhat charitably characterized as an eccentric one.

[The bottom line here was that by Mitchell's lawsuit for under $300—a lawsuit of which Neff had no idea—a very valuable piece of property came into Pennoyer's hands. So much for Action #1, and on to Action #2 concerning that land.

[Much later and in Oregon federal court safe from the political pressures present in state court, Neff sued Pennoyer in ejectment. On September 10, 1874, he filed his complaint, which alleged diversity jurisdiction in this action by a California citizen against an Oregon citizen to recover possession of wrongfully withheld land then worth $15,000. He sued in the Circuit Court of the United States for the District of Oregon, which was then the appropriate federal trial court and which sat in Portland. Its distinguished judge was Matthew P. Deady, who had been the primary author of the Oregon Code of Civil Procedure and who despised Mitchell.

[On September 12, 1874, the deputy marshal served summons and complaint by personal delivery on Pennoyer in Portland. Pennoyer promptly answered, denying Neff's title and right to possession and alleging his own good title and right to possession. Neff replied by denying Pennoyer's title and right to possession, and hence by implication collaterally attacking the earlier judgment.

[The parties having stipulated to a nonjury trial, the court tried the case on September 24–25, 1874. Neff proved his patent to the land, and then he rested. Pennoyer, over Neff's objections, established the basics as to the earlier case by showing complaint, summons, order of publication, editor's affidavit, judgment, execution, assignment, and title documents, and then he rested. Neff, over Pennoyer's objection, introduced Mitchell's affidavit from that earlier case, and then both rested.

[Upon this evidence, the outcome turned on the success of the collateral attack. Here Neff argued most fervently that the state court had been exercising neither personal jurisdiction over him nor nonpersonal jurisdiction over his land, and he also argued that Mitchell's and the editor's affidavits had been faulty. The parties thereafter submitted briefs. Therein, on the key jurisdictional point, Neff argued that pre-judgment seizure of the property had been necessary for judicial power, while Pennoyer argued that Mitchell's procedural steps had been adequate to give jurisdiction over the land.

[In 1875, Judge Deady decided the case. His opinion quickly agreed with Pennoyer that jurisdiction over the land had been available, on the theory that Oregon could and did choose to exercise nonpersonal jurisdiction with only a post-judgment seizure of in-state property. Nevertheless, he ruled for Neff because of defects in the affidavits, after lengthy exposition along the following lines. Mitchell's affidavit had violated the Oregon Code's required method of showing due diligence, in that it offered no showing at all that Mitchell had exercised any diligence in ascertaining Neff's residence, knowledge of which would have facilitated notice. The editor's affidavit had likewise violated the Code, in that proof of publication had to be made by someone literally involved in the printing process, who would likely have had personal knowledge of the fact of actual publication. Collateral attack on these grounds would have been possible in an Oregon court, and thus the Oregon federal court did not owe full faith and credit to this judgment of a state court lacking jurisdiction. Mitchell's judgment and Pennoyer's title were accordingly void. Therefore, Judge Deady ruled, Neff was entitled to recover possession from Pennoyer, plus costs.]

■ [In 1877, Pennoyer proceeded to the Supreme Court by writ of error. On January 21, 1878, JUSTICE STEPHEN J. FIELD, a champion of substantive due process as a judicial protection of property rights, delivered the opinion of the Court. See Adrian M. Tocklin, Pennoyer v. Neff: The Hidden Agenda of Stephen J. Field, 28 Seton Hall L.Rev. 75 (1997). After a very brief rendition of the facts and prior proceedings, he continued:]

The Code of Oregon provides for such service [by publication] when an action is brought against a non-resident and absent defendant, who has property within the State. It also provides, where the action is for the recovery of money or damages, for the attachment of the property of the non-resident. And it also declares that no natural person is subject to the jurisdiction of a court of the State, "unless he appear in the court, or be found within the State, or be a resident thereof, or have property therein; and, in the last case, only to the extent of such property at the time the jurisdiction attached." Construing this latter provision to mean, that, in an action for money or damages where a defendant does not appear in the court, and is not found within the State, and is not a resident thereof, but has property therein, the jurisdiction of the court extends only over such property, the declaration expresses a principle of general, if not universal, law. The authority of every tribunal is necessarily restricted by the territorial limits of the State in which it is established. Any attempt to exercise authority beyond those limits would be deemed in every other forum, as has been said by this court, an illegitimate assumption of power, and be resisted as mere abuse. D'Arcy v. Ketchum et al., 11 How. 165. In the case against the plaintiff, the property here in controversy sold under the judgment rendered was not attached nor in any way brought under the jurisdiction of the court. Its first connection with the case was caused by a levy of the execution. It was not, therefore, disposed of pursuant to any adjudication, but only in enforcement of a personal judgment, having no relation to the property, rendered against a non-resident without service of process upon him in the action, or his appearance therein. The court below did not consider that an attachment of the property was essential to its jurisdiction or to the validity of the sale, but held that the judgment was invalid from defects in the affidavit upon which the order of publication was obtained, and in the affidavit by which the publication was proved.

There is some difference of opinion among the members of this court as to the rulings upon these alleged defects. The majority are of opinion that inasmuch as the statute requires, for an order of publication, that certain facts shall appear by affidavit *to the satisfaction of the court or judge,* defects in such affidavit can only be taken advantage of on appeal, or by some other direct proceeding, and cannot be urged to impeach the judgment collaterally. The majority of the court are also of opinion that the provision of the statute requiring proof of the publication in a newspaper to be made by the "affidavit of the printer, or his foreman, or his principal clerk," is satisfied when the affidavit is made by the editor of the paper. The term "printer," in their judgment, is there used not to indicate the person who sets up the type . . . .

If, therefore, we were confined to the rulings of the court below upon the defects in the affidavits mentioned, we should be unable to uphold its decision. But it was also contended in that court, and is insisted upon here, that the judgment in the State court against the plaintiff was void for want of personal service of process on him, or of his appearance in the action in which it was rendered, and that the premises in controversy could not be subjected to the payment of the demand of a resident creditor except by a proceeding in rem; that is, by a direct proceeding against the property for that purpose. If these positions are sound, the ruling of the Circuit Court as to the invalidity of that judgment must be sustained, notwithstanding our dissent from the reasons upon which it was made. And that they are sound would seem to follow from two well-established principles of public law respecting the jurisdiction of an independent State over persons and property. The several States of the Union are not, it is true, in every respect independent, many of the rights and powers which originally belonged to them being now vested in the government created by the Constitution. But, except as restrained and limited by that instrument, they possess and exercise the authority of independent States, and the principles of public law to which we have referred are applicable to them. One of these principles is, that every State possesses exclusive jurisdiction and sovereignty over persons and property within its territory. As a consequence, every State has the power to determine for itself the civil status and capacities of its inhabitants; to prescribe the subjects upon which they may contract, the forms and solemnities with which their contracts shall be executed, the rights and obligations arising from them, and the mode in which their validity shall be determined and their obligations enforced; and also to regulate the manner and conditions upon which property situated within such territory, both personal and real, may be acquired, enjoyed, and transferred. The other principle of public law referred to follows from the one mentioned; that is, that no State can exercise direct jurisdiction and authority over persons or property without its territory. Story, Confl.Laws, c. 2; Wheat, Int.Law, pt. 2, c. 2. . . .

But as contracts made in one State may be enforceable only in another State, and property may be held by non-residents, the exercise of the jurisdiction which every State is admitted to possess over persons and property within its own territory will often affect persons and property without it. To any influence exerted in this way by a State affecting persons resident or property situated elsewhere, no objection can be justly taken; whilst any direct exertion of authority upon them, in an attempt to give ex-territorial operation to its laws, or to enforce an ex-territorial jurisdiction by its tribunals, would be deemed an encroachment upon the independence of the State in which the persons are domiciled or the property is situated, and be resisted as usurpation.

Thus the State, through its tribunals, may compel persons domiciled within its limits to execute, in pursuance of their contracts respecting property elsewhere situated, instruments in such form and with such solemnities as to transfer the title, so far as such formalities can be complied with; and the exercise of this jurisdiction in no manner interferes with the supreme control over the property by the State within which it is situated. [Citations omitted.]

So the State, through its tribunals, may subject property situated within its limits owned by non-residents to the payment of the demand of its own citizens against them; and the exercise of this jurisdiction in no respect infringes upon the sovereignty of the State where the owners are domiciled. Every State owes protection to its own citizens; and, when non-residents deal with them, it is a legitimate and just exercise of authority to hold and appropriate any property owned by such non-residents to satisfy the claims of its citizens. It is in virtue of the State's jurisdiction over the property of the non-resident situated within its limits that its tribunals can inquire into that non-resident's obligations to its own citizens, and the inquiry can then be carried only to the extent necessary to control the disposition of the property. If the non-resident have no property in the State, there is nothing upon which the tribunals can adjudicate.

[Having stated and qualified its two basic principles, the Court turned to the matters of notice and nexus.]

. . . If, without personal service, judgments in personam, obtained ex parte against non-residents and absent parties, upon mere publication of process, which, in the great majority of cases, would never be seen by the parties interested, could be upheld and enforced, they would be the constant instruments of fraud and oppression. Judgments for all sorts of claims upon contracts and for torts, real or pretended, would be thus obtained, under which property would be seized, when the evidence of the transactions upon which they were founded, if they ever had any existence, had perished.

Substituted service by publication, or in any other authorized form, may be sufficient to inform parties of the object of proceedings taken where property is once brought under the control of the court by seizure or some equivalent act. The law assumes that property is always in the possession of its owner, in person or by agent; and it proceeds upon the theory that its seizure will inform him, not only that it is taken into the custody of the court, but that he must look to any proceedings authorized by law upon such seizure for its condemnation and sale. Such service may also be sufficient in cases where the object of the action is to reach and dispose of property in the State, or of some interest therein, by enforcing a contract or a lien respecting the same, or to partition it among different owners, or, when the public is a party, to condemn and appropriate it for a public purpose. In other words, such service may answer in all actions which are substantially proceedings in rem. [The Court then shifted from notice to nexus.] Process from the tribunals of one State cannot run into another State, and summon parties there domiciled to leave its territory and respond to proceedings against them. Publication of process or notice within the State where the tribunal sits cannot create any greater obligation upon the non-resident to appear. . . .

The want of authority of the tribunals of a State to adjudicate upon the obligations of non-residents, where they have no property within its limits, is not denied by the court below; but the position is assumed, that, where they have property within the State, it is immaterial whether the property is in the first instance brought under the control of the court by attachment or some other equivalent act, and afterwards applied by its judgment to the satisfaction of demands against its owner; or such demands be first established in a personal action, and the property of the non-resident be afterwards seized and sold on execution. But the answer to this position has already been given in the statement, that the jurisdiction of the court to inquire into and determine his obligations at all is only incidental to its jurisdiction over the property. Its jurisdiction in that respect cannot be made to depend upon facts to be ascertained after it has tried the cause and rendered the judgment. If the judgment be previously void, it will not become valid by the subsequent discovery of property of the defendant, or by his subsequent acquisition of it. The judgment, if void when rendered, will always remain void: it cannot occupy the doubtful position of being valid if property be found, and void if there be none. Even if the position assumed were confined to cases where the non-resident defendant possessed property in the State at the commencement of the action, it would still make the validity of the proceedings and judgment depend upon the question whether, before the levy of the execution, the defendant had or had not disposed of the property. If before the levy the property should be sold, then, according to this position, the judgment would not be binding. This doctrine would introduce a new element of uncertainty in judicial proceedings. The contrary is the law: the validity of every judgment depends upon the jurisdiction of the court before it is rendered, not upon what may occur subsequently.

[Before finally applying all this learning to the lack of nexus for Mitchell's judgment, the Court spent the following five paragraphs discussing the means to challenge nexus in a different sovereign's court or in the rendering state itself.]

The force and effect of judgments rendered against non-residents without personal service of process upon them, or their voluntary appearance, have been the subject of frequent consideration in the courts of the United States and of the several States, as attempts have been made to enforce such judgments in States other than those in which they were rendered, under the provision of the Constitution requiring that "full faith and credit shall be given in each State to the public acts, records, and judicial proceedings of every other State;" and the act of Congress providing for the mode of authenticating such acts, records, and proceedings, and declaring that, when thus authenticated, "they shall have such faith and credit given to them in every court within the United States as they have by law or usage in the courts of the State from which they are or shall be taken."[a] In the earlier cases, it was supposed that the act gave to all judgments the same effect in other States which they had by law in the State where rendered. But this view was afterwards qualified so as to make the act applicable only when the court rendering the judgment had jurisdiction of the parties and of the subject-matter, and not to preclude an inquiry into the jurisdiction of the court in which the judgment was rendered, or the right of the State itself to exercise authority over the person or the subject-matter. . . .

. . . In all the cases brought in the State and Federal courts, where attempts have been made under the act of Congress to give effect in one State to personal judgments rendered in another State against non-residents, without service upon them, or upon substituted service by

---

a   Now 28 U.S.C. § 1738.

publication, or in some other form, it has been held, without an exception, so far as we are aware, that such judgments were without any binding force, except as to property, or interests in property, within the State, to reach and affect which was the object of the action in which the judgment was rendered, and which property was brought under control of the court in connection with the process against the person. The proceeding in such cases, though in the form of a personal action, has been uniformly treated, where service was not obtained, and the party did not voluntarily appear, as effectual and binding merely as a proceeding in rem, and as having no operation beyond the disposition of the property, or some interest therein. . . .

. . . In several of the cases, the decision has been accompanied with the observation that a personal judgment thus recovered has no binding force without the State in which it is rendered, implying that in such State it may be valid and binding. But if the court has no jurisdiction over the person of the defendant by reason of his non-residence, and, consequently, no authority to pass upon his personal rights and obligations; if the whole proceeding, without service upon him or his appearance, is coram non judice and void; if to hold a defendant bound by such a judgment is contrary to the first principles of justice,—it is difficult to see how the judgment can legitimately have any force within the State. The language used can be justified only on the ground that there was no mode of directly reviewing such judgment or impeaching its validity within the State where rendered; and that, therefore, it could be called in question only when its enforcement was elsewhere attempted. In later cases, this language is repeated with less frequency than formerly, it beginning to be considered, as it always ought to have been, that a judgment which can be treated in any State of this Union as contrary to the first principles of justice, and as an absolute nullity, because rendered without any jurisdiction of the tribunal over the party, is not entitled to any respect in the State where rendered. [State citations omitted.]

Be that as it may, the courts of the United States are not required to give effect to judgments of this character when any right is claimed under them. Whilst they are not foreign tribunals in their relations to the State courts, they are tribunals of a different sovereignty, exercising a distinct and independent jurisdiction, and are bound to give to the judgments of the State courts only the same faith and credit which the courts of another State are bound to give to them.

Since the adoption of the Fourteenth Amendment to the Federal Constitution,[b] the validity of such judgments may be directly questioned, and their enforcement in the State resisted, on the ground that proceedings in a court of justice to determine the personal rights and obligations of parties over whom that court has no jurisdiction do not

---

b   By a concurrent resolution dated July 21, 1868, Congress declared that the required three-fourths of the state legislatures had ratified the Fourteenth Amendment.

constitute due process of law. Whatever difficulty may be experienced in giving to those terms a definition which will embrace every permissible exertion of power affecting private rights, and exclude such as is forbidden, there can be no doubt of their meaning when applied to judicial proceedings. They then mean a course of legal proceedings according to those rules and principles which have been established in our systems of jurisprudence for the protection and enforcement of private rights. To give such proceedings any validity, there must be a tribunal competent by its constitution—that is, by the law of its creation—to pass upon the subject-matter of the suit; and, if that involves merely a determination of the personal liability of the defendant, he must be brought within its jurisdiction by service of process within the State, or his voluntary appearance.

Except in cases affecting the personal status of the plaintiff [such as marital status], and cases in which that mode of service may be considered to have been assented to in advance [as where a non-resident agrees by contract to receive some mode of service,] the substituted service of process by publication, allowed by the law of Oregon and by similar laws in other States, where actions are brought against non-residents, is effectual only where, in connection with process against the person for commencing the action, property in the State is brought under the control of the court, and subjected to its disposition by a process adapted to that purpose, or where the judgment is sought as a means of reaching such property or affecting some interest therein; in other words, where the action is in the nature of a proceeding in rem. . . .

It is true that, in a strict sense, a proceeding in rem is one taken directly against property, and has for its object the disposition of the property, without reference to the title of individual claimants; but, in a larger and more general sense, the terms are applied to actions between parties, where the direct object is to reach and dispose of property owned by them, or of some interest therein. Such are cases commenced by attachment against the property of debtors, or instituted to partition real estate, foreclose a mortgage, or enforce a lien. So far as they affect property in the State, they are substantially proceedings in rem in the broader sense which we have mentioned.

It is hardly necessary to observe, that in all we have said we have had reference to proceedings in courts of first instance, and to their jurisdiction, and not to proceedings in an appellate tribunal to review the action of such courts. The latter may be taken upon such notice, personal or constructive, as the State creating the tribunal may provide. They are considered as rather a continuation of the original litigation than the commencement of a new action. [Citation omitted.]

It follows from the views expressed that the personal judgment recovered in the State court of Oregon against the plaintiff herein, then a non-resident of the State, was without any validity, and did not authorize a sale of the property in controversy.

. . . .

Judgment affirmed.

■ [The dissenting opinion of JUSTICE HUNT is omitted. He argued that, as recognized in existing statutory and case law, a state could constitutionally allow a plaintiff to sue any defendant for damages and then levy on any of the latter's property in the state, as long as the defendant received reasonable notice and opportunity to be heard.]

———

CLOSSON v. CHASE, 158 Wis. 346, 149 N.W. 26 (1914). In an action on promissory notes, where the plaintiff claimed no pre-existing lien on or interest in any property of the nonresident defendant, the plaintiff proceeded by an action against the defendant's Wisconsin land. The relevant Wisconsin statute provided: "Service of the summons may be made without the state or by publication upon a defendant against whom a cause of action appears to exist . . . on obtaining an order therefor . . . in . . . the following cases: (1) When such defendant is a nonresident of this state . . . and . . . has property within the state . . . ." The attorney's affidavit supporting such service stated "that the defendant was the owner of real estate within this state" and then described the land. The court ordered service by publication upon the defendant.

Upon the defendant's subsequent challenge to this procedure, the appellate court said in part: "The issuance of a writ of attachment and levy upon property thereunder is not essential to competency to make service on a defendant by publication. Gallun v. Weil, 116 Wis. 236, 92 N.W. 1091. The statutory requisite of property of the defendant within this state, existing and duly brought to the attention of the court, is all that is necessary in respect to the property feature. Such an action is regarded as one in rem. The judgment when rendered is good only against the property described in the moving papers. . . . It is the res within the jurisdiction of the court that is essential to jurisdiction, not actual seizure of it, or even constructive seizure, unless description of the property in the [action's] moving papers and [the therein] recorded purpose of the plaintiff to burden it with payment of the debt should be regarded as such seizure. Jarvis v. Barrett, 14 Wis. 591; Winner v. Fitzgerald, 19 Wis. 393; Disconto Gesellschaft v. Terlinden, 127 Wis. 651, 106 N.W. 821.

"The foregoing sufficiently answers, if any be necessary, after express and implied approval of the statute in question for more than sixty years, the suggestion that it is unconstitutional under the doctrine of Pennoyer v. Neff, 95 U.S. 714."

———

COLLATERAL ATTACK

Under current law, federal or state, lack of jurisdiction may be raised not only in the ordinary course of review in the trial and appellate courts but even sometimes in subsequent litigation, as by collateral attack. What is a collateral attack? If a party uses a prior judgment in a new action as the basis for a claim (as where, in enforcing a judgment, the plaintiff brings suit upon the judgment in another state) or as the basis for a defense (as where a defendant pleads res judicata), and if the other party in turn attacks the prior judgment to prevent its use, we have a collateral attack.

The rule is that collateral attack will succeed only if the prior judgment contains certain, very serious errors. So, suppose an action in federal court has proceeded to final judgment upon default, and the plaintiff has brought suit upon the judgment elsewhere. The defendant now contends that the court that rendered the judgment lacked jurisdiction. If she can establish that such a defect indeed existed, the collateral-attack court generally will refuse to enforce the judgment.

Change the problem to this extent: suppose an action in federal court has proceeded to final judgment, but in that action the defendant raised and litigated the question of the court's subject-matter jurisdiction and the court decided that it had jurisdiction. In a suit upon the judgment, is it open to the second court to reexamine the question of the first court's subject-matter jurisdiction and refuse to enforce the judgment, assuming it is convinced that the first court erred in its decision on its own jurisdiction? Generally not, because res judicata works to foreclose relitigation of a prior determination of jurisdiction. This question we shall treat in Topic E of Part 4.

Questions: (1) Which law should govern the question of whether there was subject-matter jurisdiction in the court that rendered judgment, upon a collateral attack in a court of a different sovereign? Should it be the law of the first court's sovereign or that of the second court's sovereign? See Restatement (Second) of Conflict of Laws § 105 cmt. b (Am. Law Inst. 1971) (first court's sovereign).

(2) To what extent should one be able to go beyond the record and look to extrinsic evidence establishing a lack of subject-matter jurisdiction, on either appeal or collateral attack? See Restatement (Second) of Judgments § 77 (Am. Law Inst. 1982) (liberal admissibility). Should we say that here the governing law on evidence shifts to that of the second court's sovereign?

(3) Who should have the burden of proof on subject-matter jurisdiction, in either the rendering court or the collateral-attack court? Should we say that merely the burden of production shifts to the attacker when the scene changes to collateral attack or to some similar procedure for relief from a rendered judgment?

———

SECTION 2.   JURISDICTION OVER THINGS— TRADITIONAL THEORY

(a) NATURE OF SUCH JURISDICTION

Tyler v. Judges of the Court of Registration

Supreme Judicial Court of Massachusetts, 1900.
175 Mass. 71, 55 N.E. 812, writ of error dismissed, 179 U.S. 405 21 S.Ct. 206 (1900).

■ HOLMES, C.J. This is a petition [by Tyler] for a writ of prohibition against the judges of the Court of Registration established by St.1898, c. 562 [and today called the Land Court, sitting in Boston], and is brought to prevent their proceeding upon an application [captioned In re Application of Gould] concerning land [claimed by Gould in Middlesex County] in which the petitioner claims an interest. The ground of the petition is that the act establishing the court is unconstitutional. [The ground] is that the original registration deprives all persons except the registered owner of any interest in the land without due process of law. There is no dispute that the object of the system, expressed in § 38, is that the decree of registration "shall bind the land and quiet the title thereto," and "shall be conclusive upon and against all persons," whether named in the proceedings or not, subject to few and immaterial exceptions. And this being admitted, it is objected that there is no sufficient process against, or notice to, persons having adverse claims, in a proceeding intended to bar their possible rights.

The application for registration is to be in writing and signed and sworn to. It is to contain an accurate description of the land, to set forth clearly other outstanding estates or interests known to the petitioner [whether admitted or denied], to identify the deed by which he obtained title, to state the name and address of the occupant if there is one, and also to give the names and addresses so far as known of the [owners and] occupants of all lands adjoining. § 21. As soon as it is filed, a memorandum containing a copy of the description of the land concerned is to be filed in the registry of deeds. § 20. The case is immediately referred to an examiner (appointed by the judge, § 12), who makes as full an investigation as he can and reports to the court. § 29. If in the opinion of the examiner the applicant has a good title as alleged, or if the applicant after an adverse opinion elects to proceed further, the recorder is to publish a notice by order of the court in some newspaper published in the district where any portion of the land lies. This notice is to be addressed by name to all persons known to have an adverse interest, and to the adjoining owners and occupants so far as known, and to all whom it may concern. It is to contain a description of the land, the name of the applicant, and the time and place of the hearing. § 31. A copy is to be mailed to every person named in the notice whose address is known, and a duly attested copy is to be posted in a conspicuous place on each parcel of land included in the application, by a sheriff or deputy sheriff, fourteen days at least before the return day. Further notice may be ordered by the court. § 32.

. . . .

If [this process] does not satisfy the Constitution, a judicial proceeding to clear titles against all the world hardly is possible, for the very meaning of such a proceeding is to get rid of unknown as well as known claims,—indeed certainty against the unknown may be said to be its chief end,—and unknown claims cannot be dealt with by personal service upon the claimant. It seems to have been the impression of the Supreme Court of Ohio, in the case most relied upon by the petitioner, that such a judicial proceeding is impossible in this country. State v. Guilbert, 56 Ohio St. 575, 629, 47 N.E. 551. But we cannot bring ourselves to doubt that the Constitutions of the United States and of Massachusetts at least permit it as fully as did the common law. Prescription or a statute of limitations may give a title good against the world and destroy all manner of outstanding claims without any notice or judicial proceeding at all. Time and the chance which it gives the owner to find out that he is in danger of losing rights are due process of law in that case. . . .

. . . .

Looked at either from the point of view of history or of the necessary requirements of justice, a proceeding in rem dealing with a tangible res may be instituted and carried to judgment without personal service . . . and not encounter any provision of either Constitution. Jurisdiction is secured by the power of the court over the res. As we have said, such a proceeding would be impossible, were this not so, for it hardly would do to make a distinction between the constitutional rights of claimants who were known and those who were not known to the plaintiff, when the proceeding is to bar all. Pennoyer v. Neff, 95 U.S. 714, 727. [Other citations omitted.] In Hamilton v. Brown, 161 U.S. 256, 16 S.Ct. 585, a judgment of escheat was held conclusive upon persons notified only by advertisement to all persons interested. It is true that the statute under consideration required the petition to name all known claimants, and personal service to be made on those so named. But that did the plaintiffs no good, as they were not named. So a decree allowing or disallowing a will binds everybody, although the only notice of the proceedings given be a general notice to all persons interested. And in this case, as in that of escheat just cited, the conclusive effect of the decree is not put upon the ground that the State has an absolute power to determine the persons to whom a man's property shall go at his death, but upon the characteristics of a proceeding in rem. Bonnemort v. Gill, 167 Mass. 338, 340, 45 N.E. 768. See 161 U.S. 256, 263, 274, 16 S.Ct. 585. Admiralty proceedings need only to be mentioned in this connection, and further citation of cases seems unnecessary.

Speaking for myself, I see no reason why what we have said as to proceedings in rem in general should not apply to such proceedings concerning land. [Chief Justice Oliver Wendell Holmes suggested that for proceedings in rem, notice by publication sufficed.]

But it is said that this is not a proceeding in rem. It is certain that no phrase has been more misused. In the past it has had little more significance than that the right alleged to have been violated was a right in rem. Austin thinks it necessary to quote Leibnitz for the sufficiently obvious remark that every right to restitution is a right in personam. So as to actions. If the technical object of the suit is to establish a claim against some particular person, with a judgment which generally, in theory at least, binds his body, or to bar some individual claim or objection, so that only certain persons are entitled to be heard in defence, the action is in personam, although it may concern the right to or possession of a tangible thing. Mankin v. Chandler, 2 Brock. 125, 127, Fed.Cas. No. 9,030. If, on the other hand, the object is to bar indifferently all who might be minded to make an objection of any sort against the right sought to be established, and if any one in the world has a right to be heard on the strength of alleging facts which, if true, show an inconsistent interest, the proceeding is in rem. Freem. Judgments, (4th ed.) § 606 ad fin. All proceedings, like all rights, are really against persons. Whether they are proceedings or rights in rem depends on the number of persons affected. Hence the res need not be personified and made a party defendant, as happens with the ship in the admiralty; it need not even be a tangible thing at all, as sufficiently appears by the case of the probate of wills. Personification and naming the res as defendant are mere symbols, not the essential matter. They are fictions, conveniently expressing the nature of the process and the result, nothing more.

. . . .

Then as to seizure of the res. It is convenient in the case of a vessel, in order to secure its being on hand to abide judgment, although in the case of a suit against a man jurisdiction is regarded as established by service without the need of keeping him in prison to await judgment. It is enough that the personal service shows that he could have been seized and imprisoned. Seizure, to be sure, is said to be notice to the owner. [Citations omitted.] But fastening the process or a copy to the mast would seem not necessarily to depend for its effect upon the continued custody of the vessel by the marshal. However this may be, when we come to deal with immovables there would be no sense whatever in declaring seizure to be a constitutional condition of the power of the Legislature to make a proceeding against land a proceeding in rem. Hamilton v. Brown, 161 U.S. 256, 274, 16 S.Ct. 585. The land cannot escape from the jurisdiction, and, except as security against escape, seizure is a mere form, of no especial sanctity, and of much possible inconvenience.

I do not wish to ignore the fact that seizure, when it means real dispossession, is another security for actual notice. But when it is considered how purely formal such an act may be, and that even adverse possession is possible without ever coming to the knowledge of a reasonably alert owner, I cannot think that the presence or absence of the form makes a constitutional difference; or rather, to express my view still more cautiously, I cannot but think that the immediate recording of the claim is entitled to equal effect from a constitutional point of view. I am free to confess, however, that, with the rest of my brethren, I think the act ought to be amended in the direction of still further precautions to secure actual notice before a decree is entered, and that, if it is not amended, the judges of the court ought to do all that is in their power to satisfy themselves that there has been no failure in this regard before they admit a title to registration.[c]

The quotations which we have made show the intent of the statute to bind the land, and to make the proceedings adverse to all the world, even if it were not stated in § 35, or if the amendment of 1899 did not expressly provide that they should be proceedings in rem. St.1899, c. 131, § 1. Notice is to be posted on the land just as admiralty process is fixed to the mast. Any person claiming an interest may appear and be heard. § 34.

But perhaps the classification of the proceeding is not so important as the course of the discussion thus far might seem to imply. I have pursued that course as one which is satisfactory to my own mind, but for the purposes of decision a majority of the court prefer to assume that in cases in which, under the constitutional requirements of due process of law, it heretofore has been necessary to give to parties interested actual notice of the pending proceeding by personal service or its equivalent in order to render a valid judgment against them, it is not in the power of the Legislature, by changing the form of the proceeding from an action in personam to a suit in rem, to avoid the necessity of giving such a notice, and to assume that under this statute personal rights in property are so involved and may be so affected that effectual notice and an opportunity to be heard should be given to all claimants who are known or who by reasonable effort can be ascertained.

. . . With regard to claimants . . . remaining undiscovered, notice by publication must suffice of necessity. As to claimants . . . known, the question seems to come down to whether we can say that there is a constitutional difference between sending notice of a suit by a messenger and sending it by the post office beside publishing in a newspaper, recording in the registry, and posting on the land. It must be remembered that there is no constitutional requirement that the summons, even in a

---

[c]   The present statute, Mass.Gen.Laws Ann. ch. 185, § 39, enlarges on § 32 of the 1898 Act by adding: "The court shall, so far as it considers it possible, require proof of actual notice to all adjoining owners and to all persons who appear to have any interest in or claim to the land included in the complaint. Notice to such persons by mail shall be by registered letter."

personal action, shall be served by an officer, or that the copy served shall be officially attested. Apart from local practice, it may be served by any indifferent person. It may be served on residents by leaving a copy at the last and usual place of abode. When we are considering a proceeding of this kind, it seems to us within the power of the Legislature to say that the mail . . . is a sufficient messenger to convey the notice, when other means of notifying the party, like publishing and posting, also are required. We agree that such an act as this is not to be upheld without anxiety. But the difference in degree between the case at bar and one in which the constitutionality of the act would be unquestionable seems to us too small to warrant a distinction. If the statute is within the power of the Legislature, it is not for us to criticise the wisdom or expediency of what the Legislature has done.

. . . .

Petition denied.[d]

■ [The dissenting opinion of JUSTICE LORING, with whom Justice Lathrop joined, is omitted.]

Garfein v. McInnis

Court of Appeals of New York, 1928.
248 N.Y. 261, 162 N.E. 73.

■ LEHMAN, J. In an action [in New York Supreme Court] for the specific performance of an alleged contract to convey real estate in the State of New York [Westchester County], service of the summons and complaint has been made in the State of Connecticut, upon a resident of that State. The motion of the defendant to set aside such service has been denied. [The defendant-appellant, who was the seller named McInnis, argued: "An action for the specific performance of a contract is an action in equity, and in the absence of a statute giving jurisdiction in rem, equity acts in personam merely."]

In an action "where the complaint demands judgment that the defendant be excluded from a vested or contingent interest in or lien upon specific real or personal property within the State or that such an interest or lien in favor of either party be enforced, regulated, defined or limited, or otherwise affecting the title to such property," the summons may be served out of the State. (Sections 232 and 235, Civ.Prac.Act.) The language of the statute is sufficiently broad to cover an action for specific performance. Service without the State is sufficient to give the court jurisdiction to grant a judgment in rem binding upon a non-resident

---

d　　The U.S. Supreme Court later dismissed a writ of error because "the plaintiff in error has not the requisite interest to draw in question" the validity of the statute, 179 U.S. 405, 21 S.Ct. 206 (1900). Tyler was an owner of land adjoining, along a disputed boundary, the parcel to be registered; but he had actual notice of the registration proceedings.

defendant so served. It does not, however, bring the non-resident defendant's person within the jurisdiction of the court. A decree in personam can be supported against a person who is not a citizen or resident of the State in which it is rendered only by actual service upon him within its jurisdiction. (Hart v. Sansom, 110 U.S. 151, 3 S.Ct. 586.) The question presented by this appeal is whether a judgment in an action for specific performance is only a decree in personam against the party who has agreed to convey property, or whether the court in such an action may grant a judgment which will operate upon the property itself and result in a transfer of the title to a successful party though the defendant fail or refuse to obey a command of the judgment directed to him.

That a court of chancery acts only upon the person is a recognized maxim of equity jurisprudence. [Citations omitted.] "A decree of chancery spoke in terms of personal command to the defendant, but its directions could only be carried into effect by his personal act. . . ." (Pomeroy on Equity Jurisprudence, § 428.) In jurisdictions where the decrees of a court of equity still retain the traditional form and effect of a mere command, a court of equity cannot obtain jurisdiction over a non-resident by service without the State. [Citations omitted.]

It has been doubted whether the jurisdiction of courts of equity was ever subject to any inherent limitation that its decrees must operate solely in personam, though the early chancellors adopted the "method of acting, as they said, upon the conscience of defendants." In this country "the statutes of the several states have virtually abolished the ancient doctrine that the decrees in equity can only act upon the person of a party, and have generally provided that in all cases where the ends of justice require such an effect, and where it is possible, a decree shall either operate ex proprio vigore to create, transfer, or vest the intended right, title, estate, or interest, or else that the acts required to be done in order to accomplish the object of the decree shall be performed by an [appointed] officer of the court acting for and in the name of the party against whom the adjudication is made." (Pomeroy's Equity Jurisprudence, § 135.) "A bill for the specific execution of a contract to convey real estate is not strictly a proceeding in rem, in ordinary cases; but where such a procedure is authorized by statute, on publication, without personal service of process, it is, substantially, of that character." (Boswell's Lessee v. Otis, 50 U.S. 336.)

[The court explained that although some states' equity courts have found quasi in rem remedies to be within their inherent powers, New York need not face that question because it has a statute of the "appointive" type.]

In this State the Legislature has provided in section 979 of the Civil Practice Act that where a "judgment directs a party . . . to convey real property, if the direction is disobeyed, the court, by order, besides punishing the disobedience as a contempt, may require the sheriff . . . to convey the real property, in conformity with the direction of the court." A decree of the court is enforceable not merely by punishment of a disobedient party but may be carried into effect by action of the sheriff operating directly upon the property. It may be that the primary purpose of the Legislature was to grant additional force to a decree in a case where the court had acquired jurisdiction of the person of a disobedient party. Its effect extends beyond such a case. It has changed the nature of the action from an action in personam, to an action substantially in rem. Though the court cannot by [out-of-state] service obtain jurisdiction of the person of a non-resident defendant and cannot compel such a defendant to obey its decree, where the court has the power to make a decree which will affect the interests of a party in property within the State, whether that party obeys the decree or not, the action is not purely in personam. The court's decree acts upon the property as well as the person of the non-resident defendant. In such case the objection that the court by [out-of-state] service obtains no jurisdiction over the person of a non-resident is without force. The Legislature has expressly provided that in an action for specific performance a court may enforce its decree by other means than direction to the defendant.

The order should be affirmed, with costs . . . .

■ CARDOZO, CH. J., POUND, CRANE, ANDREWS and O'BRIEN, JJ., concur; KELLOGG, J., dissents.

————

Questions: (4) *B,* a resident of New York, entered into a contract with *S,* a resident of Connecticut, by which *S* undertook to convey to *B* certain real estate situated in New York. *S* refused to perform. What, if any, equitable relief can *B* obtain from a Connecticut court, *S* having been personally served in Connecticut and having actively contested the suit there?

(5) The decree of the Connecticut court orders *S* to convey the New York land, and *S* fails to do so. Can the Connecticut court, given the existence of a Connecticut statute of either the "appointive" or the "vesting" type, give *B* title to the land? See Fall v. Eastin, 215 U.S. 1, 30 S.Ct. 3 (1909) (no).

(6) The Connecticut court enters a decree simply ordering *S* to convey the New York land, and *S* leaves the Northeast without doing so. Thereafter *B* brings an action against *S* in New York for enforcement of the Connecticut decree. What should be the result of the action?

(7) Now assume instead that *B* agreed to buy and *S* agreed to sell certain real estate situated in Connecticut. *B* refused to perform. *B* is not subject to personal jurisdiction in Connecticut and has no other property there. What, if any, relief can *S* obtain from a Connecticut court? See Prudential Ins. Co. v. Berry, 153 S.C. 496, 151 S.E. 63 (1930) (cutting off *B*'s equitable interest in the land).

————

Harris v. Balk

Supreme Court of the United States, 1905.
198 U.S. 215, 25 S.Ct. 625.

The plaintiff in error brings the case here in order to review the judgment of the Supreme Court of North Carolina, affirming a judgment of a lower court against him for $180, with interest, as stated therein. The case has been several times before the Supreme Court of that State, and is reported in 122 N.Car. 64; again, 124 N.Car. 467; the opinion delivered at the time of entering the judgment now under review, is to be found in 130 N.Car. 381; see also 132 N.Car. 10.

The facts are as follows: The plaintiff in error, Harris, was a resident of North Carolina at the time of the commencement of this action in 1896, and prior to that time was indebted to the defendant in error, Balk, also a resident of North Carolina, in the sum of $180, for money borrowed from Balk by Harris during the year 1896, which Harris verbally promised to repay, but there was no written evidence of the obligation. During the year above mentioned one Jacob Epstein, a resident of Baltimore, in the State of Maryland, asserted that Balk was indebted to him in the sum of [$344 for the wholesale purchase of general merchandise]. In August, 1896, Harris visited Baltimore for the purpose of purchasing merchandise, and while he was in that city temporarily on August 6, 1896, Epstein caused to be issued out of a proper court in Baltimore a foreign or non-resident writ of attachment against Balk, attaching the debt due Balk from Harris, which writ the sheriff at Baltimore laid in the hands of Harris, with a summons to appear in the court at a day named. With that attachment, a writ of summons and a short declaration against Balk (as provided by the Maryland statute), were also delivered to the sheriff and by him set up at the court house door, as required by the law of Maryland. Before the return day of the attachment writ Harris left Baltimore and returned to his home in North Carolina. He did not contest the garnishee process, which was issued to garnish the debt which Harris owed Balk. After his return Harris made an affidavit on August 11, 1896, that he owed Balk $180, and stated that the amount had been attached by Epstein of Baltimore, and by his counsel in the Maryland proceeding Harris consented therein to an order of condemnation against him as such garnishee for $180, the amount of his debt to Balk. Judgment was thereafter entered against the garnishee and in favor of the plaintiff, Epstein, for $180. After the entry of the garnishee judgment, condemning the $180 in the hands of the garnishee, Harris paid the amount of the judgment to one Warren, an attorney of Epstein, residing in North Carolina. On August 11, 1896, Balk commenced an action against Harris before a justice of the peace in North Carolina, to recover the $180 which he averred Harris owed him. The plaintiff in error, by way of answer to the suit, pleaded in bar the recovery of the Maryland judgment and his payment thereof, and contended that it was conclusive against the defendant in error in this action, because that judgment was a valid judgment in Maryland, and was therefore entitled to full faith and credit in the courts of North Carolina. This contention was not allowed by the trial court, and judgment was accordingly entered against Harris for the amount of his indebtedness to Balk, and that judgment was affirmed by the Supreme Court of North Carolina.[e] The ground of such judgment was that the Maryland court obtained no jurisdiction to attach or garnish the debt due from Harris to Balk, because Harris was but temporarily in the State, and [therefore] the situs of the debt [remained] in North Carolina.

■ MR. JUSTICE PECKHAM, after making the foregoing statement, delivered the opinion of the court.

The state court of North Carolina has refused to give any effect in this action to the Maryland judgment; and the Federal question is, whether it did not thereby refuse the full faith and credit to such judgment which is required by the Federal Constitution. If the Maryland court had jurisdiction to award it, the judgment is valid and entitled to the same full faith and credit in North Carolina that it has in Maryland as a valid domestic judgment.

The defendant in error contends that the Maryland court obtained no jurisdiction to award the judgment of condemnation, because the garnishee, although at the time in the State of Maryland, and personally served with process therein, was a non-resident of that State, only casually or temporarily within its boundaries; that the situs of the debt due from Harris, the garnishee, to the defendant in error herein was in North Carolina, and did not accompany Harris to Maryland; that, consequently, Harris, though within the State of Maryland, had not possession of any property of Balk, and the Maryland state court therefore obtained no jurisdiction over any property of Balk in the attachment proceedings, and the consent of Harris to the entry of the judgment was immaterial. The plaintiff in error, on the contrary, insists that, though the garnishee were but temporarily in Maryland, yet the laws of that State provide for an attachment of this nature, if the debtor, the garnishee, is found in the State and the court obtains jurisdiction over him by the service of process therein; that the judgment, condemning the debt from Harris to Balk, was a valid judgment, provided Balk could himself have sued Harris for the debt in Maryland. This it is asserted, he could have done, and the judgment was therefore entitled to full faith and credit in the courts of North Carolina.

. . . .

We regard the contention of the plaintiff in error as the correct one. . . .

---

[e]   It seems that Epstein was financing Harris's litigation, for the reason that "the legal question is of considerable importance to the mercantile and business world." Brief for Plaintiff in Error at 5.

Attachment is the creature of the local law; that is, unless there is a law of the State providing for and permitting the attachment it cannot be levied there. If there be a law of the State providing for the attachment of the debt, then if the garnishee be found in that State, and process be personally served upon him therein, we think the court thereby acquires jurisdiction over him, and can garnish the debt due from him to the debtor of the plaintiff and condemn it, provided the garnishee could himself be sued by his creditor in that State. We do not see how the question of jurisdiction vel non can properly be made to depend upon the so-called original situs of the debt, or upon the character of the stay of the garnishee, whether temporary or permanent, in the State where the attachment is issued. . . .

. . . .

It thus appears that Balk could have sued Harris in Maryland to recover his debt . . . ; it also appears that the municipal law of Maryland permits the debtor of the principal debtor to be garnished, and therefore if the court of the State where the garnishee is found obtains jurisdiction over him, through the service of process upon him within the State, then the judgment entered is a valid judgment. . . .

. . . The importance of the fact of the right of the original creditor to sue his debtor in the foreign State, as affecting the right of the creditor of that creditor to sue the debtor or garnishee, lies in the nature of the attachment proceeding. The plaintiff, in such proceeding in the foreign State is able to sue out the attachment and attach the debt due from the garnishee to his (the garnishee's) creditor, because of the fact that the plaintiff is really in such proceeding a representative of the creditor of the garnishee, and therefore if such creditor himself had the right to commence suit to recover the debt in the foreign State his representative has the same right, as representing him, and may garnish or attach the debt, provided the municipal law of the State where the attachment was sued out permits it.

It seems to us, therefore, that the judgment against Harris in Maryland, condemning the $180 which he owed to Balk, was a valid judgment, because the court had jurisdiction over the garnishee by personal service of process within the State of Maryland.

It ought to be and it is the object of courts to prevent the payment of any debt twice over. Thus, if Harris owing a debt to Balk, paid it under a valid judgment against him, to Epstein, he certainly ought not to be compelled to pay it a second time, but should have the right to plead his payment under the Maryland judgment. . . .

[The Court further ruled that Balk had received adequate notice of the attachment proceeding.]

Reversed.

■ MR. JUSTICE HARLAN and MR. JUSTICE DAY dissented.

(b) PROCEDURE FOR SUCH JURISDICTION

Consideration of some of the procedural incidents of jurisdiction over things may help to clarify the nature of such jurisdiction, whether of the in rem variety as in Tyler or the two quasi in rem varieties of Garfein (subtype 1) and Harris (subtype 2).

For example, consider the implications of Restatement (Second) of Judgments § 32 cmt. c, illus. 1 (Am. Law Inst. 1982): "A brings an action against B to recover damages for breach of contract. Personal jurisdiction over B is not established, but an automobile worth $500 belonging to him is attached and he is personally notified of the proceeding. Judgment by default is rendered in favor of A for his damages to be assessed. The jury impanelled to assess the damages gives a verdict of $500 and judgment is rendered for A for $500 and $50 costs, to be paid out of the proceeds of the sale of the automobile. The automobile is sold for $500, which sum is paid to A. Of this sum $50 is applicable to the payment of the costs and $450 toward the payment of A's claim. B is not liable for the deficiency. However, in a new action brought by A against B on the original claim, A will be entitled, if successful, to recover whatever damages may be awarded in that action, which may be more or less than $500, less the sum of $450, plus the costs of the new action." By contrast, if B successfully defends the second action on the ground that he did not breach the contract, that outcome will not affect the prior proceeding and the court will not direct A to restore his earlier recovery.

Now consider the implications of CME Media Enterprises B.V. v. Zelezny, 2001 WL 1035138 (S.D.N.Y. Sept. 10, 2001). In Amsterdam, CME obtained an arbitration award against Dr. Vladimir Zelezny in the principal amount of $23.35 million. Then in the United States, with representation by a major law firm, CME petitioned a federal court for a judgment confirming and enforcing the award. Counsel did not contend that the court had personal jurisdiction over Zelezny, who was a citizen and resident of the Czech Republic, but that the court had jurisdiction because Zelezny had assets in New York—funds in an account at Citibank. "At the time this action was commenced, however, Zelezny's Citibank account had a balance of only $69.65. Moreover, because Citibank thereafter deducted certain charges from the account, there is now a balance of only $0.05. . . . For the reasons that follow, Zelezny's motion to dismiss is denied and the petition is granted, but only to the extent of the assets that form the basis for quasi in rem jurisdiction—the $0.05 in the Account. The Court does not have jurisdiction to confirm an award in the amount of $23.35 million; CME may enforce the award only against the assets of $0.05." Incidentally, CME argued that Zelezny "may have other assets in New York. But quasi in rem jurisdiction cannot be based on speculation about the possible existence of other property. . . . Zelezny is not before the Court; only the limited assets in the Account—

$0.05—are before the Court. For these reasons, petitioner's request for discovery to locate other assets in this jurisdiction is denied."

––––––

FEDERAL ACTIONS UNDER 28 U.S.C. § 1655

For in rem and some quasi in rem cases, § 1655 works to authorize territorial jurisdiction. Courts have long held this statute to apply only to a lien or title existing prior to the suit—and not to one created by the institution of the suit itself, as for example through attachment or garnishment. The real or personal property must be present within the district.

A defendant must receive notice sufficient to satisfy procedural due process. There must in addition be subject-matter jurisdiction—ordinarily, diversity of citizenship or a federal question.

If the absent defendant does not appear, the judgment affects only the property that is the subject of the action. The defendant can make the equivalent of a "special appearance" for the purpose of challenging the court's jurisdiction over the property without submitting himself to a personal judgment. Whether he can make a "limited appearance" for the purpose of defending on the merits the claim involving the property without subjecting himself to personal jurisdiction is a question addressed in the upcoming Campbell case. As you know, personal jurisdiction is the ordinary type of territorial jurisdiction, which we shall soon study in depth.

––––––

FEDERAL ACTIONS UNDER RULE 4(n)(2)

For many years there was no provision for commencing an original federal action on the basis of only attachment or garnishment, that is, without personal jurisdiction over the defendant and without a pre-existing lien or title as under § 1655. See Big Vein Coal Co. v. Read, 229 U.S. 31, 33 S.Ct. 694 (1913).[f] The case of Davis v. Ensign-Bickford Co., 139 F.2d 624 (8th Cir.1944), held that Rule 64 did not effect any change, because it deals with security rather than jurisdiction; and Rosenthal v. Frankfort Distillers Corp., 193 F.2d 137 (5th Cir.1951), rejected the contention that Erie required a different result to accord with state law.

In 1963, the federal rulemakers closed the lacuna by amending Rule 4 to allow original quasi in rem and in rem jurisdiction to the extent authorized in the courts of the state where the federal court sits. Of

––––––

[f]   Removal was a different matter. A suit in a state court with attachment or garnishment as the sole basis of territorial jurisdiction was removable if the usual requirements for removal were met. Incidentally, removal by itself is not a general appearance, so the removing defendant lost no rights to special and limited appearances.

course, adequate notice must be given, and jurisdiction over the subject matter must exist.

By a 1993 amendment, the rulemakers limited the use of nonpersonal jurisdiction under Rule 4(n)(2) to circumstances where personal jurisdiction is not available. However, as should eventually become clear to you, this change had a relatively minor effect, really affecting only those few plaintiffs who in their selected federal court had a choice between invoking attachment-variety quasi in rem jurisdiction and invoking personal jurisdiction and who preferred the former.

The amended Rule 4(n)(2) presents its problems of interpretation, but these too should be minor. For example, who has to make the required showing with respect to the unavailability of personal jurisdiction, and by what standard of proof—and how does the scheme work in case of default? Probably the courts will work these problems out by following the usual and soon-to-be-studied practice on personal jurisdiction challenges and showings.

———

Campbell v. Murdock

United States District Court, Northern District of Ohio, 1950.
90 F.Supp. 297.

■ JONES, CHIEF JUDGE. This is an action to foreclose a mechanic's lien on land owned by defendant Murdock and for other relief.

It appears from the complaint that plaintiff expended considerable labor and materials in the improvement of Murdock's land pursuant to a contract between plaintiff and defendant McMahon, the duly authorized agent of Murdock. Plaintiff, even though he has joined McMahon as a party defendant, does not pray for relief as against him.

Plaintiff, Murdock and McMahon are respectively residents of Pennsylvania, South Carolina and Ohio. This Court has jurisdiction because of the diversity of citizenship and the provisions of 28 U.S.C.A. § 1655, formerly 28 U.S.C.A. § 118.

. . . Murdock, appearing specially and for the purpose of challenging this court's jurisdiction moves to dismiss the action against her, in so far as it asks for personal judgment and, appearing solely for the purpose of defending her interest in the property, moves for a more definite statement of the complaint.

. . . .

[Section 1655] provides in actions to enforce liens on property within the district for service on non-resident defendants by personal service where possible or by publication. The defendant is ordered to appear but if he does not, the final judgment can affect only the property which is the subject of the action.

Murdock claims that this section does not authorize a personal judgment against a non-resident defendant who does not make a general appearance, and she appears specially to move to dismiss the action insofar as it asks for personal judgment. The ultimate question to be decided, then, is whether Section 1655 permits personal judgments when jurisdiction is based solely on the fact that the property in controversy is located within the District.

We have been able to find only one case where the question has been squarely presented. In Bede Steam Shipping Co. v. New York Trust Co., 2 Cir., 54 F.2d 658, the court held that the non-resident defendant has but two choices. He could elect not to appear or he could make a general appearance and subject himself to the general jurisdiction of the court on all claims against him. The court specifically held that the defendant could not appear only for the purpose of defending his interest in the property.

This ruling seems reasonable and correct. The statute, it is true, limits the situations in which the court has in rem jurisdiction. But the statute does not prohibit the taking of personal judgments if the defendant appears, and it also provides, if the defendant does not appear, that the court's adjudication shall affect only the property before it. This leaves the inference that if the defendant does appear, the court may try the entire controversy between the parties.

There has been some suggestion that the personal judgment must be limited to such relief as is related to the in rem feature of the action which originally gives the court jurisdiction. The Bede case lends itself to such an interpretation. (See also 2 Cylo.Fed.Pro. 620–621) Even with this limitation a personal judgment may be had in this action. A personal judgment on the debt which gives rise to the lien in this action does not seem so incidental to the foreclosure of the lien as to defeat the jurisdiction of the court under section 1655. It is not necessary to decide what types of personal relief cannot be coupled with the actions listed in 1655, for the personal relief here is too closely related to the in rem feature of this case . . . .

. . . .

In the circumstances, the defendant Murdock's motion to dismiss will be overruled.

The motion for a more definite statement will be granted. It is unopposed and failure to oppose may be taken as implied consent to the court's favorable ruling on the motion.

———

Limited Appearance

A general appearance by the defendant in an action has the effect of waiving any threshold defenses of lack of territorial authority to adjudicate or lack of notice with respect to any currently asserted claims. By contrast, a special appearance is a procedural technique by which the defendant can raise lack of territorial authority to adjudicate or lack of notice without waiving those defenses.

Quasi in rem inherently differs from in rem in that a personal claim against a person is asserted along with the nonpersonal claim. Thus, a general appearance in a quasi in rem action would submit the defendant to personal jurisdiction for that claim against the person. By contrast, a limited appearance, if allowed, is a procedural technique by which the defendant restricts her appearance to defending the nonpersonal claim on the merits without submitting to personal jurisdiction on any personal claim.

Campbell's difficult problem of whether to allow a limited appearance arises in state actions, removed actions, and federal actions under Rule 4(n)(2). See generally I. Daniel Stewart, Jr., Note, Limited Appearances, 7 Utah L.Rev. 369 (1961). In drafting Rule 4(n)(2), the rulemakers decided not to resolve the problem, but instead to remit it to "the molecular process of litigation." Benjamin Kaplan, Amendments of the Federal Rules of Civil Procedure, 1961–63 (I), 77 Harv.L.Rev. 601, 628 (1964).

The Campbell approach seems efficient. But contrast with Campbell the following situation: in state court, plaintiff brings a contract claim against a foreigner not subject to personal jurisdiction, and so bases territorial jurisdiction on the attachment of unrelated property belonging to defendant and worth less than the claim. One leading decision held that defendant on these facts could choose to (1) sacrifice his property by default, (2) make a limited appearance, or (3) enter a general appearance that would convert the jurisdiction to in personam. Cheshire Nat'l Bank v. Jaynes, 224 Mass. 14, 112 N.E. 500 (1916). Here the wider choice seems fair, because the contract claim is unrelated to the attached property. The Campbell decision itself recognized this difference, at its second reference to the Bede precedent.

Putting Cheshire together with Campbell would suggest allowing a limited appearance if but only if it would be unreasonable for the forum to exercise personal jurisdiction with respect to the additional claim concurrently with hearing the nonpersonal action.

Question: (8) Note that the Campbell decision seems to have proceeded on the assumption that federal law governed the limited-appearance question. Some commentators disagree, and they would look instead in the circumstances of that case to state law. See Wright & Miller § 1123. What arguments can you make each way?

In an action commenced on a basis other than personal jurisdiction, the defendant in federal court need not plead any counterclaims that she might happen to have. See Rule 13(a)(2)(B), which was added by amendment in 1963. This apparently holds true even if the defendant makes a general appearance; but if the defendant chooses to assert any of her counterclaims, then the compulsory counterclaim Rule comes back into normal operation.

SECTION 3. JURISDICTION OVER PERSONS—EVOLVING THEORY

(a) PRESENCE AS BASIS FOR JURISDICTION

DARRAH v. WATSON, 36 Iowa 116 (1873). Darrah sued Watson in Iowa upon a judgment of a Virginia state court. Watson contended that the Virginia court had not acquired jurisdiction over him for that prior judgment because, when he had received in-hand service of process in Virginia, he was a citizen and resident of Pennsylvania and was in Virginia only for a few hours on business; and after that service Watson had left Virginia, before rendition of the default judgment against him. The Iowa court held that the Virginia court had acquired jurisdiction over Watson's person, and that the Virginia judgment was therefore entitled to full faith and credit under the Constitution and the laws of the United States.

ENFORCEMENT OF JUDGMENTS IN OTHER STATES

A judgment for the plaintiff (or a judgment for the defendant for costs or on her own counterclaim) may be enforced in the state where it is rendered. In addition, a party with a judgment may wish to enforce it in another state, as did Darrah. But Darrah could not simply request an Iowa sheriff to levy execution on Watson's property in Iowa in order to satisfy the Virginia judgment. The Iowa sheriff would have no authority to do so, and he would be guilty of conversion if he seized the property on bare faith in a Virginia judgment. So what could Darrah do? The traditional way to enforce a judgment in another state has been to bring there an action upon the judgment, with the aim being to obtain a new judgment and then to enforce that new, domestic judgment.

Testing jurisdiction of the judgment-rendering court.—In such an action upon a judgment, the forum court will, on collateral attack as in Darrah v. Watson, inquire into the possible lack of validity of the judgment of the rendering court. If the Iowa court had decided that the Virginia judgment was not valid, it would not have allowed recovery thereon. But the Iowa court could not, and did not, look into the merits of the underlying claim for mere error by the Virginia court.

Some broad generalizations on validity are helpful here. Generally, for a judgment to be valid and hence enforceable, first, the court must have had a sufficient basis for exercising adjudicatory authority over the defendant or other target of the action;[g] second, the persons to be legally affected must have received an opportunity to be heard;[h] and, third, it must have been rendered by a court with subject-matter jurisdiction to render it.[i] So, for example, a personal judgment rendered by a court of a state with no basis for exercising jurisdiction over the defendant is not valid, and this is what Watson was contending.

Question: (9) Do not be led into thinking that such an issue can be raised only on collateral attack. Suppose that in the original action Watson, instead of defaulting, had challenged Virginia's jurisdiction over him. (As we shall see later, the Virginia court would have permitted him to appear specially for the purpose of raising the defense of lack of jurisdiction over his person without submitting himself generally to the jurisdiction of that state.) If the trial court had rejected the challenge and given judgment for Darrah, and the highest court of the state had affirmed, would Watson have a basis for review of the jurisdictional point by the Supreme Court of the United States? What of the argument that it is only the enforcement and not the rendition of the judgment that violates Watson's constitutional rights?

However, the Iowa court did find that the Virginia judgment was valid. It held that in-hand service of process in Virginia had authorized the exercise of jurisdiction over Watson (while also satisfying the demands of procedural due process). The contention of Watson thus being overcome, Iowa had to give the Virginia judgment full faith and credit. Subject only to rare exception, the mandate of the Full Faith and Credit Clause in Article IV, Section 1 of the U.S. Constitution and of its implementing statute at 28 U.S.C. § 1738 is that a state give the same effect to a valid judgment that it has in the state that rendered the judgment.[j] This general principle of retroversion applies to all judgments as between state and federal courts. If the first judgment is from a state court and the second action is in a federal court, § 1738 ("every court within the United States") compels the same result. If the first judgment is from a federal court and the second action is in a state court, the analogous result of looking to the judgment's effect in the rendering court follows because federal law, including the federal common law of full faith and credit, is applicable and binding in the state court under the Supremacy Clause of Article VI. Finally, if both actions are in federal courts, the second court must give like respect to the judgment of the first

---

[g]   The principal concern here has been substantive due process, which permeates the doctrine called territorial jurisdiction, adjudicatory jurisdiction, judicial jurisdiction, nexus, or amenability. This is the main focus of study for this Topic A.

[h]   The principal concern here is procedural due process. We deal with this concern in passing throughout this Topic A and shall give it detailed study in Topic B of this Part. At this stage, the student should make an effort to distinguish the concept of procedural due process from substantive due process.

[i]   Topic C of this Part will treat subject-matter jurisdiction, or competency, expanding on Section 6 of Topic B of Part 1.

[j]   In Mills v. Duryee, 11 U.S. (7 Cranch) 481 (1813), Francis Scott Key, as counsel, contended plausibly that full faith and credit required only that the judgment be weighed along with the evidence, but the Court held that at least the implementing statute required giving it a binding effect.

because both courts are arms of the same sovereign and that sovereign respects res judicata.

In an action upon a nondomestic judgment, the law to be applied by the forum court in determining the validity of the judgment is the law of the judgment-rendering sovereign, but that law is subject to some very real constitutional limitations. Thus, Iowa had to look to Virginia law to see if Virginia had acquired jurisdiction over Watson, and then inquire whether this acquisition had been consistent with the Due Process Clause of the Fourteenth Amendment to the U.S. Constitution.

If valid, the judgment is entitled to "recognition" by the forum court as well as "enforcement." In deciding the range of effects that recognition entails, the forum court must apply the res judicata law that the rendering court would apply, again a law that includes any externally imposed constraints. However, with respect to the method of enforcement, the forum will apply its own law, subject to the requirement that the method not be so complex or expensive as to burden unduly the enforcement of nondomestic judgments.

Acquiring jurisdiction in the judgment-enforcing court.—To bring an action upon a judgment, the plaintiff must satisfy the usual requirements for suit, including acquisition of territorial jurisdiction. The plaintiff with a money judgment could go to where the defendant has any assets and then proceed by quasi in rem jurisdiction of the attachment variety; or when the judgment treats specific property, the plaintiff can go to where the property is and proceed quasi in rem to assert his interest in that property. Alternatively, the plaintiff can go to where personal jurisdiction exists over the defendant and get a fresh personal judgment to enforce; and the enforcement could lead to orders against the defendant personally and enforceable by contempt, such as an order that the defendant turn over assets that might be located anywhere.

There have been attempts to facilitate enforcement of nondomestic judgments by creating alternative methods of enforcement. In 1948, on the federal level, Congress enacted 28 U.S.C. § 1963. This statute dispensed with the necessity of an action upon a judgment by providing for registration of a district-court judgment "for the recovery of money or property" in any other district court, with the effect of automatically making the judgment so registered enforceable like a judgment of the court where it was registered. In addition to saving time and expense, this statute avoids the venue requirement for an action upon the judgment. It avoids as well the jurisdictional problems of an action upon the judgment: no need exists to acquire territorial jurisdiction, and the judgment may be registered even though an action upon the judgment would have failed for lack of subject-matter jurisdiction in the registering court.[k] Finally, it removes the availability of a collateral attack by the

---

[k]   Subject-matter jurisdiction is otherwise a serious concern because an action upon a federal judgment does not arise under the Constitution or laws of the United States, despite the

defendant, who must instead take the initiative to seek any desired relief from the judgment on the ground of invalidity by making a Rule 60(b) motion or instituting an independent action, normally in the rendering court. See Moore §§ 130.31–.35; Wright & Miller § 2787.

Question: (10) Does this registration procedure strike a fair balance between the parties' interests?

The National Conference of Commissioners on Uniform State Laws in 1948 approved a Uniform Enforcement of Foreign Judgments Act providing for registration in the enacting state of federal or sister-state judgments. In 1964 the Commissioners approved a revision that further facilitated enforcement of such judgments by providing a procedure very similar to the federal statute, although the Uniform Act required giving notice of registration to the judgment debtor. The 1964 version has been adopted in almost all states.

———

GRACE v. MacARTHUR, 170 F.Supp. 442 (E.D.Ark.1959). Arkansas citizens brought a diversity action in the Eastern District of Arkansas against three defendants on a claim arising in Arkansas. A marshal served one of the defendants, who was from Tennessee, by handing him the papers on a nonstop flight from Memphis, Tennessee, to Dallas, Texas, at a time when the plane was flying directly over the Eastern District of Arkansas. The defendant moved to quash the service, arguing that at the time of service he was not within the territorial limits of Arkansas as required by the predecessor to Federal Rule 4(k)(1)(A). The motion was denied.

———

WYMAN v. NEWHOUSE, 93 F.2d 313 (2d Cir.1937), cert. denied, 303 U.S. 664, 58 S.Ct. 831 (1938). Mr. N, domiciled in New York, had had meretricious relations over a period of years with Mrs. W, a widow domiciled in Florida. Mrs. W telegraphed, wrote, and telephoned Mr. N stating that her mother was dying in Ireland, that she was leaving the United States to go to her mother and would not return, and that she wanted to see him once more before she left; she added that she loved him and entreated him to come to Florida for a last visit. These statements were essentially false. Upon his arrival at the Miami airport, Mr. N was served in-hand with process in Mrs. W's Florida state-court action for money loaned to him and for seduction under promise of marriage. Mr. N did not appear in the action, and the court entered a judgment against him upon his default.

In the present action upon the Florida judgment in a federal court in New York, Mr. N set up the foregoing matter as a defense. Was the defense valid? The court thought it was. The court indicated that Florida

fact that there was federal-question subject-matter jurisdiction for rendering the judgment in the original action. See Metcalf v. Watertown, 128 U.S. 586, 9 S.Ct. 173 (1888).

law generally governed. The facts showed that Mr. N had been fraudulently enticed into the Florida jurisdiction for the sole purpose of service of process. This made the judgment invalid, and subject to collateral attack, in the state of rendition. But Mr. N did not need to assert his defense of fraud in the Florida action or to attack the judgment in Florida. The judgment was open to collateral attack when sued upon in another jurisdiction. Moreover, in the present action, Mr. N did not need to show that he had a defense on the merits to the Florida action.

———

FRAUD AND FORCE

Restatement (Second) of Conflict of Laws § 82 (Am. Law Inst. 1971) says: "A state will not exercise judicial jurisdiction, which has been obtained by fraud or unlawful force, over a defendant or his property."

Comment f to that section states that this prevailing rule is "not jurisdictional," that is, the rule represents only a self-imposed limitation on the state's exercise of its utmost constitutional powers. Accordingly, if a state instead chooses to exercise judicial jurisdiction in such circumstances involving fraud or unlawful force, other states must honor its choice.

Questions: (11) New York follows the rule of § 82. See, e.g., Terlizzi v. Brodie, 38 A.D.2d 762, 329 N.Y.S.2d 589 (1972) (New Jersey defendants were telephoned at home and falsely told that they had been chosen to receive two Broadway tickets as a promotional venture to get their opinion of the new 7:30 p.m. curtain time; they were served in the theater by the man sitting behind them; motion to vacate service granted). But the prevailing rule, in New York and elsewhere, is that it is permissible to resort to subterfuge in order to serve a person who is voluntarily in the state. See, e.g., Gumperz v. Hofmann, 245 A.D. 622, 283 N.Y.S. 823 (1935), aff'd, 271 N.Y. 544, 2 N.E.2d 687 (1936) (defendant, an Argentine doctor sojourning in a New York City hotel, was telephoned by a process server who falsely represented himself to be a Dr. Goldman with a letter from the president of the New York County Medical Society to be personally delivered; they arranged to meet in the hotel lobby, where service was made; motion to vacate service denied). What difference accounts for the two rules?

(12) It has also been held that service is invalid in the following circumstances. Husband, an attorney, accompanied his wife to a New York dockside, whence she was to sail to California to visit her mother. During an affectionate farewell, he gave her a wrapped box, telling her it contained a present for her mother, but in reality it contained process for a divorce action. She sailed without opening it, and she consequently defaulted. Bulkley v. Bulkley, 6 Abb.Pr. 307 (N.Y.Sup.Ct.1858). How can you reconcile this case with Gumperz?

(13) Prospective defendant is in New York only for settlement negotiations with potential plaintiff. Negotiations break down. Plaintiff continues the conference for a few hours, not to conduct good-faith

negotiations but rather as an artifice to make service on defendant in a New York state-court action by awaiting the arrival of the process server. Now there is a motion to vacate service. What decision?

———

IMMUNITY FROM SERVICE OF PROCESS

The customary doctrine has long been that a nonresident party, witness, or counsel is immune from service of process when present in a state for attendance at litigation and for a reasonable time to go to and fro. The rule has been criticized in its entirety, see, e.g., John Martinez, Discarding Immunity from Service of Process Doctrine, 40 Ohio N.U.L.Rev. 87 (2013), and has been qualified or given restrictive application, see, e.g., Wangler v. Harvey, 41 N.J. 277, 196 A.2d 513 (1963).

Again, the immunity rule is in the nature of a self-imposed limitation, which the state may choose not to adopt. See Restatement (Second) of Conflict of Laws § 83 cmt. b (Am. Law Inst. 1971).

Questions: (14) Are the considerations different as between a witness and a party? as between counsel and party? as between a plaintiff and a defendant?

(15) Should it matter whether the two actions involve related facts? whether the pending action for which the person comes in is criminal or civil? whether presence is for attending trial or some other phase of litigation?

(16) What, if any, effect on the immunity rule should there be if the person who claims immunity is subjectable to personal jurisdiction on some basis other than her presence in the state? (Renew consideration of this question after studying the rest of this Section.)

———

(b) DOMICILE AS BASIS FOR JURISDICTION

MILLIKEN v. MEYER, 311 U.S. 457, 61 S.Ct. 339 (1940). Milliken sued Meyer in a Wyoming state court to recover profits from certain Colorado oil properties. Meyer was domiciled in Wyoming at all relevant times. He received in-hand service of process in Colorado pursuant to a Wyoming statute. He did not appear in the action, and the court rendered judgment against him.

Subsequently Meyer sued Milliken in a Colorado state court to enjoin Milliken from enforcing the Wyoming judgment and to obtain a decree that the Wyoming judgment was invalid for want of jurisdiction over Meyer. Milliken appeared and defended. The Colorado Supreme Court eventually granted Meyer relief. On certiorari, the Supreme Court of the United States reversed, holding that the Wyoming judgment was valid and entitled to full faith and credit in Colorado. The unanimous Court, by Justice Douglas, said: "Domicile in the state is alone sufficient to bring an absent defendant within the reach of the state's jurisdiction for purposes of a personal judgment by means of appropriate substituted service."

The Court first discussed notice: "Substituted service in such cases has been quite uniformly upheld where the absent defendant was served at his usual place of abode in the state [citations omitted] as well as where he was personally served without the state. [Citation omitted.] That such substituted service may be wholly adequate to meet the requirements of due process was recognized by this Court in McDonald v. Mabee, 243 U.S. 90, 37 S.Ct. 343,[1] despite earlier intimations to the contrary. See Pennoyer v. Neff, 95 U.S. 714, 733; [other citation omitted]. Its adequacy so far as due process is concerned is dependent on whether or not the form of the substituted service provided for such case and employed is reasonably calculated to give him actual notice of the proceedings and an opportunity to be heard. If it is, the traditional notions of fair play and substantial justice (McDonald v. Mabee, supra) implicit in due process are satisfied. Here there can be no question on that score."

The Court then addressed nexus: "Certainly then Meyer's domicile in Wyoming was a sufficient basis for that extraterritorial service. As in case of the authority of the United States over its absent citizens (Blackmer v. United States, 284 U.S. 421, 52 S.Ct. 252), the authority of a state over one of its citizens is not terminated by the mere fact of his absence from the state. The state which accords him privileges and affords protection to him and his property by virtue of his domicile may also exact reciprocal duties."

EXTENDING THE BASIS

The old common law generally did not recognize domicile as a basis for personal jurisdiction, and state courts have therefore usually held that they cannot exercise jurisdiction on this basis unless authorized to do so by the legislature. See, e.g., Duncan v. McDonough, 105 N.H. 308, 199 A.2d 104 (1964). But again, if a state's courts were authoritatively to decide that such statutory authorization was unnecessary, their judgments on this basis would be entitled to full faith and credit.

Note that domicile, like physical presence, can act as a basis of personal jurisdiction for any claim against the defendant. There is no

---

[1]   This 1917 case is much cited, chiefly for the statement of Justice Holmes: "The foundation of jurisdiction is physical power . . . ." It held that service by publication, if "substituted" for personal delivery of notice, would not yield a valid personal judgment against a person who, although technically domiciled in the state, had left it intending to establish his home elsewhere. The Court apparently believed that the notice, and not necessarily the nexus, was fatally defective. In this connection, Justice Holmes for the Court said: "To dispense with personal service the substitute that is most likely to reach the defendant is the least that ought to be required if substantial justice is to be done."

requirement of relatedness of the claim to the state. Perhaps, then, the legislatures and the courts should act with restraint in extending this sort of "general" jurisdiction.

Questions: (17) What if the defendant was a domiciliary of the forum state when the claim arose and when the action was commenced, but ceased to be before service was made? See Allen v. Superior Court, 41 Cal.2d 306, 259 P.2d 905 (1953) (jurisdiction exists pursuant to statute, for claim arising in state).

(18) What if the defendant was a domiciliary when the claim arose, but ceased to be before the action was commenced and service was made? See Owens v. Superior Court, 52 Cal.2d 822, 345 P.2d 921 (1959) (jurisdiction exists pursuant to statute, for claim arising in state).

(19) What if, at all relevant times, the defendant was a resident but not a domiciliary?

————

(c) CONSENT AS BASIS FOR JURISDICTION

Consent to personal jurisdiction for an action before the action is brought is generally effective. It typically comes as part of a contract the breach of which is the subject of the action.[m]

A defendant may also effectively consent to personal jurisdiction after the action is brought. This may be done by accepting or waiving service, even though he would not otherwise be subject to personal jurisdiction and even though he is physically outside the state when he does the acts constituting the acceptance or waiver.[n] Or the defendant may confer jurisdiction over the person by the entry of a general appearance in the action, doing so in person or by his authorized attorney.

Question: (20) What other action by the defendant or his authorized attorney would be effective in a federal court to confer jurisdiction over his person?

————

HESS v. PAWLOSKI, 274 U.S. 352, 47 S.Ct. 632 (1927). In 1923 Massachusetts enacted a statute, the material parts of which were these:

---

[m]   Sometimes such consent poses serious problems—turning in part on whether the defendant voluntarily, intelligently, and knowingly consented—but we reserve these problems for consideration in Topic B of this Part.

[n]   There may be a question of interpretation whether the defendant has consented to something or has merely admitted that process has been served upon him. For instance, if he writes on the summons, "I acknowledge that this summons was handed to me in State Y," this is not a consent to personal jurisdiction in an action commenced in State X. In contrast, if he writes, "I acknowledge due and personal service of this summons upon me and waive further service upon me," this is such a consent. See Restatement (Second) of Conflict of Laws § 32 cmt. d, illus. 7–8 (Am. Law Inst. 1971). Given consent, another level of distinction exists between consenting to personal jurisdiction and merely agreeing not to contest the form of summons or the manner of transmitting notice.

"[T]he operation by a non-resident of a motor vehicle on a public way in the commonwealth . . . shall be deemed equivalent to an appointment by such non-resident of the registrar [of motor vehicles], or his successor in office, to be his true and lawful attorney upon whom may be served all lawful processes in any action or proceeding against him, growing out of any accident or collision in which said non-resident may be involved while operating a motor vehicle on such a way, and said . . . operation shall be a signification of his agreement that any such process against him which is so served shall be of the same legal force and validity as if served on him personally. Service of such process shall be made by leaving a copy of the process with a fee of two dollars in the hands of the registrar, or in his office, and such service shall be sufficient service upon the said non-resident; provided, that notice of such service and a copy of the process are forthwith sent by registered mail by the plaintiff to the defendant, and the defendant's return receipt and the plaintiff's affidavit of compliance herewith are appended to the [summons] and entered with the [complaint]. The court in which the action is pending may order such continuances as may be necessary to afford the defendant reasonable opportunity to defend the action."

In a later lawsuit, the Pennsylvania defendant challenged, as violative of due process, service made in compliance with this statute. The Supreme Judicial Court of Massachusetts held the statute to be a valid exercise of the state's police power. On writ of error the Supreme Court of the United States affirmed unanimously. After citing Pennoyer v. Neff, McDonald v. Mabee, and other decisions, Justice Butler for the Court continued:

"Motor vehicles are dangerous machines; and, even when skillfully and carefully operated, their use is attended by serious dangers to persons and property. In the public interest the State may make and enforce regulations reasonably calculated to promote care on the part of all, residents and non-residents alike, who use its highways. The measure in question operates to require a non-resident to answer for his conduct in the State where arise causes of action alleged against him, as well as to provide for a claimant a convenient method by which he may sue to enforce his rights. Under the statute the implied consent is limited to proceedings growing out of accidents or collisions on a highway in which the non-resident may be involved. It is required that he shall actually receive and receipt for notice of the service and a copy of the process. And it contemplates such continuances as may be found necessary to give reasonable time and opportunity for defense. It makes no hostile discrimination against non-residents but tends to put them on the same footing as residents. Literal and precise equality in respect of this matter is not attainable; it is not required. Canadian Northern Ry. Co. v. Eggen, 252 U.S. 553, 561–562, 40 S.Ct. 402. The State's power to regulate the use of its highways extends to their use by non-residents as well as by residents. Hendrick v. Maryland, 235 U.S. 610, 622, 35 S.Ct.

140. And, in advance of the operation of a motor vehicle on its highway by a non-resident, the State may require him to appoint one of its officials as his agent on whom process may be served in proceedings growing out of such use. Kane v. New Jersey, 242 U.S. 160, 167, 37 S.Ct. 30.° That case recognizes power of the State to exclude a non-resident until the formal appointment is made. And, having the power so to exclude, the State may declare that the use of the highway by the non-resident is the equivalent of the appointment of the registrar as agent on whom process may be served. [Citations omitted.] The difference between the formal and implied appointment is not substantial so far as concerns the application of the due process clause of the Fourteenth Amendment."

————

Questions: (21) Suppose Massachusetts amended the statute in Hess v. Pawloski so that, instead of calling for service of process upon a public official within the state and for notice by registered mail to the defendant, it required only service by registered mail to the out-of-state defendant. Would that statute be constitutional?

(22) Suppose Massachusetts amended the statute in Hess v. Pawloski by changing the operative words "on a public way in the commonwealth" to "within the commonwealth." Would it be valid as applied to a nonresident involved in an accident on private property? See Sipe v. Moyers, 353 Pa. 75, 44 A.2d 263 (1945) (yes). Why?

————

FLEXNER v. FARSON, 248 U.S. 289, 39 S.Ct. 97 (1919). In Jefferson County, Kentucky, Bernard Flexner entered into a contract to purchase bonds from Farson, Son & Company, a partnership engaged in the business of trading in securities; one Washington Flexner acted as the agent of the partnership during the negotiations. Bernard Flexner, seemingly an older brother, later commenced suit in a Kentucky state court against the individual partners for breach of the contract. The partners being domiciled and residing outside Kentucky, he made service in Jefferson County upon Washington Flexner as their agent, in attempted compliance with the following Kentucky statute: "In actions against an individual residing in another state, or a partnership, association, or joint stock company, the members of which reside in another state, engaged in business in this state, the summons may be served on the manager, or agent of, or person in charge of, such business in this state, in the county where the business is carried on, or in the county where the cause of action occurred." Defendants defaulted, and plaintiff obtained a money judgment.

° In this 1916 case, the New Jersey statute required a nonresident motorist before driving in the state to file a document appointing the N.J. secretary of state as his agent for service of process in proceedings arising out of his driving within the state. The statute was enacted in 1908, so one need not visualize traffic on the New Jersey Turnpike.

In an action upon the judgment against one of the partners in an Illinois state court, the defendant partner urged that the Kentucky judgment was invalid for want of jurisdiction over the partners' persons. The plaintiff argued that the quoted statute had been implicitly incorporated into the contract and that the partners had thereby effectively consented to service in actions arising from business conducted in Kentucky. The Illinois courts denied effect to the Kentucky judgment. On writ of error the Supreme Court of the United States affirmed unanimously. The entire legal discussion in the opinion by Justice Holmes for the Court follows:

"It is argued that the pleas tacitly admit that Washington Flexner was agent of the firm at the time of the transaction sued upon in Kentucky,[p] and the Kentucky statute is construed as purporting to make him agent to receive service in suits arising out of the business done in that State. On this construction it is said that the defendants by doing business in the State consented to be bound by the service prescribed. The analogy of suits against insurance companies based upon such service is invoked. Mutual Reserve Fund Life Association v. Phelps, 190 U.S. 147, 23 S.Ct. 707. But the consent that is said to be implied in such cases is a mere fiction, founded upon the accepted doctrine that the States could exclude foreign corporations altogether, and therefore could establish this obligation as a condition to letting them in. Lafayette Ins. Co. v. French, 18 How. 404. Pennsylvania Fire Ins. Co. v. Gold Issue Mining & Milling Co., 243 U.S. 93, 96, 37 S.Ct. 344. The State had no power to exclude the defendants[q] and on that ground without going farther the Supreme Court of Illinois rightly held that the analogy failed, and that the Kentucky judgment was void. If the Kentucky statute purports to have the effect attributed to it, it cannot have that effect in the present case. New York Life Ins. Co. v. Dunlevy, 241 U.S. 518, 522, 523, 36 S.Ct. 613."

――――――

(d) ACTS AS BASIS FOR JURISDICTION

HENRY L. DOHERTY & CO. v. GOODMAN, 294 U.S. 623, 55 S.Ct. 553 (1935). In Des Moines, Iowa, Goodman entered into a contract to

――――――

[p]   Plaintiff alleged in the Illinois action that Washington Flexner was the partners' agent at the time of the transaction of sale and at the time of the service upon him in the Kentucky action. The defendant partner's plea, to which plaintiff demurred, alleged that Washington Flexner was not their agent at the time of the service, but did not allege that Washington Flexner was not their agent at the time of the transaction.

[q]   The Court in Hess v. Pawloski elaborated the distinction between nonresident individuals (like Farson) and foreign corporations (like those insurance companies), by explaining that a state's constitutional power to exclude from doing intrastate business is lesser for individuals than for corporations because the Privileges and Immunities Clause of Article IV, Section 2 applies to individuals but not to corporations. The Hess Court summarized and distinguished the holding of the earlier Flexner v. Farson thus: "The mere transaction of business in a state by nonresident natural persons does not imply consent to be bound by the process of its courts."

purchase stock from Henry L. Doherty, a major financier engaged in the securities business and trading under the name and style of Henry L. Doherty & Company; a salesman operating from the defendant's Des Moines office negotiated the sales contract. Goodman later brought suit in an Iowa state court against Mr. Doherty for damages arising out of the contract. Doherty being a citizen and resident of New York, service was made on King, the district manager in charge of the Des Moines office, in attempted compliance with Iowa Code § 11079 (in effect since 1851), which provided: "When a corporation, company, or individual has, for the transaction of any business, an office or agency in any county other than that in which the principal resides, service may be made on any agent or clerk employed in such office or agency, in all actions growing out of or connected with the business of that office or agency."

Doherty appeared specially and challenged on constitutional grounds the jurisdiction over his person. The Iowa court upheld the service, and Doherty made no further defense. The Iowa Supreme Court affirmed, pointing out that the statute did not violate the Privileges and Immunities Clause because it applied equally to residents of other counties in Iowa and to nonresidents of Iowa. On appeal the Supreme Court of the United States affirmed. Justice McReynolds for the unanimous Court said in part:

"Iowa treats the business of dealing in corporate securities as exceptional and subjects it to special regulation. Laws 1913, c. 137; Laws 1921, c. 189; Laws 1929, c. 10, approved Mar. 19, 1929. . . . Doherty voluntarily established an office in Iowa and there carried on this business. Considering this fact, and accepting the construction given to § 11079, we think to apply it as here proposed will not deprive him of any right guaranteed by the Federal Constitution.

"Flexner v. Farson, 248 U.S. 289, 39 S.Ct. 97, much relied upon, does not sustain appellant's position. There the service was made upon one not then agent for the defendants; here the situation is different. King was manager of the appellant's office when the sale contract was made; also when process was served upon him. Moreover, under the laws of Iowa, neither her citizens nor non-residents could freely engage in the business of selling securities.

"The power of the States to impose terms upon non-residents, as to activities within their borders, recently has been much discussed. Hess v. Pawloski, 274 U.S. 352, 47 S.Ct. 632; Wuchter v. Pizzutti, 276 U.S. 13, 48 S.Ct. 259; Young v. Masci, 289 U.S. 253, 53 S.Ct. 599. Under these opinions it is established doctrine that a State may rightly direct that non-residents who operate automobiles on her highways shall be deemed to have appointed the Secretary of State as agent to accept service of process, provided there is some 'provision making it reasonably probable that notice of the service on the Secretary will be communicated to the non-resident defendant who is sued.'

"So far as it affects appellant, the questioned statute goes no farther than the principle approved by those opinions permits. Only rights claimed upon the present record are determined. The limitations of § 11079 under different circumstances we do not consider."

––––––––

Question: (23) What vitality remained in Flexner v. Farson after the decision in the Doherty case?

––––––––

ADAM v. SAENGER, 303 U.S. 59, 58 S.Ct. 454 (1938). *X* brought an action against *Y* in a California state court for goods sold and delivered. *X* had no connection with California other than institution of the action against *Y*. In accordance with the California Code of Civil Procedure, *Y* chose to bring a permissive "cross-action" against *X*, alleging conversion by repossession of the goods in dispute and serving the "cross-complaint" upon *X*'s attorney of record in the pending action. Judgment in the cross-action went by default against *X*; subsequently the court dismissed the main action by *X* for want of prosecution.

Y then brought an action in a Texas state court to enforce his judgment. The Texas court dismissed, holding that the California judgment was invalid because California had not acquired jurisdiction over *X* for the purposes of the cross-action. Appeal within the state system resulted in the dismissal's affirmance. On certiorari the United States Supreme Court reversed without dissent. Justice Stone for the Court said on the jurisdictional point:

"There is nothing in the Fourteenth Amendment to prevent a state from adopting a procedure by which a judgment in personam may be rendered in a cross-action against a plaintiff in its courts, upon service of process or of appropriate pleading upon his attorney of record. The plaintiff having, by his voluntary act in demanding justice from the defendant, submitted himself to the jurisdiction of the court, there is nothing arbitrary or unreasonable in treating him as being there for all purposes for which justice to the defendant requires his presence. It is the price which the state may exact as the condition of opening its courts to the plaintiff."

––––––––

Questions: (24) Why would physical presence, as a basis for personal jurisdiction, not suffice to reach the Adam v. Saenger holding?

(25) *P-1* and *P-2* bring an action against *D* in a court of State *A*, which has rules concerning counterclaims and crossclaims identical with those found in the Federal Rules. *D* asserts a permissive counterclaim against *P-1*. Is there then jurisdiction over *P-1*? *P-1* next brings a crossclaim, arising out of the transaction that is the subject matter of the counterclaim, against *P-2*. *P-2* has no connection with State *A* other than her institution of the

action against *D*. Is there jurisdiction over *P-2* for the purposes of the crossclaim?

———

APPEARANCE AS DEFENDANT

If the defendant does not want to submit to personal jurisdiction, he plainly would not enter, or authorize his attorney to enter, a general appearance. If he is confident that jurisdiction over his person is lacking, he may, in theory at least, simply ignore the lawsuit entirely. Here is an illustration. Seeking money damages, *P* commences an action against *D* in a court of State *X* for an alleged tort committed by *D* in State *Y*. *D* resides in State *Y*, and he has never set foot in nor had any other connection with State *X*. *P* delivers process to *D* in State *Y*. In short, State *X* has not acquired jurisdiction over *D*'s person. If the court enters judgment against *D* upon his default, and *P* attempts to enforce the judgment in State *Y* or elsewhere, it is generally thought that *D* can set up the lack of jurisdiction in a collateral attack.

But *D* may wish to contest State *X*'s jurisdiction over his person in the original action. He may be in genuine doubt whether State *X* has acquired jurisdiction over him, or he may not relish the prospect of an overhanging judgment against him even though he is convinced it is invalid. And note that if *D* chooses to stay away, he may on collateral attack argue only the invalidity of the default judgment (defective competency, nexus, or notice), not the merits of the underlying claim. So, intuition suggests that, instead of staying away, *D* may come into the original action to challenge the jurisdiction. In doing so, what procedural problems might he encounter?

A state apparently, at least under hoary case law, has the power to treat *any* appearance by the defendant or his authorized attorney as a conferral of jurisdiction over his person. On this idea, a Texas statute built a particularly cruel trapdoor, which was not dismantled until fairly recently. Under the statute, an appearance carefully denominated as special for the purpose of challenging the jurisdiction would nevertheless constitute a submission to the jurisdiction and thus nullify what might have been a perfectly good objection to the jurisdiction. If the defendant had instead stayed away, he could have challenged the judgment as invalid for lack of jurisdiction when the plaintiff sought to enforce it in Texas or elsewhere; but a special appearance would remove this option. Accordingly, in a Texas action the defendant had to choose between (1) coming in and fighting the action on the merits and (2) staying away entirely and later challenging personal jurisdiction. The Supreme Court refused to hold that the state's imposition of this dilemma violated the Fourteenth Amendment. York v. Texas, 137 U.S. 15, 11 S.Ct. 9 (1890).

Despite the acquiescence of the Supreme Court, the Texas approach found little favor in other states.[r] The other states permitted the device of a special appearance. The defendant, at the outset, would file a notice that he was appearing solely for the purpose of challenging the jurisdiction and not submitting generally to the jurisdiction. Moreover, he had to be careful to take no action looking like a general appearance, for the court might well treat such action as evidence of waiver.[s] The details of state practice in making jurisdictional objections varied widely, and still do. Costly and even irretrievable mistakes may result from failure to master local procedure.

Under the Federal Rules and the numerous state rules patterned upon them, there is no provision for a so-called special appearance. But the rules achieve a similar result. See Rule 12(b)(2) (using "personal" broadly to mean "territorial"); see also Rule 12(b)(3) (covering venue), 12(b)(4) (covering defects in the form of summons), and 12(b)(5) (covering defects in the manner of transmitting notice). A defendant may raise a jurisdictional defense by including it in a motion in advance of answer or by including it in his answer along with all other defenses and objections. As Judge Maris said in Orange Theatre Corp. v. Rayherstz Amusement Corp., 139 F.2d 871, 874 (3d Cir.1944): "He is no longer required at the door of the federal courthouse to intone that ancient abracadabra of the law, de bene esse,[t] in order by its magic power to enable himself to remain outside even while he steps within." This is not, of course, to say that a defendant may not still waive a jurisdictional defense by failure to present it in timely fashion. See Rule 12(g) and (h).

Questions: (26) *P* sues *D* in federal district court. *D* moves successfully under Rule 6(b)(1) for an extension of time to answer or move before the original time expired, and then within the extended time *D* moves to dismiss under Rule 12(b)(2). Has *D* waived this jurisdictional defense?

(27) *P* sues *D* in federal district court to enjoin appropriation of trade secrets and to recover damages. *P* moves for a preliminary injunction. *D* participates in four days of contested hearings on this motion. *D* then files a motion to dismiss under Rule 12(b)(2), within the time prescribed by Rule 12(a). *P* argues that participation in the hearing on the preliminary injunction waived this jurisdictional defense. Should this argument prevail? See Wyrough & Loser, Inc. v. Pelmor Labs., 376 F.2d 543 (3d Cir.1967) (yes).

---

[r]   Texas abrogated its statute in 1962, doing so by Tex.R.Civ.P. 120a. Mississippi, the only other state to build that trapdoor, has since given it up, doing so in Mladinich v. Kohn, 250 Miss. 138, 164 So.2d 785 (1964).

[s]   An ironic example lies in Jackson v. National Grange Mutual Liability Co., 299 N.Y. 333, 87 N.E.2d 283 (1949), where the defendant urged both lack of jurisdiction over his person and lack of jurisdiction over the subject matter. The court held that the challenge to subject-matter jurisdiction, which was unsuccessful, constituted a waiver of the challenge to personal jurisdiction, which would have been good. New York undid this result by statute two years later, but some states might still adhere to it.

[t]   The reference was to a practice peculiar to the courts of Pennsylvania. "The legitimate purpose of the appearance de bene esse is to enable the defendant to deny the jurisdiction of the court without submitting to it." 1 Standard Pennsylvania Practice 410 (1935).

Thus, a special appearance or a Rule 12(b) defense enables the defendant to circumvent the dilemma involved in York v. Texas. But there may be another dilemma lurking down the road. Suppose the defendant has properly challenged personal jurisdiction in the original action, but the court has overruled his challenge. If he then defends on the merits, does he waive his right to renew the jurisdictional challenge on appeal?

On the one hand, a few states have answered this question in the affirmative. Unless such a state permits an interlocutory appeal, a defendant faces a hard choice between (1) defending on the merits and thereby forgoing any appeal as to personal jurisdiction and (2) standing on his jurisdictional objection alone, submitting to an adverse judgment that forecloses the merits, and then appealing the jurisdictional ruling. It appears that a state's imposition of this dilemma does not offend due process. See W. Life Indem. Co. v. Rupp, 235 U.S. 261, 35 S.Ct. 37 (1914). In justification of this approach, it has been said that a defendant who insists he is not properly before the court should not be able to do anything inconsistent with his contention. Moreover, allowing a defense on the merits to be followed by reversal for lack of personal jurisdiction upon the defendant's appeal from a final decision, an appeal that comes after much time and litigation have elapsed, could work severe hardship on the plaintiff.

On the other hand, the federal courts and most states have removed this dilemma as well. They allow the defendant to challenge the jurisdiction, defend on the merits, and then appeal the adverse decisions on the jurisdiction and on the merits. Thus, the dominant American rule is the quite pro-defendant one prescribed for the federal courts in Harkness v. Hyde, 98 U.S. 476, 479 (1879): "The right of the defendant to insist upon the objection to the illegality of the service was not waived by the special appearance of counsel for him to move the dismissal of the action on that ground, or what we consider as intended, that the service be set aside; nor, when that motion was overruled, by their answering for him to the merits of the action. Illegality in a proceeding by which jurisdiction is to be obtained is in no case waived by the appearance of the defendant for the purpose of calling the attention of the court to such irregularity; nor is the objection waived when being urged it is overruled, and the defendant is thereby compelled to answer. He is not considered as abandoning his objection because he does not submit to further proceedings without contestation. It is only where he pleads to the merits in the first instance, without insisting upon the illegality, that the objection is deemed to be waived."

Question: (28) *P* sues *D* in federal district court. *D* moves to dismiss under Rule 12(b)(2), but the trial court overrules his challenge. *D* then answers, including a counterclaim for which there is independent subject-matter jurisdiction. Claim and counterclaim are litigated and decided.

(a) If *D* loses on the main claim, may he on appeal from that judgment still assert lack of jurisdiction over his person or has he waived the jurisdictional defense? Does it matter whether the counterclaim was compulsory or permissive?

(b) In the case law, asserting a permissive counterclaim bestows jurisdiction over the defendant. Indeed, most courts rule that litigating a compulsory counterclaim will defeat any appeal by the defendant grounded on lack of personal jurisdiction, even though that puts the defendant in a new dilemma. If *D* is in one of the minority of courts that do allow appellate review on the jurisdictional defense and if the appellate court reversed the judgment on the main claim for lack of jurisdiction, what consequence if any should this have for the judgment on a compulsory counterclaim? Does it matter whether *D* won or lost on the counterclaim? See Dragor Shipping Corp. v. Union Tank Car Co., 378 F.2d 241 (9th Cir.1967).

In summary, just as intuition probably suggested, the defendant usually has a choice today between (1) coming into the original action to challenge personal jurisdiction as well as the merits and (2) staying away to await raising the jurisdictional point on collateral attack. But he cannot raise jurisdiction both ways. If he loses his challenge in the original action and fails to upset the result by appeal, then the doctrine of res judicata will preclude his relitigating the point on collateral attack. This rule is further explored in Topic E of Part 4.

Question: (29) *P* brings an automobile-accident action against *D-1* and *D-2* in a court of State *A*, which has rules concerning crossclaims identical with those found in the Federal Rules. *D-2* makes a general appearance. *D-1* then appears, and she brings a crossclaim within Rule 13(g) against *D-2*. *D-2* has no connection with State *A* other than his general appearance in *P*'s action against him. Is there jurisdiction over *D-2* for the purposes of the crossclaim? What if *D-1* joined an unrelated claim against *D-2* under Rule 18(a)? See Restatement (Second) of Judgments § 9 (Am. Law Inst. 1982) (building on the rationale for curtailing limited appearances, and providing that a state has power over anyone who has appeared as a party in a pending action in a court of the state and that it can exercise this power with respect to an additional claim related to the original action unless determining it concurrently would be unreasonable).

———

DUBIN v. CITY OF PHILADELPHIA, 34 Pa.D. & C. 61 (C.P.1939). A Pennsylvania statute provided that a nonresident owner or user of real estate and the footways and curbs adjacent thereto, by the ownership and use thereof, made the Secretary of the Commonwealth the nonresident's agent for service of process in any civil action arising out of any accident or injury involving such real estate, footways, or curbs. In addition to the service upon the Secretary, there was a provision for registered-mail notice to the defendant at its last known address.

The plaintiff sued in a Pennsylvania court for injuries from a fall on a broken sidewalk in Philadelphia. The owner of the abutting property was served in accordance with the statute. That owner, who lived in New Jersey, appeared specially to challenge on constitutional grounds the jurisdiction over her person. Presiding Judge Bok said that the statute created "another exception to the rule of personal service in personal actions" and was "a reasonable procedural requirement of a nonresident" who elected to own real estate in Pennsylvania. He therefore held it constitutional.

———

HESS v. PAWLOSKI, 274 U.S. 352, 47 S.Ct. 632 (1927). The Hess case was included in the preceding Subsection because the Massachusetts legislature drew the statute in terms of implied consent. This transparent fiction was a useful first step in escaping the rigors of Pennoyer, but it proved troublesome in other contexts. For instance, some cases held that "consent" to suit in a state under a nonresident motorist statute was a waiver of objection to improper venue in the local federal court. (This was before Congress amended the general venue statute to make the district in which the claim arose a proper venue.) Finally, in Olberding v. Illinois Central Railroad Co., 346 U.S. 338, 340–41, 74 S.Ct. 83, 85 (1953), Justice Frankfurter, observing that this venue problem "is a horse soon curried,"[u] put the fiction to rest in these words:

"It is true that in order to ease the process by which new decisions are fitted into pre-existing modes of analysis there has been some fictive talk to the effect that the reason why a non-resident can be subjected to a state's jurisdiction is that the non-resident has 'impliedly' consented to be sued there. In point of fact, however, jurisdiction in these cases does not rest on consent at all. See Scott, Jurisdiction over Nonresident Motorists, 39 Harv.L.Rev. 563. The defendant may protest to high heaven his unwillingness to be sued and it avails him not. The liability rests on the inroad which the automobile has made on the decision of Pennoyer v. Neff, 95 U.S. 714, as it has on so many aspects of our social scene. The potentialities of damage by a motorist, in a population as mobile as ours, are such that those whom he injures must have opportunities of redress against him provided only that he is afforded an opportunity to defend himself.... But to conclude from [Hess v. Pawloski] that the motorist, who never consented to anything and whose consent is altogether immaterial, has actually agreed to be sued and has thus waived his federal venue rights is surely to move in the world of Alice in Wonderland."

———

[u]   For a metric comment on Justice Frankfurter's fondness for unusual words and phrases, see Richard H. Field, Frankfurter, J., Concurring . . . , 71 Harv.L.Rev. 77 (1957).

(e) Jurisdiction over Corporations

Domestic Corporations: Suing Them in the Place of Incorporation

Having examined four bases of personal jurisdiction, we now consider how these bases translate into the corporate setting. To begin, we are talking about jurisdiction over the corporate entity. This differs from jurisdiction over its officials and workers, as the Supreme Court made clear in Riverside & Dan River Cotton Mills v. Menefee, 237 U.S. 189, 35 S.Ct. 579 (1915).

Menefee, a citizen of North Carolina, sued defendant, a Virginia corporation, in a North Carolina state court for injuries sustained while working as defendant's employee in its Virginia cotton mill. Defendant had never transacted any business in North Carolina and had no property there. In-hand service was made in North Carolina on one of defendant's directors, who resided in North Carolina but had never transacted any business in that state for defendant. The North Carolina state courts overruled the corporation's challenge to the propriety of the jurisdiction. On writ of error the U.S. Supreme Court reversed, holding that any judgment against the corporation based on such service entailed a denial of substantive due process. (Incidentally, the Court expressly rejected the argument that it was only the enforcement of judgment, and not the exercise of jurisdiction to render judgment, that would violate the Due Process Clause.)

Instead, Menefee should have gone to the corporation's Virginia home to sue. Jurisdiction always exists over a domestic corporation. Incorporation in a state gives that state a basis for the exercise of jurisdiction over the corporation in any action brought against it there, regardless of where the claim arose. This basis of jurisdiction thus assures that there is always a place at which a corporation is amenable to suit. (Procedural due process requires, of course, employing an adequate method to give the corporation notice of the action.)

Foreign Corporations: Background of the International Shoe Case

Introduction.—Originally no action looking to a personal judgment lay against a corporation outside the place of its incorporation—unless, perhaps, the corporation actually consented. The notion on which this doctrine went appears from Chief Justice Taney's statement in Bank of Augusta v. Earle, 38 U.S. (13 Pet.) 519, 588 (1839): "It is very true that a corporation can have no legal existence out of the boundaries of the sovereignty by which it is created." But bear in mind that back then corporations were very few and primarily localized in operation. Subsequently, corporate activities steadily increased and broadened because of the many advantages of the corporate form. Meanwhile, public and judicial attitudes toward nondomestic corporations oscillated between favor and disfavor, causing an ebb and flow in the law of jurisdiction over corporations.

Actual consent.—Taney's restrictive doctrine failed to meet evolving needs and protectionist attitudes, and so courts had to overcome it. They first managed this in the nineteenth century by manipulating the idea of "consent." If a state could exclude a foreign corporation from doing local, as distinguished from interstate, business in the state, why could it not authorize the foreign corporation to do local business on the condition that the corporation explicitly consent to personal jurisdiction in the courts of the state? This device worked, *and still works at the present time*, like this: if the state requires the foreign corporation doing local business in the state to appoint an agent upon whom service of process may be made or to suffer consequences, and if the corporation does appoint such an agent, this consent provides a basis for the state's rendering valid personal judgments against the corporation. The consent is no less effective because somewhat coerced. Nor is it material that the agent so appointed is a public official, such as the Secretary of State or Commissioner of Corporations, as long as the corporation itself receives due process notice of the lawsuit. As an example, N.Y.Bus.Corp.Law § 1301(b) defines the trigger of local business by the corporation as being more than such activities as merely conducting litigation, holding directors or shareholders meetings, maintaining bank accounts, or maintaining offices or agencies for transferring or holding its securities in New York.

Fictitious consent.—The foreign corporation might refuse to signify its consent in an explicit manner, however. The next step was to provide statutorily that if the foreign corporation did local business within the state, plaintiffs might bring personal actions against it, by service of process in a prescribed manner, irrespective of any explicit indication of consent. The cases held that this provided a basis for the state's assuming jurisdiction. Thus the consent idea became attenuated. Suppose now that the foreign corporation in question was doing only interstate business in the state. The cases held that jurisdiction existed for actions growing out of that business done in the state. Here the courts were pushing the implied consent fiction to the breaking point, for the state did not have the constitutional power to exclude the corporation from doing interstate business within the state. Reconsider Flexner v. Farson.

Corporate presence.—In the face of these difficulties, courts formulated a nominally different idea, that of corporate "presence." In Philadelphia & Reading Railway Co. v. McKibbin, 243 U.S. 264, 265, 37 S.Ct. 280, 280 (1917), Justice Brandeis for the Court said: "A foreign corporation is amenable to process to enforce a personal liability, in the absence of consent, only if it is doing business within the State in such manner and to such extent as to warrant the inference that it is present there." Again, this theory presented the promise of providing nexus. But yet again, fiction had its costs.

General jurisdiction.—What about claims unrelated to the out-of-state corporation's ties to the state? For fictitious consent and corporate presence, the cases did not clearly answer the question of how far a foreign corporation doing business in a state would be subject, in the absence of explicit and complete consent, to personal actions on claims not arising from business done in the state. On the one hand, courts frequently cited Old Wayne Mutual Life Ass'n v. McDonough, 204 U.S. 8, 27 S.Ct. 236 (1907), and Simon v. Southern Railway Co., 236 U.S. 115, 35 S.Ct. 255 (1915), for the proposition that it was not constitutionally permissible for the courts of a state to hold a foreign corporation amenable to suit, without its actual consent, on a claim unconnected with the business done in the state. Both of these cases involved statutes providing that if a foreign corporation doing some business in the state failed to designate an agent for service of process, service might be made upon a public official. In each case, no designation of an agent having been made, the Court held service upon a public official insufficient to subject the corporation to suit on a claim arising elsewhere. However, it was not wholly clear whether the decisions turned upon statutory interpretation or constitutional power. Moreover, mention was made in both cases of the fact that no notice to the corporation was required or given. On the other hand, Tauza v. Susquehanna Coal Co., 220 N.Y. 259, 115 N.E. 915 (1917) (Cardozo, J.), as well as some U.S. Supreme Court cases, tended to affirm a state's authority over a foreign corporation doing business in the state, even as to a claim unconnected with that business, if service of process was made anywhere with statutory authorization upon an appropriate corporate official or agent. In Tauza, the defendant coal company was incorporated in Pennsylvania, but it had a branch office in New York City headed by a sales agent who had under him eight salesmen and also other stenographic and clerical personnel; sales in New York were subject to confirmation by the home office in Pennsylvania, customer payments were made to the treasurer in Pennsylvania, and shipments were made from Pennsylvania. The court held this activity to constitute doing business in New York and to make the corporation amenable to suit in New York on a claim having no relation to its New York business, and so it therefore upheld service on the sales agent in accordance with the New York service law.

What if the corporation has actually consented to service for unrelated claims, doing so pursuant to the state's appointment-of-agent statute? There may be a question of statutory interpretation as to whether the consent, and hence jurisdiction over the corporation, comprehends only those lawsuits arising from business done within the state or is broad enough to cover all personal actions. On familiar principles, the highest court of the state is the final authority on this question of interpretation. If the state has adopted the latter statutory construction, it might not be exceeding constitutionally permissible limits, see Pa. Fire Ins. Co. v. Gold Issue Mining & Milling Co., 243 U.S. 93, 37 S.Ct. 344 (1917), although this particular question is still not settled, see Brown v. Lockheed Martin Corp., 814 F.3d 619 (2d Cir.2016); Zachary D. Clopton, Procedural Retrenchment and the States, 106 Calif.L.Rev. 411, 441–42 (2018). Settled it must soon be, because plaintiffs today are increasingly relying on this route to bring corporations into courts of the plaintiffs' choosing. See Oscar G. Chase, Consent to Judicial Jurisdiction, 73 N.Y.U.Ann.Surv.Am.L. 159 (2018).

Summary.—So, although the limits imposed by substantive due process were unclear, the consent and corporate presence theories seemed to be running up against those limits. Indeed, in the early twentieth century the growing tendency to look directly at the acts of transacting or doing business as the relevant due process test facilitated the increasingly conservative courts' restricting the states' powers over foreign corporations, a restriction that the courts could tighten simply by raising the threshold of in-state activity necessary for jurisdiction. But then, a depression and another war set the stage for abandoning the pro-business, laissez-faire attitudes that had come to dominate. Once again, it became evident that social, economic, political, and other such forces shape jurisdictional law. See generally Joseph J. Kalo, Jurisdiction as an Evolutionary Process: The Development of Quasi In Rem and In Personam Principles, 1978 Duke L.J. 1147.

International Shoe Co. v. Washington

Supreme Court of the United States, 1945.
326 U.S. 310, 66 S.Ct. 154.

■ MR. CHIEF JUSTICE STONE delivered the opinion of the Court.

The questions for decision are (1) whether, within the limitations of the due process clause of the Fourteenth Amendment, appellant, a Delaware corporation, has by its activities in the State of Washington rendered itself amenable to proceedings in the courts of that state to recover unpaid contributions to the state unemployment compensation fund exacted by state statutes, Washington Unemployment Compensation Act, Washington Revised Statutes, § 9998–103a through § 9998–123a, 1941 Supp., and (2) whether the state can exact those contributions consistently with the due process clause of the Fourteenth Amendment.

The statutes in question set up a comprehensive scheme of unemployment compensation, the costs of which are defrayed by contributions required to be made by employers to a state unemployment compensation fund. The contributions are a specified percentage of the wages payable annually by each employer for his employees' services in the state. The assessment and collection of the contributions and the fund are administered by appellees. Section 14(c) of the Act . . . authorizes appellee Commissioner to issue an order and notice of assessment of delinquent contributions upon prescribed personal service of the notice upon the employer if found within the state, or, if not so found, by mailing the notice to the employer by registered mail at his last known address.[v] That section also authorizes the Commissioner to collect the assessment by distraint if it is not paid within ten days after service of the notice. By §§ 14e and 6b the order of assessment may be administratively reviewed by an appeal tribunal within the office of unemployment upon petition of the employer, and this determination is by § 6i made subject to judicial review on questions of law by the state Superior Court, with further right of appeal in the state Supreme Court as in other civil cases.

In this case notice of assessment for the years in question was personally served upon a sales solicitor employed by appellant in the State of Washington, and a copy of the notice was mailed by registered mail to appellant at its address in St. Louis, Missouri. Appellant appeared specially before the office of unemployment and moved to set aside the order and notice of assessment on the ground that the service upon appellant's salesman was not proper service upon appellant; that appellant was not a corporation of the State of Washington and was not doing business within the state; that it had no agent within the state upon whom service could be made; and that appellant is not an employer and does not furnish employment within the meaning of the statute.

The motion was heard on evidence and stipulation of facts by the appeal tribunal which denied the motion and ruled that appellee Commissioner was entitled to recover the unpaid contributions. That action was affirmed by the Commissioner; both the Superior Court and the Supreme Court affirmed. 22 Wash.2d 146, 154 P.2d 801. Appellant in each of these courts assailed the statute as applied, as a violation of the due process clause of the Fourteenth Amendment, and as imposing a constitutionally prohibited burden on interstate commerce. The cause comes here on appeal under § 237(a) of the Judicial Code, 28 U.S.C. § 344(a),[w] appellant assigning as error that the challenged statutes as applied infringe the due process clause of the Fourteenth Amendment and the commerce clause.

---

[v] Section 14(c) of the Act stated: "At any time after the Commissioner shall find that any contribution or the interest thereon have become delinquent, the Commissioner may issue a notice of assessment specifying the amount due, which notice of assessment shall be served upon the delinquent employer in the manner prescribed for the service of summons in a civil action, except that if the employer cannot be found within the state, said notice will be deemed served when mailed to the delinquent employer at his last known address by registered mail." The Washington statute governing service of summons in a civil action upon a foreign corporation doing business in the state provided that the summons be served by delivery of a copy to any in-state agent, cashier, or secretary thereof. The state here used both the in-state and the out-of-state methods of service referred to in § 14(c). See Int'l Shoe Co. v. State, 22 Wash.2d 146, 151, 154 P.2d 801, 803 (1945). For more factual background on this case, see Christopher D. Cameron & Kevin R. Johnson, Death of a Salesman? Forum Shopping and Outcome Determination Under International Shoe, 28 U.C.Davis L.Rev. 769 (1995).

[w] The current version appears as 28 U.S.C. § 1257.

The facts as found by the appeal tribunal and accepted by the state Superior Court and the Supreme Court, are not in dispute. Appellant is a Delaware corporation, having its principal place of business in St. Louis, Missouri, and is engaged in the manufacture and sale of shoes and other footwear. It maintains places of business in several states, other than Washington, at which its manufacturing is carried on and from which its merchandise is distributed interstate through several sales units or branches located outside the State of Washington.

Appellant has no office in Washington and makes no contracts either for sale or purchase of merchandise there. It maintains no stock of merchandise in that state and makes there no deliveries of goods in intrastate commerce. During the years from 1937 to 1940, now in question, appellant employed eleven to thirteen salesmen under direct supervision and control of sales managers located in St. Louis. These salesmen resided in Washington; their principal activities were confined to that state; and they were compensated by commissions based upon the amount of their sales. The commissions for each year totaled more than $31,000. Appellant supplies its salesmen with a line of samples, each consisting of one shoe of a pair, which they display to [merchants as] prospective purchasers. On occasion they rent permanent sample rooms, for exhibiting samples, in business buildings, or rent rooms in hotels or business buildings temporarily for that purpose. The cost of such rentals is reimbursed by appellant.

The authority of the salesmen is limited to exhibiting their samples and soliciting orders from prospective buyers, at prices and on terms fixed by appellant. The salesmen transmit the orders to appellant's office in St. Louis for acceptance or rejection, and when accepted the merchandise for filling the orders is shipped f.o.b. from points outside Washington to the purchasers within the state. All the merchandise shipped into Washington is invoiced at the place of shipment from which collections are made. No salesman has authority to enter into contracts or to make collections.

The Supreme Court of Washington was of opinion that the regular and systematic solicitation of orders in the state by appellant's salesmen, resulting in a continuous flow of appellant's product into the state, was sufficient to constitute doing business in the state so as to make appellant amenable to suit in its courts. But it was also of opinion that there were sufficient additional activities shown to bring the case within the rule frequently stated, that solicitation within a state by the agents of a foreign corporation plus some additional activities there are sufficient to render the corporation amenable to suit brought in the courts of the state to enforce an obligation arising out of its activities there. International Harvester Co. v. Kentucky, 234 U.S. 579, 587, 34 S.Ct. 944, 946; People's Tobacco Co. v. American Tobacco Co., 246 U.S. 79, 87, 38 S.Ct. 233, 235; Frene v. Louisville Cement Co., 77 U.S.App.D.C. 129, 134 F.2d 511, 516. The court found such additional activities in the salesmen's display of samples sometimes in permanent display rooms, and the salesmen's residence within the state, continued over a period of years, all resulting in a substantial volume of merchandise regularly shipped by appellant to purchasers within the state. The court also held that the statute as applied did not invade the constitutional power of Congress to regulate interstate commerce and did not impose a prohibited burden on such commerce.

Appellant's argument, renewed here, that the statute imposes an unconstitutional burden on interstate commerce need not detain us. For 53 Stat. 1391, 26 U.S.C. § 1606(a) provides that "No person required under a State law to make payments to an unemployment fund shall be relieved from compliance therewith on the ground that he is engaged in interstate or foreign commerce, or that the State law does not distinguish between employees engaged in interstate or foreign commerce and those engaged in intrastate commerce." It is no longer debatable that Congress, in the exercise of the commerce power, may authorize the states, in specified ways, to regulate interstate commerce or impose burdens upon it. [Citations omitted.]

Appellant also insists that its activities within the state were not sufficient to manifest its "presence" there and that in its absence the state courts were without jurisdiction, that consequently it was a denial of due process for the state to subject appellant to suit. It refers to those cases in which it was said that the mere solicitation of orders for the purchase of goods within a state, to be accepted without the state and filled by shipment of the purchased goods interstate, does not render the corporation seller amenable to suit within the state. See Green v. Chicago, B. & Q.R. Co., 205 U.S. 530, 533, 27 S.Ct. 595, 596; International Harvester Co. v. Kentucky, supra, 234 U.S. 586, 587, 34 S.Ct. 946; Philadelphia & Reading R. Co. v. McKibbin, 243 U.S. 264, 268, 37 S.Ct. 280; People's Tobacco Co. v. American Tobacco Co., supra, 246 U.S. 87, 38 S.Ct. 235. And appellant further argues that since it was not present within the state, it is a denial of due process to subject it to taxation or other money exaction. It thus denies the power of the state to lay the tax or to subject appellant to a suit for its collection.

Historically the jurisdiction of courts to render judgment in personam is grounded on their de facto power over the defendant's person. Hence his presence within the territorial jurisdiction of a court was prerequisite to its rendition of a judgment personally binding him. Pennoyer v. Neff, 95 U.S. 714, 733. But now that the capias ad respondendum has given way to personal service of summons or other form of notice, due process requires only that in order to subject a defendant to a judgment in personam, if he be not present within the territory of the forum, he have certain minimum contacts with it such that the maintenance of the suit does not offend "traditional notions of fair play and substantial justice." Milliken v. Meyer, 311 U.S. 457, 463, 61 S.Ct. 339, 343. See Holmes, J., in McDonald v. Mabee, 243 U.S. 90, 91,

37 S.Ct. 343. Compare Hoopeston Canning Co. v. Cullen, 318 U.S. 313, 316, 319, 63 S.Ct. 602, 604, 606. See Blackmer v. United States, 284 U.S. 421, 52 S.Ct. 252; Hess v. Pawloski, 274 U.S. 352, 47 S.Ct. 632; Young v. Masci, 289 U.S. 253, 53 S.Ct. 599.

Since the corporate personality is a fiction, although a fiction intended to be acted upon as though it were a fact, Klein v. Board of Supervisors, 282 U.S. 19, 24, 51 S.Ct. 15, 16, it is clear that unlike an individual its "presence" without, as well as within, the state of its origin can be manifested only by activities carried on in its behalf by those who are authorized to act for it. To say that the corporation is so far "present" there as to satisfy due process requirements, for purposes of taxation or the maintenance of suits against it in the courts of the state, is to beg the question to be decided. For the terms "present" or "presence" are used merely to symbolize those activities of the corporation's agent within the state which courts will deem to be sufficient to satisfy the demands of due process. L. Hand, J., in Hutchinson v. Chase & Gilbert, 45 F.2d 139, 141. Those demands may be met by such contacts of the corporation with the state of the forum as make it reasonable, in the context of our federal system of government, to require the corporation to defend the particular suit which is brought there. An "estimate of the inconveniences" which would result to the corporation from a trial away from its "home" or principal place of business is relevant in this connection. Hutchinson v. Chase & Gilbert, supra, 45 F.2d 141.

"Presence" in the state in this sense has never been doubted when the activities of the corporation there have not only been continuous and systematic, but also give rise to the liabilities sued on, even though no consent to be sued or authorization to an agent to accept service of process has been given. St. Clair v. Cox, 106 U.S. 350, 355, 1 S.Ct. 354, 359; Connecticut Mutual Life Ins. Co. v. Spratley, 172 U.S. 602, 610–11, 19 S.Ct. 308, 311–12; Pennsylvania Lumbermen's Mut. Fire Ins. Co. v. Meyer, 197 U.S. 407, 414–415, 25 S.Ct. 483, 484–85; Commercial Mutual Accident Co. v. Davis, 213 U.S. 245, 255–256, 29 S.Ct. 445, 448; International Harvester Co. v. Kentucky, supra; cf. St. Louis S.W.R. Co. v. Alexander, 227 U.S. 218, 33 S.Ct. 245. Conversely it has been generally recognized that the casual presence of the corporate agent or even his conduct of single or isolated items of activities in a state in the corporation's behalf are not enough to subject it to suit on causes of action unconnected with the activities there. St. Clair v. Cox, supra, 106 U.S. 359, 360, 1 S.Ct. 362, 363; Old Wayne Mut. Life Ass'n v. McDonough, 204 U.S. 8, 21, 27 S.Ct. 236, 240; Frene v. Louisville Cement Co., supra, 134 F.2d 515, and cases cited. To require the corporation in such circumstances to defend the suit away from its home or other jurisdiction where it carries on more substantial activities has been thought to lay too great and unreasonable a burden on the corporation to comport with due process.

While it has been held, in cases on which appellant relies, that continuous activity of some sort within a state is not enough to support the demand that the corporation be amenable to suits unrelated to that activity, Old Wayne Mut. Life Ass'n v. McDonough, supra; Green v. Chicago, B. & Q.R. Co., supra; Simon v. Southern R. Co., 236 U.S. 115, 35 S.Ct. 255; People's Tobacco Co. v. American Tobacco Co., supra; cf. Davis v. Farmers' Co-operative Co., 262 U.S. 312, 317, 43 S.Ct. 556, 558, there have been instances in which the continuous corporate operations within a state were thought so substantial and of such a nature as to justify suit against it on causes of action arising from dealings entirely distinct from those activities. See Missouri, K. & T.R. Co. v. Reynolds, 255 U.S. 565, 41 S.Ct. 446; Tauza v. Susquehanna Coal Co., 220 N.Y. 259, 115 N.E. 915; cf. St. Louis S.W.R. Co. v. Alexander, supra.

Finally, although the commission of some single or occasional acts of the corporate agent in a state sufficient to impose an obligation or liability on the corporation has not been thought to confer upon the state authority to enforce it, Rosenberg Bros. & Co. v. Curtis Brown Co., 260 U.S. 516, 43 S.Ct. 170, other such acts, because of their nature and quality and the circumstances of their commission, may be deemed sufficient to render the corporation liable to suit. Cf. Kane v. New Jersey, 242 U.S. 160, 37 S.Ct. 30; Hess v. Pawloski, supra; Young v. Masci, supra. True, some of the decisions holding the corporation amenable to suit have been supported by resort to the legal fiction that it has given its consent to service and suit, consent being implied from its presence in the state through the acts of its authorized agents. Lafayette Insurance Co. v. French, 18 How. 404, 407; [other citations omitted]. But more realistically it may be said that those authorized acts were of such a nature as to justify the fiction. Smolik v. Philadelphia & Reading Co., 222 F. 148, 151. Henderson, The Position of Foreign Corporations in American Constitutional Law, 94–95.

It is evident that the criteria by which we mark the boundary line between those activities which justify the subjection of a corporation to suit, and those which do not, cannot be simply mechanical or quantitative. The test is not merely, as has sometimes been suggested, whether the activity, which the corporation has seen fit to procure through its agents in another state, is a little more or a little less. [Citations omitted.] Whether due process is satisfied must depend rather upon the quality and nature of the activity in relation to the fair and orderly administration of the laws which it was the purpose of the due process clause to insure. That clause does not contemplate that a state may make binding a judgment in personam against an individual or corporate defendant with which the state has no contacts, ties, or relations. Cf. Pennoyer v. Neff, supra; Minnesota Commercial Ass'n v. Benn, 261 U.S. 140, 43 S.Ct. 293.

But to the extent that a corporation exercises the privilege of conducting activities within a state, it enjoys the benefits and protection of the laws of that state. The exercise of that privilege may give rise to obligations, and, so far as those obligations arise out of or are connected with the activities within the state, a procedure which requires the corporation to respond to a suit brought to enforce them can, in most instances, hardly be said to be undue. [Citations omitted.]

Applying these standards, the activities carried on in behalf of appellant in the State of Washington were neither irregular nor casual. They were systematic and continuous throughout the years in question. They resulted in a large volume of interstate business, in the course of which appellant received the benefits and protection of the laws of the state, including the right to resort to the courts for the enforcement of its rights. The obligation which is here sued upon arose out of those very activities. It is evident that these operations establish sufficient contacts or ties with the state of the forum to make it reasonable and just, according to our traditional conception of fair play and substantial justice, to permit the state to enforce the obligations which appellant has incurred there. Hence we cannot say that the maintenance of the present suit in the State of Washington involves an unreasonable or undue procedure.

We are likewise unable to conclude that the service of the process within the state upon an agent whose activities establish appellant's "presence" there was not sufficient notice of the suit, or that the suit was so unrelated to those activities as to make the agent an inappropriate vehicle for communicating the notice. It is enough that appellant has established such contacts with the state that the particular form of substituted service adopted there gives reasonable assurance that the notice will be actual. [Citations omitted.] Nor can we say that the mailing of the notice of suit to appellant by registered mail at its home office was not reasonably calculated to apprise appellant of the suit. [Citations omitted.]

Only a word need be said of appellant's liability for the demanded contributions to the state unemployment fund. The Supreme Court of Washington, construing and applying the statute, has held that it imposes a tax on the privilege of employing appellant's salesmen within the state measured by a percentage of the wages, here the commissions payable to the salesmen. This construction we accept for purposes of determining the constitutional validity of the statute. The right to employ labor has been deemed an appropriate subject of taxation in this country and England, both before and since the adoption of the Constitution. [Citation omitted.] And such a tax imposed upon the employer for unemployment benefits is within the constitutional power of the states. [Citation omitted.]

Appellant having rendered itself amenable to suit upon obligations arising out of the activities of its salesmen in Washington, the state may maintain the present suit in personam to collect the tax laid upon the exercise of the privilege of employing appellant's salesmen within the state. For Washington has made one of those activities, which taken together establish appellant's "presence" there for purposes of suit, the taxable event by which the state brings appellant within the reach of its taxing power. The state thus has constitutional power to lay the tax and to subject appellant to a suit to recover it. The activities which establish its "presence" subject it alike to taxation by the state and to suit to recover the tax. [Citations omitted.]

Affirmed.

■ MR. JUSTICE JACKSON took no part in the consideration or decision of this case.

■ MR. JUSTICE BLACK delivered the following opinion.

. . . Nor is the further ground advanced on this appeal, that the State of Washington has denied appellant due process of law, any less devoid of substance [than the claim that imposition of the tax violates the Commerce Clause]. It is my view, therefore, that we should dismiss the appeal as unsubstantial, Seaboard Air Line R. Co. v. Watson, 287 U.S. 86, 90, 92, 53 S.Ct. 32, 34, 35, and decline the invitation to formulate broad rules as to the meaning of due process, which here would amount to deciding a constitutional question "in advance of the necessity for its decision." Alabama State Federation of Labor v. McAdory, 325 U.S. 450, 461, 65 S.Ct. 1384, 1389.

Certainly appellant cannot in the light of our past decisions meritoriously claim that notice by registered mail and by personal service on its sales solicitors in Washington did not meet the requirements of procedural due process. And the due process clause is not brought in issue any more by appellant's further conceptualistic contention that Washington could not levy a tax or bring suit against the corporation because it did not honor that State with its mystical "presence." For it is unthinkable that the vague due process clause was ever intended to prohibit a State from regulating or taxing a business carried on within its boundaries simply because this is done by agents of a corporation organized and having its headquarters elsewhere. To read this into the due process clause would in fact result in depriving a State's citizens of due process by taking from the State the power to protect them in their business dealings within its boundaries with representatives of a foreign corporation. Nothing could be more irrational or more designed to defeat the function of our federative system of government. Certainly a State, at the very least, has power to tax and sue those dealing with its citizens within its boundaries, as we have held before. Hoopeston Canning Co. v. Cullen, 318 U.S. 313, 63 S.Ct. 602 [(1943) (deciding that N.Y. can regulate out-of-state insurance companies doing business in N.Y. by insuring property in N.Y.)]. Were the Court to follow this principle, it would provide a workable standard for cases where, as here, no other questions are involved. The Court has not chosen to do so, but instead has engaged in an unnecessary discussion in the course of which it has announced vague Constitutional criteria applied for the first time to the issue before us. It has thus introduced uncertain elements confusing the simple pattern and tending to curtail the exercise of State powers to an extent not justified by the Constitution.

The criteria adopted insofar as they can be identified read as follows: Due Process does permit State courts to "enforce the obligations which appellant has incurred" if it be found "reasonable and just according to our traditional conception of fair play and substantial justice." And this in turn means that we will "permit" the State to act if upon "an 'estimate of the inconveniences' which would result to the corporation from a trial away from its 'home' or principal place of business," we conclude that it is "reasonable" to subject it to suit in a State where it is doing business.

It is true that this Court did use the terms "fair play" and "substantial justice" in explaining the philosophy underlying the holding that it could not be "due process of law" to render a personal judgment against a defendant without notice and an opportunity to be heard. Milliken v. Meyer, 311 U.S. 457, 61 S.Ct. 339. In McDonald v. Mabee, 243 U.S. 90, 91, 37 S.Ct. 343, cited in the Milliken case, Mr. Justice Holmes, speaking for the Court, warned against judicial curtailment of this opportunity to be heard and referred to such a curtailment as a denial of "fair play," which even the common law would have deemed "contrary to natural justice." And previous cases had indicated that the ancient rule against judgments without notice had stemmed from "natural justice" concepts. These cases, while giving additional reasons why notice under particular circumstances is inadequate, did not mean thereby that all legislative enactments which this Court might deem to be contrary to natural justice ought to be held invalid under the due process clause. None of the cases purport to support or could support a holding that a State can tax and sue corporations only if its action comports with this Court's notions of "natural justice." I should have thought the Tenth Amendment settled that.

I believe that the Federal Constitution leaves to each State, without any "ifs" or "buts," a power to tax and to open the doors of its courts for its citizens to sue corporations whose agents do business in those States. Believing that the Constitution gave the States that power, I think it a judicial deprivation to condition its exercise upon this Court's notion of "fair play," however appealing that term may be. Nor can I stretch the meaning of due process so far as to authorize this Court to deprive a State of the right to afford judicial protection to its citizens on the ground that it would be more "convenient" for the corporation to be sued somewhere else.

There is a strong emotional appeal in the words "fair play," "justice,"[x] and "reasonable." But they were not chosen by those who wrote the

---

[x]   Justice Holmes wrote to Dr. John C.H. Wu on July 1, 1929, "I have said to my brethren many times that I hate justice, which means that I know if a man begins to talk about that, for one reason or another he is shirking thinking in legal terms." Justice Oliver Wendell Holmes: His Book Notices and Uncollected Letters and Papers 201 (Harry C. Shriver ed., 1936).

original Constitution or the Fourteenth Amendment as a measuring rod for the Court to use in invalidating State or Federal laws passed by elected legislative representatives. No one, not even those who most feared a democratic government, ever formally proposed that courts should be given power to invalidate legislation under any such elastic standards. Express prohibitions against certain types of legislation are found in the Constitution, and under the long-settled practice, courts invalidate laws found to conflict with them. This requires interpretation, and interpretation, it is true, may result in extension of the Constitution's purpose. But that is no reason for reading the due process clause so as to restrict a State's power to tax and sue those whose activities affect persons and businesses within the State, provided proper service can be had. Superimposing the natural justice concept on the Constitution's specific prohibitions could operate as a drastic abridgment of democratic safeguards they embody, such as freedom of speech, press and religion, and the right to counsel. This has already happened. Betts v. Brady, 316 U.S. 455, 62 S.Ct. 1252 [(1942) (balancing to determine due process right to appointed counsel in criminal case), overruled, Gideon v. Wainwright, 372 U.S. 335, 83 S.Ct. 792 (1963) (rejecting balancing in favor of a rule); other citation omitted]. For application of this natural law concept, whether under the terms "reasonableness," "justice," or "fair play," makes judges the supreme arbiters of the country's laws and practices. [Citations omitted.] This result, I believe, alters the form of government our Constitution provides. I cannot agree.

True, the State's power is here upheld. But the rule announced means that tomorrow's judgment may strike down a State or Federal enactment on the ground that it does not conform to this Court's idea of natural justice. I therefore find myself moved by the same fears that caused Mr. Justice Holmes to say in 1930:

"I have not yet adequately expressed the more than anxiety that I feel at the ever increasing scope given to the Fourteenth Amendment in cutting down what I believe to be the constitutional rights of the States. As the decisions now stand, I see hardly any limit but the sky to the invalidating of those rights if they happen to strike a majority of this Court as for any reason undesirable." Baldwin v. Missouri, 281 U.S. 586, 595, 50 S.Ct. 436, 439.

———

ADDITIONAL CONSTITUTIONAL LIMITATIONS: COMMERCE CLAUSE AND FIRST AMENDMENT

As suggested by the International Shoe case, constitutional bounds on a state's exercise of judicial authority over a foreign corporation may exist quite apart from the Due Process Clause. In Davis v. Farmers' Co-operative Equity Co., 262 U.S. 312, 43 S.Ct. 556 (1923), a Kansas plaintiff sued a Kansas railroad corporation in a Minnesota state court for a cause of action arising in Kansas. The railroad did not own or operate any lines in Minnesota, but it did maintain an agent there solely for the solicitation of traffic. The Supreme Court, without reaching the due process question, held that a statute authorizing service on the agent "imposes upon interstate commerce a serious and unreasonable burden which renders the statute obnoxious to the commerce clause." A district court more recently so relied on the Commerce Clause as an alternative ground for dismissal in Bryson v. Northlake Hilton, 407 F.Supp. 73 (M.D.N.C.1976). Otherwise, courts have very rarely invoked the Commerce Clause for such purpose, and its continuing vitality as an independent limitation on a state's exercise of judicial authority is in doubt. It seems unlikely that the Commerce Clause could work so to dismiss in a situation satisfying the current interpretation of the Due Process Clause. But see John F. Preis, The Dormant Commerce Clause as a Limit on Personal Jurisdiction, 102 Iowa L.Rev. 121 (2016) (arguing that a nonresident plaintiff's invocation of an appointment-of-agent statute to sue a business on a claim unrelated to in-state business violates the Commerce Clause).

The First Amendment also has sometimes been thought to place a limitation on a state's exercise of territorial jurisdiction over a foreign corporation, this limitation helping, for example, to ensure the free flow of information throughout the country. In New York Times Co. v. Connor, 365 F.2d 567, 572 (5th Cir.1966), which was a libel case against the newspaper, the Fifth Circuit described its view of the way in which the First Amendment restricts a state court's jurisdiction: "First Amendment considerations surrounding the law of libel require a greater showing of contact to satisfy the due process clause than is necessary in asserting jurisdiction over other types of tortious activity." While agreeing that the First Amendment has a role in this area, the Second Circuit, in Buckley v. New York Post Corp., 373 F.2d 175 (2d Cir.1967), took a slightly different approach by suggesting that, with respect to a state's authority to entertain a libel case, the First Amendment imposed a restriction independent of the usual one imposed by the Due Process Clause. Cf. Lamb v. Turbine Design, Inc., 273 Ga. 154, 538 S.E.2d 437 (2000) (holding that mere dealings with a federal regulatory agency do not expose defendant to a related private tort action brought at the agency's site, in view of First Amendment right to petition for redress of grievances); Hilaire H. Butler, Note, The Government Contacts Exception to the District of Columbia Long-Arm Statute: Portrait of a Legal Morass, 36 Cath.U.L.Rev. 745 (1987). However, the Supreme Court now has put a damper on such approaches, at least in libel cases. Calder v. Jones, 465 U.S. 783, 104 S.Ct. 1482 (1984) ("We . . . reject the suggestion that First Amendment concerns enter into the jurisdictional analysis. The infusion of such considerations would needlessly complicate an already imprecise inquiry. [Citation omitted.] Moreover, the potential chill on protected First Amendment activity stemming from libel and defamation actions is already taken into account in the constitutional limitations on the substantive law governing such suits.");

see also Keeton v. Hustler Magazine, Inc., 465 U.S. 770, 104 S.Ct. 1473 (1984) (holding that a nonresident individual can seek damages suffered throughout the country in a libel action against a nondomestic magazine in New Hampshire, where there was a uniquely long statute of limitations but where sales of the magazine were only ten to fifteen thousand per month).

To summarize the current but unclear law, the policies underlying the Commerce Clause and some First Amendment concerns might occasionally work to restrict state jurisdiction, but probably doing so indirectly by weighing on the due process balance.

———

Perkins v. Benguet Consolidated Mining Co.

Supreme Court of the United States, 1952.
342 U.S. 437, 72 S.Ct. 413.

■ MR. JUSTICE BURTON delivered the opinion of the Court.

This case calls for an answer to the question whether the Due Process Clause of the Fourteenth Amendment to the Constitution of the United States precludes Ohio from subjecting a foreign corporation to the jurisdiction of its courts in this action in personam. The corporation has been carrying on in Ohio a continuous and systematic, but limited, part of its general business. Its president, while engaged in doing such business in Ohio, has been served with summons in this proceeding. The cause of action sued upon did not arise in Ohio and does not relate to the corporation's activities there. For the reasons hereafter stated, we hold that the Fourteenth Amendment leaves Ohio free to take or decline jurisdiction over the corporation.

After extended litigation elsewhere petitioner, Idonah Slade Perkins, a non-resident of Ohio, filed two actions in personam in the Court of Common Pleas of Clermont County, Ohio, against the several respondents. Among those sued is the Benguet Consolidated Mining Company, here called the mining company. It is styled a "sociedad anonima" under the laws of the Philippine Islands, where it owns and has operated profitable gold and silver mines. In one action petitioner seeks approximately $68,400 in dividends claimed to be due her as a stockholder. In the other she claims $2,500,000 damages largely because of the company's failure to issue to her certificates for 120,000 shares of its stock.[y]

In each case the trial court sustained a motion to quash the service of summons on the mining company. Ohio Com.Pl., 99 N.E.2d 515. The

---

[y]   The briefs explain that behind these two actions lay a marital dispute. Essentially, Mrs. Perkins was claiming that the mining company (pronounced BEN-get) should have paid certain cash and stock dividends, when declared before World War II, to her rather than to her husband.

Court of Appeals of Ohio affirmed that decision, 88 Ohio App. 118, 95 N.E.2d 5, as did the Supreme Court of Ohio, 155 Ohio St. 116, 98 N.E.2d 33. The cases were consolidated and we granted certiorari . . . . 342 U.S. 808, 72 S.Ct. 33.

We start with the holding of the Supreme Court of Ohio, not contested here, that, under Ohio law, the mining company is to be treated as a foreign corporation. Actual notice of the proceeding was given to the corporation in the instant case through regular service of summons upon its president while he was in Ohio acting in that capacity. Accordingly, there can be no jurisdictional objection based upon a lack of notice to a responsible representative of the corporation.

The answer to the question of whether the state courts of Ohio are open to a proceeding in personam, against an amply notified foreign corporation, to enforce a cause of action not arising in Ohio and not related to the business or activities of the corporation in that State rests entirely upon the law of Ohio, unless the Due Process Clause of the Fourteenth Amendment compels a decision either way.

The suggestion that federal due process *compels* the State to open its courts to such a case has no substance.

> "Provisions for making foreign corporations subject to service in the state is a matter of legislative discretion, and a failure to provide for such service is not a denial of due process. Still less is it incumbent upon a state in furnishing such process to make the jurisdiction over the foreign corporation wide enough to include the adjudication of transitory actions not arising in the state." Missouri P.R. Co. v. Clarendon Boat Oar Co., 257 U.S. 533, 535, 42 S.Ct. 210, 211.

. . . .

A more serious question is presented by the claim that the Due Process Clause of the Fourteenth Amendment *prohibits* Ohio from granting such relief against a foreign corporation. The . . . report of the case below, while denying the relief sought, does not indicate whether the Supreme Court of Ohio rested its decision on Ohio law or on the Fourteenth Amendment. . . .

. . . .

. . . Accordingly, for us to allow the judgment to stand as it is would risk an affirmance of a decision which might have been decided differently if the court below had felt free, under our decisions, to do so.

. . . .

The essence of the issue here, at the constitutional level, is . . . general fairness to the corporation. . . .

. . . .

It remains only to consider, in more detail, the issue of whether, as a matter of federal due process, the business done in Ohio by the respondent mining company was sufficiently substantial and of such a nature as to *permit* Ohio to entertain a cause of action against a foreign corporation, where the cause of action arose from activities entirely distinct from its activities in Ohio. See International Shoe Co. v. Washington, [326 U.S. 310, 318, 66 S.Ct. 154, 159 (1945)].

The Ohio Court of Appeals summarized the evidence on the subject. 88 Ohio App. at pages 119–125, 95 N.E.2d at pages 6–9. From that summary the following facts are substantially beyond controversy: The company's mining properties were in the Philippine Islands. Its operations there were completely halted during the occupation of the Islands by the Japanese. During that interim the president, who was also the general manager and principal stockholder of the company, returned to his home in Clermont County, Ohio. There he maintained an office in which he conducted his personal affairs and did many things on behalf of the company. He kept there office files of the company. He carried on there correspondence relating to the business of the company and to its employees. He drew and distributed there salary checks on behalf of the company, both in his own favor as president and in favor of two company secretaries who worked there with him. He used and maintained in Clermont County, Ohio, two active bank accounts carrying substantial balances of company funds. A bank in Hamilton County, Ohio, acted as transfer agent for the stock of the company. Several directors' meetings were held at his office or home in Clermont County. From that office he supervised policies dealing with the rehabilitation of the corporation's properties in the Philippines and he dispatched funds to cover purchases of machinery for such rehabilitation. Thus he carried on in Ohio a continuous and systematic supervision of the necessarily limited wartime activities of the company. He there discharged his duties as president and general manager, both during the occupation of the company's properties by the Japanese and immediately thereafter. While no mining properties in Ohio were owned or operated by the company, many of its wartime activities were directed from Ohio and were being given the personal attention of its president in that State at the time he was served with summons [in 1947]. Consideration of the circumstances which, under the law of Ohio, ultimately will determine whether the courts of that State will choose to take jurisdiction over the corporation is reserved for the courts of that State. Without reaching that issue of state policy, we conclude that, under the circumstances above recited, it would not violate federal due process for Ohio either to take or decline jurisdiction of the corporation in this proceeding. This relieves the Ohio courts of the restriction ... which may have influenced the judgment of the court below.

Accordingly, the judgment of the Supreme Court of Ohio is vacated and the cause is remanded to that court for further proceedings in the light of this opinion.

It is so ordered.[z]

■ MR. JUSTICE BLACK concurs in the result.

■ [The dissenting opinion of JUSTICE MINTON, with whom Chief Justice Vinson joined, is omitted.]

———————

GENERAL JURISDICTION: PERKINS' PROGENY

Within the category of personal jurisdiction, the kind invoked in Perkins is called general jurisdiction. It gives the state the power to adjudicate any personal claim whether or not arising from, or even related to, the defendant's contacts with the forum state. The distinction is to specific jurisdiction, by which lesser contacts give the state power to adjudicate only those personal claims related to the contacts.

You will recall that the domicile basis yields general jurisdiction. Also, an individual's physical presence in the state when served with process works that way. Perkins (and International Shoe) said that if a corporation's in-state business activities are, at the time of process serving, extensively continuous and systematic—which courts phrased as "doing business" rather than merely "transacting business"—then the corporation is subject to jurisdiction even for claims wholly unrelated to the in-state business activities. In fact, the states built enthusiastically on this idea, greatly expanding general jurisdiction. A big corporation could be sued in many states on any claim.

1. This kind of "doing business" jurisdiction came before the Supreme Court in Helicópteros Nacionales de Colombia, S.A. v. Hall, 466 U.S. 408, 104 S.Ct. 1868 (1984). The facts of this Texas state court wrongful-death action involved American pipeline workers killed when the Colombian defendant's helicopter crashed in Peru. The defendant was providing transportation services there pursuant to a contract negotiated with Texans in Texas, and it received payment from Texas. It had bought its helicopters and parts in Texas, and its helicopter pilots and workers had received training in Texas. These Texan contacts were substantial, but not substantial enough for general jurisdiction according to the Supreme Court's view of the Due Process Clause. So the Court reversed, over Justice Brennan's dissent.

2. Then, in Goodyear Dunlop Tires Operations, S.A. v. Brown, 564 U.S. 915, 131 S.Ct. 2846 (2011), North Carolinian parents of young sons killed in a bus accident on the way to the airport in France outside Paris had sued a U.S. tire company and three of its foreign-country subsidiaries

———————

[z]   On remand, the court denied defendant's motion to quash the service of summons, 158 Ohio St. 145, 107 N.E.2d 203 (1952).

in a North Carolina state court. The subsidiaries made tires designed for the European and Asian markets, although a small percentage of their output traveled by the stream of commerce to North Carolina in response to custom orders. The subsidiaries had unsuccessfully challenged North Carolina's exercise of general jurisdiction. But on certiorari, the U.S. Supreme Court unanimously reversed for denial of due process, in an opinion by Justice Ginsburg:

"A court may assert general jurisdiction over foreign (sister-state or foreign-country) corporations to hear any and all claims against them when their affiliations with the State are so 'continuous and systematic' as to render them essentially at home in the forum State. . . .

" . . . For an individual, the paradigm forum for the exercise of general jurisdiction is the individual's domicile; for a corporation, it is an equivalent place, one in which the corporation is fairly regarded as at home. . . .

"Measured against Helicopteros and Perkins, North Carolina is not a forum in which it would be permissible to subject petitioners to general jurisdiction."

The Court indicated that a corporation was "essentially at home" in its place of incorporation and its principal place of business, but not everywhere it sells its products. "Under the sprawling view of general jurisdiction urged by respondents and embraced by the North Carolina Court of Appeals, any substantial manufacturer or seller of goods would be amenable to suit, on any claim for relief, wherever its products are distributed."

The most interesting thing about the Goodyear opinion is that the Court suggested a discontinuity exists between specific and general jurisdiction. Instead of the continuum implied in International Shoe, with the required contacts smoothly increasing with the claim's unrelatedness to those contacts, general jurisdiction might require not only much higher but also qualitatively different contacts. "The North Carolina court's stream-of-commerce analysis elided the essential difference between case-specific and all-purpose (general) jurisdiction. Flow of a manufacturer's products into the forum, we have explained, may bolster an affiliation germane to *specific* jurisdiction. [Citation omitted.] But ties serving to bolster the exercise of specific jurisdiction do not warrant a determination that, based on those ties, the forum has *general* jurisdiction over a defendant."

3. Daimler AG v. Bauman, 571 U.S. 117, 134 S.Ct. 746 (2014), spelled out the implications of Goodyear. Argentinian plaintiffs sued the German corporation Daimler in California for human rights violations allegedly committed in Argentina by its Argentinian subsidiary. Personal jurisdiction rested on the Californian activities of Daimler's U.S. subsidiary, which was incorporated in Delaware with its principal place

of business in New Jersey but which distributed in California 2.4% of all of the Mercedes vehicles that Daimler manufactured.

The federal district court granted Daimler's motion to dismiss. The Ninth Circuit reversed. On certiorari, the U.S. Supreme Court emphatically reversed the Ninth Circuit, in another opinion by Justice Ginsburg. (Justice Sotomayor concurred in the judgment, reaching reversal by a different route.) The Court found Daimler's level of California activity to fall far short of that required by the Fourteenth Amendment for general jurisdiction, even if one assumed that the U.S. subsidiary's acts could be attributed to the parent company.

Recognizing specific jurisdiction as the centerpiece of modern personal jurisdiction and treating general jurisdiction as a different animal, the Court restricted general jurisdiction over corporations to the place of incorporation (in the sense of nerve center, according to recent cases rather than policy considerations) and the principal place of business (if it is in the United States). Nonetheless, in a footnote it left open the rare possibility that "a corporation's operations in a forum other than its formal place of incorporation or principal place of business may be so substantial and of such a nature as to render the corporation at home in that State."

Confronted by Justice Sotomayor with the fact in the Perkins record that by 1947 Benguet had resumed its mining operations in the Philippines and had significant operational and management activities outside Ohio including in California, Justice Ginsburg suggested that Perkins might have been one of those exceptional cases for general jurisdiction outside the place of incorporation and the principal place of business. But ultimately Justice Ginsburg held her ground, saying more directly that Ohio was the principal, if temporary, place of business: "All of Benguet's activities were directed by the company's president from within Ohio."

4.   The level of corporate activities required to produce general jurisdiction, which would allow suit on any claim whatsoever, is now very high indeed. The Court forbade general jurisdiction in BNSF Railway Co. v. Tyrrell, 137 S.Ct. 1549, 1558–59 (2017) (holding that out-of-state employees cannot sue the employer-railroad in Montana, where it merely transacts business, for injuries suffered elsewhere), over Justice Sotomayor's dissent. The lower courts are applying the new test strictly, cutting back the implications of Perkins.

In sum, general jurisdiction assures the plaintiff a forum for bringing any claim against the defendant. That jurisdiction is based on the defendant's connections to the forum state at the time of service of process. For an individual defendant, that forum is either the domicile or the place of physical presence of the defendant. The corporate analogies are the defendant's place of incorporation (as an analog of domicile) and its worldwide principal place of business (as a revival of corporate presence). For an unincorporated association, general jurisdiction exists only at its worldwide principal place of business.

However, as Justice Ginsburg observed, most of the action in extending territorial jurisdiction came in connection with specific jurisdiction. So we now return to that story.

McGee v. International Life Insurance Co.

Supreme Court of the United States, 1957.
355 U.S. 220, 78 S.Ct. 199.

■ MR. JUSTICE BLACK delivered the opinion of the Court.

Petitioner, Lulu B. McGee, recovered a judgment in a California state court against respondent, International Life Insurance Company, on a contract of insurance. Respondent was not served with process in California but by registered mail at its principal place of business in Texas. The California court based its jurisdiction on a state statute which subjects foreign corporations to suit in California on insurance contracts with residents of that State even though such corporations cannot be served with process within its borders.[1]

Unable to collect the judgment in California petitioner went to Texas where she filed suit on the judgment in a Texas court. But the Texas courts refused to enforce her judgment holding it was void under the Fourteenth Amendment because service of process outside California could not give the courts of that State jurisdiction over respondent. Since the case raised important questions, not only to California but to other States which have similar laws, we granted certiorari. 352 U.S. 924, 77 S.Ct. 239. It is not controverted that if the California court properly exercised jurisdiction over respondent the Texas courts erred in refusing to give its judgment full faith and credit. 28 U.S.C. § 1738.

The material facts are relatively simple. In 1944, Lowell Franklin, a resident of California, purchased a life insurance policy from the Empire Mutual Insurance Company, an Arizona corporation. In 1948 the respondent agreed with Empire Mutual to assume its insurance obligations. Respondent then mailed a reinsurance certificate to Franklin in California offering to insure him in accordance with the terms of the policy he held with Empire Mutual. He accepted this offer and from that time until his death in 1950 paid premiums by mail from his California home to respondent's Texas office. Petitioner, Franklin's mother, was the beneficiary under the policy.[aa] She sent proofs of his death to the respondent but it refused to pay claiming that he had committed suicide.

---

[1]   Cal.Insurance Code, West's Anno. §§ 1610–1620. [The statute authorizes specific jurisdiction over an insurer who solicits, issues, delivers, or collects premiums on a policy that covers a resident or property present in California at the time of issuance or delivery.—Ed.]

[aa]   She was a California resident. See McGee v. Int'l Life Ins. Co., 288 S.W.2d 579, 580 (Tex.Civ.App.1956).

It appears that neither Empire Mutual nor respondent has ever had any offices or agents in California. And so far as the record before us shows, respondent has never solicited or done any insurance business in California apart from the policy involved here.

Since Pennoyer v. Neff, 95 U.S. 714, this Court has held that the Due Process Clause of the Fourteenth Amendment places some limit on the power of state courts to enter binding judgments against persons not served with process within their boundaries. But just where this line of limitation falls has been the subject of prolific controversy, particularly with respect to foreign corporations. . . . More recently in International Shoe Co. v. State of Washington, 326 U.S. 310, 66 S.Ct. 154, the Court decided that "due process requires only that in order to subject a defendant to a judgment in personam, if he be not present within the territory of the forum, he have certain minimum contacts with it such that the maintenance of the suit does not offend 'traditional notions of fair play and substantial justice.' " Id., 326 U.S. at page 316, 66 S.Ct. at page 158.

Looking back over this long history of litigation a trend is clearly discernible toward expanding the permissible scope of state jurisdiction over foreign corporations and other nonresidents. In part this is attributable to the fundamental transformation of our national economy over the years. Today many commercial transactions touch two or more States and may involve parties separated by the full continent. With this increasing nationalization of commerce has come a great increase in the amount of business conducted by mail across state lines. At the same time modern transportation and communication have made it much less burdensome for a party sued to defend himself in a State where he engages in economic activity.

Turning to this case we think it apparent that the Due Process Clause did not preclude the California court from entering a judgment binding on respondent. It is sufficient for purposes of due process that the suit was based on a contract which had substantial connection with that State. Cf. Hess v. Pawloski, 274 U.S. 352, 47 S.Ct. 632; Henry L. Doherty & Co. v. Goodman, 294 U.S. 623, 55 S.Ct. 553; Pennoyer v. Neff, 95 U.S. 714, 735. The contract was delivered in California, the premiums were mailed from there and the insured was a resident of that State when he died. It cannot be denied that California has a manifest interest in providing effective means of redress for its residents when their insurers refuse to pay claims. These residents would be at a severe disadvantage if they were forced to follow the insurance company to a distant State in order to hold it legally accountable. When claims were small or moderate individual claimants frequently could not afford the cost of bringing an action in a foreign forum—thus in effect making the company judgment proof. Often the crucial witnesses—as here on the company's defense of suicide—will be found in the insured's locality. Of course there may be inconvenience to the insurer if it is held amenable to suit in California where it had this contract but certainly nothing which amounts to a denial of due process. [Citation omitted.] There is no contention that respondent did not have adequate notice of the suit or sufficient time to prepare its defense and appear.

The California statute became law in 1949, after respondent had entered into the agreement with Franklin to assume Empire Mutual's obligation to him. Respondent contends that application of the statute to this existing contract improperly impairs the obligation of the contract. We believe that contention is devoid of merit. The statute was remedial, in the purest sense of that term, and neither enlarged nor impaired respondent's substantive rights and obligations under the contract. It did nothing more than to provide petitioner with a California forum to enforce whatever substantive rights she might have against respondent. At the same time respondent was given a reasonable time to appear and defend on the merits after being notified of the suit. Under such circumstances it had no vested right not to be sued in California. [Citations omitted.]

The judgment is reversed and the cause is remanded to the Court of Civil Appeals of the State of Texas, First Supreme Judicial District, for further proceedings not inconsistent with this opinion.

It is so ordered.

■ THE CHIEF JUSTICE [WARREN, Governor of California 1943–1953,] took no part in the consideration or decision of this case [leaving Justice Black, as the senior Justice in the majority, to designate the opinion-writer].

———

SPECIFIC JURISDICTION: MCGEE'S PROGENY

The major focus of the preceding cases was the constitutional limits on state jurisdiction. The essential limits come from the Due Process Clause. Subsequently excerpted cases will further specify those restraints of substantive due process, but already apparent is that the Clause interplays an idea of power (whether the defendant had "minimum contacts" with the state, in light of the relatedness or unrelatedness of the claim to those contacts) with an idea of reasonableness (more of an all-interests-considered inquiry into fundamental fairness as encapsulated in "fair play and substantial justice").

1. As a matter of power, if the claim is unrelated, the only possible kind of personal jurisdiction is general jurisdiction. If the claim is related, however, specific jurisdiction based on the defendant's state-directed acts might be available.

A frustrating thing about the Helicópteros opinion on general jurisdiction was that the Court expressly decided not to reach the more difficult question of whether specific jurisdiction existed. The case thus left unclear whether it mattered that the particular claim was at least somewhat connected to the Texan contacts. International Shoe authorized specific jurisdiction not only for claims that "arise from" contacts with the forum state but also for claims that "relate to" those contacts. One could theorize that state-directed activity by the defendant could still be related even if only parallel (i.e., similar state-directed behavior toward people other than the plaintiff or toward the plaintiff on other occasions) or incidental (i.e., minor state-directed steps taken to facilitate liability-generating acts elsewhere) to the activities from which the plaintiff's claim actually arose. As the relation between the state-directed activity and the claim gets weaker, however, due process would demand a higher level of state-directed activity to justify jurisdiction. The result would be a sliding scale.

That sliding-scale approach is no more, after the major decision in Bristol-Myers Squibb Co. v. Superior Court, 137 S.Ct. 1773 (2017). The Court explicitly rejected any reading of International Shoe that would produce a sliding scale: "Our cases provide no support for this approach, which resembles a loose and spurious form of general jurisdiction."

In the BMS case, the California courts had allowed nonresident tort plaintiffs to sue an out-of-state drug company in California, a state where the plaintiffs neither acquired the blood-thinning drug nor were injured, and where the defendant did not develop or make the drug but heavily marketed it to other consumers and maintained fairly substantial research and lobbying operations. The U.S. Supreme Court reversed. Justice Alito wrote for eight Justices that the nonresidents' claims were insufficiently related to the defendant's Californian activities. (Justice Sotomayor dissented, finding the relation sufficient.) A completely Californian plaintiff could of course invoke specific jurisdiction in California against the drug company, but these nonresidents could not.

The post-BMS result is that power exists for specific jurisdiction if state-directed acts are (a) closely enough related to the claim and (b) substantial enough to get over a threshold quite low compared to general jurisdiction's threshold of being at home. Together those two requirements ensure a rational basis of the sovereign's power to adjudicate the litigation. A further consequence is that specific and general jurisdiction are now completely distinguishable, just as the Goodyear and Daimler cases had suggested.

(a) How "closely enough related" must the claim be to fit within specific jurisdiction? The Court indicated that the relation of the claim to the defendant's state-directed activity required more than parallel or incidental activity:

The mere fact that *other* plaintiffs were prescribed, obtained, and ingested Plavix in California—and allegedly sustained the same injuries as did the nonresidents—does not allow the State to assert specific jurisdiction over the nonresidents' claims. As we have explained, "a defendant's relationship with a . . . third party, standing alone, is an insufficient basis for jurisdiction." Walden [v. Fiore, 571 U.S. 277, 286, 134 S.Ct. 1115, 1123 (2014)]. This remains true even when third parties (here, the plaintiffs who reside in California) can bring claims similar to those brought by the nonresidents. Nor is it sufficient—or even relevant— that BMS conducted research in California on matters unrelated to Plavix.

The defendant BMS had argued that the state-directed activity needs to have played a causal role in creating the claim. But the BMS Court declined to pin down the required relation. It just said that in order for a state court to exercise specific jurisdiction, the claim must relate to the forum through the defendant's contacts with the forum. "When there is no such connection, specific jurisdiction is lacking regardless of the extent of a defendant's unconnected activities in the State."

(b) How "substantial enough" must the state-directed activity be for specific jurisdiction? Specific jurisdiction will exist for related claims as long as the activity is above some pretty low level. The defendant must have performed acts directed to the forum state with a purpose, as International Shoe said, to avail itself of "the benefits and protection of the laws of that state." The cases you have read and will soon read spell out this requirement. International Shoe said to consider the "quality and nature" of the defendant's state-directed activity. McGee authorized jurisdiction based on minimal in-state acts when the burden on the defendant was slight, the forum state's interest was considerable, the plaintiff would avoid severe disadvantage, and the witnesses would be convenienced.

Certainly, these ideas add up to mean that some real limits on specific jurisdiction exist. We can use the McGee facts to sketch the current law. The bottom line is that a state cannot reach just anyone, despite Justice Black's words.

Imagine that the McGee facts were that Lowell Franklin lived in Arizona and conducted all his insurance affairs there, but his alleged suicide occurred while visiting Lulu McGee in California: there would be no jurisdiction in California, because defendant did not do enough directed at California, even though both plaintiff and California have plenty of interests in going forward there. Indeed, the result would remain the same even if defendant had insured some others in California: plaintiff's claim must relate more closely to defendant's state-directed activity to establish specific jurisdiction.

2. There remains that idea of reasonableness. This idea had implicitly worked to expand power in cases like Hess, Doherty, and McGee. But International Shoe had suggested that reasonableness could limit power too.

Thus, even if defendant has minimum contacts, they will not always suffice if a separate reasonableness test applies. Imagine on the actual McGee facts that the insurance company instead sued the beneficiary in Texas for a declaration of nonliability: there might be no jurisdiction in Texas, in view of the unreasonableness of the burden on Lulu and the presence of all the evidence in California, even though Lulu through Lowell as her "agent" had contacts with Texas related to the insurance policy. If this example seems too complicated, an alternative might be the commonsense rule you could intuit from your own life: even if a consumer might be able to bring at home a tort or contract action arising from a one-shot purchase of clothes from a big mail-order seller, we should not allow the seller to exert unreasonable jurisdiction over the consumer in the seller's state in a suit for nonpayment. The upcoming cases will clarify the role for reasonableness.

The McGee hypotheticals also raise the question of the kinds of defendants reachable by the state. The International Shoe case speaks primarily in terms of foreign corporations, although its reasoning seems equally applicable to nonresident individuals. The same is true of the Perkins case. The defendant in McGee was an insurance company, but Justice Black refers to the then clearly discernible trend "toward expanding the permissible scope of state jurisdiction over foreign corporations and other nonresidents."

(f) JURISDICTIONAL STATUTES

For separation-of-powers reasons, the states generally hold that a state court must be authorized by state statute to exercise the various bases of jurisdictional power, except for the bases of presence and consent which were recognized at common law. Accordingly, once International Shoe and its immediate progeny suggested the possible extent of state reach, all the states enacted statutes, often called long-arm statutes, to extend their territorial jurisdiction.

However, a state is certainly not required to extend its jurisdiction all the way to constitutionally permissible limits. Of great practical importance is the fact that to the extent a state long-arm statute falls short of authorizing all the jurisdiction permitted by the Constitution, the statute serves in effect to restrict the state court's jurisdiction. Many assertions of jurisdiction fail because the situation in suit does not come within the statute.

Illinois Revised Statutes Chapter 110

§ 17.   *Act submitting to jurisdiction—Process*[bb]

(1) Any person, whether or not a citizen or resident of this State, who in person or through an agent does any of the acts hereinafter enumerated, thereby submits said person, and, if an individual, his personal representative, to the jurisdiction of the courts of this State as to any cause of action arising from the doing of any of said acts:

(a) The transaction of any business within this State;

(b) The commission of a tortious act within this State;

(c) The ownership, use, or possession of any real estate situated in this State;

(d) Contracting to insure any person, property or risk located within this State at the time of contracting.

(2) Service of process upon any person who is subject to the jurisdiction of the courts of this State, as provided in this section, may be made by personally serving the summons upon the defendant outside this State, as provided in this Act, with the same force and effect as though summons had been personally served within this State.

(3) Only causes of action arising from acts enumerated herein may be asserted against a defendant in an action in which jurisdiction over him is based upon this section.

(4) Nothing herein contained limits or affects the right to serve any process in any other manner now or hereafter provided by law.

As to defendants reached, most modern jurisdictional statutes in fact cover individuals as well as corporations, and no case suggests that the standards are different in substance. In Forbes v. Wells Beach Casino, Inc., 219 A.2d 542 (Me.1966), an action for specific performance of a contract in which the movant (defendant Elias Loew of Massachusetts) had been served with process in Massachusetts pursuant to the Maine long-arm statute, he argued that, at least in the case of a "human nonresident," recent Supreme Court decisions did not go to the length of upholding personal jurisdiction in respect to "activities of a kind which the State of Maine has not regarded as exceptional and has not subjected to special and unique regulation." This contention the Maine court rejected.

[bb]   This is the original version of the statute, enacted in 1955 as the first comprehensive long-arm statute in the nation. The statute has since been amended, as we shall see.

SECTION 4.   COMPLEX RELATIONSHIPS TO THE FORUM STATE—THEORETICAL REFINEMENT

(a) A RONDEL

Mullane v. Central Hanover Bank & Trust Co.

Supreme Court of the United States, 1950.
339 U.S. 306, 70 S.Ct. 652.

■ MR. JUSTICE JACKSON delivered the opinion of the Court.

This controversy questions the constitutional sufficiency of notice to beneficiaries on judicial settlement of accounts by the trustee of a common trust fund established under the New York Banking Law, Consol. Laws, c. 2. The New York Court of Appeals considered and overruled objections that the statutory notice contravenes requirements of the Fourteenth Amendment and that by allowance of the account beneficiaries were deprived of property without due process of law. The case is here on appeal under 28 U.S.C. § 1257.

Common trust fund legislation is addressed to a problem appropriate for state action. Mounting overheads have made administration of small trusts undesirable to corporate trustees. In order that donors and testators of moderately sized trusts may not be denied the service of corporate fiduciaries, the District of Columbia and some thirty states other than New York have permitted pooling small trust estates into one fund for investment administration. The income, capital gains, losses and expenses of the collective trust are shared by the constituent trusts in proportion to their contribution. By this plan, diversification of risk and economy of management can be extended to those whose capital standing alone would not obtain such advantage.

Statutory authorization for the establishment of such common trust funds is provided in the New York Banking Law, § 100–c, c. 687, L.1937, as amended by c. 602, L.1943, and c. 158, L.1944. Under this Act a trust company may, with approval of the State Banking Board, establish a common fund and, within prescribed limits, invest therein the assets of an unlimited number of estates, trusts or other funds of which it is trustee. Each participating trust shares ratably in the common fund, but exclusive management and control is in the trust company as trustee, and neither a fiduciary nor any beneficiary of a participating trust is deemed to have ownership in any particular asset or investment of this common fund. The trust company must keep fund assets separate from its own, and in its fiduciary capacity may not deal with itself or any affiliate. Provisions are made for accountings twelve to fifteen months after the establishment of a fund and triennially thereafter. The decree in each such judicial settlement of accounts is made binding and conclusive as to any matter set forth in the account upon everyone having any interest in the common fund or in any participating estate, trust or fund.

In January, 1946, Central Hanover Bank and Trust Company established a common trust fund in accordance with these provisions, and in March, 1947, it petitioned the Surrogate's Court for settlement of its first account as common trustee. During the accounting period a total of 113 trusts, approximately half inter vivos and half testamentary, participated in the common trust fund, the gross capital of which was nearly three million dollars. The record does not show the number or residence of the beneficiaries, but they were many and it is clear that some of them were not residents of the State of New York.

The only notice given beneficiaries of this specific application was by publication in a local newspaper in strict compliance with the minimum requirements of N.Y. Banking Law § 100–c(12): "After filing such petition [for judicial settlement of its account] the petitioner shall cause to be issued by the court in which the petition is filed and shall publish not less than once in each week for four successive weeks in a newspaper to be designated by the court a notice or citation addressed generally without naming them to all parties interested in such common trust fund and in such estates, trusts or funds mentioned in the petition, all of which may be described in the notice or citation only in the manner set forth in said petition and without setting forth the residence of any such decedent or donor of any such estate, trust or fund." Thus the only notice required, and the only one given, was by newspaper publication setting forth merely the name and the date of establishment of the common trust fund, and a list of all participating estates, trusts or funds.

At the time the first investment in the common fund was made on behalf of each participating estate, however, the trust company, pursuant to the requirements of § 100–c(9), had notified by mail each person of full age and sound mind whose name and address was then known to it and who was "entitled to share in the income therefrom . . . [or] . . . who would be entitled to share in the principal if the event upon which such estate, trust or fund will become distributable should have occurred at the time of sending such notice." Included in the notice was a copy of those provisions of the Act relating to the sending of the notice itself and to the judicial settlement of common trust fund accounts.

Upon the filing of the petition for the settlement of accounts, appellant was, by order of the court pursuant to § 100–c(12), appointed special guardian and attorney for all persons known or unknown not otherwise appearing who had or might thereafter have any interest in the income of the common trust fund; and appellee Vaughan was appointed to represent those similarly interested in the principal. There were no other appearances on behalf of any one interested in either interest or principal.

Appellant appeared specially, objecting that notice and the statutory provisions for notice to beneficiaries were inadequate to afford due process under the Fourteenth Amendment, and therefore that the court was without jurisdiction to render a final and binding decree. Appellant's objections were entertained and overruled, the Surrogate holding that the notice required and given was sufficient. 75 N.Y.S.2d 397. A final decree accepting the accounts has been entered, affirmed by the Appellate Division of the Supreme Court, In re [Accounting of] Central Hanover Bank & Trust Co., 275 App.Div. 769, 88 N.Y.S.2d 907, and by the Court of Appeals of the State of New York, 299 N.Y. 697, 87 N.E.2d 73.

The effect of this decree, as held below, is to settle "all questions respecting the management of the common fund." We understand that every right which beneficiaries would otherwise have against the trust company, either as trustee of the common fund or as trustee of any individual trust, for improper management of the common trust fund during the period covered by the accounting is sealed and wholly terminated by the decree. [Citations omitted.]

We are met at the outset with a challenge to the power of the State—the right of its courts to adjudicate at all as against those beneficiaries who reside without the State of New York. It is contended that the proceeding is one in personam in that the decree affects neither title to nor possession of any res, but adjudges only personal rights of the beneficiaries to surcharge their trustee for negligence or breach of trust. Accordingly, it is said, under the strict doctrine of Pennoyer v. Neff, 95 U.S. 714, the Surrogate is without jurisdiction as to nonresidents upon whom personal service of process was not made.

Distinctions between actions in rem and those in personam are ancient and originally expressed in procedural terms what seems really to have been a distinction in the substantive law of property under a system quite unlike our own. Buckland and McNair, Roman Law and Common Law, 66; Burdick, Principles of Roman Law and Their Relation to Modern Law, 298. The legal recognition and rise in economic importance of incorporeal or intangible forms of property have upset the ancient simplicity of property law and the clarity of its distinctions, while new forms of proceedings have confused the old procedural classification. American courts have sometimes classed certain actions as in rem because personal service of process was not required, and at other times have held personal service of process not required because the action was in rem. See cases collected in Freeman on Judgments, § 1517 et seq. (5th ed.).

Judicial proceedings to settle fiduciary accounts have been sometimes termed in rem, or more indefinitely quasi in rem, or more vaguely still, "in the nature of a proceeding in rem." It is not readily apparent how the courts of New York did or would classify the present proceeding, which has some characteristics and is wanting in some features of proceedings both in rem and in personam. But in any event we think that the requirements of the Fourteenth Amendment to the

Federal Constitution do not depend upon a classification for which the standards are so elusive and confused generally and which, being primarily for state courts to define, may and do vary from state to state. Without disparaging the usefulness of distinctions between actions in rem and those in personam in many branches of law, or on other issues, or the reasoning which underlies them, we do not rest the power of the State to resort to [out-of-state] service in this proceeding upon how its courts or this Court may regard this historic antithesis. It is sufficient to observe that, whatever the technical definition of its chosen procedure, the interest of each state in providing means to close trusts that exist by the grace of its laws and are administered under the supervision of its courts is so insistent and rooted in custom as to establish beyond doubt the right of its courts to determine the interests of all claimants, resident or nonresident, provided its procedure accords full opportunity to appear and be heard.

■ [The portion of the majority's opinion reversing for inadequacy of notice, and JUSTICE BURTON's dissent with respect thereto, are reprinted in the next Topic. JUSTICE DOUGLAS did not participate.]

Hanson v. Denckla

Supreme Court of the United States, 1958.
357 U.S. 235, 78 S.Ct. 1228.

[On March 25, 1935, Mrs. Dora Browning Donner, then a Pennsylvania domiciliary, purported to create a trust naming the Wilmington Trust Co., a Delaware corporation, as trustee. The corpus consisted of securities. The trust instrument reserved a life estate to Mrs. Donner and empowered her to appoint the remainder interest either by inter vivos instrument or by will. In 1944 she established her domicile in Florida, and there on December 3, 1949, she exercised her power of appointment under the trust and separately executed a will. She died domiciled in Florida in 1952, and her will was probated there, with her daughter Elizabeth Hanson as executrix.

[The issue presented by this litigation was whether the trust assets passed pursuant to the appointment or in accordance with the residuary clause of the will. This in turn depended upon whether Mrs. Donner had reserved such extensive powers over the trust assets as to make the trust invalid. If the trust were valid, the appointment would be effective, and trust assets totaling $400,000 would pass to trusts of which the Delaware Trust Co., a Delaware corporation, was trustee and of which Mrs. Hanson's children, Donner Hanson and Joseph Winsor, were the beneficiaries; several other appointees would receive minor amounts of the trust assets. If the trust were invalid, all these assets would pass under the will to two of Mrs. Donner's other daughters, Katherine

Denckla and Dorothy Stewart, who were Mrs. Hanson's half-sisters and who as residuary legatees had already received over $500,000 each.

[Mrs. Denckla and Mrs. Stewart, both residents of Florida, brought a declaratory judgment action in Florida for the purpose of establishing that the assets passed under the will. The plaintiffs secured jurisdiction over Mrs. Hanson, Donner Hanson, and Joseph Winsor, all Florida residents, by personal service in Florida. The plaintiffs also named as defendants the Wilmington Trust Co., the Delaware Trust Co., and certain of the other appointees; notice was given to these nonresidents by ordinary mail, and publication was made in a Palm Beach newspaper pursuant to Florida law; none of these nonresidents appeared. The Florida trial court held under Florida law that the assets passed pursuant to the will.

[Meanwhile, Mrs. Hanson instituted a declaratory judgment action in Delaware to determine the persons who were entitled to the assets. The parties were substantially the same as in Florida. The nonresident defendants, including Mrs. Denckla and Mrs. Stewart, were notified by registered mail; only Mrs. Denckla did not appear. After the Florida decree, a guardian ad litem for the incompetent Mrs. Stewart unsuccessfully urged it as res judicata. The Delaware trial court held under Delaware law that the assets passed pursuant to the appointment.

[Next the Supreme Court of Florida and then the Supreme Court of Delaware sustained on the merits the determinations of their lower courts. The Florida Supreme Court also held that the Florida courts could exercise "substantive" jurisdiction over the absent defendants; but, as the Supreme Court of the United States was later to note, "[w]hether this meant jurisdiction over the person of the defendants or jurisdiction over the trust assets is open to doubt." The Delaware Supreme Court also rejected the contention that it was bound to give full faith and credit to the Florida decree.

[These inconsistent judgments came before the Supreme Court of the United States.]

■ MR. CHIEF JUSTICE WARREN delivered the opinion of the Court.

. . . .

The issues for our decision are, first, whether Florida erred in holding that it had jurisdiction over the nonresident defendants, and second, whether Delaware erred in refusing full faith and credit to the Florida decree. . . .

No. 107, The Florida Appeal. [The Court first ruled that the proper mode of review here was by petition for certiorari, but that it would treat the appeal as a petition. The Court then granted certiorari.]

Relying upon the principle that a person cannot invoke the jurisdiction of this Court to vindicate the right of a third party, appellees urge that appellants lack standing to complain of a defect in jurisdiction over the nonresident trust companies, who have made no appearance in this action. Florida adheres to the general rule that a trustee is an indispensable party to litigation involving the validity of the trust. In the absence of such a party a Florida court may not proceed to adjudicate the controversy. Since state law required the acquisition of jurisdiction over the nonresident trust company[8] before the court was empowered to proceed with the action, any defendant affected by the court's judgment has that "direct and substantial personal interest in the outcome" that is necessary to challenge whether that jurisdiction was in fact acquired. Chicago v. Atchison, T. & S.F.R. Co., 357 U.S. 77, 78 S.Ct. 1063.

Appellants charge that this judgment is offensive to the Due Process Clause of the Fourteenth Amendment because the Florida court was without jurisdiction. There is no suggestion that the court failed to employ a means of notice reasonably calculated to inform nonresident defendants of the pending proceedings, or denied them an opportunity to be heard in defense of their interests. The alleged defect is the absence of those "affiliating circumstances"[11] without which the courts of a State may not enter a judgment imposing obligations on persons (jurisdiction in personam) or affecting interests in property (jurisdiction in rem or quasi in rem).[12] While the in rem and in personam classifications do not exhaust all the situations that give rise to jurisdiction,[13] they are adequate to describe the affiliating circumstances suggested here, and accordingly serve as a useful means of approach to this case.

In rem jurisdiction. Founded on physical power, McDonald v. Mabee, 243 U.S. 90, 91, 37 S.Ct. 343, the in rem jurisdiction of a state court is limited by the extent of its power and by the coordinate authority of sister States. The basis of the jurisdiction is the presence of the subject property within the territorial jurisdiction of the forum State. [Citations omitted.] Tangible property poses no problem for the application of this rule, but the situs of intangibles is often a matter of controversy. In considering restrictions on the power to tax, this Court has concluded that

---

[8]   Hereafter the terms "trust," "trust company" and "trustee" have reference to the trust established in 1935 with the Wilmington Trust Co., the validity of which is at issue here. It is unnecessary to determine whether the Delaware Trust Co., to which the $400,000 remainder interest was appointed and was paid after Mrs. Donner's death, is also an indispensable party to this proceeding.

[11]   Sunderland, The Problem of Jurisdiction, Selected Essays on Constitutional Law, 1270, 1272.

[12]   A judgment in personam imposes a personal liability or obligation on one person in favor of another. A judgment in rem affects the interests of all persons in designated property. A judgment quasi in rem affects the interests of particular persons in designated property. The latter is of two types. In one the plaintiff is seeking to secure a pre-existing claim in the subject property and to extinguish or establish the nonexistence of similar interests of particular persons. In the other the plaintiff seeks to apply what he concedes to be the property of the defendant to the satisfaction of a claim against him. Restatement, Judgments, 5–9. For convenience of terminology this opinion will use "in rem" in lieu of "in rem and quasi in rem."

[13]   E.g., Mullane v. Central Hanover Bank & Trust Co., 339 U.S. 306, 312, 70 S.Ct. 652, 656; Williams v. North Carolina, 317 U.S. 287, 297, 63 S.Ct. 207, 212 [(1942) (divorce)]. Fraser, Jurisdiction by Necessity, 100 U. of Pa.L.Rev. 305.

"jurisdiction" over intangible property is not limited to a single State. [Citations omitted.] Whether the type of "jurisdiction" with which this opinion deals may be exercised by more than one State we need not decide. The parties seem to assume that the trust assets that form the subject matter of this action[16] were located in Delaware and not in Florida. We can see nothing in the record contrary to that assumption, or sufficient to establish a situs in Florida.[17]

The Florida court held that the presence of the subject property was not essential to its jurisdiction. Authority over the probate and construction of its domiciliary's will, under which the assets might pass, was thought sufficient to confer the requisite jurisdiction. But jurisdiction cannot be predicated upon the contingent role of this Florida will. Whatever the efficacy of a so-called "in rem" jurisdiction over assets admittedly passing under a local will, a State acquires no in rem jurisdiction to adjudicate the validity of inter vivos dispositions simply because its decision might augment an estate passing under a will probated in its courts. If such a basis of jurisdiction were sustained, probate courts would enjoy nationwide service of process to adjudicate interests in property with which neither the State nor the decedent could claim any affiliation. The settlor-decedent's Florida domicile is equally unavailing as a basis for jurisdiction over the trust assets. For the purpose of jurisdiction in rem the maxim that personalty has its situs at the domicile of its owner[19] is a fiction of limited utility. [Citation omitted.] The maxim is no less suspect when the domicile is that of a decedent. In analogous cases, this Court has rejected the suggestion that the probate decree of the State where decedent was domiciled has an in rem effect on personalty outside the forum State that could render it conclusive on the interests of nonresidents over whom there was no personal jurisdiction. [Citations omitted.] The fact that the owner is or was domiciled within the forum State is not a sufficient affiliation with the property upon which to base jurisdiction in rem. . . .

. . . .

In personam jurisdiction. Appellees' stronger argument is for in personam jurisdiction over the Delaware trustee. They urge that the

---

[16]   This case does not concern the situs of a beneficial interest in trust property. These appellees were contesting the validity of the trust. Their concern was with the legal interest of the trustee or, if the trust was invalid, the settlor. Therefore, the relevant factor here is the situs of the stocks, bonds, and notes that make up the corpus of the trust. Properly speaking such assets are intangibles that have no "physical" location. But their embodiment in documents treated for most purposes as the assets themselves makes them partake of the nature of tangibles. [Citation omitted.]

[17]   The documents evidencing ownership of the trust property were held in Delaware, [citation omitted], by a Delaware trustee who was the obligee of the credit instruments and the record owner of the stock. The location of the obligors and the domicile of the corporations do not appear. The trust instrument was executed in Delaware by a settlor then domiciled in Pennsylvania. Without expressing any opinion on the significance of these or other factors unnamed, we note that none relates to Florida.

[19]   We assume arguendo for the purpose of this discussion that the trust was invalid so that Mrs. Donner was the "owner" of the subject property.

circumstances of this case amount to sufficient affiliation with the State of Florida to empower its courts to exercise personal jurisdiction over this nonresident defendant. Principal reliance is placed upon McGee v. International Life Ins. Co., 355 U.S. 220, 78 S.Ct. 199. In McGee the Court noted the trend of expanding personal jurisdiction over nonresidents. As technological progress has increased the flow of commerce between States, the need for jurisdiction over nonresidents has undergone a similar increase. At the same time, progress in communications and transportation has made the defense of a suit in a foreign tribunal less burdensome. In response to these changes, the requirements for personal jurisdiction over nonresidents have evolved from the rigid rule of Pennoyer v. Neff, 95 U.S. 714, to the flexible standard of International Shoe Co. v. Washington, 326 U.S. 310, 66 S.Ct. 154. But it is a mistake to assume that this trend heralds the eventual demise of all restrictions on the personal jurisdiction of state courts. See Vanderbilt v. Vanderbilt, 354 U.S. 416, 418, 77 S.Ct. 1360, 1362 [(1957) (holding that Nevada divorce court had no personal jurisdiction over New York wife)]. Those restrictions are more than a guarantee of immunity from inconvenient or distant litigation. They are a consequence of a territorial limitations on the power of the respective States. However minimal the burden of defending in a foreign tribunal, a defendant may not be called upon to do so unless he has had the "minimal contacts" with that State that are a prerequisite to its exercise of power over him. See International Shoe Co. v. Washington, 326 U.S. 310, 319, 66 S.Ct. 154, 159.

We fail to find such contacts in the circumstances of this case. The defendant trust company has no office in Florida, and transacts no business there. None of the trust assets has ever been held or administered in Florida, and the record discloses no solicitation of business in that State either in person or by mail. Cf. International Shoe Co. v. Washington, 326 U.S. 310, 66 S.Ct. 154; McGee v. International Life Ins. Co., 355 U.S. 220, 78 S.Ct. 199; Travelers Health Ass'n v. Virginia ex rel. State Corporation Comm., 339 U.S. 643, 70 S.Ct. 927 [(1950) (holding that continuous business activities subjected insurance company to specific jurisdiction)].

The cause of action in this case is not one that arises out of an act done or transaction consummated in the forum State. In that respect, it differs from McGee v. International Life Ins. Co., 355 U.S. 220, 78 S.Ct. 199, and the cases there cited. In McGee, the nonresident defendant solicited a reinsurance agreement with a resident of California. The offer was accepted in that State, and the insurance premiums were mailed from there until the insured's death. Noting the interest California has in providing effective redress for its residents when nonresident insurers refuse to pay claims on insurance they have solicited in that State, the Court upheld jurisdiction because the suit "was based on a contract which had substantial connection with that State." In contrast, this action involves the validity of an agreement that was entered without any connection with the forum State. The agreement was executed in Delaware by a trust company incorporated in that State and a settlor domiciled in Pennsylvania. The first relationship Florida has to the agreement was years later when the settlor became domiciled there, and the trustee remitted the trust income to her in that State. From Florida Mrs. Donner carried on several bits of trust administration that may be compared to the mailing of premiums in McGee. But the record discloses no instance in which the *trustee* performed any acts in Florida that bear the same relationship to the agreement as the solicitation in McGee. Consequently, this suit cannot be said to be one to enforce an obligation that arose from a privilege the defendant exercised in Florida. Cf. International Shoe Co. v. Washington, 326 U.S. 310, 319, 66 S.Ct. 154, 159. This case is also different from McGee in that there the State had enacted special legislation (Unauthorized Insurers Process Act, West's Ann.Cal.Insurance Code § 1610 et seq.) to exercise what McGee called its "manifest interest" in providing effective redress for citizens who had been injured by nonresidents engaged in an activity that the State treats as exceptional and subjects to special regulation. Cf. Travelers Health Ass'n v. Virginia ex rel. State Corporation Comm., 339 U.S. 643, 647–649, 70 S.Ct. 927, 929–930; Doherty & Co. v. Goodman, 294 U.S. 623, 627, 55 S.Ct. 553, 554; Hess v. Pawloski, 274 U.S. 352, 47 S.Ct. 632.

The execution in Florida of the powers of appointment under which the beneficiaries and appointees claim does not give Florida a substantial connection with the contract on which this suit is based. It is the validity of the trust agreement, not the appointment, that is at issue here. For the purpose of applying its rule that the validity of a trust is determined by the law of the State of its creation, Florida ruled that the appointment amounted to a "republication" of the original trust instrument in Florida. For choice-of-law purposes such a ruling may be justified, but we think it an insubstantial connection with the trust agreement for purposes of determining the question of personal jurisdiction over a nonresident defendant. The unilateral activity of those who claim some relationship with a nonresident defendant cannot satisfy the requirement of contact with the forum State. The application of that rule will vary with the quality and nature of the defendant's activity, but it is essential in each case that there be some act by which the defendant purposefully avails itself of the privilege of conducting activities within the forum State, thus invoking the benefits and protections of its laws. International Shoe Co. v. Washington, 326 U.S. 310, 319, 66 S.Ct. 154, 159. The settlor's execution in Florida of her power of appointment cannot remedy the absence of such an act in this case.

It is urged that because the settlor and most of the appointees and beneficiaries were domiciled in Florida the courts of that State should be able to exercise personal jurisdiction over the nonresident trustees. This is a non-sequitur. With personal jurisdiction over the executor, legatees, and appointees, there is nothing in federal law to prevent Florida from adjudicating concerning the respective rights and liabilities of those parties. But Florida has not chosen to do so. As we understand its law, the trustee is an indispensable party over whom the court must acquire jurisdiction before it is empowered to enter judgment in a proceeding affecting the validity of a trust. It does not acquire that jurisdiction by being the "center of gravity" of the controversy, or the most convenient location for litigation. The issue is personal jurisdiction, not choice of law. It is resolved in this case by considering acts of the trustee. As we have indicated, they are insufficient to sustain the jurisdiction.

Because it sustained jurisdiction over the nonresident trustees, the Florida Supreme Court found it unnecessary to determine whether Florida law made those defendants indispensable parties in the circumstances of this case. Our conclusion that Florida was without jurisdiction over the Delaware trustee, or over the trust corpus held in that State, requires that we make that determination in the first instance. As we have noted earlier, the Florida Supreme Court has repeatedly held that a trustee is an indispensable party without whom a Florida court has no power to adjudicate controversies affecting the validity of a trust. For that reason the Florida judgment must be reversed not only as to the nonresident trustees but also as to appellants, over whom the Florida court admittedly had jurisdiction.

No. 117, The Delaware Certiorari. The same reasons that compel reversal of the Florida judgment require affirmance of the Delaware one. Delaware is under no obligation to give full faith and credit to a Florida judgment invalid in Florida because offensive to the Due Process Clause of the Fourteenth Amendment. . . .

. . . .

The judgment of the Delaware Supreme Court is affirmed, and the judgment of the Florida Supreme Court is reversed and the cause is remanded for proceedings not inconsistent with this opinion.

It is so ordered.

■ Mr. Justice Black, whom Mr. Justice Burton and Mr. Justice Brennan join, dissenting.

I believe the courts of Florida had power to adjudicate the effectiveness of the appointment made in Florida by Mrs. Donner with respect to all those who were notified of the proceedings and given an opportunity to be heard without violating the Due Process Clause of the Fourteenth Amendment. If this is correct, it follows that the Delaware courts erred in refusing to give the prior Florida judgment full faith and credit. U.S.Const., Art. IV, § 1; 28 U.S.C. § 1738.

. . . .

. . . This disposition, which was designed to take effect after her death, had very close and substantial connections with that State. Not only was the appointment made in Florida by a domiciliary of Florida, but the primary beneficiaries also lived in that State. In my view it could hardly be denied that Florida had sufficient interest so that a court with jurisdiction might properly apply Florida law, if it chose, to determine whether the appointment was effectual. [Citations omitted.] True, the question whether the law of a State can be applied to a transaction is different from the question whether the courts of that State have jurisdiction to enter a judgment, but the two are often closely related and to a substantial degree depend upon similar considerations. It seems to me that where a transaction has as much relationship to a State as Mrs. Donner's appointment had to Florida its courts ought to have power to adjudicate controversies arising out of that transaction, unless litigation there would impose such a heavy disproportionate burden on a nonresident defendant that it would offend what this Court has referred to as "traditional notions of fair play and substantial justice." Milliken v. Meyer, 311 U.S. 457, 463, 61 S.Ct. 339, 342, 343; International Shoe Co. v. Washington, 326 U.S. 310, 316, 66 S.Ct. 154, 158. So far as the nonresident defendants here are concerned I can see nothing which approaches that degree of unfairness. Florida, the home of the principal contenders for Mrs. Donner's largess, was a reasonably convenient forum for all.[3] Certainly there is nothing fundamentally unfair in subjecting the corporate trustee to the jurisdiction of the Florida courts. It chose to maintain business relations with Mrs. Donner in that State for eight years regularly communicating with her with respect to the business of the trust including the very appointment in question.

. . . .

The Court's decision that Florida did not have jurisdiction over the trustee (and inferentially the nonresident beneficiaries) stems from principles stated the better part of a century ago in Pennoyer v. Neff, 95 U.S. 714. That landmark case was decided in 1878, at a time when business affairs were predominantly local in nature and travel between States was difficult, costly and sometimes even dangerous. There the Court laid down the broad principle that a State could not subject nonresidents to the jurisdiction of its courts unless they were served with process within its boundaries or voluntarily appeared, except to the extent they had property in the State. But as the years have passed the constantly increasing ease and rapidity of communication and the tremendous growth of interstate business activity have led to a steady and inevitable relaxation of the strict limits on state jurisdiction announced in that case. In the course of this evolution the old jurisdictional landmarks have been left far behind so that in many instances States may now properly exercise jurisdiction over nonresidents not amenable to service within their borders. Yet further relaxation seems certain. Of course we have not reached the point where

---

[3]   The suggestion is made that Delaware was a more suitable forum, but the plain fact is that none of the beneficiaries or legatees has ever resided in that State.

state boundaries are without significance, and I do not mean to suggest such a view here. There is no need to do so. For we are dealing with litigation arising from a transaction that had an abundance of close and substantial connections with the State of Florida.

Perhaps the decision most nearly in point is Mullane v. Central Hanover Bank & Trust Co., 339 U.S. 306, 70 S.Ct. 652. In that case the Court held that a State could enter a personal judgment in favor of a trustee against nonresident beneficiaries of a trust even though they were not served with process in that State. So far as appeared, their only connection with the State was the fact that the trust was being administered there.[5] In upholding the State's jurisdiction the Court emphasized its great interest in trusts administered within its boundaries and governed by its laws. Id., 339 U.S. at page 313, 70 S.Ct. at page 656. Also implicit in the result was a desire to avoid the necessity for multiple litigation with its accompanying waste and possibility of inconsistent results. It seems to me that the same kind of considerations are present here supporting Florida's jurisdiction over the nonresident defendants.

. . . .

■ MR. JUSTICE DOUGLAS, dissenting.

. . . .

. . . Florida has such a plain and compelling relation to these out-of-state intangibles [citation omitted], and the nexus between the settlor and trustee is so close, as to give Florida the right to make the controlling determination even without personal service over the trustee and those who claim under it. We must remember this is not a suit to impose liability on the Delaware trustee or on any other absent person. It is merely a suit to determine interests in those intangibles. Cf. Mullane v. Central Hanover Trust Co., supra, 339 U.S. at page 313, 70 S.Ct. at page 656. Under closely analogous facts the California Supreme Court held in Atkinson v. Superior Court, 49 Cal.2d 338, 316 P.2d 960, that California had jurisdiction over an absent trustee. I would hold the same here. . . .

Shaffer v. Heitner

Supreme Court of the United States, 1977.
433 U.S. 186, 97 S.Ct. 2569.

■ MR. JUSTICE MARSHALL delivered the opinion of the Court.

The controversy in this case concerns the constitutionality of a Delaware statute that allows a court of that State to take jurisdiction of a lawsuit by sequestering any property of the defendant that happens to

---

[5]   There was no basis for in rem jurisdiction since the litigation concerned the personal liability of the trustee and did not involve the trust property.

be located in Delaware. Appellants contend that the sequestration statute as applied in this case violates the Due Process Clause of the Fourteenth Amendment both because it permits the state courts to exercise jurisdiction despite the absence of sufficient contacts among the defendants, the litigation, and the State of Delaware and because it authorizes the deprivation of defendants' property without providing adequate procedural safeguards. We find it necessary to consider only the first of these contentions.

I

Appellee Heitner, a nonresident of Delaware, is the owner of one share of stock in the Greyhound Corporation, a business incorporated under the laws of Delaware with its principal place of business in Phoenix, Ariz. On May 22, 1974, he filed a [multimillion dollar] shareholder's derivative suit in the Court of Chancery for New Castle County, Del., in which he named as defendants Greyhound . . . and 28 present or former officers or directors of [Greyhound].cc In essence, Heitner alleged that the individual defendants had violated their duties to Greyhound by causing it . . . to engage in actions that resulted in [its] being held liable for substantial damages in a private antitrust suit and a large fine in a criminal contempt action. The activities which led to these penalties took place in Oregon.

Simultaneously with his complaint, Heitner filed a motion for an order of sequestration of the Delaware property of the individual defendants pursuant to 10 Del.C. § 366.[4] This motion was accompanied by a supporting affidavit of counsel which stated that the individual defendants were nonresidents of Delaware.dd . . . The requested

---

cc   A subsidiary of Greyhound was also involved in this action, but nothing in the case turns on this. For the story of the Shaffer case, see Wendy Collins Perdue, "The Story of Shaffer: Allocating Jurisdictional Authority Among the States," in Civil Procedure Stories 135 (Kevin M. Clermont ed., 2d ed. 2008).

    4   10 Del.C. § 366 provides:

"(a) If it appears in any complaint filed in the Court of Chancery that the defendant or any one or more of the defendants is a nonresident of the State, the Court may make an order directing such nonresident defendant or defendants to appear by a day certain to be designated. Such order shall be served on such nonresident defendant or defendants by mail or otherwise, if practicable, and shall be published in such manner as the Court directs, not less than once a week for 3 consecutive weeks. The Court may compel the appearance of the defendant by the seizure of all or any part of his property, which property may be sold under the order of the Court to pay the demand of the plaintiff, if the defendant does not appear, or otherwise defaults. Any defendant whose property shall have been so seized and who shall have entered a general appearance in the cause may, upon notice to the plaintiff, petition the Court for an order releasing such property or any part thereof from the seizure. The Court shall release such property unless the plaintiff shall satisfy the Court that because of other circumstances there is a reasonable possibility that such release may render it substantially less likely that plaintiff will obtain satisfaction of any judgment secured. If such petition shall not be granted, or if no such petition shall be filed, such property shall remain subject to seizure and may be sold to satisfy any judgment entered in the cause. The Court may at any time release such property or any part thereof upon the giving of sufficient security.

    . . . ."

dd   Nine states appeared in the affidavit's list of the individual defendants' last known addresses. However, nine of those addresses were in Arizona and eight in California.

sequestration order was signed the day the motion was filed. Pursuant to that order, the sequestrator "seized" approximately 82,000 shares of Greyhound common stock belonging to 19 of the defendants,[7] and options belonging to another two defendants.[8] These seizures were accomplished by placing "stop transfer" orders or their equivalents on the books of the Greyhound Corporation. So far as the record shows, none of the certificates representing the seized property was physically present in Delaware. The stock was considered to be in Delaware, and so subject to seizure, by virtue of 8 Del.C. § 169, which makes Delaware the situs of ownership of all stock in Delaware corporations.

All 28 defendants were notified of the initiation of the suit by certified mail directed to their last known addresses and by publication in a New Castle County newspaper. The 21 defendants whose property was seized (hereafter referred to as appellants) responded by entering a special appearance for the purpose of moving to quash service of process and to vacate the sequestration order. They contended that the ex parte sequestration procedure did not accord them due process of law and that the property seized was not capable of attachment in Delaware. In addition, appellants asserted that under the rule of International Shoe Co. v. Washington, 326 U.S. 310, 66 S.Ct. 154 (1945), they did not have sufficient contacts with Delaware to sustain the jurisdiction of that State's courts.

The Court of Chancery rejected these arguments . . . .

On appeal, the Delaware Supreme Court affirmed the judgment of the Court of Chancery. Greyhound Corp. v. Heitner, 361 A.2d 225 (1976). . . .

Appellants' claim that the Delaware courts did not have jurisdiction to adjudicate this action received . . . cursory treatment. The court's analysis of the jurisdictional issue is contained in two paragraphs:

> "There are significant constitutional questions at issue here but we say at once that we do not deem the rule of International Shoe to be one of them. . . . The reason, of course, is that jurisdiction under § 366 remains . . . quasi in rem founded on the presence of capital stock here, not on prior contact by defendants with this forum. Under 8 Del.C. § 169 the 'situs of the ownership of the capital stock of all corporations existing under the laws of this State . . . [is] in this State,' and that provides the initial basis for jurisdiction. Delaware may constitutionally establish situs of such shares here, . . . it has

---

[7] The closing price of Greyhound stock on the day the sequestration order was issued was $14 3/8. New York Times, May 23, 1974, at 62. Thus, the value of the sequestered stock was approximately $1.2 million.

[8] . . . .

The remaining defendants apparently owned no property subject to the sequestration order.

done so and the presence thereof provides the foundation for § 366 in this case. . . .

"We hold that seizure of the Greyhound shares is not invalid because plaintiff has failed to meet the prior contacts tests of International Shoe." 361 A.2d, at 229.

We noted probable jurisdiction. 429 U.S. 813, 97 S.Ct. 52.[12] We reverse.

II

The Delaware courts rejected appellants' jurisdictional challenge by noting that this suit was brought as a quasi in rem proceeding. Since quasi in rem jurisdiction is traditionally based on attachment or seizure of property present in the jurisdiction, not on contacts between the defendant and the State, the courts considered appellants' claimed lack of contacts with Delaware to be unimportant. This categorical analysis assumes the continued soundness of the conceptual structure founded on the century-old case of Pennoyer v. Neff, 95 U.S. 714 (1878).

. . . .

From our perspective, the importance of Pennoyer is not its result, but the fact that its principles and corollaries derived from them became the basic elements of the constitutional doctrine governing state-court jurisdiction. . . . [U]nder Pennoyer state authority to adjudicate was based on the jurisdiction's power over either persons or property. This fundamental concept is embodied in the very vocabulary which we use to describe judgments. If a court's jurisdiction is based on its authority over the defendant's person, the action and judgment are denominated "in personam" and can impose a personal obligation on the defendant in favor of the plaintiff. If jurisdiction is based on the court's power over property within its territory, the action is called "in rem" or "quasi in rem." The effect of a judgment in such a case is limited to the property that supports jurisdiction and does not impose a personal liability on the property owner, since he is not before the court.[17] In Pennoyer's terms, the owner is affected only "indirectly" by an in rem judgment adverse to his interest in the property subject to the court's disposition.

. . . .

The Pennoyer rules generally favored nonresident defendants by making them harder to sue. This advantage was reduced, however, by the ability of a resident plaintiff to satisfy a claim against a nonresident defendant by bringing into court any property of the defendant located in

---

12   Under Delaware law, defendants whose property has been sequestered must enter a general appearance, thus subjecting themselves to in personam liability, before they can defend on the merits. See Greyhound Corp. v. Heitner, supra, at 235–236 . . . .

17   [The Court here quoted from footnote 12 of Hanson v. Denckla, 357 U.S. 235, 78 S.Ct. 1228 (1958), and adopted the convention that "we will for convenience generally use the term 'in rem' in place of 'in rem and quasi in rem.'"]

the plaintiff's State. [Citation omitted.] For example, . . . Harris v. Balk, 198 U.S. 215, 25 S.Ct. 625 (1905). . . .

[The Court here traced developments from Pennoyer to International Shoe, closing with extensive quotations from the latter.[ee]]

. . . Thus, the relationship among the defendant, the forum, and the litigation, rather than the mutually exclusive sovereignty of the States on which the rules of Pennoyer rest, became the central concern of the inquiry into personal jurisdiction.[20] The immediate effect of this departure from Pennoyer's conceptual apparatus was to increase the ability of the state courts to obtain personal jurisdiction over nonresident defendants. [Citations omitted.]

No equally dramatic change has occurred in the law governing jurisdiction in rem. There have, however, been intimations that the collapse of the in personam wing of Pennoyer has not left that decision unweakened as a foundation for in rem jurisdiction. Well-reasoned lower court opinions have questioned the proposition that the presence of property in a State gives that State jurisdiction to adjudicate rights to the property regardless of the relationship of the underlying dispute and the property owner to the forum. [Citations omitted.] The overwhelming majority of commentators have also rejected Pennoyer's premise that a proceeding "against" property is not a proceeding against the owners of that property. Accordingly, they urge that the "traditional notions of fair play and substantial justice" that govern a State's power to adjudicate in personam should also govern its power to adjudicate personal rights to property located in the State. [Citations omitted.]

. . . Moreover, in Mullane [v. Central Hanover Bank & Trust Co., 339 U.S. 306, 70 S.Ct. 652 (1950),] we held that Fourteenth Amendment rights cannot depend on the classification of an action as in rem or in personam, since that is

> "a classification for which the standards are so elusive and confused generally and which, being primarily for state courts to define, may and do vary from state to state." 339 U.S., at 312, 70 S.Ct., at 656.

It is clear, therefore, that the law of state-court jurisdiction no longer stands securely on the foundation established in Pennoyer. We think that

---

[ee] In the course of its discussion, the Court noted that "the International Shoe Court believed that the standard it was setting forth governed actions against natural persons as well as corporations, and we see no reason to disagree. . . . The differences between individuals and corporations may, of course, lead to the conclusion that a given set of circumstances establishes state jurisdiction over one type of defendant but not over the other."

[20] Nothing in Hanson v. Denckla, supra, is to the contrary. The Hanson Court's statement that restrictions on state jurisdiction "are a consequence of territorial limitations on the power of the respective States," id., 357 U.S., at 251, 78 S.Ct., at 1238, simply makes the point that the States are defined by their geographical territory. After making this point, the Court in Hanson determined that the defendant over which personal jurisdiction was claimed had not committed any acts sufficiently connected to the State to justify jurisdiction under the International Shoe standard.

the time is ripe to consider whether the standard of fairness and substantial justice set forth in International Shoe should be held to govern actions in rem as well as in personam.

III

The case for applying to jurisdiction in rem the same test of "fair play and substantial justice" as governs assertions of jurisdiction in personam is simple and straightforward. It is premised on recognition that "[t]he phrase, 'judicial jurisdiction over a thing,' is a customary elliptical way of referring to jurisdiction over the interests of persons in a thing." Restatement (Second) of Conflict of Laws § 56, Introductory Note (1971).[22] This recognition leads to the conclusion that in order to justify an exercise of jurisdiction in rem, the basis for jurisdiction must be sufficient to justify exercising "jurisdiction over the interests of persons in a thing."[23] The standard for determining whether an exercise of jurisdiction over the interests of persons is consistent with the Due Process Clause is the minimum-contacts standard elucidated in International Shoe.

This argument, of course, does not ignore the fact that the presence of property in a State may bear on the existence of jurisdiction by providing contacts among the forum State, the defendant, and the litigation. For example, when claims to the property itself are the source of the underlying controversy between the plaintiff and the defendant,[24] it would be unusual for the State where the property is located not to have jurisdiction. In such cases, the defendant's claim to property located in the State would normally[25] indicate that he expected to benefit from the State's protection of his interest. The State's strong interests in assuring the marketability of property within its borders and in providing a procedure for peaceful resolution of disputes about the possession of that property would also support jurisdiction, as would the likelihood that important records and witnesses will be found in the State. The presence of property may also favor jurisdiction in cases, such as suits for injury suffered on the land of an absentee owner, where the

---

[22]   "All proceedings, like all rights, are really against persons. Whether they are proceedings or rights in rem depends on the number of persons affected." Tyler v. Court of Registration, 175 Mass. 71, 76, 55 N.E. 812, 814 (Holmes, C.J.), appeal dismissed, 179 U.S. 405, 21 S.Ct. 206 (1900).

[23]   It is true that the potential liability of a defendant in an in rem action is limited by the value of the property, but that limitation does not affect the argument. The fairness of subjecting a defendant to state-court jurisdiction does not depend on the size of the claim being litigated. . . .

[24]   This category includes true in rem actions and the first type of quasi in rem proceedings. See n. 17, supra.

[25]   In some circumstances the presence of property in the forum State will not support the inference suggested in text. Cf., e.g., Restatement (Second) of Conflict of Laws § 60, Comments c, d; [other citation omitted]; Note, The Power of a State to Affect Title in a Chattel Atypically Removed to It, 47 Colum.L.Rev. 767 (1947).

defendant's ownership of the property is conceded but the cause of action is otherwise related to rights and duties growing out of that ownership.[29]

It appears, therefore, that jurisdiction over many types of actions which now are or might be brought in rem would not be affected by a holding that any assertion of state-court jurisdiction must satisfy the International Shoe standard. For the type of quasi in rem action typified by Harris v. Balk and the present case, however, accepting the proposed analysis would result in significant change. These are cases where the property which now serves as the basis for state-court jurisdiction is completely unrelated to the plaintiff's cause of action. Thus, although the presence of the defendant's property in a State might suggest the existence of other ties among the defendant, the State, and the litigation, the presence of the property alone would not support the State's jurisdiction. If those other ties did not exist, cases over which the State is now thought to have jurisdiction could not be brought in that forum.

Since acceptance of the International Shoe test would most affect this class of cases, we examine the arguments against adopting that standard as they relate to this category of litigation. Before doing so, however, we note that this type of case also presents the clearest illustration of the argument in favor of assessing assertions of jurisdiction by a single standard. For in cases such as Harris and this one, the only role played by the property is to provide the basis for bringing the defendant into court. Indeed, the express purpose of the Delaware sequestration procedure is to compel the defendant to enter a personal appearance. In such cases, if a direct assertion of personal jurisdiction over the defendant would violate the Constitution, it would seem that an indirect assertion of that jurisdiction should be equally impermissible.

The primary rationale for treating the presence of property as a sufficient basis for jurisdiction to adjudicate claims over which the State would not have jurisdiction if International Shoe applied is that a wrongdoer

> "should not be able to avoid payment of his obligations by the expedient of removing his assets to a place where he is not subject to an in personam suit." Restatement (Second) of Conflict of Laws § 66, Comment a.

[Citation omitted.] This justification, however, does not explain why jurisdiction should be recognized without regard to whether the property is present in the State because of an effort to avoid the owner's obligations. Nor does it support jurisdiction to adjudicate the underlying

---

[29]   Cf. Dubin v. City of Philadelphia, 34 Pa.D. & C. 61 (1938). If such an action were brought under the in rem jurisdiction rather than under a long-arm statute, it would be a quasi in rem action of the second type. See n. 17, supra. [New York has used this idea to allow attachment jurisdiction in the "gap" where personal jurisdiction would be constitutional but where New York's strictly construed long-arm statute does not reach. Banco Ambrosiano, S.P.A. v. Artoc Bank & Trust Ltd., 62 N.Y.2d 65, 464 N.E.2d 432, 476 N.Y.S.2d 64 (1984).—Ed.]

claim. At most, it suggests that a State in which property is located should have jurisdiction to attach that property, by use of proper procedures, as security for a judgment being sought in a forum where the litigation can be maintained consistently with International Shoe. [Citations omitted.] Moreover, we know of nothing to justify the assumption that a debtor can avoid paying his obligations by removing his property to a State in which his creditor cannot obtain personal jurisdiction over him. The Full Faith and Credit Clause, after all, makes the valid in personam judgment of one State enforceable in all other States.[36]

It might also be suggested that allowing in rem jurisdiction avoids the uncertainty inherent in the International Shoe standard and assures a plaintiff of a forum.[37] See Folk & Moyer, [Sequestration in Delaware: A Constitutional Analysis, 73 Colum.L.Rev.] 749, 767 (1973). We believe, however, that the fairness standard of International Shoe can be easily applied in the vast majority of cases. Moreover, when the existence of jurisdiction in a particular forum under International Shoe is unclear, the cost of simplifying the litigation by avoiding the jurisdictional question may be the sacrifice of "fair play and substantial justice." That cost is too high.

We are left, then, to consider the significance of the long history of jurisdiction based solely on the presence of property in a State. Although the theory that territorial power is both essential to and sufficient for jurisdiction has been undermined, we have never held that the presence of property in a State does not automatically confer jurisdiction over the owner's interest in that property. This history must be considered as supporting the proposition that jurisdiction based solely on the presence of property satisfies the demands of due process, [citation omitted], but it is not decisive. "[T]raditional notions of fair play and substantial justice" can be as readily offended by the perpetuation of ancient forms that are no longer justified as by the adoption of new procedures that are inconsistent with the basic values of our constitutional heritage. [Citations omitted.] The fiction that an assertion of jurisdiction over property is anything but an assertion of jurisdiction over the owner of the property supports an ancient form without substantial modern justification. Its continued acceptance would serve only to allow state-court jurisdiction that is fundamentally unfair to the defendant.

---

[36]　Once it has been determined by a court of competent jurisdiction that the defendant is a debtor of the plaintiff, there would seem to be no unfairness in allowing an action to realize on that debt in a State where the defendant has property, whether or not that State would have jurisdiction to determine the existence of the debt as an original matter. . . .

[37]　This case does not raise, and we therefore do not consider, the question whether the presence of a defendant's property in a State is a sufficient basis for jurisdiction when no other forum is available to the plaintiff.

We therefore conclude that all assertions of state-court jurisdiction must be evaluated according to the standards set forth in International Shoe and its progeny.[39]

IV

The Delaware courts based their assertion of jurisdiction in this case solely on the statutory presence of appellants' property in Delaware. Yet that property is not the subject matter of this litigation, nor is the underlying cause of action related to the property. Appellants' holdings in Greyhound do not, therefore, provide contacts with Delaware sufficient to support the jurisdiction of that State's courts over appellants. If it exists, that jurisdiction must have some other foundation.

Appellee Heitner did not allege and does not now claim that appellants have ever set foot in Delaware. Nor does he identify any act related to his cause of action as having taken place in Delaware. Nevertheless, he contends that appellants' positions as directors and officers of a corporation chartered in Delaware provide sufficient "contacts, ties, or relations," International Shoe Co. v. Washington, supra, 326 U.S., at 319, 66 S.Ct., at 160, with that State to give its courts jurisdiction over appellants in this stockholder's derivative action. This argument is based primarily on what Heitner asserts to be the strong interest of Delaware in supervising the management of a Delaware corporation. That interest is said to derive from the role of Delaware law in establishing the corporation and defining the obligations owed to it by its officers and directors. In order to protect this interest, appellee concludes, Delaware's courts must have jurisdiction over corporate fiduciaries such as appellants.

This argument is undercut by the failure of the Delaware Legislature to assert the state interest appellee finds so compelling. Delaware law bases jurisdiction not on appellants' status as corporate fiduciaries, but rather on the presence of their property in the State. Although the sequestration procedure used here may be most frequently used in derivative suits against officers and directors, Hughes Tool Co. v. Fawcett Publications, Inc., 290 A.2d 693, 695 (Del.Ch.1972), the authorizing statute evinces no specific concern with such actions. Sequestration can be used in any suit against a nonresident, [citations omitted], and reaches corporate fiduciaries only if they happen to own interests in a Delaware corporation, or other property in the State. But as Heitner's failure to secure jurisdiction over seven of the defendants named in his complaint demonstrates, there is no necessary relationship between holding a position as a corporate fiduciary and owning stock or other interests in the corporation. If Delaware perceived its interest in securing jurisdiction over corporate fiduciaries to be as great as Heitner

---

[39]   It would not be fruitful for us to re-examine the facts of cases decided on the rationales of Pennoyer and Harris to determine whether jurisdiction might have been sustained under the standard we adopt today. To the extent that prior decisions are inconsistent with this standard, they are overruled.

suggests, we would expect it to have enacted a statute more clearly designed to protect that interest.

Moreover, even if Heitner's assessment of the importance of Delaware's interest is accepted, his argument fails to demonstrate that Delaware is a fair forum for this litigation. The interest appellee has identified may support the application of Delaware law to resolve any controversy over appellants' actions in their capacities as officers and directors. But we have rejected the argument that if a State's law can properly be applied to a dispute, its courts necessarily have jurisdiction over the parties to that dispute. [The Court here quoted Hanson v. Denckla.]

Appellee suggests that by accepting positions as officers or directors of a Delaware corporation, appellants performed the acts required by Hanson v. Denckla. He notes that Delaware law provides substantial benefits to corporate officers and directors, and that these benefits were at least in part the incentive for appellants to assume their positions. It is, he says, "only fair and just" to require appellants, in return for these benefits, to respond in the State of Delaware when they are accused of misusing their powers. Brief, at 15.

But like Heitner's first argument, this line of reasoning establishes only that it is appropriate for Delaware law to govern the obligations of appellants to Greyhound and its stockholders. It does not demonstrate that appellants have "purposefully avail[ed themselves] of the privilege of conducting activities within the forum State," Hanson v. Denckla, supra, 357 U.S., at 253, 78 S.Ct., at 1240, in a way that would justify bringing them before a Delaware tribunal. Appellants have simply had nothing to do with the State of Delaware. Moreover, appellants had no reason to expect to be haled before a Delaware court. Delaware, unlike some States, has not enacted a statute that treats acceptance of a directorship as consent to jurisdiction in the State. And "[i]t strains reason . . . to suggest that anyone buying securities in a corporation formed in Delaware 'impliedly consents' to subject himself to Delaware's . . . jurisdiction on any cause of action." Folk & Moyer, supra, at 785. Appellants, who were not required to acquire interests in Greyhound in order to hold their positions, did not by acquiring those interests surrender their right to be brought to judgment only in States with which they had had "minimum contacts."

The Due Process Clause

"does not contemplate that a state may make binding a judgment . . . against an individual or corporate defendant with which the state has no contacts, ties, or relations." International Shoe Co. v. Washington, supra, 326 U.S., at 319, 66 S.Ct., at 160.

Delaware's assertion of jurisdiction over appellants in this case is inconsistent with that constitutional limitation on state power. The judgment of the Delaware Supreme Court must, therefore, be reversed.

It is so ordered.

■ Mr. Justice Rehnquist took no part in the consideration or decision of this case.

■ Mr. Justice Powell, concurring.

. . . .

I would explicitly reserve judgment . . . on whether the ownership of some forms of property whose situs is indisputably and permanently located within a State may, without more, provide the contacts necessary to subject a defendant to jurisdiction within the State to the extent of the value of the property. In the case of real property, in particular, preservation of the common law concept of quasi in rem jurisdiction arguably would avoid the uncertainty of the general International Shoe standard without significant cost to " 'traditional notions of fair play and substantial justice.' " . . .

Subject to the foregoing reservation, I join the opinion of the Court.

■ Mr. Justice Stevens, concurring in the judgment.

The Due Process Clause affords protection against "judgments without notice." International Shoe Co. v. Washington, 326 U.S. 310, 324, 66 S.Ct. 154, 162 (opinion of Black, J.). . . .

The requirement of fair notice also, I believe, includes fair warning that a particular activity may subject a person to the jurisdiction of a foreign sovereign. If I visit another State, or acquire real estate or open a bank account in it, I knowingly assume some risk that the State will exercise its power over my property or my person while there. My contact with the State, though minimal, gives rise to predictable risks.

. . . .

One who purchases shares of stock on the open market can hardly be expected to know that he has thereby become subject to suit in a forum remote from his residence and unrelated to the transaction. . . . I therefore agree with the Court that on the record before us no adequate basis for jurisdiction exists and that the Delaware statute is unconstitutional on its face.

How the Court's opinion may be applied in other contexts is not entirely clear to me. I agree with Mr. Justice Powell that it should not be read to invalidate quasi in rem jurisdiction where real estate is involved. I would also not read it as invalidating other long-accepted methods of acquiring jurisdiction over persons with adequate notice of both the particular controversy and the fact that their local activities might subject them to suit. My uncertainty as to the reach of the opinion, and my fear that it purports to decide a great deal more than is necessary to dispose of this case, persuade me merely to concur in the judgment.

■ MR. JUSTICE BRENNAN, concurring in part and dissenting in part.

I join Parts I–III of the Court's opinion. I fully agree that the minimum contacts analysis developed in International Shoe Co. v. Washington, 326 U.S. 310, 66 S.Ct. 154 (1945), represents a far more sensible construct for the exercise of state court jurisdiction than the patchwork of legal and factual fictions that has been generated from the decision in Pennoyer v. Neff, 95 U.S. 714 (1878). It is precisely because the inquiry into minimum contacts is now of such overriding importance, however, that I must respectfully dissent from Part IV of the Court's opinion.

[Justice Brennan thought that the Court did not need to reach and should not have reached the issue in Part IV.]

Nonetheless, because the Court rules on the minimum contacts question, I feel impelled to express my view. While evidence derived through discovery might satisfy me that minimum contacts are lacking in a given case, I am convinced that as a general rule a state forum has jurisdiction to adjudicate a shareholder derivative action centering on the conduct and policies of the directors and officers of a corporation chartered by that State. Unlike the Court, I therefore would not foreclose Delaware from asserting jurisdiction over appellants were it persuaded to do so on the basis of minimum contacts.

It is well settled that a derivative lawsuit as presented here does not inure primarily to the benefit of the named plaintiff. Rather, the primary beneficiaries are the corporation and its owners, the shareholders. "The cause of action which such a plaintiff brings before the court is not his own but the corporation's. . . . Such a plaintiff often may represent an important public and stockholder interest in bringing faithless managers to book." Koster v. Lumbermens Mutual Casualty Co., 330 U.S. 518, 522, 524, 67 S.Ct. 828, 831, 832 (1947).

Viewed in this light, the chartering State has an unusually powerful interest in insuring the availability of a convenient forum for litigating claims involving a possible multiplicity of defendant fiduciaries and for vindicating the State's substantive policies regarding the management of its domestic corporations. I believe that our cases fairly establish that the State's valid substantive interests are important considerations in assessing whether it constitutionally may claim jurisdiction over a given cause of action.

In this instance, Delaware can point to at least three interrelated public policies that are furthered by its assertion of jurisdiction. First, the State has a substantial interest in providing restitution for its local corporations that allegedly have been victimized by fiduciary misconduct, even if the managerial decisions occurred outside the State. . . . Second, state courts have legitimately read their jurisdiction expansively when a cause of action centers in an area in which the forum State possesses a manifest regulatory interest. . . . Finally, a State like Delaware has a recognized interest in affording a convenient forum for supervising and overseeing the affairs of an entity that is purely the creation of that State's law. . . .

To be sure, the Court is not blind to these considerations. It notes that the State's interests "may support the application of Delaware law to resolve any controversy over appellants' actions in their capacities as officers and directors." . . . But this, the Court argues, pertains to choice of law, not jurisdiction. I recognize that the jurisdictional and choice-of-law inquiries are not identical. Hanson v. Denckla, 357 U.S. 235, 254, 78 S.Ct. 1228, 1240 (1958). But I would not compartmentalize thinking in this area quite so rigidly as it seems to me the Court does today, for both inquiries "are often closely related and to a substantial degree depend upon similar considerations." Id., at 258, 78 S.Ct., at 1242 (Black, J., dissenting). In either case an important linchpin is the extent of contacts between the controversy, the parties, and the forum State. While constitutional limitations on the choice of law are by no means settled, see, e.g., Home Ins. Co. v. Dick, 281 U.S. 397, 50 S.Ct. 338 (1930), important considerations certainly include the expectancies of the parties and the fairness of governing the defendants' acts and behavior by rules of conduct created by a given jurisdiction. See, e.g., Restatement (Second) of Conflict of Laws § 6. These same factors bear upon the propriety of a State's exercising jurisdiction over a legal dispute. At the minimum, the decision that it is fair to bind a defendant by a State's laws and rules should prove to be highly relevant to the fairness of permitting that same State to accept jurisdiction for adjudicating the controversy.

Furthermore, I believe that practical considerations argue in favor of seeking to bridge the distance between the choice-of-law and jurisdictional inquiries. Even when a court would apply the law of a different forum, as a general rule it will feel less knowledgeable and comfortable in interpretation, and less interested in fostering the policies of that foreign jurisdiction, than would the courts established by the State that provides the applicable law. [Citations omitted.] Obviously, such choice-of-law problems cannot entirely be avoided in a diverse legal system such as our own. Nonetheless, when a suitor seeks to lodge a suit in a State with a substantial interest in seeing its own law applied to the transaction in question, we could wisely act to minimize conflicts, confusion, and uncertainty by adopting a liberal view of jurisdiction, unless considerations of fairness or efficiency strongly point in the opposite direction.

This case is not one where, in my judgment, this preference for jurisdiction is adequately answered. Certainly nothing said by the Court persuades me that it would be unfair to subject appellants to suit in Delaware. The fact that the record does not reveal whether they "set foot" or committed "act[s] related to [the] cause of action" in Delaware . . . is not decisive, for jurisdiction can be based strictly on out-of-state acts having foreseeable effects in the forum State. [Citations omitted.] I have little difficulty in applying this principle to nonresident fiduciaries whose alleged breaches of trust are said to have substantial damaging effect on the financial posture of a resident corporation. Further, I cannot understand how the existence of minimum contacts in a constitutional sense is at all affected by Delaware's failure statutorily to express an interest in controlling corporate fiduciaries. . . . To me this simply demonstrates that Delaware did not elect to assert jurisdiction to the extent the Constitution would allow.[5] Nor would I view as controlling or even especially meaningful Delaware's failure to exact from appellants their consent to be sued. . . . Once we have rejected the jurisdictional framework created in Pennoyer v. Neff, I see no reason to rest jurisdiction on a fictional outgrowth of that system such as the existence of a consent statute, expressed or implied.[6]

I, therefore, would approach the minimum contacts analysis differently than does the Court. Crucial to me is the fact that appellants voluntarily associated themselves with the State of Delaware, "invoking the benefits and protections of its laws," Hanson v. Denckla, supra, 357 U.S., at 253, 78 S.Ct., at 1240; International Shoe Co. v. Washington, supra, 326 U.S., at 319, 66 S.Ct., at 159, by entering into a long-term and fragile relationship with one of its domestic corporations. They thereby elected to assume powers and to undertake responsibilities wholly derived from that State's rules and regulations, and to become eligible for those benefits that Delaware law makes available to its corporations' officials. E.g., 8 Del.C. § 143 (interest-free loans); § 145 (indemnification). While it is possible that countervailing issues of judicial efficiency and the like might clearly favor a different forum, they do not appear on the meager record before us; and, of course, we are concerned solely with "minimum" contacts, not the "best" contacts. I thus do not believe that it is unfair to insist that appellants make themselves available to suit in a competent forum that Delaware might create for vindication of its important public policies directly pertaining to appellants' fiduciary associations with the State.

---

[5]   In fact, it is quite plausible that the Delaware Legislature never felt the need to assert direct jurisdiction over corporate managers precisely because the sequestration statute heretofore has served as a somewhat awkward but effective basis for achieving such personal jurisdiction. . . .

[6]   Admittedly, when one consents to suit in a forum, his expectation is enhanced that he may be haled into that State's courts. To this extent, I agree that consent may have bearing on the fairness of accepting jurisdiction. But whatever is the degree of personal expectation that is necessary to warrant jurisdiction should not depend on the formality of establishing a consent law. Indeed, if one's expectations are to carry such weight, then appellants here might be fairly charged with the understanding that Delaware would decide to protect its substantial interests through its own courts, for they certainly realized that in the past the sequestration law has been employed primarily as a means of securing the appearance of corporate officials in the State's courts. Supra, at n. 5. Even in the absence of such a statute, however, the close and special association between a state corporation and its managers should apprise the latter that the state may seek to offer a convenient forum for addressing claims of fiduciary breach of trust.

———

Question: (30) Thirteen days after the Shaffer decision the Delaware legislature had passed and the Governor had signed a bill providing that henceforth a nonresident's accepting a directorship or continuing in the position of director of a Delaware corporation would be deemed consent to the appointment of the registered agent of such corporation as his agent for service of process in connection with suits such as Shaffer; the statute also required direct notice of suit to the nonresident by registered mail. See Del.Code Ann. tit. 10, § 3114 (now covering corporate officers too). Is this jurisdictional statute constitutional? See Armstrong v. Pomerance, 423 A.2d 174 (Del.1980) (yes, on the ground that the new statute gave fair warning, so that serving as a director constituted purposeful availment). (Shortly after the enactment, Greyhound reincorporated in Arizona to avoid the new statute. See David L. Ratner & Donald E. Schwartz, The Impact of Shaffer v. Heitner on the Substantive Law of Corporations, 45 Brook.L.Rev. 641, 653–54 (1979) (noting, however, "that, while Delaware makes it easy for a minority shareholder to sue, it makes it very difficult to recover").)

———

ATKINSON v. SUPERIOR COURT, 49 Cal.2d 338, 316 P.2d 960 (1957), appeals dismissed and cert. denied, 357 U.S. 569, 78 S.Ct. 1381 (1958). Class actions were brought in a California state court on behalf of the employees of various motion picture and phonograph record companies, attacking the validity of the collective bargaining agreements between their employers and the American Federation of Musicians, and also attacking certain related trust agreements. The gist of the complaints was that the A.F.M., in violation of its duty as the employees' collective bargaining agent, had agreed with the employers that the latter should periodically turn over certain royalty payments to a New York trustee for named trust purposes, instead of to the employees who claimed the payments as wages earned in California; they further alleged that the employers were willing to make payment to the employees but for their agreements with the A.F.M. to make payment to the trustee, and that the officers of the A.F.M. had wrongfully negotiated the arrangement for the selfish purpose of perpetuating themselves in office. The complaints sought a declaration of the collective bargaining agreements' invalidity and of the employees' right to the payments, and also damages from the A.F.M.; they further asked for the appointment of a receiver to collect future royalty payments and for a preliminary injunction to prevent the employers from making payment to the trustee.

The plaintiffs named as defendants the employers, the A.F.M., and the trustee. They obtained personal jurisdiction over the employers and the A.F.M. in California. The trustee was served in New York, but did not appear. The trial court ruled the trustee an indispensable party and dismissed for lack of personal jurisdiction over the trustee. The Supreme Court of California, speaking through Justice Traynor, reversed, concluding that "service upon the trustee in New York was sufficient to give the court jurisdiction to adjudicate his right to receive payments under the contracts here involved."

———

Questions: (31) Appraise the Atkinson decision sequentially in the light of Mullane v. Central Hanover Bank & Trust Co., Hanson v. Denckla, and Shaffer v. Heitner.

(32) If the Atkinson case were to arise for the first time today, what position would you advise the defendant employers to take on the jurisdictional question?

(b) THE FRAMEWORK—RESTRUCTURED OR RESURRECTED?

KULKO v. SUPERIOR COURT, 436 U.S. 84, 98 S.Ct. 1690 (1978). Some time after Sharon Horn and first one and later the other of her children had moved to California, she sued her former husband, Dr. Ezra Kulko, for child support in a California court. The defendant still lived in New York City but had consented to the children's living with her in California. Upon the defendant's special appearance, the California courts, just before the Shaffer decision, upheld personal jurisdiction as "reasonable."

On certiorari, the Supreme Court of the United States held that here jurisdiction violated due process because the defendant lacked the minimum contacts with California required by the power test, even though he had visited the state a couple of times. Justice Marshall, writing for the Court, cited Hanson v. Denckla liberally. He generalized that personal jurisdiction demands "a sufficient connection between the defendant and the forum State to make it fair to require defense of the action in the forum. . . . While the interests of the forum State and of the plaintiff in proceeding with the cause in the plaintiff's forum of choice are, of course, to be considered, see McGee v. International Life Insurance Co., . . . an essential criterion in all cases is whether the 'quality and nature' of the defendant's activity is such that it is 'reasonable' and 'fair' to require him to conduct his defense in that State. International Shoe Co. v. Washington . . . ." Here the defendant "did not purposefully derive benefit from any activities relating to the State" and "lacks any other relevant contact with the State."

Justice Brennan, joined by Justices White and Powell, dissented.

———

RUSH v. SAVCHUK, 444 U.S. 320, 334, 100 S.Ct. 571, 580 (1980). In January 1972 Rush, who was the driver from Indiana, and Savchuk, the passenger also from Indiana, were in a single-car accident in Indiana. However, Indiana's guest statute would have barred a claim by the injured Savchuk.

In June 1973 Savchuk moved with his parents to Minnesota. In May 1974 he brought a $125,000 negligence action against Rush in

Minnesota, which would apply its more favorable tort law. State Farm Mutual Automobile Insurance Company insured the car, owned by Rush's father, under a policy issued in Indiana. Savchuk invoked quasi in rem jurisdiction by garnishing State Farm's contractual obligation to defend and indemnify Rush, and he arranged service upon Rush in Indiana. State Farm, an insurer operating nationwide, had supposedly consented to general jurisdiction in Minnesota. Rush moved to dismiss for lack of territorial jurisdiction. The trial court denied the motion, and the state supreme court affirmed the existence of quasi in rem jurisdiction.

Savchuk's jurisdictional gambit was authorized by a specific Minnesota statute, which in turn had been based on the jurisdictional theory generated in Seider v. Roth, 17 N.Y.2d 111, 216 N.E.2d 312, 269 N.Y.S.2d 99 (1966). So-called Seider jurisdiction conceptually reified the insurer's obligation to the insured as an in-state debt that would support quasi in rem jurisdiction, given authorization to garnish and given the insurer's amenability to suit—somewhat oddly, however, the plaintiff had to be a forum-state resident, and the liability of even an appearing defendant-insured could not exceed the policy's liability limit.

On appeal, the Supreme Court of the United States reversed for lack of territorial jurisdiction. Justice Marshall, writing for the Court, cited Shaffer v. Heitner liberally. He apparently felt that Minnesota was not reasonable in categorizing this action as quasi in rem and thus evading the restrictions on personal jurisdiction. At any rate, he applied a constitutional test for personal jurisdiction, under which Rush lacked minimum contacts with the forum state.

Irrelevant to the Court were, on the one hand, the possible unreasonableness of Seider's highly conceptual reification and, on the other hand, the possible overall fairness of going forward with this suit in Minnesota.

The Court also refused to treat this suit as being essentially against State Farm and hence the functional equivalent of a so-called direct action, whereby under a few states' law an injured plaintiff can sue the liability insurer directly without joining the insured. The Court observed that Minnesota formally required suit to be against the insured. Moreover, the insured was more than a merely nominal defendant, as the Court noted that the insured's reputation, insurability, and other interests could suffer detriment from the suit.

Justices Brennan and Stevens dissented. Excerpts from Justice Brennan's opinion appear after World-Wide Volkswagen Corp. v. Woodson, which follows below.

———

Question: (33) As part of its enforcement scheme, available even for registered out-of-state judgments, New York now allows the judgment creditor to utilize personal jurisdiction over a third party, if such jurisdiction otherwise exists in New York, to institute a proceeding for an order that the third party turn over debt or personal property located outside New York and owned by the judgment debtor but possessed by the third party—without regard to the existence of connections between New York and the judgment creditor, the judgment debtor, their dispute, or the asset. See Koehler v. Bank of Berm. Ltd., 12 N.Y.3d 533, 911 N.E.2d 825, 883 N.Y.S.2d 763 (2009). This innovation by New York uses personal jurisdiction over a garnishee to extend the ordinary reach of enforcement. The policy of such aggressive enforcement is questionable, but is it even constitutional? Given that Shaffer and Rush held that a state cannot unreasonably substitute quasi in rem jurisdiction for personal jurisdiction, can New York so use personal jurisdiction as a substitute for quasi in rem jurisdiction over in-state assets? Or is New York simply adding an in personam remedy to the enforcement process, in a converse replay of Garfein's addition of a quasi in rem remedy to equity?

World-Wide Volkswagen Corp. v. Woodson

Supreme Court of the United States, 1980.
444 U.S. 286, 100 S.Ct. 559, 580.

■ MR. JUSTICE WHITE delivered the opinion of the Court.

The issue before us is whether, consistently with the Due Process Clause of the Fourteenth Amendment, an Oklahoma court may exercise in personam jurisdiction over a nonresident automobile retailer and its wholesale distributor in a products liability action, when the defendants' only connection with Oklahoma is the fact that an automobile sold in New York to New York residents became involved in an accident in Oklahoma.

I

Respondents Harry and Kay Robinson purchased a new Audi automobile from petitioner Seaway Volkswagen, Inc. (Seaway) in Massena, N.Y., in 1976. The following year the Robinson family, who resided in New York, left that State for a new home in Arizona. As they passed through [Creek County in] the State of Oklahoma, another car struck their Audi in the rear, causing a fire which severely burned Kay Robinson and her two children.

The Robinsons subsequently brought a products liability action in the District Court for Creek County, Okla., claiming that their injuries resulted from defective design and placement of the Audi's gas tank and fuel system. They joined as defendants the automobile's manufacturer, Audi NSU Auto Union Aktiengesellschaft (Audi); its importer, Volkswagen of America, Inc. (Volkswagen); its regional distributor, petitioner World-Wide Volkswagen Corporation (World-Wide); and its retail dealer, petitioner Seaway. Seaway and World-Wide entered special appearances,[3] claiming that Oklahoma's exercise of jurisdiction over them would offend the limitations on the State's jurisdiction imposed by the Due Process Clause of the Fourteenth Amendment.

The facts presented to the District Court showed that World-Wide is incorporated and has its business office in New York. It distributes vehicles, parts, and accessories, under contract with Volkswagen, to retail dealers in New York, New Jersey, and Connecticut. Seaway, one of these retail dealers, is incorporated and has its place of business in New York. Insofar as the record reveals, Seaway and World-Wide are fully independent corporations whose relations with each other and with Volkswagen and Audi are contractual only. Respondents adduced no evidence that either World-Wide or Seaway does any business in Oklahoma, ships or sells any products to or in that State, has an agent to receive process there, or purchases advertisements in any media calculated to reach Oklahoma. In fact, as respondents' counsel conceded at oral argument, Tr. of Oral Arg. 32, there was no showing that any automobile sold by World-Wide or Seaway has ever entered Oklahoma with the single exception of the vehicle involved in the present case.

Despite the apparent paucity of contacts between petitioners and Oklahoma, the District Court rejected their constitutional claim and reaffirmed that ruling in denying petitioners' motion for reconsideration. Petitioners then sought a writ of prohibition in the Supreme Court of Oklahoma to restrain the District Judge, respondent Charles S. Woodson, from exercising in personam jurisdiction over them. They renewed their contention that because they had no "minimal contacts," App. 32, with the State of Oklahoma, the actions of the District Judge were in violation of their rights under the Due Process Clause.

The Supreme Court of Oklahoma denied the writ, 585 P.2d 351 (1978), holding that personal jurisdiction over petitioners was authorized by Oklahoma's "Long-Arm" Statute, Okla.Stat., Tit. 12, § 1701.03(a)(4) (1971).[7] Although the Court noted that the proper approach was to test jurisdiction against both statutory and constitutional standards, its analysis did not distinguish these questions, probably because § 1701.03(a)(4) has been interpreted as conferring jurisdiction to the

---

[3]   Volkswagen also entered a special appearance in the District Court, but unlike World-Wide and Seaway did not seek review in the Supreme Court of Oklahoma and is not a petitioner here. Both Volkswagen and Audi remain as defendants in the litigation pending before the District Court in Oklahoma. [The latter two were, respectively, New Jersey and German citizens.—Ed.]

[7]   This subsection provides:

"A court may exercise personal jurisdiction over a person, who acts directly or by an agent, as to a cause of action or claim for relief arising from the person's . . . causing tortious injury in this state by an act or omission outside this state if he regularly does or solicits business or engages in any other persistent course of conduct, or derives substantial revenue from goods used or consumed or services rendered, in this state. . . ."

The State Supreme Court rejected jurisdiction based on § 1701.03(a)(3), which authorizes jurisdiction over any person "causing tortious injury in this state by an act or omission in this state." Something in addition to the infliction of tortious injury was required.

limits permitted by the United States Constitution. The Court's rationale was contained in the following paragraph, 585 P.2d, at 354:

> "In the case before us, the product being sold and distributed by the petitioners is by its very design and purpose so mobile that petitioners can foresee its possible use in Oklahoma. This is especially true of the distributor, who has the exclusive right to distribute such automobile [sic] in New York, New Jersey and Connecticut. The evidence presented below demonstrated that goods sold and distributed by the petitioners were used in the State of Oklahoma, and under the facts we believe it reasonable to infer, given the retail value of the automobile, that the petitioners derive substantial income from automobiles which from time to time are used in the State of Oklahoma. This being the case, we hold that under the facts presented, the trial court was justified in concluding that the petitioners derive substantial revenue from goods used or consumed in this State."

We granted certiorari, 440 U.S. 907, 99 S.Ct. 1212 (1979), to consider an important constitutional question with respect to state-court jurisdiction and to resolve a conflict between the Supreme Court of Oklahoma and the highest courts of at least four other States. We reverse.

II

The Due Process Clause of the Fourteenth Amendment limits the power of a state court to render a valid personal judgment against a nonresident defendant. Kulko v. Superior Court, 436 U.S. 84, 91, 98 S.Ct. 1690, 1696 (1978). A judgment rendered in violation of due process is void in the rendering State and is not entitled to full faith and credit elsewhere. Pennoyer v. Neff, 95 U.S. 714, 732–733 (1878). Due process requires that the defendant be given adequate notice of the suit, Mullane v. Central Hanover Trust Co., 339 U.S. 306, 313–314, 70 S.Ct. 652, 657 (1950), and be subject to the personal jurisdiction of the court, International Shoe Co. v. Washington, 326 U.S. 310, 66 S.Ct. 154 (1945). In the present case, it is not contended that notice was inadequate; the only question is whether these particular petitioners were subject to the jurisdiction of the Oklahoma courts.

[The constitutional limit on state jurisdiction] can be seen to perform two related, but distinguishable, functions. It protects the defendant against the burdens of litigating in a distant or inconvenient forum. And it acts to ensure that the States, through their courts, do not reach out beyond the limits imposed on them by their status as coequal sovereigns in a federal system.

The protection against inconvenient litigation is typically described in terms of "reasonableness" or "fairness." We have said that the defendant's contacts with the forum State must be such that maintenance of the suit "does not offend 'traditional notions of fair play and substantial justice.'" International Shoe Co. v. Washington, supra, at 316, 66 S.Ct., at 158, quoting Milliken v. Meyer, 311 U.S. 457, 463, 61 S.Ct. 339, 342 (1940). The relationship between the defendant and the forum must be such that it is "reasonable . . . to require the corporation to defend the particular suit which is brought there." 326 U.S., at 317, 66 S.Ct., at 158. Implicit in this emphasis on reasonableness is the understanding that the burden on the defendant, while always a primary concern, will in an appropriate case be considered in light of other relevant factors, including the forum State's interest in adjudicating the dispute, see McGee v. International Life Ins. Co., 355 U.S. 220, 223, 78 S.Ct. 199, 201 (1957); the plaintiff's interest in obtaining convenient and effective relief, see Kulko v. Superior Court, supra, at 92, 98 S.Ct., at 1697, at least when that interest is not adequately protected by the plaintiff's power to choose the forum, cf. Shaffer v. Heitner, 433 U.S. 186, 211, n. 37, 97 S.Ct. 2569, 2583, n. 37 (1977); the interstate judicial system's interest in obtaining the most efficient resolution of controversies; and the shared interest of the several States in furthering fundamental substantive social policies, see Kulko v. Superior Court, supra, at 93, 98, 98 S.Ct., at 1697, 1700.

The limits imposed on state jurisdiction by the Due Process Clause, in its role as a guarantor against inconvenient litigation, have been substantially relaxed over the years. As we noted in McGee v. International Life Ins. Co., supra, at 222–223, 78 S.Ct., at 201, this trend is largely attributable to a fundamental transformation in the American economy:

> "Today many commercial transactions touch two or more States and may involve parties separated by the full continent. With this increasing nationalization of commerce has come a great increase in the amount of business conducted by mail across state lines. At the same time modern transportation and communication have made it much less burdensome for a party sued to defend himself in a State where he engages in economic activity."

The historical developments noted in McGee, of course, have only accelerated in the generation since that case was decided.

Nevertheless, we have never accepted the proposition that state lines are irrelevant for jurisdictional purposes, nor could we and remain faithful to the principles of interstate federalism embodied in the Constitution. The economic interdependence of the States was foreseen and desired by the Framers. In the Commerce Clause, they provided that the Nation was to be a common market, a "free trade unit" in which the States are debarred from acting as separable economic entities. H.P. Hood & Sons, Inc. v. Du Mond, 336 U.S. 525, 538, 69 S.Ct. 657, 665 (1949). But the Framers also intended that the States retain many essential attributes of sovereignty, including, in particular, the sovereign power to try causes in their courts. The sovereignty of each State, in turn, implied a limitation on the sovereignty of all of its sister States—a limitation express or implicit in both the original scheme of the Constitution and the Fourteenth Amendment.

Hence, even while abandoning the shibboleth that "[t]he authority of every tribunal is necessarily restricted by the territorial limits of the State in which it is established," Pennoyer v. Neff, supra, at 720, we emphasized that the reasonableness of asserting jurisdiction over the defendant must be assessed "in the context of our federal system of government," International Shoe Co. v. Washington, supra, at 317, 66 S.Ct., at 158, and stressed that the Due Process Clause ensures, not only fairness, but also the "orderly administration of the laws," id., at 319, 66 S.Ct., at 159. As we noted in Hanson v. Denckla, 357 U.S. 235, 250–251, 78 S.Ct. 1228, 1238 (1958):

> " . . . But it is a mistake to assume that this trend [from Pennoyer to International Shoe] heralds the eventual demise of all restrictions on the personal jurisdiction of state courts. [Citation omitted.] Those restrictions are more than a guarantee of immunity from inconvenient or distant litigation. They are a consequence of territorial limitations on the power of the respective States."

Thus, the Due Process Clause "does not contemplate that a state may make binding a judgment in personam against an individual or corporate defendant with which the state has no contacts, ties, or relations." International Shoe Co. v. Washington, supra, at 319, 66 S.Ct., at 159. Even if the defendant would suffer minimal or no inconvenience from being forced to litigate before the tribunals of another State; even if the forum State has a strong interest in applying its law to the controversy; even if the forum State is the most convenient location for litigation, the Due Process Clause, acting as an instrument of interstate federalism, may sometimes act to divest the State of its power to render a valid judgment. Hanson v. Denckla, supra, at 251, 254, 78 S.Ct., at 1238, 1240.

III

Applying these principles to the case at hand, we find in the record before us a total absence of those affiliating circumstances that are a necessary predicate to any exercise of state-court jurisdiction. Petitioners carry on no activity whatsoever in Oklahoma. They close no sales and perform no services there. They avail themselves of none of the privileges and benefits of Oklahoma law. They solicit no business there either through salespersons or through advertising reasonably calculated to reach the State. Nor does the record show that they regularly sell cars at wholesale or retail to Oklahoma customers or residents or that they indirectly, through others, serve or seek to serve the Oklahoma market. In short, respondents seek to base jurisdiction on one, isolated occurrence and whatever inferences can be drawn therefrom: the fortuitous circumstance that a single Audi automobile, sold in New York to New

York residents, happened to suffer an accident while passing through Oklahoma.

It is argued, however, that because an automobile is mobile by its very design and purpose it was "foreseeable" that the Robinsons' Audi would cause injury in Oklahoma. Yet "foreseeability" alone has never been a sufficient benchmark for personal jurisdiction under the Due Process Clause. In Hanson v. Denckla, supra, it was no doubt foreseeable that the settlor of a Delaware trust would subsequently move to Florida and seek to exercise a power of appointment there; yet we held that Florida courts could not constitutionally exercise jurisdiction over a Delaware trustee that had no other contacts with the forum State. In Kulko v. Superior Court, supra, it was surely "foreseeable" that a divorced wife would move to California from New York, the domicile of the marriage, and that a minor daughter would live with the mother. Yet we held that California could not exercise jurisdiction in a child-support action over the former husband who had remained in New York.

If foreseeability were the criterion, a local California tire retailer could be forced to defend in Pennsylvania when a blowout occurs there, see Erlanger Mills, Inc. v. Cohoes Fibre Mills, Inc., 239 F.2d 502, 507 (C.A.4 1956); a Wisconsin seller of a defective automobile jack could be haled before a distant court for damage caused in New Jersey, Reilly v. Phil Tolkan Pontiac, Inc., 372 F.Supp. 1205 (NJ 1974); or a Florida soft drink concessionaire could be summoned to Alaska to account for injuries happening there, see Uppgren v. Executive Aviation Services, Inc., 304 F.Supp. 165, 170–171 (Minn.1969). Every seller of chattels would in effect appoint the chattel his agent for service of process. His amenability to suit would travel with the chattel. We recently abandoned the outworn rule of Harris v. Balk, 198 U.S. 215, 25 S.Ct. 625 (1905), that the interest of a creditor in a debt could be extinguished or otherwise affected by any State having transitory jurisdiction over the debtor. Shaffer v. Heitner, supra, 433 U.S. 186, 97 S.Ct. 2569 (1977). Having interred the mechanical rule that a creditor's amenability to a quasi in rem action travels with his debtor, we are unwilling to endorse an analogous principle in the present case.[11]

This is not to say, of course, that foreseeability is wholly irrelevant. But the foreseeability that is critical to due process analysis is not the mere likelihood that a product will find its way into the forum State.

---

[11]   Respondents' counsel, at oral argument, see Tr. of Oral Arg. 19–22, 29, sought to limit the reach of the foreseeability standard by suggesting that there is something unique about automobiles. It is true that automobiles are uniquely mobile, see Tyson v. Whitaker & Son, Inc., 407 A.2d 1, 6, and n. 11 (Me.1979) (McKusick, C.J.), that they did play a crucial role in the expansion of personal jurisdiction through the fiction of implied consent, e.g., Hess v. Pawloski, 274 U.S. 352, 47 S.Ct. 632 (1927), and that some of the cases have treated the automobile as a "dangerous instrumentality." But today, under the regime of International Shoe, we see no difference for jurisdictional purposes between an automobile and any other chattel. The "dangerous instrumentality" concept apparently was never used to support personal jurisdiction; and to the extent it has relevance today it bears not on jurisdiction but on the possible desirability of imposing substantive principles of tort law such as strict liability.

Rather, it is that the defendant's conduct and connection with the forum State are such that he should reasonably anticipate being haled into court there. See Kulko v. Superior Court, supra, at 97–98, 98 S.Ct., at 1699–1700; Shaffer v. Heitner, supra, at 216, 97 S.Ct., at 2586; and see id., at 217–219, 97 S.Ct., at 2586–2587 (Stevens, J., concurring in judgment). The Due Process Clause, by ensuring the "orderly administration of the laws," International Shoe Co. v. Washington, 326 U.S., at 319, 66 S.Ct., at 159, gives a degree of predictability to the legal system that allows potential defendants to structure their primary conduct with some minimum assurance as to where that conduct will and will not render them liable to suit.

When a corporation "purposefully avails itself of the privilege of conducting activities within the forum State," Hanson v. Denckla, supra, at 253, 78 S.Ct., at 1240, it has clear notice that it is subject to suit there, and can act to alleviate the risk of burdensome litigation by procuring insurance, passing the expected costs on to customers, or, if the risks are too great, severing its connection with the State. Hence if the sale of a product of a manufacturer or distributor such as Audi or Volkswagen is not simply an isolated occurrence, but arises from the efforts of the manufacturer or distributor to serve, directly or indirectly, the market for its product in other States, it is not unreasonable to subject it to suit in one of those States if its allegedly defective merchandise has there been the source of injury to its owner or to others. The forum State does not exceed its powers under the Due Process Clause if it asserts personal jurisdiction over a corporation that delivers its products into the stream of commerce with the expectation that they will be purchased by consumers in the forum State. Compare Gray v. American Radiator & Standard Sanitary Corp., 22 Ill.2d 432, 176 N.E.2d 761 (1961).

But there is no such or similar basis for Oklahoma jurisdiction over World-Wide or Seaway in this case. Seaway's sales are made in Massena, N.Y. World-Wide's market, although substantially larger, is limited to dealers in New York, New Jersey, and Connecticut. There is no evidence of record that any automobiles distributed by World-Wide are sold to retail customers outside this tri-State area. It is foreseeable that the purchasers of automobiles sold by World-Wide and Seaway may take them to Oklahoma. But the mere "unilateral activity of those who claim some relationship with a nonresident defendant cannot satisfy the requirement of contact with the forum State." Hanson v. Denckla, supra, at 253, 78 S.Ct., at 1239–1240.

In a variant on the previous argument, it is contended that jurisdiction can be supported by the fact that petitioners earn substantial revenue from goods used in Oklahoma. The Oklahoma Supreme Court so found, 585 P.2d, at 354–355, drawing the inference that because one automobile sold by petitioners had been used in Oklahoma, others might have been used there also. While this inference seems less than compelling on the facts of the instant case, we need not question the Court's factual findings in order to reject its reasoning.

This argument seems to make the point that the purchase of automobiles in New York, from which the petitioners earn substantial revenue, would not occur *but for* the fact that the automobiles are capable of use in distant States like Oklahoma. Respondents observe that the very purpose of an automobile is to travel, and that travel of automobiles sold by petitioners is facilitated by an extensive chain of Volkswagen service centers throughout the country, including some in Oklahoma. However, financial benefits accruing to the defendant from a collateral relation to the forum State will not support jurisdiction if they do not stem from a constitutionally cognizable contact with that State. See Kulko v. Superior Court, supra, at 94–95, 98 S.Ct., at 1698–1699. In our view, whatever marginal revenues petitioners may receive by virtue of the fact that their products are capable of use in Oklahoma is far too attenuated a contact to justify that State's exercise of in personam jurisdiction over them.

Because we find that petitioners have no "contacts, ties, or relations" with the State of Oklahoma, International Shoe Co. v. Washington, supra, at 319, 66 S.Ct., at 159, the judgment of the Supreme Court of Oklahoma is

Reversed.

■ MR. JUSTICE BRENNAN, dissenting [in this case and in Rush v. Savchuk, which precedes this case].

The Court holds that the Due Process Clause of the Fourteenth Amendment bars the States from asserting jurisdiction over the defendants in these two cases. In each case the Court so decides because it fails to find the "minimum contacts" that have been required since International Shoe Co. v. Washington, 326 U.S. 310, 316, 66 S.Ct. 154, 158 (1945). Because I believe that the Court reads International Shoe and its progeny too narrowly, and because I believe that the standards enunciated by those cases may already be obsolete as constitutional boundaries, I dissent.

I

[Justice Brennan argued that the defendant had minimum contacts.] Surely International Shoe contemplated that the significance of the contacts necessary to support jurisdiction would diminish if some other consideration helped establish that jurisdiction would be fair and reasonable. The interests of the State and other parties in proceeding with the case in a particular forum [and lesser burdens on the defendant in defending in the forum] are such considerations. McGee v. International Life Insurance Co., 355 U.S. 220, 223, 78 S.Ct. 199, 201 (1957) . . . .

. . . .

II

[He next argued that exercise of personal jurisdiction would satisfy the cumulative test of reasonableness.]

III

It may be that affirmance of the judgments in these cases would approach the outer limits of International Shoe's jurisdictional principle. But that principle, with its almost exclusive focus on the rights of defendants, may be outdated. . . .

International Shoe inherited its defendant focus from Pennoyer v. Neff, 95 U.S. 714 (1878), and represented the last major step this Court has taken in the long process of liberalizing the doctrine of personal jurisdiction. Though its flexible approach represented a major advance, the structure of our society has changed in many significant ways since International Shoe was decided in 1945. . . .

In answering the question whether or not it is fair and reasonable to allow a particular forum to hold a trial binding on a particular defendant, the interests of the forum State and other parties loom large in today's world and surely are entitled to as much weight as are the interests of the defendant. The "orderly administration of the laws" provides a firm basis for according some protection to the interests of plaintiffs and States as well as of defendants. Certainly, I cannot see how a defendant's right to due process is violated if the defendant suffers no inconvenience. . . .

The conclusion I draw is that constitutional concepts of fairness no longer require the extreme concern for defendants that was once necessary. Rather, as I wrote in dissent from Shaffer v. Heitner, . . . (emphasis added), minimum contacts must exist "among the *parties,* the contested transaction, and the forum State." The contacts between any two of these should not be determinative. . . .

. . . .

■ [The dissenting opinions of JUSTICES MARSHALL and BLACKMUN, not taking issue with the majority's approach but arguing that Seaway and World-Wide had sufficient contacts with Oklahoma to satisfy International Shoe, are omitted. Interestingly, however, Justice Blackmun began his opinion with this paragraph: "I confess that I am somewhat puzzled why the plaintiffs in this litigation are so insistent that the regional distributor and the retail dealer, the petitioners here, who handled the ill-fated Audi automobile involved in this litigation, be named defendants. It would appear that the manufacturer and the importer, whose subjectability to Oklahoma jurisdiction is not challenged before this Court, ought not to be judgment-proof. It may, of course, ultimately amount to a contest between insurance companies that, once begun, is not easily brought to a termination. Having made this much of an observation, I pursue it no further."][ff]

Questions: (34) How are all the Court's jurisdictional cases to be read together?

(a) To start with the case you just read, World-Wide seemed to make the following argument: The restriction that emerges from the early progeny of International Shoe, especially Mullane, rests on a concept of venue in a loose sense—the multifactor determination of "reasonableness" with respect to the litigation (a standard that was pro-plaintiff in the early days but is ultimately more party-neutral) puts the emphasis on *fairness* in selecting the forum. However, the restriction that re-emerges from the later progeny of International Shoe, beginning with Hanson, represents the law of territorial jurisdiction in a strict sense—the conceptual concern with "power" over the target of the action (a standard now seemingly pro-defendant in effect) puts the emphasis on governmental *structure* in limiting the states' power.

(b) In fact, Shaffer had earlier seemed to apply that same scheme: The two constitutional restrictions of reasonableness and power apply cumulatively, as the Shaffer Court showed by holding in Part III of its opinion that the exercise of in rem or quasi in rem power must also be reasonable, and then by holding in Part IV of its opinion that even a reasonable forum must have power in order to exercise personal jurisdiction (previously the cumulative relation of the two restrictions had sometimes gone unrecognized, as perhaps exemplified by Mullane). Incidentally, Shaffer also demonstrated by this treatment that the Pennoyer tripartite construct of in rem, quasi in rem, and in personam jurisdiction is alive and well (this despite the Shaffer Court's lip service to the Mullane heresy, or reform, that would have abolished the tripartite categorization as a constitutional matter).

(35) How should the Court further shape the doctrine now? Are the reasonableness and power tests bound eventually to coalesce, leaving some sort of reasonableness test as the survivor? Is the tripartite categorization then doomed?

[ff]   Soon after the Court's decision, the remaining defendants removed to a federal district court from the state court known for high verdicts. The Robinsons then lost at trial. They made numerous further attempts to recover from Audi, including trying to reopen the judgment by alleging Audi's fraud in the initial litigation, but none was successful. For a heart-rending description of the accident and the litigation, see Charles W. Adams, World-Wide Volkswagen v. Woodson—The Rest of the Story, 72 Neb.L.Rev. 1122 (1993). According to later newspaper accounts, when the Robinsons lost their bid for review by the Supreme Court of that fraud suit in January 1996, almost twenty years after the accident, see Robinson v. Audi Aktiengesellschaft, 516 U.S. 1045, 116 S.Ct. 705 (1996), denying cert. to 56 F.3d 1259, 1268 (10th Cir.1995), they decided to give up. Instead of living in the home they originally purchased in Tucson near a golf course, they were living in a mobile home on the other side of town. Sadly, they say that their original attorney never told them that Audi had offered to settle the case for $1 million. See Hipolito R. Corella, Tucsonans Lose Battle Against Audi, Ariz. Daily Star, Jan. 9, 1996, at 1A.

BURGER KING CORP. v. RUDZEWICZ, 471 U.S. 462, 105 S.Ct. 2174 (1985). Burger King is a Florida corporation whose principal offices are in Miami. This huge restaurant organization operates primarily through a franchise system, which entails a twenty-year contract whereby the company lends its name, restaurant facility, and advice in exchange for an initial fee, monthly payments, and submission to exacting regulation. Burger King sets corporate policy and makes significant decisions in Miami, while its ten district offices conduct day-to-day monitoring of franchisees.

John Rudzewicz (pronounced roo-JE-vich), an accountant from Michigan, wanted to invest by opening a Burger King restaurant in Michigan. He applied for a franchise to Burger King's district office in Michigan. Protracted negotiations followed, mainly with the district office but also with the Miami headquarters. Although Rudzewicz obtained limited concessions in the final contract, he did obligate himself to pay amounts to headquarters exceeding a million dollars over the twenty-year relationship and agreed to the standard provisions, including submission to regulation by Burger King and application of Florida law in construing the contract.

Rudzewicz's restaurant soon foundered, and he fell behind in payments. Unsuccessful negotiations led to Burger King's terminating the franchise and ordering him to vacate. Rudzewicz refused and continued to operate the facility as a Burger King restaurant until well into the ensuing lawsuit.

Burger King brought that lawsuit as a diversity action in the Southern District of Florida, including a claim against Rudzewicz for breach of the obligation to make required payments. Burger King served him by invoking, under the predecessor of Federal Rule 4(k)(1)(A), the provision of Florida's long-arm statute that specifically treats causes of action arising from a breach of contract in Florida by failure to perform acts required by the contract to be performed in Florida. Rudzewicz moved unsuccessfully to dismiss for lack of personal jurisdiction. He then answered, with a counterclaim for violations of Michigan's franchise investment law. The court found him liable for $228,875 in contract damages and found for Burger King on the counterclaim. On appeal, a divided panel of the Eleventh Circuit reversed the whole judgment on the ground that exercise of personal jurisdiction offended fundamental fairness.

On certiorari, the Supreme Court in turn reversed, concluding there was no offense to due process. Justice Brennan delivered the opinion of the Court, following a narration of the facts and prior proceedings with an explanation of the relevant principles:

"The Due Process Clause protects an individual's liberty interest in not being subject to the binding judgments of a forum with which he has established no meaningful 'contacts, ties, or relations.' International Shoe Co. v. Washington, 326 U.S. [310, 319, 66 S.Ct. 154, 160 (1945)]. By requiring that individuals have 'fair warning that a particular activity may subject [them] to the jurisdiction of a foreign sovereign,' Shaffer v. Heitner, 433 U.S. 186, 218, 97 S.Ct. 2569, 2587 (1977) (Stevens, J., concurring in judgment), the Due Process Clause 'gives a degree of predictability to the legal system that allows potential defendants to structure their primary conduct with some minimum assurance as to where that conduct will and will not render them liable to suit,' World-Wide Volkswagen Corp. v. Woodson, 444 U.S. 286, 297, 100 S.Ct. 559, 567 (1980).

"Where a forum seeks to assert specific jurisdiction over an out-of-state defendant who has not consented to suit there, this 'fair warning' requirement is satisfied if the defendant has 'purposefully directed' his activities at residents of the forum, Keeton v. Hustler Magazine, Inc., 465 U.S. 770, 774, 104 S.Ct. 1473, 1478 (1984), and the litigation results from alleged injuries that 'arise out of or relate to' those activities, Helicopteros Nacionales de Colombia, S.A. v. Hall, 466 U.S. 408, 414, 104 S.Ct. 1868, 1872 (1984). Thus '[t]he forum State does not exceed its powers under the Due Process Clause if it asserts personal jurisdiction over a corporation that delivers its products into the stream of commerce with the expectation that they will be purchased by consumers in the forum State' and those products subsequently injure forum consumers. World-Wide Volkswagen Corp. v. Woodson, supra, at 297–298, 100 S.Ct., at 567–568. Similarly, a publisher who distributes magazines in a distant State may fairly be held accountable in that forum for damages resulting there from an allegedly defamatory story. Keeton v. Hustler Magazine, Inc., supra; see also Calder v. Jones, 465 U.S. 783, 104 S.Ct. 1482 (1984) (suit against author and editor). And with respect to interstate contractual obligations, we have emphasized that parties who 'reach out beyond one state and create continuing relationships and obligations with citizens of another state' are subject to regulation and sanctions in the other State for the consequences of their activities. Travelers Health Assn. v. Virginia, 339 U.S. 643, 647, 70 S.Ct. 927, 929 (1950). See also McGee v. International Life Insurance Co., 355 U.S. 220, 222–223, 78 S.Ct. 199, 200–201 (1957).

. . . .

"This 'purposeful availment' requirement ensures that a defendant will not be haled into a jurisdiction solely as a result of 'random,' 'fortuitous,' or 'attenuated' contacts, Keeton v. Hustler Magazine, Inc., supra, at 774, 104 S.Ct., at 1478; World-Wide Volkswagen Corp. v. Woodson, 444 U.S., at 299, 100 S.Ct., at 568, or of the 'unilateral activity of another party or a third person,' Helicopteros Nacionales de Colombia, S.A. v. Hall, supra, at 417, 104 S.Ct., at 1873. Jurisdiction is proper, however, where the contacts proximately result from actions by the defendant *himself* that create 'a substantial connection' with the forum State. McGee v. International Life Insurance Co., supra, at 223, 78 S.Ct., at 201; [other citation omitted]. Thus where the defendant 'deliberately' has engaged in significant activities within a State, Keeton v. Hustler Magazine, Inc., 465 U.S., at 781, 104 S.Ct., at 1481, or has created 'continuing obligations' between himself and residents of the forum, Travelers Health Assn. v. Virginia, 339 U.S., at 648, 70 S.Ct., at 929, he manifestly has availed himself of the privilege of conducting business there, and because his activities are shielded by 'the benefits and protections' of the forum's laws it is presumptively not unreasonable to require him to submit to the burdens of litigation in that forum as well."

After so treating power, Justice Brennan explained reasonableness:

"Once it has been decided that a defendant purposefully established minimum contacts within the forum State, these contacts may be considered in light of other factors to determine whether the assertion of personal jurisdiction would comport with 'fair play and substantial justice.' International Shoe Co. v. Washington, 326 U.S., at 320, 66 S.Ct., at 160. Thus courts in 'appropriate case[s]' may evaluate 'the burden on the defendant,' 'the forum State's interest in adjudicating the dispute,' 'the plaintiff's interest in obtaining convenient and effective relief,' 'the interstate judicial system's interest in obtaining the most efficient resolution of controversies,' and the 'shared interest of the several States in furthering fundamental substantive social policies.' World-Wide Volkswagen Corp. v. Woodson, supra, at 292, 100 S.Ct., at 564. These considerations sometimes serve to establish the reasonableness of jurisdiction upon a lesser showing of minimum contacts than would otherwise be required. See, e.g., Keeton v. Hustler Magazine, Inc., supra, at 780, 104 S.Ct., at 1481; Calder v. Jones, supra, 465 U.S., at 788–89, 104 S.Ct., at 1486–87; McGee v. International Life Insurance Co., supra, at 223–224, 78 S.Ct., at 201–202. On the other hand, where a defendant who purposefully has directed his activities at forum residents seeks to defeat jurisdiction, he must present a compelling case that the presence of some other considerations would render jurisdiction unreasonable. Most such considerations usually may be accommodated through means short of finding jurisdiction unconstitutional. For example, the potential clash of the forum's law with the 'fundamental substantive social policies' of another State may be accommodated through application of the forum's choice-of-law rules. Similarly, a defendant claiming substantial inconvenience may seek a change of venue. Nevertheless, minimum requirements inherent in the concept of 'fair play and substantial justice' may defeat the reasonableness of jurisdiction even if the defendant has purposefully engaged in forum activities. World-Wide Volkswagen Corp. v. Woodson, 444 U.S., at 292, 100 S.Ct., at 564; see also Restatement (Second) of Conflict of Laws §§ 36–37 (1971). As we previously have noted, jurisdictional rules may not be employed in such a way as to make litigation 'so gravely difficult and inconvenient' that a party unfairly is at a 'severe disadvantage' in comparison to his opponent. The Bremen v. Zapata Off-Shore Co., 407 U.S. 1, 18, 92 S.Ct. 1907, 1917 (1972) (re forum-selection provisions); McGee v. International Life Insurance Co., supra, at 223–224, 78 S.Ct., at 201–202."

Applying those principles to this case, the Court noted that John Rudzewicz had reached out to negotiate with a Florida corporation and agreed by long-term contract to be regulated from Florida, to make payments to Florida, and to have disputes governed by the laws of Florida. The Court thus held that the record and the law supported the district court's determination that the defendant had purposefully established minimum contacts with Florida.

Similarly, the Court upheld the district court's findings and conclusions to the effect that jurisdiction was not so unfair as to be unconstitutionally unreasonable, at least in this particular case.

However, Justice Stevens, with whom Justice White joined, dissented on the ground that "there is a significant element of unfairness in requiring a franchisee to defend a case of this kind in the forum chosen by the franchisor." Justice Powell did not participate in the case.

––––––

Question: (36) Is there any limit on what factors enter into the unreasonableness test? Consider Lynda Wray Black, The Long-Arm's Inappropriate Embrace, 91 St.John's L.Rev. 1 (2017), which criticizes a Mississippi case using the state's long-arm statute to apply its alienation-of-affections tort law on behalf of an out-of-state plaintiff against out-of-staters who had in-state sex, and which argues that Mississippi's so applying its outdated law via its long-arm is an unreasonable denial of due process.

––––––

ASAHI METAL INDUSTRY CO. v. SUPERIOR COURT, 480 U.S. 102, 107 S.Ct. 1026 (1987). Gary Zurcher was severely injured and his wife killed in a motorcycle accident in California, allegedly caused by the explosion of the cycle's defective rear tire. There he sued among others Cheng Shin, the Taiwanese manufacturer of the tube. Cheng Shin impleaded Asahi, allegedly the Japanese manufacturer of the tube's valve assembly. The main claims were eventually settled, leaving only Cheng Shin's indemnity claim against Asahi.

Before that settlement, Asahi had moved unsuccessfully to quash service. Asahi made its valves in Japan and sold some of them to Cheng Shin in Taiwan, where Cheng Shin made its tubes with valves by Asahi or other suppliers and then sold them throughout the world, with Cheng Shin selling a fair number in California, perhaps including the one in suit. Other Asahi valves in other manufacturers' tubes similarly came into California. Asahi apparently had no other contacts with California. The California courts ultimately upheld personal jurisdiction over Asahi as being within the state's long-arm statute and consistent with due process.

On certiorari, the Supreme Court reversed because jurisdiction here violated due process. On the one hand, five Justices suggested that power would exist over this defendant, which put its goods into the stream of commerce flowing into the forum state and thereby "purposefully availed." On the other hand, eight Justices held that exercising jurisdiction would be unreasonable, considering the severe burdens on Asahi of defending in a foreign legal system, the supposedly slight interests of Cheng Shin and California in the exercise of jurisdiction, and the international interests in not subjecting this foreign corporation to an indemnification offshoot of a products liability action in an American court. In short, here is one of those rare cases where personal jurisdiction is held unconstitutional because, even though it might pass the power test, it fails the unreasonableness test.

The complex breakdown of the Justices' opinions is perhaps telling, as indicated by this schema:

	O'Connor Rehnquist Powell	Scalia	Brennan White Marshall Blackmun	Stevens White Blackmun
(i)	no power, under standard requiring that defendant had purpose to serve California market	no power, applying O'Connor standard	power exists, under standard requiring only defendant's actual awareness that product was being regularly sold in California	power seemingly exists, regardless of whether Brennan's mere-awareness standard or O'Connor's awareness-plus standard governs
(ii)	unreasonable	no opinion on unreasonableness	unreasonable	unreasonable

———

Question: (37) In Burnham v. Superior Court, 495 U.S. 604, 110 S.Ct. 2105 (1990), a New Jersey couple separated by agreement, with the wife and the two children moving to California. Six months later, the husband visited California for three days on business and to see his children. The wife had him served with process for a California suit seeking divorce and monetary relief. He returned to New Jersey. He then tried to quash service for lack of personal jurisdiction. The California courts refused, relying on his transient physical presence. The United States Supreme Court unanimously affirmed, but the Justices split so badly in their opinions as to rob the case of most precedential significance. Justice Scalia, writing for a minority, opined that the basis of physical presence always suffices thanks to its history—without any regard to its possible unreasonableness; Justice Brennan, writing for a different minority, agreed that personal jurisdiction existed in most cases founded on physical presence because the defendant gets some benefits while in the state and is on notice of amenability to suit there—but a defendant in a particular case could attempt to show that transient jurisdiction would be unreasonable. So, what do you think would be the result if Grace v. MacArthur, supra p. 492, now came before the Supreme Court? See Sarieddine v. Moussa, 820 S.W.2d 837, 840 (Tex.Ct.App.1991) (suggesting weakly that transient jurisdiction is constitutional only where its application is not so outlandish as to be unreasonable in the particular circumstances). But see Daimler AG v. Bauman, 571 U.S. 117, 139 n.20, 134 S.Ct. 746, 762 n.20 (2014) (suggesting weakly that the unreasonableness test does not apply to general jurisdiction).

J. McINTYRE MACHINERY, LTD. v. NICASTRO, 564 U.S. 873, 131 S.Ct. 2780 (2011). Plaintiff Nicastro seriously injured his hand while using a metal-shearing machine in New Jersey that the defendant English corporation had manufactured in England. Plaintiff brought a products liability action in a New Jersey state court.

The defendant unsuccessfully challenged New Jersey's exercise of personal jurisdiction. The state supreme court, conscious of globalization, upheld statutory and constitutional jurisdiction as long as the manufacturer knew or reasonably should have known that its products were being distributed by a U.S. system that might lead to sales in any state. Three facts concerning the defendant were prominent: a U.S. distributor had agreed to sell its machines in this country; its officials had annually attended a trade show in various states, albeit not in New Jersey; and the machine at issue, and perhaps a couple other of its machines, had ended up in New Jersey.

On certiorari, the U.S. Supreme Court reversed for denial of due process, by a series of opinions that were still seriously split on stream-of-commerce jurisdiction twenty-four years and eight new Justices after Asahi:

Kennedy	Ginsburg	Breyer
Roberts	Sotomayor	Alito
Scalia	Kagan	
Thomas		

| no power, applying the O'Connor standard, arguing that a stream-of-commerce doctrine has not displaced the purposeful-availment requirement, observing that defendant's activities in New Jersey did not reveal an intent to invoke or benefit from the protection of its laws, and saying, "The defendant's | power exists, applying in dissent a standard that would uphold jurisdiction in the state of injury if the manufacturer purposefully | no power, under Brennan or O'Connor test, because there was no regular flow of the product into New Jersey, as well as no special |

Kennedy	Ginsburg	Breyer
Roberts	Sotomayor	Alito
Scalia	Kagan	
Thomas		

| transmission of goods permits the exercise of jurisdiction only where the defendant can be said to have targeted the forum; as a general rule, it is not enough that the defendant might have predicted that its goods will reach the forum State." | served the U.S. market, whether or not it used an independent distributor | purpose to serve the state's market |

———

Question: (38) Daniel Klerman, *Personal Jurisdiction and Product Liability*, 85 S.Cal.L.Rev. 1551 (2012), uses economic analysis to argue for allowing the injured consumer to sue where he purchased the product. Does the economic argument address the power requirement?

———

INTENTIONALLY DIRECTED EFFECTS

The time has come to define more carefully the threshold for specific jurisdiction based on state-directed activity. Recall the Keeton and Calder cases, which raised First Amendment concerns. In particular, the unanimous Calder Court in 1984 allowed the entertainer Shirley Jones to sue for libel in her home state of California against the National Enquirer's writer and editor living and working in Florida. The Court stressed that the defendants had "intentionally directed" their Florida acts at California while knowing that their conduct would have "effects" there.

In Walden v. Fiore, 571 U.S. 277, 134 S.Ct. 1115 (2014), however, the Court unanimously concluded that a defendant did not have constitutionally sufficient contacts with Nevada to support specific jurisdiction. The defendant was a DEA agent who in Georgia allegedly submitted a knowingly false affidavit to support the forfeiture of cash that had been seized at the Atlanta airport from the plaintiffs, who were gamblers returning from a casino in Puerto Rico. They later sued in federal court at their Nevada residence for delay in returning the funds. The Court held that the *defendant*, not the plaintiffs, must create a sufficient contact with the *forum state*, not with the resident plaintiffs. "Rather, it is the defendant's conduct that must form the necessary connection with the forum State that is the basis for its jurisdiction over him."

The difficulty lay in reconciling Calder. Justice Thomas's opinion in Walden stressed that the Calder defendants researched and prepared a California-focused article for circulation in California and for impact on third parties there, so that more was in play than simply a plaintiff who felt effects while in California. Instead of such state-directed acts, Anthony Walden in Georgia inflicted an effect on plaintiffs who he knew would be residing in Nevada when they felt the delay in getting back the funds. "The proper question is not where the plaintiff experienced a particular injury or effect but whether the defendant's conduct connects him to the forum in a meaningful way."

That last phrase does not in fact give much guidance as to jurisdiction based on out-of-state acts with in-state effects (but without a physical entry into the forum state directly attributable to the defendant, like shooting a gun intentionally across a state line). The plaintiff cannot simply get to choose to sue where injured. The jurisdictional focus is on the defendant. Calder/Walden appears to demand that the defendant meant to connect with the forum state. So where to draw the line more precisely?

Hanson had fleshed out the metaphor of minimum contacts by generalizing that power exists for specific jurisdiction over a defendant who has purposefully availed itself "of the privilege of conducting activities within the forum State, thus invoking the benefits and protections of its laws." Kulko later said, "an essential criterion in all cases is whether the 'quality and nature' of the defendant's activity is such that it is 'reasonable' and 'fair' to require him to conduct his defense in that State." The defendant's state-directed activity must make it fair for the sovereign to exercise jurisdiction over the defendant. Burger King added, "considerations sometimes serve to establish the reasonableness of jurisdiction upon a lesser showing of minimum contacts than would otherwise be required." It seems that the required level for the defendant's activity could lower in light of the case's reasonableness factors favorable to the plaintiff. Echoing the old doctrine of fictional consent, this so-called purposeful availment now seems to work as a sort of tacit submission to foreseeable jurisdiction, a volitional tie to the forum, that makes jurisdiction fair for the defendant. Cf. J. McIntyre Mach., Ltd. v. Nicastro, 564 U.S. 873, 881, 131 S.Ct. 2780, 2787 (2011) (plurality opinion) (testing for "circumstances, or a course of conduct, from which it is proper to infer an intention to benefit from and thus an intention to submit to the laws of the forum State"); Armstrong v. Pomerance, 423 A.2d 174 (Del.1980) (approving, after passage of consent statute, personal jurisdiction over out-of-state directors of Delaware corporations).

Hence, purposeful availment has come to include out-of-state acts directed toward the forum state with a purpose to get benefits through effects there. This development explains the line of cases invoking the stream of commerce.

How much other jurisdiction based on out-of-state acts with in-state effects does purposeful availment include? What of a foreign defendant intentionally dumping pollutants into a river, which happens to flow into the forum state: can the damaged persons sue at home? What of the defendant intentionally setting a forest fire, which unexpectedly spreads wind-borne across the state line? What of a negligently set fire? What of a malicious computer virus that unintentionally gets loose? Although such jurisdiction would not be unreasonable, whence comes the power? Some courts measure power by a test requiring that the defendant allegedly (1) committed an intentional act, (2) expressly aimed at the forum state, (3) that caused harm the defendant knew was likely to be suffered in the forum state. See Hydentra HLP Int. Ltd. v. Sagan Ltd., ___ F.App'x ___, ___, 2019 WL 3492486 (9th Cir.2019).

SECTION 5. STATE JURISDICTIONAL LAW

NELSON v. MILLER, 11 Ill.2d 378, 143 N.E.2d 673 (1957). In this action involving alleged negligence in unloading a truck in Illinois during a delivery by an out-of-state defendant, the Illinois Supreme Court upheld the Illinois jurisdictional statute reprinted after the McGee case above. The court said sweepingly that the entire statute reflected "a conscious purpose to assert jurisdiction over nonresident defendants to the extent permitted by the due-process clause."

The defendant had argued that jurisdiction under the words "commission of a tortious act within this State" depended upon proof of all the facts necessary to spell out ultimate liability in tort. The Illinois Supreme Court rejected this construction, holding the jurisdictional requirement satisfied "when the defendant, personally or through an agent, is the author of acts or omissions within the State, and when the complaint states a cause of action in tort arising from such conduct."

The rejected construction of the statute would have produced anomalous results, as explained in detail by Kevin M. Clermont, Jurisdictional Fact, 91 Cornell L.Rev. 973 (2006): A preliminary hearing on jurisdiction would entail a minitrial on the merits as to all issues of liability. If the defendant were to lose the minitrial, a redo of liability at any trial on the merits would be necessary to avoid troublesome problems regarding jury right and preclusion. If the defendant were to win the minitrial, he would get not a conclusive judgment on the merits but only a threshold dismissal for lack of jurisdiction—and he would have relinquished his right not to have to litigate the merits in that forum. If instead he were to default, upon enforcement elsewhere he could force a trial on all the issues of liability because these would be jurisdictional facts subject to collateral attack—and thus the statutory objective of forcing the defendant, when appropriate, to defend his conduct in the state where it took place would be nullified.

GRAY v. AMERICAN RADIATOR & STANDARD SANITARY CORP., 22 Ill.2d 432, 176 N.E.2d 761 (1961). The explosion in Illinois of a hot-water heater injured the plaintiff. She sued the American Radiator & Standard Sanitary Corp. and the Titan Valve Manufacturing Co. Her claim was that Titan had negligently constructed a safety valve in Ohio and sold it to American Radiator, which manufactured the heater and attached the safety valve thereto in Pennsylvania. The heater was sold to an Illinois purchaser in the course of commerce. American Radiator set up a crossclaim against Titan for indemnification by reason of certain warranties made by Titan.

Titan moved to dismiss the complaint and the crossclaim for lack of jurisdiction. There was no showing that Titan had had any other contact with Illinois, directly or indirectly, nor that it had any agent there. The trial court granted the motion, and the plaintiff appealed. The questions presented were (1) whether a tortious act was committed in Illinois within the meaning of the Illinois statute and (2) whether the statute, if so construed, was consistent with due process of law. In reversing, the Illinois Supreme Court said:

"The first aspect to which we must direct our attention is one of statutory construction. Under section 17(1)(b) jurisdiction is predicated on the committing of a tortious act in this State. It is not disputed, for the purpose of this appeal, that a tortious act was committed. The issue depends on whether it was committed in Illinois, so as to warrant the assertion of personal jurisdiction by service of summons in Ohio.

"The wrong in the case at bar did not originate in the conduct of a servant physically present here, but arose instead from acts performed at the place of manufacture. Only the consequences occurred in Illinois. It is well established, however, that in law the place of wrong is where the last event takes place which is necessary to render the actor liable. (Restatement, Conflict of Laws, sec. 377.) A second indication that the place of injury is the determining factor is found in rules governing the time within which an action must be brought. In applying statutes of limitation our court has computed the period from the time when the injury is done. [Citations omitted.] We think it is clear that the alleged negligence in manufacturing the valve cannot be separated from the resulting injury; and that for present purposes, like those of liability and limitations, the tort was committed in Illinois.

"Titan seeks to avoid this result by arguing that instead of using the word 'tort,' the legislature employed the term 'tortious act'; and that the latter refers only to the act or conduct, separate and apart from any consequences thereof. We cannot accept the argument. To be tortious an act must cause injury. The concept of injury is an inseparable part of the phrase. In determining legislative intention courts will read words in their ordinary and popularly understood sense. [Citations omitted.] We think the intent should be determined less from technicalities of definition than from considerations of general purpose and effect. To adopt the criteria urged by defendant would tend to promote litigation over extraneous issues concerning the elements of a tort and the territorial incidence of each, whereas the test should be concerned more with those substantial elements of convenience and justice presumably contemplated by the legislature. As we observed in Nelson v. Miller . . . , the statute contemplates the exertion of jurisdiction over nonresident defendants to the extent permitted by the due-process clause."

The court likewise answered the second question in the affirmative, after observing: "In the case at bar defendant does not claim that the present use of its product in Illinois is an isolated instance. While the record does not disclose the volume of Titan's business or the territory in which appliances incorporating its valves are marketed, it is a reasonable inference that its commercial transactions, like those of other manufacturers, result in substantial use and consumption in this State."

————

Question: (39) If this case had come before the Supreme Court of the United States for review, what arguments would you have made for reversal? What, if any, facts in addition to those summarized above would you have considered relevant? Given your assumed facts, what do you think would be the result? See Russell v. SNFA, 987 N.E.2d 778 (Ill.2013) (conceding there would be no power if only a single item reached Illinois or if the foreign supplier were unaware of its products' Illinois destination).

————

LONGINES-WITTNAUER WATCH CO. v. BARNES & REINECKE, INC., 15 N.Y.2d 443, 209 N.E.2d 68, 261 N.Y.S.2d 8 (1965). The court decided three cases under this caption. In one of these, Feathers v. McLucas, the plaintiffs had suffered injury by the explosion of a tractor-drawn propane gas tank, en route from Pennsylvania to Vermont, on a highway near their home in New York. They sued, among others, the Darby Corporation, which had manufactured the mobile tank in Kansas and sold it, through an intermediary, to a Pennsylvania corporation that was an interstate carrier licensed by several states including New York. The plaintiffs charged Darby with negligence and breach of warranty in the manufacture of the tank.

Darby contended that no jurisdiction existed. There was no showing that Darby had had any other contact with New York, directly or indirectly, nor that it had any agent there. The plaintiffs asserted jurisdiction over Darby by NY CPLR § 302(a)(2), which like the Illinois statute says that jurisdiction extends to a defendant who "commits a tortious act within the state."[gg]

Reversing the court below, the Court of Appeals of New York sided with Darby. It rejected the view that the legislature had intended to go

————

[gg]   The current New York long-arm statute, along with service provisions, appears in the statutory section of the Rules booklet.

to the limits of the Due Process Clause. Looking to the wording of the statute, the court said: "The language of paragraph 2 . . . is too plain and precise to permit it to be read, as has the Appellate Division, as if it were synonymous with 'commits a tortious act *without* the state which causes injury within the state.' " The court found further support for its reading in the legislative history, before concluding that expansion of the statute's scope "is a matter for the Legislature rather than the courts."

————

Question: (40) *P* of Illinois has brought a paternity action against *D* of Ohio in an Illinois court. *P* alleges, in essence, that *D* sired her child out of wedlock and has failed in his duty to provide support. More specifically, she alleges that "during the time biologically certain to have been the instant of conception, your Plaintiff had sexual intercourse with your Defendant in Cook County, Illinois, and with no other person." *P* alleges no other connection of *D* to Illinois. *D* received in-hand service of process in Ohio pursuant to the Illinois long-arm statute reprinted above. He has now, by his attorney, submitted a motion to dismiss for lack of personal jurisdiction. *D*'s papers in support deny those allegations of the complaint and further argue that, even if they were true, such facts would not sustain jurisdiction over the person. *P*'s papers take the opposite positions. How should the motion be decided? Compare Poindexter v. Willis, 87 Ill.App.2d 213, 231 N.E.2d 1 (1967), enforced, 23 Ohio Misc. 199, 256 N.E.2d 254 (C.P.1970), with Anonymous v. Anonymous, 49 Misc.2d 675, 268 N.Y.S.2d 710 (Fam.Ct.1966). (Note that since those decisions, Illinois and New York, like all other states, have enacted a statute that would reach this kind of case. See, e.g., the provision that New York enacted in 1997 as N.Y.Fam.Ct.Act § 580–201(6) ("the individual engaged in sexual intercourse in this state and the child may have been conceived by that act of intercourse").)

————

Uniform Interstate and International Procedure Act[hh]

§ 1.03.   *[Personal Jurisdiction Based upon Conduct]*

(a) A court may exercise personal jurisdiction over a person, who acts directly or by an agent, as to a [cause of action] [claim for relief] arising from the person's

———

[hh]   This Uniform Act—approved by the National Conference of Commissioners on Uniform State Laws in 1962 but withdrawn in 1977 because all states had gone at least as far—presented a comprehensive code treating state litigation with interstate or international incidents. In addition to these provisions extending personal jurisdiction over persons not within the forum state, it supplanted earlier Uniform Acts for the taking of depositions outside the state, the determination of foreign law, and the proof of official records. A number of states adopted it.

The brackets generally suggest to state legislatures a choice in the form of words to conform to state usage. Section 1.03(a)(6) is in brackets because many states have similar and more

(1)   transacting any business in this state;

(2)   contracting to supply services or things in this state;

(3)   causing tortious injury by an act or omission in this state;

(4)   causing tortious injury in this state by an act or omission outside this state if he regularly does or solicits business or engages in any other persistent course of conduct in this state or derives substantial revenue from goods or services used or consumed in this state; [or]

(5)   having an interest in, using, or possessing real property in this state[; or

(6)   contracting to insure any person, property, or risk located within this state at the time of contracting].

. . . .

Questions: (41) What differences do you see between the Uniform Act and subsection (1) of the above-reprinted Illinois statute? What is the significance of these differences? What would have been the result if the Gray case (or Feathers v. McLucas) had arisen under the Uniform Act?

(42) Defendant makes false representations outside the state communicated by telephone or mail to plaintiff within the state, intending that they should be relied on there to plaintiff's injury. Defendant has no other connection with the state. Is there sufficient basis for jurisdiction under the above-reprinted Illinois statute? Cf. Se. Guar. Trust Co. v. Rodman & Renshaw, Inc., 358 F.Supp. 1001 (N.D.Ill.1973) (yes). Is there sufficient basis for jurisdiction under NY CPLR § 302(a)(2)? Cf. Bauer Indus., Inc. v. Shannon Luminous Materials Co., 52 A.D.2d 897, 383 N.Y.S.2d 80 (1976) (no). Is there sufficient basis for jurisdiction under a statute derived from the Uniform Act? See Murphy v. Erwin-Wasey, Inc., 460 F.2d 661 (1st Cir.1972) (yes, in case from Massachusetts).

(43) Defendant by his out-of-state website misleads plaintiff (or defames her, or infringes her trademark). Defendant has no other connection with plaintiff's home state. Does that state have sufficient constitutional basis for jurisdiction? Is a passive home page, which merely provides information, any different from defendant's having a telephone with a recorded message in defendant's home? Or is this internet situation more like defendant's mailing a letter to plaintiff's home as part of a mass mailing? Are such analogies useful? What, if any, additional information would you consider relevant? See Kevin M. Clermont, Principles of Civil Procedure 290–93 (5th ed. 2018) (treating internet jurisdiction).

---

explicit provisions in their insurance laws, as illustrated in McGee v. International Life Insurance Co.

New York Update

The Feathers result would not prevail today. To avoid it, the New York legislature added NY CPLR § 302(a)(3) in 1966, which extended specific jurisdiction over a defendant who "commits a tortious act without the state causing injury to person or property within the state" and has a sufficient business connection with New York.

In Penguin Group (USA) Inc. v. American Buddha, 2009 WL 1069158 (S.D.N.Y. Apr. 21, 2009), a Delaware corporation, with its principal place of business in New York, sued a nonprofit Oregon corporation for copyright infringement through its publishing complete copies of four of the plaintiff's books on the defendant's website. Although the plaintiff did not allege any viewing or downloading in New York, other than by the plaintiff's attorney, the plaintiff asserted jurisdiction by § 302(a)(3). The defendant contended that no jurisdiction existed.

The district court dismissed the action. It construed the statute to require a direct injury in New York caused by the alleged tort, not merely a derivative financial loss suffered at home by a New Yorker. In other words, "in cases of injury caused by infringement of intellectual property, the intellectual property owner suffers injury where the infringement occurs," which would be Oregon, in the absence of any alleged infringement in New York. On appeal, however, the Second Circuit certified a question to the New York Court of Appeals, which held the statutory situs of injury in these circumstances was the New York location of the copyright owner.

On the subsequent remand by the Second Circuit, and after jurisdictional discovery, the district court nevertheless dismissed again. Now the district court said that the non-money-making defendant did not meet § 302(a)(3)(ii)'s requirement of "deriv[ing] substantial revenue from interstate or international commerce," 2013 WL 865486 (S.D.N.Y. Mar. 7, 2013).

————

California Code of Civil Procedure

§ 410.10 *Basis*

A court of this state may exercise jurisdiction on any basis not inconsistent with the Constitution of this state or of the United States.

————

Question: (44) A California plaintiff brings an action in a California court against a Nebraska defendant for damages arising out of a vehicular accident, occurring in Nevada near the California border and involving plaintiff's car and defendant's truck. Defendant, an interstate trucker, was en route to California to deliver and receive cargo when the accident occurred; during the seven years preceding the accident he made about 20 trips per year into California; and he was licensed to haul freight by several states including California. Is there sufficient basis for personal jurisdiction under the California statute? See Cornelison v. Chaney, 16 Cal.3d 143, 545 P.2d 264, 127 Cal.Rptr. 352 (1976) (yes).

———————

Cook Associates v. Lexington United Corp.

Supreme Court of Illinois, 1981.
87 Ill.2d 190, 429 N.E.2d 847.

■ WARD, JUSTICE:

This appeal arises out of an action for breach of contract brought in the circuit court of Cook County. The plaintiff, Cook Associates, an Illinois corporation, brought the action against Lexington United Corporation, a Delaware corporation not licensed to do business in Illinois. Lexington is a dinnerware manufacturer whose principal place of business is St. Louis, Missouri. Lexington filed a special appearance to contest the court's in personam jurisdiction (Ill.Rev.Stat.1977, ch. 110, par. 20), but its motion to quash service of process was denied. Thereafter, Lexington answered, discovery was taken, and subsequently summary judgment was granted in favor of Cook. The appellate court reversed the judgment (86 Ill.App.3d 909, 407 N.E.2d 944), holding that the circuit court lacked personal jurisdiction over Lexington. Because of the disposition it made, the appellate court did not consider the propriety of the summary judgment. We granted Cook's petition for leave to appeal.

Cook is an employment agency whose offices are in Chicago. From July 1973 to July 1976, it also maintained a branch office in Massachusetts, which was operated by Edith McIntosh. Cook specializes in the placement of executive and professional employees with employers who pay Cook a fee if a person referred by Cook is hired. On May 12, 1976, Joseph Runza, a Lexington executive, phoned McIntosh, with whom he had done business before, at Cook's Massachusetts office. He requested assistance in filling a sales management position at Lexington. The record is unclear as to the title of the position discussed. It appears that Runza had first described it as "national sales manager" but later changed the description to "field sales manager."

On May 13, 1976, McIntosh sent Runza the names and resumes of some prospective employees, one of whom was Gregg Hoegemeir. Her accompanying letter stated: "As you know from our previous correspondence, these men, like all of our candidates, are being submitted to you upon the understanding that if they are employed, our fee will be paid by you in accordance with the enclosed schedule." Cook's fee schedule indicated its Chicago address on the letterhead, and stated that the fee would be 20% of one year's salary for positions paying $15,000 per year or more. The schedule also stated: "A fee will be due from you as to any applicant you hire within two years of our disclosure of his identity, or of our submission or referral of him, to you."

Runza communicated with Hoegemeir and arranged to meet him in Chicago. Hoegemeir's resume discloses that he was then a regional sales manager for a Chicago manufacturer and that he resided in Ballwin, Missouri. At the meeting, Runza offered Hoegemeir the position of "field sales manager" at an annual salary of $22,000. Hoegemeir rejected the offer, and the record reflects that there were no further contacts between Lexington and him for several months.

McIntosh's employment by Cook terminated in July 1976. About three months later, she opened her own employment search and placement service in Massachusetts. It appears that soon thereafter, Runza communicated with McIntosh at her home and advised he was seeking a sales manager for Lexington. This time, it appears, the position would be that of "national sales manager" at a salary in excess of $22,000. McIntosh, acting for her own agency, submitted the names of a number of candidates, including that of Hoegemeir. After several interviews with Hoegemeir, Runza offered him the position at a salary of $25,000 and Hoegemeir accepted. The record does not show whether any of the negotiations which led to Hoegemeir's employment took place in Illinois, nor does it make clear where the contract for his employment was made.

Hoegemeir began working for Lexington in December 1976, and Lexington paid McIntosh a $5,000 fee for her services. Cook later became aware of the hiring of Hoegemeir, and it demanded a $5,000 fee, representing 20% of Hoegemeir's starting salary. When Lexington refused to pay the commission, Cook filed the action for breach of contract in July 1977.

Process was served on Lexington's president, Frank Ivitch, when he was attending a trade show in Chicago. Ivitch and several other company officials were appearing in a week-long housewares exhibit of Lexington. Exhibitors were prohibited from selling merchandise at the exhibition. Less than $50,000 in orders was taken by Lexington at the exhibit, according to the answer to an interrogatory, and were later accepted at Lexington's St. Louis office. Officials of Lexington had attended two other trade shows in Chicago in 1976 and 1977. At each of them, a similar volume of orders was received and later accepted.

Lexington's other contacts with Illinois were listed in an affidavit of Ivitch, and in Lexington's answers to interrogatories. Lexington did not have an office or an employee in this State. It had no Illinois telephone number. It did not advertise in Illinois, except in connection with the trade shows held in Chicago. Lexington merchandise was sold by an independent manufacturer's representative in Illinois to his Illinois accounts. The record does not reflect the volume of those sales. The representative sold merchandise of other manufacturers as well. Working strictly on a commission basis, he received no salary from Lexington. In the year preceding the filing of this action an employee of

Lexington accompanied the representative on three or four occasions, but the employee did not make any sales.

The appellate court held, on due process grounds, that the circuit court of Cook County lacked personal jurisdiction over Lexington.

When arguing before the appellate court the parties were not in agreement as to the test or standard to be applied for determining whether there was personal jurisdiction. Lexington submitted that our long-arm statute provides the only means of acquiring jurisdiction over a nonresident corporate defendant. . . . Lexington contended that the requirements of the statute were not satisfied, because the action did not arise from "the transaction of any business" by Lexington in Illinois.

Cook, on the other hand, contended that the long-arm statute does not prohibit the acquiring of jurisdiction according to the doing-business doctrine. Under that doctrine, a foreign corporation is deemed to have submitted to our jurisdiction by doing business in Illinois. . . . Cook urged that Lexington's contacts with Illinois rendered the corporation subject to the jurisdiction of the circuit court of Cook County under the "doing business" view, or under the due process standard of "minimum contacts."

. . . .

Under the due process clause of the fourteenth amendment there are limits to which a State is confined in asserting in personam jurisdiction over a nonresident corporate defendant. . . .

It is important to recognize that this due process standard represents only the outer limits beyond which a State may not go to acquire jurisdiction over nonresidents. A State is free to set its own limits in acquiring this jurisdiction within the perimeters allowed by the due process clause. [Citations omitted.] We recently stressed that the boundaries or limits under our statute are not to be equated with the "minimum contacts" test under the due process clause. In Green v. Advance Ross Electronics Corp. (1981), 86 Ill.2d 431, 436, 427 N.E.2d 1203, 1206, we stated, in reference to the Illinois long-arm statute:

> "In Nelson v. Miller (1957), 11 Ill.2d 378, 389 [143 N.E.2d 673], this court said that the Illinois long-arm statute reflects a conscious purpose to assert jurisdiction over nonresidents to the extent permitted by the due process clause. We do not, however, regard this observation as the equivalent of declaring that the construction and application of section 17(1)(b) depend entirely upon decisions determining in what circumstances due process requirements would permit long-arm jurisdiction. Neither do we read Nelson to say that in applying section 17(1)(b) we should not construe the meaning and intent of our own statute irrespective of the due process limitations generally applicable to State long-arm statutes. *A statute worded in the way ours is should have a fixed meaning without regard to changing*

concepts of due process, except, of course, that an interpretation which renders the statute unconstitutional should be avoided, if possible. Thus, instead of turning to the array of tests which have been articulated to assist in determining whether long-arm statutes as applied exceed permissible constitutional boundaries, we prefer to resolve this appeal by looking to the meaning of our statute." (Emphasis added.)

We conclude that Lexington is not amenable to the jurisdiction of our courts under either the Illinois long-arm statute or under the doctrine of submitting to jurisdiction by virtue of doing business in Illinois.

Lexington is not amenable to service under the long-arm statute because the cause of action did not arise from the transaction of business in Illinois. Cook argues, however, that a contract between Lexington and Cook was formed in Illinois at the time of Hoegemeir's interview with Lexington. Alternatively, it says that this action arose out of Lexington's activities in Illinois because the interview with Hoegemeir in Chicago was an essential first step in a process of negotiations that culminated in the hiring of Hoegemeir. The contentions do not persuade. Hoegemeir rejected the offer of employment when he was interviewed in Illinois, and of course no contract was formed. Too, it cannot be said that the Chicago interview was any part in the negotiations that led to the hiring of Hoegemeir. The positions involved were different. Hoegemeir rejected the position of field sales manager. He later was hired as national sales manager, but there is no indication whatever in the record that the interview had any influence on his hiring. It was in the fall of 1976 that Runza asked McIntosh, who was then operating her own agency, for prospects to fill the position of national sales manager. There was no communication between Runza and Hoegemeir until McIntosh referred his name to Lexington in behalf of her own agency.

  . . . .

The doing-business standard, of course, continues to be used in determining questions of jurisdiction over foreign corporations not licensed in Illinois (e.g., St. Louis-San Francisco Ry. v. Gitchoff (1977), 68 Ill.2d 38, 369 N.E.2d 52), as it was early recognized that the doctrine was not preempted by the long-arm statute. (See Lindley v. St. Louis-San Francisco Ry. Co. (7th Cir.1968), 407 F.2d 639.) In fact, it complements the long-arm statute because if a foreign, unlicensed corporation is found to be doing business in this State, it is amenable to the jurisdiction of courts of Illinois even for causes of action not arising from the defendant's transactions of business in Illinois. See Hertz Corp. v. Taylor (1959), 15 Ill.2d 552, 155 N.E.2d 610.

  . . . .

We consider that Lexington was not doing business in Illinois through having an exhibit at three trade shows in Chicago, and its fruitless interview. . . . The independent manufacturer's representative

resides in Illinois. The scant references to him in the record are inadequate for us to conclude that because of its association with him Lexington should be deemed to have submitted itself to our jurisdiction
. . . .

. . . .

Judgment affirmed.

———

IMPUTED CONTACTS

All these statutes expose the fundamental problem of when to attribute another's acts to the defendant for jurisdictional purposes. A general proposition is that to justify personal jurisdiction over a principal, the court can attribute the state-directed acts of the principal's agent. To determine whether an agent-principal relationship exists, the court looks to the ordinary law of agency, asking whether the defendant has empowered an agent and whether the agent has acted within the scope of that authority. To establish challenged jurisdiction, then, the plaintiff must make a prima facie showing of the principal's vicarious liability under the applicable substantive law. The rationale is that if the principal would be substantively liable for the agent's acts, then those acts can contribute to a finding of jurisdiction over the principal.

Indeed, courts have extended or surpassed that rationale in a variety of contexts. See Lea Brilmayer & Kathleen Paisley, Personal Jurisdiction and Substantive Legal Relations: Corporations, Conspiracies, and Agency, 74 Calif.L.Rev. 1 (1986). Of those contexts, the one giving courts the greatest difficulty is the attribution of state-directed acts by a validly incorporated and formally separate corporation that, along with the corporate defendant, constitutes part of a modern multistate or multinational enterprise. If the affiliate corporation has an agent-principal relationship to the defendant, then the courts will attribute the affiliate's contacts to the defendant. But some courts have gone perceptibly beyond the "agency" standard, coming up with tests that ask, for example, whether the state-directed acts are sufficiently important to the defendant that it would have performed them itself in the affiliate's absence. Such a test seems to be a confused stab at a standard that still conforms to the rationale of tying jurisdictional attribution to substantive liability. A more coherent formulation of an "alter ego" test maintains that if substantive liability would exist—taking the courts into corporate law by asking whether the defendant would be liable for all of the affiliate's activities under the doctrine of piercing the corporate veil, which, in special situations of common control, overcomes the usual limited liability of corporations and merges the corporate entities—then the activities of the affiliate can contribute to a finding of jurisdiction over the defendant. See Lonny Sheinkopf Hoffman, The Case Against Vicarious Jurisdiction, 152 U.Pa.L.Rev. 1023 (2004) (arguing, however, for a jurisdictional rather than substantive test that directly asks whether the defendant has created, albeit partly through others, a sufficient connection to the forum).

―――――

ILLINOIS UPDATE

The Cook result would not necessarily prevail today. The court there was applying an Illinois long-arm statute basically the same as the original one earlier reprinted. On September 7, 1989, Illinois amended its long-arm statute. See generally Keith H. Beyler, The Illinois Long Arm Statute: Background, Meaning, and Needed Repairs, 12 S.Ill.U.L.J. 293 (1988). With that amendment's major changes shown below, the statute now appears as 735 Ill.Comp.Stat.Ann. 5/2–209 (the somewhat redundant new clauses (a)(6) and (a)(8) derived from separate but almost simultaneous bills):

(a) Any person, whether or not a citizen or resident of this State, who in person or through an agent does any of the acts hereinafter enumerated, thereby submits such person, and, if an individual, his or her personal representative, to the jurisdiction of the courts of this State as to any cause of action arising from the doing of any of such acts:

(1) The transaction of any business within this State;

(2) The commission of a tortious act within this State;

(3) The ownership, use, or possession of any real estate situated in this State;

(4) Contracting to insure any person, property or risk located within this State at the time of contracting;

(5) With respect to actions of dissolution of marriage, *declaration of invalidity of marriage* and legal separation, the maintenance in this State of a matrimonial domicile at the time this cause of action arose or the commission in this State of any act giving rise to the cause of action;

(6) With respect to actions brought under the Illinois Parentage Act of 1984, as now or hereafter amended, the performance of an act of sexual intercourse within this State during the possible period of conception;

(7) *The making or performance of any contract or promise substantially connected with this State;*

(8) *The performance of sexual intercourse within this State which is claimed to have resulted in the conception of a child who resides in this State;*

(9) *The failure to support a child, spouse or former spouse who has continued to reside in this State since the*

person either formerly resided with them in this State or directed them to reside in this State;

(10) The acquisition of ownership, possession or control of any asset or thing of value present within this State when ownership, possession or control was acquired;

(11) The breach of any fiduciary duty within this State;

(12) The performance of duties as a director or officer of a corporation organized under the laws of this State or having its principal place of business within this State;

(13) The ownership of an interest in any trust administered within this State; or

(14) The exercise of powers granted under the authority of this State as a fiduciary.

(b) A court may exercise jurisdiction in any action arising within or without this State against any person who:

(1) Is a natural person present within this State when served;

(2) Is a natural person domiciled or resident within this State when the cause of action arose, the action was commenced, or process was served;

(3) Is a corporation organized under the laws of this State; or

[A clause (4), basing general jurisdiction on "doing business" in Illinois, was declared unconstitutional in 2017. A clause (5), on suing foreign-country defamation plaintiffs, was added in 2008.]

(c) A court may also exercise jurisdiction on any other basis now or hereafter permitted by the Illinois Constitution and the Constitution of the United States.

(d)(b) Service of process upon any person who is subject to the jurisdiction of the courts of this State, as provided in this Section, may be made by personally serving the summons upon the defendant outside this State, as provided in this Act, with the same force and effect as though summons had been personally served within this State.

(e)(c) . . . .

(f)(d) Only causes of action arising from acts enumerated herein may be asserted against a defendant in an action in which jurisdiction over him or her is based upon *subsection (a)* this Section.

(g)(e) Nothing herein contained limits or affects the right to serve any process in any other manner now or hereafter provided by law.

Incidentally, on November 30, 1990, the Supreme Court of Illinois decided Rollins v. Ellwood, 141 Ill.2d 244, 565 N.E.2d 1302 (1990). In that case, Illinois police had arrested Sylvester Rollins for speeding and then detained him on a Maryland fugitive warrant for child abuse. John Ellwood, a Baltimore police sergeant, then went to Illinois and took him back to Maryland, where a judge found that all this had been a matter of mistaken identity. So, back in Illinois, Rollins sued Ellwood in tort. The defendant moved to quash service for lack of personal jurisdiction. The lower courts denied the motion. The Illinois Supreme Court reversed. It explained that jurisdiction over Ellwood existed under subsection (a)(2) of the state long-arm statute and under the Federal Due Process Clause, but not under the state constitution's due process clause. In the "fair, just, and reasonable" standard implicit in the latter provision, the court found a "fiduciary shield doctrine," which protected an employee from personal jurisdiction based on the employee's acts taken on behalf of the employer and not out of personal interest. Thus, the Illinois court could not exercise personal jurisdiction over this defendant.

––––––––

Questions: (45) Plaintiff brings an action in her home state of Illinois against an out-of-state lawyer for damages from alleged malpractice while representing her in prior litigation arising and conducted outside plaintiff's state. Plaintiff solicited that representation from her state. Defendant briefly visited plaintiff's state in the course of discovery and frequently communicated by mail, telephone, and e-mail with her at home and periodically received billed fees from her, but had no other contacts with her state. Is there sufficient basis for personal jurisdiction? What, if any, additional information would you consider relevant? See Cassandra Burke Robertson, Personal Jurisdiction in Legal Malpractice Litigation, 6 St.Mary's J.Legal Malpractice & Ethics 2 (2016),

(46) Back in the lawyer's state, would there be a sufficient basis for personal jurisdiction over the client for owed fees? What, if any, additional information would you consider relevant?

––––––––

SECTION 6.   ACTIONS IN FEDERAL COURT

We have considered statutory and constitutional limitations on the exercise of territorial jurisdiction, and in doing so we have dealt both with state cases and with federal cases (such as Burger King and Walden). The time has come, however, to examine with a finer focus this issue of amenability to suit in the context of actions in federal court.

The federal courts can constitutionally reach much farther than can the state courts in exercising territorial jurisdiction.[ii] Nevertheless, the federal government has decided that ordinarily its courts are not to

––––––––––––––––––––––––––––

[ii]   See supra pp. 273–277.

assert their utmost constitutional powers of adjudication, but instead are to act within certain limits specified by Rule 4.

———

DeJames v. Magnificence Carriers

United States District Court, District of New Jersey, 1980.
491 F.Supp. 1276, aff'd, 654 F.2d 280 (3d Cir.),
cert. denied, 454 U.S. 1085, 102 S.Ct. 642 (1981).

■ COHEN, SENIOR JUDGE:

Plaintiff, Joseph DeJames, a New Jersey citizen, has brought suit under the admiralty jurisdiction of the court, 28 U.S.C. § 1333, to recover damages for personal injuries suffered while working aboard the vessel M.V. Magnificence Venture. The injuries allegedly occurred on January 26, 1977, while the vessel was moored at a pier in Camden, New Jersey.

According to the pleadings defendant, Hitachi Shipbuilding and Engineering Company, Ltd. (Hitachi), entered into a contract in Japan with defendants Magnificence Carriers [and the other charterers of the vessel], whereby Hitachi agreed to convert the vessel into an automobile carrier. Plaintiff alleges in his complaint that the conversion work performed by Hitachi was defective and was the direct cause of his injuries.

Presently before the court is a motion by Hitachi to dismiss the complaint against it for insufficiency of service and for lack of in personam jurisdiction.[jj] Hitachi contends that it does not maintain the requisite contacts with New Jersey to enable this court to render a binding personal judgment against it. In support thereof, Hitachi has submitted an affidavit from Kiyoshi Ohno, manager of its ship repair business department located in Tokyo, Japan. According to the affidavit, Hitachi completed all work on the vessel at issue in its Japanese shipyard and had no further contact or involvement with the ship once it left Osaka, Japan. The affidavit further states that Hitachi does not maintain an office in New Jersey, nor does it have an agent of any type there or transact any business in the State.

At the outset it should be noted that when a federal court is asked to exercise personal jurisdiction over a defendant sued on a claim arising out of federal law, federal law under the due process clause of the fifth amendment is controlling. See Honeywell, Inc. v. Metz Apparatewerke, [509] F.2d 1137, 1143 (7th Cir.1975); Fraley v. Chesapeake and Ohio Railway Company, 397 F.2d 1, 3–4 (3d Cir.1968); Alco Standard Corp. v. Benalal, 345 F.Supp. 14, 24–25 (E.D.Pa.1972). That is not to say, however, that the analysis employed in diversity jurisdiction cases arising under the fourteenth amendment has no bearing on our decision in this case. In this regard, the Court of Appeals for the Third Circuit has

———

[jj]   Hitachi was served in Japan.

remarked that the standard of due process set forth by the Supreme Court in International Shoe Co. v. Washington, 326 U.S. 310, 66 S.Ct. 154, 90 L.Ed. 95 (1945) and its progeny is equally applicable in cases grounded on a federal claim. See Fraley, 397 F.2d at 3; [other citations omitted].

In response to Hitachi's motion to dismiss, plaintiff argues first, that Hitachi's contacts with New Jersey are sufficient for the purposes of jurisdiction, and second, that where, as here, the court is to determine whether it has jurisdiction over a defendant who is being sued on a federal claim, it may consider not only the defendant's contacts with the forum state, but also the aggregate contacts of the defendant with the United States as a whole. We take up these arguments in turn.

[The court concluded that under the International Shoe and World-Wide cases, Hitachi lacked minimum contacts with New Jersey.]

The earliest case adopting the national contacts approach is First Flight Co. v. National Carloading Corp., 209 F.Supp. 730 (E.D.Tenn.1962). That court held that the proper inquiry in determining personal jurisdiction in a case involving federal rights is one related to the contacts with the sovereignty in question, the United States. Id. at 738. The theoretical basis behind this approach is that the restrictions of the fourteenth amendment upon state jurisdiction have no application to a cause of action arising under federal law. Instead, the argument runs, the fifth amendment due process clause controls, and a defendant's national contacts may be aggregated to satisfy that standard. [Citations omitted.] As described by one court, "it is not the territory in which a court sits that determines the extent of its jurisdiction, but rather the geographical limits of the unit of government of which the court is a part." Cryomedics, Inc. v. Spembly, Ltd., 397 F.Supp. 287, 291 (D.Conn.1975); accord, Holt v. Klosters Rederi A/S, 355 F.Supp. 354, 357 (W.D.Mich.1973); [other citations omitted].

Although the fifth amendment test is sometimes expressed in more general "fairness" terms, see, e.g., Honeywell, Inc., 509 F.2d at 1143 (citing Galvan v. Press, 347 U.S. 522, 530, 74 S.Ct. 737, 742, 98 L.Ed. 911 (1954)), the International Shoe line of cases . . . provides the foundation for the test, and the analysis is substantially similar. See Honeywell, Inc., 509 F.2d at 1143; First Flight, 209 F.Supp. at 738 (E.D.Tenn.1962). Accordingly, the standard which has been applied by those courts adopting the national contacts approach is whether defendant "has such minimum contacts with the United States that the exercise of jurisdiction does not offend traditional notions of fair play and substantial justice." Holt v. Klosters Rederi A/S, 355 F.Supp. at 357 n. 2 (quoting First Flight, 209 F.Supp. at 738); [other citations omitted].

. . . .

Since the First Flight opinion discussed the national contacts theory in 1962, several jurisdictions have considered the approach in federal question cases. But most courts which have analyzed the theory have refused to apply it and have instead looked solely to state contacts as a basis for jurisdiction. While these courts generally acknowledge the logic of inquiring into a defendant's contacts with the United States where the suit is based upon a federally created right, they reason that they must have a federal rule or statute authorizing nationwide or worldwide service of process before doing so. See, e.g., Wells Fargo & Co. v. Wells Fargo Exp. Co., 556 F.2d 406, 418 (9th Cir.1977) (refused to aggregate national contacts since Lanham Act did not grant the court broad service of process powers); [other citations omitted].

A review of the pertinent case law reveals that the overwhelming majority of courts which have considered the national contacts approach have rejected its application in the absence of statutory authority for service of process. After careful analysis of the rationale underlying these decisions, the court finds that it must join their ranks. We, therefore, reject plaintiff's contention in the instant matter that defendant Hitachi's national contacts may be aggregated as a basis for the exercise of jurisdiction over Hitachi.

The court's opinion in the case at bar, however, should not be construed as a total rejection of the national contacts theory. On the contrary, the court believes that it is not unfair nor unreasonable as a matter of due process to consider the nationwide contacts of an alien defendant in determining whether jurisdiction exists. As noted by Judge Wilson in his opinion in First Flight,

> One fundamental principle of the Anglo-American law of jurisdiction is that a sovereignty has personal jurisdiction over any defendant within its territorial limits, and that it may exercise that jurisdiction by any of its courts able to obtain service upon the defendant.

209 F.Supp. at 736. This court also believes that many good policy reasons exist for applying the national contacts theory, particularly in those federal question cases involving alien defendants. . . .

We also recognize, however, that the United States has by the enactment of the Federal Rules of Civil Procedure imposed restrictions upon the exercise of personal jurisdiction by its courts. One such restriction, relevant to the case at bar, is that imposed by Rule 4(e), which provides that when substituted service is made pursuant to a state's long-arm statute, the service be made "under the circumstances and in the manner prescribed in the statute." Fed.R.Civ.P. 4(e)(2).[kk] That portion of the Rule has been interpreted to mean that service under a valid state long-arm statute in a federal court is only possible in those situations where the in-state activities of the defendant would be sufficient to invoke the long-arm statute had the defendant been sued in state court. See, e.g., Hydraulics Unlimited Mfg. Co. v. B/J Manufacturing Co., 449

[kk]   The operative part of this provision now lies in Rule 4(k)(1)(A).

F.2d 775, 777 (10th Cir.1971); [other citations omitted]. Thus, where service of process is effected by means of a state statute, a federal court is forced to look to the state in which the district is located to determine whether jurisdiction may be asserted over an out-of-state defendant.

. . . .

Plaintiff has urged the court to exercise jurisdiction on the ground that New Jersey's long-arm rule, R. 4:4–4, N.J.Court Rules (the rule employed in the case at bar) has been construed as extending New Jersey's jurisdictional reach to its constitutional limits. See Avdel v. Mecure, 58 N.J. 264, 268, 277 A.2d 207, 209 (1971). The power of the State of New Jersey, however, is still limited by the due process requirements of the fourteenth amendment. There must still be some contact of a defendant with the forum state.

It is important to note that our rejection of the national contacts approach in the instant matter is limited to those factual situations where service of process must be made pursuant to a state statute. We believe that where service can be effected through wholly federal means, a defendant's national contacts may still be a viable basis for jurisdiction in a federal question case. Thus, for instance, where Congress has provided for nationwide service of process, we can perceive of no impediment to the application of the national contacts theory with the exception of the fifth amendment's "fairness" standard. There would be no need to make reference to any state law in making service, . . . and concomitantly, no need to consider any fourteenth amendment or state restrictions on that service. See, e.g., Alco Standard Corp. v. Benalal, 345 F.Supp. 14, 25 (E.D.Pa.1972) (In action brought under [1934 Securities] Exchange Act, which provides for nationwide service of process, court ruled that since the Act is national in scope, the court's jurisdictional inquiry should focus on a defendant's national contacts.) . . .

Since Congress has not enacted a federal statute authorizing nationwide service of process in admiralty actions, and since the district court's power in the present matter is therefore limited by the Federal Rules of Civil Procedure and, through them, the laws of New Jersey, we find the relevant jurisdictional inquiry to be the extent of the defendant Hitachi's contacts with New Jersey. And since we have determined that Hitachi lacks sufficient contacts with New Jersey to satisfy the jurisdictional standards set forth in International Shoe and its progeny, defendant Hitachi's Motion to Dismiss must be granted.[ll]

[ll]   This decision was affirmed, 654 F.2d 280 (3d Cir.), cert. denied, 454 U.S. 1085, 102 S.Ct. 642 (1981). The Third Circuit made this observation of particular interest:

"We will accept for purposes of this appeal DeJames' position that if service can be made by wholly federal means all of Hitachi's contacts with the United States may be aggregated to support jurisdiction in the District of New Jersey, even if these contacts are limited exclusively to Hawaii, to Alaska, or to a few states on the west coast. . . . [W]e are not sure that some geographic limit short of the entire United States might not be incorporated into the 'fairness'

———

FURTHER ON FEDERAL RULE 4

As you have just seen, Rule 4(k)(1)(A) provides that a party is amenable to federal suit whenever the party would be amenable to suit in the courts of the state in which the district court sits. That is, this provision authorizes the federal court to reach only as far as the forum state could under the Fourteenth Amendment and the state's long-arm provisions. See Cofield v. Randolph Cty. Comm'n, 844 F.Supp. 1499 (M.D.Ala.1994).

The rest of Rule 4(k) comprises federal-law extensions of the federal courts' reach, but these are available only in special situations. Recall, for example, the 100-mile "bulge" provision of Rule 4(k)(1)(B).

Questions: (47) Plaintiff brings suit on a state-created claim in a federal court located in State A. There is an attempt to bring in an additional corporate defendant under Rule 19, with service being made on one of its officers in neighboring State B in accordance with the "bulge" provision of Rule 4(k). The additional defendant is transacting business in the "bulge" located in State B, but it has no connection at all with State A. May the "bulge" provision operate at all in this situation? If so, should federal or state law govern amenability? (If state law is to control, should the federal court look to the law of State A or State B? If the law of State B is to control, what happens if the facts are changed so that the additional defendant is transacting business in State B but is not transacting business in and has no other connection with that part of State B constituting the "bulge," except the presence of its officer in the "bulge" when served?

(48) Change the facts of the preceding question so that the suit is on a federally created claim. Should federal or state law govern amenability? (If a federal standard is to control, how should that standard be defined? See Benjamin Kaplan, Amendments of the Federal Rules of Civil Procedure, 1961–1963 (I), 77 Harv.L.Rev. 601, 632–33 (1964).)

Rule 4(k)(1)(C) picks up the relatively rare federal statutes that extend the federal courts' reach. The particular federal service statute prescribes amenability to the federal suit. For example, under 28 U.S.C. § 2361 an interpleader claimant may be served anywhere in the United States, and then the federal court can exercise personal jurisdiction to the limits of the Fifth Amendment Due Process Clause. Another example would be the federal securities act mentioned in the DeJames case.

---

component of the fifth amendment. For a discussion of possible fifth amendment limitations, see Oxford First Corp. v. PNC Liquidating Corp., 372 F.Supp. 191, 198–204 (E.D.Pa.1974)."

This additional limitation, which would allow the defendant to defeat jurisdiction by showing unreasonableness, has been adopted in later cases. E.g., Peay v. BellSouth Med. Assistance Plan, 205 F.3d 1206 (10th Cir.2000) ("Accordingly, we hold that in a federal question case where jurisdiction is invoked based on nationwide service of process, the Fifth Amendment requires the plaintiff's choice of forum to be fair and reasonable to the defendant.").

Question: (49) Try finally to formulate explicitly the ultimate constitutional constraints on federal courts' territorial authority to adjudicate, working in the context of the following hypothetical case:

> Consider a small business in Hawaii that produces a small amount of toxic waste as a by-product of its operations. This firm maintains its headquarters in Hawaii and does business in both Hawaii and California. It maintains no adequate disposal facilities of its own, so it has contracted with a California waste disposal firm over the past ten years for disposal of its wastes. The California disposal firm maintains its headquarters in California and engages in waste disposal throughout most of the United States. It owns a number of advanced disposal sites, including one in California and one in New Jersey. The Hawaiian firm's contract has always required that its waste be safely disposed of at the California site. In the first year of the contract, though, the wastes were shipped to the New Jersey site because the California waste disposal site was temporarily inactive. It is now discovered that the New Jersey site is leaking wastes into the environment.

> The EPA responds by using "Superfund" to fund the cleanup operations necessitated by the toxic waste spill, and sues to recover its cleanup costs under section 107 of CERCLA, which imposes liability for these costs on both the generator and disposer of the toxic waste. Under CERCLA, venue for this action lies in "any district in which the release or damages occurred, or in which the defendant resides, may be found, or has his principal office." The EPA follows its usual practice of initiating suit at the site of the waste spill, and brings the action in New Jersey federal court, naming the California waste-disposal firm and the Hawaiian corporation as defendants. [CERCLA also provides for nationwide service of process, and so the Federal Environmental Protection Agency serves the defendants at their home offices.] The Hawaiian firm appears specially to challenge personal jurisdiction.

James J. Connors, II, Note, Nationwide Service of Process Under the Comprehensive Environmental Response, Compensation, and Liability Act: The Need for Effective Fairness Constraints, 73 Va.L.Rev. 631, 653–54 (1987). What result?

———

OMNI CAPITAL INTERNATIONAL v. RUDOLF WOLFF & CO., 484 U.S. 97, 108 S.Ct. 404 (1987). Fairly complex proceedings essentially involved disgruntled Louisiana investors suing New York financial managers (collectively referred to as "Omni") under the Federal Commodity Exchange Act for fraud in connection with a trading program on the London Metals Exchange, and Omni then impleading by out-of-state service its London traders (Wolff and Gourlay) on the basis of allegedly improper trading activities. The latter two individuals moved to dismiss for lack of personal jurisdiction. The United States District Court for the Eastern District of Louisiana at first denied the motion, but on reconsideration dismissed the claims against Wolff and Gourlay. The en banc Fifth Circuit affirmed (9–6).

In the Supreme Court on certiorari, Omni argued that in this sort of case the only limits on the district court's exercise of personal jurisdiction derive from the Due Process Clause of the Fifth Amendment. Wolff and Gourlay countered that, additionally, a statute or rule must authorize service. Omni responded that, if necessary, federal courts should fashion a gap-filling service provision.

The unanimous Supreme Court decided that personal jurisdiction was lacking and therefore affirmed. Justice Blackmun's opinion for the Court addressed the three points raised by the parties' contentions.

First, although the Court agreed that the requirement of personal jurisdiction flows from that Due Process Clause, it rejected Omni's argument that due process is the sole concern: "Before a federal court may exercise personal jurisdiction over a defendant, the procedural requirement of service of summons must be satisfied. '[S]ervice of summons is the procedure by which a court having venue and jurisdiction of the subject matter of the suit asserts jurisdiction over the person of the party served.' Mississippi Publishing Corp. v. Murphree, 326 U.S. 438, 444–445, 66 S.Ct. 242, 245–246 (1946). Thus, before a court may exercise personal jurisdiction over a defendant, there must be more than notice to the defendant and a constitutionally sufficient relationship between the defendant and the forum. There also must be a basis for the defendant's amenability to service of summons. Absent consent, this means there must be authorization for service of summons on the defendant."

Second, the Court ruled that what is now Rule 4(k)(1) governed and that it required either a federal statute or a forum-state law authorizing out-of-state service in the circumstances of the case. However, the Commodity Exchange Act did not itself authorize long-arm service explicitly or implicitly. Moreover, as held below and as conceded by Omni, Wolff and Gourlay were beyond Louisiana's long-arm statute, because they had no statutorily sufficient connection to Louisiana. Thus, even for federally created claims such as these, and despite the third-party defendants' extensive contacts with the United States, "neither part of [the] Rule . . . authorizes the service of summons on Wolff and Gourlay."

Third, the Court decided against any practice of judicial ad hoc authorization of service, even to fill a possibly inadvertent gap by "authorizing service on an alien in a federal-question case when the alien is not amenable to service under the applicable state long-arm statute." Such a practice would be unwise, as well as possibly beyond the courts' power. The solution should instead come by congressional act or "from those who propose the Federal Rules of Civil Procedure."

———

Question: (50) Would the resultant Rule 4(k)(2) have changed the outcome in DeJames or in the Omni case itself? Note that it was unclear in both cases whether the defendants' contacts were substantial with respect to any state. See United States v. Swiss Am. Bank, 191 F.3d 30, 35 (1st Cir.1999) (in avoiding Rule 4(k)(2), defendant has the burden of production in showing that some specific state had personal jurisdiction), dismissed on remand, 116 F.Supp.2d 217 (D.Mass.2000), aff'd, 274 F.3d 610 (1st Cir.2001).

––––––––

FURTHER ON FEDERAL/STATE LAW

As we said back in Part 1, with understatement, "Rule 4 is somewhat intricate because, by the nature of its historical growth, it combines specific federal regulations with adopted features of state law."

Before its 1993 rewriting, Rule 4 was even more intricate. It failed to specify the governing law on amenability in some circumstances. It thereby sometimes posed the Erie issue of whether federal or state law governed amenability in a federal suit based on a state-created claim. The cases held for state law. E.g., Arrowsmith v. UPI, 320 F.2d 219, 226 (2d Cir.1963) (in banc) ("State statutes determining what foreign corporations may be sued, for what, and by whom, are not mere whimsy; like most legislation they represent a balancing of various considerations—for example, affording a forum for wrongs connected with the state and conveniencing resident plaintiffs, while avoiding the discouragement of activity within the state by foreign corporations.").

On some issues closely related to the one involved in Arrowsmith, the Erie balance seems to come out the other way. For example, federal law determines which acts committed in the course of litigating will confer jurisdiction over the person, so that federal law will determine whether a defendant has made a general appearance.

Similarly, the cases have generally held federal law to govern in all actions in federal court the questions both of immunity from service of process and of the effect of fraud or force in the attempted acquisition of territorial jurisdiction. However, recent developments on the Erie front make some of these results now seem doubtful. There are a number of other issues where it is difficult to determine which law governs. We touch upon a few of these issues in the following questions.

Questions: (51) Plaintiff brings suit against a foreign corporation in state court on a federally created claim, service being made within the state on an officer of the defendant. The defendant removes the case to federal court and then moves to dismiss under Rule 12(b)(2), as is permissible. Should federal or state law govern this jurisdictional issue? Does it matter whether the defendant is served again after removal under 28 U.S.C. § 1448 and in accordance with a federal nationwide-service provision? See Wright & Miller § 1082.

(52) Change the facts of the preceding question so that there was no removal. In what circumstances, if any, would the state court have to apply federal amenability law under the reverse-Erie doctrine? See David S.

Welkowitz, Beyond Burger King: The Federal Interest in Personal Jurisdiction, 56 Fordham L.Rev. 1, 49–51 (1987).

———

PENDENT PERSONAL JURISDICTION

1.   One further aspect of the interplay between federal and state law on amenability may merit mention. Consider as an example the situation in which the plaintiff joins a substantial federal claim with a state claim in a federal action, service being made in accordance with a federal statute providing nationwide service for the federal claim. Assuming that supplemental subject-matter jurisdiction would exist for the state claim, but that the nationwide-service provision is the sole basis for exercising jurisdiction over the defendant, is there personal jurisdiction for the purposes of the state claim? A careful reading of the applicable statutes reveals no congressional intent to extend nationwide service of process to state claims. However, the policies of judicial economy, convenience, and fairness underlying the exercise of supplemental jurisdiction suggest that some degree of "pendent personal jurisdiction" should exist. The courts over time have split on this problem. But the judicial trend supports reaching a related state claim, the trend having accelerated after the Advisory Committee's allusion to the approach in its note on the 1993 amendment to Rule 4(k)(2). See Action Embroidery Corp. v. Atl. Embroidery, Inc., 368 F.3d 1174 (9th Cir.2004).

(a)   Going beyond the extension of specific jurisdiction from federal causes to related state causes, consider the horizontal reach under a long-arm statute, whether in federal or state court, from one claim within the sovereign's specific jurisdiction to another claim by the same plaintiff against the same defendant that alone would not be within the sovereign's specific jurisdiction. If the second claim is unrelated, not being based on the same nucleus of operative fact, *pendent-claim* personal jurisdiction will not apply. There would simply be no logic in a doctrine that would allow an unrelated claim to piggy-back on a claim within specific jurisdiction. See Charles W. "Rocky" Rhodes & Cassandra Burke Robertson, Toward a New Equilibrium in Personal Jurisdiction, 48 U.C.Davis L.Rev. 207, 244–45 (2014). In fact, long-arm statutes often expressly limit their reach to interrelated causes of action. See the above-quoted 735 Ill.Comp.Stat.Ann. 5/2–209(f).

(b)   By contrast, the jurisdictional reach does seem to go all the way to the limits of "claim" or "case." A related second count based on the same nucleus of operative fact can thus rest on the first count's specific jurisdiction. Long-arm statutes often so imply, and the Constitution would so permit. See Linda Sandstrom Simard, Exploring the Limits of Specific Personal Jurisdiction, 62 Ohio St.L.J. 1619 (2001); cf. Wright & Miller § 1069.7 (discussing Erie implications). Here is an example: a New Hampshire plaintiff can sue at home against a Massachusetts author who slandered him during a book reading in Massachusetts, as long as the plaintiff joins a count for libel by the book, which was distributed in New Hampshire. See Riley v. Harr, 292 F.3d 282, 288 n.8 (1st Cir.2002); cf. Miller Pipeline Corp. v. British Gas plc, 901 F.Supp. 1416 (S.D.Ind.1995) (exercising personal jurisdiction for a patent infringement count, as pendent to a related antitrust count for which there was statutory nationwide service). An example involving dispersed harm comes from Keeton v. Hustler Magazine, Inc., 465 U.S. 770, 104 S.Ct. 1473 (1984) (holding that a nonresident individual can seek damages suffered throughout the country in a libel action against a nondomestic magazine in New Hampshire, where there was a uniquely long statute of limitations but where sales of the magazine were only ten to fifteen thousand per month).

2. A different problem arises when there are multiple parties. Multiple parties means multiple claims.

(a) If a plaintiff sues two or more defendants for the same wrong, personal jurisdiction must independently exist over each defendant. In our country, personal jurisdiction is a personal defense that each defendant can assert. Likewise, suit fails where *P-1* sues *D-1* within specific jurisdiction and *P-2* sues *D-2* without independent specific jurisdiction (additionally, this configuration constitutes improper joinder under Rule 20).

(b) If *P-1* and *P-2* sue the same *D*, where specific jurisdiction exists for *P-1*'s claim but not for *P-2*'s claim, we have a case squarely posing the question of *pendent-party* personal jurisdiction. Say, a Californian sues a Delawarean drug company for injuries suffered in California, and a New Yorker injured in New York tries to go along for the ride. Without more connections, it is initially difficult to see any argument for allowing to the New Yorker this pendent personal jurisdiction in California. An argument might be that the defendant's activity directed at California made jurisdiction foreseeable there. But was jurisdiction invoked by a New Yorker foreseeable? If so, why could the New Yorker not bring her own suit alone in California? In any event, no cases have approved this sort of pendent-party personal jurisdiction.

(c) Yet, a variety of pendent personal jurisdiction has long been the norm in plaintiff-class actions. Recall that courts have considered only the named parties, not the absentee members, in determining jurisdictional questions. But even if the class-action idea seems to authorize this approach to personal jurisdiction over the defendant, why is such jurisdiction still constitutional under the latest cases? It may be that the structuring of class actions so that the absentees are not actually parties before the court dispenses with the need for them to acquire personal jurisdiction, justifying such formalism with the thought that the court will afford procedural due process to the defendant. See Fitzhenry-Russell v. Dr. Pepper Snapple Grp., Inc., 2017 WL 4224723, at *5 (N.D.Cal. Sept. 22, 2017).

————

TRIBAL COURTS

The territorial reach of a Native American tribal court is similar to all this law on territorial jurisdiction, but is not quite the same as the law for state courts and not quite the same as the law for federal courts.

The tribes are not bound by the Fifth or Fourteenth Amendment. However, Congress in 1968 enacted the Indian Civil Rights Act, which imposes constraints that mirror many provisions in the Bill of Rights, including due process. 25 U.S.C. § 1302(a)(8) ("No Indian tribe in exercising powers of self-government shall . . . deprive any person of liberty or property without due process of law.").

Application of this constraint is left to the tribal courts, apparently without the possibility of review by any federal court. Within that constraint, tribal courts have variably developed their territorial jurisdiction as a matter of tribal law. See generally David A. Castleman, Comment, Personal Jurisdiction in Tribal Courts, 154 U.Pa.L.Rev. 1253 (2006).

————

SECTION 7. INTERNATIONAL LITIGATION

We have considered statutory and constitutional limitations on the exercise of territorial jurisdiction, and in doing so we have dealt with both domestic cases and international cases. The international cases came from both state court (Perkins, Helicópteros, Goodyear, Asahi, and Nicastro) and federal court (DeJames, Omni, and Daimler). The basic lesson was that international cases are not so special jurisdictionally. The time has come, however, to examine with a still finer focus this issue of amenability to suit in the context of international litigation.

————

Kadic v. Karadžić

United States Court of Appeals, Second Circuit, 1995.
70 F.3d 232, cert. denied, 518 U.S. 1005, 116 S.Ct. 2524 (1996).

■ Before NEWMAN, CHIEF JUDGE, FEINBERG and WALKER, CIRCUIT JUDGES.

■ JON O. NEWMAN, CHIEF JUDGE:

Most Americans would probably be surprised to learn that victims of atrocities committed in Bosnia are suing the leader of the insurgent Bosnian-Serb forces in a United States District Court in Manhattan. [The court expressed the view—prevalent before the Supreme Court in Kiobel v. Royal Dutch Petroleum Co., 569 U.S. 108, 133 S.Ct. 1659 (2013), sharply limited the extraterritorial application of the Alien Tort Statute, 28 U.S.C. § 1350—that the statute provided federal subject-matter] jurisdiction for suits alleging torts committed anywhere in the world against aliens in violation of the law of nations. The pending appeals pose additional significant issues as to . . . whether a person, otherwise liable for a violation of the law of nations, is immune from service of process because he is present in the United States as an invitee of the United Nations.

These issues arise on appeals by two groups of plaintiffs-appellants from the November 19, 1994, judgment of the United States District Court for the Southern District of New York (Peter K. Leisure, Judge), dismissing, for lack of subject-matter jurisdiction, their suits against defendant-appellee Radovan Karadžić . . . . For the reasons set forth below, we hold that subject-matter jurisdiction exists . . . and that he is not immune from service of process. We therefore reverse and remand.

Background

The plaintiffs-appellants are Croat and Muslim citizens of the internationally recognized nation of Bosnia-Herzegovina, formerly a republic of Yugoslavia. Their complaints, which we accept as true for purposes of this appeal, allege that they are victims, and representatives of victims, of various atrocities . . . carried out by Bosnian-Serb military forces as part of a genocidal campaign conducted in the course of the Bosnian civil war. Karadžić, formerly a citizen of Yugoslavia and now a citizen of Bosnia-Herzegovina, is the President of a three-man presidency of the self-proclaimed Bosnian-Serb republic within Bosnia-Herzegovina, sometimes referred to as "Srpska," which claims to exercise lawful authority, and does in fact exercise actual control, over large parts of the territory of Bosnia-Herzegovina. In his capacity as President, Karadžić possesses ultimate command authority over the Bosnian-Serb military forces, and the injuries perpetrated upon plaintiffs were committed as part of a pattern of systematic human rights violations that was directed by Karadžić and carried out by the military forces under his command. . . .

The two groups of plaintiffs asserted causes of action for genocide, rape, forced prostitution and impregnation, torture and other cruel, inhuman, and degrading treatment, assault and battery, sex and ethnic inequality, summary execution, and wrongful death. They sought compensatory and punitive damages, attorney's fees, and, in one of the cases, injunctive relief. . . .

In early 1993, Karadžić was admitted to the United States on three separate occasions as an invitee of the United Nations. According to affidavits submitted by the plaintiffs, Karadžić was personally served with the summons and complaint . . . while he was physically present in Manhattan. . . .

In the District Court, Karadžić moved for dismissal of both actions on the grounds of insufficient service of process, lack of personal jurisdiction, lack of subject-matter jurisdiction, and nonjusticiability of plaintiffs' claims. . . .

     . . . .

Appellants aver that Karadžić was personally served with process while he was physically present in the Southern District of New York. In the Doe action, the affidavits detail that on February 11, 1993, process servers approached Karadžić in the lobby of the Hotel Intercontinental at 111 East 48th St. in Manhattan, called his name and identified their purpose, and attempted to hand him the complaint from a distance of two feet, that security guards seized the complaint papers, and that the papers fell to the floor. Karadžić submitted an affidavit of a State Department security officer, who generally confirmed the episode, but stated that the process server did not come closer than six feet of the defendant. In the Kadic action, the plaintiffs obtained from Judge Owen an order for alternate means of service, directing service by delivering the complaint to a member of defendant's State Department security detail, who was ordered to hand the complaint to the defendant. The security officer's affidavit states that he received the complaint and handed it to Karadžić outside the Russian Embassy in Manhattan. Karadžić's statement confirms that this occurred during his second visit to the United States, sometime between February 27 and March 8, 1993. Appellants also allege that during his visits to New York City, Karadžić stayed at hotels outside the "headquarters district" of the United Nations and engaged in non-United Nations-related activities such as fund-raising.

[Federal Rule 4] authorizes personal service of a summons and complaint upon an individual physically present within [the state], and such personal service comports with the requirements of due process for the assertion of personal jurisdiction. See Burnham v. Superior Court of California, 495 U.S. 604, 110 S.Ct. 2105, 109 L.Ed.2d 631 (1990).

Nevertheless, Karadžić maintains that his status as an invitee of the United Nations during his visits to the United States rendered him immune from service of process. He relies on both the Agreement Between the United Nations and the United States of America Regarding the Headquarters of the United Nations, reprinted at 22 U.S.C. § 287 note (1988) ("Headquarters Agreement"), and a claimed federal common law immunity. We reject both bases for immunity from service.

A.   Headquarters Agreement

The Headquarters Agreement provides for immunity from suit only in narrowly defined circumstances. First, "service of legal process . . . may take place within the headquarters district only with the consent of and under conditions approved by the Secretary-General." Id. § 9(a). This provision is of no benefit to Karadžić, because he was not served within the well-defined confines of the "headquarters district," which is bounded by Franklin D. Roosevelt Drive, 1st Avenue, 42nd Street, and 48th Street, see id. annex 1. Second, certain representatives of members of the United Nations, whether residing inside or outside of the "headquarters district," shall be entitled to the same privileges and immunities as the United States extends to accredited diplomatic envoys. Id. § 15. This provision is also of no benefit to Karadžić, since he is not a designated representative of any member of the United Nations.

A third provision of the Headquarters Agreement prohibits federal, state, and local authorities of the United States from "impos[ing] any impediments to transit to or from the headquarters district of . . . persons invited to the headquarters district by the United Nations . . . on official business." Id. § 11. Karadžić maintains that allowing service of process upon a United Nations invitee who is on official business would violate this section, presumably because it would impose a potential burden— exposure to suit—on the invitee's transit to and from the headquarters district. However, this Court has previously refused "to extend the immunities provided by the Headquarters Agreement beyond those explicitly stated." See Klinghoffer v. S.N.C. Achille Lauro, 937 F.2d 44, 48 (2d Cir.1991). We therefore reject Karadžić's proposed construction of section 11, because it would effectively create an immunity from suit for United Nations invitees where none is provided by the express terms of the Headquarters Agreement.[9]

The parties to the Headquarters Agreement agree with our construction of it. In response to a letter from plaintiffs' attorneys opposing any grant of immunity to Karadžić, a responsible State Department official wrote: "Mr. Karadžić's status during his recent visits to the United States has been solely as an 'invitee' of the United Nations, and as such he enjoys no immunity from the jurisdiction of the courts of the United States." Letter from Michael J. Habib, Director of Eastern

---

[9]   Conceivably, a narrow immunity from service of process might exist under section 11 for invitees who are in *direct* transit between an airport (or other point of entry into the United States) and the Headquarters District. Even if such a narrow immunity did exist—which we do not decide—Karadžić would not benefit from it since he was not served while traveling to or from the Headquarters District.

European Affairs, U.S. Dept. of State, to Beth Stephens (Mar. 24, 1993) ("Habib Letter"). Counsel for the United Nations has also issued an opinion stating that although the United States must allow United Nations invitees access to the Headquarters District, invitees are not immune from legal process while in the United States at locations outside of the Headquarters District. See In re Galvao, [1963] U.N.Jur.Y.B. 164 (opinion of U.N. legal counsel); see also Restatement (Third) [of the Foreign Relations Law of the United States] § 469 reporter's note 8 (U.N. invitee "is not immune from suit or legal process outside the headquarters district during his sojourn in the United States").

B.   Federal common law immunity

Karadžić nonetheless invites us to fashion a federal common law immunity for those within a judicial district as a United Nations invitee. He contends that such a rule is necessary to prevent private litigants from inhibiting the United Nations in its ability to consult with invited visitors. Karadžić analogizes his proposed rule to the "government contacts exception" to the District of Columbia's long-arm statute, which has been broadly characterized to mean that "mere entry [into the District of Columbia] by non-residents for the purpose of contacting federal government agencies cannot serve as a basis for in personam jurisdiction," Rose v. Silver, 394 A.2d 1368, 1370 (D.C.1978); [other citation omitted]. He also points to a similar restriction upon assertion of personal jurisdiction on the basis of the presence of an individual who has entered a jurisdiction in order to attend court or otherwise engage in litigation. See generally 4 Charles A. Wright & Arthur R. Miller, Federal Practice and Procedure § 1076 (2d ed. 1987).

. . . .

. . . [W]e decline the invitation to create a federal common law immunity as an extension of the precise terms of a carefully crafted treaty that struck the balance between the interests of the United Nations and those of the United States.

. . . .mm

———

Suits in U.S. courts.—The U.S. Supreme Court has largely elaborated the country's law of territorial jurisdiction by deciding cases that arose on the interstate level, and in fact it has decided no international jurisdiction cases other than those you have encountered herein. The United States has no general treaties on international jurisdiction.

---

mm   Default followed by jury trials on compensatory and punitive damages in 2000 resulted in unappealed, but unenforced, judgments for $745 million and an injunction in Kadic and for $4.5 billion in Doe. Nat'l L.J., Feb. 19, 2001, at C25. For background, see Maria T. Vullo, Prosecuting Genocide, 2 Chi.J.Int'l L. 495 (2001).

Consider a suit against a Frenchwoman in a court here. In the absence of a specific treaty, international law imposes no significant restrictions on state-court territorial jurisdiction beyond those restrictions already imposed by the Due Process Clause of the Fourteenth Amendment. Likewise, in the absence of a specific treaty, international law imposes no significant restrictions on federal-court territorial jurisdiction beyond those restrictions already imposed by the Due Process Clause of the Fifth Amendment.

Thus, the Frenchwoman is treated just like anyone else, with no special international protections. Indeed, one might instead wonder why she can even invoke the U.S. constitutional protections. After all, every provision of the Constitution does not extend protection to foreigners who are outside the U.S. territory. Nevertheless, the U.S. Supreme Court has always assumed that a person subject to suit in our courts can demand treatment consistent with the Constitution. Accordingly, the lower courts, and Rule 4(k)(2) too, extend to foreign defendants all the jurisdictional protections given to U.S. defendants. See Gary B. Born, Reflections on Judicial Jurisdiction in International Cases, 17 Ga.J.Int'l & Comp.L. 1, 21–22 (1987).

Suits in foreign courts.—A quick look at the European approach to territorial jurisdiction serves to show how the law can work out differently, given different origins.

Roman law, enjoying unlimited power, embraced the idea of venue restrained with at least some spirit of fairness. *Actor sequitur forum rei,* or the plaintiff follows the forum of the defendant or the property in suit. Generally, then, the plaintiff had to go to the defendant's domicile, where the courts could entertain any cause of action against the defendant. Eventually, there was additional provision for long-arm-like jurisdiction in actions of tort and contract, so that, for example, a plaintiff could sue for a tort at the place of wrongful conduct. In other words, the Roman law and its direct descendant, the civil law, generated a decent scheme that avoided the headaches of the U.S. territorial power dogma.

Development of national law for international cases.—The civil-law courts long ago developed jurisdictional rules for international cases, usually by the method of extending the venue rules that they applied to domestic cases. Modern French law, for example, builds on the Roman restraint idea. Domicile is thus the foundation of French jurisdiction. But socio-economic-political pressures similar to those prevailing in the United States, as well as the usual procedural policies of accuracy, fairness, and efficiency, have pushed France to reach foreign defendants whose acts have caused harm in France.

The territorial power idea was absent from France, with telling implications. On the one hand, without the impulses of that power idea, France has not produced such excesses as tag or attachment jurisdiction. On the other hand, without the restraints of that power idea, France has succumbed even more blatantly to parochial impulses, so that article 14 of its Civil Code as construed authorizes territorial jurisdiction over virtually any action brought by a plaintiff of French nationality. Thus, a French person can sue at home on any cause of action, whether or not the events in suit related to France and regardless of the defendant's connections and interests. This French approach to jurisdiction has emigrated with French law to other countries. The forum-shopping potential of jurisdiction based on the plaintiff's nationality is evident, even though in practice this exorbitant jurisdiction is not abused all that often.

A different example, from the German system, further shows that foreign is not always better than American when it comes to jurisdiction. Germany follows the usual civil-law approach, which does not make our distinction between jurisdiction over things and jurisdiction over persons, but gets to a similar result through the notion of exclusive local jurisdiction for certain kinds of suits that intrinsically involve things. Going much further, however, article 23 of Germany's Code of Civil Procedure authorizes ordinary *personal jurisdiction* given only the presence in Germany of a tangible or intangible thing belonging to the defendant, thus outpacing the U.S. authorization in certain circumstances of *jurisdiction over a thing* based upon presence of the thing. Recovery in a German case founded on presence of goods is not limited to the value of the goods, although the plaintiff might have trouble enforcing the judgment outside Germany. Traditionally the cause of action did not have to relate to the thing or even to Germany, although the Federal Court of Justice has now imposed on the code a requirement that the cause of action be linked to Germany by a "domestic connection," such as the plaintiff's being domiciled in Germany. At least in theory, such property-based jurisdiction could create worrisome opportunities for forum-shopping, as many enterprises have assets in countries with German-based law.

Still, when all is said and done, the civil law of today is not so different from the common law of territorial jurisdiction, at least if one ignores the exorbitant bases of jurisdiction on both sides. This evolution demonstrates how different legal systems tend toward so-called convergence, given similar influences.

Even in the doctrinal details of exorbitant jurisdiction, where national peculiarities peak, the differences are smaller than they first appear. French nationality-based jurisdiction or German property-based jurisdiction may not look much like U.S. tag or attachment jurisdiction, but in fact they share a common core: all nations have tended to disregard defendants' interests in order to give their own people a way to sue at home, letting them try to enforce the resulting judgment locally. See Kevin M. Clermont & John R.B. Palmer, Exorbitant Jurisdiction, 58 Me.L.Rev. 473 (2006).

Imposition of supranational law.—More recently European lawmakers, acting from above, have step-by-step acted to preempt these rules for international cases. They first did so by an enlightened, albeit far from perfect, treaty signed in 1968. That treaty was the Brussels Convention on Jurisdiction and the Enforcement of Judgments in Civil and Commercial Matters, which eventually morphed into a European Union regulation. The European Court of Justice has supranational authority to decide questions arising under the treaty and regulation.

By the Brussels Convention, the member states agreed to provide virtually automatic recognition and enforcement of the judgments of the other member states. This provision was like the Full Faith and Credit Clause of the U.S. Constitution. In order to make this agreement on judgments acceptable, the Brussels Convention was a "double convention" that also defined the bases of territorial jurisdiction— jurisdiction being the doctrine that must, in any judgment-respecting agreement, serve to ensure adjudicative restraint. That is, the European member states could give respect to the others' judgments because they knew that the Brussels Convention restricted the others to appropriately limited jurisdictional reach. This latter restriction worked as the Due Process Clause does in the United States. (The European Convention on Human Rights art. 6 (Right to a Fair Trial) protects procedural due process.)

Today, the Brussels Regulation's jurisdictional bases follow the civil-law approach. The defendant's domicile is the usual place for suit. There is additionally long-arm-like jurisdiction for tort and contract actions; tort actions can be brought "where the harmful event occurred or may occur," and contract actions at "the place of performance of the obligation in question." Certain disadvantaged plaintiffs, such as consumers, often can sue at home. Moreover, there is authorization for forum selection clauses, and there is exclusive local jurisdiction in actions concerning real property and the like.

Further on the prohibited side, each member state gave up its exorbitant jurisdiction, so that for example France gave up its personal jurisdiction based on the plaintiff's French nationality, and Germany gave up its property-based jurisdiction. The United Kingdom had to give up tag jurisdiction and attachment jurisdiction upon its accession in 1978. The Brussels Regulation not only prohibits exorbitant jurisdiction, but also makes mandatory the permissible bases of jurisdiction. So, the United Kingdom had to abandon its judicial practice of sometimes declining jurisdiction on expressly discretionary grounds such as forum non conveniens.

Comparative evaluation.—As already said, the Brussels Regulation is enlightened but imperfect. For one thing, its jurisdictional restraint applies only to defendants domiciled in another member state. Indeed, it openly discriminates against outsiders. Accordingly, although the Brussels Regulation prevents France from using its exorbitant jurisdiction against a German domiciliary, France can still use it in a suit by a French national or domiciliary against an American domiciliary instead. Moreover, the resulting French judgment now gets recognition and enforcement in Germany and elsewhere in the European Union against the American or the American's assets there. Admittedly, this example is an extreme one, without much actual use in practice to date, but it works to illustrate the legal context.

Moreover, any suggestion that European Union law on jurisdiction has achieved markedly greater certainty than U.S. law seems unfounded and even naive. This suggestion is improbable on its face. The Brussels regime attempts to satisfy and reconcile the needs of a variety of different countries and legal systems, using vague and simple formulas sometimes foggily drafted and always in multiple languages. It necessitates the complicated interplay of European and national laws, raising many Erie-like problems. In actual application, the picture is no prettier. There is a lot of litigating throughout the European Union about where to litigate. So the European Union is nowhere close to the perfect-certainty end of the spectrum running from uncertainty to certainty. It may be that the European Union enjoys somewhat greater certainty in its jurisdictional law, but in fact the United States is not really that far behind.

After all, jurisdictional problems remain problems because they are hard problems. A nice way to demonstrate this point is to reconsider comparatively two of the classically unclear cases from the U.S. Supreme Court: World-Wide Volkswagen Corp. v. Woodson and Asahi Metal Industry Co. v. Superior Court.

In World-Wide, which supposedly engendered a jurisdictional law that is "a hopeless mess," Patrick J. Borchers, Comparing Personal Jurisdiction in the United States and the European Community: Lessons for American Reform, 40 Am.J.Comp.L. 121, 143 (1992), the Court made the close call that Oklahoma did not have constitutional power over New York car dealers if the plaintiffs drove the car to Oklahoma and had a horrific accident there, because the defendants had not conducted sufficient Oklahoma-directed activities. The European result, imagining analogous facts subject to the Brussels Regulation, would apparently be different under its provision for tort jurisdiction "where the harmful event occurred." But the European Union achieved that "clear" result only after suffering through judicial creation of redundant jurisdiction at the places of act and of injury, and after addressing such questions as whether products liability actions involve tort or contract, whether such harm is sufficiently direct, and whether supranational or national law governs such issues. Incidentally, without the power test, the U.S. Constitution, like the European Union's law, would allow jurisdiction in the World-Wide setting (and properly so).

The European Union's relative clarity starts disappearing as one wades deeper into stream-of-commerce cases, such as Asahi. In that case brought by an injured motorcyclist, the U.S. Supreme Court made the close call that California's exercise of jurisdiction was constitutionally unreasonable in the peculiar circumstances involving a third-party claim by a Taiwanese manufacturer against a Japanese supplier. Curiously, on analogous facts involving a claim that happened to arrive by third-party procedure, jurisdiction would clearly exist under Brussels Regulation article 8, which by simple fiat extends jurisdiction to reach certain *additional* defendants, including third-party defendants. But that result is clarity by the circumstantial fluke of impleader, and it is not necessarily a desirable outcome. Consider instead the more general circumstances of the motorcyclist as tort victim suing the Japanese supplier. Although jurisdiction at the place of a sufficiently direct tortious harm would seem to exist under the construed words of the Brussels Regulation, it is hard to know what the European Court of Justice would actually do with regard to the stream of commerce as it dilutes in this way. For what it is worth, the national law of some European Union countries would likely view such unlimited jurisdiction as impermissibly exorbitant. The current U.S. approach seems about as clear as the European Union approach, while both stumble toward permitting foreseeable and fair, and only foreseeable and fair, jurisdiction in the general stream-of-commerce situation (and properly so).

SECTION 8.   VENUE

(a) GENERAL PROVISIONS

Recall Part 1's discussion of the rules of venue, which specify where the sovereign is willing to exercise its territorial jurisdiction. By now the nature of venue, and its pursuit of convenience and efficiency, should reappear to you with considerably greater clarity. A few additional observations should consolidate and expand your understanding.

FEDERAL PROVISIONS

Federal venue is a personal privilege of the defendant, so only the defendant as to whom venue appears improper may raise the point. See Camp v. Gress, 250 U.S. 308, 39 S.Ct. 478 (1919) (holding that resident defendant may not pursue point that another defendant is nonresident of district). The defendant may choose to waive a defect in venue and, in any event, will waive one not asserted in timely fashion. See Rule 12(g) and (h). Unlike some defects in subject-matter jurisdiction, territorial jurisdiction, and opportunity to be heard, defective venue does not render a judgment invalid and subject to collateral attack.

Question: (53) How can this last sentence, stating traditional doctrine, be explained?

When a plaintiff brings an action, the plaintiff waives in advance any venue objection to counterclaims—even permissive ones. See Gen. Elec. Co. v. Marvel Rare Metals Co., 287 U.S. 430, 53 S.Ct. 202 (1932). Reading the venue statutes' restrictions on where an action "may be brought" to refer only to the original main action, subsequent case law more broadly holds that those already parties cannot block counterclaims or crossclaims on venue grounds. As to newly joined parties, there may be an emergent doctrine of "supplemental" venue, which thus far is understood to mean that if a claim is within the supplemental subject-matter jurisdiction of the federal court, then there is no ground for objection to venue with respect to that claim. See generally Wright & Miller § 3808.

———

STATE PROVISIONS

The place of trial of civil actions in state courts within each state is governed very largely by statute, and the statutes of the several states do not exhibit any uniform pattern. Professor George N. Stevens, in Venue Statutes: Diagnosis and Proposed Cure, 49 Mich.L.Rev. 307 (1951), listed some thirteen items that appear in various statutory schemes as grounds of venue, including the following: where the subject of action is situated; where the cause of action arose; where "some fact" is present or happened; where defendant resides; where defendant is doing business; where defendant has a place of business; where plaintiff resides; where plaintiff is doing business; where defendant may be found; where defendant may be summoned or served; and where the seat of government is located. Indeed, provisions exist that allow plaintiff to lay venue in any county designated in the complaint or, more simply, in any county. Professor Stevens criticized the existing confused situation and proposed a model venue code.

To concretize your vision of state venue, you should examine NY CPLR art. 5, most of which appears in the statutory section of the Rules booklet.

———

Question: (54) What is, after all, the difference between territorial jurisdiction and venue? The answers seem different for federal and state courts.

———

LOCAL ACTIONS

Most states perpetuate an ancient, confusing, and unsound judge-made doctrine that overrides the usual venue statutes and requires any of a rather arbitrary group of actions to be brought in the county or other subdivision where the subject of the action is located. These "local actions" contrast with "transitory actions" that can be brought anywhere satisfying the usual rules of territorial jurisdiction and venue. Local actions involve claims that supposedly could take place in only one locale, which usually means that local actions include proceedings in rem and those within subtype one of quasi in rem, as well as certain personal actions such as trespass to land, negligent damage to land, and abatement of nuisance. The scope of the doctrine varies from state to state.

Note that if the subject of a local action is not located within the state, the plaintiff cannot sue in that state. So, this venue doctrine can restrict territorial authority to adjudicate on an interstate level. Thus, there remains some contention that the local-action doctrine falls within the realm of territorial jurisdiction, or even subject-matter jurisdiction, but the better view would classify it as a venue rule.

A few states have drastically curtailed or even eliminated the doctrine, either by decision as in Minnesota in 1896 or by statute as in New York in 1913. See Moore § 110.20[2].

The federal courts had long perpetuated this doctrine, requiring local actions to be brought in the district where the subject of the action was located. The federal doctrine derived from case law. The classic case was Livingston v. Jefferson, 15 F.Cas. 660 (C.C.D.Va.1811) (No. 8411), in which Edward Livingston of New York sued Thomas Jefferson of Virginia in a Virginia federal court, alleging trespass to land in New Orleans by the President when he sent in troops to seize the land of a political opponent. The case was dismissed for improper venue. Venue lay only where the land was, even though in those old days Jefferson was not amenable to service of process issuing from there.

However, the Federal Courts Jurisdiction and Venue Clarification Act of 2011, Pub.L. No. 112–63, 125 Stat. 758, abolished the federal doctrine on local actions.

Question: (55) A state court of Virginia still would not permit a trespass action to be maintained on the facts of Livingston v. Jefferson, deeming it a local action for venue purposes. Should the United States District Court for the Western District of Virginia today permit an action to be maintained in such circumstances? What if the case reached the federal court by removal from the state court of Virginia?

———

(b) DISMISSAL OR TRANSFER

FORUM NON CONVENIENS

In Gulf Oil Corp. v. Gilbert, 330 U.S. 501, 67 S.Ct. 839 (1947), a diversity action in the Southern District of New York, a Virginia plaintiff sued a Pennsylvania corporation, which was viewed as having actually consented to general jurisdiction in New York, for alleged negligence in causing to burn the plaintiff's warehouse in Lynchburg, Virginia. Defendant sought dismissal under the doctrine of forum non conveniens, claiming that Virginia was the appropriate place for trial because plaintiff lived there, defendant transacted some business there, and all the events giving rise to the suit occurred there. The doctrine thus invoked is a discretionary one, typically said to come into play when jurisdiction and venue are proper but the court decides that it should dismiss, or sometimes just stay, the case because of the serious inappropriateness of the chosen forum and because of the availability of a substantially more appropriate forum.

The district court dismissed, considering itself bound under Erie by New York law. The court of appeals reversed, disagreeing as to the controlling effect of New York law and taking a restrictive view of the entire doctrine. On certiorari, the Supreme Court, with four dissents, reversed the court of appeals and ordered dismissal. Finding no difference between New York and federal law, it did not pursue the Erie question. Justice Jackson for the majority continued:

"Wisely, it has not been attempted to catalogue the circumstances which will justify or require either grant or denial of remedy. The doctrine leaves much to the discretion of the court to which plaintiff resorts, and experience has not shown a judicial tendency to renounce one's own jurisdiction so strong as to result in many abuses.

"If the combination and weight of factors requisite to given results are difficult to forecast or state, those to be considered are not difficult to name. An interest to be considered, and the one likely to be most pressed, is the private interest of the litigant. Important considerations are the relative ease of access to sources of proof; availability of compulsory process for attendance of unwilling, and the cost of obtaining attendance of willing, witnesses; possibility of view of premises, if view would be appropriate to the action; and all other practical problems that make trial of a case easy, expeditious and inexpensive. There may also be questions as to the enforcibility of a judgment if one is obtained. The court will weigh relative advantages and obstacles to fair trial. It is often said that the plaintiff may not, by choice of an inconvenient forum, 'vex,' 'harass,' or 'oppress' the defendant by inflicting upon him expense or trouble not necessary to his own right to pursue his remedy. But unless the balance is strongly in favor of the defendant, the plaintiff's choice of forum should rarely be disturbed.

"Factors of public interest also have place in applying the doctrine. Administrative difficulties follow for courts when litigation is piled up in congested centers instead of being handled at its origin. Jury duty is a burden that ought not to be imposed upon the people of a community which has no relation to the litigation. In cases which touch the affairs of many persons, there is reason for holding the trial in their view and reach rather than in remote parts of the country where they can learn of it by report only. There is a local interest in having localized controversies decided at home. There is an appropriateness, too, in having the trial of a diversity case in a forum that is at home with the state law that must govern the case, rather than having a court in some other forum untangle problems in conflict of laws, and in law foreign to itself."

THE § 1404(a) TRANSFER PROVISION

In 1948 Congress enacted 28 U.S.C. § 1404(a), which read: "For the convenience of parties and witnesses, in the interest of justice, a district court may transfer any civil action to any other district or division where it might have been brought." The reviser's note explained the provision by saying: "Subsection (a) was drafted in accordance with the doctrine of forum non conveniens, permitting transfer to a more convenient forum, even though the venue is proper." But the statute changed the remedy from dismissal of the federal action to transfer of the action to the more convenient federal forum.

Because prior to 1948 the Supreme Court had indicated that the special venue act for FELA cases precluded dismissal on the basis of forum non conveniens, Baltimore & Ohio Railroad Co. v. Kepner, 314 U.S. 44, 62 S.Ct. 6 (1941), the question soon arose whether a federal court could transfer an FELA case under § 1404(a). The Supreme Court held that such transfer was allowable, Ex parte Collett, 337 U.S. 55, 69 S.Ct. 944 (1949).

Then, in Norwood v. Kirkpatrick, 349 U.S. 29, 75 S.Ct. 544 (1955), while declining to set aside transfer of three FELA cases, the Supreme Court held that § 1404(a) permits transfer upon a lesser showing of inconvenience than forum non conveniens had required for its remedy of dismissal. The Court added: "This is not to say that the relevant factors have changed or that the plaintiff's choice of forum is not to be considered, but only that the discretion to be exercised is broader." (This sentence appeared to give an emphasis different from Justice Jackson's statement in the Gilbert case: "But unless the balance is strongly in favor of the defendant, the plaintiff's choice of forum should rarely be disturbed." The three dissenters took the view that the Court's interpretation did violence to the intent of Congress and was inconsistent with the reviser's note.) Today, courts still struggle over the appropriate way to verbalize how significantly more convenient a venue the transferee court must be.

The statute worked other changes. Forum non conveniens had been a defendant's remedy. With transfer substituted for dismissal, § 1404(a) became attractive to plaintiffs as well. After some early authority that "Section 1404(a) is not available to plaintiffs who voluntarily choose their own forum," Barnhart v. John B. Rogers Producing Co., 86 F.Supp. 595 (N.D.Ohio 1949), the federal courts came to accept that transfer was available to any plaintiff in a proper case. (Forum non conveniens could be invoked on the court's own motion, and apparently the same is now true for § 1404(a) in rare circumstances.)

Questions: (56) What would be a proper case for transfer upon plaintiff's motion?

(57) What remains of the doctrine of forum non conveniens in federal court, after the enactment of § 1404(a)?

The hottest controversy under § 1404(a) concerned limiting transfer of a case to districts "where it might have been brought." Could a plaintiff obtain a transfer to a district where venue would have been improper or where service of process on the defendant would have been impossible? No. But since venue is a personal privilege of the defendant and since the defendant may consent to service, could a defendant waive any restriction implicit in the "where it might have been brought" requirement and obtain a transfer to a district where venue or service would otherwise be objectionable as to her?

———

HOFFMAN v. BLASKI, 363 U.S. 335, 80 S.Ct. 1084 (1960). In two cases the district courts ordered transfer to a more convenient district on defendants' motion. The Seventh Circuit granted mandamus, ruling that § 1404(a) did not authorize these transfers. On certiorari, the Supreme Court affirmed.

Justice Whittaker explained for the Court: "Petitioners concede that these actions were properly brought in the respective transferor forums; that statutory venue did not exist over either of these actions in the respective transferee districts, and that the respective defendants were not within the reach of the process of the respective transferee courts. . . .

"Petitioners' 'thesis' and sole claim is that § 1404(a), being remedial, Ex parte Collett, 337 U.S. 55, 71, 69 S.Ct. 944, 946, should be broadly construed, and, when so construed, the phrase 'where it might have been brought' should be held to relate not only to the time of the bringing of the action, but also to the time of the transfer; and that 'if at such time the transferee forum has the power to adjudicate the issues of the action, it is a forum in which the action might *then* have been brought.' (Emphasis added.) They argue that in the interim between the bringing of the action and the filing of a motion to transfer it, the defendants may move their residence to . . . some other district, and if such is done, the phrase 'where it might have been brought' should be construed to empower the District Court to transfer the action, on motion of the defendants, to such other district; and that, similarly, if, as here, the defendants move to transfer the action to some other district and consent to submit to the jurisdiction of such other district, the latter district should be held one 'in which the action might *then* have been brought.' (Emphasis added.)

"We do not agree. We do not think the § 1404(a) phrase 'where it might have been brought' can be interpreted to mean, as petitioners' theory would require, 'where it may now be rebrought, with defendants' consent.' This Court has said, in a different context, that § 1404(a) is 'unambiguous, direct [and] clear,' Ex parte Collett, 337 U.S. at page 58, 69 S.Ct. at page 946, and that the 'unequivocal words of § 1404(a) and the legislative history . . . [establish] that Congress indeed meant what it said.' United States v. National City Lines, Inc., 337 U.S. 78, 84, 69 S.Ct. 955, 958. Like the Seventh Circuit, . . . we think the dissenting opinion of Judges Hastie and McLaughlin in Paramount Pictures, Inc. v. Rodney, 3 Cir., 186 F.2d 111, 119, correctly answered this contention:

> 'But we do not see how the conduct of a defendant after suit has been instituted can add to the forums where "it might have been brought." In the normal meaning of words this language of Section 1404(a) directs the attention of the judge who is considering a transfer to the situation which existed when suit was instituted.'

. . . .

"The thesis urged by petitioners would not only do violence to the plain words of § 1404(a), but would also inject gross discrimination. That thesis, if adopted, would empower a District Court, upon a finding of convenience, to transfer an action to any district desired by the *defendants* and in which they were willing to waive their statutory defenses as to venue and jurisdiction over their persons, regardless of the fact that such transferee district was not one in which the action 'might have been brought' by the plaintiff. Conversely, that thesis would not permit the court, upon motion of the *plaintiffs* and a like showing of convenience, to transfer the action to the same district, without the consent and waiver of venue and personal jurisdiction defenses by the defendants. Nothing in § 1404(a), or in its legislative history, suggests such a unilateral objective and we should not, under the guise of interpretation, ascribe to Congress any such discriminatory purpose."

Justice Frankfurter in dissent, joined by Justices Harlan and Brennan, countered:

"One would have to be singularly unmindful of the treachery and versatility of our language to deny that as a mere matter of English the words 'where it might have been brought,' may carry more than one meaning. For example, under Rule 3 of the Federal Rules of Civil Procedure, civil actions are 'commenced' by filing a complaint with the court. As a matter of English there is no reason why 'commenced' so used should not be thought to be synonymous with 'brought' as used in § 1404(a), so that an action 'might have been brought' in any district where a complaint might have been filed, or perhaps only in districts with jurisdiction over the subject matter of the litigation. As a matter of English alone, the phrase might just as well be thought to refer either to those places where the defendant 'might have been' served with process, or to those places where the action 'might have been brought' in light of the applicable venue provision, for those provisions speak generally of where actions 'may be brought.' Or the phrase may be thought as a matter of English alone to refer to those places where the action 'might have been brought' in light of the applicable statute of limitations, or other provisions preventing a court from reaching the merits of the litigation. On the face of its words alone the phrase may refer to any one of these considerations, i.e., venue, amenability to service, or period of limitations, to all of them or to none of them, or to others as well. And to the extent that these are matters which may or may not be raised at the defendant's election, the English of the phrase surely does not tell whether the defendant's actual or potential waiver or failure to raise such objections is to be taken into account in determining whether a district is one in which the action 'might have been brought,' or whether the phrase refers only to those districts where the plaintiff 'might have brought' the action even over a timely objection on the part of the defendant, that is, where he had 'a right' to bring it.

. . . .

"Surely, the Court creates its own verbal prison in holding that 'the plain words' of § 1404(a) dictate that transfer may not be made in this case although transfer concededly was in the interest of 'convenience' and 'justice.' . . .

. . . .

"In summary, . . . the statute . . . contains ambiguities which must be resolved by considerations relevant to the problem with which the statute deals. Moreover, the most obvious significance for the set of words here in question, considered as self-contained words, is that they have regard for the limitations contained in the regular statutory rules of venue. Those rules, it is beyond dispute, take into account the consent of the defendant to proceed in the forum, even if it is not a forum designated by statute. And the doctrine of forum non conveniens 'in accordance with' which § 1404(a) was drafted, also took into account the defendant's consent to proceed in another forum to which he was not obligated to submit. Nor can a decision against transfer be rested upon notions of 'discrimination' or of unfairness to the plaintiff in wrenching him out of the forum of his choice to go forward in a place to which he objects. In the proper administration of § 1404(a), such consequences cannot survive the necessity to find transfer to be in the interests of 'convenience' and 'justice,' before it can be made. On the other hand, to restrict transfer as the Court does to those very few places where the defendant was originally amenable to process and could have had no objection to the venue is drastically to restrict the number of situations in which § 1404(a) may serve the interests of justice by relieving the parties from a vexatious forum. And it is to restrict the operation of the section capriciously, for such a drastic limitation is not counseled by any legitimate interest of the plaintiff, or by any interest of the federal courts in their jurisdiction. The defendant's interest of course is not involved because he is the movant for transfer."

———

Questions: (58) The American Law Institute, after considerable study and noting that substantial sentiment exists for simply eliminating the transfer statute's key six words, concluded against proposing a change: "For fear of the bugs beneath, this stone is here left unturned." Federal Judicial Code Revision Project § 1404(a) (Am. Law Inst. 2004). Nevertheless, Congress amended § 1404(a) in 2011 by appending at the end "or to any district or division to which all parties have consented." What is now the continuing significance of Hoffman?

(59) Does the Hoffman reading of § 1404(a) prevent the transfer of in rem and quasi in rem actions? See Wright & Miller § 3843, at 39–42 (citing cases that allow, surprisingly enough, transfer to where personal jurisdiction exists).

———

VAN DUSEN v. BARRACK, 376 U.S. 612, 84 S.Ct. 805 (1964). A large number of plaintiffs properly sued in the District Court for the Eastern District of Pennsylvania for wrongful deaths resulting from an air crash in Boston Harbor on takeoff of a flight to Philadelphia. (Many others brought similar actions in the District Court for the District of Massachusetts.) The defendants moved to transfer the Pennsylvania federal actions to Massachusetts under § 1404(a), and the court ordered the transfer.

The plaintiffs brought mandamus proceedings in the Court of Appeals for the Third Circuit, in which they successfully contended that the appellate court should vacate the district court's order because Massachusetts, although venue and jurisdiction were proper there, was not a district where the actions "might have been brought": the plaintiffs, being the decedents' personal representatives who had not obtained the appointments necessary to qualify them to initiate actions in Massachusetts, did not have an unqualified right to bring suit there. On certiorari, the Supreme Court reversed and remanded, holding "that the words 'where it might have been brought' must be construed with reference to the federal laws delimiting the districts in which such an action 'may be brought,' " without regard to laws concerning the capacity of fiduciaries to sue.

Another critical issue was what the applicable choice-of-law rule would be upon transfer. A possible difference in substantive law was at stake: Massachusetts based recovery in wrongful-death cases on the degree of the defendant's culpability and limited recovery to a $20,000 maximum, while Pennsylvania allowed compensatory damages without limitation as to amount.[nn] On this issue, the Supreme Court said that the transferee district court, after transfer on defendants' motion, would have to apply the state law that would have been applied if there had been no change of venue, thus closing the door to any defendants' shopping for favorable law.[oo] The explanation in part was that there is nothing "in the language or policy of § 1404(a) to justify its use by defendants to defeat the advantages accruing to plaintiffs who have chosen a forum which, although it was inconvenient, was a proper venue." Moreover, "our interpretation of that statute fully accords with and is supported by the policy underlying Erie," in that the result in federal court will conform to what would have been the result in the filing state. A change of venue in pursuit of convenience, concluded Justice Goldberg for the unanimous Court, "generally should be, with respect to state law, but a change of courtrooms.[40]"

Question: (60) *P* properly brings a diversity action against *D* for injuries to *P*, a guest passenger in *D*'s automobile, in a federal court of State *X*, which is *D*'s residence. The court properly transfers it to a federal court of State *Y*, *P*'s residence, pursuant to § 1404(a) upon *P*'s motion. The law of State *X* holds that a host driver is liable to his guest passenger for lack of ordinary care, regardless of where the accident occurred. The law of State *Y* holds that the duty of care is measured by the law of the place where the accident occurred, in this case State *Y*, where a guest passenger may recover only upon proof of gross negligence. What should be the governing law as to standard of care in this case?

FERENS v. JOHN DEERE CO., 494 U.S. 516, 110 S.Ct. 1274 (1990). A Pennsylvania man working on his farm lost his hand allegedly in a combine harvester manufactured by defendant, which is incorporated in Delaware with its principal place of business in Illinois but which does business widely. He and his wife delayed three years before bringing a

---

[nn]　On the one hand, the federal court sitting in Pennsylvania would of course apply the Pennsylvania choice-of-law rule, under Klaxon Co. v. Stentor Electric Manufacturing Co., 313 U.S. 487, 61 S.Ct. 1020 (1941). At that time, it was unclear what choice-of-law rule Pennsylvania would adopt for such an action arising in another state; but shortly after the Supreme Court's decision, Pennsylvania in a different crash case held that it would apply its own rule of compensatory damages without limitation as to amount, Griffith v. United Air Lines, 416 Pa. 1, 203 A.2d 796 (1964).

On the other hand, the plaintiffs feared and the defendants hoped that the transferee federal court sitting in Massachusetts would apply the Massachusetts choice-of-law rule and hence the Massachusetts law on damages, which, according to the plaintiffs, would be highly prejudicial to them and not "in the interest of justice."

[oo]　Do you think this rule would make transfer generally more likely or less likely? At any rate, after remand and the further consideration ordered by the Supreme Court in the light of its decision, the district court denied transfer of these cases. Popkin v. E. Air Lines, 253 F.Supp. 244 (E.D.Pa.1966).

[40]　Of course the transferee District Court may apply its own rules governing the conduct and dispatch of cases in its court. We are only concerned here with those state laws of the transferor State which would significantly affect the outcome of the case.

diversity action, sounding in contract and warranty, in the Western District of Pennsylvania. Relying on the defendant's prior consent to Mississippi's general jurisdiction, they then brought another diversity action in the Southern District of Mississippi, sounding in negligence and products liability, because that court would apply Mississippi's six-year statute of limitations rather than Pennsylvania's two-year statute for torts. The plaintiffs next moved to transfer the second case to the Western District of Pennsylvania under § 1404(a), the defendant put up no opposition, and the court granted the motion.

The transferee court, however, dismissed the tort case by applying the Pennsylvania statute of limitations. The court of appeals affirmed. On certiorari, the Supreme Court reversed, adopting the simple rule that transferor law applies regardless of who moves to transfer under § 1404(a). Justice Kennedy for the majority argued that the core reasons behind the Van Dusen decision carried over to the context of the plaintiffs' motion. Anticipating Justice Scalia's dissent, which Justices Brennan, Marshall, and Blackmun joined, the Court's opinion further argued that the plaintiffs' opportunity to forum-shop by this file-and-transfer ploy results from our federal system, and not from § 1404(a).

———

Question: (61) If a transferred case involves disputed questions of federal law, should the transferee court apply the transferor court's interpretation of federal law or exercise independent judgment as to federal law? Cases are split, but most are now going the latter route. Why? See Richard L. Marcus, Conflicts Among Circuits and Transfers Within the Federal Judicial System, 93 Yale L.J. 677, 720 (1984) ("transferee court is fully competent to decide issues of federal law"). But what if the federal law is meant to be geographically nonuniform, as are some statutes of limitations? See McMasters v. United States, 260 F.3d 814 (7th Cir.2001) (dictum to effect that transferor law applies).

———

THE § 1406(a) TRANSFER PROVISION

A quite different statute came before the Court in Goldlawr, Inc. v. Heiman, 369 U.S. 463, 82 S.Ct. 913 (1962). Plaintiff had sued several defendants in the Eastern District of Pennsylvania for treble damages and other relief under the antitrust laws, doing so within the federal statute of limitations. On motion by two of the corporate defendants to dismiss for improper venue and lack of personal jurisdiction, the district court, passing only on the venue contention, found venue improper as to them. By this time, the statute of limitations had run. Refusing to dismiss, the court under 28 U.S.C. § 1406(a) ordered transfer of the action as against the two defendants to the Southern District of New York, where venue would be proper and personal jurisdiction would be obtainable.

The transferee court, however, granted dismissal on the ground that the transferor court, lacking personal jurisdiction, had no power to transfer. The Court of Appeals for the Second Circuit affirmed. On certiorari, the Supreme Court reversed (5–2), holding that § 1406(a) authorized such transfer—so giving the plaintiff who has filed in the wrong court the benefit of that filing date when the transferee court applies its statute of limitations.

Justice Black for the majority said: "The language of § 1406(a) is amply broad enough to authorize the transfer of cases, however wrong the plaintiff may have been in filing his case as to venue, whether the court in which it was filed had personal jurisdiction over the defendants or not. The section is thus in accord with the general purpose which has prompted many of the procedural changes of the past few years—that of removing whatever obstacles may impede an expeditious and orderly adjudication of cases and controversies on their merits. When a lawsuit is filed, that filing shows a desire on the part of the plaintiff to begin his case and thereby toll whatever statutes of limitation would otherwise apply."

Justice Harlan in dissent, joined by Justice Stewart, said: "The notion that a District Court may deal with an in personam action in such a way as possibly to affect a defendant's substantive rights without first acquiring jurisdiction over him is not a familiar one in federal jurisprudence. No one suggests that Congress was aware that 28 U.S.C. § 1406(a) might be so used when it enacted that statute."

Question: (62) *P* brings a diversity action against *D* for injuries to *P*, a guest passenger in *D*'s automobile, in a federal court of State *X*, which *P* alleges to be *D*'s residence. When it appears that *D* is not a resident of State *X*, the court correctly transfers it to a federal court of State *Y*, *P*'s residence, pursuant to § 1406(a). The law of State *X* holds that the duty of care is measured by the law of the defendant's residence, in this case State *Z*, where a guest passenger may recover only upon proof of gross negligence. The law of State *Y* holds that the duty of care is measured by the law of the place where the accident occurred, in this case State *Y*, where a host driver is liable to his guest passenger for lack of ordinary care. What should be the governing law?

MARTIN v. STOKES, 623 F.2d 469 (6th Cir.1980). In March 1975 a Virginia personal-injury plaintiff filed a diversity action against Kentucky and California defendants in her home district, the Western District of Virginia, which was a proper venue under the then-current version of 28 U.S.C. § 1391. After personal service in their home districts, defendants moved to quash process. The district court without explanation refused to quash and ordered transfer to the Western

District of Kentucky, where the automobile accident had occurred in August 1973.

The transferee court, however, granted defendants' request to dismiss on the basis of Kentucky's one-year statute of limitations, even though the transferor court would have applied Virginia's two-year statute. Plaintiff appealed.

The court of appeals ruled that (1) on state-law questions transferor law applies after a § 1404(a) transfer (which would defeat the limitations defense), but transferee law applies after a § 1406(a) transfer (which would sustain the limitations defense); (2) the two statutes being mutually exclusive but complementary, § 1404(a) operates only where the transferor court is a proper forum, but § 1406(a) can operate where the transferor court cannot acquire personal jurisdiction although venue is proper; and (3) this case should be remanded to the Western District of Kentucky to make the critical determination of whether the Virginia court obtained personal jurisdiction.

————

Questions: (63) Suppose that a federal court of State *X* would apply a one-year statute of limitations to a particular action if commenced there, while a federal court of State *Y* would apply a two-year statute if the same case were commenced there. Can plaintiff, after transfer from an improper forum under § 1406(a), maintain that action over a limitations defense in the following situations? (a) Federal suit is brought in forum *X* nineteen months after accrual of the cause of action; transfer to forum *Y* is made one month later. (b) Federal suit is brought in forum *X* six months after accrual; transfer to forum *Y* is made nineteen months later. (c) Federal suit is brought in forum *X* nineteen months after accrual; transfer to forum *Y* is made six months later. (d) Federal suit is brought in forum *X* twenty-five months after accrual; transfer to forum *Y* is made one month later. See generally John D. Currivan, Note, Choice of Law in Federal Court After Transfer of Venue, 63 Cornell L.Rev. 149 (1977); Roberto Finzi, Note, The 28 U.S.C. § 1406(a) Transfer of Time-barred Claims, 79 Cornell L.Rev. 975 (1994).

(64) Can plaintiff transfer from a federal court lacking subject-matter jurisdiction to a federal court with subject-matter jurisdiction? See 28 U.S.C. § 1631; Jeffrey W. Tayon, The Federal Transfer Statute: 28 U.S.C. § 1631, 29 S.Tex.L.Rev. 189 (1987).

(65) Should there be transfer between courts of different states? Think of the various ways we could implement and design such a system. One method that does not necessitate federal involvement would have states enact uniform transfer laws. In fact, the Uniform Transfer of Litigation Act, approved by the National Conference of Commissioners on Uniform State Laws in 1991 but withdrawn as obsolete in 2015 without being enacted anywhere, provided that the enacting state's courts could make or receive a transfer in cooperation with any other sovereign's court; the Act permitted transfer by a court with subject-matter and territorial jurisdiction to a consenting court that had subject-matter jurisdiction, and also permitted

transfer by a court lacking jurisdiction to a consenting court that had subject-matter and territorial jurisdiction; and the Act contained provisions regularizing some subsidiary concerns such as appellate review and statute of limitations. See also Leonard J. Feldman, The Interstate Compact: A Cooperative Solution to Complex Litigation in State Courts, 12 Rev.Litig. 137 (1992).

———

Kevin M. Clermont, "The Story of Piper: Forum Matters"

Civil Procedure Stories 199 (Kevin M. Clermont ed., 2d ed. 2008),
with case documents at http://civprostories.law.cornell.edu.

Any study of the forum's authority to adjudicate would be incomplete without considering venue. Nonetheless, the definition of venue is frustratingly murky. Venue concerns the subconstitutional doctrines that work to site litigation in particular, and presumably appropriate, courts among the several of the sovereign's courts that have constitutional authority—or venue can conceivably work to oust any or all such courts of authority. Venue naturally includes so-called venue statutes and doctrines, but it also includes or at least abuts transfer provisions, forum selection clauses, and forum non conveniens, as well as restrictions on serving process and other of the sovereign's self-imposed limitations such as door-closing statutes and lis pendens doctrines.

Broadly conceived in that way, venue's varied limitations are theoretically critical to understanding the judicial branch. They also relate to an essential part of the litigator's arsenal [as I have earlier written]:

> The name of the game is forum-shopping. In the American civil litigation system today, few cases reach trial. After perhaps some initial skirmishing, most cases settle. Yet all cases entail forum selection, which has a major impact on outcome.

The legal system's task is to site litigation in a fashion that puts appropriate constraints on the litigators' gaming. In the United States, the Constitution puts an outer limit on the list of available forums with territorial authority to adjudicate a litigation that has nonlocal elements. But the Constitution's minimal requirements produce a list of forums that is too long to be optimal or even acceptable. Legal systems therefore utilize the various strands of venue law to narrow the list, not necessarily to the best forum but at least to a shorter list of appropriate forums. In doing so, legal systems face one huge legal-process issue: should they accomplish this narrowing by a set of preconceived legislative rules that rigidly treat categories of cases or by general standards that judges apply in an ad hoc way to the particular case? Once past that threshold issue, the legal system must resolve a host of other questions in order to generate a law of venue.

An ideal vehicle for studying the whole subject of venue is Piper Aircraft Co. v. Reyno. "The fact pattern permits a review of virtually the whole of forum-selection—an impressive array of issues relating to personal jurisdiction, subject matter jurisdiction, venue, transfer, choice of law . . . . At the end of the day, in my opinion, Piper is the greatest teaching case in the civil procedure curriculum."[4] Piper does, however, feature most prominently forum non conveniens, so discussion must start there.

In theory, forum non conveniens allows a court discretionarily to decline existing authority to adjudicate if the court is a seriously inappropriate forum and if a substantially more appropriate forum is available to the plaintiff. The doctrine is relatively recent in origin and mainly Anglo-American in adoption. Most but not all U.S. states have adopted this important doctrine, usually by court decision but sometimes by statute. Analogously, a federal district court, without any statutory authority, may discretionarily decline existing authority to adjudicate if the court is a seriously inappropriate forum, if a substantially more appropriate (normally foreign but conceivably state) forum is available to the plaintiff, and if transfer of venue to a more convenient federal forum is not an adequate remedy.

In practice, the doctrine of forum non conveniens has proven quite troublesome in application. It entails three significant precepts. *First*, forum non conveniens may be invoked on the defendant's motion or on the court's own motion. The plaintiff obviously would oppose forum non conveniens. The burden of proof does not rest on the plaintiff. *Second*, in passing on the motion, the court balances the interests of both the private parties and the public for and against litigating elsewhere. Examples of relevant private factors include residence of the parties, relative ease of access to sources of proof, and problems of judgment enforcement; examples of relevant public factors include which sovereign's law will apply, relative burdens on the court system from hearing the case, and relative benefits to the polity from deciding the case. All these incommensurable factors go onto the balance for the court to determine, by a very imprecise process, the direction of tilt. Critically, however, the court gives the plaintiff's choice of forum great deference, so that the court will decline to hear the case only in an extreme situation, when the balance tilts strongly toward the alternative forum. *Third*, if the court grants the motion, the remedy is ultimately dismissal, either outright or conditional upon the defendant's waiving defenses (such as personal jurisdiction or the statute of limitations) that would impede suit in the more appropriate forum. Courts indeed may impose various other conditions.

Piper restated this whole doctrine of forum non conveniens, and so is its central text. No procedural doctrine is so encapsulated in a single

---

[4]   Richard D. Freer, Refracting Domestic and Global Choice-of-Forum Doctrine Through the Lens of a Single Case, 2007 BYU L.Rev. 959, 960–61 (2007).

opinion that is so ill-conceived. That is a boldly harsh statement. Let me try to support it in brief compass.

Social and Legal Background

Three socio-legal influences set the scene for Piper.

First, the twentieth century saw the development of a substantive and procedural scheme in the United States that was quite favorable to plaintiffs. On the substantive side, mention might be made of strict liability and generous damages in tort, simply by way of illustration. On the procedural side, weapons like notice pleading, liberal joinder, broad discovery, and nonmutual collateral estoppel were added to a system already featuring the civil jury, the contingent fee, and the nonreimbursement of the winner's attorney's fees. Meanwhile, territorial authority to adjudicate was becoming much more expansive, albeit more discretionary in effect. All these changes contributed mightily to the consternation of defendants.

Second, foreign plaintiffs woke up to the possibility of invoking the U.S. system to their advantage. "As a moth is drawn to the light, so is a litigant drawn to the United States. If he can only get his case into their courts, he stands to win a fortune."[7]

Third, U.S. judges became obsessed with docket control, as they rode out what they saw as a litigation crisis. There is good reason to question the size and the cause of the increase in caseloads, but there is no denying the courts' drive for docket control.

These three influences combined to create pitched battles in personal-injury lawsuits brought here by foreign plaintiffs against U.S. corporate defendants—battles over where to litigate—in which plaintiffs and defendants had intensely opposed interests and in which the courts were not altogether neutral bystanders. . . .

Factual Background

The fatal flight set out that overcast day of July 27, 1976. The pilot, a twenty-two-year-old Scot named Eric Massie Scott who had obtained his commercial license less than three months before, was flying a commercial charter for a minor air taxi company called McDonald Aviation, Ltd. When he initially left Perth, Scotland, at 7:10 a.m. on a small Piper Aztec aircraft, he had three or four stops to make on that day's circuit. However, after he landed in Blackpool, England, he was forced to change aircraft because of a problem with the plane. The pilot leased an identical Piper from Air Navigation and Trading Co., Ltd., a Blackpool company that owned and maintained the plane. Both McDonald and Air Navigation were British companies, and the British-

---

[7]   Smith Kline & French Labs. Ltd. v. Bloch, [1983] 1 W.L.R. 730, 733 (C.A.1982) (Eng.) (Lord Denning, M.R.); see Peter F. Schlosser, Lectures on Civil-Law Litigation Systems and American Cooperation with Those Systems, 45 U.Kan.L.Rev. 9, 37 (1996) (characterizing U.S. courts as "the plaintiff's heaven").

registered plane leased in Blackpool was a six-seat twin-engine Piper Aztec Model PA-23.

When the leased plane returned from Leeds to Blackpool later that day, the original plane was still out of commission. Therefore, as the pilot left Blackpool to return to Perth at 5:13 p.m., he flew the leased plane. He carried five Scottish passengers: William and Liam Stuart Fehilly (44-year-old father and 11-year-old son), David Vincent Moran, Peter Cunningham Scott, and William James McDougall Storm. The pilot was flying by visual flight rules over the Scottish highlands at about 3,000 feet, way too low in the view of McDonald's manual. Less than an hour after takeoff, at 5:56 p.m., the plane entered into a tailspin and crashed vertically into mountainous terrain about 2,500 feet high just south of Edinburgh near Talla, or about eight miles northeast of Moffat, Scotland. All six aboard died on impact. There were no distress or emergency transmissions from the aircraft, and there were no witnesses.

The wreckage was stored in England. The British Department of Trade investigated the crash a few months later. Its investigators provisionally suggested mechanical failure in the plane (manufactured in Lock Haven, which is in the Middle District of Pennsylvania, by Piper Aircraft Company in 1968; then sold to an Ohio dealer; and a few years later somehow brought to England) or in a propeller (manufactured in Ohio by Hartzell Propeller, Inc.), because four mounting bolts for the propeller's governor were found with loose nuts, which might have led to port engine failure. On review by way of a nine-day adversary hearing in December 1978 at Hartzell's request, the Department's Review Board— finding insufficient evidence of equipment defect and instead raising the possibility of pilot error—determined the probable cause to be loss of control from shutting down the port engine, which the pilot may have done because it was running rough.

The Scottish survivors of the five passengers later sued in the United Kingdom against McDonald, Air Navigation, the pilot's estate, and the Civil Aviation Authority, doing so in July 1978, just before the Scottish two-year statute of limitations expired. Also, the pilot's representative sued in the United Kingdom in July 1978 against Piper, Hartzell, McDonald, and Air Navigation.[11]

This factual background is admittedly sparse. The key point is that the U.S. Supreme Court knew nothing more, and indeed probably less.

Prior Proceedings

1.　Trial Courts. A Scottish law firm referred the five passengers' survivors to a U.S. lawyer, Daniel Cathcart. His prominent L.A. law firm—Magaña, Cathcart & McCarthy—specialized in aviation-injury

---

[11]　Despite my considerable efforts, the outcomes of these two lawsuits remain unknown. However, Air Navigation reports: "As far as I am aware the Lawsuits in the UK did not come to fruition." E-mail from Russell Whyham (Sept. 3, 2007) (Mr. Whyham is Director of the company).

cases, from its office at 1801 Avenue of the Stars. Indeed, Cathcart, then a forty-four-year-old USC law graduate and a certified pilot, is the author of the book Aircrash Litigation Techniques.

Suit. As is not that unusual in connection with wrongful death lawsuits on behalf of foreigners, Cathcart arranged for a California probate court to appoint his legal secretary, Gaynell Reyno, as local administratrix of the passengers' estates. Within a couple of weeks, on July 21, 1977, she sued Piper and Hartzell for compensatory and punitive damages for wrongful death, unspecified in amount but for millions of dollars in effect, in the Superior Court of the State of California for the County of Los Angeles.[15] The plaintiff's lawyer showed his preference for the state court in California by so selecting it.

Removal. In an adversary system, the plaintiff's preference meant that the defendants disliked the forum, in fact a lot. The plaintiff's forum-shopping triggered a spate of forum-shopping by the defendants. Their initial move was to remove on the basis of diversity to the United States District Court for the Central District of California on August 24, 1977. Reyno was a citizen of California, Piper of Pennsylvania, and Hartzell of Ohio.

Transfer. Then, by arguing that this product liability case would best be heard at the place of manufacture, over strenuous opposition, Piper managed by motion under 28 U.S.C. § 1404(a) to transfer the case against it to the Middle District of Pennsylvania, where the case might have been brought. Simultaneously, on December 21, 1977, Hartzell [who alone raised the point] managed to quash service for lack of personal jurisdiction in California, but the federal court nevertheless used 28 U.S.C. § 1406(a) to transfer the case against it to the Middle District of Pennsylvania, where Hartzell could be and later was served with process. This difference added another layer of complexity to the case, because § 1404(a) called for the application of the law that the transferor court would have applied to Piper while § 1406(a) called for the application of the law that the transferee court would apply to Hartzell.

Dismissal. Finally, arguing with new information . . . , the defendants moved the Pennsylvania district court on May 15, 1978, to dismiss on the ground of forum non conveniens. As a lawyer for the plaintiff said at oral argument of the motion on September 13, 1978, in Harrisburg: "I hesitate to think where we will go if we get to Scotland." Nevertheless, the district court dismissed on October 19, 1979, finding that the private and public factors overwhelmingly pointed to Scotland. The court conditioned the dismissal on Piper's and Hartzell's waiving any personal jurisdiction or statute of limitations defenses in Scotland.

---

[15]   Reyno also sued the engine maker, Avco Lycoming Engine Group, but agreed to the California district court's dismissal of Avco in November 1977.

2. *Appellate Courts.* The plaintiff appealed on November 15, 1979. The parties orally argued on May 22, 1980. The Third Circuit reversed on July 24, 1980, on the grounds that:

> (1) the district court had abused its discretion in balancing the factors, by weighing too heavily the Scotland-leaning factors and too lightly the interests of the plaintiff in choice of forum and the interests of Pennsylvania and Ohio in regulating their manufacturers, and

> (2) dismissal is improper when a plaintiff would then be subject to less favorable law, such as the Scottish tort law that lacked strict liability and compensated the estates only for funeral expense (and the passengers' survivors only for loss of support and loss of society, without recovery for emotional loss or award of punitive damages).

Certiorari. The U.S. Supreme Court granted certiorari on February 23, 1981. Faced with a broadly phrased petition, the Court expressly limited the question presented, agreeing to decide only whether a court must deny a forum non conveniens dismissal that would inflict an unfavorable change in law on the plaintiff. Even so limited, the case was obviously an important one, generating an amicus brief from three major U.S. aircraft manufacturers and an opposing amicus brief from a plaintiffs' law firm.

Briefs. The difference in substantive law between the United States and Scotland was what this whole procedural fight was about. The plaintiff at least was candid: "Respondent does not attempt to hide the fact that her prospective recovery in the courts of the United States is much greater than in those of Scotland. It is openly conceded that the choice of a United States forum was made precisely because the jurisdictions in this country allow the cause of action for strict liability for manufacture of defective products . . . . It can only be concluded that Petitioners desire to have this matter heard in [a foreign] jurisdiction precisely because of the limitation on applicable causes of action, as well as the unavoidable fact that Petitioners stand to have a larger monetary judgment entered against them here."

For briefing in the Supreme Court, Piper and Hartzell switched from their local counsel to specialists from Washington, D.C., firms. On whether the change in law should defeat a forum non conveniens dismissal, Piper in its wide-ranging brief in the Supreme Court argued thus:

> The approach taken by the court of appeals just makes no sense, especially where, as here, the real plaintiff parties in interest are nonresident aliens who retain the right and the ability to proceed in and invoke the protection of their home forum. There is nothing unfair about remitting foreign plaintiffs to the remedies afforded by their own legal system. But it is

unfair to subject American defendants, as the court of appeals would do, to the double burden not only of an inconvenient forum but also of harsher rules of liability than would apply in the foreign plaintiffs' own home forum where the accident occurred.

. . . [T]he decision below amounts to an open-door policy toward foreign claimants, the predictable result of which will be to induce essentially foreign litigation to be brought here rather than abroad. The net effect of the decision below would be to encourage and facilitate the exploitation of the American legal system by nonresident aliens, to the detriment of American citizens and American courts alike.

The trial lawyer Cathcart remained the plaintiff's lead counsel. His briefs were not especially effective. He took a number of preliminary shots that missed their mark. As he zeroed in to respond on the issue of change in law, he did not help the plaintiff by embracing the Third Circuit's approach in the following terms:

The weight to be accorded the plaintiff's choice of a forum . . . is considerable. The reasons are many, but beyond all of the irrefutable and uncontradicted arguments in favor of bestowing upon the injured plaintiff the right to seek redress wherever he sees fit, there is a further, highly just and desirable benefit to be derived from according the plaintiff his choice of a forum: The defendant accused of wrongdoing will always be held to the highest available standard of accountability for his actions and resulting injuries and damages. In this way are persons and entities such as the defendant manufacturers now before this Court made aware of the extent to which they may be answerable for a panoply of wrongful acts—in this instance the dissemination of defective products into the worldwide mainstream of commerce and industry.

The public policy to be advanced by this vehicle is obvious. As between a jurisdiction holding manufacturers only to the standard of due care (Scotland), and a jurisdiction holding the same manufacturers to the standard of strict liability (United States), the latter can clearly be seen to better advance a policy of deterrence of wrongful conduct, while at the same time provide the injured plaintiff with the best opportunity for compensatory redress.

Thus, to look at the law of a particular forum only in terms of its "favorability" to the plaintiff is to eclipse the other, highly important half of the same concept, the ability of that forum to insure that the actions of prospective defendants are within the limits of acceptable conduct within the jurisdiction.

In replying, Hartzell pounced:

> There runs through respondent's arguments a conviction that the judicial system can operate fairly only when it produces the maximum prospect of recovery for the plaintiff and the largest liability for the defendant. We, to the contrary, have supposed as a general proposition that the judicial system is supposed to be neutral as between plaintiff and defendant. We submit that none of respondent's arguments for the virtual inviolability of her choice of forum could appeal to a neutral tribunal.

Oral Argument. On October 14, 1981, James M. Fitzsimons of Mendes & Mount in New York City, Piper's national product liability counsel, argued for that company in his first and only appearance before the Court. The highly experienced Warner W. Gardner of Shea & Gardner in Washington argued for Hartzell. Their oral arguments started out focused on the change-in-law question before the Court. However, the few questions from the Justices, which were neither focused nor probing questions, caused the arguments to meander into more general consideration of the forum non conveniens balance of factors.

During his responding argument, in this his sole appearance before the Court, Cathcart sharply observed: "We have, then, the manufacturers trying to use a procedural rule to bring about a substantive result."[28] Justice Thurgood Marshall, who would write the Court's opinion, chimed in with his only real contribution by expressing concern that Cathcart's position meant that anyone injured by a U.S. product anywhere in the world could sue in U.S. courts. Cathcart fleetingly conceded that unfavorable change in law should not be determinative, but should be a factor that goes onto the balance. And he argued that if the Supreme Court were to overturn the Third Circuit on the determinative role of change in law, the Court still should not reverse the decision below because it could stand on the alternative holding that the district court had abused its discretion in balancing all the factors.

Worth noting is that it was in the defendants' interests, but not the plaintiff's, to lead the Supreme Court into reviewing the lower courts' application of the discretionary balance. The defendants thought the Third Circuit's holding on the change-in-law question to be so clearly wrong that there would be little difficulty in persuading the Supreme Court to overturn that holding. Their real problem would be in getting the Supreme Court to dismiss outright, instead of vacating on the basis

---

[28]　In Justice Blackmun's handwritten notes during oral argument, he kept track of the lawyers this way:

- Fitzsimons—grey 55
- Gardner—older-grey 72
- Cathcart—younger, Cal smooth blond 49

Notes, Oct. 14, 1981, Harry A. Blackmun Papers (Library of Congress), Box 343, Folder 8.

of the change-in-law question and then remanding for rebalancing. They sensed that the Third Circuit, if given a chance, was likely to reinstate its result. So, their briefs and arguments pressed for outright dismissal.

Ready for Decision? The key point that emerges from this review of the prior proceedings is that the case arrived for Supreme Court decision in a remarkably undeveloped and unfocused condition. The Court had tried to limit review to one issue, but neither the parties nor the Justices seemed willing or able so to limit themselves. The briefs were all over the place, especially those of the defendants, and the two sides did not really join issue with each other. The oral argument revealed almost nothing. Throughout the process, what was really at issue (and the arguments bearing directly thereon) received only glancing treatment. The prior proceedings did not bode well for sound decision.

Piper Aircraft Co. v. Reyno

Supreme Court of the United States, 1981.
454 U.S. 235, 102 S.Ct. 252.

■ JUSTICE MARSHALL delivered the opinion of the Court.

[Part I set out the facts and prior proceedings.]

II

The Court of Appeals erred in holding that plaintiffs may defeat a motion to dismiss on the ground of forum non conveniens merely by showing that the substantive law that would be applied in the alternative forum is less favorable to the plaintiffs than that of the present forum. The possibility of a change in substantive law should ordinarily not be given conclusive or even substantial weight in the forum non conveniens inquiry.

We expressly rejected the position adopted by the Court of Appeals in our decision in Canada Malting Co. v. Paterson Steamships, Ltd., 285 U.S. 413, 52 S.Ct. 413 (1932). . . .

It is true that Canada Malting was decided before [Gulf Oil Corp. v. Gilbert, 330 U.S. 501, 67 S.Ct. 839 (1947)], and that the doctrine of forum non conveniens was not fully crystallized until our decision in that case.[13] However, Gilbert in no way affects the validity of Canada Malting. Indeed, by holding that the central focus of the forum non conveniens

---

[13]   . . . .

In previous forum non conveniens decisions, the Court has left unresolved the question whether under Erie R. v. Tompkins, 304 U.S. 64, 58 S.Ct. 817 (1938), state or federal law of forum non conveniens applies in a diversity case. [Three citations, including Gilbert, omitted.] The Court did not decide this issue because the same result would have been reached in each case under federal or state law. The lower courts in this case reached the same conclusion: Pennsylvania and California law on forum non conveniens dismissals are virtually identical to federal law. See 630 F.2d at 158. Thus, here also, we need not resolve the Erie question.

inquiry is convenience, Gilbert implicitly recognized that dismissal may not be barred solely because of the possibility of an unfavorable change in law. Under Gilbert, dismissal will ordinarily be appropriate where trial in the plaintiff's chosen forum imposes a heavy burden on the defendant or the court, and where the plaintiff is unable to offer any specific reasons of convenience supporting his choice.[15] If substantial weight were given to the possibility of an unfavorable change in law, however, dismissal might be barred even where trial in the chosen forum was plainly inconvenient.

The Court of Appeals' decision is inconsistent with this Court's earlier forum non conveniens decisions in another respect. Those decisions have repeatedly emphasized the need to retain flexibility. . . . If central emphasis were placed on any one factor, the forum non conveniens doctrine would lose much of the very flexibility that makes it so valuable.

In fact, if conclusive or substantial weight were given to the possibility of a change in law, the forum non conveniens doctrine would become virtually useless. Jurisdiction and venue requirements are often easily satisfied. As a result, many plaintiffs are able to choose from among several forums. Ordinarily, these plaintiffs will select that forum whose choice-of-law rules are most advantageous. Thus, if the possibility of an unfavorable change in substantive law is given substantial weight in the forum non conveniens inquiry, dismissal would rarely be proper.

. . . .

The Court of Appeals' approach is not only inconsistent with the purpose of the forum non conveniens doctrine, but also poses substantial practical problems. If the possibility of a change in law were given substantial weight, deciding motions to dismiss on the ground of forum non conveniens would become quite difficult. Choice-of-law analysis would become extremely important, and the courts would frequently be required to interpret the law of foreign jurisdictions. First, the trial court would have to determine what law would apply if the case were tried in the chosen forum, and what law would apply if the case were tried in the alternative forum. It would then have to compare the rights, remedies, and procedures available under the law that would be applied in each forum. Dismissal would be appropriate only if the court concluded that the law applied by the alternative forum is as favorable to the plaintiff as that of the chosen forum. The doctrine of forum non conveniens, however, is designed in part to help courts avoid conducting complex exercises in comparative law. As we stated in Gilbert, the public interest factors point towards dismissal where the court would be required to

---

[15]   In other words, Gilbert held that dismissal may be warranted where a plaintiff chooses a particular forum, not because it is convenient, but solely in order to harass the defendant or take advantage of favorable law. This is precisely the situation in which the Court of Appeals' rule would bar dismissal.

"untangle problems in conflict of laws, and in law foreign to itself." Gilbert, supra, 330 U.S. at 509, 67 S.Ct., at 843.

Upholding the decision of the Court of Appeals would result in other practical problems. . . . The American courts, which are already extremely attractive to foreign plaintiffs, would become even more attractive. The flow of litigation into the United States would increase and further congest already crowded courts.[19]

The Court of Appeals based its decision, at least in part, on an analogy between dismissals on grounds of forum non conveniens and transfers between federal courts pursuant to § 1404(a). In Van Dusen v. Barrack, 376 U.S. 612, 84 S.Ct. 805 (1964), this Court ruled that a § 1404(a) transfer should not result in a change in the applicable law. . . . However, § 1404(a) transfers are different than dismissals on the ground of forum non conveniens.

Congress enacted § 1404(a) to permit change of venue between federal courts. Although the statute was drafted in accordance with the doctrine of forum non conveniens, [citations omitted], it was intended to be a revision rather than a codification of the common law. Norwood v. Kirkpatrick, 349 U.S. 29, 75 S.Ct. 544 (1955). District courts were given more discretion to transfer under § 1404(a) than they had to dismiss on grounds of forum non conveniens. Id., at 31–32, 75 S.Ct., at 546.

The reasoning employed in Van Dusen v. Barrack is simply inapplicable to dismissals on grounds of forum non conveniens. That case did not discuss the common-law doctrine. Rather, it focused on "the construction and application" of § 1404(a). 376 U.S. at 613, 84 S.Ct., at 807–08. Emphasizing the remedial purpose of the statute, Barrack concluded that Congress could not have intended a transfer to be accompanied by a change in law. Id., at 622, 84 S.Ct., at 812. The statute was designed as a "federal housekeeping measure," allowing easy change of venue within a unified federal system. Id., at 613, 84 S.Ct., at 807–08. The Court feared that if a change in venue were accompanied by a change in law, forum-shopping parties would take unfair advantage of the

---

[19]   In holding that the possibility of a change in law unfavorable to the plaintiff should not be given substantial weight, we also necessarily hold that the possibility of a change in law favorable to defendant should not be considered. Respondent suggests that Piper and Hartzell filed the motion to dismiss, not simply because trial in the United States would be inconvenient, but also because they believe the laws of Scotland are more favorable. She argues that this should be taken into account in the analysis of the private interests. We recognize, of course, that Piper and Hartzell may be engaged in reverse forum-shopping. However, this possibility ordinarily should not enter into a trial court's analysis of the private interests. If the defendant is able to overcome the presumption in favor of plaintiff by showing that trial in the chosen forum would be unnecessarily burdensome, dismissal is appropriate—regardless of the fact that defendant may also be motivated by a desire to obtain a more favorable forum. Cf. Kloeckner Reederei und Kohlenhandel v. A/S Hakedal, 210 F.2d 754, 757 (CA2), cert. dismissed by stipulation, 348 U.S. 801, 75 S.Ct. 17 (1954) (defendant not entitled to dismissal on grounds of forum non conveniens solely because the law of the original forum is less favorable to him than the law of the alternative forum).

relaxed standards for transfer. The rule was necessary to ensure the just and efficient operation of the statute.

We do not hold that the possibility of an unfavorable change in law should *never* be a relevant consideration in a forum non conveniens inquiry. Of course, if the remedy provided by the alternative forum is so clearly inadequate or unsatisfactory that it is no remedy at all, the unfavorable change in law may be given substantial weight; the district court may conclude that dismissal would not be in the interests of justice.[22] In these cases, however, the remedies that would be provided by the Scottish courts do not fall within this category. Although the relatives of the decedents may not be able to rely on a strict liability theory, and although their potential damages award may be smaller, there is no danger that they will be deprived of any remedy or treated unfairly.

III

The Court of Appeals also erred in rejecting the District Court's Gilbert analysis. The Court of Appeals stated that more weight should have been given to the plaintiff's choice of forum, and criticized the District Court's analysis of the private and public interests. However, the District Court's decision regarding the deference due plaintiff's choice of forum was appropriate. Furthermore, we do not believe that the District Court abused its discretion in weighing the private and public interests.

A

The District Court acknowledged that there is ordinarily a strong presumption in favor of the plaintiff's choice of forum, which may be overcome only when the private and public interest factors clearly point towards trial in the alternative forum. It held, however, that the presumption applies with less force when the plaintiff or real parties in interest are foreign.

The District Court's distinction between resident or citizen plaintiffs and foreign plaintiffs is fully justified. In Koster, the Court indicated that a plaintiff's choice of forum is entitled to greater deference when the plaintiff has chosen the home forum. Koster [v. (Am.) Lumbermens Mut. Cas. Co., 330 U.S. 518, 524, 67 S.Ct. 828, 831–32 (1947)].[23] When the

---

[22]   At the outset of any forum non conveniens inquiry, the court must determine whether there exists an alternative forum. Ordinarily, this requirement will be satisfied when the defendant is "amenable to process" in the other jurisdiction. Gilbert, supra, 330 U.S. at 506–507, 67 S.Ct., at 842. In rare circumstances, however, where the remedy offered by the other forum is clearly unsatisfactory, the other forum may not be an adequate alternative, and the initial requirement may not be satisfied. Thus, for example, dismissal would not be appropriate where the alternative forum does not permit litigation of the subject matter of the dispute. Cf. Phoenix Canada Oil Co. Ltd. v. Texaco, Inc., 78 F.R.D. 445 (D.C.Del.1978) (court refuses to dismiss, where alternative forum is Ecuador, it is unclear whether Ecuadorean tribunal will hear the case, and there is no generally codified Ecuadorean legal remedy for the unjust enrichment and tort claims asserted).

[23]   . . . .

home forum has been chosen, it is reasonable to assume that this choice is convenient. When the plaintiff is foreign, however, this assumption is much less reasonable. Because the central purpose of any forum non conveniens inquiry is to ensure that the trial is convenient, a foreign plaintiff's choice deserves less deference.

B

The forum non conveniens determination is committed to the sound discretion of the trial court. It may be reversed only when there has been a clear abuse of discretion; where the court has considered all relevant public and private interest factors, and where its balancing of these factors is reasonable, its decision deserves substantial deference. Gilbert, supra, 330 U.S. at 511–512, 67 S.Ct., at 844–45; Koster, supra, 330 U.S. at 531, 67 S.Ct., at 835. Here, the Court of Appeals expressly acknowledged that the standard of review was one of abuse of discretion. In examining the District Court's analysis of the public and private interests, however, the Court of Appeals seems to have lost sight of this rule, and substituted its own judgment for that of the District Court.

(1)

In analyzing the private interest factors, the District Court stated that the connections with Scotland are "overwhelming." 479 F.Supp. at 732. This characterization may be somewhat exaggerated. Particularly with respect to the question of relative ease of access to sources of proof, the private interests point in both directions. As respondent emphasizes, records concerning the design, manufacture, and testing of the propeller and plane are located in the United States. She would have greater access to sources of proof relevant to her strict liability and negligence theories if trial were held here.[25] However, the District Court did not act unreasonably in concluding that fewer evidentiary problems would be posed if the trial were held in Scotland. A large proportion of the relevant evidence is located in Great Britain.

. . . .

The District Court correctly concluded that the problems posed by the inability to implead potential third-party defendants clearly supported holding the trial in Scotland. Joinder of the pilot's estate, Air Navigation, and McDonald is crucial to the presentation of petitioners' defense. If Piper and Hartzell can show that the accident was caused not by a design defect, but rather by the negligence of the pilot, the plane's owners, or the charter company, they will be relieved of all liability. It is

---

A citizen's forum choice should not be given dispositive weight, however. [Citations omitted.] Citizens or residents deserve somewhat more deference than foreign plaintiffs, but dismissal should not be automatically barred when a plaintiff has filed suit in his home forum. As always, if the balance of conveniences suggests that trial in the chosen forum would be unnecessarily burdensome for the defendant or the court, dismissal is proper.

[25]   In the future, where similar problems are presented, district courts might dismiss subject to the condition that defendant corporations agree to provide the records relevant to the plaintiff's claims.

true, of course, that if Hartzell and Piper were found liable after a trial in the United States, they could institute an action for indemnity or contribution against these parties in Scotland. It would be far more convenient, however, to resolve all claims in one trial. The Court of Appeals rejected this argument. Forcing petitioners to rely on actions for indemnity or contributions would be "burdensome" but not "unfair." 630 F.2d at 162. Finding that trial in the plaintiff's chosen forum would be burdensome, however, is sufficient to support dismissal on grounds of forum non conveniens.

(2)

The District Court's review of the factors relating to the public interest was also reasonable. On the basis of its choice-of-law analysis, it concluded that if the case were tried in the Middle District of Pennsylvania, Pennsylvania law would apply to Piper and Scottish law to Hartzell. . . . The Court of Appeals found that the District Court's choice-of-law analysis was incorrect, and that American law would apply to both Hartzell and Piper. . . . Even if the Court of Appeals' conclusion is correct, however, all other public interest factors favored trial in Scotland.

. . . Respondent argues that American citizens have an interest in ensuring that American manufacturers are deterred from producing defective products, and that additional deterrence might be obtained if Piper and Hartzell were tried in the United States, where they could be sued on the basis of both negligence and strict liability. However, the incremental deterrence that would be gained if this trial were held in an American court is likely to be insignificant. The American interest in this accident is simply not sufficient to justify the enormous commitment of judicial time and resources that would inevitably be required if the case were to be tried here.

IV

. . . Thus, the judgment of the Court of Appeals is

Reversed.

THE SUPREME COURT DECISION

This reversal of the court of appeals came on December 8, 1981. Justice Marshall reinstated the district court's dismissal, holding that:

> (1) a change in law was not a determinative factor barring dismissal, so that the plaintiff had no entitlement to avoid Scotland's less favorable law, and

> (2) the showing to get dismissal in the district court was sufficient, such showing being generally easier to make than the court of appeals imagined.

It was unclear why Justice Marshall's opinion reached the second issue, which was outside the grant of certiorari. He tried to explain in footnote 12, which he added after circulation of his initial draft but which is omitted from our excerpt of the long opinion. In it, he maintained that once the court found error on the first issue, it had to consider the second to determine whether dismissal was justified. "An order limiting the grant of certiorari does not operate as a jurisdictional bar. We may consider questions outside the scope of the limited order when resolution of those questions is necessary for the proper disposition of the case."

Chief Justice Burger and Justices Blackmun and Rehnquist, who would hardly be considered the Court's liberal wing, joined Marshall's opinion. Justice Powell recused himself because his former law firm was counsel for the respondent in a similar pending case, and so he took no part in the decision of this case. Having just been appointed to replace Justice Stewart, Justice O'Connor took no part in the case's consideration or decision.

Justice White partly concurred in the majority opinion and partly dissented. Justice Stevens, joined by Justice Brennan, dissented. Both these separate opinions, although differently characterized, made the same point. While agreeing with the part of the Court's opinion that dealt with change in law, they rightly maintained that the Court should not have reviewed the lower courts' application of the discretionary balance in this case because of the limited question on which the Court had granted certiorari. The parties, and especially the plaintiff, had not had a full chance to address the second issue; and reviewing a circuit court's review of district-court abuse does not seem to be the Supreme Court's calling. Justice Stevens said: "Having decided [the first] question, I would simply remand the case to the Court of Appeals for further consideration of the question whether the District Court correctly decided that Pennsylvania was not a convenient forum in which to litigate a claim against a Pennsylvania company that a plane was defectively designed and manufactured in Pennsylvania."

The Papers of Justices Marshall and Blackmun flesh out the story. It seems that Chief Justice Burger and Justices Blackmun and Rehnquist formed the core of those pushing to grant certiorari. Their interest lay in addressing the Third Circuit's change-in-law holding—which would hobble forum non conveniens in its capacity to toss foreign plaintiffs' suits against corporate defendants out of U.S. courts—but not in getting bogged down on review of a mere balancing issue. So, they limited the grant of certiorari, with Justices Stewart and Powell going along. Interestingly, Justice Marshall voted with the liberals against granting certiorari.

The day after the oral argument, which had strayed from the limited issue, Justice Blackmun got the inkling, from chatting separately with Justice Brennan's, Justice White's, and Justice Marshall's law clerks, that some Justices were thinking of dismissing the writ as improvidently granted because the Third Circuit would likely have come out the same way without its change-in-law holding. He wrote the Chief Justice to warn him of the possible turn of events: "I thought I should tell you what I heard to forestall any surprise at Conference."

At that Friday conference, October 16, 1981, Justices Brennan and White did indeed push to dismiss, and Justice Stevens echoed their regret at limiting the grant of certiorari. Of course, Chief Justice Burger and Justices Blackmun and Rehnquist wished to decide the case, despite the mistake in limiting the grant; they wanted to reverse the Third Circuit's change-in-law holding, but they now saw the need to address balancing in order to ensure that the Third Circuit would not rebalance in the plaintiff's favor. So, it came down to Justice Marshall. Justice Blackmun's handwritten conference notes curiously conveyed Justice Marshall's position: "tell them Scotland." And so the vote went 4–3.

The Chief Justice assigned the opinion to Justice Marshall. Subsequently, the other Justices in the majority kept an eye on his drafts of the opinion, making small suggestions on how to beef it up. Most interesting was another memo from Justice Blackmun to the Chief, recommending that he join in the opinion, faulting the opinion for being "unusually long and detailed," and observing: "While only the first holding lies squarely within the limited grant . . . , I think the opinion will educate the lower courts considerably by reaching and deciding the [balancing] issue."

1. *Unfavorable change in law.*—As to changing law, the Piper Court said: "The possibility of a change in substantive law should ordinarily not be given conclusive or even substantial weight in the forum non conveniens inquiry." But:

> We do not hold that the possibility of an unfavorable change in law should *never* be a relevant consideration in a forum non conveniens inquiry. Of course, if the remedy provided by the alternative forum is so clearly inadequate or unsatisfactory that it is no remedy at all, the unfavorable change in law may be given substantial weight; the district court may conclude that dismissal would not be in the interests of justice. In [this case], however, the remedies that would be provided by the Scottish courts do not fall within this category. Although the relatives of the decedents may not be able to rely on a strict liability theory, and although their potential damages award may be smaller, there is no danger that they will be deprived of any remedy or treated unfairly.

Thus, a change in substantive law should not "ordinarily" be given "substantial weight," and the decision should instead depend on the balance of conveniences. But if the alternative forum's remedy is so clearly inadequate or unsatisfactory "that it is no remedy at all," then the change in law *may* be given substantial weight. Right there, the Court dropped its footnote 22 saying that the lower court *must* determine whether an alternative forum exists and that a lack of remedy *may* fail that requirement and thereby preclude dismissal.

The Papers of Justice Marshall help to clarify the difficulties of the quoted paragraph. During the drafting process, Justice Rehnquist wrote Justice Marshall:

> On the whole, I agree with your analysis of the forum non conveniens issue in [this case]. I am troubled, however, by the last paragraph of Section II. In my mind, the paragraph gives too much latitude for the domestic forum to evaluate the legal system of the alternate forum. As written, a district court here could examine the sufficiency of the causes of action permitted by the alternate forum. This paragraph thus undercuts the point that a district court should have [sic] to engage in "complex exercises in comparative law." We should not permit a plaintiff to defeat a forum non conveniens motion by arguing that the foreign forum's substantive law is "unsatisfactory" by American standards. Rather, the district court's analysis of the law to be applied by the foreign forum should be limited to determining whether that forum would permit litigation on the subject matter in dispute.

In response, Justice Marshall changed the opinion's phrasing from "that it approaches no remedy at all" to the above-quoted "that it is no remedy at all," explaining:

> I recognize that even with the change in wording, the paragraph suggests that plaintiffs may ask the courts to conduct at least a limited exercise in comparative law. My answer to this is that such exercises are necessary. If it really is true that the remedy in the alternative forum is completely inadequate, dismissal should be barred. Requiring the court to make this determination should not be unduly burdensome; it should be able to decide fairly quickly whether the alternative remedy is wholly inadequate.

Thus, the Court's opinion really did mean to confine the consideration of change in law to determining the threshold question of whether an alternative forum exists. Once the lower court gets beyond that threshold question, the change in law does not go onto the balance.

As for Justice Marshall's confusing use of "may," when he wrote that "the unfavorable change in law may be given substantial weight," he did not thereby mean that courts have general permission to consider change in law in deciding on balance *not* to dismiss. Instead, his words meant only what close examination reveals that they actually said, namely, that the lower court must consider change in law in determining whether an alternative forum exists, but nevertheless may still decide *to dismiss* for forum non conveniens even in the absence of an alternative forum. He revealed this by further explaining privately to Justice Rehnquist:

"Where the forum chosen by the plaintiff was plainly inconvenient, and where it appears that he purposely delayed filing suit until the limitations period had run in the alternative forum, a decision to dismiss might be warranted. In the typical case, however, dismissal would not be appropriate."

Clear, then, was the Court's intent to constrain consideration of change in law, restricting it to a nondeterminative threshold question. Accordingly, post-Piper lower courts often say that they will not put on the subsequent balance any effect of dismissal in changing law unfavorably to the plaintiff.

Nevertheless, the post-Piper lower courts' behavior does not conform to their words. Change in law does appear to have an effect on courts' decisions—directly or in the judicial manipulation of the doctrine's precepts—even though the result is that the courts must dip their toes further into sometimes "complex exercises in comparative law." The reasons for their so considering change in law are several.

First, even if precedential blinders force the parties to argue mainly in terms of convenience, the parties' real motive in moving for or fighting against a forum non conveniens dismissal is its substantive impact on the case's outcome. And no trial judge could put this critical consideration completely out of mind. Thus, as a matter of psychology, change in law will be an active concern behind the scenes despite Piper.

Second, as a matter of policy, the law should overlook a relevant and important factor only when it can somehow neutralize it. Good policy would seem to dictate that the only situation in which the dismissing court could justify focusing only on convenience factors would be where it could neutralize change in law by ensuring that its applicable law would carry over to the new court. The key difference between the transfer-of-venue statute and the forum non conveniens doctrine is that § 1404(a) can indeed neutralize the change-in-law factor by requiring the federal system's courts to apply transferor law, but forum non conveniens cannot feasibly achieve the equivalent. Despite that fact, under a literal reading of Piper's forum non conveniens doctrine, the plaintiff would just take his or her lumps on the merits while the trial court aridly pursues its notions of convenience. "A dismissal . . . permitted for reasons of convenience . . . without considering the difference in law which would be applied . . . could amount to directing a verdict on the merits without examining them." Brief for Amicus Curiae in Support of Respondent at 12. Ignoring an outcome-determinative change in law, and then dismissing mainly on the basis of conveniences, seems downright bizarre.

Third, as a matter of doctrine, it is hard to see why change in law deserves the special denigration that Piper dealt it. After all, onto the forum non conveniens balance go a variety of Court-blessed private and public factors, some of them being clearly much less important than the content of the applicable law (e.g., the location of the wreckage or the need to translate documents) and some clearly concerning matters other than conveniences (e.g., the sovereigns' interests in applying their own law and in hearing the case). A coherent doctrine would call for balancing change in law too.

Fourth, as a matter of logic, it is hard to believe that Piper could succeed in rendering change in law irrelevant. The opinion's language concedes that an extremely unfavorable change in law remains highly relevant. So a trial court should not send a plaintiff off to no remedy at all. Yet it is hard to discern when a poor remedy deteriorates into an inadequate one. Apparently dismissal to a less generous system such as Scotland's can reduce a $10 million claim to $100 thousand, while a trial court will usually not allow forum non conveniens to reduce a $100 thousand claim to a legal worth of zero because that would be no remedy at all. That is illogical. Simply put, a change in law should not, and will not, lose all influence just because it falls short of that extreme of no remedy.

Is there a way to reconcile the Court's clear intent to constrain the change-in-law factor with the lower courts' more desirable flexibility? One could argue that because a dismissal will result virtually always in a substantive-law change disadvantageous to the plaintiff, Piper's larger purpose in knocking down the Third Circuit's supposedly wooden approach to change in law was ensuring some availability of forum non conveniens. The Court also had the purpose to remove any rigidity from forum non conveniens, in order to ensure that it really was a discretionary doctrine. Consistent with those sensible purposes, a lower court arguably should adopt the sole sensible way to read Piper: an unfavorable change in law does not, by itself, block dismissal—but, to avoid rigidity, the unfavorable change in law otherwise remains relevant to the discretionary balance. Nonetheless, honesty compels admitting that this approach would violate the Court's holding. The law-abiding lower federal court should look instead at ways to adjust the balancing process.

2. *Discretionarily balancing the factors.*—It is true that the Piper Court intended forum non conveniens to be a discretionary balancing doctrine. The trial judge should, on a case-by-case basis, ensure that the lawsuit ends up in an appropriate court, rather than leaving the venue entirely to forum-shopping by plaintiff or defendant. This implies that no rigid rules should exist, despite the long-persisting judicial urge to forge a few. Instead, the balance should rule.

The Supreme Court, however, also wished to encourage lower courts to grant forum non conveniens dismissals, by easing the decisional standard for how strongly the balance must tilt toward the alternative forum. So the Court reached the second issue. And in doing so, the Court itself suggested rigidities. Or at least the Piper Court's language deepened the confusion about the discretionary doctrine's oxymoronic rules. Consider the following five mysteries (and, after each, a tentative paragraph on the mystery's solution).

First, consider the aforementioned mysterious rule, which Piper recited without any real clarification but in seemingly narrow terms, that a prerequisite to dismissal is the existence of an **alternative forum**. Lower courts almost always recite that another court, at least able to offer some remedy with a modicum of fairness, must be available. But as already explained, this unclear and even illogical rule is nonbinding. An alternative forum turns out in very rare situations not to be an absolute prerequisite, its absence being overlooked when the tilt of the balance toward dismissal is utterly overwhelming.[pp]

In any event, the way courts apply the supposed rule means that the prerequisite of an alternative forum might be more a useful verbiage than a working rule. When courts today apply the prerequisite in denying dismissal, they usually do so as a shorthand expression in extreme cases, to sum up the obvious conclusion that the balance of factors indicates that dismissal would be very unjust. Other than in that situation, courts invoke the prerequisite in the course of conditioning dismissal on the defendants' waiving the defenses of personal jurisdiction and the statute of limitations. In the end, the prerequisite of an alternative forum is not really a rule, and its flexible application is illustrative of the way courts can still take changing law into account.

Second, courts take changing law into account more globally by that technique of **conditioned dismissal**. Here Piper was particularly mysterious. The Court said that considering changes in law was ordinarily off the table, but it seemed to approve conditioning dismissal on the defendants' waiving jurisdictional and limitations defenses—two aspects of the alternative forum's quasi-substantive law that can be strikingly unfavorable to the plaintiff. Going further, the Court suggested in its footnote 25 a possible condition that defendants agree to discovery along U.S. lines, as by agreeing "to provide the records relevant to the plaintiff's claims"—a condition that would temper unfavorable procedural law in the foreign court. The Court never explained why courts should so consider foreign law, or when they should force such concessions from the moving party.

No rule on conditions exists, consequently. Today courts in some cases impose quite a variety of conditions, ranging from a substantive

---

[pp]   See, e.g., Islamic Republic of Iran v. Pahlavi, 62 N.Y.2d 474, 467 N.E.2d 245, 478 N.Y.S.2d 597, 57 A.L.R.4th 955 (1984) (dismissing case against former Shah of Iran), discussed in Ann Alexander, Note, Forum Non Conveniens in the Absence of an Alternative Forum, 86 Colum.L.Rev. 1000 (1986); cf. John P. Dobrovich, Jr., Dismissal Under Forum Non Conveniens: Should the Availability Requirement Be a Threshold Issue When Applied to Nonessential Defendants, 12 Widener L.Rev. 561, 579–83 (2006) (arguing that the prerequisite does not require a forum against those defendants not necessary for adequate relief); Michael Wallace Gordon, Forum Non Conveniens Misconstrued: A Response to Henry Saint Dahl, 38 U.Miami Inter-Am.L.Rev. 141, 183–84 (2006) (arguing that U.S. courts should ignore certain Latin American countries' blocking statutes, which provide that the country will not entertain cases dismissed for forum non conveniens); Joel H. Samuels, When Is an Alternative Forum Available? Rethinking the Forum Non Conveniens Analysis, 85 Ind.L.J. 1059 (2010) (showing more generally that courts are tending to ignore the alternative forum requirement).

condition that the defendant waive the right to contest liability in exchange for escaping U.S. damages law to the peculiarly ill-advised procedural condition that the defendant consent to U.S.-style discovery in the new court.[qq] Although the lower courts' approach for imposing conditions is understandably unarticulated, it appears that they impose a condition whenever necessary for offsetting an unfair change in substantive or procedural law sufficiently to keep the dismissal from being its own miscarriage of justice.

Third, the courts have spoken of a **plaintiff presumption** or, in other words, the great weight given the plaintiff's choice of forum. For dismissal, the balance of other factors must not merely tilt toward the alternative forum, but must tilt strongly in that direction. The effect is that a plaintiff must have done something worse than forum-shopping to get dislodged: the plaintiff must have abused the opponent and the court in selecting this forum. The Piper Court acknowledged that there is this considerable presumption in favor of the plaintiff's choice when the real plaintiff is a U.S. citizen or resident, rather than a foreigner. Justice Marshall justified this in terms of the convenience of the "home forum." He said that this presumption substantially lessens in strength when the plaintiff is foreign. However: (a) The most obvious problem of application would involve a U.S. person suing in a district court far from his or her actual home. As to which of the two levels of presumption to apply, the Court's language is perfectly ambiguous, and so the lower courts have since struggled on whether to treat such a plaintiff as local or foreign or something in-between. (b) It is difficult to mesh a bifurcated (or trifurcated) presumption with a flexible balancing doctrine. Bifurcation is an on/off switch that will create discontinuities in result. (c) Whatever the detailed bounds and workings of the rule, this presumption does create the risk of xenophobic discrimination, perhaps even in violation of treaty. This risk of discrimination against outsiders has been realized in at least some cases.

The bifurcation in treatment is unnecessary. Under normal balancing, a plaintiff's choice could get great weight, especially when the plaintiff is an American and the venue lies at the plaintiff's actual home, because this choice reflects the plaintiff's interest in convenience as well as America's interest in providing its citizens and residents with a forum. Contrariwise, a foreign plaintiff arrives under suspicion of blatant forum-shopping, so that the weight should substantially lessen as appropriate. Perhaps this is all that Piper meant. That is, it did not establish the supposed rule of a bifurcated presumption, but rather was generally

---

[qq]   See, e.g., In re Union Carbide Corp. Gas Plant Disaster at Bhopal, India in Dec., 1984, 809 F.2d 195 (2d Cir.1987) (dismissing case in favor of India's courts, but reversing imposition of this discovery condition), discussed in John Bies, Comment, Conditioning Forum Non Conveniens, 67 U.Chi.L.Rev. 489 (2000); cf. Gross v. British Broad. Corp., 386 F.3d 224, 234–35 (2d Cir.2004) (disapproving conditions of waiving UK fee rules); Thomas Orin Main, Toward a Law of "Lovely Parting Gifts": Conditioning Forum Non Conveniens Dismissals, 18 Sw.J.Int'l L. 475 (2012).

expressing an intelligent approach on weighing the interests that go onto the forum non conveniens balance. Legitimate reasons for choice of forum should receive appropriate weight; nationality and even residence correlate imperfectly with that relevant concern of legitimate forum choice. The real message, then, is that the weight given to the plaintiff's choice of forum should decline over a continuum that runs from those legitimate reasons down to undesirable tactics.[rr]

Fourth, because forum non conveniens thus turns out to be little more than a discretionary balancing doctrine, the appellate court exercises only **deferential review**, once the trial judge has muddled through these supposed rules and declared a result of the balancing. Piper reaffirmed this standard by holding that the Third Circuit was too activist in its review, even asserting that the court of appeals had "substituted its own judgment for that of the District Court." The Supreme Court said that the proper standard of review was "abuse of discretion." Yet in the single paragraph of its opinion on this point, the confused Court managed also to state the standard as "clear abuse of discretion," which is a different and highly deferential standard of review.

Whatever the Court meant, most appellate courts normally do take a hands-off approach to review of the balancing process.[ss] The consequence is that an inconsistent pattern of ad hoc trial-court decisions constitutes the uncertain law of forum non conveniens. For this consequence there is no ready cure. Instead, this consequence of inconsistency is an indictment of forum non conveniens itself.

Fifth, Piper's footnote 13 said that the question of **governing law**, state or federal, is unresolved. It further said that in this case, given the similarity between federal forum non conveniens law and potentially applicable state law, "we need not resolve the Erie question." This simply cannot be. The Court necessarily had to resolve the Erie question: the Court was going to resolve disputed points of forum non conveniens law (e.g., what factors—such as unfavorable change in law—may be considered), and so was not merely applying settled law to facts. The

---

[rr]   See, e.g., Iragorri v. United Techs. Corp., 274 F.3d 65 (2d Cir.2001) (en banc) (declining to dismiss in favor of Colombia's courts, when Floridians had sued at defendants' Connecticut home), discussed in John R. Wilson, Note, Coming to America to File Suit: Foreign Plaintiffs and the Forum Non Conveniens Barrier in Transnational Litigation, 65 Ohio St.L.J. 659 (2004); cf. Brett J. Workman, Note, Deference to the Plaintiff in Forum Non Conveniens Cases, 86 Fordham L.Rev. 871, 895 (2017) ("Although useful, citizenship and residency are only indirect estimates of whether a plaintiff's choice of forum was motivated by genuine convenience as opposed to forum-shopping opportunism.").

[ss]   See Wright & Miller § 3828.5, at 732–38. Compare Creative Tech., Ltd. v. Aztech Sys. Pte, Ltd., 61 F.3d 696 (9th Cir.1995) (affirming forum non conveniens dismissal in favor of Singaporean courts of an action between two Singaporean corporations over copyright violation in the United States, because it was an action between two foreigners), with Guidi v. Inter-Continental Hotels Corp., 224 F.3d 142 (2d Cir.2000) (reversing dismissal of an action brought by U.S. victims of shooting in Egyptian hotel against hotel operator, because inconvenience and emotional burden of dismissal on plaintiffs outweighed greater convenience of litigating in Egypt).

Court could not duck the choice of law by hiding behind the similarity of state law: the state law could not be the same as the federal law both before and after the Court resolved a difficult point of either state or federal forum non conveniens law. The Court was shaping forum non conveniens law, and it had to be resolving what the *federal* law was to be because it can shape only federal law: it had no constitutional authority to resolve state law (and did not even allude to state law's cloudy content on the issues before the Court), so it must have been applying federal law. In short, this case forced the Piper Court to choose the governing law, and the Court chose to apply federal law: federal law governs forum non conveniens in federal court.

At any rate, although the lower federal courts still respectfully say that this Erie question is not completely settled, the strong trend in these courts favors federal doctrine as the governing law on forum non conveniens in federal court. Application of federal law conforms with the general rule that federal courts do not look to state law concerning the provisions of venue. Analogously, at least so far, state law governs forum non conveniens in state court, where the doctrine is a very important one in almost all states.[tt] To get to this Erie result, forum non conveniens is viewed as a procedural and discretionary doctrine to be governed by the court's own law, a view fostered by Piper's emphasis on balancing conveniences but a view belied by the doctrine's impact in reality.

3. The immediate impact of Piper.—Upon remand, on March 5, 1982, the United States District Court for the Middle District of Pennsylvania dismissed the action:

> It must have seemed like a bizarre good news/bad news joke to the plaintiff. Imagine the lawyer's explanation:
>
>> Well, we served the defendant with a summons at its place of business in the forum. We sued the defendant in one of the places in which Congress in the venue statute said a defendant may be sued. We were even able to persuade the court that our choice of forum was a reasonable one under the due process clause of the Constitution since the defendant could reasonably anticipate being haled into court here. Best of all, we convinced the court that it should apply the forum's pro-plaintiff law because the forum state has the most significant relationship to the controversy. However, I must tell you that the case was dismissed because the judge didn't think this was an appropriate forum.

[tt] See Am. Dredging Co. v. Miller, 510 U.S. 443 (1994) (admiralty case, rather than a transnational case, in state court); George A. Bermann, Transnational Litigation in a Nutshell 103–06 (2003).

In response to the client's astonished question—"Can't we appeal?"—the lawyer somewhat sheepishly explains that they have already lost in the Supreme Court of the United States.[uu]

That imaginary exchange nicely conveys Piper's bottom line. U.S. courts declined to exercise their authority over U.S. defendants. Most of the rest of the world considers the defendants' home as the natural forum, but not here. The forum was to be Scotland. There Reyno could not sue, so the passengers' survivors would be the plaintiffs. The value of their lawsuit, as measured in likely damages, vastly diminished. Cathcart urged the referring firm in Scotland to go forward and offered to help, but the Scottish firm had no financial incentive. The plaintiffs applied for legal aid in Scotland, but it was never granted. And so the suit never progressed after the U.S. Supreme Court's decision.

The anticlimactic outcome was not an aberration. In actual practice, forum non conveniens tends to be fatal in application. In a survey of the plaintiffs' lawyers in the 180 reported transnational cases that the federal courts dismissed on forum non conveniens grounds from 1947 to 1984, responses covered 85 cases; of those 85, not one resulted in a plaintiff's win in the foreign court; most cases were abandoned or settled for little.[vv] So if the defendant wins the all-important forum-shopping battle, almost always the case is over.

With such a stark effect of forum non conveniens on outcome, is it fair then for the court both to ignore an unfavorable change in applicable law and to dismiss readily on the basis of mere inconvenience? The Piper Court seemed to think so, taking change in law off the table and declaring that "the central focus of the forum non conveniens inquiry is convenience." But, concisely put, that is unfair.

Before Piper, the lower courts were treating forum non conveniens as a doctrine to curb forum-shopping abuse. The Third Circuit held that Reyno's suit at the defendants' home was not an abuse. The Supreme Court used her case to push forum non conveniens, in a poorly expressed way, toward a doctrine to mitigate inconvenience of forum. That move was the Court's critical mistake.

Forum non conveniens should not expand into a doctrine of inconvenience but instead should remain a doctrine of abuse. The properly restrained doctrine should call for dismissal only when the plaintiff has abused the privilege of forum selection, as by exploiting loose jurisdictional law and malleable choice-of-law doctrine in an unrelated forum, to the extent that going forward here rather than there would be

---

[uu]   Allan R. Stein, Forum Non Conveniens and the Redundancy of Court-Access Doctrine, 133 U.Pa.L.Rev. 781, 781 (1985).

[vv]   See David W. Robertson, Forum Non Conveniens in America and England: "A Rather Fantastic Fiction," 103 Law Q.Rev. 398, 418–20 (1987); see also David W. Robertson, The Federal Doctrine of Forum Non Conveniens: "An Object Lesson in Uncontrolled Discretion," 29 Tex.Int'l L.J. 353 (1994) (arguing for reliable rules to temper judicial discretion and otherwise to narrow forum non conveniens).

a miscarriage of justice. Such abuse by the plaintiff, albeit by one who has sued in a technically proper court, is what makes it fair to inflict the change in law on the plaintiff.

4. *The continuing importance of Piper today.*—Academic musing to the side, the doctrine of forum non conveniens is whatever the trial courts are actually doing in their discretion. Yet it is difficult to measure the current practice empirically. Foreign personal-injury plaintiffs may have been hard hit since Piper, but otherwise the post-Piper trial courts might be edging back toward a doctrine of abuse. That is, facing real litigants in real cases, the trial courts seem to be intuitively producing outcomes that would mostly please the academic.[ww]

So, what many trial judges seem to be doing is balancing all interests (except perhaps for nonextreme changes in law), and dismissing with restraint and only when in their subjective opinion the balance tilts beyond this tough standard for dismissal: *the plaintiff has so abused the privilege of forum selection that going forward would be a miscarriage of justice.* In fact, almost half the time the judge conditions any such dismissal on the defendant's varied concessions, so as to offset an unfair change in substantive or procedural law sufficiently to keep the dismissal from being its own miscarriage of justice. In sum, those two sentences convey the not-so-complicated-after-all law of forum non conveniens.

This practice is consistent with Piper. The Court ruled explicitly against routine consideration of change in law, but ultimately was vague as to the required tilt of the balance. By requiring a strong showing by the defendant, the lower courts can still counter the change of law. Now, if forum non conveniens has indeed so reverted most of the way to a doctrine of abuse, then Piper will have turned out to be merely an inelegant rephrasing of the old doctrine—a rephrasing that might be easily misunderstood in dangerous ways and might risk the doctrine's occasional overuse, but that today seems to work passably well in practice.

Yet, one could argue that even this restrained version of forum non conveniens does not make much sense. If once again it is in the main merely a doctrine of abuse, what does it contribute beyond the unreasonableness test for territorial jurisdiction, a test discovered by the Supreme Court in the Due Process Clauses in the years since the birth of forum non conveniens? Not much, besides (a) multiplying costs, (b)

[ww]   See, e.g., Tuazon v. R.J. Reynolds Tobacco Co., 433 F.3d 1163 (9th Cir.2006) (affirming the Western District of Washington's denying of forum non conveniens dismissal, in a products-liability action brought by a Philippine smoker who had become a resident of Washington after diagnosis); Bhatnagar v. Surrendra Overseas Ltd., 52 F.3d 1220 (3d Cir.1995) (affirming denial of dismissal because alternative forum of India had backlog of cases greatly delaying resolution in that system, in a U.S. lawsuit brought by Indians who had become local residents since shipping accident); cf. R. Maganlal & Co. v. M.G. Chem. Co., 942 F.2d 164 (2d Cir.1991) (reversing dismissal of contract action by Indian corporate buyer against New York corporate seller). But see, e.g., In re Factor VIII or IX Concentrate Blood Prods. Litig., 484 F.3d 951 (7th Cir.2007) (affirming dismissal of action against American manufacturers of blood-clotting products, brought by infected hemophiliac foreigners).

increasing uncertainty, and (c) facilitating discrimination against foreigners. In other words, forum non conveniens often raises intricate questions, requiring extensive investigation and research as well as wasteful litigation on a mere threshold issue; the judicial decision involved is blatantly discretionary and hence unpredictable; and the Supreme Court's ambiguous blessing of various rules and presumptions can skew that discretion away from fairness. Although some judicial flexibility in rejecting jurisdiction might be desirable, the Constitution's unreasonableness test provides it, while at the same time subjecting it to nondeferential appellate review.[xx]

Nevertheless, a counterarguer might ask, does not forum non conveniens tend to narrow the currently overbroad law of territorial authority to adjudicate? Yes, but the system should openly and directly pursue the desirable course of narrowing territorial reach by legislatively reforming venue rules on the federal and the state levels, rather than surreptitiously and dangerously narrowing reach by an activist judicial embrace of forum non conveniens. For example, the very substantive decision on whether U.S. and multinational corporations should be amenable to foreigners' suits here should not be delegated to the haphazard quilt work of trial judges' discretion and biases. In short, a decent venue scheme would eliminate the need for a doctrine of forum non conveniens, by narrowing in advance and by rule the plaintiff's choice of forum to a smaller list of appropriate courts.

That new venue scheme need not merely codify a doctrine of abuse. The U.S. system might very well decide to tighten access to its courts aggressively, creating a venue law that cuts off much more than the most abusive excesses of forum-shopping. The flaw in forum non conveniens lies not in its results, but rather in the manner by which the system achieves them. A general venue statute's restrictive listing of appropriate courts substantially differs from a judge's whim that sends a particular plaintiff in an otherwise proper court off to a certain death. Even when much of the other law on territorial authority to adjudicate remains judge-made and ad hoc, special legal-process dangers lie in manufacturing a doctrine of forum non conveniens.

Alternatively but more specifically stated, closing the courthouse doors to cases like Piper might not be unjust. Maybe the Scots' lawsuit, even though against U.S. defendants, did not belong in this country. But if so, a venue rule should have so provided, not an ad hoc judicial exclusion uncertainly applied through the retrospective lens of litigation. Narrowing the law of territorial authority to adjudicate is a laudable goal, but the doctrine of forum non conveniens is not a defensible means to the end.

Thus, rethinking Piper sufficiently to cut its overstatements down to size makes one reconsider the reconstructed forum non conveniens

---

xx   See Maggie Gardner, Retiring Forum Non Conveniens, 92 N.Y.U.L.Rev. 390 (2017).

doctrine itself. Maybe we do not need it at all, at least in the federal courts.

In any event, removal, transfer, and forum non conveniens, as seen at play in Piper, integrate state and federal court systems, and such devices also take a step toward integrating U.S. and foreign court systems. That integration is so complex that until Piper is mastered, one has no clue how the various judicial systems really work, or what federalism and globalization really mean in the judicial context.

————

LIS PENDENS

Under the vague doctrine called lis alibi pendens ("suit elsewhere pending"), or just lis pendens, a federal or state court may stay its own proceedings in deference to another court's, if the related proceedings are in a more appropriate forum. This discretionary power has been judicially created as an incident to the courts' inherent power to control their own dockets. But both the circuits' and the states' case law is split, as the local precedent either emphasizes the court's obligation to proceed with the case by narrowly limiting the court's power to stay its proceedings or gives the court considerable discretion to decide on an all-things-considered basis whether to stay its proceedings. When a court so stays itself, it is exercising self-restraint with respect to its territorial jurisdiction. Indeed, this doctrine is very similar to forum non conveniens dismissal, the differences for lis pendens being that the alternative proceedings must be pending, that the showing of greater appropriateness is usually easier to make, and that stayed proceedings are much more easily revived if necessary than dismissed proceedings.

Interestingly, while Europeans have traditionally detested forum non conveniens, they liberally use lis pendens to defer to the court "first seised." Indeed, they make part of the doctrine nondiscretionary: Brussels Regulation article 29 provides that "where proceedings involving the same cause of action and between the same parties are brought in the courts of different Member States, any court other than the court first seised shall of its own motion stay its proceedings."

TOPIC B

OPPORTUNITY TO BE HEARD

SECTION 1.   GENERAL OBSERVATIONS

Mullane v. Central Hanover Bank & Trust Co.

Supreme Court of the United States, 1950.
339 U.S. 306, 70 S.Ct. 652.

■ [The facts appear in the portion of the majority's opinion reprinted supra p. 534. For the legal background of the case's story, see John Leubsdorf, Unmasking Mullane: Due Process, Common Trust Funds, and the Class Action Wars, 66 Hastings L.J. 1693 (2015). After finding adequate nexus, JUSTICE JACKSON proceeded to the question of notice:]

Quite different from the question of a state's power to discharge trustees is that of the opportunity it must give beneficiaries to contest. Many controversies have raged about the cryptic and abstract words of the Due Process Clause but there can be no doubt that at a minimum they require that deprivation of life, liberty or property by adjudication be preceded by notice and opportunity for hearing appropriate to the nature of the case.

In two ways this proceeding does or may deprive beneficiaries of property. It may cut off their rights to have the trustee answer for negligent or illegal impairment of their interests. Also, their interests are presumably subject to diminution in the proceeding by allowance of fees and expenses to one who, in their names but without their knowledge, may conduct a fruitless or uncompensatory contest. Certainly the proceeding is one in which they may be deprived of property rights and hence notice and hearing must measure up to the standards of due process.

Personal service of written notice within the jurisdiction is the classic form of notice always adequate in any type of proceeding. But the vital interest of the State in bringing any issues as to its fiduciaries to a final settlement can be served only if interests or claims of individuals who are outside of the State can somehow be determined. A construction of the Due Process Clause which would place impossible or impractical obstacles in the way could not be justified.

Against this interest of the State we must balance the individual interest sought to be protected by the Fourteenth Amendment. This is defined by our holding that "The fundamental requisite of due process of law is the opportunity to be heard." Grannis v. Ordean, 234 U.S. 385, 394, 34 S.Ct. 779, 783. This right to be heard has little reality or worth unless one is informed that the matter is pending and can choose for himself whether to appear or default, acquiesce or contest.

The Court has not committed itself to any formula achieving a balance between these interests in a particular proceeding or determining when constructive notice may be utilized or what test it must meet. Personal service has not in all circumstances been regarded as indispensable to the process due to residents, and it has more often been held unnecessary as to nonresidents. We disturb none of the established rules on these subjects. No decision constitutes a controlling or even a very illuminating precedent for the case before us. But a few general principles stand out in the books.

An elementary and fundamental requirement of due process in any proceeding which is to be accorded finality is notice reasonably calculated, under all the circumstances, to apprise interested parties of the pendency of the action and afford them an opportunity to present their objections. Milliken v. Meyer, 311 U.S. 457, 61 S.Ct. 339; Grannis v. Ordean, 234 U.S. 385, 34 S.Ct. 779; Priest v. Board of Trustees of Town of Las Vegas, 232 U.S. 604, 34 S.Ct. 443; Roller v. Holly, 176 U.S. 398, 20 S.Ct. 410. The notice must be of such nature as reasonably to convey the required information, Grannis v. Ordean, supra, and it must afford a reasonable time for those interested to make their appearance, Roller v. Holly, supra, and cf. Goodrich v. Ferris, 214 U.S. 71, 29 S.Ct. 580. But if with due regard for the practicalities and peculiarities of the case these conditions are reasonably met, the constitutional requirements are satisfied. "The criterion is not the possibility of conceivable injury, but the just and reasonable character of the requirements, having reference to the subject with which the statute deals." American Land Co. v. Zeiss, 219 U.S. 47, 67, 31 S.Ct. 200, 207; and see Blinn v. Nelson, 222 U.S. 1, 7, 32 S.Ct. 1, 2.

But when notice is a person's due, process which is a mere gesture is not due process. The means employed must be such as one desirous of actually informing the absentee might reasonably adopt to accomplish it. The reasonableness and hence the constitutional validity of any chosen method may be defended on the ground that it is in itself reasonably certain to inform those affected, compare Hess v. Pawloski, 274 U.S. 352, 47 S.Ct. 632, with Wuchter v. Pizzutti, 276 U.S. 13, 48 S.Ct. 259, or, where conditions do not reasonably permit such notice, that the form chosen is not substantially less likely to bring home notice than other of the feasible and customary substitutes.

It would be idle to pretend that publication alone, as prescribed here, is a reliable means of acquainting interested parties of the fact that their rights are before the courts. It is not an accident that the greater number of cases reaching this Court on the question of adequacy of notice have been concerned with actions founded on process constructively served through local newspapers. Chance alone brings to the attention of even a local resident an advertisement in small type inserted in the back pages of a newspaper, and if he makes his home outside the area of the newspaper's normal circulation the odds that the information will never reach him are large indeed. The chance of actual notice is further reduced when, as here, the notice required does not even name those whose attention it is supposed to attract, and does not inform acquaintances who might call it to attention. In weighing its sufficiency on the basis of equivalence with actual notice we are unable to regard this as more than a feint.

Nor is publication here reinforced by steps likely to attract the parties' attention to the proceeding. It is true that publication traditionally has been acceptable as notification supplemental to other action which in itself may reasonably be expected to convey a warning. The ways of an owner with tangible property are such that he usually arranges means to learn of any direct attack upon his possessory or proprietary rights. Hence, libel of a ship, attachment of a chattel or entry upon real estate in the name of law may reasonably be expected to come promptly to the owner's attention. When the state within which the owner has located such property seizes it for some reason, publication or posting affords an additional measure of notification. A state may indulge the assumption that one who has left tangible property in the state either has abandoned it, in which case proceedings against it deprive him of nothing, [citations omitted], or that he has left some caretaker under a duty to let him know that it is being jeopardized. [Citations omitted.] As phrased long ago by Chief Justice Marshall in The Mary, 9 Cranch 126, 144, "It is the part of common prudence for all those who have any interest in [a thing], to guard that interest by persons who are in a situation to protect it."

In the case before us there is, of course, no abandonment. On the other hand these beneficiaries do have a resident fiduciary as caretaker of their interest in this property. But it is their caretaker who in the accounting becomes their adversary. Their trustee is released from giving notice of jeopardy, and no one else is expected to do so. Not even the special guardian is required or apparently expected to communicate with his ward and client, and, of course, if such a duty were merely transferred from the trustee to the guardian, economy would not be served and more likely the cost would be increased.

This Court has not hesitated to approve of resort to publication as a customary substitute in another class of cases where it is not reasonably possible or practicable to give more adequate warning. Thus it has been recognized that, in the case of persons missing or unknown, employment of an indirect and even a probably futile means of notification is all that the situation permits and creates no constitutional bar to a final decree foreclosing their rights. [Citations omitted.]

Those beneficiaries represented by appellant whose interests or whereabouts could not with due diligence be ascertained come clearly within this category. As to them the statutory notice is sufficient. However great the odds that publication will never reach the eyes of such unknown parties, it is not in the typical case much more likely to fail than any of the choices open to legislators endeavoring to prescribe the best notice practicable.

Nor do we consider it unreasonable for the State to dispense with more certain notice to those beneficiaries whose interests are either conjectural or future or, although they could be discovered upon investigation, do not in due course of business come to knowledge of the common trustee. Whatever searches might be required in another situation under ordinary standards of diligence, in view of the character of the proceedings and the nature of the interests here involved we think them unnecessary. We recognize the practical difficulties and costs that would be attendant on frequent investigations into the status of great numbers of beneficiaries, many of whose interests in the common fund are so remote as to be ephemeral; and we have no doubt that such impracticable and extended searches are not required in the name of due process. The expense of keeping informed from day to day of substitutions among even current income beneficiaries and presumptive remaindermen, to say nothing of the far greater number of contingent beneficiaries, would impose a severe burden on the plan, and would likely dissipate its advantages. These are practical matters in which we should be reluctant to disturb the judgment of the state authorities.

Accordingly we overrule appellant's constitutional objections to published notice insofar as they are urged on behalf of any beneficiaries whose interests or addresses are unknown to the trustee.

As to known present beneficiaries of known place of residence, however, notice by publication stands on a different footing. Exceptions in the name of necessity do not sweep away the rule that within the limits of practicability notice must be such as is reasonably calculated to reach interested parties. Where the names and post office addresses of those affected by a proceeding are at hand, the reasons disappear for resort to means less likely than the mails to apprise them of its pendency.

The trustee has on its books the names and addresses of the income beneficiaries represented by appellant, and we find no tenable ground for dispensing with a serious effort to inform them personally of the accounting, at least by ordinary mail to the record addresses. Cf. Wuchter v. Pizzutti, supra. Certainly sending them a copy of the statute months and perhaps years in advance does not answer this purpose. The trustee periodically remits their income to them, and we think that they might reasonably expect that with or apart from their remittances word might come to them personally that steps were being taken affecting their interests.

We need not weigh contentions that a requirement of personal service of citation on even the large number of known resident or nonresident beneficiaries would, by reasons of delay if not of expense, seriously interfere with the proper administration of the fund. Of course personal service even without the jurisdiction of the issuing authority serves the end of actual and personal notice, whatever power of compulsion it might lack. However, no such service is required under the circumstances. This type of trust presupposes a large number of small interests. The individual interest does not stand alone but is identical with that of a class. The rights of each in the integrity of the fund and the fidelity of the trustee are shared by many other beneficiaries. Therefore notice reasonably certain to reach most of those interested in objecting is likely to safeguard the interests of all, since any objections sustained would inure to the benefit of all. We think that under such circumstances reasonable risks that notice might not actually reach every beneficiary are justifiable. "Now and then an extraordinary case may turn up, but constitutional law like other mortal contrivances has to take some chances, and in the great majority of instances no doubt justice will be done." Blinn v. Nelson, supra, 222 U.S. at page 7, 32 S.Ct. at page 2.

The statutory notice to known beneficiaries is inadequate not because in fact it fails to reach everyone, but because under the circumstances it is not reasonably calculated to reach those who could easily be informed by other means at hand. However it may have been in former times, the mails today are recognized as an efficient and inexpensive means of communication. Moreover, the fact that the trust company has been able to give mailed notice to known beneficiaries at the time the common trust fund was established is persuasive that postal notification at the time of accounting would not seriously burden the plan.

In some situations the law requires greater precautions in its proceedings than the business world accepts for its own purposes. In few, if any, will it be satisfied with less. Certainly it is instructive, in determining the reasonableness of the impersonal broadcast notification here used, to ask whether it would satisfy a prudent man of business, counting his pennies but finding it in his interest to convey information to many persons whose names and addresses are in his files. We are not satisfied that it would. Publication may theoretically be available for all the world to see, but it is too much in our day to suppose that each or any individual beneficiary does or could examine all that is published to see if something may be tucked away in it that affects his property interests. We have before indicated in reference to notice by publication that, "Great caution should be used not to let fiction deny the fair play that can be secured only by a pretty close adhesion to fact." McDonald v. Mabee, 243 U.S. 90, 91, 37 S.Ct. 343.

We hold that the notice of judicial settlement of accounts required by the New York Banking Law § 100–c(12) is incompatible with the requirements of the Fourteenth Amendment as a basis for adjudication depriving known persons whose whereabouts are also known of substantial property rights. Accordingly the judgment is reversed and the cause remanded for further proceedings not inconsistent with this opinion.

Reversed.

■ MR. JUSTICE DOUGLAS took no part in the consideration or decision of this case.

■ MR. JUSTICE BURTON, dissenting.

These common trusts are available only when the instruments creating the participating trusts permit participation in the common fund. Whether or not further notice to beneficiaries should supplement the notice and representation here provided is properly within the discretion of the State. The Federal Constitution does not require it here.

———

Question: (1) What changes in the statute would you, as counsel to the appropriate committee of the New York legislature, recommend for adoption? See N.Y. Banking Law § 100–c(6), as amended by 1951 N.Y. Laws ch. 778, § 3, by which New York sought to meet the defects revealed by the Mullane case.

———

MENNONITE BOARD OF MISSIONS v. ADAMS, 462 U.S. 791, 103 S.Ct. 2706 (1983). In the course of lengthy proceedings to sell certain real property consequent to the owner's nonpayment of taxes, notice was posted in the county courthouse and published a number of times. Also, the county sent notice by certified mail to the owner. After title had passed, cutting off a recorded mortgage on the property, the mortgagee learned of the proceedings. The tax-sale purchaser then brought suit to quiet title, during which the mortgagee challenged the adequacy of notice of the tax sale. The Indiana courts upheld the prescribed procedure that had been employed.

On appeal, the United States Supreme Court reversed. Justice Marshall for the Court began by discussing Mullane and continued:

"In subsequent cases, this Court has adhered unwaveringly to the principle announced in Mullane. In Walker v. City of Hutchinson, 352 U.S. 112, 77 S.Ct. 200 (1956), for example, the Court held that notice of condemnation proceedings published in a local newspaper was an inadequate means of informing a landowner whose name was known to the city and was on the official records. Similarly, in Schroeder v. City of New York, 371 U.S. 208, 83 S.Ct. 279 (1962), the Court concluded that publication in a newspaper and posted notices were inadequate to apprise a property owner of condemnation proceedings when his name and address were readily ascertainable from both deed records and tax rolls. Most recently, in Greene v. Lindsey, 456 U.S. 444, 102 S.Ct. 1874 (1982), we held that posting a summons on the door of a tenant's apartment was an inadequate means of providing notice of forcible entry and detainer actions. [Citations omitted.]

"This case is controlled by the analysis in Mullane. To begin with, a mortgagee possesses a substantial property interest that is significantly affected by a tax sale. . . .

"Since a mortgagee clearly has a legally protected property interest, he is entitled to notice reasonably calculated to apprise him of a pending tax sale. [Citation omitted.] When the mortgagee is identified in a mortgage that is publicly recorded, constructive notice by publication must be supplemented by notice mailed to the mortgagee's last known available address, or by personal service. But unless the mortgagee is not reasonably identifiable, constructive notice alone does not satisfy the mandate of Mullane.

. . . .

"Personal service or mailed notice is required even though sophisticated creditors have means at their disposal to discover whether property taxes have not been paid and whether tax sale proceedings are therefore likely to be initiated. . . . It is true that particularly extensive efforts to provide notice may often be required when the State is aware of a party's inexperience or incompetence. [Citations omitted.] But it does not follow that the State may forgo even the relatively modest administrative burden of providing notice by mail to parties who are particularly resourceful. [Citation omitted.] Notice by mail or other means as certain to ensure actual notice is a minimum constitutional precondition to a proceeding which will adversely affect the liberty or property interests of *any* party, whether unlettered or well versed in commercial practice, if its name and address are reasonably ascertainable."

Justice O'Connor, joined by Justices Powell and Rehnquist, dissented. She argued that the Court was departing from Mullane by adopting a rigid rule against constructive notice, rather than using a balancing approach in circumstances where the mortgagee could have protected its own interest.

———

PROCEDURAL DUE PROCESS

Procedural due process normally requires that a person or his representative receive notice and opportunity to be heard before governmental action unduly impairs his property or liberty interests. The Fourteenth Amendment extends these protections to action by a state government, while the Fifth Amendment covers action by the federal government.

In order to satisfy this constitutional prerequisite for civil adjudication, fair notice of the pendency of the lawsuit must go to any person whose interests are to be so affected or to his representative, unless waived. Fair notice must be suitably formal in tenor and informative in content. Also, fair notice must be either actual notice or notice that is reasonably calculated to result in actual notice.

If the person entitled to notice duly challenges its adequacy, the court will pass on the constitutional requirement. The typical setting where such a challenge might succeed is the defendant's attack after a default judgment. Here the Constitution generally requires the courts to provide relief from judgment if there was a violation of procedural due process, whether or not the defendant has a meritorious defense on the merits. See Peralta v. Heights Med. Ctr., Inc., 485 U.S. 80, 108 S.Ct. 896 (1988).

On the one hand, authority persists for the somewhat surprising proposition that if the method of notification prescribed by statute, rule, or order is not reasonably calculated to result in actual notice, then notice in the particular case is invalid even if the person in one way or another received actual notice. See 1 Robert C. Casad, William M. Richman & Stanley E. Cox, Jurisdiction in Civil Actions § 2–7[2][a] (4th ed. 2014). The idea is that we care about the steps that the government prescribes officially, and so we bestow standing to challenge not only the notice in the case but also the legal scheme for giving notice.

On the other hand, if a reasonable method of notification was prescribed and employed, mere failure to achieve actual notice will not undermine the validity of a default judgment. However, if the plaintiff employs an otherwise reasonable prescribed means of notice that she knows to be substantially less likely to give actual notice in the circumstances than another prescribed means, the failure to achieve actual notice will invalidate the resulting default judgment. See Restatement (Second) of Judgments § 2 (Am. Law Inst. 1982).

A fair opportunity to be heard is also critical to procedural due process. Notice to a defendant of a claim being made against him is of no value to him if he gets no opportunity to defend the action. See Roller v. Holly, 176 U.S. 398, 20 S.Ct. 410 (1900). Indeed, it would seem that the real concern of procedural due process here is opportunity to be heard. Notice is merely the means to make possible the exercise of that right.

———

SERVICE OF PROCESS

Descending from the constitutional level, we encounter the regulations for serving process. State law lays out these regulations for state court, while Federal Rule 4 does so for federal court.

How inflexible are the prescribed procedures for service? NY CPLR § 308(5) provides for so-called expedient service in cases where service cannot practicably be made in the usual way (namely, service in hand; delivering process to a person of suitable age and discretion at defendant's abode or place of business, plus mailing to last known residence or to place of business; or affixing process to the door of defendant's abode or place of business, plus mailing). Pursuant to this subsection, expedient service may be made "in such manner as the court, upon motion without notice, directs."

In Dobkin v. Chapman, 21 N.Y.2d 490, 236 N.E.2d 451, 289 N.Y.S.2d 161 (1968), the New York Court of Appeals unanimously upheld the constitutionality of service in three automobile-accident cases against the contention that the methods provided by court order did not give the absent defendants sufficient chance of receiving actual notice of the commencement of the actions (the uninsured motorist fund and the insurance company involved had challenged the service). The manner of notice ordered in the first case was ordinary mail to the address from which registered mail had been returned unclaimed; in the second case, one publication in a designated newspaper after registered mail had been returned unclaimed; and in the third case, where the defendant was known to be insured, delivery of copies of summons and complaint to the insurance carrier plus ordinary mail to the defendant's last known New York address. The court pointed out that in these cases it was the conduct of the defendants themselves—their removal without informing anyone of their whereabouts—that prevented service of process by the usual means. Chief Judge Fuld for the court said: "Indeed, in an automobile case, no defendant need be without notice unless he chooses and wants to be; many an injured plaintiff, however, will go without recompense if, in a proper case, the standards of informative notice may not be relaxed." The court relied upon Mullane, among other cases. It also referred to NY CPLR § 317, which gives a defendant served other than by personal delivery one year after learning of entry of judgment, but in no event more than five years after such entry, to come in and defend upon a finding that he did not actually receive timely notice and has a meritorious defense on the merits. See also Federal Rules 4(f)(3) and 55(c); Rio Props., Inc. v. Rio Int'l Interlink, 284 F.3d 1007 (9th Cir.2002) (approving court-ordered service by e-mail on an elusive Costa Rican defendant).

Local law may strictly enforce some of the nonconstitutional requirements of service for asserting jurisdiction and for giving notice and opportunity to be heard. For example, before judgment a defendant may succeed in attacking service if the summons inaccurately named him or if the manner of service did not precisely comply with the statute, rule, or order. However, the trend is away from an overly strict approach, with courts now tending to ignore service irregularities where there was actual notice of suitable tenor and content and where the manner of transmitting and form of process substantially complied with the prescribed procedure. See Restatement (Second) of Judgments §§ 2–3 (Am. Law Inst. 1982). Indeed, local law may dispense altogether with the requirement of formal service of process in some circumstances, as is done for example in connection with jurisdiction over plaintiffs for counterclaims.

SECTION 2.   NOTICE BEFORE SEIZING PROPERTY

SNIADACH v. FAMILY FINANCE CORP. OF BAY VIEW, 395 U.S. 337, 89 S.Ct. 1820 (1969). Plaintiff finance company sued Christine Sniadach (pronounced SNEE-dek) on a $420 promissory note in a Wisconsin state court, garnishing defendant's employer in order to secure any judgment that it might win. The garnishee answered, stating that it had $63.18 of the defendant's wages, earned and unpaid, and that it would pay the defendant one-half thereof as a subsistence allowance and hold the other half subject to the order of the court, as provided in a Wisconsin statute. Under that statute, the court clerk issues the garnishment summons at the request of the plaintiff's lawyer, who by serving the garnishee can then freeze the wages; the defendant must be served with the summons and complaint within ten days of service on the garnishee; if the defendant wins the main suit on the merits, the wages are restored to her, but in the interim she is deprived of them. The defendant moved to dismiss the garnishment proceedings for failure to provide procedural due process. The Wisconsin courts approved the garnishment procedure.

On certiorari, the Supreme Court reversed. After noting that wages are "a specialized type of property presenting distinct problems in our economic system," Justice Douglas for the Court held that the Wisconsin procedure violated the Fourteenth Amendment by failure to provide notice and opportunity to be heard before the garnishment. Justice Black was the lone dissenter.

FUENTES v. SHEVIN, 407 U.S. 67, 92 S.Ct. 1983 (1972). In Florida, Mrs. Fuentes purchased a stove and a stereo under conditional sales contracts that provided for monthly payments and for repossession by the seller in case of any default in payment by the buyer. Under the contracts, the seller retained a U.C.C. security interest in the goods pending full payment, but the buyer was entitled to possession absent default. The total cost of the stove and stereo was about $500, plus a financing charge of over $100. More than a year later, after a dispute over servicing the stove, Fuentes stopped making payments while still owing about $200 under the contracts. The seller initiated an action for repossession in small-claims court, simultaneously obtaining a writ of replevin ordering state agents to seize the stove and stereo. The same day a deputy sheriff went with the seller's employee to Fuentes' home, served her, and seized the disputed goods. The relevant Florida statute provides for summary issuance of a writ of replevin upon ex parte application to the court clerk by someone suing on a claim to possession of "wrongfully detained" property and upon the plaintiff's posting a bond for double the value of the property; the agent who makes the seizure holds the property for three days, during which time the defendant may regain possession of the property upon posting her own bond for double the property's value; if the defendant does not so act, the property then passes to the plaintiff, pending the final disposition of the underlying repossession action. Shortly after the seizure, Fuentes sued in federal court, challenging the replevin proceedings on procedural due process grounds.[a] Relief was denied.

On appeal, the Supreme Court reversed, holding by Justice Stewart, joined by Justices Douglas, Brennan, and Marshall, that the Florida procedure (and the similar Pennsylvania procedure involved in a companion case) violated the Fourteenth Amendment by failure to provide notice and opportunity to be heard before deprivation of a possessory interest in property. The required hearing would at least aim at establishing the probable validity of the underlying claim, given that the statute required no special showing. Justice White, joined by Chief Justice Burger and Justice Blackmun, filed a dissenting opinion. He argued that due process calls for a more flexible approach, that the process and outcome values served by pre-seizure notice and opportunity to be heard should be weighed against other interests, and that in the real world the illusory benefits of such procedure do not match the considerable costs to the public, creditors, consumers, and even debtors. Newly appointed Justices Powell and Rehnquist did not participate.

———

MITCHELL v. W.T. GRANT CO., 416 U.S. 600, 94 S.Ct. 1895 (1974). In Louisiana, W.T. Grant sold a refrigerator, range, stereo, and washer to Mr. Mitchell under installment sales contracts. About a year later, Grant sued in city court for the overdue and unpaid balance of $574.17, Mitchell having paid less than one-quarter of his total principal obligation; Grant alleged having a vendor's lien on the goods securing the unpaid balance, which lien would under state law expire if Mitchell transferred possession. Grant simultaneously obtained a writ of sequestration ordering state agents to seize the goods. Soon thereafter the constable served Mitchell at home and, at the same time, seized the disputed goods. The relevant Louisiana statute allows sequestration if the plaintiff claims ownership or right to possession of property or a lien thereon and if it would otherwise be within the defendant's power to dispose of or remove the property during the pendency of the action; the plaintiff must state specific facts by affidavit supporting issuance of the writ and must file a bond sufficient to protect the defendant against any damage resulting from wrongful issuance; ex parte application to a judge accomplishes issuance; the defendant may immediately seek dissolution of the writ, which the court must then order unless the plaintiff proves the grounds upon which the writ issued—the existence of the debt, lien,

---

[a]   For background on this important case, see C. Michael Abbott & Donald C. Peters, *Fuentes v. Shevin: A Narrative of Federal Test Litigation in the Legal Services Program*, 57 Iowa L.Rev. 955 (1972).

and delinquency; the defendant may also regain possession upon posting his own bond for 125% of the lesser of the value of the property or the amount of the claim. Mitchell moved to dissolve the writ of sequestration for failure to provide procedural due process. The Louisiana courts approved the sequestration procedure.

On certiorari, the Supreme Court affirmed, with Justices Powell and Rehnquist joining the three Fuentes dissenters to form a new majority. Justice White delivered the opinion of the Court, which declared in part: "In our view, this statutory procedure effects a constitutional accommodation of the conflicting interests of the parties. We cannot accept petitioner's broad assertion that the Due Process Clause of the Fourteenth Amendment guaranteed to him the use and possession of the goods until all issues in the case were judicially resolved after full adversary proceedings had been completed." Justice Powell issued a concurring opinion. The former majority in Fuentes was now in dissent, arguing that the Fuentes decision controlled.

———

NORTH GEORGIA FINISHING, INC. v. DI-CHEM, INC., 419 U.S. 601, 95 S.Ct. 719 (1975). Di-Chem filed suit against the corporate defendant in a Georgia state court for goods sold and delivered in the amount of $51,279.17, simultaneously obtaining process for garnishing the defendant's bank account. The relevant Georgia statute provides for garnishment upon the plaintiff's or his attorney's submitting to the court clerk an affidavit stating the amount claimed and reason to apprehend loss; the plaintiff must file a bond for double the amount claimed to protect the defendant against any damage resulting from wrongful issuance; the defendant may dissolve the garnishment by filing a bond for the amount claimed. Right after service of process, the defendant filed a bond to dissolve the garnishment. Then it moved to dismiss the garnishment proceedings and discharge its bond, arguing violation of procedural due process. The Georgia courts approved the garnishment procedure.

On certiorari, the Supreme Court reversed on Fourteenth Amendment grounds. Justice White switched sides to join the Mitchell dissenters and delivered the opinion of the Court. His opinion seemed to resuscitate Fuentes. He distinguished Mitchell by noting the Louisiana statute's requirement of a plaintiff's affidavit going beyond mere conclusory allegations and setting out clearly the facts entitling the plaintiff to seizure, its requirement of issuance by a judge, and its provision of a hearing immediately after seizure where the plaintiff must prove the grounds for the writ's issuance. In this Georgia case, the affidavit asserted the debt and "reason to apprehend the loss of said sum or some part thereof unless process of Garnishment issues," a court clerk issued the writ, and there was no provision for an early hearing where the plaintiff had "to demonstrate at least probable cause for the garnishment. . . . It may be that consumers deprived of household appliances will more likely suffer irreparably than corporations deprived of bank accounts, but the probability of irreparable injury in the latter case is sufficiently great so that some procedures are necessary to guard against the risk of initial error. We are no more inclined now than we have been in the past to distinguish among different kinds of property in applying the Due Process Clause. Fuentes v. Shevin, 407 U.S., at 89–90, 92 S.Ct., at 1998–1999." He concluded his brief opinion: "Enough has been said, we think, to require the reversal of the judgment of the Georgia Supreme Court."

Justice Stewart concurred just to observe: "It is gratifying to note that my report of the demise of Fuentes v. Shevin [citation omitted] seems to have been greatly exaggerated." Justice Powell concurred in the judgment, incidentally arguing that issuance by a court clerk would suffice under a Mitchell-type statute.

Justice Blackmun, joined by Justice Rehnquist and Chief Justice Burger, observed in dissent: "Neither do I conclude that, because this is a garnishment case, rather than a lien or vendor-vendee case, it is automatically controlled by Sniadach. Sniadach, as has been noted, concerned and reeks of wages. North Georgia Finishing is no wage earner. It is a corporation engaged in business. It was protected (a) by the fact that the garnishment procedure may be instituted in Georgia only after the primary suit has been filed or judgment obtained by the creditor, thus placing on the creditor the obligation to initiate the proceedings and the burden of proof, and assuring a full hearing to the debtor; (b) by the respondent's statutorily required and deposited double bond; and (c) by the requirement of the respondent's affidavit of apprehension of loss. It was in a position to dissolve the garnishment by the filing of a single bond. These are transactions of a day-to-day type in the commercial world. They are not situations involving contracts of adhesion or basic unfairness, imbalance, or inequality. See D.H. Overmyer Co. v. Frick Co., 405 U.S. 174, 92 S.Ct. 775 (1972); Swarb v. Lennox, 405 U.S. 191, 92 S.Ct. 767 (1972). The clerk-judge distinction, relied on by the Court, surely is of little significance so long as the court officer is not an agent of the creditor. The Georgia system, for me, affords commercial entities all the protection that is required by the Due Process Clause of the Fourteenth Amendment."

———

Questions: (2) What would Di-Chem have to show in the hearing required by the Supreme Court?

(3) If Georgia had had an applicable Mitchell-type statute, with which Di-Chem had complied, would the result have been different (even though Di-Chem had no pre-existing interest in the bank account)?

———

Connecticut v. Doehr

Supreme Court of the United States, 1991.
501 U.S. 1, 111 S.Ct. 2105.

■ JUSTICE WHITE delivered an opinion, Parts I, II, and III of which are the opinion of the Court.

This case requires us to determine whether a state statute that authorizes prejudgment attachment of real estate without prior notice or hearing, without a showing of extraordinary circumstances, and without a requirement that the person seeking the attachment post a bond, satisfies the Due Process Clause of the Fourteenth Amendment. We hold that, as applied to this case, it does not.

I

On March 15, 1988, petitioner John F. DiGiovanni submitted an application to the Connecticut Superior Court for an attachment in the amount of $75,000 on respondent Brian K. Doehr's home in Meriden, Connecticut. DiGiovanni took this step in conjunction with a civil action for assault and battery that he was seeking to institute against Doehr in the same court. The suit did not involve Doehr's real estate nor did DiGiovanni have any pre-existing interest either in Doehr's home or any of his other property.

Connecticut law authorizes prejudgment attachment of real estate without affording prior notice or the opportunity for a prior hearing to the individual whose property is subject to the attachment. The State's prejudgment remedy statute provides, in relevant part:

> "The court or a judge of the court may allow the prejudgment remedy to be issued by an attorney without hearing as provided in sections 52–278c and 52–278d upon verification by oath of the plaintiff or of some competent affiant, that there is probable cause to sustain the validity of the plaintiff's claim and (1) that the prejudgment remedy requested is for an attachment of real property[; or (2) that there is reasonable likelihood that the defendant (A) neither resides in nor maintains an office or place of business in this state and is not otherwise subject to jurisdiction over his person by the court, or (B) has hidden or will hide himself so that process cannot be served on him or (C) is about to remove himself or his property from this state or (D) is about to fraudulently dispose of or has fraudulently disposed of any of his property with intent to hinder, delay, or defraud his creditors or (E) has fraudulently hidden or withheld money, property, or effects which should be liable to the satisfaction of his debts or (F) has stated he is insolvent or has stated he is

unable to pay his debts as they mature.] . . ." Conn.Gen.Stat. § 52–278e(a) (1991).[b]

The statute does not require the plaintiff to post a bond to insure the payment of damages that the defendant may suffer should the attachment prove wrongfully issued or the claim prove unsuccessful.

As required, DiGiovanni submitted an affidavit in support of his application. In five one-sentence paragraphs, DiGiovanni stated that the facts set forth in his previously submitted complaint were true; that "I was willfully, wantonly and maliciously assaulted by the defendant, Brian K. Doehr"; that "[s]aid assault and battery broke my left wrist and further caused an ecchymosis to my right eye, as well as other injuries"; and that "I have further expended sums of money for medical care and treatment." The affidavit concluded with the statement, "In my opinion, the foregoing facts are sufficient to show that there is probable cause that judgment will be rendered for the plaintiff."

On the strength of these submissions the Superior Court judge, by an order dated March 17, found "probable cause to sustain the validity of the plaintiff's claim" and ordered the attachment on Doehr's home "to the value of $75,000." The sheriff attached the property four days later, on March 21. Only after this did Doehr receive notice of the attachment. He also had yet to be served with the complaint, which is ordinarily necessary for an action to commence in Connecticut. [Citation omitted.] As the statute further required, the attachment notice informed Doehr that he had the right to a hearing: (1) to claim that no probable cause existed to sustain the claim; (2) to request that the attachment be vacated, modified, or dismissed or that a bond be substituted; or (3) to claim that some portion of the property was exempt from execution. Conn.Gen.Stat. § 52–278e(b) (1991).

Rather than pursue these options, Doehr filed suit against DiGiovanni in Federal District Court, claiming [with similarly situated joined parties] that § 52–278e(a)(1) was unconstitutional under the Due Process Clause of the Fourteenth Amendment. The District Court upheld the statute and granted summary judgment in favor of DiGiovanni. Pinsky v. Duncan, 716 F.Supp. 58 (Conn.1989). On appeal, a divided panel of the United States Court of Appeals for the Second Circuit reversed. Pinsky v. Duncan, 898 F.2d 852 (1990).[3] Judge Pratt, who wrote the opinion for the court, concluded that the Connecticut statute violated due process in permitting ex parte attachment absent a showing of extraordinary circumstances. "The rule to be derived from Sniadach and its progeny, therefore, is not that postattachment hearings are generally

---

[b]   As a consequence of this decision by the U.S. Supreme Court, Connecticut rewrote this statute, so that today it preserves only (2)(B)–(E) as "exigent circumstances" that excuse pre-seizure notice and hearing. In addition, the defendant now may request that the court in its discretion require the plaintiff to post a bond. Other statutes deal with foreclosing a lien.

[3]   The Court of Appeals invited Connecticut to intervene pursuant to 28 U.S.C. § 2403(b) after oral argument. The State elected to intervene in the appeal, and has fully participated in the proceedings before this Court.

acceptable provided that the plaintiff files a factual affidavit and that a judicial officer supervises the process, but that a prior hearing may be postponed where exceptional circumstances justify such a delay, *and where* sufficient additional safeguards are present." Id., at 855. This conclusion was deemed to be consistent with our decision in Mitchell v. W.T. Grant Co., 416 U.S. 600, 94 S.Ct. 1895 (1974), because the absence of a preattachment hearing was approved in that case based on the presence of extraordinary circumstances.

A further reason to invalidate the statute, the court ruled, was the highly factual nature of the issues in this case. In Mitchell, there were "uncomplicated matters that len[t] themselves to documentary proof" and "[t]he nature of the issues at stake minimize[d] the risk that the writ [would] be wrongfully issued by a judge." Id., at 609–610, 94 S.Ct., at 1901. Similarly, in Mathews v. Eldridge, 424 U.S. 319, 343–344, 96 S.Ct. 893, 907 (1976), where an evidentiary hearing was not required prior to the termination of disability benefits, the determination of disability was "sharply focused and easily documented." Judge Pratt observed that in contrast the present case involved the fact-specific event of a fist fight and the issue of assault. He doubted that the judge could reliably determine probable cause when presented with only the plaintiff's version of the altercation. "Because the risk of a wrongful attachment is considerable under these circumstances, we conclude that dispensing with notice and opportunity for a hearing until after the attachment, without a showing of extraordinary circumstances, violates the requirements of due process." 898 F.2d at 856. . . .

    . . . .

The dissent's conclusion accorded with the views of the Connecticut Supreme Court, which had previously upheld § 52–278e in Fermont Division, Dynamics Corp. of America v. Smith, 178 Conn. 393, 423 A.2d 80 (1979). We granted certiorari to resolve the conflict of authority. 498 U.S. 809, 111 S.Ct. 42 (1990).

II

With this case we return to the question of what process must be afforded by a state statute enabling an individual to enlist the aid of the State to deprive another of his or her property by means of the prejudgment attachment or similar procedure. Our cases reflect the numerous variations this type of remedy can entail. [The Court here described the Sniadach, Fuentes, Mitchell, and Di-Chem cases.]

These cases "underscore the truism that '[d]ue process, unlike some legal rules, is not a technical conception with a fixed content unrelated to time, place and circumstances.' " Mathews v. Eldridge, supra, 424 U.S., at 334, 96 S.Ct., at 902 (quoting Cafeteria Workers v. McElroy, 367 U.S. 886, 895, 81 S.Ct. 1743, 1748 (1961)). In Mathews, we drew upon our prejudgment remedy decisions to determine what process is due when the government itself seeks to effect a deprivation on its own initiative.

Mathews, 424 U.S., at 334, 96 S.Ct., at 902. That analysis resulted in the now familiar threefold inquiry requiring consideration of "the private interest that will be affected by the official action"; "the risk of an erroneous deprivation of such interest through the procedures used, and the probable value, if any, of additional or substitute safeguards"; and lastly "the Government's interest, including the function involved and the fiscal and administrative burdens that the additional or substitute procedural requirement would entail." Id., at 335, 96 S.Ct., at 903.

Here the inquiry is similar but the focus is different. Prejudgment remedy statutes ordinarily apply to disputes between private parties rather than between an individual and the government. Such enactments are designed to enable one of the parties to "make use of state procedures with the overt, significant assistance of state officials," and they undoubtedly involve state action "substantial enough to implicate the Due Process Clause." Tulsa Professional Collection Services, Inc. v. Pope, 485 U.S. 478, 486, 108 S.Ct. 1340, 1345 (1988). Nonetheless, any burden that increasing procedural safeguards entails primarily affects not the government, but the party seeking control of the other's property. See Fuentes v. Shevin, supra, 407 U.S., at 99–101, 92 S.Ct., at 2003–2005 (White, J., dissenting). For this type of case, therefore, the relevant inquiry requires, as in Mathews, first, consideration of the private interest that will be affected by the prejudgment measure; second, an examination of the risk of erroneous deprivation through the procedures under attack and the probable value of additional or alternative safeguards; and third, in contrast to Mathews, principal attention to the interest of the party seeking the prejudgment remedy, with, nonetheless, due regard for any ancillary interest the government may have in providing the procedure or forgoing the added burden of providing greater protections.

We now consider the Mathews factors in determining the adequacy of the procedures before us, first with regard to the safeguards of notice and a prior hearing, and then in relation to the protection of a bond.

III

We agree with the Court of Appeals that the property interests that attachment affects are significant. For a property owner like Doehr, attachment ordinarily clouds title; impairs the ability to sell or otherwise alienate the property; taints any credit rating; reduces the chance of obtaining a home equity loan or additional mortgage; and can even place an existing mortgage in technical default where there is an insecurity clause. Nor does Connecticut deny that any of these consequences occurs.

Instead, the State correctly points out that these effects do not amount to a complete, physical, or permanent deprivation of real property; their impact is less than the perhaps temporary total deprivation of household goods or wages. See Sniadach, supra, 395 U.S., at 340, 89 S.Ct., at 1822; Mitchell, supra, 416 U.S., at 613, 94 S.Ct., at 1903. But the Court has never held that only such extreme deprivations trigger due process concern. [Citation omitted.] To the contrary, our cases show that even the temporary or partial impairments to property rights that attachments, liens, and similar encumbrances entail are sufficient to merit due process protection. Without doubt, state procedures for creating and enforcing attachments, as with liens, "are subject to the strictures of due process." Peralta v. Heights Medical Center, Inc., 485 U.S. 80, 85, 108 S.Ct. 896, 899 (1988) (citing Mitchell, supra, 416 U.S., at 604, 94 S.Ct., at 1898; [other citation omitted]).[4]

We also agree with the Court of Appeals that the risk of erroneous deprivation that the State permits here is substantial. By definition, attachment statutes premise a deprivation of property on one ultimate factual contingency—the award of damages to the plaintiff which the defendant may not be able to satisfy. [Citations omitted.] For attachments before judgment, Connecticut mandates that this determination be made by means of a procedural inquiry that asks whether "there is probable cause to sustain the validity of the plaintiff's claim." Conn.Gen.Stat. § 52–278e(a). The statute elsewhere defines the validity of the claim in terms of the likelihood "that judgment will be rendered in the matter in favor of the plaintiff." Conn.Gen.Stat. § 52–278c(a)(2) (1991) . . . .

. . . .

. . . As the record shows, and as the State concedes, only a skeletal affidavit need be and was filed. The State urges that the reviewing judge normally reviews the complaint as well, but concedes that the complaint may also be conclusory. It is self-evident that the judge could make no realistic assessment concerning the likelihood of an action's success based upon these one-sided, self-serving, and conclusory submissions. And as the Court of Appeals said, in a case like this involving an alleged assault, even a detailed affidavit would give only the plaintiff's version of the confrontation. Unlike determining the existence of a debt or delinquent payments, the issue does not concern "ordinarily uncomplicated matters that lend themselves to documentary proof." Mitchell, 416 U.S., at 609, 94 S.Ct., at 1901. The likelihood of error that results illustrates that "fairness can rarely be obtained by secret, one-sided determination of facts decisive of rights. . . . [And n]o better instrument has been devised for arriving at truth than to give a person in jeopardy of serious loss notice of the case against him and an

---

[4]   Our summary affirmance in Spielman-Fond, Inc. v. Hanson's Inc., 417 U.S. 901, 94 S.Ct. 2596 (1974), does not control. In Spielman-Fond, the District Court held that the filing of a mechanic's lien did not amount to the taking of a significant property interest. 379 F.Supp. 997, 999 (Ariz.1973) (three-judge court) (per curiam). A summary disposition does not enjoy the full precedential value of a case argued on the merits and disposed of by a written opinion. Edelman v. Jordan, 415 U.S. 651, 671, 94 S.Ct. 1347, 1359 (1974). The facts of Spielman-Fond presented an alternative basis for affirmance in any event. Unlike the case before us, the mechanic's lien statute in Spielman-Fond required the creditor to have a pre-existing interest in the property at issue. 379 F.Supp., at 997. As we explain below, a heightened plaintiff interest in certain circumstances can provide a ground for upholding procedures that are otherwise suspect. . . .

opportunity to meet it." Joint Anti-Fascist Refugee Committee v. McGrath, 341 U.S. 123, 170–172, 71 S.Ct. 624, 647–649 (1951) (Frankfurter, J., concurring).

What safeguards the State does afford do not adequately reduce this risk. Connecticut points out that the statute also provides an "expeditiou[s]" postattachment adversary hearing, § 52–278e(c); notice for such a hearing, § 52–278e(b); judicial review of an adverse decision, § 52–278*l*(a); and a double damages action if the original suit is commenced without probable cause, § 52–568(a)(1). Similar considerations were present in Mitchell where we upheld Louisiana's sequestration statute despite the lack of predeprivation notice and hearing. But in Mitchell, the plaintiff had a vendor's lien to protect, the risk of error was minimal because the likelihood of recovery involved uncomplicated matters that lent themselves to documentary proof, [citation omitted], and plaintiff was required to put up a bond. None of these factors diminishing the need for a predeprivation hearing is present in this case. It is true that a later hearing might negate the presence of probable cause, but this would not cure the temporary deprivation that an earlier hearing might have prevented. . . .

Finally, we conclude that the interests in favor of an ex parte attachment, particularly the interests of the plaintiff, are too minimal to supply such a consideration here. Plaintiff had no existing interest in Doehr's real estate when he sought the attachment. His only interest in attaching the property was to ensure the availability of assets to satisfy his judgment if he prevailed on the merits of his action. Yet there was no allegation that Doehr was about to transfer or encumber his real estate or take any other action during the pendency of the action that would render his real estate unavailable to satisfy a judgment. Our cases have recognized such a properly supported claim would be an exigent circumstance permitting postponing any notice or hearing until after the attachment is effected. See Mitchell, supra, 416 U.S., at 609, 94 S.Ct., at 1901; Fuentes, supra, 407 U.S., at 90–92, 92 S.Ct., at 1999–2000; Sniadach, 395 U.S., at 339, 89 S.Ct., at 1821. Absent such allegations, however, the plaintiff's interest in attaching the property does not justify the burdening of Doehr's ownership rights without a hearing to determine the likelihood of recovery.

No interest the government may have affects the analysis. The State's substantive interest in protecting any rights of the plaintiff cannot be any more weighty than those rights themselves. Here the plaintiff's interest is de minimis. Moreover, the State cannot seriously plead additional financial or administrative burdens involving predeprivation hearings when it already claims to provide an immediate postdeprivation hearing. [Citations omitted.]

. . . .

IV

. . . .

Although a majority of the Court does not reach the issue, Justices Marshall, Stevens, O'Connor, and I deem it appropriate to consider whether due process also requires the plaintiff to post a bond or other security in addition to requiring a hearing or showing of some exigency.

As noted, the impairments to property rights that attachments affect merit due process protection. Several consequences can be severe, such as the default of a homeowner's mortgage. In the present context, it need only be added that we have repeatedly recognized the utility of a bond in protecting property rights affected by the mistaken award of prejudgment remedies. Di-Chem, 419 U.S., at 610, 611, 95 S.Ct., at 724, 725 (Powell, J., concurring in judgment); id., at 619, 95 S.Ct., at 728 (Blackmun, J., dissenting); Mitchell, 416 U.S., at 606, n. 8, 94 S.Ct., at 1899, n. 8.

Without a bond, at the time of attachment, the danger that these property rights may be wrongfully deprived remains unacceptably high even with such safeguards as a hearing or exigency requirement. The need for a bond is especially apparent where extraordinary circumstances justify an attachment with no more than the plaintiff's ex parte assertion of a claim. We have already discussed how due process tolerates, and the States generally permit, the otherwise impermissible chance of erroneously depriving the defendant in such situations in light of the heightened interest of the plaintiff. Until a postattachment hearing, however, a defendant has no protection against damages sustained where no extraordinary circumstance in fact existed or the plaintiff's likelihood of recovery was nil. Such protection is what a bond can supply. Both the Court and its individual members have repeatedly found the requirement of a bond to play an essential role in reducing what would have been too great a degree of risk in precisely this type of circumstance. [Citations to Fuentes, Mitchell, and Di-Chem omitted.]

But the need for a bond does not end here. A defendant's property rights remain at undue risk even when there has been an adversarial hearing to determine the plaintiff's likelihood of recovery. At best, a court's initial assessment of each party's case cannot produce more than an educated prediction as to who will win. This is especially true when, as here, the nature of the claim makes any accurate prediction elusive. See Mitchell, supra, 416 U.S., at 609–610, 94 S.Ct., at 1901. In consequence, even a full hearing under a proper probable-cause standard would not prevent many defendants from having title to their homes impaired during the pendency of suits that never result in the contingency that ultimately justifies such impairment, namely, an award to the plaintiff. Attachment measures currently on the books reflect this concern. All but a handful of States require a plaintiff's bond despite also affording a hearing either before, or (for the vast majority, only under extraordinary circumstances) soon after, an attachment takes place. . . .

Bonds have been a similarly common feature of other prejudgment remedy procedures that we have considered, whether or not these procedures also included a hearing. [Citations omitted.]

. . . .

Nor is there any appreciable interest against a bond requirement. . . .

. . . .

V

Because Connecticut's prejudgment remedy provision, Conn.Gen.Stat. § 52–278e(a)(1), violates the requirements of due process by authorizing prejudgment attachment without prior notice or a hearing, the judgment of the Court of Appeals is affirmed, and the case is remanded to that court for further proceedings consistent with this opinion.

It is so ordered.

. . . .

■ [CHIEF JUSTICE REHNQUIST and JUSTICES BLACKMUN, KENNEDY, and SOUTER joined only Parts I, II, and III, and JUSTICE SCALIA joined only Parts I and III. Chief Justice Rehnquist, joined by Justice Blackmun, wrote a concurring opinion, which is omitted; he explained that the Court did not have to reach the issue of Part IV in order to decide this case; nevertheless, by way of an aside he offered his view that in the Spielman-Fond situation, with the heightened plaintiff's interest implicit in a mechanic's lien, due process required neither pre-seizure notice and hearing nor a plaintiff's bond. Justice Scalia's concurrence, which did not specifically address the bond issue, is also omitted. For the background story of the Doehr case, see Robert G. Bone, "The Story of Connecticut v. Doehr: Balancing Costs and Benefits in Defining Procedural Rights," in Civil Procedure Stories 159 (Kevin M. Clermont ed., 2d ed. 2008).]

———

Question: (4) If DiGiovanni were suing on some other cause of action to protect a pre-existing interest in the real estate (imagine his filing a mechanic's lien without notice or hearing, but without exigent circumstances, while trying to recover for repairs he made to Doehr's house), would the constitutional result have been different? See Shaumyan v. O'Neill, 987 F.2d 122 (2d Cir.1993) (yes).

———

SCOPE OF SNIADACH'S PROGENY

The foregoing cases deal with the extension of procedural due process standards to regulate pre-judgment seizures of property for security. In this context and in others, the general requirement that fair notice and opportunity to be heard must be given before the government unduly impairs a person's property interest—or that at least the procedures of a Mitchell-type or Mitchell-like statute must be followed in the case of a pre-judgment seizure for security where plaintiff has a pre-existing interest in the property or where exigent circumstances endanger security—raises several more problems of definition.

For example, what kind of impaired property interest will trigger this protection? These cases show an expansive view of the impairment of property interest that is regulated by the Due Process Clauses. The property involved certainly need not be a necessity of life, and the interest may be only possessory. The deprivation might be only temporary or partial.

Sniadach and its progeny are immediately concerned only with pre-judgment seizures of property for security. It is obvious, however, that they should have an influence in many other contexts—such as termination of welfare benefits, loss of driver's license, and suspension from school—although the strength of that influence will not always be clear. Compare Goldberg v. Kelly, 397 U.S. 254, 90 S.Ct. 1011 (1970), discussed by Judith Resnik, "The Story of Goldberg: Why This Case Is Our Shorthand," in Civil Procedure Stories 473 (Kevin M. Clermont ed., 2d ed. 2008), with Mathews v. Eldridge, 424 U.S. 319, 96 S.Ct. 893 (1976), discussed in Topic C of Part 1.

To consider a particular context, courts had in the past treated pre-judgment attachments and garnishments of property to obtain in rem or quasi in rem jurisdiction as not being subject to the procedural due process dictates of the foregoing cases. They grounded such treatment on the theory that there is strong public interest in obtaining jurisdiction and that this consideration colors the seizure as an "extraordinary situation" beyond the reach of Sniadach's progeny. Cf. Calero-Toledo v. Pearson Yacht Leasing Co., 416 U.S. 663, 94 S.Ct. 2080 (1974) (holding that seizure of a drug-running yacht for forfeiture proceedings is such an "extraordinary situation"). But more recent cases have held that a general exception of this sort is illogical and unwise, and they have applied the Sniadach line of cases to run-of-the-mill seizures for jurisdictional purposes. Cf. United States v. James Daniel Good Real Property, 510 U.S. 43, 114 S.Ct. 492 (1993) (holding that seizure of a drug dealer's house for forfeiture proceedings without notice and hearing is invalid without a showing of "exigent circumstances"). See generally Karen Nelson Moore, Procedural Due Process in Quasi In Rem Actions After Shaffer v. Heitner, 20 Wm. & Mary L.Rev. 157 (1978).

Another context in which the Sniadach line might have an impact is that of seizures of property to enforce judgments. Here a leading case has held, however, that a wage garnishment for enforcement need not be preceded by notice of the garnishment and opportunity to be heard on the garnishment's propriety; the court reasoned that the state's interest in facilitating the enforcement of its judgments and the creditor's interest in satisfying his judgment outweighed the debtor's interests, given that the debtor had had notice and opportunity to be heard before judgment and given that the debtor would under the state law have the opportunity of a prompt post-garnishment hearing. Brown v. Liberty Loan Corp., 539 F.2d 1355 (5th Cir.1976). Yet, more recent cases have emphasized that due process generally does require prompt post-seizure notice and opportunity to be heard. E.g., Finberg v. Sullivan, 634 F.2d 50 (3d Cir.1980) (en banc). See generally Virginia C. Patterson, Commentary, Due Process and Postjudgment Enforcement Procedures: Where Do We Stand?, 37 Ala.L.Rev. 759 (1986).

Question: (5) What protection does procedural due process afford in connection with seizure of property to obtain quasi in rem jurisdiction when the purpose of exercising that jurisdiction is to enforce an out-of-state personal judgment?

GOVERNMENTAL ACTION

Impairments of property interests invoke the Due Process Clauses only when they result from governmental action. However, such action need not involve direct action by government officials. Action by private persons that the government compels or significantly encourages may qualify as governmental action. See Reitman v. Mulkey, 387 U.S. 369, 87 S.Ct. 1627 (1967). And action by private persons that is taken under authority delegated by the government and is traditionally an exclusively public function may constitute governmental action. See Marsh v. Alabama, 326 U.S. 501, 66 S.Ct. 276 (1946). Nevertheless, to attribute private action to the government, there must be significant governmental involvement, something more than mere neutral enforcement of laws. See generally Laurence H. Tribe, American Constitutional Law 1688– 720 (2d ed. 1988).

At any rate, state action was clearly present in the foregoing cases of official pre-judgment seizures of property for security. See Lugar v. Edmondson Oil Co., 457 U.S. 922, 102 S.Ct. 2744 (1982). But self-help might open an end-run on Sniadach's progeny.

Question: (6) U.C.C. § 9–609 provides that upon default a secured party may repossess collateral in the debtor's possession without judicial process, as long as this can be done without breach of the peace. Would such repossession under § 9–609 constitute state action for the purposes of the Fourteenth Amendment? See Flagg Bros. v. Brooks, 436 U.S. 149, 98 S.Ct. 1729 (1978) (holding that a sale under U.C.C. § 7–210 does not constitute state action for the purposes of the Fourteenth Amendment (§ 7–210 provides that a warehouseman may enforce his lien on stored goods—which lien the law gives him for charges due for that storage—by selling the goods in a commercially reasonable manner without judicial process)).

It should be noted that constitutional provisions other than the Federal Due Process Clauses may contribute to the regulation of seizure procedures. For example, in Blair v. Pitchess, 5 Cal.3d 258, 486 P.2d 1242, 96 Cal.Rptr. 42 (1971), the California Supreme Court found that the warrantless seizure of property by state agents, in a Fuentes-type situation, violated the Search and Seizure Clause of the Fourth Amendment. More pertinently, in Svendsen v. Smith's Moving & Trucking Co., 54 N.Y.2d 865, 429 N.E.2d 411, 444 N.Y.S.2d 904 (1981), the New York Court of Appeals found U.C.C. § 7–210 unconstitutional under the due process clause of the state's constitution, thanks to its broader view of state action. Most importantly, federal and state legislative and administrative provisions may, of course, further restrict seizure procedures even in the absence of governmental involvement in the seizure. The courts stand ready to enforce all this law, sometimes even by awarding damages in a tort action, say, for unlawful attachment. See Thomas D. Crandall, Richard B. Hagedorn & Frank W. Smith, Jr., Debtor-Creditor Law Manual ¶ 6.04[5][b] (1985); Dean Gloster, Comment, Abuse of Process and Attachment: Toward a Balance of Power, 30 UCLA L.Rev. 1218 (1983).

SECTION 3.   CONSENT IN ADVANCE

D.H. Overmyer Co. v. Frick Co.

Supreme Court of the United States, 1972.
405 U.S. 174, 92 S.Ct. 775.

■ MR. JUSTICE BLACKMUN delivered the opinion of the Court.

This case presents the issue of the constitutionality, under the Due Process Clause of the Fourteenth Amendment, of the cognovit note authorized by Ohio Rev.Code § 2323.13.

The cognovit is the ancient legal device by which the debtor consents in advance to the holder's obtaining a judgment without notice or hearing, and possibly even with the appearance, on the debtor's behalf, of an attorney designated by the holder. It was known at least as far back as Blackstone's time. 3 W. Blackstone, Commentaries *397. In a case applying Ohio law, it was said that the purpose of the cognovit is "to permit the note holder to obtain judgment without a trial of possible defenses which the signers of the notes might assert." Hadden v. Rumsey Products, Inc., 196 F.2d 92, 96 (C.A.2 1952). And long ago the cognovit method was described by the Chief Justice of New Jersey as "the loosest way of binding a man's property that ever was devised in any civilized country." Alderman v. Diament, 7 N.J.L. 197, 198 (1824). Mr. Dickens noted it with obvious disfavor. Pickwick Papers, c. 47. The cognovit has been the subject of comment, much of it critical.

Statutory treatment varies widely. Some States specifically authorize the cognovit. Others disallow it. Some go so far as to make its employment a misdemeanor. The majority, however, regulate its use and many prohibit the device in small loans and consumer sales.

. . . .

The argument that a provision of this kind is offensive to current notions of Fourteenth Amendment due process is, at first glance, an appealing one. However, here, as in nearly every case, facts are important. [Overmyer was a warehousing enterprise with many warehouses in many states. It contracted with Frick for an automatic refrigeration system in a warehouse under construction in Ohio. Overmyer fell behind in its progress payments, and Frick stopped its work. After negotiations, Frick resumed the work under new installment-payment terms and completed it to Overmyer's then satisfaction. Later Overmyer requested additional time to make its installment payments. Negotiations finally resulted in a new agreement, which, unlike the earlier agreements, included the execution of a note with a cognovit provision. As the Supreme Court was later to observe, the execution and delivery of this note "were for an adequate consideration and were the product of negotiations carried on by corporate parties with the advice of competent counsel." Later Overmyer ceased to make the required monthly payments under the note, asserting a breach by Frick of the original contract. Frick caused judgment for the balance due on the note to be entered in an Ohio court without prior notice: an Ohio attorney, not known to Overmyer, appeared for Overmyer "by virtue of the warrant of attorney" in the note, and then waived service of process and confessed judgment. As required by Ohio law, the court clerk notified Overmyer of entry of judgment on the cognovit note. Overmyer moved to vacate judgment, and it tendered an answer and counterclaim. The Ohio court denied the motion, and the state appellate courts affirmed. Certiorari was granted.]

[Overmyer argues] that due process requires reasonable notice and an opportunity to be heard, citing Boddie v. Connecticut, 401 U.S. 371, 378, 91 S.Ct. 780, 786 (1971). It is acknowledged, however, that the question here is in a context of "contract waiver, before suit has been filed, before any dispute has arisen" and "whereby a party gives up in advance his constitutional right to defend any suit by the other, to notice and an opportunity to be heard, no matter what defenses he may have, and to be represented by counsel of his own choice."[9] In other words, Overmyer's position here specifically is that it is "unconstitutional to waive in advance the right to present a defense in an action on the note."[10] It is conceded that in Ohio a court has the power to open the judgment upon a proper showing. Bellows v. Bowlus, 83 Ohio App. 90, 93, 82 N.E.2d 429, 432 (1948). But it is claimed that such a move is discretionary and ordinarily will not be disturbed on appeal, and that it may not prevent execution before the debtor has notice, Griffin v. Griffin,

---

9   Brief for Petitioners 16.
10   Trans. of Oral Arg. 17.

327 U.S. 220, 231–232, 66 S.Ct. 556, 561–562 (1946). Goldberg v. Kelly, 397 U.S. 254, 90 S.Ct. 1011 (1970), and Sniadach v. Family Finance Corp., 395 U.S. 337, 89 S.Ct. 1820 (1969), are cited.

The due process rights to notice and hearing prior to a civil judgment are subject to waiver. In National Equipment Rental, Ltd. v. Szukhent, 375 U.S. 311, 84 S.Ct. 411 (1964), the Court observed:

> "[I]t is settled . . . that parties to a contract may agree in advance to submit to the jurisdiction of a given court, to permit notice to be served by the opposing party, or even to waive notice altogether." Id., at 315–316, 84 S.Ct., at 414.

And in Boddie v. Connecticut, supra, the Court acknowledged that "the hearing required by due process is subject to waiver." 401 U.S., at 378–379, 91 S.Ct., at 786.

This, of course, parallels the recognition of waiver in the criminal context where personal liberty, rather than a property right, is involved. Illinois v. Allen, 397 U.S. 337, 342–343, 90 S.Ct. 1057, 1060 (1970) (right to be present at trial); Miranda v. Arizona, 384 U.S. 436, 444, 86 S.Ct. 1602, 1612 (1966) (rights to counsel and against compulsory self-incrimination); Fay v. Noia, 372 U.S. 391, 439, 83 S.Ct. 822, 849 (1963) (habeas corpus); Rogers v. United States, 340 U.S. 367, 371, 71 S.Ct. 438, 440 (1951) (right against compulsory self-incrimination).

Even if, for present purposes, we assume that the standard for waiver in a corporate-property-right case of this kind is the same standard applicable to waiver in a criminal proceeding, that is, that it be voluntary, knowing, and intelligently made, Brady v. United States, 397 U.S. 742, 748, 90 S.Ct. 1463, 1468 (1970); Miranda v. Arizona, 384 U.S., at 444, 86 S.Ct., at 1612, or "an intentional relinquishment or abandonment of a known right or privilege," Johnson v. Zerbst, 304 U.S. 458, 464, 58 S.Ct. 1019, 1023 (1938); Fay v. Noia, 372 U.S., at 439, 83 S.Ct., at 849, and even if, as the Court has said in the civil area, "[w]e do not presume acquiescence in the loss of fundamental rights," Ohio Bell Tel. Co. v. Public Utilities Comm'n, 301 U.S. 292, 307, 57 S.Ct. 724, 731 (1937), that standard was fully satisfied here.

. . . .

We therefore hold that Overmyer, in its execution and delivery to Frick of the second installment note containing the cognovit provision, voluntarily, intelligently, and knowingly waived the rights it otherwise possessed to prejudgment notice and hearing, and that it did so with full awareness of the legal consequences.

. . . .

Some concluding comments are in order:

1. Our holding necessarily means that a cognovit clause is not, per se, violative of Fourteenth Amendment due process. Overmyer could prevail here only if the clause were constitutionally invalid. The facts of

this case, as we observed above, are important, and those facts amply demonstrate that a cognovit provision may well serve a proper and useful purpose in the commercial world and at the same time not be vulnerable to constitutional attack.

2.   Our holding, of course, is not controlling precedent for other facts of other cases. For example, where the contract is one of adhesion, where there is great disparity in bargaining power, and where the debtor receives nothing for the cognovit provision, other legal consequences may ensue.

3.   Overmyer, merely because of its execution of the cognovit note, is not rendered defenseless. It concedes that in Ohio the judgment court may vacate its judgment upon a showing of a valid defense and, indeed, Overmyer had a post-judgment hearing in the Ohio court. If there were defenses such as prior payment or mistaken identity, those defenses could be asserted. And there is nothing we see that prevented Overmyer from pursuing its breach-of-contract claim against Frick in a proper forum. . . .

The judgment is affirmed.

■ [The concurring opinion of JUSTICE DOUGLAS, with whom Justice Marshall joined, is omitted. JUSTICES POWELL and REHNQUIST did not participate.]

————

Question: (7) Overmyer went bankrupt in 1973, so you can sense what is sometimes at stake here for the creditor. Yet the Overmyer case clearly suggests that a contractual waiver of notice and opportunity to be heard may sometimes be invalid in a consumer setting, as indeed the court held in Gonzalez v. County of Hidalgo, Texas, 489 F.2d 1043 (5th Cir.1973). As the attorney for a seller of consumer goods, how would you draft waiver provisions in a conditional sales contract so as to meet the requirements suggested by the Overmyer case? As the attorney for the buyer, what would you counterargue to establish the unconstitutionality of those provisions?

————

CHOICE OF LAW AND FORUM

As you have seen, the parties have significant powers to select the governing law and, of special interest here in this Part on authority to adjudicate, to select the forum. As indicated by the quotation in Overmyer from National Equipment Rental, Ltd. v. Szukhent, 375 U.S. 311, 315–16, 84 S.Ct. 411, 414 (1964), the defendant can in the proper circumstances waive in advance objections to territorial jurisdiction.

Question: (8) Should the same principle be applied to venue, so that pursuant to waiver in advance an action may proceed in a place improper under the venue statute, or so that pursuant to agreement in advance an action may proceed only in a certain place despite the more permissive provisions of the venue statute? Compare The Bremen v. Zapata Off-Shore Co., 407 U.S. 1, 92 S.Ct. 1907 (1972) (generally yes), with Carnival Cruise Lines, Inc. v. Shute, 499 U.S. 585, 111 S.Ct. 1522 (1991) (even more expansively enforcing agreement, seemingly recognizing as exceptions only fraud in inclusion of clause or an unconscionably chosen forum). See generally Nw. Nat'l Ins. Co. v. Donovan, 916 F.2d 372, 376 (7th Cir.1990) (Posner, J.) ("We are persuaded that the only good reason for treating a forum selection clause differently from any other contract (specifically, from the contract in which the clause appears) is the possibility of adverse effects on third parties. Where that possibility is slight, the clause should be treated like any other contract. What is more, if any inconvenience to third parties can be cured by a change of venue under section 1404(a), that is the route to follow, rather than striking down the clause.").

Thus, the parties may consent in advance to territorial jurisdiction not otherwise existing, and they may waive in advance the restrictions of venue and other doctrines of self-restraint. Under modern law, courts will usually give effect to such "prorogation" agreements, apparently subject to ordinary contract law and the requirement that the forum not be an unconscionable one.

Conversely, the parties generally may, by a "derogation" agreement, give up permissible forums and thus restrict any potential litigation to one or more courts. That is, the law, in a further show of self-restraint, allows the parties themselves to restrict territorial authority to adjudicate.

The law of the forum where suit is brought will govern enforceability of the forum selection clause. Even if the parties also included a choice-of-law clause, the chosen law should not govern enforceability of the forum selection clause, although it should govern interpretation. The question remains open whether federal law or state law governs the forum selection clause for a state-created cause of action in federal court. See Wong v. PartyGaming Ltd., 589 F.3d 821, 826–28 (6th Cir.2009) (deciding in favor of federal law on enforceability, but noting that a few circuits favor state law). In the meantime, international treaties giving effect to forum selection clauses are emerging.

The federal law on enforceability of forum selection clauses is supportive, but ultimately discretionary. Accordingly, if public-interest factors overwhelmingly favor transfer, 28 U.S.C. § 1404(a) could override any otherwise enforceable forum selection clause, allowing the selected court rarely to transfer to another federal court where the case might have been brought absent the clause. As usual, transferor choice of law would apply. See Stewart Org. v. Ricoh Corp., 487 U.S. 22, 108 S.Ct. 2239 (1988). In international cases, a federal court may entertain the rare possibility that forum non conveniens trumps an otherwise enforceable forum selection clause agreeing on suit in that federal court. See Kelvion, Inc. v. PetroChina Canada Ltd., 918 F.3d 1088 (10th Cir.2019).

If, conversely, the plaintiff lays federal venue in accordance with the federal venue laws but in violation of the forum selection clause, and the defendant moves to transfer, the court normally should transfer under § 1404(a) to the selected forum. *But transferee law would then be applicable.* See Atl. Marine Constr. Co. v. U.S. Dist. Court, 571 U.S. 49, 65–66, 134 S.Ct. 568, 583 (2013) ("The court in the contractually selected venue should not apply the law of the transferor venue to which the parties waived their right."). In international cases, forum non conveniens would be in play.

The Atlantic Marine case explained that the "wrongness" of venue in the transferor court necessary for triggering 28 U.S.C. § 1406(a) demands violation of the federal venue laws. So, transfer for improper venue would come under § 1406(a) only if the transferor forum violates the federal venue laws and is unauthorized by an otherwise enforceable forum selection clause. Then the transferee court, whose law would apply, normally should be the selected forum.

Overall, American courts have shifted with time from a view that territorial authority to adjudicate is largely a matter for the sovereign and not the parties to decide, through a grudging acceptance of party agreements, and toward a perhaps overly enthusiastic embrace of freedom of contract even in the face of uneven bargaining capabilities and powers. Where the optimum lies and where American law will end up are still matters of debate and evolution.

Question: (9) Should a similar principle be applied to subject-matter jurisdiction, so that pursuant to agreement in advance, an action that is not within exclusive federal jurisdiction may proceed in state court but not in federal court? See Michael D. Moberly, Judicial Protection of Forum Selection: Agreements to Litigate in State Court, 1 Phoenix L.Rev. 1 (2008) (yes).

Whatever the future holds, forum selection clauses are currently becoming more and more important. Good lawyers try increasingly by agreement to contract their clients' way around the morass of the law on authority to adjudicate, and to do so in a way that advantages their clients. Lots of litigated cases, however, turn on how to interpret these clauses, most often as a result of the lawyers' failings. Office lawyers need to know a lot of law, including choice of law, to negotiate and write a forum selection clause effectively and clearly.

———

CUSTOMIZED LITIGATION

If, as Overmyer suggests, the parties can waive important procedural protections by consent in advance, then they can likewise choose to customize their litigation, or at least do so up to some vaguely defined limits. In short, the normal rules of procedure are no more than default contractual rules, many of which the parties can extensively modify through negotiation.

The parties might attempt to restrict joinder or discovery, alter the rules of evidence or waive jury trial, or restrict or waive appeal. In fact, they could try to make litigation look a lot like a peculiarly effective brand of arbitration, or they might agree to abide by some set of transnationally "neutral" rules of procedure. Perhaps that prospect should raise some caution flags, or perhaps not. Perhaps the governing law should step in to specify or tighten the limits on freedom of contract, or perhaps not. See generally Robert G. Bone, Party Rulemaking: Making Procedural Rules Through Party Choice, 90 Tex.L.Rev. 1329 (2012).

The debate now focuses on distinguishing noncore procedures over which the parties can bargain from core procedures not subject to party bargains. The core procedures might be those that protect the rights of third parties and those that limit burdens on the court or enable performance of the adjudicator's essential decisionmaking.

Question: (10) For a state-created cause of action in federal court, should the enforceability of a procedural waiver be governed by state or federal law? Cf. In re Cty. of Orange, 784 F.3d 520 (9th Cir.2015) ("[W]e find that the law governing pre-dispute jury trial waivers is procedural under Erie, and so federal courts should apply federal law to determine the validity of a waiver. But we also conclude that the federal 'knowing and voluntary' standard does not necessarily conflict with California's [anti-waiver rule]. We hold, therefore, that Erie's federalism principle requires federal courts sitting in diversity to import, as the federal rule, state law governing jury trial waivers where, as here, state law is even more protective than federal law of the jury trial right. Applying California law, we hold that the parties' contractual jury trial waiver is unenforceable.").

TOPIC C

JURISDICTION OVER SUBJECT MATTER

SECTION 1. GENERAL OBSERVATIONS

Restatement of Judgments (Am. Law Inst. 1942) used the expression "competency of the court" more or less interchangeably with "the court's jurisdiction over the subject matter." We propose to use these two catch phrases interchangeably. We can convey the general notion underlying both, although imperfectly, by this single question: has the sovereign properly given this court power to entertain this type of action?

As examples of lack of competence, Restatement of Judgments § 7 cmt. b (Am. Law Inst. 1942) gave the following: "There are many situations in which a court lacks competency to render a judgment. Thus, although a State has jurisdiction to grant a divorce of parties domiciled within the State, a decree of divorce rendered by a court which is not empowered to entertain suits for divorce is void. Similarly, a judgment rendered by a justice of the peace is void if under the law of the State such justices are not empowered to deal with the subject matter of the action; as, for example, where the action is one for tort and justices of the peace are given no power except in actions of contract. So also, where a court is given power to deal with actions involving no more than a designated amount, the statute limiting the amount is ordinarily construed not merely to make erroneous a judgment rendered by such a court in excess of its power, but to make such judgment void."

The last example suggests that, in a particular court, the failure to satisfy a minimum amount-in-controversy requirement might be a mere error, rather than a defect of competency rendering any judgment void. In fact, any particular court system might give varying treatment to the scope of competency in different situations. There seems to be no all-purpose clear-cut definition as to which legal requirements the concept of competency encompasses. Lack of competency shades off into other kinds of defects, either procedural or on the merits.

To the extent that such other defects entail the same consequences to the litigants as lack of competency, it may be unimportant to make sharp distinctions. But under current law there are situations where the court's categorization of a defect as one of competency becomes crucial.

Going beyond matters of definition, Restatement (Second) of Judgments § 11 cmt. b (Am. Law Inst. 1982) further elaborates subject-matter jurisdiction: "The rules of subject matter jurisdiction of a court are generally prescribed by the political authority that has created the court. (However, a superior political authority may impose limits on that authority. Thus, state law rather than federal law invests a state's courts with authority to adjudicate particular types of controversies, but federal law through preemption may supersede that authority). The prescriptions of subject matter jurisdiction express divisions of functions among the organs of that government, separating courts from other branches of government and differentiating one court from another."

The federal courts are particularly sensitive to questions of their own jurisdiction over the subject matter. Thus, it is possible at any stage of the federal litigation for either party to raise, or for the court on its own motion to consider, a question of competency. Rule 12(h)(3) in its original form made the explicit statement that "*whenever* it appears by suggestion of the parties *or otherwise* that the court lacks jurisdiction of the subject matter, the court shall dismiss the action." (Emphasis added.) That is still the thrust of Rule 12(h)(3).

Dismissal for want of such jurisdiction might come in the trial court or in an appellate court. Recall Louisville & Nashville Railroad Co. v. Mottley, supra p. 256, where the Supreme Court itself dismissed the federal suit, even though the federal issue in the case could reappear on review of an action on the same claim initiated in a state court (as indeed the Court did, supra p. 272).

The proposition that a federal court is bound to consider its own jurisdiction, regardless of the attitude or conduct of the parties, opens the door to strategic manipulations and wasted resources. Nevertheless, according to Mansfield, Coldwater & Lake Michigan Railway Co. v. Swan, 111 U.S. 379, 382, 4 S.Ct. 510, 511 (1884), the proposition springs from the limited nature of the judicial power of the United States under Article III, Section 2 of the Constitution. In that case the Supreme Court, noting that the record showed lack of diversity jurisdiction, ordered the action remanded to state court, although the only asserted grounds of appeal were alleged errors at trial.

Many cases declare that the parties cannot confer jurisdiction over the subject matter by *consent* or *collusion*. For instance, in Jackson v. Ashton, 33 U.S. (8 Pet.) 148 (1834), the Supreme Court dismissed for lack of diversity jurisdiction where both sides were eager for the Court to hear the appeal, and where counsel for the plaintiffs-appellants argued that jurisdiction existed and counsel for the defendant-appellee expressly renounced any objection to jurisdiction.

Similarly, any party—even the party who invoked federal jurisdiction in the first place—will at a late stage be heard to say that the case should be dismissed for want of competency. In Mansfield, Coldwater, remand worked to the benefit of the defendant-appellants, who had themselves invoked federal jurisdiction by removal from state court. In American Fire & Casualty Co. v. Finn, 341 U.S. 6, 71 S.Ct. 534 (1951), a defendant who had invoked federal jurisdiction by removal and had resisted a motion to remand was allowed to challenge subject-matter jurisdiction on appeal from an adverse judgment. That is to say, there is no general doctrine of *waiver* in connection with objections to federal jurisdiction. But see Caterpillar Inc. v. Lewis, 519 U.S. 61, 71–73, 117 S.Ct. 467, 474–75 (1996) (referring to a doctrine that prohibits, for plaintiffs and defendants alike, a late raising of any statutory bar to removal if the case is within original federal jurisdiction).

Next suppose that *A* sues *B* in federal court, alleging herself to be a citizen of State *X* and *B* to be a citizen of State *Y*. *B*'s answer admits these allegations. After the running of the statute of limitations so as to bar a new action, *B* moves to dismiss for lack of subject-matter jurisdiction and satisfies the court that the parties were in fact both citizens of State *X* when suit was brought. Is the court bound to dismiss for lack of competency? Yes, as there seems to be no general doctrine of equitable *estoppel* in connection with objections to federal jurisdiction. But cf. Itel Containers Int'l Corp. v. P.R. Marine Management, 108 F.R.D. 96 (D.N.J.1985) (imposing monetary sanctions for such behavior, payable to the court and to the plaintiff by the defendant and its counsel).

Questions: (1) What would you think of the constitutionality and desirability of a federal statute allowing any claim, if timely brought in federal court but dismissed for lack of subject-matter jurisdiction, to be asserted in a new action in a proper state court if the now applicable statute of limitations would not have barred the original action and if the new action is brought "within thirty days after dismissal" or within such longer period as might be available under applicable state law? See Study of the Division of Jurisdiction Between State and Federal Courts § 1386(b) commentary at 373–74, 453–57 (Am. Law Inst. 1969); cf. Jinks v. Richland Cty., 538 U.S. 456, 123 S.Ct. 1667 (2003) (upholding similar federal tolling statute for certain state-law claims).

(2) What would you think of a federal statute setting up a cutoff date in any federal action after which the court could not consider, on its own motion or at the instance of any party, a newly raised question of jurisdiction over the subject matter, unless (a) a party is raising the issue and is relying upon facts the party did not know, and could not be expected to have discovered in the exercise of reasonable diligence, at an earlier stage in the proceedings, or is relying on a change in jurisdictional law, or (b) there was collusion between opposing parties in concealing a known jurisdictional defect? Would it be constitutional for a federal court so to proceed to adjudication of a case for which there was in fact no subject-matter jurisdiction under the congressional grants of jurisdiction? See Study of the Division of Jurisdiction Between State and Federal Courts § 1386(a) commentary at 366–73 (Am. Law Inst. 1969). How about where there was no subject-matter jurisdiction under the Constitution itself? See Jessica Berch, Waiving Jurisdiction, 36 Pace L.Rev. 853 (2016).

Means and Ends

"The mechanism of law—what courts are to deal with which causes and subject to what conditions—cannot be dissociated from the ends that law subserves. So-called jurisdictional questions treated in isolation from the purposes of the legal system to which they relate become barren pedantry. After all, procedure is instrumental; it is the means of effectuating policy. Particularly true is this of the federal courts. The Judiciary Acts, the needs which urged their enactment, the compromises which they embodied, the consequences which they entailed, the changed conditions which in turn modified them, are the outcome of continuous interaction of traditional, political, social, and economic forces. In common with other courts, the federal courts are means for securing justice through law. But in addition and transcending this in importance, the legislation governing the structure and function of the federal judicial system is one means of providing the accommodations necessary to the operation of a federal government. The happy relation of States to Nation—constituting as it does our central political problem—is to no small extent dependent upon the wisdom with which the scope and limits of the federal courts are determined." Felix Frankfurter & James M. Landis, The Business of the Supreme Court 2 (1927).

"The law of federal courts in general, and judicial federalism in particular, is especially vulnerable to the charge that law is merely politics by another name. It is an area where decisions often have substantive implications, yet those implications are oblique, indirect, and uncertain. In addition, the rulings can readily be explained in neutral terms, no matter what their real motivation. Furthermore, much of the doctrine is so recondite that the average person, even the average lawyer, is never quite sure what is going on in a federal courts opinion. For many judges of all political stripes, the temptation to manipulate jurisdictional principles to serve substantive ends, while concealing the dirty deed behind a cloud of Federalist or Nationalist rhetoric, is too great to resist. This happens often enough to justify the assertion that naked politics explains most of the law of judicial federalism." Michael Wells, Rhetoric and Reality in the Law of Federal Courts: Professor Fallon's Faulty Premise, 6 Const. Comment. 367, 381–82 (1989).

———

Section 2.   Federal Questions

Federal question jurisdiction rests on the first clause of Article III, Section 2 of the Constitution. What is the meaning of the term "arising under" that there appears? The Supreme Court, early on, sweepingly construed it to cover all cases of which a federal question forms an "ingredient." Osborn v. Bank of the United States, 22 U.S. (9 Wheat.) 738 (1824) (Marshall, C.J.) (holding that the "arising under" language of Article III authorized a then-existing statute bestowing jurisdiction on the federal courts over all actions brought by the federally chartered bank, because any such action would have as an ingredient the minor federal question of whether the bank under its charter had the power to sue).

Congress for the most part tracked the constitutional language in the Act of March 3, 1875, ch. 137, § 1, 18 Stat. 470, 470, the statute that really for the first time gave the federal courts in general terms original jurisdiction over federal question cases. That Act, with no changes of true substance, now appears as 28 U.S.C. § 1331. What is the meaning of the term "arising under" that there delineates the original jurisdiction? Courts have construed it much more narrowly than the same constitutional language. The courts have read a series of restrictions into the statutory language. In fact, we have already seen one such restriction, the well-pleaded complaint rule, in the first Louisville & Nashville Railroad Co. v. Mottley case.

On the one hand, reading Article III expansively is desirable, because Congress thereby retains the power to bestow original jurisdiction over special kinds of cases that present a need for federal jurisdiction but possess merely a federal ingredient, and because the appellate jurisdiction of the Supreme Court thereby remains broad enough to cover all state cases that finally turn upon an issue of federal law. On the other hand, reading § 1331 narrowly is defensible, because Congress probably did not intend to inundate the lower federal courts with all the cases having a mere federal ingredient.

At any rate, there is an accepted difference in scope between the constitutional and the statutory language. Indeed, we have already observed that difference in the second Louisville & Nashville Railroad Co. v. Mottley case, when the Supreme Court ultimately exercised its appellate jurisdiction over federal questions to review an issue of federal law decided in state court, even though it had earlier held that the issue of federal law did not support original federal question jurisdiction. The restrictions read into § 1331 make it narrower than the same language in Article III.

Besides the well-pleaded complaint rule, what are the other restrictions that the courts have read into "arising under" in § 1331? One critical restriction deals with the relationship of the case to its federal element. It is clear, as already suggested, that to satisfy the statute the federal element must be more than a mere ingredient. Beyond that, it is difficult to be precise—no single definition that would encompass all the decided cases is evident. But some have nevertheless attempted a formulation. A famous one is that of Justice Holmes, who argued: "A suit arises under the law that creates the cause of action."[a] This test yields many correct answers: for important examples, an action for patent

---

[a]   Am. Well Works Co. v. Layne & Bowler Co., 241 U.S. 257, 260, 36 S.Ct. 585, 586 (1916).

infringement does arise under federal law, but an action to recover contractual royalties for use of a patent does not.

There are problem cases, such as Shoshone Mining Co. v. Rutter, 177 U.S. 505, 20 S.Ct. 726 (1900) (holding that federal jurisdiction does not exist for suit to determine right to possession of mining claim; a federal statute authorized this type of suit, but directed that local law should govern the rights involved). Still, one can be fairly confident that a claim created by federal law falls within § 1331. One should be less confident that a claim created by state law falls outside § 1331. The courts recognize exceptional cases, such as in Smith v. Kansas City Title & Trust Co., 255 U.S. 180, 41 S.Ct. 243 (1921) (holding that federal jurisdiction exists for suit by a trust company's shareholder to enjoin the trust company from investing in certain federal bonds; state law limited permissible investment to legal securities, but plaintiff claimed that the federal statute authorizing the bonds' issuance was unconstitutional). In order for a state-law claim to fall within § 1331, the test now appears to impose three requirements: "does a state-law claim [1] necessarily raise a stated federal issue, [2] actually disputed and substantial, which a federal forum may entertain [3] without disturbing any congressionally approved balance of federal and state judicial responsibilities." Grable & Sons Metal Prods., Inc. v. Darue Eng'g & Mfg., 545 U.S. 308, 314, 125 S.Ct. 2363, 2368 (2005).

Therefore, an accurate overall formulation would necessarily be fuzzier that that of Holmes. Professor Mishkin's definition in the leading article on the subject is a "claim founded 'directly' upon federal law."[b] Consequently, the American Law Institute, faced with the jumble of cases, did not attempt definition but instead retained the "arising under" term.[c]

Question: (3) It has been argued that this absence of a precise definition is an advantage, because it frees the courts to determine the jurisdictional point on the basis of pragmatic considerations, such as: "the extent of the caseload increase for federal trial courts if jurisdiction is recognized; the extent to which cases of this class will, in practice, turn on issues of state or federal law; the extent of the necessity for an expert federal tribunal to handle issues of federal law that do arise; the extent of the necessity for a sympathetic federal tribunal in cases of this class." William Cohen, The Broken Compass: The Requirement That a Case Arise "Directly" Under Federal Law, 115 U.Pa.L.Rev. 890, 916 (1967). The Supreme Court now seems receptive to some version of this argument. See Grable & Sons Metal Prods., Inc. v. Darue Eng'g & Mfg., 545 U.S. 308, 312, 125 S.Ct. 2363, 2367 (2005) (justifying "resort to the experience, solicitude, and hope of uniformity that a federal forum offers" on important federal issues). What do you think of such an approach? Cf. Jonathan Remy Nash, On the Efficient

---

[b]   Paul J. Mishkin, The Federal "Question" in the District Courts, 53 Colum.L.Rev. 157, 168 (1953).

[c]   See Study of the Division of Jurisdiction Between State and Federal Courts § 1311(a) commentary at 178–79 (Am. Law Inst. 1969).

Deployment of Rules and Standards to Define Federal Jurisdiction, 65 Vand.L.Rev. 509 (2012) (arguing that the outer reach of federal jurisdiction should find expression in categorical rules, while federal courts should employ discretionary standards in declining sometimes to exercise the jurisdiction).

———

Bell v. Hood

Supreme Court of the United States, 1946.
327 U.S. 678, 66 S.Ct. 773.

■ MR. JUSTICE BLACK delivered the opinion of the Court.

Petitioners brought this suit [on April 7, 1943] in a federal district court to recover damages in excess of [the then jurisdictional amount for federal question cases of] $3,000 from the respondents who are agents of the Federal Bureau of Investigation. The complaint alleges that the Court's jurisdiction is founded upon federal questions arising under the Fourth and Fifth Amendments. It is alleged that the damages were suffered as a result of the respondents imprisoning the petitioners in violation of their Constitutional right to be free from deprivation of their liberty without due process of law, and subjecting their premises to search and their possessions to seizure, in violation of their Constitutional right to be free from unreasonable searches and seizures.[1]

Respondents moved to dismiss the complaint for failure to state a cause of action for which relief could be granted and for summary judgment on the grounds that the federal agents acted within the scope

---

[1]   The complaint stated in part:

"That on or about the 17th day of December, 1942, defendant R.B. Hood and each of the other defendants, unlawfully conspired with each other to act beyond their authority as said Federal Bureau of Investigation agents and police officers respectively, and agreed that they would abridge the Constitutional rights of the plaintiffs as guaranteed by the Fourth and Fifth Amendments to the Constitution of the United States to be free from the deprivation of liberty and property without due process of law, and to be free from unreasonable searches and seizures, and agreed unlawfully to simultaneously, in the early morning of December 18th, 1942, search the homes of the individual plaintiffs herein without any warrants of search or seizure, and unlawfully to seize the papers, documents and effects of said plaintiffs and of 'Mankind United,' and falsely to imprison the individual plaintiffs by unlawfully arresting some of the individual plaintiffs without a warrant of arrest and unreasonably to delay the taking of all the individual plaintiffs before a committing officer, in order to effectuate the unlawful searches and seizures aforesaid.

"That thereafter, and on the 18th day of December, 1942, . . . the defendants and each of them, in order to carry out the terms and conditions of the illegal conspiracy aforesaid, and solely for the purpose of carrying out said terms and conditions, did arrest and imprison the individual plaintiffs herein, and did search the homes of said plaintiffs, and seize and carry away books, papers and effects of said individual plaintiffs and of said 'Mankind United.' "

. . . .

" . . . by reason of the deprivation of . . . [their] Constitutional rights . . . [plaintiffs had] suffered damages." [For further development of the factual background, see United States v. Bell, 48 F.Supp. 986 (S.D.Cal.1943) (related criminal case involving this pacifist religious cult).—Ed.]

of their authority as officers of the United States and that the searches and seizures were incidental to lawful arrests and were therefore valid. Respondents filed affidavits in support of their motions and petitioners filed counter-affidavits. After hearing the motions the district judge did not pass on them but, on his own motion, dismissed the suit [on March 20, 1944] for want of federal jurisdiction on the ground that this action was not one that " . . . arises under the Constitution or laws of the United States . . ." as required by 28 U.S.C. § 41(1).[d] The Circuit Court of Appeals affirmed on the same ground. 9 Cir., 150 F.2d 96 [(June 7, 1945)]. At the same time it denied a motion made by petitioners asking it to direct the district court to give petitioners leave to amend their complaint in order to make it still more clearly appear that the action was directly grounded on violations of rights alleged to stem from the Fourth and Fifth Amendments. We granted certiorari because of the importance of the jurisdictional issue involved.

Respondents make the following argument in support of the district court's dismissal of the complaint for want of federal jurisdiction. First, they urge that the complaint states a cause of action for the common law tort of trespass made actionable by state law and that it therefore does not raise questions arising "under the Constitution or laws of the United States." Second, to support this contention, respondents maintain that petitioners could not recover under the Constitution or laws of the United States, since the Constitution does not expressly provide for recovery in money damages for violations of the Fourth and Fifth Amendments and Congress has not enacted a statute that does so provide. A mere reading of the complaint refutes the first contention and, as will be seen, the second one is not decisive on the question of jurisdiction of the federal court.

Whether or not the complaint as drafted states a common law action in trespass made actionable by state law, it is clear from the way it was drawn that petitioners seek recovery squarely on the ground that respondents violated the Fourth and Fifth Amendments. It charges that the respondents conspired to do acts prohibited by these amendments and alleges that respondents' conduct pursuant to the conspiracy resulted in damages in excess of $3,000. It cannot be doubted therefore that it was the pleaders' purpose to make violation of these Constitutional provisions the basis of this suit. Before deciding that there is no jurisdiction, the district court must look to the way the complaint is drawn to see if it is drawn so as to claim a right to recover under the Constitution and laws of the United States. For to that extent "the party who brings a suit is master to decide what law he will rely upon, and . . . does determine whether he will bring a 'suit arising under' the . . . [Constitution or laws] of the United States by his declaration or bill." The Fair v. Kohler Die & Specialty Co., 228 U.S. 22, 25, 33 S.Ct. 410, 411. Though the mere failure to set out the federal or Constitutional claims

---

d   Now 28 U.S.C. § 1331.

as specifically as petitioners have done would not always be conclusive against the party bringing the suit, where the complaint, as here, is so drawn as to seek recovery directly under the Constitution or laws of the United States, the federal court, but for two possible exceptions later noted [at the end of the next paragraph], must entertain the suit. . . .

Jurisdiction . . . is not defeated as respondents seem to contend, by the possibility that the averments might fail to state a cause of action on which petitioners could actually recover. For it is well settled that the failure to state a proper cause of action calls for a judgment on the merits and not for a dismissal for want of jurisdiction. Whether the complaint states a cause of action on which relief could be granted is a question of law and just as issues of fact it must be decided after and not before the court has assumed jurisdiction over the controversy. If the court does later exercise its jurisdiction to determine that the allegations in the complaint do not state a ground for relief, then dismissal of the case would be on the merits, not for want of jurisdiction. [Citations omitted.] The previously carved out exceptions are that a suit may sometimes be dismissed for want of jurisdiction [1] where the alleged claim under the Constitution or federal statutes clearly appears to be immaterial and made solely for the purpose of obtaining jurisdiction or [2] where such a claim is wholly insubstantial and frivolous. . . .

But as we have already pointed out the alleged violations of the Constitution here are not immaterial but form rather the sole basis of the relief sought. Nor can we say that the cause of action alleged is so patently without merit as to justify, even under the qualifications noted, the court's dismissal for want of jurisdiction. The Circuit Court of Appeals correctly stated that "the complaint states strong cases, and if the allegations have any foundation in truth, the plaintiffs' legal rights have been ruthlessly violated." Petitioners' complaint asserts that the Fourth and Fifth Amendments guarantee their rights to be free from unauthorized and unjustified imprisonment and from unreasonable searches and seizures. They claim that respondents' invasion of these rights caused the damages for which they seek to recover and point further to 28 U.S.C. § 41(1), which authorizes the federal district courts to try "suits of a civil nature" where the matter in controversy "arises under the Constitution or laws of the United States," whether these are suits in "equity" or at "law."[e] Petitioners argue that this statute authorizes the Court to entertain this action at law and to grant recovery for the damages allegedly sustained. Respondents contend that the Constitutional provisions here involved are prohibitions against the federal government as a government and that 28 U.S.C. § 41(1) does not authorize recovery in money damages in suits against unauthorized officials who according to respondents are in the same position as individual trespassers.

---

[e]   Compare the language of the present provision, § 1331.

Respondents' contention does not show that petitioners' cause is insubstantial or frivolous, and the complaint does in fact raise serious questions, both of law and fact, which the district court can decide only after it has assumed jurisdiction over the controversy. The issue of law is whether federal courts can grant money recovery for damages said to have been suffered as a result of federal officers violating the Fourth and Fifth Amendments. That question has never been specifically decided by this Court. That the issue thus raised has sufficient merit to warrant exercise of federal jurisdiction for purposes of adjudicating it can be seen from the cases where this Court has sustained the jurisdiction of the district courts in suits brought to recover damages for depriving a citizen of the right to vote in violation of the Constitution. And it is established practice for this Court to sustain the jurisdiction of federal courts to issue injunctions to protect rights safeguarded by the Constitution and to restrain individual state officers from doing what the 14th Amendment forbids the state to do. Moreover, where federally protected rights have been invaded, it has been the rule from the beginning that courts will be alert to adjust their remedies so as to grant the necessary relief. And it is also well settled that where legal rights have been invaded, and a federal statute provides for a general right to sue for such invasion, federal courts may use any available remedy to make good the wrong done. Whether the petitioners are entitled to recover depends upon an interpretation of 28 U.S.C. § 41(1), and on a determination of the scope of the Fourth and Fifth Amendments' protection from unreasonable searches and deprivations of liberty without due process of law. Thus, the right of the petitioners to recover under their complaint will be sustained if the Constitution and laws of the United States are given one construction and will be defeated if they are given another. For this reason the district court has jurisdiction. Gully v. First National Bank, 299 U.S. 109, 112, 113, 57 S.Ct. 96, 97; Smith v. Kansas City Title & Trust Co., 255 U.S. 180, 199, 200, 41 S.Ct. 243, 244, 245.

Reversed.

■ [The concurring opinion of JUSTICE REED is omitted.]

■ MR. JUSTICE JACKSON took no part in the consideration or decision of this case.

■ MR. CHIEF JUSTICE STONE and MR. JUSTICE BURTON, dissenting.

The district court is without jurisdiction as a federal court unless the complaint states a cause of action arising under the Constitution or laws of the United States. Whether the complaint states such a cause of action is for the court, not the pleader, to say. When the provision of the Constitution or federal statute affords a remedy which may in some circumstances be availed of by a plaintiff, the fact that his pleading does not bring him within that class as one entitled to the remedy, goes to the sufficiency of the pleading and not to the jurisdiction. [Citations omitted.] But where as here, neither the constitutional provision nor any act of Congress affords a remedy to any person, the mere assertion by a plaintiff that he is entitled to such a remedy cannot be said to satisfy jurisdictional requirements. Hence we think that the courts below rightly decided that the district court was without jurisdiction because no cause of action under the Constitution or laws of the United States was stated.

The only effect of holding, as the Court does, that jurisdiction is conferred by the pleader's unfounded assertion that he is one who can have a remedy for damages arising under the Fourth and Fifth Amendments is to transfer to the federal court the trial of the allegations of trespass to person and property, which is a cause of action arising wholly under state law. For even though it be decided that petitioners have no right to damages under the Constitution, the district court will be required to pass upon the question whether the facts stated by petitioners give rise to a cause of action for trespass under state law. See Hurn v. Oursler, 289 U.S. 238, 53 S.Ct. 586.

———

Questions: (4) In a case such as Bell v. Hood, what difference does it make whether defendants faced with a meritless federal claim win on Rule 12(b)(1) grounds or by means of Rule 12(b)(6)? Would you not expect the defendants to prefer a decision on the merits under the latter Rule? What then were Hood et al. up to?

(5) A building contractor brings an action in federal district court against certain unions, alleging that their strike aimed at compelling him to employ union labor is a conspiracy to restrain interstate commerce in violation of the antitrust laws. This legal contention, once an open question, has been squarely rejected by two prior Supreme Court cases. The plaintiff invokes jurisdiction on the ground that the case arises under federal antitrust law, but the defendants move for dismissal under Rule 12(b)(1). What decision on the motion? See Levering & Garrigues Co. v. Morrin, 289 U.S. 103, 53 S.Ct. 549 (1933) (grant).

———

SECTION 3. SUPPLEMENTAL JURISDICTION

Federal district courts can hear some state claims that are related to claims within the federal jurisdiction. Because the pertinent doctrines thus allow a federal court to hear a claim that would otherwise be only a state claim, they effectively constitute a separate basis, or "head," of federal jurisdiction. But they do require as a support some claim that comes within a more traditional head of federal jurisdiction, such as federal question or diversity jurisdiction, from which they can hang.

———

PENDENT JURISDICTION

Backing up a bit, it is clear that if federal question jurisdiction exists for a "claim," the district court has the power to decide not only the federal question but also any other questions, be they federal or state in nature, the resolution of which is necessary to decision on the claim. After all, a court of original jurisdiction must have this power to function practically, because such a court decides whole cases and not just isolated questions (as recognized in the constitutional reference to "cases" and in the statutory references to "civil actions"). So, for example, the Osborn case indicated that if the Bank of the United States brought a claim on an ordinary contract, federal question jurisdiction would exist, and moreover the federal court would be empowered to decide all nonfederal-law questions it ran into when disposing of the contract claim on the merits.

According to a thorough researcher, old English cases had recognized the need for this judicial power. Indeed, from this need, the old cases built a judge-made doctrine that allowed a plaintiff to assert an additional claim against the defendant that would otherwise be beyond the court's subject-matter jurisdiction but that should be entertained in the interests of fairness and the like as an incident to deciding the claim within its jurisdiction. Such notions migrated to our young country and emerged in numerous American cases. See Mary Brigid McManamon, Dispelling the Myths of Pendent and Ancillary Jurisdiction: The Ramifications of a Revised History, 46 Wash. & Lee L.Rev. 863 (1989).

Hurn v. Oursler, 289 U.S. 238, 53 S.Ct. 586 (1933), crystallized from these cases the federal doctrine called pendent jurisdiction. This doctrine empowered a district court, given jurisdiction over a federal question claim, to entertain the plaintiff's additional state claim against the defendants that did not independently satisfy federal jurisdictional requirements. The Hurn plaintiffs joined three claims in the same complaint: (1) for infringement of the copyright in a play entitled "The Evil Hour," a claim arising under a federal statute; (2) for unfair competition in unauthorized use of the same play, which would be a claim arising under state law; and (3) for unfair competition through interference with the plaintiffs' rights in an uncopyrighted, revised version of the play, which would also be a claim arising under state law. At the close of the evidence in a bench trial, the trial court dismissed that first claim for failure of proof of infringement and the other two claims for lack of jurisdiction. The Supreme Court held that it was error so to dismiss the second claim, saying: "The distinction to be observed is between a case where two distinct grounds in support of a single cause of action are alleged, one only of which presents a federal question, and a case where two separate and distinct causes of action are alleged, one only of which is federal in character." On this test, the Court held that the claim for unfair competition with regard to the copyrighted play constituted the same cause of action as the copyright infringement claim and hence required decision on the merits, but the claim as to the uncopyrighted revision of the play was a separate and distinct cause of action and hence was properly dismissed for lack of jurisdiction.

Question: (6) Upon remand, the district court in Bell v. Hood granted defendants' motion to dismiss the complaint on the ground that it failed to state a claim upon which relief could be granted, 71 F.Supp. 813 (S.D.Cal.1947). In doing so, it first decided that no federal claim was stated,[f] and it then concluded that consequently the pendent state trespass claim now being urged should be dismissed for lack of jurisdiction. Was this latter holding consistent with Hurn v. Oursler?

The lower courts had trouble in applying the Hurn "single cause of action" test, especially after the liberal joinder provisions of the Federal Rules came onto the scene. Although the desirability of the Hurn extension of jurisdiction seemed fairly apparent, some courts would take jurisdiction of the state claim only when there was a virtually complete identity of facts in the two claims.

In 1948 Congress purportedly codified the Hurn holding in § 1338(b) of title 28. The codification aggravated the difficulties instead of solving them. In the first place, the statute refers to a state "claim ... when joined with a substantial and related [federal] claim." So the statute, like the Federal Rules, avoids the term "cause of action," which was the touchstone of the Hurn test. But does "claim" in the statute mean the same as "cause of action"? What meaning is to be given to "substantial" and to "related"? The statutory formulation is broader than Hurn's, but how much broader? In the second place, the statute refers only to a claim of unfair competition joined to a claim under certain federal laws. Here, the subsequent cases were clear in recognizing that the statute did not abolish pendent jurisdiction in other areas of law.

UNITED MINE WORKERS v. GIBBS, 383 U.S. 715, 86 S.Ct. 1130 (1966). Plaintiff sued the union in a federal district court, alleging that the union improperly interfered in his contractual relations with the coal company that employed him. He claimed damage from secondary boycotts under § 303 of the Labor Management Relations Act, 29 U.S.C. § 187, and also damage from the same unlawful acts under the common law of the state. The trial court dismissed the federal claim on judgment

---

[f]   The Supreme Court has since decided, contrary to the district court in Bell v. Hood, that violation of the Fourth Amendment by federal agents acting under the color of their authority can give rise to a federal cause of action within 28 U.S.C. § 1331 for damages resulting from their unconstitutional conduct. Bivens v. Six Unknown Named Agents of Fed. Bureau of Narcotics, 403 U.S. 388, 91 S.Ct. 1999 (1971). Justice Black, who wrote the opinion in Bell v. Hood, dissented, along with Chief Justice Burger and Justice Blackmun.

Later, the Supreme Court decided that violation of the Due Process Clause of the Fifth Amendment similarly can give rise to a federal cause of action for damages within § 1331. Davis v. Passman, 442 U.S. 228, 99 S.Ct. 2264 (1979). But more recently, the Supreme Court has backed away from Bivens' message. See, e.g., Minneci v. Pollard, 565 U.S. 118, 132 S.Ct. 617 (2012) (refusing a Bivens action against employees of a privately operated federal prison for violating the Eighth Amendment's prohibition against cruel and unusual punishment, and listing multiple instances where the Court in recent years has refused Bivens actions for other constitutional violations).

n.o.v., but it allowed the plaintiff's verdict on the state claim to stand. The court of appeals affirmed.

In likewise holding that the court had properly entertained jurisdiction over the pendent state claim, Justice Brennan for the Supreme Court first characterized the prevailing approach of lower courts to pendent jurisdiction as "unnecessarily grudging." Rephrasing the inquiry as whether the relationship between the federal question claim and the state claim was close enough to permit "the conclusion that the entire action before the court comprises but one constitutional 'case,'" he then explained: "The state and federal claims must derive from a common nucleus of operative fact. But if, considered without regard for their federal or state character, a plaintiff's claims are such that he would ordinarily be expected to try them all in one judicial proceeding, then, assuming substantiality of the federal issues, there is *power* in federal courts to hear the whole.

"That power need not be exercised in every case in which it is found to exist. It has consistently been recognized that pendent jurisdiction is a doctrine of discretion, not of plaintiff's right. Its justification lies in considerations of judicial economy, convenience and fairness to litigants; if these are not present a federal court should hesitate to exercise jurisdiction over state claims, even though bound to apply state law to them, Erie R. Co. v. Tompkins, 304 U.S. 64, 58 S.Ct. 817. Needless decisions of state law should be avoided both as a matter of comity and to promote justice between the parties, by procuring for them a surer-footed reading of applicable law. . . . [I]f it appears that the state issues substantially predominate, whether in terms of proof, of the scope of the issues raised, or of the comprehensiveness of the remedy sought, the state claims may be dismissed without prejudice and left for resolution to state tribunals. There may, on the other hand, be situations in which the state claim is so closely tied to questions of federal policy that the argument for exercise of pendent jurisdiction is particularly strong. In the present case, for example, the allowable scope of the state claim implicates the federal doctrine of pre-emption; while this interrelationship does not create statutory federal question jurisdiction, Louisville & N.R. Co. v. Mottley, 211 U.S. 149, 29 S.Ct. 42, its existence is relevant to the exercise of discretion. Finally, there may be reasons independent of jurisdictional considerations, such as the likelihood of jury confusion in treating divergent legal theories of relief, that would justify separating state and federal claims for trial, Fed.Rule Civ.Proc. 42(b). If so, jurisdiction should ordinarily be refused.

"The question of power will ordinarily be resolved on the pleadings. But the issue whether pendent jurisdiction has been properly assumed is one which remains open throughout the litigation."

———

Questions: (7) Considering the *power* of a federal court under Gibbs to hear a state claim pendent to a claim arising under federal law, what constitutional arguments could have been made against the existence of such power? What arguments could have been made on the basis of the various congressional grants of federal question jurisdiction?

(8) Considering the role of *discretion* in choosing under Gibbs whether or not to hear such a state claim, is it desirable that the federal courts should have discretion so to define their own jurisdiction? See generally Gene R. Shreve, Pragmatism Without Politics—A Half Measure of Authority for Jurisdictional Common Law, 1991 BYU L.Rev. 767.

––––––––

ANCILLARY JURISDICTION

Having the same historical roots as pendent jurisdiction, ancillary jurisdiction was another judge-made doctrine that allowed a party to assert an additional claim that would otherwise be beyond the court's subject-matter jurisdiction but that should be entertained in the interests of fairness and the like as an incident to deciding the claim within its jurisdiction.

Ancillary jurisdiction was classically a doctrine of necessity. A court of original jurisdiction must have the power to handle certain incidental matters in order to function as a court of justice. For example, in Freeman v. Howe, 65 U.S. (24 How.) 450 (1861), the Supreme Court said that a federal court had jurisdiction over a claim by mortgagees to the mortgaged property in the form of railroad cars—where that property had previously been brought under the court's control by attachment in a diversity action to which the endangered mortgagees were not parties— even though there was no independent jurisdictional ground for the nondiverse mortgagees' claim. The reasoning was that a state court could not interfere with the federal control of the property, and this in turn necessitated a federal forum for the mortgagees in order not to leave them remediless. Accordingly, the federal court would hear their claim under the theory that it was "ancillary and dependent, supplementary merely to the original suit."

The doctrine perceptibly shifted gears in Moore v. New York Cotton Exchange, 270 U.S. 593, 46 S.Ct. 367 (1926), where the Court seemed to embrace a doctrine of convenience. In this federal antitrust suit complaining of the Exchange's restrictions on access to its cotton price quotations, the Exchange counterclaimed seeking an injunction against the plaintiff's wrongfully obtaining those quotations. The counterclaim fell within the compulsory counterclaim provision of the Equity Rules of 1912. Although there was no independent jurisdictional ground for that counterclaim, the Court held that it fell within the federal court's ancillary jurisdiction.

This embrace of convenient jurisdiction for procedurally permissible claims expanded the doctrine of ancillary jurisdiction. Its scope further increased, albeit to an uncertain extent, with the broadening of provisions for joinder of claims and parties under the Federal Rules of Civil Procedure. Thus, the doctrine's historical point of departure and the subsequent accommodation to expansionist pressures justified calling ancillary jurisdiction a "child of necessity and sire of confusion." Jay C. Baker, Note, Federal Practice: Jurisdiction of Third-Party Claims, 11 Okla.L.Rev. 326, 329 (1958).

———

REVERE COPPER & BRASS INC. v. AETNA CASUALTY & SURETY CO., 426 F.2d 709 (5th Cir.1970). Revere Copper & Brass, a Maryland corporation, brought suit in federal court against Aetna, surety on performance bonds on construction contracts, alleging that Aetna's principal, a Maryland corporation named Fuller, had failed to perform its obligations under the contracts. There was diversity of citizenship between Revere and Aetna, and Revere sought to recover $2,045,000. Aetna denied Revere's allegations and impleaded Fuller under Rule 14(a), alleging that Fuller had agreed to indemnify Aetna for all losses from its suretyship. Fuller admitted Aetna's allegations, but Fuller denied the allegations in Revere's complaint and made claim against Revere, seeking to recover $1,328,880 on the basis of the same disputed contracts.

Revere moved to dismiss Fuller's claim against it on the ground that there was no diversity of citizenship between them. The district court found the claim to be within its ancillary jurisdiction, and it therefore denied Revere's motion. An interlocutory appeal under 28 U.S.C. § 1292(b) followed, and the court of appeals affirmed:

"The theoretical basis which underlies the modern doctrine of ancillary jurisdiction appears to be fairly well settled. . . .

"The exact criteria to be used to detect the presence of ancillary jurisdiction, however, is more elusive. The leading case on the modern doctrine of ancillarity is Moore v. New York Cotton Exchange, 270 U.S. 593, 46 S.Ct. 367, 70 L.Ed. 750 (1926), which held that a compulsory counterclaim under old Equity Rule 30 need not be supported by an independent basis of federal jurisdiction, but was ancillary to the main cause of action since it arose out of the transaction which was the subject matter of the original suit. In defining what it meant by the word 'transaction', the Court said:

'Transaction' is a word of flexible meaning. It may comprehend a series of many occurrences, depending not so much upon the immediateness of their connection as upon their *logical relationship*.

. . . .

"It would be fair to say, therefore, that a claim is ancillary when it bears a logical relationship to the aggregate core of operative facts which constitutes the main claim over which the court has an independent basis of federal jurisdiction. However, the type of relationship contemplated by the phrase 'logical relationship' remains somewhat clouded. Perhaps the simplest way to determine the type of the nexus that must necessarily exist between the main claim and another claim for the other claim to be considered ancillary is to examine the present extent of the application of the doctrine to the various devices of the Federal Rules allowing joinder of claims.

"While it is well established that a compulsory counterclaim under Rule 13(a) is within the ancillary jurisdiction since it necessarily arises out of the same transaction or occurrence as the original claim, Moore v. New York Cotton Exchange, supra, a permissive counterclaim under Rule 13(b) requires an independent ground of federal jurisdiction since it does not arise out of the same transaction or occurrence as the original claim, Camper & Nicholsons, Ltd. v. Yacht 'Fontainebleau II', S.D.Fla., 1968, 292 F.Supp. 734, except where a setoff is involved. Fraser v. Astra Steamship Corp., S.D.N.Y., 1955, 18 F.R.D. 240; [other citation omitted]. Contra, Robinson Bros. & Co. v. Tygart Steel Products Co., W.D.Pa., 1949, 9 F.R.D. 468.[7] Crossclaims under Rule 13(g) are considered ancillary since, under the Rule, they must arise 'out of the transaction or occurrence that is the subject matter either of the original action or of a counterclaim therein or relating to any property that is the subject matter of the original action.' Childress v. Cook, 5 Cir., 1957, 245 F.2d 798. An impleader action under Rule 14(a) is considered ancillary even though such an action does not, as a general rule, directly involve the aggregate of operative facts upon which the original claim is based, but arises out of that claim in the sense that the impleader action, such as the action for indemnity here brought by Aetna against Fuller, would not exist without the threat of liability arising out of the original claim. Waylander-Peterson Co. v. Great Northern Ry. Co., 8 Cir., 1953, 201 F.2d 408; Lesnik v. Public Industrials Corp., 2 Cir., 1944, 144 F.2d 968. Likewise, intervention as of right under Rule 24(a), available 'when the applicant claims an interest relating to the property or transaction which is the subject of the action and he is so situated that the disposition of the action may as a practical matter impair or impede his ability to protect that interest, unless the applicant's interest is adequately represented by existing parties,' is regarded as ancillary to the original claim and need not be supported by an independent ground of federal jurisdiction. Formulabs, Incorporated v. Hartley Pen Company, 9 Cir.,

---

[7]   The treatment of permissive counterclaims involving set-offs is an exception to the logical relationship test in that they are independent from the original claim and can be said to be ancillary only in the sense that they are limited by the amount of the original claim. The ancillary status given set-offs is best explained historically from their source in English statute, 2 Geo. 2, c. 22, § 13 (1729). See, Note "Diversity Requirements In Multi-Party Litigation", [58 Colum.L.Rev. 548, 553–55 (1958); see also William A. Fletcher, "Common Nucleus of Operative Fact" and Defensive Set-Off: Beyond the Gibbs Test, 74 Ind.L.J. 171 (1998)—Ed.].

1963, 318 F.2d 485, 492, cert. den. 375 U.S. 945, 84 S.Ct. 352, 11 L.Ed.2d 275.

"From the application of the doctrine of ancillary jurisdiction to these joinder devices, it appears that a claim has a logical relationship to the original claim if it *arises* out of the same aggregate of operative facts as the original claim in two senses: (1) that the same aggregate of operative facts serves as the basis of both claims; or (2) that the aggregate core of facts upon which the original claim rests activates additional legal rights in a party defendant that would otherwise remain dormant.

"Before proceeding, another aspect of the Moore decision, supra, must be mentioned, and that is the Court's concern with the need to provide complete relief to the counterclaiming defendant. 270 U.S. at 610, 46 S.Ct. 367, 70 L.Ed. 750. A cursory review of the joinder situations to which ancillary jurisdiction is applied reveals that, generally, it is made available to litigants in a defensive posture, who would otherwise be prevented or greatly burdened in adequately protecting their interests. There is much to be said for allowing parties who are involuntarily brought into federal court to defend against a claim, or who must be allowed to intervene in a federal action as a defendant to secure their interests, to assert all their claims arising out of the controversy in one proceeding and that this is, or ought to be, one of the factors to be considered in determining the existence of ancillary jurisdiction. See, Note, 'Diversity Requirements in Multiparty Litigation', supra, n.[7], at 561.

"It is easily seen that Fuller's claim arises out of the aggregate of operative facts which forms the basis of Revere's claim in such a way to put their logical relationship beyond doubt. The two claims are but two sides of the same coin. The construction was not completed before the time provided in the two contracts. If Revere is not responsible for the delay, as Fuller alleges, Fuller must at least be guilty of breach of contract, not to mention the other allegations of fault in Revere's complaint. To paraphrase the Supreme Court in Moore v. New York Cotton Exchange, supra: so close is the connection between the case sought to be stated in Revere's complaint and that set up in Fuller's Rule 14(a) counterclaim that it only needs the failure of the former to establish the foundation for the latter.

"Not only is the parallel between a Rule 14(a) counterclaim and a compulsory counterclaim under Rule 13(a) so close as to be persuasive on the question of ancillarity, the parallel between the instant case and cases dealing with the ability of an intervenor of right under Rule 24(a) to counterclaim against the original plaintiff without an independent basis of federal jurisdiction removes any substantial doubt. It is well established that a contractor who has agreed to indemnify his surety on a performance bond can intervene as a party defendant as of right in a suit on the performance bond against the surety and then assert his counterclaim against the plaintiff, even in the absence of an independent ground of federal jurisdiction. United States, to Use and Benefit of Foster Wheeler Corp. v. American Surety Co., 2 Cir., 1944, 142 F.2d 726; Coleman Capital Corp. v. Fidelity & Deposit Co. of Md., S.D.N.Y., 1967, 43 F.R.D. 407. It would be anomalous to hold that Fuller could have asserted its counterclaim against Revere free of any jurisdictional impediment if it had taken the initiative of intervening, and yet hold that since Fuller was brought into this action involuntarily as a third-party defendant, its counterclaim must satisfy the requirements of strict diversity and thus fail.

. . . .

"Revere also argues that the recognition of ancillary jurisdiction in the present situation would be an unwarranted extension of federal diversity jurisdiction in contravention of Rule 82, F.R.C.P., and the general trend to restrict this head [of] jurisdiction. [Citations omitted.] In answer to this argument, it should be noted that the Federal Rules do not expand ancillary jurisdiction, but provide opportunities for involving the doctrine, which, as has been seen, was already well established when the rules became effective, in additional situations."

––––––––

Question: (9) What should happen to an ancillary claim if the original claim on which federal jurisdiction is based is disposed of by voluntary dismissal? by settlement? by summary judgment? by dismissal for failure to state a claim upon which relief can be granted? See Stamford Bd. of Educ. v. Stamford Educ. Ass'n, 697 F.2d 70, 72–73 (2d Cir.1982) (recognizing role for discretion, with timing and nature of dismissal being factors). What if the dismissal of the original claim is for lack of subject-matter jurisdiction? See Estate of Harshman v. Jackson Hole Mountain Resort Corp., 379 F.3d 1161 (10th Cir.2004) (requiring dismissal of ancillary claim).

––––––––

Owen Equipment & Erection Co. v. Kroger

Supreme Court of the United States, 1978.
437 U.S. 365, 98 S.Ct. 2396.

■ MR. JUSTICE STEWART delivered the opinion of the Court.

In an action in which federal jurisdiction is based on diversity of citizenship, may the plaintiff assert a claim against a third-party defendant when there is no independent basis for federal jurisdiction over that claim? The Court of Appeals for the Eighth Circuit held in this case that such a claim is within the ancillary jurisdiction of the federal courts. We granted certiorari, 434 U.S. 1008, 98 S.Ct. 715, because this decision conflicts with several recent decisions of other Courts of Appeals.

I

On January 18, 1972, James Kroger was electrocuted when the boom of a steel crane next to which he was walking came too close to a high tension electric power line. The respondent (his widow, who is the administratrix of his estate) filed a wrongful death action in the United States District Court for the District of Nebraska against the Omaha Public Power District (OPPD). Her complaint alleged that OPPD's negligent construction, maintenance and operation of the power line had caused Kroger's death. Federal jurisdiction was based on diversity of citizenship, since the respondent was a citizen of Iowa and OPPD was a Nebraska corporation.

OPPD then filed a third-party complaint pursuant to Fed.Rule Civ.Proc. 14(a) against the petitioner, Owen Equipment and Erection Company (Owen), alleging that the crane was owned and operated by Owen, and that Owen's negligence had been the proximate cause of Kroger's death.[3] OPPD later moved for summary judgment on the respondent's complaint against it. While this motion was pending, the respondent was granted leave to file an amended complaint naming Owen as an additional defendant. Thereafter, the District Court granted OPPD's motion for summary judgment in an unreported opinion. The case thus went to trial between the respondent and the petitioner alone.

The respondent's amended complaint alleged that Owen was "a Nebraska corporation with its principal place of business in Nebraska." Owen's answer admitted that it was "a corporation organized and existing under the Laws of the State of Nebraska," and denied every other allegation of the complaint. On the third day of trial, however, it was disclosed that the petitioner's principal place of business was in Iowa, not Nebraska,[5] and that the petitioner and the respondent were thus both citizens of Iowa. The petitioner then moved to dismiss the complaint for lack of jurisdiction. The District Court reserved decision on the motion, and the jury thereafter returned a verdict in favor of the respondent. In an unreported opinion issued after the trial, the District Court denied the petitioner's motion to dismiss the complaint.

---

[3]   Under Rule 14(a), a third-party defendant may not be impleaded merely because he may be liable to the *plaintiff*. [Citations omitted.] While the third-party complaint in this case alleged merely that Owen's negligence caused Kroger's death, and the basis of Owen's alleged liability *to OPPD* is nowhere spelled out, OPPD evidently relied upon the state common-law right of contribution among joint tortfeasors. See Dairyland Ins. Co. v. Mumert, 212 N.W.2d 436, 438 (Iowa); Best v. Yerkes, 247 Iowa 800, 77 N.W.2d 23. The petitioner has never challenged the propriety of the third-party complaint as such.

[5]   The problem apparently was one of geography. Although the Missouri River generally marks the boundary between Iowa and Nebraska, Carter Lake, Iowa, where the accident occurred and where Owen had its main office, lies west of the river, adjacent to Omaha, Neb. Apparently the river once avulsed at one of its bends, cutting Carter Lake off from the rest of Iowa.

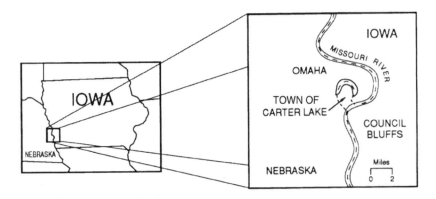

The judgment was affirmed on appeal. 558 F.2d 417. The Court of Appeals held that under this Court's decision in Mine Workers v. Gibbs, 383 U.S. 715, 86 S.Ct. 1130, the District Court had jurisdictional power, in its discretion, to adjudicate the respondent's claim against the petitioner because that claim arose from the "core of 'operative facts' giving rise to both [respondent's] claim against OPPD and OPPD's claim against Owen." 558 F.2d at 424. It further held that the District Court had properly exercised its discretion in proceeding to decide the case even after summary judgment had been granted to OPPD, because the petitioner had concealed its Iowa citizenship from the respondent. . . .

II

It is undisputed that there was no independent basis of federal jurisdiction over the respondent's state-law tort action against the petitioner, since both are citizens of Iowa. And although Fed.Rule Civ.Proc. 14(a) permits a plaintiff to assert a claim against a third-party defendant, . . . it does not purport to say whether or not such a claim requires an independent basis of federal jurisdiction. Indeed, it could not determine that question, since it is axiomatic that the Federal Rules of Civil Procedure do not create or withdraw federal jurisdiction.

In affirming the District Court's judgment, the Court of Appeals relied upon the doctrine of ancillary jurisdiction, whose contours it believed were defined by this Court's holding in Mine Workers v. Gibbs, supra. The Gibbs case differed from this one in that it involved pendent jurisdiction, which concerns the resolution of a plaintiff's federal and state law claims against a single defendant in one action. By contrast, in this case there was no claim based upon substantive federal law, but rather state-law tort claims against two different defendants. Nonetheless, the Court of Appeals was correct in perceiving that Gibbs and this case are two species of the same generic problem: Under what circumstances may a federal court hear and decide a state-law claim arising between citizens of the same State?[8] But we believe that the

---

[8]   No more than in Aldinger v. Howard, 427 U.S. 1, 96 S.Ct. 2413, is it necessary to determine here "whether there are any 'principled' differences between pendent and ancillary

Court of Appeals failed to understand the scope of the doctrine of the Gibbs case.

. . . .

It is apparent that Gibbs delineated the constitutional limits of federal judicial power. But even if it be assumed that the District Court in the present case had constitutional power to decide the respondent's lawsuit against the petitioner,[10] it does not follow that the decision of the Court of Appeals was correct. Constitutional power is merely the first hurdle that must be overcome in determining that a federal court has jurisdiction over a particular controversy. For the jurisdiction of the federal courts is limited not only by the provisions of Art. III of the Constitution, but by Acts of Congress. [Citations omitted.]

That statutory law as well as the Constitution may limit a federal court's jurisdiction over nonfederal claims[11] is well illustrated by . . . Aldinger v. Howard, 427 U.S. 1, 96 S.Ct. 2413 . . . . In Aldinger the Court held that a federal district court lacked jurisdiction over a state-law claim against a county, even if that claim was alleged to be pendent to one against county officials under 42 U.S.C. § 1983. . . . [D]espite the fact that federal and nonfederal claims arose from a "common nucleus of operative fact," the Court held that the statute [28 U.S.C. § 1343(a)(3)] conferring jurisdiction over the federal claim did not allow the exercise of jurisdiction over the nonfederal claim.

. . . Aldinger . . . thus make[s] clear that a finding that federal and nonfederal claims arise from a "common nucleus of operative fact," the test of Gibbs, does not end the inquiry into whether a federal court has power to hear the nonfederal claims along with the federal ones. Beyond this constitutional minimum, there must be an examination of the posture in which the nonfederal claim is asserted and of the specific statute that confers jurisdiction over the federal claim, in order to determine whether "Congress in [that statute] has . . . expressly or by implication negated" the exercise of jurisdiction over the particular nonfederal claim. Aldinger v. Howard, supra, 427 U.S., at 18, 96 S.Ct., at 2422.

III

The relevant statute in this case, 28 U.S.C. § 1332(a)(1), confers upon federal courts jurisdiction over "civil actions where the matter in

---

jurisdiction; or, if there are, what effect Gibbs had on such differences." Id., at 13, 96 S.Ct., at 2420.

[10]   Federal jurisdiction in Gibbs was based upon the existence of a question of federal law. The Court of Appeals in the present case believed that the "common nucleus of operative fact" test also determines the outer boundaries of constitutionally permissible federal jurisdiction when that jurisdiction is based upon diversity of citizenship. We may assume without deciding that the Court of Appeals was correct in this regard. See also n. 13, infra.

[11]   As used in this opinion, the term "nonfederal claim" means one as to which there is no independent basis for federal jurisdiction. Conversely, a "federal claim" means one as to which an independent basis for federal jurisdiction exists.

controversy exceeds the sum or value of [the then jurisdictional amount for diversity cases of] $10,000 . . . and is between . . . citizens of different States." This statute and its predecessors have consistently been held to require complete diversity of citizenship.[13] That is, diversity jurisdiction does not exist unless *each* defendant is a citizen of a different State from *each* plaintiff. Over the years Congress has repeatedly re-enacted or amended the statute conferring diversity jurisdiction, leaving intact this rule of complete diversity. Whatever may have been the original purposes of diversity of citizenship jurisdiction, this subsequent history clearly demonstrates a congressional mandate that diversity jurisdiction is not to be available when any plaintiff is a citizen of the same State as any defendant. Cf. Snyder v. Harris, 394 U.S. 332, 338–339, 89 S.Ct. 1053, 1057–1058.[16]

Thus it is clear that the respondent could not originally have brought suit in federal court naming Owen and OPPD as codefendants, since citizens of Iowa would have been on both sides of the litigation. Yet the identical lawsuit resulted when she amended her complaint. Complete diversity was destroyed just as surely as if she had sued Owen initially. In either situation, in the plain language of the statute, the "matter in controversy" could not be "between . . . citizens of different States."

It is a fundamental precept that federal courts are courts of limited jurisdiction. The limits upon federal jurisdiction, whether imposed by the Constitution or by Congress, must be neither disregarded nor evaded. Yet under the reasoning of the Court of Appeals in this case, a plaintiff could defeat the statutory requirement of complete diversity by the simple expedient of suing only those defendants who were of diverse citizenship and waiting for them to implead nondiverse defendants.[17] If, as the Court of Appeals thought, a "common nucleus of operative fact"

---

[13]   E.g., Strawbridge v. Curtiss, 3 Cranch 267; Coal Company v. Blatchford, 11 Wall. 172; Indianapolis v. Chase National Bank, 314 U.S. 63, 69, 62 S.Ct. 15, 16; American Fire & Cas. Co. v. Finn, 341 U.S. 6, 17, 71 S.Ct. 534, 541. It is settled that complete diversity is not a constitutional requirement. State Farm Fire & Cas. Co. v. Tashire, 386 U.S. 523, 530–531, 87 S.Ct. 1199, 1203–1204.

[16]   Notably, Congress enacted § 1332 as part of the Judicial Code of 1948, 62 Stat. 930, shortly after Rule 14 was amended in 1946. When the Rule was amended, the Advisory Committee noted that "in any case where the plaintiff could not have joined the third party originally because of jurisdictional limitations such as lack of diversity of citizenship, the majority view is that any attempt by the plaintiff to amend his complaint and assert a claim against the impleaded third party would be unavailing." 28 U.S.C.App., p. 7752. The subsequent re-enactment without relevant change of the diversity statute may thus be seen as evidence of congressional approval of that "majority view."

[17]   This is not an unlikely hypothesis, since a defendant in a tort suit such as this one would surely try to limit his liability by impleading any joint tortfeasors for indemnity or contribution. Some commentators have suggested that the possible abuse of third-party practice could be dealt with under 28 U.S.C. § 1359, which forbids collusive attempts to create federal jurisdiction. See, e.g., 3 Moore's Federal Practice ¶ 14.27[1], at 14–571 (2d ed. 1974); 6 C. Wright & A. Miller, Federal Practice and Procedure § 1444, at 231–232 (1971); Note, Rule 14 Claims and Ancillary Jurisdiction, 57 Va.L.Rev. 265, 274–275 (1971). The dissenting opinion today also expresses this view. . . . But there is nothing necessarily collusive about a plaintiff selectively suing only those tortfeasors of diverse citizenship, or about the named defendants' desire to implead joint tortfeasors. Nonetheless, the requirement of complete diversity would be eviscerated by such a course of events.

were the only requirement for ancillary jurisdiction in a diversity case, there would be no principled reason why the respondent in this case could not have joined her cause of action against Owen in her original complaint as ancillary to her claim against OPPD. Congress' requirement of complete diversity would thus have been evaded completely.

It is true, as the Court of Appeals noted, that the exercise of ancillary jurisdiction over nonfederal claims has often been upheld in situations involving impleader, cross-claims or counterclaims. But in determining whether jurisdiction over a nonfederal claim exists, the context in which the nonfederal claim is asserted is crucial. See Aldinger v. Howard, 427 U.S., at 14, 96 S.Ct., at 2420. And the claim here arises in a setting quite different from the kinds of nonfederal claim that have been viewed in other cases as falling within the ancillary jurisdiction of the federal courts.

First, the nonfederal claim in this case was simply not ancillary to the federal one in the same sense that, for example, the impleader by a defendant of a third-party defendant always is. A third-party complaint depends at least in part upon the resolution of the primary lawsuit. See n. 3, supra. Its relation to the original complaint is thus not mere factual similarity but logical dependence. Cf. Moore v. New York Cotton Exchange, 270 U.S. 593, 610, 46 S.Ct. 367, 371. The respondent's claim against the petitioner, however, was entirely separate from her original claim against OPPD, since the petitioner's liability to her depended not at all upon whether or not OPPD was also liable. Far from being an ancillary and dependent claim, it was a new and independent one.

Second, the nonfederal claim here was asserted by the plaintiff, who voluntarily chose to bring suit upon a state-law claim in a federal court. By contrast, ancillary jurisdiction typically involves claims by a defending party haled into court against his will, or by another person whose rights might be irretrievably lost unless he could assert them in an ongoing action in a federal court. A plaintiff cannot complain if ancillary jurisdiction does not encompass all of his possible claims in a case such as this one, since it is he who has chosen the federal rather than the state forum and must thus accept its limitations. "[T]he efficiency plaintiff seeks so avidly is available without question in the state courts." Kenrose Mfg. Co. v. Fred Whitaker Co., 512 F.2d 890, 894 (CA4).[20]

---

[20]   Whether Iowa's statute of limitations would now bar an action by the respondent in an Iowa court is, of course, entirely a matter of state law. See Iowa Code § 614.10. Compare 558 F.2d, at 420, with id., at 432 n. 42 (Bright, J., dissenting); cf. Burnett v. New York Central R. Co., 380 U.S. 424, 431–432, and n. 9, 85 S.Ct. 1050, 1056–1057, and n. 9. [In fact, despite this uncertainty that the Supreme Court was willing to accept when ordering dismissal, the widow sued again in state court and overcame the statute of limitations, eventually settling the case on favorable terms. For the background story of the Owen Equipment case, see John B. Oakley, "The Story of Owen Equipment v. Kroger: A Change in the Weather of Federal Jurisdiction," in Civil Procedure Stories 81 (Kevin M. Clermont ed., 2d ed. 2008).—Ed.]

It is not unreasonable to assume that, in generally requiring complete diversity, Congress did not intend to confine the jurisdiction of federal courts so inflexibly that they are unable to protect legal rights or effectively to resolve an entire, logically entwined lawsuit. Those practical needs are the basis of the doctrine of ancillary jurisdiction. But neither the convenience of litigants nor considerations of judicial economy can suffice to justify extension of the doctrine of ancillary jurisdiction to a plaintiff's cause of action against a citizen of the same State in a diversity case. Congress has established the basic rule that diversity jurisdiction exists under 28 U.S.C. § 1332 only when there is complete diversity of citizenship. "The policy of the statute calls for its strict construction." Healy v. Ratta, 292 U.S. 263, 270, 54 S.Ct. 700, 703; [other citations omitted]. To allow the requirement of complete diversity to be circumvented as it was in this case would simply flout the congressional command.[21]

Accordingly, the judgment of the Court of Appeals is reversed.

It is so ordered.

■ Mr. Justice White, with whom Mr. Justice Brennan joins, dissenting.

The Court today states that "[i]t is not unreasonable to assume that, in generally requiring complete diversity, Congress did not intend to confine the jurisdiction of federal courts so inflexibly that they are unable . . . effectively to resolve an entire, logically entwined lawsuit." . . . In spite of this recognition, the majority goes on to hold that in diversity suits federal courts do not have the jurisdictional power to entertain a claim asserted by a plaintiff against a third-party defendant, no matter how entwined it is with the matter already before the court, unless there is an independent basis for jurisdiction over that claim. Because I find no support for such a requirement in either Art. III of the Constitution or in any statutory law, I dissent from the Court's "unnecessarily grudging"[1] approach.

. . . .

. . . [Gibbs'] language and reasoning were broad enough to cover the instant factual situation. . . . Accordingly, as far as Art. III of the Constitution is concerned, the District Court had power to entertain Mrs. Kroger's claim against Owen.

The majority correctly points out, however, that the analysis cannot stop here. As Aldinger v. Howard, 427 U.S. 1, 96 S.Ct. 2413 (1976), teaches, the jurisdictional power of the federal courts may be limited by

---

[21]   Our holding is that the District Court lacked power to entertain the respondent's lawsuit against the petitioner. Thus, the asserted inequity in the respondent's alleged concealment of its citizenship is irrelevant. Federal judicial power does not depend upon "prior action or consent of the parties." American Fire & Cas. Co. v. Finn, 341 U.S. 6, 18, 71 S.Ct. 534, 542.

[1]   See Mine Workers v. Gibbs, 383 U.S. 715, 725, 86 S.Ct. 1130, 1138 (1966).

Congress, as well as by the Constitution. In Aldinger, . . . the Court held that the District Court did not have pendent jurisdiction over the state claim, for, under the Court's precedents at that time, it was thought that Congress had specifically determined not to confer on the federal courts jurisdiction over civil rights claims against cities and counties. . . .

In the present case, the only indication of congressional intent that the Court can find is that contained in the diversity jurisdictional statute . . . . Because this statute has been interpreted as requiring complete diversity of citizenship between each plaintiff and each defendant, Strawbridge v. Curtiss, 3 Cranch 267 (1806), the Court holds that the District Court did not have ancillary jurisdiction over Mrs. Kroger's claim against Owen. In so holding, the Court unnecessarily expands the scope of the complete-diversity requirement while substantially limiting the doctrine of ancillary jurisdiction.

The complete-diversity requirement, of course, could be viewed as meaning that in a diversity case, a federal district court may adjudicate only those claims that are between parties of different States. Thus, in order for a defendant to implead a third-party defendant, there would have to be diversity of citizenship; the same would also be true for cross-claims between defendants and for a third-party defendant's claim against a plaintiff. Even the majority, however, refuses to read the complete-diversity requirement so broadly; it recognizes with seeming approval the exercise of ancillary jurisdiction over nonfederal claims in situations involving impleader, cross-claims and counterclaims. . . . Given the Court's willingness to recognize ancillary jurisdiction in these contexts, despite the requirements of § 1332(a), I see no justification for the Court's refusal to approve the District Court's exercise of ancillary jurisdiction in the present case.

It is significant that a plaintiff who asserts a claim against a third-party defendant is not seeking to add a new party to the lawsuit. In the present case, for example, Owen had already been brought into the suit by OPPD, and, that having been done, Mrs. Kroger merely sought to assert against Owen a claim arising out of the same transaction that was already before the court. Thus the situation presented here is unlike that in Aldinger, supra . . . .

Because in the instant case Mrs. Kroger merely sought to assert a claim against someone already a party to the suit, considerations of judicial economy, convenience, and fairness to the litigants—the factors relied upon in Gibbs, supra—support the recognition of ancillary jurisdiction here. Already before the court was the whole question of the cause of Mr. Kroger's death. Mrs. Kroger initially contended that OPPD was responsible; OPPD in turn contended that Owen's negligence had been the proximate cause of Mr. Kroger's death. In spite of the fact that the question of Owen's negligence was already before the District Court, the majority requires Mrs. Kroger to bring a separate action in state court in order to assert that very claim. Even if the Iowa Statute of

Limitations will still permit such a suit, . . . considerations of judicial economy are certainly not served by requiring such duplicative litigation.

The majority, however, brushes aside such considerations of convenience, judicial economy, and fairness because it concludes that recognizing ancillary jurisdiction over a plaintiff's claim against a third-party defendant would permit the plaintiff to circumvent the complete-diversity requirement and thereby "flout the congressional command." Since the plaintiff in such a case does not bring the third-party defendant into the suit, however, there is no occasion for deliberate circumvention of the diversity requirement, absent collusion with the defendant. In the case of such collusion, of which there is absolutely no indication here,[5] the court can dismiss the action under the authority of 28 U.S.C. § 1359. In the absence of such collusion, there is no reason to adopt an absolute rule prohibiting the plaintiff from asserting those claims that he may properly assert against the third-party defendant pursuant to Fed.Rule Civ.Proc. 14(a). The plaintiff in such a situation brings suit against the defendant only with absolutely no assurance that the defendant will decide or be able to implead a particular third-party defendant. Since the plaintiff has no control over the defendant's decision to implead a third party, the fact that he could not have originally sued that party in federal court should be irrelevant. Moreover, the fact that a plaintiff in some cases may be able to foresee the subsequent chain of events leading to the impleader does not seem to me to be a sufficient reason to declare that a district court does not have the *power* to exercise ancillary jurisdiction over the plaintiff's claims against the third-party defendant.[7]

We have previously noted that "[s]ubsequent decisions of this Court indicate that Strawbridge is not to be given an expansive reading." State Farm Fire & Cas. Co. v. Tashire, 386 U.S. 523, 531 n. 6, 87 S.Ct. 1199, 1203 n. 6 (1967). In light of this teaching, it seems to me appropriate to view § 1332 as requiring complete diversity only between the plaintiff and those parties he actually brings into the suit. Beyond that, I would hold that in a diversity case the District Court has power, both constitutional and statutory, to entertain all claims among the parties arising from the same nucleus of operative fact as the plaintiff's original, jurisdiction-conferring claim against the defendant. Accordingly, I dissent from the Court's disposition of the present case.

---

[5]   When Mrs. Kroger brought suit, it was believed that Owen was a citizen of Nebraska, not Iowa. Therefore, had she desired at that time to make Owen a party to the suit, she would have done so directly by naming Owen as a defendant.

[7]   Under the Gibbs analysis, recognition of the District Court's power to hear a plaintiff's nonfederal claim against a third-party defendant in a diversity suit would not mean that the court would be required to entertain such claims in all cases. The District Court would have the discretion to dismiss the nonfederal claim if it concluded that the interests of judicial economy, convenience, and fairness would not be served by the retention of the claim in the federal lawsuit. See Gibbs, 383 U.S., at 726, 86 S.Ct., at 1139. Accordingly, the majority's concerns that lead it to conclude that ancillary jurisdiction should not be recognized in the present situation could be met on a case-by-case basis, rather than by the absolute rule it adopts.

ORTIZ v. UNITED STATES GOVERNMENT, 595 F.2d 65 (1st Cir.1979). Puerto Rican plaintiffs sued the United States in a federal district court for medical malpractice under the Federal Tort Claims Act, 28 U.S.C. § 1346(b), which puts such claims against the U.S. government within exclusive federal jurisdiction. The United States impleaded a Puerto Rican hospital. Then plaintiffs attempted to assert a nonfederal claim against the hospital under Rule 14(a). On interlocutory appeal, the court of appeals held that "pendent" jurisdiction could be exercised over such a claim.

CODIFICATION

Finley bluster.—Suppose *P* sues *D-1* in a federal district court on a claim for which there is federal question jurisdiction. Does the federal court have discretion to hear a closely related state-law claim against *D-2* that *P* attempts to join under Rule 20?

The lower federal courts were embracing an affirmative answer when the Supreme Court blustered in with Finley v. United States, 490 U.S. 545, 109 S.Ct. 2003 (1989). In that case, plaintiff's family died in an airplane crash while landing. She sued the United States in a federal district court for negligence in the airport's operation, invoking exclusive jurisdiction under 28 U.S.C. § 1346(b). She tried to join nonfederal claims against a municipality and a corporation that were also involved in the airport's operation. In holding against the exercise of this form of pendent jurisdiction, Justice Scalia for the Supreme Court attempted to explain:

"Analytically, petitioner's case is fundamentally different from Gibbs in that it brings into question what has become known as pendent-*party* jurisdiction, that is, jurisdiction over parties not named in any claim that is independently cognizable by the federal court. We may assume, without deciding, that the constitutional criterion for pendent-party jurisdiction is analogous to the constitutional criterion for pendent-claim jurisdiction, and that petitioner's state-law claims pass that test. Our cases show, however, that with respect to the addition of parties, as opposed to the addition of only claims, we will not assume that the full constitutional power has been congressionally authorized, and will not read jurisdictional statutes broadly. . . .

. . . .

" . . . [O]ur cases do not display an entirely consistent approach with respect to the necessity that jurisdiction be explicitly conferred. The Gibbs line of cases was a departure from prior practice, and a departure that we have no intent to limit or impair. But Aldinger indicated that the Gibbs approach would not be extended to the pendent-party field, and we decide today to retain that line. Whatever we say regarding the scope of jurisdiction conferred by a particular statute can of course be changed by Congress. What is of paramount importance is that Congress be able to legislate against a background of clear interpretive rules, so that it may know the effect of the language it adopts."

Justice Blackmun dissented, as did Justice Stevens, with whom Justices Brennan and Marshall joined. They stressed the widely recognized desirability of jurisdiction here, the proposition that Aldinger stood for presuming congressional intent to favor pendent jurisdiction unless Congress indicated otherwise in a specific context, and the confusion that the Finley opinion would sow with regard to additional parties under ancillary jurisdiction.

Statutory intercession.—The upshot was that Congress quickly enacted a new provision on so-called supplemental jurisdiction. Judicial Improvements Act of 1990, Pub.L. No. 101–650, tit. III, § 310, 104 Stat. 5089, 5113. This provision, now 28 U.S.C. § 1367, overturned the holding of Finley v. United States by combining and codifying the doctrines of pendent and ancillary jurisdiction. Congress explained its statute, drafted quickly in subcommittee with some academic input, in H.R.Rep. No. 101–734: "This section would authorize jurisdiction in a case like Finley, as well as essentially restore the pre-Finley understandings of the authorization for and limits on other forms of supplemental jurisdiction. In federal question cases, it broadly authorizes the district courts to exercise supplemental jurisdiction over additional claims, including claims involving the joinder of additional parties. In diversity cases, the district courts may exercise supplemental jurisdiction, except when doing so would be inconsistent with the jurisdictional requirements of the diversity statute. In both cases, the district courts, as under current law, would have discretion to decline supplemental jurisdiction in appropriate circumstances.

"Subsection [(a)] generally authorizes the district court to exercise jurisdiction over a supplemental claim whenever it forms part of the same constitutional case or controversy as the claim or claims that provide the basis of the district court's original jurisdiction.[15] In providing for supplemental jurisdiction over claims involving the addition of parties, subsection (a) explicitly fills the statutory gap noted in Finley v. United States.

"Subsection [(b)] prohibits a district court in a case over which it has jurisdiction founded solely on the general diversity provision, 28 U.S.C. § 1332, from exercising supplemental jurisdiction in specified circumstances.[16] In diversity-only actions the district courts may not hear plaintiffs' supplemental claims when exercising supplemental

---

[15] In so doing, subsection (a) codifies the scope of supplemental jurisdiction first articulated by the Supreme Court in United Mine Workers v. Gibbs, 383 U.S. 715, 86 S.Ct. 1130 (1966).

[16] The net effect of subsection (b) is to implement the principal rationale of Owen Equipment & Erection Co. v. Kroger, 437 U.S. 365, 98 S.Ct. 2396 (1978).

jurisdiction would encourage plaintiffs to evade the jurisdictional requirement of 28 U.S.C. § 1332 by the simple expedient of naming initially only those defendants whose joinder satisfies section 1332's requirements and later adding claims not within original federal jurisdiction against other defendants who have intervened or been joined on a supplemental basis. In accord with case law, the subsection also prohibits the joinder or intervention of persons as plaintiffs if adding them is inconsistent with section 1332's requirements. The section is not intended to affect the jurisdictional requirements of 28 U.S.C. § 1332 in diversity-only class actions, as those requirements were interpreted prior to Finley.[17]

"Subsection (b) makes one small change in pre-Finley practice. Anomalously, under current practice, the same party might intervene as of right under Federal Rule of Civil Procedure 24(a) and take advantage of supplemental jurisdiction, but not come within supplemental jurisdiction if parties already in the action sought to effect the joinder under Rule 19. Subsection (b) would eliminate this anomaly, excluding Rule 24(a) plaintiff-intervenors to the same extent as those sought to be joined as plaintiffs under Rule 19.

"If this exclusion threatened unavoidable prejudice to the interests of the prospective intervenor if the action proceeded in its absence, the district court should be more inclined not merely to deny the intervention but to dismiss the whole action for refiling in state court under the criteria of Rule 19(b).

"Subsection [(c)] codifies the factors that the Supreme Court has recognized as providing legitimate bases upon which a district court may decline jurisdiction over a supplemental claim, even though it is empowered to hear the claim. Subsection (c)(1)–(3) codifies the factors recognized as relevant under current law. Subsection (c)(4) acknowledges that occasionally there may exist other compelling reasons for a district court to decline supplemental jurisdiction, which the subsection does not foreclose a court from considering in exceptional circumstances. As under current law, subsection (c) requires the district court, in exercising its discretion, to undertake a case-specific analysis."

Question: (10) *P* of State *A* sues *D* of State *B* in a federal district court on a $101,000 claim for which diversity of citizenship is the only basis of jurisdiction. Assume that *D* impleads *T-1* of State *A*. Then *T-1* asserts a nonfederal claim against *P* under Rule 14(a)(2)(D), which prompts a nonfederal counterclaim by *P* against *T-1* under Rule 13(a). Is supplemental jurisdiction authorized for this counterclaim? Compare Gibson v. Chrysler Corp., 261 F.3d 927, 938 (9th Cir.2001) (dictum) (yes, and noting that "our reading gives specific meaning to the last phrase of § 1367(b) [the proviso of 'when exercising supplemental jurisdiction over such claims would be inconsistent with the jurisdictional requirements of section 1332'], for it

---

[17]   See Supreme Tribe of Ben Hur v. Cauble, 255 U.S. 356, 41 S.Ct. 338 (1921); Zahn v. International Paper Co., 414 U.S. 291, 94 S.Ct. 505 (1973).

preserves a small slice of supplemental jurisdiction that would otherwise have been lost"), with Wright & Miller § 3567.2 (no).

Future reform.—While overturning Finley was an excellent idea, the execution of drafting § 1367 was not an unqualified success. Consequently, the American Law Institute proposed a complete overhaul of that statute. Federal Judicial Code Revision Project pt. I (Am. Law Inst. 2004). Here is its proposed amendment to the particularly troublesome § 1367(b):

> *Restriction of supplemental jurisdiction in diversity litigation.* When the jurisdiction of a district court over a supplemental claim depends upon a freestanding claim that is asserted in the same pleading and that qualifies as a freestanding claim solely on the basis of the jurisdiction conferred by section 1332 of this title, the court shall have jurisdiction of the supplemental claim . . . only if it—
>
> > (1) is asserted representatively by or against a class of additional unnamed parties; or
> >
> > (2) would be a freestanding claim on the basis of section 1332 of this title but for the value of the claim; or
> >
> > (3) has been joined to the action by the intervention of a party whose joinder is not indispensable to the litigation of the action.
>
> ["Asserted in the same pleading" means that the relevant claims have been asserted in one or more of the following ways: (1) by the pleading as originally filed with the court, (2) by amendment of the pleading, (3) by order of the court reformulating the pleading to compel joinder of parties, (4) by the pleader's assertion of a claim (other than a counterclaim or a claim for indemnity or contribution) against a third party impleaded previously in response to the pleading, or (5) by the assertion of the claim or defense of an intervenor who seeks to be treated as if the pleading had asserted a claim by or against that intervenor.]

Question: (11) *P* of State *A* sues *D* of State *B* in a federal district court on a $101,000 claim for which diversity of citizenship is the only basis of jurisdiction. Assume that *D* asserts a compulsory counterclaim against *P*, which prompts *P* to implead *T-2* of State *A*. Is there supplemental jurisdiction for the impleader under § 1367? See Chase Manhattan Bank v. Aldridge, 906 F.Supp. 866 (S.D.N.Y.1995) (no, because of the wording of § 1367(b)); Guaranteed Sys., Inc. v. Am. Nat'l Can Co., 842 F.Supp. 855 (M.D.N.C.1994) (no, because of the wording of § 1367(b), even when the case had initially arrived in federal court by *D*'s removal); Peter Raven-Hansen, The Forgotten Proviso of § 1367(b) (and Why We Forgot), 74 Ind.L.J. 197, 204–05 (1998) ("the 'plainer' meaning of the listed proscriptions of § 1367(b) is likely to overshadow the murkier and anachronistic assignment of decisional authority to the courts by the Proviso"). Would there be under the ALI's proposed statute?

————

EXECUTIVE SOFTWARE NORTH AMERICA, INC. v. UNITED STATES DISTRICT COURT, 24 F.3d 1545 (9th Cir.1994) (2–1 decision). Donna Page, as an African American woman formerly employed by an allegedly Scientology-dominated company, brought federal and state discrimination claims in a California state-court case. Defendants removed. The federal district court chose not to retain jurisdiction over the state-law claims, the court possibly concerned about mere docket congestion but simply citing to its Gibbs discretion. The federal court of appeals granted mandamus.

The court of appeals ordered reconsideration, after taking a position in a statutory-construction dispute that has since seriously split the circuits. Elaborating on the effect of codification on judge-made law, the Ninth Circuit explained its view that 28 U.S.C. § 1367 had narrowed the scope of Gibbs discretion:

"Therefore, under the regime established by Gibbs ... and ... progeny, whether pendent jurisdiction should be exercised in a given circumstance depended on the district court assessing whether doing so 'would most sensibly accommodate' the values of 'economy, convenience, fairness, and comity.' Although the specific examples given in Gibbs informed the determination of when the particular balance of these factors was likely to point against (or in favor) of retaining jurisdiction, courts by no means found these specific illustrations to exhaust Gibbs's underlying values.

. . . .

"Section 1367 retains the basic division, reflected in Gibbs, between the power of a court to entertain a pendent claim and the authority of a court, in its discretion, to decline to exercise that power. However, Congress, in codifying supplemental jurisdiction, has chosen to codify as well the discretionary factors that warrant declining jurisdiction. Section 1367(a), providing that 'the district courts shall have supplemental jurisdiction over all other claims that are so related to claims in the action within such original jurisdiction that they form part of the same case or controversy under Article III of the United States Constitution,' ... confers power to entertain supplemental jurisdiction in mandatory terms. By use of the word 'shall,' the statute makes clear that if power is conferred under section 1367(a), and its exercise is not prohibited by section 1367(b), a court can decline to assert supplemental jurisdiction over a pendent claim only if one of the four categories specifically enumerated in section 1367(c) applies. . . .

" . . . Not only is this conclusion supported by the legislative history, see H.R. No. 734, 101st Cong., 2d Sess. 29 (1990), . . . but a contrary reading of the statute would appear to render section 1367(c) superfluous. . . .

"A consequence of the statutory structure chosen by Congress is that section 1367(c) somewhat changes the nature of the Gibbs discretionary inquiry. . . .

"The statute . . . channels the application of the underlying values to a greater degree than the Gibbs regime, although section 1367(c) continues to recognize the doctrine's dynamic aspects. Subsections (c)(1)–(c)(3) appear to codify concrete applications of the underlying Gibbs values recognized in preexisting case law. . . .

"By codifying [most of the] preexisting applications of Gibbs in subsections (c)(1)–(3), however, it is clear that Congress intended the exercise of discretion to be triggered by the court's identification of a factual predicate that corresponds to one of the section 1367(c) categories. Once that factual predicate is identified, the exercise of discretion, of course, still is informed by whether remanding the pendent state claims comports with the underlying objective of 'most sensibly accommodat[ing]' the values of 'economy, convenience, fairness, and comity.' [Citations omitted, including Carnegie-Mellon Univ. v. Cohill, 484 U.S. 343, 108 S.Ct. 614 (1988).]

"We believe that the 'catchall,' Palmer v. Schwan's Sales Enters., Inc., 1993 WL 390053, 1993 U.S. Dist. LEXIS 14069, at *7 (D.Kan. Sep. 27, 1993), provided by subsection (c)(4) should be interpreted in a similar manner. Subsection (c)(4) permits a discretionary remand of pendent claims when 'in exceptional circumstances, there are other compelling reasons for declining jurisdiction.' . . . Congress's use of the word 'other' to modify 'compelling reasons' indicates that what ought to qualify as 'compelling reasons' for declining jurisdiction under subsection (c)(4) should be of the same nature as the reasons that gave rise to the categories listed in subsections (c)(1)–(3). . . . [W]e believe that 'compelling reasons' for the purposes of subsection (c)(4) similarly should be those that lead a court to conclude that declining jurisdiction 'best accommodate[s] the values of economy, convenience, fairness, and comity.' Carnegie-Mellon, 484 U.S. at 351, 108 S.Ct. at 619.

"We do not believe, however, that Congress has replicated unaltered the command of the Carnegie-Mellon Court that the 'Judicial Branch is to shape and apply [the doctrine of pendent jurisdiction] in [light of this objective].' Id. By providing that an exercise of discretion under subsection 1367(c)(4) ought to be made only in 'exceptional circumstances' Congress has sounded a note of caution that the bases for declining jurisdiction should be extended beyond the circumstances identified in subsections (c)(1)–(3) only if the circumstances are quite unusual. In short, although we find that 'other compelling reasons' clearly refers the district court back to the subsection (c)(1)–(3) categories, and thus requires the court to balance the underlying values that they embody, we think 'exceptional circumstances' requires an additional inquiry."

The Ninth Circuit held "that declining jurisdiction outside of subsection (c)(1)–(3) should be the exception, rather than the rule." The language chosen by Congress requires "factual circumstances that truly are unusual."

"Therefore, to the extent that Gibbs and Carnegie-Mellon were interpreted as permitting courts to extend the doctrine's underlying values beyond previously recognized applications whenever doing so was consistent with those values, [citation omitted], we believe that section 1367(c)(4) more carefully channels courts' discretion by requiring the court to identify how the circumstances that it confronts, and in which it believes the balance of the Gibbs values provides 'compelling reasons' for declining jurisdiction, are 'exceptional.'"

––––––––––

Question: (12) Henceforth, is the outer limit on supplemental jurisdiction to be delineated according to a Revere-like set of categorical rules or a Gibbs-like flexible standard? Although § 1367(b) seems to impose some woodenness in its realm of application, how should courts read the more generally applicable § 1367(a)?

(a) For example, imagine permissive counterclaims by defendant: will all of them fall outside § 1367(a), or could some have a sufficiently close logical relationship to qualify? Even here some courts proceed with flexibility. See, e.g., Jones v. Ford Motor Credit Co., 358 F.3d 205, 213 (2d Cir.2004) (extending supplemental jurisdiction for debt-collection counterclaims to an Equal Credit Opportunity Act class action, as the court observed: "Whether or not the Gibbs 'common nucleus' standard provides the outer limit of an Article III 'case,' and is therefore a requirement for entertaining a permissive counterclaim that otherwise lacks a jurisdictional basis, the facts of Ford Credit's counterclaims and those of the Plaintiffs' ECOA claims satisfy that standard, even though the relationship is not such as would make the counterclaims compulsory.").

(b) For a converse example, imagine impleader claims by defendant: will all such claims automatically fall within § 1367(a), or might some upon a case-by-case analysis fail the constitutional-case test because the impleader does not directly involve the same aggregate of operative facts? See Hartford Accident & Indem. Co. v. Sullivan, 846 F.2d 377, 382 (7th Cir.1988) (Posner, J.) (doubting the existence of a universal rule "that *any* 14(a) claim is within the ancillary jurisdiction of the federal courts").

––––––––––

SECTION 4.   JURISDICTIONAL AMOUNT

Various statutes impose a jurisdictional amount requirement, but by far the most important is the requirement in 28 U.S.C. § 1332(a) that "the matter in controversy exceeds the sum or value of $75,000, exclusive of interest and costs." The purpose of such a requirement is to keep petty controversies out of the federal courts. However, what this statutory creation seems to do best is to create litigation over how it should be applied.

Snyder v. Harris
(Gas Service Co. v. Coburn)
Supreme Court of the United States, 1969.
394 U.S. 332, 89 S.Ct. 1053.

[In order to resolve a conflict among the courts of appeals, the Supreme Court granted certiorari in two cases.

[In Snyder, 390 F.2d 204 (8th Cir.1968), plaintiff brought a class action, grounded on diversity of citizenship, for herself and all others similarly situated, against members of the board of directors of Missouri Fidelity Union Trust Life Insurance Co., alleging that the defendants had sold their shares of the company's stock far in excess of fair market value, the excess representing payment to obtain control of the company, and that under Missouri law this excess should be distributed among all the shareholders. Plaintiff's own claim was for $8740 in damages; the total claim of all the 4000-odd shareholders would be about $1,200,000. The district court and the court of appeals refused to permit aggregation.

[In Gas Service Co., 389 F.2d 831 (10th Cir.1968), also a diversity action, Coburn brought a class action alleging that Gas Service Co. had billed and illegally collected a city franchise tax from him and others living outside city limits. Plaintiff alleged damages to himself of $7.81; the total claim of about 18,000 customers living outside city limits was allegedly over the then jurisdictional amount of $10,000. The district court and the court of appeals permitted aggregation, relying on the major 1966 amendment to Rule 23.]

■ MR. JUSTICE BLACK delivered the opinion of the Court.

. . . The issue presented by these two cases is whether separate and distinct claims presented by and for various claimants in a class action may be added together to provide the $10,000 jurisdictional amount in controversy.

. . . .

The first congressional grant to district courts to take suits between citizens of different States fixed the requirement for the jurisdictional amount in controversy at $500. In 1887 this jurisdictional amount was increased to $2,000; in 1911 to $3,000; and in 1958 to $10,000. The traditional judicial interpretation under all of these statutes has been from the beginning that the separate and distinct claims of two or more plaintiffs cannot be aggregated in order to satisfy the jurisdictional amount requirement. Aggregation has been permitted only (1) in cases in which a single plaintiff seeks to aggregate two or more of his own claims against a single defendant and (2) in cases in which two or more plaintiffs unite to enforce a single title or right in which they have a common and undivided interest. It is contended, however, that the adoption of a 1966 amendment to Rule 23 effectuated a change in this jurisdictional doctrine. . . .

The doctrine that separate and distinct claims could not be aggregated was never, and is not now, based upon . . . any rule of procedure. That doctrine is based rather upon this Court's interpretation of the statutory phrase "matter in controversy." . . . Nothing in the amended Rule 23 changes this doctrine. The class action plaintiffs in the two cases before us argue that since the new Rule will include in the judgment all members of the class who do not ask to be out by a certain date, the "matter in controversy" now encompasses all the claims of the entire class. But it is equally true that where two or more plaintiffs join their claims under the joinder provisions of Rule 20, each and every joined plaintiff is bound by the judgment. And it was in joinder cases of this very kind that the doctrine that distinct claims could not be aggregated was originally enunciated. Troy Bank v. G.A. Whitehead & Co., 222 U.S. 39, 32 S.Ct. 9 (1911); Pinel v. Pinel, 240 U.S. 594, 36 S.Ct. 416 (1916).[g] . . .

     . . . .

. . . It is urged, however, that this Court should now overrule its established statutory interpretation and hold that "matter in controversy" encompasses the aggregation of all claims that can be brought together in a single suit, regardless of whether any single plaintiff has a claim that exceeds the required jurisdictional amount. It is argued in behalf of this position that (1) the determination of whether claims are "separate and distinct" is a troublesome question that breeds uncertainty and needless litigation, and (2) the inability of parties to aggregate numerous small claims will prevent some important questions from being litigated in federal courts. And both of these factors, it is

---

[g]   Pinel held that there could be no aggregation of claims by two children seeking to establish their interests in their father's estate, when the children were alleging that he had unintentionally omitted them from his will. Contrast this with the holding of Shields v. Thomas, 58 U.S. (17 How.) 3 (1855), that an estate's distributees, such as children of the decedent, could aggregate their claims against the person who allegedly converted the estate, because they had a common and undivided interest in a single title or right.

Thus, common and undivided interests, which can be aggregated, represent a small property-based category of ancient lineage that seems virtually undefinable. One can delineate it by precedential examples like Pinel and Shields. See Wright & Miller § 3704 for more cases treating this category of common and undivided interests. Or one can try to generalize. Fitting within this category requires much more than relatedness among the claims. Indeed, the emerging consensus is that the category is quite narrow, comprising only disputes over (1) a common fund, created by a single occurrence, to which the claimants assert (2) a joint interest, such that the shares of the remaining claimants increase if one claimant cannot or does not collect a share, as opposed to a situation where a group of plaintiffs litigate individual claims that would be unaffected by the amounts obtained by fellow plaintiffs. See Travelers Prop. Cas. v. Good, 689 F.3d 714, 718–22 (7th Cir.2012).

argued, will tend to undercut the attempt of the Judicial Conference to promulgate efficient and modernized class action procedures. We think that whatever the merit of these contentions, they are not sufficient to justify our abandonment of a judicial interpretation of congressional language that has stood for more than a century and a half.

. . . .

. . . Moreover, while the class action device serves a useful function across the entire range of legal questions, the jurisdictional amount requirement applies almost exclusively to controversies based upon diversity of citizenship. A large part of those matters involving federal questions can be brought, by way of class actions or otherwise, without regard to the amount in controversy. Suits involving issues of state law and brought on the basis of diversity of citizenship can often be most appropriately tried in state courts. . . . There is no compelling reason for this Court to overturn a settled interpretation of an important congressional statute in order to add to the burdens of an already overloaded federal court system. Nor can we overlook the fact that the Congress that permitted the federal rules to go into effect was assured before doing so that none of the rules would either expand or contract the jurisdiction of federal courts. If there is a present need to expand the jurisdiction of those courts we cannot overlook the fact that the Constitution specifically vests that power in the Congress, not in the courts.

. . . .

■ MR. JUSTICE FORTAS, with whom MR. JUSTICE DOUGLAS joins, dissenting.

The Court today refuses to conform the judge-made formula for computing the amount in controversy in class actions with the 1966 amendment to Rule 23 of the Federal Rules of Civil Procedure. The effect of this refusal is substantially to undermine a generally welcomed and long-needed reform in federal procedure.

. . . .

Permitting aggregation in class action cases does not involve any violation of the principle, expressed in Rule 82 and inherent in the whole procedure for the promulgation and amendment of the Federal Rules, that the courts cannot by rule expand their own jurisdictions. While the Rules cannot change subject-matter jurisdiction, changes in the forms and practices of the federal courts through changes in the Rules frequently and necessarily will affect the occasions on which subject-matter jurisdiction is exercised because they will in some cases make a difference in what cases the federal courts will hear and who will be authoritatively bound by the judgment. For example, the development of the law of joinder and ancillary jurisdiction under the Federal Rules has influenced the "jurisdiction" of the federal courts in this broader sense. . . . Making judicial rules for calculating jurisdictional amount responsive to the new structure of class actions is not an extension of the jurisdiction of the federal courts, but a recognition that the procedural framework in which the courts operate has been changed by a provision having the effect of law.

. . . .

The new Rule 23, by redefining the law of class actions, has, with the effect of statute, provided for a decision by the district courts that the nominally separate and legally "several" claims of individuals may be so much alike that they can be tried all at once, as if there were just one claim, in a single proceeding in which most members of the class asserting the claim will not be personally present at all. When that determination has been made in accordance with the painstaking demands of Rule 23, there is authorized to be brought in the federal courts a single litigation, in which, both practically and in legal theory, the thing at stake, the "matter in controversy," is the total, combined, aggregated claim of the whole class. When that happens the courts do not obey, but violate, the jurisdictional statutes if they continue to impose an ancient and artificial judicial doctrine to fragment what is in every other respect a single claim, which the courts are commanded to stand ready to hear.

For these reasons, I would measure the value of the "matter in controversy" in a class action found otherwise proper under the amended Rule 23 by the monetary value of the claim of the whole class.

———

Question: (13) Does it seem wise to you to allow *P* of State *A* to sue *D* of State *B* in federal court upon two wholly unrelated claims for $37,000 and $39,000 respectively, but not to allow *P-1* and *P-2* of State *A* to aggregate their separate and distinct claims against *D* for $37,000 and $39,000 respectively arising out of the same transaction or occurrence, such as an automobile accident?

———

GALLO v. HOMELITE CONSUMERS PRODUCTS, 371 F.Supp.2d 943 (N.D.Ill.2005). A diverse consumer brought a state-court action against the manufacturer and the distributor of a weed trimmer. He alleged negligence, strict liability, and breach of express and implied warranty resulting in his burns. Each of the claims was somewhat under $75,000. Defendants removed. Plaintiff moved to remand.

The court remanded, ruling: "However, where two or more claims are alternative theories of recovery for the same harm, they may not be aggregated. . . . Compare Hill v. United Insurance Co. of America, 998 F.Supp. 1333, 1337 (M.D.Ala.1998) ('As clear as it is that a plaintiff may recover both in contract and tort for the same events, it is also clear that a plaintiff may not get a "double recovery" . . . . [W]hatever items of damage are compensated for as damage resulting from the breach of contract may not also be compensated for as damages in a tort claim.'), with Connolly v. Volvo Trucks North America, Inc., 208 F.R.D. 600, 601 (N.D.Ill.2002) (aggregating the ad damnum's of plaintiff's three claims because each claim asserted its own basis for compensation—Count I sought damages for decedent's pain and suffering prior to death, Count II sought damages for survivors' pecuniary loss due to decedent's death, and Count III sought damages for medical and funeral expenses as a result of decedent's death)."

———

ZAHN v. INTERNATIONAL PAPER CO., 414 U.S. 291, 94 S.Ct. 505 (1973). Plaintiffs brought a class action, grounded on diversity of citizenship, on behalf of certain lake-front property owners and lessees, against an alleged polluter. The named plaintiffs' claims each exceeded the jurisdictional amount of $10,000. However, the district court and the court of appeals ruled that jurisdiction did not extend to absent class members whose claims did not individually satisfy the jurisdictional amount requirement.

On certiorari, the Supreme Court affirmed. Justice White explained that the aggregation rules require "dismissal of those litigants whose [separate and distinct] claims do not satisfy the jurisdictional amount, even though other litigants assert claims sufficient to invoke the jurisdiction of the federal court."

Justice Brennan, joined by Justices Douglas and Marshall, dissented. He argued that ancillary jurisdiction should apply here.

———

Exxon Mobil Corp. v. Allapattah Services, Inc.
(Ortega v. Star-Kist Foods, Inc.)

Supreme Court of the United States, 2005.
545 U.S. 546, 125 S.Ct. 2611.

[In order to resolve a sharp conflict among the courts of appeals, the Supreme Court granted certiorari in two cases.

[In Exxon, 333 F.3d 1248 (11th Cir.2003), several representatives of some 10,000 gasoline dealers brought a diversity class action under Rule 23, alleging that Exxon had overcharged them all. The court of appeals affirmed the verdict and judgment for plaintiffs, upholding the exercise of supplemental jurisdiction over the claims of all class members, even though some of the absentees' claims did not reach the jurisdictional amount.

[In Ortega, 370 F.3d 124 (1st Cir.2004), also a diversity action, a nine-year-old girl sued a food company, seeking damages for severe injuries from slicing her finger on a tuna can. Her family joined as plaintiffs under Rule 20, seeking damages for smallish medical expenses and damages for emotional distress that the lower courts ruled did not fill the gap to reach the jurisdictional amount. The court of appeals affirmed the summary judgment for defendant as to the family members, by rejecting the exercise of supplemental jurisdiction over their claims.]

■ JUSTICE KENNEDY delivered the opinion of the Court.

These consolidated cases present the question whether a federal court in a diversity action may exercise supplemental jurisdiction over additional plaintiffs whose claims do not satisfy the minimum amount-in-controversy requirement, provided the claims are part of the same case or controversy as the claims of plaintiffs who do allege a sufficient amount in controversy. Our decision turns on the correct interpretation of 28 U.S.C. § 1367. . . .

We hold that, where the other elements of jurisdiction are present and at least one named plaintiff in the action satisfies the amount-in-controversy requirement, § 1367 does authorize supplemental jurisdiction over the claims of other plaintiffs in the same Article III case or controversy, even if those claims are for less than the jurisdictional amount specified in the statute setting forth the requirements for diversity jurisdiction. . . .

. . . .

. . . No sound canon of interpretation requires Congress to speak with extraordinary clarity in order to modify the rules of federal jurisdiction within appropriate constitutional bounds. Ordinary principles of statutory construction apply. In order to determine the scope of supplemental jurisdiction authorized by § 1367, then, we must examine the statute's text in light of context, structure, and related statutory provisions.

. . . The single question before us, therefore, is whether a diversity case in which the claims of some plaintiffs satisfy the amount-in-controversy requirement, but the claims of other plaintiffs do not, presents a "civil action of which the district courts have original jurisdiction." . . .

We now conclude the answer must be yes. When the well-pleaded complaint contains at least one claim that satisfies the amount-in-controversy requirement, and there are no other relevant jurisdictional defects, the district court, beyond all question, has original jurisdiction over that claim. The presence of other claims in the complaint, over which the district court may lack original jurisdiction, is of no moment. If the court has original jurisdiction over a single claim in the complaint, it has original jurisdiction over a "civil action" within the meaning of § 1367(a), even if the civil action over which it has jurisdiction comprises fewer claims than were included in the complaint. Once the court determines it has original jurisdiction over the civil action, it can turn to the question whether it has a constitutional and statutory basis for exercising supplemental jurisdiction over the other claims in the action.

. . . The terms of § 1367 do not acknowledge any distinction between pendent jurisdiction and the doctrine of so-called ancillary jurisdiction. Though the doctrines of pendent and ancillary jurisdiction developed separately as a historical matter, the Court has recognized that the doctrines are "two species of the same generic problem," [Owen Equip. & Erection Co. v. Kroger, 437 U.S. 365, 370, 98 S.Ct. 2396, 2401 (1978)]. Nothing in § 1367 indicates a congressional intent to recognize, preserve, or create some meaningful, substantive distinction between the jurisdictional categories we have historically labeled pendent and ancillary.

. . . While § 1367(b) qualifies the broad rule of § 1367(a), it does not withdraw supplemental jurisdiction over the claims of the additional parties at issue here. The specific exceptions to § 1367(a) contained in § 1367(b), moreover, provide additional support for our conclusion that § 1367(a) confers supplemental jurisdiction over these claims. Section 1367(b), which applies only to diversity cases, withholds supplemental jurisdiction over the claims of plaintiffs proposed to be joined as indispensable parties under Federal Rule of Civil Procedure 19, or who seek to intervene pursuant to Rule 24. Nothing in the text of § 1367(b), however, withholds supplemental jurisdiction over the claims of plaintiffs permissively joined under Rule 20 (like the additional plaintiffs in [Ortega]) or certified as class-action members pursuant to Rule 23 (like the additional plaintiffs in [Exxon]). The natural, indeed the necessary, inference is that § 1367 confers supplemental jurisdiction over claims by Rule 20 and Rule 23 plaintiffs. This inference, at least with respect to Rule 20 plaintiffs, is strengthened by the fact that § 1367(b) explicitly excludes supplemental jurisdiction over claims against defendants joined under Rule 20.

We cannot accept the view, urged by some of the parties, commentators, and Courts of Appeals, that a district court lacks original jurisdiction over a civil action unless the court has original jurisdiction over every claim in the complaint. As we understand this position, it requires assuming either that all claims in the complaint must stand or fall as a single, indivisible "civil action" as a matter of definitional necessity—what we will refer to as the "indivisibility theory"—or else that the inclusion of a claim or party falling outside the district court's original jurisdiction somehow contaminates every other claim in the complaint, depriving the court of original jurisdiction over any of these claims—what we will refer to as the "contamination theory."

The indivisibility theory is easily dismissed, as it is inconsistent with the whole notion of supplemental jurisdiction. . . .

. . . .

The contamination theory . . . can make some sense in the special context of the complete diversity requirement because the presence of nondiverse parties on both sides of a lawsuit eliminates the justification for providing a federal forum. The theory, however, makes little sense with respect to the amount-in-controversy requirement, which is meant to ensure that a dispute is sufficiently important to warrant federal-court attention. The presence of a single nondiverse party may eliminate the fear of bias with respect to all claims, but the presence of a claim that falls short of the minimum amount in controversy does nothing to reduce the importance of the claims that do meet this requirement.

It is fallacious to suppose, simply from the proposition that § 1332 imposes both the diversity requirement and the amount-in-controversy requirement, that the contamination theory germane to the former is also relevant to the latter. There is no inherent logical connection between the amount-in-controversy requirement and § 1332 diversity jurisdiction. . . .

. . . .

. . . The omission of Rule 20 plaintiffs from the list of exceptions in § 1367(b) may have been an "unintentional drafting gap," Meritcare [Inc. v. St. Paul Mercury Ins. Co., 166 F.3d 214, 221 & n.6 (3d Cir.1999)]. If that is the case, it is up to Congress rather than the courts to fix it. The omission may seem odd, but it is not absurd. . . .

. . . .

And so we circle back to the original question. When the well-pleaded complaint in district court includes multiple claims, all part of the same case or controversy, and some, but not all, of the claims are within the court's original jurisdiction, does the court have before it "any civil action of which the district courts have original jurisdiction"? It does. . . . Though the special nature and purpose of the diversity requirement mean that a single nondiverse party can contaminate every other claim in the lawsuit, the contamination does not occur with respect to jurisdictional defects that go only to the substantive importance of individual claims.

It follows from this conclusion that the threshold requirement of § 1367(a) is satisfied in cases, like those now before us, where some, but not all, of the plaintiffs in a diversity action allege a sufficient amount in controversy. We hold that § 1367 by its plain text overruled . . . Zahn and authorized supplemental jurisdiction over all claims by diverse parties arising out of the same Article III case or controversy, subject only to enumerated exceptions not applicable in the cases now before us.

. . . .

The proponents of the alternative view of § 1367 insist that the statute is at least ambiguous and that we should look to other interpretive tools, including the legislative history of § 1367, which supposedly demonstrate Congress did not intend § 1367 to overrule Zahn. We can reject this argument at the very outset simply because § 1367 is not ambiguous. . . .

. . . .

■ [JUSTICE STEVENS, joined by Justice Breyer, wrote a dissent, which is omitted. He urged greater reliance on the legislative history.]

■ JUSTICE GINSBURG, with whom JUSTICE STEVENS, JUSTICE O'CONNOR, and JUSTICE BREYER join, dissenting.

. . . .

The Court adopts a plausibly broad reading of § 1367, a measure that is hardly a model of the careful drafter's art. There is another plausible reading, however, one less disruptive of our jurisprudence regarding supplemental jurisdiction. If one reads § 1367(a) to instruct, as the statute's text suggests, that the district court must first have "original jurisdiction" over a "civil action" before supplemental jurisdiction can attach, then [cases such as] Zahn are preserved, and supplemental jurisdiction does not open the way for joinder of plaintiffs, or inclusion of class members, who do not independently meet the amount-in-controversy requirement. For the reasons that follow, I conclude that this narrower construction is the better reading of § 1367.

. . . .

. . . § 1367(a) addresses "civil action[s] of which the district courts have original jurisdiction," a formulation that, in diversity cases, is sensibly read to incorporate the rules on joinder and aggregation tightly tied to § 1332 at the time of § 1367's enactment. On this reading, a complaint must first meet that "original jurisdiction" measurement. If it does not, no supplemental jurisdiction is authorized. If it does, § 1367(a) authorizes "supplemental jurisdiction" over related claims. In other words, § 1367(a) would preserve undiminished, as part and parcel of § 1332 "original jurisdiction" determinations, both the "complete diversity" rule and the decisions restricting aggregation to arrive at the amount in controversy. Section 1367(b)'s office, then, would be "to prevent the erosion of the complete diversity [and amount-in-controversy] requirement[s] that might otherwise result from an expansive application of what was once termed the doctrine of ancillary jurisdiction." See Pfander, Supplemental Jurisdiction and Section 1367: The Case for a Sympathetic Textualism, 148 U.Pa.L.Rev. 109, 114 (1999) . . . .

. . . .

The less disruptive view I take of § 1367 also accounts for the omission of Rule 20 plaintiffs and Rule 23 class actions in § 1367(b)'s text. . . . [P]laintiffs who do not meet the amount-in-controversy requirement would fail at the § 1367(a) threshold. Congress would have no reason to resort to a § 1367(b) exception to turn such plaintiffs away from federal court, given that their claims, from the start, would fall outside the court's § 1332 jurisdiction. See Pfander, 148 U.Pa.L.Rev., at 148.

. . . .

Question: (14) *P-1* of State *A* sues *D-1* of State *B* and *D-2* of State *B* in a federal district court on a $101,000 claim for which diversity of citizenship is the only basis of jurisdiction. Does the federal court have discretion to hear a related nonfederal claim for $4000 that *P-2* of State *A,* joining under Rule 20, has against *D-1* and *D-2*? In other words, would the presence of multiple defendants put the Ortega situation within the reach of § 1367(b)?

MEASURING THE JURISDICTIONAL AMOUNT

How is the district court to determine whether the case meets any applicable jurisdictional amount requirement? Why not wait until the end of trial to see how much the plaintiff recovers? If instead it is deemed desirable to apply the test at the outset of the case, why not have a hearing to determine the probable recovery? If instead it is deemed desirable to avoid holding a hearing, why not take the plaintiff at his word, as spoken in his ad damnum clause?

Saint Paul Mercury Indemnity Co. v. Red Cab Co., 303 U.S. 283, 58 S.Ct. 586 (1938), is the leading case. Red Cab sued St. Paul for failure to pay workers' compensation claims as required by the contract of insurance covering injuries to Red Cab's employees, as a result of which Red Cab allegedly had to pay or obligate itself to pay the sum of $4000. St. Paul removed the case to the federal district court on the basis of diversity of citizenship. Thereafter Red Cab filed an amended complaint still claiming $4000 in damages, but with an attached exhibit that listed the names of the injured employees and the amounts claimed totaling $1380.89. On a trial without jury, the court entered judgment for Red Cab in the amount of $1162.98.

St. Paul appealed on the merits. The court of appeals on its own refused to decide the merits, saying that, as the record showed Red Cab's claim did not exceed the jurisdictional amount of $3000, the district court should have remanded the case to the state court. On certiorari, the Supreme Court reversed. Justice Roberts said without dissent:

"The intent of Congress drastically to restrict federal jurisdiction in controversies between citizens of different states has always been rigorously enforced by the courts. The rule governing dismissal for want of jurisdiction in cases brought in the federal court is that, unless the law gives a different rule, the sum claimed by the plaintiff controls if the claim is apparently made in good faith. It must appear to a legal certainty that the claim is really for less than the jurisdictional amount to justify dismissal. The inability of plaintiff to recover an amount adequate to give the court jurisdiction does not show his bad faith or oust the jurisdiction. Nor does the fact that the complaint discloses the existence of a valid defense to the claim. But if, from the face of the pleadings, it is apparent, to a legal certainty, that the plaintiff cannot recover the amount claimed, or if, from the proofs, the court is satisfied to a like certainty that the plaintiff never was entitled to recover that amount, and that his claim was therefore colorable for the purpose of conferring jurisdiction, the suit will be dismissed. Events occurring subsequent to the institution of suit which reduce the amount recoverable below the statutory limit do not oust jurisdiction.

. . . .

"The present case well illustrates the propriety of the rule that subsequent reduction of the amount claimed cannot oust the district court's jurisdiction. Suit was instituted in the state court June 5, 1934. The lump sum claimed was largely in excess of $3,000, exclusive of interest and costs. The items which went to make up the respondent's demand for indemnity were numerous and each, in turn, was itself the total of several items of expenditure or liability. There is nothing to indicate that all of the sums for which reimbursement was claimed had actually been expended prior to the beginning of suit or that the sums thereafter to be expended had been ascertained. Not until the ... amended complaint was filed in the United States court, in November 1934, did the respondent furnish a statement of the particulars of its claim. That statement is not inconsistent with the making of a claim in good faith for over $3,000 when the suit was instituted."

The much-quoted words of Justice Roberts, and subsequent decisions of the courts pursuant thereto,[h] have made it clear that the "legal certainty" test poses little problem for the plaintiff seeking to invoke federal jurisdiction. Because the jurisdictional amount and the merits overlap, courts ask for no more than a very modest factual showing to establish jurisdiction. To satisfy the jurisdictional amount requirement in a diversity case where the plaintiff has pleaded a claim for more than $75,000 against the defendant, the plaintiff needs to be able only to show a legal possibility that the judgment could exceed $75,000 under the applicable *law*. Plaintiffs can pass this test very easily, especially in unliquidated tort cases involving pain and suffering, because jurisdiction will exist even though a recovery over $75,000 is highly unlikely on the *facts*. In order to rebut legal certainty, the plaintiff need establish only that a reasonable factfinder could award more than the jurisdictional amount or, in other words, a reasonable possibility.

Accordingly, given that the amount claimed by the plaintiff will be controlling except in flagrant circumstances, plaintiffs have often greatly inflated their claims for relief in order to circumvent the jurisdictional amount requirement. When Congress increased the amount for diversity cases from $3000 to $10,000 in 1958, it also provided a costs sanction giving the court discretionary power to deny costs to the plaintiff and in

---

[h] For example, "The test of the plaintiff's 'good faith' is not his subjective state of mind but a very strict objective standard. . . . Thus, there is but one test; good faith and legal certainty are equivalents rather than two separate tests." Jones v. Landry, 387 F.2d 102, 104 (5th Cir.1967).

addition to impose costs upon him, if he recovered less than $10,000. 28 U.S.C. § 1332(b) (now reflecting later increases of jurisdictional amount). Because courts have used this power very rarely and because costs are not likely to be sizable anyway, this sanction has plainly not deterred plaintiffs' lawyers from making excessive claims in order to get into a federal forum. "The records of the Administrative Office of judgments after trial in diversity cases terminated in the fiscal year 1961 (some few of which were probably filed before the 1958 increase in jurisdictional amount from $3,000 to $10,000 became effective) show that 614 out of 1,268 reported judgments [for plaintiff], 48 per cent of the total, were for less than $10,000, and that the amount of the median judgment in these [614] cases was $3,793. The amount of the median claim in these same cases was $32,200. While it is obvious that there are a good many cases where counsel might reasonably hope for a judgment over $10,000 and obtain one for substantially less than that, it seems clear that the jurisdiction is being abused." Study of the Division of Jurisdiction Between State and Federal Courts 120 (Am. Law Inst. 1969).

Question: (15) Would you expect Rule 11 to be effective in this regard?

The case below reflects the widely held concern over the inflation of the claimed amount in controversy. Although it is not an isolated example, as illustrated by the Ortega decision reversed by the Exxon Court, we should emphasize that it applies the St. Paul test with much more rigor than the general run of personal-injury actions. It raises the bar, in effect by nudging the standard of proof from a reasonable possibility up to a substantial possibility. It accords with the Twombly-Iqbal spirit, but the relevant question remains whether Nelson's approach is authorized, desirable, and workable.

Nelson v. Keefer

United States Court of Appeals, Third Circuit, 1971.
451 F.2d 289.

■ Before VAN DUSEN, ALDISERT and GIBBONS, CIRCUIT JUDGES.

■ ALDISERT, CIRCUIT JUDGE. These appeals question the propriety of dismissing a personal injury diversity action at pre-trial because the district court concluded that it appeared "to a legal certainty" that the claims were "really for less than the jurisdictional amount" of $10,000.

[The court summarized the damage claims of the three plaintiffs, husband, wife, and minor son, based on the automobile accident. The claims were mostly for injuries such as whiplash, the most substantial claim being the husband's which included questionably related medical bills of $603.50 and also property damage of $727.69.]

It is our intention to require removal from the trial list of those "flagrant" cases where it can be determined in advance "with legal certainty" that the congressional mandate of a $10,000 minimum was not satisfied. . . .

We are not persuaded by the argument that a termination prior to trial deprives a "plaintiff of his present statutory right to a jury trial." See Deutsch v. Hewes Street Realty Corp., [359 F.2d 96, 100 (2d Cir.1966)]. Indeed, such an argument begs the question, for the precise issue is whether plaintiff has a statutory right to enter the courtroom for any trial, jury or otherwise. The corollary suggestion that the remedy lies with Congress is similarly specious, for the reality is that Congress *did* act in 1958 in raising the amount in controversy from $3,000 to $10,000.

. . . .

Given the congressional intention to eliminate trials of unsubstantial diversity cases, and mindful that personal injury actions comprise a majority—at least 60 per cent—of diversity controversies, and that the intangible factor of pain, suffering, and inconvenience usually constitutes the largest single item of damages in personal injury claims, we have no difficulty in concluding that Congress intended that trial judges exercise permissible discretion prior to trial in adjudicating challenges to jurisdiction.

. . . .

Analogizing the authority of the court to reject a jury's verdict [by giving a new trial for its being excessive], we have no difficulty in recognizing a corollary power in that same court to evaluate a case prior to trial where sufficient information has been made available through pre-trial discovery and comprehensive pre-trial narrative statements which disclose medical reports. Assuming that claimed tangible items of damage legally related to the cause of action will be taken as true, the court should be able to determine . . . the "upper limit" of a permissible award that includes tangible recoverable items such as medical special and lost wages damage items as well as the intangibles of pain, suffering, and inconvenience. . . .

. . . .

Our scope of review under these circumstances is similar to that which is utilized in review of a trial court's determination that a verdict is "excessive" or "capricious." [Citations omitted.] Accordingly, although we must "give the benefit of every doubt to the judgment of the trial judge," we must "make a detailed appraisal of the evidence bearing on damages." Having done so, we find that the district court gave plaintiffs ample opportunity, at the pre-trial stage, to justify their jurisdictional claim. Convinced to a legal certainty that the evidence would not permit it to sustain a verdict for [any of the] plaintiffs of $10,000 or more, the district court did not—and indeed could not—allow the case to proceed to trial.

. . . And since plaintiffs' legally recoverable ceiling did not at its apex reach the federal jurisdictional floor, the judgment of the district court will be affirmed.

————

Questions: (16) *P* seeks an injunction against *D* in a federal district court on the basis of diversity of citizenship. Normally, the amount in controversy in such an action is the value of the relief requested. But what if it is stipulated that the benefit to *P* will be worth less than the jurisdictional amount, but the cost to *D* of complying with the requested relief will be greatly in excess of that figure: is the jurisdictional amount requirement met? What if the benefit to the plaintiff is more than the jurisdictional amount, but the cost to the defendant less? Should it matter whether *P* institutes the action in federal court or *D* brings it there by removal? See Charles Alan Wright & Mary Kay Kane, Law of Federal Courts § 34 (8th ed. 2017).

(17) *P* of State *A* sues *D* of State *B* in a court of State *A* on a state-law claim for $70,000. Knowing that state law permits recovery in excess of the amount demanded except in default cases and believing that P wants big damages, *D* removes to the federal court under 28 U.S.C. § 1441(a). *P* moves to remand. What decision on that motion? See 28 U.S.C. § 1446(c)(2), amended in 2011 to allow the removing defendant to show by a preponderance that, as the legislative history says, "the true amount in controversy" exceeds the jurisdictional amount.

————

SECTION 5.   REMOVAL JURISDICTION

Question: (18) *P* of Delaware sues *D* of Texas in a Delaware state court on a state-law claim for $4000. *D* counterclaims for $101,000. *D* removes to the federal court under 28 U.S.C. § 1441(a). *P* moves to remand. What decision on that motion? Should it matter whether or not *D*'s counterclaim arises out of the same transaction or occurrence as *P*'s claim? If so, should it matter whether or not Delaware has a compulsory counterclaim provision like Rule 13(a)? See Kevin M. Clermont, Principles of Civil Procedure 264–65 (5th ed. 2018).

————

SHAMROCK OIL & GAS CORP. v. SHEETS, 313 U.S. 100, 61 S.Ct. 868 (1941). *P* of Delaware sued *D* of Texas in a Texas state court on a contract claim for more than the federal jurisdictional amount. As was permitted by Texas law, *D* counterclaimed on a wholly unrelated contract claim also in excess of the federal jurisdictional amount. *P* immediately removed to the federal district court on the basis of diversity of citizenship. *D* moved to remand. The district court denied that motion, and after trial it gave judgment for *P* on the claim and the counterclaim. The Fifth Circuit reversed, ordering the case remanded to state court.

On certiorari the Supreme Court affirmed the court of appeals' decision, on the basis that § 1441(a) speaks of removal "by the defendant or the defendants" and it means what it says. The Court implied that it was irrelevant whether the counterclaim was compulsory or permissive under state law, and whether or not the counterclaim was factually related to the main claim. Indeed, the Court went out of its way to say that its conclusion that plaintiffs cannot remove was independent of whether the main claim was for more or less than the jurisdictional amount.

———

Questions: (19) Does the Shamrock reading of § 1441(a) make any sense? See Study of the Division of Jurisdiction Between State and Federal Courts §§ 1304(c), 1312(a)(3) commentary at 147–48, 196–97 (Am. Law Inst. 1969).

(20) Could *P* instead have promptly dismissed the initial claim voluntarily, then quickly removed the remaining counterclaim as the sole defendant, and finally repleaded the initial claim as a counterclaim in federal court? See Home Depot U.S.A., Inc. v. Jackson, 139 S.Ct. 1743 (2019) (implying no, reaffirming Shamrock, and defining "defendant" as a person joined as a defendant by the original plaintiff).

———

REMOVAL UNDER 28 U.S.C. § 1441(c)

This narrow and difficult statute, with a long and convoluted history, now allows removal of a claim within the general federal question statute when joined with a nonremovable claim. That is, the defendants to the plaintiffs' federal question claim can remove even though the plaintiffs have joined a claim that those defendants could not have removed if it stood by itself. The additional claim might be nonremovable because some federal statute so provides, or because the additional nondiversity state-law claim is completely unrelated to the facts of the federal question claim ("separate and independent" in the words of former versions of § 1441(c)).

So, § 1441(c) provides a slim opportunity to remove a federal question claim not removable under § 1441(a) because the whole case is not within the federal district court's original jurisdiction. Given such joinder of removable and nonremovable claims, the entire case becomes removable via § 1441(c). But the federal district court must remand the nonremovable claim once the entire case comes before it. For example, if a plaintiff sues nondiverse *D* in a state court on a federal civil rights claim and joins a completely unrelated contract claim against *D*, *D* can remove the whole case, but the court will remand the contract claim.

Question: (21) If *P* of State *A* sues *D-1* of State *B* in a court of State *A* on a federal civil rights claim and joins a completely unrelated contract claim for $200,000 against *D-1* and *D-2*, also of State *B*, and if *D-1* but not *D-2* wishes to remove, can *D-1* properly do so? See Fravel v. Stankus, 936 F.Supp. 474, 479 (N.D.Ill.1996) (yes).

Think, now, of that same *P* of State *A* suing *D* of State *B* in a court of State *A* on an FELA claim and joining a completely unrelated small contract claim against *D*. Removal is impermissible by virtue of 28 U.S.C. § 1445(a). The federal question claim itself must be removable.

Question: (22) *P* sues *D* in a state court on a federal civil rights claim and joins a completely unrelated FELA claim against *D*. Can *D* properly remove despite § 1445(a)? If so, must the district court remand the FELA claim under § 1441(c)?

The wording of the statute's current version still presents numerous difficulties. Think, for example, about who may invoke § 1441(c). Think of *P* suing *D* in a state court on a small contract claim and *D* counterclaiming with a completely unrelated federal civil rights claim. Can *P* now avoid the Shamrock rule by invoking § 1441(c)? The cases hold in the negative on this point, although the statute does not obviously require that result. More generally, despite a close policy call in the circumstances of certain additional claims, courts tend to read § 1441(c) narrowly as not applying to claims other than those joined by original plaintiffs against original defendants, even when the counterclaim, crossclaim, or third-party claim is arguably separate and independent. See Wright & Miller § 3722.3, at 610, 616–26.

Question: (23) *P* sues *D* in a state court on a small contract claim. Under state joinder rules, *D* impleads *T* on an indemnity claim and joins a completely unrelated federal civil rights claim against *T*. Can *T* properly remove? See Haden P. Gerrish, Note, Third-Party Removal Under Section 1441(c), 52 Fordham L.Rev. 133, 156–58 (1983) (arguing yes, but only in this most extreme setting of an unrelated claim).

Finally, § 1441(c) apparently now interlocks with supplemental, or pendent, jurisdiction to provide for removal of almost any federal question case. Consider a plaintiff's federal question claim that would be removable if sued upon alone, joined with an ordinary state-law claim against the defendant who is nondiverse. On the one hand, if the state claim falls within pendent jurisdiction, the federal and state claims being factually related, then the defendant can remove the whole case under § 1441(a). On the other hand, if the state claim does not come within pendent jurisdiction, then § 1441(c) should kick in. And if the plaintiff joins (1) the federal question claim, (2) the pendent state claim, and (3) the separate and independent state claim, the defendant can still remove under § 1441(c), although the court must remand the third claim and, as we shall see next, it may remand the second claim for relief with its discretion guided by the standards of 28 U.S.C. § 1367(c).

———

CARNEGIE-MELLON UNIVERSITY v. COHILL, 484 U.S. 343, 108 S.Ct. 614 (1988). Based on an allegedly wrongful termination of employment, plaintiffs sued co-citizen defendants in Pennsylvania state court under federal and state age-discrimination laws and on various contract and tort theories. Defendants properly removed under § 1441(a), utilizing the doctrine of pendent jurisdiction. Plaintiffs did not contest removal, but six months later they (1) moved to amend their complaint by deleting certain untenable allegations, including age discrimination, and (2) moved, conditional upon that amendment, to remand. The district court granted both motions. The sharply divided Third Circuit denied a petition for mandamus.

On certiorari to resolve a conflict among circuits, the Supreme Court affirmed, upholding the power to remand. Justice Marshall for the Court acknowledged that neither 28 U.S.C. § 1447(c) (because removal jurisdiction was proper) nor § 1441(c) (because the claims were not separate and independent) applied to give that power. But he explained that pendent jurisdiction itself entails discretion to decline jurisdiction by *dismissing* the removed state claims in some circumstances and hence implies the discretionary power to *remand* in such circumstances. Thus, when the federal claim that justifies removal is eliminated, the district court can remand the remaining pendent state claims to the state court in pursuit of "economy, convenience, fairness, and comity."

Justice White, joined by Chief Justice Rehnquist and Justice Scalia, dissented by arguing in support of the general rule that Congress must have statutorily authorized remand.

Borough of West Mifflin v. Lancaster
United States Court of Appeals, Third Circuit, 1995.
45 F.3d 780.

■ Before STAPLETON, GARTH, and PRATT,* CIRCUIT JUDGES.

■ PRATT, CIRCUIT JUDGE:

FACTS AND BACKGROUND

The operative facts giving rise to this mandamus application are set forth in the civil complaint of respondents Alan D. Lindsey and Randall Coughanour. In September 1991 Lindsey and Coughanour were involved in disputes with security guards at an indoor shopping mall on Route 51 in West Mifflin Borough, just south of Pittsburgh, Pa. They had travelled to the mall to shop, but upon their arrival, they were "harassed, threatened, and assaulted" by the security guards. When the guards refused their request that the police be summoned, Lindsey and Coughanour themselves telephoned the West Mifflin Police Department requesting assistance. West Mifflin Police Officer Evan, one of the petitioners in this mandamus application, responded to the call. Evan

---

*   Honorable George C. Pratt, United States Circuit Judge for the Second Circuit, sitting by designation.

refused to arrest or admonish any of the guards, but told Lindsey and Coughanour to leave the mall and never come back; otherwise, they would be arrested.

The following day, Lindsey returned to the mall in an attempt to talk to someone from the DeBartolo organization, which owned the mall, to find out why he had been accosted and why he was not permitted on the mall without permission. During the next three weeks Lindsey repeatedly and unsuccessfully attempted to contact Sam Vindovich, the mall manager, one of the defendants in the underlying action, to find out why he and Coughanour were banned from the mall. Lindsey finally consulted his present counsel, who advised him that the law permitted his entrance to the mall as long as the mall was open to the public.

On September 27, 1991, Lindsey and Coughanour returned to the mall to shop, but were accosted and handcuffed in the mall men's room, and then dragged through the mall corridor to mall offices to await the arrival of Officer Evan.

Evan then wrote out summary offense citations for disorderly conduct and defiant trespass. Lindsey and Coughanour were photographed by a Polaroid camera, and the photographs were attached to printed forms that said "DEFIANT TRESPASS". These paper forms contained, among other things a warning that, if Lindsey and Coughanour came onto the mall property again, they would be arrested. These preprinted forms were then displayed on a bulletin board in the mall at the security offices for everyone passing in front of the board to see.

The handcuffs were then removed, and Lindsey and Coughanour were ordered to leave the mall, separately, which they did. They were prosecuted and convicted in Common Pleas Court on charges stemming from the incidents at the mall, but on February 26, 1993, a three judge panel of the Superior Court of Pennsylvania vacated the convictions and discharged them.

Lindsey and Coughanour then filed a seven count complaint in the Court of Common Pleas of Allegheny County, Pennsylvania, claiming that they had committed no crimes while at the mall and that they had been maliciously abused and prosecuted. As defendants, they named the Borough of West Mifflin and Officer Evan ("the municipal defendants"), . . . as well as the owners, supervisors, and security officers of the mall ("the DeBartolo defendants"). Specifically, Lindsey and Coughanour alleged: (1) state law claims of malicious prosecution, malicious abuse of process, assault, and conspiracy against all defendants; (2) a negligence claim against the municipal defendants; (3) a negligence claim against the DeBartolo defendants; and (4) a federal claim under 42 U.S.C. § 1983 which alleged that the municipal defendants and the DeBartolo defendants conspired to deprive Lindsey and Coughanour of their civil rights through harassment, assault, false arrest, malicious prosecution, and abuse of process in violation of the 4th, 5th, and 14th amendments.

Relying on the federal civil rights claim, the . . . defendants filed a notice of removal from the state court to the United States District Court for the Western District of Pennsylvania. Lindsey and Coughanour then moved to remand the case back to state court. Magistrate Judge Kenneth J. Benson recommended a remand under 28 U.S.C. § 1441(c) of the entire case, including the § 1983 claim. He found that

> [t]he issues of state law clearly predominate in this matter. Not only do they predominate with respect to the state law claims, but there is also a predominance of state law issues with respect to the single claim pursuant to § 1983.

United States District Judge Gary L. Lancaster adopted the report and recommendation "as the opinion of the court" and entered a two page Memorandum and Order granting Lindsey and Coughanour's motion to remand the entire case.

The . . . defendants now seek in this court a writ of mandamus to compel Judge Lancaster to accept jurisdiction of this action, which, they contend, was properly removed under § 1441(a) . . . . They argue that by remanding the entire case under § 1441(c), Judge Lancaster exceeded his authority.

DISCUSSION

[After concluding that the remand order was reviewable, the court ruled that] Lindsey and Coughanour rely on the same series of events for all counts of their complaint, including the federal § 1983 count; therefore, the federal claim is not separate and independent under § 1441(c), and the district court had no authority to remand the case under that section.

. . . .

The plaintiffs insist that, even if the district court was not authorized to remand this entire case under § 1441(c), its action should be sustained under the authority of 28 U.S.C. § 1367(c) which gives a district court discretion to decline to hear certain state claims it would have supplemental jurisdiction to entertain under § 1367(a). We disagree for two reasons. First, nothing in § 1367(c) authorizes a district court to decline to entertain a claim over which it has original jurisdiction and, accordingly, that section clearly does not sanction the district court's remand of this entire case, including the civil rights claims, to the state court.

Further, § 1367(c) cannot legitimately be invoked to affirm even the district court's remand of the state claims to the state court. While we agree with plaintiffs that the discretion bestowed by § 1367(c) exists with respect to removed claims as well as claims filed initially in the district court, it is apparent that the district court has not exercised that discretion in this case. The magistrate judge's opinion, adopted by the district court, refers only to § 1441(c) and it is apparent from that opinion that the court remanded the entire case based solely on the authority of that section. Moreover, the result of an exercise of discretion under § 1367(c) in circumstances like those before the district court would have been two parallel proceedings, one in federal court and one in the state system, and a district court cannot properly exercise its discretion under § 1367(c) without taking that fact into account. The district court's § 1441(c) analysis accordingly cannot serve as a surrogate for a § 1367(c) analysis that was not conducted.

. . . .

As we have noted, the "substantially predominates" standard of § 1367(c)(2) comes from Gibbs. It is important to recognize that this standard was fashioned as a limited exception to the operation of the doctrine of pendent jurisdiction—a doctrine that seeks to promote judicial economy, convenience, and fairness to litigants by litigating in one case all claims that arise out of the same nucleus of operative fact. When a district court exercises its discretion not to hear state claims under § 1367(c)(2), the advantages of a single suit are lost. For that reason, § 1367(c)(2)'s authority should be invoked only where there is an important countervailing interest to be served by relegating state claims to the state court. This will normally be the case only where "a state claim constitutes the real body of a case, to which the federal claim is only an appendage," Gibbs, 383 U.S. at 727, 86 S.Ct. at 1140—only where permitting litigation of all claims in the district court can accurately be described as allowing a federal tail to wag what is in substance a state dog.

. . . .

In short, while we do not foreclose the parties from hereafter arguing, and the district court from hereafter considering, the issue posed by § 1367(c)(2), we think it unlikely that either will be able to point to a countervailing interest that would justify bifurcating this case into a federal and a state suit that will essentially duplicate each other.

. . . .

Accordingly, the petition for a writ of mandamus is granted.

———

Question: (24) If state claims constitute the real body of a removed case, to which the federal claim is merely the tail, remand of the whole case would be desirable to avoid duplicative proceedings. Some authorities have accordingly argued that such a case calling for discretionary dismissal of the state claims was never in the district court's "original jurisdiction" and so was not properly removable under § 1441(a), and thus the court must remand the whole case under § 1447(c) rather than settle for partial remand. Was the Third Circuit correct in seemingly rejecting this argument and concluding that the federal claim had to remain in the federal court even if the state claims were remanded?

———

Section 6. Diverse Citizenship

Marshall v. Marshall

Supreme Court of the United States, 2006.
547 U.S. 293, 126 S.Ct. 1735.

■ JUSTICE GINSBURG delivered the opinion of the Court.

. . . Among longstanding limitations on federal jurisdiction otherwise properly exercised are the so-called "domestic relations" and "probate" exceptions. Neither is compelled by the text of the Constitution or federal statute. Both are judicially created doctrines stemming in large measure from misty understandings of English legal history. . . . In Ankenbrandt v. Richards, 504 U.S. 689, 112 S.Ct. 2206 (1992), this Court reined in the "domestic relations exception." Earlier, in Markham v. Allen, 326 U.S. 490, 66 S.Ct. 296 (1946), the Court endeavored similarly to curtail the "probate exception."

Nevertheless, the Ninth Circuit in the instant case read the probate exception broadly to exclude from the federal courts' adjudicatory authority "not only direct challenges to a will or trust, but also questions which would ordinarily be decided by a probate court in determining the validity of the decedent's estate planning instrument." 392 F.3d 1118, 1133 (C.A.9 2004). The Court of Appeals further held that a State's vesting of exclusive jurisdiction over probate matters in a special court strips federal courts of jurisdiction to entertain any "probate related matter," including claims respecting "tax liability, debt, gift, [or] tort." Id., at 1136. We hold that the Ninth Circuit had no warrant from Congress, or from decisions of this Court, for its sweeping extension of the probate exception.

I

Petitioner, Vickie Lynn Marshall (Vickie), also known as Anna Nicole Smith, is the surviving widow of J. Howard Marshall II (J. Howard). Vickie and J. Howard met in October 1991. After a courtship lasting more than two years, they were married on June 27, 1994. J. Howard died on August 4, 1995. Although he lavished gifts and significant sums of money on Vickie during their courtship and marriage, J. Howard did not include anything for Vickie in his will. According to Vickie, J. Howard intended to provide for her financial security through a gift . . . .

Respondent, E. Pierce Marshall (Pierce), one of J. Howard's sons, was the ultimate beneficiary of J. Howard's estate plan, which consisted of a living trust and a "pourover" will. Under the terms of the will, all of J. Howard's assets not already included in the trust were to be transferred to the trust upon his death.

Competing claims regarding J. Howard's fortune ignited proceedings in both state and federal courts. In January 1996, while J. Howard's estate was subject to ongoing proceedings in Probate Court in Harris County, Texas, Vickie filed for bankruptcy under Chapter 11 of the Bankruptcy Code, 11 U.S.C. § 1101 et seq., in the United States Bankruptcy Court for the Central District of California. See 275 B.R. 5, 8 (C.D.Cal.2002). In June 1996, Pierce filed a proof of claim in the federal bankruptcy proceeding, id., at 9; see 11 U.S.C. § 501, alleging that Vickie had defamed him when, shortly after J. Howard's death, lawyers representing Vickie told members of the press that Pierce had engaged in forgery, fraud, and overreaching to gain control of his father's assets, 275 B.R., at 9. Pierce sought a declaration that the debt he asserted in that claim was not dischargeable in bankruptcy. Ibid. Vickie answered, asserting truth as a defense. She also filed counterclaims, among them a claim that Pierce had tortiously interfered with a gift she expected. Ibid.; see App. 23–25. Vickie alleged that Pierce prevented the transfer of his father's intended gift to her by, among other things: effectively imprisoning J. Howard against his wishes; surrounding him with hired guards for the purpose of preventing personal contact between him and Vickie; making misrepresentations to J. Howard; and transferring property against J. Howard's expressed wishes. Id., at 24.

[The bankruptcy court rejected Pierce's attack on subject-matter jurisdiction over Vickie's tort counterclaim. It found for Vickie, awarding her $449 million in compensatory damages and $25 million in punitive damages.

[Next, the Texas probate court found Pierce's living trust and J. Howard's will both valid. It entered judgment to that effect.

[Then, the United States District Court for the Central District of California, treating the bankruptcy court's decision as proposed findings of fact and conclusions of law to be reviewed de novo, found Pierce's behavior willful, malicious, and fraudulent. It entered judgment for $44.3 million in compensatory damages and $44.3 million in punitive damages. But the court of appeals reversed for lack of federal subject-matter jurisdiction over Vickie's claim, which it saw as a thinly veiled will contest. The Supreme Court granted certiorari.]

II

In Ankenbrandt v. Richards, 504 U.S. 689, 112 S.Ct. 2206 (1992), we addressed both the derivation and the limits of the "domestic relations exception" to the exercise of federal jurisdiction. Carol Ankenbrandt, a citizen of Missouri, brought suit in Federal District Court on behalf of her daughters, naming as defendants their father (Ankenbrandt's former husband) and his female companion, both citizens of Louisiana. Id., at 691, 112 S.Ct. 2206. Ankenbrandt's complaint sought damages for the defendants' alleged sexual and physical abuse of the children. Ibid. Federal jurisdiction was predicated on diversity of citizenship. Ibid. (citing 28 U.S.C. § 1332). The District Court dismissed the case for lack of subject-matter jurisdiction, holding that Ankenbrandt's suit fell within "the 'domestic relations' exception to diversity jurisdiction." 504 U.S., at

692, 112 S.Ct. 2206. The Court of Appeals agreed and affirmed. Ibid. We reversed the Court of Appeals' judgment. Id., at 706–707, 112 S.Ct. 2206.

Holding that the District Court improperly refrained from exercising jurisdiction over Ankenbrandt's tort claim, id., at 704, 112 S.Ct. 2206, we traced explanation of the current domestic relations exception to Barber v. Barber, 21 How. 582 (1859). See Ankenbrandt, 504 U.S., at 693–695, 112 S.Ct. 2206. In Barber, the Court upheld federal-court authority, in a diversity case, to enforce an alimony award decreed by a state court. In dicta, however, the Barber Court announced—without citation or discussion—that federal courts lack jurisdiction over suits for divorce or the allowance of alimony. 21 How., at 584–589; see Ankenbrandt, 504 U.S., at 693–695, 112 S.Ct. 2206.

Finding no Article III impediment to federal-court jurisdiction in domestic relations cases, id., at 695–697, 112 S.Ct. 2206, the Court in Ankenbrandt anchored the exception in Congress' original provision for diversity jurisdiction, id., at 698–701, 112 S.Ct. 2206. Beginning at the beginning, the Court recalled:

> "The Judiciary Act of 1789 provided that 'the circuit courts shall have original cognizance, concurrent with the courts of the several States, of *all suits of a civil nature at common law or in equity, where the matter in dispute exceeds*, exclusive of costs, the sum or value of *five hundred dollars*, and . . . an alien is a party, or the suit is *between a citizen of the State where the suit is brought, and a citizen of another State.*' " Id., at 698, 112 S.Ct. 2206 (quoting Act of Sept. 24, 1789, § 11, 1 Stat. 78; emphasis added in Ankenbrandt).

The defining phrase, "all suits of a civil nature at common law or in equity," the Court stressed, remained in successive statutory provisions for diversity jurisdiction until 1948, when Congress adopted the more economical phrase, "all civil actions." 504 U.S., at 698, 112 S.Ct. 2206; 1948 Judicial Code and Judiciary Act, 62 Stat. 930, 28 U.S.C. § 1332.

The Barber majority, we acknowledged in Ankenbrandt, did not expressly tie its announcement of a domestic relations exception to the text of the diversity statute. 504 U.S., at 698, 112 S.Ct. 2206. But the dissenters in that case made the connection. They stated that English courts of chancery [as opposed to ecclesiastical courts] lacked authority to issue divorce and alimony decrees. Because "the jurisdiction of the courts of the United States in chancery is bounded by that of the chancery in England," Barber, 21 How., at 605 (opinion of Daniel, J.), the dissenters reasoned, our federal courts similarly lack authority to decree divorces or award alimony, ibid. Such relief, in other words, would not fall within the diversity statute's original grant of jurisdiction over "all suits of a civil nature at common law or in equity." We concluded in Ankenbrandt that "it may be inferred fairly that the jurisdictional limitation recognized by the [Barber] Court rested on th[e] statutory basis" indicated by the dissenters in that case. 504 U.S., at 699, 112 S.Ct. 2206.

We were "content" in Ankenbrandt "to rest our conclusion that a domestic relations exception exists as a matter of statutory construction not on the accuracy of the historical justifications on which [the exception] was seemingly based." Id., at 700, 112 S.Ct. 2206. "[R]ather," we relied on "Congress' apparent acceptance of this construction of the diversity jurisdiction provisions in the years prior to 1948, when the statute limited jurisdiction to 'suits of a civil nature at common law or in equity.'" Ibid. (quoting 1 Stat. 78). We further determined that Congress did not intend to terminate the exception in 1948 when it "replace[d] the law/equity distinction with the phrase 'all civil actions.'" 504 U.S., at 700, 112 S.Ct. 2206. Absent contrary indications, we presumed that Congress meant to leave undisturbed "the Court's nearly century-long interpretation" of the diversity statute "to contain an exception for certain domestic relations matters." Ibid.

We nevertheless emphasized in Ankenbrandt that the exception covers only "a narrow range of domestic relations issues." Id., at 701, 112 S.Ct. 2206. The Barber Court itself, we reminded, "sanctioned the exercise of federal jurisdiction over the enforcement of an alimony decree that had been properly obtained in a state court of competent jurisdiction." 504 U.S., at 702, 112 S.Ct. 2206. Noting that some lower federal courts had applied the domestic relations exception "well beyond the circumscribed situations posed by Barber and its progeny," id., at 701, 112 S.Ct. 2206, we clarified that only "divorce, alimony, and child custody decrees" remain outside federal jurisdictional bounds, id., at 703, 704, 112 S.Ct. 2206. While recognizing the "special proficiency developed by state tribunals . . . in handling issues that arise in the granting of [divorce, alimony, and child custody] decrees," id., at 704, 112 S.Ct. 2206, we viewed federal courts as equally equipped to deal with complaints alleging the commission of torts, ibid.[i]

III

Federal jurisdiction in this case is premised on 28 U.S.C. § 1334, the statute vesting in federal district courts jurisdiction in bankruptcy cases and related proceedings. Decisions of this Court have recognized a "probate exception," kin to the domestic relations exception, to otherwise proper federal jurisdiction. See Markham, 326 U.S., at 494, 66 S.Ct. 296; see also Sutton v. English, 246 U.S. 199, 38 S.Ct. 254 (1918); Waterman v. Canal-Louisiana Bank & Trust Co., 215 U.S. 33, 30 S.Ct. 10 (1909). Like the domestic relations exception, the probate exception has been linked to language contained in the Judiciary Act of 1789.

---

[i]   For commentary on the domestic relations exception, see, e.g., Judith Resnik, "Naturally" Without Gender: Women, Jurisdiction, and the Federal Courts, 66 N.Y.U.L.Rev. 1682 (1991); Mark Strasser, Congress, Federal Courts, and Domestic Relations Exceptionalism, 12 Conn.Pub.Int.L.J. 193 (2012).

[English equity in 1789 did not extend to probate matters.]

[The Court tied the probate exception to] the general principle that, when one court is exercising in rem jurisdiction over a res, a second court will not assume in rem jurisdiction over the same res. See, e.g., Penn General Casualty Co. v. Pennsylvania ex rel. Schnader, 294 U.S. 189, 195–196, 55 S.Ct. 386 (1935); Waterman, 215 U.S., at 45–46, 30 S.Ct. 10. Thus, the probate exception reserves to state probate courts the probate or annulment of a will and the administration of a decedent's estate; it also precludes federal courts from endeavoring to dispose of property that is in the custody of a state probate court. But it does not bar federal courts from adjudicating matters outside those confines and otherwise within federal jurisdiction.

A

As the Court of Appeals correctly observed, Vickie's claim does not "involve the administration of an estate, the probate of a will, or any other purely probate matter." 392 F.3d, at 1133. Provoked by Pierce's claim in the bankruptcy proceedings, Vickie's claim, like Carol Ankenbrandt's, alleges a widely recognized tort. [Citations omitted.] Vickie seeks an in personam judgment against Pierce, not the probate or annulment of a will. Cf. Sutton, 246 U.S., at 208, 38 S.Ct. 254 (suit to annul a will found "supplemental to the proceedings for probate of the will" and therefore not cognizable in federal court). Nor does she seek to reach a res in the custody of a state court. See Markham, 326 U.S., at 494, 66 S.Ct. 296.

. . . .

B

. . . .

Texas courts have recognized a state-law tort action for interference with an expected inheritance or gift . . . . It is clear, under Erie R. Co. v. Tompkins, 304 U.S. 64, 58 S.Ct. 817 (1938), that Texas law governs the substantive elements of Vickie's tortious interference claim. It is also clear, however, that Texas may not reserve to its probate courts the exclusive right to adjudicate a transitory tort. We have long recognized that "a State cannot create a transitory cause of action and at the same time destroy the right to sue on that transitory cause of action in any court having jurisdiction." Tennessee Coal, Iron & R. Co. v. George, 233 U.S. 354, 360, 34 S.Ct. 587 (1914). Jurisdiction is determined "by the law of the court's creation and cannot be defeated by the extraterritorial operation of a [state] statute . . . , even though it created the right of action." Ibid. Directly on point, we have held that the jurisdiction of the federal courts, "having existed from the beginning of the Federal government, [can]not be impaired by subsequent state legislation creating courts of probate." McClellan v. Carland, 217 U.S. 268, 281, 30 S.Ct. 501 (1910) (upholding federal jurisdiction over action by heirs of decedent, who died intestate, to determine their rights in the estate (citing Waterman, 215 U.S. 33, 30 S.Ct. 10)).

. . . .

IV

[Because the court of appeals considered only subject-matter jurisdiction, Pierce's arguments concerning preclusion remain open on remand.]

For the reasons stated, the judgment of the Court of Appeals for the Ninth Circuit is reversed, and the case is remanded for further proceedings consistent with this opinion.

It is so ordered.[j]

■ [JUSTICE STEVENS, concurring in part and concurring in the judgment, argued for eliminating the probate exception.]

_____

DEVICES TO MANIPULATE FEDERAL JURISDICTION

Devices to create jurisdiction.—In order to get a case into federal court, a potential plaintiff will sometimes assign his claim to someone whose citizenship is different from the defendant's, or use some analogous tactic such as naming a diverse representative for a potential party. However, such tactics will often fail. First, courts ignore the citizenship of any named party whose interest at stake is strictly nominal, such as a purely formal obligee, regardless of the motive in naming the party. The diversity statute itself was amended in 1988, by adding § 1332(c)(2), to prevent manipulation by appointment of legal representatives of infants, incompetents, and decedents. Second, 28 U.S.C. § 1359 says to ignore the citizenship of any party "improperly or collusively" named. In applying § 1359, courts look for a motive to manufacture federal jurisdiction; but as the named party's interest at stake becomes more substantial, the motive necessary for triggering § 1359 must increasingly be a blatant one. See Kramer v. Caribbean Mills, Inc., 394 U.S. 823, 89 S.Ct. 1487 (1969).

Indeed, if the named party has a very real or even exclusive interest, and bears no resemblance whatsoever to a straw party, then her citizenship is considered, as motive in naming the party again becomes irrelevant. A complete and absolute transfer of interest will thus affect

_____

[j]   On remand, the court of appeals ruled that the district court was precluded by the contrary factual findings of the probate court, 600 F.3d 1037 (9th Cir.2010), aff'd sub nom. Stern v. Marshall, 564 U.S. 462, 131 S.Ct. 2594 (2011) (Roberts, C.J.) (5–4) (holding that the bankruptcy court, as contrasted to an Article III district court, had no constitutional authority to enter its 2000 judgment on a claim like Vickie's without waiver or consent, and that therefore the probate court's 2001 judgment constituted res judicata in the other federal proceedings, which were subsequent to 2001). The latest in all the later litigation is In re Marshall, 2019 WL 410324 (9th Cir. Jan. 31, 2019) (rejecting Vickie's estate's Rule 60(b) motion). In the end, the estate of Vickie, who had died in 2007 at age 39, recovered nothing from the estate of Pierce, who had died in 2006 at age 67.

jurisdiction. Recall Baker v. Keck, supra p. 259 (holding that the plaintiff could establish a new domicile, even with the purpose of creating diversity jurisdiction), and the Black & White Taxicab case, supra p. 373 (upholding diversity jurisdiction after the plaintiff had reincorporated in a different state).

Devices to defeat jurisdiction.—In order to prevent the defendant from removing the action to federal court, a potential plaintiff will sometimes try to destroy complete diversity by joining a party whose state citizenship is the same as an opposing party's. If the joined party is not nominal, this device will often work, because there is no general equivalent of § 1359 that would prohibit obstruction of federal jurisdiction. See Mecom v. Fitzsimmons Drilling Co., 284 U.S. 183, 52 S.Ct. 84 (1931). So, picture *P*, a citizen of Maine, suing *D*, an Oregon citizen, in a Maine state court for breach of contract. Before bringing his action, *P* had assigned 1/100 of his claim to an Oregon citizen, a law-school classmate of *P*'s attorney, for a consideration of $9. The potential value of the claim was about $300,000. The Oregon assignee joined with *P* as co-plaintiff. *P*'s attorney conceded that the sole purpose of the assignment was to defeat an anticipated removal by destroying diversity of citizenship. *D* removed under 28 U.S.C. § 1441(a). *P* moved to remand. The court remanded in Ridgeland Box Mfg. Co. v. Sinclair Refining Co., 82 F.Supp. 274 (E.D.S.C.1949).

Nevertheless, some courts of late have invoked a power supposedly inherent in the judiciary to reject artificial devices that would defeat jurisdiction, shaping the so-called fraudulent joinder doctrine into a kind of converse § 1359. The fraudulent joinder doctrine worked to facilitate removal of diversity cases by ignoring a joined party, but traditionally took a narrow form analogous to the Bell v. Hood rule. That is, to invoke it, the defendant had to show that the claim involving the joined party who impeded removal was factually or legally frivolous and pretextual: more precisely, the defendant had the burden of showing that the merits position as to the joined party was strong enough to remove reasonable doubt, and also that the plaintiff had the equivalent of an intent to deceive. See Wecker v. Nat'l Enameling & Stamping Co., 204 U.S. 176, 27 S.Ct. 184 (1907) (upholding removal because one of the defendants was wrongfully joined for the sole purpose of defeating the defendants' right to remove). However, of late, some lower courts have expanded the fraudulent joinder doctrine: they seem to be moving toward putting the burden on even an innocent plaintiff to make a reasonably possible showing on the facts and a full showing on the law regarding the joined party. See, e.g., Rose v. Giamatti, 721 F.Supp. 906 (S.D.Ohio 1989) (upholding removal on the ground that the real controversy was the Ohio plaintiff against the defendant baseball commissioner from New York, rather than against the Ohio defendants, namely, the Cincinnati Reds and Major League Baseball). This amorphous expansion, although seemingly consistent with other judicial efforts to defeat any party's trick that destroys federal jurisdiction, has come without any statutory authorization and may be undesirably activist.

———

SECTION 7. HYPOTHETICAL JURISDICTION

Ruhrgas AG v. Marathon Oil Co.

Supreme Court of the United States, 1999.
526 U.S. 574, 119 S.Ct. 1563.

■ JUSTICE GINSBURG delivered the opinion of the Court.

This case concerns the authority of the federal courts to adjudicate controversies. Jurisdiction to resolve cases on the merits requires both authority over the category of claim in suit (subject-matter jurisdiction) and authority over the parties (personal jurisdiction), so that the court's decision will bind them. In Steel Co. v. Citizens for Better Environment, 523 U.S. 83, 118 S.Ct. 1003 (1998), this Court adhered to the rule that a federal court may not hypothesize subject-matter jurisdiction for the purpose of deciding the merits. Steel Co. rejected a doctrine, once approved by several Courts of Appeals, that allowed federal tribunals to pretermit jurisdictional objections "where (1) the merits question is more readily resolved, and (2) the prevailing party on the merits would be the same as the prevailing party were jurisdiction denied." Id., at 93, 118 S.Ct. 1003. Recalling "a long and venerable line of our cases," id., at 94, 118 S.Ct. 1003, Steel Co. reiterated: "The requirement that jurisdiction be established as a threshold matter . . . is 'inflexible and without exception,'" id., at 94–95, 118 S.Ct. 1003 (quoting Mansfield, C. & L.M.R. Co. v. Swan, 111 U.S. 379, 382, 4 S.Ct. 510 (1884)); for "[j]urisdiction is power to declare the law," and " '[w]ithout jurisdiction the court cannot proceed at all in any cause,'" 523 U.S., at 94, 118 S.Ct. 1003 (quoting Ex parte McCardle, 7 Wall. 506, 514 (1868)). The Court, in Steel Co., acknowledged that "the absolute purity" of the jurisdiction-first rule had been diluted in a few extraordinary cases, 523 U.S., at 101, 118 S.Ct. 1003, and Justice O'Connor, joined by Justice Kennedy, joined the majority on the understanding that the Court's opinion did not catalog "an exhaustive list of circumstances" in which exceptions to the solid rule were appropriate, id., at 110, 118 S.Ct. 1003.

Steel Co. is the backdrop for the issue now before us: If, as Steel Co. held, jurisdiction generally must precede merits in dispositional order, must subject-matter jurisdiction precede personal jurisdiction on the decisional line? Or, do federal district courts have discretion to avoid a difficult question of subject-matter jurisdiction when the absence of personal jurisdiction is the surer ground? The particular civil action we confront was commenced in state court and removed to federal court. The specific question on which we granted certiorari asks "[w]hether a federal district court is absolutely barred in all circumstances from dismissing a removed case for lack of personal jurisdiction without first deciding its subject-matter jurisdiction." Pet. for Cert. i.

We hold that in cases removed from state court to federal court, as in cases originating in federal court, there is no unyielding jurisdictional hierarchy. Customarily, a federal court first resolves doubts about its jurisdiction over the subject matter, but there are circumstances in which a district court appropriately accords priority to a personal jurisdiction inquiry. The proceeding before us is such a case.

I

The underlying controversy stems from a venture to produce gas in the Heimdal Field of the Norwegian North Sea. In 1976, respondents Marathon Oil Company and Marathon International Oil Company acquired Marathon Petroleum Company (Norway) (MPCN) and respondent Marathon Petroleum Norge (Norge). See App. 26.[1] Before the acquisition, Norge held a license to produce gas in the Heimdal Field; following the transaction, Norge assigned the license to MPCN. . . . In 1981, MPCN contracted to sell 70% of its share of the Heimdal gas production to a group of European buyers, including petitioner Ruhrgas AG. . . .

II

Marathon Oil Company, Marathon International Oil Company, and Norge (collectively, Marathon) filed this lawsuit against Ruhrgas in Texas state court on July 6, 1995, asserting state-law claims of fraud, tortious interference with prospective business relations, participation in breach of fiduciary duty, and civil conspiracy. See App. 33–40. Marathon Oil Company and Marathon International Oil Company alleged that Ruhrgas and the other European buyers induced them with false promises of "premium prices" and guaranteed pipeline tariffs to invest over $300 million in MPCN for the development of the Heimdal Field and the erection of a pipeline to Ruhrgas' plant in Germany. . . . Norge alleged that Ruhrgas' effective monopolization of the Heimdal gas diminished the value of the license Norge had assigned to MPCN. . . . Marathon asserted that Ruhrgas had furthered its plans at three meetings in Houston, Texas, and through a stream of correspondence directed to Marathon in Texas. . . .

Ruhrgas removed the case to the District Court for the Southern District of Texas. See 145 F.3d 211, 214 (C.A.5 1998). In its notice of removal, Ruhrgas asserted three bases for federal jurisdiction: diversity of citizenship, see 28 U.S.C. § 1332 (1994 ed. and Supp. III), on the theory that Norge, the only nondiverse plaintiff, had been fraudulently joined; federal question, see § 1331, because Marathon's claims "raise[d]

---

[1]   Ruhrgas is a German corporation; Norge is a Norwegian corporation. See App. 21, 22. Marathon Oil Company, an Ohio corporation, and Marathon International Oil Company, a Delaware corporation, moved their principal places of business from Ohio to Texas while the venture underlying this case was in formation. . . . [As a signatory to the Heimdal Gas Agreement, MPCN's claims were subject to binding arbitration in Europe.—Ed.]

substantial questions of foreign and international relations, which are incorporated into and form part of the federal common law," App. 274; and 9 U.S.C. § 205, which authorizes removal of cases "relat[ing] to" international arbitration agreements. . . . Ruhrgas moved to dismiss the complaint for lack of personal jurisdiction. Marathon moved to remand the case to the state court for lack of federal subject-matter jurisdiction. . . .

After permitting jurisdictional discovery, the District Court dismissed the case for lack of personal jurisdiction [on the ground that Ruhrgas had constitutionally insufficient contacts with Texas].

A panel of the Court of Appeals for the Fifth Circuit concluded that "respec[t]" for "the proper balance of federalism" impelled it to turn first to "the formidable subject matter jurisdiction issue presented." 115 F.3d [315, 318 (5th Cir.1997)]. After examining and rejecting each of Ruhrgas' asserted bases of federal jurisdiction . . . , the Court of Appeals vacated the judgment of the District Court and ordered the case remanded to the state court . . . . This Court denied Ruhrgas' petition for a writ of certiorari, which was limited to the question whether subject-matter jurisdiction existed under 9 U.S.C. § 205. See 522 U.S. 967, 118 S.Ct. 413 (1997).

The Fifth Circuit, on its own motion, granted rehearing en banc, thereby vacating the panel decision. See 129 F.3d 746 (C.A.5 1997). In a 9-to-7 decision, the en banc court held that, in removed cases, district courts must decide issues of subject-matter jurisdiction first, reaching issues of personal jurisdiction "only if subject-matter jurisdiction is found to exist." 145 F.3d, at 214. . . .

We granted certiorari, 525 U.S. 1039, 119 S.Ct. 589 (1998), to resolve a conflict between the Circuits and now reverse.

III

Steel Co. held that Article III generally requires a federal court to satisfy itself of its jurisdiction over the subject matter before it considers the merits of a case. "For a court to pronounce upon [the merits] when it has no jurisdiction to do so," Steel Co. declared, "is . . . for a court to act ultra vires." 523 U.S., at 101–102, 118 S.Ct. 1003. The Fifth Circuit incorrectly read Steel Co. to teach that subject-matter jurisdiction must be found to exist, not only before a federal court reaches the merits, but also before personal jurisdiction is addressed. See 145 F.3d, at 218.

A

The Court of Appeals accorded priority to the requirement of subject-matter jurisdiction because it is nonwaivable and delimits federal-court power, while restrictions on a court's jurisdiction over the person are waivable and protect individual rights. See id., at 217–218. The character of the two jurisdictional bedrocks unquestionably differs. Subject-matter limitations on federal jurisdiction serve institutional interests. They keep the federal courts within the bounds the Constitution and Congress have prescribed. Accordingly, subject-matter delineations must be policed by the courts on their own initiative even at the highest level. See Steel Co., 523 U.S., at 94–95, 118 S.Ct. 1003; Fed.Rule Civ.Proc. 12(h)(3) ("Whenever it appears . . . that the court lacks jurisdiction of the subject matter, the court shall dismiss the action."); 28 U.S.C. § 1447(c) (1994 ed., Supp. III) ("If at any time before final judgment [in a removed case] it appears that the district court lacks subject matter jurisdiction, the case shall be remanded.").

Personal jurisdiction, on the other hand, "represents a restriction on judicial power . . . as a matter of individual liberty." Insurance Corp. of Ireland v. Compagnie des Bauxites de Guinee, 456 U.S. 694, 702, 102 S.Ct. 2099 (1982). Therefore, a party may insist that the limitation be observed, or he may forgo that right, effectively consenting to the court's exercise of adjudicatory authority. See Fed.Rule Civ.Proc. 12(h)(1) (defense of lack of jurisdiction over the person waivable); Insurance Corp. of Ireland, 456 U.S., at 703, 102 S.Ct. 2099 (same).

These distinctions do not mean that subject-matter jurisdiction is ever and always the more "fundamental." Personal jurisdiction, too, is "an essential element of the jurisdiction of a district . . . court," without which the court is "powerless to proceed to an adjudication." Employers Reinsurance Corp. v. Bryant, 299 U.S. 374, 382, 57 S.Ct. 273 (1937). In this case, indeed, the impediment to subject-matter jurisdiction on which Marathon relies—lack of complete diversity—rests on statutory interpretation, not constitutional command. Marathon joined an alien plaintiff (Norge) as well as an alien defendant (Ruhrgas). If the joinder of Norge is legitimate, the . . . diversity required by 28 U.S.C. § 1332 (1994 ed. and Supp. III), but not by Article III, see State Farm Fire & Casualty Co. v. Tashire, 386 U.S. 523, 530–531, 87 S.Ct. 1199 (1967), is absent. In contrast, Ruhrgas relies on the constitutional safeguard of due process to stop the court from proceeding to the merits of the case. See Insurance Corp. of Ireland, 456 U.S., at 702, 102 S.Ct. 2099 ("The requirement that a court have personal jurisdiction flows . . . from the Due Process Clause.").

While Steel Co. reasoned that subject-matter jurisdiction necessarily precedes a ruling on the merits, the same principle does not dictate a sequencing of jurisdictional issues. "[A] court that dismisses on . . . non-merits grounds such as . . . personal jurisdiction, before finding subject-matter jurisdiction, makes no assumption of law-declaring power that violates the separation of powers principles underlying Mansfield and Steel Company." In re Papandreou, 139 F.3d 247, 255 (C.A.D.C.1998). It is hardly novel for a federal court to choose among threshold grounds for denying audience to a case on the merits. Thus, as the Court observed in Steel Co., district courts do not overstep Article III limits when they decline jurisdiction of state-law claims on discretionary grounds without determining whether those claims fall within their pendent jurisdiction, see Moor v. County of Alameda, 411 U.S. 693, 715–716, 93 S.Ct. 1785

(1973), or abstain under Younger v. Harris, 401 U.S. 37, 91 S.Ct. 746 (1971), without deciding whether the parties present a case or controversy, see Ellis v. Dyson, 421 U.S. 426, 433–434, 95 S.Ct. 1691 (1975). See Steel Co., 523 U.S., at 100–101, n. 3, 118 S.Ct. 1003; cf. Arizonans for Official English v. Arizona, 520 U.S. 43, 66–67, 117 S.Ct. 1055 (1997) (pretermitting challenge to appellants' standing and dismissing on mootness grounds).

B

Maintaining that subject-matter jurisdiction must be decided first even when the litigation originates in federal court . . . , Marathon sees removal as the more offensive case, on the ground that the dignity of state courts is immediately at stake. If a federal court dismisses a removed case for want of personal jurisdiction, that determination may preclude the parties from relitigating the very same personal jurisdiction issue in state court. See Baldwin v. Iowa State Traveling Men's Assn., 283 U.S. 522, 524–527, 51 S.Ct. 517 (1931) (personal jurisdiction ruling has issue-preclusive effect).

Issue preclusion in subsequent state-court litigation, however, may also attend a federal court's subject-matter determination. . . .

Most essentially, federal and state courts are complementary systems for administering justice in our Nation. Cooperation and comity, not competition and conflict, are essential to the federal design. A State's dignitary interest bears consideration when a district court exercises discretion in a case of this order. If personal jurisdiction raises "difficult questions of [state] law," and subject-matter jurisdiction is resolved "as eas[ily]" as personal jurisdiction, a district court will ordinarily conclude that "federalism concerns tip the scales in favor of initially ruling on the motion to remand." Allen v. Ferguson, 791 F.2d 611, 616 (C.A.7 1986). In other cases, however, the district court may find that concerns of judicial economy and restraint are overriding. See, e.g., Asociacion Nacional de Pescadores v. Dow Quimica, 988 F.2d 559, 566–567 (C.A.5 1993) (if removal is nonfrivolous and personal jurisdiction turns on federal constitutional issues, "federal intrusion into state courts' authority . . . is minimized"). The federal design allows leeway for sensitive judgments of this sort. . . .

The Fifth Circuit and Marathon posit that state-court defendants will abuse the federal system with opportunistic removals. A discretionary rule, they suggest, will encourage manufactured, convoluted federal subject-matter theories designed to wrench cases from state court. . . . This specter of unwarranted removal, we have recently observed, "rests on an assumption we do not indulge—that district courts generally will not comprehend, or will balk at applying, the rules on removal Congress has prescribed. . . . The well-advised defendant . . . will foresee the likely outcome of an unwarranted removal—a swift and nonreviewable remand order, see 28 U.S.C. §§ 1447(c), (d), attended by the displeasure of a district court whose authority has been improperly invoked." Caterpillar Inc. v. Lewis, 519 U.S. 61, 77–78, 117 S.Ct. 467 (1996).

C

. . . [W]e recognize that in most instances subject-matter jurisdiction will involve no arduous inquiry. See 145 F.3d, at 229 ("engag[ing]" subject-matter jurisdiction "at the outset of a case . . . [is] often . . . the most efficient way of going"). In such cases, both expedition and sensitivity to state courts' coequal stature should impel the federal court to dispose of that issue first. See Cantor Fitzgerald, L.P. v. Peaslee, 88 F.3d 152, 155 (C.A.2 1996) (a court disposing of a case on personal jurisdiction grounds "should be convinced that the challenge to the court's subject-matter jurisdiction is not easily resolved"). Where, as here, however, a district court has before it a straightforward personal jurisdiction issue presenting no complex question of state law, and the alleged defect in subject-matter jurisdiction raises a difficult and novel question, the court does not abuse its discretion by turning directly to personal jurisdiction.

* * *

For the reasons stated, the judgment of the Court of Appeals is reversed, and the case is remanded for proceedings consistent with this opinion.

It is so ordered.[k]

———

SCOTT C. IDLEMAN, THE EMERGENCE OF JURISDICTIONAL RESEQUENCING IN THE FEDERAL COURTS, 87 Cornell L.Rev. 1, 31–35 (2001). "[O]ne of the most critical premises in Ruhrgas is that personal jurisdiction is materially as *essential* as subject-matter jurisdiction to a court's power to decide cases. Yet the Court arrives at this premise—and the conclusion that personal jurisdiction can be decided first—not by unearthing and comparing the theoretical elements of each type of jurisdiction, but simply by proclaiming it to be true. . . .

"Consider again, however, the starkness of these distinctions between subject-matter and personal jurisdiction. The former is a nonwaivable, structural limitation on a court's power to act at all; the latter, a waivable, personal liberty interest that merely limits a court's ability to bind a particular defendant with the otherwise valid exercise of judicial power. . . . Thus, while '[a] judge has no power to decide a case

---

[k]   On remand, the court of appeals affirmed the district court's finding of a lack of personal jurisdiction, 182 F.3d 291 (5th Cir.1999). Under res judicata law, a finding of no jurisdiction does not produce a valid judgment and so should not be binding in another action, except to defeat jurisdiction in any attempt to sue again in a court where exactly the same jurisdictional issue arises. The court has authority to determine its lack of authority, and so for that latter limited purpose the judgment is a valid one. Accordingly, the federal judgment in Ruhrgas's favor would preclude later suit in a Texas state court, just as Justice Ginsburg suggested.

over which he lacks subject-matter jurisdiction, . . . he *can* decide a case though he lacks personal jurisdiction over the defendant, if the defendant waives the issue of personal jurisdiction.' To be sure, courts regularly describe their relationship to subject-matter jurisdiction in hortatory terms—noting 'their nondelegable duty to police the limits of federal jurisdiction with meticulous care,' their 'independent, constitutional obligation to protect the jurisdictional limits of the federal courts,' and 'the duty of the federal courts to assure themselves that their jurisdiction is not being exceeded'—while characterizing the requirements of personal jurisdiction as 'merely the[ ] personal privileges' of the parties, or collectively as 'an individual right,' or as 'procedural requirements' or 'affirmative defenses' akin to the interposition of a statute of limitations. In turn, one would think that the Court might be interested in *why* each type of jurisdiction bears different characteristics and whether these reasons indicate anything about their respective importance.

"Perhaps the most significant consideration in this regard, which the Ruhrgas Court neither noted nor explored, is the respective constitutional source of each jurisdictional requirement. Subject-matter jurisdiction ultimately derives from Article III, although its affirmation, particularly in the lower courts, is typically by statute. As such, subject-matter jurisdiction is properly characterized as an *internal* limitation on the existence of federal judicial power and thus the sovereignty of the federal government. In turn, without subject-matter jurisdiction, a federal court is entirely without power to adjudicate a dispute, irrespective of the parties' wishes. Personal jurisdiction, by comparison, is essentially the exercise of jurisdiction over a particular defendant as long as such exercise complies with the Fifth Amendment Due Process Clause. Personal jurisdiction, accordingly, is best characterized as an *external* limitation on the exercise of federal judicial power, without which a court is simply precluded from binding the defendant absent some form of consent. . . .

"This distinction is important in at least two respects, one of judicial practice, the other of constitutional theory. First, as a matter of standard judicial practice, challenges premised on the internal limits on federal power ought, analytically, to precede challenges premised on the external limits on the same, assuming that the parties have presented both and that the court must address at least one. The more fundamental question, after all, is whether the federal government has the power to act in the first place, not whether its exercise of this alleged power, if it even exists, happens to transgress an external limitation. Second, this respective sequencing of internal and external power issues reflects the more basic principle that maintaining the limited nature of federal authority is, along with federalism and the separation of powers, more theoretically central to American constitutionalism than the imposition of external limits, such as due process, on the exercise of federal power otherwise delegated. In the day-to-day existence of citizens, of course, the latter is no less important and often may seem to be the Constitution's raison d'être. By their office and tenure, however, judges are obligated to view the Constitution in its architectural totality, drawing upon the historical events and philosophical understandings that gave rise to it and that have sustained its integrity over time. This is particularly true where, as in Ruhrgas, the ultimate question is not one of individual liberty as such, but rather of federal judicial power. And from this architectural perspective, it is clear not only that structural features—such as the principles of internally limited federal power, the separation of powers, and federalism—are at the core of American constitutionalism, but that the protection of liberty is, in the first instance, very much tied to their maintenance.

"To be sure, it is primarily the different constitutional sources underlying the two jurisdictional forms that explain the distinctive characteristics of each form, characteristics which the Court itself noted but inexplicably deemed irrelevant."[1]

———

Questions: (25) In the D.C. federal district court, P sued D from New York on a defamation claim arising in New York City. D forwarded a number of defenses, including lack of personal jurisdiction and failure to state a claim. Without reaching personal jurisdiction, the district court dismissed the action, on the merits, for failure to state a claim. P appealed. The court of appeals seemed to say that the jurisdictional motion must be decided first and so remained open on appeal, that personal jurisdiction was clearly lacking, and that the appellate court therefore need not reach the more difficult issues on the merits. So, the court affirmed the dismissal in favor of D, but did so on the ground of personal jurisdiction. Does this decision make good sense? Compare Forras v. Rauf, 812 F.3d 1102, 1105 (D.C.Cir.2016), with Kevin M. Clermont, Sequencing the Issues for Judicial Decisionmaking: Limitations from Jurisdictional Primacy and Intrasuit Preclusion, 63 Fla.L.Rev. 301, 311–15 (2011) (arguing that although subject-matter jurisdiction cannot be bypassed to dismiss on the merits, personal jurisdiction may be bypassed to dismiss on the merits with fully preclusive effect).

(26) In the N.J. federal district court, P sued D on a fraud claim. D forwarded a number of defenses, including subject-matter jurisdiction and claim preclusion. Without reaching subject-matter jurisdiction, the district court dismissed the action on the ground that P had lost an earlier suit for failure to state this same claim. P appealed. The court of appeals seemed to say that application of claim preclusion does not "technically" produce a new judgment on the merits but merely a determination that the merits have already been adjudicated elsewhere. So, the court affirmed the dismissal in

---

[1]   Despite these concerns, the Supreme Court has expanded the resequencing option. Now, a federal court may skip over a challenge to subject-matter jurisdiction (or to Article III justiciability) to decide on another jurisdiction or justiciability ground or on abstention, exhaustion, class certification, or venue. Upon upholding one of these threshold defenses, the court gives a binding decision on the threshold issue, without precluding the merits of the claim.

favor of *D*, saying that the district court could resequence claim preclusion and so dismiss without first deciding whether it had subject-matter jurisdiction. Does this decision make good sense? Compare Hoffman v. Nordic Naturals, Inc., 837 F.3d 272, 277–78 (3d Cir.2016), with Kevin M. Clermont, Sequencing the Issues for Judicial Decisionmaking: Limitations from Jurisdictional Primacy and Intrasuit Preclusion, 63 Fla.L.Rev. 301, 328–29 (2011) (arguing that a court cannot bypass subject-matter jurisdiction to dismiss on a ground that disposes preclusively of the claim).

PART 4

FORMER ADJUDICATION

GENERAL OBSERVATIONS

We have already encountered a number of problems regarding rules designed to treat or prevent repetitious litigation. The purpose of this Part is to examine these problems systematically in a single place and to evaluate the policies that appear to mold decision. Our primary interest will be the centrally important doctrine of res judicata, which treats the effects of previously rendered adjudication on a subsequent adjudication.

Res judicata, or res adjudicata by its older name, is a classic common-law doctrine. It does the work of defining "judgment." *First*, responding to felt needs, every legal system has produced at least a core of res judicata law. "The doctrine of res judicata is a principle of universal jurisprudence forming part of the legal systems of all civilized nations."[a] But each jurisdiction generates its own distinctive body of law, as has been done independently by each of the states, by the federal system, and by other countries. American res judicata is distinctively a good deal more expansive than res judicata law in other countries. *Second*, American res judicata is an almost entirely judge-made body of law. Courts responded to the needs they most acutely felt by formulating, revising, and complexifying a doctrine. It is true that constitutions, legislation, and rulemaking can override the judicial doctrine. The U.S. Constitution has a real albeit limited impact on res judicata doctrine; in many jurisdictions, statutes deal with small parts of the subject; most court rules avoid most of the subject. The belief is that in general it is just too complex a subject for successful codification. *Third*, res judicata is policy-driven. Despite first impression, it comprises principles or flexible standards as much as fixed rules and exceptions. As a result, it has been a surprisingly contentious and uncertain area of law. Some questions of res judicata have not been authoritatively resolved, and there is considerable dissatisfaction with some of the solutions that have been given. Indeed, there has been a certain uneasiness with the whole doctrine, even in the courts, as exemplified by Judge Clark's aphorism: "The defense of res judicata is universally respected, but actually not very well liked."[b] And there has long been strong advocacy of drastic change. Yet, as we shall see, the modern Supreme Court seems to have embraced res judicata with renewed affection.

Some basic propositions.—Res judicata's key propositions nevertheless can be simply stated.

If a plaintiff sues and obtains a valid and final personal judgment in his favor, generally res judicata extinguishes his claim and merges it in

---

[a]   2 A.C. Freeman, A Treatise of the Law of Judgments § 627, at 1321 (5th ed. 1925).

[b]   Riordan v. Ferguson, 147 F.2d 983, 988 (2d Cir.1945) (dissenting opinion).

the judgment. "Merger" means that he cannot relitigate the claim in hopes of winning a more favorable decision against the defendant, either in the same jurisdiction or elsewhere. The judgment stands in place of the claim, and it is only the judgment that he can then seek to enforce. (The plaintiff can get enforcement of the judgment where rendered. If necessary, he can sue upon the judgment in another jurisdiction, attempting to obtain a fresh judgment to enforce there. If he does so, the first judgment is not merged into and so precluded by the second. He can seek to enforce either or both, even in a third state by another action upon either judgment. But he is of course limited to one satisfaction. See Moore v. Justices of the Mun. Court, 291 Mass. 504, 197 N.E. 487 (1935).)

Similarly, if a plaintiff sues but judgment goes against him, then generally his claim is extinguished and barred by the judgment. "Bar" means that he cannot relitigate the same claim.[c] (What is signified by these statements about merger and bar is that if the plaintiff attempts relitigation of the same claim, the defendant may successfully plead res judicata. Here is another instance where rules of law are not self-executing. What happens when the defense of res judicata is not pleaded, and the court renders a second judgment inconsistent with the first, is considered later in this Part.)

How does the principle against relitigation apply to actions where the claims are different? Unlike the doctrines of merger and bar, which operate to preclude the whole claim without regard to what issues were in reality litigated in the first suit, an additional branch of res judicata makes preclusive between the parties the prior determination of an issue, but only if the same issue was actually litigated and determined in the original action and, moreover, only if the determination of that issue was essential to the first judgment. This doctrine, applicable between different claims, is termed "collateral estoppel" by many courts and commentators.

If an exception to claim preclusion applies so that a claim may be relitigated, a doctrine identical to collateral estoppel acts to preclude relitigation of issues in any subsequent action on the same claim. This doctrine is termed "direct estoppel."[d]

For clarity of analysis it is useful to distinguish claim preclusion from issue preclusion, but courts too often in their thinking have lumped these doctrines together. Furthermore, courts have frequently confused the picture by using idiosyncratic terminology and categorization to subdivide the subject of res judicata; most confusingly, some courts persist in using the general term "res judicata" to encompass only claim preclusion and not issue preclusion too.

---

[c]   The two doctrines, merger and bar, now are collectively named "claim preclusion."

[d]   The two doctrines, collateral and direct estoppel, now are collectively named "issue preclusion."

Rejecting the old muddle, the Restatement (Second) of Judgments § 17 (Am. Law Inst. 1982) presents its basic provision on res judicata this way, stating the general rules along with references to its more detailed provisions:

> A valid and final personal judgment is conclusive between the parties, except on appeal or other direct review, to the following extent:
>
> > (1) If the judgment is in favor of the plaintiff, the claim is extinguished and merged in the judgment and a new claim may arise on the judgment (see § 18);
> >
> > (2) If the judgment is in favor of the defendant, the claim is extinguished and the judgment bars a subsequent action on that claim (see § 19);
> >
> > (3) A judgment in favor of either the plaintiff or the defendant is conclusive, in a subsequent action between them on the same or a different claim, with respect to any issue actually litigated and determined if its determination was essential to that judgment (see § 27).

We largely devote the rest of this Part to exploring the hidden depths of this basic provision on res judicata. But here, for orientation purposes, let us first take a preliminary look at some of the rather obvious implications of § 17—even though several of our tentative statements require later elaboration and qualification.

General context: second action.—The doctrine of res judicata specifies certain binding effects, in subsequent litigation, of a previously rendered judgment. Generally speaking, then, res judicata can apply only when an attempt is made in a second action to foreclose relitigation of a matter already adjudicated in a previous action. Res judicata therefore has no application to an attempt in the original action at correcting error in the judgment, as by motion for a new trial or by appeal.[e]

For example, compare Thompson v. Washington National Bank, 68 Wash. 42, 122 P. 606 (1912), with Louisville & Nashville Railroad Co. v. Whitley County Court, 100 Ky. 413, 38 S.W. 678 (1897). In Thompson, the plaintiff sued for payment on a contract to lay a tile floor and lost on the ground that he had not substantially performed his contract, in that the tiled floor had been left in a discolored condition. Eight months after the judgment he sued again on the same contract, eager to show that after the first judgment the defendant had removed the discoloration at a cost of only $12 and that therefore the contract had been substantially performed. In Louisville & Nashville, posttrial events similarly showed

---

[e]   There is a doctrine called law of the case, which stands for the sensible proposition that a court, and courts coordinate with or inferior to it, will normally not depart from a ruling declared by it in a particular case if the point is again presented in the same case. However, this flexible and limited doctrine, although very similar to stare decisis, is distinguishable from res judicata, which applies more rigidly and broadly in later actions. See generally Wright & Miller § 4478.

that the judgment was erroneous, and the aggrieved party moved for a new trial on the ground of newly discovered evidence. In Thompson, res judicata blocked suit; in Louisville & Nashville, res judicata was not involved because the motion was made in the original action, so the movant got relief. Had Thompson promptly moved for a new trial instead of suing again, he could have avoided the application of res judicata.

First prerequisite: validity.—These rules of res judicata are applicable, as said in § 17, only to "valid" judgments. A judgment is valid for this purpose unless the person against whom it is invoked obtains relief from judgment, such as by a collateral attack launched in the second action. Generally speaking, a collateral attack lies on, and only on, the ground that the court rendering the prior judgment failed to satisfy the requirement of subject-matter jurisdiction, territorial jurisdiction, or opportunity to be heard.

On the one hand, if such a defect in competence, nexus, or notice can be shown, the judgment will normally be deemed not valid. Although those defects are rather rare, relief from judgment is available, even by collateral attack. Thus, the attacker can defeat the invocation of res judicata.

On the other hand, the fact that the judgment may have been otherwise erroneous is usually immaterial with respect to res judicata. Mere error, as opposed to the three basic defects, does not affect a judgment's validity. Mere error can be corrected only on appeal or other direct review. Indeed, the failure to honor an erroneous but valid judgment rendered by a court of another American jurisdiction is, in our federal system, an impermissible denial of full faith and credit.

Second prerequisite: finality.—These rules of res judicata are applicable, as we have also seen, only to "final" judgments. The law does not want to preclude on the basis of the tentative, contingent, or provisional. But what constitutes finality for this purpose? It is not precisely the same as "final" in the statute providing for appellate review of "final decisions of the district courts." 28 U.S.C. § 1291.

First, the rules of claim preclusion stick pretty closely to the strict formulation of finality for appellate review that applied traditionally: the court rendering the prior judgment must ordinarily have said its last word on the claim, except for award of costs and enforcement of judgment. By contrast, for appellate review, modern courts have stretched this strict concept of finality so as to provide immediate review in some situations where deemed necessary.

Second, when issue preclusion is involved, there is a cautious tendency to be somewhat more willing to find finality than in the case of claim preclusion. If the first court has firmly decided an issue after adequate hearing and full deliberation, a second court has discretion to give the decision preclusive effect despite its lack of finality in the strict sense. Of course, if the decision were avowedly tentative in the first court, it would not receive such effect. In Lummus Co. v. Commonwealth Oil Refining Co., 297 F.2d 80, 89 (2d Cir.1961), Judge Friendly put this discretionary relaxation of the finality standard in these words: " 'Finality' in the context here relevant may mean little more than that the litigation of a particular issue has reached such a stage that a court sees no really good reason for permitting it to be litigated again." In the Lummus case, the second court gave preclusive effect on an issue of fraud in the inducement of a contract to an earlier decision of the Court of Appeals for the First Circuit in litigation related to the same contract, by which decision the First Circuit had reversed a preliminary injunction staying arbitration between the parties. Restatement (Second) of Judgments § 13 (Am. Law Inst. 1982) adopts Friendly's view, but in fact even this short description of Lummus reveals it to have been a peculiarly appropriate case for preclusion.

Questions: (1) Should finality depend on whether the earlier determination was immediately appealable, as had been the situation in Lummus? See Avondale Shipyards v. Insured Lloyd's, 786 F.2d 1265, 1269–72 (5th Cir.1986) (yes, although also generally disapproving modern relaxation of finality for issue preclusion).

(2) For personal injuries in an automobile accident, *A* sues *B* in a jurisdiction where the issues as to liability are determined first, and the damage issues are heard later by another jury if liability is found. The jury goes for *A* on liability, by finding *B* negligent. Should this determination before the ultimate judgment, which would have to await the assessment of damages, now be controlling in a personal-injury action by *B* against *A*, wherein *A* pleads contributory negligence and res judicata? Should this determination be controlling, by way of merger or otherwise, in another action by *A* against *B* on the same claim, now seeking property damages?

Under the res judicata law of most American jurisdictions, a judgment otherwise final for res judicata purposes does not lose finality because time still exists for attack in the trial court, as by motion for a new trial, or because a party has actually made such an attack. Likewise, the fact that the time for appeal has not expired, or that a party has taken a still pending appeal, normally does not prevent a judgment from being final for res judicata purposes.

More specifically as to appeal, Restatement of Judgments § 41 cmt. d (Am. Law Inst. 1942) considered loss of finality pending appeal to depend on whether taking the appeal "vacates" the judgment, as taking an appeal in equity did. That approach seems to have little relevance today. Restatement (Second) of Judgments § 13 cmt. f (Am. Law Inst. 1982) rejects it and says: "The better view is that a judgment otherwise final remains so despite the taking of an appeal unless what is called an appeal actually consists of a trial de novo . . . ." If there is to be a trial de novo in a higher court, the original decision does lose its finality pending the appeal.

In brief, claim preclusion and issue preclusion require a judgment's finality, but finality does not mean that direct review of the judgment is complete. Obviously, this early finality can create problems, and so sometimes needs a cure. If direct review eventually overturns the judgment, relief from a second judgment—which res judicata produced in the meantime—normally will be available by appropriate proceedings. See, e.g., Rule 60(b)(5).

Temporary focus: personal judgment between the parties.— For the moment, we are concerned only with the res judicata effects of ordinary judgments and indeed only with those effects between the parties thereto. Special rules for the effects of a judgment resting on jurisdiction over a thing are prescribed in Restatement (Second) of Judgments §§ 30, 32 (Am. Law Inst. 1982). Similarly, the effects of claim and issue preclusion on persons not parties to the prior judgment, and other special effects, are examined later in this Part.

Some closing thoughts.—Res judicata is a profoundly important doctrine. It is not merely a technical set of rules on the conduct of litigation. It fundamentally defines what a court has decided, what bundle of aspects constitute a judgment, what the product of the judicial branch is to be.

Strong policies underlie the scope of res judicata. Efficiency argues for avoiding wasteful litigation and possibly inconsistent adjudication, and also for achieving the certainty and stability of repose. Fairness looks to the burden on res judicata's invoker of conducting renewed litigation and to the opponent's fault in causing it, as well as to the reliance interests at stake. These policies deserve consideration in connection with both the instant case and the long run of cases. Substantive policies also demand consideration, sometimes adding to the arguments for broad res judicata.

Nevertheless, all those policies can cut the other way too. There are the "direct costs" of litigating about res judicata, while the fear of future preclusion might produce overlitigation in the initial action. Also, there are the inefficient "error costs" of deciding to live with an incorrect judgment. By way of illustration of the possible harshness in the operation of res judicata, we shall summarize a much-cited case.

In Jacobson v. Mutual Benefit Health & Accident Ass'n, 73 N.D. 108, 11 N.W.2d 442 (1943), the plaintiff had sued for $2000 on her husband's policy insuring against his accidental death. Part A of the policy entitled her to $2000 on the insured's accidental death; Part B provided that each year's renewal of the policy would add $200 to the death benefit, and there had been nine such renewals. That suit had resulted in judgment for the plaintiff for $2000. The plaintiff's lawyer apparently had neglected to read the policy's Part B.

Later, becoming aware of the error, Clara Jacobson, with the same lawyer, brought a new suit for the additional $1800. The defendant insurer pleaded the prior judgment as res judicata. The court held that the plaintiff was seeking improperly to split her cause of action; that there had been but one cause of action, in solido, for the $3800; that this cause of action had been extinguished by the prior judgment; and that the second action therefore could not be maintained.

The Jacobson result is not compelled by logic or by the nature of things, although it is one by which lawyers would not be surprised in the light of past decisions of the courts, and by which judicial economy is arguably served through the message sent to future plaintiffs. Much can be said against exacting such a penalty from the plaintiff, and correspondingly giving such a windfall to the insurance company, because of counsel's failure to read the policy with care.

At any rate, returning from policy to doctrine, the Jacobson decision shows how essential it is, in applying the principle that judgment extinguishes the cause of action, to determine the precise dimensions of the thing extinguished. So the question of the measure of "cause of action," or "claim" in modern usage, reappears in a new context. Why does the law say that a suit on the policy's Part A extinguishes rights under Part B? This question we shall examine in the next Section.

CLAIM PRECLUSION

SECTION 1.   DIMENSIONS OF A CLAIM

Williamson v. Columbia Gas & Electric Corp.

United States Court of Appeals, Third Circuit, 1950.
186 F.2d 464, cert. denied, 341 U.S. 921, 71 S.Ct. 743 (1951).

■ Before GOODRICH, KALODNER and HASTIE, CIRCUIT JUDGES.

■ GOODRICH, CIRCUIT JUDGE. This case involves the application of the rules of res judicata to a civil suit brought by the plaintiff, through its trustee in bankruptcy, for injuries alleged to have been sustained because of the defendant's violation of the anti-trust laws.

This action, which we shall call action No. 1, was begun on February 14, 1938. It charged that the defendant, conspiring with certain other persons, had, in violation of the provisions of the anti-trust laws, inflicted great injury upon the plaintiff [Inland Gas Corporation, by acquiring control of it in order to destroy it as a competitor]. But as the complaint was amended it sought recovery against Columbia Gas and Electric Corporation alone, although other parties were named as having conspired with Columbia in the various transactions of which complaint is made.

Subsequently, on September 16, 1938, the plaintiff brought in the same court (the United States District Court for the District of Delaware) another action against the defendant charging injury in violation of the anti-trust laws. This we shall call action No. 2. In this action the charge did not read in terms of conspiracy but alleged Columbia alone as the wrongdoer.

Thus we have two actions pending by the same plaintiff against the same defendant in the same court, each involving a suit for recovery of injuries alleged to have been sustained by action on the part of the defendant in violation of the anti-trust laws of the United States. Later to be examined is the identity, or substantial identity, of these suits.

The No. 2 action came to a conclusion first. On April 29, 1939, the court ordered "That the complaint in the . . . cause be and it hereby is dismissed. . . ."

The whole question with which we have to do in this case involves the effect of this judgment for the defendant upon the plaintiff's No. 1 action. In the District Court, the defendant moved [for summary judgment in] action No. 1 because of its victory in action No. 2. The motion was granted and the plaintiff appeals. Our discussion of the main question will be divided into consideration of the several issues presented.

Assume for the moment that the subject-matter of action No. 1 is identical with the subject-matter No. 2 so as to amount to the same "cause of action." Then we have two questions which may be disposed of first to clear the way for the most difficult thing about the case which is the assumption of identity just stated. The two questions are: (1) Does it matter for purposes of application of res judicata that the No. 2 action, later begun, was finished first? The answer to this question is no. The point is so well settled on authority that it is not a serious matter of contention in this case. (2) The second question is, what of the fact that the recital contained in the order of dismissal . . . mentioned a stipulation between the parties and the further fact that that stipulation had to do with the time in which the alleged cause of action accrued?

Here is what had occurred. Prior to the dismissal of action No. 2 the parties had entered into a stipulation. That stipulation provided that "The alleged right of action sued upon in this cause accrued not later than January 1, 1931." It was further agreed that if the court should consider the action barred by any applicable statute of limitations the pending motion to dismiss was to be granted. The plaintiff's theory at that time was that his action was not barred by the Delaware statute of limitations, and he evidently felt sufficiently confident of his position to enter into the stipulation which posed the legal issue of its correctness.

Subsequent events proved plaintiff's theory to be incorrect. Both the District Court and this Court held that the Delaware statute was applicable and the plaintiff's suit was begun too late.[5]

Does the fact that the judgment was entered for the defendant in action No. 2 on the basis that the action was barred by lapse of time preclude the application of res judicata to action No. 1, still assuming that the causes of action are identical? The answer to this question is likewise no. The adjudication in favor of the defendant operates as a bar to another suit on the same cause of action in the same jurisdiction. The fact that the case was tried upon stipulation of fact does not make it any the less a final adjudication of the plaintiff's claim.

With these minor points out of the way we now get to the main question in the case which was hypothetically assumed in the discussion just preceding. That question is whether action 1 and action 2 are substantially identical. If they are the rule of law is clear enough. "Where a valid and final personal judgment is rendered on the merits in favor of the defendant, the plaintiff cannot thereafter maintain an action on the

---

[5]   Williamson v. Columbia Gas & Electric Corp., D.C.Del.1939, 27 F.Supp. 198, affirmed, 3 Cir.1939, 110 F.2d 15, certiorari denied, 1940, 310 U.S. 639, 60 S.Ct. 1087, 84 L.Ed. 1407.

original cause of action."[7] The general principle is well known and undisputed. The difficulty comes in its application to varying sets of facts.

The best way to find out what is involved in the two actions is to look at the claims made by the plaintiff. Neither case went to trial on the facts so all we have is what the plaintiff charges, plus the supplementary affidavits, motions, and the like, which led up to the action of the Trial Judge dismissing plaintiff's action No. 1. The plaintiff alleges its organization and entry into the gas business. It says that the defendant, seeking to crush out a competitor, acquired the controlling shareholder interest in the plaintiff company and proceeded to manipulate its affairs to the disadvantage of the plaintiff and the advantage of the defendant. It says that after the plaintiff went into receivership the defendant named and controlled the receiver and the final result was that the plaintiff was forced into bankruptcy. . . .

The complaint in action No. 1 alleged that all this had been done as part of a continuing conspiracy in violation of Sections 1 and 2 of the Sherman Act, but, as amended, named only Columbia as defendant. The complaint in action No. 2, filed 7 months later, alleged that all that had transpired was in violation of Section 7 of the Clayton Act. The information set forth in the two complaints is substantially identical, plaintiff merely using words of conspiracy in the first action and replacing them with allegations that defendant did the same things on its own or through its agents in the second action. The wrongful acts alleged on the part of the defendant and the damages alleged to have been sustained by the plaintiff are practically identical in both suits. Indeed, the identity of the damage claims is almost startling, for except for a few figures with regard to interest the allegations of the particular items of damage are alike to the penny.

Nevertheless, plaintiff says the causes of action are different. We therefore proceed to examine the reasons stated to show the difference.

One alleged difference is that action No. 2 was a claim against Columbia as a sole tortfeasor and action No. 1 is a claim against Columbia as a conspirator. It is true that the complaint in No. 1 contains allegations of conspiracy and the complaint in action No. 2 did not. We do not think, however, that this constitutes a difference if the other elements alleged by the plaintiff are the same. Columbia was sought to be held as the party defendant in both suits. Whether Columbia is sought to be held as a sole tortfeasor or sued singly as one of several tortfeasors, assuming the injury is the same, does not matter. Several people getting together to do wrong to another do not commit a tort at the time they make their agreement, although they may commit a crime. The tort action arises when harm is done to the plaintiff. Then he may hold all the conspirators responsible for things done in pursuance of the conspiracy

---

[7] Restatement, Judgments § 48 (1942). Cromwell v. County of Sac, 1876, 94 U.S. 351, 352, 24 L.Ed. 195.

by any of them. But if he seeks to hold only one conspirator liable, as he may for the tort, since the liability is joint and several, he has not claimed anything substantially different from what he claims if he sues the sole conspirator as an individual tortfeasor. So we think, therefore, the presence of conspiracy allegations in action No. 1 and their absence in action No. 2 does not change the substance of the two claims.

Another difference claimed by the plaintiff in the two actions is that one suit is said to rest on the Sherman Act and the other on the Clayton Act. This argument carries no weight. While the rule may not have been clear at one time, we think it is now the law that the fact that different statutes are relied on does not render the claims different "causes of action" for purposes of res judicata. . . .

Also not in point, we think, are the cases cited by plaintiff in which the question involved was whether a plaintiff is required to state in separate counts claims based on the Sherman Act and the claims based on the Clayton Act. The purpose of the requirement of separate counts is to clarify the issues and simplify the trial, and thus the considerations in determining what are separate "causes of action" or claims for that purpose are not the same as those when the question is res judicata. As has often been said, the phrase "cause of action" means different things in different contexts.

Does action No. 1 differ from action No. 2 because the conspiracy charged in action No. 1 is alleged to be a continuing one? In a civil conspiracy suit each invasion of plaintiff's interest resulting from the conspiracy creates a new cause of action when the question is the application of the bar of the statute of limitations. This rule would be controlling if the issue here was whether the statute of limitations bars all or a part of the damages claimed by plaintiff as a result of a continuing conspiracy. But if the cause of action is the same, the principle of res judicata prevents our reaching that question, not because it was actually decided in action No. 2, but because the judgment is a final determination of not only what was actually in issue but what might have been in issue had it been raised. . . .

The purpose of the principle of res judicata is to end litigation. The theory is that parties should not have to litigate issues which they have already litigated or had a reasonable opportunity to litigate. A reading of the early cases as compared with recent ones makes it clear that the meaning of "cause of action" for res judicata purposes is much broader today than it was earlier. Formerly the whole aim in pleading, and in the elaborate system of writs, was to frame one single legal issue. That being the guiding principle, the phrase "cause of action" came to have a very narrow meaning. If the theory in the second suit was unavailable under the writ used in the first suit, the plaintiff had no opportunity to litigate it there and so plaintiff was not barred by res judicata. The force of the rule is still operative but the scope of its operation has been greatly limited by the modernization of our procedure. The principle which pervades the modern systems of pleading, especially the federal system, as exemplified by the free permissive joinder of claims, liberal amendment provisions, and compulsory counterclaims, is that the whole controversy between the parties may and often must be brought before the same court in the same action. The instant case presents an excellent example of one of the things these rules were designed to avoid. As pointed out above, the acts complained of and the demand for recovery are the same. The only thing that is different is the theory of recovery. The same witnesses and documents will be necessary in the trial in both cases. No material fact is alleged in action No. 1 that was not alleged in action No. 2, save the allegations of conspiracy. Everything that plaintiff was entitled to ask for from defendant was included in action No. 2.

Reference to the basic theory of tort liability substantiates the position taken here. To put it in rather elementary tort language, the basis of the plaintiff's recovery is liability-creating conduct on the part of defendant, the invasion of a legally protected interest of the plaintiff and the necessary causal connection between defendant's acts and plaintiff's injury. The plaintiff having alleged operative facts which state a cause of action because he tells of defendant's misconduct and his own harm has had his day in court. He does not get another day after the first lawsuit is concluded by giving a different reason than he gave in the first for recovery of damages for the same invasion of his rights. The problem of his rights against the defendant based upon the alleged wrongful acts is fully before the court whether all the reasons for recovery were stated to the court or not.

The points discussed here were all treated in the well-considered opinion of the District Judge. What we do is put in our own words our reason for thinking that he was right. The judgment will be affirmed.

———

Question: (1) In reading a mysterious case, it is often critical to worry about why the parties took the actions they took.

(a) The plaintiff faced a potentially serious but perhaps partially avoidable limitations defense in action No. 1. The likely applicable Delaware statute provided: "No action of trespass, no action of replevin, no action of detinue, no action of debt not found upon a record or specialty, no action of account, no action of assumpsit, and no action upon the case shall be brought after the expiration of three years from the accruing of the cause of such action." The new Federal Rules were coming into effect, with Rule 2 abolishing the common-law forms of action for the federal courts. So the plaintiff brought a new action subject to Rule 2, arguing that "since the 'civil action' provided for by the Federal Rules of Civil Procedure . . . has abolished all distinctions in the forms of actions the state statutes of limitations based upon differences in forms of action no longer apply" and that therefore Delaware's twenty-year backup statute applied. Was this stratagem worth a shot?

(b) There is a defense named "prior pending action." This defense will result in dismissal without prejudice if another action on the same claim between the same parties was pending in the same court system (in the same state or in the same or another federal district) when the present action was commenced and if that other action is still pending. (If the second action was brought elsewhere, the defendant could move to stay the second action.) Why did the defendant in action No. 2 not immediately raise prior pending action?

———

SMITH v. KIRKPATRICK, 305 N.Y. 66, 111 N.E.2d 209 (1953). Plaintiff Smith originally sued defendant in New York state court for money due him under an oral contract of employment. His complaint alleged that the contract required him to devote his full time to soliciting export accounts for defendant; that his remuneration was to be 50% of the income derived from the business procured by him; that he procured business from which defendant derived or would derive $26,000; and that defendant failed to pay him as agreed. Defendant obtained summary judgment for the reason that the agreement pleaded did not comply with the statute of frauds' requirement of a writing.

Plaintiff was granted leave to amend to quantum meruit, so as to recover the reasonable value of services rendered by him to defendant at defendant's request. But he chose not to seek the modest recovery of that theory. Instead he set forth in his amended complaint two causes of action, in pursuit of an accounting and other relief. The first alleged an informal oral agreement terminable at will whereby plaintiff conducted some of his business through defendant's office, paying to defendant for such use of his office 50% of the gross profits of plaintiff's business so conducted. The second alleged an oral agreement of joint venture substantially to the same effect. A trial without jury was held, after which the trial judge dismissed the amended complaint on the merits because "plaintiff has failed to establish his causes of action by a fair preponderance of the credible evidence." Although the now alleged agreements escaped the statute of frauds, the judge said: "It is clear to the court that the original position taken by the plaintiff correctly represented the relationship between the parties but, unfortunately for the plaintiff, that action was barred by the statute of frauds. . . . It ought to be stated, however, in fairness to the plaintiff, that the defendant was clearly guilty of overreaching the plaintiff, but the bar of the statute of frauds and the failure on the part of the plaintiff to proceed on the theory of quantum meruit have given to the defendant a windfall which in business morals and good conscience he is not entitled to."

Plaintiff took no appeal, or any other ameliorative procedural step. Instead he brought a second action, the present quantum meruit action. The trial court denied a motion to dismiss on the ground of res judicata. The appellate division reversed and dismissed the complaint. The New York Court of Appeals in turn reversed the appellate division and affirmed the order of the trial court.

Judge Conway for the unanimous New York Court of Appeals conceded that deciding what constitutes the same or different causes of action is difficult. Quoting with approval earlier opinions holding that the number and variety of the facts alleged do not establish more than one cause of action so long as their result is the violation of but one right by a single legal wrong, he continued: "The two actions involve different 'rights' and 'wrongs'. The requisite elements of proof and hence the evidence necessary to sustain recovery vary materially. The causes of action are different and distinct and the rights and interests established by the previous adjudication will not be impaired by a recovery, if that be the outcome, in quantum meruit."[a]

Question: (2) Is this case consistent with Williamson? Does it reach a desirable result, either as to the merits of the immediate case or as to res judicata doctrine that must consider efficiency and fairness over the long-run too?

O'BRIEN v. CITY OF SYRACUSE, 54 N.Y.2d 353, 429 N.E.2d 1158, 445 N.Y.S.2d 687 (1981). In 1973 plaintiffs sued defendants in New York state court for de facto appropriation, alleging that in the course of urban rehabilitation the defendant city authorities had so seriously interfered with plaintiffs' property rights as to constitute a de facto taking. A 1975 nonjury trial resulted in dismissal for failure to establish a de facto taking, which was affirmed on appeal. However, the appellate division did indicate that plaintiffs had suffered serious economic loss and that defendants' acts might have constituted trespass.

In 1978 plaintiffs brought a new suit against the same defendants for trespass to the same property at various times from 1967 to 1978. Defendants moved to dismiss on grounds of res judicata and failure to

---

[a]   The court further held that plaintiff had not, by reason of the doctrine of election of remedies, lost his right to sue in quantum meruit by attempting and failing to succeed on the contract causes involved in the first action. The two types of remedies were not, said the court, so inconsistent or irreconcilable that the choice of the one precluded resort to the other.

What is this doctrine of election of remedies? Today much of the doctrine is substantive law. A person who originally had a choice of remedies may by his conduct before any action is brought disentitle himself to one or more of them. For instance, a defrauded person may lose the remedy of rescission, which involves a tender of return of the article purchased and a recovery of the purchase price, by material alteration of the article after discovery of the fraud, which would confine the defrauded party to the remedy of damages in an action for deceit.

Sometimes it has been held that mere commencement of an action seeking a particular remedy is itself an election preventing resort to another remedy deemed to be inconsistent. Under the Federal Rules and other modern procedural systems, however, such result should now be rare. As an example of today's procedural spirit, in federal court a party may pursue alternative and inconsistent remedies, subject always to the obligations of Rule 11, and may postpone the choice among them until a late stage of the action, even after findings of fact on the alternatives.

In any event, election of remedies, when properly viewed as a consequence of conduct, is distinguishable from res judicata, which is preclusion by judgment. See generally Wright & Miller § 4476.

serve a timely notice of claim. The trial court denied the motion. The appellate division reversed, applying res judicata to dismiss the complaint. The unanimous New York Court of Appeals affirmed the appellate division on a somewhat different basis, as Chief Judge Cooke explained:

"In analyzing the complaint, plaintiffs' allegations fall into two categories: (1) those concerning activities underlying the 1973 litigation; and (2) those asserting trespass generally. Only the claims encompassed by the first category are definitely barred by res judicata.

"This State has adopted the transactional analysis approach in deciding res judicata issues (Matter of Reilly v. Reid, 45 N.Y.2d 24, 407 N.Y.S.2d 645, 379 N.E.2d 172 [(1978)]). Under this address, once a claim is brought to a final conclusion, all other claims arising out of the same transaction or series of transactions are barred, even if based upon different theories or if seeking a different remedy (id., at pp. 29–30, 407 N.Y.S.2d 645, 648–49, 379 N.E.2d 172, 175–76). Here, all of defendants' conduct falling in the first category was also raised during the 1973 suit as the basis for that litigation. That proceeding having been brought to a final conclusion, no other claim may be predicated upon the same incidents.

"Plaintiffs, relying on Smith v. Kirkpatrick, 305 N.Y. 66, 111 N.E.2d 209, . . . urge that de facto appropriation and trespass are actions having different theoretical bases and requiring different evidentiary proof. This contention, however, erroneously characterizes the bases of the two causes. . . . [D]e facto appropriation, in the context of physical invasion, is based on showing that the government has intruded onto the citizen's property and interfered with the owner's property rights to such a degree that the conduct amounts to a constitutional taking requiring the government to purchase the property from the owner . . . . In effect, de facto appropriation may be characterized as an aggravated form of trespass. The pertinent evidence in both actions is the same. The basic distinction lies in the egregiousness of the trespass and whether it is of such intensity as to amount to a taking.

"In any event, even if it were assumed that the two actions involved materially different elements of proof, the second suit would be barred as to the claim predicated upon the first category allegations. When alternative theories are available to recover what is essentially the same relief for harm arising out of the same or related facts such as would constitute a single 'factual grouping' (Restatement, Judgments 2d, § 61 [Tent. Draft No. 5]), the circumstance that the theories involve materially different elements of proof will not justify presenting the claim by two different actions.[1] Consequently, plaintiffs' action is barred by the

---

[1]   To the extent Smith v. Kirkpatrick, 305 N.Y. 66, 111 N.E.2d 209, supra may be to the contrary, it is overruled.

doctrine of res judicata insofar as the allegations in the first category are concerned.

"Finally, the second category of allegations—the general trespass allegations—are not barred by res judicata to the extent that they describe acts occurring after [commencement of] the 1973 lawsuit. They are, however, barred by reason of plaintiffs' failure to serve timely a notice of claim."

The court further explained that a condition precedent to bringing a tort claim against a municipality is a timely notice of claim providing information sufficient to permit investigation of the claim, and that the notice preceding the second suit had failed to mention any trespassory acts other than those underlying the 1973 lawsuit and so was ineffective with respect to the "claim" stemming from the second category of allegations.

Questions: (3) Plaintiff brought an FELA action against a railroad and lost on the ground that he was not an employee of the railroad at the time of his injury. He now sues the railroad in the same court for the same injury, basing his claim on common-law negligence, a theory available only if he was not an employee. The railroad pleads bar. What decision on bar? (Reserve for later consideration the question of issue preclusion as to issues decided in the first action.) Compare Restatement (Second) of Judgments § 25 cmt. k (Am. Law Inst. 1982) (bar, thus counseling future litigants to plead in the alternative in the first suit), with People ex rel. Chi. & E. Ill. R.R. Co. v. Fleming, 42 Ill.2d 231, 246 N.E.2d 275 (1969) (no bar, under older view of "claim").

(4) An information technology provider brought an action on a negotiated settlement agreement and lost on the ground that there had been no meeting of the minds on settling. It then sued for the underlying services rendered, under both breach of oral contract and quantum meruit theories. By O'Brien, is there bar? See Funny Guy, LLC v. Lecego, LLC, 293 Va. 135, 795 S.E.2d 887 (2017) (4–3 decision) (yes). But do the alleged facts of the settlement agreement constitute the same transaction as the underlying dispute? Do we want to incentivize joinder of such disputes in future cases, or to punish the nonjoinder in this case?

HENNEPIN PAPER CO. v. FORT WAYNE CORRUGATED PAPER CO., 153 F.2d 822 (7th Cir.1946). The plaintiff-seller first sued in the United States District Court for the Northern District of Indiana, alleging the defendant-buyer's failure to take and pay for 800 tons of corrugating material monthly. A written contract of July 1, 1941, provided: "Owner agrees to sell Customer, and Customer agrees to purchase, all of Customer's needs of .009 Corrugating Material that Customer will purchase monthly from the outside up to 600 tons, more or less." On the apparent assumption that this language was ambiguous and hence that evidence of contemporaneous negotiations would be admissible to clarify the meaning, plaintiff pleaded certain negotiations at about the time of the execution of the contract showing that the parties had intended a commitment to buy a minimum of 600 tons per month. Plaintiff also alleged that by oral agreement during October 1941 the parties had changed the minimum amount to 800 tons per month. On defendant's motion, the court struck out the allegations of the complaint regarding the negotiations contemporaneous with the written contract on the ground that the contract was unambiguous and parol evidence could not be used to vary its terms, and ruled that defendant was committed by the contract to buy only the amount it required. The case thus stood upon the written contract as allegedly modified by the oral agreement of October 1941. On this claim, defendant had verdict and judgment. Plaintiff took no appeal.

Thereafter, plaintiff brought the present action in the United States District Court for the Northern District of Illinois to reform the written contract, so as to make it correspond with the "true intent and understanding of both parties," and to recover upon the contract as reformed. The alleged intent and understanding appeared from the negotiations contemporaneous with the written contract, i.e., a commitment to buy 600 tons monthly. The court granted defendant's motion for summary judgment, which was supported by affidavits setting forth the proceedings in the first action. Plaintiff appealed. The court of appeals affirmed.

Although in the old days the court system allowed and indeed often required separate actions for legal and equitable remedies, such as damages and reformation respectively, times have changed. "Under the Federal Rules of Civil Procedure [8(d)(3) and 18(a)], and under the law of Indiana, the plaintiff had the right, in the first action, to, by proper pleading, ask that the written contract of July 1, 1941, be reformed and redrawn, as it is attempting to do in the second action. It certainly knew the same facts at the time the district court struck out paragraph 5 of the complaint in the first action [the allegations concerning the contemporaneous negotiations] as it knew at the time it drafted the complaint in the second action, and it should have filed either an amended complaint or an additional count or paragraph in that action so as to have presented all issues in the same action." Thus, "the plaintiff could have, in the first action, sought a reformation of the contract, and it was its duty to have done so if it desired to litigate that question. Not having done so, and having sought an entirely different and inconsistent remedy in that action, it cannot now maintain the second action."

———

Questions: (5) Suppose a plaintiff sues in a state court for unfair competition, even though diversity of citizenship exists and more than the jurisdictional amount is at stake, but loses on the merits. She then alleges the same basic wrong in a federal-court action under the federal antitrust laws, an action over which the federal courts have exclusive jurisdiction. The defendant pleads bar. What decision on bar? (Assume that a generic law of res judicata applies here, but the choice-of-law rule in an interjurisdictional setting is to apply the res judicata law of the court that rendered the first judgment.) See Cream Top Creamery v. Dean Milk Co., 383 F.2d 358 (6th Cir.1967) (no bar, because antitrust theory was unavailable in state court and the plaintiff was not obliged to switch to federal court); Restatement (Second) of Judgments § 26(1)(c) (Am. Law Inst. 1982) (recognizing exception where the "plaintiff was unable to rely on a certain theory of the case or to seek a certain remedy or form of relief in the first action because of the limitations on the subject matter jurisdiction of the courts or restrictions on their authority to entertain multiple theories or demands for multiple remedies or forms of relief in a single action").

(6) Reverse the situation in the preceding question, so that the first action was in the federal court under the federal antitrust laws, with no reference to the claim of unfair competition, and the second in the state court. Should the state-court action be barred by res judicata? Does the existence of diversity jurisdiction determine your answer? In the absence of diversity, what of supplemental jurisdiction? See Restatement (Second) of Judgments § 25 cmt. e (Am. Law Inst. 1982) (bar).

(7) Finally, assume that the plaintiff first sues in a state court for unfair competition, the suit is removed to federal court on the basis of diversity jurisdiction, and the plaintiff then loses on the merits, there never having been reference by amendment or otherwise to any federal antitrust claim. She later brings a second action in a federal court under the federal antitrust laws. Should the second action be barred by res judicata?

Sutcliffe Storage & Warehouse Co. v. United States

United States Circuit Court of Appeals, First Circuit, 1947.
162 F.2d 849.

■ Before CLARK,[1] MAHONEY and WOODBURY, CIRCUIT JUDGES.

■ CLARK, CIRCUIT JUDGE. The present four appeals were filed in four actions instituted in the district court on February 18, 25, 26, and 28, 1946, respectively, each claiming sums due, with interest, for the use and occupancy of the same realty in Boston, over different periods of time from June 15, 1942, to December 31, 1945. The first action covered the period from June 15, 1942, to June 30, 1943, the second and third each covered a succeeding year, and the fourth covered the final six months to the end in 1945. In all four the amounts claimed are computed at identical rates per square foot for the various parcels involved. In the latter three actions the district court has granted the defendant's motions to dismiss on the ground that they were brought for inseparable parts of the claim set forth in the first action. D.C.Mass., 68 F.Supp. 446. In the

---

[1]   Judge Clark of the Second Circuit, serving by designation.

first action the defendant has made no motion and the court has entered no order.

Normally the district court would be acting quite within its discretion in taking steps to consolidate or otherwise avoid the duplication of such closely similar cases, whatever the substantive rights of the parties. Compare Rule 42(a), Federal Rules of Civil Procedure . . . . But the situation here is different because of the jurisdictional provisions of the Tucker Act. The first three actions claim amounts between eight and ten thousand dollars each; the last claims an amount in excess of four thousand dollars. The district court's jurisdiction of claims against the United States is limited to $10,000; for greater claims resort must be had to the Court of Claims in Washington. 28 U.S.C.A. § 41(20).[b] The plaintiff asserts a desire and right to sue for all amounts due in the courts of its own locality, asserting that the Tucker Act so permits and also relying on the facts alleged as showing four separate claims. And it is so entitled to sue if its contention is correct; otherwise it must either waive the excess or go to Washington to sue. The particular facts it relies upon are that on April 13, 1942, it executed a lease running until June 30, 1943, of certain premises it controlled to the United States Navy, and that this contract was renewed by separate renewal leases for periods identical with those covered by the last three actions. Plaintiff's contention—duly pleaded in each action—is that beginning about June 15, 1942, the Navy occupied and used a greater area than was designated in the lease for the period in question and that therefore the plaintiff is entitled to the reasonable value of the use and occupancy of the additional area for each period.

The defendant, however, asserts that the general rule against "splitting causes of action" applies to the Government as defendant equally with all other litigants, and that the existence of separate renewal leases for the adjoining premises does not affect the nature of the plaintiff's claims, and, indeed, is important only in connection with the defendant's own defenses. For defendant has filed answers which both claim possession of the additional premises as being actually included in the leases and alternatively assert that if this is not the case the leases failed to include the additional premises by mistake and should now be reformed to include them. In the last three actions the answers also state as a separate defense the pendency of the first action. It was this defense, made the subject of a separate motion for preliminary hearing and adjudication, which was sustained by the court below.

As Professor Moore succinctly states, "The pendency of a prior pending action in the same federal court is ground for abatement of the second action." 1 Moore's Federal Practice 237; United States v. The Haytian Republic, 154 U.S. 118, 14 S.Ct. 992, 38 L.Ed. 930; [other citations omitted]. There is no reason why a court should be bothered or

---

[b]   See the Tucker Act in present 28 U.S.C. § 1346(a)(2).

a litigant harassed with duplicating lawsuits on the same docket; it is enough if one complete adjudication of the controversy be had. As a matter of fact, it is often an advantage to the plaintiff to have the issue of double suits settled before he finds himself barred from full recovery by a partial but final judgment in one action. Thus here the plaintiff may count itself in luck to have the matter settled before a portion of its rights is irretrievably lost. For the test as ordinarily stated is whether the claims set up are legally the same so that judgment in one is a bar to the others. United States v. The Haytian Republic, supra, 154 U.S. 118, 129, 14 S.Ct. 992, 38 L.Ed. 930.

It is an ancient and well-settled legal principle that claims for amounts due on running accounts or as installment payments, such as rent under a lease, must include all amounts due at the time action is brought. [Citations omitted.] The same rule has been applied to claims for royalties under a patent, Buchanan v. General Motors Corp., 2 Cir., 158 F.2d 728, to claims affecting realty, as for continuing trespasses, Evans v. Durango Land & Coal Co., 8 Cir., 80 F. 433, 437, appeal dismissed Durango Land & Coal Co. v. Evans, 19 S.Ct. 875, 43 L.Ed. 1178, and to claims in quantum meruit for the occupancy of land, See v. See, 294 Mo. 495, 242 S.W. 949, 24 A.L.R. 880, with note collecting cases, 885–897. The doctrine is a salutary one in forcing the trial of identical matters together and affording a defendant once sued the protection of the doctrine of res judicata. Ordinarily there is no reason why a plaintiff cannot make all his claims on a running account at one time without piecemeal presentation. The fact that here involved are questions of federal jurisdiction is not a sufficient basis for departing from these usual rules as to the splitting of legal claims. The congressional policy is that all large claims must be presented in the one court in Washington, and in every practical sense there is here presented such a claim. Even though the plaintiff's own convenience might be served by adjudication in its vicinage, the congressional policy seems clearly opposed.

. . . .

Finally the particular facts urged by plaintiff do not vary the principle. That the plaintiff had separate leases for the adjoining property covering each fiscal year is not a sufficient basis to allow it to divide its claim for use and occupation of the particular premises here involved into four parts. In very truth its basic legal position depends upon its assertion that there were no leases covering these premises; once the existing leases are shown to affect them, the defendant has a solid basis for the assertion of its defenses. The plaintiff cannot in the same breath repudiate the leases and yet rely upon them as operating to separate its claim into parts.

The consequence of this conclusion is that there will be an affirmance of the dismissal of the latter three cases, Nos. 4238–4240 in this court. Since no action has been taken by the district court with reference to the earlier instituted action, No. 4241 in this court, there is nothing from which an appeal can be taken and we have no jurisdiction to consider it. [Citation omitted.] The plaintiff asks us, in the event of our affirmance of dismissal in the other three cases, to order dismissal also of this action to avoid what it terms its anomalous position in having one indivisible cause of action for an amount beyond the court's jurisdictional limit. But even if we had jurisdiction, no such action would be justified; for plaintiff has its own choice to make, whether it wishes to waive the greater amount and remain in the District Court for the District of Massachusetts, United States v. Johnson, 9 Cir., 153 F.2d 846, or now move that court for dismissal without prejudice under Rule 41(a)(2), F.R.C.P.[c] . . .

     . . . .

OTHER WAYS TO SPLIT A CLAIM

Judge Charles Clark refers above to the "ancient and well-settled legal principle that claims for amounts due on running accounts . . . must include all amounts due at the time action is brought." Suppose D is P's tenant under a lease calling for monthly payments. P sues for the May rent and obtains judgment. She cannot, because of the "ancient and well-settled legal principle," sue later for the earlier March or April rent.

Change the facts and suppose that D gave P a series of promissory notes, one payable each month, for the rental under the lease. P obtains a judgment on a note falling due on May 1. May she sue thereafter on other notes in the series due on the earlier March 1 and April 1? Is this case different from the previous example? See Restatement (Second) of Judgments § 24 cmt. d (Am. Law Inst. 1982) (yes).

There is a conflict of authority as to whether the splitting rule precludes a person from bringing successive actions for property damage and for personal injury suffered in the same automobile accident. Compare Dearden v. Hey, 304 Mass. 659, 24 N.E.2d 644 (1939) (second action precluded), with Clancey v. McBride, 338 Ill. 35, 169 N.E. 729 (1929) (second action not precluded, under Illinois's then-prevailing old-style view of "claim"). Which is the preferable rule?

Much more difficult problems exist in this realm. For example, in the case of a toxic tort (such as exposure to asbestos), where the plaintiff has sued successfully for incurred injury (from asbestosis) but chosen not to sue for considerably increased risk of injury (from cancer), can the plaintiff sue again when the risk later becomes reality? See Robert C. Casad & Kevin M. Clermont, Res Judicata 71–78 (2001).

---

[c]   An additional option became available in 1960: transfer between the district court and the Court of Claims (which has since become the Court of Federal Claims). See present 28 U.S.C. § 1631. Problems of jurisdictional division persist. See Gregory C. Sisk, The Jurisdiction of the Court of Federal Claims and Forum Shopping in Money Claims Against the Federal Government, 88 Ind.L.J. 83 (2013).

Questions: (8) Judge Clark says that "the plaintiff may count itself in luck to have the matter settled before a portion of its rights is irretrievably lost." He apparently is suggesting that the attorney for the government might have let one of the four cases go to judgment and then have pleaded res judicata to the other three. Would this be an ethically permissible course of action by the government attorney? Would your answer be the same if it were done by an attorney for a private party? Indeed, would it be ethically permissible for a privately employed attorney not to use such a tactic if available?

(9) Can you make an argument that Judge Clark's suggested res judicata tactic ought not to be successful? See Todd v. Cent. Petroleum Co., 155 Kan. 249, 124 P.2d 704 (1942) (looking to acquiescence in splitting by the defendant's failure to plead prior pending action); Restatement (Second) of Judgments § 26(1)(a) (Am. Law Inst. 1982) (recognizing exception where the "parties have agreed in terms or in effect that the plaintiff may split his claim, or the defendant has acquiesced therein").

RESTATEMENT OF JUDGMENTS

The traditional approach held that more than one "cause of action" could regularly arise out of the same transaction. Harking back to the days of the forms of action and the separation of law and equity, or to the days of code pleading, courts tended to equate a cause of action with a single theory or ground of recovery, to allow successive actions when the court concluded that different "rights" or "primary rights" had been simultaneously infringed, or otherwise to subdivide a transaction. For example, in Smith v. Kirkpatrick, the court strained to manipulate the terminology so as not to deny redress to a deserving plaintiff with misguided counsel.

Restatement of Judgments §§ 61–67 (Am. Law Inst. 1942) reflected that judicial attitude, but at the same time tried to set forth a series of black-letter rules that would bring order to a confused situation. The effort was not conspicuously successful.

Restatement (Second) of Judgments § 24 (Am. Law Inst. 1982) opts instead for a transactional view of "claim," providing that "the claim extinguished includes all rights of the plaintiff to remedies against the defendant with respect to all or any part of the transaction, or series of connected transactions, out of which the action arose" and also that the factual grouping constituting a "transaction" or a "series" is "to be determined pragmatically, giving weight to such considerations as whether the facts are related in time, space, origin, or motivation, whether they form a convenient trial unit, and whether their treatment as a unit conforms to the parties' expectations or business understanding or usage." The general rule of this section is exemplified in the Second Restatement's § 25 (along the lines of the Williamson and Sutcliffe cases), but it is subject to the exceptions stated in § 26 (including the exceptions suggested by Cream Top Creamery v. Dean Milk Co. and Todd v. Central Petroleum Co., cited in the questions above).

Question: (10) Does it matter whether a court proceeds (a) by defining "claim" narrowly so as to avoid claim preclusion or (b) by avoiding otherwise applicable claim preclusion through recognition of some exception thereto, such as defendant's agreement to claim-splitting?

This transactional approach of the Second Restatement puts pressure on the plaintiff not to overlook or withhold from his initial complaint any grievance he has relating to the transaction in question regardless of differences in "evidence," "grounds," "theories," "remedies," or "forms of relief." Should he err in the first instance, he will, given a modern procedural system, almost certainly have an opportunity to amend as the case unfolds. But failing that, he risks losing the unasserted portion of his claim.

Questions: (11) Do you see any likely problems for counsel in applying the Second Restatement's definition of the factual grouping that constitutes a "transaction" or a "series"?

(12) Does the punishment for splitting a claim fit the crime? Professor Cleary thought not. He would ordinarily have penalized the splitter by requiring reimbursement of the increase in the opponent's expenses due to using two lawsuits to do the work of one, rather than by complete loss of the right to further recovery. See Edward W. Cleary, Res Judicata Reexamined, 57 Yale L.J. 339, 349–50 (1948). But is that penalty a sufficient deterrent?

The Second Restatement is unarguably a work of high quality, although of course it is not perfect. It merits careful study because it manages to bring much order to the field and because it has so influenced the courts. It is thus worthy of debate.

Here, it should be emphasized that although there is considerable and increasing case support for the Second Restatement's transactional approach, some state courts still adhere to the older and narrower views. See Alan M. Trammell, Transactionalism Costs, 100 Va.L.Rev. 1211, 1270–75 (2014) (listing fewer than a dozen states conforming to the same-evidence test, while California follows the primary-rights test).

———

Harrington v. Vandalia-Butler Board of Education

United States Court of Appeals, Sixth Circuit, 1981.
649 F.2d 434.

■ Before GEORGE CLIFTON EDWARDS, JR., CHIEF JUDGE, ENGEL and BOYCE F. MARTIN, JR., CIRCUIT JUDGES.

■ BOYCE F. MARTIN, JR., CIRCUIT JUDGE.

In 1974, Jeanne Harrington filed suit in the United States District Court for the Southern District of Ohio against the Vandalia-Butler Board of Education, alleging sex discrimination in [former] employment and seeking relief under Title VII of the Civil Rights Act of 1964, 42 U.S.C. § 2000e, et seq. After a bench trial in June, 1976, the court found that [by reason of inferior work facilities for the teaching of girls' physical education in junior high school] she had been discriminated against in violation of Title VII and awarded compensatory damages [of $6000] and attorney's fees [of $2000]. Harrington v. Vandalia-Butler Board of Education, 418 F.Supp. 603 (S.D.Ohio 1976). On appeal to this Court, the factual finding of discrimination was sustained. However, we reversed the judgment on the grounds that Title VII does not authorize compensatory damages and that the finding of discrimination, standing alone, did not support an award of attorney's fees. Harrington v. Vandalia-Butler Board of Education, 585 F.2d 192 (6th Cir.1978), cert. denied, 441 U.S. 932, 99 S.Ct. 2053, 60 L.Ed.2d 660 (1979).

In 1978, while Harrington's appeal was pending in this court, the Supreme Court decided Monell v. Department of Social Services, 436 U.S. 658, 98 S.Ct. 2018, 56 L.Ed.2d 611 (1978). That decision overruled Monroe v. Pape, 365 U.S. 167, 81 S.Ct. 473, 5 L.Ed.2d 492 (1961), insofar as the latter held that municipalities are not "persons" subject to liability under 42 U.S.C. § 1983. Immediately after Monell was decided, Harrington brought this action against the Board of Education, school principal Ralph Clay, and school superintendent Blutcher P. Gibson, alleging employment discrimination and seeking relief under § 1983.

The defendant Board of Education moved for summary judgment on the ground that the plaintiff's claim was barred by the doctrine of res judicata. On June 7, 1979, the District Court granted this motion, holding that the plaintiff had ample opportunity during the previous litigation to raise a claim for relief based on the alleged violation of § 1983.

. . . .

Harrington next contends that the defense of res judicata may not be invoked in this case because her present claim under § 1983 could not have been raised at the time the first suit was filed. She argues that the change in the law brought about by Monell precludes the availability of the defense. We disagree.

It is undisputed that appellant's earlier Title VII action and the present § 1983 suit are based on the same discriminatory acts. When two successive suits seek recovery for the same injury, "a judgment on the merits operates as a bar to the later suit, even though a different legal theory of recovery is advanced in the second suit." Cemer v. Marathon Oil Company, 583 F.2d 830, 832 (6th Cir.1978). [Other citations omitted.] This principle applies even if an intervening decision effects a change in the law which bears directly on the legal theory advanced in the second suit.

. . . Section 1983 was not "unavailable" to appellant when she filed her Title VII action. She was free to challenge the validity of Monroe v. Pape to the extent that it exempted municipalities from the ambit of

§ 1983. Moreover, it is clear that if she had brought the § 1983 claim initially and lost it on the basis of Monroe v. Pape, she would not be entitled to reassert the § 1983 claim in the aftermath of Monell. She would be bound by the prior judgment on the merits.[d] That prior judgment is no less binding against her here merely because she elected not to advance a § 1983 claim in her first action.

. . . .

In summary, the thrust of the decisions discussed above is this: generally, a judgment on the merits—even if erroneous—will be deprived of its conclusive effect only if it is vacated, reversed, or set aside on direct appeal. [Citations omitted.]

We are convinced, therefore, that the change in the law wrought by Monell, standing alone, does not preclude the application of res judicata to this case. That conclusion does not, however, end our inquiry, for "This court has held . . . that '[n]either collateral estoppel nor res judicata is rigidly applied. Both rules are qualified or rejected when their application would contravene an overriding public policy or result in manifest injustice.' Tipler v. E.I. du Pont de Nemours and Co., 443 F.2d 125, 128 (6th Cir.1971)." Bronson v. Board of Education, 525 F.2d 344 (6th Cir.1975), cert. denied, 425 U.S. 934, 96 S.Ct. 1665, 48 L.Ed.2d 175 (1976). See also United States v. LaFatch, 565 F.2d 81 (6th Cir.1977), cert. denied, 435 U.S. 971, 98 S.Ct. 1611, 56 L.Ed.2d 62 (1978); Ferguson v. Winn Parish Police Jury, 589 F.2d 173, 176 n. 6 (5th Cir.1979).

. . . .

In Bronson v. Board of Education, supra, we addressed the problem of res judicata in the context of school desegregation litigation. For our purposes in the present case, it is sufficient to recall our conclusion that the strong public policy against perpetuating racial segregation in public schools does not necessarily preclude the application of res judicata and collateral estoppel to school desegregation cases. 525 F.2d 349.

Finally, United States v. LaFatch, supra, involved an attempt by a corporation to recover $50,000.00 it had paid to Anthony LaFatch. According to the corporation, the money was paid in cooperation with the FBI and under its surveillance. The transaction had provided the basis for an extortion indictment against LaFatch. After the District Court dismissed the extortion charge at the close of the government's case, the corporation filed suit in an Ohio court to recover the $50,000.00. It obtained a verdict against LaFatch for only $15,000.00. The federal District Court, which had retained custody of the money, found that the Ohio court's judgment was res judicata as to the ownership of the money and granted LaFatch's motion asking for its return. We, however, held

---

[d]   Unlike a civil rights action under § 1983, Title VII then gave only equitable relief. Congress has since provided for limited compensatory and punitive damages in Title VII actions for intentional discrimination. Civil Rights Act of 1991, Pub.L. No. 102–166, tit. I, § 102, 105 Stat. 1071, 1072. But likewise, res judicata would prevent Harrington from suing again for damages under amended Title VII.

that res judicata should not be applied for reasons of overriding public policy. We said that if the corporation's claim that it made the payment in cooperation with the FBI were true, the application of res judicata would violate the public policy of encouraging cooperation with law enforcement authorities in thwarting attempts at bribery and extortion. 565 F.2d at 84.

. . . .

... The policy at issue here—the availability of compensatory damages for violations of Title VII rights—does not, in our view, rise to the degree of overall importance to our society which Bronson and LaFatch suggest is necessary to avoid the preclusive effect of judgments.

We realize that in the circumstances of this case the doctrine of res judicata seems to work an unfair result. Appellant has established that she was discriminated against; the defendant's "vindication" on the merits was attributable only to the remedial limits of Title VII. Compare Bronson, supra, at 349. When she filed her Title VII action, appellant had good reason to believe that she could not successfully sue a school board under § 1983, which permits the award of damages for violations of constitutional and statutory rights. Upon learning from Monell that a municipality is now considered a "person" for the purposes of § 1983, appellant filed another suit which raised the § 1983 claim for the first time. There is undoubtedly an element of injustice in the application of res judicata to preclude that claim. However, we believe that the decisions of the Supreme Court and of this circuit, together with the policies underlying the doctrine of res judicata, compel that result.

Manifest injustice of the type necessary to except a case from the application of the doctrine is simply not present here. A mere showing that the second litigation, if allowed to proceed, would produce a different result than the first is not a showing of manifest injustice. Because the doctrine of res judicata effects a balance between competing interests, a certain degree of inequity is inevitable. Res judicata ensures the finality of judicial decisions. It encourages reliance on those decisions, thereby establishing certainty in legal relations. It bars vexatious litigation and promotes economy of judicial time and effort. Brown v. [Felsen, 442 U.S. 127, 131, 99 S.Ct. 2205, 2209 (1979)]. If the Supreme Court had decided, subsequent to appellant's Title VII suit, that compensatory damages could indeed be awarded under that statute, appellant would nevertheless be barred from reasserting her Title VII claim to collect such damages. That result would be no more or less fair than the one achieved here. The injustice inherent in either result is a necessary by-product of the general rule that judgments are final. In our opinion, that general rule must prevail here.

[This part of the opinion resulted in affirmance. Other parts of the opinion are omitted.]

Questions: (13) Could the plaintiff have pressed a § 1983 count in her original suit without violating former Rule 11? Even if so, would the legal system have wanted to encourage her to do so? Did, then, her having originally "elected not to advance a § 1983 claim" really constitute a basis for the court's application of res judicata?

(14) Similarly, when the Sixth Circuit said, "Section 1983 was not 'unavailable' to appellant when she filed her Title VII action," did it mean to imply that claim preclusion would not have applied if Rule 11 had made a § 1983 count unavailable? Did, then, it matter at all whether or not she could have elected to advance a § 1983 claim before Monell?

(15) If she had brought a § 1983 count in her original suit and lost, then the Supreme Court changed the law in Monell, and so she sued again, the Sixth Circuit said the result would have been the same. Therefore, whether she had failed to assert, could not have asserted, or had asserted a § 1983 count, res judicata would have precluded a second suit. The Sixth Circuit was just alluding to the plaintiff's "failures" to make its harsh result go down more easily. What, then, is the Harrington case's real rationale?

SECTION 2.   ADJUDICATION NOT ON THE MERITS

Waterhouse v. Levine

Supreme Judicial Court of Massachusetts, 1903.
182 Mass. 407, 65 N.E. 822.

CONTRACT for goods sold and delivered. Writ in the Municipal Court of the City of Boston dated April 13, 1901.

On appeal to the Superior Court the case was tried before Sherman, J., without a jury. The defence pleaded and relied upon was a former judgment. The judge refused to rule that the judgment was a bar to this action, and made the ruling stated by the court, admitting evidence to show the issue tried in the former action. He found for the plaintiff[s] in the sum of $336.04; and the defendant alleged exceptions.

■ BARKER, J. The defendant contends that the plaintiffs cannot maintain this action because judgment was rendered for the defendant upon a trial in a previous action between the same parties and for the same cause of action. Evidence was admitted in this action against the defendant's exception that the former judgment was upon the ground that the first suit was prematurely brought, the goods for the price of which both suits were brought having been sold upon a credit which had not expired when the first action was begun. The judge found as a fact that the only issue decided in the former action was whether that action was prematurely brought, and that the former judgment was entered because the action was prematurely brought and for that reason alone.

The only answer in the former action was a general denial. But under that answer the defence that the goods were bought upon a credit not expired when the suit was begun was open. [Citations omitted.] Whether oral evidence would be admissible to show that a former judgment went solely upon an issue which strictly could not have been tried upon the pleadings as they stood, but was in fact tried with the assent of all parties, is a question upon which we express no opinion.

It is only when rendered upon the merits that a judgment constitutes an absolute bar to a subsequent action for the same cause and the parties are concluded upon all issues which might have been tried. . . .

. . . .

Exceptions overruled.

————

Questions: (16) To what extent, if any, should evidence extrinsic to the record be admissible to show that a prior judgment went solely on an issue that was not open on the pleadings but was tried by consent pursuant to Rule 15(b)(2)?

(17) If there was evidence at the first trial on each of two alternative issues and the trial judge's decision did not show upon which issue he decided, would his testimony on this point be admissible in the second action?

————

Keidatz v. Albany

Supreme Court of California, 1952.
39 Cal.2d 826, 249 P.2d 264.

■ TRAYNOR, JUSTICE. In this action to recover damages for fraud, plaintiffs alleged that they were induced to buy a newly-constructed home from defendants by certain false and fraudulent representations respecting the character of the construction of the house and its location on the described real property. They further alleged that the representations were known by defendants to be false and were made to induce plaintiffs to purchase the property and that the contract price of $6,500 exceeded the value of the property by $3,000. In their answer defendants denied the allegations of fraud and pleaded affirmatively that plaintiffs' action was barred by two former adjudications between the parties. Defendants then made a motion for summary judgment supported by affidavits setting out the following undisputed facts: In 1949, plaintiffs brought an action to rescind the contract for fraud and failure of consideration. A demurrer to the second amended complaint was sustained with leave to amend. Plaintiffs failed to amend within the time allowed, and judgment was entered for defendants for costs. Thereafter plaintiffs unsuccessfully sought relief from the judgment under section 473 of the Code of Civil Procedure. No appeal was taken, however, from the judgment or from the order denying relief under section 473. Approximately four months after the judgment in the rescission action was entered, plaintiff brought this action for damages for fraud. The trial court granted defendants' motion for summary judgment and plaintiffs have appealed.

Plaintiffs contend that their unsuccessful attempt to secure rescission of the contract does not bar their present action for damages for fraud. Defendants, on the other hand, contend that the former judgment is res judicata of all issues presented here. Since the former judgment was entered after a general demurrer had been sustained with leave to amend, it is necessary to determine the scope of the doctrine of res judicata in such circumstances. The procedural effect of such a judgment appears to be sui generis. It is a judgment on the merits to the extent that it adjudicates that the facts alleged do not constitute a cause of action, and will, accordingly, be a bar to a subsequent action alleging the same facts. [Citations omitted.] Moreover, even though different facts may be alleged in the second action, if the demurrer was sustained in the first action on a ground equally applicable to the second, the former judgment will also be a bar. [Citations omitted.] If, on the other hand, new or additional facts are alleged that cure the defects in the original pleading, it is settled that the former judgment is not a bar to the subsequent action whether or not plaintiff had an opportunity to amend his complaint. [Citations omitted]; Restatement, Judgments, § 50, Comments c and e.

In plaintiffs' first action they sought rescission of the contract. In addition to alleging certain fraudulent representations whereby they were induced to enter into the contract, they alleged that they had offered to restore everything of value they had received, and sought the return of the payments they had made. It appeared from the complaint, however, that the alleged defects in construction became apparent to plaintiffs over a year before they sought to rescind, and defendants successfully demurred on the ground that the action was barred by laches and by failure to rescind promptly. [Citations omitted.] Whether or not the complaint stated a cause of action for rescission, the demurrer should have been overruled if a cause of action for damages was stated. [Citations omitted.] Plaintiffs' complaint did not, however, allege that the property was worth less than the price they agreed to pay for it, Civ.Code § 3343, and accordingly, it did not state a cause of action for damages for fraud. [Citations omitted.] In the present action, plaintiffs have added this allegation that was absent from their former complaint, and accordingly, under the rule hereinabove stated, the former judgment is not a bar to this action.

Defendants contend, however, that Wulfjen v. Dolton, 24 Cal.2d 891, 151 P.2d 846, establishes the rule that a party claiming to have been defrauded must seek all the relief to which he may be entitled in one action, and that he may not, after having failed in an action to rescind a contract for fraud, thereafter bring a second action for damages. In the Wulfjen case, however, the judgment in the rescission action had not been entered on demurrer, but had followed a full trial on the merits, and the court applied the rule that such a judgment is res judicata not only as to issues actually raised, but as to issues that could have been raised in support of the action. See, Sutphin v. Speik, 15 Cal.2d 195, 202, 99 P.2d 652, 101 P.2d 497. As has been pointed out above, however, it has been the settled rule in this state that a judgment entered on demurrer does not have such broad res judicata effect. [On the one hand, Justice Traynor conceded that there are forceful arguments, in view of the liberal rules relating to amendments to the pleadings, for requiring the plaintiff to set forth in one action all the facts relating to his dispute.] On the other hand less prejudice is suffered by a defendant who has had only to attack the pleadings, than by one who has been forced to go to trial . . . , and the hardship suffered by being forced to defend against a new action, instead of against an amended complaint, is not materially greater. [Citation omitted.] We do not feel, however, that at this time we should reweigh the conflicting arguments over the wisdom of the rule we apply. Since it is a settled rule of procedure upon which parties are entitled to rely in conducting their litigation, any change therein should be made by the Legislature and not by this court.

. . . .

The judgment is reversed.

■ SCHAUER, J., concurs in the judgment.

———

DISMISSAL FOR INSUFFICIENCY OF COMPLAINT

As Justice Traynor suggested, the position of Restatement of Judgments § 50 (Am. Law Inst. 1942) was essentially as follows:

1.   After judgment sustaining a demurrer on the ground that the facts stated were insufficient to constitute a cause of action, a new action on a complaint in which the defect has been corrected is not barred. It does not matter that the plaintiff failed in the first action to avail himself of permission to amend.

2.   However, judgment sustaining a demurrer on such ground precludes a new action alleging the same, or virtually the same, facts as alleged in the first action. This was seen as an application of direct estoppel, which precludes repetitively litigating the same issue.

3.   Also, judgment sustaining a demurrer precludes a new action where the defect in the first action was "an entire failure to state a cause of action" rather than "merely the omission of an essential allegation." If, for example, the plaintiff sued for invasion of privacy and the court dismissed on the ground that the state recognized no such right, a new action on the same cause is barred even if the state has meanwhile altered its views on the right of privacy.

Question: (18) Should this last rule be inexorably applied, or are there extraordinary situations where relitigation ought to be allowed? Suppose, for instance, that a board of education set up plans for reduction of the teaching force as part of a school desegregation program and that a group of African American teachers brought an action seeking to enjoin the plans as racially discriminatory. On demurrer, the court upheld the plans and dismissed the action. There was no appeal. Subsequently, in an identical case arising in another state, the Supreme Court of the United States declares the plans to be unconstitutional. Should those original teachers be able to maintain a new action over the defendant's plea of res judicata? See Restatement (Second) of Judgments § 26(1)(d) (Am. Law Inst. 1982) (recognizing exception where the "judgment in the first action was plainly inconsistent with the fair and equitable implementation of a statutory or constitutional scheme").

There persists limited support for the First Restatement's view, as in California today. Some courts departed from it to the extent of barring a new action if, after the demurrer was sustained in the first action, the plaintiff was expressly granted leave to amend and he neglected or refused to amend. E.g., Elfman v. Glaser, 313 Mass. 370, 47 N.E.2d 925 (1943). And other courts viewed even this revised version of the First Restatement's position as inconsistent with the modern rules of pleading and especially the freedom to amend, and hence as not going far enough toward embracing bar. See Osserman v. Jacobs, 369 Mass. 200, 339 N.E.2d 193 (1975) (Kaplan, J.) (precluding in absence of express leave to amend); Developments in the Law—Res Judicata, 65 Harv.L.Rev. 818, 836–37 (1952).

Therefore, Restatement (Second) of Judgments § 19 cmt. d (Am. Law Inst. 1982) abandons the position of the First Restatement, by providing in effect that a judgment for insufficiency of the complaint normally operates as a bar unless the rendering court otherwise specifies by order. Most states have followed suit. In this connection, consider the effect of a rule like Federal Rule 41(b), discussed in the following case and in Wright & Miller § 4435.

Rinehart v. Locke

United States Court of Appeals, Seventh Circuit, 1971.
454 F.2d 313.

[Plaintiff, by his attorney, sued in 1969 under 42 U.S.C. § 1983, claiming that his arrest by the defendants—private detectives and police officers—deprived him of his constitutional rights. The Federal Rule 12(b)(6) dismissal by District Judge Julius J. Hoffman was based upon the failure to allege lack of probable cause. Plaintiff sought leave to amend to include such an allegation, but the judge denied leave, stating no reason. Plaintiff did not appeal.

[More than a year later (and nearly six years after the events in suit), plaintiff brought a second action based on the same arrest, the complaint being identical in substance to the first except that it included an allegation of lack of probable cause. The same district court, this time by Judge Joseph S. Perry, sustained the defense of res judicata and dismissed. Plaintiff appealed.]

■ Before SWYGERT, CHIEF JUDGE, and FAIRCHILD and STEVENS, CIRCUIT JUDGES.

■ FAIRCHILD, CIRCUIT JUDGE.

. . . .

Plaintiff contends that the May, 1969 dismissal did not establish that defendants were not liable to him under § 1983 on account of the 1964 arrest, but established only that he had no cause of action unless he was able to plead and prove lack of probable cause.

[The court stated that the traditional rule supported plaintiff's position, citing Gould v. Evansville & Crawfordsville R.R. Co., 91 U.S. 526 (1876), and Restatement of Judgments § 50 cmt. c (Am. Law Inst. 1942).]

Arguably Rule 41(b), F.R.C.P., may have changed this rule where the earlier judgment, as in this case, was entered in a federal court. The Rule provides in part: "Unless the court in its order for dismissal otherwise specifies, a dismissal under this subdivision and any dismissal not provided for in this rule, other than a dismissal for lack of jurisdiction, for improper venue, or for failure to join a party under Rule 19, operates as an adjudication upon the merits."

It has been held that the list in Rule 41(b) of types of dismissal which are not presumptively adjudications on the merits is not exclusive, and that the situations where dismissals not provided for in Rule 41 are to operate as adjudication on the merits are those "in which the defendant must incur the inconvenience of preparing to meet the merits because there is no initial bar to the Court's reaching them."[2] The same decision indicates that a dismissal for failure to fulfill a "precondition" for consideration of the merits is not a decision on the merits.

With this gloss upon the Rule, the question remains a close one, but we are persuaded that under the Rule an order of a district court which dismisses a complaint for failure to state a claim, but which does not specify that the dismissal is without prejudice, is res judicata as to the then existing claim which it appears plaintiff was attempting to state. This view places upon a plaintiff in a case like the 1969 case in this

---

[2]   Costello v. United States, 365 U.S. 265, 286, 81 S.Ct. 534, 545, 5 L.Ed.2d 551 (1961). [This case held that a dismissal of a denaturalization proceeding for failure to file a required affidavit of good cause with the complaint, where the dismissal order did not specify whether it was with or without prejudice, was not "an adjudication upon the merits" despite the wording of Rule 41(b). The Court reached this result by ruling that the Rule's term "lack of jurisdiction" is not to be read technically or narrowly, and that this dismissal was for "lack of jurisdiction."— Ed.]

instance the burden of persuading the district court either to include a specification that the dismissal is without prejudice or to permit an amendment. If plaintiff is unsuccessful, his recourse is to appeal. We think this view is consistent with the expedient purpose of the Rules.

[The other part of the opinion, to the effect that the action was also barred by the statute of limitations, is omitted.]

The judgment appealed from is affirmed.

———

Question: (19) There is an exception to claim preclusion where the "court in the first action has expressly reserved the plaintiff's right to maintain the second action." See Restatement (Second) of Judgments § 26(1)(b) (Am. Law Inst. 1982). May a district court instead specify that its dismissal for lack of jurisdiction is "with prejudice" or is "an adjudication upon the merits"? See id. § 20 cmt. d; Wright & Miller § 2373.

———

DISMISSAL FOR FAILURE TO PROSECUTE

Does a dismissal for failure to prosecute, or failure to obey a court order or rule, operate as an adjudication on the merits? In this situation, there has not been in a literal sense an adjudication on the merits—there usually has been no consideration whatever of the merits—but the dismissal nevertheless operates as a bar unless the rendering court otherwise specifies by order. Such is the result that is suggested by Rule 41(b), which has its counterpart in a majority of the states, and is more generally provided by Restatement (Second) of Judgments § 19 cmt. e (Am. Law Inst. 1982). The justification for the harsh result to the litigant deprived of a chance to establish his claim lies in the interests of his opponent and those of litigants generally in having the court effectively control its docket and enforce its procedure.

Dismissal on these grounds is reviewable on appeal for abuse of discretion. In most instances where abuse of discretion is the test, the appellate court strains to uphold the decision of the lower court. Here, however, appellate judges do not look with favor upon the sanction of dismissal. As the appellate court said in Industrial Building Materials, Inc. v. Interchemical Corp., 437 F.2d 1336, 1339 (9th Cir.1970): "Application of the remedy rests within the sound discretion of the court, but since it may severely punish a party not responsible for the alleged dereliction of his counsel, the rule should only be invoked in extreme circumstances. In reviewing the propriety of dismissal under Rule 41(b) we should, we think, look to see whether the court might have first adopted other, less drastic alternatives." See also Russell G. Vineyard, Note, Dismissal with Prejudice for Failure to Prosecute: Visiting the Sins of the Attorney upon the Client, 22 Ga.L.Rev. 195 (1987).

———

"ON THE MERITS"

Restatement of Judgments § 48 (Am. Law Inst. 1942) stated that a valid and final personal judgment for the defendant acts as a bar only if it was "on the merits." But, over time and in response to considerations of fairness and efficiency, the rule of bar has come to apply more broadly, with judgments not passing directly on the substance of the claim acting as a bar.

Restatement (Second) of Judgments § 19 (Am. Law Inst. 1982) consequently omits the phrase "on the merits," and comment a thereto explains that the phrase was no longer descriptive of the many situations in which bar applies. But, of course, this omission does not mean that under the Second Restatement *any* valid and final personal judgment for the defendant acts as a bar: the remains of the on-the-merits condition became the set of not-on-the-merits exceptions laid out in § 20.

————

Restatement (Second) of Judgments
(Am. Law Inst. 1982).

§ 20.   *Judgment for Defendant—Exceptions to the General Rule of Bar*

(1) A personal judgment for the defendant, although valid and final, does not bar another action by the plaintiff on the same claim:

(a) When the judgment is one of dismissal for lack of jurisdiction, for improper venue, or for nonjoinder or misjoinder of parties; or

(b) When the plaintiff agrees to or elects a nonsuit (or voluntary dismissal) without prejudice or the court directs that the plaintiff be nonsuited (or that the action be otherwise dismissed) without prejudice; or

(c) When by statute or rule of court the judgment does not operate as a bar to another action on the same claim, or does not so operate unless the court specifies, and no such specification is made.

(2) A valid and final personal judgment for the defendant, which rests on the prematurity of the action or on the plaintiff's failure to satisfy a precondition to suit, does not bar another action by the plaintiff instituted after the claim has matured, or the precondition has been satisfied, unless a second action is precluded by operation of the substantive law.

————

Question: (20) Should Restatement (Second) of Judgments § 20(2) (Am. Law Inst. 1982) apply to permit a second action even where the dismissal of the first action came not at the threshold but only after full-blown trial? Or instead should there be another exception to the exception, providing for bar where it would be "manifestly unfair" to subject the defendant to the second action? See John E. Eichhorst, Symposium Note, Res Judicata Effects of Involuntary Dismissals: When Involuntary Dismissals Based upon Prematurity or Failure to Satisfy a Precondition to Suit Should Bar a Second Action, 70 Cornell L.Rev. 667 (1985).

————

DISMISSAL FOR STATUTE OF LIMITATIONS

The courts have developed a special rule, seen in Williamson, for dismissal on limitations grounds. It will apply if the plaintiff later brings a recast action in an attempt to circumvent the statute of limitations: a dismissal on limitations grounds acts as a bar in the same jurisdiction and in foreign courts applying the same jurisdiction's limitations law—but, for reasons difficult to fathom, it may not act as a bar to suit somewhere else on the same claim.

Perhaps the way to explain this rule is to resort to issue preclusion rather than claim preclusion. Although the first judgment may not have bar effect, it did determine the broad issue of the particular limitations law's application to that particular claim, however the claim is repleaded. The expiration of the statutory period for that claim was litigated and determined in dismissing the first suit, and relitigation of that issue should be foreclosed by principles of direct estoppel where, but only where, that same limitations law applies.

Nevertheless, courts persist in speaking in terms of bar or no bar: "bar" to express the broad preclusion applied with respect to the same jurisdiction's limitations law, but "no bar" otherwise. Restatement (Second) of Judgments § 19 cmt. f, reporter's note (Am. Law Inst. 1982) restates this traditional doctrine, while questioning the soundness of the part of the doctrine permitting a second action in another jurisdiction after a judgment of dismissal based on the statute of limitations.

Some slippage from the nonpreclusion-elsewhere rule occurs in courts more conscious that they are applying, as for all other judgments, the res judicata law of the rendering court. The second jurisdiction must uncover the first court's res judicata law for a statute-of-limitations dismissal. But extraterritorially phrased res judicata law does not, of course, exist: the first court's law will treat domestic statute-of-limitations dismissals as domestically preclusive, but will not hold with respect to their preclusive effect elsewhere. So the second court must uncover what the first court thought it was deciding and thus how it would have expected its statute-of-limitations dismissal to be treated elsewhere. The second court would do so by looking at the first court's statute-of-limitations law to see, principally, if it views its statute as a statute of repose eliminating the plaintiff's substantive right or as a mere statute of limitations denying the plaintiff a remedy. If the former, the first court would have expected its judgment to have bar effect elsewhere. If the latter, the first court would have expected its judgment to have no bar effect but only direct estoppel effect, precluding the issue of the applicability of the limitations law that the first court applied but allowing suit to proceed under a different limitations law in another jurisdiction. See Newman v. Krintzman, 723 F.3d 308, 313–15 (1st Cir.2013) (applying bar); cf. CTS Corp. v. Waldburger, 573 U.S. 1, 134 S.Ct. 2175 (2014) (explaining that statutes of limitations promote justice by encouraging plaintiffs to pursue claims diligently and start to run when a claim accrues, while the statutes-of-repose subtype frees a defendant from liability strictly without regard to equities after a set amount of time that runs from the defendant's last culpable act or omission).

In fact, more direct and coherent undermining of the traditional doctrine is now occurring. Courts seem increasingly willing to accord bar effect to all foreign dismissals based on the statute of limitations. See, e.g., AmBase Corp. v. City Investing Co. Liquidating Trust, 326 F.3d 63, 72 (2d Cir.2003). Their reasons are many. First, the plaintiff has had his day in court, and the defendant should not have to suffer another. Fairness and efficiency are at stake. Second, the limitations defense is indistinguishable in policy from many defenses that are unquestionably on the merits such as the statute of frauds, especially as the realm of bar has expanded to reach defenses like failure to state a claim. The usual rule is that when a plaintiff has lost under the law of one jurisdiction, that plaintiff faces bar in another jurisdiction even though under its law he would have won. Third, given that the limitations dismissal is a bar in the first jurisdiction, according a different effect in the second jurisdiction is at least anomalous, if not actually in conflict with the principles of full faith and credit. If the dismissal is a bar in the first jurisdiction, then it should be a bar in the second. It appears, then, that the wave of the future will be to treat limitations dismissals like other dismissals on the merits, that is, as creating a bar.

––––––––

SECTION 3.   COUNTERCLAIM

Counterclaim pleaded.—Once a defendant pleads a counterclaim, the principles of former adjudication generally apply to it just as they apply to an original claim in a complaint. See Restatement (Second) of Judgments §§ 21(1), 23 (Am. Law Inst. 1982).

The one exception to this rule applies when the defendant counterclaims, but the defendant cannot obtain full recovery because the action was brought in a court that was not empowered to give the defendant full recovery on his counterclaim (such as a court of limited jurisdiction with a ceiling on damages) and because no procedural devices were available by which the defendant might readily have obtained full recovery (such as transferring the entire case to another court in the same legal system). In this very narrow situation, the defendant's claim is not extinguished by the judgment, and he may seek recovery on the remainder of his claim by a subsequent action in a competent court. Cf. id. § 21(2).

Permissive counterclaim not pleaded.—Whenever applicable law permits a counterclaim to be asserted but does not make it compulsory, a defendant has the choice between responding to the plaintiff's claim with an answer that includes the counterclaim and reserving the subject matter of the potential counterclaim for an independent action.

This rule is usually straightforward enough, but complications ensue when the same facts constitute both a ground of defense to the plaintiff's claim and a basis for counterclaim. If these facts are not used as a defense, the main action may be lost, and therefore the defendant will almost certainly so use them. But suppose that the defendant nevertheless wishes to reserve his affirmative claim in order to bring it as an independent action, perhaps in another forum that is more convenient or might apply more favorable law. Should the defendant be free to rely on the common facts as a defense, without pleading a counterclaim, and still bring an independent action based on those same facts?

Schwabe v. Chantilly, Inc.

Supreme Court of Wisconsin, 1975.
67 Wis.2d 267, 226 N.W.2d 452.

■ WILKIE, CHIEF JUSTICE. This is a landlord-tenant case presenting a question of civil procedure. In a prior action, the landlord, Chantilly, Inc., sued the tenants, James and Mary Schwabe, for nonpayment of rent. The Schwabes set up the affirmative defense that they were fraudulently induced to sign the lease, but they did not counterclaim. Judgment was awarded to the Schwabes based upon this defense. Now in the present action they seek compensatory and punitive damages against Chantilly and Chantilly's managing officer, Abraham Wolinsky, based upon the fraud and upon malicious prosecution. Chantilly and Wolinsky moved to strike the causes of action based on fraud, arguing that by setting up the affirmative defense in the first action the Schwabes obliged themselves to also counterclaim in that action or else lose the claim completely. The trial court agreed and ordered the fraud causes of action struck from the complaint. The Schwabes appeal. We reverse.

    . . . .

The sole question presented here is whether plaintiffs are barred from maintaining these causes of action for fraud because they raised fraud as an affirmative defense to the prior rent-collection action brought by Chantilly, one of the defendants here. This court considered a related problem in Wm. H. Heinemann Creameries v. Milwaukee Automobile Ins. Co.[3] arising from personal injury litigation following an auto collision between A and B. In the first action where A sued B, the suit was dismissed by court order upon stipulation of the parties. Then in a subsequent action, B sued A and one question raised on appeal was whether B's action was barred on principles of res judicata because B had not counterclaimed in the first suit. Relying on sec. 263.14(1), Stats., making all counterclaims permissive, and sec. 58 of the Restatement of Judgments, the court held B's action not barred on this ground. Sec. 263.14(1), Stats., provides:

> "A defendant *may* counterclaim any claim which he has against a plaintiff, upon which a judgment may be had in the action." (Emphasis supplied.)

Sec. 58 of the Restatement of Judgments provides, at page 230:

> "Where the defendant does not interpose a counterclaim although he is entitled to do so, he is not precluded thereby from subsequently maintaining an action against the plaintiff on the cause of action which could have been set up as a counterclaim."

In discussing this section, the court in Heinemann particularly relied on comments b and f. However, comments c and d following this section apply to the facts in the instant case where plaintiffs set up an affirmative defense but not a counterclaim in the first action.

The comments distinguish between situations where the plaintiff in the second action lost in the first case and where he won. Where he loses in the first case, he is barred from commencing a new action. As comment c to sec. 58 provides:

> "*Defense and counterclaim—Judgment for plaintiff—Collateral estoppel.* Where the same facts constitute a ground of defense to the plaintiff's claim and also a ground for a counterclaim, and the defendant alleges these facts as a defense but not as a counterclaim, and after litigation of the defense judgment is given for the plaintiff, the defendant is precluded from maintaining an action against the plaintiff based on these facts. This is in accordance with the rule as to collateral estoppel stated in sec. 68, that where a question of fact essential to a judgment is actually litigated and determined by the judgment, the determination is conclusive between the parties in a subsequent action on a different cause of action."

---

[3]   (1955), 270 Wis. 443, 71 N.W.2d 395, 72 N.W.2d 102.

However, where the party wins in the first action, based on the affirmative defense, it is permissible then to start a new action. He is then not in the position of attacking facts previously established. As comment d indicates:

> "*Defense and counterclaim—Judgment for defendant—Splitting Claims.* Where the same facts constitute a defense to the plaintiff's claim and also a ground for counterclaim, and the defendant sets up these facts as a defense but not as a counterclaim, and after litigation of the defense judgment is given for the defendant, the defendant is not precluded from maintaining a subsequent action against the plaintiff based upon these facts. In such a case he is not improperly splitting his cause of action (compare sec. 62), although he uses the same facts first as a defense to the plaintiff's claim and later as the basis of an action against the plaintiff. In the subsequent action, the judgment in the prior action is conclusive as to the facts actually litigated and determined in the first action (see sec. 68)."

. . . Because judgment was rendered for the Schwabes in the first case they may now sue for damages caused by the fraud. Their present action does not seek to upset the determination reached in the first case and, in fact, affirms it. If they had lost, however, in the first action, under comment c a different result would be reached.

Defendants argue that plaintiffs' action is barred based primarily upon . . . Vukelic v. Upper Third Street Savings & Loan Asso.[6] . . . .

In Vukelic, A sued B in a mortgage foreclosure action, and the court determined that approximately $15,000 was due under the mortgage. Then in a second action B sued A alleging as a "cause of action" that B had never received approximately $11,000 under the mortgage and that the amount due should be reduced accordingly. The court held B's action barred on the grounds that the first judgment was res judicata as to the amount due. For two reasons, however, Vukelic is not persuasive in the case at bar. First, the second action commenced by B really amounted to an attack on the first judgment. In the instant case the two actions involved are completely consistent. Second, although Vukelic contains language indicating that an unused counterclaim is lost unless it is a " 'distinct cause of action,' " "one having no connection with the matters involved in the former cause of action; one not involving the same subject matter," such is no longer the law. Vukelic was decided in 1936, and in 1943 this court adopted [by court rule] the present version of sec. 263.14(1), Stats., making all counterclaims optional. . . . The statement in Vukelic that the only unused counterclaims that survive are those with no connection to the subject matter of the first action is thus consistent with the federal rule, but not the present rule in Wisconsin.

---

6   (1936), 222 Wis. 568, 269 N.W. 273.

. . . .

We conclude that the instant case seeking damages based on fraud is not barred . . . .

. . . .

Order reversed and cause remanded for further proceedings not inconsistent with this opinion.

———

Questions: (21) If the Schwabes had affirmatively sought in the first action to rescind the fraudulently induced lease, would their fraud causes of action for damages have been precluded? See Restatement (Second) of Judgments § 22 cmt. d, illus. 6 (Am. Law Inst. 1982) (indicating that claim preclusion would apply, because defendants had asserted a counterclaim for rescission).

(22) Instead, if without provoking any objection the Schwabes had presented evidence in the first action of the extent of damages caused by the fraud, would their fraud causes of action for damages have been precluded? See Wickenhauser v. Lehtinen, 302 Wis.2d 41, 734 N.W.2d 855 (2007) (indicating no, apparently unless parties and court treated the case as if an actual counterclaim were asserted).

Compulsory counterclaim not pleaded.—As conceded in Schwabe when distinguishing Vukelic, there are two situations in which a defendant does not have a free choice between bringing a counterclaim and bringing an independent action. Whenever one of these two important situations occurs, a defendant who could have but did not interpose his claim as a counterclaim will be barred from maintaining a subsequent action thereon.

1.   One such situation occurs when the plaintiff's claim and the defendant's claim are related in such a way that if the defendant were to prevail on his claim in any subsequent action, the effect would be to nullify or undo the prior judgment. This "common-law compulsory counterclaim rule" applies whether or not the jurisdiction has a compulsory counterclaim statute or rule of court, and whether or not the prior judgment is by default. Indeed, it is this doctrine that makes default judgments mean something.

Perhaps the scope of this somewhat imprecisely stated doctrine can be best conveyed by example. On the one hand, Restatement (Second) of Judgments § 22(2)(b) cmt. f, illus. 9 (Am. Law Inst. 1982) offers this example: "A brings an action against B for failure to pay the contract price for goods sold and delivered and recovers judgment by default. After entry of final judgment and payment of the price, B brings an action against A to rescind the contract for mutual mistake, seeking restitution of the contract price and offering to return the goods. The action is precluded." On the other hand, *D* normally may default in *P*'s personal-injury action and then bring his own action against *P* for injuries sustained in the same accident, the idea being that a judgment for D would not "nullify" P's prior judgment. The line lies somewhere between these two examples.

The doctrine's scope is also suggested by consideration of its genesis, which reveals the doctrine to be a specific aspect of a broad principle of claim preclusion called defense preclusion: a valid and final personal judgment generally precludes the defendant from later asserting mere defenses to the claim. Therefore, the defendant cannot later pursue an action that is essentially a way to defend anew against an already adjudicated claim. See generally Kevin M. Clermont, Common-Law Compulsory Counterclaim Rule: Creating Effective and Elegant Res Judicata Doctrine, 79 Notre Dame L.Rev. 1745 (2004).

————

MENARD, INC. v. LITEWAY LIGHTING PRODUCTS, 282 Wis.2d 582, 698 N.W.2d 738 (2005). For six years Liteway sold lights to Menard. Often the buyer held money back for defective products it returned. But the relationship fizzled, with no more sales or returns after 1999 but with a persisting dispute over how much the buyer still owed. In 2000, Liteway sued Menard on the unpaid invoices and soon recovered about $355,000 by a default judgment.

Then, in 2001, Menard sued Liteway for failing to reimburse fully for the earlier returns. Liteway asserted claim preclusion as an affirmative defense and moved for summary judgment. The trial court denied the motion and, by nonjury trial, awarded Menard about $140,000. The court of appeals reversed. The Supreme Court of Wisconsin (5–2) affirmed that reversal, even though Wisconsin still has no compulsory counterclaim statute or rule of court, because "Menard's suit is merely an attempt to collaterally attack the original judgment by raising defenses and counterclaims to Liteway's original suit."

"Moreover, we conclude that Menard's claims fall under the common-law compulsory counterclaim rule because allowing Menard to proceed with its present suit would impair Liteway's rights as determined in the original action and would undermine the validity of the judgment Liteway obtained. Both suits involve the amount of money Menard owed Liteway, and Liteway could not have recovered the price of goods sold to Menard if those goods were defective."

————

Questions: (23) Some argue that the Menard result should be embodied in an express rule of court. See Donald Leo Bach, Landing in A.B.C.G. Soup: The Compulsory Counterclaim Trap, Wis.Law., Mar. 2006, at 12, 48–49 ("Although the statutes indicate exactly the opposite, certain counterclaims are mandated by case law. This not only presents a trap for the unwary but also continues to generate confusion, uncertainty, and litigation over whether a claim must be (or must have been) brought."). However, it seems that the minimal core of res judicata, shared by all legal systems—that a claimant does not get a second shot to win a "claim" (however defined) and a defendant does not get a second shot at defeating the claim, which means that a valid and final judgment cannot collaterally be undone by claimant or defendant—is so intuitive that an express rule is unnecessary. Does that justify not expressing in Federal Rule 18(a) the claimant's duty to state the whole claim?

(24) Contrariwise, why should the whole doctrine of claim preclusion not be reduced to court rules similar to Rule 13(a) (and somewhat analogous to the compulsory party-joinder provisions of Rule 19)? See Wright & Miller § 4407, at 163–69.

2.   The second situation occurs when the potential counterclaim falls within the express terms of a compulsory counterclaim statute or rule of court. After a case goes to judgment, a failure to have asserted an available counterclaim will preclude bringing a subsequent action thereon.

––––––––––

HORNE v. WOOLEVER, 170 Ohio St. 178, 163 N.E.2d 378 (1959), cert. denied, 362 U.S. 951, 80 S.Ct. 861 (1960). Woolever sued Horne in an Ohio court in February 1957, seeking $150,000 for personal injuries resulting from a collision between their two automobiles. Horne removed the action to the United States District Court for the Northern District of Ohio on diversity grounds, and he thereafter filed in the federal court an answer that was in effect a general denial. He did not plead a counterclaim.

Subsequently, in August 1957, while that federal action was pending, Horne sued Woolever in an Ohio court for $65,000 for his own injuries sustained in the same accident.

In March 1958, Horne paid Woolever $25,000 to settle the latter's claim in the first lawsuit. The attorneys filed a stipulation in the federal court for dismissal of Woolever's action with prejudice, and the federal judge so ordered.

Thereafter, Woolever used his federal judgment to defeat Horne's Ohio action. Ultimately, the Supreme Court of Ohio affirmed, holding the federal judgment to be a bar. Judge Taft explained that Federal Rule 13(a) had required Horne to assert his own claim as a counterclaim in Woolever's action in the federal court, whether that action was originally instituted in that court or was removed from the state court, and even though Ohio then had no statute or rule comparable to Rule 13(a). See Rule 81(c). He added: "To the extent to which a judgment of a federal court operates as res adjudicata in that court, it operates as res adjudicata in the courts of this state."

––––––––––

Question: (25) If the Horne case were decided the other way, would the Supreme Court of the United States have jurisdiction to review the final judgment of the Ohio court? (Of what, if any, relevance is the fact that Rule 13 is not an act of Congress but a rule of court promulgated pursuant to the Rules Enabling Act? Of what, if any, significance is the fact that the Rules Enabling Act provides that the Rules shall govern only procedural matters and not affect substantive rights?) If the Supreme Court of the United States were to hear this imagined case, how should it decide?

Dindo v. Whitney

United States Court of Appeals, First Circuit, 1971.
451 F.2d 1.

■ Before ALDRICH, CHIEF JUDGE, MCENTEE and COFFIN, CIRCUIT JUDGES.

■ ALDRICH, CHIEF JUDGE. Following remand of this case with our order vacating the district court's sustaining of the defense of the statute of limitations, 429 F.2d 25,[e] the defendant pleaded, successfully, that the action was barred by reason of plaintiff's having failed to assert it as a compulsory counterclaim, pursuant to F.R.Civ.P. 13(a), in a prior action. This question we had raised ourselves, but declined to resolve because of lack of briefing, and because of its possible complexity. In now granting defendant's motion to dismiss on this ground, the court had before it certain testimony by way of depositions to which it made reference in its opinion, 52 F.R.D. 194. We accordingly consider the case in terms of a motion for summary judgment. . . .

Briefly, plaintiff Dindo alleges that defendant Whitney was a passenger in a car belonging to Whitney, but driven by Dindo; that the car went off the road, severely injuring Dindo, and that the cause of the accident was Whitney's putting his hand through the steering wheel in reaching for a flashlight on the steering shaft. Suit was brought in the district court of New Hampshire on October 29, 1968, within the New Hampshire period for suit, the accident having occurred on October 30, 1965. Dindo and Whitney had long been friends, Dindo living in Vermont

---

[e]   In this action No. 2, Vermont plaintiff-driver Dindo and New Hampshire defendant-owner-passenger Whitney, en route to a hunting trip in northern Maine, had an accident in the Province of Quebec. When suit was brought in the New Hampshire federal court, the Quebec statute of limitations had run but the New Hampshire statute (and the Vermont statute) had not. The district court dismissed. In its cited 1970 decision, the court of appeals reversed, saying that the relation of the parties to Quebec was most fortuitous, and that the application of the Quebec statute would further no Quebec interest but would frustrate New Hampshire's interests to some degree.

In 1952 the New Hampshire Supreme Court on similar facts had applied the Quebec statute of limitations. However, in a 1966 case involving husband and wife who had had an accident in Vermont on the way from their New Hampshire home to another part of New Hampshire, that court had applied New Hampshire law, which allowed a guest passenger to recover from a host driver for ordinary negligence, instead of Vermont law, which required gross negligence. The federal court of appeals concluded that the 1966 decision had implicitly overruled the 1952 case, and that the New Hampshire Supreme Court would have applied the New Hampshire statute of limitations in the instant case.

and Whitney in New Hampshire. In June, 1966 Whitney sued Dindo in the district court of Vermont. Dindo gave the papers to his insurance agent, who forwarded them to Whitney's insurer which, by virtue of a clause in the policy, insured Dindo as a driver of Whitney's car with Whitney's permission. The insurer retained counsel, but informed Dindo that he should retain his own counsel as well, as the ad damnum [$150,000] exceeded the coverage [$50,000]. Dindo did not do so. In March, 1967 [after an answer, including the defense of contributory negligence, was filed,] the insurer paid Whitney a sum within the policy limit in settlement [$45,000], and an entry was made on the court docket, "Settled and discontinued." The present action is defended by the same insurer, Whitney, as the car's owner, being covered by the policy that had included coverage of Dindo.

It is clear on the record that before insurance company counsel settled the case they conferred with Dindo on a number of occasions, and apparently saw no defense to the suit. All that was said is not entirely clear. The [N.H. district] court made findings of fact which may have been the most reasonable resolution, but which went beyond permissible bounds on a motion for summary judgment. It was proper for it to find that Dindo did not request counsel to file a counterclaim against Whitney, and that there had been time to do so, but we must accept Dindo's position that he did not realize, until he spoke with new counsel in September 1968, that he had a basis for so doing, namely, Whitney's conduct in reaching for the flashlight. Dindo, assertedly, had thought that because he was driving the car he could have no claim.

[The court here quoted from Rule 13(a).] The accident, by whomever caused, was obviously the same transaction or occurrence. Dindo claims, however, that the compulsory rule is inapplicable to him since the original case was settled, rather than pursued to final judgment on the merits. Alternatively, he says that it is inequitable to assert the rule against him when he had not realized he had a counterclaim until afterwards.

The bar arising out of Rule 13(a) has been characterized variously. Some courts have said that a judgment is res judicata of whatever could have been pleaded in a compulsory counterclaim. Dragor Shipping Corp. v. Union Tank Car Co., 9 Cir., 1967, 378 F.2d 241; United States v. Eastport S.S. Corp., 2 Cir., 1958, 255 F.2d 795. Other courts have viewed the rule not in terms of res judicata, but as creating an estoppel or waiver. Lawhorn v. Atlantic Refining Co., 5 Cir., 1962, 299 F.2d 353; Dow Chemical Co. v. Metlon Corp., 4 Cir., 1960, 281 F.2d 292. The latter approach seems more appropriate, at least when the case is settled rather than tried. The purposes of the rule are "to prevent multiplicity of actions and to achieve resolution in a single lawsuit of all disputes arising out of common matters." Southern Constr. Co. v. Pickard, 1962, 371 U.S. 57, 60, 83 S.Ct. 108, 110, 9 L.Ed.2d 31. If a case has been tried, protection both of the court and of the parties dictates that there should be no further directly related litigation. But if the case is settled, normally the court has not been greatly burdened, and the parties can protect themselves by demanding cross-releases. In such circumstances, absent a release, better-tailored justice seems obtainable by applying principles of equitable estoppel.

If, in the case at bar, Dindo, clearly having opportunity to assert it, cf. LaFollette v. Herron, D.C.Tenn., 1962, 211 F.Supp. 919, knew of the existence of a right to counterclaim, the fact that there was no final judgment on the merits should be immaterial, and a Rule 13(a) bar would be appropriate. His conscious inaction not only created the very additional litigation the rule was designed to prevent it exposed the insurer to double liability. We are not persuaded that a final judgment is a sine qua non to invocation of the bar; there is nothing in the rule limning the term "judgment."

However, on a motion for summary judgment this factual finding could not be made on the present record. We are not prepared to say at this time what lesser facts would compel a conclusion of estoppel as a matter of law. There should be a hearing on the merits, the facts to be found by the jury. United States ex rel. Westinghouse Electric v. James Stewart Co., 9 Cir., 1964, 336 F.2d 777, subject to instructions by the court, Home Indemnity Co. of New York v. Allen, 7 Cir., 1951, 190 F.2d 490. . . .

The judgment of the district court is vacated and the action remanded for further proceedings consistent herewith.

––––––––––

Question: (26) What did the court mean when it said that allowing this extra suit would expose the insurance company to "double liability"?

––––––––––

INSURER-INSURED CONFLICTS OF INTEREST

The Dindo case points up some of the numerous problems that exist when counsel for a liability insurance company represents its insured, as the interests of insurer and insured are likely not identical. A converse conflict of interest arises when the insured is interested in pressing a compulsory counterclaim, but the insurer has no interest in doing so. This kind of problem stimulated great criticism in Maine upon the adoption of a rule identical to Rule 13(a). After less than a year of experience under that rule, it was amended to except motor vehicle tort cases from its reach. See 1 Richard H. Field, Vincent L. McKusick & L. Kinvin Wroth, Maine Civil Practice 263–64 (2d ed. 1970).

––––––––––

ESTOPPEL

Equitable estoppel, sometimes called estoppel in pais, generally provides that a party may not take a position in litigation when that position is inconsistent with earlier conduct and the change would unfairly burden another party who has detrimentally relied. For an example of when this many-faceted doctrine might apply, consider the situation of a person having recovered worker's compensation for an accident and then in subsequent tort litigation unfairly trying to deny that she was an employee. Obviously, this loose doctrine presents a risk of expanding to punish merely unseemly behavior. See generally Wright & Miller § 4477.

Contrasted with res judicata, the looser doctrine of equitable estoppel looks to the party's earlier out-of-court or in-court conduct, rather than to a prior judicial decision. Equitable estoppel can therefore play a role complementary to res judicata. For instance, failure to interpose a compulsory counterclaim in a proceeding that ended by a voluntary dismissal, rather than in an actual judgment, may nevertheless equitably estop the defendant from later pursuing the counterclaim.

Another doctrine that some people confuse with res judicata is judicial estoppel. This minor but controversial doctrine, which varies widely from jurisdiction to jurisdiction and which is even rejected outright in a good number of states, usually holds that a litigant cannot unfairly take factual positions that are directly inconsistent with positions previously taken by the person in a prior proceeding. See generally New Hampshire v. Maine, 532 U.S. 742, 121 S.Ct. 1808 (2001).

Judicial estoppel aims to prevent abuse of the judicial machinery. It differs from equitable estoppel in that it treats only in-court conduct but does not require detrimental reliance. It differs from the issue-precluding effect of res judicata in that it can estop a successful party and does not require the prior rendering of a judicial decision.

TOPIC C

ISSUE PRECLUSION

SECTION 1.   REQUIREMENTS OF THE RULE

Little v. Blue Goose Motor Coach Co.

Supreme Court of Illinois, 1931.
346 Ill. 266, 178 N.E. 496.

[Dr. Robert M. Little, while driving his automobile in East St. Louis, Illinois, collided with a bus owned and operated by Blue Goose Motor Coach Company. Blue Goose sued Dr. Little in a justice of the peace court for damage to its bus caused by the collision and, after nonjury trial, recovered judgment for $139.35. Dr. Little's appeal to the county court was dismissed for lack of prosecution on April 2, 1926.

[During the pendency of that suit before the justice of the peace, Dr. Little commenced an action against Blue Goose in the city court of East St. Louis for personal injuries suffered by him in the collision. Dr. Little died on May 25, 1926, and his wife as executrix was substituted as plaintiff. Her new declaration alleged in the first count that Dr. Little's death had been caused by the defendant's negligence, and in the second count that his death had been caused by the defendant's willful and wanton negligence. Blue Goose then set up as a defense the justice of the peace proceedings, contending that they constituted an "estoppel by verdict." Blue Goose introduced evidence, including testimony by the justice of the peace himself, bearing on what had occurred in the proceedings before the justice of the peace. The plaintiff had verdict and judgment for $5000.

[On appeal from the latter judgment to the Appellate Court of Illinois, that court reversed with the following finding of fact: "The Court finds that appellant sued Dr. Robert M. Little, appellee's testate, before a Justice of the Peace for damages to its bus in the collision which occurred on November 1, 1925, and recovered a judgment therefor in the sum of $139.35; that in the rendition of said judgment it was necessarily determined that the collision and damages occasioned to the bus were due to the negligence of Dr. Little and that immediately prior to his death he could not have maintained an action for personal injuries growing out of the same collision."]

■ PER CURIAM.

. . . .

The first question arises on the ruling of the Appellate Court invoking against the claim of plaintiff in error the doctrine of estoppel by verdict. It is argued on behalf of plaintiff in error that where a former adjudication is relied on as a bar to a subsequent action it is essential that there be identity both of the subject matter and of the parties, and that in the instant case the subject matter is not the same, as this is the action for death by wrongful act for the benefit of the widow and next of kin, while the former suit was a claim for damages for injury to personal property. The issue on which this case is bottomed was the issue of fact which lay at the base of the judgment recovered before the justice of the peace. The allegation of the special plea is that the issue there raised was one of negligence on the part of Dr. Little on one hand and the defendant in error on the other, and that issue having been determined against Dr. Little, the fact is forever settled between these parties or their privies. Estoppel by verdict arises when a material fact in any litigation has been determined in a former suit between the same parties or between parties with whom the parties to the subsequent suit are in privity, where the fact was also material to the issue. The Appellate Court found as a matter of fact that the issue tried before the justice of the peace was an issue of negligence and was the same issue, arising on the same facts as those relied upon in the action for the wrongful death of Dr. Little, and that the issue of negligence was necessarily determined in the suit by the defendant in error against Dr. Little. That question of fact was tried before the city court in this case, and on the evidence there adduced the Appellate Court made its finding of fact. That issue of fact therefore is not open here, and we are to proceed to further consideration of the cause under the established fact that the issue of negligence, at least under the first count of the declaration, is the same issue tried before the justice of the peace.

While on appeal to the county court the trial, had there been one, would have been de novo, yet when the appeal was dismissed and a procedendo was issued to the justice of the peace, the judgment of the justice of the peace became a final determination of that issue between the parties, and is conclusive not only upon the immediate parties to that suit but also upon all persons in privity with them, and cannot be litigated again between the parties to that case or their privies in any subsequent action in the same or other court where that question arises, whether upon the same or a different cause of action or whatever may have been the nature or purpose of the action in which the judgment was rendered or of that in which the estoppel is set up. [Citations omitted.] It follows that Dr. Little could not during his lifetime maintain the action filed by him against the defendant in error, and since plaintiff in error's right to recover damages under the Injuries Act depends upon Dr. Little's right, during his lifetime, to recover damages for injuries arising out of the same collision, plaintiff in error cannot recover here. [Citation omitted.] In a suit under the Injuries Act, the cause of action is the wrongful act and not merely the death itself. [Citations omitted.] Plaintiff in error therefore was not entitled to recover under the first count of her declaration, and the Appellate Court did not err in so holding.

It is contended, however, that as the second count of the declaration charges wanton and willful negligence on the part of defendant in error, contributory negligence on the part of Dr. Little is not a defense, and that the judgment of the city court was therefore right. Contributory negligence is not a defense to willful and wanton conduct, but it does not follow that the judgment of the city court was right because of that fact. In all cases charging willful and wanton negligence it is necessary to make proof of such negligence, and where there is no such proof no recovery under such charge can be had. [Citation omitted.] The finding of the Appellate Court that the collision was caused by the negligence of Dr. Little necessarily was a finding of fact on the willful negligence count as well as the general negligence count. Thus the rule that contributory negligence on the part of the plaintiff is not a defense to a charge of willful negligence does not apply. Whether Dr. Little or the bus driver was responsible for the accident was, as we have seen, settled. The judgment for $139.35 necessarily decided that the bus driver was not guilty of willful negligence.[a]

. . . .

Judgment affirmed.

————

Question: (1) In Illinois it was held that two causes of action arise when a negligent act causes a person to suffer both personal injury and property damage, so that a judgment for property damage did not block a later action for personal injury by claim preclusion. Clancey v. McBride, supra p. 776. Suppose Dr. Little, and not Blue Goose, had brought suit in the justice of the peace court for property damage and, after trial, he had won judgment. What should be the effect of these proceedings in the later city court action by the executrix?

————

DIMENSIONS OF AN ISSUE

In applying the doctrine of issue preclusion, there predictably arises the difficult problem of defining the scope of the "issue" foreclosed. Restatement (Second) of Judgments § 27 cmt. c (Am. Law Inst. 1982) does not essay a precise definition of issue, but instead proposes several factors to consider in resolving whether a matter to be presented in the second action and a matter presented in the first action constitute the same issue. Most notable among these factors is the degree of overlap, with respect to the two matters, between the evidence and legal argument advanced in the first action and that to be advanced in the second. This approach is then applied in illustrations 4 and 6:

————

[a]   Under then applicable Illinois law, the plaintiff in an ordinary negligence action had to plead and prove his own due care. Illinois has no compulsory counterclaim rule.

"4. A brings an action against B to recover for personal injuries in an automobile accident. A seeks to establish that B was negligent in driving at an excessive rate of speed. After trial, verdict and judgment are given for B. In a subsequent action by B against A for injuries in the same accident, A is precluded from setting up B's negligence as a defense, whether or not the alleged negligence is based on an assertion of excessive speed. It is reasonable to require A to bring forward all evidence in support of the alleged negligence in the initial proceeding. (It is assumed in this Illustration that the forum has no applicable compulsory counterclaim rule. See § 22.)

"6. A brings an action against B to recover an installment payment due under a contract. B's sole defense is that the contract is unenforceable under the statute of frauds. After trial, judgment is given for A, the court ruling that an oral contract of the kind sued upon is enforceable. In a subsequent action by A against B to recover a second installment falling due after the first action was brought, B is precluded from raising the statute of frauds as a defense, whether or not on the basis of arguments made in the prior action, but is not precluded from asserting as a defense that the installment is not owing as a matter of law on any other ground."

Jacobson v. Miller

Supreme Court of Michigan, 1879.
41 Mich. 90, 1 N.W. 1013.

[Miller sued two persons in Michigan state court for installments of rent then due under a written lease. The general issue was pleaded, but there was no denial under oath of the execution of the lease as required by court rule if execution was to be disputed. Jacobson contended at the jury trial that he was not liable because the other defendant, and not he, had occupied the premises during the period for which rent was claimed. The plaintiff had verdict and judgment.

[Thereafter Miller sued for subsequent installments of rent now due under the same lease. Jacobson, by the requisite statement under oath, denied execution of the lease. The plaintiff offered the prior judgment as conclusive proof of execution, and the trial judge received it as such over the defendant's objection. The correctness of this ruling was the principal question on appeal from judgment for the plaintiff.]

■ COOLEY, J.

. . . .

It is not denied by the defendant that if the execution and delivery of the lease had been disputed in the first suit, the determination of the issue would have been conclusive upon the parties in any subsequent litigation involving the right to rents under the same lease. . . .

But the execution of the lease was not denied in the former suit. No issue was made upon it, and the defendant, by not denying it, suffered a default in respect to it which left it wholly outside the issue made and actually passed upon. Consequently it was not and could not have been considered by the court as a point which in that suit was open to controversy. The defendants, by their pleadings, made the actual existence of the lease an immaterial fact, and had the lease counted upon been a known forgery, the case must nevertheless have proceeded with its existence and genuineness admitted.

It is said, however, that the defendants in the first suit were at liberty to put the execution of the lease in issue, and that it was their duty to do so then if they proposed to contest it at all. This is upon the ground that public policy will not suffer the withholding of a defense with a view to further litigation, when a single suit might determine the whole controversy. This is no doubt true where the defense is sought to be made use of in the retrial of a dispute respecting the same subject matter of the former litigation. Pierce v. Kneeland, 9 Wis. 23, 31. The question now is, whether the proposition is applicable to a case where the subject matter of the second suit is different. In other words, where one is sued in respect to one subject matter, must he bring forward all his defenses, at the peril, if he fails to do so, of being debarred of them in any subsequent litigation which may involve the same questions, though relating to a different subject matter? We think not.

The precise point was before the Supreme Court of the United States in Cromwell v. County of Sac, 94 U.S. 351, 356, in which Mr. Justice Field, delivering the opinion of the court, says: "Various considerations, other than the actual merits, may govern a party in bringing forward grounds of recovery or defense in one action, which may not exist in another action upon a different demand, such as the smallness of the amount or the value of the property in controversy, the difficulty of obtaining the necessary evidence, the expense of the litigation, and his own situation at the time. . . ."

. . . .

The judgment must be reversed, with costs, and a new trial ordered.

■ [The concurring opinion of JUSTICE GRAVES is omitted.]

———

Questions: (2) If one were to feel that policies favored preclusion, even though nonexecution was not "actually litigated and determined," what doctrinal arguments could be made to change the Jacobson result? See Denio v. City of Huntington Beach, 74 Cal.App.2d 424, 168 P.2d 785 (1946) (suggesting preclusion of a more broadly defined issue, such as the obligation to pay rent under the lease); cf. Wright & Miller § 4414, at 378–81 (arguing for preclusion of unraised defenses).

(3) Assuming an issue has been properly raised, by the pleadings or otherwise, should it be deemed actually litigated and determined if it is

disposed of via total absence of proof? judgment as a matter of law? summary judgment? demurrer? stipulation? admission? default?

_____

RES JUDICATA AND THE MECHANICS OF SETTLEMENT

When a prospective defendant settles a claim by payment of an agreed sum before action is brought, it is routine practice for him to condition his payment upon the execution by the intending plaintiff of a release of the claim. If the plaintiff has already brought a suit, the defendant will still insist upon a release as part of the settlement, but there is the additional problem of disposing of the pending lawsuit. The defendant is likely to insist upon a disposition on the record that will protect him as fully as possible against further litigation on the claim. In that way, if the plaintiff does bring a later action on the same claim, the defendant may plead not only the release as a defense but also res judicata.

At common law a voluntary nonsuit or discontinuance by the plaintiff was not a bar to a new suit. However, there was a common-law device called a retraxit, a voluntary renunciation of the claim by the plaintiff in open court, which both terminated the particular action and barred relitigation of the same cause. It may be assumed that in usual practice the plaintiff made such a renunciation only after reaching a settlement.

Under present-day practice a mere voluntary dismissal is not a bar, nor is a dismissal by stipulation of the parties, unless the notice or order of dismissal or the stipulation states otherwise. See Federal Rule 41(a). There is, however, some authority in state courts to the effect that a dismissal shown on its face to be by agreement is a bar to a new suit. E.g., Doan v. Bush, 130 Ark. 566, 198 S.W. 261 (1917).

Another way to dispose of a lawsuit that has been settled is to enter a consent judgment for the plaintiff in the agreed amount, with a further entry of "Judgment satisfied." But the parties who have adjusted their differences may prefer not to spread upon the record the details of their arrangement. They may therefore file a consent judgment for the plaintiff in a nominal amount, with a "judgment satisfied" entry. Or the defendant may insist, as a condition of the settlement, that the entry be "Judgment for the defendant." All these forms of consent judgment terminate the pending action and normally preclude another suit upon the same claim by merger or bar.

A consent judgment is satisfactory enough when there is no possibility of an action upon a different claim involving the same issues. As just suggested, a consent judgment, like a judgment by default, has claim-preclusive effect so far as the same claim is concerned, even though nothing was in fact ever litigated. But when assertion of a different claim involving the same issues is possible, one must give attention to collateral estoppel.

The customary statement of the rule of collateral estoppel specifies that the issue must have been actually litigated and determined in order for there to be collateral estoppel effect. It is all very well to say conformably, as Professor Fleming James, Jr., convincingly did in Consent Judgments as Collateral Estoppel, 108 U.Pa.L.Rev. 173 (1959), that consent judgments ought not to have collateral estoppel effect. The fact remains that in some states, apparently a minority, the law is otherwise, as shown by Sheldon R. Shapiro, Annotation, Modern Views of State Courts as to Whether Consent Judgment Is Entitled to Res Judicata or Collateral Estoppel Effect, 91 A.L.R.3d 1170, 1183–91 (1979). The flawed theory of these states' approach is that all the facts alleged by the plaintiff and necessary to the recovery are raised by the plaintiff's pleading, and the defendant should not be able to escape the consequence of judgment by waiving the right to contest them.

Failure by counsel to take into account this risk involved in a consent judgment has produced unintended and serious consequences for the client in a later action. In Biggio v. Magee, 272 Mass. 185, 172 N.E. 336 (1930), for example, Magee's suit against Biggio for injuries from an automobile accident had been settled by Biggio's attorney, actually an attorney retained and paid by his liability insurer, with an entry on the court record of judgment for Magee in a substantial sum by agreement of the parties and with a further entry of "judgment satisfied." When Biggio, this time represented by counsel of his own choosing, sued Magee for his own injuries, the court held him collaterally estopped by the consent judgment.[b]

How, then, should the parties effectuate their agreed settlement if they wish to avoid all risk of collateral estoppel? A consent judgment is in large part a contract of the parties, acknowledged in court and ordered to be recorded. The parties are free, unless a statute or rule of court otherwise provides, to include in this contract such terms as they wish. Just as they could efficaciously manifest their intention to wind up the entire controversy (i.e., give collateral estoppel effect to the judgment), see Restatement (Second) of Judgments § 27 cmt. e (Am. Law Inst. 1982), so can they provide that the agreement is to have no effect on any other claim.

Another approach is for the parties to agree on "Judgment for neither party, no further action to be brought on this claim." Such an entry should terminate the pending action and preclude a new suit by

---

[b]   Massachusetts promptly enacted a statute to undo the result of this decision in actions within that state's compulsory automobile insurance law, unless the settlement agreement was signed by the defendant himself. 1932 Mass.Acts ch. 130, § 1 (current version at Mass.Gen.Laws Ann. ch. 231, § 140A). Incidentally, Massachusetts had no applicable compulsory counterclaim provision.

the plaintiff upon the same claim, but it should have no collateral estoppel effect. See Gendron v. Hovey, 98 Me. 139, 56 A. 583 (1903).

Question: (4) How would entry of a judgment for neither party have affected Horne v. Woolever? Might it therefore be better for courts to analyze consent judgments exclusively in contractual terms, looking directly to the parties' intent and discarding the res judicata analysis?

———

Cambria v. Jeffery

Supreme Judicial Court of Massachusetts, 1940.
307 Mass. 49, 29 N.E.2d 555.

TORT. Writ in the First District Court of Eastern Middlesex dated April 4, 1938.

On removal to the Superior Court, the action was tried before Greenhalge, J. The finding of the judge of the District Court in the [earlier] action of Jeffery v. Cambria was as follows: "Defendant was clearly negligent. The only question is as to the due care of the plaintiff operator. Taking all the circumstances into consideration including the fact that Concord Avenue on which defendant was driving is the more important street, I find that Ernest Jeffery did not use due care in entering the intersection."

■ LUMMUS, J. Two automobiles, one owned by the plaintiff Cambria and operated by his servant, the other owned and operated by the defendant Jeffery, had a collision.

Jeffery brought in a District Court an action of tort for alleged negligence against Cambria to recover for bodily injury and damage to Jeffery's automobile. The judge found that the collision was caused by negligence of both operators, and therefore judgment was rendered in favor of the then defendant Cambria.

Afterwards the present action of tort, for alleged negligence of Jeffery causing damage to Cambria's automobile, was tried. The jury returned a verdict in favor of the plaintiff Cambria for $838.35; but the judge under leave reserved (G.L. [Ter.Ed.] c. 231, § 120) entered a verdict for the defendant Jeffery on the ground that the earlier judgment had adjudicated that the present plaintiff Cambria through his servant was guilty of contributory negligence, and reported the case.

A fact merely found in a case becomes adjudicated only when it is shown to have been a basis of the relief, denial of relief, or other ultimate right established by the judgment. [Citations omitted.]

The earlier judgment was in effect that Jeffery could not recover against Cambria. The sole basis for that judgment was the finding that Jeffery was guilty of contributory negligence. The further finding that Cambria's servant was negligent had no effect, and could have none, in producing that judgment. Therefore that judgment did not adjudicate that Cambria's servant was negligent.

Verdict under leave reserved set aside.

Judgment upon the verdict returned by the jury.

———

LOOSENING THE REQUIREMENTS

Courts could expand the reach of issue preclusion by loosening its requirements. For example, Home Owners Federal Savings & Loan Ass'n v. Northwestern Fire & Marine Insurance Co., 354 Mass. 448, 238 N.E.2d 55 (1968) (4–3 decision), involved facts analogous to Cambria v. Jeffery. But the Supreme Judicial Court modified the "essential to the judgment" requirement, making it more flexible in these words: "[O]ur holding expands the applicability of the doctrine to encompass certain findings not strictly essential to the final judgment in the prior action. Cf. Restatement, Judgments, § 68. Such findings may be relied upon if it is clear that the issues underlying them were treated as essential to the prior case by the court and the party to be bound. Stated another way, it is necessary that such findings be the product of full litigation and careful decision. Cf. Cambria v. Jeffery, 307 Mass. 49, 29 N.E.2d 555. This limited expansion of the class of findings within the ambit of the doctrine of collateral estoppel does no violence to the policies underlying the rule of the Cambria case, supra. See James, Civil Procedure, . . . at p. 583. We deem this limited extension of the rule warranted in view of the strong and oft-stated public policy of limiting each litigant to one opportunity to try his case on the merits."

Nevertheless, courts should recognize that fairness, efficiency, and substantive policies might counsel a somewhat constrained approach to issue preclusion. This doctrine is, after all, much more broadly applicable than claim preclusion.

Question: (5) If the reach of issue preclusion is allowed to expand to some matters not really considered in the prior action—which may be done by enlarging the dimensions of the "same issue" or by relaxing the "actually litigated and determined" requirement—what differences, if any, would remain between the doctrines of issue preclusion and claim preclusion? See Wright & Miller § 4406, at 154 ("The distinction is one of emphasis and degree, no more."); id. § 4417, at 469 ("If different theories and consequences are to apply, care must be taken in seeking the most useful distinction possible."); cf. David P. Currie, Res Judicata: The Neglected Defense, 45 U.Chi.L.Rev. 317, 336–42 (1978).

Most courts, then, maintain the three requirements of issue preclusion. For example, in Rudow v. Fogel, 376 Mass. 587, 382 N.E.2d 1046 (1978) (alternative holding) (Kaplan, J.), the Supreme Judicial Court unanimously returned, a decade after Home Owners, to the unmodified Cambria rule. The retention of the three requirements, though, means that each will continue to present difficulties of application.

Questions: (6) *A* sues *B* for interest on a note. *B* alleges fraud in the execution of the note (a defense to both interest and principal obligations) and a later release of the obligation to pay any interest (a legally and factually distinct defense applicable only to interest obligations). Upon trial, *A* gets verdict and judgment. After maturity, *A* sues *B* for the note's principal, and the only issue raised by *B* is the fraud. Is the prior judgment conclusive on the question of fraud?

(7) If instead there had been a general verdict and judgment for *B* in that first action, could *B* make effective use of the judgment in the subsequent action for the principal?

(8) What if *B*'s victory in the first action had come upon a special verdict and judgment for *B* on both issues? (Or, equivalently, if that result came in express findings after a bench trial?)

————

ALTERNATIVE DETERMINATIONS

In the case of the preceding question, where a party prevails upon each of two issues and where either determination standing alone would be sufficient to support judgment in his favor, Restatement of Judgments § 68 cmt. n (Am. Law Inst. 1942) took the position that the judgment is binding on both issues. The judgment is not based on one issue more than on the other, so it must be said that it is conclusive as to both issues or as to neither. The comment continued: "It seems obvious that it should not be held that neither is material, and hence both should be held to be material."

Questions: (9) Why is it obvious?

(10) How is this situation different from Cambria v. Jeffery?

In Halpern v. Schwartz, 426 F.2d 102 (2d Cir.1970), Evelyn Halpern had been involuntarily adjudicated a bankrupt on each of three different grounds, only one of which had involved a finding of actual intent to hinder, delay, or defraud creditors. In a later proceeding Halpern sought a discharge in bankruptcy. The Bankruptcy Act provided that the court could not grant a discharge if it finds the bankrupt acted with that particular intent. The court denied Halpern her discharge on the ground that the prior determination of intent was preclusive. The court of appeals reversed, holding, contrary to the First Restatement, that a judgment resting on alternative grounds (here three) is not preclusive as to any of the grounds.

Questions: (11) What arguments can you make in support of this decision?

(12) Should there be, under the Halpern approach, a difference in result if there was an appeal in the prior case and the appellate court expressly

affirmed on one of two alternative grounds? on both of the two alternative grounds?

Restatement (Second) of Judgments § 27 cmts. i, o (Am. Law Inst. 1982) likewise takes a position contrary to the First Restatement, by providing that neither determination is preclusive unless there was an appellate-court determination. The reporter's note thereon says that the question is a close and difficult one, but that the reasoning in Halpern v. Schwartz is highly persuasive.

Question: (13) Assume that you as counsel have two alternative grounds of defense (or recovery) in each of which you have confidence. Assume further that you foresee the likelihood of later litigation involving one of the grounds and that the Halpern approach is governing authority. Accordingly, you perceive that you will be worse off winning on both grounds than on the one. What, then, should your tactics at trial be?

Trying to chart a middle course in Malloy v. Trombley, 50 N.Y.2d 46, 52, 405 N.E.2d 213, 216, 427 N.Y.S.2d 969, 973 (1980) (4–3 decision), the New York Court of Appeals decided that the Halpern approach should not be applied rigidly and held "in this instance that the rule of issue preclusion is applicable notwithstanding that in a precise sense the issue precluded was the subject of only an alternative determination by the trial court. The issue was fully litigated, and the party precluded had full opportunity to be heard and was in no way, motivationally or procedurally, restricted or inhibited in the presentation of his position. Additionally, and critically in our view, the decision of the trial court gives significant internal evidence of the thorough and careful deliberation by that court, both in its consideration of the proof introduced and of the applicable law, and the determination made, although recognized to be an alternative, served a substantial operational purpose in the judicial process, thus negativing any conclusion that the trial court's resolution was casual or of any lesser quality than had the outcome of the trial depended solely on this issue."

Question: (14) *A* sues *B* for interest on a note. *B* alleges fraud in the execution of the note and a later release of the obligation to pay any interest. In the trial court, *B* gets judgment upon a special verdict favorable on both issues (or by general verdict). There is no appeal. Later, *A* sues *B* for a subsequent installment of interest on the note. Can *B* invoke issue preclusion based on the prior judgment?

Noteworthily, the Halpern approach has received only limited acceptance in the courts, and even the Second Circuit has since backed away from it. After considering all these arguments pro and con, and the implications of and reactions to the Halpern rule regarding alternative determinations, what do you think? Might we be better off returning to the First Restatement rule, while trying to treat the relatively few cases of inappropriate collateral estoppel by means of exceptions to issue preclusion? See Monica Renee Brownewell, Note, Rethinking the

Restatement View (Again!): Multiple Independent Holdings and the Doctrine of Issue Preclusion, 37 Val.U.L.Rev. 879 (2003).

Question: (15) *A* sues *B* for a note's principal in a First Restatement jurisdiction. *B* alleges prematurity of the action and also fraud in the execution of the note. In the trial court, *B* gets judgment upon a special verdict that is favorable on both issues. There is no appeal. After maturity, *A* sues *B* again for the note's principal. Can *B* invoke either claim or issue preclusion based on the prior judgment? Compare Restatement (Second) of Judgments § 20 cmt. e (Am. Law Inst. 1982) (no bar), and Hawksbill Sea Turtle v. FEMA, 126 F.3d 461, 475 (3d Cir.1997) (" 'If a first decision is supported by findings that deny the power of the court to decide the case on the merits and by findings that reach the merits, preclusion is inappropriate as to the findings on the merits.' " (quoting Wright & Miller § 4421)), with Jo Desha Lucas, The Direct and Collateral Estoppel Effects of Alternative Holdings, 50 U.Chi.L.Rev. 701, 707–18 (1983) (approving both bar and direct estoppel).

————

INCONSISTENT JUDGMENTS

Question: (16) *A* sues *B* for interest on a note. *B* alleges a release of the obligation to pay any interest. Upon trial, *A* gets judgment. Later, *A* sues *B* for a subsequent installment of interest on the note. *B* alleges the release. Upon trial, *B* gets judgment on that ground. Later, *A* sues *B* yet again for a subsequent installment of interest on the note. *B* alleges the release. Are the prior judgments now conclusive on the question of release?

In Donald v. J.J. White Lumber Co., 68 F.2d 441 (5th Cir.1934), a taxpayer brought several successive tax actions, each action relating to a different tax year. The computation of the tax each year depended upon the determination of the depletion allowance for standing timber. This in turn depended upon the value as of March 1, 1913, the effective date of the first modern income tax law, of standing timber on land acquired by the taxpayer before that date. The higher that value was, the greater the depletion allowance and hence the lower the tax. In the first action, the Board of Tax Appeals valued the standing timber on March 1, 1913, at $5.34 per thousand feet—and the tax for the year in question was figured on that basis. In the second action, a federal district court adjudged the value on March 1, 1913, to be $7.00 per thousand feet—and the tax for the year involved was computed accordingly. No reference was made to the valuation of the timber in the prior action. There was no appeal from the decision in either case. In a third action, covering a third tax year, the government contended that the $5.34 valuation of the first action was binding, but the taxpayer contended that the $7.00 valuation of the second action controlled. The court of appeals held that the last judgment in time is controlling.

Question: (17) Why should the rule not be that neither determination is binding?

Suppose, however, that judgments of different states are involved. The same last-in-time rule ordinarily prevails and, indeed, is compelled by full faith and credit. But imagine: First, *A* wins on an issue against *B* in State *X*. Second, *A* later relies upon that judgment in a case involving the same issue in State *Y*, arguing the judgment is entitled to full faith and credit. The court of State *Y* wrongly rejects that argument and decides in favor of *B*. After appealing unsuccessfully in State *Y*, *A* seeks certiorari from the Supreme Court of the United States, but it is denied. Third, *A* then commences another case involving the same issue in State *X*, and *B* relies upon the State *Y* judgment as preclusive. Should the State *Y* judgment be controlling? Yes, says the case law.

Question: (18) Do the Federal Rules require a defendant relying upon the collateral estoppel effect of a prior judgment to set it up in her pleading? See Rule 8(c)(1). How about a plaintiff? See Wright & Miller § 4405, at 87–117.

Berlitz Schools of Languages of America v. Everest House

United States Court of Appeals, Second Circuit, 1980.
619 F.2d 211.

[The facts, simplified to their essence, were as follows. Berlitz Schools and Berlitz Publications had sued certain defendants, including Charles Berlitz, in New York state court for unfair competition and trademark dilution under state law. In 1974 the court, although recognizing in accord with prior litigation that Charles Berlitz could not identify himself as author of language materials unless he made clear that he was not connected with the plaintiffs in any way, had found that the following book-cover disclaimer on his "Passport" series of language books sufficed to dispel confusion: "Charles Berlitz, world-famous linguist and author of more than 100 language teaching books, is the grandson of the founder of the Berlitz Schools. Since 1967, Mr. Berlitz has not been connected with the Berlitz Schools in any way." That state judgment had been affirmed on appeal.

[Later Charles Berlitz authored the new "Step-By-Step" series of language books, on the cover of which were his name and that disclaimer. Those same plaintiffs sued in the United States District Court for the Southern District of New York for trademark infringement and unfair competition under the Lanham Act, 15 U.S.C. §§ 1051–1127. The defendants' answer pleaded collateral estoppel. The district court granted defendants' motion for summary judgment on the basis of collateral estoppel in 1979. Plaintiffs appealed.]

■ Before LUMBARD, MANSFIELD and NEWMAN, CIRCUIT JUDGES.

■ LUMBARD, CIRCUIT JUDGE:

. . . .

. . . The question is whether the issues finally and necessarily determined in the state proceedings are identical to those presented to the district court for determination.

The sine qua non of an action for trademark infringement, dilution of a trademark or unfair competition, is a showing by the plaintiff of the likelihood of confusion as to the origin of the goods in issue at the consumer level. [Citations omitted.] Indeed, this is precisely the claim made by plaintiffs in the district court as well as in . . . the prior state proceedings.

. . . .

Plaintiffs' principal objection to the application of [collateral estoppel] is that the facts presented herein differ substantially from those before the state court in the prior proceedings. Thus, the principal question before us is: is the legend of Charles Berlitz's name and the disclaimer on the cover of the "Step-By-Step" language books substantially different from that which was given the blessing of the New York courts? This mixed question of fact and law was decided in favor of the defendants by the district court. We cannot say that the judgment of the district court was erroneous. On the contrary, the judgment is supported by the record and the applicable law.

Reproductions of book covers—as submitted to the Second Circuit in Joint Appendix to the briefs and indistinctly showing the disclaimer at the bottom of each front cover

The appellants argue that on the "Step-By-Step" cover the name "Charles Berlitz" is larger in proportion to the disclaimer which consequently is less noticeable, and that these factual differences are sufficient to justify the relief they seek. We disagree.

It is true that the legend "Charles Berlitz" is slightly larger on the "Step-By-Step" volumes than it was on the "Passport" series, and that the disclaimer legend is slightly reduced in size. These proportional modifications are, however, so minuscule as to be hardly detectable on visual inspection. The differences are not so great as to warrant another judicial proceeding. Of course, substantially greater discrepancies in the presentation of the name "Charles Berlitz" and the disclaimer of his association with Berlitz schools may give rise to claims which might not be barred by principles of res judicata and collateral estoppel.

. . . .

Regarding plaintiffs' assertion that they are entitled to de novo determination of their federally created Lanham Act rights in a federal court [because they did not assert those rights in the state proceedings], it is enough to say that their state and federal claims all involved the issue of the likelihood of confusion. The state courts have concurrent jurisdiction to determine those claims, and having determined them adversely to the plaintiffs, that is the end of the matter. . . .

Accordingly, . . . the judgment which dismissed the complaint is affirmed.

———

Question: (19) Given such differences in circumstances between two actions, is the proper question in the second action (a) whether the same issue of law-application is involved or (b) whether the different circumstances should trigger an exception to otherwise applicable issue preclusion? Does this distinction have any significance?

———

SECTION 2.   EXCEPTIONS TO THE RULE

UNITED STATES v. MOSER, 266 U.S. 236, 45 S.Ct. 66 (1924). Moser was a cadet at the Naval Academy during the Civil War. Upon retirement forty years later, he sued in the Court of Claims based on the difference between the pay of a captain and a rear admiral pursuant to a statute of the United States providing that "any officer of the Navy, with a creditable record, who served during the civil war shall, when retired, be retired with the rank and three-fourths the sea pay of the next higher grade." The government contended that service at the Naval Academy did not constitute service during the Civil War within the meaning of the statute, but the Court of Claims rejected the contention and decided in Moser's favor.

Later in a suit by another claimant similarly situated, one Jasper, the Court of Claims had its attention called to another retirement statute, previously overlooked, and by reference to that statute denied Jasper recovery.

In two subsequent actions by Moser for later installments of salary, the Court of Claims declined to follow the Jasper case, holding that by reason of its decision in the first Moser case the question was concluded as to Moser. In the present (fourth) action by Moser, the Court of Claims again held for him on the same ground. It ruled, alternatively, that its decision in the Jasper case was unsound as a matter of statutory interpretation and should be abandoned.

The Supreme Court affirmed. "We find it unnecessary to consider the latter ruling, since we are of opinion that the court was clearly right in its application of the doctrine of res judicata." Justice Sutherland explained for the Court:

"The contention of the Government seems to be that the doctrine of res judicata does not apply to questions of law; and, in a sense, that is true. It does not apply to unmixed questions of law. Where, for example, a court in deciding a case has enunciated a rule of law, the parties in a subsequent action upon a different demand are not estopped from insisting that the law is otherwise, merely because the parties are the same in both cases. But a *fact, question* or *right* distinctly adjudged in the original action cannot be disputed in a subsequent action, even though the determination was reached upon an erroneous view or by an erroneous application of the law. That would be to affirm the principle in respect of the thing adjudged but, at the same time, deny it all efficacy by sustaining a challenge to the grounds upon which the judgment was based. [Citations omitted.] A determination in respect of the status of an individual upon which his right to recover depends is as conclusive as a decision upon any other matter."

———

MONTANA v. UNITED STATES, 440 U.S. 147, 99 S.Ct. 970 (1979). Montana imposed a 1% gross-receipts tax upon contractors on public, but not private, construction projects in Montana. The United States had been involved in launching a state-court challenge to the tax on the ground that it discriminated against the United States in violation of the Federal Constitution. The Montana Supreme Court ultimately upheld the tax in 1973 ("Kiewit I"), and further appeal was abandoned.

Asserting a new claim that arose in connection with similar federal contracts, the United States challenged the Montana tax anew in the United States District Court for the District of Montana. The United States prevailed below. But the Supreme Court of the United States reversed, as Justice Marshall explained for the Court:

"A fundamental precept of common-law adjudication, embodied in the related doctrines of collateral estoppel and res judicata, is that a 'right, question or fact distinctly put in issue and directly determined by a court of competent jurisdiction . . . cannot be disputed in a subsequent suit between the same parties or their privies . . . .' Southern Pacific R. Co. v. United States, 168 U.S. 1, 48–49, 18 S.Ct. 18, 27 (1897). Under res judicata, a final judgment on the merits bars further claims by parties or their privies based on the same cause of action. Cromwell v. County of Sac, 94 U.S. 351, 352 (1877); Lawlor v. National Screen Service Corp., 349 U.S. 322, 326, 75 S.Ct. 865, 867 (1955); 1B J. Moore, Federal Practice ¶ 0.405[1], pp. 621–624 (2d ed. 1974) (hereinafter 1B Moore); Restatement (Second) of Judgments § 47 (Tent. Draft No. 1, Mar. 28, 1973) (merger); id., § 48 (bar). Under collateral estoppel, once an issue is actually and necessarily determined by a court of competent jurisdiction, that determination is conclusive in subsequent suits based on a different cause of action involving a party to the prior litigation. Parklane Hosiery Co. v. Shore, 439 U.S. 322, 326 n. 5, 99 S.Ct. 645, 649 n. 5 (1979); Scott, Collateral Estoppel by Judgment, 56 Harv.L.Rev. 1, 2–3 (1942); Restatement (Second) of Judgments § 68 (Tent. Draft No. 4, Apr. 15, 1977) (issue preclusion). Application of both doctrines is central to the purpose for which civil courts have been established, the conclusive resolution of disputes within their jurisdictions. Southern Pacific R. Co., supra, 168 U.S., at 49, 18 S.Ct., at 27; Hart Steel Co. v. Railroad Supply Co., 244 U.S. 294, 299, 37 S.Ct. 506, 507 (1917). To preclude parties from contesting matters that they have had a full and fair opportunity to litigate protects their adversaries from the expense and vexation attending multiple lawsuits, conserves judicial resources, and fosters reliance on judicial action by minimizing the possibility of inconsistent decisions.

. . . .

"To determine the appropriate application of collateral estoppel in the instant case necessitates three further inquiries: first, whether the issues presented by this litigation are in substance the same as those resolved against the United States in Kiewit I; second, whether controlling facts or legal principles have changed significantly since the state-court judgment; and finally, whether other special circumstances warrant an exception to the normal rules of preclusion.

A

"A review of the record in Kiewit I dispels any doubt that the plaintiff there raised and the Montana Supreme Court there decided the precise constitutional [challenges advanced here]. . . .

. . . .

"Thus, the 'question expressly and definitely presented in this suit is the same as that definitely and actually litigated and adjudged' adversely to the Government in state court. United States v. Moser, 266 U.S. 236, 242, 45 S.Ct. 66, 67 (1924). Absent significant changes in controlling facts or legal principles since Kiewit I, or other special circumstances, the Montana Supreme Court's resolution of these issues is conclusive here.

B

"Relying on Commissioner of Internal Revenue v. Sunnen, 333 U.S. 591, 68 S.Ct. 715 (1948), the United States argues that collateral estoppel extends only to contexts in which 'the controlling facts and applicable legal rules remain unchanged.' Id., at 600, 68 S.Ct., at 720. In the Government's view, factual stasis is missing here because the contract at issue in Kiewit I contained a critical provision which the contracts involved in the instant litigation do not.

[The Court concluded that the Montana Supreme Court had not essentially predicated its opinion in Kiewit I on the existence of that particular contractual provision and that therefore the change in facts did not suffice to avoid issue preclusion.]

"Thus, unless there have been major changes in the law governing intergovernmental tax immunity since Kiewit I, the Government's reliance on Commissioner of Internal Revenue v. Sunnen, 333 U.S. 591, 68 S.Ct. 715 (1948), is misplaced. Sunnen involved the tax status of certain income generated by a license agreement during a particular tax period. Although previous litigation had settled the status of income from the same agreement during earlier tax years, the Court declined to give collateral estoppel effect to the prior judgment because there had been a significant 'change in the legal climate.' Id., at 606, 68 S.Ct., at 723. Underlying the Sunnen decision was a concern that modifications in 'controlling legal principles,' id., at 599, 68 S.Ct., at 720, could render a previous determination inconsistent with prevailing doctrine, and that

'[i]f such a determination is then perpetuated each succeeding year as to the taxpayer involved in the original litigation, he is accorded a tax treatment different from that given to other taxpayers of the same class. As a result, there are inequalities in the administration of the revenue laws, discriminatory distinctions in tax liability, and a fertile basis for litigious confusion. [Collateral estoppel] is not meant to create vested rights in decisions that have become obsolete or erroneous with time, thereby causing inequities among taxpayers.' Ibid. (citations omitted).

No such considerations obtain here. The Government does not contend and the District Court did not find that a change in controlling legal principles had occurred between Kiewit I and the instant suit. That the Government's amended complaint in this action replicates in substance the legal argument advanced by the . . . complaint in Kiewit I further suggests the absence of any major doctrinal shifts since the Montana Supreme Court's decision.

"Because the factual and legal context in which the issues of this case arise has not materially altered since Kiewit I, normal rules of preclusion should operate to relieve the parties of 'redundant litigation [over] the identical question of the statute's application to the taxpayer's status.' Tait v. Western Maryland R. Co., 289 U.S. 620, 624, 53 S.Ct. 706, 707 (1933). [Other citation omitted.]

C

"The sole remaining question is whether the particular circumstances of this case justify an exception to general principles of estoppel. Of possible relevance is the exception which obtains for 'unmixed questions of law' in successive actions involving substantially unrelated claims. United States v. Moser, 266 U.S. 236, 242, 45 S.Ct. 66, 67 (1924). . . . Thus, when issues of law arise in successive actions involving unrelated subject matter, preclusion may be inappropriate. See Restatement (Second) of Judgments § 68.1, Reporter's Note, pp. 43–44 (Tent. Draft No. 4, Apr. 15, 1977); 1B Moore ¶ 0.448, p. 4235; Scott, 56 Harv.L.Rev., at 10. This exception is of particular importance in constitutional adjudication. Unreflective invocation of collateral estoppel against parties with an ongoing interest in constitutional issues could freeze doctrine in areas of the law where responsiveness to changing patterns of conduct or social mores is critical. To be sure, the scope of the Moser exception may be difficult to delineate, particularly where there is partial congruence in the subject matter of successive disputes. But the instant case poses no such conceptual difficulties. Rather, as the preceding discussion indicates, the legal 'demands' of this litigation are closely aligned in time and subject matter to those in Kiewit I.

. . . .

"Finally, the Government has not alleged unfairness or inadequacy in the state procedures to which it voluntarily submitted.[11] We must conclude therefore that it had a full and fair opportunity to press its constitutional challenges in Kiewit I. Accordingly, the Government is estopped from seeking a contrary resolution of those issues here."

Justice Rehnquist concurred in "the Court's opinion on the customary understanding that its references to . . . drafts or finally adopted versions of the Restatement of Judgments are not intended to bind the Court to the views expressed therein on issues not presented by the facts of this case."

Justice White dissented on the grounds that the change in facts sufficed to avoid issue preclusion and that the tax was unconstitutional.

———

Questions: (20) In a government action to recover customs duties from Importer *A* Corp., the court determines that the articles in question fall within a classification that makes them duty-free. In a later government

---

[11]   Redetermination of issues is warranted if there is reason to doubt the quality, extensiveness, or fairness of procedures followed in prior litigation. See Restatement (Second) of Judgments § 68.1(c) (Tent. Draft No. 4, Apr. 15, 1977); [other citations omitted].

action against Importer *B* Corp., the court determines that articles of the same kind fall within a classification requiring payment of a substantial duty. Then *A* imports additional articles of the same kind. Is the judgment in the first action preclusive on the issue of classification? See United States v. Stone & Downer Co., 274 U.S. 225, 47 S.Ct. 616 (1927) (suggesting no).

(21) Ex-cadet Moser continued for life to have his pension fixed at the higher rate dictated by the result of United States v. Moser. Ex-cadet Jasper continued for life to have his pension fixed at the lower rate, despite an ingenious effort by his administrator to alter the result by a retroactive appointment to a higher rank. Was the continued disparity of treatment of Moser and Jasper more justifiable than allowing *A* in the preceding question a permanent built-in competitive advantage over *B*?

(22) If Jasper had again sued the United States to get later installments at the higher rate, could he have avoided the rule of collateral estoppel by invoking the Sunnen exception based on intervening change in legal climate?

————

COURTS OF LIMITED JURISDICTION

It frequently happens that issue preclusion is asserted in an action that would be outside the jurisdiction of the court that rendered the prior judgment. Should issue preclusion effect extend to such a situation? The decisions are widely divergent. Consider the illustrative cases set forth below, which are designed to suggest that a flat answer either way is an unduly rigid approach.

1.   *A* sues *B* for negligently inflicted property damage in a county court with jurisdiction limited to $10,000. Should a judgment holding *B* negligent and *A* in the exercise of due care receive collateral estoppel effect from a court of general jurisdiction, in *B*'s action against *A* for $100,000 damages sustained in the same accident? See Gollner v. Cram, 258 Minn. 8, 102 N.W.2d 521 (1960) (giving preclusive effect).

2.   Same as the preceding case, except that the first court is a small-claims court that has a $1000 limit and operates informally without counsel, pleadings, or strict rules of evidence. Does this make a difference? See Sanderson v. Niemann, 17 Cal.2d 563, 110 P.2d 1025 (1941) (denying preclusive effect); cf. N.Y.City Civ.Ct.Act § 1808 ("A judgment obtained under this [small-claims] article shall not be deemed an adjudication of any fact at issue or found therein in any other action or court; except that a subsequent judgment obtained in another action or court involving the same facts, issues and parties shall be reduced by the amount of a judgment awarded under this article.").

3.   A surrogate's court—the jurisdiction of which is limited to wills, administration of estates, guardianship, and the like—decides in favor of an attorney claiming sizable fees against an estate, with the court necessarily determining that he did not commit a certain alleged fraud while administering the estate. Should this determination receive

collateral estoppel effect from a court of general jurisdiction, in a suit for damages for the fraud brought against the attorney by an adverse party to the prior proceeding? See United States v. Silliman, 167 F.2d 607 (3d Cir.1948) (giving preclusive effect).

4. A family court—the jurisdiction of which is limited to support, custody, and the like—denies a woman's support petition on the ground that the parties are not legally married because the man obtained a foreign divorce. Should this determination receive collateral estoppel effect from a court of general jurisdiction with exclusive jurisdiction over divorce and the like, in the woman's suit to declare the divorce's noneffect? See Loomis v. Loomis, 288 N.Y. 222, 42 N.E.2d 495 (1942) (denying preclusive effect, because of legislative intent); cf. Vanderveer v. Erie Malleable Iron Co., 238 F.2d 510 (3d Cir.1956) (giving preclusive effect to state-court adjudication of patent issues).

UNFORESEEABILITY OF FUTURE LITIGATION

In Evergreens v. Nunan, 141 F.2d 927, 929 (2d Cir.1944), Judge Learned Hand said: "Were the law to be recast, it would . . . be a pertinent inquiry whether the conclusiveness . . . of facts decided in the first [suit] might not properly be limited to future controversies which could be thought reasonably in prospect when the first suit was tried. . . . Logical relevance is of infinite possibility; there is no conceivable limit which can be put to it. Defeat in one suit might entail results beyond all calculation by either party; a trivial controversy might bring utter disaster in its train." However, Judge Hand did not feel free to recast the law in this way. Instead, in an attempt to place a reasonable restriction upon the extent to which a determination in the first suit precluded its relitigation in a second, Judge Hand drew a distinction between "ultimate facts" and "mediate data" at issue in the second suit: only ultimate facts in the second suit could be conclusively established by prior determination; mediate data, being merely premises from which the ultimate facts could be inferred, were beyond the reach of issue preclusion. Precluding only ultimate facts would help to ensure that the second suit is not too remote and that preclusion accomplishes significant work. Hand's distinction has received some support. Strangely enough, other authorities would instead limit preclusion to determinations that were ultimate facts in the *first* action.

The distinction between ultimate facts and mediate data is, however, vague and difficult to apply. It has been criticized by several commentators, who have suggested that truer hazards lie in making conclusive henceforth a determination that was not seriously contested and in imposing the risk of completely unforeseeable consequences. See, e.g., Geoffrey C. Hazard, Jr., John Leubsdorf & Debra Lyn Bassett, Civil Procedure 639–40 (6th ed. 2011). This alternative of recasting the law in terms of foreseeability has received some judicial support. In an early and prominent example, Hyman v. Regenstein, 258 F.2d 502, 511 (5th Cir.1958) (dictum), the court said that "collateral estoppel by judgment is applicable only when it is evident from the pleadings and record that determination of the fact in question was necessary to the final judgment and it was foreseeable that the fact would be of importance in possible future litigation."

It seems, indeed, that Judge Hand's actual decision in Evergreens will prove less influential than his dictum concerning foreseeability. Today, a typical court will not apply issue preclusion if such application was unforeseeable at the time of the initial action and such unforeseeability may have affected the effort therein by the party sought to be precluded. But such exceptional cases should be rare, and relitigation should follow only a clear and convincing showing of need. An example of where this constrained exception for unforeseeability would apply: the tax court's prior adjudication of the value of specific property would not be preclusive if it were later to acquire tremendously greater financial significance for the taxpayer's future returns because of an amendment to the tax code's depletion provisions. Creating an exception for this situation is necessary because there is no other way to escape inappropriate issue preclusion—the change in circumstances has not created a different issue as to value, and this purely *factual* issue falls outside the Sunnen exception designed to avoid persons' unequal *legal* treatment.

Question: (23) Although *un*foreseeability creates an exception under today's doctrine, should foreseeability have the effect of extending the rule of collateral estoppel beyond essential issues actually litigated and determined, as in cases like Jacobson v. Miller where the prospect of future litigation was apparent at the time of the first action? See Developments in the Law—Res Judicata, 65 Harv.L.Rev. 818, 841 (1952).

————

Restatement (Second) of Judgments
(Am. Law Inst. 1982).

§ 28.   *Exceptions to the General Rule of Issue Preclusion*

Although an issue is actually litigated and determined by a valid and final judgment, and the determination is essential to the judgment, relitigation of the issue in a subsequent action between the parties is not precluded in the following circumstances:

(1) The party against whom preclusion is sought could not, as a matter of law, have obtained review of the judgment in the initial action; or

(2) The issue is one of law and (a) the two actions involve claims that are substantially unrelated, or (b) a new

determination is warranted in order to take account of an intervening change in the applicable legal context or otherwise to avoid inequitable administration of the laws; or

(3) A new determination of the issue is warranted by differences in the quality or extensiveness of the procedures followed in the two courts or by factors relating to the allocation of jurisdiction between them; or

(4) The party against whom preclusion is sought had a significantly heavier burden of persuasion with respect to the issue in the initial action than in the subsequent action; the burden has shifted to his adversary; or the adversary has a significantly heavier burden than he had in the first action; or

(5) There is a clear and convincing need for a new determination of the issue (a) because of the potential adverse impact of the determination on the public interest or the interests of persons not themselves parties in the initial action, (b) because it was not sufficiently foreseeable at the time of the initial action that the issue would arise in the context of a subsequent action, or (c) because the party sought to be precluded, as a result of the conduct of his adversary or other special circumstances, did not have an adequate opportunity or incentive to obtain a full and fair adjudication in the initial action.

————

Question: (24) These exceptions have some major consequences. They provide another escape that serves to keep res judicata from freezing the meaning of the Constitution and other laws. See also Whole Woman's Health v. Hellerstedt, 136 S.Ct. 2292 (2016) (holding that changed circumstances avoided claim preclusion, where the first action was a facial attack on the Texas abortion statute before its effective date and the second action was an as-applied attack in which the plaintiffs could show the actual adverse consequences of its enforcement). Do you see how the Restatement's exceptions also help to produce the precept that issue preclusion normally does not bind the winner of a judgment?

————

Spilker v. Hankin

United States Court of Appeals, District of Columbia Circuit, 1951.
188 F.2d 35.

[Spilker gave her attorney Hankin a series of seven notes in payment for legal services in a matrimonial action. The first was a demand note for $500; and the others, each in the amount of $250, became due at three-month intervals thereafter. Spilker paid the demand note. When she failed to pay the second note, Hankin sued thereon in the Municipal

Court for the District of Columbia. Spilker pleaded duress, alleged that the note in suit was for an exorbitant and unconscionable fee, and further alleged that she had already overpaid Hankin. She also filed a counterclaim seeking a determination that the amount already paid was to be considered full payment for his services and asking that the remaining notes be declared void. In a trial without jury, Hankin won judgment on the note and also prevailed against the counterclaim, without specific findings or conclusions. She took no appeal.

[Later Hankin brought the present action in the same court on the five remaining notes, all of which had now become due. Spilker's chief defense was misrepresentation in inducing execution of the notes, and she again urged that she had paid Hankin all his professional services were worth. The plaintiff's motion for summary judgment on the ground that the prior judgment precluded the defendant was denied by the same judge who had rendered the prior judgment. There was a jury trial leading to a verdict and judgment for the defendant. The Municipal Court of Appeals reversed and ordered judgment for the plaintiff. The defendant appealed to the federal court of appeals, as was then permitted.]

■ Before [BENNETT] CLARK, FAHY and WASHINGTON, CIRCUIT JUDGES.

■ WASHINGTON, CIRCUIT JUDGE.

. . . .

We agree with much that the learned Municipal Court of Appeals has said with regard to the principles of res judicata. We agree, for example, that in successive suits on a series of notes, defenses failing in the first suit ordinarily are foreclosed to the defendant in subsequent litigation. Restatement, Judgments § 68, Comments c, m, Illustration 5. But, with all respect to that court, we consider that weight should have been given to a factor not mentioned in its discussion of the case, that is, the fiduciary relationship of attorney and client which existed between the parties. In a very real sense attorneys are officers of the courts in which they practice; and clients are wards of the court in regard to their relationship with their attorneys. This factor is one of high significance in the present context.

The doctrine of res judicata is but the technical formulation of the "Public policy . . . that there be an end of litigation; that those who have contested an issue shall be bound by the result of the contest; and that matters once tried shall be considered forever settled as between the parties." Baldwin v. Iowa State Traveling Men's Ass'n, 283 U.S. 522, 525, 51 S.Ct. 517, 518, 75 L.Ed. 1244. This policy has long been a tenet of the common law, and even finds expression in the Constitution of the United States, in the full faith and credit clause. Experience has taught that as a general rule there is no reason why the doctrine of res judicata "should not apply in every case where one voluntarily appears, presents his case and is fully heard . . . ." [Id.] But rules and policies such as these must be weighed against competing necessities: situations may arise which call for exceptions. . . .

. . . [R]es judicata, as the embodiment of a public policy, must, at times, on occasion, yield to other policies.

Fee contracts between attorney and client are a subject of special interest and concern to the courts. . . .

Ordinarily the matter of a fee will be litigated but once, and the first determination will be conclusive. Were this merely a suit upon the original judgment we would, of course, consider res judicata to be applicable. But here we have a series of notes, one brought into litigation prior to the others. The original suit was for a much smaller amount, and some of the issues here in question were only indirectly involved in it. And it is the attorney who seeks further court aid with regard to his fee. The fee arrangement in question was reduced to promissory notes shortly before the termination of the litigation in which the attorney acted for the client, and appears to have been required by the attorney as a condition of his remaining in the case. While we do not mean to imply that an attorney can never protect himself with regard to his fee by making an arrangement of this sort, we consider that when under such circumstances the attorney twice brings the matter into court, the requirements of justice are better served by permitting reexamination of the merits than by treating the prior suit as foreclosing the matter. We think that the client should be permitted to make any legal or equitable defense to the remaining notes which appeals to the conscience of the court.

. . . .

Reversed . . . .

Question: (25) Should the general rule of issue preclusion be applied more flexibly, with a greater willingness to recognize exceptions, than the general rule of claim preclusion?

FEDERATED DEPARTMENT STORES v. MOITIE, 452 U.S. 394, 101 S.Ct. 2424 (1981). A number of plaintiffs each brought similar price-fixing actions against certain department stores. Treating the actions together, the district court dismissed for failure to state a claim. Plaintiffs in five of the actions appealed. But the plaintiff in another action instead chose to bring a new action with a complaint based on a different theory; the same district court dismissed on the ground of claim preclusion; and that plaintiff appealed.

The court of appeals then reversed in the five suits, indicating that they had stated a claim under the antitrust laws as interpreted by an intervening Supreme Court decision. Later the court of appeals reversed in the other case as well, ruling "that non-appealing parties may benefit from a reversal when their position is closely interwoven with that of appealing parties" and that the otherwise applicable claim preclusion must give way to simple justice and public policy.

On certiorari in the latter case, the Supreme Court reversed. Justice Rehnquist for the Court rejected any "interwoven" exception to claim preclusion. He further explained, in an opinion that seemed to use "res judicata" as a synonym for claim preclusion:

"The Court of Appeals also rested its opinion in part on what it viewed as 'simple justice.' But we do not see the grave injustice which would be done by the application of accepted principles of res judicata. 'Simple justice' is achieved when a complex body of law developed over a period of years is evenhandedly applied. The doctrine of res judicata serves vital public interests beyond any individual judge's ad hoc determination of the equities in a particular case. There is simply 'no principle of law or equity which sanctions the rejection by a federal court of the salutary principle of res judicata.' Heiser v. Woodruff, 327 U.S. 726, 733, 66 S.Ct. 853, 856 (1946). The Court of Appeals' reliance on 'public policy' is similarly misplaced. This Court has long recognized that '[p]ublic policy dictates that there be an end of litigation; that those who have contested an issue shall be bound by the result of the contest, and that matters once tried shall be considered forever settled as between the parties.' Baldwin v. Traveling Men's Association, 283 U.S. 522, 525, 51 S.Ct. 517, 518 (1931). We have stressed that '[the] doctrine of res judicata is not a mere matter of practice or procedure inherited from a more technical time than ours. It is a rule of fundamental and substantial justice, "of public policy and of private peace," which should be cordially regarded and enforced by the courts . . . .' Hart Steel Co. v. Railroad Supply Co., 244 U.S. 294, 299, 37 S.Ct. 506, 507 (1917). The language used by this Court half a century ago is even more compelling in view of today's crowded dockets:

> 'The predicament in which respondent finds himself is of his own making . . . . [W]e cannot be expected, for his sole relief, to upset the general and well-established doctrine of res judicata, conceived in the light of the maxim that the interest of the state requires that there be an end to litigation—a maxim which comports with common sense as well as public policy. And the mischief which would follow the establishment of precedent for so disregarding the salutary doctrine against prolonging strife would be greater than the benefit which would result from relieving some case of individual hardship.' Reed v. Allen, [286 U.S. 191, 198–99, 52 S.Ct. 532, 533 (1932)]."

Justice Blackmun, joined by Justice Marshall, concurred in the judgment. Justice Brennan dissented on other grounds.

EXCEPTIONS BASED ON POSTURE OF PARTY

A party does not always come within the reach of the rules of claim and issue preclusion that we have studied so far. A party may find himself in a special posture in the litigation so that he does not have a full and fair opportunity to litigate certain aspects of the case, and so that to a certain extent the application of res judicata would be inappropriate. It could be said that, to such extent, the person will be deemed to have been a nonparty.

For example, Restatement (Second) of Judgments § 36(2) (Am. Law Inst. 1982) provides: "A party appearing in an action in one capacity, individual or representative, is not thereby bound by or entitled to the benefits of the rules of res judicata in a subsequent action in which he appears in another capacity." Thus, an individual will not normally be precluded by determinations in a prior action that she litigates as a trustee. This exception frees the fiduciary to litigate that first action without the influence of personal interest.

On a somewhat different point, the rules of res judicata that we have studied so far do not normally apply between parties who were not on opposite sides of the relevant claim—although issue preclusion can apply if they in actuality did litigate the issue fully and fairly as adversaries to each other. See id. § 38.

Questions: (26) *W*, administratrix of *H*'s estate, sues *D* for wrongful death of *H* in an automobile accident wherein *H* and *D* were drivers. *D* wins, with the court finding that *D* was not negligent. *W* then sues *D* for her own personal injuries sustained in the same accident as a passenger. May *D* invoke res judicata?

(27) An automobile passenger sues Driver *A* and Driver *B*, and she recovers against both. Then Driver *A* sues Driver *B*, who pleads contributory negligence. Is the prior judgment controlling on the issues of the two drivers' negligence? See Schwartz v. Pub. Adm'r, 24 N.Y.2d 65, 246 N.E.2d 725, 298 N.Y.S.2d 955 (1969) (giving issue-preclusive effect). Why?

TOPIC D

EFFECTS ON PERSONS NOT PARTIES

SECTION 1.   PERSONS BOUND BY PRIOR JUDGMENT

A judgment not only will preclude the parties thereto in the various ways already considered, but also will have similar effects upon persons who are not parties but who stand in a relation of "privity" to them. "Privity" is a term of art, and it does not necessarily follow that a person who is a privy of a party for another purpose is a privy for the purpose of res judicata. Indeed, Restatement of Judgments § 83 cmt. a (Am. Law Inst. 1942) called the word "privity" in this context "a short method of stating that under the circumstances and for the purpose of the case at hand [a nonparty] is bound by and entitled to the benefits of all or some of the rules of res judicata."

By contrast, the Second Restatement does not use the term "privity" and, instead, treats in more than twenty separate sections the specific classes of nonparties falling to some degree within the reach of the binding rules of res judicata, classifying them thematically (1) as persons having substantive legal relationships with parties justifying preclusion, (2) as persons whose conduct justifies preclusion, or (3) as persons represented by parties. Nevertheless, if the word "privity" is clearly recognized as being conclusory, it remains useful as a general descriptive term.

The premise in common to all findings of privity is that there was some substantial reason to bind a nonparty. Conventionally, privies include among others the following core examples of the three themes:

1. *Successors in interest to a party's property involved in an action.* This one is intuitive. For example, *A* brings an action to quiet title to Blackacre against an assertion by *B* that *B* holds a mortgage on the land. Judgment goes for *B*, adjudging the mortgage to be good. *A* conveys to *C* after judgment. The judgment bars a later attempt by *C* to quiet title, given that *A* in a sense represented *C*. Incidentally, if judgment had been for *A* in the first action, *C* would similarly have been entitled to benefit from the judgment.

2. *Nonparties who control the prosecution or defense of an action.* Such a person is bound by issue preclusion as if he were himself the party whose position he espouses. For example, *A* brings an action against *B* for infringement of *A*'s patent in connection with *B*'s manufacturing certain goods. *B* has a license from *O* to manufacture the goods under *O*'s patent. *O* controls the defense of the *A* versus *B* action. If *A* gets a judgment of infringement against *B*, that determination will be

preclusive in a later action between *A* and *O*. By contrast, one who participates as an amicus curiae is neither a party nor a controlling nonparty, and is not thereby bound by any res judicata effects of the judgment.

3.   *Persons who are actually represented by a party to an action.* This one is potentially broad. For example, beneficiaries of an express trust will normally be bound by a judgment in an action to which the trustee, in her character as trustee, was a party. This principle is not limited to formal trusts or to fiduciary relationships such as that between administrator and beneficiaries of an estate, but extends at least to situations of representation in the nature of principal-agent.

————

Restatement (Second) of Judgments

(Am. Law Inst. 1982).

§ 52.   *Bailee and Bailor*

(1) A judgment in an action by either bailee or bailor against a third party for interference with ownership or destruction of or damage to property that is the subject of a bailment precludes a subsequent action by either, except that:

(a) Where the claim is limited to the claimant's own loss in the property it does not preclude an action by the other for his loss;

(b) If the action is by the bailee it does not preclude an action by the bailor if the judgment was based on a defense not available against the bailor;

(c) An action by the bailee against the third party for claims arising out of the transaction in which the loss occurred does not preclude an action by the bailor for his loss if the third party was on notice that the bailee's action did not seek recovery for the bailor's interest.

(2) The determination of issues in an action by either bailee or bailor is not preclusive against the other of them in a subsequent action between the latter and the third party.

————

INDEMNITY

There are numerous situations where either by contract or by operation of law a person is entitled to indemnity from another source against loss. The most familiar illustration of indemnity by contract, which figured in the Dindo case, is the liability insurance contract: the insurer undertakes to pay certain kinds of judgments against its insured and his attendant expenses, up to specified policy limits. (Under the typical policy, the insurer also undertakes to defend at its own expense claims made against the insured, and the insured obligates himself to give prompt notice of any accident and to cooperate in the defense.) An instance of indemnity by operation of law, already dealt with supra p. 288, is that of an employee whose negligent conduct in carrying out his employer's business is the sole basis of the employer's liability to a third person: the employee is legally bound to indemnify the employer for its loss. (In an ordinary automobile accident in which liability insurance protects the employer, the protection of the policy extends to the employee as well, pursuant to a standard policy provision covering, in addition to the named insured, any person operating a motor vehicle with the owner's express or implied consent.)

When either type of indemnity prevails, the indemnitee who is sued may "vouch in" the indemnitor, a still-available common-law device whereby the indemnitee gives the indemnitor simple notice of the action and offers it control of the defense. Once so vouched in, whether or not it accepts control of the defense, the indemnitor normally will be bound by the judgment on the questions of the indemnitee's liability. However, the indemnitor normally remains free to litigate in a later action the separate issue of whether and to what extent it is obligated by contract or by operation of law to indemnify that liability.

Instead of vouching in the indemnitor and so making it a privy, the indemnitee may, in a federal court or in a state court with a rule like Rule 14, go further by invoking impleader to make the indemnitor an actual party. This course allows the indemnitee to retain control of the defense and also to bring the indemnitor into the action and so obtain a judgment against it. The effectiveness of impleader is limited, however, by the requirement of service—whereas, according to the better view, a vouched-in entity need not be within the reach of the court's process.

If the indemnitee neither vouches in nor impleads the indemnitor, he does not thereby lose his right to indemnity. He must, however, establish his claim all over again, unless a contract provides otherwise. In the second action, the indemnitee faces having to offer practically the same proof previously relied upon by the injured person. This may leave the indemnitee the loser because of differing views of the evidence by the two factfinders, and in any event it is a needless expense to him.

———

SHOW-WORLD CENTER v. WALSH, 438 F.Supp. 642 (S.D.N.Y.1977). A landlord (303 Corp.) unsuccessfully sued New York City officials twice in state court to challenge a safety order and later an eviction order that was enforced against only one of its many tenants, a sex shop. The landlord alleged that the orders were unconstitutional parts of a campaign to ban sex-oriented activity from the Times Square area.

Next the tenant (Show-World) sued New York City officials in federal court to challenge the eviction on similar grounds under 42 U.S.C. § 1983. District Judge Motley rejected the application of res judicata for this reason:

"During all of these proceedings . . . 303 Corp. was represented by Ralph J. Schwarz, Jr. (Schwarz) who is also general counsel to Show-World. When Schwarz perceived that the Buildings Department was acting solely against Show-World, he decided that Show-World should be separately represented and called in outside counsel on its behalf. Mr. Herald Price Fahringer has since represented Show-World.

. . . .

"A threshold issue of critical importance to disposition of the preliminary questions in this case . . . is the nature of the relationship between Show-World, the plaintiff in this action, and 303 Corp., the plaintiff in the two State court proceedings. The only clear, undisputed facts on this issue are that Show-World was a tenant of 303 Corp., and that both corporations have had dealings with one attorney, Ralph Schwarz. Mr. Schwarz has been General Counsel to Show-World since 1974, when he handled that entity's incorporation and negotiated its lease with 303 Corp. During the lease negotiation, 303 Corp. was represented in the main by its President and sole shareholder, Wallace Katz, who looked to another lawyer for legal advice on that occasion. Mr. Katz owns no part of Show-World and 303 Corp. owns no part of Show-World.

"During the State court proceedings, Mr. Schwarz represented only 303 Corp. although, on two occasions in the State court, he did identify himself as being also the attorney for Show-World, allegedly to provide support for his assertion of personal knowledge of some of the facts there in issue. He admitted at the hearing in the instant case that he kept his client, Show-World, informed as to the course of the [administrative] proceedings . . . . However, he made clear in this court that he at no time represented Show-World *as a party* in the State courts.

"On the basis of these facts adduced at the hearings thus far in the case, the court finds no privity between Show-World and 303 Corp. such as to equate the interests of the two entities in the State proceedings, and, thereby, to preclude the litigation by Show-World in this court.

"Assuming, without deciding, that Show-World might have had standing to intervene in either or both of the State proceedings to date, that fact alone would not be sufficient to bar this action. The fact that a party has a right to intervene, which it chooses not to exercise, is not enough to make it bound by a judgment in the proceeding in which it possessed such a right. Brown v. Wright, 137 F.2d 484, 487 (4th Cir.1943); Western Union Telegraph Company v. Foster, 247 U.S. 105, 38 S.Ct. 438, 62 L.Ed. 1006 (1918).

"Moreover, the mere existence of a landlord-tenant (lessor-lessee) relationship is insufficient to bind the tenant to the adjudication in the prior litigation to which the landlord only was a party. While there is language in the two cases cited to the court by defendants which would tend to indicate that under some circumstances, the 'privity of estate' between landlord and tenant may cause the latter to be bound by prior judgments to which the landlord only was a party, Kruger & Birch, Inc. v. DuBoyce, 241 F.2d 849, 854 (3d Cir.1957); Fouke v. Schenewerk, 197 F.2d 234, 236 (5th Cir.1952) (dictum), those cases appear to involve only disputes relating to either title to, or right to possession of, real property. See 50 C.J.S. Judgments § 801 and cases cited therein; [other citations omitted]. Certainly this court has been cited no authority for the proposition that a landlord's derivative assertion of his tenant's constitutional rights in a proceeding to which the tenant was not a party should bind the tenant in a later proceeding in which the tenant seeks to raise those important rights directly. In view of the possible conflict of interest between landlord and tenant, whose rights a landlord might, at least hypothetically, be willing to sacrifice, there appears to be no basis for binding the tenant to the former adjudication on the basis of its relation to the landlord qua landlord.

"Finally, and most clearly, privity is not established from the mere fact that Show-World may happen to be 'interested' in the same question at issue in the earlier proceedings in the New York courts, whether by way of establishing a proposition of law, or by proving or disproving some state of facts. [Citations omitted.] Nor does the fact that the prior decision might affect Show-World's action in this court as a favorable or unfavorable judicial precedent cause Show-World to be considered a privy to 303 Corp. in the earlier proceeding."

———

TAYLOR v. STURGELL, 553 U.S. 880, 128 S.Ct. 2161 (2008), rev'g Taylor v. Blakey, 490 F.3d 965 (D.C.Cir.2007). By this case, the Supreme Court conformed to the suggestion in Show-World's last paragraph and so pretty much killed off virtual representation as a route to privity. The court of appeals had described the case this way:

"Brent Taylor requested certain documents from the Federal Aviation Administration under the Freedom of Information Act. The FAA denied his request and Taylor sued to compel disclosure. The district court dismissed the case, holding res judicata barred Taylor's claim because Greg Herrick, a 'close associate' of Taylor's, had been his 'virtual representative' in a prior FOIA case Herrick had brought unsuccessfully seeking the same documents. We affirm that judgment.

"Herrick, a member of the Antique Aircraft Association (AAA) and the owner of an F-45 aircraft manufactured by a predecessor of the Fairchild Corporation, filed a request under the FOIA seeking the plans and specifications for the F-45. Herrick v. Garvey, 298 F.3d 1184, 1188

(10th Cir.2002). After conferring with Fairchild, the FAA determined the requested material was a trade secret and withheld the information pursuant to Exemption 4 of the FOIA. See 5 U.S.C. § 552(b)(4). [The district court and the Tenth Circuit decided against Herrick.]

"Approximately one month after the Tenth Circuit issued its decision in Herrick, Taylor, the executive director of the AAA, filed a FOIA request for the same documents relating to the F-45 that Herrick had sought. . . . Taylor, represented by the lawyer who had represented Herrick in his litigation, . . . argu[ed] the trade secret status of the F-45 documents . . . .

    . . . .

" . . . [Taylor] added that he did not know of Herrick's FOIA request until after the Tenth Circuit's decision. Also, he said Herrick and Taylor sought the information for different reasons—Herrick to restore his F-45 and Taylor more generally 'for the public and in the interest of the preservation of antique aircraft heritage.' "

The court of appeals then explained its approach to virtual representation of Taylor this way: "An appropriate test for virtual representation must consider and balance competing interests in due process and efficiency. Too readily to find virtual representation risks infringing upon the nonparty's right to due process of law and departs from our 'deep-rooted historic tradition that everyone should have his own day in court.' Richards [v. Jefferson Cty., 517 U.S. 793, 798, 116 S.Ct. 1761, 1766 (1996)]. To find virtual representation under only very narrow circumstances, on the other hand, would expose defendants to the burden of relitigation, raise the possibility of inconsistent results, and compromise the public interest in judicial economy. [Citations omitted.] We believe these competing concerns can best be addressed by considering five factors . . . . [W]e believe identity of interests and adequate representation are necessary conditions. We do not, however, believe they are sufficient . . . . We therefore require in addition a showing of at least one of the other factors . . . : a close relationship between the present party and his putative representative, or substantial participation by the present party in the first case, or tactical maneuvering on the part of the present party to avoid preclusion by the prior judgment. As this approach clarifies, there can be no virtual representation absent an affirmative link between the later litigant and either the prior party or the prior case."

The court of appeals eventually concluded that "there is record evidence that: (1) Taylor and Herrick had identical interests, even when viewed in terms of incentives, and (2) Taylor's interest was adequately represented in Herrick, in addition to which (3) Herrick and Taylor had a close working relationship relative to these successive cases. There is no countervailing evidence. We therefore conclude Herrick served as Taylor's virtual representative in the litigation for the F-45 documents."

The Supreme Court unanimously vacated the court of appeals' judgment, and remanded for further proceedings on whether Taylor was in fact acting as Herrick's undisclosed agent in relitigating. Justice Ginsburg explained that the background rule is that nonparties are not bound—subject to quite limited and relatively rigid extensions of privity. Virtual representation was not to be one of those extensions under the federal common law of res judicata.

As to the recognized extensions resting on representation, she said they required certain protections that are at least "grounded in due process": "A party's representation of a nonparty is 'adequate' for preclusion purposes only if, at a minimum: (1) the interests of the nonparty and her representative are aligned, see Hansberry [v. Lee, 311 U.S. 32, 43, 61 S.Ct. 115, 119 (1940)]; and (2) either the party understood herself to be acting in a representative capacity or the original court took care to protect the interests of the nonparty, see Richards, 517 U.S., at 801–802, 116 S.Ct. 1761 .... In addition, adequate representation sometimes requires (3) notice of the original suit to the persons alleged to have been represented, see Richards, 517 U.S., at 801, 116 S.Ct. 1761. In the class-action context, these limitations are implemented by the procedural safeguards contained in Federal Rule of Civil Procedure 23."

Furthermore she warned against framing extensions in the loose terms of a balancing approach: "Preclusion doctrine, it should be recalled, is intended to reduce the burden of litigation on courts and parties. [Citation omitted.] 'In this area of the law,' we agree, ' "crisp rules with sharp corners" are preferable to a round-about doctrine of opaque standards.' Bittinger v. Tecumseh Products Co., 123 F.3d 877, 881 (C.A.6 1997)."

NEENAN v. WOODSIDE ASTORIA TRANSPORTATION CO., 261 N.Y. 159, 184 N.E. 744 (1933). Judge Crane, for the court, said in part:

"On February 7, 1929, at the corner of Seventeenth avenue and Jamaica avenue, in the borough of Queens, New York City, a collision occurred between the automobile owned and operated by John J. Huppmann and a bus of the Woodside Astoria Transportation Co., Inc. Huppmann sued the transportation company for damages [in New York state court] and proved that the collision was due solely to the negligence of its driver to which no carelessness on his part contributed. He recovered a judgment of $2,153.75 against the company.

"Later, a passenger in the bus, Mary Neenan, sued both Huppmann and the Woodside Astoria Transportation Co., Inc., for the damages due to personal injuries received in the collision and, strange as it may seem, recovered a judgment of $1,500 against both defendants. Huppmann sought to introduce the judgment roll in his action against the transportation company, but of course it was not res judicata as to the passenger, Mary Neenan, as she was not a party to that action. She was free to prove that Huppmann was also negligent. If this were not so a responsible party might by collusion shift the liability upon an irresponsible person who cared little about a judgment against him. A plaintiff may hold all joint tort feasors. There was no error in excluding the judgment roll in the action of Mary Neenan."

––––––––

Questions: (1) Would a holding that Mary Neenan was bound by the prior judgment be consistent with due process of law?

(2) NYCPA § 211–a, in force at the time of the Neenan case, provided that a defendant who had paid more than his pro rata share of a judgment (i.e., the amount of the judgment divided by the number of defendants jointly liable under the judgment) could obtain contribution to the extent of the excess from the other defendants. If Woodside satisfied Mary Neenan's judgment in full and sued Huppmann for contribution, what if any effect should be given to the judgment in the prior action of Huppmann v. Woodside?

(3) Would your answer to the preceding question be different under New York's new contribution statute, NY CPLR art. 14, enacted in 1974? (New York adopted comparative negligence between plaintiff and defendant in 1975.) The contribution statute provides that a defendant who has paid more than his equitable share of a judgment (i.e., a share determined in accordance with his culpability relative to that of the other persons subject to liability for the injury) can obtain contribution to the extent of the excess from those other persons. The defendant can assert the contribution claim either by crossclaim or impleader or by separate action.

––––––––

SECTION 2.   PERSONS BENEFITED BY PRIOR JUDGMENT

Prevalence of mutuality.—By definition, only parties and their privies are bound by a prior judgment, although of course the categories of "privies" are susceptible to stretching. Sound policy does not countenance binding other nonparties, who may be termed "strangers." Parties and their privies may also benefit from a prior judgment under the rules of res judicata. But may strangers benefit from the judgment, even though they are not bound?

First of all, collateral estoppel holds the greatest promise of benefits for such a person not a party or a privy. Involvement of strangers implies a different claim. Usually, then, only parties and their privies may obtain the benefits of the other rules of res judicata, as in the example already given of a successor in interest who could invoke bar based on her predecessor's successful quiet-title action against a rival claimant.

So let us first think in terms of a stranger's use of collateral estoppel. The traditional approach derived from the general rule that estoppels must be mutual—because a stranger to a prior judgment could not be bound by it, letting the stranger benefit from it would be unfair.

Mutuality's bounds.—The Restatement of Judgments (Am. Law Inst. 1942) followed the generally prevailing case law in taking mutuality's narrow approach, but tempered it with exceptions to meet exigent situations. The result was a rather grudging retreat from mutuality of estoppel, and one that ignored a growing body of decisions espousing broader extensions of preclusion.

For a classic problem, which is critically important to understanding this whole area, consider once more the above-described employment-indemnity problem. Imagine that S, driving her employer M's car on M's business, is in a collision with a car owned and driven by T. The master-servant relation makes M liable to T for S's negligence, if any; as between M and S, S is obliged (in theory at least) to make good to M any liability M suffers by S's negligence. Assume that T sues S, and S wins. Next T sues M, relitigating the issues of S's negligence and T's due care, and this time T recovers. That poses a dilemma: on the one hand, if M is now free to get indemnity from S, S would have to pay as a result of a trial to which she was not a party, when she had already achieved exoneration from liability in a trial to which she was a party; on the other hand, if M is not free to recover from S, M would have lost his right of indemnity as a result of a trial to which he was not a party. The natural way around this dilemma would have been to allow M to plead res judicata against T based on the prior judgment for S. But if T had won against S, T could not have used the judgment against M, who had never had his day in court. The mutuality rule therefore prohibited that natural solution.

Mutuality's purity was too much for the First Restatement. Thus, an extension of preclusion was created to the extent necessary to protect both S's victory and M's right of indemnity: M, the indemnitee, was allowed to use the judgment in favor of S, the indemnitor, as a defense to a second suit by T. See Restatement of Judgments §§ 96–97 (Am. Law Inst. 1942). (The First Restatement provided for the same result whether S had won the first suit as defendant or plaintiff, and so did the case law, e.g., Good Health Dairy Prods. Corp. v. Emery, 275 N.Y. 14, 9 N.E.2d 758 (1937).[a] However, the First Restatement, but not all courts, refused to allow M to invoke nonmutual preclusion offensively as a plaintiff in a second suit, rather than defensively as a defendant.)

But what if T's first suit were instead against M for S's negligence, and M won? Because it was S who was obliged to indemnify M and not the other way around, the right of indemnity was not in the mix when T next sued S and so posed no dilemma. Here the First Restatement stuck with the mutuality requirement and refused to let S take advantage of the first judgment. The result gave T a second chance on the same issues

---

[a]   A judgment for T against S for \$200 fixed that as the maximum liability of M if T, not having satisfied his judgment against S, sued M. See Pinnix v. Griffin, 221 N.C. 348, 20 S.E.2d 366 (1942).

by merely shifting adversaries. Yet there was already authority contrary to the First Restatement's position, e.g., Giedrewicz v. Donovan, 277 Mass. 563, 179 N.E. 246 (1932), and much more thereafter.

Question: (4) What would the Massachusetts court do, in the light of Giedrewicz v. Donovan, if T successfully sued M for S's negligence (with T winning after a trial at which S testified as a witness for M) and then S sued T for her own injuries? See Pesce v. Brecher, 302 Mass. 211, 19 N.E.2d 36 (1939) (no res judicata). Why?

Nevertheless, Restatement of Judgments § 99 (Am. Law Inst. 1942) recognized another breach in the wall of mutuality, which went beyond the indemnity situation and which seemed to go beyond the demands of compelling need. This broader exception is illustrated by American Button Co. v. Warsaw Button Co., 31 N.Y.S.2d 395 (Sup.Ct.1941) (alternative holding), aff'd mem., 265 A.D. 905, 38 N.Y.S.2d 570 (1942). In a prior action A had sued B for breach of contract, and had lost. Then A sued W for inducing B to breach that contract with A. The court held the prior judgment to preclude A from recovering against W. The First Restatement generalized the result: a judgment in favor of a person charged with commission of a tort or with breach of a contract normally precluded recovery by the same plaintiff against another defendant who was responsible for the conduct of the former defendant.

Rise of nonmutual estoppel.—For years almost all courts avoided a frontal attack on mutuality, living instead within its framework by an increasing recognition of such extensions of the preclusion rule, whose coverage eventually reached all the permutations of these secondary-liability cases. When the frontal attack finally came, it precipitated great controversy and great change in the law in most jurisdictions, a process that is still not fully played out.

———

COCA-COLA CO. v. PEPSI-COLA CO., 36 Del. 124, 172 A. 260 (Super.Ct.1934). Pepsi-Cola offered a $10,000 reward for information leading to the detection of any dealer substituting Pepsi-Cola for any other five-cent drink. Coca-Cola sued Pepsi-Cola, claiming the reward and alleging that it had made known to Pepsi-Cola instances where certain dealers had substituted Pepsi-Cola for Coca-Cola, a five-cent drink. Pepsi-Cola pleaded res judicata, asserting that the identical issues had been decided against Coca-Cola in prior actions brought by Coca-Cola against the dealers in Delaware state court. Coca-Cola demurred to this plea. The court considered res judicata to be universally applicable against any prior plaintiff, saying: "[W]e are of the opinion that a plaintiff who deliberately selects his forum and there unsuccessfully presents his proofs, is bound by such adverse judgment in a second suit involving all the identical issues already decided. The requirement of mutuality must yield to public policy."

———

Bernhard v. Bank of America National Trust & Savings Ass'n

Supreme Court of California, 1942.
19 Cal.2d 807, 122 P.2d 892.

[Sather authorized Cook to deposit money for her in the defendant bank. Cook did so, but later withdrew it, deposited it in his name, and used it for his own purposes. Sather died, appointing Cook her executor. In Cook's final accounting to the probate court, no mention was made of this money. Helen Bernhard and other beneficiaries under Sather's will filed objections to Cook's account, claiming that Cook had embezzled the money from Sather. The probate court after a hearing found that Sather in her lifetime had made a gift to Cook of the money in question, and so it allowed Cook's account and discharged him as executor.

[Thereafter Helen Bernhard was appointed administratrix with the will annexed. She brought this suit against the bank, seeking to recover the deposit for the estate on the ground that Sather had never authorized its withdrawal. According to the bank, however, the fact that it had paid the money to Cook with the consent of Sather was res judicata by virtue of the probate court's finding that she had made a gift of it to Cook. The trial court gave judgment for the defendant on this ground. The plaintiff appealed.]

■ TRAYNOR, J.

   . . . .

Plaintiff contends that the doctrine of res judicata does not apply because the defendant who is asserting the plea was not a party to the previous action nor in privity with a party to that action and because there is no mutuality of estoppel.

   . . . .

Many courts have stated the facile formula that the plea of res judicata is available only when there is privity and mutuality of estoppel. [Citations omitted.] Under the requirement of privity, only parties to the former judgment or their privies may take advantage of or be bound by it. . . . The estoppel is mutual if the one taking advantage of the earlier adjudication would have been bound by it, had it gone against him. [Citations omitted.]

The criteria for determining who may assert a plea of res judicata differ fundamentally from the criteria for determining against whom a plea of res judicata may be asserted. The requirements of due process of law forbid the assertion of a plea of res judicata against a party unless he was bound by the earlier litigation in which the matter was decided. [Citations omitted.] He is bound by that litigation only if he has been a party thereto or in privity with a party thereto. [Citation omitted.] There is no compelling reason, however, for requiring that the party asserting the plea of res judicata must have been a party, or in privity with a party, to the earlier litigation.

No satisfactory rationalization has been advanced for the requirement of mutuality. Just why a party who was not bound by a previous action should be precluded from asserting it as res judicata against a party who was bound by it is difficult to comprehend. (See 7 Bentham's Works (Bowring's ed.) 171.[b]) Many courts have abandoned the requirement of mutuality and confined the requirement of privity to the party against whom the plea of res judicata is asserted. (Coca-Cola Co. v. Pepsi-Cola Co., [36 Del. 124, 172 A. 260 (Super.Ct.1934)]; Liberty Mutual Ins. Co. v. George Colon & Co., 260 N.Y. 305, 183 N.E. 506; Atkinson v. White, 60 Me. 396;[c] Eagle, etc., Ins. Co. v. Heller, 149 Va. 82, 140 S.E. 314, 57 A.L.R. 490; Jenkins v. Atlantic Coast Line R. Co., 89 S.C. 408, 71 S.E. 1010; United States v. Wexler, 8 F.2d 880. See Good Health Dairy Food Products Corp. v. Emery, 275 N.Y. 14, 9 N.E.2d 758, 112 A.L.R. 401.) The commentators are almost unanimously in accord. [Citations omitted.] The courts of most jurisdictions have in effect accomplished the same result by recognizing a broad exception to the requirements of mutuality and privity, namely, that they are not necessary where the liability of the defendant asserting the plea of res judicata is dependent upon or derived from the liability of one who was exonerated in an earlier suit brought by the same plaintiff upon the same facts. [Citations omitted.] Typical examples of such derivative liability are master and servant, principal and agent, and indemnitor and indemnitee. Thus, if a plaintiff sues a servant for injuries caused by the servant's alleged negligence within the scope of his employment, a judgment against the plaintiff on the grounds that the servant was not negligent can be pleaded by the master as res judicata if he is subsequently sued by the same plaintiff for the same injuries. Conversely, if the plaintiff first sues the master, a judgment against the plaintiff on the grounds that the servant was not negligent can be pleaded by the servant as res judicata if he is subsequently sued by the plaintiff. In each of these situations the party asserting the plea of res judicata was not a party to the previous action nor in privity with such a party under the accepted definition of a privy . . . . Likewise, the estoppel is not mutual since the party asserting the plea, not having been a party or in privity with a party to the former

---

[b]   Bentham there attacked the rule of mutuality as "a maxim which one would suppose to have found its way from the gaming-table to the bench." But see Note, A Probabilistic Analysis of the Doctrine of Mutuality of Collateral Estoppel, 76 Mich.L.Rev. 612, 616 n.15 (1978) (noting that Bentham's book was proposing use of judgments as evidence, not for preclusion); Michael J. Waggoner, Fifty Years of Bernhard v. Bank of America Is Enough: Collateral Estoppel Should Require Mutuality but Res Judicata Should Not, 12 Rev.Litig. 391, 430–31 (1993) (noting that words were not Bentham's but his editor's, a very young John Stuart Mill).

[c]   In this 1872 case the court said, 60 Me. at 399: "[Mutuality] was adopted when parties could not be witnesses, and from a very tender care of suitors, lest by possibility injustice might be done. For it is said, and this appears to be the only reason on which the law is founded, that 'if the adverse party was not also a party to the judgment offered in evidence, it may have been obtained upon his own testimony; in which case, to allow him to derive benefit from it would be unjust.'"

action, would not have been bound by it had it been decided the other way. The cases justify this exception on the ground that it would be unjust to permit one who has had his day in court to reopen identical issues by merely switching adversaries.

    ... In re Estate of Smead, 219 Cal. 572, 28 P.2d 348; Silva v. Hawkins, 152 Cal. 138, 92 P. 72, and People v. Rodgers, 118 Cal. 393, 46 P. 740, 50 P. 668, to the extent that they are inconsistent with this opinion, are overruled.

    In the present case, therefore, the defendant is not precluded by lack of privity or of mutuality of estoppel from asserting the plea of res judicata against the plaintiff. Since the issue as to the ownership of the money is identical with the issue raised in the probate proceeding, and since the order of the probate court settling the executor's account was a final adjudication of this issue on the merits [citations omitted], it remains only to determine whether the plaintiff in the present action was a party or in privity with a party to the earlier proceeding. The plaintiff has brought the present action in the capacity of administratrix of the estate. In this capacity she represents the very same persons and interests that were represented in the earlier hearing on the executor's account. In that proceeding plaintiff and the other legatees who objected to the executor's account represented the estate of the decedent. They were seeking not a personal recovery but, like the plaintiff in the present action, as administratrix, a recovery for the benefit of the legatees and creditors of the estate, all of whom were bound by the order settling the account. (Prob.Code, sec. 931. See cases cited in 12 Cal.Jur. 62, 63.) The plea of res judicata is therefore available against plaintiff as a party to the former proceeding, despite her formal change of capacity. . . .

    The judgment is affirmed.

    Nonmutual collateral estoppel's rule.—The immediate impact of Justice Traynor's root-and-branch demolition of mutuality was not significant. But later it came to have widespread repercussions in many states, thanks in no small part to an influential article by Professor Brainerd Currie, Mutuality of Collateral Estoppel: Limits of the Bernhard Doctrine, 9 Stan.L.Rev. 281 (1957).

    The notion that a party ought not to enjoy the luxury of a second trial on an issue he has already litigated and lost had growing appeal in days of crowded dockets and increased costs of maintaining the judicial system.

    Nonetheless, the litigation-saving aspect of the Bernhard rule is not as obvious as it superficially appears. If courts completely abrogate mutuality, an adverse judgment will preclude a party on every litigated and determined issue essential to the judgment with respect to *all* persons; consequently, a prudent litigant may feel bound to fight a case to the utmost in both trial and appellate courts, even though he would treat the case or a particular issue less determinedly if its sole effects regarded the immediate adversaries and their privies. Also, extending nonmutuality has complicated the law, routinely producing litigation about whether to preclude relitigation. The effect on the volume of litigation is thus not susceptible of clear proof. We just do not know.

Moreover, there are concerns of basic fairness cutting both ways, as we soon shall see. See also James Wm. Moore & Thomas S. Currier, Mutuality and Conclusiveness of Judgments, 35 Tul.L.Rev. 301 (1961), which gives a stout defense of the doctrine of mutuality with "certain dispensing exceptions shown to be sound by theory and experience."

So, in this darkness, how far should the law go with Bernhard's disputable approach? Most of the courts influenced by Bernhard have stopped short of accepting the full sweep of Justice Traynor's dictum. There has, however, been a contrariety of views as to where the proper stopping point is. To explore this question, the four possible patterns in which the question arises deserve separate consideration. (For convenience, P = plaintiff in first action; D = defendant in first action; NP = new plaintiff, not a party or privy to first action; and ND = new defendant, not a party or privy to first action.)

1. P sues D, D wins. Then loser P sues ND. Can ND use collateral estoppel?

This is the strongest case for collateral estoppel. P chose the court and the adversary in the first action. (How important is this?) P now tries again against a new adversary, who wants to use the prior judgment defensively. This category includes Coca-Cola Co. v. Pepsi-Cola Co.

Question: (5) Is it fair to Coca-Cola to use against it in an action against Pepsi-Cola its defeat in a suit against a small dealer, who would presumably have had the factfinder's sympathy? When a party has had a day in court, is it relevant to ask, "A day in court against whom?" Indeed, because traditionally an adjudication is an often close decision of a specific dispute involving particular litigants, where special factors off the merits may influence the outcome, could not one say generally that fairness requires a day in court against the present opponent? Or instead should one say that adjudication yields a free-floating truth?

2. P sues D, P wins. Then loser D sues ND. Can ND use collateral estoppel?

This situation also involves a defensive use of collateral estoppel, the difference being that here the party to the prior action did not have the initiative and so did not choose the court or the adversary in that action.

Question: (6) Driver's car collides with a car driven by T. A passenger in Driver's car sues T and wins (T negligent). Then T sues Driver. Is it just to preclude T on the issue of her contributory negligence? What of the jury's likely sympathy for the first plaintiff, or indeed for most plaintiffs?

3. P sues D, D wins. Then NP sues loser P. Can NP use collateral estoppel?

This is offensive use of collateral estoppel. (Is the difference between using a prior judgment as a sword rather than as a shield significant?) Note that *P*, the party against whom collateral estoppel is invoked, chose the court and the adversary in the first action.

Question: (7) *T* sues Driver and loses (*T* contributorily negligent). Then a passenger in Driver's car sues *T*. Is it just to preclude *T* on the issue of her negligence? Is this a harder case than the preceding situation to justify the use of collateral estoppel?

4.   *P* sues *D, P* wins. Then *NP* sues loser *D.* Can *NP* use collateral estoppel?

This is the hardest case of all for collateral estoppel. *NP* wants to use the prior judgment offensively, and here the party to the prior action did not choose the court or the adversary in that action. This situation encompasses the favorite classroom hypothetical case called by Professor Currie the multiple-claimant anomaly. Assume there are forty passengers injured in a bus accident. If *P-1* sues the bus company and loses, presumably no other passenger can be bound by the result (see the Neenan case). So if *P-2, P-3,* and *P-4* all also sue and lose, but *P-5* has the good fortune to win, does this mean that *P-6* through *P-40* can win by collateral estoppel? If so, bear in mind that plaintiffs who might normally join in a single action would have strong incentive to hang back and hope for a case with a favorable result. Bear in mind also the likely tactic of planning the first suit to be on behalf of the most appealing of the potential plaintiffs.

Question: (8) Is there a practical way to take care of this anomaly? What of denying collateral estoppel effect to a later plaintiff if the bus company has prevailed in any of the prior actions? That seems to be a good but incomplete approach. To handle the situation where *P-1* won, should the law also deny collateral estoppel effect if there has been only one plaintiff victory so far? See Aaron Gershonowitz, Issue Preclusion: The Return of the Multiple Claimant Anomaly, 14 U.Balt.L.Rev. 227 (1985).

Nonmutual collateral estoppel's exceptions.—Many modern cases have extended preclusion to all four of those patterns. But even Justice Traynor balked at giving unrestricted effect to his own dictum. There have to be exceptions.

In the case of Taylor v. Hawkinson, 47 Cal.2d 893, 306 P.2d 797 (1957), Mr. Taylor obtained a verdict of $63.06 for property damage, the driver of his car won $65.00 for personal injuries, and Mrs. Taylor won $371.94 for personal injuries. Only Mrs. Taylor moved for a new trial for insufficiency of damages, and she succeeded on her motion. Thereafter the judgment for the other plaintiffs became final. Mrs. Taylor then sought to limit her retrial to damages, on the ground that the Bernhard rule precluded the issue of liability. Nevertheless, the trial court submitted all issues to the jury, which returned a verdict for the defendant. The judgment thereon was affirmed. Justice Traynor, for the court, said: "There is ample evidence to support the trial court's implied finding that the verdicts following the first trial were compromise verdicts and that the jury did not determine the issue of liability." Justice Carter, alone in dissent, said: "It is no answer to say that the judgment is not res judicata because being based on a compromise verdict the issue of liability was not determined. [Citation omitted.] If the jury did not decide that issue, it decided nothing, and the judgment entered on its verdict would not be binding on the parties thereto. To say it did not decide the issue is to ignore the pleadings, verdict and judgment, and to permit a collateral attack on the judgment which is not permitted."

Questions: (9) Does the Taylor holding mean that the first trial is always subject to reexamination to see whether the verdict appears to have been a compromise?

(10) Early on, there was some tendency to draw the line between defensive and offensive use of nonmutual collateral estoppel, allowing only the former. E.g., Albernaz v. City of Fall River, 346 Mass. 336, 191 N.E.2d 771 (1963). Is such a rule a more desirable solution than the flexibility implicit in the Taylor exception? See Aetna Cas. & Sur. Co. v. Niziolek, 395 Mass. 737, 481 N.E.2d 1356 (1985) (abandoning the Albernaz line).

Blonder-Tongue Laboratories v. University of Illinois Foundation

Supreme Court of the United States, 1971.
402 U.S. 313, 91 S.Ct. 1434.

[The rule in patent infringement cases in the federal courts had been, ever since Triplett v. Lowell, 297 U.S. 638, 56 S.Ct. 645 (1936), that a determination of invalidity of a patent in an action by the patentee against an alleged infringer did not preclude the patentee in a second action against another alleged infringer. Triplett was decided late in the heyday of the mutuality doctrine.

[In the present case, the lower courts followed Triplett to permit the Foundation, as patentee, to maintain and win a second action after losing its first action. But, on certiorari, the Supreme Court undertook sua sponte to reexamine Triplett.]

■ MR. JUSTICE WHITE delivered the opinion for a unanimous Court.

. . . .

The cases and authorities discussed above connect erosion of the mutuality requirement to the goal of limiting relitigation of issues where that can be achieved without compromising fairness in particular cases. The courts have often discarded the rule while commenting on crowded dockets and long delays preceding trial. Authorities differ on whether the public interest in efficient judicial administration is a sufficient ground in and of itself for abandoning mutuality, but it is clear that more than crowded dockets is involved. The broader question is whether it is any longer tenable to afford a litigant more than one full and fair opportunity for judicial resolution of the same issue. The question in these terms includes as part of the calculus the effect on judicial administration, but it also encompasses the concern exemplified by Bentham's reference to the gaming table in his attack on the principle of mutuality of estoppel. In any lawsuit where a defendant, because of the mutuality principle, is forced to present a complete defense on the merits to a claim which the plaintiff has fully litigated and lost in a prior action, there is an arguable misallocation of resources. To the extent the defendant in the second suit may not win by asserting, without contradiction, that the plaintiff had fully and fairly, but unsuccessfully, litigated the same claim in the prior suit, the defendant's time and money are diverted from alternative uses—productive or otherwise—to relitigation of a decided issue. And, still assuming that the issue was resolved correctly in the first suit, there is reason to be concerned about the plaintiff's allocation of resources. Permitting repeated litigation of the same issue as long as the supply of unrelated defendants holds out reflects either the aura of the gaming table or "a lack of discipline and of disinterestedness on the part of the lower courts, hardly a worthy or wise basis for fashioning rules of procedure." Kerotest Mfg. Co. v. C-O-Two Co., 342 U.S. 180, 185, 72 S.Ct. 219, 222 (1952). Although neither judges, the parties, nor the adversary system performs perfectly in all cases, the requirement of determining whether the party against whom an estoppel is asserted had a full and fair opportunity to litigate is a most significant safeguard.

Some litigants—those who never appeared in a prior action—may not be collaterally estopped without litigating the issue. They have never had a chance to present their evidence and arguments on the claim. Due process prohibits estopping them despite one or more existing adjudications of the identical issue which stand squarely against their position. See Hansberry v. Lee, 311 U.S. 32, 40, 61 S.Ct. 115, 117 (1940); Bernhard [v. Bank of Am. Nat'l Trust & Sav. Ass'n, 19 Cal.2d 807, 811, 122 P.2d 892, 894 (1942)]. Also, the authorities have been more willing to permit a defendant in a second suit to invoke an estoppel against a plaintiff who lost on the same claim in an earlier suit than they have been to allow a plaintiff in the second suit to use offensively a judgment obtained by a different plaintiff in a prior suit against the same defendant. But the case before us involves neither due process nor "offensive use" questions. Rather, it depends on the considerations weighing for and against permitting a patent holder to sue on his patent after it has once been held invalid following opportunity for full and fair trial.

[The Court concluded (1) that the Triplett rule was not essential to effectuate the purposes of the patent system; (2) that the economic costs of continuing adherence to Triplett were substantial in terms of (a) costs to both sides of repetitive litigation and (b) economic disruption flowing from the multiple opportunities for holders of invalid patents to exact licensing agreements from alleged infringers, who will often pay royalties under a license rather than bear the costly burden of challenging the patent; and (3) that although any burden placed on the judiciary by Triplett was an incidental matter in comparison to the other economic costs of following Triplett, its abrogation would save some judicial time, if collateral estoppel fairly disposed of even a few relatively lengthy patent suits.]

Moreover, we do not suggest, without legislative guidance, that a plea of estoppel by an infringement or royalty suit defendant must automatically be accepted once the defendant in support of his plea identifies the issue in suit as the identical question finally decided against the patentee or one of his privies in previous litigation. Rather, the patentee-plaintiff must be permitted to demonstrate, if he can, that he did not have "a fair opportunity procedurally, substantively and evidentially to pursue his claim the first time." Eisel v. Columbia Packing Co., 181 F.Supp. 298, 301 (Mass.1960). This element in the estoppel decision will comprehend, we believe, the important concerns about the complexity of patent litigation and the posited hazard that the prior proceedings were seriously defective.

Determining whether a patentee has had a full and fair chance to litigate the validity of his patent in an earlier case is of necessity not a simple matter. In addition to the considerations of choice of forum and incentive to litigate . . . , certain other factors immediately emerge. For example, . . . appropriate inquiries would be . . . whether the opinions filed by the District Court and the reviewing court, if any, indicate that the prior case was one of those relatively rare instances where the courts wholly failed to grasp the technical subject matter and issues in suit; and whether without fault of his own the patentee was deprived of crucial evidence or witnesses in the first litigation. But as so often is the case, no one set of facts, no one collection of words or phrases, will provide an automatic formula for proper rulings on estoppel pleas. In the end, decision will necessarily rest on the trial courts' sense of justice and equity.

. . . .

It is clear that judicial decisions have tended to depart from the rigid requirements of mutuality. In accordance with this trend, there has been a corresponding development of the lower courts' ability and facility in dealing with questions of when it is appropriate and fair to impose an estoppel against a party who has already litigated an issue once and lost. As one commentator has stated:

> "Under the tests of time and subsequent developments, the Bernhard decision has proved its merit and the mettle of its author. The abrasive action of new factual configurations and of actual human controversies, disposed of in the common-law tradition by competent courts, far more than the commentaries of academicians, leaves the decision revealed for what it is, as it

was written: a shining landmark of progress in justice and law administration." Currie, [Civil Procedure: The Tempest Brews, 53 Calif.L.Rev. 25, 37 (1965)].

. . . [I]t is apparent that the uncritical acceptance of the principle of mutuality of estoppel expressed in Triplett v. Lowell is today out of place. Thus, we conclude that Triplett should be overruled to the extent it forecloses a plea of estoppel by one facing a charge of infringement of a patent that has once been declared invalid.

. . . .

Res judicata and collateral estoppel are affirmative defenses that must be pleaded. Fed.Rule Civ.Proc. 8(c). The purpose of such pleading is to give the opposing party notice of the plea of estoppel and a chance to argue, if he can, why the imposition of an estoppel would be inappropriate. Because of Triplett v. Lowell, petitioner did not plead estoppel and [the Foundation] never had an opportunity to challenge the appropriateness of such a plea on the grounds [that the patentee did not have "a full and fair chance to litigate the validity of his patent" in the prior case]. Petitioner should be allowed to amend its pleadings in the District Court to assert a plea of estoppel. [The Foundation] must then be permitted to . . . supplement the record with any evidence showing why an estoppel should not be imposed in this case. If necessary, petitioner may also supplement the record. In taking this action, we intimate no views on the other issues presented in this case. The judgment of the Court of Appeals is vacated and the cause is remanded to the District Court for further proceedings consistent with this opinion.[d]

Parklane Hosiery Co. v. Shore

Supreme Court of the United States, 1979.
439 U.S. 322, 99 S.Ct. 645.

■ MR. JUSTICE STEWART delivered the opinion of the Court.

This case presents the question whether a party who has had issues of fact adjudicated adversely to it in an equitable action may be collaterally estopped from relitigating the same issues before a jury in a subsequent legal action brought against it by a new party.

The respondent brought this stockholder's class action against the petitioners in a federal district court. The complaint alleged that the petitioners, Parklane Hosiery Company, Inc. (Parklane) and 12 of its officers, directors, and stockholders, had issued a materially false and

---

[d]   Upon remand, the same district judge found that the Foundation failed to make the requisite showing to escape the defense of estoppel and entered summary judgment for the defendant, 334 F.Supp. 47 (N.D.Ill.1971) (Hoffman, J.), aff'd per curiam, 465 F.2d 380 (7th Cir.), cert. denied, 409 U.S. 1061, 93 S.Ct. 559 (1972).

misleading proxy statement in connection with a merger. The proxy statement, according to the complaint, had violated [various federal securities laws]. The complaint sought damages, rescission of the merger, and recovery of costs.

Before this action came to trial, the SEC filed suit against the same defendants in a federal district court, alleging that the proxy statement that had been issued by Parklane was materially false and misleading in essentially the same respects as those that had been alleged in the respondent's complaint. Injunctive relief was requested. After a four-day trial, the District Court found that the proxy statement was materially false and misleading in the respects alleged, and entered a declaratory judgment to that effect. Securities and Exchange Commission v. Parklane Hosiery Co., 422 F.Supp. 477. The Court of Appeals for the Second Circuit affirmed this judgment. 558 F.2d 1083.

The respondent in the present case then moved for partial summary judgment against the petitioners, asserting that the petitioners were collaterally estopped from relitigating the issues that had been resolved against them in the action brought by the SEC.[2] The District Court denied the motion on the ground that such an application of collateral estoppel would deny the petitioners their Seventh Amendment right to a jury trial. The Court of Appeals for the Second Circuit reversed, holding that a party who has had issues of fact determined against him after a full and fair opportunity to litigate in a nonjury trial is collaterally estopped from obtaining a subsequent jury trial of these same issues of fact. 565 F.2d 815. The appellate court concluded that "the Seventh Amendment preserves the right to jury trial only with respect to issues of fact, [and] once those issues have been fully and fairly adjudicated in a prior proceeding, nothing remains for trial, either with or without a jury." Id., at 819. Because of an intercircuit conflict, we granted certiorari. 435 U.S. 1006, 98 S.Ct. 1875.

I

The threshold question to be considered is whether, quite apart from the right to a jury trial under the Seventh Amendment, the petitioners can be precluded from relitigating facts resolved adversely to them in a prior equitable proceeding with another party under the general law of collateral estoppel. Specifically, we must determine whether a litigant who was not a party to a prior judgment may nevertheless use that judgment "offensively" to prevent a defendant from relitigating issues resolved in the earlier proceeding.

---

[2]   A private plaintiff in an action under the proxy rules is not entitled to relief simply by demonstrating that the proxy solicitation was materially false and misleading. The plaintiff must also show that he was injured and prove damages. [Citation omitted.] Since the SEC action was limited to a determination of whether the proxy statements contained materially false and misleading statements, the respondent conceded that he would still have to prove these other elements of his prima facie case in the private action. The petitioners' right to a jury trial on those remaining issues is not contested.

A

[The Court here reviewed the rejection of the mutuality requirement by the Blonder-Tongue decision.]

B

The Blonder-Tongue case involved defensive use of collateral estoppel—a plaintiff was estopped from asserting a claim that the plaintiff had previously litigated and lost against another defendant. The present case, by contrast, involves offensive use of collateral estoppel—a plaintiff is seeking to estop a defendant from relitigating the issues which the defendant previously litigated and lost against another plaintiff. In both the offensive and defensive use situations, the party against whom estoppel is asserted has litigated and lost in an earlier action. Nevertheless, several reasons have been advanced why the two situations should be treated differently.

First, offensive use of collateral estoppel does not promote judicial economy in the same manner as defensive use does. Defensive use of collateral estoppel precludes a plaintiff from relitigating identical issues by merely "switching adversaries." Bernhard v. Bank of America Nat. Trust & Savings Assn., 19 Cal.2d 807, 813, 122 P.2d 892, 895 (1942). Thus defensive collateral estoppel gives a plaintiff a strong incentive to join all potential defendants in the first action if possible. Offensive use of collateral estoppel, on the other hand, creates precisely the opposite incentive. Since a plaintiff will be able to rely on a previous judgment against a defendant but will not be bound by that judgment if the defendant wins, the plaintiff has every incentive to adopt a "wait and see" attitude, in the hope that the first action by another plaintiff will result in a favorable judgment. [Citations omitted.] Thus offensive use of collateral estoppel will likely increase rather than decrease the total amount of litigation, since potential plaintiffs will have everything to gain and nothing to lose by not intervening in the first action.

A second argument against offensive use of collateral estoppel is that it may be unfair to a defendant. If a defendant in the first action is sued for small or nominal damages, he may have little incentive to defend vigorously, particularly if future suits are not foreseeable. Evergreens v. Nunan, 141 F.2d 927, 929; cf. Berner v. British Commonwealth Pac. Airlines, 346 F.2d 532 (application of offensive collateral estoppel denied where defendant did not appeal an adverse judgment awarding damages of $35,000 and defendant was later sued for over $7 million). Allowing offensive collateral estoppel may also be unfair to a defendant if the judgment relied upon as a basis for the estoppel is itself inconsistent with one or more previous judgments in favor of the defendant. Still another situation where it might be unfair to apply offensive estoppel is where the second action affords the defendant procedural opportunities unavailable in the first action that could readily cause a different result.[15]

C

We have concluded that the preferable approach for dealing with these problems in the federal courts is not to preclude the use of offensive collateral estoppel, but to grant trial courts broad discretion to determine when it should be applied. The general rule should be that in cases where a plaintiff could easily have joined in the earlier action or where, either for the reasons discussed above or for other reasons, the application of offensive estoppel would be unfair to a defendant, a trial judge should not allow the use of offensive collateral estoppel.

In the present case, however, none of the circumstances that might justify reluctance to allow the offensive use of collateral estoppel is present. The application of offensive collateral estoppel will not here reward a private plaintiff who could have joined in the previous action, since the respondent probably could not have joined in the injunctive action brought by the SEC even had he so desired.[17] Similarly, there is no unfairness to the petitioners in applying offensive collateral estoppel in this case. First, in light of the serious allegations made in the SEC's complaint against the petitioners, as well as the foreseeability of subsequent private suits that typically follow a successful government judgment, the petitioners had every incentive to litigate the SEC lawsuit fully and vigorously. Second, the judgment in the Commission action was not inconsistent with any previous decision. Finally, there will in the respondent's action be no procedural opportunities available to the petitioners that were unavailable in the first action of a kind that might be likely to cause a different result.[19]

We conclude, therefore, that none of the considerations that would justify a refusal to allow the use of offensive collateral estoppel is present in this case. Since the petitioners received a "full and fair" opportunity to

---

[15]   If, for example, the defendant in the first action was forced to defend in an inconvenient forum and therefore was unable to engage in full scale discovery or call witnesses, application of offensive collateral estoppel may be unwarranted. Indeed, differences in available procedures may sometimes justify not allowing a prior judgment to have estoppel effect in a subsequent action even between the same parties, or where defensive estoppel is asserted against a plaintiff who has litigated and lost. The problem of unfairness is particularly acute in cases of offensive estoppel, however, because the defendant against whom estoppel is asserted typically will not have chosen the forum in the first action. See Restatement (Second) of Judgments (Tent. Draft No. 2, 1975) § 88(2) and Comment d.

[17]   Securities and Exchange Commission v. Everest Management Corp., 475 F.2d 1236, 1240 ("the complicating effect of the additional issues and the additional parties outweighs any advantage of a single disposition of the common issues"). Moreover, consolidation of a private action with one brought by the SEC without its consent is prohibited by statute. 15 U.S.C. § 78u(g).

[19]   It is true, of course, that the petitioners in the present action would be entitled to a jury trial of the issues bearing on whether the proxy statement was materially false and misleading had the SEC action never been brought—a matter to be discussed in Part II of this opinion. [And the petitioners did not have a right to a jury trial in the equitable suit brought by the SEC.—Ed.] But the presence or absence of a jury as factfinder is basically neutral, quite unlike, for example, the necessity of defending the first lawsuit in an inconvenient forum.

litigate their claims in the SEC action, the contemporary law of collateral estoppel leads inescapably to the conclusion that the petitioners are collaterally estopped from relitigating the question of whether the proxy statements were materially false and misleading.

II

The question that remains is whether, notwithstanding the law of collateral estoppel, the use of offensive collateral estoppel in this case would violate the petitioners' Seventh Amendment right to a jury trial.

[The Court here rejected the petitioners' argument and affirmed the court of appeals. The Court ruled that because in 1791 an equitable determination could have collateral estoppel effect in a subsequent legal action, such estoppel by itself entails no violation of the Seventh Amendment. And even though England in 1791 permitted collateral estoppel only when there was mutuality, collateral estoppel is permissible in the circumstances of this case because the Seventh Amendment's protection of the fundamental elements of the jury right did not mandate the exact procedural incidents and details associated with jury trial in 1791 and so did not inhibit the subsequent evolution of collateral estoppel.]

■ [The decision drew a passionate dissent from JUSTICE REHNQUIST. He argued that the majority was condoning a violation of the Seventh Amendment by permitting nonmutual collateral estoppel to destroy a jury right. Moreover, he argued that simply as a matter of res judicata law, collateral estoppel should be denied here because it "runs counter to the strong federal policy favoring jury trials" and because "the opportunity for a jury trial in the second action could easily lead to a different result from that obtained in the first action before the court and therefore . . . it is unfair to estop petitioners from relitigating the issues before a jury." He closed by observing:]

The ultimate irony of today's decision is that its potential for significantly conserving the resources of either the litigants or the judiciary is doubtful at best. . . . It is . . . probable that today's decision will have the result of coercing defendants to agree to consent orders or settlements in agency enforcement action in order to preserve their right to jury trial in the private actions. In that event, the Court, for no compelling reason, will have simply added a powerful club to the administrative agencies' arsenals that even Congress was unwilling to provide them.[e]

––––––––––

Question: (11) What would have happened if the district court had invoked its "discretion" to determine that collateral estoppel should not apply

––––––––––

[e]   For the background story of the Parklane case, see Lewis A. Grossman, "The Story of Parklane: The 'Litigation Crisis' and the Efficiency Imperative," in Civil Procedure Stories 405, 436 (Kevin M. Clermont ed., 2d ed. 2008) (noting that the parties eventually settled the class action for $258,000).

on the ground that the petitioners had not had a full and fair opportunity to litigate, instead of resting on the jury right? That is, what should be the scope of the trial court's discretion in this context? See Wright & Miller § 4465, at 713–15 (showing that appellate courts differ).

————

Rethinking of nonmutual collateral estoppel.—Restatement (Second) of Judgments § 29 (Am. Law Inst. 1982) provides that issue preclusion, subject to all its usual requirements and exceptions, may be invoked by a nonparty against a party to the prior action, "unless the fact that he lacked full and fair opportunity to litigate the issue in the first action or other circumstances justify affording him an opportunity to relitigate the issue." The section goes on to mention some of the numerous such circumstances that should be considered as factors in applying this exception, including whether the nonparty could have joined in the prior action, whether the prior determination is itself inconsistent with some other determination of the same issue, whether relationships among the parties to the first action that are absent in the second seem to have affected the prior determination, and whether preclusion may complicate the second action or prejudice another party thereto. Indeed, the final sentence of the reporter's note thereon states: "The ultimate question is whether there is good reason, all things considered, to allow the party to relitigate the issue."

Questions: (12) Is the purpose of res judicata in putting an end to litigation defeated by such an approach that invites litigation over whether to apply res judicata? Might one argue that we would be better off with the bare minimum of preclusion than with a flexible doctrine of res judicata? See generally Maurice J. Holland, Modernizing Res Judicata: Reflections on the Parklane Doctrine, 55 Ind.L.J. 615 (1980).

(13) More specifically, was not the mutuality rule with a few defined extensions of preclusion (such as in secondary-liability circumstances) preferable in terms of workability to the Second Restatement's more extensive preclusion that requires fuzzy exceptions entailing case-by-case inquiry into fairness and efficiency? Cf. Janet S. Ellis, Note, Nonmutuality: Taking the Fairness Out of Collateral Estoppel, 13 Ind.L.Rev. 563, 596 (1980) ("Perhaps all nonmutuality runs too great a risk of unfairness because fairness cannot be unerringly determined. If fairness is the prime concern of courts, then requiring mutuality may be the best method of meeting this concern. Mutuality guarantees fairness to the party by restricting the effect of the judgment to parties with whom the original party has actually litigated. A nonparty who has not litigated has lost nothing when he is denied the use of a judgment for lack of mutuality.").

————

UNITED STATES v. MENDOZA, 464 U.S. 154, 104 S.Ct. 568 (1984). By a 1975 decision of the District Court for the Northern District of California, a number of Filipino war veterans established that the United States had denied them due process by its spotty administration of the statute regarding the naturalization in the Philippines in 1945 and 1946 of noncitizens who had served in the American armed forces during World War II, a decision the United States did not appeal.

In 1978, another Filipino war veteran petitioned for naturalization. Sergio Mendoza was now an elderly resident of the U.S. subject to deportation, but he had served as an army doctor until he was captured by the Japanese, and he had then survived their notorious Bataan Death March. The District Court for the Central District of California and the Court of Appeals for the Ninth Circuit held that the prior decision collaterally estopped the United States on the constitutional issue. On certiorari, a unanimous Supreme Court reversed, holding that "nonmutual offensive collateral estoppel is not to be extended to the United States." Justice Rehnquist explained for the Court:

"We have long recognized that 'the Government is not in a position identical to that of a private litigant,' INS v. Hibi, 414 U.S. 5, 8, 94 S.Ct. 19, 21 (1973) (per curiam), both because of the geographic breadth of government litigation and also, most importantly, because of the nature of the issues the government litigates. It is not open to serious dispute that the government is a party to a far greater number of cases on a nationwide basis than even the most litigious private entity; in 1982, the United States was a party to more than 75,000 of the 206,193 [civil] filings in the United States District Courts. Administrative Office of the United States Courts, Annual Report of the Director 98 (1982). In the same year the United States was a party to just under 30% of the civil cases appealed from the District Courts to the Court of Appeals. Id., at 79, 82. Government litigation frequently involves legal questions of substantial public importance; indeed, because the proscriptions of the United States Constitution are so generally directed at governmental action, many constitutional questions can arise only in the context of litigation to which the government is a party. Because of those facts the government is more likely than any private party to be involved in lawsuits against different parties which nonetheless involve the same legal issues.

"A rule allowing nonmutual collateral estoppel against the government in such cases would substantially thwart the development of important questions of law by freezing the first final decision rendered on a particular legal issue. Allowing only one final adjudication would deprive this Court of the benefit it receives from permitting several courts of appeals to explore a difficult question before this Court grants certiorari. [Citations omitted.] Indeed, if nonmutual estoppel were routinely applied against the government, this Court would have to revise its practice of waiting for a conflict to develop before granting the government's petitions for certiorari. See Sup.Ct.R. [10].

"The Solicitor General's policy for determining when to appeal an adverse decision would also require substantial revision. The Court of Appeals faulted the government in this case for failing to appeal a decision that it now contends is erroneous. . . . But the government's litigation conduct in a case is apt to differ from that of a private litigant. Unlike a private litigant who generally does not forego an appeal if he believes that he can prevail, the Solicitor General considers a variety of factors, such as the limited resources of the government and the crowded dockets of the courts, before authorizing an appeal. Brief for the United States, at 30–31. The application of nonmutual estoppel against the government would force the Solicitor General to abandon those prudential concerns and to appeal every adverse decision in order to avoid foreclosing further review.

"In addition to those institutional concerns traditionally considered by the Solicitor General, the panoply of important public issues raised in governmental litigation may quite properly lead successive Administrations of the Executive Branch to take differing positions with respect to the resolution of a particular issue. While the Executive Branch must of course defer to the Judicial Branch for final resolution of questions of constitutional law, the former nonetheless controls the progress of government litigation through the federal courts. It would be idle to pretend that the conduct of government litigation in all its myriad features, from the decision to file a complaint in the United States District Court to the decision to petition for certiorari to review a judgment of the Court of Appeals, is a wholly mechanical procedure which involves no policy choices whatever.

     . . . .

"The Court of Appeals did not endorse a routine application of nonmutual collateral estoppel against the government, because it recognized that the government does litigate issues of far-reaching national significance which in some cases, it concluded, might warrant relitigation. But in this case it found no 'record evidence' indicating that there was a 'crucial need' in the administration of the immigration laws for a redetermination of the due process question decided in [the 1975 case] and presented again in this case. . . . The Court of Appeals did not make clear what sort of 'record evidence' would have satisfied it that there *was* a 'crucial need' for redetermination of the question in this case, but we pretermit further discussion of that approach; we believe that the standard announced by the Court of Appeals for determining when relitigation of a legal issue is to be permitted is so wholly subjective that it affords no guidance to the courts or to the government. Such a standard leaves the government at sea because it can not possibly anticipate, in determining whether or not to appeal an adverse decision, whether a court will bar relitigation of the issue in a later case. . . .

"We hold, therefore, that nonmutual offensive collateral estoppel simply does not apply against the government in such a way as to preclude relitigation of issues such as those involved in this case. The conduct of government litigation in the courts of the United States is sufficiently different from the conduct of private civil litigation in those courts so that what might otherwise be economy interests underlying a broad application of collateral estoppel are outweighed by the constraints which peculiarly affect the government. We think that our conclusion will better allow thorough development of legal doctrine by allowing litigation in multiple forums. Indeed, a contrary result might disserve the economy interests in whose name estoppel is advanced by requiring the government to abandon virtually any exercise of discretion in seeking to review judgments unfavorable to it. . . .

"Our holding in this case is consistent with each of our prior holdings to which the parties have called our attention, and which we reaffirm. Today in a companion case we hold that the government may be estopped under certain circumstances from relitigating a question when the parties to the two lawsuits are the same. United States v. Stauffer Chemical Co., 464 U.S. 165, 104 S.Ct. 575 (1984); see also Montana v. United States, [440 U.S. 147, 99 S.Ct. 970 (1979)]; United States v. Moser, 266 U.S. 236, 45 S.Ct. 66 (1924). . . .

"The concerns underlying our disapproval of collateral estoppel against the government are for the most part inapplicable where mutuality is present, as in Stauffer Chemical, Montana, and Moser. The application of an estoppel when the government is litigating the same issue with the same party avoids the problem of freezing the development of the law because the government is still free to litigate that issue in the future with some other party. And, where the parties are the same, estopping the government spares a party that has already prevailed once from having to relitigate—a function it would not serve in the present circumstances. We accordingly hold that the Court of Appeals was wrong in applying nonmutual collateral estoppel against the government in this case."

———

Question: (14) Congress can get involved. On the one hand, six years later it bestowed citizenship on the Filipino war veterans directly. See Antonio Raimundo, Comment, The Filipino Veterans Equity Movement: A Case Study in Reparations Theory, 98 Calif.L.Rev. 575 (2010). On the other hand, and with a totally different impulse, some versions of the proposed Federal Product Liability Act, which would have supplanted state law, forbade preclusion on issues of fact between different claimants' products liability actions "unless both actions were based on harm caused by the same event in which two or more persons were harmed." E.g., S. 2631, 97th Cong., 2d Sess. § 4(d) (1982). What do you think of that proposal? See Michael D. Green, The Inability of Offensive Collateral Estoppel to Fulfill Its Promise: An Examination of Estoppel in Asbestos Litigation, 70 Iowa L.Rev. 141 (1984).

———

Note, A Probabilistic Analysis of the Doctrine of Mutuality of Collateral Estoppel

76 Mich.L.Rev. 612, 619, 622–24, 640–43, 645, 679 (1978).

Using probability theory as an aid to analysis, this Note will demonstrate that the mutuality doctrine is designed to allocate trial risks in a manner consistent with the burden of persuasion in civil litigation. Thus, the abandonment of mutuality strikes at the heart of the trial process. Where a single party (hereinafter the "common party") faces multiple opponents on a common question, the abandonment of mutuality can significantly alter the common party's probability of success. Bernhard thus amounts to little more than an instruction to the trier of fact to find against the common party simply because he is the common party, a fact entirely unrelated to the merits of the case.

. . . .

. . . [T]he burden of persuasion in civil litigation embodies a strategy designed to minimize the number of erroneous verdicts. . . . Absent some peculiar and cognizable virtue inhering in one of the parties, there is no reason to prefer an error in one direction over an error in the other. Consequently, the preponderance-of-the-evidence test instructs the factfinder to follow the error-minimizing strategy to choose the verdict most likely to be the truth. . . . The burden of persuasion is thus not merely a rule of convenience to be discarded or modified lightly. It embodies the fundamental assumption of civil litigation that, without regard to the merits, neither party is the more deserving of a favorable judgment.

. . . .

The central theme of mutuality is the fair apportionment of trial risks. By potentially precluding either party (if both would have been bound) or neither party (if either party would not have been bound), mutuality allows litigation risks to reflect only the merits of the cases. The abandonment of mutuality alters the litigation risks by forcing only one party to face the potential of preclusion in subsequent litigation, thus shifting additional risks to that party. In addition to altering the distribution of risks between the parties, the Bernhard doctrine affects the measure of trial efficacy by generally increasing the error rate.

To see more clearly and to what extent mutuality and Bernhard affect the allocation of litigation risks, consider the result in two hypothetical multiple litigation situations that differ only with respect to the presence or absence of the mutuality requirement. Because Currie initially suggested that Bernhard produces no objectionable results when the common party is the protagonist, as have other commentators, it will be assumed in both hypotheticals that a common party plaintiff seeks to assert related claims[80] against a series of defendants. As will become apparent, this assumption does not affect the alteration of trial risks produced by Bernhard.

Assume also that the plaintiff has a fifty percent probability of winning his case, that is, that if the case were tried indefinitely, the plaintiff would be successful fifty per cent of the time. . . . It is assumed that the plaintiff has ten claims, each liquidated in the amount of $100. . . .

[The Note's author, David Gruber, thus makes a number of assumptions to create a model. The aim is to see if, all else being held equal, nonmutual collateral estoppel has a tendency—one effect among many, but one overlooked in prior simplistic analyses of fairness and efficiency—to stack the odds against one party. He also assumes that nonmutual collateral estoppel is "operating mechanically," an assumption that increases the size of the effect but not its direction.]

Finally, assume that no defendant is in privity with any other defendant, so that under the traditional mutuality doctrine, as well as under Bernhard, the common party plaintiff will not be able to use a favorable judgment against one defendant to preclude any other defendant from relitigating the common issue. Given this set of assumptions, if each case is tried separately and preclusive effect is denied for lack of mutuality, all ten cases will be litigated. By hypothesis, the plaintiff can expect to win fifty percent of his cases for a total expected recovery of $500. This result is illustrated in the mutuality column of Table I.

---

[80]   "Related claims" denotes claims with a sufficient common basis to create a collateral estoppel problem. For the sake of simplicity, it is assumed that the common questions are dispositive of each case.

TABLE I

				Mutuality		**Bernhard**	
Trial	Recovery if win trial	Probability of winning trial	Expected Recovery	Cumulative Expected Recovery	Probability of winning trial	Expected Recovery	Cumulative Expected Recovery
1	$100	.5	$50	$50	.500	$50.00	$50.00
2	$100	.5	$50	$100	.250	$25.00	$75.00
3	$100	.5	$50	$150	.125	$12.50	$87.50
4	$100	.5	$50	$200	.063	$6.30	$93.80
5	$100	.5	$50	$250	.031	$3.10	$96.90
6	$100	.5	$50	$300	.016	$1.60	$98.50
7	$100	.5	$50	$350	.008	$.80	$99.30
8	$100	.5	$50	$400	.004	$.40	$99.70
9	$100	.5	$50	$450	.002	$.20	$99.90
10	$100	.5	$50	$500	.001	$.10	$100.00

Total expected recovery $500 $100.00

On the other hand, under Bernhard, once the plaintiff loses one case, he will be precluded from litigating the remaining cases. While the probability of winning any single case that is litigated is still fifty percent, the preclusive effect of a single loss makes the probability of ever litigating a case dependent upon the outcome of previous cases. This cumulative effect reduces the common party's expected recovery from $500 to $100, as illustrated in the Bernhard column of Table I.

When the probability of winning a single case is initially assumed to be fifty percent, each successive claim under Bernhard is worth only half as much to the plaintiff as its predecessor because it is that much less likely that he will be able to recover. The presence of the preceding claims decreases the probability that the common party will recover on succeeding claims. The impact of the Bernhard doctrine is dramatic and can be evaluated in terms of expected recovery rather than mere conjecture.

. . . .

The argument advanced by one commentator—that the result produced by Bernhard is no worse than forcing a common party to litigate all claims at once so that any recovery is dependent upon that single outcome[91]—is, as Professor Currie argued, incorrect. If, in the hypotheticals, all defendants were joined in a single suit so that each would be bound by an adverse judgment as well as benefitted by a favorable one, the plaintiff's expected recovery would be $500. Thus, the expected recovery when all of the defendants are joined in a single action is the same as it would be if the suits were tried separately under mutuality, but it is not the same as it would be if they were tried under Bernhard. There is a vast difference between compelling a litigant to accept an all-or-nothing bet with even odds, as joinder rules do, and weighting the odds heavily in favor of his opponent, as the Bernhard doctrine does.

. . . .

This Note began by demonstrating, with the aid of probability theory, that the burden of persuasion in civil litigation embodies a strategy designed to minimize the total number of erroneous judgments and that this strategy is based on the various disutilities society attaches to the different possible outcomes of litigation. This Note then established that the abandonment of mutuality causes a statistically certain decrease in the recovery of a party facing multiple opponents on related claims. This effect of Bernhard is of concern to more than just the common party, for the mutuality doctrine is designed to allocate trial risks in a manner consistent with the burden of persuasion, that is, in a manner designed to minimize the total number of errors. Thus, the abandonment of mutuality harms the system of civil sanctions by weakening the causal link between culpable conduct and trial outcome. This Note also demonstrated [in omitted passages] that the objections to the abandonment of a mutuality requirement are not met by a requirement that the common party be precluded only if he has previously enjoyed a full and fair opportunity to litigate. Both the full and fair opportunity test and the mutuality requirement should be satisfied before the common party is precluded.

Finally, it was demonstrated [in other omitted passages] that the traditional [extensions of preclusion, such as in all the secondary-liability circumstances,] are entirely consistent with an error minimizing strategy.

———

Questions: (15) Evaluate the argument that "the major shortcoming with the breakdown of mutuality is that it does not go far enough to relieve court congestion and operates as a one-way street to the serious disadvantage of parties to litigation." Thus, the argument runs, there should be "a return to mutuality, but a new kind of mutuality" under which collateral estoppel expands to bind as well as benefit strangers. Michael A. Berch, A Proposal to Permit Collateral Estoppel of Nonparties Seeking

---

[91] See Comment, [Privity and Mutuality in the Doctrine of Res Judicata, 35 Yale L.J. 607, 610–11 (1926)].

Affirmative Relief, 1979 Ariz.St.L.J. 511, 530–31. This change could be achieved by stretching the categories of privies or, more frankly, by abandoning the requirement of privity. Due process would be satisfied by looking to the stranger's earlier failure to intervene or, more aptly albeit shakily, by looking retrospectively to a party's adequate representation of the stranger. Apparent excesses could be controlled by delimiting the rule of preclusion or, similarly, by developing exceptions thereto. Taken to its logical conclusion, the new regime would give effects by collateral estoppel analogous to those of a class action. See Lawrence C. George, Sweet Uses of Adversity: Parklane Hosiery and the Collateral Class Action, 32 Stan.L.Rev. 655 (1980); cf. Robert G. Bone, Rethinking the "Day in Court" Ideal and Nonparty Preclusion, 67 N.Y.U.L.Rev. 193 (1992). Note that this argument runs along lines similar to how the less binding stare decisis already works. See EEOC v. Trabucco, 791 F.2d 1 (1st Cir.1986); cf. Amy Coney Barrett, Stare Decisis and Due Process, 74 U.Colo.L.Rev. 1011 (2003).

(16) Evaluate the argument that the most mainstream alternative to achieve nonmutuality's aim of eliminating relitigation would be to expand mandatory joinder of all the concerned persons. This route would efficiently dispose of common matters in one shot, but in a fair shot. The joined parties would be bound, but only after being heard. Their common opponent would be bound if it lost, but if it won it would win against all the joined parties. By so equating the parties' litigating risk, this procedural technique would restore procedural neutrality. Nevertheless, society has chosen, after balancing benefits and costs, to follow this mandatory joinder route no further than society has gone in such provisions as Federal Rule 19 on compulsory joinder. Because society has in fact chosen not to pursue this joinder alternative or any other alternative, the choice by the courts to adopt on their own the inferior reform of nonmutuality arguably looks even more questionable. See generally Elinor P. Schroeder, Relitigation of Common Issues: The Failure of Nonparty Preclusion and an Alternative Proposal, 67 Iowa L.Rev. 917 (1982).

———

SECTION 3.   STRETCHING STRANGERS' BENEFITS

Collateral estoppel based on criminal proceedings.—Res judicata is an important topic in criminal law, even finding partial expression in the Double Jeopardy Clause. Generally speaking, though, criminal res judicata has developed independently from the civil doctrine and has ended up playing a more limited role. For example, nonmutual collateral estoppel does not normally apply in criminal cases at all.

But what about res judicata in civil cases based on a prior criminal judgment? Imagine that after trial, *A* is convicted of arson for having intentionally destroyed his own property by fire. Thereafter, he sues the *B* Fire Insurance Co. on its policy covering the property. Should the criminal conviction preclude *A* in the civil action?

The traditional answer was no. The reason usually given for denying preclusion was lack of mutuality: the parties in the two actions were not the same.

While recognizing that the customary answer to this question was in the negative, Eagle, Star & British Dominions Insurance Co. v. Heller, 149 Va. 82, 140 S.E. 314 (1927), nevertheless held that there should be preclusion, saying that the contrary result "would be a reproach to the administration of justice." The retreat from mutuality heralded by Bernhard has led many more courts to give preclusive effect to a conviction, subject to the usual requirements and exceptions of issue preclusion. E.g., Teitelbaum Furs, Inc. v. Dominion Ins. Co., 58 Cal.2d 601, 375 P.2d 439, 25 Cal.Rptr. 559 (1962). See generally Jonathan C. Thau, Collateral Estoppel and the Reliability of Criminal Determinations: Theoretical, Practical, and Strategic Implications for Criminal and Civil Litigation, 70 Geo.L.J. 1079 (1982).

Where a criminal conviction does not so receive preclusive effect in a subsequent civil action, one might ask whether it is admissible therein as probative evidence on a common issue. As a general matter, a judgment either has preclusive effect under the rules of res judicata or has no effect at all, being inadmissible on hearsay grounds as a prior statement offered for its truth. See generally Hiroshi Motomura, Using Judgments as Evidence, 70 Minn.L.Rev. 979 (1986). Accordingly, the traditional rule was that when the court had denied res judicata effect, the admission of evidence of a prior criminal conviction was reversible error. E.g., Silva v. Silva, 297 Mass. 217, 7 N.E.2d 601 (1937).

Yet the heavier burden of proof and other protections in criminal cases would seem to make it reasonable to give a conviction at least some effect in a civil case. As a result, a number of states have adopted a half-way rule making a conviction admissible but not preclusive evidence, even against strangers, although there has been a tendency in those states to limit admissibility to convictions for serious offenses. Federal Evidence Rule 803(22) makes admissible in federal court proof of conviction of a felony, demonstrating the same doubt concerning the reliability of convictions for lesser offenses. The Advisory Committee's note thereto explains that this hearsay exception is to have no effect on the operation of res judicata.

Questions: (17) Should a conviction upon a guilty plea be preclusive in a subsequent civil action? See David L. Shapiro, Should a Guilty Plea Have Preclusive Effect?, 70 Iowa L.Rev. 27 (1984). Should such a conviction be admissible as evidence? See McCormick on Evidence §§ 257, 298 (Kenneth S. Broun gen. ed., 7th ed. 2013).

(18) Should an acquittal in a criminal case be preclusive in a subsequent civil action? Should an acquittal be admissible as evidence?

Allen v. McCurry

Supreme Court of the United States, 1980.
449 U.S. 90, 101 S.Ct. 411.

■ JUSTICE STEWART delivered the opinion of the Court.

At a hearing before his criminal trial in a Missouri court, the respondent, Willie McCurry, invoked the Fourth and Fourteenth Amendments to suppress evidence that had been seized by the police. The trial court denied the suppression motion in part, and McCurry was subsequently convicted after a jury trial. The conviction was later affirmed on appeal. State v. McCurry, 587 S.W.2d 337 (Mo.Ct.App.). Because he did not assert that the state courts had denied him a "full and fair opportunity" to litigate his search and seizure claim, McCurry was barred by this Court's decision in Stone v. Powell, 428 U.S. 465, 96 S.Ct. 3037, from seeking a writ of habeas corpus in a federal district court. Nevertheless, he sought federal court redress for the alleged constitutional violation by bringing a damage suit under 42 U.S.C. § 1983 against the officers who had entered his home and seized the evidence in question. We granted certiorari to consider whether the unavailability of federal habeas corpus prevented the police officers from raising the state courts' partial rejection of McCurry's constitutional claim as a collateral estoppel defense to the § 1983 suit against them for damages. 444 U.S. 1070, 100 S.Ct. 1012.

I

In April 1977, several undercover police officers, following an informant's tip that McCurry was dealing in heroin, went to his house in St. Louis, Mo., to attempt a purchase. Two officers, petitioners Allen and Jacobsmeyer, knocked on the front door, while the other officers hid nearby. When McCurry opened the door, the two officers asked to buy some heroin "caps." McCurry went back into the house and returned soon thereafter, firing a pistol at and seriously wounding Allen and Jacobsmeyer. After a gun battle with the other officers and their reinforcements, McCurry retreated into the house; he emerged again when the police demanded that he surrender. Several officers then entered the house without a warrant, purportedly to search for other persons inside. One of the officers seized drugs and other contraband that lay in plain view, as well as additional contraband he found in dresser drawers and in auto tires on the porch.

McCurry was charged with possession of heroin and assault with intent to kill. At the pretrial suppression hearing, the trial judge excluded the evidence seized from the dresser drawers and tires, but denied suppression of the evidence found in plain view. McCurry was convicted of both the heroin and assault offenses.

McCurry subsequently filed the present § 1983 action for $1 million in damages against petitioners Allen and Jacobsmeyer [and other police]. The complaint alleged a conspiracy to violate McCurry's Fourth

Amendment rights, an unconstitutional search and seizure of his house, and an assault on him by unknown police officers after he had been arrested and handcuffed. The petitioners moved for summary judgment. The District Court apparently understood the gist of the complaint to be the allegedly unconstitutional search and seizure and granted summary judgment, holding that collateral estoppel prevented McCurry from relitigating the search and seizure question already decided against him in the state courts. McCurry v. Allen, 466 F.Supp. 514 (E.D.Mo.1978).[2]

The Court of Appeals reversed the judgment and remanded the case for trial. McCurry v. Allen, 606 F.2d 795 (C.A.8 1979).[3] The appellate court said it was not holding that collateral estoppel was generally inapplicable in a § 1983 suit raising issues determined against the federal plaintiff in a state criminal trial. Id., at 798. But noting that Stone v. Powell, supra, barred McCurry from federal habeas corpus relief, and invoking "the special role of the federal courts in protecting civil rights," id., at 799, the court concluded that the § 1983 suit was McCurry's only route to a federal forum for his constitutional claim and directed the trial court to allow him to proceed to trial unencumbered by collateral estoppel.

II

The federal courts have traditionally adhered to the related doctrines of res judicata and collateral estoppel. Under res judicata, a final judgment on the merits of an action precludes the parties or their privies from relitigating issues that were or could have been raised in that action. Cromwell v. County of Sac, 94 U.S. 351, 352. Under collateral estoppel, once a court has decided an issue of fact or law necessary to its judgment, that decision may preclude relitigation of the issue in a suit on a different cause of action involving a party to the first case. Montana v. United States, 440 U.S. 147, 153, 99 S.Ct. 970, 973.[5] As this Court and

---

[2]   The merits of the Fourth Amendment claim are discussed in the opinion of the Missouri Court of Appeals. State v. McCurry, 587 S.W.2d 337 (Mo.Ct.App.). The state courts upheld the entry of the house as a reasonable response to emergency circumstances, but held illegal the seizure of any evidence discovered as a result of that entry except what was in plain view. Id., at 340. McCurry therefore argues here that even if the doctrine of collateral estoppel generally applies to this case, he should be able to proceed to trial to obtain damages for the part of the seizure declared illegal by the state courts. The petitioners contend, on the other hand, that the complaint alleged essentially an illegal entry, adding that only the entry could possibly justify the $1 million prayer. Since the state courts upheld the entry, the petitioners argue that if collateral estoppel applies here at all, it removes from trial all issues except the alleged assault. The United States Court of Appeals, however, addressed only the broad question of the applicability of collateral estoppel to § 1983 suits brought by plaintiffs in McCurry's circumstances, and questions as to the scope of collateral estoppel with respect to the particular issues in this case are not now before us.

[3]   Beyond holding that collateral estoppel does not apply in this case, the Court of Appeals noted that the District Court had overlooked the conspiracy and assault charges. 606 F.2d, at 797, and n. 1.

[5]   The Restatement of Judgments now speaks of res judicata as "claim preclusion" and collateral estoppel as "issue preclusion." Restatement of Judgments (Second) § 74 (Tent. Draft No. 3, 1976). Some courts and commentators use "res judicata" as generally meaning both forms

other courts have often recognized, res judicata and collateral estoppel relieve parties of the cost and vexation of multiple lawsuits, conserve judicial resources, and, by preventing inconsistent decisions, encourage reliance on adjudication. Id., at 153–154, 99 S.Ct., at 973–974.

In recent years, this Court has reaffirmed the benefits of collateral estoppel in particular, finding the policies underlying it to apply in contexts not formerly recognized at common law. Thus, the Court has eliminated the requirement of mutuality in applying collateral estoppel to bar relitigation of issues decided earlier in federal court suits, Blonder-Tongue Laboratories, Inc. v. University of Illinois Foundation, 402 U.S. 313, 91 S.Ct. 1434, and has allowed a litigant who was not a party to a federal case to use collateral estoppel "offensively" in a new federal suit against the party who lost on the decided issue in the first case, Parklane Hosiery Co. v. Shore, 439 U.S. 322, 99 S.Ct. 645.[6] But one general limitation the Court has repeatedly recognized is that the concept of collateral estoppel cannot apply when the party against whom the earlier decision is asserted did not have a "full and fair opportunity" to litigate that issue in the earlier case. Montana v. United States, supra, 440 U.S., at 153, 99 S.Ct., at 973; Blonder-Tongue Laboratories, Inc. v. University of Illinois Foundation, supra, 402 U.S., at 328–329, 91 S.Ct., at 1443.[7]

The federal courts generally have also consistently accorded preclusive effect to issues decided by state courts. E.g., Montana v. United States, supra; Angel v. Bullington, 330 U.S. 183, 67 S.Ct. 657. Thus, res judicata and collateral estoppel not only reduce unnecessary litigation and foster reliance on adjudication, but also promote the comity between state and federal courts that has been recognized as a bulwark of the federal system. See Younger v. Harris, 401 U.S. 37, 43–45, 91 S.Ct. 746, 750–51.

Indeed, though the federal courts may look to the common law or to the policies supporting res judicata and collateral estoppel in assessing the preclusive effect of decisions of other federal courts, Congress has specifically required all federal courts to give preclusive effect to state-court judgments whenever the courts of the State from which the judgments emerged would do so .... 28 U.S.C. § 1738 ...; [citations omitted]. It is against this background that we examine the relationship

---

of preclusion. ... [The Supreme Court soon came to adopt this modern terminology. See Migra v. Warren City Sch. Dist. Bd. of Educ., 465 U.S. 75, 77 n.1, 104 S.Ct. 892, 894 n.1 (1984).—Ed.]

[6]   In Blonder-Tongue the Court noted other trends in the state and federal courts expanding the preclusive effects of judgments, such as the broadened definition of "claim" in the context of res judicata and the greater preclusive effect given criminal judgments in subsequent civil cases. Blonder-Tongue Laboratories, Inc. v. University of Illinois Foundation, 402 U.S. 313, 326, 91 S.Ct. 1434, 1441.

[7]   Other factors, of course, may require an exception to the normal rules of collateral estoppel in particular cases. E.g., Montana v. United States, 440 U.S. 147, 162, 99 S.Ct. 970, 978 (unmixed questions of law in successive actions between the same parties on unrelated claims).

... It must be emphasized that the question whether any exceptions or qualifications within the bounds of that doctrine might ultimately defeat a collateral estoppel defense in this case is not before us. See n. 2, supra.

of § 1983 and collateral estoppel, and the decision of the Court of Appeals in this case.

III

This Court has never directly decided whether the rules of res judicata and collateral estoppel are generally applicable to § 1983 actions. But in Preiser v. Rodriguez, 411 U.S. 475, 497, 93 S.Ct. 1827, 1840, the Court noted with implicit approval the view of other federal courts that res judicata principles fully apply to civil rights suits brought under that statute. [Citations omitted.] And the virtually unanimous view of the Courts of Appeals since Preiser has been that § 1983 presents no categorical bar to the application of res judicata and collateral estoppel concepts. These federal appellate court decisions have spoken with little explanation or citation in assuming the compatibility of § 1983 and rules of preclusion, but the statute and its legislative history clearly support the courts' decisions.

Because the requirement of mutuality of estoppel was still alive in the federal courts until well into this century, see Blonder-Tongue Laboratories, Inc. v. University of Illinois Foundation, supra, 402 U.S., at 322–323, 91 S.Ct., at 1439–1440, the drafters of the 1871 Civil Rights Act, of which § 1983 is a part, may have had less reason to concern themselves with rules of preclusion than a modern Congress would. Nevertheless, in 1871 res judicata and collateral estoppel could certainly have applied in federal suits following state-court litigation between the same parties or their privies, and nothing in the language of § 1983 remotely expresses any congressional intent to contravene the common-law rules of preclusion or to repeal the express statutory requirements of . . . 28 U.S.C. § 1738 . . . . Section 1983 creates a new federal cause of action. It says nothing about the preclusive effect of state-court judgments.[12]

Moreover, the legislative history of § 1983 does not in any clear way suggest that Congress intended to repeal or restrict the traditional doctrines of preclusion. The main goal of the Act was to override the corrupting influence of the Ku Klux Klan and its sympathizers on the

---

[12]   By contrast, the roughly contemporaneous statute extending the federal writ of habeas corpus to state prisoners expressly rendered "null and void" any state-court proceeding inconsistent with the decision of a federal habeas court, Act of Feb. 5, 1867, ch. 28, § 1, 14 Stat. 385, 386 (1867) (current version at 28 U.S.C. § 2254), and the modern habeas statute also expressly adverts to the effect of state-court criminal judgments by requiring the applicant for the writ to exhaust his state-court remedies, 28 U.S.C. § 2254(b), and by presuming a state court resolution of a factual issue to be correct except in eight specific circumstances, id., § 2254(d). In any event, the traditional exception to res judicata for habeas corpus review, see Preiser v. Rodriguez, supra, 411 U.S., at 497, 93 S.Ct., at 1840, provides no analogy to § 1983 cases, since that exception finds its source in the unique purpose of habeas corpus—to release the applicant for the writ from unlawful confinement. Sanders v. United States, 373 U.S. 1, 8, 83 S.Ct. 1068, 1073. [Although res judicata itself supposedly does not apply in habeas corpus proceedings, the Supreme Court of late has pursued similar policies in developing such doctrines as "abuse of the writ," which blocks repetitive petitions. See, e.g., McCleskey v. Zant, 499 U.S. 467, 111 S.Ct. 1454 (1991). Similarly, Congress has further tightened the habeas statute to reduce repetitive litigation. Antiterrorism and Effective Death Penalty Act of 1996, Pub.L. No. 104–132, tit. I, §§ 104, 106, 110 Stat. 1214, 1218, 1220.—Ed.]

governments and law enforcement agencies of the Southern States, see Monroe v. Pape, 365 U.S. 167, 174, 81 S.Ct. 473, 477, and of course the debates show that one strong motive behind its enactment was grave congressional concern that the state courts had been deficient in protecting federal rights, Mitchum v. Foster, 407 U.S. 225, 241–242, 92 S.Ct. 2151, 2161–2162; Monroe v. Pape, supra, 365 U.S., at 180, 81 S.Ct., at 480. But in the context of the legislative history as a whole, this congressional concern lends only the most equivocal support to any argument that, in cases where the state courts have recognized the constitutional claims asserted and provided fair procedures for determining them, Congress intended to override § 1738 or the common-law rules of collateral estoppel and res judicata. Since repeals by implication are disfavored, Radzanower v. Touche Ross & Co., 426 U.S. 148, 154, 96 S.Ct. 1989, 1993, much clearer support than this would be required to hold that § 1738 and the traditional rules of preclusion are not applicable to § 1983 suits.

As the Court has understood the history of the legislation, Congress realized that in enacting § 1983 it was altering the balance of judicial power between the state and federal courts. See Mitchum v. Foster, supra, 407 U.S., at 241, 92 S.Ct., at 2161. But in doing so, Congress was adding to the jurisdiction of the federal courts, not subtracting from that of the state courts. See Monroe v. Pape, supra, 365 U.S., at 183, 81 S.Ct., at 481 ("The federal remedy is supplementary to the state remedy . . . ."). The debates contain several references to the concurrent jurisdiction of the state courts over federal questions, and numerous suggestions that the state courts would retain their established jurisdiction so that they could, when the then current political passions abated, demonstrate a new sensitivity to federal rights.

To the extent that it did intend to change the balance of power over federal questions between the state and federal courts, the 42d Congress was acting in a way thoroughly consistent with the doctrines of preclusion. In reviewing the legislative history of § 1983 in Monroe v. Pape, supra, the Court inferred that Congress had intended a federal remedy [inter alia] . . . where state procedural law was inadequate to allow full litigation of a constitutional claim, and where state procedural law, though adequate in theory, was inadequate in practice. 365 U.S., at 173–174, 81 S.Ct., at 476–477. In short, the federal courts could step in where the state courts were unable or unwilling to protect federal rights. Id., at 176, 81 S.Ct., at 478. This understanding of § 1983 might well support an exception to res judicata and collateral estoppel where state law did not provide fair procedures for the litigation of constitutional claims, or where a state court failed to even acknowledge the existence of the constitutional principle on which a litigant based his claim. Such an exception, however, would be essentially the same as the important general limit on rules of preclusion that already exists: Collateral estoppel does not apply where the party against whom an earlier court decision is asserted did not have a full and fair opportunity to litigate the claim or issue decided by the first court. . . . But the Court's view of § 1983 in Monroe lends no strength to any argument that Congress intended to allow relitigation of federal issues decided after a full and fair hearing in a state court simply because the state court's decision may have been erroneous.

. . . The Court of Appeals . . . concluded that since Stone v. Powell had removed McCurry's right to a hearing of his Fourth Amendment claim in federal habeas corpus, collateral estoppel should not deprive him of a federal judicial hearing of that claim in a § 1983 suit.

Stone v. Powell does not provide a logical doctrinal source for the court's ruling. This Court in Stone assessed the costs and benefits of the judge-made exclusionary rule within the boundaries of the federal courts' statutory power to issue writs of habeas corpus, and decided that the incremental deterrent effect that the issuance of the writ in Fourth Amendment cases might have on police conduct did not justify the cost the writ imposed upon the fair administration of criminal justice. 428 U.S., at 489–496, 96 S.Ct., at 3050–3053. The Stone decision concerns only the prudent exercise of federal court jurisdiction under 28 U.S.C. § 2254. It has no bearing on § 1983 suits or on the question of the preclusive effect of state-court judgments.

The actual basis of the Court of Appeals' holding appears to be a generally framed principle that every person asserting a federal right is entitled to one unencumbered opportunity to litigate that right in a federal district court, regardless of the legal posture in which the federal claim arises. But the authority for this principle is difficult to discern. It cannot lie in the Constitution, which makes no such guarantee, but leaves the scope of the jurisdiction of the federal district courts to the wisdom of Congress. And no such authority is to be found in § 1983 itself. For reasons already discussed at length, nothing in the language or legislative history of § 1983 proves any congressional intent to deny binding effect to a state-court judgment or decision when the state court, acting within its proper jurisdiction, has given the parties a full and fair opportunity to litigate federal claims, and thereby has shown itself willing and able to protect federal rights. And nothing in the legislative history of § 1983 reveals any purpose to afford less deference to judgments in state criminal proceedings than to those in state civil proceedings. There is, in short, no reason to believe that Congress intended to provide a person claiming a federal right an unrestricted opportunity to relitigate an issue already decided in state court simply because the issue arose in a state proceeding in which he would rather not have been engaged at all.[23]

---

[23] The Court of Appeals did not suggest that the prospect of collateral estoppel in a § 1983 suit would deter a defendant in a state criminal case from raising Fourth Amendment claims, and it is difficult to imagine a defendant risking conviction and imprisonment because he hoped to win a later civil judgment based upon an allegedly illegal search and seizure.

Through § 1983, the 42d Congress intended to afford an opportunity for legal and equitable relief in a federal court for certain types of injuries. It is difficult to believe that the drafters of that Act considered it a substitute for a federal writ of habeas corpus, the purpose of which is not to redress civil injury, but to release the applicant from unlawful physical confinement, Preiser v. Rodriguez, supra, 411 U.S., at 484, 93 S.Ct., at 1833; Fay v. Noia, 372 U.S. 391, 399, n. 5, 83 S.Ct. 822, 827, n. 5,[24] particularly in light of the extremely narrow scope of federal habeas relief for state prisoners in 1871.

The only other conceivable basis for finding a universal right to litigate a federal claim in a federal district court is hardly a legal basis at all, but rather a general distrust of the capacity of the state courts to render correct decisions on constitutional issues. It is ironic that Stone v. Powell provided the occasion for the expression of such an attitude in the present litigation, in view of this Court's emphatic reaffirmation in that case of the constitutional obligation of the state courts to uphold federal law, and its expression of confidence in their ability to do so. [Citations omitted.]

The Court of Appeals erred in holding that McCurry's inability to obtain federal habeas corpus relief upon his Fourth Amendment claim renders the doctrine of collateral estoppel inapplicable to his § 1983 suit. Accordingly, the judgment is reversed, and the case is remanded to the Court of Appeals for proceedings consistent with this opinion.

It is so ordered.[f]

■ JUSTICE BLACKMUN, with whom JUSTICE BRENNAN and JUSTICE MARSHALL join, dissenting.

The legal principles with which the Court is concerned in this civil case obviously far transcend the ugly facts of respondent's criminal convictions in the courts of Missouri for heroin possession and assault.

The Court today holds that notions of collateral estoppel apply with full force to this suit brought under 42 U.S.C. § 1983. In my view, the Court, in so ruling, ignores the clear import of the legislative history of that statute and disregards the important federal policies that underlie its enforcement. It also shows itself insensitive both to the significant differences between the § 1983 remedy and the exclusionary rule, and to the pressures upon a criminal defendant that make a free choice of forum illusory. I do not doubt that principles of preclusion are to be given such

---

[24]   Under the modern statute, federal habeas corpus is bounded by a requirement of exhaustion of state remedies and by special procedural rules, 28 U.S.C. § 2254, which have no counterparts in § 1983, and which therefore demonstrate the continuing illogic of treating federal habeas and § 1983 suits as fungible remedies for constitutional violations.

[f]   After remand and the application of collateral estoppel against McCurry, and upon trial of the remaining issues, the judge directed a verdict against McCurry on his claim, and the jury rendered a $105,000 verdict against him on Jacobsmeyer's counterclaim for battery. The judgment was affirmed, 688 F.2d 581 (8th Cir.1982). Incidentally, McCurry made a bid to use collateral estoppel for establishing that part of the seizure had been illegal, but he failed on the ground that the defendants were strangers to the state proceedings.

effect as is appropriate in a § 1983 action. In many cases, the denial of res judicata or collateral estoppel effect would serve no purpose and would harm relations between federal and state tribunals. Nonetheless, the Court's analysis in this particular case is unacceptable to me. It works injustice on this § 1983 plaintiff, and it makes more difficult the consistent protection of constitutional rights, a consideration that was at the core of the enacters' intent. Accordingly, I dissent.

. . . .

. . . Although the legislators of the 42d Congress did not expressly state whether the then-existing common-law doctrine of preclusion would survive enactment of § 1983, they plainly anticipated more than the creation of a federal statutory remedy to be administered indifferently by either a state or a federal court. The legislative intent, as expressed by supporters and understood by opponents, was to restructure relations between the state and federal courts. Congress deliberately opened the federal courts to individual citizens in response to the States' failure to provide justice in their own courts. Contrary to the view presently expressed by the Court, the 42d Congress was not concerned solely with procedural regularity. Even where there was procedural regularity, which the Court today so stresses, Congress believed that substantive justice was unobtainable. The availability of the federal forum was not meant to turn on whether, in an individual case, the state procedures were adequate. Assessing the state of affairs as a whole, Congress specifically made a determination that federal oversight of constitutional determinations through the federal courts was necessary to ensure the effective enforcement of constitutional rights.

That the new federal jurisdiction was conceived of as concurrent with state jurisdiction does not alter the significance of Congress' opening the federal courts to these claims. Congress consciously acted in the broadest possible manner. The legislators perceived that justice was not being done in the States then dominated by the Klan, and it seems senseless to suppose that they would have intended the federal courts to give full preclusive effect to prior state adjudications. That supposition would contradict their obvious aim to right the wrongs perpetuated in those same courts.

. . . .

. . . [M]y understanding of the policies underlying § 1983 would lead me to consider all relevant factors in each case before concluding that preclusion was warranted.

In this case, the police officers seek to prevent a criminal defendant from relitigating the constitutionality of their conduct in searching his house, after the state trial court had found that conduct in part violative of the defendant's Fourth Amendment rights and in part justified by the circumstances. I doubt that the police officers, now defendants in this

§ 1983 action, can be considered to have been in privity with the State in its role as prosecutor. Therefore, only "issue preclusion" is at stake.

The following factors persuade me to conclude that this respondent should not be precluded from asserting his claim in federal court. . . .

. . . [T]he process of deciding in a state criminal trial whether to exclude or admit evidence is not at all the equivalent of a § 1983 proceeding. The remedy sought in the latter is utterly different. In bringing the civil suit the criminal defendant does not seek to challenge his conviction collaterally. At most, he wins damages. In contrast, the exclusion of evidence may prevent a criminal conviction. A trial court, faced with the decision whether to exclude relevant evidence, confronts institutional pressures that may cause it to give a different shape to the Fourth Amendment right from what would result in civil litigation of a damages claim. Also, the issue whether to exclude evidence is subsidiary to the purpose of a criminal trial, which is to determine the guilt or innocence of the defendant, and a trial court, at least subconsciously, must weigh the potential damage to the truth-seeking process caused by excluding relevant evidence. [Citations omitted.]

A state criminal defendant cannot be held to have chosen "voluntarily" to litigate his Fourth Amendment claim in the state court. The risk of conviction puts pressure upon him to raise all possible defenses. . . . To hold that a criminal defendant who raises a Fourth Amendment claim at his criminal trial "freely and without reservation submits his federal claims for decision by the state courts," see England v. Medical Examiners, [375 U.S. 411, 419, 84 S.Ct. 461, 466 (1964)], is to deny reality. The criminal defendant is an involuntary litigant in the state tribunal, and against him all the forces of the State are arrayed. To force him to a choice between forgoing either a potential defense or a federal forum for hearing his constitutional civil claim is fundamentally unfair.

I would affirm the judgment of the Court of Appeals.

———

Question: (19) An African American venireperson is the subject of a peremptory challenge by the prosecution in a state criminal case. The defendant objects, arguing that the prosecution based the challenge on race, thereby violating the venireperson's equal protection rights, which the defendant has third-party standing to assert. The prosecution responds that it had nondiscriminatory grounds for the challenge. The judge rules that there was no constitutional violation. The eventually convicted defendant loses a full appeal. If the would-be juror then brings a federal § 1983 action, will she be precluded from relitigating whether her civil rights were violated? See Shaw v. Hahn, 56 F.3d 1128 (9th Cir.1995) (yes).

———

Nonmutual claim preclusion.—As already explained, usually parties and their privies are the only ones who can benefit from the rules of res judicata other than collateral estoppel, because for a stranger a different claim is necessarily involved. There remains the question of the unusual: when can a stranger use the other rules of res judicata?

Sometimes a stranger can use a former party's victory to bar a new assertion of the opposing party's claim against the stranger. A ready example lies in the old indemnitor-indemnitee situation. If the injured person litigates with the employee and loses—the employee being found not negligent—everyone agrees that the employer can invoke nonmutual collateral estoppel in the injured person's later action against the employer. But what if the injured party lost the prior action by failure to prosecute? The same indemnity dilemma argues for allowing the employer to use the prior judgment, even though this use would be an instance of nonmutual claim preclusion.

But how far should the law go with this new idea?

———

Fagnan v. Great Central Insurance Co.

United States Court of Appeals, Seventh Circuit, 1978.
577 F.2d 418, cert. denied, 439 U.S. 1004, 99 S.Ct. 615 (1978).

■ Before TONE and BAUER, CIRCUIT JUDGES, and CAMPBELL, SENIOR DISTRICT JUDGE.*

■ TONE, CIRCUIT JUDGE.

The issue presented is whether the federal compulsory counterclaim rule, Rule 13(a), Fed.R.Civ.P., precludes an action against an insurance company under the Wisconsin direct action statute, when an action directly against the insured would be barred by the rule. The District Court answered this question in the negative and entered judgment against the insurance company. We reverse.

The collision of two automobiles in Wisconsin resulted in the death of one of the drivers, Robert Thompson, and injuries to his passenger, David Harness [of California]. The driver of the other automobile, Duane Fagnan [of Wisconsin], was also injured.

Harness, Thompson's passenger, brought an action against the administrator of Thompson's estate [with Minnesota citizenship] in the United States District Court for the District of Minnesota. The administrator filed a third party claim for contribution against Fagnan, who filed an answer to that claim. Later Harness filed a claim under Rule 14(a) against Fagnan, which Fagnan also answered. In addition, Fagnan

---

*   The Honorable William J. Campbell, Senior District Judge of the United States District Court for the Northern District of Illinois, is sitting by designation.

cross-claimed against the administrator for contribution. The case was settled without a trial, and the court dismissed the action. Under the last sentence of Rule 41(b), Fed.R.Civ.P., the dismissal operated as an adjudication upon the merits.[1]

A few months after the action in Minnesota was dismissed, Duane Fagnan and his father, Raymond Fagnan, sued in a Wisconsin state court against Thompson's insurer, Great Central Insurance Company, under the Wisconsin direct action statute. Raymond Fagnan's claim was for medical expenses and care of his minor child incurred as a result of the [collision].[2] Also named as a defendant was Thompson's father, Darrold Thompson. The defendants removed the case to the United States District Court for the Western District of Wisconsin, where a trial before a jury resulted in a directed verdict in favor of Darrold Thompson, from which no appeal is taken, and verdicts [finding Thompson 100% negligent] in favor of both Duane Fagnan and Raymond Fagnan against the insurer, who appeals.

Relying on Rule 13(a), the insurer argues that any claim of Duane Fagnan against Robert Thompson's estate was disposed of by the judgment in the Minnesota action. The insurer now concedes that the award to Raymond Fagnan of damages for the medical expenses and care of Duane Fagnan cannot properly be challenged, since Raymond Fagnan was not a party to the Minnesota action. Accordingly, the judgment in his favor is not subject to attack.

I.

At the time of the accident in this case, Wisconsin's direct action statutes were Wis.Stat. §§ 204.30(4) and 260.11(1). Section 204.30(4) was substantive and created "direct liability between the in[j]ured third person and the insurer," while § 260.11(1) provided the procedural vehicle by which the insurer could be made a party defendant. [Citations omitted.] However,

> [t]he fact that a third party can sue an insurer of a motor vehicle direct ... without first recovering a judgment against the insured defendant does not enlarge the coverage afforded by such policy or determine the insure[r]'s liability thereunder. The third party can only recover from the insurer by virtue of the contract existing between it and its insured.

---

[1]   The court's order of dismissal recited that the court had been reliably informed that the case had been settled but the attorneys had "been negligent for some time in getting a stipulation of dismissal signed and filed." The court, therefore, sua sponte dismissed the action, retaining jurisdiction for 10 days, within which the parties could move to vacate. A stipulation to dismiss with prejudice had already been signed, the record before us shows, although it was apparently never filed with the court. The order of dismissal became final at the expiration of the 10 days and fell within the final category, "any dismissal not provided for in this rule," of Rule 41(b) and as such operated as an adjudication upon the merits.

[2]   Under Wisconsin law a parent's liability for the medical expense and care of his minor child are separate causes of action from the child's personal injury claims and can only be asserted by the parent. Sulkowski v. Schaefer, 31 Wis.2d 600, 143 N.W.2d 512, 515 (1966).

Nichols v. U.S.F. & Guaranty Co., 13 Wis.2d 491, 109 N.W.2d 131, 136 (1961).

Therefore, an insurance company's liability under the Wisconsin direct action statute is derivative, i.e., the "insurer is not liable unless the assured is." Hunt v. Dollar, 224 Wis. 48, 271 N.W. 405, 409 (1937). Thus the insurer is liable in this action only if the insured, Robert Thompson's administrator, is liable.

II.

[The court here quoted Rule 13(a).] A compulsory counterclaim that is not asserted is barred by the judgment. Baker v. Gold Seal Liquors, Inc., 417 U.S. 467, 469 n. 1, 94 S.Ct. 2504, 41 L.Ed.2d 243 (1974); Pipeliners Local Union No. 798, Tulsa, Okl. v. Ellerd, 503 F.2d 1193, 1198 (10th Cir.1974).

Duane Fagnan's claim against Robert Thompson's administrator existed at the time the pleadings were served in the Minnesota action,[5] arose out of the same transaction or occurrence that was the subject of that action, and did not require for its adjudication the presence of third parties. It was therefore a compulsory counterclaim and was extinguished by the judgment in that action.

Because Duane Fagnan's claim against the administrator is barred, his claim against the insurer is also barred. The judgment in favor of Duane Fagnan against Great Central must therefore be reversed.

Affirmed in part and reversed in part. Each side will bear its own costs.

MICHAEL J. WAGGONER, FIFTY YEARS OF BERNHARD v. BANK OF AMERICA IS ENOUGH: COLLATERAL ESTOPPEL SHOULD REQUIRE MUTUALITY BUT RES JUDICATA SHOULD NOT, 12 Rev.Litig. 391, 396, 440 (1993). "These ancient [secondary-liability] exceptions to the mutuality requirement should be extended to produce a general rule that mutuality is not required for [claim preclusion]. Res judicata should be a defense, not only to claims against the defendant in the prior case, but also to claims against persons who could have been made defendants in that case, if the other requirements for res judicata are met. A person having claims arising from the same transaction against both agent and principal, or against alternative defendants, should be required to proceed against all at once, or forego the claims against those omitted."

The author even more startlingly generalized: "Nonmutual [claim preclusion] should be implemented because it is both fair and efficient.

---

[5]   Duane Fagnan also could have asserted his direct action against the insurer, which Minnesota law permitted him to do in view of the existence of the Wisconsin direct action statute. Myers v. Government Employees' Insurance Company, 302 Minn. 359, 225 N.W.2d 238 (1974).

Nonmutual collateral estoppel in civil cases should be rejected, because even where it might be fair and efficient nonmutual [claim preclusion] is more so, and because in other areas it is unfair. The authority in favor of nonmutual collateral estoppel is, upon careful examination, far weaker than it might initially appear, so weak that even at this late date reconsideration of the question whether to require mutuality for collateral estoppel should still be open."

———

Comparative lessons.—U.S. res judicata law is distinctively a good deal more expansive than the res judicata law of other countries, including civil-law countries. For a somewhat representative example, we can take a quick look at France.

In France, res judicata (authority of *la chose jugée*, or the thing adjudged) finds embodiment in *Code civil* [C. civ.] art. 1355, which originated in a part of the code treating presumptions. That is to say, French res judicata proceeds upon a presumption of correctness: when raised by a party, a prior judgment is presumed to be correct and should not be contradicted in a subsequent suit. By virtue of the prior decision, the judgment has established what the law will treat as truth, if the judgment is final and valid.

A final judgment on the merits acquires the authority of res judicata immediately upon rendition, according to *Code de procédure civile* [C.P.C.] art. 480. A reversal will deprive the judgment of its res judicata effect, while an affirmance will render stronger the presumptive force of res judicata. The judgment becomes irrebuttable when the means of direct attack have expired.

A French court today will treat a prior judgment, even a foreign judgment, as valid if it did not entail violation of either international standards for jurisdiction or French exclusive jurisdiction or violation of either fundamental procedural fairness or basic public policy. Formerly, France gave foreign judgments much more suspicious treatment.

A French judgment must set out the parties' positions, the court's very briefly stated reasons (*les motifs*), and the decree announcing the court's decision on the parties' positions (*le dispositif*). While res judicata is said to attach only to the *dispositif*, there is long-running debate over the extent to which one can look to the *motifs* in determining the judgment's effect. It remains fair to say that although a court might look to the *motifs* in order to interpret the *dispositif*, it is only the latter that has preclusive effect.

To specify further the current scope of res judicata, take an actual look at C. civ. art. 1355:

> *L'autorité de la chose jugée n'a lieu qu'à l'égard de ce qui a fait l'objet du jugement. Il faut que la chose demandée soit la même; que la demande soit fondée sur la même cause; que la*

demande soit entre les mêmes parties, et formée par elles et contre elles en la même qualité. [The authority of res judicata extends only to what was the subject matter of the judgment. The thing claimed must be the same; the action must be based on the same ground; the action must be between the same parties, and brought by and against them in the same capacities.]

It requires three identities between the successive lawsuits: identity of the parties, of the object demanded, and of the *cause*:

  1. Identity of parties requires not physical identity but identity of quality, or legal capacity. Thus, privies represented in the prior suit have the same identities as the parties, but the same person who later sues in a different capacity does not.

  2. The second required identity is the identity of object demanded, or the end the action has in view. This difficult concept has meant that the suits must involve generally the same juridical right sought as to the same matter. For close but contrary examples, a person who lost an action in which he claimed title to a building could later sue freely for a life estate, but a person who has unsuccessfully claimed a debt owing could not later sue for interest thereon.

  3. The last required identity, and probably even more troublesome, is the identity of *cause*. On the one hand, it was generally accepted that this concept of *cause* was broader than the old common-law concept of cause of action, or theory of recovery. *Cause* referred to the ultimate facts and legal principle upon which the action was grounded, such that collection on a loan was a *cause*. On the other hand, all agreed that the concept of *cause* remained more restrictive than the new common-law transactional view of a claim. For two examples, a party who unsuccessfully attacked a will for a defect of form could renew the attack for lack of testamentary capacity, but that party could not raise different formal defects in successive actions.

If these three identities are present, res judicata attaches, both preventing the losing party from asserting new evidence or theories to change the outcome and also preventing the winning party from relitigating to improve position.

In a much-noted 2006 decision, the Court of Cassation (France's highest court for civil and criminal matters) surprisingly reread the code, appearing to collapse the requirements of identity of object demanded and *cause*. Then, in a 2007 decision, the court stated that it is incumbent upon each party to make in the first action all the arguments capable of justifying its claim or defense. These decisions reflect at the least a principle of *concentration des moyens*, i.e., that each party is expected to make all available arguments in support of its position. They may also reflect a principle of *concentration des demandes*, i.e., that a claimant must assert against the opponent all available demands arising from the relevant event. Especially if the broad view wins out, French preclusion law might be converging with U.S. claim preclusion, which readily extinguishes previously unasserted demands and defenses in the name of efficiency.

In summary, the wellspring of French res judicata law was the desire to avoid undoing the judgment, with the law emphasizing the *dispositif* and the required identities to create a concept that looked a little like direct estoppel. That is, preclusion reached only the ultimate issue actually decided. The French law later developed the claim-preclusive effect described above, knocking out matters that might have been urged. Both old and new approaches are sometimes referred to as the "negative effect" of the judgment. Authority for a "positive effect" of the judgment, one that would resemble collateral estoppel, remains sparse and speculative in France.

By a different path to a similarly restrained scope in another civil-law country, Japanese res judicata law has more overtly comprised a variant of claim preclusion, albeit one applicable only to asserted claims narrowly conceived. See Minsohō [Code of Civil Procedure] arts. 114–115 (Japan); Takaaki Hattori & Dan Fenno Henderson, Civil Procedure in Japan § 7.09[8] (Yasuhei Taniguchi, Pauline C. Reich & Hiroto Miyake eds., rev. 2d ed. 2009); Robert C. Casad, Issue Preclusion and Foreign Country Judgments: Whose Law?, 70 Iowa L.Rev. 53, 66–67 (1984); cf. J. Mark Ramseyer & Minoru Nakazato, Japanese Law: An Economic Approach 144–45 (1999) (attributing the narrowness of Japanese preclusion law to the low cost of proving anew in a system that relies largely on documentary evidence and operates without juries). In some recent cases, however, the Japanese courts seem to be introducing some narrow notions of issue preclusion.

In further explanation, we are locating the civil-law systems within U.S. terminology. That terminology sees res judicata as increasing in breadth from direct estoppel (the branch of issue preclusion applicable to the same claim) all the way to broad claim preclusion, with collateral estoppel (the branch of issue preclusion applicable to a different claim) being an orthogonal development that the civil law has not followed. Direct estoppel precludes the ultimate point that the judgment disposed of, that is, whether this cause of action succeeded or failed. Claim preclusion, in the U.S. sense, also precludes matters that could have been but were not decided. In other words, direct estoppel can be seen as an especially narrow approach to claim preclusion. France does not employ the term "direct estoppel" and instead thinks of itself as applying a kind of claim preclusion, but to American eyes it is precluding only the precise point of the judgment. This is like direct estoppel. By contrast, Japan at least speaks in terms of precluding a whole (albeit narrowly defined) claim, including any matters not decided. This is more like claim preclusion.

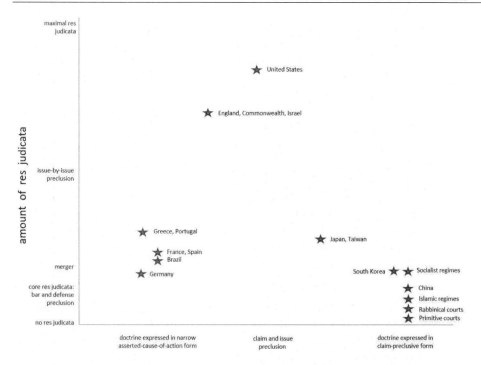

In order to affect other causes of action as well as other persons, civil-law countries broadly allow an evidential use of prior judgments, rather than expand their preclusive doctrine of res judicata. One could argue that the United States should have relaxed its hearsay rule in order to follow the same evidential route as the civilians, and so could have avoided its battles over scope of claim and over nonmutuality of estoppel. Following that evidential route in this country would entail giving to all rulings a persuasive effect similar to the effect that stare decisis gives to legal rulings. However, there are arguments against extending evidential weight to factual findings: first, combining a past decision with new evidence, especially new oral evidence, is a bit like combining apples and oranges; second, our juries especially would have trouble in weighing a past decision; and, third, the evidential approach lacks res judicata's advantage of altogether avoiding trial, an especially burdensome procedural stage in our system. Therefore, the United States has in the main rejected this civilian solution.

CREDIT DUE TO VALID AND FINAL JUDGMENTS

SECTION 1.   JUDGMENTS OF U.S. ADJUDICATORS

Fauntleroy v. Lum

Supreme Court of the United States, 1908.
210 U.S. 230, 28 S.Ct. 641.

[Fauntleroy brought action in a state court of Mississippi upon a Missouri judgment. The defendant pleaded that the original controversy arose in Mississippi out of a speculative transaction in cotton futures between two Mississippi citizens, which was illegal under Mississippi law;[a] that the parties submitted the controversy to arbitration in Mississippi, the question of illegality not being included in the submission, and the plaintiff won an award against the defendant; and that the plaintiff brought suit on the award in a Missouri state court, serving the defendant with process while he was temporarily in Missouri, and the Missouri trial court did not allow the defendant to show the nature of the transaction, and hence its illegality under Mississippi law, and eventually entered verdict and judgment for the plaintiff. On demurrer, the Mississippi trial court ordered judgment for the plaintiff. The Mississippi Supreme Court reversed, ruling that the Missouri judgment was not entitled to full faith and credit. The case came to the Supreme Court of the United States on a writ of error.]

■ MR. JUSTICE HOLMES delivered the opinion of the court.

. . . .

The doctrine laid down by Chief Justice Marshall was "that the judgment of a state court should have the same credit, validity, and effect in every other court in the United States which it had in the state where it was pronounced, and that whatever pleas would be good to a suit thereon in such state, and none others, could be pleaded in any other court in the United States." Hampton v. M'Connel, 3 Wheat. 234 [(1818) (discussing what is now 28 U.S.C. § 1738, on which see supra p. 490)]. . . .

. . . .

. . . Whether the award would or would not have been conclusive, and whether the ruling of the Missouri court upon that matter was right or wrong, there can be no question that the judgment was conclusive in Missouri on the validity of the cause of action. Pitts v. Fugate, 41 Mo.

---

[a]   The statutes of Mississippi made dealing in futures a misdemeanor and provided that such a contract "shall not be enforced by any court."

405; State ex rel. Hudson v. Trammel, 106 Mo. 510, 17 S.W. 502; Re Copenhaver, 118 Mo. 377, 40 Am.St.Rep. 382, 24 S.W. 161. A judgment is conclusive as to all the media concludendi (United States v. California & O. Land Co., 192 U.S. 355, 24 S.Ct. 266); and it needs no authority to show that it cannot be impeached either in or out of the state by showing that it was based upon a mistake of law. Of course, a want of jurisdiction over either the person or the subject-matter might be shown. Andrews v. Andrews, 188 U.S. 14, 23 S.Ct. 237; Clarke v. Clarke, 178 U.S. 186, 20 S.Ct. 873. But, as the jurisdiction of the Missouri court is not open to dispute, the judgment cannot be impeached in Mississippi even if it went upon a misapprehension of the Mississippi law. [Citations omitted.]

We feel no apprehensions that painful or humiliating consequences will follow upon our decision. No court would give judgment for a plaintiff unless it believed that the facts were a cause of action by the law determining their effect. Mistakes will be rare. In this case the Missouri court no doubt supposed that the award was binding by the law of Mississippi. If it was mistaken, it made a natural mistake. The validity of its judgment, even in Mississippi, is, as we believe, the result of the Constitution as it always has been understood, and is not a matter to arouse the susceptibilities of the states, all of which are equally concerned in the question and equally on both sides.

Judgment reversed.

■ [The dissenting opinion of JUSTICE WHITE, with whom Justices Harlan, McKenna, and Day joined, is omitted.]

———

Questions: (1) Would the Supreme Court of the United States have had jurisdiction to review the Missouri judgment? If so, and the Supreme Court had heard the case, how should it have been decided? See William B. Sohn, Note, Supreme Court Review of Misconstructions of Sister State Law, 98 Va.L.Rev. 1861 (2012) (criticizing the rule that the Supreme Court could reverse only if Missouri was constitutionally compelled to apply Mississippi law and yet ignored or seriously misconstrued it).

(2) Why is the obligation to recognize and enforce sister-state judgments so much more demanding than the respect owing by choice of law to sister-state laws?

———

JAMES v. GRAND TRUNK WESTERN RAILROAD CO., 14 Ill.2d 356, 152 N.E.2d 858, cert. denied, 358 U.S. 915, 79 S.Ct. 288 (1958). The plaintiff administratrix sued the railroad in an Illinois court under the Michigan Wrongful Death Act, based on a fatal collision in Cass County, Michigan, where the plaintiff resided. She believed, with some reason, that she could not obtain a fair trial in Cass County. Thereafter a Cass County court granted the railroad an injunction restraining her from prosecuting the Illinois action;[b] but she did not appeal because no stay was available. Instead, she sought in Illinois a counter-injunction enjoining the railroad from enforcing the Michigan injunction. After denial of relief in the lower courts and an appeal by the plaintiff, the Illinois Supreme Court, in a 4–3 decision, restrained the enforcement of the Michigan injunction. It held that the Illinois court, having acquired jurisdiction first, was free not only to disregard an out-of-state injunction but also to protect its jurisdiction from usurpation by issuance of a counter-injunction, and that neither full faith and credit nor rules of comity prevented this result. The dissenters, while agreeing that the Michigan injunction was not entitled to full faith and credit, took the view that just as the first injunction sired the second, so the second might sire a third, and so forth, and that therefore the counter-injunction should be denied.

In fact, the U.S. Supreme Court has approved only rare and narrow exceptions to full faith and credit where recognition or enforcement would so grossly and improperly interfere with the second state's important interests as to create a national interest against such recognition or enforcement, that is, where the rendering state has purported directly to transfer title to land in the second state or, as here, has enjoined a person from pursuing litigation in the second state's courts on the ground of inconvenience. See Baker v. Gen. Motors Corp., 522 U.S. 222, 235–36, 118 S.Ct. 657, 665 (1998).

———

Questions: (3) Would the Supreme Court of the United States have jurisdiction to review the Illinois decree granting the injunction against the railroad? If so, and the Supreme Court were to hear the case, how should it be decided? See Restatement (Second) of Conflict of Laws § 103 cmt. b (Am. Law Inst. 1971) (amended 1988) ("The Supreme Court of the United States has the final voice in determining what exceptions there are to full faith and credit, and the nature of these exceptions.").

(4) Suppose that instead of going to the U.S. Supreme Court, the railroad initiates contempt proceedings in Michigan when the plaintiff continues to prosecute the Illinois action. What should the Michigan court do? See id. § 113 (1971) (indicating that the later Illinois injunction against enforcement would be entitled to full faith and credit, even though the Michigan injunction was not).

———

---

[b]   The Illinois court was to say that "the Michigan injunction was apparently issued pursuant to the policy of the State embodied in a Michigan venue statute restricting venue in suits against railroads to the county in which plaintiff resides, if the railroad lines traverse that county." On the limited propriety of issuing such interstate injunctions in the first place, see Edward Dumbauld, Judicial Interference with Litigation in Other Courts, 74 Dick.L.Rev. 369 (1970); James P. George, Parallel Litigation, 51 Baylor L.Rev. 769 (1999). Problems increase in the federal-state setting, as is suggested by the existence of 28 U.S.C. § 2283. See generally Charles A. Wright & Mary Kay Kane, Law of Federal Courts §§ 46–47 (7th ed. 2011).

KREMER v. CHEMICAL CONSTRUCTION CORP., 456 U.S. 461, 102 S.Ct. 1883 (1982). As already suggested, a "judgment" is entitled not only to enforcement but also to recognition, which means getting res judicata effects. In this case, the Supreme Court decided that "a federal court in a Title VII case should give preclusive effect to a decision of a [New York] state court upholding a state administrative agency's rejection of an employment discrimination claim as meritless when the state court's decision would be [preclusive] in the state's own courts."

After overcoming a number of the plaintiff's arguments, Justice White for the Court observed:

"The more serious contention is that even though administrative proceedings and judicial review are legally sufficient to be given preclusive effect in New York, they should be deemed so fundamentally flawed as to be denied recognition under § 1738. We have previously recognized that the judicially created doctrine of collateral estoppel does not apply when the party against whom the earlier decision is asserted did not have a 'full and fair opportunity' to litigate the claim or issue . . . .

"Our previous decisions have not specified the source or defined the content of the requirement that the first adjudication offer a full and fair opportunity to litigate. But for present purposes, where we are bound by the statutory directive of § 1738, state proceedings need do no more than satisfy the minimum procedural requirements of the Fourteenth Amendment's Due Process Clause in order to qualify for the full faith and credit guaranteed by federal law. It has long been established that § 1738 does not allow federal courts to employ their own rules of res judicata in determining the effect of state judgments. Rather, it goes beyond the common law and commands a federal court to accept the rules chosen by the State from which the judgment is taken . . . .

"The State must, however, satisfy the applicable requirements of the Due Process Clause. A State may not grant preclusive effect in its own courts to a constitutionally infirm judgment, and other state and federal courts are not required to accord full faith and credit to such a judgment. Section 1738 does not suggest otherwise; other state and federal courts would still be providing a state court judgment with the 'same' preclusive effect as the courts of the State from which the judgment emerged. In such a case, there could be no constitutionally recognizable preclusion at all.

" . . . We must bear in mind that no single model of procedural fairness, let alone a particular form of procedure, is dictated by the Due Process Clause. . . .

. . . .

"In our system of jurisprudence the usual rule is that merits of a legal claim once decided in a court of competent jurisdiction are not subject to redetermination in another forum. Such a fundamental departure from traditional rules of preclusion, enacted into federal law, can be justified only if plainly stated by Congress. Because there is no 'affirmative showing' of a 'clear and manifest' legislative purpose in Title VII to deny res judicata or collateral estoppel effect [in federal court] to a state court judgment affirming that a claim of employment discrimination is unproved, and because the procedures provided in New York for the determination of such claims offer a full and fair opportunity to litigate the merits, the judgment of the Court of Appeals is affirmed."

Justice Blackmun, with whom Justices Brennan and Marshall joined, and Justice Stevens dissented. They argued that Congress had intended mere judicial review of this sort to be nonpreclusive in this setting.

The Supreme Court later applied the Kremer majority's approach in an antitrust case, Marrese v. American Academy of Orthopaedic Surgeons, 470 U.S. 373, 105 S.Ct. 1327 (1985), and in a securities case, Matsushita Electrical Industrial Co. v. Epstein, 516 U.S. 367, 116 S.Ct. 873 (1996), both of which are within exclusive federal jurisdiction. Thus, in considering the preclusive effects of an earlier state judgment on a state claim, the federal court must apply the state res judicata law even though a state court could not have heard the federal claim.

––––––––

Question: (5) Evaluate this position: A federal court in determining the effects of a state-court judgment must normally apply the preclusion law that the rendering state would apply, which includes some federal law such as the transsubstantive dictates of due process; this retroverse approach is, however, subject to rare and primarily congressional exceptions to § 1738 providing in substance-specific settings for less (or conceivably, by statute, more) credit to the state-court judgment in federal court. Does this position represent what the cases require or policy suggests, or both or neither?

––––––––

UNIVERSITY OF TENNESSEE v. ELLIOTT, 478 U.S. 788, 106 S.Ct. 3220 (1986). In this case, the Supreme Court had to decide whether a federal court in a Title VII and § 1983 action should give preclusive effect to a state administrative adjudicatory finding that racial prejudice had not motivated the firing.

Justice White for the Court premised: "Title 28 U.S.C. § 1738 governs the preclusive effect to be given the judgments and records of state courts, and is not applicable to the unreviewed state administrative factfinding at issue in this case. However, we have frequently fashioned federal common-law rules of preclusion in the absence of a governing statute." (Here his cited cases included Blonder-Tongue and Parklane Hosiery. Elsewhere, he cited Alexander v. Gardner-Denver Co., 415 U.S. 36, 94 S.Ct. 1011 (1974), which had held that unreviewed arbitration proceedings were not within § 1738 and, under the federal common law of preclusion, did not preclude a federal Title VII action. He failed to cite McDonald v. City of West Branch, 466 U.S. 284, 104 S.Ct. 1799 (1984), which had held that unreviewed arbitration proceedings did not preclude a federal § 1983 action.)

As to the Title VII claim in the instant case, Justice White found by the statute's language and legislative history that Congress had evidently intended unreviewed state administrative proceedings to have no preclusive effect on a Title VII claim in federal court, regardless of state preclusion law.

As to the § 1983 claim, he found no such intent. In formulating the consequently applicable federal common law, he observed, first, that giving issue preclusion effect to federal or state administrative factfinding serves the value of repose and, second: "Having federal courts give preclusive effect to the factfinding of state administrative tribunals also serves the value of federalism. Significantly, all of the opinions in Thomas v. Washington Gas Light Co., 448 U.S. 261, 100 S.Ct. 2647 (1980), express the view that the Full Faith and Credit Clause compels the States to give preclusive effect to the factfindings of an administrative tribunal in a sister State. . . . The Full Faith and Credit Clause is of course not binding on federal courts, but we can certainly look to the policies underlying the Clause in fashioning federal common-law rules of preclusion. 'Perhaps the major purpose of the Full Faith and Credit Clause is to act as a nationally unifying force,' id., at 289, 100 S.Ct., at 2664 (White, J., concurring in judgment), and this purpose is served by giving preclusive effect to state administrative factfinding rather than leaving the courts of a second forum, state or federal, free to reach conflicting results. Accordingly, we hold that when a state agency 'acting in a judicial capacity . . . resolves disputed issues of fact properly before it which the parties have had an adequate opportunity to litigate,' [United States v. Utah Constr. & Mining Co., 384 U.S. 394, 422, 86 S.Ct. 1545, 1560 (1966)], federal courts must give the agency's factfinding the same preclusive effect to which it would be entitled in the State's courts."

Justice Marshall did not participate. Justice Stevens, with whom Justices Brennan and Blackmun joined, dissented from authorizing preclusion on the § 1983 claim. See also Daan Braveman & Richard Goldsmith, Rules of Preclusion and Challenges to Official Action: An Essay on Finality, Fairness, and Federalism, All Gone Awry, 39 Syracuse L.Rev. 599 (1988). But the Court later elevated its favor for issue preclusion by administrative determination to a presumption, which prevails in the absence of congressional prohibition, in B & B Hardware, Inc. v. Hargis Industries, Inc., 135 S.Ct. 1293 (2015).

Unlike its cases under § 1738 such as Kremer, however, the Court's opinion in Elliott did not indicate that its rationale would apply to authorize claim preclusion as well as issue preclusion. Indeed, most lower courts have since ruled that, under the federal common law of preclusion, unreviewed state administrative proceedings do not have claim preclusion effect on a § 1983 action. E.g., Gjellum v. City of Birmingham, 829 F.2d 1056 (11th Cir.1987).

———

Hart v. American Airlines
(Landano v. American Airlines)
(Kirchstein v. American Airlines)

Supreme Court of New York, New York County, 1969.
61 Misc.2d 41, 304 N.Y.S.2d 810.

■ HARRY B. FRANK, JUSTICE. Defendant American Airlines moves pursuant to CPLR, Section 602(a), for an order directing that all issues of liability in the death actions brought by plaintiffs Landano and Kirchstein be joined for trial with the 20 other American Airlines cases [including the Hart case] subject to joint trial under an order of the Appellate Division dated November 10, 1967. (See 28 A.D.2d 986.)

The actions all arise out of the crash, in Kentucky on November 8, 1965, of an American Airlines aircraft while the plane was en route from La Guardia Airport, New York to an airport in Covington, Kentucky. The crash resulted in the death of 58 out of the 62 persons aboard and, in addition to the multiple actions pending in this court, comparable actions have been instituted in other states and in various United States District Courts.

Of the various actions instituted as a result of the crash, the first case to be tried to conclusion was that brought in the United States District Court, Northern District of Texas (Creasy v. American Airlines, Inc.), which resulted in a [$175,000] verdict in favor of the plaintiff therein against the defendant American Airlines. On a prior motion brought in the Hart case herein, the opinion of Mr. Justice Quinn, dated May 15, 1968, noted that in the Creasy trial, which lasted some 19 days, the Texas court applied the Kentucky wrongful death statute and submitted the question of American Airlines' liability on the basis of the substantive law of Kentucky relating to negligence. Reference to the pleadings in the two actions here sought to be joined for trial indicates that the basis for the recovery sought against defendant American Airlines is similarly predicated, and it is undisputable from the pleadings and papers herein that the issue of defendant airline's liability in these cases is identical to the issue in that regard determined in the Texas action.

In light of the Texas result which has now been affirmed on appeal, plaintiffs Landano and Kirchstein oppose defendant's motion for a joint trial by cross-moving for summary judgment on the issue of liability which, if granted, would obviate a trial on such issue and necessarily require a denial of defendant's motion.

Plaintiffs contend that while, concededly, they were not parties to the Texas action, nevertheless the determination in that action of defendant's liability for the plane crash of November 8, 1965 is, under the doctrine of collateral estoppel, conclusive on the issue of defendant's liability for such crash in the actions brought by these plaintiffs.

In its recent decision in Schwartz v. Public Administrator, 24 N.Y.2d 65, 298 N.Y.S.2d 955, 246 N.E.2d 725, our Court of Appeals definitively crystalized the controlling considerations governing the doctrine of collateral estoppel in this State and "arrived at a modern and stable statement of the law of res judicata" grounded on "the sound principle that, where it can be fairly said that a party has had a full opportunity to litigate a particular issue, he cannot reasonably demand a second one" . . . . "There must be an identity of issue which has necessarily been decided in the prior action and is decisive of the present action, and, second, there must have been a full and fair opportunity to contest the decision now said to be controlling."

No extended discussion is necessary to demonstrate that such requirements are amply met in the instant cases. As already indicated, the issue of defendant airline's liability for the crash in which plaintiffs' decedents perished is identical to the issue of liability litigated in the Texas action where defendant was similarly charged with responsibility for that same accident. Indeed, in an airplane crash there are absent any of the problems with respect to "identity of issue" on liability which might arise in other types of accidents involving multiple participants such as automobile accident cases. With respect to the second requirement, it is in no way disputed that defendant had a full and fair opportunity to contest the issue of its liability in the course of the 19 day trial in the Texas action, and in order to defeat collateral estoppel on this ground the burden rests on the defendant to show that it had no such opportunity.

While defendant presents various arguments as to why the finding on liability should not be applied in these cases, it relies most heavily upon the prior decision of Mr. Justice Quinn in the Hart matter, hereinbefore referred to, which was affirmed without opinion by the Appellate Division, 31 A.D.2d 896, 297 N.Y.S.2d 587. Although defendant concedes that such decision is not "in a strict sense" the law of the case here, it nevertheless contends that such decision compels a denial of plaintiffs' motion for summary judgment. This court disagrees. Contrary to defendant's assertions, the controlling factor in the Hart decision was the non-domiciliary status of the plaintiffs therein involved and the unwillingness of the court to apply the New York law of collateral estoppel with respect to a Texas determination on behalf of "non-domiciliary dependents of a deceased non-domiciliary 'bread winner'" having no significant contacts with New York.[c] While such result will undoubtedly be effective to discourage possible "forum shopping" by non-residents, it does not, as defendant argues, preclude the application of

---

[c]　Unlike the cases of Landano and Kirchstein, the companion Hart case involved only nonresidents. Justice Quinn there refused to extend collateral estoppel in favor of the New Jersey and Connecticut plaintiffs and decedents, looking to the state law of Texas which then followed the rule of mutuality of estoppel. N.Y.L.J., May 20, 1968, at 2, excerpted in 36 U.S.L.W. 2736.

the New York doctrine of collateral estoppel in an action brought by New York dependents of deceased New York residents. As was pointed out in Kilberg v. Northeast Airlines, 9 N.Y.2d 34, 39, 211 N.Y.S.2d 133, 135, 172 N.E.2d 526, 527–528, which involved a death action arising out of an airplane crash where decedent had been a New York resident, "The place of injury becomes entirely fortuitous. Our courts should if possible provide protection for our own State's people against unfair and anachronistic treatment of the lawsuits which result from these disasters." The state of Texas has no legitimate interest in imposing its rules on collateral estoppel upon these New York residents and a holding that permits such result would indeed constitute the "anachronistic treatment" warned against in Kilberg. The fact that the plaintiffs herein involved are New York domiciliaries, as were their decedents, sufficiently establishes this state's superior interest in the issue of collateral estoppel. It may be observed that these plaintiffs occupy much the same relationship to the state of Texas as the non-resident Hart plaintiffs do to New York, and the unavailability of the New York rule on collateral estoppel to the Hart plaintiffs is equally relevant in holding the instant resident plaintiffs outside the scope of the Texas rule on that issue.

Defendant's reliance on "full faith and credit" to defeat the application of collateral estoppel herein is misplaced. This is not a situation where the judgment, as such, of the Texas court is sought to be enforced. What is here involved is a policy determination by our courts that " 'One who has had his day in court should not be permitted to litigate the question anew' " (B.R. DeWitt, Inc. v. Hall, 19 N.Y.2d 141, 144, 278 N.Y.S.2d 596, 599, 225 N.E.2d 195, 197 . . .), and, further, refusal "to tolerate a condition where, on relatively the same set of facts, one fact-finder, be it court or jury" may find a party liable while another exonerates him leading to the "inconsistent results which are always a blemish on a judicial system" (Schwartz v. Public Administrator, 24 N.Y.2d 65, 74, 298 N.Y.S.2d 955, 962, 246 N.E.2d 725, 730, supra). It is in order to carry out these policy determinations in the disposition of cases in this jurisdiction that . . . use is being made of a particular issue determination made in the Texas action.

. . . .

Accordingly, plaintiffs' cross motion for summary judgment is granted and defendant's motion for a joint trial is denied. Settle order providing for an assessment of damages.

———

Questions: (6) Should the law that the rendering court would apply or the law of the forum court govern the basic res judicata effects of a prior state judgment? See Restatement (Second) of Conflict of Laws §§ 94–95 (Am. Law Inst. 1971) (amended 1988) (rendering court).

(7) Should the Full Faith and Credit Clause and statute be read to permit a state to give a sister state's judgment *more* credit than it would be

given where rendered? Is the giving of more credit fair to the party to be burdened? See Farmland Dairies v. Barber, 65 N.Y.2d 51, 478 N.E.2d 1314, 489 N.Y.S.2d 713 (1985) (giving same credit).

(8) Should federal law or state law govern the res judicata effects of a prior judgment rendered by a federal court sitting in diversity, such as the Creasy judgment?

————

Semtek International Inc. v. Lockheed Martin Corp.

Supreme Court of the United States, 2001.
531 U.S. 497, 121 S.Ct. 1021.

■ JUSTICE SCALIA delivered the opinion of the Court.

This case presents the question whether the claim-preclusive effect of a federal judgment dismissing a diversity action on statute-of-limitations grounds is determined by the law of the State in which the federal court sits.

I

Petitioner filed a complaint against respondent in California state court, alleging breach of contract and various business torts. Respondent [a Maryland citizen] removed the case to the United States District Court for the Central District of California on the basis of diversity of citizenship . . . , and successfully moved to dismiss petitioner's claims as barred by California's 2-year statute of limitations. In its order of dismissal, the District Court, adopting language suggested by respondent, dismissed petitioner's claims "in [their] entirety on the merits and with prejudice." . . . Without contesting the District Court's designation of its dismissal as "on the merits," petitioner appealed to the Court of Appeals for the Ninth Circuit, which affirmed the District Court's order. 168 F.3d 501 (1999) (table). Petitioner also brought suit against respondent in the State Circuit Court for Baltimore City, Maryland, alleging the same causes of action, which were not time barred under Maryland's 3-year statute of limitations. . . . Following a hearing, the Maryland state court granted respondent's motion to dismiss on the ground of res judicata. . . . The Court of Special Appeals affirmed, holding that, regardless of whether California would have accorded claim-preclusive effect to a statute-of-limitations dismissal by one of its own courts, the dismissal by the California federal court barred the complaint filed in Maryland, since the res judicata effect of federal diversity judgments is prescribed by federal law, under which the earlier dismissal was on the merits and claim preclusive. 128 Md.App. 39, 736 A.2d 1104 (1999). After the Maryland Court of Appeals declined to review the case, we granted certiorari. 530 U.S. 1260, 120 S.Ct. 2715 (2000).

II

Petitioner contends that the outcome of this case is controlled by Dupasseur v. Rochereau, 21 Wall. 130, 135 (1875), which held that the res judicata effect of a federal diversity judgment "is such as would belong to judgments of the State courts rendered under similar circumstances," and may not be accorded any "higher sanctity or effect." Since, petitioner argues, the dismissal of an action on statute-of-limitations grounds by a California state court would not be claim preclusive, it follows that the similar dismissal of this diversity action by the California federal court cannot be claim preclusive. While we agree that this would be the result demanded by Dupasseur, the case is not dispositive because it was decided under the Conformity Act of 1872, 17 Stat. 196, which required federal courts to apply the procedural law of the forum State in nonequity cases. That arguably affected the outcome of the case. [Citations omitted.]

Respondent, for its part, contends that the outcome of this case is controlled by Federal Rule of Civil Procedure 41(b) . . . .

. . . .

In short, it is no longer true that a judgment "on the merits" is necessarily a judgment entitled to claim-preclusive effect; and there are a number of reasons for believing that the phrase "adjudication upon the merits" does not bear that meaning in Rule 41(b). To begin with, Rule 41(b) sets forth nothing more than a default rule for determining the import of a dismissal (a dismissal is "upon the merits," with the three stated exceptions, unless the court "otherwise specifies"). This would be a highly peculiar context in which to announce a federally prescribed rule on the complex question of claim preclusion, saying in effect, "All federal dismissals (with three specified exceptions) preclude suit elsewhere, unless the court otherwise specifies."

And even apart from the purely default character of Rule 41(b), it would be peculiar to find a rule governing the effect that must be accorded federal judgments by other courts ensconced in rules governing the internal procedures of the rendering court itself. Indeed, such a rule would arguably violate the jurisdictional limitation of the Rules Enabling Act: that the Rules "shall not abridge, enlarge or modify any substantive right," 28 U.S.C. § 2072(b). Cf. Ortiz v. Fibreboard Corp., 527 U.S. 815, 842, 119 S.Ct. 2295 (1999) (adopting a "limiting construction" of Federal Rule of Civil Procedure 23(b)(1)(B) in order to "minimiz[e] potential conflict with the Rules Enabling Act, and [to] avoi[d] serious constitutional concerns"). In the present case, for example, if California law left petitioner free to sue on this claim in Maryland even after the California statute of limitations had expired, the federal court's extinguishment of that right (through Rule 41(b)'s mandated claim-preclusive effect of its judgment) would seem to violate this limitation.

Moreover, as so interpreted, the Rule would in many cases violate the federalism principle of Erie R. Co. v. Tompkins, 304 U.S. 64, 78–80, 58 S.Ct. 817 (1938), by engendering " 'substantial' variations [in outcomes] between state and federal litigation" which would "[l]ikely . . . influence the choice of a forum," Hanna v. Plumer, 380 U.S. 460, 467–468, 85 S.Ct. 1136 (1965). See also Guaranty Trust Co. v. York, 326 U.S. 99, 108–110, 65 S.Ct. 1464 (1945). Cf. Walker v. Armco Steel Corp., 446 U.S. 740, 748–753, 100 S.Ct. 1978 (1980). . . .

Finally, if Rule 41(b) did mean what respondent suggests, we would surely have relied upon it in our cases recognizing the claim-preclusive effect of federal judgments in federal-question cases. Yet for over half a century since the promulgation of Rule 41(b), we have not once done so. [Citations omitted.]

. . . .

We think, then, that the effect of the "adjudication upon the merits" default provision of Rule 41(b)—and, presumably, of the explicit order in the present case that used the language of that default provision—is simply that, unlike a dismissal "without prejudice," the dismissal in the present case barred refiling of the same claim in the United States District Court for the Central District of California. That is undoubtedly a necessary condition, but it is not a sufficient one, for claim-preclusive effect in other courts.

III

Having concluded that the claim-preclusive effect, in Maryland, of this California federal diversity judgment is dictated neither by Dupasseur v. Rochereau, as petitioner contends, nor by Rule 41(b), as respondent contends, we turn to consideration of what determines the issue. Neither the Full Faith and Credit Clause, U.S. Const., Art. IV, § 1, nor the full faith and credit statute, 28 U.S.C. § 1738, addresses the question. By their terms they govern the effects to be given only to state-court judgments (and, in the case of the statute, to judgments by courts of territories and possessions). And no other federal textual provision, neither of the Constitution nor of any statute, addresses the claim-preclusive effect of a judgment in a federal diversity action.

It is also true, however, that no federal textual provision addresses the claim-preclusive effect of a federal-court judgment in a federal-question case, yet we have long held that States cannot give those judgments merely whatever effect they would give their own judgments, but must accord them the effect that this Court prescribes. See Stoll v. Gottlieb, 305 U.S. 165, 171–172, 59 S.Ct. 134 (1938); Gunter v. Atlantic Coast Line R. Co., 200 U.S. 273, 290–291, 26 S.Ct. 252 (1906); Deposit Bank v. Frankfort, 191 U.S. 499, 514–515, 24 S.Ct. 154 (1903). The reasoning of that line of cases suggests, moreover, that even when States are allowed to give federal judgments (notably, judgments in diversity cases) no more than the effect accorded to state judgments, that disposition is by direction of this Court, which has the last word on the claim-preclusive effect of all federal judgments . . . .

. . . In short, federal common law governs the claim-preclusive effect of a dismissal by a federal court sitting in diversity. See generally R. Fallon, D. Meltzer, & D. Shapiro, Hart and Wechsler's The Federal Courts and the Federal System 1473 (4th ed. 1996); Degnan, Federalized Res Judicata, 85 Yale L.J. 741 (1976).

It is left to us, then, to determine the appropriate federal rule. And despite the sea change that has occurred in the background law since Dupasseur was decided—not only repeal of the Conformity Act but also the watershed decision of this Court in Erie—we think the result decreed by Dupasseur continues to be correct for diversity cases. Since state, rather than federal, substantive law is at issue there is no need for a uniform federal rule. And indeed, nationwide uniformity in the substance of the matter is better served by having the same claim-preclusive rule (the state rule) apply whether the dismissal has been ordered by a state or a federal court. This is, it seems to us, a classic case for adopting, as the federally prescribed rule of decision, the law that would be applied by state courts in the State in which the federal diversity court sits. [Citations omitted.] As we have alluded to above, any other rule would produce the sort of "forum-shopping . . . and . . . inequitable administration of the laws" that Erie seeks to avoid, Hanna, 380 U.S., at 468, 85 S.Ct. 1136, since filing in, or removing to, federal court would be encouraged by the divergent effects that the litigants would anticipate from likely grounds of dismissal. See Guaranty Trust Co. v. York, 326 U.S., at 109–110, 65 S.Ct. 1464.

This federal reference to state law will not obtain, of course, in situations in which the state law is incompatible with federal interests. If, for example, state law did not accord claim-preclusive effect to dismissals for willful violation of discovery orders, federal courts' interest in the integrity of their own processes might justify a contrary federal rule. No such conflict with potential federal interests exists in the present case. Dismissal of this state cause of action was decreed by the California federal court only because the California statute of limitations so required; and there is no conceivable federal interest in giving that time bar more effect in other courts than the California courts themselves would impose.

* * *

Because the claim-preclusive effect of the California federal court's dismissal "upon the merits" of petitioner's action on statute-of-limitations grounds is governed by a federal rule that in turn incorporates California's law of claim preclusion (the content of which we do not pass upon today), the Maryland Court of Special Appeals erred in holding that the dismissal necessarily precluded the bringing of this action in the Maryland courts. The judgment is reversed, and the case remanded for further proceedings not inconsistent with this opinion.

It is so ordered.[d]

Q INTERNATIONAL COURIER, INC. v. SMOAK, 441 F.3d 214 (4th Cir.2006). "Glenn Smoak filed an action in Virginia state court ('the first action') against Q International Courier, Inc. ('Quick') seeking a declaration that Quick used an improper basis appraising the value of Smoak's stock after Smoak exercised his option requiring Quick to purchase his stock. Quick removed this first action to federal district court in the Eastern District of Virginia based on diversity jurisdiction. Quick also filed a counterclaim against Smoak, alleging that Smoak used an improper basis for his stock appraisal and breached the parties' stock option agreement. After a bench trial, the district court entered judgment substantially in favor of Quick." However, the court, for lack of proof, denied Quick the damages it sought for Smoak's suing rather than following the stock appraisal method specified in the parties' stock option agreement.

Four months after the first action concluded, Quick filed "the second action" in the same federal district court, seeking damages against Smoak, his lawyer, and his other advisors for their conspiracy not to follow that specified stock appraisal method. The district court, by a different district judge, dismissed the second action based on the federal law of res judicata. In its ruling from the bench, the district court stated: "I think the record is clear that there was a common core of operative facts that were fully litigated in that first case that [Quick] is trying to essentially relitigate in this case."

The court of appeals said: "Quick now appeals, asserting that the district court erred in applying the federal law of res judicata rather than the Virginia law of res judicata, and that its claims are not subject to dismissal under the Virginia law of res judicata. For the following reasons, we reverse and remand."

The court of appeals ruled that Semtek required looking to Virginia res judicata law. While leaving the details to the district court on remand, the appellate court indicated that the answer lay in the compulsory counterclaim rule: "Although the parties agree [on the broad outlines of] the Virginia law of res judicata, neither party has argued that Virginia also has a specific res judicata rule for cases—like the instant one—in which the first action was litigated in federal district court. In such a circumstance, the initial question under Virginia law is whether the claims filed in the second action would have been considered compulsory counterclaims in the first action under Federal Rule of Civil Procedure

---

d   On remand, the court denied the res judicata defense and then proceeded to the merits, 2002 WL 32500569 (Md.Cir.Ct. Mar. 20, 2002).

13(a). See Nottingham v. Weld, 237 Va. 416, 377 S.E.2d 621, 623 (1989) ('[W]e look to the federal courts' constructions of the preclusive effect of a failure to file a compulsory counterclaim in the federal court'). If the claims asserted in the second action would have been considered compulsory counterclaims under Rule 13(a) in the first action, the claims will be precluded in the second action."

———

Questions: (9) In what sense, if any, is the court of appeals applying Virginia res judicata law? The court in Horne, supra p. 797, directly applied a uniform federal law of compulsory counterclaims rather than Ohio res judicata law. But was compulsoriness even in play here, given that Quick had actually counterclaimed? In any event, the district judge in oral proceedings on remand dismissed Quick's action for res judicata reasons, seemingly relying on Virginia's issue preclusion law rather than on Federal Rule 13(a).

(10) Did the court of appeals in Fagnan, supra p. 873, properly handle the initial choice-of-res-judicata-law question?

———

TRIBAL COURTS

The Full Faith and Credit Clause in the Constitution covers only "States" and so does not apply to Native American tribes. By contrast, 28 U.S.C. § 1738 has a broader coverage. Is not a tribal court, just like "every court within the United States and its Territories and Possessions," bound by § 1738 to give full faith and credit? But does a tribal court count as a court of "any State, Territory, or Possession of the United States" whose judgments are entitled to receive full faith and credit under § 1738?

The only sure answers are that "how much credit and deference state and federal courts must extend to the decisions of tribal courts, and vice versa, presents an ongoing and difficult legal question that has received sporadic attention from courts and commentators." Craig Smith, Comment, Full Faith and Credit in Cross-Jurisdictional Recognition of Tribal Court Decisions Revisited, 98 Calif.L.Rev. 1393, 1393–94 (2010) (arguing for the position that tribes are "territories" within the full faith and credit statute). There are, however, some specifically applicable provisions, both federal, e.g., 25 U.S.C. § 1911(d) ("The United States, every State, every territory or possession of the United States, and every Indian tribe shall give full faith and credit to the public acts, records, and judicial proceedings of any Indian tribe applicable to Indian child custody proceedings . . . ."), and state, e.g., Wyo.Stat.Ann. § 5–1–111 (requiring Wyoming state courts to give full faith and credit to valid "judgments by the courts of the Eastern Shoshone and Northern Arapaho Tribes of the Wind River Reservation" if the tribal court is a court of record and gives full faith and credit to Wyoming state judgments).

―――――

SECTION 2.   JUDGMENTS FROM FOREIGN NATIONS

Hilton v. Guyot

Supreme Court of the United States, 1895.
159 U.S. 113, 16 S.Ct. 139.[e]

[French plaintiffs invoked diversity jurisdiction to sue United States citizens in a circuit court of the United States in New York upon a French judgment. The defendants denied any indebtedness and contended that the merits of the case should be examined, because at that time French courts would do so in a suit in France upon an American judgment against a French national. The circuit court entered judgment for the French plaintiffs without examining the merits.]

■ MR. JUSTICE GRAY, after stating the case, delivered the opinion of the court.

. . . .

The most certain guide, no doubt, for the decision of such questions is a treaty or a statute of this country. But when, as is the case here, there is no written law upon the subject, the duty still rests upon the judicial tribunals of ascertaining and declaring what the law is, whenever it becomes necessary to do so, in order to determine the rights of parties to suits regularly brought before them. In doing this, the courts must obtain such aid as they can from judicial decisions, from the works of jurists and commentators, and from the acts and usages of civilized nations. [Citations omitted.]

No law has any effect, of its own force, beyond the limits of the sovereignty from which its authority is derived. The extent to which the law of one nation, as put in force within its territory, whether by executive order, by legislative act, or by judicial decree, shall be allowed to operate within the dominion of another nation, depends upon what our greatest jurists have been content to call "the comity of nations." Although the phrase has been often criticised, no satisfactory substitute has been suggested.

"Comity," in the legal sense, is neither a matter of absolute obligation, on the one hand, nor of mere courtesy and good will, upon the other. But it is the recognition which one nation allows within its territory to the legislative, executive or judicial acts of another nation, having due regard both to international duty and convenience, and to the

---

[e]   This case, covering 122 pages in the U.S. Reports, has been very drastically edited. For the background story of Hilton v. Guyot (pronounced gwee-YOH), see Louise Ellen Teitz, "The Story of Hilton: From Gloves to Globalization," in Civil Procedure Stories 445 (Kevin M. Clermont ed., 2d ed. 2008).

rights of its own citizens or of other persons who are under the protection of its laws.

. . . .

In view of all the authorities upon the subject, and of the trend of judicial opinion in this country and in England, following the lead of Kent and Story, we are satisfied that, where there has been opportunity for a full and fair trial abroad before a court of competent jurisdiction, conducting the trial upon regular proceedings, after due citation or voluntary appearance of the defendant, and under a system of jurisprudence likely to secure an impartial administration of justice between the citizens of its own country and those of other countries, and there is nothing to show either prejudice in the court, or in the system of laws under which it was sitting, or fraud in procuring the judgment, or any other special reason why the comity of this nation should not allow it full effect, the merits of the case should not, in an action brought in this country upon the judgment, be tried afresh, as on a new trial or an appeal, upon the mere assertion of the party that the judgment was erroneous in law or in fact. The defendants, therefore, cannot be permitted, upon that general ground, to contest the validity or the effect of the judgment sued on.

. . . .

It is next objected that in [the French] courts one of the plaintiffs was permitted to testify not under oath, and was not subjected to cross-examination by the opposite party, and that the defendants were, therefore, deprived of safeguards which are by our law considered essential to secure honesty and to detect fraud in a witness; and also that documents and papers were admitted in evidence, with which the defendants had no connection, and which would not be admissible under our own system of jurisprudence. But it having been shown by the plaintiffs, and hardly denied by the defendants, that the practice followed and the method of examining witnesses were according to the laws of France, we are not prepared to hold that the fact that the procedure in these respects differed from that of our own courts is, of itself, a sufficient ground for impeaching the foreign judgment.

[The Court next discussed whether a foreign judgment may be impeached on the ground that it rested on fraudulent evidence, and the Court cited English cases holding that it may be so impeached.]

But whether those decisions can be followed in regard to foreign judgments, consistently with our own decisions as to impeaching domestic judgments for fraud, it is unnecessary in this case to determine, because there is a distinct and independent ground upon which we are satisfied that the comity of our nation does not require us to give conclusive effect to the judgments of the courts of France; and that ground is, the want of reciprocity, on the part of France, as to the effect to be given to the judgments of this and other foreign countries.

[An extended review of the law of many countries as to the recognition of foreign judgments is omitted.]

The reasonable, if not the necessary, conclusion appears to us to be that judgments rendered in France, or in any other foreign country, by the laws of which our own judgments are reviewable upon the merits, are not entitled to full credit and conclusive effect when sued upon in this country, but are prima facie evidence only of the justice of the plaintiffs' claim [which means that a plaintiff seeking enforcement can introduce a valid and final foreign judgment to show there is presumptively a judgment debt, but the defendant can then induce full and free reexamination of the merits of the claim].

In holding such a judgment, for want of reciprocity, not to be conclusive evidence of the merits of the claim, we do not proceed upon any theory of retaliation upon one person by reason of injustice done to another; but upon the broad ground that international law is founded upon mutuality and reciprocity, and that by the principles of international law recognized in most civilized nations, and by the comity of our own country, which it is our judicial duty to know and to declare, the judgment is not entitled to be considered conclusive.

■ [The judgment was reversed. The dissenting opinion of CHIEF JUSTICE FULLER, with whom Justices Harlan, Brewer, and Jackson joined, is omitted. He would have treated foreign judgments like American judgments and rejected a reciprocity rule.]

———

Questions: (11) Should a state court, in considering whether to give conclusive effect to a French judgment in a case like Hilton v. Guyot, regard the questions as ones of federal law? See John Norton Moore, Federalism and Foreign Relations, 1965 Duke L.J. 248, 265.

(12) The New York courts, like those of most states, have given conclusive effect to judgments of foreign nations without regard to any question of reciprocity, thus rejecting the Hilton rule. Johnston v. Compagnie Générale Transatlantique, 242 N.Y. 381, 152 N.E. 121 (1926). In a diversity action upon a foreign judgment in a federal court in New York, like Hilton but commenced after Erie, must the New York rule be followed? See Bank of Montreal v. Kough, 612 F.2d 467 (9th Cir.1980) (yes). But see John D. Brummett, Jr., Note, The Preclusive Effect of Foreign Country Judgments in the United States and Federal Choice of Law: The Role of the Erie Doctrine Reassessed, 33 N.Y.L.Sch.L.Rev. 83 (1988).

———

UNIFORM ACT

New York, long the preeminent state in matters of enforcing foreign judgments, codified its liberal law in 1970 by enacting NY CPLR art. 53 on recognition and enforcement of foreign judgments. It did so primarily to provide a ready means of demonstrating its liberality to any reciprocity-minded foreign court contemplating a New York judgment. The codification proceeded by enacting, as most other states have done, a version of the Uniform Foreign-Country Money Judgments Recognition Act.

The National Conference of Commissioners on Uniform State Laws had approved this Uniform Act in 1962 and clarified it by revision in 2005. That Act now provides that a recognized judgment is "enforceable in the same manner and to the same extent as a judgment rendered in this state." It requires recognition of a foreign money judgment that is "final, conclusive, and enforceable" under the rendering country's law. Recognition means that the judgment is "conclusive between the parties to the same extent as the judgment of a sister state entitled to full faith and credit in this state would be conclusive," which "means that the foreign-country judgment generally will be given the same effect in the forum state that it has in the foreign country where it was rendered."

The new Uniform Act rightly imposes a recognition precondition that necessitates judicial approval either in the course of an action upon the judgment based on personal jurisdiction or attachment jurisdiction or in connection with the judgment's invocation as res judicata in some other kind of lawsuit. But the enacting states have not enacted the Uniform Act uniformly. Some states have even experimented with a registration procedure for enforcement of foreign-country judgments, much like the procedure for U.S. judgments described supra p. 492.

Section 4 of the current Uniform Act specifies mandatory and discretionary grounds for nonrecognition:

> (b) A court of this state may not recognize a foreign-country judgment if:
>
> > (1) the foreign-country judgment was rendered under a judicial system that does not provide impartial tribunals or procedures compatible with the requirements of due process of law;
> >
> > (2) the foreign court did not have personal jurisdiction over the defendant; or
> >
> > (3) the foreign court did not have jurisdiction over the subject matter.
>
> (c) A court of this state need not recognize a foreign-country judgment if:
>
> > (1) the defendant in the proceeding in the foreign court did not receive notice of the proceeding in sufficient time to enable the defendant to defend;
> >
> > (2) the foreign-country judgment was obtained by fraud that deprived the losing party of an adequate opportunity to present its case;

(3) the foreign-country judgment or the [cause of action] [claim for relief] on which the foreign-country judgment is based is repugnant to the public policy of this state or of the United States;

(4) the judgment conflicts with another final and conclusive judgment;

(5) the proceeding in the foreign court was contrary to an agreement between the parties under which the dispute in question was to be determined otherwise than by proceedings in that foreign court;

(6) in the case of jurisdiction based only on personal service, the foreign court was a seriously inconvenient forum for the trial of the action;

(7) the foreign-country judgment was rendered in circumstances that raise substantial doubt about the integrity of the rendering court with respect to the foreign-country judgment; or

(8) the specific proceeding in the foreign court leading to the foreign-country judgment was not compatible with the requirements of due process of law.

The brackets suggest to state legislatures a choice in the form of words to conform to state usage.

Section 5 restricts the especially important testing of personal jurisdiction, by essentially spelling out when the U.S. standards of substantive due process must be deemed satisfied:

(a) A foreign-country judgment may not be refused recognition for lack of personal jurisdiction if:

(1) the defendant was served with process personally in the foreign country;

(2) the defendant voluntarily appeared in the proceeding, other than for the purpose of protecting property seized or threatened with seizure in the proceeding or of contesting the jurisdiction of the court over the defendant;

(3) the defendant, before the commencement of the proceeding, had agreed to submit to the jurisdiction of the foreign court with respect to the subject matter involved;

(4) the defendant was domiciled in the foreign country when the proceeding was instituted or was a corporation or other form of business organization that had its principal place of business in, or was organized under the laws of, the foreign country;

(5) the defendant had a business office in the foreign country and the proceeding in the foreign court involved a [cause of action] [claim for relief] arising out of business done by the defendant through that office in the foreign country; or

(6) the defendant operated a motor vehicle or airplane in the foreign country and the proceeding involved a [cause of action] [claim for relief] arising out of that operation.

(b) The list of bases for personal jurisdiction in subsection (a) is not exclusive, and the courts of this state may recognize other bases of personal jurisdiction as sufficient to support a foreign-country judgment.

The Uniform Act covers foreign-country court judgments granting or denying "recovery of a sum of money," other than judgments for taxes, for a fine or other penalty, or for support in domestic relations matters. Although the Uniform Act's application is thus to certain money judgments only, many states look to it for guidance in treating nonmonetary judgments as well. Indeed, the Restatement (Fourth) of Foreign Relations Law of the United States §§ 481–487 (Am. Law Inst. 2018) builds on the Uniform Act's approach by applying it to more kinds of judgments.

SOCIETY OF LLOYD'S v. ASHENDEN, 233 F.3d 473 (7th Cir.2000). Plaintiff in this diversity action invoked the Illinois version of the Uniform Act to collect on big money judgments obtained in England. The defendants collaterally attacked on the ground that the judgments rested on two contractual clauses so onerous as to deny due process, but the United States District Court for the Northern District of Illinois granted summary judgment to the plaintiff. The Seventh Circuit affirmed, per Judge Posner, in whose view "the key question is not the fairness of Lloyd's [contractual] measures but the fairness of the English court":

"The defendants . . . asked the district court not to recognize the English judgments as being enforceable in Illinois. They argued that those judgments had denied them due process of law and therefore were not enforceable under the foreign money-judgments recognition act, which makes a judgment rendered by a court outside the United States unenforceable in Illinois if 'the judgment was rendered under a *system* which does not provide impartial tribunals or procedures compatible with the requirements of due process of law.' . . .

"We have italicized the word that defeats the defendants' argument. The judgments about which they complain were rendered by the Queen's Bench Division of England's High Court, which corresponds to our federal district courts; they were affirmed by the Court of Appeal, which corresponds to the federal courts of appeals; and the Appellate

Committee of the House of Lords, which correspond[ed] to the U.S. Supreme Court, denied the defendants' petition for review. Any suggestion that this system of courts 'does not provide impartial tribunals or procedures compatible with the requirements of due process of law' borders on the risible. . . .

"Not that the English concept of fair procedure is identical to ours; but we cannot believe that the Illinois statute is intended to bar the enforcement of all judgments of any foreign legal system that does not conform its procedural doctrines to the latest twist and turn of our courts regarding, for example, the circumstances under which due process requires an opportunity for a hearing in advance of the deprivation of a substantive right rather than afterwards. See Hilton v. Guyot, 159 U.S. 113, 205, 16 S.Ct. 139, 40 L.Ed. 95 (1895); Ingersoll Milling Machine Co. v. Granger, 833 F.2d 680, 687–88 (7th Cir.1987). It is a fair guess that no foreign nation has decided to incorporate our due process doctrines into its own procedural law; and so we interpret 'due process' in the Illinois statute (which, remember, is a uniform act, not one intended to reflect the idiosyncratic jurisprudence of a particular state) to refer to a concept of fair procedure simple and basic enough to describe the judicial processes of civilized nations, our peers. The statute requires only that the foreign procedure be '*compatible* with the requirements of due process of law,' and we have interpreted this to mean that the foreign procedures are 'fundamentally fair' and do not offend against 'basic fairness.' Id. at 687–88; see also Hilton v. Guyot, supra, 159 U.S. at 202–03, 16 S.Ct. 139; [other citations omitted].

"We'll call this the 'international concept of due process' to distinguish it from the complex concept that has emerged from American case law. . . .

"It is true that no evidence was presented in the district court on whether England *has* a civilized legal system, but that is because the question is not open to doubt. We need not consider what kind of evidence would suffice to show that a foreign legal system 'does not provide impartial tribunals or procedures compatible with the requirements of due process of law' if the challenged judgment had been rendered by Cuba, North Korea, Iran, Iraq, Congo, or some other nation whose adherence to the rule of law and commitment to the norm of due process are open to serious question, [citations omitted], as England's are not. It is anyway not a question of fact. It is not, strictly speaking, a question of law either, but it is a question about the law of a foreign nation, and in answering such questions a federal court is not limited to the consideration of evidence that would be admissible under the Federal Rules of Evidence; any relevant material or source may be consulted. Fed.R.Civ.P. 44.1; [other citations omitted]."

Questions: (13) If Fauntleroy v. Lum had been an action to enforce an English judgment, rather than that of a sister state, how should the case have been decided? See Restatement (Second) of Conflict of Laws § 117 cmt. c (Am. Law Inst. 1971).

(14) Assuming that the required circumstances exist for recognizing a judgment from a foreign nation, what should be the extent of recognition? That is, should the res judicata effects of the prior judgment be governed by the foreign law, by the usual res judicata rules of domestic law, or by some special set of res judicata rules for international judgments (for example, a rule to apply the foreign res judicata law unless it goes too far to be fair in the domestic view)? Is it significant that res judicata rules in American legal systems generally are considerably broader in effect than those elsewhere? See Robert C. Casad, Issue Preclusion and Foreign Country Judgment: Whose Law?, 70 Iowa L.Rev. 53 (1984).

(15) After invoking personal jurisdiction to bring a successful action in U.S. State A to recognize and enforce her foreign-country judgment, can P successfully bring an action upon her State A judgment in U.S. State B (or register the State A judgment in State B) in order to apply more assets toward satisfying the judgment debt? What if State B would not have accepted the foreign-country judgment on reciprocity or on public policy grounds?

———

INTERNATIONAL LAW

Current law.—International law itself plays no real role in U.S. treatment of foreign judgments, except to the extent that the U.S. approach is already a manifestation of any generally recognized principles that constitute part of international law. The United States has not a single treaty on the subject. So, for foreign judgments, no binding law comparable to full faith and credit exists to take them out of the normal background rule: the acts of foreign governments have no effect within another government's territory, unless the latter government *chooses* to give them effect.

Yet U.S. courts at the federal and state level do give respect to foreign judgments, not only because finality is a fair and efficient policy even as to foreign judgments, but also because U.S. courts hope to encourage abroad similar respect for their own judgments. That is, freed from constitutional, statutory, and treaty obligations but motivated by similar policies, U.S. courts generally respect foreign judgments that are valid and final under the foreign law. Accordingly, the foreign res judicata law should be applicable, and the foreign judgment should be enforceable, in the United States.

The U.S. courts' approach to foreign judgments can still be somewhat flexible, precisely because their respect flows from "comity" rather than from external legal obligation. A closer look at the actual holdings and opinions suggests that U.S. courts apply somewhat different standards to judgments of foreign nations, as compared to those they apply to domestic, state, or federal judgments. The principal reason for the difference is that a U.S. court has no guarantee that a foreign judgment, although comporting with the basic requirements of the foreign nation, is minimally acceptable to Americans. The foreign laws concerning validity vary widely. Moreover, the Due Process Clause and the rest of the U.S. Constitution do not control foreign sovereigns, of course, and so the workings of the foreign legal system could be too foreign to tolerate.

From this realistic insight follow four corollaries. First, while a U.S. court will ask whether jurisdiction existed under the foreign law, the U.S. court more importantly may examine whether the foreign assertion of jurisdiction satisfied the U.S. tests of substantive due process. A U.S. court, for example, would disregard a French judgment for which personal jurisdiction was based solely on the plaintiff's French nationality. Second, a U.S. court will give no respect to a foreign judgment that it views as repugnantly unfair. A U.S. court will not recognize or enforce a foreign judgment resulting from proceedings that failed to meet the basic notions of U.S. procedural due process, such as adequate notice, and so prevented the parties from having a fair day in court. Third, a U.S. court might apply other limitations, such as refusing recognition or enforcement if the prior judgment resulted from fraud extrinsic to the merits or if the original claim is directly contrary to strong local public policy. For a procedural example of those limitations, a foreign default judgment rendered contrary to a forum selection clause's derogation might fall within the public policy exception, even where Uniform Act § 4(c)(5) is not in force. For a substantive example, a U.S. court would reject an English judgment for defamation that impinges on U.S. principles of free speech with respect to U.S.-linked speech; also, U.S. courts would generally not regard judgments of foreign countries imposing tax obligations or penal sanctions as entitled to recognition or enforcement. Fourth, in principle not often applied in actual practice, a U.S. court may require reciprocity. In sum, U.S. courts treat judgments of foreign nations pretty much like U.S. judgments, but not quite. See generally S.I. Strong, Recognition and Enforcement of Foreign Judgements in U.S. Courts: Problems and Possibilities, 33 Rev.Litig. 45 (2014).

This U.S. behavior is nevertheless fairly generous compared to most other nations'. Most other nations appear to demonstrate a relatively heightened notion of sovereignty in this regard. Even if the U.S. judgment passes the foreign court's jurisdictional reexamination, which very well might involve meeting all the standards of the foreign jurisdictional law, the foreign court tends to reexamine the merits to ensure that the applied law conformed to local policy. And as to the extent of any recognition, the foreign court tends to apply its own, narrower res judicata law. See generally Samuel P. Baumgartner, How Well Do U.S. Judgments Fare in Europe?, 40 Geo.Wash.Int'l L.Rev. 173 (2008).

Treaty possibilities.—European countries appear ahead of the United States on the treatment of foreign judgments or, rather, on their treatment of European judgments. As already explained, the European Union has an enlightened, albeit far from perfect, jurisdiction-and-judgments system. By that so-called Brussels Regulation, the member states must provide virtually automatic recognition and enforcement of the judgments of the other member states, if rendered on specified jurisdictional bases.

The European Union does not appear superior in all regards, however. It discriminates against outsiders in matters of jurisdiction. The virtually automatic recognition and enforcement understandably does not extend to judgments rendered by countries that are not member states. The European countries, in fact, have traditionally been and continue to be rather stingy in extending respect to foreign judgments not covered by treaty, such as U.S. judgments. In brief, Americans are being whipsawed by the European Union approach. Not only are they still subject (in theory) to the far-reaching jurisdiction of European courts and the wide recognition and enforceability of those courts' resulting judgments, but also U.S. judgments tend (in practice) to receive short shrift in European courts.

The overall international situation, as exacerbated by the Brussels Regulation, is unacceptable in the long run for the United States. Therefore, in 1992 the United States initiated a push to conclude a worldwide convention on jurisdiction and judgments, naturally choosing to work through the Hague Conference on Private International Law. Drafting and agreeing on a multilateral convention could yield great returns for the United States. A convention would rationalize both jurisdiction law and judgments law on an international level. A convention would also resolve the whipsawing predicament in which Americans today find themselves regarding exercise of jurisdiction as well as treatment of judgments. As to the jurisdictional side, a convention would require nations to renounce their own exorbitant jurisdiction. It also could substantively improve U.S. jurisdiction law in international cases. In the specific matter of treatment of foreign judgments, a convention would more unarguably be desirable for the United States. It would mean that the United States could get returns for the respect the United States is already according other nations' judgments.

The proposed convention would have been very similar to the Brussels Regulation. Under it, the United States would abandon—on the international level, but not necessarily with respect to its courts' actions against its own habitual residents—attachment jurisdiction (Europeans oppose the remnants still available, except when used for security or enforcement), tag jurisdiction (seen as an unnecessary relic of the power theory), doing business (opposed when used as a basis for general jurisdiction other than at the principal place of business), and much of forum non conveniens (seen as too discretionary). The Europeans' objection is to the U.S. proclivity to base general jurisdiction on rather thin contacts, namely, allowing unrelated causes of action to be brought on the basis of the defendant's property ownership, physical presence, or doing business in the forum. They do not object to specific jurisdiction as a concept, as long as a rules-based approach makes its application nondiscretionary. Thus, jurisdiction would exist at the unconsenting defendant's habitual residence or where a specific part of the events in suit occurred, but would not extend to the broader bases of jurisdiction now authorized by U.S. law. In sum, the general convention would have agreed on certain bases of territorial jurisdiction, but chiefly those palatable to the Europeans—and judgments based thereon would then receive virtually automatic recognition and enforcement in other signatory countries (except those judgments that the Europeans consider too generous or punitive).

Will such a broad jurisdiction-and-judgments convention—as opposed to narrower conventions treating important but special problem areas (such as judgments resulting from business-to-business contracts containing choice-of-court agreements that select forums for disputes to the exclusion of other forums, on which treaty not yet in force see Ronald A. Brand & Paul Herrup, The 2005 Hague Convention on Choice of Court Agreements (2008))—come into existence? Not in the near future. The United States has little bargaining power under the current regime. It needs a convention, while the Europeans have little to gain over their presently favorable situation. Consequently, the general talks at The Hague broke down after a decade of effort.

In 2011, though, those Hague talks resumed. They produced a so-called single convention that would treat recognition and enforcement of judgments (as the Uniform Act does) without trying to agree on a double convention that would also codify the grounds for jurisdiction (as the Brussels Regulation does). The 2019 Hague Convention on the Recognition and Enforcement of Foreign Judgments in Civil or Commercial Matters, not yet in force, would indeed work much like our Uniform Act. See Hague Conference on Private Int'l Law, The Judgments Project, https://www.hcch.net/en/projects/legislative-projects/judgments.

The fruits of negotiation to date have definitely been worth the effort. Merely negotiating a draft double convention taught all sides a lot about jurisdiction. For example, exorbitant jurisdiction looks different when viewed through foreign eyes. In particular, the effort has revealed to the United States the possibility of untangling on its own the jurisdictional law that it applies in domestic cases.

––––––––

SECTION 3.   VALIDITY VERSUS FINALITY

As just suggested once again, a judgment must be deemed "valid" in order to have any res judicata effects. To be so deemed, the judgment must be of sufficient quality to withstand attack launched in the form of a request for relief from judgment.

As we shall see in this Section, relief from judgment lies by various procedural techniques. The attacker can raise an array of grounds for relief by each technique, with more grounds available by, say, motion in the rendering court than by, say, collateral attack in a second action— but with relief ultimately resting on a discretionary balancing of equities. Consequently, one cannot define validity by specifying certain attributes of the judgment, but only as the outcome of the process of relief from judgment.

Such a definition of validity might seem frustratingly circular, but it is not. It is what is called an operational definition. Although it is not the usual kind of definition by categorization, specifying a process to determine validity is an entirely defensible sort of definition.

GROUNDS FOR ATTACK

Generally, relief from judgment, which could come by various procedures in subsequent litigation outside the ordinary course of review in the trial and appellate courts, will lie on grounds set by the judgment-rendering sovereign. Of course, that sovereign's law is subject to any applicable external restraints, an example being where due process and other federal provisions are imposed on and become part of state law.

So in, say, an action to enforce a default judgment of a state court, that state's law governs the grounds for collateral attack. At least traditionally, the common formulation of state law provided that the judgment was not valid in these circumstances if and only if the rendering court had failed to satisfy the requirement of (1) subject-matter jurisdiction, (2) territorial jurisdiction, or (3) opportunity to be heard.

If, instead, the defaulting party had proceeded promptly to the rendering court to move for relief from judgment, the list of grounds would have been slightly longer. Relief then would have lain in a situation of extraordinary injustice, such as in a case where the opponent procured the judgment by fraudulent means extrinsic to the merits. The party might thus get relief for extrinsic fraud, as by preventing the party from litigating—in contrast to intrinsic fraud, as by using fraudulent evidence.

There have been some inroads on this traditional doctrine, and hence on its relative certainty. Among some theorists and in some cases, relief from judgment should turn more expressly on a discretionary balancing of equities. Various factors would determine the availability of relief: (1) the nature and importance of the judgment's alleged infirmity; (2) the procedural technique of relief from judgment employed, this factor being based on the view that such techniques form a spectrum and that the list of available grounds for relief should contract as the mode, place, and time of attack become more distant from the initial action; (3) the impact of the relief requested; and (4) the position of the parties, including diligence in seeking relief and reliance on the judgment.

This fluid approach approximates the traditional doctrine. But there are divergences. Sometimes and for some purposes, taking into account the fluid factors, judgments not meeting the three requirements of competence and nexus and notice nevertheless would have effect (even on motion in the rendering court, as in Gschwind v. Cessna Aircraft Co., 232 F.3d 1342 (10th Cir.2000) (disallowing Federal Rule 60(b)(4) motion despite a jurisdictional defect under the diversity statute)), and other judgments meeting those requirements would have no effect (even in an out-of-state action upon the judgment, as in Lee v. Carroll, 146 So.2d 242 (La.Ct.App.1962) (allowing collateral attack on an extrinsic fraud ground)).

Consider how well the traditional and fluid approaches explain the next three cases.

———

Bank of Montreal v. Olafsson

United States Court of Appeals, Sixth Circuit, 1981.
648 F.2d 1078, cert. denied, 454 U.S. 1084, 102 S.Ct. 641 (1981).

■ Before ENGEL and MERRITT, CIRCUIT JUDGES and PHILLIPS, SENIOR CIRCUIT JUDGE.

■ PER CURIAM.

The plaintiff is a Canadian corporation, and the defendant a citizen of Iceland. The issue here is whether the trial court erred in setting aside a default judgment it had entered more than a year earlier. The ground for setting it aside was that it had no subject matter jurisdiction because the requisite diversity of citizenship was lacking.

The Bank of Montreal filed suit March 2, 1978 [in the Eastern District of Michigan] against Thorhallur G. Olafsson to recover $34,572 due it through promissory notes and an overdraft. On May 31, 1978 the District Court granted a default judgment. The Bank then filed liens on Michigan realty held in the name of Olafsson's wife, and the property was sold to the Bank in satisfaction of its judgment. On June 7, 1979 Olafsson moved to set aside the judgment on two grounds: (1) because he was never personally served with a copy of the complaint, and (2) because he had filed for bankruptcy in Canada on March 28, 1978,[2] and under Canada law it is illegal to pursue claims while bankruptcy proceedings are pending.

In argument on the motion, Olafsson raised the diversity question. The district court rendered its opinion from the bench, finding that the

---

[2]   In that proceeding the Bank was named as a creditor.

bank was a Canadian corporation and that Olafsson was not a citizen of the United States either. It stated that the Bank knew or should have known of the citizenship of Olafsson. It recognized that the Bank had taken action in reliance on the default but found the policy against granting judgments in cases in which the court has no jurisdiction to be overriding. It noted that it had never before addressed the jurisdictional question and concluded that the default judgment should be vacated under Fed.R.Civ.P. 60(b)(4) or 60(b)(6) because it was entered "in excess of the power of this court." The court set aside the default judgment and "all liens, writs of levy and execution, and sheriff's sales," and dismissed the suit.

The grant of motions made under rule 60(b) is a matter of discretion for the district court, and its decision is to be set aside only if it constitutes an abuse of discretion. Wright & Miller, Federal Practice and Procedure: Civil § 2872; 7 Moore's Federal Practice ¶ 60.19. The competing values implicated in the decision are on the one hand the interest in finality of judgments and on the other the interest in maintaining federal constitutional jurisdictional limitations.

[Feeling that voidness under Rule 60(b)(4) was merely "arguable," the court of appeals decided to rely on Rule 60(b)(6).] The district court also relied on rule 60(b)(6), which allows for a weighing of equities, in setting aside the judgment. See Wright & Miller, § 2864; 7 Moore's ¶ 60.27[2]. It discounted the Bank's reliance interest because of its finding that the Bank "knew or reasonably should have known" of Olafsson's citizenship. Olafsson's stated reason for not responding to the Bank's suit was that he had forwarded the complaint to his bankruptcy trustee with the understanding that he would take care of it.

. . . .

Given the lack of federal jurisdiction in the case, and considering the equities of the case under rule 60(b), we agree with the district court that the default judgment should be set aside and the case dismissed for lack of subject matter jurisdiction. The dispute between the parties over the promissory notes, overdraft, and liens can be more fairly and completely adjudicated in the Canadian bankruptcy court, in the country where the loan was made, the bank is located and Olafsson's bankruptcy is pending.

Accordingly, the judgment of the district court is affirmed.

————

Marshall v. Lockhead

Court of Civil Appeals of Texas, 1952.
245 S.W.2d 307, writ of error refused n.r.e.

■ Hale, Justice.

Appellant sued appellee [in the 134th Judicial District Court of Dallas County] to set aside a prior judgment rendered in a former suit for the collection of delinquent taxes and to recover the title and possession of a certain lot sold and conveyed to appellee under an order of sale issued on the judgment in the prior tax suit. The present case was tried before the court below without a jury and resulted in judgment that appellant take nothing.

Appellant says the judgment in the tax suit was invalid and void in so far as he is concerned, because he was not served with citation and did not enter any appearance in the former suit, and hence he insists the Court did not acquire jurisdiction over his person. On the other hand, appellee says the judgment was not void and hence is not subject to collateral attack in this suit, and that appellant, by accepting the benefits accruing to him under the same, is estopped from asserting in this suit that such judgment is void or invalid.

The record before us discloses that on May 10, 1945, a final judgment was rendered in the 44th Judicial District Court of Dallas County, whereby the court found the amount of delinquent taxes, penalties and interest due and owing to the State of Texas and certain of its political subdivisions by reason of the ownership of the two lots therein described, being hereafter referred to as Lots 6 and 18. The judgment recites that defendants, C.B. Marshall and wife, Isabelle Marshall, had been duly cited in terms of law to appear but had wholly made default. The court found the amount of taxes, penalties and interest due against each of the two lots, decreed a foreclosure of the tax lien on each lot as against the defendants and directed that an order of sale be issued for each lot.

In pursuance of an order of sale issued on the above judgment, the sheriff of Dallas County sold Lot 6 to one George A. Harnack on July 3, 1945 for the sum of $1160.00. Of this amount the sum of $530.59 was paid to the State of Texas and others in satisfaction of the taxes due on Lot 6, and the balance thereof in the sum of $626.41 was paid into the registry of the court for the former owner of said lot. Thereafter, on April 6, 1948, C.B. (Bruce) Marshall, the appellant herein, applied to the 44th Judicial District Court for an order granting him permission to withdraw such excess money from the registry of the court as the former owner of Lot 6. The court granted the application, appellant withdrew said sum of $626.41 from the registry of the court, appropriated the same to his own use and benefit, and he has not returned or offered to return the same, or any part thereof, into court. In pursuance of another order of sale issued on the above judgment, the sheriff of Dallas County sold and conveyed Lot 18 to appellee and it is this lot which appellant seeks to recover in the present suit.

. . . .

. . . [I]t is generally held upon sound principles of equity that one who accepts and retains the fruits of a judgment is estopped thereafter to assert its invalidity. [Citations omitted.] This just rule applies to cases where the asserted invalidity arises from a lack of jurisdiction of the court over the person of a party to the suit. Therefore, even though the C.B.

Marshall who was served with citation in the tax suit here involved was not in fact the same person as the appellant in this cause, nevertheless it appears to us that the appellant herein, by reason of his conduct in procuring and retaining the sum of $626.41 paid into the registry of the court under the judgment rendered in the tax suit, conclusively estopped himself from successfully asserting in this suit that the tax judgment or either of the sales emanating therefrom was void or invalid. [Citations omitted.]

Consequently, all of appellant's points of error are overruled and the judgment appealed from is affirmed.

Britton v. Gannon

Supreme Court of Oklahoma, 1955.
285 P.2d 407, cert. denied, 350 U.S. 886, 76 S.Ct. 140 (1955).

■ ARNOLD, JUSTICE.

Mark Gannon brought this action in the District Court of Pontotoc County against W.R. Britton [on February 2, 1952] on a foreign judgment rendered in favor of said Gannon against Britton [on October 20, 1951] in the Circuit Court of Fayette County, Illinois, in the sum of $18,000.

Defendant filed answer consisting of a general denial and allegations to the effect that Mark Gannon was only a nominal party; that the real party in interest was Roy or "Spike" Gannon, brother of Mark Gannon; that said "Spike" Gannon had advised defendant that he was filing suit to recover certain personal property owned by him and defendant which had been sold pursuant to mortgage foreclosure proceedings and that Britton was a necessary defendant, but that no judgment would be taken against him, and relying on these representations, although served with summons, Britton made no effort to defend such suit and did not know that judgment had been taken against him until the instant suit was filed. Upon motion of plaintiff and over the objections and exceptions of defendant all allegations of defendant's answer except his general denial were stricken.

[At trial, plaintiff proved his claim based upon the Illinois judgment, but defendant's evidence of extrinsic fraud was not admitted.]

The court found that under the full faith and credit clause of the Constitution of the United States, art. 4, § 1, it had no right to hear and determine the validity of the defendant's defense . . . and entered judgment in favor of plaintiff for the amount prayed for.

Defendant contends that the court erred in refusing to allow him to present evidence to the effect that the judgment in Illinois, the basis of the present suit, was procured by extrinsic fraud and therefore not entitled to full faith and credit in Oklahoma.

The general rule is that a state court is not required to recognize the judgment of a court of another state, territory, or country subject to the jurisdiction of the United States, where the court rendering the judgment was without jurisdiction or judgment was obtained by extrinsic fraud. Stephens v. Thomasson, 63 Ariz. 187, 160 P.2d 338, and cases therein cited. Whatever plea would be good in the state in which the judgment was rendered may be pleaded in suit on the judgment in any other court in the United States. Ibid. Extrinsic fraud has been defined as any fraudulent conduct of the successful party which was practiced outside of an actual adversary trial directly and affirmatively on the defeated party whereby he was prevented from presenting fully and fairly his side of the cause. Included in such definition are false representations that the defeated party is merely a nominal party against whom no relief is sought, false promises of compromise, concealment of the suit, kidnapping of witnesses, and the like. Calkin v. Wolcott, 182 Okl. 278, 77 P.2d 96. In such cases a court of equity had power to annul the decree so obtained. Ibid. See also American Ry. Express Co. v. Murphy, 234 Ill.App. 346, Village of Hartford v. First National Bank of Wood River, 307 Ill.App. 447, 30 N.E.2d 524. Some cases, as United States v. Throckmorton, 98 U.S. 61, 25 L.Ed. 93, put this on the ground that in such cases there has never been a real contest in the hearing of the case; others, such as Williams v. State of North Carolina, 325 U.S. 226, 65 S.Ct. 1092, 89 L.Ed. 1577, cited as authority in Stephens v. Thomasson, supra, on the ground that such conduct on the part of the successful party prevented the court from having jurisdiction to render the judgment which was rendered. Others, such as Levin v. Gladstein, 142 N.C. 482, 55 S.E. 371, 32 L.R.A.,N.S., 905, put it on the ground that a foreign court is not required to give greater faith and credit to the judgment than it is entitled to at home, and when the state in which the judgment was rendered would enjoin the enforcement of such judgment because of the circumstances under which it was obtained, the sister state may do likewise.

Regardless of the reason assigned for the rule, the weight of authority is overwhelming that a defense of extrinsic fraud of the nature here sought to be plead and proved may be interposed in a suit on a foreign judgment, not for the purpose of reviewing, setting aside, modifying, or annulling the judgment of the sister state, but to prevent its enforcement in the collateral court. [Citations omitted.] The trial court erred in refusing the proffered evidence of extrinsic fraud.

Reversed and remanded for a new trial.[f]

---

[f]   In a different action, brought in 1956 while the Oklahoma state action was still pending on remand, the Oklahoma federal court denied relief by collateral attack on the same Illinois judgment. Gannon v. American Airlines, 251 F.2d 476, 482 (10th Cir.1957) (2–1 decision) (holding that the judgment was "not open to collateral attack in this proceeding upon the ground of fraud not going to the jurisdiction of the court"), vacated per stipulation, 251 F.2d 486 (10th Cir.1958).

PROCEDURES FOR ATTACK

Three primary techniques lead to relief from judgment:

1.   A party or privy may attack the judgment in the rendering court by a motion for relief from judgment. Bank of Montreal v. Olafsson provides an example, which involves Federal Rule 60(b). Such a motion is technically a continuation of the initial action. Nevertheless, it lies only in fairly extraordinary situations of injustice, designedly not serving as a cure for carelessness. See generally Wright & Miller §§ 2857–2866. In appropriate cases, however, it is the preferred means of giving relief from judgment, being the most direct and orderly technique.

2.   If adequate relief from judgment is unavailable by motion because of any applicable limits on use of such motion, a person may properly bring an independent suit against the judgment-holder to nullify or to enjoin the enforcement of the judgment. The essence here is a separate claim, but one aimed directly at the prior judgment. The suit is preferably, but not necessarily, brought in the rendering court. An example, which shows the difficulty of definition, comes when Britton alleges extrinsic fraud to obtain relief from judgment by equitable counterclaim or defense—given the ground for relief, this would probably equate to an independent claim under the traditional classification, according to Restatement (Second) of Judgments § 80 cmt. a, reporter's note (Am. Law Inst. 1982).

3.   If someone in a subsequent action relies on a prior judgment as a basis for claim or defense (as where the plaintiff sues upon the judgment to enforce it or where the defendant pleads res judicata), and if adequate relief from judgment is not available and more convenient by another procedural technique, then the other party may properly launch a collateral attack on the prior judgment to prevent its use. The term "collateral attack" is used in distinction to a "direct attack," which comes as a challenge to a judgment in a proceeding brought specially for that purpose. A tricky example is Bruce Marshall's unsuccessful attack upon Lockhead's use of the prior judgment as a defense against recovery of land—given the main objective of the subsequent action, this would probably be a collateral attack in traditional terms, according to id. ch. 5 introductory note, at 141–42.

In brief, direct attacks in the form of motions and independent suits for relief from judgment have traditionally been limited to cases of extraordinary injustice, although not quite as limited as collateral attack with its focus on subject-matter and territorial jurisdiction and opportunity to be heard.

Notice that all three of the preceding illustrative cases involved an attack on a default judgment. In nondefault situations, res judicata (and waiter) may work to foreclose attack by any of these techniques. Such concerns are the focus of the next Section.

———

SECTION 4. "JURISDICTION TO DETERMINE JURISDICTION"—JURISDICTIONAL FINDINGS AS RES JUDICATA

Affirmative rulings on jurisdiction can preclude the parties from attacking the resultant judgment on that ground in subsequent litigation. The impact of this so-called jurisdiction to determine jurisdiction doctrine is a bit shocking upon first impression. After all, seemingly implicit in the concept of due process embodied in the Fifth and Fourteenth Amendments of the U.S. Constitution is the principle that one cannot be bound by a judgment of a court that lacked jurisdiction. This validity principle would seem to imply both that a basically defective judgment should not be entered against the person or the person's property and also that any such judgment will not be enforced or recognized as a valid judgment would be. The fact is, however, that such a validity principle does not exist.

———

Baldwin v. Iowa State Traveling Men's Ass'n
Supreme Court of the United States, 1931.
283 U.S. 522, 51 S.Ct. 517.

■ MR. JUSTICE ROBERTS delivered the opinion of the Court.

A writ of certiorari was granted herein to review the affirmance by the Circuit Court of Appeals of a judgment for respondent rendered by the District Court for Southern Iowa. The action was upon the record of a judgment rendered in favor of the petitioner against the respondent in the United States District Court for Western Missouri.[g]

The defense was lack of jurisdiction of the person of the respondent in the court which entered the judgment. After hearing, in which a jury was waived, this defense was sustained and the action dismissed. The first suit was begun in a Missouri state court and removed to the District Court. Respondent appeared specially and moved to quash and dismiss for want of service. The court quashed the service, but refused to dismiss. An alias summons was issued and returned served, whereupon it again appeared specially, moved to set aside the service, quash the return, and dismiss the case for want of jurisdiction of its person. After a hearing on affidavits and briefs, the motion was overruled, with leave to plead within thirty days. No plea having been filed within that period, the

———

[g]   On the option of registration of federal judgments, which became available in 1948, see supra p. 491.

cause proceeded and judgment was entered for the amount claimed. Respondent did not move to set aside the judgment nor sue out a writ of error.

The ground of the motion made in the first suit is the same as that relied on as a defense to this one, namely, that the respondent is an Iowa corporation, that it never was present in Missouri, and that the person served with process in the latter State was not such an agent that service on him constituted a service on the corporation. The petitioner objected to proof of these matters, asserting that the defense constituted a collateral attack and a retrial of an issue settled in the first suit. The overruling of this objection and the resulting judgment for respondent are assigned as error.

The petitioner suggests that Article IV, Section 1 of the Constitution forbade the retrial of the question determined on respondent's motion in the Missouri District Court; but the full faith and credit required by that clause is not involved, since neither of the courts concerned was a state court. (Compare Cooper v. Newell, 173 U.S. 555, 567,[h] 19 S.Ct. 506; Supreme Lodge, Knights of Pythias v. Meyer, 265 U.S. 30, 33,[i] 44 S.Ct. 432.) The respondent, on the other hand, insists that to deprive it of the defense which it made in the court below, of lack of jurisdiction over it by the Missouri District Court, would be to deny the due process guaranteed by the Fourteenth Amendment; but there is involved in that doctrine no right to litigate the same question twice [citations omitted].

The substantial matter for determination is whether the judgment amounts to res judicata on the question of the jurisdiction of the court which rendered it over the person of the respondent. It is of no moment that the appearance was a special one expressly saving any submission to such jurisdiction. That fact would be important upon appeal from the judgment, and would save the question of the propriety of the court's decision on the matter even though after the motion had been overruled the respondent had proceeded, subject to a reserved objection and exception, to a trial on the merits. Harkness v. Hyde, 98 U.S. 476; [other citations omitted]. The special appearance gives point to the fact that the respondent entered the Missouri court for the very purpose of litigating the question of jurisdiction over its person. It had the election not to appear at all. If, in the absence of appearance, the court had proceeded to judgment and the present suit had been brought thereon, respondent could have raised and tried out the issue in the present action, because it would never have had its day in court with respect to jurisdiction. [Omitted citations include Pennoyer.] It had also the right to appeal from

---

[h]   "And the courts of the United States are bound to give to the judgments of the state courts the same faith and credit that the courts of one State are bound to give to the judgments of the courts of her sister States."

[i]   "While the judicial proceedings of the federal courts are not within the terms of the constitutional provision, such proceedings, nevertheless, must be accorded the same full faith and credit by state courts as would be required in respect of the judicial proceedings of another State."

the decision of the Missouri District Court, as is shown by Harkness v. Hyde, supra, and the other authorities cited. It elected to follow neither of those courses, but, after having been defeated upon full hearing in its contention as to jurisdiction, it took no further steps, and the judgment in question resulted.

Public policy dictates that there be an end of litigation; that those who have contested an issue shall be bound by the result of the contest, and that matters once tried shall be considered forever settled as between the parties. We see no reason why this doctrine should not apply in every case where one voluntarily appears, presents his case and is fully heard, and why he should not, in the absence of fraud, be thereafter concluded by the judgment of the tribunal to which he has submitted his cause.

. . . .

Reversed [and remanded].

————

Questions: (16) Would the result have been different if the prior judgment against the respondent had been entered after a general appearance and the issue of personal jurisdiction had not been raised, litigated, or determined?

(17) What law should govern the res judicata effects of jurisdictional findings, the law that the rendering court would apply or the law of the forum court? What if the prior judgment came from a foreign nation? See Nippon Emo-Trans Co. v. Emo-Trans, Inc., 744 F.Supp. 1215, 1227 (E.D.N.Y.1990) ("the determination of a foreign court as to jurisdiction is to be treated with circumspection").

(18) In a second action a party launches a collateral attack for lack of personal jurisdiction in the first action, and the court sustains or rejects the attack. If in a third action the same question of personal jurisdiction again arises on collateral attack on the first judgment, what result and why? See Arecibo Radio Corp. v. Puerto Rico, 825 F.2d 589 (1st Cir.1987) (second decision has normal issue preclusion effect).

————

Chicot County Drainage District v. Baxter State Bank

Supreme Court of the United States, 1940.
308 U.S. 371, 60 S.Ct. 317.

■ MR. CHIEF JUSTICE HUGHES delivered the opinion of the Court.

Respondents brought this suit [on July 24, 1937] in the United States District Court for the Western Division of the Eastern District of Arkansas to recover on fourteen bonds of $1,000 each, which had been issued in 1924 by the petitioner, Chicot County Drainage District, organized under statutes of Arkansas, and had been in default since 1932.

In its answer, petitioner pleaded a decree of the same District Court in a proceeding instituted by petitioner to effect a plan of readjustment of its indebtedness under the Act of May 24, 1934, providing for "Municipal-Debt Readjustments". The decree recited that a plan of readjustment had been accepted by the holders of more than two-thirds of the outstanding indebtedness and was fair and equitable; that to consummate the plan and with the approval of the court petitioner had issued and sold new serial bonds to the Reconstruction Finance Corporation in the amount of $193,500 and that these new bonds were valid obligations; that, also with the approval of the court, the Reconstruction Finance Corporation had purchased outstanding obligations of petitioner to the amount of $705,087.06 which had been delivered in exchange for new bonds and canceled; that certain proceeds had been turned over to the clerk of the court and that the disbursing agent had filed his report showing that the Reconstruction Finance Corporation had purchased all the old bonds of petitioner other than the amount of $57,449.30. The decree provided for the application of the amount paid into court to the remaining old obligations of petitioner, that such obligations might be presented within one year, and that unless so presented they should be forever barred from participating in the plan of readjustment or in the fund paid into court. Except for the provision for such presentation, the decree canceled the old bonds and the holders were enjoined from thereafter asserting any claim thereon.

Petitioner pleaded this decree, which was entered in March, 1936, as res judicata. Respondents demurred to the answer. Thereupon the parties stipulated for trial without a jury.

The evidence showed respondents' ownership of the bonds in suit and that respondents had notice of the proceeding for debt readjustment. The record of that proceeding, including the final decree, was introduced. The District Court ruled in favor of respondents and the Circuit Court of Appeals affirmed. 8 Cir., 103 F.2d 847. The decision was placed upon the ground that the decree was void because, subsequent to its entry, this Court in a proceeding relating to a municipal district in Texas had declared the statute under which the District Court had acted to be unconstitutional. Ashton v. Cameron County District, 298 U.S. 513, 56 S.Ct. 892 [(1936)]. In view of the importance of the question we granted certiorari. October 9, 1939. 308 U.S. 532, 60 S.Ct. 84.

. . . .

First. Apart from the contention as to the effect of the later decision as to constitutionality, all the elements necessary to constitute the defense of res judicata are present. It appears that the proceedings in the District Court to bring about a plan of readjustment were conducted in complete conformity to the statute. The Circuit Court of Appeals observed that no question had been raised as to the regularity of the court's action. The answer in the present suit alleged that the plaintiffs (respondents here) had notice of the proceeding and were parties, and the evidence was to the same effect, showing compliance with the statute in that respect. As parties, these bondholders had full opportunity to present any objections to the proceeding, not only as to its regularity, or the fairness of the proposed plan of readjustment, or the propriety of the terms of the decree, but also as to the validity of the statute under which the proceeding was brought and the plan put into effect.[j] Apparently no question of validity was raised and the cause proceeded to decree on the assumption by all parties and the court itself that the statute was valid. There was no attempt to review the decree. If the general principles governing the defense of res judicata are applicable, these bondholders, having the opportunity to raise the question of invalidity, were not the less bound by the decree because they failed to raise it. Cromwell v. County of Sac, 94 U.S. 351, 352; [other citations omitted].

Second. The argument is pressed that the District Court was sitting as a court of bankruptcy, with the limited jurisdiction conferred by statute, and that, as the statute was later declared to be invalid, the District Court was without jurisdiction to entertain the proceeding and hence its decree is open to collateral attack. We think the argument untenable. The lower federal courts are all courts of limited jurisdiction, that is, with only the jurisdiction which Congress has prescribed. But none the less they are courts with authority, when parties are brought before them in accordance with the requirements of due process, to determine whether or not they have jurisdiction to entertain the cause and for this purpose to construe and apply the statute under which they are asked to act. Their determinations of such questions, while open to direct review, may not be assailed collaterally.

. . . This rule applies equally to the decrees of the District Court sitting in bankruptcy, that is, purporting to act under a statute of Congress passed in the exercise of the bankruptcy power. The court has the authority to pass upon its own jurisdiction and its decree sustaining jurisdiction against attack, while open to direct review, is res judicata in a collateral action. Stoll v. Gottlieb, 305 U.S. 165, 171, 172, 59 S.Ct. 134, 137.

Whatever the contention as to jurisdiction may be, whether it is that the boundaries of a valid statute have been transgressed, or that the statute itself is invalid, the question of jurisdiction is still one for judicial determination. If the contention is one as to validity, the question is to be considered in the light of the standing of the party who seeks to raise the question and of its particular application. In the present instance it is suggested that the situation of petitioner, Chicot County Drainage District, is different from that of the municipal district before the court

---

       [j]   The briefs in this case indicate that while other bondholders did appear in the bankruptcy proceeding, the respondents themselves never appeared in person or by attorney. The court below likewise observed this fact, 103 F.2d at 848.

in the Ashton case. Petitioner contends that it is not a political subdivision of the State of Arkansas but an agent of the property owners within the District. See Drainage District No. 7 of Poinsett County v. Hutchins, 184 Ark. 521, 42 S.W.2d 996. We do not refer to that phase of the case as now determinative but merely as illustrating the sort of question which the District Court might have been called upon to resolve had the validity of the Act of Congress in the present application been raised. As the question of validity was one which had to be determined by a judicial decision, if determined at all, no reason appears why it should not be regarded as determinable by the District Court like any other question affecting its jurisdiction. There can be no doubt that if the question of the constitutionality of the statute had actually been raised and decided by the District Court in the proceeding to effect a plan of debt readjustment in accordance with the statute, that determination would have been final save as it was open to direct review upon appeal. Stoll v. Gottlieb, supra.

The remaining question is simply whether respondents, having failed to raise the question in the proceeding to which they were parties and in which they could have raised it and had it finally determined, were privileged to remain quiet and raise it in a subsequent suit. Such a view is contrary to the well-settled principle that res judicata may be pleaded as a bar, not only as respects matters actually presented to sustain or defeat the right asserted in the earlier proceeding, "but also as respects any other available matter which might have been presented to that end". Grubb v. Public Utilities Commission, [281 U.S. 470, 479, 50 S.Ct. 374, 378 (1930); other citation omitted].

The judgment is reversed and the cause is remanded to the District Court with direction to dismiss the complaint.

Reversed.

Questions: (19) Would the rule of Chicot—that lack of subject-matter jurisdiction generally cannot be raised on collateral attack even though it was not actually litigated in the prior action—apply if a prior judgment were invoked merely for issue preclusion on a litigated and determined merits issue?

(20) Would the rule of Chicot apply if the prior judgment resulted from a complete default by all defendants (or by the sole defendant if sued alone)? See Restatement (Second) of Judgments § 12 cmt. f (Am. Law Inst. 1982) (no).

(21) A federal statute provides that during the pendency of a farmer's bankruptcy proceedings in federal court, the state courts shall have no jurisdiction to foreclose a mortgage on the farmer's land. Imagine that in a contested state-court proceeding, at a time when federal bankruptcy proceedings are pending, the state court erroneously either assumes or decides that it has jurisdiction and decrees foreclosure of the mortgage of *K*'s

farm. The property is sold to the mortgagee at a sheriff's foreclosure sale, and the sheriff evicts *K*. In a new action in the same state court, *K* sues the mortgagee-purchaser for cancellation of the sheriff's deed and restoration of possession. Is the foreclosure decree subject to attack in this new proceeding? See Kalb v. Feuerstein, 308 U.S. 433, 60 S.Ct. 343 (1940) (yes), which is generalized by Restatement (Second) of Judgments § 12 (Am. Law Inst. 1982) (providing exceptions when: "(1) The subject matter of the action was so plainly beyond the court's jurisdiction that its entertaining the action was a manifest abuse of authority; or (2) Allowing the judgment to stand would substantially infringe the authority of another tribunal or agency of government; or (3) The judgment was rendered by a court lacking capability to make an adequately informed determination of a question concerning its own jurisdiction and as a matter of procedural fairness the party seeking to avoid the judgment should have opportunity belatedly to attack the court's subject matter jurisdiction."), which in turn is criticized by Karen Nelson Moore, Collateral Attack on Subject Matter Jurisdiction: A Critique of the Restatement (Second) of Judgments, 66 Cornell L.Rev. 534 (1981).

———

DURFEE v. DUKE, 375 U.S. 106, 84 S.Ct. 242 (1963). Durfee, a Nebraska citizen, sued Duke, a Missouri citizen, in a Nebraska state court to quiet title to certain bottom land situated on the Missouri River, the main channel of which forms the boundary between Nebraska and Missouri. The Nebraska court had jurisdiction only if the land in question was in Nebraska; whether the land was Nebraska land depended entirely upon the factual question of whether a shift in the river's course had been caused by avulsion or accretion; when the change in the channel of a river is sudden (avulsion), the state boundary remains as before, but when the change is gradual (accretion), the boundary moves with the channel. Duke appeared in the Nebraska court and fully litigated the issues, explicitly contesting the court's jurisdiction. The court found the land to be in Nebraska by application of the rule of avulsion, and it ordered that title to the land be quieted in Durfee. On appeal, the Supreme Court of Nebraska affirmed. Duke did not petition for certiorari.

Two months later Duke sued in a Missouri state court to quiet title to the same land, alleging it to be in Missouri. Durfee removed to the federal district court by reason of diversity of citizenship. The district court, although expressing the view that on the evidence the land was in Missouri, found for Durfee on the ground that the Nebraska judgment was entitled to full faith and credit. On appeal, the Eighth Circuit reversed. The Supreme Court of the United States granted certiorari.

The Supreme Court in turn reversed the court of appeals, holding that the Nebraska judgment was entitled to full faith and credit when the jurisdictional issue had been fully and fairly litigated and finally determined in the Nebraska courts and when Nebraska would therefore not permit collateral attack. Justice Stewart, for the Court, said that the general rule of finality of litigated jurisdictional determinations, unambiguously established in the Baldwin case with respect to jurisdiction over the person, was "no different when the claim is made that the original forum did not have jurisdiction over the subject matter."

―――――

Questions: (22) Did this case really involve a question of subject-matter jurisdiction? Compare Restatement (Second) of Judgments §§ 10, 12 (Am. Law Inst. 1982), with Restatement (Second) of Conflict of Laws §§ 96–97 (Am. Law Inst. 1971) (amended 1988).

(23) In what circumstances should lack of opportunity to be heard survive as a ground for collateral attack?

(24) If the Nebraska court had dismissed for lack of jurisdiction because it had found the land to be in Missouri, could Duke have used this finding against Durfee in the later action in Missouri? See Ruhrgas AG v. Marathon Oil Co., supra p. 749 note k (discussing jurisdiction to determine no jurisdiction).

―――――

SECTION 5. "JURISDICTION TO DETERMINE JURISDICTION"—POWER TO PUNISH DISOBEDIENCE OF IMPROPER COURT ORDER

The other side of the collateral attack coin is the so-called collateral bar rule, which holds that in subsequent litigation one cannot correct errors in a valid judgment, no matter how important or obvious the error. But surely, in the tradition of civil disobedience, one can violate any seriously improper court order, and still avoid punishment if one proves to have been in the right, right? No. Although for centuries one could argue fundamental error in the order when the court tried later to punish disobedience, today that is no longer allowed.

―――――

United States v. United Mine Workers
Supreme Court of the United States, 1947.
330 U.S. 258, 67 S.Ct. 677.

[In October 1946 the United States was in possession of, and operating, most of the nation's bituminous coal mines pursuant to an executive order of the President issued upon his determination that labor disputes were interrupting the production of coal necessary for the operation of the economy during the transition from war to peace. Terms and conditions of employment were controlled by an agreement between Secretary of the Interior Julius A. Krug, as Coal Mines Administrator, and John L. Lewis, as president of the United Mine Workers. A dispute arose as to the union's power to terminate the Krug-Lewis agreement, and Lewis gave notice to Krug on November 15 of termination as of

November 20, circulating to the mine workers a copy of his letter to Krug for their "official information."

[On November 18 the United States, contending that Lewis and the union had no power unilaterally to terminate the agreement, filed a complaint against them in the United States District Court for the District of Columbia, seeking a declaratory judgment to that effect and a temporary restraining order and preliminary injunction enjoining the defendants from encouraging the mine workers to strike and from taking any action that would interfere with the court's jurisdiction and its determination of the case. Jurisdiction was based on 28 U.S.C. § 1345. The court immediately issued without notice a temporary restraining order, to expire on November 27 when it would hold the hearing on a preliminary injunction. The complaint and restraining order were served on the defendants on November 18. A gradual walkout by the miners commenced that same day, and by midnight of November 20, consistent with the miners' "no contract, no work" policy, a full-blown strike was in progress. Mines furnishing most of the nation's bituminous coal were idle.

[On November 21 the United States, alleging a willful violation of the restraining order, filed a petition for a rule to show cause why the defendants should not be punished for contempt. The rule issued. On November 25, its return date, the defendants denied the "jurisdiction" of the court to issue the restraining order and subsequently moved to discharge the rule to show cause. They contended that the Norris-LaGuardia Act prohibited the granting of injunctive relief. Section 4 of the Act, 29 U.S.C. § 104, provided that "[n]o court of the United States shall have jurisdiction to issue any restraining order or temporary or permanent injunction in any case involving or growing out of any labor dispute" against various specified acts, including what the defendants had done. It seemed apparent that the Act would apply if the dispute were between the defendants and a private employer, but the United States urged that the Act did not apply to the government as employer. On November 27 the district judge extended the restraining order, and on November 29 he overruled the motion to discharge the rule and held that the restraining order was not affected by the Norris-LaGuardia Act. The bench trial for contempt proceeded, and both defendants were found guilty of both criminal and civil contempt. On December 4 Lewis was fined $10,000 and the union $3,500,000, without any apportionment between criminal and civil contempt. On the same day the judge issued a preliminary injunction in terms similar to those of the restraining order, effective until termination of the case.

[On December 5 Lewis sent the miners back to work. On the same day the defendants appealed to the court of appeals, and the judgments of contempt were stayed pending appeal. The United States asked for certiorari under 28 U.S.C. § 1254(1), which allows either party to do so prior to judgment in the court of appeals, and next the defendants also sought certiorari. Certiorari was granted, "[p]rompt settlement of this case being in the public interest." The Supreme Court rendered decision on March 6, 1947.]

■ MR. CHIEF JUSTICE VINSON delivered the opinion of the Court.

[Part I of the opinion held that the Norris-LaGuardia Act did not apply to a labor dispute with the government.]

II.

Although we have held that the Norris-LaGuardia Act did not render injunctive relief beyond the jurisdiction of the District Court, there are alternative grounds which support the power of the District Court to punish violations of its orders as criminal contempt.

. . . .

In the case before us, the District Court had the power to preserve existing conditions while it was determining its own authority to grant injunctive relief. The defendants, in making their private determination of the law, acted at their peril. Their disobedience is punishable as criminal contempt.

Although a different result would follow were the question of jurisdiction frivolous and not substantial, such contention would be idle here. The applicability of the Norris-LaGuardia Act to the United States in a case such as this had not previously received judicial consideration, and both the language of the Act and its legislative history indicated the substantial nature of the problem with which the District Court was faced.

Proceeding further, we find impressive authority for the proposition that an order issued by a court with jurisdiction over the subject matter and person must be obeyed by the parties until it is reversed by orderly and proper proceedings. This is true without regard even for the constitutionality of the Act under which the order is issued. In Howat v. Kansas, 258 U.S. 181, 189–90, 42 S.Ct. 277, 280–81 (1922), this Court said:

> "An injunction duly issuing out of a court of general jurisdiction with equity powers upon pleadings properly invoking its action, and served upon persons made parties therein and within the jurisdiction, must be obeyed by them however erroneous the action of the court may be, even if the error be in the assumption of the validity of a seeming but void law going to the merits of the case. It is for the court of first instance to determine the question of the validity of the law, and until its decision is reversed for error by orderly review, either by itself or by a higher court, its orders based on its decision are to be respected, and disobedience of them is contempt of its lawful authority, to be punished."

Violations of an order are punishable as criminal contempt even though the order is set aside on appeal, Worden v. Searls, 121 U.S. 14, 7 S.Ct. 814 (1887), or though the basic action has become moot, Gompers v. Buck's Stove & Range Co., 221 U.S. 418, 31 S.Ct. 492 (1911).

We insist upon the same duty of obedience where, as here, the subject matter of the suit, as well as the parties, was properly before the court; where the elements of federal jurisdiction were clearly shown; and where the authority of the court of first instance to issue an order ancillary to the main suit depended upon a statute, the scope and applicability of which were subject to substantial doubt. The District Court on November 29 affirmatively decided that the Norris-LaGuardia Act was of no force in this case and that injunctive relief was therefore authorized. Orders outstanding or issued after that date were to be obeyed until they expired or were set aside by appropriate proceedings, appellate or otherwise. Convictions for criminal contempt intervening before that time may stand.

It does not follow, of course, that simply because a defendant may be punished for criminal contempt for disobedience of an order later set aside on appeal, that the plaintiff in the action may profit by way of a fine imposed in a simultaneous proceeding for civil contempt based upon a violation of the same order. The right to remedial relief falls with an injunction which events prove was erroneously issued, [citations omitted]; and a fortiori when the injunction or restraining order was beyond the jurisdiction of the court. . . . If the Norris-LaGuardia Act were applicable in this case, the conviction for civil contempt would be reversed in its entirety.

[In subsequent Parts of the opinion, the Court rejected the contention that procedural errors required reversal of the contempt judgments. The defendants urged that the criminal and civil contempts should not have been heard together, and that they had been deprived of their procedural rights for criminal contempt under Federal Rule of Criminal Procedure 42. The Court found that the defendants had been accorded all the rights owing to defendants in criminal contempt proceedings. The Court conceded that it might be "the better practice" to try criminal contempt alone, but found no substantial prejudice requiring reversal.

[Finally, the Court ordered the $10,000 fine imposed on Lewis to stand as punishment for criminal contempt, but found that $3,500,000 was excessive as to the union and instead imposed a $700,000 fine for criminal contempt with the balance of $2,800,000 for civil contempt being conditioned on the defendant's failure to purge itself within five days by publicly withdrawing its notice of termination.]

■ [Only Justices Reed and Burton concurred fully in the Chief Justice's opinion. Professor Chafee called this case "a masterpiece of judicial logrolling." Zechariah Chafee, Jr., Some Problems of Equity 366 (1950). The various separate opinions are omitted.

[JUSTICES FRANKFURTER and JACKSON separately opined that the Norris-LaGuardia Act applied to the government and forbade the injunction. But they acquiesced in Part II of the opinion, justifying the reduced punishment by criminal contempt for violation of an order made to preserve the status quo while the court was determining its own jurisdiction to grant injunctive relief. This made a shaky majority of five for resort to criminal contempt, which the Chief Justice plainly wanted.

[For the ultimate combination of a sanction partly criminal and partly civil, the Chief Justice needed the support of JUSTICES BLACK and DOUGLAS. In a joint opinion, those two agreed that the Norris-LaGuardia Act was inapplicable and that civil contempt sanctions in the full amounts were therefore authorized. But feeling that a criminal contempt sanction here was inconsistent with the principle that in contempt proceedings courts should never exercise more than "the least possible power adequate to the end proposed," they found it unnecessary to deal with the problems of Part II.

[JUSTICES MURPHY and RUTLEDGE in separate opinions dissented all the way, noting that the rule of Part II authorizing punishment for disobedience of orders issued in excess of "jurisdiction" was contrary to the long-settled course of decision. The several opinions took up 128 pages of the U.S. Reports.]

Question: (25) As counsel for John L. Lewis, how would you have advised him before this decision? How would you have advised him if the substance of this decision were already on the books?

Walker v. City of Birmingham

Supreme Court of the United States, 1967.
388 U.S. 307, 87 S.Ct. 1824.

[In the Easter season of 1963, Rev. Martin Luther King, Jr., and a group of Birmingham, Alabama, ministers organized a campaign featuring peaceful parades and picketing to protest racial segregation. A Birmingham ordinance required that public demonstrations be licensed by the city commission, which could refuse to grant a permit only if "in its judgment the public welfare, peace, safety, health, decency, good order, morals or convenience" so required. Two attempts on April 3 and April 5 to obtain a permit from Commissioner "Bull" Connor were rebuffed,[k] but no formal written application was submitted to the full three-person commission as the ordinance stipulated.

---

[k]   A witness at the contempt hearing testified that Commissioner Connor said: "No, you will not get a permit in Birmingham, Alabama, to picket. I will picket you over to the City Jail." For a full treatment of the factual background of this case, see Alan F. Westin & Barry Mahoney,

[On Wednesday, April 10, city officials sought and obtained from a state circuit court an ex parte temporary injunction enjoining Dr. King and specified others from participating in or encouraging further mass protests without a permit. Dr. King and others who had been served with copies of the writ of injunction held a press conference the next day, declaring their intention to disobey the injunction because it was "raw tyranny under the guise of maintaining law and order."

[On Good Friday, April 12, Dr. King and his followers defied the injunction by holding a parade of about 50 or 60 persons with a crowd of 1000 to 1500 onlookers standing by, clapping and shouting. On Easter Sunday, a crowd of 1500 to 2000 congregated. A group of about 50 started down the sidewalk two abreast. Some 300 or 400 of the onlookers followed in a crowd that occupied the entire width of the street and overflowed onto the sidewalks. Violence occurred. Members of the crowd threw rocks, which injured a newspaperman and damaged a police motorcycle.

[A week later Dr. King and other leaders were convicted by the state circuit court of criminal contempt and given the statutory maximum sentence of five days in jail and a $50 fine. The judge refused to consider contentions that the injunction and the ordinance were unconstitutional and that the ordinance had previously been administered in an arbitrary and discriminatory manner, ruling that because there had been no motion to dissolve the injunction, and no attempt to comply by applying for a permit, the only issues were whether there was jurisdiction to issue the injunction and whether the defendants had knowingly violated it. The Supreme Court of Alabama affirmed, citing Howat v. Kansas, 258 U.S. 181, 42 S.Ct. 277 (1922). The Supreme Court of the United States granted certiorari.]

■ MR. JUSTICE STEWART delivered the opinion of the Court.

[After stating the case, the opinion quoted the same passage from Howat v. Kansas as did the Court in the United Mine Workers case.]

The rule of state law accepted and approved in Howat v. Kansas is consistent with the rule of law followed by the federal courts.[5]

In the present case, however, we are asked to hold that this rule of law, upon which the Alabama courts relied, was constitutionally impermissible. We are asked to say that the Constitution compelled Alabama to allow the petitioners to violate this injunction, to organize and engage in these mass street parades and demonstrations, without any previous effort on their part to have the injunction dissolved or modified, or any attempt to secure a parade permit in accordance with

---

The Trial of Martin Luther King (1974); David Benjamin Oppenheimer, Martin Luther King, Walker v. City of Birmingham, and the Letter from Birmingham Jail, 26 U.C.Davis L.Rev. 791 (1993).

    5   [In a footnote here, after citing a number of cases, the majority made its lone, unadorned citation to the United Mine Workers case.—Ed.]

its terms. Whatever the limits of Howat v. Kansas,[6] we cannot accept the petitioners' contentions in the circumstances of this case.

Without question the state court that issued the injunction had, as a court of equity, jurisdiction over the petitioners and over the subject matter of the controversy. And this is not a case where the injunction was transparently invalid or had only a frivolous pretense to validity. We have consistently recognized the strong interest of state and local governments in regulating the use of their streets and other public places. Cox v. New Hampshire, 312 U.S. 569, 61 S.Ct. 762; Poulos v. New Hampshire, 345 U.S. 395, 73 S.Ct. 760. [Other citations omitted.] When protest takes the form of mass demonstrations, parades, or picketing on public streets and sidewalks, the free passage of traffic and the prevention of public disorder and violence become important objects of legitimate state concern. . . .

The generality of the language contained in the Birmingham parade ordinance upon which the injunction was based would unquestionably raise substantial constitutional issues concerning some of its provisions. [Citations omitted.] The petitioners, however, did not even attempt to apply to the Alabama courts for an authoritative construction of the ordinance. Had they done so, those courts might have given the licensing authority granted in the ordinance a narrow and precise scope, as did the New Hampshire courts in Cox v. New Hampshire and Poulos v. New Hampshire, both supra. [Other citations omitted.] Here, just as in Cox and Poulos, it could not be assumed that this ordinance was void on its face.

The breadth and vagueness of the injunction itself would also unquestionably be subject to substantial constitutional question. But the way to raise that question was to apply to the Alabama courts to have the injunction modified or dissolved. The injunction in all events clearly prohibited mass parading without a permit, and the evidence shows that the petitioners fully understood that prohibition when they violated it.

The petitioners also claim that they were free to disobey the injunction because the parade ordinance on which it was based had been administered in the past in an arbitrary and discriminatory fashion. In support of this claim they sought to introduce evidence that, a few days before the injunction issued, requests for permits to picket had been made to a member of the city commission. One request had been rudely rebuffed, and this same official had later made clear that he was without

---

[6]   In In re Green, 369 U.S. 689, 82 S.Ct. 1114 [(1962)], the petitioner was convicted of criminal contempt for violating a labor injunction issued by an Ohio court. Relying on the preemptive command of the federal labor law, the Court held that the state courts were required to hear Green's claim that the state court was *without jurisdiction* to issue the injunction. The petitioner in Green, unlike the petitioners here, had attempted to challenge the validity of the injunction *before* violating it by promptly applying to the issuing court for an order vacating the injunction. The petitioner in Green had further offered to prove that the court issuing the injunction had agreed to its violation as an appropriate means of testing its validity. [Wright & Miller § 3537, at 22, observes that the briefs in Green made the point that state law did not permit appellate review of this temporary injunction.—Ed.]

power to grant the permit alone, since the issuance of such permits was the responsibility of the entire city commission. Assuming the truth of this proffered evidence, it does not follow that the parade ordinance was void on its face. The petitioners, moreover, did not apply for a permit either to the commission itself or to any commissioner after the injunction issued. Had they done so, and had the permit been refused, it is clear that their claim of arbitrary or discriminatory administration of the ordinance would have been considered by the state circuit court upon a motion to dissolve the injunction.

This case would arise in quite a different constitutional posture if the petitioners, before disobeying the injunction, had challenged it in the Alabama courts, and had been met with delay or frustration of their constitutional claims. But there is no showing that such would have been the fate of a timely motion to modify or dissolve the injunction. There was an interim of two days between the issuance of the injunction and the Good Friday march. The petitioners gave absolutely no explanation of why they did not make some application to the state court during that period. The injunction had issued ex parte; if the court had been presented with the petitioners' contentions, it might well have dissolved or at least modified its order in some respects. If it had not done so, Alabama procedure would have provided for an expedited process of appellate review. It cannot be presumed that the Alabama courts would have ignored the petitioners' constitutional claims. Indeed, these contentions were accepted in another case by an Alabama appellate court that struck down on direct review the conviction under this very ordinance of one of these same petitioners.[13]

. . . .

The rule of law that Alabama followed in this case reflects a belief that in the fair administration of justice no man can be judge in his own case, however exalted his station, however righteous his motives, and irrespective of his race, color, politics, or religion. This Court cannot hold that the petitioners were constitutionally free to ignore all the procedures of the law and carry their battle to the streets. One may sympathize with the petitioners' impatient commitment to their cause. But respect for judicial process is a small price to pay for the civilizing hand of law, which alone can give abiding meaning to constitutional freedom.

Affirmed.

. . . .

■ MR. CHIEF JUSTICE WARREN, whom MR. JUSTICE BRENNAN and MR. JUSTICE FORTAS join, dissenting.

. . . .

---

[13]   Shuttlesworth v. City of Birmingham, 43 Ala.App. 68, 180 So.2d 114. The case is presently pending on certiorari review in the Alabama Supreme Court.

These facts lend no support to the court's charges that petitioners were presuming to act as judges in their own case, or that they had a disregard for the judicial process. They did not flee the jurisdiction or refuse to appear in the Alabama courts. Having violated the injunction, they promptly submitted themselves to the courts to test the constitutionality of the injunction and the ordinance it parroted. They were in essentially the same position as persons who challenge the constitutionality of a statute by violating it, and then defend the ensuing criminal prosecution on constitutional grounds. It has never been thought that violation of a statute indicated such a disrespect for the legislature that the violator always must be punished even if the statute was unconstitutional. On the contrary, some cases have required that persons seeking to challenge the constitutionality of a statute first violate it to establish their standing to sue. Indeed, it shows no disrespect for law to violate a statute on the ground that it is unconstitutional and then to submit one's case to the courts with the willingness to accept the penalty if the statute is held to be valid.

The Court concedes that "[t]he generality of the language contained in the Birmingham parade ordinance upon which the injunction was based would unquestionably raise substantial constitutional issues concerning some of its provisions." . . . That concession is well-founded but minimal. I believe it is patently unconstitutional on its face. Our decisions have consistently held that picketing and parading are means of expression protected by the First Amendment, and that the right to picket or parade may not be subjected to the unfettered discretion of local officials. . . . The unconstitutionality of the ordinance is compounded, of course, when there is convincing evidence that the officials have in fact used their power to deny permits to organizations whose views they dislike. . . . The only circumstance that the court can find to justify anything other than a per curiam reversal is that Commissioner Connor had the foresight to have the unconstitutional ordinance included in an ex parte injunction issued without notice or hearing or any showing that it was impossible to have notice or a hearing . . . . This injunction was such potent magic that it transformed the command of an unconstitutional statute into an impregnable barrier, challengeable only in what likely would have been protracted legal proceedings and entirely superior in the meantime even to the United States Constitution.

I do not believe that giving this Court's seal of approval to such a gross misuse of the judicial process is likely to lead to greater respect for the law any more than it is likely to lead to greater protection for First Amendment freedoms. The ex parte temporary injunction has a long and odious history in this country, and its susceptibility to misuse is all too apparent from the facts of the case. As a weapon against strikes, it proved so effective in the hands of judges friendly to employers that Congress was forced to take the drastic step of removing from federal district courts the jurisdiction to issue injunctions in labor disputes. The labor injunction fell into disrepute largely because it was abused in precisely the same way that the injunctive power was abused in this case. Judges who were not sympathetic to the union cause commonly issued, without notice or hearing, broad restraining orders addressed to large numbers of persons and forbidding them to engage in acts that were either legally permissible or, if illegal, that could better have been left to the regular course of criminal prosecution. The injunctions might later be dissolved, but in the meantime strikes would be crippled because the occasion on which concerted activity might have been effective had passed. Such injunctions, so long discredited as weapons against concerted labor activities, have now been given new life by this Court as weapons against the exercise of First Amendment freedoms. Respect for the courts and for judicial process was not increased by the history of the labor injunction.

. . . .

It is not necessary to question the continuing validity of the holding in Howat v. Kansas, however, to demonstrate that neither it nor the Mine Workers case supports the holding of the majority in this case. In Howat the subpoena and injunction were issued to enable the Kansas Court of Industrial Relations to determine an underlying labor dispute. In the Mine Workers case, the District Court issued a temporary anti-strike injunction to preserve existing conditions during the time it took to decide whether it had authority to grant the Government relief in a complex and difficult action of enormous importance to the national economy. In both cases the orders were of questionable legality, but in both cases they were reasonably necessary to enable the court or administrative tribunal to decide an underlying controversy of considerable importance before it at the time. This case involves an entirely different situation. The Alabama Circuit Court did not issue this temporary injunction to preserve existing conditions while it proceeded to decide some underlying dispute. There was no underlying dispute before it, and the court in practical effect merely added a judicial signature to a preexisting criminal ordinance. Just as the court had no need to issue the injunction to preserve its ability to decide some underlying dispute, the city had no need of an injunction to impose a criminal penalty for demonstrating on the streets without a permit. The ordinance already accomplished that. In point of fact, there is only one apparent reason why the city sought this injunction and why the court issued it: to make it possible to punish petitioners for contempt rather than for violating the ordinance, and thus to immunize the unconstitutional statute and its unconstitutional application from any attack. I regret that this strategy has been so successful.

It is not necessary in this case to decide precisely what limits should be set to the Mine Workers doctrine in cases involving violations of the First Amendment. Whatever the scope of that doctrine, it plainly was not intended to give a State the power to nullify the United States Constitution by the simple process of incorporating its unconstitutional criminal statutes into judicial decrees. I respectfully dissent.

■ [The dissenting opinions of JUSTICES DOUGLAS and BRENNAN, each joined in by all of the dissenting Justices, are omitted.

[It is definitely worth noting, however, the later case of Shuttlesworth v. City of Birmingham, 394 U.S. 147, 89 S.Ct. 935 (1969). Rev. Fred L. Shuttlesworth, one of the ministers accompanying Dr. King in the demonstrations and later one of the petitioners in Walker v. City of Birmingham, was arrested and convicted upon jury trial of violating the ordinance there involved by leading the march on April 12, 1963. The state circuit judge sentenced him to 90 days' imprisonment at hard labor, and to an additional 48 days in default of payment of a $75 fine and $24 costs.

[The Alabama Court of Appeals overturned the conviction, as noted above in footnote 13, but the Supreme Court of Alabama later reinstated it. The latter court rejected the contention that the ordinance was an unconstitutional censorship or prior restraint upon the exercise of First Amendment freedoms. The court did so by construing the ordinance so as to limit the applicability of its broad language to protection of the public safety and convenience in the use of the streets, and thus to save it from being unconstitutional on its face. The court also ruled that there was nothing in the record tending to show that the ordinance had been applied in other than a fair and nondiscriminatory fashion.

[The Supreme Court of the United States granted certiorari. Then, in an opinion by Justice Stewart, who had written the majority opinion in Walker v. City of Birmingham, the Court unanimously reversed, holding that the ordinance "as it was written" was unconstitutional and that a person could ignore it with impunity. In light of past understanding of and practice under the ordinance, it could not be saved by narrow and precise construction. He called the Alabama court's construction "a remarkable job of plastic surgery upon the face of the ordinance" and said that it "would have taken extraordinary clairvoyance for anyone to perceive that this language meant what the Supreme Court of Alabama was destined to find that it meant more than four years later."]

Martin Luther King, Jr., in the Birmingham jail, serving the contempt sentence in early November of 1967—photographed by Wyatt Tee Walker, his cellmate and one of the jailed ministers (AP/Wide World Photos)

———

UNITED STATES v. RYAN, 402 U.S. 530, 91 S.Ct. 1580 (1971). This was a case holding that denial of a motion to quash a subpoena duces tecum commanding production of documents before a federal grand jury is not appealable or otherwise reviewable before the time for compliance.

In the course of decision, the Court pointed out that one who claims a subpoena is unduly burdensome or otherwise unlawful may refuse to comply, and then litigate those questions in the event contempt proceedings are brought against him: if his contentions are rejected in the trial court, they will then be ripe for appellate review; if on appeal his contentions are upheld, any contempt adjudication will then fall. At this point in the opinion the Court dropped the following footnote: "Walker v. Birmingham . . . is not to the contrary. Our holding that the claims there sought to be asserted were not open on review of petitioners' contempt convictions was based upon the availability of review of those claims at an earlier stage."

———

MANESS v. MEYERS, 419 U.S. 449, 95 S.Ct. 584 (1975). This was a case holding that a lawyer, representing a defendant in a state civil case, may not be held in criminal contempt for advising his client not to comply with a subpoena duces tecum that the court refused to quash, or with the court's follow-up order to comply, when the lawyer believed reasonably and in good faith that compliance might tend to incriminate his client in violation of the Fifth Amendment.

In the course of decision, the Court discussed the duty of the client to obey court orders. It began with the "basic proposition" that the "orderly and expeditious administration of justice by the courts requires" the client to comply with all court orders and then pursue review thereof. "Remedies for judicial error may be cumbersome but the injury flowing from an error generally is not irreparable . . . . When a court during trial orders a witness to reveal information, however, a different situation may be presented. Compliance could cause irreparable injury because appellate courts cannot always 'unring the bell' once the information has been released. Subsequent appellate vindication does not necessarily have its ordinary consequence of totally repairing the error." So here, although eventual review of the Fifth Amendment contention might be possible, there was no regular opportunity for review before compliance. And compliance constituted irreparable injury. Thus, the client could refuse to comply, and then raise his constitutional contention in any consequent contempt proceedings: if his contention were eventually upheld, any contempt adjudication would then fall.

———

Questions: (26) How should the courts construe this "irreparable injury" limitation to requiring pursuit of further review? If irreparable injury means merely feared infringement of a right for some time, the limitation would devour the requirement. So it must mean at least that temporary obedience would permanently and substantially impair a significant right, as subjectively anticipated by the violator and later objectively found on review. But how does that translate into practical application? What would have happened if Dr. King had litigated to the hilt in the Alabama courts until Good Friday, having no success but meeting no "delay or frustration" either, and then he decided that the critical moment had come for the movement and he therefore marched without completing the full course of review? Could he then rely on Maness? Or must he rely solely on the court's mercy in not pursuing and punishing disobedience of an arguably improper court order when the violator had acted with adequate excuse?

(27) Imagine a trial court has imposed criminal and civil contempt sanctions on someone for disobedience of what it believed to be its proper order. On appeal, the propriety of the order comes before the appellate court. That court finds the order to be beyond the trial court's power, but the circumstances are such that the criminal contempt punishment could stand under the collateral bar rule—that is, under the UMW-Walker approach that the Court explained in Ryan and Maness. Should the appellate court remand for reconsideration of the punishment in light of the finding of the order's impropriety? See Donovan v. City of Dallas, 377 U.S. 408, 84 S.Ct. 1579 (yes), on remand sub nom. City of Dallas v. Brown, 384 S.W.2d 724 (Tex.Civ.App.1964).

(28) In summary, this line of cases authorizes punishment by criminal contempt for the violation of any court order even though that order is judicially determined to have been erroneous, no matter how serious the error, including a constitutional violation or lack of subject-matter jurisdiction—unless either (a) the violator lacked opportunity to pursue full review of the improper order or lacked such opportunity without incurring "irreparable injury" or (b) the order were subject to collateral attack for lack of personal jurisdiction or notice. Should there be additional exceptions to this power to punish? For example, would it matter if the order were crazy enough to be "transparently invalid"—can the violator ignore such an order with impunity? See In re Providence Journal Co., 820 F.2d 1354 (1st Cir.1987) (en banc, per curiam) (no), cert. dismissed, 485 U.S. 693, 108 S.Ct. 1502 (1988).

INDEX

References are to Pages

(references to pages above 934 are to the casebook's unabridged edition)

———————

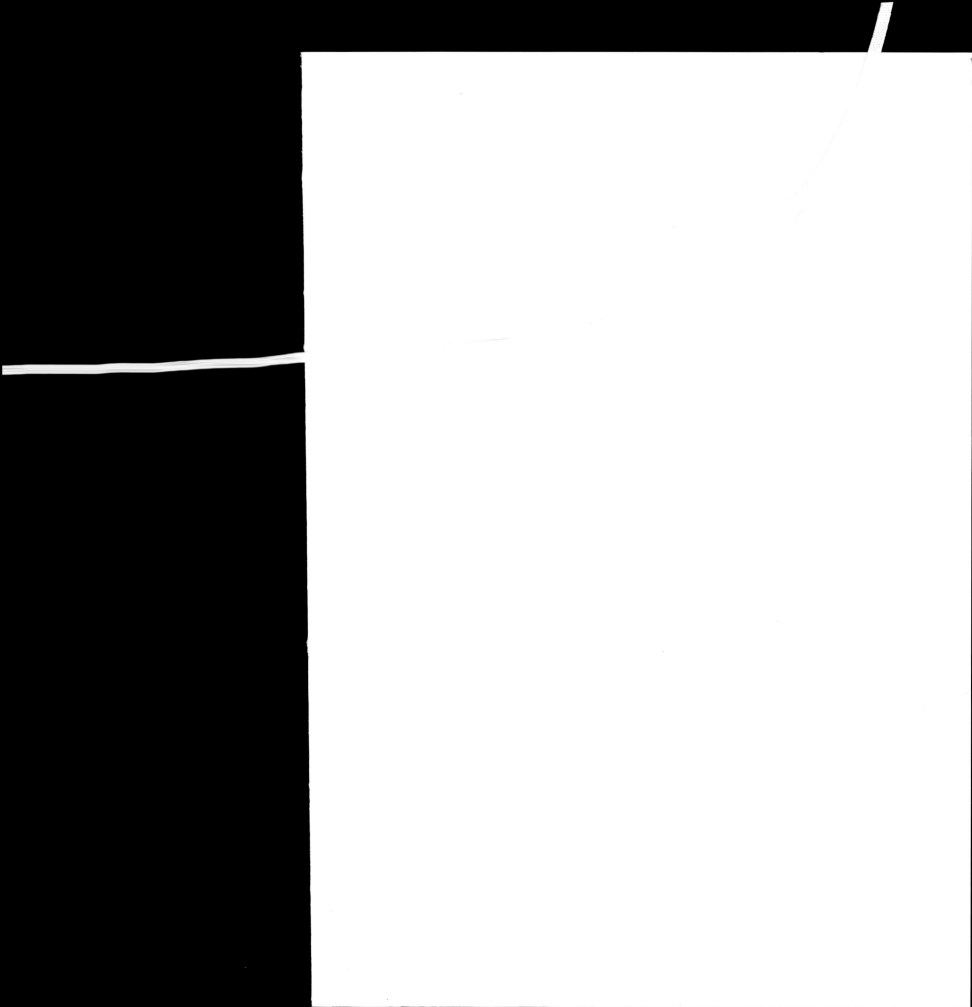